DATE DUE

			PRINTED IN U.S.A.

Literature Criticism from 1400 to 1800

Guide to Gale Literary Criticism Series

For criticism on	Consult these Gale series
Authors now living or who died after December 31, 1959	*CONTEMPORARY LITERARY CRITICISM (CLC)*
Authors who died between 1900 and 1959	*TWENTIETH-CENTURY LITERARY CRITICISM (TCLC)*
Authors who died between 1800 and 1899	*NINETEENTH-CENTURY LITERATURE CRITICISM (NCLC)*
Authors who died between 1400 and 1799	*LITERATURE CRITICISM FROM 1400 TO 1800 (LC)* *SHAKESPEAREAN CRITICISM (SC)*
Authors who died before 1400	*CLASSICAL AND MEDIEVAL LITERATURE CRITICISM (CMLC)*
Black writers of the past two hundred years	*BLACK LITERATURE CRITICISM (BLC)*
Authors of books for children and young adults	*CHILDREN'S LITERATURE REVIEW (CLR)*
Dramatists	*DRAMA CRITICISM (DC)*
Hispanic writers of the late nineteenth and twentieth centuries	*HISPANIC LITERATURE CRITICISM (HLC)*
Native North American writers and orators of the eighteenth, nineteenth, and twentieth centuries	*NATIVE NORTH AMERICAN LITERATURE (NNAL)*
Poets	*POETRY CRITICISM (PC)*
Short story writers	*SHORT STORY CRITICISM (SSC)*
Major authors from the Renaissance to the present	*WORLD LITERATURE CRITICISM, 1500 TO THE PRESENT (WLC)*

ISSN 0740-2880

Volume 27

Literature Criticism from 1400 to 1800

Excerpts from Criticism of the Works
of Fifteenth, Sixteenth, Seventeenth, and
Eighteenth-Century Novelists, Poets, Playwrights,
Philosophers, and Other Creative Writers, from
the First Published Critical Appraisals
to Current Evaluations

James E. Person, Jr., Editor

Jelena O. Krstovic´
Michael Magoulias
Associate Editors

 *Gale Research Inc.*

An International Thomson Publishing Company

OCT '95 ITP

NEW YORK • LONDON • BONN • BOSTON • DETROIT • MADRID
MELBOURNE • MEXICO CITY • PARIS • SINGAPORE • TOKYO
TORONTO • WASHINGTON • ALBANY NY • BELMONT CA • CINCINNATI OH

STAFF

James E. Person, Jr., *Editor*

Jennifer Brostrom, Jelena O. Krstović, Sean McCready, Michael Magoulias, *Associate Editors*

Dana Ramel Barnes, Catherine C. Dominic, *Assistant Editors*

Marlene H. Lasky, *Permissions Manager*
Margaret A. Chamberlain, Linda M. Pugliese, *Permissions Specialists*
Susan Brohman, Diane Cooper, Maria Franklin, Pamela A. Hayes, Arlene Johnson, Josephine M. Keene,
Michele Lonoconus, Maureen Puhl, Shalice Shah, Kimberly F. Smilay, Barbara A. Wallace,
Permissions Associates
Edna Hedblad, Tyra Y. Phillips, *Permissions Assistants*

Victoria B. Cariappa, *Research Manager*
Eva M. Felts, Mary Beth McElmeel, Tamara C. Nott, Tracie A. Richardson, Norma Sawaya, *Research Associates*
Melissa E. Brown, Maria E. Bryson, Shirley Gates, Michele P. Pica,
Amy Terese Steel, Amy Beth Wieczorek, *Research Assistants*

Mary Beth Trimper, *Production Director*
Mary Kelley, *Production Associate*

Cynthia Baldwin, *Product Design Manager*
Sherrell Hobbs, *Macintosh Artist*
Willie Mathis, *Camera Operator*

∞™ This book is printed on acid-free paper that meets the minimum requirements of American National Standard for Information Sciences—Permanence Paper for Printed Library Materials, ANSI Z39.48-1984.

Library of Congress Catalog Card Number 94-29718
ISBN 0-8103-8943-6
ISSN 0732-1864
Printed in the United States of America
Published simultaneously in the United Kingdom
by Gale Research International Limited
(An affiliated company of Gale Research Inc.)

I(T)P™   Gale Research Inc., an International Thomson Publishing Company.
ITP logo is a trademark under license.

10 9 8 7 6 5 4 3 2 1

Contents

Preface   vii

Acknowledgments   xi

Preface

Literature Criticism from 1400 to 1800 (LC) presents criticism of world authors of the fifteenth through eighteenth centuries. The literature of this period reflects a turbulent time of radical change that saw the rise of drama equal in stature to that of classical Greece, the birth of the novel and personal essay forms, the emergence of newspapers and periodicals, and major achievements in poetry and philosophy. Much of modern literature reflects the influence of these centuries. Thus the literature treated in *LC* provides insight into the universal nature of human experience, as well as into the life and thought of the past.

Scope of the Series

LC is designed to serve as an introduction to authors of the fifteenth through eighteenth centuries and to the most significant interpretations of these authors' works. The great poets, dramatists, novelists, essayists, and philosophers of this period are considered classics in every secondary school and college or university curriculum. Because criticism of this literature spans nearly six hundred years, an overwhelming amount of critical material confronts the student. *LC* therefore organizes and reprints the most noteworthy published criticism of authors of these centuries. Readers should note that there is a separate Gale reference series devoted to Shakespearean studies. For though belonging properly to the period covered in *LC,* William Shakespeare has inspired such a tremendous and ever-growing corpus of secondary material that the editors have deemed it best to give his works extensive coverage in a separate series, *Shakespearean Criticism.*

Each author entry in *LC* attempts to present a historical survey of critical response to the author's works. Early criticism is offered to indicate initial responses, later selections document any rise or decline in literary reputations, and retrospective analyses provide students with modern views. The size of each author entry is intended to reflect the author's critical reception in English or foreign criticism in translation. Articles and books that have not been translated into English are therefore excluded. Every attempt has been made to identify and include the seminal essays on each author's work and to include recent commentary providing modern perspectives.

The need for *LC* among students and teachers of literature was suggested by the proven usefulness of Gale's *Contemporary Literary Criticism (CLC), Twentieth-Century Literary Criticism (TCLC),* and *Nineteenth-Century Literature Criticism (NCLC),* which excerpt criticism of works by nineteenth- and twentieth-century authors. Because of the different time periods covered, there is no duplication of authors or critical material in any of these literary criticism series. An author may appear more than once in the series because of the great quantity of critical material available and because of the aesthetic demands of the series's *thematic organization.*

Thematic Approach

Beginning with Volume 12, all the authors in each volume of *LC* are organized in a thematic scheme. Such themes include literary movements, literary reaction to political and historical events, significant eras in literary history, and the literature of cultures often overlooked by English-speaking readers.

Organization of the Book

Each entry consists of the following elements: author or thematic heading, introduction, list of principal works (in author entries only), annotated works of criticism (each followed by a bibliographical citation), and a bibliography o further reading. Also, most author entries contain author portraits and others illustrations.

- The **Author Heading** consists of the author's full name, followed by birth and death dates. If an author wrote consistently under a pseudonym, the pseudonym is used in the author heading, with the real name given in parentheses on the first line of the biographical and critical introduction. Also located here are any name variations under which an author wrote, including transliterated forms for authors whose native languages use nonroman alphabets. Uncertain birth or death dates are indicated by question marks. The **Thematic Heading** simply states the subject of the entry.

- The **Biographical and Critical Introduction** contains background information designed to introduce the reader to an author and to critical discussion of his or her work. Parenthetical material following many of the introductions provides references to biographical and critical reference series published by Gale in which additional material about the author may be found. The **Thematic Introduction** briefly defines the subject of the entry and provides social and historical background important to understanding the criticism.

- Most *LC* author entries include **Portraits** of the author. Many entries also contain illustrations of materials pertinent to an author's career, including author holographs, title pages, letters, or representations of important people, places, and events in an author's life.

- The **List of Principal Works** is chronological by date of first book publication and identifies the genre of each work. In the case of foreign authors whose works have been translated in to English, the title and date of the first English-language edition are given in brackets beneath the foreign-language listing. Unless otherwise indicated, drama are dated by first performance, not first publication.

- **Criticism** is arranged chronologically in each author entry to provide a useful perspective on changes in critical evaluation over the years. For the purpose of easy identification, the critic's name and the composition or publication date or the critical work are given at the beginning of each piece of criticism. Unsigned criticism is preceded by the title of the source in which it appeared. All titles by the author featured in the critical entry are printed in boldface type. Publication information (such as publisher names and book prices) and parenthetical numerical references (such as footnotes or page and line references to specific editions of works) have been deleted at the editors' discretion to provide smoother reading of the text.

- Critical essays are prefaced by **Annotations** as an additional aid to students using *LC*. These explanatory notes may provide several types of useful information, including: the reputation of a critic, the importance of a work of criticism, the commentator's individual approach to literary criticism, the intent of the criticism, and the growth of critical controversy or changes in critical trends regarding an author's work. In some cases, these notes cross-reference the work of critics within the entry who agree or disagree with each other.

- A complete **Bibliographical Citation** of the original essay or book follows each piece of criticism.

- An annotated bibliography of **Further Reading** appears at the end of each entry and suggests resources for additional study of authors and themes. It also includes essays for which the editors could not obtain reprint rights.

Cumulative Indexes

Each volume of *LC* includes a cumulative **Author Index** listing all the authors that have appeared in *Contemporary Literary Criticism, Twentieth-Century Literary Criticism, Nineteenth-Century Literature Criticism, Literature Criticism from 1400 to 1800, and Classical and Medieval Literature Criticism,* along with cross-references to the Gale series *Short Story Criticism, Poetry Criticism, Children's Literature Review, Authors in the News, Contemporary Authors, Contemporary Authors Autobiography Series, Contemporary Authors Bibliographical Series, Dictionary of Literary Biography, Concise Dictionary of Literary Biography, Something about the Author, Something about the Author Autobiography Series, and Yesterday's Authors of Books for Children.* Readers will welcome this cumulative author index as a useful tool for locating an author within the various series. The index, which includes authors' birth and death dates, is particularly valuable for those authors who are identified with a certain period but whose death dates cause them to be placed in another, or for those authors whose careers span two periods. For example, F. Scott Fitzgerald is found in *TCLC,* yet a writer often associated with him, Ernest Hemingway, is found in *CLC.*

Beginning with Volume 12, *LC* includes a cumulative **Topic Index** that lists all literary themes and topics treated in *LC, NCLC* Topics volumes, *TCLC* Topics volumes, and the *CLC* Yearbook. Each volume of *LC* also includes a cumulative **Nationality Index** in which authors' names are arranged alphabetically under their respective nationalities and followed by the numbers of the volumes in which they appear.

Each volume of *LC* also includes a cumulative **Title Index,** an alphabetical listing of the literary works discussed in the series since its inception. Each title listing includes the corresponding volume and page numbers where criticism may be located. Foreign-language titles that have been translated followed by the tiles of the translation—for example, *El ingenioso hidalgo Don Quixote de la Mancha (Don Quixote).* Page numbers following these translated titles refers to all pages on which any form of the titles, either foreign-language or translated, appear. Title of novels, dramas, nonfiction books, and poetry, short story, or essays collections are printed in italics, while individual poems, short stories, and essays are printed in roman type within quotation marks.

A Note to the Reader

When writing papers, students who quote directly from any volume in the Literary Criticism Series may use the following general forms to footnote reprinted criticism. The first example pertains to material drawn from periodicals, the second to material reprinted from books.

T. S. Eliot, "John Donne," *The Nation and the Athenaeum,* 33 (9 June 1923), 321-32; excerpted and reprinted in *Literature Criticism from 1400 to 1800,* Vol. 10, ed. James E. Person, Jr. (Detroit: Gale Research, 1989), pp. 28-9.

Clara G. Stillman, *Samuel Butler: A Mid-Victorian Modern* (Viking Press, 1932); excerpted and reprinted in *Twentieth-Century Literary Criticism,* Vol. 33, ed. Paula Kepos (Detroit: Gale Research, 1989), pp. 43-5.

Suggestions Are Welcome

In response to various suggestions features have been added to *LC* since the series began, including a nationality index, a Literary Criticism Series topic index, thematic entries, a descriptive table of contents, and more extensive illustrations.

Readers who wish to suggest new features, themes or authors to appear in future volumes, or who have other suggestions, are cordially invited to write to the editor.

Acknowledgments

The editors wish to thank the copyright holders of the excerpted criticism included in this volume, the permissions managers of many book and magazine publishing companies for assisting us in securing reprint rights. We are also grateful to the staffs of the Detroit Public Library, the Library of Congress, the University of Detroit Mercy Library, Wayne State University Purdy/Kresge Library Complex, and the University of Michigan Libraries for making their resources available to us. Following is a list of the copyright holders who have granted us permission to reprint material in this volume of *LC-27*. Every effort has been made to trace copyright, but if omissions have been made, please let us know.

COPYRIGHTED EXCERPTS IN *LC*, VOLUME 27, WERE REPRINTED FROM THE FOLLOWING PERIODICALS:

Bibliotheque D'Humanisme et Renaissance, v. XXVI, 1964; v. XXXIV, 1972. Both reprinted by permission of the publisher.—*Journal of the History of Ideas,* v. XXXVIII, April-June, 1977. Copyright 1977, Journal of the History of Ideas, Inc. Reprinted by permission of the publisher.—*The Sixteenth Century Journal,* v. XV, Summer, 1984. Copyright © 1984 by The Sixteenth Century Journal Publishers, Inc., Kirksville, Missouri. All rights reserved. Reprinted by permission of the publisher.—*Soviet Studies in Philosophy,* v. VI, Fall, 1967. Reprinted with permission by M. E. Sharpe, Inc., Publisher, Armonk, NY 10504.

COPYRIGHTED EXCERPTS IN *LC*, VOLUME 27, WERE REPRINTED FROM THE FOLLOWING BOOKS:

Blau, Joseph Leon. From *The Christian Interpretation of the Cabala in the Renaissance.* Columbia University Press, 1944. Copyright 1944 Columbia University Press, New York. Renewed 1972 by Joseph Leon Blau. All rights reserved. Reprinted with the permission of the publisher.—Bornstein, Diane. From an introduction to *The Feminist Controversy of the Renaissance: Facsimile Reproductions.* By Guillaume Alexis, Sir Thomas Bird, and Henricus Cornelius Agrippa. Scholars' Facsimiles & Reprints, 1980. © 1979 Diane Bornstein. All rights reserved.—Brooks, Cleanth. From "Henry Vaughan: Quietism and Mysticism," in *Essays in Honor of Esmond Linworth Marilla.* Edited by Thomas Austin Kirby and William John Olive. Louisiana State University Press, 1970. Copyright © 1970 by Louisiana State University Press. Reprinted by permission of the publisher.—Bruno, Giordano. From the *Expulsion of the Triumphant Beast.* Edited and translated by Arthur D. Imerti. University of Nebraska Press, 1992. Copyright © 1964, renewed 1992 by Arthur D. Imerti. Reprinted by permission of the publisher.—Castiglioni, Arturo. From *Adventures of the Mind.* Translated by V. Gianturco. Knopf, 1946. Copyright 1946, renewed 1973 by Alfred A. Knopf, Inc. Reprinted by permission of Alfred A. Knopf, Inc.—Clements, Arthur L. From *Poetry of Contemplation: John Donne, George Herbert, Henry Vaughan, and the Modern Period.* State University of New York Press, 1990. © 1990 State University of New York. All rights reserved. Reprinted by permission of the publisher.—Copenhaver, Brian P. From "Natural Magic, Hermetism, and Occultism in Early Modern Science," in *Reappraisals of the Scientific Revolution.* Edited by David C. Lindberg and Robert S. Westman. Cambridge University Press, 1990. © Cambridge University Press 1990. Reprinted with the permission of the publisher and the author.—Copenhaver, Brian P., and Charles B. Schmitt. From *Renaissance Philosophy.* Oxford University Press, Oxford, 1992. © Brian P. Copenhaver and the estate of Charles B. Schmitt 1992. All rights reserved. Reprinted by permission of Oxford University Press.—Curry, Patrick. From *Prophecy and Power: Astrology in Early Modern England.* Polity Press, 1989. Copyright © Patrick Curry 1989. All rights reserved. Reprinted by permission of the publisher.—Durr, R. A. From *On the Mystical Poetry of Henry Vaughan.* Cambridge, Mass.: Harvard University Press, 1962. Copyright © 1962 by the President and Fellows of Harvard College. Renewed 1990

xi

Henry Cornelius Agrippa von Nettesheim

1486-1535

German philosopher and theologian.

INTRODUCTION

One of the most prominent of the sixteenth-century European occultists, Agrippa was an erudite and versatile scholar knowledgeable in the fields of science, medicine, magic, philosophy, and theology. Dismissed as a charlatan and self-promoter by some commentators, Agrippa has been praised by others for his role in helping to bring about the beginnings of the scientific revolution, and particularly for his steadfast and daring intellectual curiosity in the face of opposition from the ecclesiastical hierarchy. In his best-known work, *De occulta philosophia libri tres* (*Occult Philosophy*), Agrippa defends magic from its detractors, claiming that study of magic ultimately leads to knowledge of nature and of God. Alternately, in *De incertitudine et vanitate scientarium declamatio inuectiua* (*Of the Vanity and Uncertainty of Arts and Sciences*), an influential but controversial treatise ridiculing humankind's effort to gain knowledge, Agrippa attacks the pretentiousness of learned men and advocates a return to a simple form of Christian faith.

Biographical Information

Agrippa was born in Cologne into a family whose members worked for the royal house of Habsburg. After completing his education at the University of Cologne, Agrippa served in the army of Maximilian I of Germany, following him on a military campaign in Catalonia in 1509. That same year Agrippa lectured at the University of Dôle on John Reuchlin's cabalistic treatise *De Verbo mirifico*; when these lectures came to the attention of the monk John Catilinet, he accused Agrippa of heresy, forcing him to flee in order to avoid imprisonment. Agrippa accompanied Maximilian I on a diplomatic mission to England in 1510 and to Italy in 1511, remaining in Italy for seven years, supported by various noble patrons and lecturing at the University of Pavia on theology and medicine. In 1518 Agrippa was offered a post in Germany as a public defender, but he soon returned to Cologne after being publicly denounced by some monks for defending a woman accused of witchcraft. Having practiced medicine in Geneva and Freiburg, he was appointed physician to Louise of Savoy in 1524 and moved to Lyons. He left her service in 1528, apparently after a quarrel concerning a task she asked him to perform, to work as archivist and historiographer for Margaret, Duchess of Savoy. Suffering from financial difficulties for most of his life, Agrippa was imprisoned for debt in Brussels. After his release, he traveled to Cologne, Bonn, and France in search of work; he was arrested again while in France, allegedly for criticizing Lou-

ise of Savoy, but was soon released. He died in Grenoble in 1535.

Major Works

Agrippa's first published work, *Of the Vanity and Uncertainty of Arts and Sciences* (1531), was written in 1527; it was followed by *Occult Philosophy*, published that same year, but written in 1510. He had delayed publication of the latter treatise until after the appearance of the more acceptable *Of the Vanity and Uncertainty of Arts and Sciences* because he feared persecution by powerful church representatives who considered his *Occult Philosophy* a dangerous and heretical work. *Occult Philosophy* incorporates elements of the cabala and numerology into a wide-ranging compendium of magic, and presents Agrippa's theory that the universe is divided into three spheres—physics, mathematics, and theology. A mixture of Christianity, Neo-Platonism, and occult science, Agrippa's work garnered much praise from his contemporaries and proved highly influential as a landmark in the Renaissance study of magic. Agrippa also wrote several other treatises, the most notable among them *De nobilitate et praeccelentia foeminei sexus* (*The Nobility of the Feminine Sex*), published in 1532 and dedicated to Margaret of Burgundy in gratitude for her patronage. Here, Agrippa asserts the natural superiority of the female sex, marshalling evidence in support of his argument from the Bible and from philosophy. While some critics regard this work as a standard piece of flattery to a patron, others now see it as a clever plea for the equality of women. Agrippa's commentary on the works of Catalonian philosopher Raymund Llull, entitled *In artem brevem Raymundi Lullii commentaria*, published in 1598, is considered a key contribution to the development of occultism in the sixteenth century.

Critical Reception

In his own time and for several centuries afterward, Agrippa was most famous as an expert on magic. His scientific activities and philosophical explorations gave rise to many popular legends—for example, that he could conjure the dead and that he was always accompanied by a large black dog who was actually the Devil. Some scholars believe that Johann Wolfgang von Goethe used Agrippa as a model for the original Faust. Moreover, Agrippa's correspondence with scientists and philosophers from many different countries, aided by his knowledge of eight languages, encouraged theories that he belonged to a secret brotherhood of occultists. Scholars have continued to debate the seemingly contradictory relationship between *Occult Philosophy* and *Of the Vanity and Uncertainty of Arts and Sciences*, with some recent commentators suggesting ways to resolve the dilemma. For example, Charles G. Nauert, Jr. has suggested that belief in and skepticism about the occult and the limits of human knowledge were present simultaneously in all phases of Agrippa's work; Barbara C. Bowen has argued that *Of the Vanity and Uncertainty of Arts and Sciences* may be a playful example of the literary paradox genre rather than the anti-intellectual harangue that some readers have deemed it. Overall, critics agree that Agrippa's writings and his desire to unite Christianity and the occult in his works were an important contribution to philosophy, especially to the Renaissance study of magic.

PRINCIPAL WORKS

De incertitudine et vanitate scientarium declamatio inuectiua [*Of the Vanity and Uncertainty of Arts and Sciences*] (treatise) 1531
De occulta philosophia libri tres [*Occult Philosophy*] (treatise) 1531
De nobilitate et praecellentia foeminei sexus [*The Nobility of the Feminine Sex*] (treatise) 1532
In arrtem brevem Raymundi Lullii commentaria [*The Art of Raymund Llull*] (commentary) 1598

CRITICISM

Henry Cornelius Agrippa   (letter date 1510)

SOURCE: A letter to John Trithemius in the year 1510, in *Three Books of Occult Philosophy or Magic, Book One: Natural Magic* by Henry Cornelius Agrippa, edited by Willis F. Whitehead, 1897. Reprint by The Aquarian Press, 1971, pp. 28-30.

[*Here, Agrippa announces to his former teacher, John Trithemius, his intention to try to restore a respect for magic among his readers.*]

To R. P. D. John Trithemius, an Abbot of Saint James, in the Suburbs of Herbipolis, Henry Cornelius Agrippa of Nettesheim sendeth Greeting:

When I was of late, most reverend father, for a while conversant with you in your Monastery of Herbipolis, we conferred together of divers things concerning Chemistry, Magic, and Cabala, and of other things, which as yet lie hid in Secret Sciences and Arts; and then there was one great question amongst the rest—Why Magic, whereas it was accounted by all ancient philosophers to be the chiefest science, and by the ancient wise men and priests was always held in great veneration, came at last, after the beginning of the Catholic Church, to be always odious to and suspected by the holy Fathers, and then exploded by Divines, and condemned by sacred Canons, and moreover, by all laws and ordinances forbidden? Now, the cause, as I conceive, is no other than this, viz.: Because, by a certain fatal depravation of times and men, many false philosophers crept in, and these, under the name of Magicians, heaping together, through various sorts of errors and factions of false religions, many cursed superstitions and dangerous rites, and many wicked sacrileges, even to the perfection of Nature; and the same set forth in many wicked and unlawful books, to which they have by stealth prefixed the most honest name and title of Magic; hoping, by this sacred title, to gain credit to their cursed and detestable fooleries. Hence it is that this name of Magic, formerly so honorable, is now become most odious to good and honest men, and accounted a capital crime if any one dare profess himself to be a Magician, either in doctrine or works, unless haply some certain old doting woman, dwelling in the country, would be believed to be skillful and have a divine power, that she (as saith Apuleis the satirist) "can throw down the heaven, lift up the earth, harden fountains, wash away mountains, raise up ghosts, cast down the Gods, extinguish the stars, illuminate hell," or, as Virgil sings:

> She'll promise by her charms to cast great cares,
> Or ease the minds of men, and make the Stars
> For to go back, and rivers to stand still,
> And raise the nightly ghosts even at her will;
> To make the earth to groan, and trees to fall
> From the mountains—

Hence those things which Lucan relates of Thessala the Magicianess, and Homer of the omnipotency of Circe. Whereof many others, I confess, are as well of a fallacious opinion as a superstitious diligence and pernicious labor;

for when they cannot come under a wicked art yet they presume they may be able to cloak themselves under that venerable title of Magic.

These things being so, I wondered much and was not less indignant that, as yet, there had been no man who had either vindicated this sublime and sacred discipline from the charge of impiety or had delivered it purely and sincerely to us. What I have seen of our modern writers—Roger Bacon, Robert of York, an Englishman, Peter Apponus, Albertus [Magnus] the Teutonich, Arnolds de villa Nova, Anselme the Parmensian, Picatrix the Spaniard, Cicclus Asculus of Florence, and many other writers of an obscure name—when they promise to treat of Magic do nothing but relate irrational tales and superstitions unworthy of honest men. Hence my spirit was moved, and, by reason partly of admiration, and partly of indignation, I was willing to play the philosopher, supposing that I should do no discommendable work—seeing I have been always from my youth a curious and undaunted searcher for wonderful effects and operations full of mysteries—if I should recover that ancient Magic (the discipline of all wise men) from the errors of impiety, purify and adorn it with its proper lustre, and vindicate it from the injuries of calumniators; which thing, though I long deliberated of it in my mind, I never durst undertake; but after some conference betwixt us of these things, at Herbipolis, your transcending knowledge and learning, and your ardent adhortation, put courage and boldness into me. There selecting the opinions of philosophers of known credit, and purging the introduction of the wicked (who, dissemblingly, and with a counterfeited knowledge, did teach that traditions of Magicians must be learned from very reprobate books of darkness or from institutions of wonderful operations), and, removing all darkness, I have at last composed three compendious books of Magic, and titled them *Of Occult Philosophy,* being a title less offensive, which books I submit (you excelling in the knowledge of these things) to your correction and censure, that if I have wrote anything which may tend either to the contumely of Nature, offending God, or injury of religion, you may condemn the error; but if the scandal of impiety be dissolved and purged, you may defend the Tradition of Truth; and that you would do so with these books, and Magic itself, that nothing may be concealed which may be profitable, and nothing approved of which cannot but do hurt; by which means these three books, having passed your examination with approbation, may at length be thought worthy to come forth with good success in public, and may not be afraid to come under the censure of posterity.

Farewell, and pardon these my bold undertakings.

John Trithemius   (letter date 1510)

SOURCE: A letter to Henry Cornelius Agrippa on April 8, 1510, in *Three Books of Occult Philosophy or Magic,* Book One: Natural Magic by Henry Cornelius Agrippa, edited by Willis F. Whitehead, 1897. Reprint by The Aquarian Press, 1971, pp. 31-32.

[*Trithemius, who was the Abbot of Saint James, Herbipolis, was well-known as an avid and learned student of philoso-*

phy and occult science. Below, he congratulates his former pupil, Agrippa, on the excellence of his Occult Philosophy, *warning him to chose carefully with whom he communicates regarding his work.*]

John Trithemius, Abbot of Saint James of Herbipolis, formerly of Spanhemia, to his Henry Cornelius Agrippa of Nettesheim, health and love:

Your work, most renowned Agrippa, entitled **Of Occult Philosophy,** which you have sent by this bearer to me, has been examined. With how much pleasure I received it no mortal tongue can express nor the pen of any write. I wondered at your more than vulgar learning—that you, being so young, should penetrate into such secrets as have been hid from most learned men; and not only clearly and truly but also properly and elegantly set them forth. Whence first I give you thanks for your good will to me, and, if I shall ever be able, I shall return you thanks to the utmost of my power. Your work, which no learned man can sufficiently commend, I approve of. Now that you may proceed toward higher things, as you have begun, and not suffer such excellent parts of wit to be idle, I do, with as much earnestness as I can, advise, intreat and beseech you that you would exercise yourself in laboring after better things, and demonstrate the light of true wisdom to the ignorant, according as you yourself are divinely enlightened. Neither let the consideration of idle, vain fellows withdraw you from your purpose; I say of them, of whom it is said, "The wearied ox treads hard," whereas no man, to the judgment of the wise, can be truly learned who is sworn to the rudiments of one only faculty. But you have been by God gifted with a large and sublime wit, and it is not that you should imitate oxen but rather birds; neither think it sufficient that you study about particulars, but bend your mind confidently to universals; for by so much the more learned any one is thought, by how much fewer things he is ignorant of. Moreover, your wit is fully apt to all things, and to be rationally employed, not in a few or low things, but many and sublimer. Yet this one rule I advise you to observe—that you communicate vulgar secrets to vulgar friends, but higher and secret to higher and secret friends only: *Give hay to an ox, sugar to a parrot only.* Understand my meaning, lest you be trod under the oxen's feet, as oftentimes it falls out. Farewell, my happy friend, and if it lie in my power to serve you, command me, and according to your pleasure it shall without delay be done; also, let our friendship increase daily; write often to me, and send me some of your labors I earnestly pray you. Again farewell.

Henry Cornelius Agrippa   (essay date 1533)

SOURCE: A preface to *Occult Philosophy* by Henry Cornelius Agrippa, in *Three Books of Occult Philosophy or Magic,* Book One: Natural Magic by Henry Cornelius Agrippa, edited by Willis F. Whitehead, 1897. Reprint by The Aquarian Press, 1971, pp. 25-27.

[*In his preface to* Occult Philosophy, *Agrippa emphasizes his view that a magician is not a sorcerer, but "a wise man, a priest, a prophet."*]

I do not doubt but the title of our book of Occult Philosophy, or of Magic, may by the rarity of it allure many to read it, amongst which, some of a disordered judgment and some that are perverse will come to hear what I can say, who, by their rash ignorance, may take the name of Magic in the worse sense and, though scarce having seen the title, cry out that I teach forbidden Arts, sow the seed of heresies, offend the pious, and scandalize excellent wits; that I am a sorcerer, and superstitious and devilish, who indeed am a Magician: to whom I answer, that a Magician doth not, amongst learned men, signify a sorcerer or one that is superstitious or devilish; but a wise man, a priest, a prophet; and that the Sybils were Magicianesses, and therefore prophesied most clearly of Christ; and that Magicians, as wise men, by the wonderful secrets of the world, knew Christ, the author of the world, to be born, and came first of all to worship him; and that the name of Magic was received by philosophers, commended by divines, and is not unacceptable to the Gospel. I believe that the supercilious censors will object against the Sybils, holy Magicians and the Gospel itself sooner than receive the name of Magic into favor. So conscientious are they that neither Apollo nor all the Muses, nor an angel from heaven can redeem me from their curse. Whom therefore I advise that they read not our writings, nor understand them, nor remember them. For they are pernicious and full of poison; the gate of Acheron is in this book; it speaks stones—let them take heed that it beat not out their brains. But you that come without prejudice to read it, if you have so much discretion of prudence as bees have in gathering honey, read securely, and believe that you shall receive no little profit, and much pleasure; but if you shall find any things that may not please you, let them alone and make no use of them, for I do not approve of them, but declare them to you. But do not refuse other things, for they that look into the books of physicians do, together with antidotes and medicines, read also of poisons. I confess that Magic teacheth many superfluous things, and curious prodigies for ostentation; leave them as empty things, yet be not ignorant of their causes. But those things which are for the profit of men—for the turning away of evil events, for the destroying of sorceries, for the curing of diseases, for the exterminating of phantasms, for the preserving of life, honor, or fortune—may be done without offense to God or injury to religion, because they are, as profitable, so necessary. But I have admonished you that I have writ many things rather narratively than affirmatively; for so it seemed needful that we should pass over fewer things, following the judgments of Platonists and other Gentile Philosophers when they did suggest an argument of writing to our purpose. Therefore if any error have been committed, or any thing hath been spoken more freely, pardon my youth, for I wrote this being scarce a young man, that I may excuse myself, and say, whilst I was a child I spake as a child, and I understood as a child, but being become a man, I retracted those things which I did being a boy, and in my book of the vanity and uncertainty of Sciences I did, for the most part, retract this book. But here, haply, you may blame me again, saying, "Behold, thou, being a youth, didst write, and now, being old, hast retracted it; what, therefore, hast thou set forth?" I confess, whilst I was very young, I set upon the writing

of these books, but, hoping that I should set them forth with corrections and enlargements—and for that cause I gave them to Trithemius, a Neapolitanian Abbot, formerly a Spanhemensian, a man very industrious after secret things. But it happened afterwards that, the work being intercepted, before I finished it, it was carried about imperfect and impolished, and did fly abroad in Italy, in France, in Germany, through many men's hands; and some men, whether more impatiently or imprudently I know not, would have put it thus imperfect to the press, with which mischief, I, being affected, determined to set it forth myself, thinking that there might be less danger if these books came out of my hands with some amendments than to come forth, torn and in fragments, out of other men's hands. Moreover, I thought it no crime if I should not suffer the testimony of my youth to perish. Also, we have added some chapters and inserted many things which did seem unfit to pass by, which the curious reader shall be able to understand by the inequality of the very phrase, for we were unwilling to begin the work anew and to unravel all that we had done, but to correct it and put some flourish upon it. Wherefore, I pray thee, courteous reader, weigh not these things according to the present time of setting them forth, but pardon my curious youth if thou find any thing in them that may displease thee.

Desiderius Erasmus   (letter date 1533)

SOURCE: A letter to Henry Cornelius Agrippa on April 21, 1533, in *A Renaissance Treasury,* edited by Hiram Haydn and John Charles Nelson, Doubleday & Company, Inc., 1953, pp. 394-95.

[*A Dutch classical scholar, philosopher, writer, and translator, Erasmus is one of the dominant intellectual figures of Renaissance Europe. His most famous work,* The Praise of Folly *(1509), written in Latin, is a powerful satire on clerical hypocrisy. Here, he praises Agrippa's* On the Uncertainty and Vanity of the Sciences, *but warns him of the dangers of becoming embroiled in disputes with the monks who considered his work heretical.*]

I wrote to you at first in few words, to the effect that the doctrine of your book on the **Vanity of Sciences** had pleased some of the most learned in these parts. I had not then read the book, but soon afterwards, having obtained it, I bade a famulus read it aloud at supper, for I had no other vacant time, and am myself compelled to abstain after supper from all study. I liked the courage and the eloquence, nor do I see why the monks should have been so angry. As you attack the bad, you praise the good, but they like altogether to be praised. What I advised you before, I would advise you now, that if you conveniently can, you extricate yourself from this contention. Take Louis Barguin for a warning, whom nothing ruined but his simple freedom towards monks and theologians, he being a man otherwise of unstained character. I often advised him dexterously to disentangle himself from that business, but the hope of victory misled him. But if you cannot fly, and must hazard the fortune of war, see that you fight from a tower, and do not trust yourself into their hands. Of this, before everything, take heed that you do not mix me up with the matter: I am burdened with more than enough ill will, and this would trouble me, while doing you more harm than good. I asked the same of Barguin, and he promised, but deceived me, trusting more to his own courage than to my advice. You see the end. There would not have been the smallest danger had he yielded to my counsel. Many a time I harped to him that monks and theologians are not to be overcome, even if one had a better cause than St. Paul had. Now, therefore, if I have any influence with you, again and again I would warn you that the task you have undertaken leads to perilous encounters, and may cost you the power of advancing in your studies. At present I have not leisure to say more, for I am writing to several friends. Farewell.

Chambers's Edinburgh Journal   (essay date 1853)

SOURCE: "A Conjuror and a Quack of the Olden Time," in *Chambers's Edinburgh Journal*, Vol. 20, No. 517, November 26, 1853, pp. 340-42.

[*In the excerpt below, the anonymous writer considers Agrippa an example of a scientist more interested in wealth and self-promotion than in new discoveries.*]

In these days of wonder-working and new lights, it may not be amiss to turn our observation to the lights and wonders which awed and astonished our ancestors. The search after the elixir vitae and the philosopher's stone was a dignified and difficult life employment, to say the least of it; and the great alchymists should not be despised or forgotten by electro-biologists, magnetisers, and table-movers. The great physical philosophers of our own time have not been backward in acknowledging the obligations of science to those men of a by-gone age. . . .

[Our] present task is to show how some among them—men of fame and scientific repute—allowed other desires and other aims to corrupt their search after truth. . . .

In the case of Cornelius Agrippa, the desire of fame and a lofty place in the world mingled with his studies, and we are forced to rank him with the great charlatans, rather than with the great philosophers. . . .

Cornelius Agrippa was a native of Cologne. He was born in 1486, and died in 1524. Long before other men of scientific fame had ceased to study at the feet of a master, Agrippa set up claims to be an accomplished alchymist, and had his claims allowed. When he was only twenty years old, his fame had spread to Paris. The doctors and alchymists of that city sent to Cologne, inviting the young adept to come and settle among them, and to give them the benefit of his wisdom and experience in their search after the philosopher's stone. In no case of the kind do we meet with higher pretensions to extraordinary powers than in that of Cornelius Agrippa. The transmutation of metals, which others are said to have achieved after a long and laborious process, he was believed to have the power of effecting by a word. He could call upon all manner of spirits, and 'they would come when he did call on them,' as they would not at the call of Glendower, or a dozen Glendowers. His power to evoke the spirits of men long passed away from this earth, was not doubted in his own day, nor long after. Most of our readers are acquainted with the tradition alluded to by Sir Walter Scott in the *Lay*

of the Last Minstrel, which tells how the learned Erasmus, and other men of cultivation, including our English Lord Surrey, prevailed on Agrippa to call up in bodily presence before them several of the famous philosophers of Greece and Rome. On this occasion, too, he is said to have made the ghosts speak to some effect; and Cicero was induced to deliver for their benefit his famous oration for Roscius. Every lover of poetry and romance knows also the tradition which says, that Lord Surrey, then in Germany, saw, in a magic mirror presented to his eyes by Agrippa, the form of his beloved and far-distant Geraldine, as she was actually employed at the moment—namely, lying on a couch reading Lord Surrey's poems, and weeping for his return—a circumstance not likely to be forgotten, or treated lightly by the author or the lover. At the request of the Emperor Charles V., Cornelius Agrippa is said to have evoked the forms of the great Hebrew monarchs, David and Solomon. *Credat Judieus.* There is a marvellous story told of his raising to life for several hours a pupil of his, who, during his absence, had presumed to enter his sanctum, and was struck dead by the guardian spirits of the place. This resuscitation was not prompted by pity for the poor prying youth, but by his own fear of exciting the suspicions of his fellow-townsmen. These, however, he did not escape; and fearing the result of the judicial inquiries instituted, he left the city (Louvain) with undignified celerity. Throughout his life, he was a denizen of courts, and held offices under some of the most distinguished potentates of the time. Early in life, he was made secretary to the Emperor Maximilian, who gave him the command of a regiment, though he knew as much of military matters as of the true method of scientific investigation. He was afterwards appointed physician to Louisa of Savoy, mother of Francis I. He foretold a splendid fortune to the celebrated Constable of Bourbon. He was invited by Henry VIII. to take up his abode in his court, but Agrippa probably feared the caprices of the cholerie monarch, and would not put his neck in jeopardy. He was afterwards an honoured resident at the court of the Archduchess Margaret, the governess of the Netherlands; and she obtained for him the post of historiographer to the Emperor Charles V. It was while he was in her service that he resided at Louvain. For her he wrote a treatise on ***The Vanity and Nothingness of Human Knowledge,*** and another on the ***Superiority of the Female Sex,*** neither of which bears the impress of genius or talent; nor is it easy for those who have considered his character and conduct impartially, to believe that he wrote what he thought *true* in either.

After the death of his kind friend and patroness, the popular feeling against him prevailed, and he was imprisoned on a charge of sorcery at Brussels. He was set at liberty after a year, and left the Low Countries. He lived in obscurity, and, some say, in absolute poverty, until the year 1534, when he died.

In the life of Cornelius Agrippa, it is a significant fact that there is much more talk of court favour, place seeking and holding, of marvels wrought to astonish the great and win their favour, than of long years of patient study, and that earnest desire for leisure and retirement from the world which are ever characteristic of the genuine student and lover of science. . . .

The Eclectic Review   (essay date 1857)

SOURCE: "Cornelius Agrippa," in *The Eclectic Review,* n. s. Vol. 1, May, 1857, pp. 467-88.

[*In the excerpt below, an anonymous reviewer briefly describes a number of Agrippa's writings, portraying him as a misunderstood and tragic figure.*]

[Agrippa's *On the Nobleness and Superiority of the Female Sex*] is a very learned but exaggerated assertion of the superiority of women to men; every weakness—physical, mental, moral—being exalted into a merit. One can scarcely conceive such a production to be the serious accomplishment of a serious mind, its extravagant perversion of fact and argument so much resembling that grave banter which is the most pungent ridicule. Some of the items are amusing: —

> It is because she is made of purer matter that a woman, from whatever height she may look down, never turns giddy, and her eyes never have a mist before them, like the eyes of men.
>
> Even after death nature respects her inherent modesty, for a drowned woman floats on her face, and a drowned man upon his back.
>
> The noblest part of a human being is the head; but the man's head is liable to baldness, —woman is never bald.
>
> The man's face often is made so filthy with a most odious beard, and so covered with sordid hairs, that it is scarcely to be distinguished from the face of a wild beast; in women, on the other hand, the face always remains pure and decent.
>
> The gift of speech is the most excellent of human faculties. Man receives this gift from woman, from his mother or his nurse; and it is a gift bestowed upon woman herself with such liberality that the world has scarcely seen a woman who was mute. Aristotle may say that of all animals the males are stronger and wiser than the females, but St. Paul writes that '*weak things have been chosen to confound the strong.*' Adam was sublimely endowed, but woman humbled him; Samson was strong, but woman made him captive; Lot was chaste, but woman seduced him; David was religious, but woman disturbed his piety; Solomon was wise, but woman deceived him; Job was patient, and was robbed by the devil of fortune and family; ulcerated, grieved, and oppressed, nothing provoked him to anger till a woman did it, therein proving herself stronger than the devil.
>
> Was ever orator so good or so successful that a courtezan could not excel his powers of persuasion? What arithmetician by false calculation would know how to cheat a woman in the payment of a debt? What musician equals her in song and amenity of voice? Does not the old nurse very often beat the doctor?

When Cornelius compounded all these truths and trash, it ought to be told that he was in love with a certain choice sample of womanhood, a young Switzer, and that she probably sat before his imagination while he sketched his portrait of female perfection. Love coloured the picture which talent at the bidding of ambition drew. It is some satisfaction to know that the young doctor of divinity gained a good wife in consequence of his lucubration, one Jane Louisa Tyssie, of Geneva, although he failed in his more remote object, that of securing such exalted patronage as was to moor the barque of his fortunes in the haven of prosperity. . . .

His treatise on the *Vanity of Sciences,* a kind of slur on all knowledge and professions, a recantation of his own whole life, and a misanthropic satire on men and their manners, made its appearance [around 1530]. It clenched his ruin. Indiscriminate in its reprobation of pretension, folly, and wrong, it made enemies in all professions and quarters. With the courts of princes, the colleges of professors, the cloisters of cenobites, he made especially free, and this, coupled with the progress of the Reformation in Germany at large, sealed his doom. His princess-patron was also just dead, whose decease he bemoaned in a graceful and learned eulogy, so that he had no one to interpose between himself and imperial neglect or sacerdotal vengeance. His book of occult sciences, *De Philosophiâ Occultâ,* circulated widely in MS., now first saw the light: the composition, in its crude form, of a youth, the accumulation of all the intervening years, and in any case rather a summary of the opinions held upon the subject than a profession of his own belief. Of this hear his own words: —

> I confess that there are very many vain things and curious prodigies taught for the sake of ostentation in books of magic; cast them aside as emptiness, but do not refuse to know their causes. Where I err, or have too freely spoken, pardon my youth, for I was less than a youth when I composed this work, so that I might excuse myself, and say, 'When I was a child, I spoke as a child, I had knowledge as a child; but now that I am a man, I have put away from me childish things;' and a great part truly of what is in this book, I have retracted in my book upon the *Vanity and Uncertainty of Sciences.*

Why print this, then? Simply because others would print spurious copies of the work, to the great injury of his reputation and finances, if he did not anticipate their peculation; to which we may add, a paternal affection, perhaps, for the first-born of his thoughts. But though he thus studiously claimed for his publication the character of a curious compilation, in which he indulged only that half-belief which is the mongrel offspring of scepticism and science, the work afforded a handle for malignity to compass his detraction, and a ground, however false, for denouncing him as a wizard, conjuror, and whatever is most opposed to *sana fides et mores sani.* The soft and feminine side of his character, his love for dogs, was enlisted in the cause of his detractors, and his canine pets, of which he cherished almost a kennel—Monsieur, Mademoiselle, Tarot, Franza, Musa, Ciccone, Balassa—were represented as so many familiars of the magician. One was especially the agent of the devil, a black pug, which used to lie on his table, and crouching among his papers. Now if this simple fact were sufficient to condemn our learned knight, we reviewers can scarcely hope to escape like reprobation, for it is both our wont and delight to write at a large table, whereon our little Fritz protendeth himself at full length, pouring the inspiration of his love and wonder into our soul as our pen travels along the paper, out of his most expressive brown eyes. To revert to Agrippa; give a dog a bad name, and you may hang him. While the best, the most learned, independent, and generous souls were on his side, the sycophants, the sneaks, the snobs, and the snakes—a large class, who both hiss loudly and sting fatally—were against him. He is poor—he can possess no merit, said the courtiers; he does not believe in the infallibility of the church, the impeccability of divines, the impecuniosity of monks—he is the devil, said the priests. And these two large classes carried the greater part of the world with them; and the struggling scholar, the softhearted householder, the ingenious interrogator and interpreter of nature, the gentle soldier, who filled with love every creature on whom his shadow fell, down to the very brutes who revered in him the image of God, sunk beneath universal prejudice. . . .

Putnam's Monthly Magazine of American Literature, Science and Art (essay date 1857)

SOURCE: "Cornelius Agrippa – Doctor, Knight, and Magician," in *Putnam's Monthly Magazine of American Literature, Science and Art*, Vol. IX, No. XLIX, January 1857, pp. 70-79.

[*Here, an anonymous reviewer provides an overview of Henry Morley's* Life of Cornelius Agrippa Von Nettesheim *(1856), favorably commenting on several of Agrippa's works.*]

Where Agrippa is known, he is known as a magician. In the sixteenth century, everybody knew that he was in commerce with the devil, to whom he had sold his soul. Charitable Butler only says that

> Agrippa kept a Stygian pug
> I'th garb and habit of a dog,
> That was his tutor, and the cur
> Read to the occult philosopher,
> And taught him subtly to maintain
> All other sciences are vain.

But Southey copies a monkish tale describing his study:

> The letters were written with blood therein,
> And the leaves were made of dead man's
> skin.

And there was no doubt, in the days of Sir Walter Raleigh, that such was the fact, and that the wretched sorcerer had been better burnt. We shall now see, under the guidance of Mr. Morley, what basis underlay this opinion. The task should be the more grateful, as it must incidentally open up a page in the world's history which we, at all events, in fast America, are hastening to forget; also, because it can hardly fail to shed some not uncertain light upon the commencement of that great struggle for freedom of thought and opinion which we call the Reformation. Viewed from so lofty an eminence as the life of Agrippa—who, sorcerer or not, was a scholar, not second to Erasmus, a theologian of high degree, a learned physician, a famous soldier, a lawyer of note, and, perhaps, the first

physicist of his day—that memorable passage in history cannot but be seen to advantage. . . .

[Reuchlin's *Mirific Word*, on which Agrippa delivered a course of lectures at Dôle,] was a cabalistic work. "When Adam was in Paradise," said certain of the Rabbis, "the angel Raziel appeared to him and gave him a book containing all the secrets of nature, and all the divine wisdom." This book, handed down miraculously from generation to generation, reached the hands of Solomon, who learnt from it his matchless sagacity. It was lost, perhaps, or destroyed in some of the Jewish convulsions; but some stray scraps of its cunning floated down the tide of time to certain Jews of the middle ages, who embodied them in works of high and holy import. These works were said to relate to the *cabala*. They purported to furnish a key to the interpretation of the hidden meaning of scripture, which hidden meaning was to be discovered by a subtle study of the letters, words, and sentences of the chapters of the Old Testament. Especially vital was the spelling and pronunciation of names. It was by a right knowledge of names—which, the scripture tells us, are written in heaven—that the ancient prophets performed their miracles; and, above all other names in importance, was the name of Jehovah. "Whoever," said the cabalists, "knows the true pronunciation of the name Jehovah, has the world in his mouth." That "mirific word" is a spell by the aid of which all miracles can be performed.

It was upon this mirific word that the "father of the reformation," the teacher of Luther and Melancthon, Reuchlin, had composed his great cabalistic work, weaving the Jewish cabala into a sort of philosophical system, and intermingling with it whatever seemed consistent and beautiful in the doctrines of Pythagoras and Plato, together with not a little astrological science. This was the work which the soldier, Cornelius Agrippa, expounded with zealous encomium before the university of Dôle. His learning, his eloquence, his impressive delivery, carried everything before them. [His patroness] Margaret acknowledged him as her servant, and the university created him a doctor of divinity.

For the still higher honor of his noble mistress, Agrippa now composed his first great work to prove the superiority of woman over man. A few of his arguments illustrate the learning and habit of thought of the age. Man was called Adam, which means Earth; but woman Eva, which means Life. By as much, therefore, as life is better than earth, woman excels man. Next comes the idea which Burns has so prettily versified—that woman, being the last work of God, was necessarily the perfection of the adornment of the heavens and the earth. Passing to physical considerations, Agrippa asserts that woman is made of purer matter than man, as is shown by her never turning giddy from whatever height she may look down—by her superior buoyancy to man's in water—by the fact that, when a woman is washed, if she wash in a second water she will not soil it, whereas a man, if he wash in ten successive waters, will soil them all. Natural history, likewise, proves the superiority of the female sex. Among the eagles, the queens of the air, there never was a male found; while no female basilisk, the most pestilent of serpents, was ever hatched. With such arguments, intermingled with copious quotations from sacred and profane writers, gallant Agrippa undertook to prove that the lord of creation was really a lady. What success the thesis may have had with his royal mistress, we are left to conjecture; but it probably answered the author's purpose in another quarter, for we find that, within a few weeks of its completion, he married a gentle and beautiful Genevoise, Jane Louisa Tyssie.

It was during the honey-moon that the young philosopher, wholly unconscious of impending danger, began the laborious work of gathering all the magical lore, he had acquired, into a book. It was almost a forbidden topic. The church disapproved of it; witches were hanged or burnt; still, Cornelius Agrippa set about his task. "I know not," says he,

> whether it be an unpardonable presumption in me that I, a man of so very little judgment and learning, should, in my very youth, set upon a business so difficult, so hard, and so intricate as this. Wherefore, whatsoever things have here been already, and shall afterwards be, said by me, I would not have any one assent to them, nor shall I myself, any further than they shall not suffer the reprobation of the universal church and congregation of the faithful.

He divided the subject into three heads—the elementary, the celestial, and the terrestrial world. After having, in the first book, discoursed upon earth, air, fire, and water, as the four elements, and disserted upon their qualities, he goes on to show how all bodies possess "occult powers," which powers may be detected by signs. The grand principle for their detection is that "like turns to like." Therefore, "if we would obtain any property or virtue, let us look for things or animals in which such property or virtue is largely developed and use them." Thus, to promote love, take a dove; to increase boldness, take the heart or eyes of a lion or cock; to make a woman tell her secrets, lay the heart of a screech-owl over her heart when she is asleep; to live long, eat a viper. Parts of animals that are used should be taken from them while they are alive. A live duck applied to the pit of the stomach will cure colic, but the duck will die. The eye of a serpent, if the serpent be allowed to escape alive after losing his eye, will cure ophthalmia; and the tooth of a mole, which runs away alive after leaving the dentist's hands, is certain to take away toothache. The author next proceeds to show the influence of the various planets over each other, and over the earth—"not only vital, but angelical and intellectual gifts may be drawn from above." How they are to be drawn is left in some obscurity; the planets are classed and reclassed; the necessity of placing one's self in conjunction with the one whose influence it is desired to conciliate, is strongly insisted upon; but the actual modus operandi is not so clear. However, by "a right understanding of things celestial and terrestrial," notable truths may be discovered. Thus the hidden virtues of the civet-cat may be detected, namely, the power of her blood, which, sprinkled on a door, is a talisman against sorcery; the power of her eye, which, administered in a decoction, renders the person who takes it odious to all; and the power of her bowel, which, taken internally in a decoction, is a charm against

the tyranny of princes. So of swords: a bit, made out of a sword wherewith a man has been killed, will tame the fiercest horse, and wine, into which has been dipped a sword with which men have been beheaded, will cure fever and ague. The stars operate on fumes and give to them occult powers. Thus, the liver of a chameleon, burnt on the top of a house, raises showers and lightnings; the burnt hoof of a horse drives away mice; while the fume of spermaceti and lignum aloes, pepperwort, musk, saffron, and red styrax, tempered with the blood of a lapwing, will, if it be used about the graves of the dead, gather together spirits and ghosts.

The second book of magic begins with an inquiry into numbers. The Pythagoreans preferred before all others the number four; Agrippa does not condemn the choice. It signifies solidity, as the origin of a square. There are four elements, four seasons, four qualities of things, heat, cold, dryness, and moisture; four letters in the name of God, in most languages; four evangelists in the Bible, four beasts standing round the throne in Revelations. Five is the sign of wedlock, being composed of a female number, two, and a male number, three. Six stands for the world. Seven was entitled the vehicle of life, as containing body and soul, that is to say, the four elements of the body, spirit, flesh, bone, and humor, and the three elements of the soul, reason, passion, and desire. Man's life is divided into stages of seven years; with the tenth seven it ends. There are seven main parts of the body: beyond seven days, life cannot be sustained without food; beyond seven hours, it cannot continue without health. Seven is the number of rest, as the Lord rested on the seventh day: whence, it was a sacred number among the Jews: in Hebrew, to seven meant to swear. There are seven planets; seven angels round the throne; seven openings in the head. Eight signifies justice, because, when divided, it forms perfect and equal halves, each of which may be subdivided equally. So on to one hundred, each number has a significance of its own, which, rightly interpreted, and considered in conjunction with the stars, may help the understanding of many things which seem obscure or accidental.

The third and last book treats of magic as connected with religion. The creed, which the author professes, is that of the Christian church of his day, somewhat etherealized and refined. But with this he intermingles the cabala of the Hebrews, and adopts the cabalistic opinion, that certain sacred names, and others profane, such as Abracadabra, when written or pronounced in a particular manner, possess the occult power of curing diseases, evoking spirits, and performing other wonderful works.

In brief, this work of Agrippa's was an olla-podrida made of the Pythagorean, the Platonic, and the Cabalistic philosophies; an attempt to fuse them into a consistent system, and to reconcile them with the crude popular notions of the time, touching natural science—the whole designed to teach spiritual virtues, and point man heavenward. It contained, of course, many statements which one can hardly read without a smile; but, as compared with its cotemporaries, it was a prodigy of learning; and, however mistaken in many of the tenets it proposed, its main object was worthy and honorable. The whole purport of the book was expressed in a passage which occurs in one of the chapters devoted to astrology. "For," says Agrippa,

> accident can, in no case, be a prime sufficient cause, and we must, in all things, look higher, and find out a cause which may know and govern the effect. This is not material but immaterial, and may be in men's souls; in departed spirits; in celestial intelligences; or in God himself. The power of man's mind, strongly exerted, may control dead matter, and govern even the throwing of the dice aright.

That is, a doctrine which, if I mistake not, has been advanced by persons who have never been called magicians.

The work, not printed but fairly transcribed, was handed to the most learned men of the day—Trithemius, among others, then at the height of his fame—all with one accord praised it, pronounced it almost beyond praise . . . .

"All science," [writes Agrippa in *The Vanity of Sciences and Arts and the Excellence of the Word of God*],

> is vain. Letters are a delusion. Grammarians have never been able to decide whether gerunds are nouns or verbs; how many pronouns there are; or whether H is a letter. Poets have pickled the bestialities of the gods in neat verse, communicating the same to posterity, as mad dogs venom. Historians are at such variance, one with another, that it is impossible but most of them must be the greatest liars in the world. Sophists are so stupidly employed that their whole business seems to be to err. Arithmetic is such idle and uncertain labor that among arithmeticians has arisen that irreconcilable dispute—whether an odd or an even number is most to be preferred. Music is a vagrant, wandering up and down after its hire. Dancing is a part of wantonness, geometry is so uncertain that no man can square the circle. Optics is a vain and useless science, invented for ostentation and full of impostures. Geography is an endless series of contentions. Architecture is the home of vanity.

Cornelius handles astrology, magic, and the cabala more tenderly, as one who has been a disciple; still he admits that they may be turned to bad uses, and recants somewhat of his earlier work.

Turning to man, he shows how vain are the best opinions about the soul. No two philosophers can agree where it resides, or what it is. Equally uncertain are men's opinions on politics and religion. What vanity in the "greedy sacerdotal race hungry for gain, which, not only out of wood and stone, but out of the bones of the saints, make instruments of rapine and extortion!" How vain church holidays; priestly despotism, monkish depravity! As to the court, it is

> a college of giants; a convent of noble and famous knaves; a theatre of the worst satellites; a school of the most corrupt morals; an asylum for execrable sins. There none prosper but flatterers, whisperers, detractors, slanderers, sycophants, liars, authors of discord and outrage among the people, whatever there is worst in every beast seems to be brought together in the single flock

of the court-fold; there is the ferocity of the lion, the cruelty of the tiger, the roughness of the bear, the rashness of the boar, the pride of the horse, the greed of the wolf, the obstinacy of the mule, the fraud of the fox, the changefulness of the chameleon, the dog's bite, the camel's vengefulness, the cowardice of the hare, the petulance of the goat, the filthiness of the hog, the fatuity of the ox, the stupidity of the ass, and the ape's jabber.

As to merchants, Agrippa agrees with St. Chrysostom and St. Augustine, who say that no merchant can possibly be saved. Agriculture is a direct produce of the sin of Adam. War is nothing but murder and robbery by mutual consent. Nobility springs out of treason, perfidy, cruelty, massacre, and other crimes, and is maintained by worse. Physic is the art of mechanical homicide. Law, originating in sin, is infirm and subject to change. The calling of advocates is to pervert equity.

The work ends with a learned and elaborate dissertation in praise of the ass. How the brave man's spirit had been broken! . . .

Cornelius Agrippa, doctor, knight, and magician, is one more name to be added to the list of martyrs who died contending for free thought and free speech against the papal hierarchy and the darkness of the times in which he lived.

Lynn Thorndike   (essay date 1941)

SOURCE: "Agrippa and Occult Philosophy," in *A History of Magic and Experimental Science*, Vol. V, Columbia University Press, 1941, pp. 127-38.

[*Thorndike was an eminent scholar of medieval history and scientific activity in the Middle Ages. His major work is the eight-volume* A History of Magic and Experimental Science (1923). *In the following excerpt from a revised edition of that work, Thorndike presents an overview of Agrippa's life and career and offers mixed reviews of* On the Uncertainty and Vanity of the Sciences *and* Occult Philosophy.]

Neither is Henry Cornelius Agrippa of Nettesheim himself to be reckoned of much weight in intellectual history nor is his book on occult philosophy so important a work in the history of magic and experimental science as one might think at first sight. He was not a person of solid learning, regular academic standing, and fixed position, but rather one of those wayward geniuses and intellectual vagabonds so common in the later fifteenth and early sixteenth centuries. In 1509, when not yet twenty-three, he lectured at the university of Dôle on Reuchlin's *De verbo mirifico,* and had a controversy with a Franciscan who called him a Judaizing heretic on that account. Before this in 1507 he had carried on alchemical experiments at Paris and he resumed them in this same year 1509 at Avignon. From 1511 to 1517 he was in Italy, where in 1515 he lectured at Pavia on the Hermetic philosophy and Marsilio Ficino's commentary on the *Pimander.* We find him practising alchemy again at Metz in 1518 and 1519, as well as courageously defending a woman who had been hounded down by the mob and inquisitor as a witch. In 1520 he was at Cologne and at Geneva, where he married a second time. Presently he became municipal physician of Fribourg, although he had no medical degree. He never stayed anywhere long, generally contrived to get into trouble wherever he went, and, like Paracelsus, left in a huff. His interest in the doctrines of reformers and Protestants—in 1519 he corresponded with Jacques Lefèvre d'Étaples, in 1525 he possessed books of Luther and Carlstadt—also tended to lay him open to suspicion.

Failing to hold any university teaching position permanently, Agrippa turned to the illicit practice of medicine or to the life of a courtier and office seeker. Having become physician to Louise of Savoy, queen mother of France, while she was at Lyons, he was left behind without pay on her departure, although he was never quite sure whether this was because he had predicted from the stars the success of the duke of Bourbon or because a letter had been brought to her attention in which he told a third person that she abused astrological judgments and was led on by vain hope and superstitious faith. A trip to Paris in an attempt to recover his favor at court was in vain. Next he appears at Antwerp practicing medicine again without a degree during a pestilence. When the plague was over, the local physicians forced him to desist. Birds of a feather flock together, so that we are not surprised to find Agrippa in 1530 addressing to the Grand Council of the Netherlands in session at Malines a defense of Jean Thibault, a contemporary quack and astrologer, against the attack of the physicians of Antwerp, whom he calls envious pigs and defends empiricism against their foolish rational and scholastic medicine. Agrippa would even prefer that mechanical operative medicine which Thessalus said he could teach in six months and which needs no dialectic or mathematics. He asserts that Thibault cured many cases which these doctors had abandoned as hopeless, and that the reason why they did not proceed against him during the epidemic was that they fled from the city at that time.

Agrippa next obtained the post of imperial historiographer, for which he was poorly paid and did little to be paid for. He complained that his work *On the Uncertainty and Vanity of the Sciences,* now first printed in December, 1530, which aroused against him the faculties of Louvain and the Sorbonne, also lost him the imperial favor. Meanwhile in 1531 the first book of his *Occult Philosophy* was published at Antwerp and Paris, a quite inconsistent procedure, since in *De incertitudine* he had specifically recanted the views expressed in this work. But after he had withdrawn to the protection of the archbishop of Cologne, publication was resumed at that place in November, 1532. The inquisitor, Dominicans and theologians of the university of Cologne made difficulties and delayed publication, however, so that the full text of the three books appeared only in July, 1533, without name of place or printer. John Wier, who later wrote against the witchcraft delusion, was with Agrippa at Bonn in 1535 as pupil and amanuensis. The next year Agrippa again resumed his wanderings and met his death. Gesner, writing in 1545, states that Agrippa, a golden knight and doctor of both laws, had died in Grenoble within a decade or thereabouts reduced to extreme poverty. Thus his troubled, chequered career, marked by no particular distinction but by poverty and bickerings, seemed to end in failure. But he had exerted

considerable influence during his lifetime by a fairly wide correspondence with learned men, and, while his medical practice and genius had been far inferior to those of Paracelsus, he had succeeded in publishing his chief works before his death as Paracelsus had failed to do. These works rapidly became well known, perhaps more because they were generally prohibited and because they gave vent to two leading intellectual currents of the time, occultism and scepticism, than because of any intrinsic worth.

Before, however, we come to estimate the contents of Agrippa's *De occulta philosophia,* let us note further by a thumbing of his letters a few hints that all through his life the occult arts and sciences had been his major interest. Despite the professed recantation in *De incertitudine* and occasional expressed scepticism as to astrology, he was not untrue to himself in printing, despite strong opposition, as probably his last publication towards the end of his life, this work begun in his youth and of which he had presented a first draft to Trithemius in 1510.

Throughout his life Agrippa was a devotee of the Cabala. On April 30, 1512, he writes from Pavia to father Chrysostom that he sends him the cabalistic book he desired and assures him that "this is that divine science sublimer than all human striving" and that he should conceal in silence in his breast "this wholly sacred and divine art." Or in May, 1525, a friend promises to bring Agrippa "the cabalistic art with many books of Raymond Lull." Or in 1532 Agrippa writes to Bernard, majordomo of cardinal Campeggio, that he counts upon him to obtain a copy of the *De arcanis* of Petrus Galatinus, the *Cabala* of Samuel, and the ancient Hebrew alphabet. Bernard replies that he is working day and night upon his mystic cabalistic system. He sends greetings to Ludovicus Lucena, from whom he hopes to have more secret light on the significance of the Hebrew letters. Later he writes again from Bologna to Agrippa that he has already sent the Hebrew alphabet attributed to Esdras and is sending from Venice the book of Galatinus. At Padua he met Franciscus Georgius, who has other books in which they are interested but who said that the *Cabala* of Samuel was disappointing. A Hebrew scholar named Aegidius who died the past month left other books on the Cabala which Bernard will try to procure. All this shows that the unfavorable opinion of the Cabala expressed in *De incertitudine* was either merely an assumed pose to conform to the sweepingly sceptical character of that work or represented but a passing mood from which in 1532 Agrippa returned again to his former favorite field of study.

On the much less dignified, less difficult, and less divine art of geomancy Agrippa had himself composed a treatise and in 1526 sent to Metz for it and also for the work of Trithemius on steganography. In another letter of April 27, 1530 Agrippa apologizes for his delayed arrival because he knows his correspondent is eager to see a geomantic table of Scepper which he is bringing with him. Apparently Scepper's *Assertion of the Faith Against Astrologers* did not keep him from lapsing into a lower form of divination. Nor did Agrippa's own previous practice keep him from writing in *De incertitudine,* after listing earlier geomancies by Hali, Gerard of Cremona, Bartholomew of

Parma, and a certain Tundinus, "I too have written a geomancy quite different from the rest but no less superstitious and fallacious or, if you wish, I will even say 'mendacious.' "

Astrological prediction at times irked Agrippa and was called by him an unworthy artifice or idle superstition, but he seems to have done a good deal of it. Rather characteristic is the letter in which he warns a Dominican, Petrus Lavinius, that judicial astrology is a vain superstition and not for a Christian, but at the same time sends him the judgment for which he had asked. He also sent a prognostication to a friend in Chambery "from which you will judge how fine an astrologer I have become"—perhaps an ironic remark—and one to the queen mother of France, Louise of Savoy, and the next year (1527) to the duke of Bourbon. For erecting figures of the sky he preferred Regiomontanus but used the *Alfonsine Tables* for most other purposes such as the movements and aspects of the stars, although he had tried Bianchini, John de Lineriis, and others. In another letter he calls the *Speculum astronomiae* of Albertus Magnus a work not praised enough. Late in life he refers to past eclipses, comets, earthquakes, floods and more recent prodigies and signs in the sky as all pointing to one conclusion, and declares that "I predict these things to you, not by doubtful methods of conjecture nor acting under the influence of mental perturbation contrary to true reason but from true arts of vaticination, oracles, prediction and foreknowledge."

Agrippa's friends and correspondents looked on him as a fount of information concerning the occult arts. While municipal physician at Fribourg he instructed a number of prominent citizens in such sciences. In 1527 or 1528 a friend asked Agrippa to send him books of chiromancy with which to amuse himself when exhausted by the din of court life. On December 28, 1532, the majordomo of cardinal Campeggio alluded to a mirror that Agrippa had once showed him in which the dead seemed alive. Another correspondent yearned to see Agrippa, to bathe in the waters of occult philosophy, and to unravel the enigmas and secrets of Picatrix and the Cabala. Another wrote to ask for Agrippa's book of natural magic, which he said he had seen at the university of Pavia. This was what was developed by Agrippa into his three books on occult philosophy. At the time he sent an index or abstract, explaining that it would be sacrilege to publish it to the crowd, and that he reserved the key to it for himself and his friends. . . . Again in 1527 came another demand for the work.

As for alchemy, in 1526 the curé Brennonius writes from Metz to Agrippa that "our Tyrius," whose vocation was clock-making and avocation alchemy, "has discovered a sweet water in which every metal is easily dissolved by the heat of the sun." It was made from wine, for he separated the four elements and extracted from earth the nature of sulphur. Brennonius, however, had done the same from chelidonia and believed that the water could also be made from anything putrefied—eggs, flesh, bread or herbs of whatever sort. Yet four years later in *De incertitudine* Agrippa was to declare that alchemy should be prohibited.

Perhaps we can see the reason for Agrippa's persistence in occult practices despite occasional scepticism or religious qualms in the following passage.

> Oh! how many writings are read concerning the irresistible power of the magic art, concerning the prodigious images of the astrologers, the marvelous metamorphosis of the alchemists, and that blessed stone which Midas-like turns all to gold or silver at its touch. All which are found vain, fictitious and false as often as they are practiced literally. Yet they are handed down in writings by great and most grave philosophers and holy men whose traditions who will dare to call false? Nay it would be impious to believe that they have written falsehoods in those works. Hence the meaning must be other than the literal sense indicates.

Agrippa's letters also show him interested for a time at least in machines, bridges and military engines, while in *De incertitudine* he alludes to having once been put in charge of some mines by the emperor and having started to write a book on mining and metallurgy. But he was to a large extent a dabbler and trifler who did not adhere to any given interest for long, just as he did not stay in any one place. Except that always he kept coming back to occult science. Even in *De incertitudine* he gives information and reveals his knowledge of the field of occult science, devoting a score of its 85 chapters to occult arts and listing past writers on such subjects as chiromancy and natural magic. But it is of course to his *De occulta philosophia* that we especially turn for his attitude to the occult arts and sciences.

[It] is a disappointing book. It is not a practical manual or even a general theory of the subject but merely a literary description and review, full of what the author doubtless flattered himself was erudite allusion and humanistic eloquence, but vague, totally lacking in precision, and written in the pseudo-Platonic, mooning style of Iamblichus, Ficino and Reuchlin rather than the direct practical tones of Roger Bacon and Albertus Magnus. Cabalistic matter and manner far exceed any natural magic. Despite the title, there is little philosophy to the work, and the author has nothing new to say on his subject. He has read widely in its past literature and is valuable in a scattering way for its bibliography. Yet even in this respect he has failed to achieve anything like an exhaustive or systematic review. Sometimes past writers are misquoted or misunderstood, as when it is asserted that Aquinas in his third book against the Gentiles admits that the human soul can be joined with the celestial intelligence and work marvels. Or the dubious, if not spurious, *De fato* is cited to show that Aquinas held that works of art receive a certain quality from the stars, whereas really this is just what he explicitly denies in his works of undoubted authenticity. While the book is diffuse and mystical, a much better and meatier encyclopedia of ancient and medieval magic might have been composed than Agrippa's, which seems a hasty rather than thorough piece of work, despite the fact that the author had been so long occupied with it.

Sometimes Agrippa's work may preserve bits from earlier writers that otherwise would not be extant, but this is not often the case. Richard Argentinus, writing in 1563, asserts that Cornelius Agrippa in his **Occult Philosophy** stole from the libraries of magic of John Torresius of Spain and Bellisarius Petrucius magic characters which he reproduced only faultily because of his ignorance of Syriac.

The work divides into three books corresponding to the three worlds of the cabalists: elemental, celestial or mathematical, and intellectual. Magic is said to embrace the knowledge of all nature. Occult virtues are not of any element but a sequel of a thing's species and form. They are implanted in the species of things by the ideas from the world soul through the stars, and even individuals of the same species may receive different occult virtues from the stars. Sympathy and likeness are the guiding principle or key in the investigation of these occult properties. Agrippa then treats of the distribution of inferior things under the planets and how through natural things and their virtues we can attract the influences of the heavenly bodies and even penetrate to intellectual, demonic and divine forces. The last dozen chapters or so (58-70) of the first book deal with the magical possibilities of the human mind, soul and words, for although these might be regarded as more intellectual than elemental, they are presumably regarded as sunk and bound in this lower world of the elements and body.

The second book is first occupied with the symbolism and virtues of numbers and letters of the alphabet and then with astrology. If there are great occult virtues in natural objects, much more is this the case with numbers which are more purely form and closely related to the celestial bodies and separate substances. Scales are given for the numbers up to twelve. Take two, for example. For the archetype we have the name of God in two letters, in the intellectual world are angel and soul, in the celestial world sun and moon, in the elemental world earth and water, in the microcosm heart and brain, in the inferno Behemoth and Leviathan. Divination by attributing numerical values to letters, astrological images, geomantic figures, and the names of the planets to be employed in magic incantations are other features of the second book.

In an early chapter of the third book Agrippa hints that such ceremonies as excommunicating worms and locusts to save the crops or baptizing bells are relics of the perverse religions of the Chaldeans, Egyptians, Assyrians, Persians and Arabs of the past. But soon he is immersed in cabalistic lore of divine names. The subsequent discussion of demons lacks unity and is a hodge-podge from previous writers, yet by no means covers the various descriptions and classifications of them to be found in classical, patristic and later medieval writers. After some consideration of necromancy and evoking the souls of the dead, we return again to the power of the human soul, to various forms of divination and to ceremonial observances. The work ends with an injunction of secrecy.

Whatever its defects, Agrippa's **De occulta philosophia** gave a more general presentation of the subject than could be found elsewhere, at least in print. Partly on this account, partly because of its daring enunciation of certain suspect doctrines such as that of a world soul, partly because of advertising which it received by being placed on various lists of prohibited books and *Indexes,* it found a

number of editions and readers during the next two centuries. In 1565 or 1567 was added an apocryphal fourth book of an extreme magical character which appealed further to prurient ears, although Wier defended Agrippa from the attribution of it to him [in his *De praestigiis daemonum,* 1564]. Agrippa became the hero or villain of legendary tales in the handbooks on witchcraft. Delrio and Boquet tell of a pupil of his at Louvain entering the master's study during Agrippa's absence and opening a book of adjurations. A demon promptly appeared, and the youth died either of fright or because attacked by the demon. When Agrippa returned and saw the dead body, he in turn invoked the demon, whom he forced to enter the corpse, to take a few turns about the square in the presence of other scholars, and then to leave the body which fell to the ground as if the youth died only then, thus clearing Agrippa of suspicion as the cause of his death. But his flight into Lorraine soon followed. Boquet further asserts that Charles V banished Agrippa and two companions from his court and territories.

Rumor was also rife as to the relations between Agrippa and his dog. Bodin in his *Démonomanie* of 1580 called Agrippa the greatest sorcerer of his time and Wier not only his disciple but valet and servitor, "drinking, eating and sleeping with him, as he confesses, after Agrippa had repudiated his wife." Bodin added that Paul Jovius and others had written that Agrippa's black dog, which he called Monsieur, so soon as Agrippa passed away in the hospital at Grenoble, hurled itself into the river before everyone's eyes and was never seen again. Bodin concludes that Wier says that it was not Satan in the guise of a dog, as well as that he led it after Agrippa on a leash, and that the dog lay between him and Agrippa [in his *De la démonomanie des sorciers,* 1580]. Wier appears to be slandered in this passage as much as Agrippa or the dog. In the passage to which Bodin alludes, Wier refers to the report that Agrippa's dog was a demon. He states that it was a medium sized black dog called Monsieur with a bitch named Mamselle. Agrippa used to fondle Monsieur excessively, and allowed him beside him at table and in his bed at night, after he had repudiated his wife of Malines at Bonn in 1535. "And when Agrippa and I were eating or studying together, this dog always lay between us." The fact that Agrippa, without leaving his quarters, knew what was going on in foreign parts was due to letters which he received daily from learned men in various regions, but was attributed by popular report to information received from the dog, acting as his familiar demon. Of Agrippa's end Wier says merely that he went from Bonn to Lyons where he was imprisoned a while by Francis I for having written against the queen mother. "Freed by the intercession of certain persons, after some months he fell asleep in the Lord at Grenoble in Dauphiné. At that time I was in Paris" [*De praestigiis daemonum,* edition of 1583].

Cardan, in connection with the horoscope of Agrippa, gave an estimate of him which is worth repeating. Born poor, he made a pretense to knowledge. Jupiter endowed him with comradery and urbanity to the point of scurrility. Mercury made him ingenious, versatile, mutable, deceitful, tricky and studious. But the tail of the dragon in the degree of the ascendent made him not apt for disciplines. Cardan regarded his *De occulta philosophia* as full of trifles and falsehoods and deserving to be burned. As for *De vanitate scientiarum,* Cardan thought its main argument bad, and that Agrippa showed his ignorance in treating things of which he knew nothing. "Yet the book pleases many as chaff does asses" [*Opera*, 1663]. Tycho Brahe referred to Agrippa as "that most worthless fabricator of vanities" [*Astronomiae instauratae progymnasmata: Opera, III,* 1916].

Joseph Leon Blau   (essay date 1944)

SOURCE: "The Fantastic Cabala," in *The Christian Interpretation of the Cabala in the Renaissance.* Columbia University Press, 1944, pp. 78-88.

[*Blau examines Agrippa's writings in the context of sixteenth-century study of the cabala.*]

In the sixteenth century magic was well-nigh respectable. Many of the most noted men of the century dabbled in it; to some, as to Marlowe's Doctor Faustus, magic spelled power. The universities did not teach magic, but many of their students practiced it. Magic went far beyond mere formulas of incantation; its doctrines were of far greater import than its practices. Much of the most original thinking of the period is to be found in books on magic.

Among the followers and students of the magical art cabala developed considerable popularity. It became, as it were, a part of the philosophic background required of each member of this fantastic fringe of the intellectual life. It is true that often when the word "cabala" was used the doctrine in no way resembled that of the Hebrew cabala. . . .

Some, however, of the sixteenth-century devotees of the magical art actually meant cabala when they used the word, and of these the most distinguished was Henry Cornelius Agrippa of Nettesheim (1486-1535). Agrippa's interest in the cabala was stimulated by Reuchlin, whose *De verbo mirifico* the young occultist studied with great care. As early as 1509 Agrippa delivered a public exposition of Reuchlin's work. His biographer, Henry Morley, explains that by 1509 Agrippa had collected the notes for a complete treatise on magic; some, of course, were from fellow members of secret societies interested in magic, but many "were obtained from Reuchlin's Hebrew-Christian way of using the Cabala" [*The Life of Henry Cornelius Agrippa*]. In order to earn the good will of Margaret of Austria, Agrippa decided to apply what he had learned in this close study of Reuchlin's work to a series of public orations on the book in honor of her highness, whom he hoped thus to gain as his patron.

We do not know what Agrippa said about Reuchlin's book. We do know that about a year later, when he was in London on a mission on which he had been sent by the Emperor Maximilian, father of Margaret, and while he was staying at the home of Dean Colet, Agrippa responded in a very mild way to an attack made upon his orations by the monk Johannes Catilinet.

This *Expostulation* was extremely Christian in tone. It was produced at a time when the vicious attacks on

Reuchlin by the Cologne Dominicans were in the air, and when the equally vicious but somewhat more toleration-conscious defenses of Reuchlin by Ulrich von Hutten and others were being composed. Yet Agrippa quietly pointed out that he was a Christian, not a "Judaizing heretic," and that the work he defended in public auditory and for whose defense he was rewarded with "a lectureship, the position of Regent, and a salary" was that of "a Christian doctor, John Reuchlin of Pforzheim." His conclusion is that Catilinet must have erred because of a lack of knowledge of cabala and that if given the opportunity to talk with him, Agrippa could change his views. There is no record of such a conversation having taken place.

Catilinet's attacks were delivered in a series of public orations before the Princess Margaret at the beginning of Lent in 1510. Shortly before this, Agrippa had submitted to the Abbot Tritheim (1462-1516) his work *On Occult Philosophy.* In an accompanying letter he requested Tritheim's criticism and advice about publishing his book.

Tritheim kept the messenger while he read the manuscript, and immediately after completing his reading, April 8, 1510, he sent a note to Agrippa. He advised Agrippa to continue his occult studies, but not to publish his book. He wrote: "Speak of things public to the public, but of things lofty and secret only to the loftiest and the most private of your friends. Hay to an ox, and sugar to a parrot: interpret this rightly, lest you be trampled down by oxen as most others have been." How apt Tritheim's warning against public presentation of occult against ideas was can be seen from the fact that the attack of Catilinet against Agrippa's lectures followed it so closely. Agrippa took heed to his friend's advice. This work on occult philosophy was not published until 1531. By this time Reuchlin's *De arte cabalistica* had appeared, and Agrippa revised his text to include some material from Reuchlin's better book.

When the work *On Occult Philosophy* appeared, it was divided into three books. At the beginning of the first book the author asserts that there are three worlds or realms: the elementary world, the intellectual world, and the celestial world. This is the schema which Pico drew from the work of Recanati. The first book deals with the elementary world, or natural magic. Only at the end does Agrippa suggest the possiblity of magical performance by means of formulas developed from letters, of which, of course, Hebrew letters are most sacred and effective.

> But this you must not be ignorant of, that it is observed by wise men, that the Hebrew letters are the most efficacious of all, because they have the greatest similitude with the celestials and the world, and that the letters of the other tongues have not so great an efficacy because they are more distant from them.

The second book treats of the intellectual world and is chiefly concerned with a statement of the symbolism of numbers. Thus we learn that unity is not a number, but the original of all numbers. We discover, too, that as in the celestial world there is but one God, whose name is written with one letter, so there is in the intellectual world one

Supreme Intelligence. There are similar treatments of the other numbers. . . .

The year 1510, so eventful in the career of Agrippa, as we have seen, also marked the appearance of his glorification of the female sex. This was another of the author's weapons in his attempt to gain the favor of Princess Margaret. The lady had listened to Catilinet's attack on Agrippa and the cabala. Agrippa replied to his opponent not only directly, in his *Expostulation,* but also indirectly, by writing of the merits of women. In the course of this political exercise there is one passage of interest to this study; Agrippa uses the alphabetical technique of the cabalist to prove that there is a closer correspondence between the name "Eve" and the Tetragrammaton than exists between the name "Adam" and that supreme four-letter name of God.

In 1515 Agrippa fought with the Italians against the French at the battle of Marignano. As a result of the French victory he was reduced to penury. In these straits he was aided by the Marquis of Montferrat, who was repaid by receiving the dedication of two treatises, one on man, the other on the threefold way of knowing God. Only the latter has come down to us. . . .

The treatise is in six chapters; the first of these deals with the necessity for seeking to know God; the second presents the three ways of knowing Him: by contemplation of His creatures, by hearing the angels, and by listening to His Son. The next three chapters discuss these three ways in more detail. The final chapter is a more or less formal summary brought into accord with the creed of the church. In the fourth chapter, dealing with the way of knowing God through angels, Agrippa explains that in addition to the written Law handed down to Moses at Mount Sinai, God revealed to the leader of the children of Israel a complete exposition of the true Law, which is contained hermetically in the written Law. Moses, therefore, received two laws, one literal and one spiritual. In accordance with the precept of the Lord, he communicated the written Law to all the people, the spiritual Law only to the seventy elders. This spiritual Law was handed down by word of mouth from generation to generation. It was, therefore, called "cabala," reception.

Cabala is concerned with those things which may be known about God and His angels. It teaches the many names to be used for the invocation of the angels. The doctrine of the Messiah was a part of the original cabala, but since the Messiah, Jesus, has already come, cabala should now be chiefly concerned with the angels.

At this point Agrippa shows an inkling of the development of an attitude which was later to lead him to renounce all his former pursuits as vanity, when he maintains that cabalists have devoted themselves too much to magic and are thus leading to a misunderstanding of the name and purpose of cabala. Cabala in its true sense is necessary, for if one does not know the technique for looking below the surface of the Scriptures one has only the literal sense to go by. Furthermore, if knowledge is of the literal meaning only, "nothing is more ridiculous than the Law, or more like old women's fables and mere wanton talk." Since, however, Christ, the sun of all justice, has come, we no longer need this misty and indirect way of knowing God; we can know Him through His Son. God can be known through the Gospels.

In 1526 Agrippa's dissatisfaction with the conditions of his life led to the composition of a remarkable book on *The Uncertainty and Vanity of the Sciences and Arts,* half satire directed against the schools, half renunciation of all his earlier preoccupations. He attacks, in turn, all the sciences and arts and their subdivisions, showing a wide knowledge, for, at some time or other [according to Morley] "Agrippa had tried nearly every art that he had found wanting. . . . He was not a reviler from without, but a satirist from within, of the uncertainties and vanities of the imperfect art and science of his day." The treatise closes with an exhortation, largely in the words of the Scriptures, that men should attempt to become like-minded with God; and, learning from Jesus, the true Master, should be wise concerning the good, and simple concerning the evil.

Among his other renunciations is the study of cabala. He describes cabala as an ancient Hebrew tradition, known to Christians for only a short time. It is double science: half treats of cosmology, half of "Marcana,"

> which is something of a symbolic theology dealing with sublimer reflections about God, the angelic powers, and sacred names and symbols, in which letters, numbers, figures, things and the names and ornaments of letters, and lines, punctuation, and accents are names significant of most profound things and of great mysteries.

While, he says, there is no doubt that such a secret tradition was handed down to Moses, nevertheless he feels that cabala as practices by the Jews is a rhapsodical superstition, allied to theurgic magic. If there is a wonder-working name, it is Iesv, which the Jews do not recognize. Cabala is, therefore, now only a vain delusion.

This renunciation did not last; as has been seen, by 1531 Agrippa dared to publish his three books on occult philosophy in their revised form. Thus, for a brief period in his life the skeptic was uppermost in him; both before and after this period he was the credulous philosopher of magic. . . .

Arturo Castiglioni   (essay date 1946)

SOURCE: "Natural Magic," in *Adventures of the Mind,* translated by V. Gianturco, 1946. Reprint by Sampson Low, Marston & Co., Ltd., 1946, pp. 257-66.

[*Below, Castiglioni comments on Agrippa's ideas about "natural magic," commending his attempt, "with a magnificent intuition of the truth, to lead magic into the highroad of the observation of nature."*]

Throughout Europe, and particularly in Italy of the fifteenth century, with the revival of learning a first attempt is made by some great scholars to inquire into the problems of the universe, by trying to explain its mysteries rationally. The Humanist, *home doctus,* becomes the type of the new epoch, taking the place of the *homo sanctus.* . . .

The idea of the magic action of the word, of the perfection

of alphabetical characters, of the value of symbol, which . . . was fundamental to the magic of the ancients, springs up again in a new form, higher, vaster, and more complete. The value of letters, words, and symbols was derived from the shared secret, the intellectual communion, of those understanding it. Upon the basis of this idea an entire system was slowly built up at the time when culture began to spread and the return to the classic spirit became visible in Humanism, and the revival of Greek philosophy became manifest. The significance of symbol and letter, like that of the *opus magnum* of alchemists and the calculations of astrologers, is, above all, philosophical and strives for a natural explanation. Ancient magic changes with the change of ideas, with the succession of new spiritual and social events modifying the milieu: the observation of nature, which begins to attract the attention of scholars as the fundamental element of research, attains predominance. Agrippa of Nettesheim, Theophrastus Paracelsus, and G. B. della Porta are the founders or, rather, the organizers of these ideas in a system of natural magic. Restless and independent spirits overwhelmed by struggle and conflict in times of bitter religious and civil wars, thinkers both rebellious and still mystical, impassioned observers still fettered by the bonds of ancient magic beliefs, they are the towering and characteristic figures of that transitional epoch in which natural magic appears and is universally accepted.

Natural magic marks a further stage in the evolution of primitive magic towards experimental science. It detaches itself from the fundamental magic concept as well as from the religious idea, borrows its form of reasoning from philosophy, but adheres to reality in so far as its observations are concerned. Natural magic slowly develops from primitive magic, as observation proceeds and method advances according to the speed with which critical faculties subdue the emotional ones, and the human mind forsakes the notion of supernatural beings and their intervention and seeks for the explanation of nature in the forces of nature itself. Natural magic, on its way to becoming science, carries with it, for a long time, a large part of its ancestral heritage of primitive magic and with difficulty frees itself from some of its beliefs, especially from those most firmly anchored in the deepest strata of the mind. . . . [The] earliest writers, champions of the magic idea and disseminators of occult sciences, repeatedly glimpsed the necessity of criticism and of experience. In an earlier epoch only a few single, isolated individuals faced this problem. Later more and more scholars and research workers, though assuming different attitudes in regard to magical and mystical problems, created a new current of ideas. Maxwell rightly remarks [in *La Magie,* 1925] that this new orientation was earlier manifest in the domain of physical and natural problems, as they lend themselves more readily to observation and criticism.

The evolution of the psychic phenomena of witchcraft is more laborious because the problems are more complex, the causes less easy to establish, and the results less controllable. All the problems concerning the mind remain much longer under the rule of magic and mysticism, because many of them do not appear sufficiently clear. Not until our day has scientific research on the functioning of the brain and on the unconscious, determining the characteristics and origins of certain psychic states (such as hypnotism, suggestion, double personalities, dreams), raised the veil of mystery and illuminated a series of formerly occult phenomena by the light of observation and criticism.

Natural magic begins with the study of atmospheric and astral phenomena and establishes a link between the individual and the elements. It asserts that all phenomena are sympathetically co-ordinated. This doctrine of sympathy enables the practitioners of natural magic to imagine the existence of secret relations and incantational connections. The inborn secret link is asserted between things and their names, which contain the power of the things in the form of their expression. The magic strength of the word derives from its relationship with the thing it designates, and the magical properties of things originate in their forms.

Agrippa of Nettesheim (1456-1535) is the first of the great figures ushering in the new era. The history of his life is a perfect illustration of his studies and mentality. Born of an ancient noble family, he assiduously devoted himself from an early age to the study of languages and passionately collected all the literature on occult sciences, tried his hand at alchemy, and at twenty founded a society for the study of secret sciences in Paris. He lived in France, and visited England and Germany, indefatigably preaching his ideas. He was often persecuted by the ecclesiastical authorities. He wrote his *De occulta philosophia,* which made him famous, in 1510, fought with the Imperial troops against the Venetians, and was knighted on the field of battle. Later he was obliged to defend himself against the accusations of the inquisitors. At Metz, where he supported the cause of some persons who were accused of witchcraft and succeeded in saving them from the death penalty, he himself was accused of being an accomplice of the accused and was forced to flee to Lyon, where he was appointed physician to the King of France. He later became historian at the court of Margaret of Austria, and a physician in Cologne. At last he returned to Lyon, was persecuted by his enemies and misfortune, and died in 1535, famed as a sorcerer.

Among new ideas in the process of formation, and amid the conflict between ancient magic conceptions and the new way of thinking, Agrippa attempted, with a magnificent intuition of the truth, to lead magic onto the highroad of the observation of nature and to explain diabolic and supernatural phenomena as the results of natural forces. Magic occurrences appeared to him as demonstrations and applications of scientific truths; the doctrine of the "sympathy and antipathy of things," which was a fundamental part of ancient Italic philosophy, was reborn. With the decline of Galen's anatomy, of Aristotle's physics, of Ptolemy's astronomical system, ancient magic was gradually forsaken by its followers. Agrippa of Nettesheim, who was called the last of the sorcerers, but might be called the first of the naturalists, placed the idea of magic on a new basis and perceived that everything formerly attributed to magic must be assigned to nature instead.

Natural magic, according to Agrippa, is a science. He claims that a direct and reciprocal relationship exists between the highest and the lowest things, and asserts that every thing is attracted by its likes, which in turn it attracts with all its forces. These secret forces are a part of the spiritual world where ideas exist. However, according to Agrippa, ideas cannot act over things by themselves, nor can matter be put in motion by itself. A medium is necessary, a vital force that can transfer the activity of the spirit to the body, and this medium is the quintessence, the fifth essence, since it is not composed of the four elements but exists beyond and above them. It fulfils the same function in the world as the soul does in the human body, and is therefore the soul of the world. It irradiates from the planets, and the occult qualities of living substances such as minerals and metals stem from it. It may be extracted from one substance and transferred to another. Because of it fire rises towards celestial fire and water flows towards the waters; living beings convert their nourishment into the substance of their organism; and stars, precious stones, plants, and animals exert an influence over men. Its signs are marked on the earth, plants, and man's organs (*law of the signatures*).

Natural magic, according to Agrippa, must, therefore, no longer admit the performance of magic and forbidden operations with the help of the supernatural, but has to search for the secret laws of nature and the utilization of natural forces. Sorcerers, according to this conception, become the priests of science.

In such a scientific belief the magic power of words, however, is important. This doctrine, which goes back to Neoplatonic philosophy but whose beginnings may be traced to a much remoter era, claims that words and names are but the reflection of the creative power of "forms" in God's mind. The same is true of writings. A speech composed of many words has a power greater than that possessed by an isolated word. The value of a magical spell depends on enunciation, on the rhythm and the enthusiasm with which it is uttered, on the emotion and conviction of the sorcerer. Agrippa mentions the example of Orpheus, and states that incantations, uttered with vehemence and passion and under careful observation of the measure and number of their words, endow the enchanter with tremendous strength due to the impetuous outburst of his imagination, and are projected on the object of the spell, binding and directing it in accordance with the desires and words of the magician. The true instrument of spellbinding is a sort of breath, pure, harmonious, and alive, which embodies movement and will, is skilfully composed, endowed will deep feeling, and conceived by reason.

Maxwell rightly observes that Agrippa thereby voices a perfectly modern psychological idea: the idea that the strength of the spell is dependent on the emotional intensity of the spell-caster, and that magical strength dwells in the sphere of passions, whereas reason must conceive the purpose and prepare the methods to encompass it. According to Agrippa, reason's task is to calculate the position of the stars or the numerical proportions between words and things or the mutual relations of things; the task of emotion is that of imparting its direction and force to the magical action. Thus natural magic and modern psychology are closely linked in the evaluation of the power of suggestion.

Hiram Haydn   (essay date 1950)

SOURCE: "The Counter-Renaissance and the Repeal of Universal Law," in *The Counter-Renaissance,* Charles Scribner's Sons, 1950, pp. 131-75.

[*Here, Haydn briefly discusses Agrippa's repudiation of reason and the Law of Nature in* On the Uncertainty and Vanity of the Sciences.]

Agrippa, as does Montaigne after him, assails the divine origin of law and its universal application [in his *Vanitie and Uncertaintie*]. He refers to the determination of "aunciente Lawe makers" to bolster the authority of their laws by persuading ignorant people "that they did as they were taught by the Gods." This same device has served Emperor and Pope alike:

> For this cause Leo the Pope straightly commaunded all Christain people, that noman in the Church of God should presume to iudge any thinge, nor any man, to iustifie nor to discusse any matter: but by the Authoritee of the holy Counsailes, Canons, and Decretals, whose heade is the Pope. . . .

Similarly,

> The like lawe the Emperoure pretendeth to have in Philosophie, Phisicke, and other Sciences, graunting no authoritee to any knowledge, but so much as is geven them by the Skilfulnes of the Lawe. . . .

"Beholde nowe," he declares,

> Yee perceive howe this knowledge of the Lawe presumeth to beare swaye over all other Artes, and exerciseth tyrannie, and howe preferringe it selfe before all other disciplines as it were the firste begotten of the Gods doth despise them as vile and vaine, *although it be altogeather made of nothinge els but of fraile and very weake inventions and opinions of men, which things be of all other the weakest.* . . .

Thus far, Agrippa's and Montaigne's versions tally substantially, except that Montaigne, a loyal if not devout Catholic, forbears, for the most part, from attacking the Mother Church and does not discuss the Canon Law. But at this point in his argument, Agrippa, with the fideistic accent which runs so strongly through the *Vanitie and Uncertaintie,* relates the Law of Nature to the Fall of Man. This "Lawe," he continues, actually

> is altered at every chaunge of time, of the state, and of the Prince, whiche tooke the firste beginninge of the sinne of our firste parent, whiche was cause of all our miseries, from whence *the first Lawe of corrupt nature* proceeded which they tearme the Lawe of nature. . . .

Thus he, and the leaders of the Reformation after him, invalidate not only man's reason and knowledge on the premise of original sin, but also that Law of Nature which is at the heart of man's moral and political life, of all goodness and justice. Listing the "notable decrees" of the "first Lawe of corrupt Nature," he scornfully sets forth a category of the "tooth for a tooth" rights of man, and concludes,

> Finally the Lawe of Nature is that wee shoulde not dye for thirste, for hunger, for colde, and not to hurt our selves with watchinges, and laboure. Whiche abandoning all the repentaunce of Religion, and the workes of repentaunce, dothe appointe the pleasure of the *Epicure* for the chiefest felicitie.

In short, the true Law of Nature which Agrippa (and many others of the Counter-Renaissance with him) recognizes is that of an individualistic, indolent and hedonistic state of nature, wholly remote from the concepts of Thomas Aquinas and the Renaissance Christian humanists. Nor does he spare those other laws, traditionally derived from the Law of Nature:

> Afterwarde the Lawe of Nations arose from whence warre, murder, bondage were derived, & dominions separated. After this came the Civil or Popular Lawe, whiche any people maketh peculiare to himselfe: from whence have growen so many debates among menne, that as the lawes doo witnes, there have ben made more businesses, then there be names of things.

Yet, adopting the early medieval attitude of the Fathers and the Canon Lawyers, that the establishment of civil institutions was necessary, both as a result of, and the remedy for, the vicious desires of corrupt man, Agrippa continues,

> For whereas men were prone and enclined to discorde, the publishinge of iustice whiche was to be observed by meanes of the Lawes was a necessarie thinge: to the end that the boldness of naughty men might in suche wise be bridled: and among the wicked innocencie might be salfe, and the honest might live quietly emonge the dishoneste.

"And," he comments, "these be that so notable beginninges of the Lawe, wherin have benne almost innumerable Lawemakers. . . ."

Yet it must be noted that although Agrippa adopts the patristic and Canonist attitude about the need for coercive government and civil laws to restrain the corrupt natures of men, he omits the one most important emphasis of that attitude. He does not, as did the medievalists, see the establishment of civil society as a measure taken by God. He retains the theological premise of original sin, but he does not attribute the origin of the state and laws to God. On the contrary, he concludes,

> Hereof then we know that al the knowledge of the Civill Lawe dependeth upon the onely opinion and will of menne, *without any other reason urginge and enforcing to be so,* then either the honestie of manners, or commoditie of livinge, or the authoritie of the Prince or the force of armes, whiche if it be the preserveresse of good menne, and the revengeresse of wicked men, it is good discipline, finally it is a most wicked thinge for the naughtinesse which is done when the

Magistrate or the Prince neglecteth it, suffereth it, or alloweth it.

With the state and its laws stripped of their divine origin, it is but a step to the denial of the universal interdependence of law and justice. Whereas the "universal-lawists" saw justice as the purpose and the child of civil law, in its turn ultimately dependent upon the great objective verities of natural law and God, Agrippa writes,

> It is not then sufficiently declared by this alone, that all the force of the Law & Justice doth not so much depend upon the Lawes as upon the honestie and equitie of the Judge.

Here, in the "science" of natural and political law, is a position parallel to that held by Montaigne in the "science" of man. Just as Montaigne deserts and denies the efficacy of the study of universal man, so Agrippa deserts and denies that of universal law. Just as Montaigne rests his "wavering" knowledge of man upon the study of a particular one, so Agrippa finds that "the force of Law & Justice" depends upon the honesty and fairness of any particular given judge. The same completely decentralizing, individuating and relativizing process has taken place.

There is one more aspect of the repeal of universal law in which an analysis of Agrippa's work supplements that of Montaigne's-with regard to the Canon Law. "From the Civill Lawe," he explains,

> proceeded the Canon of the Popes Law, which to many may appeare most holy, so wittily it doth shadow the precepts of covetousnes, and manners of robbinge under the coloure of godlines.

He devotes many of his most scorching pronouncements to the task of excoriating the Canon Law, the Pope, and the church's pretensions to temporal authority. And in conclusion he makes the forthright assertion which we have been awaiting, that

> these Lawes and Canons come not from God, not be addressed to God: but are derived from the corrupt nature and witte of men and are invented for gaine and covetousnesse.

Agrippa includes among his alternative sanctions, "urginge and enforcinge" the Civil Law, "the authoritee of the Prince" and "the force of armes." . . .

Donald T. Atkinson   (essay date 1956)

SOURCE: "Agrippa and the Beginning of Psychiatry," in *Magic, Myth and Medicine,* The World Publishing Company, 1956, pp. 85-92.

[Atkinson explores the influence of Agrippa's ideas in the formation of attitudes toward the treatment of mentally ill patients.]

Only in recent years has man been able to banish a fear of the unseen which for thousands of years had kept him in perpetual torment. Everywhere about him in the long ago were disembodied spirits, evil, malicious, and cunning. Invisible forms, lurking in every shadow, were thought to be ready to hurl at him some great and terrible misfortune. From the storm reached the outstretched hands of the denizens of the unseen world, and malignant spirits, bent upon his undoing, leered at him from the lightning's flash. Witches with burning eyes cast malevolent glances from the darkness as they swung through the air on unholy errands bent, and salamanders, wreathing and hissing in the flames, set the sparks flying vehemently across his hearth.

Every calamity that had befallen friend or neighbor was believed to have been the culmination of the malicious design of some abominable demon. It was thought that life itself would soon have suffered a frightful termination but for the guardianship of the friendly spirits who waged a perpetual warfare against the innumerable monsters of the air.

Such beliefs were as real to the medieval mind as are the phantoms conjured up today by the imagination of the child. When we recall the visions which sometimes accompanied our childish nocturnal adventures, when every lurking shadow held a possible enemy, we can realize something of the paralyzing terror of these mental children of the past whose paths were so beset with the creatures of their imaginations. The existence of these apparitions was rarely doubted. A great fabric of evidence was at hand to prove the prevalence of such enemies of the human race. Hundreds of persons believed that they had met these demons face to face, and thousands more were thought to have gone down to untimely deaths at their hands.

During certain phases of the moon these enemies of mankind were thought to be particularly hostile, and at such times their frenzy could be allayed only by seizing upon a victim. The bodies of the seized then became the habitats of these dreaded personalities, and the resulting symptoms, which we now know to have been insanity, were but the reflected conduct of the Evil One himself. We have an illustration of this tradition in the word "epilepsy," which we get from the Greek and which literally means "seizing."

It was argued by medical men of the time that moonlight was a factor in producing disturbed mentality, because it gave the demon sufficient light to pursue his nefarious work. An echo of this delusion comes down to us in our English word "lunatic," from luna, the moon, a term used by the old masters of medicine to designate any mental departure from the normal. It was thought the moon also had the power to create physical ills and its debilitating rays were often the cause of death. It was known that the moon influenced the tides, and it was thought that at the turning of the tide death often hovered over the sickbed. We have a reminder of this weird superstition in the case of Shakespeare's Falstaff.

During this period of human history physical disorders were nearly always attributed to spirits who had evaded the protecting sylphs and forced an entrance into the body. Failing in life to accomplish their ends, it was believed, they often succeeded in getting control of the disembodied soul after death. To frighten away these unwelcome neighbors, bells were rung at nightfall. This was the origin of the curfew. As Professor Henry Draper suggests, the bells today given to children as toys had a medieval significance very different from the modern. At that time they were put into the child's hands not to afford him amusement but to act as a safeguard to his life. If these childish beliefs had not been accompanied by acts of supposed retribution, the history of this time would be of interest to us today only as an amusing study in psychology. Instead of this it gives us the most appalling examples of cruelty known to the world.

As already noted, a common belief during the Middle Ages was that of demoniacal possession of the living. Many persons, it was thought, were in league with the devil, the archenemy of mankind. Possessed persons were accused of making storms at sea, of being responsible for periods of drought, of causing hailstorms, of stunting the growth of children, and of a thousand other impossible crimes. Because of this superstition thousands upon thousands of men, women, and children suffered the most excruciating tortures. They were suspended to ceilings by their thumbs, famished in dungeons, stretched on the rack, and broken on the wheel. Only in death which left them beyond the reach of their tormentors were they to find deliverance. So fearful was the torture which usually preceded the executions of these victims that a great many confessed themselves guilty of the most impossible deeds. Accused persons were known to have admitted that they had caused children to vomit crooked pins, that they had inhabited the bodies of wild animals at night and were enabled thereby to commit the most diabolical acts. Thousands confessed themselves guilty of witchcraft, knowing that such a confession meant death.

The psychology of these confessions has long been a subject of mystery. It is probable that they were made in the hope of a few minutes surcease from pain or as a means of ending an unbearable existence. Some, no doubt, confessed because the terror occasioned by their accusation drove them insane. It is estimated by Samuel Laing that during the eighth century in German alone, over one hundred thousand persons suffered excruciating deaths for the crime of maintaining an alliance with the devil. . . .

In the treatment of the mentally deranged, as in all other things, we find the hand of evolution. By this process the execution of the insane gradually gave way to punishment without death. For centuries these unfortunates were starved, exorcised, and seared with hot irons, under the belief that the demons would find their bodies such an uncomfortable abode that they would vacate the premises for a more agreeable residence. Gradually several of these methods of punishment were supplanted by a therapeutic method with which medical history abounds for centuries. This remedial agent was the whip. So great was the belief in its merit that, until a century and a half ago, it was dispensed to the great as well as the lowly. . . .

Another method of dealing with victims diabolically possessed was "torture insomnia," the subjects of mental disorder being kept continuously awake. No form of treatment could so successfully have defeated its own end. Sleep is as necessary to the human body as food is. It is only while we sleep that brain repair goes on. During our waking hours something which may be called brain waste is stored up within us and if not eliminated by sleep will, of itself, destroy our reason. Is it a wonder that none recovered? Even if mildly insane, the victim was chained to a stake in an upright position and all the devices of perverted ingenuity were used to keep him awake. The inevitable was the result. What would have been a temporary disorder under rational treatment became a hopeless disease.

In 1486, a time when the infamy and horror so long directed toward the insane was at its peak, a child was born at Cologne who was to cross swords with the swarming myriads of ghouls and infesting spirits, and whose influence, sweeping down through the centuries, was to be the means of banishing them forever from the world. This child was Henry Cornelius Agrippa.

Agrippa was a favored son of Cologne. He lived at a time when the ninety and nine were born into feudalism, were ill-nourished, half-clothed, and poorly housed serfs whose ceaseless toil went to maintain an aristocracy and to support a brutal military employed to keep them in bondage. Agrippa, of the one per cent which history is pleased to call noble ancestry, was destined to throw away his birthright in the hope of bringing to a close the orgies of superstition and inhumanity toward the insane which so long had cursed his country. He was further destined to grope his way alone through a maze of intolerance and ignorance, maligned, opposed, and suspected. And, as a friend of the oppressed, he was to meet with a persecution that was to end only with his death.

Agrippa's accident of birth gave him the opportunity of a liberal education, which, by the way, in medieval times consisted largely in storing the mind with mistakes and studying in detail various and sundry events which had never happened. The universities turned out an insipid product taught to conform, whose thoughts followed the beaten path of convention. This, however, seems not to have affected Agrippa.

By some Agrippa is believed to have graduated from the University of Cologne. Others say that he was expelled. At any rate he carried away from his university a salutary ambition to hew out a name for himself. What appeared to be a channel to this end was soon open. The court of Emperor Maximilian I was in need of a secretary. He could fill the requirements from the standpoint of both blood and education, so he applied and was duly installed; but his new post brought him only disillusionment, and soon he left, disgusted with the jealousy and frippery of court life. In 1509 he studied divinity at the University of Dôle, in Burgundy, and later became its professor of Hebrew. Here his utterances against the popular belief in witchcraft made him enemies, but he worked on, patiently and aggressively, ever ready to strike with his caustic pen at wrongs which for centuries had been blighting humanity. Later he took up the study of medicine. He received his degree in 1515, after which he traveled in France and England.

In 1518 Agrippa became the syndic at Metz. Here he was appalled at the treatment of the insane, who were either

confined in dismal and repulsive quarters or languished in the most wretched dungeons. Incurable cases wore an iron belt about their bodies with a ring attached, through which ran an upright bar. They could sit and stand, but this unhappy contrivance prevented their lying down. In this way they were doomed to spend their miserable lives. The prisons for the insane had no drainage and no proper ventilation. Disinfection was unknown. Shut away from the sunlight, eating improper food, and drinking contaminated water, they soon sickened and died. Two or three years was the average life of an inmate.

Agrippa began to advocate the treatment of the insane with humane methods and sought to prove that the padded cell was more efficacious than the iron collar and chain then used on nearly all cases. Contending that the prevalent superstition as applied to the insane was fatal to even a moderately disturbed intellect, and impatient at the credulity of his contemporaries and the cruelties which their ignorance encouraged, he resolved at any cost to hew a path through this jungle of popular superstition.

One day a demented old woman was dragged through the streets, having been accused of witchcraft. Agrippa made an impassioned plea in her defense, upholding the view that the supposed witches were really victims of disease of the brain and that they should be treated with mercy instead of abuse. The result of this innovation was inevitable; he was openly denounced by the medical profession, his friends forsook him, and soon the mob was at his heels. Savan, the Inquisitor of Metz, was preparing to bring him before the Inquisition for disturbing a popular belief, when he fled the city. To remain would have meant death at the stake, the inevitable fate of those of the time whose personalities were not lost in conformity, or whose characters were not dominated by submission to authority.

Agrippa was still essentially an aristocrat, and in 1523 at Lyons he was made court physician to Louis of Savoy. But he was not long to enjoy peace. His enemies began their intrigues anew, and he was repaid for his services by being banished. His compensation was withheld and he again found himself a penniless wanderer. In 1528 he was once more a court physician, this time to Margaret of Austria, regent of the Netherlands, at Antwerp. Here he wrote his book, *On the Vanity of the Sciences.* This work was a general condemnation of the medical science of the time, in which the part played by the medical profession in promoting the witchcraft delusion and its resulting cruelty to the insane was set forth in scathing language. His ideas on insanity, embodied in this book, may be considered the nucleus around which has grown the science of psychiatry.

Soon after the publication of Agrippa's work he was imprisoned in Brussels. After a year he was released and returned to Lyons, where he was again thrown into prison. In the year 1535 at Grenoble, France, the great humanitarian, with a broken heart and a body wasted with disease, succumbed to an acute illness. Much prison life had done for him that from which he had given so much of his life to save others.

In 1816 Philippe Pinel at the risk of his liberty instituted the reforms which Agrippa sought to bring about nearly three hundred years earlier. Pinel succeeded in striking off the chains of insane prisoners, liberating them from close and musty cells and placing them in humane surroundings. Thus was the dream of Agrippa to become a reality.

[Agrippa] was the first man in history to strike a blow in favor of the persecuted insane. Since that time all advocates for reform in the treatment of the mentally diseased have but followed the footsteps of this great physician, humanitarian, and searcher after truth.

Charles G. Nauert, Jr. (essay date 1957)

SOURCE: "Magic and Skepticism in Agrippa's Thought," in *Journal of the History of Ideas,* Vol. XVIII, April, 1957, pp. 161-82.

[*In the following excerpt, Nauert examines the interrelationship between belief in occult science and skepticism about the limits of human knowledge, suggesting that both elements were present in all phases of Agrippa's work.*]

From his own age down to the present, Heinrich Cornelius Agrippa von Nettesheim (1486-1535) has received widely varying evaluations from students of his thought. Some have dismissed him cursorily as an intellectual lightweight or as a wicked familiar of demons. Even those who have valued him highly have often done so for most contradictory reasons. Much of this disagreement results from uncertainty about which Agrippa to believe: Agrippa the credulous magician, author of a widely used magical compilation, *De occulta philosophia libri tres,* or Agrippa the skeptical doubter, writer of *De incertitudine et vanitate scientiarum declamatio inuectiua.* This dual personality as magician and skeptic is evident not only in Agrippa's numerous writings but also in the reaction of others to these writings. To some, such as Giordano Bruno in the sixteenth century and Thomas Vaughan in the seventeenth, the exposition of a magical world, a universe the parts of which are intimately connected by occult bonds, was the fruitful element in Agrippa's thought. Bruno found in *De occulta philosophia* much of the detail of his own *De monade;* and his world-view was little different from Agrippa's except that it was more consistently worked out. To others, however, the stimulating element in Agrippa's writings was the universal doubt which in *De vanitate* he cast on all human learning. One late sixteenth-century French writer complained of the existence of a whole school of "atheists" or doubters who called themselves Agrippans, while there is no doubt that *De vanitate* furnished both ideas and illustrative material for the skeptical thought of Michel de Montaigne, especially for his "Apology for Raymond Sebond." Some of the themes of *De vanitate* also show similarity to the thought of the Libertines of seventeenth-century Italy.

The presence of these two apparently contradictory elements, magic and skepticism, in the thought of the same man made his writings disturbing to many readers. The clash between these elements and the anguished doubts of *De vanitate* helped to mold the legend which symbolizes the intellectual malaise of the sixteenth century, that of Faust. Christopher Marlowe's Doctor Faustus explicitly took Agrippa as his ideal when he renounced human sci-

ences in favor of magic. Much later, Agrippa contributed to the concept of Faust in the mind of Goethe, who admitted that as a youth he passed through an intellectual crisis after reading the pessimistic *De vanitate.* Thus the juxtaposition of magic and skepticism in Agrippa's thought has been fruitful in the artistic world; but no modern student of his writings has satisfactorily analyzed the relations between these elements and the way in which Agrippa's own thought developed them. . . .

In his brilliant though much-criticized book, *The Counter-Renaissance,* Hiram Haydn suggests a dialectical interpretation of the development of the European mind in the sixteenth century. In opposition to the orderly world-view which the Thomists and humanists shared, there arose a general skepticism concerning the power of the human mind to gain truth. This skepticism in turn produced, two results, sometimes at odds but often found in the same person: unsystematic empiricism, which granted truth only to sensory knowledge, and occultism, which appealed rather to gnostic traditions of revealed truth, especially the Hermetic and the cabalistic. Finally, these two tendencies, especially the empirical, contributed in some measure to the birth of modern scientific methodology, which restored faith in the power of the human mind, but on a different level from that of medieval rationalism. . . .

This pattern is particularly fruitful in interpreting the thought of Agrippa. In particular, it hints at quite another pattern than the credulity-incredulity-charlatanry one which has been most common, for distrust in the powers of the human mind to attain truth becomes the basic presupposition of occultism rather than the product of disgust with the results of occultism. It is not true that Agrippa represents the full course of this dialectical movement, nor is it true that his mind proceeds steadily from step to step without contradiction and without backtracking. But it is true that even *De occulta philosophia* is not the product of a man with confidence in the powers of the human mind, but rather an appeal from bankrupt reason to an occult tradition based ultimately on a divine revelation.

This first major work is highly complex. In large part it is just a compilation of facts and alleged facts from earlier writers, and as such it reveals an astounding degree of erudition (and of credulity) on the part of its author. The vast wealth of medieval literature and the rediscovered treasures of Antiquity have been laid under contribution. Authority of the past, not human powers in the present, receives the author's emphasis. Agrippa's underlying intention, although he does not adhere to it consistently, is to rediscover the truths known to the past, truths which, insofar as they concern ultimate matters, are the product not of human reason but of divine revelation to man. This revelation, traced back in the last analysis to the revelation given to Moses, supposedly included an esoteric interpretation which passed into the cabala of the Jews and into the Hermetic literature of the Egyptians, and from the latter into the philosophical mysticism of the Pythagoreans and the Platonists. This myth of a continuous esoteric tradition was a commonplace of the fifteenth-century Italian Neoplatonists, finding expression, for instance, in the writings of Gémistos Plethon, Marsilio Ficino, and Pico della Mirandola.

Although one cannot draw out of *De occulta philosophia* any explicit and coherent statement of an epistemological skepticism, it is quite clear that human reason is not primary to the work. Agrippa admits, to be sure, that man can accomplish great works, seeming miracles, and this not with the aid of demons but by natural powers. These natural powers, however, are not what we mean by the same phrase today. Sometimes Agrippa means merely "terrestrial" when he writes "natural." Generally, however, he uses the latter term to describe any thing or any event which exists or occurs without the direct action of some divine or angelic power. Thus the use of celestial influences to accomplish mighty works is "natural," in Agrippa's terminology. But man does not by his rational powers learn to use such natural forces; he depends, Agrippa argues, on divine inspiration for his control over them. Hence the *magus* may construct images which will accomplish great things; but such images are useless "unless they be so brought to life that either a natural, or celestial, or heroic, or animastic, or demonic, or angelic power is present in them or with them." The soul of the magician who employs these images draws its ability to use them not from reason but from a mystical ascent aided by ceremonial preparation but dependent for its consummation on divine illumination. More than twenty years later, writing a dedication for Book Three of *De occulta philosophia,* Agrippa repeated his assertion that the mind is unable to make this ascent to God, the ultimate truth, if it trusts in merely worldly things rather than in divine things.

Clearer proof that Agrippa saw no inconsistency between belief in the truth of the esoteric tradition and a thoroughgoing denial of the power of the human mind to grasp ultimate reality appears in a somewhat later work, *De triplici ratione cognoscendi Deum.* This book is a product of Agrippa's years in Italy, being inscribed to Guglielmo Paleologo, marquis of Monferrato, in 1516. It bears strong traces of the influence of Hermetic literature, on which Agrippa had lectured at the University of Pavia the preceding year, and also of cabala, on which he had lectured at the University of Dole in 1509. Original sin, Agrippa teaches, has so beclouded man's mind that he cannot know God by his own powers. There remain open to him three ways of knowing God. The first, the Book of Nature, depends on the power of his mind to know God as His creatures reflect Him. But this way cannot lead to knowledge of God in Himself; and even the limited knowledge that we can gain from the created world is distorted by the passions of the soul. The second way to know God is the Book of the Law, the revelation of God to Moses and the secret, revealed interpretation of it found in the cabala. But this book, even interpreted by cabala, reaches its perfection only with the coming of the Messiah, Jesus Christ, who fulfilled the Old Law and gave mankind the third way to know God, the Gospel. This Gospel, like the Old Testament, is divided into an open revelation contained in the words of Scripture and a secret revelation which interprets the published words in gnostic fashion. These last two ways, the Law and the Gospel, can truly lead man to God,

the ultimate truth, but only through faith and grace, not through the unaided powers of human reason.

The first two stages in Agrippa's development, then, were a fundamental doubt concerning the powers of the human mind, and an effort to escape this doubt by an appeal to the authority of the past, especially Antiquity. The Antiquity to which he turned was not primarily the aesthetic and reasonable Antiquity of Cicero but the mystical Antiquity of Neoplatonism, an Antiquity which included the Hermetic and cabalistic writings. Ultimately this ancient wisdom depended on an esoteric tradition supposedly based on divine revelation.

An obvious next step in Agrippa's development was the growth of doubts concerning the validity of the authorities on which his occult system was founded. The germ of this process was present even in *De occulta philosophia,* for Agrippa felt that the usual authorities in the various occult sciences, Albertus Magnus, Robert of Lincoln, Roger Bacon, Arnold of Villanova, Picatrix, Pietro d'Abano and Cecco d'Ascoli, had mixed much nonsense with their writings and so were largely responsible for the ill repute in which magic (which, to Agrippa, was the generic term for all the occult sciences) was generally held. Agrippa throughout his life appears to have searched avidly for more knowledge about occult subjects. Perhaps he never felt completely satisfied with what he knew, but continued to hope that just round the next corner, just on the next page he read, he might find satisfaction. His lecture on the *Pimander* in 1515 and his lecture on the *Symposium* of Plato, undated but probably of the same period, show no weakening of his trust in ancient occult tradition. His *Dialogus de homine,* a work about contemporary with *De triplici ratione cognoscendi Deum,* exalts man's powers almost beyond the confines of the occultist tradition.

On the other hand, Agrippa's *De originali peccato,* completed between 1516 and early 1519, shows considerable doubts about the various arts of prognostication, especially astrology, a pseudo-science which Agrippa may have questioned as early as 1509. It appears that astrology was the first of the occult sciences to suffer from the growth of doubt in Agrippa's mind. It was perhaps the weak link in his whole occult system, for Agrippa gave celestial influences a central position in his occultism. One must distinguish, however, between a form of occultism which used celestial influences to control nature and one which attempted to predict the future from the stars. Attack on astrological prophecy might well lead Agrippa to a more general renunciation of belief in occult forces coming from the stars, but this result did not necessarily follow.

An unusually frank letter of early 1519 shows both the extensiveness and the limitations of Agrippa's doubts about not only human learning but occult sciences as well. Dialectic and philosophy are "diabolical and seductive artifices and errors" [Agrippa to Theodoricus, bishop of Cyrene, Metz, February 6, 1518 (1519, n. s.), Lyons, Bibliothèque Municipale, MS. No. 48, fols. 31v-32v]. After studying dialectic, natural science, and astrology, Agrippa feels that he has wasted his time, effort, and substance and has got nothing in return but sin, "for all these are not from faith." Finally, "by the grace of God at length realizing how great [is] the vanity of human sciences," and after taking doctorates in medicine and both laws, Agrippa has turned to sacred letters. This letter contains no trace of the epistemological critique of the early chapters of his later (1526) work. *De vanitate* no extended demonstration of the vanity of arts and sciences, and no reference to the thought of ancient skepticism. It also fails to strike very clearly at any of the occult sciences but astrology, the most vulnerable one in Agrippa's estimation. In particular, it makes no attack on the gnostic myth of an esoteric revelation which justified study of Hermetic and cabalistic writings. Nevertheless, this letter does show two important facts. One is that by 1519 Agrippa had progressed far toward the rejection of human learning and had begun to question natural philosophy and astrology as well. The other is the intimate connection between his interest in the Bible and his depreciation of human learning. His thought since at least 1516 had assumed an increasing tendency to stress simple, Biblical religion; and this religious coloration of his thought was working to the detriment of human reason and of at least some of the occult sciences.

From mid-1519 to early 1526, Agrippa wrote no books at all; then in 1526 came an apparently sudden proliferation of works, especially *De vanitate,* which call in question not only the fruits of human reason but occult sciences as well, and which go far beyond the doubts which we have seen in these earlier works. It seems obvious that Agrippa's doubts must have matured gradually during these years.

When, however, lacking any books from this period, one turns to Agrippa's numerous letters, one finds few evidences of this growth of doubt, and no hint at all of the emotional and explosive rejection of learning that was to follow. Most of the letters show Agrippa following with interest (though also with a bit of amusement) the alchemical enthusiasms of his friend Tyrius at Metz; interpreting prodigies on the model of similar instances in Roman history; studying the writings of Trithemius, Ptolemy, and the unidentified Marcus Damascenus; and giving and taking opinions on occult matters. Perhaps one is justified in seeing a certain reluctance to commit himself on occult questions, but mention of such subjects is as frequent as ever. A letter of early 1524 shows Agrippa painfully aware of the contradictory doctrines and procedures of various astrological texts, but still eager to find from his correspondent an explanation which would resolve these difficulties.

One may conjecture that one source of the crisis of 1526 was his study of the great religious controversy which was unfolding. From the time he went to Metz early in 1518, Agrippa had been reading avidly the works of Erasmus, Lefèvre d'Étaples, and Martin Luther. This reading would have stimulated the anti-rational element already present in his thought, for all three writers stressed the Bible and deprecated what they regarded as the excessive and contentious rationalism of the Schoolmen. Erasmus's ideal of *philosophia Christi* was that of a reasonable faith, but not of a rationalistic one. Luther, of course, would impel his reader to an even more extreme depreciation of all human learning, for although many have exaggerated his irratio-

nalism, his own unbridled and intemperate statements are much to blame. This influence is not the only root of Agrippa's skeptical development, and in any case it is directed against rational theology rather than against the occult tradition of Hermes and the cabalists; but its general effect was adverse to any knowledge except that gained from the Bible.

Another source of the growth of skepticism in Agrippa's thought was some acquaintance, probably at second hand and perhaps in part through Erasmus's translation of Galen's *De optimo docendi genere,* with the ancient skeptical schools. Personal experience was yet another influence on this development. The inability of all his learning to relieve the want of himself and his family from early 1526 onward must have created a feeling that his studies had been futile, as well as a bitterness against court life, both elements which are very pronounced in *De vanitate.*

The year 1526 saw the full development of Agrippa's doubts concerning occultism, the maturation of his earlier depreciation of the powers of human reason, and the introduction of specific reference to the ancient skeptical schools. It was the year which produced not only two letters denouncing astrology but also two treatises which called the whole occult system into question. The first of these, *Dehortatio gentilis theologiae,* existed by June 10, 1526, and may date back to an earlier year. The composition of *De vanitate* took place in the summer of 1526 and was completed by September 16, when Agrippa mentioned the book in a letter to Chapelain. The tone of the little treatise and the much larger book is quite consistent. Both of them elaborate Agrippa's earlier skepticism about the power of human reason. What is more, both of them indicate disillusionment with the occult sources to which Agrippa had once turned for refuge from intellectual anarchy; and both contain an appeal to simple faith in the words of the Bible.

There is nothing surprising about the denunciation of pagan philosophy in the *Dehortatio.* The idea that pagan philosophers were pernicious or at best superfluous in the study of Christian theology is a commonplace of almost all of Agrippa's earlier works, and the real basis of his denunciation of scholastic theology in both his published works and his private letters. But now the distinction which he once made between profane and sacred authors in Antiquity has disappeared. The little treatise opens by reproving certain friends for urging Agrippa to expound Hermes' *Pimander,* as he had earlier done at Pavia, rather than the Epistles of Paul, as he had proposed:

> I marvel greatly and am astounded and angered that you, who have been baptized in the Gospel of Christ, who fulfill the priesthood in the church of Christ, after sacred baptism, after the sacred chrism, are seeking knowledge of God from the heathen, as if the Gospel were imperfect and it were pardonable to sin against the Holy Ghost; for whoever think they can get knowledge of God elsewhere than from the Gospel, they truly are those who attack the Holy Ghost, a blasphemy which is pardoned neither in this nor in the next world.

All truth is in the Gospel, and pagan letters are at best superfluous and usually lead to destruction. Agrippa flatly denies any special value to the doctrines of Hermes or the sibyls; and with them fall Plato, Plotinus, and Proclus, and all those who had benefitted by the Neoplatonic myth of esoteric revelation.

De vanitate goes much further. This treatise, the pungent invective and sometimes startling argumentation of which make it the one work of Agrippa which can still be read with enjoyment, contains four chief elements. The first is a full elaboration of Agrippa's denial of the power of human reason to achieve truth. This denial . . . is not wholly new, though its elaboration and development are. The second element is an attack on the occult sciences and their authorities. We shall return to this subject shortly. The third ingredient of Agrippa's declamation is a denunciation of abuses in contemporary society, both secular and ecclesiastical. The final element, which contains Agrippa's effort to resolve the problems he has raised, is his appeal to the Bible and the grace of God as the only real source of truth. In itself, this element in his thought is no innovation, for it strongly marks works produced as early as his Italian period and in a sense is presupposed by his interest in the cabalistic interpretation of Scripture expressed in *De occulta philosophia.* But the statement is much more complete than in his earlier writings.

Agrippa's *De vanitate* certainly seems to mark the end of his belief in the occult sciences. He directly recants the errors of *De occulta philosophia,* and this recantation was printed along with other similar material in an appendix to the 1533 edition of his occultist writing:

> But I while yet a youth wrote in a quite large volume three books of magical things, which I called *De occulta philosophia,* in which whatever was then erroneous because of my curious-youth, now, more cautious, I wish to retract by this recantation, for formerly I spent much time and goods on these vanities. At length I have gained this, that I know by what arguments one must dissuade others from this destruction.

Elsewhere in the same book he retracts his little treatise *In geomanticam disciplinam lectura:* "I also wrote a certain geomancy quite different from the others, but not less superstitious and fallaeious, or, if you want me to say it, even mendacious."

Agrippa then proceeds to destroy the authorities to which he once had appealed to escape the feebleness of human reason. Medieval writers on magical subjects had already received criticism in *De occulta philosophia* itself. *Dehortatio gentilis theologiae* had abolished the esoteric myth of Neoplatonism, and with it the special authority of the Hermetic writings and the Platonists and Neoplatonists. Now, in *Dè vanitate,* the authority of the Jewish cabala also falls. After a careful study of cabala, Agrippa says, he found it to be "nothing but a mere rhapsody of superstition." If it had had any real merit, he felt, God would not so long have concealed it from His church, for the Holy Ghost had abandoned the synagogue and had come to teach Christians all truth. Agrippa notes with satisfaction that since the Incarnation the Jews have been able to accomplish few if any miraculous works with divine names. He concludes:

> And so this cabala of the Jews is nothing but a certain most pernicious superstition, by which according to their own will they gather, divide, and transfer words and names, and letters placed here and there in Scripture,. ... constructing from this [practice] words, conclusions, and parables from their own imaginings; they want to fit the words of God to them, defaming the Scriptures and saying that their imaginings arise from them; they calumniate the law of God and by impudently twisted computations of words, syllables, letters, and numbers, try to infer violent and blasphemous proofs of their perfidy.

Having thus renounced the occult authorities, Agrippa felt no compunction in denouncing one by one the occult sciences as vain and superstitious: geomancy, dicing, Pythagorean lots, astronomy and astrology, physiognomy, metoposcopy, chiromancy, auspices, interpretation of dreams, prophetic madness, the various branches of magic. The several arts of divination and prognostication suffer particularly heavily. Surely, one would think, any later activity by this man in the field of occult sciences must be the work of a charlatan and swindler.

Yet the break with the occult sciences was neither so sudden nor so complete as a superficial comparison of the two major books suggests. We have already seen that Agrippa's position on astrological prognostication had long been wavering, even unfavorable to this pseudo-science. It is worth nothing that Giovanni Pico della Mirandola, like Agrippa, had directed his attack against astrology and divinatory arts, especially because they undermined the freedom of the human will. But Pico did not so attack those parts of the occult system which presented themselves as means for the human mind to use in controlling the universe. Agrippa, who cites Pico's attack on astrology in his own chapter on judicial astrology, does not really go so far as Pico, who reduced the influence of the heavens on the earth to a merely physical one. Agrippa points to the conflicts among authorities, the lack of objective existence of astrological and astronomical constructions, the ambiguity and subterfuges of those who practice astrology, and the impiety of seeking to read in the stars a future which is determined not by celestial influences but by God. This latter phrase, that "in truth, neither do the stars govern a wise man, nor a wise man the stars, but God governs both," is as close as Agrippa comes to a frontal assault on the doctrine that the stars influence terrestrial events. His main line of argument is rather that even if such influences do exist, there is no certain science of them and probably never can be one, and that anyway a desire to know the future betokens an impious lack of trust in divine providence.

Even in the case of cabala, Agrippa's break with his earlier views is neither so sudden nor so complete as one might think. He had long taught that Jewish cabala was imperfect until the coming of Jesus Christ. And he still did not deny that God gave to Moses a secret and divinely revealed interpretation of the external teachings of the old Testament. He merely denied that the currently circulating Jewish writings were a true cabala. His efforts as late as 1532 to learn of new cabalistical discoveries of his friends in Italy are not inconsistent with his dissatisfaction with what he already knew of cabala. He had serious doubts, but he still did not exclude the possibility of a true cabala.

One more example of the persistence of his old views will be illuminating, especially as it takes us out of the realm of both prognostication and mystical exegesis and into the relations of man with the natural world. Agrippa's chapter on natural magic leaves that field of endeavor almost unscathed. Just like *De occulta philosophia, De vanitate* defines natural magic as "the highest peak of natural philosophy and its most absolute consummation." It was professed not only by the Brahmans, Gymnosophists, and Zoroastrians, but also by the three Magi of the New Testament. It produces works seemingly marvellous but actually natural, though the ignorant masses think that they are miracles. Examples of its works are the growing of plants out of season, the causation of thunder, and transmutations of things. Of course Agrippa has reservations about natural magic, for all its authorities have mixed superstition with it; and its works are often impious and subject to serious misuse. The most serious abuses, however, occur in the other major subdivision of magic, the ceremonial, which consists of goetia (necromancy and witchcraft) and theurgy. These arts depend on the summoning of spirits, a most dangerous practice even if one calls on good spirits, for good angels rarely appear because they are obedient to God, while evil spirits often disguise their true nature and lure the rash conjurer to his destruction. Awareness of the admixture of superstition in natural magic appears almost as clearly in Agrippa's letter of 1510 dedicating *De occulta philosophia* to Trithemius as it does in *De vanitate.* Thus again we see the roots of Agrippa's doubts extending back to his earliest years, just as we see that his great declamation does not utterly destroy (in this case, it hardly does more than mildly criticize) his earlier teaching. Perhaps something could yet be salvaged from occult arts, though even if it could, it would be relatively unimportant, since no science, occult or not, can make any significant contribution to man's beatitude, which depends not on a rich intellect but on a virtuous will.

Agrippa's subsequent work in the occult arts (and one must never forget that his studies and researches continued through every period of his life) is nevertheless an effort at such a salvage operation. A letter written about a year after the completion of *De vanitate* suggests that mere rejection of occult sciences did not satisfy Agrippa, that he shrank back from the destruction which his critical thought had accomplished. He warned his correspondent not to be misled as others had been:

> Oh, how many writings are read about the insuperable power of the magical art, about the prodigious images of the astrologers . . . which are all found to be vain, fictitious, and false as often as they are practiced to the letter. And yet they are related and written by great and weighty philosophers and holy men. . . . Indeed it would be impious to believe that, having taken pains, they wrote lies. Therefore there is another sense

than what is given in the letters, a sense concealed by various mysteries, but up to now expounded openly by none of the masters, which sense I doubt whether anyone can attain solely by the mere reading of books without a skilled and trusty master, unless he be illuminated by a divine spirit, a thing which is granted to very few; and so, many strive in vain who pursue these most recondite secrets of nature, applying their mind to a mere course of reading.

A key exists to these secrets, Agrippa adds; and it is the human soul. But how the spirit in man can unlock these secrets is a matter not to be committed to a letter, he darkly concludes, but only to be revealed by word of mouth. A letter written later in 1527 further explains that the key to the occult sciences is the intellect, which can achieve the deification of man, but only if it is freed from the bonds of the flesh by a mystical ascent, a death to the world and to the flesh which Agrippa admits he has never achieved, offering only to point the way to others. His final refuge, then, is mysticism, as is also clear from the later chapters of *De vanitate.* Like Nicholas of Cusa, he turned to a mystical experience which he himself had never personally known.

Yet the restless mind of Cornelius Agrippa did not stop with mysticism. The real philosophical justification of his continued alchemical experiments, of his unceasing search for new books of cabala and natural magic is not just a confidence that there must be in the works of such distinguished authors a deeper truth visible only to the mind illumined by mystical experience. Even in the midst of his most critical passages, there are materials for an attempt at reconstruction on an intellectual plane. Agrippa had really never denied the validity of sensory knowledge in theory, although he felt that the passions of the soul and man's liability to error made it unreliable in practice. His real skepticism concerned rather the jump from this sensory knowledge of singulars to the higher levels of ratiocination. Thus in attacking the various occult arts of prognostication, he does not deny that there may be some factual truth in their predictions. Rather, his favorite charge against such arts as chiromancy (or palmistry) is that their defenders can allege no solid reasons but only fortuitous experiences to uphold their claims. Any higher patterns of explanations in these arts or in any science, he argues, are merely arbitrary constructs of the human mind without any objective existence. This is true of the various astronomical cycles, epicycles, signs, and houses; it is also true of metaphysical concepts. Real but possibly erroneous sensory knowledge and arbitrary intellectual patterns: after all has been said, these still survive the general intellectual wreckage produced by *De vanitate.*

How, then, could Agrippa have excused his continued practice of the occult arts had anyone in his own lifetime thought to accuse him of being a charlatan? One way, as we have seen, was the vague claim that a mystically illumined mind could see the real truth under the apparent inconsistencies. Another way was empiricism or authoritarianism, for they could be much alike: passive acceptance of brute fact as discovered by his alchemical experiments and daily observations, or passive acceptance of the reports of others concerning their observations. That he accepted many ridiculous tales in his final recension of ***De occulta philosophia*** is not surprising, for simple empiricism and skepticism do not offer an adequate basis for criticism of fact. Michel de Montaigne, a far greater skeptic than Agrippa, used many of the same anecdotes (and probably believed or half-believed many of them) that appear in Agrippa's writings. A third way of justifying his occult practices, even in their theoretical aspects, could have been Agrippa's own doctrine of the arbitrariness of mental constructs. All patterns of interpretation, he teaches, are artificial and arbitrary, the magical ones no more than any others. So one may adopt them provisionally as long as they are useful.

It is precisely on this utilitarian basis that Agrippa defends magical arts in a letter of February 13, 1528, to a friend at the French court, clearly the royal physician Chapelain. Natural sciences, metaphysical arts, and occult devices do exist, he says, whereby one can licitly defend kingdoms, increase wealth, and cure sickness. Similarly in his dedication of Book One of ***De occulta philosophia*** to Hermann von Wied, dated January 1531, Agrippa after admitting that even in its revised form the book contains much that is not true, adds that it nevertheless contains many useful and necessary things. His preface to the reader justifies its publication partly by fears of an offensive and imperfect pirated edition but also because many of the things that it contains are useful for overcoming magical spells and for the conservation of health, honor, and fortune. Agrippa urges his readers to accept what they find useful and reject the rest, for he himself merely relates the opinions of others and does not approve all that the book contains. What Agrippa is really approaching with his pragmatic attitude toward conjectures and empirical facts is an adumbration of the idea of hypothesis and its subjection to the test of facts, a procedure that characterizes the methodology of modern science. He has, of course, no clear awareness of this principle, and there is no hint of either controlled experimentation or quantitative expression; but his mind is tending in this direction.

This attempt to trace the movement of Agrippa's mind would not be complete without some mention of the restlessness of his thought. No path seemed too much out of the way to be explored, even though Agrippa might on another occasion develop its opposite just as fully. For instance, he could extol the excellences of women in ***De sacramento matrimonii*** and especially in ***De nobilitate et praecellentia fóeminei serus,*** and yet could cry out against the fickleness and gullibility of the sex during his troubles with Louise of Savoy at Lyons from 1526 to 1528, and again when he fell from the favor of Margaret of Austria in 1530.

The most striking example of the flexibility of his mind, however, appears in what one might call his minority report on the powers of the human mind. Most of the statements where he seems to exalt the power of human reason are not really rationalistic, for he is referring to the power of the divinely illuminated mind, not to native reason. But in one work his ***In artem brevem Raymundi Lullii commentaria,*** he seems to grant almost unlimited powers to

the mind of man. By the use of the Lullian art, he claims, man can easily and quickly master all sciences. This art judges all sciences and can attain all knowledge, even without the aid of Scripture. In illustrating its powers, Agrippa undertakes logical proof of even the most abstruse dogmas of religion, for example, that God contains a coeternal spirit. The mind, he argues, is perfectly justified in holding a given proposition because it seems more pleasant and reasonable than its opposite. This rationalistic tendency seems logically to fit into the earliest stage of Agrippa's intellectual development, before growing doubt had driven him first to occult traditions and then to the near-despair which his works of 1526 show. Unfortunately, there is no sure way of dating the Lullian treatise. Its dedication to Jean de Laurencin probably occurred about 1517 and certainly no later than 1523. But the book itself may well be considerably older than the dedication; and Agrippa's contact with that Andreas Canterius, whom in the preface he calls his teacher in the Lullian art, occurred early in his life, probably while he was still an undergraduate in the University of Cologne. Thus the introduction of this rationalistic element into his thought, and perhaps the composition of the treatise itself, does lie, as one would expect, near the beginning of Agrippa's intellectual development. It is true that Agrippa in 1533 published this one rationalistic work; but one may note that even this apparent contradiction of his usual epistemological pessimism requires that reason be sustained by a highly rigid (one might almost say magical) set of logical artifices and mnemonic aids.

Finally, one must not forget that Agrippa lived in the age of humanism, of enthusiasm for ancient literature, and that he spent some seven years in Italy, the center of humanistic activities. He avowed to Erasmus that he was a loyal follower of Erasmian learning. Some of the optimistic trust of the age in the value of ancient literature *(bonae literae)* is reflected in Agrippa's writings. On two occasions, he urged students to study classical letters and to return to the sources of Roman law, disregarding modern (that is, medieval) legal commentaries. In 1518, sending advice to the young Claudius Cantiuncula, he sounded very optimistic, urging his friend not to confine himself to one field of study but, trusting in the powers of the mind, to master the whole of human learning. But in a second letter to the same friend, Agrippa made it clear that while law and humane letters were praiseworthy studies, they also had their dangers and were in the last analysis vain and perishable in comparison with the study of sacred letters, to which he strongly urged his young acquaintance. Thus even in this exchange of 1518, Agrippa's optimism concerning humane letters was subservient to a stress on sacred letters.

Like so many of the northern humanists Agrippa found the best of the *bonae literae* in the Bible. Perhaps the highest recommendation of literary endeavor which Agrippa could make was that a good mastery of the three languages, Latin, Greek, and Hebrew, was necessary for a thorough mastery of the Bible and so for the education of a theologian. Grammar alone among human sciences, he said, is useful for understanding Scripture; and even in this one science of grammar, the danger of pride and of willful misinterpretation of the Bible is great. Even it can be praised only when it is confined to its most elementary stage, the understanding of a text. If one passes on to a study of elegance of diction and a critique of the language, grammar becomes like all the other human sciences: vain, uncertain, leading to perdition.

The general development of Agrippa's mind, then, proceeded not by a sudden intellectual revolution in the mid-1520's but in three stages. His early position, as represented especially by *De occulta philosophia,* already doubted the power of unaided human reason to grasp reality but found refuge from intellectual anarchy by an appeal to the wisdom of an occult Antiquity, a wisdom that came ultimately from divine revelation. The second stage in Agrippa's intellectual odyssey was the growth of doubts about the validity of those occultist writings in which he had first acknowledged ancient wisdom. Parallel to this growth was the further maturation of his early doubts about the validity of human reason. These two movements of his thought found their chief expression in his works of 1526, especially *De vanitate.* But Agrippa recoiled from the glimpse he had had of utter intellectual anarchy. So the third stage, an attempt at reconstruction, is evident even in *De vanitate* and also in some of his later writings. His attempt at reconstruction followed three lines. Most prominent of these was his fideistic appeal to the pure and unadulterated Gospel as the only source of truth. A second way of escape was the doctrine that magical writings contained a deeper meaning open only to the initiate or to the man whose mind has been illumined by an act of God's grace. The third line was an attitude of which Agrippa himself surely did not see the full implications. By continuing to uphold the reality of sense perception of singulars, by teaching that all intellectual abstractions are equally arbitrary, and by hinting that one might in practice follow any abstract system as long as it met the pragmatic test of facts, Agrippa was unconsciously moving toward the epistemological doctrines underlying modern science: sci-

entific hypothesis and its subjection to the test of facts. The only element which does not fit into this three-stage movement of Agrippa's mind is his interest in Lullian rationalism. But this interest is probably an expression of an even earlier stage of his development, for his studies of Lull almost certainly occurred during his undergraduate days at Cologne. In any case, it is a subordinate element in his thought and finds expression in only one of his works.

D. P. Walker (essay date 1958)

SOURCE: "Ficino's Magic in the 16th Century," in *Spiritual and Demonic Magic from Ficino to Campanella,* The Warburg Institute, 1958, pp. 85-144.

[*Below, Walker focuses on the ways in which Agrippa's writings called attention to demonic elements in the philosophy of Marsilio Ficino.*]

Any discussion of Agrippa's views on magic is made somewhat uncertain and complicated by the following facts. He did not publish his *De Occulta Philosophia,* which had been completed by 1510, until 1533, several years after the publication of his *De Vanitate Scientiarum* (1530), which contains a retraction of the former work and several discussions of various kinds of magic. Agrippa reprinted these at the end of the *De Occ. Phil.*; in his preface he refers the reader to them and uses Ficino's feeble words to excuse himself for printing a book he had publicly renounced: "I am merely recounting these things, not approving of them". He also says that he has made considerable additions to it.

Before giving any weight to this retraction, we must remember, first, that the *De Vanitate* is a *Declamatio Invectiva,* that is, a rhetorical set-piece, and that therefore, though much of it is seriously evangelical, by no means all of its destructive scepticism is meant to be taken in earnest; secondly that, thought it contains one formal retraction of the *De Occ. Phil.,* this is limited to magic involving bad demons, and that the other discussions of magic, though far more cautious and less favourable than the *De Occ. Phil.,* do contain a defence of natural magic and even of theurgy, by which he means the obtaining of benefits by operations directed towards angels, including planetary ones. There is, however, a real difference of attitude between the two books which indicates an unresolved conflict in Agrippa's mind. In the *De Vanitate,* and perhaps in later additions to the *De Occ. Phil.,* he is an earnest Evangelical, who is harsh on what he regards as superstitious abuses in the Catholic Church, and who is obviously wanting a Christianity as free of magic as possible. On the other hand, the chapters on magic in the *De Vanitate,* the fact of his publishing the *De Occ. Phil.,* and other evidence collected by Thorndike [in *A History of Magic and Experimental Science,* 1923-1958], show clearly that he continued to believe in the value of magic, even of the most dangerous kind.

Agrippa is the only writer I know of earlier than Paolini and Campanella to give a full exposition of the theory of Ficino's astrological magic, including the details of his planetary music. This exposition is taken, often *verbatim,* from the *De Triplici Vita,* and is combined with an Orphic

---

Preface by "J. F.," translator of the first English edition of *De occulta philosophia*:

JUDICIOUS READER: This is true and sublime Occult Philosophy. To understand the mysterious influences of the intellectual world upon the celestial, and of both upon the terrestrial; and to know how to dispose and fit ourselves so as to be capable of receiving the superior operations of these worlds, whereby we may be enabled to operate wonderful things by a natural power—to discover the secret counsels of men, to increase riches, to overcome enemies, to procure the favor of men, to expel diseases, to preserve health, to prolong life, to renew youth, to foretell future events, to see and know things done many miles off, and such like as these. These things may seem incredible, yet read but the ensuing treatise and thou shalt see the possibility confirmed both by reason and example.

J.F., in his translation of De occulta philosophia *by Henry Cornelius Agrippa, 1651.*

Conclusio of Pico and an interpretation of the Orphic Hymns as astrological invocations; but it is dispersed and embedded in Agrippa's vast survey of magic, and therefore closely associated, one might say contaminated, with quite different kinds of magic. Though the ***De Occ. Phil.*** is predominantly Neoplatonic in its terminology and underlying metaphysical scheme, it includes many strands of magical theory, some of them hopelessly unorthodox; Agrippa has no cautious timidity about angels or demons, let alone talismans and incantations.

How Ficino's spiritual magic is transformed by appearing in the rich and varied context of Agrippa's magic can best be shown by a few examples. In all of these it must be remembered that Agrippa never openly cites modern writers, but frequently quotes from them; he is skilful at doing this, so that fragments of Ficino and Pico merge smoothly into the flow of his argument and seem to become part of it.

Early in his treatise Agrippa writes a chapter on the *spiritus mundi,* largely taken from Ficino, where he explains how planetary influences are conveyed by this spirit, which is analogous to man's. This is followed by fairly harmless chapters listing the various things which, containing an abundance of spirit and subject to various planets, are to be used for acquiring celestial benefits. But then come directions for obtaining, not only celestial, "but even intellectual and divine" benefits, and this is accomplished by using these planetary things, herbs, incense, lights, sounds, to attract good demons or angels into statues, as in our familiar *Asclepius* passage, to which Agrippa refers. These directions are given without a word of caution, and moreover are said to be exactly parallel to the attraction of evil demons by obscene rites.

Part of Ficino's rules for planetary music, combined with the Pico *Conclusio* on the use of Orphic Hymns in magic, appear in a chapter on incantations. These are to be directed towards the "numina" of stars, and the planetary angels are to be given their proper names. The operator's spirit, instead of being conditioned by the music into a suitably receptive state for planetary influence, as in the ***De V.C.C.,*** is here an active instrument, which is projected "into the enchanted thing in order to constrain or direct it". Ficino's musically transformed spirit appears here, "warm, breathing, living, bearing movement, emotion and meaning with it, articulated, endowed with sense, and conceived by reason", but in Agrippa's hands it has become a means of enchanting, compelling, directing planetary angels.

Even where Agrippa is closely following Neoplatonic sources, he differs strikingly from Ficino and most later syncretists in that he makes no effort to force them into a Christian framework, or to warn the reader against the unorthodox religious ideas they contain. But he does not, like Diacceto, for example, merely omit such considerations and give what could be taken as an uncommented, historical account of Neoplatonic magical theories; he frequently, especially in the 3rd Book, discusses Christian prayers and ceremonies in relation to magic and pagan religions, and plainly regards them all as examples of the same basic activity. Magic and religion, Christian or

pagan, are for him of the same nature; the *prisca theologia* is also a *prisca magia* and is accepted in a quite exceptionally "liberal" way. It was, of course, generally held that most of the *prisci theologi* were also *magi;* astrology and magic, for those who approved of them, were part of the ancient, extra-Christian revelation. The invention of these arts is regularly ascribed to Zoroaster; . . . the importance of Hermes Trismegistus for Ficino's magic, and of Orpheus and the Neoplatonists [has been noted].

Agrippa's remarkably thorough-going syncretism can be clearly seen even in the unusually careful chapter entitled: "On the two props of ceremonial magic, religon and superstition". Here we are told that all creatures, in their own several ways, worship their creator;

> But the rites and ceremonies of religion vary with different times and places; and each religion has something good, which is directed towards God Himself the Creator; and although God approves of only the Christian religion, nevertheless He does not wholly reject other cults, practised for His sake; and does not leave them unrewarded, if not eternally, at least temporally. . . .

God's anger is directed towards the irreligious, not towards those who worship Him in a mistaken way. In so far as these other religions differ from the true religion (i. e. Christianity), they are superstitious, but they all contain some spark of the truth:

> For no religion, as Lactantius tells us, is so mistaken that it does not contain some wisdom; wherefore those may find forgiveness who fulfilled man's highest office, if not in reality, at least in intention.

Moreover, even superstition is not wholly to be rejected. It is tolerated by the Church in many cases, and can, if believed in with sufficient force, produce by this credulity miraculous effects, just as true religion does by faith. Examples of this are the excommunication of locusts in order to save crops, and the baptism of bells so that they may repell devils and storms. But, Agrippa goes on, we must remember that the *prisci magi* were idolaters, and not let their errors infect our Catholic religion. It is difficult here to tell whether Agrippa the Evangelical is having a shot at Catholic practices he thinks are superstitions, or whether Agrippa the Magician is using them to justify his own magical practices. The caution about the *prisci magi* is quite exceptional, and I strongly suspect it is one of the later additions he mentions in his preface.

Elsewhere Agrippa makes no attempt to distinguish between true religion and superstition or magic. In a series of chapters towards the end of the 3rd Book on prayers, sacraments and other religious rites, he constantly places Christian examples side by side, and on a level, with pagan or magical ones. In the chapter on prayer, for example, we are told, first, that if we are praying to God for, say, the destruction of our enemies, we should recall in our prayer the Flood, Sodom and Gomorrah, etc., and use those names of God that are expressive of anger and vengeance; secondly, that we should also address an "invocation" to the angel, star or saint, whose particular job it is to do this kind of work. The invocation is to be composed

> in accordance with the rules given when we treated of the composition of incantations. For there is no difference between them, unless it be that they are incantations in so far as they affect our soul, and dispose its passions in conformity with certain spirits (numina), and are prayers in so far as they are addressed to a certain spirit in honour and veneration of it. . . .

Agrippa also thinks that prayers and purifications will be more effective on days and at times that are astrologically favourable—it was not "without cause that our Saviour said 'Are there not twelve hours in the day?'" In this part of his book ceremonies such as the baptism of bells are not said to be superstitious; they are effective "sacred incantations", used by the "primitive Church".

One can see from all this that, although Agrippa's exposition of Ficino's spiritual magic certainly gave it a wide diffusion, it may also have frightened people away from it. He exposes what Ficino, rather feebly, had tried to conceal: that his magic was really demonic. He also mixes it up with magic that aims at transitive, thaumaturgic effects, whereas Ficino's effects were subjective and psychological. Finally, and most importantly, by treating magic, pagan religion and Christianity as activities and beliefs of exactly the same kind, he demonstrates strikingly how dangerous Neoplatonic magic was from a Christian point of view. It is also relevant to this point that the spurious 4th Book of the *De Occ. Phil.*, where the magic is evidently black, was sometimes later believed to be by Agrippa, in spite of Wier's well-founded denials [*De Praest. Daem.*, 1583], which also did not prevent belief in the sinister stories about Agrippa's black dog. Ficino has got into bad company. . . .

George H. Daniels   (essay date 1964)

SOURCE: "Knowledge and Faith in the Thought of Cornelius Agrippa," in *Bibliotheque D'Humanisme et Renaissance*, Vol. XXVI, 1964, pp. 326-40.

[*Daniels discusses inherent contradictions in Agrippa's writings, noting that his main contribution was to demonstrate "the profound difference between the [Baconian] method . . . and the method of modern science."*]

The enigmatic figure of Heinrich Cornelius Agrippa von Nettesheim (1486-1535) has been subjected to various interpretations since the early 16th Century. Even his contemporaries were never quite sure what to do with him. Lauded as a great scholar and leading man of letters on the one hand, he was condemned as a wicked practitioner of the black arts and collaborator with devils on the other. Men of later generations were equally divided. The great skeptical works of Sir Philipp Sidney and of Montaigne were consciously modeled after Agrippa's volume, *On the Uncertainty and Vanity of the Arts and Sciences,* while Giordano Bruno and Thomas Vaughan took his three books of occult philosophy as a model. For Marlowe and, to a lesser extent, for Goethe, Cornelius Agrippa was the original Faust.

THREE BOOKS
OF
Occult Philoſophy,
WRITTEN BY
Henry Cornelius Agrippa,
OF
NETTESHEIM,
Counſeller to CHARLES the Fifth,
EMPEROR of Germany:
AND
Iudge of the Prerogative Court.

Tranſlated out of the Latin into the Engliſh Tongue, By *J. F.*

London, Printed by *R. W.* for *Gregory Moule,* and are to be ſold at the Sign of the three Bibles neer the Weſt-end of *Pauls.* 1651.

Title page of the first English translation of Occult Philosophy.

The difficulty is that there has always seemed to be two Agrippas—the one who wrote *De Occulta Philosophia,* proclaiming that the world was tied together with pervasive mystic bonds and that the intelligence of man was capable of utilizing the occult qualities of the universe for his own advantage, and the other Agrippa, the author of *De Incertitudine et Vanitate Scientiarum, Declamatio Invectiva, et Excellentia Verbi Dei,* a violent declamation against all of man's learning and against the possibility of his reaching understanding through reason. On the surface at least, the two Agrippas do seem incompatible, and until very recently, historians have followed the pattern of choosing one of them and discounting the other as a fraud, or at least, the victim of a temporary intellectual aberration. A few, following Marlowe, have looked upon him as a Faustian character who, at a certain point, renounces scholarly allegiance to human sciences and turns to the black arts.

In 1957, an ingenious attempt was made by Charles G. Nauert [in his "Magic and Skepticism in Agrippa's Thought," *Journal of the History of Ideas* (April, 1957)] to unite the two strands in the character of Agrippa, by interpreting him as a paradigm of the dialectical movement of Western European thought which Hiram Haydn [in his *The Counter-Renaissance,* 1951] saw as characterizing the period.

This [essay] arose out of the conviction that an insistence upon viewing Agrippa either in terms of intellectual development or discounting one side of his thought necessitates an entirely false final evaluation of the man, and, what is more serious, a misunderstanding of his real significance in the history of thought. A comparison—implied or otherwise—of Agrippa with Faust does have a certain seductive appeal, and interpreting him as a paradigm of the dialectical movement of Haydn's "Counter-Renaissance" thesis is even more tempting. But either effort precludes a real understanding of the relationship between magic, skepticism, and modern science. . . .

[It] is evident that Agrippa, to say the least, was hardly a Faust figure. True, both Faust and Agrippa had grasped the whole range of human learning and both had found it wanting. But it is not accurate to say that Agrippa *turned* to magic—there is no dramatic turning point in his life, nor is there a series of minor turning points which can fit into any obvious rational pattern. His text on magic was written *before* and published *after* he had written his skeptical treatise; therefore, it must be considered as indicative of a continuing interest, if not commitment. His skeptical work condemns not only science, but magic as well and much more besides; and his last letters indicate that he never lost interest in either science or magic. Moreover, his commentary on Lull, his last major published work (although it was apparently written much earlier), is a highly favorable account of the intricate rational system. It has nothing about it which would indicate that its author has rejected human reason. Here we have a complex series of intellectual events that cannot be reduced to an easy systematization, but if a key to the puzzle does exist, it should be found in a formal elaboration of his doctrine of knowledge. What I propose to do in the remainder of this [essay] is to assume—with Nauert and others—that *de Vanitate* does represent Agrippa's mature thought, and after analyzing the concept of knowledge upon which it seems to be based, to try to understand the interest in magic in terms of this epistemology.

The topical arrangement of the 102 chapters of Agrippa's *de Vanitate* is a study in itself, and the book as a whole still makes fascinating reading today. In this [essay], however, I shall concern myself solely with what the book can tell us about the author's attitude toward human knowledge. This approach will undoubtedly obscure important elements in the work—Erasmus, for example, considered it to be primarily an attack upon the theologians—but interesting as these matters are, they can be ignored for our purposes.

Of the sciences in general, Agrippa tells us that all of them are evil as well as good, and that in themselves they bring no advantage to men beyond that which was promised by the Serpent, when he said, "Ye shall be as Gods, Knowing good and evil". The sciences can bring no happiness, for true happiness consists not in the knowledge of good things, but in good life; not in understanding, but in living understandingly. Thus far, the attitude expressed is anti-

intellectualism, not skepticism, but Agrippa soon advances to a more positive assertion:

> So large, however, is the liberty of the truth, and the largeness thereof so free, that it cannot be contained within the speculations of any science, nor with any compelling judgment of the senses, nor with any argument of the art of logic, with no evident proof, no syllogism of demonstration, and not with any discourse of human reason, but with faith only.

Agrippa has not, in this passage at least, ruled out the existence of truth; quite the contrary, he has merely ruled out various ways of reaching it, including the "compelling judgment of the senses", reason and logic. Furthermore, truth is to be actively pursued in every possible manner:

> . . . what a wicked tyranny it is, to bind the wits of students to prescribed authors, and to take away from scholars the freedom of searching out and following truth.

He does not seem, in this last quotation, to be talking about faith; indeed, he seems to speak of the ordinary ways scholars search out truth. It is, in effect, merely a plea for intellectual freedom. But this seems paradoxical, since in his introductory chapter Agrippa makes the flat statement that

> All sciences are nothing else but the ordinances and opinions of men; as noxious as useful, as pestilent as wholesome, as bad as good; in no respect complete, but even ambigious, full of error and contention—all of which we now hide by scattering them through the various scientific disciplines.

We are confronted, then, with the curious situation in which a scholar pleads for intellectual freedom—the freedom to employ one's wits—in one breath, and in the next castigates the fruits of this use of reason. Faith is the only avenue to Truth and, at the same time, it is a "wicked tyranny" to deprive scholars of liberty to use their mental gifts in searching out truth. Is Agrippa simply saying that it is a wicked tyranny not to allow scholars to damn themselves by the free use of their wits? Hardly—it seems, rather, that 'truth' is here given two different meanings. We have, in effect, the old familiar of all students of literature—the semantic confusion. A further analysis of the work may serve to clear it up.

In Chapter VII, Agrippa, in speaking of the scholastic doctrine of knowledge, brings out this double meaning of "Truth":

> The peripatetics suppose that nothing can stand or be understood unless it is proved by syllogisms from demonstration; that is to say, in the manner described by Aristotle. But yet he [Aristotle] never observed the method in his dogmatic opinions, for he deduced all his arguments from presupposed matters; and all the professors of sciences; imitating him, have so far not given any, or very few, true demonstrations—much less in terms of natural phenomena—but all deduce them from precedents either from their Aristotle or from some other who spoke before, whose authority to give principles of demonstra-

tion the professors keep to themselves . . . If, therefore, the principles of demonstration are not well known, and the circular argument be not admitted, certainly one can have none but very slender and uncertain knowledge. We are required to believe things shown by certain weak principles, to which we assent to known limits either on the authority of the wise, or else with experience we allow [the principles] through the senses. For every concept (as they say) has its beginning from the senses, and the proof of true statements (as Averroes says) is that they agree with sensory objects. And that thing is better known and more true about which most [men's] senses agree. Through sensory objects, then, we are led by the hand to all things that may be known by us. Since all the senses are often fallacious, we cannot prove with certainty to ourselves any genuine experience. Furthermore, since the senses cannot attain to the intellectual nature, and since the cause of inferior things, from which their natures, effects, and properties—or rather passions—should be demonstrated, are by the consent of all men altogether unknown to our senses, is it not clearly demonstrated that the way to truth is closed to the senses? Therefore all these demonstrations and sciences which are fast rooted in the senses will be uncertain, erroneous, and deceitful. What, then, is the profit of logic, and what fruit comes from that learned demonstration by principles and proofs to which we of necessity assent, as it were, to known limits? Are not these principles and proofs already assumed rather than demonstrated?

Agrippa is discussing a number of subjects in this paragraph. It contains, in very abbreviated form to be sure, his entire doctrine of knowledge. Observe first of all his attitude toward authority—he is scornful of it when the arguments are based upon "presupposed matters", and not upon demonstration in "natural phenomena". Aside from the authority of "certain weak principles", he mentions, and in part rejects, the possibility of admitting that which comes to us through the senses. He then observes Averroes' arguments for the sensory basis of proof, and poses two distinct objections to it. First of all, he cites the psychological objection that the senses can deceive us as to the reception of particulars. He does not deny that knowledge of particulars can come to us through the senses; he merely states that it is difficult to be certain one has a true perception. Significantly, he does not deny the Averroistic contention that "that thing is better known and more true, about which most men's senses agree". The psychological objection is not a serious one; it is, in fact, a truism which has nothing to do with epistemology.

But Agrippa sees a second, more serious, objection to knowledge attained through the senses. The senses, he tells us, cannot attain to the "intellectual nature", or to the causes and properties of things. This is a serious epistemological criticism similar to that later made by Hume, and here is where Agrippa's real skeptical attitude lies. When one passes from sensory perception of singulars to the higher levels of thought, he says, one has to make some kind of assumption to guide one's synthesis of particular

perceptions into a meaningful whole. This is why Agrippa observes in another place that every science "has in it some certain principles which must be believed, and cannot by any means be demonstrated". If the fundamental principles of any science be denied, no amount of logical disputation can demonstrate them. Nature, as Hume was later to put it more explicitly, gives us no objective guide for combining intuitions into any pattern. We can, though, subject to the limitation of perceptual error, rely upon our intuitions [In a footnote, the critic writes: " 'Intuition,' as used in this paper has no mystical denotation; it is used in the philosophical sense of 'immediate apprehension.' "]. Since the reach of the senses is limited and, on the other hand, "so large is the liberty of truth", we cannot perceive it even with a "compelling judgment of the senses". When we move into this kind of "Truth"—that is, the truth of patterns or judgments on the facts—immediate perception is obviously not enough, especially if one can only perceive singulars. In retaining the concept of "Truth" as opposed to the limited truths available to the senses, Agrippa moved into the fideistic position attributed to him in the beginning.

Agrippa's general position as it appears in *de Vanitate,* then, is a thorough-going dismissal of any and all constructions that can be labelled as "human", nonetheless coupled with a willingness to accept the facts of experience subject only to the limitations of perceptual error. But as the last chapter of his work indicates, he is convinced that he lives in a God-centered universe which ultimately makes some kind of sense independent of human ability to perceive the sense in it. There is thus only a very limited justification for labelling Agrippa a skeptic, even on the basis of the publication which earned him the title. The word "skepticism" has a number of common meanings, and at least two of them are incompatible with each other. As a philosophical position, skepticism involves the denial that any certainty is possible concerning the phenomena of nature. As a theological position, it involves the denial of revelation or the existence of God. As it is currently used in commonsensical discourse, it signifies a critical attitude toward any theory, statement, experiment, or phenomenon until adequate proof has been produced. It is evident that none of these definitions fit Agrippa. He never denied the existence of knowledge of nature in the realm of individual fact; he certainly never denied either revelation or God, and everyone who studies the man notices the extreme credulity manifested in his other works. It can be said, in accordance with common usage, that Agrippa exhibited a "skeptical attitude" toward certain classes of statements (constructions), but to call him a skeptic is to confuse matters, for this kind of "skeptical attitude" is characteristic of empiricism, not of skepticism. His epistemological position can best be characterized as that of the pure empiricist who also believed, on faith, that his God-centered world was ultimately meaningful, if only according to some supernatural pattern. This is the same kind of combination of Platonism with empiricism which some students have attributed to Telesio and other thinkers of the period.

If this analysis is correct, it has somehow to be made to accommodate Agrippa's extreme credulity, evidenced in his three books on occult philosophy. This is the well-known problem of "reconciling" Agrippa's belief in magic with his "skepticism". Actually there is no problem of reconciliation, once it is realized that empiricism rather than skepticism was the foundation of his epistemology. Empiricism without theoretical guidance practically guaranteed the belief he showed in magical phenomena [In a footnote, the critic writes: "It is only fair to point out that Nauert does recognize a close relationship between Agrippa's magic and what he called his 'skepticism', but within the framework of intellectual development, the notion of scientific hypothesis was called in to connect the two. The point of this [essay] is that there was no such connecting agent."]. For instance, when Aristotle asserts that the sublunar world is composed of four elements and the heavens of a fifth, Agrippa (as a hypothetical example of his reasoning) could immediately rejoin that since Aristotle cannot demonstrate this, it remains mere conjecture. On this level of argument, there was no stage in Agrippa's life when he was subservient to scholarly authority. Agrippa did appeal to the past, and he did so throughout his productive life; it can be found in the *de Vanitate* as well as in *de Occulta Philosophia.* But it was a quite different kind of appeal. Agrippa searched the records of the past for the only kind of information that he felt men could communicate to each other—individual facts. Although he could scornfully dismiss Aristotle's theoretical constructs, as he had those of the "peripatetic theology" as early as 1519, it is a different matter when he is faced, not with a construct, but with a report of an individual fact.

If, for example, Agrippa reads that a man has been revived from the dead, he has no theory to confute this reported fact. He can only argue that "the one who reported this is a liar", or "the one who reported this is guilty of perceptual error". What, though, if he finds a great number of respected authorities testifying to the same thing? He can only—as he did—remark that although the facts are hard to believe, they must be credited, inasmuch as they are certified abundantly by approved scholars. And in cases like this, of course, he would cite a great number of instances and think that he had established another "marvel" actually to have occurred. This kind of acceptance of authority signifies something quite unlike blind subservience to that authority; it is rather an example of a profound respect for brute fact and acquiescence in the weight of empirical evidence. He has, after all, no grounds for casting out the testimony, and no theory for testing its validity.

Most of the "marvels" reported in his books of magic are of this nature, and he is constantly making appeals to experience in order to establish their truth. A marvel, in its simplest definition, is only a fact that is beyond ordinary comprehension, and what is beyond ordinary comprehension varies with place and time. Science had no effective way of dealing with that which seemed to oppose itself to laws of nature until the time of David Hume. What, then, is a scholar to do at a time when he has no universal laws of nature to guide him, especially if he is committed to the belief that on the human level one can be sure only of that which is intuited? He has no choice but to place all intuitions on the same level, and as a corollary to this, to place all theoretical constructs on the same level. Many things

exist in the world, Agrippa maintains, that "no otherwise than by experience and conjecture can be inquired into by us". In another place, he notes that qualities are called "occult", simply because their causes lie beyond the reach of human intellect, and philosophers attain to knowledge of them with the help of experience alone.

Among the occult qualities that Agrippa thought experience had revealed are the fact that any substance standing for a long time with salt turns to salt, the fact that the power of the lodestone may be transferred to iron by simply rubbing the two together, and that by eating the herb ditany a wounded stag can expel the arrow from his body. Again, he accepts claims that cranes have been known to medicine themselves with bulrushes, leopards with wolfsbane, and boars with ivy. Agrippa sincerely believed all the reports and he believed that knowledge of occult qualities could be useful. For example, as a thing angrily shuns its contraries or drives it out of its presence, so rhubarb acts against bile, treacle against poison, amethyst against drunkeness, and so on for a long list. Experience is also the basis for joining earthly things to heavenly things. It is experience, for example, which informs us that asparagus is under Aries' jurisdiction and garden-basil under Scorpio's, since asparagus is generated from the shawings of rams' horns and garden-basil rubbed between two stones has been known to produce scorpions.

Among all these examples of "occult qualities", some have a sound basis in fact—the power of the lodestone, for instance, may indeed in a certain empirical sense be transmitted to the iron. Most, of course, are absurd. But the fact that this is true in the light of modern knowledge should not obscure the reality that his belief in every one of these qualities stems from the same source. Observers reported each of these "occult instances" to have been the case at a particular time. The intellectually honest man who refuses to recognize the validity of theoretical guidance has no alternative but to accept or reject both the sound and the absurd on exactly the same basis—the weight of evidence, including testimony. This, of course, creates a dilemma which Agrippa expressed in a letter written toward the end of his life:

> Oh! How many writings are read concerning the irresistible power of the magic art, concerning the prodigious images of the astrologers, the marvelous metamorphosis of the alchemists, and that blessed stone which Midas-like turns all to gold or silver at its touch. All which are found vain, fictitious and false as often as they are practiced literally. And yet they are handed down in writings by great and most weighty philosophers and holy men whose traditions who will dare to call false? Nay it would be impious to believe that they have written lies in those works. Therefore there is another sense than what is passed down in the letters, a sense concealed by various mysteries, but up to now openly expounded by none of the masters, which sense I doubt whether anyone can attain to solely by the mere reading of books without a skilled and trusty master, unless he be illuminated by a divine spirit, a thing which is granted to very few.

This is perhaps as close as Agrippa ever came to recognizing the the sterility of his empiricism even on the level of individual fact. All of his examples are statements of fact which were reported by a great number of writers—exactly the kind of facts he used in his *de Occulta Philosophia.* The alternative to accepting reported fact is not to dispute an interpretation, but—as he says—to accuse the writers of having "written falsehoods". Agrippa never hesitated to dispute anyone's interpretation—anyone's "conjecture"—but, as we have seen, he felt that facts had to be accepted if enough testimony could be accumulated in favor of them. If his own senses could err, as he realized they could, and if the weight of testimony could not be accepted, as he was on the verge of realizing here, then one must doubt even the reality of individual fact. But obviously when one doubts the reality of individual fact, one completely loses contact with the external world. In order to avoid epistemological nihilism, Agrippa retreats to his psychological insights into the nature of the human mind. Perhaps, he seems to be saying here, he just did not understand what was being said.

One cannot interpret Cornelius Agrippa as a consistent empiricist without facing the apparently contradictory fact that he offers an interpretation of his own in *de Occulta Philosophia.* Although the work is largely a catalogue of magic and occult miscellanies, Agrippa was not afraid to drawn conclusions from them. The picture that emerges from the three books is of a universe intimately connected by occult bonds in which man has a prescribed role. As for the role of the magician, Agrippa invokes the classic Renaissance belief concerning the relationship between the individual and the external world:

> Let, therefore, everyone who would work in magic, know and understand the property, virtue, measure, order, and degree of his own soul among the powers in the universe itself.

The form of Platonism characteristic of the Renaissance is evident in this sentence—microcosm mirrors macrocosm, and is affected by it, but yet through the knowledge and understanding of his soul, the magician can be as one with the mystical powers of the universe. He had expounded the philosophy of Ficino in his early years as a lecturer, and was no doubt greatly influenced by it. Neither, of course, was this empiricism at all original. He lived in the midst of the revival of ancient skeptical schools of thought, and this, too, entered into the formation of his thought.

Although Agrippa, like many other Renaissance thinkers, was able to unite these two strains of thought—that is, he did not merely report facts in his work, but commented upon them—this seeming inconsistency offers no real challenge to my interpretation. After all, even Hume, a far greater and more sophisticated empiricist than Agrippa, adopted and even defended a pattern of interpretation. The peculiarity of Agrippa is that he did not attempt to defend any of his interpretations; he merely offered them in the spirit of one who realized that all patterns were artificial and who considered them all on the same footing. Realizing that mere experience was not enough, he had said that one penetrated to the nature of things by experience and *conjecture*. His use of the word "conjecture", I

think, is significant. He was no doubt thinking of the difference between fact and conjecture when he said in the dedication of his first book of occult philosophy that while it probably contains much that is in error, it nevertheless contains many useful and necessary "things". The facts, he thought, would be useful no matter what the value of the pattern he had placed upon them.

His unusual religious attitudes—unusual at least for the time—are another indication of his undogmatic acceptance of a pattern. He had defied the authorities as early as 1519 by defending the views of Jacques LeFevre d'Etaples; in 1525, he possessed the books of Luther and Carlstadt. He never left the Roman Catholic faith and we have no reason to suspect hypocrisy [In a footnote, the critic adds: "There is not one shred of evidence which could explain why Agrippa never actually broke with the Roman faith. It is a matter of common observation, though, that while all kinds of skeptics (using the word loosely here) are usually at odds with the established order, they do not make good revolutionaries. Both Montaigne and Hume, for example, were suspect to many of their contemporaries, but both were staunch defenders of the social status quo. From the viewpoint of an empiricist, there is no reason for change—what we have at least has the virtue of being established and, presumably, tolerable, while we have no way of knowing what evils a change will bring with it. The outcome of the empirical view of reality is most clearly seen in Burke, although there were other elements involved in his case."]; yet he could write to Melancthon in a letter dated September, 1532:

> May God keep you in safety and prosper you, according to the desire of your Christian mind. Salute for me Martin Luther, that unconquered heretic, who, as Saint Paul says in the Acts, after the way which they call heresy worships the God of his fathers.

At about the same time, he was interrogated by the authorities for publicly calling Luther an "unconquered heretic". The theologians contended that since the Church had declared him wrong, Luther was, indeed, conquered. From their viewpoint, "unconquered heretic" was a contradiction in terms. Agrippa countered their argument by pointing out the absurdity of mistaking the word for the fact. Luther was, after all, making new converts daily and, however desirable that end might be, he was not conquered. The theologians could condemn him with every known invective without bringing his "conquest" any closer.

Perhaps the best way to sum up this evaluation of Cornelius Agrippa is to say that, as in the controversy over Luther, he was always willing to confront any notion with sheer fact. Whatever the pattern he might place upon the world in order to make some sense of it, the pattern had to yield to the fact. That this approach has its dangers has been shown—pursued consistently, it guarantees credulity as to reported fact, and there is a possibility that it will evolve into nihilism. But it can also, at times, produce the instances of hard-headed, commonsense realism which is apparent in his argument with the theologians.

One must ask, though, why the faith which Agrippa postulated as the only way to arrive at eternal "Truth" seemingly had so little to do with the rest of his philosophy. An answer was at least implied at the beginning of this [essay]: Faith applied to a different world from the world of fact—the world of inner connections between things, of essences, and of purpose. That this higher world existed was an article of belief for Cornelius Agrippa; his chief insight into it was that he could only conjecture about its nature. With this attitude, faith could have no relation to fact: it could only justify the use of facts in conjecture, and cause a continuing belief in "constructions" throughout all his failure to find the right one.

It is always hazardous to speculate about whether a given attitude is "scientific". Contributions to science have come from men holding such vastly different presuppositions that any generalization this broad is likely to be refuted as soon as it is made. Kepler, for example, who undoubtedly made great contributions to science, was a good deal like Agrippa. He observed facts, and by the method of trial and error tried to find a pattern that would fit them. Although he tested countless fantastic schemes before finding the right one, his ultimate success is a matter of record. Whether his success was by accident is a matter of conjecture. At any rate, without going into the broader, and perhaps insoluble question, one can give an answer to the limited question of whether the methods of trial and error is the same as the method of "scientific hypothesis and experiment".

I think that the most obvious conclusion to be drawn from this analysis of Agrippa is that the two methods, trial-and-error and scientific hypothesis, are radically different. It is, then, necessary to reject the notion that Agrippa was reaching, even unconsciously, toward the concept of scientific hypothesis and experiment. It is at the same time necessary to reject the close relationship which Haydn found between unsystematic empiricism and modern scientific methodology. While the concept of scientific hypothesis does, of course, have to do with facts, and requires a certain respect for fact, Agrippa's empirical epistemology bears no relationship to scientific hypothesis. Modern physical science owes its origin, to a great extent, to relinquishing the unquestioning acquiescence in fact which was typical of Agrippa. The making of a verifiable hypothesis, as the example of Galileo illustrated, requires that one initially leave the realm of intuited fact for the world of mathematical idealizations. Who could conceive of Agrippa studying the path of a projectile by rolling a ball down an inclined plane? Or of announcing, when the weight of empirical evidence was overwhelmingly against him, that under ideal conditions a projectile would continue in a straight line forever? He would, rather—as Galileo's Aristotelian contemporaries did—study the projectile itself, and pronounce the scientific constructs "fantastic". After all, there is no place on earth where the ideal conditions demanded by Galileo could be found to exist.

The crucial difference is at what point the respect for fact enters. The method of modern science is to subject the hypothesis to facts *after* the idealized conditions are calculated and proper allowances are made for the operation of the hypothesis under actual conditions. Pure empiricism,

however, demands that if hypotheses are introduced at all they shall be used to rationalize facts already accepted at their face value. For instance, one first accepts the "fact" that people have been raised from the dead, then elaborates a theory to explain the fact. The flitting from theory to theory, the acceptance of one occult system after another provided it can "explain" some intuition or reported fact, is the logical absolute of pure empiricism when it is held in conjunction with a faith that the world ultimately makes sense. Unsystematic and unguided trial-and-error is the only method an empiricist can regard as trustworthy, and as long as he is true to his presuppositions he will never advance beyond it.

From this point of view, Agrippa's endorsement of Lullian rationalism is perfectly understandable. So with geomancy, astrology, and innumerable other black arts, he was willing to flirt with Lullian rationalism if it could explain some of the facts of the world. According to Agrippa's empiricism, it was not required, or even expected, that the various theories he held should be related to one another. The principle of non-contradiction was simply a "construct" like all the others be tried and found wanting. "Do I contradict myself?" he might have said with Walt Whitman, "Very well then, I contradict myself". One thing should be apparent by now—whatever the chance contributions this trial-and-error procedure might make, it cannot be called "the scientific method". The real significance of Cornelius Agrippa in the history of thought is to illustrate the profound difference between the method that came to be known (if unjustly) as "Baconian", and the method of modern science.

Agrippa was a widely learned man and he was as versatile as either *l'uomo universale* or Faust. But the habitat of the universal man was Renaissance Italy and that of Goethe's Faust was a Germany modeled after Renaissance Italy. The universal man knew his place in the cosmos, and knowing this, had no doubts about his ability to penetrate to the inner nature of that cosmos by the method of human intelligence and human activity. Faust, still a Renaissance man, repudiated human science, but only to reaffirm his ability to penetrate into the meaning of the world by another method. Had Agrippa lived in Renaissance Italy, he would perhaps have been *l'uomo universale,* and in his own time and place had he been less intellectually honest, he might have been Faust. But living in Reformation Germany where two rival dogmatisms faced each other on equally insecure grounds, and having his particular blend of faith and empiricism, he was closer to the two worlds of Immanuel Kant than he was either to *l'uomo universale* or Faust.

Richard H. Popkin   (essay date 1964)

SOURCE: "The Revival of Greek Scepticism in the 16th Century," in *The History of Scepticism from Erasmus to Descartes,* revised edition, Van Gorcum & Comp., 1964, pp. 17-43.

[*Below, Popkin focuses on* On the Uncertainty and Vanity of the Sciences *as an "example of fundamentalist anti-*

intellectualism" that nevertheless played an important role in the revival of interest in ancient skepticism.]

Probably the most notorious of those who have been ranked as sceptics in [the sixteenth century] is the curious figure, Henricus Cornelius Agrippa von Nettesheim, 1486-1535. He was a man who was interested in many things, but most notably, occult science. A strange work he wrote in 1526, **De Incertitudine et vanitate scientiarum declamatio invectiva . . .** has led him to be classed as an early sceptic. The popularity of this work, its many editions in Latin, as well as Italian, French and English translations in the 16th century, plus its influence on Montaigne, have given Agrippa an undeserved stature among those who played a role in the revival of sceptical thought in the Renaissance.

The book itself is actually a long diatribe against all sorts of intellectual activity, and all types of arts. The purpose, Agrippa tells us in his preface, is to denounce those who are proud in human learning and knowledge, and who therefore despise the Sacred Scriptures as too simple and crude; those who prefer the schools of philosophy to the Church of Christ. This denunciation is accomplished by surveying the arts and sciences (including such arts and sciences as dice- playing, whoring, etc.), and announcing that they are all useless, immoral, or something of the sort. Practically no argument occurs, only condemnations of the sins that all human activities are heir to. Knowledge, we are told, was the source of Adam's troubles, and will only cause us grief if we pursue it.

> Nothinge can chaunce unto men more pestilente, then knowledge: this is the very pestilence, that putteth all mankinde to ruine, the which chaseth awaie all Innocencie, and hath made us subjecte to so many kindes of sinne, and to death also: whiche hath extinguished the light of Faith, castinge our Soules into blinde darkenesse: which condemninge the truethe, hath placed errours in the hiest throne.

The only genuine source of Truth is Faith, Agrippa announces. The sciences are simply unreliable opinions of men, which are never actually established.

Not satisfied with these pronouncements, Agrippa then discussed each science and art in turn, liberally indicting the villainies of scientists and artists. The grammarians are blamed for having caused confusion about the proper translation of Scripture; the poets and historians are accused of lying; the logicians, criticized for making everything more obscure; mathematicians are castigated for offering no aid in salvation and for failing to square the circle; musicians for wasting people's time; natural philosophers for disagreeing with each other about everything; metaphysicians for having produced heresies; physicians for killing their patients; and theologians are accused of quibbling, and ignoring the Word of God.

What Agrippa advocated instead was that one should reject all knowledge, becoming a simple believer in God's Revelation. 'It is better therefore and more profitable to be Idiotes, and knowe nothinge, to beleve by Faithe and charitee, and to become next unto God, then being lofty & prowde through the subtilties of sciences to fall into the

possession of the Serpente.' On this note, the book closes, with a final condemnation of the scientists, 'O yee fooles & wicked ones, which setting apart the giftes of ye Ghost, endevour to learne those thinges of faitheles Philosophers, and masters of errours, whiche ye ought to receive of God, and the holy Ghoste.'

This example of fundamentalist anti-intellectualism is hardly a genuine philosophical argument for scepticism regarding human knowledge, nor does it contain a serious epistemological analysis. Some commentators have questioned whether it genuinely represents Agrippa's point of view in the light of his interest in occult science. Others have considered **De vanitate** more a fit of anger than a serious attempt to present doubts about what can be known. A recent study by Nauert ["Magic and Skepticism in Agrippa's Thought," *Journal of the History of Ideas* 18, April, 1957] has tried to show the relationship of Agrippa's views about the occult and his 'scepticism.' It is indicated that because of his distrust of our human mental capacities, Agrippa sought truth by more esoteric means. On this interpretation, **De vanitate** represents a stage in the development of Agrippa's views, in which faith and the Bible were becoming more central elements in his quest for truth which he felt could not be carried on by reason and science.

However, even though Agrippa's work does not present any sceptical analysis of human knowledge, it represents a facet of the revival of ancient scepticism, and it had some influence in producing further interest in sceptical thought. Agrippa mentions Cicero and Diogenes Laertius among his sources, and apparently used Gian Francesco Pico's work. I have found no reference to Sextus Empiricus in his book, though there are some sections which look as if they may have been based on that source. As to influence, Agrippa's book was well known in the 16th century, and was used by Montaigne as one of his sources. . . .

Charles G. Nauert, Jr.   (essay date 1965)

SOURCE: "Agrippa and the End of a World" and "Fact and Fantasy: Agrippa's Position in Intellectual History," in *Agrippa and the Crisis of Renaissance Thought,* University of Illinois Press, 1965, pp. 292-321, 322-34.

[*In the following excerpt, Nauert discusses the influence of Agrippa's works, emphasizing the ways in which they "helped shatter the rational and orderly worldview of the great medieval intellectual syntheses" and pointed the way toward the scientific revolution.*]

Despite Agrippa's failure to carry through consistently the exposition of his magical world view, and despite the fact that pessimism about human reason dominated his thinking even in his early years, the universe portrayed in **De occulta philosophia** is an orderly one. If man is unable by reason to comprehend all its secrets, Agrippa felt, still he may be able to find in the divinely revealed traditions of ancient sages, especially of Hermes and the cabalists, the key to mastery of his surroundings. The idea of a closely interconnected world, a world every part of which is alive, and the idea that the divinely illuminated soul can draw down superior powers, celestial, angelic, and even divine, do not represent a break on Agrippa's part with the cultural heritage of either the remote or the more immediate past. His aim of restoring magic to its ancient purity did not at all prevent him from drawing freely on such medieval magical writers as Albertus Magnus, Arnold of Villanova, Roger Bacon, Pietro d'Abano, and *Picatrix.* The organic, animistic, aesthetic world view which Agrippa shared with these men was not, after all, alien even to the thought of the greatest minds of the Middle Ages, such as Thomas Aquinas.

Yet some elements in the thought of Agrippa were destructive and disintegrative of the medieval world view in particular and, in general, of all culture. This [essay] will consider these anarchical elements, which appear not only in Agrippa's speculative thought but also in his ethical, political, and social doctrines. This side of his thought found its chief expression in *De incertitudine et vanitate scientiarum declamatio invectiva,* just as his magical thought was expressed principally and most completely in **De** *occulta philosophia*; but elements of this tendency appear in other works as well.

It is one of the peculiarities of intellectual history that later generations have found elements of skepticism in the thought of a man who on one occasion wrote that of the three chief modes of philosophizing, the Peripatetic, the Academic, and the Skeptical, he sometimes followed the first and sometimes the second, but always shunned the Skeptics, "among whom nothing is certain that they may follow, but all things are indifferent to them, and so they dispute on both sides concerning all things. . . ." Yet such is the case with Agrippa. Almost all the standard histories of philosophy mention the presence of skeptical elements in his thought, although they generally class him among Neoplatonic occultists or theosophists, and although they agree that his skepticism is only fragmentary and not of much significance. One of the few writers who have taken the skeptical side of his thought seriously, Rossi, explains [in his *Agrippa di Nettesheym e la direzione scettica della filosofia nel Rinascimento,* 1906] this apparent contradiction by assuming a fundamental change of attitude in the eleven years between the quoted statement and the composition of *De vanitate* in 1526. Actually, however, there was no major change. The context of the earlier statement makes it clear that what Agrippa had in mind when he attacked the skeptics was those who, often pretending to give rational demonstration of Christian dogmas, often even sincerely intending to do so, actually weakened Christian faith by seeking to confine faith within the bounds of human reason. This attitude, which is strongly reminiscent of the Scotist and Occamist denial of the power of reason to grasp ultimate, divine truths, was the basis of the criticism of scholastic philosophy which fills much of *De vanitate.* For Agrippa, the essence of the skepticism which he denounced was failure to acknowledge the limitations of human reason in religious matters. He would have agreed with the statement of his contemporary, Giovanni Francesco Pico della Mirandola, that the skeptics' arguments properly ought not to have any force when turned against Christian doctrines, since those doctrines rest solely on faith and revelation and are subject

neither to proof nor to disproof [*Examen vanitatis doctrinae gentium, et veritatis christianae disciplinae,* 1520].

Even Rossi admits that Agrippa's approach to skepticism was inductive, that is, that his main line of argument was to show that all sciences as now taught are full of contradictions and so cannot be regarded as certain. It is certainly true that quantitatively speaking, Agrippa based most of his declamation against the sciences on points which are only peripheral to the main problem of human knowledge. The lines of attack are several. The most important is that a given science is uncertain because all the authorities are at odds with one another. Unlike many of his contemporaries, in particular unlike his favorite modern authors, Ficino and Pico, Agrippa appears to delight in emphasizing the disunity of the various philosophical schools. He also shows a strong inclination to discredit the great authorities of the past, most notably in his repeated aspersions against the moral and intellectual integrity of Aristotle. A second major line which his so-called inductive skepticism follows is to show that the various arts and sciences are often or even usually the source of sin, evil, and heresy. Architecture, for example, is in itself praiseworthy but has led to excessive ornateness in the design of churches and has been employed in construction of engines of war. Rhetoric, to take another instance, is unsure of its principles, subject to misuse in the interests of injustice and untruth, infamous and disgraceful, and a source of heresies such as the apostasy of the Emperor Julian or, more recently, the outbreak of the Lutheran heresy, whose heads only a few years ago were everywhere lauded for their skill in rhetoric. Painting has been misused to depict obscene and inflammatory subjects. Further, if he can think of no other accusation against a science, Agrippa calls it useless for human salvation and happiness, as in the case of mathematics or cosmography. This, of course, is completely to confuse the issue, to divert discussion from the validity of human knowledge to the question of human beatitude and salvation. Finally, Agrippa repeats the common objection that human life is too short to master even one science well, even though he himself had often advised students to master all fields of learning.

Certain aspects of this attack on the individual sciences possess considerable intrinsic interest. There is, for example, his appeal to the reports of Spanish and Portuguese navigators in order to show how baseless were the authoritative opinions of all earlier geographers. This appeal to brute fact to undermine accepted theories shows an empirical side to his thought quite in harmony with the widespread empiricism of the later sixteenth century. It is also a rather early instance of the disturbing effect of the discoveries on the European world view. The chapters on astronomy and astrology have high intrinsic interest in their own right, one of the many interesting ideas being the disquieting possibility that unknown planets and stars may exist, thus vitiating any astrological science based on present knowledge. The whole argument is an example of the influence of Pico della Mirandola north of the Alps. Agrippa's general practice of collecting the opinions of the various philosophical schools on a given point is an example of the spread of knowledge about ancient philosophy and of the unsettling effect which acquaintance with ancient philosophical controversy might have.

But if there were nothing more than these immediately apparent lines of argument in Agrippa's thought, the historians of philosophy would have the best of Rossi on the question of the significance of Agrippa's skeptical tendencies. The most one could make of such statements would be an additional instance of the widespread dissatisfaction with late medieval learning. *De vanitate* would remain nothing but a flashy bit of paradox without much significance for the history of European thought and with greatly reduced significance even for study of Agrippa's own development. Agrippa would be just Agrippa the Magician or perhaps Agrippa the Charlatan.

In reality Agrippa has at least the germ of a far more thorough-going skeptical development than anyone, even Rossi, has realized. He is quite aware of the skepticism of the Academics and the Pyrrhonists concerning the ability of man to know causes. He sees as the weakness of Peripatetic logic the fact that the force of any argumentation depends on the truth of the premises, which must come from earlier demonstrations of no greater validity, or else from an accepted authority. He had always known this fact, even in his more optimistic treatise on the Lullian art; but by 1526 he was ready to deny not only in specific cases but also in the most general terms the ability of the human mind in any way to arrive at truths which can form adequate premises for truthful as well as formally valid syllogisms: "But so great is the ample liberty of truth, and its free amplitude, that by the speculations of no science, by no urgent judgment of the senses, by no arguments of logical artifice, by no evident proof, by no demonstrating syllogism, and by no discourse of human reason can it be seized upon, but only by faith. . . ." In short, what he is arguing, and this in the most explicit terms, is that "all sciences are nothing but decisions and opinions of men. . . ." If any science is used to good purpose, the goodness comes from its inventor or its user, not from the science itself. He flatly states that anything can be disproved just as easily as it can be proved, that there is no argument so strong that a stronger cannot be presented to overturn it.

These are not mere bald statements unsupported by argumentation. How is man by his own powers to grasp truths from which to construct logical chains of reasoning? The way obviously would be by sensory means. But although Agrippa does not name any source, he here applies arguments ultimately derived from ancient skepticism and later developed, with help from Sextus Empiricus, at much greater length by Michel de Montaigne. Agrippa observes that all knowledge comes from the senses and that the test of a true proposition is whether it corresponds to the sensed object. From this source alone we get all knowledge that is possible. But in the first place, it is evident that the senses are often deceived and hence that they can give no great degree of certitude. What is more, the senses are unable to reach intellectual nature and so can teach us nothing of the causes of lower things, from which must be demonstrated their natures, effects, and properties. The most we can know from the senses is individual

objects. So all higher sciences founded on sensory knowledge can be only fallacious, since sensation cannot give us any general principles.

A way out of this dilemma should have been available to one so strongly influenced by Platonism as Agrippa; but he fails to discuss it at this point because his own doctrine of original sin had already closed this way to him. The obvious solution was to teach that the ideas of all things already pre-existed in the soul. This would at least bridge the gap between the sensory and intellectual realms. But by teaching that original sin had veiled these ideas in the human soul by causing the departure of the divine light that had once made man know all truth, Agrippa effectively blocked this means of escape from skepticism. Of course, he clearly and consistently taught that mystical illumination could restore the original condition and grant all knowledge and true wisdom to man. But this doctrine leads out of the realm of epistemology and into the field of religious experience and grace. Although never systematically stated in his earlier writings, this skeptical attitude is intimately associated with his doctrine of mystical illumination. His general message had always been that man needs grace before he can attain ultimate reality.

The theoretical presentation of true skepticism in *De vanitate* is small in bulk, far smaller than the space devoted to specific and "empirical" attacks on various sciences. When compared to this latter element, the critical analysis of the foundations of human certitude seems hurried, sketchy, and incomplete. Agrippa's declamation against human learning certainly does not mark the systematic introduction of ancient Pyrrhonism into modern philosophical discussion, an introduction foreshadowed by the younger Pico and really accomplished by Montaigne and his disciples only much later in the century. So brief is the Nettesheimer's discussion of truly epistemological issues and so small the evidence of direct contact with the works of Sextus Empiricus, that the author of an important recent work on the growth of skepticism in the Renaissance refuses to call his standpoint skeptical and prefers the phrase "fundamentalist anti-intellectualism" [Richard H. Popkin, *The History of Scepticism from Erasmus to Descartes,* 1960]. Whether one chooses to apply the term *skeptic* to Agrippa depends, of course, on how strictly one wishes to limit the term. Certainly Agrippa did not offer the detailed presentation of ancient Pyrrhonist arguments that one will find in Montaigne and his followers. Whether he drew directly on the principal ancient skeptical source, Sextus Empiricus, is debatable. But although his book does indeed give far more space to gibes against learning than to philosophical analysis (the same is true, in lesser degree, even of Montaigne's "Apology for Raymond Sebond"), his work is not entirely innocent of the profounder philosophical questions. Small in bulk though it is, he does present a brief but effective analysis, framed in terms of broad reference to the problem of man's ability to know. This general consideration of the basis of human knowledge explains why he found so much uncertainty in each of the special sciences which he studied. Furthermore, he made specific reference to the Academics and Pyrrhonists when he wrote his short general discussion of the foundations of human knowledge. This evidence suggests that alongside late medieval disdain for learning, which was re-inforced in his lifetime by the tendency of humanists and Reformers to adopt a fundamentalist anti-intellectualism, Agrippa did feel some influence of truly skeptical nature. It is not entirely wrong, therefore, to call him a skeptic, even though strictly skeptical considerations form only a very small portion of *De vanitate.*

The fundamental inability of unaided human reason to gain valid scientific knowledge of course applies also to man's knowledge of God, the highest form of knowledge. God reveals Himself in three ways, which Agrippa describes as the Book of Nature, the Book of the Law, and the Book of the Gospel. Only from the first of these does man read by use of his own cognitive powers. But the knowledge of God from creatures, while clear enough to make inexcusable anyone who does not know and honor God, cannot attain His essence as He is in Himself, separated from all things. Thus even if man were capable of forming a valid science from created things, the real essentials of a knowledge of God are not discoverable in those created things. Dialectic and philosophy are simply unable to rise to true knowledge of God. Only the purified soul, filled with grace, love, and faith, can do this. In other words, knowledge of God occurs only in the realm of grace, not in that of reason.

As early as 1516, this belief in the inability of reason to comprehend the divine nature had led Agrippa to attack contemporary theology for trying to bend divinity to human reason. Reasoning in divinity, he argues, is the source of all error. It even led to the fall of Adam, since by reasoning with the Serpent instead of blindly obeying God's commandment, Eve made it possible for him to deceive her. Reason does nothing but destroy the simplicity of faith, trying to take heaven by storm, questioning and so undermining the most most sacred beliefs. The Schoolmen, Agrippa charges, while criticizing freely all others, themselves debate the most shocking propositions imaginable. The only theology which he praises is that of the Church Fathers. Needless to say, Agrippa's study of the writings of Luther and other Reformers did not weaken this antischolastic predilection, a fact which appears clearly from *De vanitate.* It is true that much of his invective is directed against symptoms of scholastic decadence, such as the involved and oversubtle terminology of the later Scotists or the blind and narrow sectarianism of the various schools, Thomists, Albertists, Scotists, Occamists, and others. Yet he clearly believes that even in the less decadent age, of Albert, Thomas, and Scotus themselves, when at least it might have been useful to refute heretics, scholastic theology was a monstrous combination of philosophical reasons and divine revelation. He expressly compares it to a centaur. Rational proof of dogmas may be clever, he admits, but it is not pious. The only theology which he can approve is that which depends on divine illumination or which plainly expounds the text of Scripture, which itself is a product of divine illumination, not of human reasoning.

What this rejection of scholastic theology really amounts to is a restatement by Agrippa of the fideistic attitude of late medieval thinkers, especially the followers of William of Ockham. Man should not proudly strive to know by rational powers, but rather should fervently believe in revelation. In itself, fideism does not necessarily imply a thoroughgoing skepticism, only a sharper division between the realm of grace and the realm of reason than that posited by the Thomists. But Agrippa united this partial skepticism of the fideists with a more general skepticism concerning all human knowledge. This more general skepticism shows traces of a rethinking of the works of ancient skeptics as they were known to the Middle Ages; it also shows the influence of potentially skeptical elements in the thought of Nicholas of Cusa, who believed that all human knowledge is more or less arbitrary, and who compared the relation between human statements and actual truth to that between a polygon and the circle in which it is inscribed. Fideism could easily employ general skeptical arguments if these terminated in counsels to follow probability in daily living and so left the way open for an act of faith. This, for instance, was the teaching of Giovanni Francesco Pico della Mirandola, nephew of the famous Pico. This late-medieval fideism not only survived into the sixteenth century but became accentuated with the appearance of Protestantism. Indeed, this union of skepticism and fideism, already foreshadowed in certain late medieval thinkers and in the younger Pico, became a prime characteristic of French Roman Catholic disciples of Montaigne, and formed a major element in the anti-Calvinist religious polemic of the Catholic Reformation in France.

Not only theology, however, but every field of human learning came in for attack by the restless and pessimistic mind of the Nettesheimer, for his epistemological doubts seriously questioned the conformity between the abstractions of the human mind and the external objects for which they stood. Thus such abstractions as the cycles, epicycles, and spheres of the astral world became for Agrippa mere figments of the astronomer's mind. Similarly, he denied any objective existence to the abstractions of metaphysics and to those of mathematics. The same anarchy of uncontrolled opinion exists in natural philosophy, where philosophers freely put forth opinions, all equally valid and invalid, concerning all questions, ranging from the theoretical problems of the principle of all being or the plurality of worlds to the practical question of the immediate causes of observable phenomena such as earthquakes. Little remained to Agrippa but unreliable sense experience of singulars and arbitrary constructs of the human mind. In later thinkers, this attitude was eventually destined to grow into the modern theory of scientific hypothesis and its subjection to the test of facts; and Agrippa's thought contains hints that he himself was groping blindly in this direction. . . . But the general effect of Agrippa's thought, and especially of *De vanitate,* the most widely circulated of his writings, was to present only the negative moment of this philosophical development. The message of *De vanitate* was overwhelmingly destructive in nature.

A further line of attack on human learning hit not so much at the intellectual validity of the sciences as at their significance. This kind of argument, as noted above, was only peripheral to Agrippa's expression of true skepticism. Yet this argument, that even if true the sciences have no significance for the happiness and well-being of man, was in its own right a disquieting, though hardly original, element in the man's thought. Orthodox Christianity had never given ultimate value to human learning in its own right, but the moderately humanistic tendency represented by Thomas Aquinas had recognized a value, secondary but still real, in secular learning. Now Agrippa denied not only the validity of the sciences as sciences but also their relevance to man's welfare in any case. Man's true happiness, he argued, does not consist in knowledge of any sort but in a good life and a connection with God which unaided human powers cannot achieve. Not a clever mind but a virtuous will is important. Repeatedly Agrippa introduced the question of value. His chief interest regularly seems to be less in the validity of a science than in its significance for man's happiness and salvation. He did not ask whether a science makes a man more knowing but whether it makes him morally better and whether it grants him true wisdom. In his pessimism he was certain that at best human arts and sciences are irrelevant for this purpose, while more often than not they are positively harmful. Sciences do not illumine the Bible but are illumined by it. Any goodness that may be in any human science comes not from the science itself but from the goodness of its founder or of him who uses it in a given instance.

Agrippa did not try to escape this intellectual anarchy by pushing aside all philosophical considerations and stressing the value of ancient literature for its aesthetic and moral content. Despite his broad general acquaintance with classical literature and the writings of such modern authors as Petrarch, Valla, Ficino, and Pico, he was not a humanist in any broad sense of the term. He believed that Roman law should be stripped of medieval accretions; he urged students to study ancient literature; he praised the study of languages; he criticized the barbarisms of the terminology of professional philosophers. But none of these traits of humanism gave him a way out of the intellectual anarchy he had wrought. If he praised the idea of trilingual (Latin, Greek, and Hebrew) learning, it was solely for the sake of Bible study. If he praised the study of ancient authors, it was not with confidence that any ancient philosophical school would provide a system of great value, and it was almost always with an admonition about the greater value of studying sacred letters. If he himself studied ancient texts with avidity, he did so in the belief that they enshrined a secret revelation from God to man. What is more, in addition to becoming disillusioned with Hermetic and cabalistic writings as a source of divine revelation, the later Agrippa reserved some of his sharpest barbs for those who upheld the value of polite letters. He accused some of the proud literary men of scorning the Bible because of its lack of literary adornment. He denied any validity to grammar because it depends on usage rather than on reason; and he pointed out the hypercritical tendency of all grammarians. Grammarians, he said, have shown that not only George of Trebizond and Lorenzo Valla but even Cicero, Ovid, and other ancient writers have committed faults of grammar. He attacked such fields of literature as poetry and history because they tell tales both untrue and depraving, such as the stories of Arthur, Lancelot, and Tristan. Ovid to him was nothing but a teller of bawdy tales, as were Aeneas Sylvius, Dante,

Petrarch, Pontano, Leon Battista Alberti, and, above all, Boccaccio. Finally, when he said that pride in learning is the source of all heresies, when he noted that Christendom was tranquil and devout when Alexander Gallus was the only grammarian, Petrus Hispanus dominated dialectic, Laurentius Aquilegius ruled rhetoric, the ecclesiastical calendar was all the mathematics studied, and Isidore sufficed for all the rest of learning, was he not striking almost as hard against the humanists as against the Schoolmen? He concentrated more on the latter because he regarded them as the more pressing danger, but he did not leave humanistic studies and their proponents untouched by any means.

Since Agrippa had left little basis for science except the authority of the past, his readers must have found it still more disconcerting to see how everywhere he assailed the accepted authorities. This was true not only of the medieval Schoolmen and their favorite philosopher, Aristotle, but also of every ancient author. He showed that even Cicero, Demosthenes, Ovid, and the other great ancient writers erred often. If study of Plato makes a man impious, yet study of Aristotle and his followers makes one superstitious, while would-be Ciceronians become pagans. Even such revered authorities as Hippocrates in medicine came under Agrippa's attack. Even the Church Fathers, the only theologians whom he praised, erred on individual points in spite of all their sanctity. A recurring refrain in Agrippa's works is: "Every man is a liar: but only Christ, man and God, never was and never will be found untruthful. . . ." Only divine grace and revelation offer hope of release from human weakness and ignorance.

Thus Agrippa denied the ability of man to know the external world or its Creator, and cast doubt on the arts and sciences which man had constructed on the presumption that he could know reality. Agrippa cast doubt on all past authorities and so could not find satisfactory refuge in any form of ipsedixitism. And he had little use for mere external sensory knowledge of singulars. What [I have] shown, in short, is his denial of any congruity between human reason and reality. The only way in which he softened this discord was by giving a high position to the power of the divinely illuminated mind and to the Bible as the greatest of all products of divine inspiration.

Yet such denial of the powers of human reason does not necessarily call into question the orderly nature of the universe itself. A further question is whether from being a mystical romantic, as Hiram Haydn would call him [in his *The Counter-Renaissance,* 1950], Agrippa passed on to become a disillusioned naturalist: in other words, whether he denied that there is any order in creation to begin with. His attack on the power of the human mind was consciously, clearly, and pungently worked out. There was no comparable assault on the idea that the universe is orderly and meaningful. Yet there were hints in this direction. Most of these occurred as an underlying and scarcely conscious element in his treatment of specific problems, especially in the realm of practical affairs.

In one sense, of course, the magical world view which he never wholly abandoned was itself a challenge to belief in an orderly universe. The action of the *magus* and of the multitude of natural, occult, celestial, and spiritual forces which he employs represented an unruly, disorderly principle which broke through the usual hierarchical structure of reality, bending and twisting that order to make it subject to the will of man. Yet at the same time, magic depended on the sympathetic interrelationship of all ranks of being an interrelationship which was no less real merely because human reason could not grasp it but could only learn it from experience. So in a higher sense, Agrippa's acceptance of a magical world view did not really contradict belief in the goodness and orderliness of God's creation. There was still an orderliness in the world, but the order was that of a living, growing, feeling, and even intelligent animal, endowed at once with material body, intermediate spirit, and nonmaterial soul, rather than that of cold, dead matter divided into rigid, easily classified categories. The order was hidden from man's reason, at least since the sin of Adam had robbed the soul of divine illumination. But it was known to the Creator, and also known to glorified, purified man—to Adam before his fall, and to man after the action of divine grace and his own self-purification had restored the light of God to his soul.

In most respects, one must conclude that Agrippa's universe still seemed orderly even though beyond the power of human comprehension. Hence he felt that if only divine illumination would lift the veil of fleshly cares from the soul, man could attain all knowledge by immediate intuition. Such divinely inspired knowledge would also enable man to perform wondrous works, beyond the ordinary powers of nature. The belief in an orderly and interconnected universe thus had not disappeared, if only man could learn the order and connection between things and so make use of them. In criticizing alchemy, Agrippa blamed the alchemists for seeking by art to overcome nature, when art could only follow nature from afar. Its effort to make gold was not only fraudulent but also wicked, for it sought to upset a divine law in nature instituted after the fall of Adam: that man should eat his bread in the sweat of his brow. Still in lesser matters, where it has not done violence to nature but only followed it, alchemy has produced many useful things, such as dyestuffs, metallic alloys, cannon, and glass. There are also something of orderliness and a suggestion of primitivism in Agrippa's treatment of the various branches of agriculture in *De vanitate,* for although he has criticisms to make, the simpler, more natural agrarian society does not suffer the scathing criticism to which he subjects courtly and urban life. Likewise his strong preference for simples and his distaste for foreign remedies in medicine, attitudes soon to be emphasized in far greater detail by Paracelsus, are based on a confidence that if any drug were really suited to the treatment of persons living in a given climate, nature would have provided a source for it in some native plant. Belief in an orderly universe also appears in Agrippa's definition of natural magic as the highest part of natural philosophy, inspecting the sympathetic bonds between things and so understanding and using occult powers to perform apparently miraculous works. Its major failing, he thought, is that it is so easily and so often contaminated by superstition. Agrippa's world even after 1526 was peopled by good and evil spirits, which the *magus* could summon; but even more than in his earlier period, he warned

of the danger of such practices, since evil spirits often appear in the guise of good ones. The only statement which might seriously shake belief in the existence of an orderly world is Agrippa's ridiculing of the notion of the music of the spheres. This is only a peripheral matter, however. Agrippa had far too much faith in divine wisdom to teach that the universe created by God was disordered and imperfect.

Religion was no guard, however, against a contrary view in the realm of human affairs, for the doctrine of original sin could always serve as a theoretical justification for belief that society was disordered, selfish, and cruel. There are strong traces of just such a view in Agrippa's thought. The key to this belief in the anarchy of society is the chapter on moral philosophy in *De vanitate.* Here, while assuming of course that there is an absolute moral law in the realm of grace, the Nettesheimer seriously questions the existence of a moral order in the purely human sphere. Moral philosophy, he charges, "depends not so much on the reasons of philosophers as on varying usage, custom, observation, and frequent use of daily living, and is changeable according to the opinion of times, places, and men. . . ." He defends this statement first of all with reference to the varying moral standards of different peoples. Like Montaigne half a century later, he says "that what once was a vice is even regarded as virtue, and what is here a virtue is elsewhere vice." For example, the ancient Hebrews and modern Turks permitted polygamy and concubinage, a practice regarded as execrable among the Christians. The Greeks found nothing wrong, he says, with homosexuality and appearance on the stage, both held shameful by the Romans. The Romans let their wives appear in public, while the Greeks did not. The Lacedemonians and Egyptians regarded theft as honorable, while we punish it. Agrippa also explains the existence of moral relativism on the grounds of different national characteristics, which in this case he attributes to the stars. This attribution, not wholly consonant with his doubts about astral influences earlier in the same work, was more happily explained as the result of climatic conditions by Jean Bodin later in the same century. Agrippa's denunciation of the wickedness of moral philosophers, especially the depraved and miscreant Aristotle, does not add much to buttress his belief in moral relativism. More effective is his argument that even ethicians are still disagreed about the nature of the *summum bonum,* some placing it in pleasure, some in virtue, and some elsewhere. He insists on the fundamental disharmony between the teachings of moral philosophy and the teachings of Christ. Beatitude, he says, is attained "not by Stoic virtue, Academic purgation, or Peripatetic speculation but by faith and grace in the Word of God." Agrippa makes a radical contrast between the wisdom of the world and the foolishness of Christ: "Christ teaches to do good to all, to love even one's enemies, to lend freely, to take revenge on no one, to give to every one who asks; on the contrary the philosophers [teach one to aid] only those who repay benefit with benefit; besides, that it is permissible to be wrathful, to hate, to contend, to wage war, to take interest." In conclusion, Agrippa charges that those who trust in the dictates of right reason are tending toward the heresy of Pelagianism. All moral philosophy is false and vain.

Accompanying this belief in moral relativism is a picture of human nature which shows strong traces of what students of sixteenth-century thought, referring to writers like Machiavelli and Guicciardini, call an animalistic view of human nature. Anyone who reads the bitter social criticisms contained in *De vanitate* must be well aware that they are not the work of a man who believed in the goodness of human nature. Every rank of society, according to Agrippa, depends on cruelty and deceit for its being. The nobility have risen to power by warfare, another name for murder, by prostituting their wives and daughters to the lusts of the monarch, or by the basest flattery and most abject servitude to the great and powerful; and they live by oppressing the lower classes, by cheating the crown, and by selling their influence at court. Their life is a mass of vices of every sort. Most members of religious orders regard their vocation as nothing but a means to win a subsidized and idle life and a shield against prosecution for their crime and immorality. Medical doctors are ignorant charlatans who do more harm than good. Lawyers are shysters who distort good laws and worm their way into the inner councils of princes, displacing the rightful and hereditary councillors. Merchants are cheats and usurers. This sharp social criticism, of which these are but a few instances, by no means implies any truly democratic element in Agrippa's thought. If the upper classes are vicious and oppressive, he regards the lower classes as stupid, superstitious, and crude. The gnostic scorn for the rabble which underlay Agrippa's insistence on the need to conceal occult philosophy never left him. The unforgivable sin of the monks is the way in which they expose the debates of the learned to the vulgar by their vituperative sermons. Their greatest folly was, by denouncing Luther in their sermons, to force him to write in the vernacular and so to infect the common herd with his heresy. The most desperate threat which Agrippa could make was that he might write in the vulgar tongue and so carry his anticlerical attack among the masses.

There is more to Agrippa's naturalistic view of man than mere denunciation of the injustice and vice of every rank of society. His attack on human nature also passes to the theoretical sphere, though not in any single coherent expression. What is the law of nature of which political theorists prattle so greatly? It is, he says, "not to go hungry, not to go thirsty, not to be cold, not to torment oneself with vigils or labors: it places Epicurean pleasure in the place of the highest felicity, pushing aside all the penitence of religion and works of penitence." Taking up a characteristic theme of the extreme ethical pessimists of the sixteenth century, Agrippa says that "even man himself (as it is in the proverb) is a wolf to man," a judgment amply borne out by his detailed picture of the abuses of society. Elsewhere he returns to the same theme by noting that when noblemen choose animals for their coats of arms, they never choose useful beasts but always fierce and predatory ones. His view of human nature is hardly optimistic.

Moral relativism and the animalistic view of natural man almost necessarily implied the shaking of all those social institutions which made for orderliness in human affairs. Politics, a branch of applied moral philosophy, fell into ruin under Agrippa's criticism. He discussed the usual three forms of government, monarchy, aristocracy, and democracy, and showed some tendency to favor a mixed constitution combining two or more of the pure forms. But no type of constitution, he concluded, has any real value. All depends on the moral character of ruler and ruled. All forms of government are equally good in good hands, equally bad in bad hands. Thus there is no true order in the state itself; there is really no science of politics.

If Agrippa's view of political science depends chiefly on his ethical relativism, his view of law derives also from his pessimistic view of human nature. Agrippa knew quite well the many definitions of justice and expressed them fully in his *Oratio pro quodam doctorando.* But what came to his mind when he wrote on law in *De vanitate* was the harsh realities of law and government. Noting papal and imperial claims to plenitude of power, he traced the origin of all law to arbitrary acts of will on the part of lawmakers, who then cleverly gave their statutes divine sanction among the vulgar masses by pretending to have received their codes from a god. At this particular point he used only examples from gentile history, but in another place in the same chapter he discussed Moses' foundation of Jewish law in terms identical to those he used to describe the origin of gentile legal systems. Thus he seems to hint at the doctrine of the political origin of religious laws which was to become a major theme of seventeenth-century libertinism. Agrippa did not explicitly state it, however, and may not have consciously intended to include the Mosaic code among those laws whose divine sanction is the result of mere imposture. His denunciation of laws as a source of strife and contention was less weighty; but then he proceeded to analyze the binding power of laws, a power which according to him derives solely from the consent of the people, or from the consent of a prince on whom this popular power has been conferred. If an error is made, the error may itself become good law. "Hence we now know that all the prudence of the civil law depends on the mere opinion and will of men, no other reason being active except honesty of manners, or convenience of living, or the authority of the prince, or force of arms." If made for a good purpose by a good prince, a law is good; otherwise not. What is more, pettifogging lawyers and glossators often succeed in distorting even a good law, while lustful princes pervert all the laws to pander to their own unclean desires. There is no law so carefully written that lawyers cannot overturn it. And legal remedies are weak and ineffective unless the plaintiff is strong enough to assert his rights. Agrippa did not spare the canon law either, for he regarded it as arbitrary and oppressive and subject to the greatest abuse by sharp practitioners and unworthy clerics. Much of the social criticism contained in the middle chapters of *De vanitate* concerns perversion of the law by the mighty, and he made effective use of the venality of the university law faculties which pronounced in favor of the divorce of Henry VIII.

Agrippa did not accept these conditions with the coolness of a Machiavelli or a Guicciardini, although his attitude is otherwise reminiscent of the amoral view of the state which appears in the writings of the two great Florentine political theorists. The difference is partly in the passion with which Agrippa denounced the conditions which grow out of this political relativism and this bestiality of the great and powerful. But it lies mainly in the persistence in his thought of the other realm of being, the other standard of morals, that of the world of grace. All this disorder just described exists in the natural and unsanctified world, which original sin has cut off from contact with the world of the ideal. The Nettesheimer was unable and unwilling to push into the background the insistent moral imperative of Christianity. The power of the state still ideally derives from God. The holders of political power are under obligation to punish those who offend against the divine law: for instance, to repress houses of prostitution instead of favoring them and profiting by them. Similarly the claims of princes to be mortal gods are not in contradiction to man's obligation to obey the divine law. Their power derives from God, and part of man's religious duty is to obey them. The ability of kings to cure disease by touch illustrates their divine institution. Agrippa's argument that kings and nobles first arose from violence and bloodshed, that the Lord was angry with the Israelites for desiring a king, and that royal power corrupted even virtuous men, does not really contradict this ultimate derivation of authority from God. There is some inconsistency in his praising tyrannicide, but this still is not contradictory to the divine origin of authority. The unclear question is rather whether one may licitly kill the ruler who abuses the divinely instituted power. Thus one cannot say that there is no moral order in the intellectual world of Agrippa; but the order is in the realm of grace, not that of nature. The natural world is disordered and animalistic. The major positive message of *De vanitate* is that to end all these abuses in the intellectual realm and in the secular and ecclesiastical worlds, man must stop depending on his own depraved nature and instead must humbly rely on the Word of God as expressed in the illuminated soul and in the Bible. The ideal Christian is symbolized by the humble and patient ass, by the *idiota,* an ideal quite reminiscent of the *docta ignorantia* of Nicholas of Cusa, to whose work *De docta ignorantia* Agrippa expressly appealed in his defense of *De vanitate.*

De vanitate was a disturbing book. The Sorbonne and the Louvain theological faculty both condemned it, though their condemnations missed much of the point of the entire argument. The radical denial of the power of the human mind to grasp reality was one of the chief disturbing elements. Villey [in his *Les sources et l'evolution des Essais de Montaigne,* 1933], although he regards the book as a mere *jeu d'esprit,* admits that it was an important source of the skepticism of Michel de Montaigne. All that survived the wreckage of human science, aside from supernatural mysticism, was sense perception of singulars, which Agrippa thought unsuited to the foundation of a science, and the authority of the past masters of Antiquity. Even the great authorities of the past came in for attack, not only Aristotle and the medieval scholastics, but also Plato, Hermes, the Alexandrian school, the cabalists, and even, with far greater limitations, the Church Fathers. These two elements of *De vanitate,* the attack on reason and the repudiation of past authorities, undermined faith in the ability of the mind to know reality. A third major theme of the book was the shaking of belief in the orderly

nature of the universe. This attack struck not at the physical world but at the moral world, where original sin provided a theoretical justification for it. A pessimistic view of human nature combined with moral relativism to undermine the rational foundations of human institutions. The prolonged and embittered social criticism which fills much of the book was really an extended demonstration of this principle of moral anarchy in the natural world. A final disturbing element was the rabid anticlericalism which the book reflects. Despite the obvious exaggeration of many of the statements, the book is a valid expression of the author's intellectual and emotional rejection of all human arts and sciences.

It is not hard to picture the consternation which Agrippa himself must have felt at the results of his formulation of doubt. The position which he had reached could hardly have satisfied him, for his tone was not the cool mockery of a Montaigne, nor the matter-of-fact attitude of a Machiavelli, but rather the impassioned invective of a Jean-Jacques Rousseau. One can see him shrinking back from the chaos he had wrought.

His declamatory little book itself contains elements of an effort to save something out of the ruin of all learning. Most important in Agrippa's own mind was the mystical escape from intellectual anarchy. As the present study has repeatedly shown, the mystical solution ran through his thought consistently from his earliest to his latest years. If only the mind of man, having been freed from the bonds of the flesh by careful preparation, can attain mystical illumination, then all knowledge and so all power will be its own. Since Agrippa himself did not claim personal experience of this sort, he had to provide a way out for those like himself who were not mystics. This way was to follow the lead of those who had gained such union, that is, simply and humbly to follow the Bible, which is the work of such illuminates. Even for a profound understanding of Scripture, illumination is necessary; but the humbler believer can gain beatitude by merely following the letter of Holy Writ carefully, believing the essentials of the teaching of the universal church (whatever those essentials were, a point on which he was not clear, though he certainly included the two great commandments and the Apostles' Creed), and reverently praying to God. God, he was sure, will not fail such a believer. Mysticism and skepticism, far from being opposed, here exist together.

Agrippa also groped, although far less surely, toward a solution of the problem of skepticism on an intellectual plane. Sense knowledge of singulars did not perish in his attack, although he seriously questioned its accuracy in any given case. This was the empirical side of his thought. His suspicion that somehow the great authorities of Antiquity could not have been so wrong as they seemed was an effort to salvage the principle of authority by accepting allegorical interpretations. Both his attempt to return to Antiquity and his empiricism really amounted to authoritarianism, the authority of bald statement and the authority of brute fact. At the same time, the belief that all higher generalizations were equally arbitrary made it possible for him to accept any scheme of explanation provisionally as long as it seemed useful, that is, as long as it stood the test of facts. Here was an adumbration of the function of scientific hypothesis, but without any program for controlled observation or planned experiments, and of course without any idea of quantitative, mathematical expression. Here was also an invitation to question and rethink all scientific generalizations, a process which was far more important in the scientific revolution that was about to begin than was any accumulation of new data. The least that such a book could do was to encourage people to explore any new idea, however absurd it might seem. All of this later development, of course, was outside the scope of Agrippa's thought, but he stood at the threshold of it. Ernst Cassirer has long since noted [in his *Das Erkennthis problem in der Philosophie and Wissenschaft der neueren Zeit,* 1906-20] that skepticism was the first great step toward modern philosophical reconstruction. Consciously or unconsciously, this is how Agrippa was able to continue his alchemical operations and his search for recondite literature after 1526, and how he was able to publish *De occulta philosophia* as a book containing many errors of the past but also much useful information.

His own and succeeding generations were unable to see this, and for them *De vanitate* remained either a pungent and sometimes witty paradox or a very unsettling book. His complete separation of the ideal and real worlds, for instance, was intended for the disparagement of the latter, not of the former. But all now depended on an act of faith, for he had ruled out on principle any rational demonstration of religious or other significant truth. Suppose one did not choose to take the leap of faith. What remained was an unknowable world, and, as far as the moral realm was concerned, a brutal, disorderly, and amoral one. This was the danger latent in the fideists' sharp separation of the realm of grace from the realm of nature. Even John Calvin felt some alarm at the tendency of certain naturalists to exalt animal instinct and appetite in man, a tendency which recent Roman Catholic apologists have called a natural outcome of the radical split which the Protestants made between the world of grace and the world of nature.

[I have] already shown the possible germ of the libertine belief that all religious laws, even that of Moses, were the products of clever impostors who gained respect for their codes among the masses by pretending to have written at the dictate of a god. This teaching was one of the major ingredients of that seventeenth-century Italian libertinism which attracted the *esprits forts* of every part of Europe. It is by no means clear that Agrippa meant the idea to apply to anyone but the founders of gentile religious laws, and there is not the slightest hint anywhere in his writings that he regarded Jesus Christ as such an impostor. This was, of course, a common enough theme in medieval literature, expressed in the tale of the three impostors, Moses, Jesus, and Mohammed.

De vanitate also shows other traits of the later libertine teachings. One is the notion that all religions are subject to the stars in their origin, rise, and fall, though Agrippa mentioned it only to denounce it as an example of the impiety to which astrology has led. He was also well aware of the heterodox interpretation of Aristotle by the Averroists and the school of Alexander of Aphrodisias; and apparently he believed that these doctrines of the unity of the intellect, the mortality of the individual soul, and the eternity of the world represented the real teaching of Aristotle. It was precisely for this reason that he so bitterly detested and denounced the Stagirite. Still this heterodox interpretation of Aristotle was available for readers of *De vanitate,* as it was in the works of many writers of that period, most notably Pietro Pomponazzi. Agrippa also approximated Machiavelli's amoral view of the world, another ingredient of the libertine teachings. His suggestion that contradiction and error exist even in Scripture might encourage the greatest disorders among persons who did not, like him, submit the interpretation and the canon of Scripture ultimately to the judgment of the institutional church. He also knew and partly adopted the notion of natural causation of such supposedly miraculous phenomena as the stigmata of St. Francis, although he specifically refuted the idea that Christ's miracles were of this sort. The gnostical scorn for the *canaille,* which Spini regards as one of the chief proofs of the un-Christian mood of the Italian Seicento, was certainly not lacking from Agrippa's thought, although it was tempered by some compassion for their suffering at the hands of their upper-class oppressors, a compassion which even grew into a positive program of indoor poor relief as a means of suppressing sturdy beggars while aiding the impotent poor, a scheme which drew an approving marginal comment from his Elizabethan translator.

A recently discovered Agrippan imprint, known in only one copy, has raised the further question whether Agrippa was not himself the central figure of a group of libertines, who combined a truly dangerous degree of free thought with the occultist enthusiasms that characterized Agrippa's circle of friends wherever he lived. This document, discovered in the Biblioteca Colombina at Seville, is a small piece of four leaves printed in blackletter type, without indication of place or date, and entitled *Prognosticon vetus in Agrippinarum archivis inventum.* It consists of a prefatory letter entitled "Henricus Cornelius Agrippa Lectori S.D.," the *Prognosticon* itself, with an appended verse referring to Revelations 22, a French translation of the main text of the *Prognosticon* and the verse, and three Italian-language quatrains appended to the French verses. Its discoverer suggests a French origin for it, and the period 1515-1530 for date of publication. She also defends its authenticity as a work of Agrippa. For one thing, the *Ad Lectorem* or prefatory letter is textually almost identical to a letter which Agrippa wrote, probably in 1526, to an unnamed friend. In this letter, he attacked the validity of astrology. Furthermore, the same text, with only minor verbal changes, forms part of his chapter "De astrologia iudiciaria" in *De vanitate.* In his letter, the Nettesheimer himself wryly referred to a prognostication with twofold commentary which he sent so that those who demand predictions from him "may know that I, whom they think to be such an astrologer, am also such a prophet, and know how to profit by their folly." The same prophecy is surely mentioned in another letter which he sent to a friend named Conrad living at Chambéry in Savoy on 18 April 1526. Here he enclosed his *De matrimonio,* the Latin text for his friend and a French text for the friend's wife, together with "a certain prognostication, and that my own, from which you can judge what a noteworthy astrologer I have become." This letter, and especially the ironic tone in which it is written, strongly confirms Agrippa's authorship of the **Prognosticon** and makes it possible that either he or his Savoyard friend also prepared the French translation.

The **Prognosticon** itself consists of a short prophetic statement concerning four kings who are to come from the four corners of the world, and the horrors and prodigies which are to ensue. It is obviously meant to be typical of the obscure prophecies of doom which circulated frequently in Agrippa's time, and about which he himself often received requests for interpretations. Then he has added a twofold marginal interpretation, one of them speaking in a serious tone and one in a tone of folly. The serious interpretation refers the prophetic words to a great war, a terrible conqueror, religious reforms, and other favorite topics of contemporary prophecy. The jocular interpretation refers the same words to a description of a carouse by a pack of gamblers (the four kings, for instance, are in a deck of cards). Obviously, this newly discovered work is a fine example of prophetic parody, a genre which was quite popular in the early Reformation period and which had reached a climax after the dire but unfulfilled predictions of floods which were expected to result from the great planetary conjunction in the sign of Pisces in 1524. Such parody became a favorite propaganda device of humanists, and Agrippa's **Prognosticon,** probably a work of his year of crisis and disillusionment, 1526, is akin to the jocular prophecies of Rabelais just a few years later, or the anticlerical *Judicio over pronostico di mastro Pasquino quinto evangelista per l'anno 1527* by Pietro Aretino, with its delightful spoof of astrological pomposity: "Secondo la opinione di moderni interpreti dei pianeti . . . lo introito del Sole sarà ne la prima taverna ch'egli troverà. . . ."

The significance of this new Agrippan document needs to be carefully weighed. Its discoverer concludes that the publication of this document and the preservation and eventual publication of Agrippa's correspondence much later in the century were both the work of a secret brotherhood of disciples, perhaps the "Agrippans" denounced by André Thevet later in the century. Yet there is danger in pushing this argument too far. For instance, Agrippa himself preserved his own letters, as is shown not only by the publication of a few of them as appendices to his books published during his lifetime, but also by his threat to retaliate against Louise of Savoy by publishing his correspondence with various courtiers, in order to demonstrate to the world how shabbily she had treated him. Second, although there can be no doubt that the Nettesheimer was linked to an extensive network of fellow students of the occult, there is no real proof that this group was an institutionalized brotherhood, a conventicle. Perhaps his friends really did preserve his letters and were responsible for their eventual publication. On the other hand, Agrippa left several children; and one of them, at least, was a man of some learning and reputation who might well have preserved his father's papers. The phrase from the new-found **Prognosticon,** "ex archivis Agrippinarum," need not be taken too literally. Finally, the real influence of Agrippa on later libertinism did not derive chiefly from circulation

of his collected letters, only a few of which betray the mocking tone and corrosive doubt of the libertines. The principal influence of Agrippa on later free thought was not a secret one exercised through secret channels, but a public one exercised through his widely circulated, much-translated, and highly popular book, **De vanitate,** a work which as late as the eighteenth century could still unsettle the youthful optimism of a Goethe. What the new Agrippan document really does, is to confirm still further a point already evident from the Nettesheimer's known works: that even at the height of his doubts about occultism and all sciences, he still preserved a belief, or at least a tentative half-belief, in such basic occultist concepts as the emanation of mysterious influences from the stars. Like **De vanitate,** like a few letters from the same period, the **Prognosticon** reflects a serious spiritual crisis on the part of the author himself, and also, in a more general sense, on the part of the Renaissance culture in which he was so deeply learned.

Although many hints of familiarity with the doctrines of later libertine groups abound in his works, Agrippa flatly rejected most of these teachings. He was no libertine, though he was interested in all viewpoints, even the most dangerous. One is not justified in calling his rejection of libertinism insincere, for it by no means ran counter to the main stream of his thought. Nor ought one to exaggerate the role of his works, chiefly **De vanitate,** in the development of unbelief at the end of the century. The book was certainly much edited and much translated in the sixteenth and seventeenth centuries and doubtless made its contribution to the growth of such ideas not only in Italy but north of the Alps as well; but Spini has shown [in his *Ricerca dei libertini: La teoria dell'impostura delle religioni nel Seicento italiano,* 1950] that these ideas were widely spread even before the sixteenth century. In any case, the writings of Agrippa von Nettesheim furnish an example of acquaintance with some of these libertine ideas in germ north of the Alps, and so suggest a third major way in which **De vanitate,** even though unintentionally in this instance, helped shatter the rational and orderly world view of the great medieval intellectual syntheses. The other two ways were the epistemological pessimism and the moral anarchism discussed in the preceding sections of this [essay].

. . . .

Agrippa von Nettesheim is now a forgotten figure in the intellectual history of the West. Yet both as a real man and as a legend he made his contribution to the development of the modern mind; and there is besides the intrinsic interest of the picture of the European mentality in the early sixteenth century which one can form from his numerous treatises and his hundreds of surviving letters. This analysis of his intellectual world will be complete when it has suggested his influence in his own day and after, discussed the legends that grew up around his figure and their contribution to that great symbol of western man, Faust, and then related the main elements of Agrippa's thought to the general intellectual movement of his age.

Only a handful of his contemporaries had a reputation for erudition and for boldness of thought and expression that could be compared to Agrippa's during the sixteenth and seventeenth centuries, and even well into the eighteenth century. His biography shows that he was able to attract, though not to hold, the attention of the greatest princes of his age. Even the reserved and cautious Erasmus, though thinking him rash and ill-advised, still admitted his erudition and wit. Juan Luis Vives called him "the wonder of letters and of literary men," while the elder Scaliger esteemed him for his learning. Rabelais knew of him and did him the honor of satirizing him as the ridiculous astrologer and cuckold Herr Trippa of his *Tiers Livre,* a book wherein he also lampooned such figures as Lefèvre d'Étaples, Lemaire de Belges, and Tiraqueau. Agrippa's doctrine of the three types of melancholy strongly influenced his great contemporary Albrecht Dürer in his famous engraving "Melencolia I." Agrippa's pupil Johann Wier, one of the few outspoken opponents of the witchcraft delusion later in the sixteenth century, wrote respectfully of his master and refuted some of the wild legends which already were gathering around this strange figure. Paracelsus, or one of his followers writing under his name, when boasting of his knowledge of magic, claimed to surpass Agrippa, as if he were an acknowledged master. Cardan attacked *De vanitate* as a mere literary trifle but admitted that many of his contemporaries admired it.

The generation which flourished near the end of the sixteenth century had not forgotten Agrippa. The continued re-editing of his books would suggest this fact even if there were no other evidence. In 1572, the landgrave of Hesse quoted an opinion of Agrippa's on astronomy in a letter to Caspar Peucer; and although both the latter and Tycho Brahe discounted this authority, they did so perhaps as much because of his reputation for impiety as because of the error of his opinions in astronomy. Giordano Bruno's general view of the universe was much like the Nettesheimer's magical world, and was partly derived from it. Of course the great Nolan philosopher drew on other sources also; but he took much of the detail of his *De monade* straight from *De occulta philosophia,* which was perhaps the chief source for his knowledge of Cabala. He also knew *De vanitate,* which in a negative sense was the source of his satirical treatment of asininity as the chief human virtue. . . . [I] have shown repeatedly that *De vanitate* was an important source for the skeptical thought of Michel de Montaigne, who based extensive passages of his "Apology for Raymond Sebond" on the earlier work. Montaigne also borrowed some illustrative details from *De occulta philosophia.* One French writer of the late sixteenth century, André Thevet, wrote that there was a whole school of atheists who claimed to follow Agrippa, while John Calvin earlier had classed him as a mocker at religion. One need not take these complaints as accurate reflections of Agrippa's own intentions; but the preceding chapter has shown that *De vanitate* contained ideas with an affinity for the thought of later groups of libertines and freethinkers. Furthermore, if *De vanitate* became a favorite of those who mocked at all learning and even at religion, *De occulta philosophia* in both printed and manuscript forms became a standard text for students of magic in the sixteenth and seventeenth centuries, although perhaps the spurious Fourth Book, with its numerous formulae and detailed instructions for conjuring spirits, was

more influential than the three genuine books. It was chiefly as an infamous sorcerer that Jean Bodin denounced the Nettesheimer, though the occasion of the attack was rather the tendency of Agrippa and the open effort of his pupil Wier to throw discredit on the prosecution of witches.

Another important author who felt Agrippa's influence, far more strongly and positively than Bodin, was Sir Philip Sidney, whose well-known *Apologie for Poetrie* (written about 1579-1580 and posthumously published in 1595) not only referred directly to *De vanitate* but also, more important, modeled its fundamental arguments in defense of poetic fiction along lines obviously suggested by the recently translated declamation. Many other Elizabethan and Jacobean authors in England read and referred to Agrippa, including Christopher Marlowe, Francis Bacon, and Thomas Nashe.

The seventeenth century saw frequent mention of Agrippa, but in the most various ways: as an enlightened opponent of the witchcraft delusion during his residence at Metz; as a Protestant hero who had been slandered by the Papists; as a wicked sorcerer or an equally wicked mocker at religion. Few of the numerous collections of lives of scholars failed to present him in one of these guises. The mystical writer and magician Thomas Vaughan in mid-century gave to Agrippa perhaps the most extravagant praise he ever received: "He indeed is my Author, and next to God I owe all that I have unto Him " [[Thomas Vaughan:] Eugenius Philalethes, *Anthroposophia theomagica; or, A Discourse of the Nature of Man and his state after death,* 1650]. His twin brother, the poet Henry Vaughan, drew from *De vanitate* at least the symbol of the ass as the humble Christian believer, and in part perhaps his stress on humility as a Christian ideal.

Such instances could be multiplied; but these, together with the continued re-editing of Agrippa's books, should at least show that there was something in his writings and in the figure of the man himself to attract the attention of his own and succeeding ages. Even well into the eighteenth century, although Agrippa had begun to be regarded as rather quaint, his *De vanitate* could still shake the youthful optimism of Goethe and cause him to pass through an intellectual crisis.

The Nettesheimer survived in the European mind, however, as a legend as well as a real man. The legends began accumulating within a very few years after his death. The earliest to find written expression was that wherever he went, a devil in the form of a black dog accompanied him, and that on his deathbed, he removed from the neck of this dog a collar bearing magical emblems and said, "Depart, damned beast, who hast wholly ruined me," whereupon the dog ran and leaped into the river Saône and was never seen again. This devil supposedly kept him informed of news, so that even though he spent long periods without ever leaving his study, he knew all that had happened even in distant places. This tale of Paolo Giovio reappears in Thevet and many later authors. Thevet also records (but denies) early tales that Agrippa's magical practices were responsible for the military victories of Charles V; and he attributes Agrippa's many travels to repeated expulsions caused by his practice of magic. Writing no later than 1599, the Jesuit Del Rio repeated the latter claim and added two new tales. According to him, Agrippa and Faust were both notorious for paying innkeepers with coins which after their departure turned into leaves or filth. The second tale is that a curious boarder once stole into the Nettesheimer's study and, by chance repeating a phrase found in a magical book that lay open on the desk, conjured up a devil. This devil fell upon the unskillful conjurer and killed him. Shortly afterward, Agrippa returned home and, fearing prosecution for murder, made the devil enter the victim's body and transport it to the public square, where, after strolling for a time as if alive, it collapsed, apparently the victim of a natural death. To these tales an eighteenth-century polyhistor added two more, that Agrippa was able to read in the moon distant events such as the outcome of the military operations of Francis I in Italy, and that he was able to lecture from nine to ten o'clock at Fribourg (or Freiburg-im-Breisgau) and at ten to begin his lecture at Pont-à-Mousson in Lorraine. In *The Lay of the Last Minstrel,* Sir Walter Scott preserves a legend—either invented or first written down by Thomas Nashe—that the alchemist Cornelius Agrippa allowed Henry Howard, Earl of Surrey, to see his deceased sweetheart in a magic mirror.

To the European mind of the sixteenth century and after, then, Agrippa represented several things. Above all, as these legends show, and as the widespread use of **De occulta philosophia** confirms, he was the great magician who had sought out the wisdom of the remote past and had expressed some (but not all) of what he knew in **De occulta philosophia,** leaving much, however, to the conjecture of the reader or to private instruction which was handed down only by word of mouth. As later generations saw him, he was expert in the secret wisdom of the ancients, as expressed in the Orphic hymns and in the Hermetic writings. Not only Hellenistic but also Jewish culture excited the imagination of later decades, however; hence his contemporaries saw in him not just an expert in the writings of the magicians but also a rediscoverer of the still more sacred lore of the cabalists. His reputation for great learning, moreover, was not confined to these occult traditions. His works, which are rich in quotations, showed his readers that he also had a command of the ancient classics, especially the Latin ones, and of more recent authors. References to Italian authors of the fourteenth and fifteenth centuries are not uncommon in his books; and of these Italians, at least one, Pico della Mirandola, had influenced the structure of his thought considerably. The authority of Agrippa as a magician was doubtless enhanced by this familiarity with classical writings and with Italian humanistic literature.

The Agrippa who lived on in the awareness of following centuries, however, was not merely the magician and cabalist, the author of **De occulta philosophia.** He was also the radical doubter who passionately questioned the worth of all human learning, the author of **De vanitate.** . . . [These] two books are not so incompatible as they seem; but the appearance of these two elements in the thought of the Nettesheimer was nevertheless profoundly disturbing to an age which felt that all the old certainties (the

unity of Christendom, the organic balance of the three traditional classes of society, the validity of human reason, the authority of accepted intellectual heroes such as Aristotle) were falling in ruin. In Agrippa the succeeding generations saw one of the greatest scholars of his age pursue and master not only the usual classical masterpieces but also the rarest works known, works enshrining the profound wisdom of ancient Greece, ancient Egypt, ancient Israel. Here they saw a man deeply versed in all the four faculties (liberal arts, medicine, law, and theology) and claiming academic degrees in all but the latter. And then they saw this same man turn against all arts and sciences, whether rational or occult, against all classes in society, even, it was whispered despite his final appeal to the unadulterated Gospel, against Christianity itself. Here these succeeding ages saw not just a man but also a symbol of disgust with all culture, with all values, with the whole condition of man in the universe. Agrippa von Nettesheim personified all the many doubts and uncertainties of his epoch.

It is small wonder that his century made of him and of other figures like him a legend, though it was Agrippa's misfortune that men named this legend, this symbol of their own intellectual despair and struggle, after a more shadowy figure, Faust. The Jesuit Del Rio classed Agrippa and Faust together as wicked sorcerers and swindlers who paid innkeepers in false gold. Christopher Marlowe expressed this same association between the two men, for his Dr. Faustus, after denouncing all human learning, explicitly takes Agrippa for his ideal:

> Philosophy is odious and obscure,
> Both Law and Physic are for petty wits;
> Divinity is basest of the three,
> Unpleasant, harsh, contemptible, and vild:
> 'Tis Magic, Magic that hath ravished me.
> Then, gentle friends, aid me in this attempt;
> And I that have with concise syllogisms
> Gravelled the pastors of the German Church,
> And made the flowering pride of Wertenberg
> Swarm to my problems, as the infernal spirits
> On sweet Musaeus when he came to hell,
> Will be as cunning as Agrippa was,
> Whose shadows made all Europe honour him.

[Christopher Marlowe, *The Tragical History of Dr. Faustus,* Scene II, ll. 104-116]

The poet knew, as scholars long did not, that rejection of all learning was the prelude to an appeal to magic, not the product of dissatisfaction with it.

The influence of Agrippa on the other great recension of the Faust legend, that of Goethe, is even more obvious and more thoroughly established by literary scholarship. Here there is more than the general parallel between the intellectual bankruptcy of Faust and Agrippa's views in **De vanitate.** It is true that the name of Agrippa does not occur in Goethe's *Faust;* but Goethe knew **De vanitate** as a youth, when it caused him an intellectual crisis; and surely during his prolonged study of magic, the poet must have come across Agrippa's name time and time again. Certain details of the Faust character are clearly Agrippan in origin, such as the *schwarze Pudel* who attaches himself to Faust not long before the latter's first encounter with

Mephistopheles. This element is the product of Giovio's legend about Agrippa's black devil-dog and of Wier's factual account of his master's fondness for a black dog called Monsieur. Like Agrippa, Goethe's Faust mastered and came to loathe all four faculties of university learning. Both of them were supposedly makers of gold; both of them supposedly offered to enrich the Emperor Charles V. Like Agrippa in the first chapter of *De vanitate,* Goethe's Mephistopheles gives an ironic twist to the phrase "Eritis sicut Deus, scientes bonum et malum" which he writes in the young scholar's book. One authority even suggests that Goethe changed Faust's first name from the Johann of earlier versions to Heinrich because Agrippa bore the latter name. This writer concludes that although Goethe drew on numerous figures, among them the real Faust and Paracelsus, no other individual united so many of the traits of his Faust as Agrippa did [Anton Reichl, "Goethes Faust und Agrippa von Nettesheim," *Euphorion: Zeitschrift für Literaturgeschichte,* IV (1897)]. Faust's opening speech sounds almost like a summary of *De vanitate.*

The matters so far discussed represent things which the contemporaries and successors of Agrippa could see. He was the magician, the cabalist, the Faustian doubter, the living embodiment of many of the enthusiasms and most of the gnawing doubts and uncertainties and fears of his age. There were other sides to his thought which his contemporaries could not see.

Agrippa's contemporaries could not, for instance, see his interest in magic and Cabala against its proper historical background. Such an appeal to occult traditions of Antiquity should not cause the modern student to speak grandly of interest in magic or Cabala as a passing fad of no great significance, as some have done. What could be more natural, in a civilization which for centuries had looked back with respect and awe to the cultural achievements of Antiquity and which was experiencing a great revival of interest in classical literature, than to look backwards for the solution of its intellectual problems? That it looked backwards not only for literary models and moral philosophies but also for magical lore should not be surprising, for even the main stream of ancient literature contained strong elements of magical belief. Furthermore, the Neoplatonic philosophy, which was the first great philosophical rediscovery of the humanists, was highly receptive to magic; and from it Agrippa's magical world view ultimately derives.

Not only Hellenistic but also Jewish culture had its contribution to make to the age; the revival of Hebrew studies led to a search for recondite Jewish literature. This interest in Cabala, too, was a natural outgrowth of the intellectual atmosphere of the century. It was natural for a humanistic age to look back to Greek and Roman literature for a shortcut to solution of its intellectual problems. It was just as natural for a Christian age to look back to the Hebrew texts that were its sources for a solution of religious and also general intellectual problems. This meant first of all study of the Hebrew Old Testament, but interest in Jewish

Biblical commentary was a natural outgrowth of this study. Development of interest in Cabala and in the Talmud was aided by the fact that these writings often took the form of Biblical commentaries, and also by the pseudepigraphical character of much of the *corpus* of Cabala: it appeared to go back to very early times and to enshrine traditions handed down from the foundations of Judaism, even from Abraham and Moses themselves. It claimed, therefore, to be presenting not a Neoplatonizing philosophy of Alexandrian origin but the true and deeper meaning of divine revelation, as preserved from the most remote times. Christians would of course be interested in writings which presented themselves in this guise, especially since the gnostic and Neoplatonic influence on the actual authors of the cabalistic texts had led them to include materials which seemed to support such Christian doctrines as the Trinity.

Another matter which Agrippa's own age could not really understand was his relation to the Reformation, for men in the sixteenth and seventeenth centuries could not see that he stood quite apart from the movement initiated by Luther, neither wholly approving nor wholly condemning. The nearest approach to a correct understanding was that of Bayle, who felt that Agrippa like Erasmus first welcomed Luther but then felt disappointment with the Lutheran movement [*Dictionnaire historique et critique*]. Most Protestants in the sixteenth and seventeenth centuries regarded him as a man of Protestant convictions who lacked the courage to avow them openly. Few in either religious camp could realize that his bitter attacks on the institutional church were accompanied by a refusal to disavow the institution, which he wanted to see purified of abuses and reduced in temporal power, but not shattered and broken.

Contemporaries also could not see that much of the destructive portion of his thought was an outgrowth of the fideism of late scholasticism and of the skeptical tendencies found in the thought of Nicholas of Cusa and perhaps in ancient philosophical writings. These contemporaries certainly felt the insufficiency of scholastic philosophy to meet their own intellectual needs; but they could not trace the growth of these antischolastic elements as, in part, scholars like Rudolf Stadelmann, Gerhard Ritter, Ernst Cassirer, and Richard H. Popkin have done in our own century. So they could not relate Agrippa to this more general movement which was producing a sense of debility, cultural decline, and decadence, a feeling that western society was passing through a terrible crisis, perhaps through its death agony, and that the Last Day was at hand.

Finally, even Agrippa himself had no glimpse of how the European mind was preparing to rise like the legendary Phoenix from the ashes of its despair to a new sense of mission, of self-confidence, of purposeful striving for progress. So he could not see his own doubt and despair as a preparation for a synthesis on a new and higher plane. He could not realize that his emphasis on sense knowledge of singulars could ever help create a new science, or even that it was in harmony with the crude empiricism of the rising generation. He could not see that the effect of books like **De vanitate** would be to encourage a bold questioning of accepted authorities and accepted beliefs in every field of endeavor and so would prepare men's minds to accept or at least to explore new patterns of explanation for old facts. Yet this inquisitive attitude, far more than the accumulation of new data, was the key to the rise of modern science later in the sixteenth and in the seventeenth centuries. Above all, Agrippa could have had only the dimmest awareness, if any at all, of the elements of future scientific reconstruction which existed in his later thought. . . . [His] half-hearted acceptance of sense perception of singulars and his doctrine that all higher patterns of explanation are arbitrary constructs of human reason, joined to his appeal to a principle of utility to justify his continued study of magic, put him on the threshold, logically speaking, of the modern notion of scientific hypothesis and its subjection to the test of facts. He did not cross this threshold; that was the work of later generations. But his history illustrates how European thinkers were beginning to grope in the direction of the seventeenth-century resolution of the problem of human knowledge. Agrippa himself stood amid the ruin of medieval thought, a ruin which he himself did much to advance; but he also pointed tentatively and unknowingly in directions which, for some centuries to come, European mankind was to find fruitful and satisfying.

Barbara C. Bowen   (lecture date 1971)

SOURCE: "Cornelius Agrippa's *De vanitate*: Polemic or Paradox?," in *Bibliotheque D'Humanisme et Renaissance,* Vol. XXXIV, No. 2, 1972, pp. 249-56.

[*Below, Bowen elaborates on* On the Uncertainty and Vanity of the Sciences *as an example of the literary paradox, a genre popular in the sixteenth century. Bowen's remarks were originally delivered as a lecture in 1971.*]

Henry Cornelius Agrippa of Nettesheim (1486-1535), one of the most intriguing figures of the Renaissance, has received a good deal of critical attention but remains a tantalisingly shadowy figure. He has proved most interesting to historians of magic and science, because of his **De Occulta philosophia,** and to intellectual historians, because of his disputed place in the intellectual development of the Renaissance. He has been curiously neglected by literary specialists, despite his acknowledged influence on Rabelais, Montaigne, Sidney and Marlowe among others. There has been only one full-length study on him in recent years, Charles Nauert's *Agrippa and the crisis of Renaissance thought,* and this too, as its title indicates, is concerned with Agrippa's relationship to the intellectual climate of his time.

In spite of the quantity of critical work done on Agrippa, one puzzle has remained unsolved, at least for most critics.

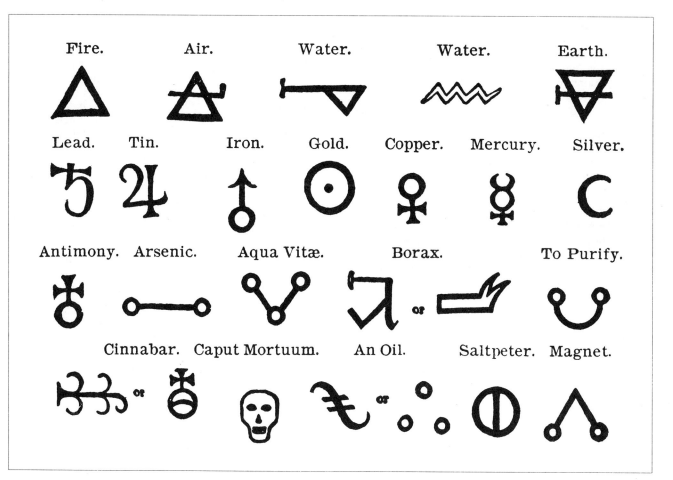

Some symbols of the Alchemists.

Why did he publish, within a few years of each other, a textbook of magic and occult philosophy (*De Occulta philosophia,* Book I 1531, first complete edition 1533) and a condemnation of all philosophy and all learning (*De Incertitudine et vanitate scientiarum,* first edition 1530)? I should like to suggest here that the literary specialist may provide the answer to this 'problem', which would never have been considered a problem at all if the early writers on Agrippa had known as much about the Renaissance as we do today.

The striking contradictions between these two works of Agrippa's have been discussed by many critics, and various ingenious solutions have been proposed. Some critics, from Morley in 1856 to Hiram Haydn in 1950, have assumed that the *De vanitate* is entirely serious in its concentration of the evils brought about by knowledge. This would imply that the *De Occulta philosophia* was the less serious, or less important, work. Other critics have gone to the other extreme, maintaining, from Pierre Villey to Richard Popkin, that the *De vanitate* is merely a joke and need not be taken seriously. Yet others, like Prost, Thorndike and Leon Blau, have assumed that Agrippa changed his mind, so that he believed what he was writing in both books at the time he wrote them. It has also been suggested that the *De vanitate* was written out of disgust and discouragement, because knowledge had not brought Agrippa success, or as a safety valve in case the *De Occulta philosophia* got him into trouble. And it has been maintained, especially by Garin, Zambelli and Nauert, that the two books are not fundamentally contradictory, but represent different aspects of the same 'Renaissance mentality.' The number and variety of these solutions show that the contradictions between Agrippa's two books do represent a serious problem for his modern readers. Let us see if by slightly re-stating this problem we can come closer to a solution.

There are, I suggest, two separate questions to be asked: 1) is the *De vanitate* a paradox? and 2) is a Renaissance paradox nothing but a frivolous rhetorical exercise?

There is, I think, no doubt whatever that the book is intended as a paradox, and there is ample external and internal evidence to prove it. The title of the 1531 Cologne edition begins as follows: *De incertitudine et vanitate scientiarum declamatio invectiva . . .* When the book was denounced by the University of Louvain and by the Sorbonne, Agrippa defended it in two works, an *Apologia* and a *Querela.* In the *Apologia* he gives the following definition of a *declamatio:*

> Proinde declamatio non judicat, non dogmatizat sed que declamationis conditiones sunt, alia joco, alia serio, alia false, alia saevere dicit: aliquando mea, aliquando aliorum sententia loquitur, quaedam vera, quaedam falsa, quaedam dubia prounnunciat . . . nec omni loco animi mei sententiam declarat . . . multa invalida argumenta adducit . . .

Now certainly he is taking care in this work to deny that the attacks on the Church contained in the *De vanitate* were serious, but his definition of a *declamatio* is borne out by Cotgrave's dictionary, which gives for the French *dec-*

lamation: "A declamation; an Oration made for a fained subject, or onely for exercise," and the O.E.D. confirms that the earliest meaning of the verb to declaim was: "to speak aloud with rhetorical expression; to make a speech on a set subject as an exercise in elocution." The French translation of the *De vanitate* by Louis Turquet de Mayerne was first published in 1582 with the title *Déclamation sur l'incertitude, vanité et abus des sciences,* and the full title of the 1608 edition runs as follows:

> *Paradoxe sur l'incertitude, vanité et abus des sciences. Traduit en françois, du latin de Henry Corneille Agrippa. Oeuvre qui peut profiter, et qui approte merveilleux contentement à ceux qui frequentent les cours des grands seigneurs, et qui veulent apprendre à discourir d'une infinité de choses contre la commune opinion.*

This contemporary acceptance of the work as a paradox, shared by Jacques Tahureau, who discusses Agrippa's "moquerie feinte et dissimulee" [*Les Dialogues de Jacques Tahureau Gentilhomme du Mans,* 1565], and by Sidney who refers to him as a "smyling rayler" [*Apologie for Poetrie*], has been obscured by the more energetic contemporary denunciations of Agrippa by bigots like Jean Bodin, who calls him "le plus grand Sorcier qui fut onques de son aage" [*De la Demonomanie des sorciers,* 1580], and André Thevet, who renders him responsible for the prevalence of atheism in his time [*Les vrais pourtraits et vies des hommes illustres,* 1584].

The *De vanitate* is not the only work of Agrippa's in the paradox *genre.* He had already published in 1529 the *De nobilitate et praecellentia foeminei sexus,* which demonstrates that women are not merely equal but superior to men. Now this is a piece of polemic of a type very common at this time. The so-called *Querelle des Femmes* lined up feminists and anti-feminists against each other, in verse and prose, Latin and French, during the whole first half of the sixteenth century, and a hundred years ago it was assumed that all these writers were seriously expounding their own point of view. We know today that the entire quarrel was more literary than real, and that most of the participants have their tongues firmly in their cheeks. Agrippa's contribution makes use of most of the stock arguments 'for' women, but some of his 'evidence' could surely not be taken seriously by the most ardent feminist in 1971 (e. g. that women are more attractive because they don't have beards, that they are more eloquent speakers than men, or that they know everything naturally).

Nor is Agrippa the only writer of his time to produce works which contradict each other. One of the participants in the Querelle des Femmes, Jean Nevizan, wrote a *Sylvae nuptialis libri sex* (1540) whose first two books attack marriage while the second two defend it, and the French writer Boaystuau wrote, and had published in one volume in 1561, a *Theatre du Monde, ou il est faict un ample discours des miseres de l'homme,* and a *Bref discours de l'excellence et dignité de l'homme* which takes exactly the opposite point of view.

This is, in fact, the great age of paradox, as literary critics have come to recognize more and more in recent years. It is an anachronism to assume that a Renaissance writer must always have his heart and soul engaged in what he is doing. Literature is still based on rhetoric, Erasmus praises Folly, French poets have imaginary mistresses, and Ortensio Landi's *Paradossi* is one of the most popular works of the age. The post-Romantic concepts of 'originality' and 'sincerity' should never have been applied to Renaissance literature.

So much, very briefly, for external evidence that the *De vanitate* is a literary paradox. Examining the work itself in the light of this, we first notice the title: *De incertitudine et vanitate . . .* One can take this as a summary of the book's intention; it will demonstrate that human knowledge is uncertain on the one hand, and vain on the other hand. But *vanitas* also means 'emptiness, nothing,' and the 'praise of nothing' is a very popular Renaissance *topos,* in both art and literature. Jean Passerat's poem *Nihil* and Shakespeare's *Much Ado about Nothing* are the best-known examples, but more relevant to Agrippa is Montaigne's essay *De la Vanité* (III, ix). The title alone would make a sixteenth century reader laugh, as this is one of his longest essays, and in the opening paragraph he plays upon the two meanings of *vanité,* 'emptiness, nothing,' and the Biblical meaning in the well-known quotation from *Ecclesiastes:* "Vanity of vanities, all is vanity."

If the 'praise of nothing' is a conventional *topos,* so too is the condemnation of arts and sciences. Villey [in his *Les Sources et l'évolution des Essais de Montaigne,* 1933] cites several contemporary authors and compilers who use it, including Ravisius Textor and Gyraldi, but there is no need to look so far afield. One of Landi's *Paradoxes* (No. 3) maintains that ignorance is better than wisdom, and a good deal of Erasmus's *Praise of Folly,* of which more in a moment, is devoted to a condemnation of learning in various forms. There is, in fact, nothing in this purely conventional subject to shock a sixteenth century reader.

The next question a literary specialist will ask is, how is the book constructed? And curiously enough I have not found a single critic who is interested in this. Since the book is called a *declamatio,* and since the conclusion is styled *Operis peroratio,* one would expect it to be constructed like a demonstrative oration, but this is not the case. There are 103 chapters (counting the conclusion), and it is quite clear from the grouping of these chapters that Agrippa intends a systematic refutation-of-knowledge-by-means-of-knowledge, as A. C. Hamilton pointed out [in his "Sidney and Agrippa," *Review of English Studies* n. s. VII (1956)]. The first ten chapters deal with the trivium: grammar (plus poetry and history), rhetoric and logic (plus sophistry and the art of memory which belong to them). Chapters 11-48 deal with the quadrivium and related subjects; thus for instance dicing (14) belongs with arithmetic (12), "Rhetoricall daunsing" (21) with music (17), perspective (26) and architecture (28) with geometry (22). Under astronomy we find the largest subgroup, comprising sixteen chapters on methods of divination and magical practices, arranged in the same order as they appear in Book I of the *De occulta philosophia* (chapters 52-60).

Chapters 49-81 are also deliberately grouped, in a roughly Aristotelian order, as follows: philosophy, physics, meta-

physics, ethics, politics, Chapter 52, *Of the Soule,* comes after *Of the Worlde* (51) and before *Of the Metaphisickes* (53), as Aristotle's *De Anima* is normally printed between the *Physics* and the *Metaphysics.* Politics occupies chapters 55-81, dealing with such diverse aspects of society as religion (in a social context), prostitution, courtiers, merchants, agriculture, fishing, war and heraldry. This apparently deliverate Aristotelian order is particularly entertaining in view of Agrippa's violent denunciations of Aristotle—referred to in chapter 52, for instance, as "the divelish Aristotle."

The remainder of the book (82-99) comprises three groups: medicine, law and "divinitie" (theology), which represent the three faculties of the University and correspond to the traditional three main preoccupations of man's life: his body, his wordly goods and his soul. In chapter 29 of Rabelais's *Tiers Livre* Pantagruel advises. Panurge to consult a theologian, a doctor and a lawyer about his marriage problem, because:

> tout ce que sommes et qu'avons consiste en trois choses, en l'ame, on corps, es biens. A la conservation de chascun des trois respectivement sont au jourd'huy destinées troys manieres de gens: les theologiens à l'ame, les medecins au corps, les jurisconsultes aux biens.

Pantagruel subsequently adds a philosopher to the group, and Agrippa has already dealt with philosophy in the previous grouping. Medicine, for Agrippa, includes such sidelines as "the crafte to cure brute beastes" (87), dieting (88), cooking (89) and even "alcumie" (90), by which he means chemistry, not the occult art. And theology comes last in this grouping because it leads naturally into his final chapter, *Of Gods Woorde.* In exactly 100 chapters he has demolished knowledge by the use of knowledge—by grouping his chapters according to the trivium, the quadrivium, the books of the Aristotelian *corpus* and the three traditional domains of human life, and of course by use of his immense erudition in each area under discussion.

The book might appear symmetrical complete at chapter 100, but Agrippa has not finished. Chapter 101, *Of Maisters of Artes in general,* resumes the entire argument and states that since all arts and sciences are "not so uncertaine as deceiptfull, as also wicked." "It is better therefore and more profitable to be Idiotes." And this is the perfect transition to chapter 102: *A digression to the praise of the Asse. Digressio,* like *declamatio,* is a rhetorical term, and the praise of the ass is yet another well-known *topos.* Agrippa ends his work with a clear reference to Erasmus' *Praise of Folly,* even in the terms he uses. The Latin title of this final chapter is *Ad encomium asini digressio,* and the title of Erasmus's work, published in 1511, not so long before Agrippa was writing his in 1526, is *Encomium Moriae.* The conclusion of the *De vanitate* makes this resemblance clearer yet. In Sanford's translation it is obviously a sermon, beginning:

> Wherefore O yee Asses, which are now with your Children under the commaundement of Christ by his Apostles the messengers and readers of true wisdome in his holy Gospel . . .

and ending:

But leaste that thorow using more woordes I shoulde declame as it is saide, beyonde the hower, let this be the ende of our Oration.

What we have just read was not a demonstrative oration, but a *sermon joyeux,* like the one preached by Erasmus's Folly. And a sermon which paradoxically undermined, not merely the evils of this world, but especially the evils of that same Church which normally preaches sermons.

I have spent so long answering my first question: is Agrippa's book a literary paradox? because it seems to me that the second question: is a Renaissance paradox merely frivolous? neither needs nor deserves a lengthy answer. The importance of Agrippa as a humanist, and his debt to the Hermetic and Italian philosophers, have been amply demonstrated, and it is quite clear from his tone that many of his condemnations of human folly and hypocrisy are genuine. The sober critical mind of the nineteenth century may have wanted to divide literature into paradoxical frivolous works on the one hand, and 'sincere' serious works on the other, but the critical mind of today no longer practises such a division, and of course the critical mind of the Renaissance never did. One of the sixteenth century's favourite quotations is Horace's *Ridentem dicere verum Quid vetat?* (*Satires*). Placed as he is between Erasmus and Rabelais, Agrippa has the right to as full recognition as they of his paradoxical technique and his many serious points of view. He is looking back to Folly's multi-level and often ambiguous attach on society, including monks and churchmen, and including arts and sciences. And for us he is looking forward to Rabelais's comic giants, heroes of folklore and pornographic exploits, and at the same time participants in the struggle of Stoic and Evangelical humanism against the Pope, Luther and the forces of repression.

In fact the 'problem' of the *De vanitate* is a false problem. Like the works in similar vein of Erasmus, Rabelais and many others, Agrippa's book is a literary paradox and at the same time a work of polemic. It is often difficult to determine which of the points of view expressed in the book represent the author's 'sincere' convictions. The evidence would suggest that Agrippa genuinely detests abuses within the Church (though this does not necessarily make him a Protestant), and that his denunciations of occult arts are artificial and produced for the purpose of the *topos*. The organisation of the book suggests that he had a sense of humour, though undoubtedly not the charming light touch of an Erasmus. And the book is still worth reading today, not as a revelation of a tormented hero's state of mind, but as a brilliantly constructed exercise on a very conventional theme.

Frances A. Yates (essay date 1979)

SOURCE: "The Occult Philosophy and Magic: Henry Cornelius Agrippa," in *The Occult Philosophy in the Elizabethan Age,* Routledge & Kegan Paul, 1979, pp. 37-47.

[*Yates is a respected writer and scholar of Renaissance philosophy and literature. Her works include* Giordano Bruno and the Hermetic Tradition *(1964),* The Rosicrucian Enlightenment *(1972), and* Astraea: The Imperial Theme *(1975). Here, she posits that Agrippa's brand of magic was "really a religion, claiming access to the highest powers, and Christian since it accepts the name of Jesus as the chief of the wonder-working Names."*]

The reputation of Henry Cornelius Agrippa (1486-1535) has been a survival from the witch-hunts of the sixteenth and seventeenth centuries in which he figured prominently as a prince of black magicians and sorcerers. The black magician of the ages of superstition became, in enlightened times, the absurd charlatan unworthy of serious attention. The same process occurred in the case of John Dee with the same result, that a figure of great historical importance disappeared in clouds of nineteenth-century ridicule, from which the scholarship of the twentieth century has slowly begun to rescue him. In the case of Agrippa, his *De occulta philosophia* is now seen as the indispensable handbook of Renaissance 'Magia' and 'Cabala', combining the natural magic of Ficino with the Cabalist magic of Pico in one convenient compendium, and, as such, playing a very important part in the spread of Renaissance Neoplatonism with its magical core.

Charles Nauert's book on Agrippa [*Agrippa and the Crisis in Renaissance Thought,* 1965] has placed the study of his life and works on a scholarly footing, and the learned articles of Paola Zambelli have added new and important material. The magician begins now to appear as something of an Erasmian evangelical, combining pre-Reformation humanism with an attempt to provide a 'powerful' philosophy to accompany evangelical reform. In this attempt, Agrippa was undoubtedly inspired by Reuchlin's Christian Cabala. In fact, Agrippa's *De occulta philosophia* can be classed as Christian Cabala for it leads up, in the third book on the supercelestial world, to the presentation of the Name of Jesus as now all-powerful, containing all the power of the Tetragrammaton, 'as is confirmed by Hebrews and Cabalists skilled in the Divine Names'. He is quoting from Pico's Cabalist Conclusions. Christian Cabala is leading to a kind of evangelicalism, supported by the occult philosophy. His attempt to combine what he believes to be Erasmian evangelicalism with a magically powerful philosophy makes of Agrippa a reformer of a strange and interesting kind.

The picture of Agrippa now emerging is thus strangely unlike the sorcerer with his black dog hunted in the witch-crazes, and serving later as the image of the nineteenth-century idea of the necromancer. In what follows I shall attempt to outline, though briefly and inadequately, Agrippa's life and work from the new points of view.

Agrippa's interest in the occult seems to date from his earliest years at Cologne; he says that one of the first texts he studied on these subjects was the *Speculum* of Albertus Magnus, also a native of Cologne. The pattern of his life as a constant traveller, mysteriously in touch with groups of people in different places, is perceptible from the start. Nauert has suggested that he and his associates formed some kind of secret society. Paola Zambelli is also of the opinion that he may have been the centre of secret societies. Such affiliations are always difficult to prove; nevertheless the groups of people always ready to receive and support Agrippa in his constant travels do suggest that there may have been some kind of organisation. The groups would seem to have been concerned with alchemy, and with the investigation of Hermetic, Neoplatonic and Cabalist literature. Quite early in his life, Agrippa is reported to have been lecturing on Reuchlin.

In 1509-10, Agrippa was in Germany, visiting the learned abbot Trithemius, and it was at about this time that he wrote the first version of the *De occulta philosophia.* The manuscript of this version exists. It is dedicated to Trithemius, who was undoubtedly an important influence on Agrippa's studies.

At this significant time in his career, when his ideas were already sufficiently formulated for him to be writing the first version of the *De occulta philosophia,* Agrippa's mysterious travels took him to England.

In 1510, in which year a dedication proves that Agrippa was in England, Henry VIII had recently ascended the throne. Erasmus was in England, and the early humanist movement around Thomas More and John Colet was spreading. Agrippa was probably only in London for a few months; we do not know whether he met Erasmus there, but he was certainly in contact with John Colet, for we hear of him studying the Epistles of St Paul with Colet. A link between Agrippa and Colet may well have been Cabala, in which Colet was certainly interested. The study of Pauline epistles with Colet, shows, according to Nauert, that Agrippa was early exposed to the Biblical Christianity which characterised Colet and the Erasmian reform movement generally. Nauert suggests that there was probably a direct connection between Agrippa's biblical studies in London and his enthusiasm for occult studies, with 'cabalistic exegetical methods serving as the link between them'.

In about 1511, Agrippa went to Italy, thus gaining the Italian experience which was so important for the northern humanist. A few years earlier, in 1506-9, Erasmus had visited Italy for the first time, and it is interesting to compare the two visits. When he went to Italy, Erasmus had been in full possession of Italian humanist scholarship and had been using it for years; on his Italian visit he saw it in action in its latest form in the Venetian circle of Aldus Manutius. Similarly, Agrippa on his first visit to Italy was in full possession of the Renaissance Magia and Cabala, stemming from Ficino and Pico, and had been using them for years. Yet the Italian visit was very important for Agrippa, as it was for Erasmus, and for the same reason, namely that he was able to meet and assimilate the tradition which he already knew, as it had been further developing in Italy. For Erasmus this was the tradition of classical scholarship, now personified in Aldus and the Aldine press. For Agrippa, it was the tradition of occult philosophy, as it had developed in Italy in recent years, that he was bent on assimilating during this visit.

Agrippa in Italy studied the Hermetic tradition and Cabala with scholars who regarded themselves as heirs of Ficino and Pico. He came in contact with Cardinal Egidius of Viterbo and with Agostino Ricci, a converted Jew, who were interested in the Catholic reform movement and were using the influences of Christian Cabala in that direc-

tion. And Agrippa was also briefly in contact with Francesco Giorgi, the Christian Cabalist Friar of Venice. All these Italian Cabalists were using Cabalist books and manuscripts now available in much larger quantities in Italy and being eagerly studied by scholars.

Thus the German Cabalist reformer made contact with Italian Christian Cabalists. Francesco Giorgi's ideas, though apparently less extreme than those of Agrippa, are actually pretty close to them, though softened by a gentler Italian colouring.

The never-stationary Agrippa next appears in the northern city of Metz where the growing influence of Luther was causing turmoil. As Nauert puts it, Agrippa in Metz has moved from the exciting and vital culture of Renaissance Italy to the exciting and vital culture of northern Europe on the eve of the Reformation. Agrippa and his friends closely followed the writings of Luther. Some of these friends afterwards became Lutheran Protestants. From Metz, Agrippa moved to Geneva where he had occultist friends. Some historians of the origins of Protestantism in Geneva have regarded Agrippa and his circle of the early 1520s 'as the seed-bed of the reformed faith.'

In 1524, Agrippa went to France where he had many friends. Here he published, in 1526, one of his two famous books, the *De vanitate scientiarum.* This book argues that all man's knowledge is vain, all sciences empty, including the occult sciences. His other famous book, the *De occulta philosophia,* the handbook of Renaissance occult sciences, was already written in its first form, but was not published until 1533. Why Agrippa published first a book on the vanity of the sciences, including the occult sciences, whilst reserving for future publication his already written book on the occult sciences, is one of the many problems of his life and work.

In France he had contacts with French doctors (he was versed in medicine), humanists, scientists, alchemists, Lullists (Lullism was one of his specialities) and the like. This world of early French humanism must have been congenial to Agrippa. Under strong Erasmian influence, the new learning was making great strides; ideas about religious reform were moving; and there were powerful Hermetic influences at work. The great French scholar and Hermeticist, Lefevre d'Etaples, was in contact with Agrippa, and Rabelais mentions 'Herr Trippa'.

In 1528 Agrippa was in Antwerp, getting his books printed, including the *De occulta philosophia* (1533), and a reissue of the *De vanitate.* The publication of his books increased his fame. The imperial ambassador to the English court wrote to him that all learned men in London were praising his *De vanitate* and his *De occulta philosophia,* and urged him to take up the defence of Queen Catherine of Aragon, repudiated as his wife by the king, Henry VIII. It was said that Queen Catherine herself had wanted to have Agrippa to defend her. However, he refrained from involving himself in this controversy, unlike Francesco Giorgi, who, as we have seen, became much involved in it on the king's side. Judging by Giorgi's experience it was perhaps as a Hebrew scholar that Agrippa's advice would have been sought, for the problem necessitated appeal to Jewish law on divorce.

At about this time there is evidence of contact between Erasmus and Agrippa. Erasmus wrote to Agrippa, asking him to advise a student of the occult whom he (Erasmus) was not able to satisfy, adding that the *De vanitate* had caused Agrippa's name to be very well-known, though he has heard that the book is rather daring. Agrippa replied eagerly, protesting that he was an Erasmian and obedient to the Church, and asking for Erasmus's opinion of the *De vanitate.* Erasmus did not reply until 1533, when he praised the book but warned Agrippa to be careful, urging him not to involve him (Erasmus) in his controversies because he already had enough ill-will against him.

Though Erasmus had at first encouraged Reuchlin, whom he admired as a scholar, his views on Cabala later hardened into a strong aversion for 'Judaising' studies, an aversion not untinged with antisemitism. Erasmus particularly disliked the attempt of the occult philosophy to increase the magic in Christian ceremonies as a way to strengthen religion through the 'more powerful' philosophy. This is really the theme of the third book of Agrippa's *De occulta philosophia* which is on 'ceremonial magic'. The aim of the occult philosophy of reform through increasing the power of 'ceremonial magic' was diametrically opposed to reform through the Erasmian kind of 'Christian philosophy'. Yet it is possible that Agrippa himself, and perhaps some of his followers, may not have quite clearly grasped the basic difference between Agrippan and Erasmian ideas of reform.

Erasmus, Luther, Agrippa, exhibit different facets of the spiritual force which was breaking down the past and ushering in the future.

. . . .

In [the striking *De vanitate*], Agrippa surveys all human intellectual effort and decides that all is empty, all man's learning is of no account, nothing can be certainly known about anything. Like the preacher in Ecclesiastes, from which he quotes, Agrippa decides that all is vanity of vanities and there is nothing new under the sun. Was he then a total sceptic? He has been treated as such by some modern scholars, but this is a mistake. Agrippa was not a sceptic, as more attentive reading of his work clearly reveals.

The first chapter begins in an atmosphere of Hermetic 'Egyptianism' with reference to 'Theut' and 'Thamus' evoking the Hermetic dialogue on Egyptian mysteries. It then states the book's theme of the uncertainty of all man's learning. The list of vain sciences includes, grammar, poetry, the art of memory, dialectic, Lullism, arithmetic, music, geometry, cosmography, architecture, astronomy, magic, Cabala, physics, metaphysics, ethics, monkish superstition, medicine, alchemy, jurisprudence. These selected titles indicate the curious scope of the work. It is not only against occult sciences, such as magic, Cabala, alchemy. It is against the sciences of number, arithmetic, geometry, architecture, astronomy. It is against physics and metaphysics and the intellectual framework of the scholastic tradition. And there is an indication in 'monkish su-

perstition' that the author is writing at a time when the storms of Reformation are beginning to blow.

The following chapters demolish the sciences in detail, a process in which Agrippa shows a great deal of knowledge of all this range of learning. He dwells much on magic and its divisions. There is a natural magic and a mathematical magic. There is a bad magic which calls on bad demons; there is a good magic which calls on angels through Cabala. There is a natural philosophy which discusses questions such as Can there be a plurality of worlds? and What is the soul? This leads on to metaphysics and moral philosophy. By the time he reaches the one hundredth chapter, Agrippa would appear to a sixteenth-century reader to have covered practically everything. All is vain, save one thing only, namely the Word of God in the Scriptures through which we may come to know Jesus Christ. The title of the one hundredth chapter is *De verbo Dei.*

Agrippa is not an atheist; he is an evangelical. He frequently refers to the Epistles of St Paul, and from one of these the title of his sermon could have been taken: 'I am determined to know nothing among you save Christ Jesus.' Agrippa's evangelical convictions come out, not only in the impressive statements in the hundredth chapter, but incidentally throughout the work. In chapter 54 it is stated that only Christ can teach moral philosophy; this is an evangelical reaction against scholasticism. In chapter 97 on scholastic theology it is stated that, though formerly taught by good men, this subject has now degenerated into sophisms and is to be superseded. In the chapter on images (chapter 25) the use of images in the Church is criticised; we are to learn the truth not from these but from the Scriptures, which prohibit idolatry. All these asides throughout the book breathe the spirit of reform, the spirit of Erasmian evangelical reform. The statements of the hundredth chapter are but a summing up of this theme.

There is no other key to knowledge, says this chapter, but the Word of God. The writer of Ecclesiastes was right when he said that all learning is vanity. We must confess our ignorance and think of ourselves as asses. Then follows Agrippa's famous Praise of the Ass. Christ entered Jerusalem upon an ass. Apuleius in *The Golden Ass* tells how his hero was not initiated into the mysteries of Isis until he had become an ass. These Christian and Hermetic-Egyptian examples of holy ignorance sum up Agrippa's theme of the insufficiency of worldly learning. This theme is basically mystical, to be found in medieval mystical writings such as *The Cloud of Unknowing* which describes the negative mystical experience. And Agrippa no doubt had in mind the great philosophical statement of the theme in Nicolas of Cusa's work *On learned ignorance.* But the closest analogue to Agrippa's *De vanitate* is much nearer to him in time and belongs precisely to the movement of Erasmian evangelicalism. It is, in fact, a work by Erasmus himself, the famous *Praise of Folly.* Agrippa's *Encomium Asini* is a counterpart of the *Encomium Moriae* by his great contemporary.

Erasmus wrote his *Praise of Folly* (*Encomium Moriae*) when he was living in the household of Thomas More in London during that momentous visit to England from

1508 to 1513. It will be remembered that Agrippa was in London in 1510 and in contact with a member of the More circle, John Colet. There is no evidence that Agrippa met Erasmus on that visit, or knew that he was writing *The Praise of Folly,* but we have seen that in later years Agrippa was particularly anxious to have Erasmus's views on his own *De vanitate,* perhaps because he hoped that Erasmus might see a kinship between Vanity and Folly. At any rate, it is very instructive to compare the two works.

Erasmus's Folly is a woman who laughs at all the sciences, at Grammar, Rhetoric, Mathematics, Astronomy, Physics; she passes them all by; the ideas and figures and arguments of the philosophers all seem to her absurd. Though she is mainly concerned with exposing the emptiness of orthodox learning, she also mentions some occult sciences, magic and alchemy, as vain. Her distrust of learning is closely associated with her pre-Reform attitudes. She mocks at pardoners and indulgences, at the sermons of monks and friars. The Erasmian wit is very fully deployed in this brilliant work which had an immense vogue as the expression of irritation against the old order of things and the longing for reform. Folly quotes Ecclesiastes on vanity of vanities, all is vanity. She quotes St Paul on science which puffs up pride. The Christian religion, she says, is a doctrine of simplicity, and the man absorbed in the love of heavenly things can look a fool.

The moral is very close to that of Agrippa's *De vanitate.* After surveying all the sciences, Folly finds security only in the Gospel. In both books, the attack on the vanity of learning is also a satire on the vanity of monkish learning. Erasmus has much less than Agrippa on the vanity of the occult sciences, but he does include them. And Agrippa is not only concerned with the vanity of occult sciences but also with the emptiness of scholastic learning. The conclusion of both is that only in the simplicity of the Gospel is security.

The parallel was noted by Philip Sidney who remarks in his *Defence of Poetry:*

> Agrippa will be as merry in showing the vanity of science as Erasmus was in the defending of folly. Neither shall any man or matter escape some touch of these smiling railers. . . . But for Erasmus and Agrippa, they had another foundation than the superficial part would promise.

I suppose that this 'other foundation' would be the Gospel, alone exempt from scepticism according to both Erasmus and Agrippa.

Erasmus did not throw away his classical and patristic scholarship nor discontinue his life-work as a humanist scholar because of the *Praise of Folly.* Nor did Agrippa abandon the occult sciences because of his praise of the Ass. On the contrary a few years after the publication of the *De vanitate* he published *De occulta philosophia,* his full-scale positive treatment of the occult philosophy.

. . . .

I have made efforts in other books to present in some moderately lucid form the contents of [*De occulta philosophia*], and I must now make the attempt again.

In the first two chapters, Agrippa lays down the outline. The universe is divided into three worlds, the elemental world, the celestial world, the intellectual world. Each world receives influences from the one above it; so that the virtue of the Creator descends through the angels in the intellectual world, to the stars in the celestial world, and thence to the elements and all things composed of them in the terrestrial world. In accordance with this outlook, Agrippa's work is divided into three books. The first book is about natural magic, or magic in the elemental world; it teaches how to arrange substances in accordance with the occult sympathies between them, so as to effect operations in natural magic. The second book is about celestial magic, or how to attract and use influences of the stars. Agrippa calls this kind of magic mathematical magic because its operations depend on number. The third book is about ceremonial magic or magic directed towards the supercelestial world of angelic spirits, beyond which is the One opifex or the creator himself.

Agrippa is summarising the disciplines of Renaissance magic; the Hermetic magic taught by Ficino, and the Cabalist magic introduced by Pico della Mirandola.

As was discovered by D. P. Walker, Ficino's magic was ultimately based on that taught by the supposed Egyptian age, Hermes Trismegistus, whom Ficino believed to be a contemporary of Moses and a prophet of Christianity [*Spiritual and Demonic Magic*]. Ficino describes his magic in his book *De vita coelitus comparanda,* the most popular and widely read of all his works. It is based very largely, as Walker showed, on the *Asclepius,* supposedly by Hermes Trismegistus, which describes how the Egyptians attracted celestial influences into the statues of their gods.

Ficino describes how to attract influences of the planets, by using arrangements of substances, by incantations, and by talismans inscribed with the images of the planets and supposed to contain, or attract, their virtues. It is the Ficinian magic which Agrippa teaches in his first book, though he teaches it in a much bolder way. Ficino was nervous of the magic; he was anxious to keep his magic 'natural', concerned only with elemental substances in their relations to the stars and avoiding the 'star demons', the spirits connected with the stars. It was really not possible to teach astral magic whilst avoiding the star demons, as Agrippa saw and boldly accepted the challenge.

Agrippa's second book is on celestial magic, dealing with the stars, not only through their influences on the elements, but ascending to the 'middle' celestial world to grapple with them. This involves number and the celestial magic becomes a mathematical magic. He states the necessity of mathematical disciplines for mathematical magic. The magical statues of the *Asclepius* depended, he says, on number. Miraculous effects can be obtained with geometry and optics. Pythagoras taught the prime importance of number, and physics has a mathematical basis. Ficino had not discussed mathematical magic (he would have avoided it because of his avoidance of star demons), but for Agrippa 'mathematical magic' held a profound attraction.

In the third book, Agrippa boldly advances into the intellectual and angelic world, and sets out schemes for reaching angels and spirits through Cabalist magic. This depends on manipulation of Hebrew letters, which have numerical values, so this again is a kind of mathematical magic though aiming much higher. This book deals with the ceremonies of religions; it is a religious magic, and the magus who reaches this point in his studies has gone far beyond natural magic and mathematical magic. He has drawn close to the Creator himself and knows how to call upon the Names of God.

Agrippa certainly believes himself to be a Christian Cabalist, for the third book leads up to the Name of Jesus as the final mystery. Pico had said in his Cabalist Conclusions that the only name with which the Cabalist can now operate is the Name of Jesus. Agrippa repeats this, word for word. The famous magician undoubtedly believed that, like Pico della Mirandola, he could qualify as a Christian Cabalist.

In fact, I believe that Agrippa's aim is precisely that of providing the technical procedures for acquiring the more powerful and 'wonder-working' philosophy which Reuchlin had called for, a philosophy ostensibly Neoplatonic but including a magical Hermetic-Cabalist core. Constantly on Agrippa's lips in the *De occulta philosophia* are the names of Plato, Plotinus, Proclus, and other Neoplatonists, and, of course, 'Hermes Trismegistus'. He is expounding in matter-of-fact text-book terms the 'wonder-working' Neoplatonism which Reuchlin had desired to encourage in place of dry and barren scholasticism as the philosophy to accompany Christianity.

If one re-reads the *De occulta philosophia* attentively one will notice that in each of the three worlds Agrippa brings in Hebrew names and formulae. This happens in the exposition of magic in the elemental world and in the celestial world, as well as in the supercelestial world where Cabala naturally belongs. Agrippa probably believes that he is both strengthening natural magic and celestial magic by bringing them into contact with powerful Hebrew magic, and also purifying these magics, making them safe by associating them with holy Cabalist influences. Like Reuchlin (and Pico) by associating all the magics with holy influences he makes them safe. He makes sure that only good and holy angelic influences are invoked, and that the stardemons are made harmless through their help. Agrippa's occult philosophy is intended to be a very white magic. In fact it is really a religion, claiming access to the highest powers, and Christian since it accepts the name of Jesus as the chief of the wonder-working Names.

. . . Agrippa's outlook seems very close indeed to that of Francesco Giorgi, though in the *De harmonia mundi* Giorgi is slightly more cautious (he is much bolder in the *Problemata*). His Franciscan affiliations would no doubt have made him seem less alarming than Agrippa, the strange wanderer with no religious home.

The function of Cabala as Agrippa saw it was not only to provide the highest 'supercelestial' magic, but to guarantee the safety of the operator against demons at all levels. The fear of demons had haunted Ficino, but Cabala eliminates this fear. It is an insurance against demons, a guarantee that bold attempts after unlimited knowledge and power will not lead to damnation.

Though the genuine Hebrew Cabalist might be shocked by Agrippa's interpretation of Cabala solely as white magic, yet this interpretation served a purpose in fortifying man for intellectual and spiritual endeavour.

Diane Bornstein   (essay date 1980)

SOURCE: An introduction to *The Feminist Controversy of the Renaissance: Facsimile Reproductions,* by Guillaume Alexis, Sir Thomas Bird, and Henry Cornelius Agrippa, Scholars' Facsimiles & Reprints, 1980, pp. v-xiii.

[*In the following excerpt, Bornstein discusses* The Nobility of the Feminine Sex, *concluding that it is "an eloquent plea for the education and liberation of women."*]

[Agrippa's *De nobilitate et praecellentia foeminei sexus* was written] in 1509, [and] it was dedicated to Margaret of Austria to win her favor. Agrippa did not have a chance to present the treatise to Margaret and did not publish it until almost twenty years later. He had to leave the University of Dôle, where he had been lecturing, because of an attack on the orthodoxy of his lectures by Jean Catilinet, provincial superior of the Franciscans in Burgundy. Agrippa was deeply involved in cabalistic studies and had a reputation as a magician. He served as the model for Faustus in Marlowe's *Dr. Faustus.*

Agrippa's cabalistic studies are reflected in the abstruse etymologies found in *De nobilitate.* According to the cabalists, the names of things were taken to be reflections of their essence. He also used the Neoplatonic idea of a hierarchy of creatures. He states that since woman was created last, she is the superior creature. His Hebrew studies are reflected in his frequent use of examples from the Old Testament.

Although Agrippa did not get to present *De nobilitate* to its intended patron, it enjoyed considerable popularity, particularly in England, where it was translated three times. It was translated into prose by David Clapam as *A Treatise of the Nobilitie and Excellencye of Woman Kynde* (1542). This English prose translation was turned into heroic couplets in a version entitled *The Glory of Women or a Looking Glasse for Ladies* (1652). An independent translation from the Latin entitled *Female Preeminence, or the Dignity and Excellency of that Sex above the Male* (1670) was made by Henry Care. The translation by Care is here reprinted. Care, a political writer and journalist, was accused of being sycophantic because of his extravagant dedication to Queen Catherine.

Although the work is not written in debate form, it is strongly polemic. Agrippa musters arguments from etymology, physiology, scripture, history, and contemporary life to demonstrate the superiority of women. His etymologies are entirely fanciful, although some of them were taken seriously in his day. His physiology is inaccurate and sometimes comic. For instance, he says that when women drown, they float face down in the water, whereas men float face (and private parts) up. This shows the natural modesty of women. Some of his arguments are trivial, although ingenious. Another argument he uses to show the modesty of women is that their hair covers their private parts. He uses many exempla from traditional antifeminist literature but changes their import, stating that these tales reflect against men and that men blame women for their own failures and weaknesses. Some of the biblical examples used in this way are the stories of Samson, Lot, David, and Solomon.

Throughout much of the work one is struck by Agrippa's wit but one doubts his seriousness. Toward the end, however, when the reader is amused and off guard, Agrippa's argument becomes more serious. Using biblical examples, he states that men were the first sinners; they introduced drunkenness, polygamy, and murder into the world; they are tyrannical and aggressive and have created many evils, whereas women have created the peaceful arts. This contribution of women is symbolized by the Muses and by female goddesses. Women are more chaste, faithful, and refined; they held all kinds of offices in ancient times, serving as priestesses, doctors, scholars, and rulers; they learn just as quickly as men and have just as many abilities. The only thing that holds women back is the tyranny of men and an education that confines them to the trivialities of life. Agrippa ends with an eloquent plea for the education and liberation of women. . . .

Linda Woodbridge   (essay date 1984)

SOURCE: "The Early Tudor Controversy," in *Women and the English Renaissance: Literature and the Nature of Womankind, 1540-1620,* University of Illinois Press, 1984, pp. 18-48.

[*Woodbridge comments on* The Nobility of the Feminine Sex *in the context of the early Tudor debate about women. She notes that in "sensing the [debate's] ultimate irrelevance to women's struggles, [Agrippa] stood virtually alone."*]

When the great Heinrich Cornelius Agrippa von Nettesheim, scholar of international reputation, theorist of magic, at once humanist and critic of humanist pursuits, undertook a defense of women, something out of the ordinary was to be expected. It is true that his defense, *De nobilitate et praecellentia Foemenei sexus,* called in Clapham's 1542 translation *A Treatise of the Nobilitie and excellencye of woman kynde,* is more generously endowed than any other early Renaissance defense with tedious lists of great women in biblical and classical history: women who inspired the love of Greek gods, beautiful women in the Bible, good wives of the Bible and the classics, great female names in religion, philosophy (Diotima *et al*), prophecy (the Sybils *et al*), oratory and poetry (Sappho *et al*), government (Semiramis, Dido, the Amazons), warfare, invention, and even—an Agrippan touch—magic. (Circe and Medea are, eccentrically, praised as better magicians than the male Zoroaster.) The Virgin puts in her statutory appearance, along with the women to whom Christ first showed himself after the resurrection, who serve as a contrast to the all male cast of malefactors involved in his trial and crucifixion. And Agrippa promotes a view of parents that cannot help striking the mod-

ern reader as painfully unfair to both sexes: the "chiefest offyce and duetye of woman," he declares (now ignoring Sappho, the Amazons, and the rest) "is to conceyue" in the course of defending childrearing as a worthy occupation, Agrippa avers that fathers have little influence on children, that mothers love children more than fathers do because they correctly perceive that children have "more of theyr mothers substance, than of theyr fathers" and that children love their mothers more than their fathers. He furthers stereotype by noting that women are more pitying and merciful than men: women, to whom milk is given, are nourishers by nature. (Woman's milk as a symbol of her gentle, nurturing qualities was a commonplace; Shakespeare twice employs it in ironic reversal: two of his least nurturing female characters, Goneril and Lady Macbeth, accuse their husbands of "milky gentleness" and of being "too full o' the milk of human kindness.")

But if Agrippa's treatise is predictable in these particulars, it is predictable in no others. His initial flat statement of the complete spiritual and intellectual equality of the sexes sparkles in an age when other defenders contended themselves mainly with shaming the unchivalrousness of detractors. Dismissing physical differences between the sexes as negligible, Agrippa announces a credo: "The woman hathe that same mynd that a man hath, that same reason and speche, she gothe to the same ende of blysfulnes. . . . Betwene man and woman by substance of the soule, one hath no higher preemynence of nobylytye aboue the other, but both of them naturally haue equall libertie of dignitie and worthynesse." This, however unorthodox, is nothing to what follows: the rest of the essay argues the superiority of women in every area except equality of divine substance. The arguments Agrippa marshalls in support of this amazing thesis are ingenious if not outrageous: many have that bright casuistical flair that characterizes the work of Neoplatonists; a few are almost certainly tongue-in-cheek.

On the sticky problem of our first mother, Agrippa expends a good deal of ingenuity. Eve was God's last and hence highest creation (since God was clearly working his way up the Great Chain of Being); she was made of nobler material, formed, unlike Adam, of animate substance. In explaining away Eve's part in the unpleasantness of the apple, Agrippa with a lawyer's mind locates a loophole: God forbade eating the fruit *before* Eve's creation; the stricture therefore did not apply to her. God deliberately declined to deny the fruit to Eve; he wished her, as a superior being, to be free of the rules governing the inferior Adam: "For god wolde [i. e., willed] her to be fre[e] from the begynning. Therefore the manne sinned in eatynyge, not the woman. And all we synned in Adam, not in Eva." This astonishing, thoroughly heretical, and perfectly delightful theory is not persuasive, and Agrippa must have known it was not. Although it is true that Adam is warned away from the fruit before Eve's creation, Eve demonstrates in her conversation with the serpent that she has been informed of the rules: "But of the fruit of the tree which is in the midst of the garden, God hath said, Ye shall not eat of it, neither shall ye touch it, lest ye die." Eve clearly believes that "ye" includes herself, and since she does die, there is no doubt that God intended her to be included. Although Agrippa tries to buttress his argument by maintaining that "the man knew well he dyd amisse; but the woman being deceyued, erred ignorantly," he accomplishes no more than to render gullible his supposed superior creature. The argument remains the purest sophistry. Considering that Agrippa's argument has no smaller effect than to recreate Woman as a separate species, exempt from original sin, it is difficult to believe that his intention was other than to amuse his readers with the joy of outrageous ingenuity exercised for its own sake. Among all the defenses of Eve, it remains my personal favorite; but I cannot believe it was meant to be taken seriously.

No more can one take seriously Agrippa's treatment of the ghastly Old Testament episodes where God commands the victorious Israelites to kill all male captives and keep the women as prizes; Agrippa considers this evidence of the excellency of womankind! And then there is hair. Agrippa's contention that women are given long hair for modesty's sake was a commonplace: it went along with the argument that women's privy parts are more privy than men's; women are more modest than men by nature. What smacks of ingenuity for its own sake is the treatment of baldness and beards: first, women are superior because they do not go bald, baldness being an affront to human dignity by spoiling the appearance of that seat of reason, the head; second (diametrically opposed to the baldness argument), men are inferior because they possess beards: excessive hairiness reduces a human being to the animal level. The manifest absurdity of these arguments, particularly when taken together, militates against serious intent.

Human physicality calls forth more logical curiosities: women are cleaner than men (Agrippa claims that men dirty the bathwater more), and women are finer because it is worthier to void "superfluous humours" by "secrete partes" than by the face, "the moste worthy part of a mannes body." (This somewhat obscure remark seems to mean that menstruation is less disgusting than spitting.)

One of Agrippa's pleasantest moments is his defense of that universally-rued vice of womankind, talkativeness. "And is not a womãn better spoke, more eloquent, more copious and plentyfull of wordes than a man?" he unblushingly inquires, no doubt fully cognizant of the chagrined agreement to be expected from most readers. His defense is humanistic: "Is it not right faire and commendable, that women shulde excelle men in that thing, in whiche men chiefly passe all other beastes?" The argument is far from unreasonable: it is a logical extension of the humanist glorification of speech as a distinctive attribute of humankind; but it must have struck contemporaries, accustomed to satiric diatribes on women's irrepressible prattling, as perverse. Again, the argument is almost certainly facetious.

The real shock is Agrippa's contention that, given women's superiority, Christ as God would surely have descended to earth in female form had it not been necessary to exhibit humility, since the sin he had come to expiate was pride: "He toke vpon hym manhode, as the more humble and lower kynde, and not womankynde, the more hygher and noble." One can imagine clergymen fainting in their studies upon reading such a passage. And if one

were not already convinced that Agrippa's tongue is planted firmly in his cheek, one could be left in very little doubt after encountering those venerable biblical bogey-women, Delilah, Lot's daughters, and Job's wife, now metamorphosed into examples of the superior power of womankind. When all this is capped with fantastic natural history (all eagles and the phoenix are female, all basilisks are male) one feels that here is no more than a rival "iest."

A later translator, Henry Care, who in 1670 refurbished this work as a rejoinder to a recent work listing women's imperfections alphabetically, took it as an elaborate jest, placing it in the classical tradition (revived in the Renaissance) of rhetorical paradox. The translator's preface suggests that the piece might gain pardon if not applause in an age of extravagant opinions and wild conceits; it is no worse than the paradoxical praises of tyranny, injustice, ugliness, and folly (here he names Erasmus's *The Praise of Folly*) which have gone before. Agrippa wrote it, Care suggests, for love of perversity: he enjoyed "stemming the impetuous Tide of popular opinion," as witness **The Vanity of the Arts and Sciences,** Agrippa's attack on humanist learning.

I see nothing in Agrippa's essay to preclude its being a rhetorical paradox. Agrippa called the work an oration. In form it is close to an epideictic oration, though an occasional foray into *refutatio* brings it closer at times to the more typical judicial oration. But Agrippa's use of this god-praising oration for that which is seldom praised, his outrageous arguments, his main thesis that flies in the face of received opinion, would seem to establish the work as rhetorical paradox. It is similar in kind to Montaigne's *Apology of Raymond Sebonde,* that trenchant argument for the superiority of animals to mankind that George Boas has discussed as part of the paradox tradition [in his *The Happy Beast in French Thought of the Seventeeth Century*]. Such a view gains strength, if anything, from the pains Agrippa takes to deny that his arguments are sophistical: this seems a hint to the reader to view the work in a certain light. But Henry Care is unjust in assuming that the paradox's motive is love of perversity, its main purpose wit for its own sake. Paradoxical literature from Montaigne's *Apology* to Erasmus's *The Praise of Folly* exhibits serious intent: the need for such outlandish arguments to maintain an extreme opinion is meant to reflect on the outlandishness of argument that would be necessary to maintain the opposite extreme. Montaigne's argument for animal superiority undermines extravagant humanist claims for the superiority of mankind, while Erasmus's panegyrics to folly call into question the age's complacent reliance on the wisdom of this world. The rhetorical paradox is an overcorrection, pointing up the untenable nature of one extreme position by demonstrating the feasibility of arguing its opposite. Paradox is not like the mock-heroic mode, where the inadequacies of the subject are exposed by the inflated terms in which it is celebrated; Agrippa's hyperbolic praise of women is not an ironic vehicle for laying bare the sex's unworthiness but a graphic demonstration of the absurdities one must resort to if one claims superiority for either sex.

Like the sonnet, paradoxical works contain a *volta,* a point at which the author takes leave of outlandish argument and outrageous example and quietly asserts the mean between extremes that must represent the attitude of the reasonable thinker. Montaigne leaves behind tales of enamored elephants and soberly objects to human presumption; Erasmus's lively and ironic enumeration of human follies yields to devout reflections on the foolishness of mankind and the wisdom of God. And Agrippa, as if his ingenuity had reached its outer limit with the eagles, phoenix, and basilisks, turns sober and begins arguing straightforwardly what was always the real issue—the case for equality.

Agrippa now decries the double standard of sexual morality, argues that women's evil has been overestimated because most writers are male, and reminds the reader (with a near-anthropological modernity) that women's social and political inferiority in contemporary Europe is not based on natural law and has not, at other times and in other cultures, invariably obtained. He recalls marital equality in ancient Rome, Roman legal guarantees for joint ownership and disposal of marital property and for wives' right of inheritance; he notes ancient arguments for women's equality and rights, citing Lycurgus and Plato. Adducing other cultures where women had more rights than they now have—the Cantabrians, Scythians, Thracians—he observes, "That is nowe forbydden by lawes, abolished by custome, extincted by education. For anon as a woman is borne euen from her infancy, she is kept at home in ydelnes, & as thoughe she were vnmete for any hygher busynesse, she is p[er]mitted to know no farther, than her nedle and her threede." Women are forbidden to hold office, plead a case at law, be guardians or tutors, preach God's word (here he notes women preachers in the Bible). In his ringing conclusion, Agrippa stands head and shoulders above his contemporaries as a realist in the study of sexual politics. Controversialists seldom went farther than to judge women good or bad by the degree of their conformity to a code of behavior seen as part of the natural order. Agrippa questioned the existence of "natural" order, viewing women's condition as a product of forces less natural than cultural: "And thus by these lawes, the women being subdewed as it were by force of armes, are constrained to giue place to men, and to obeye theyr subdewers, not by no naturall, no diuyne necessitie or reason, but by custome, education, fortune, and a certayne Tyrannicall occasion." In the light of this statement, Agrippa's lists of great women in history take on new meaning: women have done more in the past than they are doing now, because contemporary society denies them the education and the legal rights they must have to perform what they are capable of. Not content with praising or blaming Woman as she now exists, Agrippa suggests reasons for the actual inferiority of so potentially excellent a creature. His initial coy disavowal of sophistry contrasts strikingly with the gravity of his final affirmation: "For neyther Ambition, nor the cause of myne own commendation, but my dutie and the very truthe moued me to wryte." The serious turn the work has taken, and the accuracy of his social analysis, incline me to believe him.

When Agrippa recognizes the opposition, he does not characterize it as misogynistic insult and jesting detrac-

tion: "There be somme men," he tells us, "whyche by relygion, clayme authoritie ouer women, and they proue theyr tyranny by holy scripture." The enemy, Agrippa sees, is not the misogynist but the male supremacist. The distinction is crucial: many men who have loved women have been male supremacists; open misogyny has always been less difficult for women to deal with than has well-intentioned paternalism of the sort in which defenders themselves indulged. The formal controversy's potential usefulness was undermined by the way defenders of women persistently depicted literary misogyny, "malicious detraction," as the major obstacle to women's happiness. Agrippa could play the literary game as well as any—better than most; but in sensing the game's ultimate irrelevance to women's struggles for freedom and dignity, he stood virtually alone. He saw that women suffer less from literary insults than from being "constrained to give place to men, and to obeye theyr subdewers."

The rhetorical paradox is itself a kind of jest—an intricate and exquisite jest, preëminently vulnerable to misinterpretation. Agrippa's feminist use of this mode reminds us that while composition of a defense is no guarantee of true authorial concern about the woman question, neither does literary sophistication evidence lack of such concern. One sometimes senses authorial "sincerity" in controversialist works, as I do with Agrippa; such impressions may frequently be wrong. But whatever the author's personal attitude toward women, it remains clear that the formal controversy, for all its preoccupation with stylistic finesse, could occasionally produce a thinker capable of laying philosophic foundations for modern feminism. . . .

FURTHER READING

Hamilton, A. C. "Sidney and Agrippa." *The Review of English Studies* VII, No. 26 (April 1956): 151-57.

> Demonstrates that Agrippa's *Of the Vanity and Uncertainty of Arts and Sciences* "provides a framework within which Sidney attacks the vanity of the arts and sciences and defends the art of poetry."

Judson, Alexander C. "Cornelius Agrippa and Henry Vaughan." *Modern Language Notes* XLI, no. 3 (March 1926): 178-81.

> Discusses the influence of Agrippa's ideas on Vaughan's poem "The Ass."

Kozicki, Henry. "Browning, *Pauline*, and Cornelius Agrippa: The Protagonist as Magus." *Victorian Poetry* 28, No. 1 (Spring 1990): 17-38.

> Asserts that "Browning knew occultist thought . . . and that [Agrippa's] *Occulta* provides the conceptual underpinning of *Pauline*."

Yates, Frances A. "Giordano Bruno: The Secret of *Shadows*." In her *The Art of Memory*, 199-230. Chicago: University of Chicago Press, 1966.

> Briefly explores Agrippa's *On the Vanity and Uncertainty of Arts and Sciences* as one of the main sources for Bruno's *De umbris idearum* (1582).

————. "Renaissance Philosophers in Elizabethan England: John Dee and Giordano Bruno." In *History & Imagination: Essays in Honor of H. R. Trevor-Roper*, edited by Hugh Lloyd-Jones, Valerie Pearl, and Blair Worden, pp. 104-14. New York: Holmes & Meier Publishers, 1981.
    Compares the attitudes of Dee and Bruno toward Agrippa's *Occult Philosophy*.

Giordano Bruno

1548-1600

Italian philosopher.

INTRODUCTION

Known for his unorthodox views regarding the nature of the universe, Bruno was a philosopher who challenged traditional cosmological beliefs held by the Roman Catholic Church and sixteenth-century society. From the sixteenth through the twentieth century, scholars have repeatedly examined Giordano Bruno's status as a heretic, scientist, pantheist, and poet. Some contend that his ideas influenced philosopher Benedictus de Spinoza and scientist Galileo Galilei and argue that Bruno was the greatest philosopher of the Renaissance. Much of the controversial nature of Bruno's works, among them *La cena de le ceneri* (1584; *The Ash Wednesday Supper*) and *Lo spaccio de la bestia trionfante* (1584; *The Expulsion of the Triumphant Beast*) stem from the social, political, and religious reform that they suggest. Many of Bruno's ideas were considered heretical by the Church, as his cosmological model was based on a Copernican rather than an Aristotelian foundation. Bruno's teachings on mnemonics, believed by many to be a form of black magic, were also a source of concern for the religious community. Despite the suspicion surrounding his views, neither in his lectures nor in his writings did Bruno compare his philosophy with Roman Catholic doctrine. Furthermore, Bruno claimed never to have taught directly against the Church's beliefs. Nevertheless, he was executed on the grounds of heresy.

Biographical Information

Born in Nola, Italy, in 1548, Bruno was given the name Filippo, which he later changed to Giordano upon entering a Dominican monastery as a teenager. Bruno fled the monastery in 1576 due to accusations of heresy. After a period of travelling and lecturing, Bruno arrived in England in 1583 and resided with the French ambassador until 1585. During this time, Bruno published several of his more well-known philosophical works, including *La cena de le ceneri, Lo spaccio de la bestia trionfante,* and *De gli eroici furori* (1585; *The Heroic Frenzies*). For several years, Bruno journeyed through France and Germany, arriving in Frankfurt in 1590. There, in 1591, he published his last works, among them *De imaginum signorum et idearum compositione* (1591; *On the Composition of Images, Signs and Ideas*), a controversial book on the art of memory. While in Frankfort, Bruno received an invitation from a Venetian gentleman, Giovanni Mocenigo, to serve as an instructor in this art. Bruno accepted and returned to Italy in 1592. Mocenigo soon turned Bruno over to the Holy Tribunal for examination on the grounds of heresy. Following the Venetian Inquisition, Bruno was sent to the Supreme Tribunal of the Holy Office of Rome for trial in

1593. He was imprisoned until 1599. Some scholars believe that during this period Bruno's inquisitors tortured him in an effort to make him admit his heresy and recant. Bruno did neither. He was sentenced to death and burned at the stake on February 17, 1600.

Major Works

Many of Bruno's works are structured in the form of a dialogue and combine discussion of societal, political, or religious issues with philosophical arguments. The setting of *La cena de le ceneri* is the home of an English nobleman, to which Bruno is invited for a discussion of the movements of the earth and sun and their relationship to the universe. Additionally, some social and political issues are mentioned or alluded to as Bruno describes the problems he encounters on the way to the nobleman's home. In *Lo spaccio de la bestia trionfante*, human vice is embodied in the "triumphant beast" which lives, argues Bruno, in everyone. Bruno explains that in order to overcome his vice, man must employ reason, gained through an understanding of the laws of nature. *De la causa, principio et uno* (1584; *Concerning the Cause, Principle, and One*) outlines Bruno's metaphysical beliefs. He provides detailed arguments concerning the nature of God, the universe, and man's relationship to both. Bruno further develops his ideas pertaining to the physical universe in *De l'infinito universo et mondi* (1584). This work focuses on the infinity of the universe as an image of an infinite God. *De gli eroici furori* reveals Bruno's ethical doctrine regarding heroic love as compared to human, or vulgar love. Bruno argues that heroic love leads one's soul toward a union with God, and that this union cannot be achieved in one's present life.

Critical Reception

During his lifetime, Roman Catholic Inquisitors examined Bruno's writings in search of heretical statements. Others, such as Johannes Kepler, turned to Bruno for different reasons. Kepler indicated that Bruno's ideas on the plurality of inhabited worlds influenced his own thought. Scholars such as Dorothea Waley Singer contend that Spinoza and Galileo may have also been influenced, directly or indirectly, by Bruno, as his cosmological ideas are often mirrored in their work. In an analysis of Bruno's beliefs, Paul Oskar Kristeller states that the body of the philosopher's work contains ambiguities regarding form and matter, the physical and the metaphysical, and the distinction between the universe and God. Other scholars have noted similar inconsistencies. Bruno's use of poetry as a means of strengthening his philosophical arguments has been a source of discussion for critics as well. Frances Yates contends that in *De gli eroici furori* Bruno uses the sonnet form as well as Petrarchan conceits to discuss the striving of man toward union with the divine. Giancarlo Maiorino insists that the subject of Bruno's "literary stature" has been evaded by most scholars. Maiorino goes on to compare Bruno's views on poetic and philosophical thought and argues that Bruno's poetics are grounded in a commitment to free thought and expression. In its complexity, Bruno's work offers endless opportunities for religious, social, and scientific analysis. He has been admired for his cosmological insights, developed through logic and analogies, for speaking out against social, political, and religious corruption, and for his unshakable faith in his own ideas.

PRINCIPAL WORKS

"*Ars memoriae*" (philosophy) 1582
Cantus circaeus (philosophy) 1582
Il Candelaio (comedy) 1582
De compendiosa architectura et complemento artis Lullii (philosophy) 1582
"*De umbris idearum*" (philosophy) 1582
De la causa, principio et uno (dialogues) 1584 [*Concerning the Cause, Principle, and One*, 1950]
La cena de le ceneri (dialogues) 1584 [*The Ash Wednesday Supper*, 1975]
De l'infinito universo et mondi (philosophy) 1584 [*On Infinite Universe and its Worlds*, 1950]
Lo spaccio de la bestia trionfante (dialogues) 1584 [*The Expulsion of the Triumphant Beast*, 1964]

Cabala del cavallo Pegaseo con L'aggiunta dell' asino cellencio (philosophy) 1585
De gli eroici furori (philosophy) 1585 [*The Heroic Frenzies*, 1964]
Articuli centum et sexaginta adversus huius tempestatis mathematicos atque philosophos (philosophy) 1588
Oratio valedictoria (speech) 1588
De magia (philosophy) 1590
Medicina Lulliana (philosophy) 1590
De imaginum signorum et idearum compositione (philosophy) 1591 [*On the Composition of Images, Signs and Ideas*, 1991]
De innumerabilibus immenso et infigurabili; sue de universo et mundis (poem) 1591
De monade, numero et figura (poem) 1591
De triplicia minimo et mensura ad trium speculativarum scientiarum et multarum activarum atrium pricipie (poem) 1591

CRITICISM

Walter Pater (essay date 1889)

SOURCE: "Giordano Bruno," in *The Fortnightly Review*, Vol. XLVI No. CCLXXII, August 1, 1889, pp. 234-44.

[*A nineteenth-century essayist, novelist, and critic, Pater is regarded as one of the most famous proponents of aestheticism in English literature. Distinguished as the first major English writer to formulate an explicitly aesthetic philosophy of life, he advocated the "love of art for art's sake" as life's greatest offering, a belief which he exemplified in his influential* Studies in the History of the Renaissance (1873) *and elucidated in his novel* Marius the Epicurean (1885) *and other works. In this essay, Pater discusses the monastic background and pantheistic philosophy of Bruno in an examination of the philosopher's 1586 speech delivered in Paris.*]

It was on the afternoon of the Feast of Pentecost that news of the death of Charles the Ninth went abroad promptly. To his successor the day became a sweet one, to be noted unmistakably by various pious and other observances; and it was on a Whit-Sunday afternoon that curious Parisians had the opportunity of listening to one who, as if with some intentional new version of the sacred event then commemorated, had a great deal to say concerning the Spirit; above all, of the freedom, the independence of its operation. The speaker, though understood to be a brother of the Order of St. Dominic, had not been present at the mass—the usual university mass, *De Spiritu Sancto*, said to-day according to the natural course of the season in the chapel of the Sorbonne, by the Italian Bishop of Paris. It was the reign of the Italians just then, a doubly refined, somewhat morbid, somewhat, ash-coloured, Italy in France, more Italian still. Men of Italian birth, "to the great suspicion of simple people," swarmed in Paris, already "flightier, less constant, than the girouettes on its steeples," and it was love for Italian fashions that had brought king and courtiers here to-day, with great *éclat,* as they said, frizzed and starched, in the beautiful, minutely considered dress of the moment, pressing the university into a perhaps not unmerited background; for the promised speaker, about whom tongues had been busy, not only in the Latin quarter, had come from Italy. In an age in which all things about which Parisians much cared must be Italian there might be a hearing for Italian philosophy. Courtiers at least would understand Italian, and this speaker was rumoured to possess in perfection all the curious arts of his native language. And of all the kingly qualities of Henry's youth, the single one that had held by him was that gift of eloquence, which he was able also to value in others—inherited perhaps; for in all the contemporary and subsequent historic gossip about his mother, the two things certain are, that the hands credited with so much mysterious ill-doing were fine ones, and that she was an admirable speaker.

Bruno himself tells us, long after he had withdrawn himself from it, that the monastic life promotes the freedom of the intellect by its silence and self-concentration. The prospect of such freedom sufficiently explains why a young man who, however well found in worldly and personal advantages, was conscious above all of great intellectual possessions, and of fastidious spirit also, with a remarkable distaste for the vulgar, should have espoused poverty, chastity, obedience, in a Dominican cloister. What liberty of mind may really come to in such places, what daring new departures it may suggest to the strictly monastic temper, is exemplified by the dubious and dangerous mysticism of men like John of Parma and Joachim of Flora, reputed author of the new "Everlasting Gospel," strange dreamers, in a world of sanctified rhetoric, of that later dispensation of the spirit, in which all law must have passed away; or again by a recognised tendency in the great rival Order of St. Francis, in the so-called "spiritual" Franciscans, to understand the dogmatic words of faith *with a difference.*

The three convents in which Bruno lived successively, at Naples, at Citta di Campagna, and finally the *Minerva* at Rome, developed freely, we may suppose, all the mystic qualities of a genius in which, from the first, a heady southern imagination took the lead. But it was from beyond conventional bounds he would look for the sustenance, the fuel, of an ardour born or bred within them. Amid such artificial religious stillness the air itself becomes generous in undertones. The vain young monk (vain of course!) would feed his vanity by puzzling the good, sleepy heads of the average sons of Dominic with his neology, putting new wine into old bottles, teaching them their own business—the new, higher, truer sense of the most familiar terms, the chapters they read, the hymns they sang, above all, as it happened, every word that referred to the Spirit, the reign of the Spirit, its excellent freedom. He would soon pass beyond the utmost limits of his brethren's sympathy, beyond the largest and freest interpretation those words would bear, to thoughts and words on an altogether different plane, of which the full scope was only to be felt in certain old pagan writers, though approached, perhaps, at first, as having a kind of natural, preparatory kinship with Scripture itself. The Do-

minicans would seem to have had well-stocked, liberally-selected, libraries; and this curious youth, in that age of restored letters, read eagerly, easily, and very soon came to the kernel of a difficult old author—Plotinus or Plato; to the purpose of thinkers older still, surviving by glimpses only in the books of others—Empedocles, Pythagoras, who had enjoyed the original divine sense of things, above all, Parmenides, that most ancient assertor of God's identity with the world. The affinities, the unity, of the visible and the invisible, of earth and heaven, of all things whatever, with each other, through the consciousness, the person, of God the Spirit, who was at every moment of infinite time, in every atom of matter, at every point of infinite space, ay! *was* everything in turn: that doctrine—*l'antica filosofia Italiana*—was in all its vigour there, a hardy growth out of the very heart of nature, interpreting itself to congenial minds with all the fulness of primitive utterance. A big thought! yet suggesting, perhaps, from the first, in still, small, immediately practical, voice, some possible modification of, a freer way of taking, certain moral precepts: say! a primitive morality, congruous with those larger primitive ideas, the larger survey, the earlier, more liberal air.

Returning to this ancient "pantheism," after so long a reign of a seemingly opposite faith, Bruno unfalteringly asserts "the vision of all things in God" to be the aim of all metaphysical speculation, as of all inquiry into nature: the Spirit of God, in countless variety of forms, neither above, nor, in any way, without, but intimately within, all things—really present, with equal integrity, in the sunbeam ninety millions of miles long, and the wandering drop of water as it evaporates therein. The divine consciousness would have the same relation to the production of things, as the human intelligence to the production of true thoughts concerning them. Nay! those thoughts are themselves God in man: a loan, there, too, of his assisting Spirit, who, in truth, creates all things in and by his own contemplation of them. For Him, as for man in proportion as man thinks truly, thought and being are identical, and things existent only in so far as they are known. Delighting in itself, in the sense of its own energy, this sleepless, capacious, fiery intelligence, evokes all the orders of nature, all the revolutions of history, cycle upon cycle, in ever new types. And God the Spirit, the soul of the world, being really identical with his own soul, Bruno, as the universe shapes itself to his reason, his imagination, ever more and more articulately, shares also the divine joy in that process of the formation of true ideas, which is really parallel to the process of creation, to the evolution of things. In a certain mystic sense, which some in every age of the world have understood, he, too, is creator, himself actually a participator in the creative function. And by such a philosophy, he assures us, it was his experience that the soul is greatly expanded: *con questa filosofia l'anima, mi s'aggrandisce: mi se magnifica l'intelletto!*

For, with characteristic largeness of mind, Bruno accepted this theory in the whole range of its consequences. Its more immediate corollary was the famous axiom of "indifference," of "the coincidence of contraries." To the eye of God, to the philosophic vision through which God sees in man, nothing is really alien from Him. The differences of things, and above all, those distinctions which schoolmen and priests, old or new, Roman or Reformed, had invented for themselves, would be lost in the length and breadth of the philosophic survey; nothing, in itself, either great or small; and matter, certainly, in all its various forms, not evil but divine. Could one choose or reject this or that? If God the Spirit had made, nay! was, all things indifferently, then, matter and spirit, the spirit and flesh, heaven and earth, freedom and necessity, the first and the last, good and evil, would be superficial rather than substantial differences. Only, were joy and sorrow also to be added to the list of phenomena really coincident or indifferent, as some intellectual kinsmen of Bruno have claimed they should?

The Dominican brother was at no distant day to break far enough away from the election, the seeming "vocation" of his youth, yet would remain always, and under all circumstances, unmistakably a monk in some predominant qualities of temper. At first it was only by way of thought that he asserted his liberty—delightful, late-found privilege!—traversing, in mental journeys, that spacious circuit, as it broke away before him at every moment into ever-new horizons. Kindling thought and imagination at once, the prospect draws from him cries of joy, a kind of religious joy, as in some new "canticle of the creatures," a new monkish hymnal or antiphonary. "Nature" becomes for him a sacred term. "Conform thyself to Nature"—with what sincerity, what enthusiasm, what religious fervour, he enounces the precept to others, to himself! Recovering, as he fancies, a certain primeval sense of Deity broadcast on things, in which Pythagoras and other inspired theorists of early Greece had abounded, in his hands philosophy becomes a poem, a sacred poem, as it had been with them. That Bruno himself, in "the enthusiasm of the idea," drew from his axiom of the "indifference of contraries" the practical consequence which is in very deed latent there, that he was ready to sacrifice to the antinomianism, which is certainly a part of its rigid logic, the purities of his youth for instance, there is no proof. The service, the sacrifice, he is ready to bring to the great light that has dawned for him, which occupies his entire conscience with the sense of his responsibilities to it, is that of days and nights spent in eager study; of a plenary, disinterested utterance of the thoughts that arise in him, at any hazard, at the price, say! of martyrdom. The work of the divine Spirit, as he conceives it, exalts, inebriates him, till the scientific apprehension seems to take the place of prayer, sacrifice, communion. It would be a mistake, he holds, to attribute to the human soul capacities merely passive or receptive. She, too, possesses, not less than the soul of the world, initiatory power, responding with the free gift of a light and heat that seem her own.

Yet a nature so opulently endowed can hardly have been lacking in purely physical ardours. His pantheistic belief that the Spirit of God was in all things, was not inconsistent with, might encourage, a keen and restless eye for the dramatic details of life and character for humanity in all its visible attractiveness, since there, too, in truth, divinity lurks. From those first fair days of early Greek speculation, love had occupied a large place in the conception of philosophy; and in after days Bruno was fond of develop-

ing, like Plato, like the Christian platonist, combining something of the peculiar temper of each, the analogy between intellectual enthusiasm and the flights of physical love, with an animation which shows clearly enough the reality of his experience in the latter. The ***Eroici Furori,*** his book of books, dedicated to Philip Sidney, who would be no stranger to such thoughts, presents a singular blending of verse and prose, after the manner of Dante's *Vita Nuova.* The supervening philosophic comment reconsiders those earlier physical impulses which had prompted the sonnet in voluble Italian, entirely to the advantage of their abstract, incorporeal equivalents. Yet if it is after all but a prose comment, it betrays no lack of the natural stuff out of which such mystic transferences must be made. That there is no single name of preference, no Beatrice or Laura, by no means proves the young man's earlier desires merely "Platonic;" and if the colours of love inevitably lose a little of their force and propriety by such deflection, the intellectual purpose as certainly finds its opportunity thereby, in the matter of borrowed fire and wings. A kind of old, scholastic pedantry creeping back over the ardent youth who had thrown it off so defiantly (as if Love himself went in for a degree at the University) Bruno develops, under the mask of amorous verse, all the various stages of abstraction, by which, as the last step of a long ladder, the mind attains actual "union." For, as with the purely religious mystics, union, the mystic union of souls with each other and their Lord, nothing less than union between the contemplator and the contemplated—the reality, or the sense, or at least the name of it—was always at hand. Whence that instinctive tendency, if not from the Creator of things himself, who has doubtless prompted it in the physical universe, as in man? How familiar the thought that the whole creation longs for God, the soul as the hart for the water-brooks! To unite oneself to the infinite by breadth and lucidity of intellect, to enter, by that admirable faculty, into eternal life—this was the true vocation of the spouse, of the rightly amorous soul—"à filosofia ènecessario amore." There would be degrees of progress therein, as of course also of relapse: joys and sorrows, therefore. And, in interpreting these, the philosopher, whose intellectual ardours have superseded religion and love, is still a lover and a monk. All the influences of the convent, the heady, sweet incense, the pleading sounds, the sophisticated light and air, the exaggerated humour of gothic carvers, the thick stratum of pagan sentiment beneath sympathies, tender inspirations, attraction, repulsion, dryness, zeal, desire, recollection: he finds a place for them all; knows them all well in their unaffected simplicity, while he seeks the secret and secondary, or, as he fancies, the primary, form and purport of each.

A light on actual life, or mere barren scholastic subtlety, never before had the pantheistic doctrine been developed with such completeness, never before connected with so large a sense of nature, so large a promise of the knowledge of it as it really is. The eyes that had not been wanting to visible humanity turned with equal liveliness on the natural world in that region of his birth, where all its force and colour is twofold. Nature is not only a thought in the divine mind; it is also the perpetual energy of that mind, which, ever identical with itself, puts forth and absorbs in turn all the successive forms of life, of thought, of language even. But what seemed like striking transformations of matter were in truth only a chapter, a clause, in the great volume of the transformations of the Spirit. To that mystic recognition that all is divine had succeeded a realisation of the largeness of the field of concrete knowledge, the infinite extent of all there was actually to know. Winged, fortified, by this central philosophic faith, the student proceeds to the reading of nature, led on from point to point by manifold lights, which will surely strike on him, by the way, from the intelligence in it, speaking directly, sympathetically, to the intelligence in him. The earth's wonderful animation, as divined by one who anticipates by a whole generation the "philosophy of experience:" in that, the bold, flighty, pantheistic speculation became tangible matter of fact. Here was the needful book for man to read, the full revelation, the detailed story of that one universal mind, struggling, emerging, through shadow, substance, manifest spirit, in various orders of being—the veritable history of God. And nature, together with the true pedigree and evolution of man also, his gradual issue from it, was still all to learn. The delightful tangle of things! it would be the delightful task of man's thoughts to disentangle that. Already Bruno had measured the space which Bacon would fill, with room perhaps for Darwin also. That Deity is everywhere, like all such abstract propositions, is a two-edged force, depending for its practical effect on the mind which admits it, on the peculiar perspective of that mind. To Dutch Spinosa, in the next century, faint, consumptive, with a hold on external things naturally faint, the theorem that God was in all things whatever, annihilating, their differences suggested a somewhat chilly withdrawal from the contact of all alike. In Bruno, eager and impassioned, an Italian of the Italians, it awoke a constant, inextinguishable appetite for every form of experience—a fear, as of the one sin possible, of limiting, for oneself or another, that great stream flowing for thirsty souls, that wide pasture set ready for the hungry heart.

Considered from the point of view of a minute observation of nature, the Infinite might figure as "the infinitely little;" no blade of grass being like another, as there was no limit to the complexities of an atom of earth, cell; sphere, within sphere. But the earth itself, hitherto seemingly the privileged centre of a very limited universe, was, after all, itself but an atom in an infinite world of starry space, then lately displayed to the ingenuous intelligence, which the telescope was one day to verify to bodily eyes. For if Bruno must needs look forward to the future, to Bacon, for adequate knowledge of the earth—the infinitely little; he looked back, gratefully, to another daring mind, which had already put the earth into its modest place, and opened the full view of the heavens. If God is eternal, then, the universe is infinite and worlds innumerable. Yes! one might well have supposed what reason now demonstrated, indicating those endless spaces which sidereal science would gradually occupy, an echo of the creative word of God himself,

> Qui innumero numero innumerorum nomina dicit.

That the stars are suns: that the earth is in motion: that the earth is of like stuff with the stars: now the familiar

knowledge of children, dawning on Bruno as calm assurance of reason on appeal from the prejudice of the eye, brought to him an inexpressibly exhilarating sense of enlargement of the intellectual, nay! the physical atmosphere. And his consciousness of unfailing unity and order did not desert him in that larger survey, making the utmost one could ever know of the earth seem but a very little chapter in that endless history of God the Spirit, rejoicing so greatly in the admirable spectacle that it never ceases to evolve from matter new conditions. The immovable earth beneath one's feet! one almost felt the movement, the respiration of God in it. And yet how greatly even the physical eye, the *sensible* imagination (so to term it) was flattered by the theorem. What joy in that motion, the prospect, the music, the music of the spheres! —he could listen to it in a perfection such as had never been conceded to Plato, to Pythagoras even.

> Veni, Creator Spiritus,
> Mentes tuorum visita,
> Imple superna gratia,
> Quæ tu creasti pectora!

Yes! the grand old Christian hymns, perhaps the grandest of them, seemed to blend themselves in the chorus, to deepen immeasurably under this new intention. It is not always, or often, that men's abstract ideas penetrate the temperament, touch the animal spirits, affect conduct. It was what they did with Bruno. The ghastly spectacle of the endless material universe, infinite dust, in truth, starry as it may look to our terrestrial eyes—that prospect from which Pascal's faithful soul recoiled so painfully—induced in Bruno only the delightful consciousness of an ever-widening kinship and sympathy, since every one of those infinite worlds must have its sympathetic inhabitants. Scruples of conscience, if he felt such, might well be pushed aside the "excellency" of such knowledge as this. To shut the eyes, whether of the body or the mind, would be a kind of dark ingratitude; the one sin, to believe directly or indirectly in any absolutely dead matter anywhere, because involving denial of the indwelling spirit. A free spirit, certainly, as of old! Through all his pantheistic flights, from horizon to horizon, it was still the thought of liberty that presented itself to the infinite relish of this "prodigal son" of Dominic. God the Spirit had made all things indifferently, with a largeness, a beneficence, impiously belied by any theory of restrictions, distinctions, absolute limitations. Touch, see, listen, eat freely of all the trees of the garden of Paradise with the voice of the Lord God literally everywhere: here was the final counsel of perfection. The world was even larger than youthful appetite, youthful capacity. Let theologian and every other theorist beware how he narrowed either. The plurality of worlds! how petty in comparison seemed the sins, to purge which was the chief motive for coming to places like this convent, whence Bruno, with vows broken, or obsolete for him, presently departed. A sonnet, expressive of the joy with which he returned to so much more than the liberty of ordinary men, does not suggest that he was driven from it. Though he must have seemed to those who surely had loved so lovable a creature there to be departing, like the prodigal of the Gospel, into the furthest of possible far countries, there is no proof of harsh treatment, or even of an effort to detain him.

It happens, of course most naturally, that those who undergo the shock of spiritual or intellectual change sometimes fail to recognise their debt to the deserted cause: how much of the heroism, or other high quality, of their rejection has really been the growth of what they reject? Bruno, the escaped monk, is still a monk: his philosophy, impious as it might seem to some, a new religion. He came forth well fitted by conventual influences to play upon men as he was played upon. A challenge, a war-cry, an alarum; everywhere he seemed to be the creature of some subtly materialised spiritual force, like that of the old Greek prophets, like the primitive "enthusiasm" he was inclined to set so high, or impulsive Pentecostal fire. His hunger to know, fed at first dreamily enough within the convent walls as he wandered over space and time an indefatigable reader of books, would be fed physically now by ear and eye, by large matter-of-fact experience, as he journeys from university to university; yet still, less as a teacher than a courtier, a citizen of the world, a knight-errant of intellectual light. The philosophic need to try all things had given reasonable justification to the stirring desire for travel common to youth, in which, if in nothing else, that whole age of the later Renaissance was invincibly young. The theoretic recognition of that mobile spirit of the world, ever renewing its youth, became, sympathetically, the motive of a life as mobile, as ardent, as itself; of a continual journey, the venture and stimulus of which would be the occasion of ever new discoveries, of renewed conviction.

The unity, the spiritual unity, of the world: —that must involve the alliance, the congruity, of all the things with each other, great reinforcements of sympathy, of the teacher's personality with the doctrine he had to deliver, the spirit of that doctrine with the fashion of his utterance. In his own case, certainly, as Bruno confronted his audience at Paris, himself, his theme, his language, were the fuel of one clear spiritual flame, which soon had hold of his audience also; alien, strangely alien, as it might seem from the speaker. It was *intimate* discourse, in magnetic touch with every one present, with his special point of impressibility; the sort of speech which, consolidated into literary form as a book, would be a dialogue according to the true Attic genius, full of those diversions, passing irritations, unlooked-for appeals, in which a solicitous missionary finds his largest range of opportunity, and takes even dull wits unaware. In Bruno, that abstract theory of the perpetual motion of the world was a visible person talking with you.

And as the runaway Dominican was still in temper a monk, so he presented himself in the comely Dominican habit. The eyes which in their last sad protest against stupidity would mistake, or miss altogether, the image of the Crucified, were to-day, for the most part, kindly observant eyes, registering every detail of that singular company, all the physiognomic lights which come by the way on people, and, through them, on things, the "shadows of ideas" in men's faces (**"De Umbris Idearum"** was the title of his discourse), himself pleasantly animated by them, in turn.

There was "heroic gaiety" there; only, as usual with gaiety, the passage of a peevish cloud seemed all the chillier. Lit up, in the agitation of speaking, by many a harsh or scornful beam, yet always sinking, in moments of repose, to an expression of high-bred melancholy, it was a face that looked, after all, made for suffering—already half pleading, half defiant—as of a creature you could hurt, but to the last never shake a hair's breadth from its estimate of yourself.

Like nature, like nature in that country of his birth, the Nolan, as he delighted to proclaim himself, loved so well that, born wanderer as he was, he must perforce return thither sooner or later, at the risk of life, he gave *plenis manibus,* but without selection, and, with all his contempt for the "asinine" vulgar, was not fastidious. His rank, unweeded eloquence, abounding in a play of words, rabbinic allegories, verses defiant of prosody, in the kind of erudition he professed to despise, with a shameless image here or there, product not of formal method, but of Neapolitan improvisation, was akin to the heady wine, the sweet, coarse odours, of that fiery, volcanic soil, fertile in the irregularities which manifest power. Helping himself indifferently to all religious for rhetoric illustration, his preference was still for that of the soil, the old pagan one, the primitive Italian gods, whose names and legends haunt his speech, as they do the carved and pictorial work of the age, according to the fashion of that ornamental paganism which the Renaissance indulged. To excite, to surprise, to move men's minds, as the volcanic earth is moved, as if in travail, and, according to the Socratic fancy, bring them to the birth, was the true function of the teacher, however unusual it might seem in an ancient university. *Fantastic,* from first to last that was the descriptive epithet, and the very word, carrying us to Shakespeare, reminds one how characteristic of the age such habit was, and that it was pre-eminently due to Italy. A bookman, yet with so vivid a hold on people and things, the traits and tricks of the audience seemed to revive in him, to strike from his memory all the graphic resources of his old readings. He seemed to promise some greater matter than was then actually exposed; himself to enjoy the fulness of a great outlook, the vague suggestion of which did but sustain the curiosity of the listeners. And still, in hearing him speak you seemed to see that subtle spiritual fire to which he testified kindling from word to word. What Parisians then heard was, in truth, the first fervid expression of all those contending apprehensions, out of which his written works would afterwards be compacted, with much loss of heat in the process. Satiric or hybrid growths, things due to υβρι insolence, insult, all that those fabled satyrs embodied—the volcanic South is kindly prolific of this, and Bruno abounded in mockeries: it was by way of protest. So much of a Platonist, for Plato's genial humour he had nevertheless substituted the harsh laughter of Aristophanes. Paris, teeming, beneath a very courtly exterior, with mordent words, in unabashed criticism of all real or suspected evil, provoked his utmost powers of scorn for the "triumphant beast," the "constellation of the Ass," shining even there, amid the university folk, those intellectual bankrupts of the Latin Quarter, who had so long passed between them gravely a worthless "parchment and paper" currency. In truth, Aristotle, as the supplanter of Plato, was still in possession, pretending to determine heaven and earth by precedent, hiding the proper nature of things from the eyes of men. Habit—the last word of his practical philosophy—indolent habit! what would this mean in the intellectual life, but just that sort of dead judgments which are most opposed to the essential freedom and quickness of the Spirit, because the mind, the eye, were no longer really at work in them?

To Bruno, a true son of the Renaissance, in the light of those large, antique, pagan ideas, the difference between Rome and the Reform would figure, of course, as but an insignificant variation upon some deeper, more radical antagonism between two tendencies of men's minds. But what about an antagonism deeper still? between Christ and the world, say! Christ and the flesh? —that so very ancient antagonism between good and evil? Was there any place for imperfection in a world wherein the minutest atom, the lightest thought, could not escape from God's presence? Who should note the crime, the sin, the mistake, in the operation of that eternal spirit, which could have made no misshapen births? In proportion as man raised himself to the ampler survey of the divine work around him, just in that proportion did the very notion of evil disappear. There were no weeds, no "tares," in the endless field. The truly illuminated mind, discerning spiritually, might do what it would. Even under the shadow of monastic walls, that had ever been the precept, which the larger theory of "inspiration" had bequeathed to practice. "Of all the trees of the garden thou mayst freely eat! If you take up any deadly thing, it shall not hurt you! And I think that I, too, have the spirit of God."

Bruno, the citizen of the world, Bruno at Paris, was careful to warn off the vulgar from applying the decisions of philosophy beyond its proper speculative limits. But a kind of secresy, an ambiguous atmosphere, encompassed, from the first, alike the speaker and the doctrine; and in that world of fluctuating and ambiguous characters, the alerter mind certainly, pondering on this novel reign of the spirit—what it might actually be—would hardly fail to find in Bruno's theories a method of turning poison into food, to live and thrive thereon; an art, surely, no less opportune in the Paris of that hour, intellectually or morally, than had it related to physical poisons. If Bruno himself was cautious not to suggest the ethic or practical equivalent to his theoretic positions, there was that in his very manner of speech, in his rank, unweeded eloquence, which seemed naturally to discourage any effort at selection, any sense of fine difference, of *nuances* or proportion, in things. The loose sympathies of his genius were allied to nature, nursing, with equable maternity of soul, good, bad, and indifferent, rather than to art, distinguishing, rejecting, refining. Commission and omission; sins of the former surely had the preference. And how would Paolo and Francesca have read the lesson? How would this Henry the Third, and Margaret of the "Memoirs," and other susceptible persons then present, read it, especially if the opposition between practical good and evil traversed another distinction, to the "opposed points," the "fenced opposites" of which many, certainly, then present, in that Paris of the last of the Valois, could never by any possibility become "indifferent," between the precious and the base,

aesthetically—between what was right and wrong, as matter of art?

Swinburne reveals his thoughts on Bruno in a poem:

GIORDANO BRUNO.
JUNE 9TH, 1889.
I.
Not from without us, only from within,
　　Comes or can ever come upon us light
　　Whereby the soul keeps ever truth in sight.
No truth, no strength, no comfort man may win,
No grace for guidance, no release from sin,
　　Save of his own soul's giving. Deep and bright
　　As fire enkindled in the core of night
Burns in the soul where once its fire has been
The light that leads and quickens thought, inspired
　　To doubt and trust and conquer. So he said
　　Whom Sidney, flower of England, lordliest head
Of all we love, loved: but the fates required
A sacrifice to hate and hell, ere fame
Should set with his in heaven Giordano's name.
II.
Cover thine eyes and weep, O child of hell,
　　Grey spouse of Satan, Church of name abhorred.
　　Weep, withered harlot, with thy weeping lord,
Now none will buy the heaven thou hast to sell
At price of prostituted souls, and swell
　　Thy loveless list of lovers. Fire and sword
　　No more are thine: the steel, the wheel, the cord,
The flames that rose round living limbs, and fell
In lifeless ash and ember, now no more
　　Approve thee godlike. Rome, redeemed at last
　　From all the red pollution of thy past,
Acclaims the grave bright face that smiled of yore
　　Even on the fire that caught it round and clomb
　　To cast its ashes on the face of Rome.

Algernon Charles Swinburne in The Athenaeum, *June 15, 1889.*

William Boulting   (essay date 1914)

SOURCE: "The Early Works," in *Giordano Bruno: His Life, Thought, and Martyrdom,* Kegan Paul, Trench, Trubner, & Co., Ltd., 1914, pp. 66-80.

[*In this excerpt, Boulting analyzes several of Bruno's early works, including philosophical writings and the comedy,* Il Candelaio, *commenting on the relevance of these works in the early twentieth century.*]

I. THE SHADOWS OF IDEAS

In 1582, Gorbin, whose shop was under the sign of "Hope," produced the second of Bruno's printed works, but the first which has been preserved down to our own time. **"De Umbris Idearum"—"The Shadows of Ideas"**—

was dedicated to Henry and issued "with his privilege." Now Chicus Æsculanus asserted in his commentary "In Spheram" that Solomon wrote a work on the shadows of ideas, and perhaps this statement suggested the title to Bruno; for more than once he refers to Solomon and his Song in in this book. The work aimed at setting before the King, men of cultured mind, scholars and students an improved art of remembering; but, since the mnemonic system displayed is loosely associated with metaphysical bases, the latter are treated of in the first part of the book as **"Shadows of Ideas."** while the second part is entitled the **"Art of Memory."** The first part is frankly Neo-Platonic. Bruno had absorbed much Neo-Platonism; it was a popular doctrine in his time. It is true that he despised its Italian exponent, Pico della Mirandola; but the symbolic doctrine of the One True Light approached so near to the conceptions he was forming, or had already formed as to the immanence of God that he had no scruple in using it. He accepts, too, the doctrine of universal animism, which was held by the ancient world and generally received by thinkers of his own age. The **"Art of Memory,"** following the philosophic treatise, is in three divisions which contain some rudimentary psychology and an attempt at mental analysis. The notions which Lully conceived to be irreducible are replaced by an increased number of concepts, chosen for their convenience in illustrating mnemonic method. Bruno retains Lully's mechanical arrangements, the various compartments bearing symbolic labels for economy and concentration of thought. There is, however, little serious attempt at systematic treatment. Severe orderly arrangement would seem to have been repellent to all the men of the Renaissance, and it was by no means conformable with the swoop and circlings of Bruno on the wing. The book was intended to be generally acceptable; and therefore its author reserved much which must have been maturing in his brain. His thought was to be quickened and strengthened by the clarifying stimulus of opposition and contumely; his bold and penetrative insight to be sharpened by the obtuse folly of his foes. His present object was to arouse the mind of his reader without incensing him unduly.

Eastern ideas reached Plato, and he endeavoured to formulate them; but Neo-Platonism retranslated thought into imagery. Bruno never entirely departed from the Neo-Platonic method. He often associates his concepts with a mystic symbolism which is not always a mere aid to memory, but implies some subtle and profound cosmic sympathy. Words, nay alphabets, he holds are the shades of things, and things are the vestiges of the Being of beings. Throughout, he presupposes an ultimate identity of thought and thing; of memory and nature; of what is knowable and the unknown; of fact and power. This opinion has been pretty generally held by the profounder thinkers. The age was so convinced of the reality of a single principle that it sought eagerly for the Elixir of Life and the Philosopher's stone.

It had been shown by the later Greeks that sense-perception was not to be depended on for the discovery of truth. The Neo-Platonists therefore relied on the directness of intuition concerning high matters; they regarded intuition as having the force of perception on a higher plane. This was also characteristic of the mystics and it greatly influenced Bruno. But he held man to be incapable of achieving the very truth. We are but shadows of the Ineffable One; for the light which reaches us is confused and contradictory and mixed with darkness; we perceive good and evil together and in contrast, the beautiful associated with the ugly to which it is in opposition. Looked at from the eternal point of view, all, even the worst evils are perfection; everything descends from the perfect and everything strives to wing a homeward flight. The human soul is to the human body as is a pilot to the ship: it is in it, but not of it, and, being associated with body, the soul perceives truth confusedly and as in flux. But the Idea draws us on; and, in itself, it is not abstract but concrete and articulated. Our ideas, we must remember, are as an admixture of light and shadow and not that absolute truth which they can never reach; but nonetheless the mind can rise above the things of sense, perceiving unity in plurality. Mystic union with the Divinity was experienced by Plotinus and others. From the acceptance of this mystical experience thus avowed in this early work, Bruno never departed. But in his later works, wherein he reproduces far less Neo-Platonism and becomes vastly more original, he proclaims that by the exercise of reason also we can attain comprehensive contact with the Absolute, Who is at once the source and object of our search.

God is immanent as well as transcendent; for does not man share a measure of the Ineffable Light? The interconnection of ideas naturally corresponds with that of things. But memory is apt to break down, and, where it does so, we may mend it by working on the lines of its natural operation. He feels the significance of the principle of the Association of Ideas, which Aristotle was the first to indicate, and uses it. He also culls the best from all writers of his time on mnemonics, as he told us in the preface he intended to do. Our ideas being shadows of truth, we use shadows of these shadows in mnemonics. We can economize thought by means of signs the nature of which is that they are shadows or traces.

> **Prolixity and the grossly grotesque entertained [Bruno's] age: they bore ours. All is overdone: there is not a thought of repose. Penetrative insight, soaring imagination, novel wisdom, severe thought have a setting of jest and jeer, clumsy buffoonery and sheer indecency. He [Bruno] was justified in being sure of himself; but his bombastic self-assertion repels the modern reader.**
>
> **—*William Boulting***

To fix attention, maintain interest and arouse emotional force, he introduces mythological subjects.

Imagine what a good "draw" a really useful tool for unearthing the buried treasures of the mind would be to men who found books so hard to come at! But Bruno was endowed with a prodigious memory, and he falsely attributed his natural power to the artifices he employed. Probably the expectations he excited were not fulfilled. There is no great novelty in his mnemonics; he was one of the "celestial thieves" of his generation. There are, in **"De Umbris,"** foreshadowings of his philosophic syncretism; but he has not yet welded the conclusions of others into a vital whole or made them live anew in his own completer thought; the work is tentative and contains only the germ of the Bruno that was presently to appear; but such remarks as the one that religious mysteries are mere institutions to train human eyes for the perception of "the steep passage from darkness to light" are truly Brunian.

He introduces symbolic verse of his own composition and gives us brisk dialogue between Hermes, Philotimus and Logifer, with thrusts, less severe than those which were to follow, at the doctors and masters of the schools.

Scholars had travelled a far road from the elegant Latin of Cicero. Bruno's Latin is full of neologisms; his syntax is bad; his prosody, abominable. In a later work he acknowledges that his Latin is coarse and rough. But it is alive. One finds the elements of Bruno's manner in this early work and they may be conveniently examined here.

He delights in brisk and varied dialogue which knows no curb. Sometimes the thread of mystical symbolism which runs through it finds a natural expression in metre; every here and there he breaks into verse, which, no less than prose, he writes with impetuous fury. At its worst, one is reminded that he came from the land of *improvvisatori*. He is far too much in a hurry to be over careful as to style, and never dreams of polish; for the thing he has to declare is infinitely more important than the manner of declaring it. Later, he hinted at being too diffuse, but failed to amend his ways. In his verses, there is little of craftsman-like skill. His pen flows as rapidly as his thought; his mind is full to bursting point; he indulges in wide circlings and side-long sweeps. He casts about for the most unlikely allegory; for to him, as to Dante and Swedenborg and Emerson, all nature and all the products of the human mind are symbolic of higher truth; and in this he fell into line with the conviction of his century, perceiving deep analogies in fact and fable, whether sacred or profane. Hence, in an age of respect for authority, he supports an argument by drawing on his own vast lore; he lugs in learning by the ears, not for display but to reinforce his meaning. He does this quite impartially: the Bible, the Pre-Socratic philosophers, the Cabala and classic myth are introduced as of equal weight. There is real unity underlying each of his works; but all give the impression of disorder. For, each trivial occasion, each intruding half-thought is as a spark which he allows to burst into vivid and vagrant flame: his imagination plays riotously round his immediate theme, and then suddenly leaps aside. Sometimes this is a trick, done of set purpose. If the men of the Renaissance rejoiced in life, towards the close of the period they expressed their vigour in violence. Hence Bruno lost no opportunity of keeping his readers awake by the oddness of his antics; he surprises them by bombardments and unexpected raking fires. He

thinks to throw each noble design, each lofty thought into relief by the dodge (not wholly unknown to modern authors) of smart paradox. Prolixity and the grossly grotesque entertained his age: they bore ours. All is overdone: there is not a thought of repose. Penetrative insight, soaring imagination, novel wisdom, severe thought have a setting of jest and jeer, clumsy buffoonery and sheer indecency. He was justified in being sure of himself; but his bombastic self-assertion repels the modern reader. He delights in contrast and invective. His polemic is implacable and often unjust, but less so than that of his contemporaries and immediate successors; and he flies less readily than they to the final argument of abuse. As Tocco remarks, his motive is always noble; he "made no thought of life" and proved it by sacrifice and suffering and sealing his faith in death.

II. THE INCANTATION OF CIRCE

Books of the period bore odd titles to catch the eye. Bruno called his next work the *Cantus Circaeus—The Incantation Of Circe.* The Homeric sorceress, who transforms men into beasts, discusses with her handmaiden the human vice which each kind of beast represents, and each beast and its vice are memorised under initial letters. Now the nature of memory is occult, and the recalling of ideas may be regarded as a sort of magical process. So the art of memory may be regarded as a fascinating incantation. The dialogue is full of bitter satire on human depravity. A second dialogue follows with different interlocutors. It treats more directly and precisely than the previous **"Art of Memory"** of that subject. There is an attempt to localise the functions of the brain as the physical conditions of mental process. The principle of the association of ideas is more closely followed than in **"De Umbris"** and copious illustrations of method are given. The work abounds in obscurities, which were as attractive to superior minds in that age as in our own. Later on Bruno found it convenient to be occasionally obscure where it was wiser to suggest merely to those few who had the capacity really to understand perilous doctrine. But Bruno never erred on the side of over-caution!

III. THE LULLIAN ARCHITECTURE

In the same year appeared a third book, the *Brief Architecture Of The Art of Lully With Its Completion* [*De compendiosa architectura et complemento artis Lullii*]. It was published by Gorbin and was little more than a reproduction of Lully's "Great Art." But Bruno thought that art a key to the structure of the universe and the ready way to a complete philosophy, proceeding from foundations of all knowledge; he conceived of it as a demonstration of unity, the shortest of roads for thought and memory, and a useful symbolic logic. Of the value of Inference in extending knowledge, Bruno had little more notion than had Lully. For, although Lully worked outside scholasticism and exhibited much of that spontaneous originality which we find in Scotus Erigena before scholasticism began, mediaeval thought was harnessed in the syllogism and employed itself in ceaseless rotation, like a donkey round a grinding mill, but mostly grinding philosophic chaff. In Bruno's time Lully captured many able minds and had a great vogue. Before Kant, it was not possible to work from other than dogmatic premises; certain concepts were posited as fundamental and ultimate; there was no notion of submitting them to criticism. For Bruno, the art of Lully was alive; for us, it has become dead and valueless.

Lully tried to prove the dogmas of the Church by human reason [in *De Articulis Fidei*] Bruno, in this work, [*Brief Architecturs of the Art of Lully with its Completion*] denies that they are reasonable: any attempt to prove their truth is a blunder; for Christianity is irrational, contrary to philosophy and in disagreement with other religions. We only accept it by faith and through revelation. As a Neo-Platonist and syncretist he relies on and quotes pagan authority as freely as Christian.

Berti thinks that at some time before Bruno left France he wrote a book, never published, of which all we know is that, two years later, he promised to send his English friend Smith his "*Purgatory of Hell,* wherein you shall see the fruit of redemption." One judges from the context that the redemption was from scientific and philosophic error.

IV. THE CHANDLER

The same year (1582) saw another work from Bruno's rapid pen. This time he wrote in Italian, and the book was printed by an Italian who had settled in Paris, Guglielmo Giuliano by name. Bruno tells us it was the fruit of "a few burning days." It differs wholly from his other writings, for it is a stage-play, full of rattling, roaring fun and furnished with a satiric probe for credulity, pedantry and pretence. Its world is full of the pursuers and hucksters of illusions; rogues abound, and fools are duped by miracle-mongers, alchemists and pretenders to magic arts. This comedy is entitled *Il Candelajo,* which may be translated as *The Chandler.* In Bruno's time the person who supplied candles also made them. Now the manufacture of tallow-dips is a noisome and undignified trade. Bruno, like Dante, loved to load words with more than their surface-meaning. "Behold," he says in the dedication, "behold in the candle borne by this Chandler, to whom I gave birth, that which shall clarify certain shadows of ideas." This product of imagination which shall set forth truth is dedicated with a letter to the lady Morgana, a name very suggestive of *Fata Morgana*—the mirage—which is illusion. In this dedication a multitude of ideas surge pellmell; they only get themselves out as obscure half-hints; the language is tortuous and the syntax involved. Priests and pedants may banish his body and make chaos of his life, but they shall not shackle his soul or obscure its vision. Here he presents some shifting shadows, but all the moving shadows of the Universe are really the expression of One Reality. "I need not instruct you of my belief: Time gives all and takes all away; everything changes but nothing perishes; One only is immutable, eternal and ever endures, one and the same with itself. With this philosophy my spirit grows, my mind expands. Whereof, however obscure the night may be, I await daybreak, and they who dwell in day look for night. . . . Rejoice therefore, and keep whole, if you can, and return love for love."

The characters of the play, being vicious, are inversions of virtue, integrals in the scheme of things, fulfilling an office to higher ends, as does the one who gives the play its title,

our provider of gross matter which shall furnish shining flame. The title of the play is repeated in three of its scenes. In the two first of these our protagonist, who aims at writing amorous poetry, is told, to his great perplexity, that he is trying to change himself from chandler to goldsmith. In the last, it is related how all the folk with a bee in the bonnet, who hanker after miracle-mongering priests and their "water of St. Peter the Martyr, seed of St. John, heaven-sent food of St. Andrew and marrow from the bones of St. Piantorio" are wont to consult an ancient dame who poses as a wise-woman. An intended bride, doubtful as to her marriage, goes to this old lady. The dialogue, though only recorded by one of the characters, may be translated as fairly illustrative of Bruno's brisk and vigorous dramatic manner. It reminds us to that of Plautus and Molière.

> "Mother mine, they want me to marry Bonifacio Trucco. He is well off." "Have him!" "Yes, but he is too old." "My daughter, don't have him!" "But my parents advise me to." "Have him!" "But he don't please me too well." "Then don't have him!" "I know he comes of good blood." "Have him!" "But I hear he has not teeth enough to bite a bean." "Don't have him!" "They tell me he has a pure-bred greyhound." "Have him!" "But, oh dear me, I hear he is only a chandler." "Don't have him!" "Everybody thinks him mad." "Take him! Take him! seven times over! His being a chandler doesn't count; it's no concern of yours if he can't eat; if he doesn't please you, no matter; what if he be old; but he is mad, so take him [Act V, Sc. xxiv]."

Herein are furtive thrusts all round.

The play begins with a few verses. Then comes the mock-dedication. By a convention dating from classic times every play required a prologue. Bruno will none of this. A love of buffoonery pervaded his age, so our author next gives us a synopsis of the characters and of the three closely interwoven but distinct plots of his comedy for prologue and follows this up with an anti-prologue, then with a pro-prologue and finally, before the curtain rises, there is a speech from the beadle; all this, excepting the synopsis, being done in that spirit of humorous provocation so characteristic of Rabelais.

The play has five acts and eighteen characters, whereof Bonifacio, an elderly, amorous miser; Bartolomeo, an avaricious seeker after the philosopher's stone, and Manfurio, pedant and fool, are chief.

The pedant is of poor but pretentious intelligence; naturally a vessel of mean capacity, which bursts into absurdities when crammed with more than it was designed to hold. His ineptitude overflows in affectation and self-conceit, and he speaks in inappropriate Latin or latinized Italian. He is a man of words and phrases, of subtle distinctions with no value in them, and of painstaking accuracy about trumpery matters. He lugs in classical lore at every breath. He is unmarried and is specially attached to his pupil Pollula: it is significant that a female name is given to the boy. Manfurio has a hand in everything that is going on and understands nothing of it; he is fooled and laughed at, eventually falls into the clutch of a sham watch, and is soundly thrashed, as are the other protagonists.

Bonifacio, married to the youthful Carubina, is in love with Vittoria, a lady no better than she should be, who only pretends to return his affection in order to bleed his purse. He commits endless absurdities in order to keep her to himself, and goes to a professor of magic to help him. This gentleman drains him dry; whereupon Vittoria manages to substitute Carubina for herself. Bonifacio, in the dress of Bernardo, a painter, who is also in love with Carubina, is thus confronted by his own wife dressed in Vittoria's clothes. The pretended watch appear and force Bonifacio to give a bribe to their captain; meanwhile Carubina is tête-à-tête with the painter. Finally the deceived husband has to entreat his wife to pardon him, and sails into more tranquil waters "by the grace of the Lord and the Madonna."

The third protagonist, Bartolomeo, trusts himself to the direction of a designing alchemist who well-nigh exhausts his lean purse. A mixture, which contains a fictitious "powder of Christ" fails to work; and after amusing scenes of roguery, the false watch appear and, by threatening prison, make their profit.

The play is a series of pictures of the seamy side of Neapolitan life and repeats the coarse talk which Bruno would have heard as a boy. He may have written the work when he was in the monastery: certain references and its fresh and vigorous touches smack of the direct transcript of recent impressions. But a reference to a recent event shows that it received at least finishing strokes in France, if not in Paris. In his castigation of vice, the very unpleasant is unduly prominent; but the play is not so foul as those of Machiavelli, Bibbiena and Aretino. It must be admitted that this comedy exhibits a great knowledge of the seamy side of life and is a queer product of monastic discipline. But not so many years before a Prince of the Church had officiated at the altar of the Cyprian as well as at that of Christ, and his comedy brought a blush to the face of that by no means severe prude, Isabella D'Este, while Erasmus tells us of a priest who took a part in a Latin play. Even in Bruno's stricter days of Catholic Reform the full effect of the Council of Trent was not felt, and no great blame attached to such lapses. We must not press too heavily on the fault. The Renaissance found frank indecency attractive; we have become more "delicately indelicate." Natural instincts held in leash are apt to manifest themselves in this vicarious and disagreeable way, and a "virile" young man, in a "virile" century at least, will roll in the obscene with the unconstrained gratification of a puppy dog. Moreover, many young men indulge in obscene speculation for precisely the same reason that lunatic maidens are said to utter foul oaths: there is fascination in the repellent and it is apt to produce an undue impression on the mind.

The plot is unduly complicated and reminds the reader of the Spanish stage. The characters are abstract types, like those of Ben Jonson and dramatists of the second rank; but they are drawn with rare felicity. The dialogue is quite as vivacious and clever as any by Aretino. *The Chandler* is quite *sui generis*—a new development in comedy. It is easy, spontaneous, the overflow of an ardent and imaginative temperament. Both the obscenity and buffoonery of the play are half intended to keep the audience amused; buffoonery and indelicacy are also introduced with this purpose in Bruno's more serious writings.

The rediscovery of the classics led, in time, to degenerate humanists: Bruno is less tender to these pedants than to knaves—probably because he had suffered more at their hands. Philosophical theory peeps out in the play here and there.

He believes that his enemies rejoice at his exile; but he is convinced he will obtain his due, "if not under one hood, then under another; if not in one life yet in another"; a remark which some have thought to show that he believed in an immortality not guaranteed by the mere pantheistic Neo-Platonism he had so far expounded.

In a somewhat earlier and more liberal age, Machiavelli expressed his contempt for the miraculous. Guicciardini thought those wonders which were best attested to be examples of natural phenomena not yet understood. This was Bruno's attitude, as is clear from many passages in his books. In *The Chandler* he pours his scorn on the trickery of the priesthood. He hints at the miseries of monastic discipline.

He is aware of his own originality and declares it; he does not disguise his Horatian contempt for the herd.

There is no evidence that the play was ever performed; but, influenced by prior productions, it left its mark in its turn on those which followed. The comedies of that many-sided genius, Giambattista della Porta (who was a Neapolitan and a contemporary of Bruno), which were published more than twenty years later than the *Candelajo,* show a singular resemblance to it. Within two generations, a French adaptation, entitled *Boniface et le Pédant,* was staged, and this was followed by Cyrano de Bergerac's *Le Pédant joué.* Cyrano concentrated Bruno's trifold plot to the advantage of the play; but he missed much of the vivacity of the original dialogue. He indirectly admits this, for he vows that "Italian twins would joke in their mother's womb." These adaptations influenced Molière; he extracted what suited him from Cyrano's version, saying

---

T.S. Eliot in a review of William Boulting's biography of Bruno:

Bruno's life is more interesting than his work is important. A violent, somewhat undisciplined temperament, a life of varied wandering, a spectacular death, and a series of romantically attractive writings provide excellent material—of which Mr. Boulting has made the most. Bruno's philosophy was not very clearly thought out, and its permanent value is slight, but the personality and career of the man are of enduring interest.

T. S. Eliot in The New Statesman, *October 21, 1916.*

that he had a right to it: "On reprend son bien partout on le trouve." Prof. Adamson suggested that Manfurio was the prototype of Holofernes in Shakespeare's "Love's Labour's Lost."

Frances A. Yates   (essay date 1943)

SOURCE: "The Emblematic Conceit in Giordano Bruno's *De gli eroici furori* and in the Elizabethan Sonnet Sequences," in *Journal of the Warburg and Courtauld Institutes,* 1943. Reprinted in *Lull & Bruno: Collected Essays, Vol. I.* Routledge & Kegan Paul, 1982, pp. 180-209.

[*An English educator, historian, and author, Yates is best known and widely respected for her books on the Renaissance. In the following essay, Yates examines Bruno's use of emblems in* Eroici furori, *arguing that by describing the divine with Petrarchan conceits, Bruno establishes a link between his work and Elizabethan poetry.*]

The influence of Petrarch upon English poetry begins before the Elizabethan period, but its most powerful development comes in the last decade of the sixteenth century, during which were published sonnet sequences on the Petrarchan model by Sir Philip Sidney, who inspires and leads the whole movement, by Daniel, Constable, Lodge, Barnes, Drayton, Spenser, and others. Those of Shakespeare were not published until later, but they really also belong to the period of this sonneteering fashion.

Modern English students of this poetry have tended to examine it mainly from two angles, which one might characterize as the personal and the literary. The critic interested in the human side asks himself how far the language of Petrarchism is sincere, by which he means: Does it express real feeling for individual women loved by these poets or is it only an artificial fashion? On the whole it has been felt that language so stilted and conventional as that of the majority of these sonnets cannot be the vehicle of genuine human feeling. The literary approach has concentrated on the tracing of sources, and has proved that the Elizabethan sonneteers borrow their conceits and phrasing, not only from Petrarch himself, but also from his many Italian imitators, and, above all, from the French Petrarchists of the school of Ronsard.

This poetry can, however, be studied from yet another angle, making the centre of interest neither the personal experiences of the poets nor their foreign sources, but the sonnet language in itself as an artistic phenomenon. In a recent book the conventional conceits used by the Elizabethan poets are discussed and a table provided by which the use of each conceit by different poets can be traced. Such a study brings out the fact that Petrarchism is really a kind of picture language, and that the chief interest of the individual Petrarchist is in the pictures or *concetti* for their own sake.

It is indeed probable that this last approach brings us nearer to the Elizabethan manner of reading the poetry than the other two. And it might be carried a stage further by inquiring what this picture language of the Petrarchan conceit meant to the Elizabethans. One is emboldened to pose this daring question by the fact that Giordano Bruno,

the Italian philosopher who came to England at a time when Elizabethan Petrarchism was on the point of bursting forth, and who knew Sir Philip Sidney, uses the Petrarchan conceit in a manner which connects it with the emblem.

The dialogue entitled *De gli eroici furori* was written by Bruno whilst he was living at the French embassy in London and was published in London in 1585 with a dedication to Sir Philip Sidney.

The *Eroici furori* is arranged in sections. Each section usually consists of an emblem or device which is described in words, this description taking the place of what would be a plate in an illustrated emblem book; a poem, generally in sonnet form, in which the forms used visually in the emblem occur as poetic conceits; and finally, an exposition or commentary in which the spiritual or philosophical meanings latent in the imagery which has been presented both in the emblem and in the poem are expounded.

The following is an example of the method. The emblem consists of two stars in the form of two radiant eyes, with the motto *Mors et vita*.

The sonnet which accompanies this emblem is built round one of the commonest clichés of Petrarchist poetry, that of the lady's eyes as stars which the lover prays may be turned upon him although he knows that their glance has power to kill him. This central convention is supported by other equally conventional ideas. There is the worn face of the lover upon which his sufferings are to be discerned:

> Writ by the hand of love may each behold
> Upon my face the story of my woes. . . .

There is the pride and cruelty of the lady who seems deliberately at times to torment the lover:

> But thou, so that thy pride no curb may know
> . . . Thou dost torment. . . .

This leads up to the image which is the foundation of the whole poem, that of the lady's eyes as lights or stars:

> Thou dost torment, by hiding from my view
> Those lovely lights beneath the beauteous lids.
> Therefore the troubled sky's no more serene.

Finally, there is the prayer to the lady, as to a goddess, to relent from her unkindness and turn her eyes upon the suffering lover, even though her glance may kill him:

> Render thyself, oh Goddess, unto pity! . . .
> Open, oh lady, the portals of thine eyes,
> And look on me if thou wouldst give me death!

The conceit dominating the whole sonnet, which is a tissue of Petrarchist phraseology, is that of the stars-eyes which had already been presented in the emblem.

In the commentary which follows the meanings are explained. The face upon which the story of the lover's woes is written is the soul seeking God. Here Bruno quotes metaphors from the Psalms: 'My soul thirsteth after thee as a weary land', and, 'I opened my mouth wide and panted; for I longed for thy commandments' [Psalms CXLII, v. 6 and CXIX, v. 131]. The image of the worn face of the lover in the sonnet is, he says, intended to have the same meaning as that which the Psalmist conveys when he speaks of the thirst and the panting of the soul. The pride of the lady is a metaphor, as God is sometimes said to be jealous, angry or asleep, signifying how often he withholds the vision of himself. 'So the lights are covered with the eyelids, the troubled sky of the human mind does not clear itself by the removal of the metaphors and enigmas. By praying that the eyes should open, the lover is praying that the divine light should show itself. And the death which the glance of the eyes can give signifies the mystical death of the soul 'which same is eternal life, which a man may anticipate in this life and enjoy in eternity'.

The commentary thus provides a key to the meaning both of the sonnet with its prayer to the death-dealing stars-eyes of the lady and of the emblem of the stars-eyes with its motto *Mors et vita*. The emblem and the conceit are vitally linked together because they both have the same hidden meaning. In short, *the conceit is an emblem.*

There is not space to work out any other emblem-conceits from the *Eroici furori* as fully as this. But the following are a few more examples of the method in abridged form, giving only the leading ideas of the figures described, without the subtleties of the detailed interpretation.

The emblem consists of two stars, below which is a head with four faces which blow towards the four corners of the heavens and which represent the winds. There is a sonnet in which the same imagery is used, and the commentary explains that the winds are spiritual aspiration, and that the two stars are divine beauty and goodness towards which the lover or enthusiast aspires. If these divine stars are visible they calm the tempest of his soul; but if invisible he will be troubled and harassed. They have the power to kill the enthusiast, a power which is benevolent because it causes him to die to everything except his divine object.

It will be observed that the meaning of this emblem and sonnet is really exactly the same as that of the stars-eyes emblem conceit, although the imagery is slightly different. The worn face of the lover, the panting breath of the Psalmist, the tempestuous winds in the breast of the enthusiast, are all hieroglyphs with the same meaning—that of spiritual aspiration. And this second emblem-conceit of the stars above the winds expresses the experience of a soul painfully in search of vision and passing through alternate moods of insight and obscurity, as the stars are now visible, now invisible.

The arrow is an image which Bruno uses very freely and in various forms. For example, the arrow-pierced heart:

> One object only I regard,
> One face alone my mind does fill,
> One beauty keeps me fixed and still;
> *One arrow pierced my heart.*

That is to say, explains the commentary, the will of the enthusiast is fixed on one divine object, and 'from thence alone he derives that barb which, killing him, constitutes the consummation of perfection'.

A variant form of the arrow emblem-conceit is the figure of two radiating arrows upon a target, with the motto: *Vicit instans.* Here the target symbolizes the hard, ada-

mantine heart pierced in an instant by the arrows of divine love. Again, he uses the figure of an arrow with a burning point. This combines the metaphors of a piercing and at the same time burning agency. Roughly speaking, Bruno means by the arrow impressions made by the divine upon the soul; the piercing arrow is the burning ray of divine beauty which wounds the lover.

A large number of the conventional sonnet images are used by Bruno in this way, that is to say as emblems of mystical experience. Yet if the poetry of the *Eroici furori* were to be printed by itself, without the prose emblems and the explanatory prose commentaries, we should have what would appear to be a kind of sonnet sequence (although not all the verses are in sonnet form), very obscure and difficult to follow, yet highly conventional in the conceits and images which it uses.

In the dedication to Sidney of the *Eroici furori,* Bruno is at pains to impress fully upon Sidney and his other readers what he is doing. This dedication opens with a violent attack on Petrarchism in the sense of worship of some human mistress, or, as he puts it, of 'distilling the elixir of the brain' in conceits which display to the public view the tortures and torments suffered under the tyranny of an unworthy object, that is of a human and not a divine object. His own poetry, so he explains to Sidney, is concerned solely with the divine. In fact he had intended to make this quite clear by entitling his book a canticle, for its meaning is the same as that of Solomon's poem, 'which under cover of ordinary loves and affections contains similar divine and heroic enthusiasms'. But he refrained from giving it this title for two reasons. First, the fear of censure. And second because there is an external dissimilarity between the form of the *Song of Songs* and these *Eroici furori* 'although the same mystery, the same substance of soul, is shadowed forth within them both':

> For in the one case the figures of speech are openly and manifestly but figures, and the metaphorical sense is known, so that it is undeniably metaphorical when thou hearest of those dove's eyes, that neck like a tower, that tongue under which is milk, that fragrance of incense, those teeth like a flock of sheep which come up from the washing, that hair which is like a flock of goats that appear from Mount Gilead; but this poem does not present an appearance which thus obviously urges thee to seek a latent and occult meaning, for in it are used ordinary modes of speech and similitudes more accommodated to common sense, such as witty lovers generally use and well-known poets are accustomed to put into verse and rhyme, with sentiments such as are used by those who speak of Citherea, or Licoris, of Doris, Cynthia, Lesbia, Corinna, Laura, and others. Whence each reader might easily be persuaded that my fundamental meaning and primary intention was addressed to an ordinary love, who had dictated to me such conceits; which love afterwards, by force of disdain, had taken to itself wings and become heroic; as it is possible to convert any fable, romance, dream, or prophetic enigma, and to transfer it, by virtue of metaphor and a pretext of allegory, into the significance of anything that may please a mind

which has an aptitude for wresting sentiments to any meaning, and of making everything out of everything, since all is in all, as the profound Anaxagoras says. But though he may think what he will and what pleases him, in the end each reader, whether he likes it or not, ought in justice to understand and define this matter as I myself understand and define it, and not force me to understand and define it as he thinks fit: for as the enthusiasms of that wise Hebrew have their own modes, orders, and titles which no one can understand or better declare than he himself, if he were present; so these Canticles have their proper title, order, and mode, which no one can better make plain and understand than I myself, when I am not absent.

One might perhaps express in other words the difference in form between his poetry and that of Solomon which Bruno is here describing by saying that it is the difference between an *allegorical* and an *emblematic* mode of speech. The allegorical mode, by its very strangeness and unnaturalness, will not allow the mind to rest in it without seeking a further explanation. But the emblematic mode may lull the reader into taking it at its face value.

It would be valuable to compare the medieval commentaries on the Canticle with Bruno's commentaries on his poems—a task not impossible since in three instances he points out in detail which passages of the Canticle correspond to which passages of the *Eroici furori*. For example, his third dialogue, he says, shows the force of the will beginning to conquer in the spiritual conflict and corresponds to those verses of the Canticle which speak of the winter being past and the rainy season over, and that the time of the flowers and singing birds has come. Such a comparison might help to trace in some detail the processes by which the allegories of medieval mystical theology were transposed in a Renaissance mind into the emblematic mode of speech.

Since Bruno uses Petrarchan conceits as emblems, and in conjunction with emblems, it seems obvious that the best way of trying to get at the historical flavour of his Petrarchism would be to relate his emblems to the history of emblem literature. In one of its aspects the *Eroici furori* is an unillustrated emblem book and as such has, or should have, a place in the history of emblem literature. The following attempt to suggest that place must be regarded as tentative.

The vast sixteenth-century literature of emblem and device first takes its characteristic form with the *Emblematum liber* (1531) of Andrea Alciati. This was one of the most influential books of the sixteenth century; it went through innumerable editions and learned men wrote commentaries upon it. The book initiated an immense fashion for similar productions; outstanding names of emblematists in the sixteenth-century are those of Paolo Giovio, Ruscelli, Contile, but their number is legion. The fashion spread through Europe and in the seventeenth century the genre continued with unabated popularity, though now chiefly in the form of the religious emblem book, a very favourite weapon of the Jesuits.

The emblem literature, trivial though it may sometimes seem at first sight to be, is deeply rooted in the thought of the time. The Renaissance type of emblem seems to have originated in the study of Egyptian hieroglyphs by the humanists. The hieroglyph was believed by them to be a picture with a hidden divine meaning, and since they also believed that both the Graeco-Roman and the Hebraeo-Christian traditions were indissolubly linked with Egypt, it followed that (to their minds) the study of the hieroglyphs was fundamentally a study of divine secrets. Understood in this way, the hieroglyphs became one with Catholic symbolism; the medieval allegories could be translated into hieroglyphs, and vice versa. The emblems of Alciati and the rest were really invented hieroglyphs, expansions of the picture language which drew material from all kinds of sources, one of which was the poetry of Petrarch.

We shall now take a few examples from sixteenth- and seventeenth-century emblem books, illustrating the development of the Petrarchan emblem, in order to compare them with the emblems of the *Eroici furori*.

The picture of a butterfly burning itself in a flame which is to be found in Camillo Camilli's *Imprese illustri* is a typical example of a plate from an Italian illustrated book of devices. The motto 'M'è piu grato il morir che il viver senza', that is 'I would rather die than live without it', is taken, as Camilli points out in his commentary, from Petrarch. Petrarch, says Camilli, meant by this image of the butterfly and the flame that he died in his mistress's presence, but nevertheless felt such sweetness in this that he preferred it to remaining alive in her absence. But in this emblem or device the flame means science for which the bearer of the device renounces all pleasure and eats up his life, yet feels a secret delight in doing this.

This is an example of how emblematists drew on Petrarch as a source of 'potential emblems'. The butterfly and flame image is a very common one in the emblem books.

Turning now to the *Eroici furori,* we find the following:

> What is the meaning of that butterfly which flutters round the flame, and almost burns itself?
> and what means that legend, 'Hostis non hostis?'

Reading this after looking at the example of an illustrated emblem from Camilli one understands how true it is to describe the *Eroici furori* as an 'unillustrated emblem book'. Bruno in these words places before the reader an imaginary illustration, and, in this case, one which would be very familiar to those well versed in the emblem literature. In the commentary he explains the meaning with which he is using the image.

Several of the devices in Ruscelli's collection are based on Petrarch. For example, the one which shows an eagle gazing at the sun with the motto 'Chi mi puo far di vera gloria lieta,' 'That which (that is, the sun) can make me happy with true glory,' is according to Ruscelli, a modification of the 'sacred precept of Petrarch' which he quotes thus:

> Tien pur gli occhi qual' Aquila in quel Sole,
> Che ti puó far d'eterna gloria degno
>
> (Keep your eyes fixed, like the Eagle, on that
>   Sun
> which can make you worthy of true glory.)

The interpretation of this impresa, which was adopted by Irene Castriota, Princess of Bisignano, is, says Ruscelli, that all the lady's thoughts and desires are fixed upon God, the Sun who illuminates the darkness of the soul. But others, he adds, have thought that the meaning is the devotion of the lady towards her husband.

This device and its meaning is characteristic of Ruscelli's treatment of Petrarchan emblems. The sense is mainly religious but at the same time it retains human undertones. Ruscelli has the humanist and courtly respect for the ideal type of human love as in itself already half divine and is without Bruno's 'anti-Petrarchist' spirit which demands an entirely abstract use of the Petrarchan emblem. It is in this respect that Bruno's emblems look forward to the seventeenth century. Their technique is that of Ruscelli and the whole sixteenth-century literature of emblem and device; but in spirit they belong to the baroque rather than to the Renaissance.

In the early seventeenth century emblem books there is a split between the 'profane' and the 'sacred' uses of the love conceit. One of the most striking examples of this is to be found in the two emblem books of Otto van Veen, or Vaenius, published at Antwerp in 1608 and 1615 respectively. The first is a book of 'profane' love emblems which gives vivid pictorial presentations of the conceits so familiar to us from the sonnet writers. The second is a book of 'sacred' love emblems in which the conceits are used in the service of religion. In the first set of pictures the actors in the drama are the profane Cupid, the lady, and the lover. In the second the actors have changed to Divine Love and the soul. But the conceits in which the spiritual drama is expressed are very close indeed to the 'profane' conceits.

This can best be studied by looking attentively at some examples.

One 'profane' emblem shows love being burned at the stake whilst the proud lady cruelly stirs the flames in which he suffers. Yet in the midst of his torments he turns upon the lady a humble and gentle gaze of resignation. The motto is 'Ny mesme la mort', and the meaning that the lover loves to suffer and even in death does not lack constancy.

The companion picture to this in the 'sacred' series shows the soul being burned at the stake whilst the executioner stirs the flames. But the soul is sustained in her torments by divine love, who clasps her hand encouragingly.

Another profane emblem shows Cupid shooting arrows at a breastplate. The motto is 'Amour passe tout' and the meaning that neither iron nor steel keeps out love's arrows.

In the sacred version the divine Cupid and the soul are seen shooting arrows at a breastplate and a shield. The meaning, of course, is the penetrating power of divine love.

Another picture in the profane series is a literal interpretation of the conceit of the darts from the lady's eyes. The lady sweeps forward in proud beauty whilst the lover lies stricken and wounded by the arrows from her eyes.

Equally literal is the presentation of the divine lover inflaming the breast of the soul with rays from his sun-like halo. The soul is here pierced by the ray of divine love just as the lover in the other picture is pierced by the arrows from the eyes. The allusion to arrows is present in the sacred emblem, for the divine Cupid is fully armed with bow and quiver.

The sacred emblem book thus uses the profane conceits as emblems of spiritual experience. And the tone of the whole series is set by the first picture in the book which shows Divine Love raising the soul. This picture is accompanied by a quotation from the Canticle: 'Rise up, my love, my fair one, and come away. For, lo, the winter is past, the rain is over and gone; the flowers appear on the earth; the time of the singing birds is come.' The whole composition is obviously meant to illustrate this imagery. It will be remembered that this very passage from the Canticle is one of those which, thirty years earlier, Bruno had told Sidney that he was transferring into the language of the Petrarchan conceit.

Let us think over for a moment the resemblances and differences between Vaenius' procedure and that of Bruno. Bruno means by the eyes of the lady, divine beauty and goodness; by her pride and the torments which she inflicts on her lover, the painful processes of spiritual progress and experience; by Cupid's piercing arrows, which burn as well as pierce, the influences of the divine working upon the soul. These are the meanings which are made explicit in Vaenius's sacred emblems. But Bruno uses the *profane* emblems with such meanings implicit in them. As he himself says, his language is not obviously sacred in intention, like that of the Canticle, but might be mistaken for an 'ordinary love'. Bruno's usage is thus more truly emblematic than that of Vaenius, for the sacred emblems of Vaenius are really sacred pictures, which quite obviously must have an allegorical meaning. But to use the ordinary conceit with the other meaning, as Bruno does, is to use it as a genuine emblem—that is to say, as a picture which secretly refers to something other than that which it appears on the surface to represent.

The sacred emblem book, of which the one illustrated by Vaenius is an early and striking example, was to have an enormous future in the literature of seventeenth-century devotion and became in the hands of the Jesuits an instrument of Counter Reformation propaganda. The Jesuit emblem books are cruder in style but they carry on the same principle of applying the conceit to the sacred emblem. Take, for example, the heart pierced by an arrow from the divine lover's bow in van Haeften's *Schola cordis* which is based entirely on conceits of the heart.

The same book contains an emblem of a winged heart. This is one which Bruno also uses and in a manner curiously like, though in some respects unlike, the form in which it is found years later in these Jesuit emblem books.

The emblem which Bruno describes consists of a winged heart escaping from a cage up into the sky. On its upward flight the heart is guided by a blind Cupid. In the accompanying sonnet he uses the same imagery, except that he now addresses his heart as an escaping bird. In the commentary he explains that the cage represents the impediments to the spiritual life caused externally in a thousand different ways and internally by natural weakness. The heart is dismissed from it to more celestial surroundings, and its wings are the powers of the soul, as the Platonists describe them. The god who guides it is Love, who has power to transform the seeker into that nature towards which he aspires. The whole episode closes with quotations from Petrarch, the Canticle, and the Psalms.

A near approach to this is to be found in one of the best known and most influential of the Jesuit emblem books, namely Herman Hugo's *Pia desideria* (first edition in 1624). One of his emblems shows the soul being released from the cage of sense by divine love, with an allusion in the empty cage hanging on the tree from which a bird has just escaped to the theme of the escaping bird. This is very close indeed to Bruno's emblem, although there are certain differences. The author of *Pia desideria* felt the emblem of the winged heart to be so typical of his aims that he uses a winged and burning heart on his title-page.

The fact that the *Eroici furori* cannot be illustrated from sixteenth-century examples alone but demands also incursions into the seventeenth century suggests that its place in the history of emblem-book literature might be that of a late Renaissance anticipation of the baroque. Bruno's emblematics would appear to use the Renaissance technique of secret allusion to convey a spirit of baroque fervour. In his hands, the courtly Petrarchan 'device', with its many-sided allusions, is used in the spirit of the future—that seventeenth-century future in which the sacred emblem was to play such a dominating role in the European imagination.

It will be remembered that in outlining Bruno's methods in the *Eroici furori* the point was emphasized that he uses emblems in conjunction with poems. He describes the conceit in visual form in the emblem, and sings it in aural form in the poem. There is thus some organic connection between pictorial emblems and poetic conceits, and it follows that to place the emblems historically is also to place the sonnets. If, as we have said before, the poems of the *Eroici furori* were to be printed without the emblems and the commentaries, they would appear as a kind of sonnet sequence. This sonnet sequence would belong to the same climate as the emblems; that is to say, however much it might appear to be addressed to an 'ordinary love', it would in fact be a record of spiritual experience, a translation of the images of the Canticle into Petrarchan conceits used as hieroglyphs, and, historically speaking, it would reflect a moment in the late sixteenth century in which the forces of the coming age were beginning to use these images with a different spiritual accent.

But there is another side to Bruno's use of the Petrarchan conceit—and one which must be mentioned, however inadequately—and that is its connections with his philosophy.

The attitude of mind which sees the universe itself as a hieroglyph or emblem in which divine truth is hidden is profoundly characteristic of Bruno. The sun, the planets, the moon, the earth, are indirect reflections of the Godhead, enigmatic pictures with a hidden meaning. The universe is constructed on the same principle as an emblem or device; that is to say, it secretly shadows forth spiritual truths in terms of objects perceived by the senses. One seventeenth-century theorist on emblematics saw the sky as 'a vast cerulean Shield, on which skilful Nature draws what she meditates: forming heroical Devices, and mysterious and witty Symbols of her secrets' [E. Tesauro, *Il Cannochiale Aristotelico,* 1655]. This attitude of mind must be realized in order to understand how it is that the sonnet conceits, as Bruno uses them, become, as it were, interchangeable with his philosophy. The witty conceits of lovers are used as emblems of spiritual truth, and therefore such emblems are merely variant ways of expressing the one divine truth which God has wittily concealed in the phenomena of the universe. Bruno's use of metaphysics is really as emblematic as his use of poetic images; hence the ease with which he modulates from the one form of expression into the other.

This is brought home by comparing a predominantly poetic dialogue, such as the *Eroici furori,* with a predominantly philosophical dialogue, such as the *Cena de le ceneri.* Yet there are many metaphysical symbols in the *Furori* and some lyrical symbols in the *Cena.* In the *Furori* the poetic emblems are dominant, though with an undercurrent of metaphysics to show their relation to the metaphysical system. In the *Cena,* the opposite is the case; the metaphysical emblems are dominant, though here and there their connection with the lyrical images is noted. We will quote one example of this correlation from the *Cena.*

One of the most characteristic and striking expositions of the philosophy in the *Cena* is that passage where Bruno in spirit breaks through the restraining Ptolemaic spheres into what he takes to be the infinity of the Copernican universe:

> Behold now, standing before you, the man who has pierced the air and penetrated the sky, wended his way amongst the stars and overpassed the margins of the world, who has broken down those imaginary divisions between the spheres, the first, the eighth, the ninth, the tenth, or what you will . . .

This passage is prefaced by a quotation from love poetry, not, indeed, that of Petrarch but that of Ariosto:

> Chi salirà per me, Madonna, in cielo
> A riportarne il mio perduto ingegno.
> > (*Orlando Furioso,* XXXV, i)

> Mistress who shall for me to heaven upfly
> To bring again from thence my wandering wit.

Here one sees how the philosophical disquisition is related to the lyrical cry, and that both are, as it were, *emblems* of ascent, of spiritual flight into realms unknown. The Ptolemaic spheres are, so to speak, the wires of an imprisoning cage whence the winged heart escapes into Copernican infinity.

One might also illustrate the interchangeability of lyrical and philosophical emblems from the woodcut which, in the *Cena de le ceneri* accompanies the argument in favour of the movement of the earth from the analogy of a stone dropped from the mast of a moving ship on to its deck. This woodcut is ostensibly a diagram. But the points marked by letters in the text are not shown on it, whilst the two flames which are visible on the sail-yards of the ship are a curious feature and seem to suggest some possible emblematic meaning.

If this woodcut is indeed an emblem it might be connected with Alciati's forty-third emblem of *Spes proxima*. In Mignault's commentary upon this emblem we are told that the two stars (in the top left-hand corner) are Castor and Pollux whose appearance means that the tempest in which the ship is tossing is about to abate, hence the motto *Spes proxima,* Hope is at hand. This emblem is perhaps the nearest thing one can find to Bruno's emblem in the *Eroici furori* of the two stars above the four winds, which, as will be remembered, was connected with the stars-eyes theme, signifying spiritual calm when the stars of divine beauty and goodness were visible and spiritual tempest when they were obscured. And it might also be connected with the woodcut in the *Cena* of the ship with the two flames on the sail-yards, for Mignault explains that, according to a well-known legend, the saving presence of the twin stars Castor and Pollux was made known to distressed mariners by the appearance of two lights on the sail-yards of their ship. The same story is told by Ruscelli in his commentary on one of the devices in his collection which is based on Alciati's *Spes proxima*. In the device shown by Ruscelli the two stars are actually on the sail-yard, though still in the form of stars and not of flames.

The woodcut in the *Cena* thus seems indirectly, through the two flames on the sail-yards, to suggest an allusion to the calming and hope-inspiring appearance of the twin stars amidst the tempest, and, if really designed by Bruno or chosen by him from an already existing design, would indicate (what is certainly in itself true) that the Copernican theory which this picture is supposed to illustrate as a diagram, meant to him an emblem of divine revelation corresponding in its meaning to the lyrical emblems, such as the one of the stars-eyes in the *Eroici furori.* But too much importance must not be attached to an argument based on this woodcut, owing to the habit of sixteenth-century printers of using the same wood-block indiscriminately in different publications.

This side of Bruno's thought connects him with the philosophy of the Renaissance. It is necessary to approach the emblems in the *Eroici furori* from this point of view in order to balance the impression gained from the realization that they anticipate the sacred emblems of the seventeenth century. Bruno's use of the Petrarchan conceits is certainly baroque in feeling, but it is a kind of metaphysical baroque, a blend of Renaissance philosophical and religious liberalism with baroque intensity and fervour.

Such was the emblem book which was dedicated to Sir Philip Sidney, the initiator of the Elizabethan poetic Renaissance. Its qualities were bound to appeal strongly to the passionate and profound Elizabethan temperament, and it indicated to the rising generation of English poets a way of using Petrarchism which would make of it, not a delayed imitation of a fashion now nearly 200 years old, but a channel for the spiritual life of Europe in its present-day manifestations.

We now come to the English poets, and here our attempts will be very modest. It is proposed to take only the very few conceits which have been studied (and which represent, of course, but a tiny fraction of the Petrarchan vocabulary) and to quote and discuss some examples of them from four sonnet writers, namely—Sidney, Daniel, Greville, and Drayton. It must be remembered that the English sonnet writers have not left us, like Bruno, commentaries on their sonnets. All we have is the poems as they stand and in pondering upon them we are no longer on the same firm ground as with Bruno, who explains what he is doing.

Before coming to the quotations from Sidney's sonnets, something must be said about the evidence for the connections between Bruno and Sidney.

Two of Bruno's works (*Lo spaccio della bestia trionfante,* 1584, and *De gli eroici furori,* 1585) are dedicated to Sidney, whilst in the *Cena de le ceneri* (1584) he speaks of having known Sidney 'first by reputation when I was in Milan and in France, and now, since I have been in this country, through having met him in the flesh'.

Sidney's sonnet sequence to 'Stella' was first published in 1591, after his death, but the dates at which he actually composed the poems cannot be exactly fixed. It is generally supposed that they must have been written in the earlier half of the 1580 decade, perhaps from 1581 onwards. (Sidney was killed at Zutphen in 1586.) A fact which is now certainly known about the sequence is that it was addressed to Penelope Devereux, Lady Rich.

In view of the uncertainty as to the actual date of composition of Sidney's sonnets, and in view also of the fact that they were definitely addressed to a real woman, can one assume them to be influenced by Bruno's 'anti-Petrarchist' emblematics?

In answer to this, the following points may be emphasized.

At the end of the *Eroici furori* dedication Bruno exempts from his anti-Petrarchist tirades those ladies who are connected with Sidney; these, he says, are worthy objects of devotion since they are divine nymphs, formed of celestial substance, like the divine Diana (Queen Elizabeth) who reigns over them. He repeats these praises in a sonnet to the ladies of England, in which he says that these ladies are like stars on earth:

> E siete in terra quel ch'in ciel le stelle.

One would be tempted to conjecture from these remarks that Bruno was alluding to Sidney's sonnets to 'Stella'. And such a conjecture is absolutely and categorically confirmed by John Florio, who, eighteen years later, addressed a dedication to two ladies connected with Sidney—namely his daughter, the Countess of Rutland, and Lady Rich, the original of 'Stella'. In this dedication the following words are to be found:

> Or as my fellow *Nolano* in his heroycall furies
> wrote (noble Countesse) to your most heroicke

father, and in a Sonnet to you Ladies of *England, You are not women, but in their likenesse Nymphs, Goddesses, and of Celestiall substance,*

Et siete in terra quel' ch'in ciel' le stelle.

Florio is here reminding Sidney's daughter, the Countess of Rutland, of her heroic father to whom Nolano (that is Bruno) had dedicated his ***Eroici furori;*** and in the next breath he reminds Lady Rich of the line on 'stelle' in Bruno's sonnet to the ladies of England. It is perfectly clear that Florio associates Lady Rich, and therefore the 'Stella' of Sidney's sonnet sequence, with Bruno's ***Eroici furori.***

This dedication is accompanied by a sonnet by Matthew Gwinne, addressed to Lady Rich, which is a tissue of epithets drawn from Sidney's sonnets. Matthew Gwinne and John Florio are both mentioned by name by Bruno in his ***Cena de le ceneri*** as his close associates, so they were in a position to know the truth—and the truth, to them, evidently is that there is a very close connection between Sidney's sonnets to 'Stella' and the ***Eroici furori.***

By excepting Sidney's sonnets to 'Stella', and the poetic worship of Queen Elizabeth as the 'divine' Diana, from his invectives against 'ordinary' Petrarchism, Bruno thus seems to include the rising school of English poets as Petrarchists in the emblematic sense. He suggests that the meanings inherent in his own poetry must also be implicit in the poetry of the heroic nobleman to whom he is addressing his own heroic enthusiasms. It follows that Sidney's devotion to Lady Rich must have had broader implications than the purely personal, and that the aspiration towards a divine object is somehow bound up with his cult of 'Stella'.

It is a point of great significance that Sidney himself professes a kind of 'anti-Petrarchism' in his sonnets. He will not, he says, imitate the poets who borrow conceits and phrases from Petrarch; he will not write in that artificial style at all but will derive all his inspiration from 'Stella'.

> You that do search for every purling spring
> Which from the ribs of old Parnassus flows;
> And every flower, not sweet perhaps, which grows
> Near thereabouts, into your poesy wring:
> You that do dictionary's methods bring
> Into your rhymes running in rattling rows;
> You that poor Petrarch's long deceasèd woes,
> With newborn sighs and denizened wit do sing:
> You take wrong ways! Those far-fet helps be such
> As do bewray a want of inward touch;
> And sure at length, stolen goods do come to light.
> But if (both for your love and skill) your name
> You seek to nurse at fullest breasts of Fame:
> STELLA behold! and then begin to endite.

The same intention is expressed in the first sonnet of the sequence, in which he says that after 'oft turning others' leaves' in search of ideas for his poetry his Muse bade him leave that barren study and turn inwards for inspiration:

'Fool!' said my Muse, 'Look in thy heart, and write!'

It has been a great disappointment, and also something of a puzzle, to those in search of 'sincerity' in the sonnet sequences, that after giving himself such admirable advice Sidney does not follow it. For his sonnets are full of the usual Petrarchan conceits—a fact which must have been perfectly patent both to himself and to his readers. Why then does he announce so solemnly that he is *not* going to Petrarchize, and then proceed to do that very thing most assiduously?

Surely, it is in Bruno's dedication to him of the *Furori,* where one learns how an anti-Petrarchist could yet make use of the conceits as emblems, that an answer to this might be found. Does it not seem probable, in the light of that dedication, that Sidney's anti-Petrarchist profession combined with Petrarchist practice means that he also is using the conceits emblematically?

In order to work this suggestion out fully the whole range of imagery used by Bruno in the *Furori* and by Sidney in *Astrophel and Stella* ought to be carefully compared. Here one can only quote a few examples from Sidney of the conceit which we chose to study as an example of Bruno's method—namely that of the stars-eyes.

This is, in fact, the dominating conceit of Sidney's sequence. Here is an example:

> Soul's joy! bend not those morning stars
> from me!
> Where Virtue is made strong by Beauty's might,
> Where Love is Chasteness, Pain doth learn Delight,
> And Humbleness grows on with Majesty:
> Whatever may ensue, O let me be
> Co-partner of the riches of that sight!
> Let not mine eyes be hell-driven from that light!
> O look! O shine! O let me die and see!
> For though I oft myself of them bemoan,
> That through my heart their beamy darts be gone;
> Whose cureless wounds, even now, most freshly bleed:
> Yet since my death wound is already got;
> Dear Killer! spare not thy sweet cruel shot!
> A kind of grace it is to slay with speed.

We gain no mental image from this of any particular woman's face, nor even of any face at all. We see only two eyes in the form of two stars. These eyes are the seat of virtues. The lover prays vehemently that their light may not be taken from him. Yet the eyes have power to kill him with death-dealing darts. Knowing this, he yet prays that they may be turned upon him so that he may die with speed.

Could anything be closer than this to Bruno's emblem of the two eyes in the form of two radiant stars with the motto *Mors et vita,* with its accompanying sonnet in which he prays that the cruel lady will not turn her eyes from him but will open them and give him death? In Bruno's case his commentary tells us the meanings—the eyes, divine beauty and goodness, the prayer to them a prayer that the divine light may show itself and clear the troubled sky of the human mind (compare Sidney 'let not mine eyes be hell-driven from that light'), the death from the mystical death of the soul, which is eternal life.

The sonnet has exactly the device-like quality with which Bruno uses the conceits. Sidney does not present this conceit in the form of the little dramatic scene which Vaenius illustrates. That scene is indeed implicit in his sonnet, but is suggested rather by the more economical methods of the device. As in Bruno's treatment of the theme, we see here little more than the two stars in the form of two radiant eyes towards which the lover bends all his will in prayer. It is an emblematic statement of the direction of the will towards a sublime object in self-effacing humility and pain, the heroic device of an heroic enthusiast.

Almost exactly the same set of images is found also in this sonnet:

> O eyes! which do the spheres of beauty move;
> Whose beams be joys; whose joys, all virtues be;
> Who while they make Love conquer, conquer
>   Love.
> The schools where Venus hath learned chastity.
>   O eyes! where humble looks most glorious
>   prove;
> Only, loved tyrants! just in cruelty,
> Do not! O do not from poor me remove!
> Keep still my zenith! Ever shine on me!
>   For though I never see them, but straight-
>   ways
> My life forgets to nourish languisht sprites;
> Yet still on me, O eyes! dart down your rays!
>   And if from majesty of sacred lights
> Oppressing mortal sense, my death proceed:
> Wracks, triumphs be; which love (high set) doth
>   breed.

The emblematic nature of the eyes is here more clearly indicated. The eyes have conquered the terrestrial Venus; they are 'sacred lights'. From them proceed the death-dealing and at the same time life-giving rays. (The paradoxical 'Wracks, triumphs be' of the last line has a motto-like precision and is a statement in variant terms of the prevailing theme of *Mors et vita.*) The emphasis in this emblem-sonnet is on the ray image rather than on the dart image, in contrast to the one first quoted where the emphasis is on the darts from the eyes (though the ray theme is present in the adjective 'beamy' in 'beamy darts'). This suits the more explicit statement of this sonnet; Cupid's darts, shot from the eyes, have openly become the divine rays streaming from the 'sacred lights'.

In succeeding sonnets there is a complaint that, in spite of these prayers, favour has been withdrawn from the lover. The more he cries, the less 'grace she doth impart'. We must here remember how, with Bruno, the pride of the lady is a metaphor, as God is sometimes said to be jealous, angry, or asleep. The sense of woe and desolation is conveyed by Sidney in an interesting use of the worn face image:

> Stella oft sees the very face of woe
> Painted in my beclouded stormy face . . .

It will be remembered that in one of his sonnets Bruno uses the worn face of the lover as an emblem of aspiration,

and in another he conveys the same meaning by tempestuous winds beneath the stars. Sidney seems here to combine these two ideas by describing the sadness of the lover's face in terms of cloud and tempest, thus producing the beautiful image of the 'beclouded stormy face' to express a mood in which 'the troubled sky of the human mind does not clear itself by the removal of metaphors and enigmas'.

Read in the light of the *Eroici furori,* Sidney's sonnets are seen to be, like Bruno's, a spiritual autobiography, reflecting in terms of Petrarchan emblems, the moods of a soul seeking God. Bruno's commentary on his own poems cannot take the place of a commentary by Sidney himself on the *Astrophel and Stella* sequence, and there are still obscurities and problems in the latter, the most puzzling of which is that the poet sometimes reproaches himself for his devotion to Stella and a moral conflict arises in his mind. We never find this in the *Eroici furori* where, although the lover passes through many conflicts and sufferings, he is always certain of the rightness and full divinity of his object. To Sidney, on the other hand, whilst Stella is usually the completely virtuous and divine object (as in the stars-eyes emblem-sonnets which we have quoted) at other times she seems not to represent the highest possible good, but something less exalted from which he must tear himself away. In the absence of a sonnet-by-sonnet explanation from Sidney of the various shades of mood and meaning in his sequence, this problem must remain a dark one.

Sidney himself issues a warning against reading into his poetry meanings which have not the author's sanction:

> You that with allegory's curious frame,
> Of others' children, changelings use to make:
> With me, those pains for God's sake do not take.
> I list not dig so deep for brazen fame.
>   When I say Stella! I do mean the same
> Princess of Beauty; for whose only sake
> The reins of love I love, though never slack:
> And joy therein, though nations count it shame.

These lines, which might appear at first sight to smash our arguments, are on the contrary one of the points in the *Astrophel and Stella* sequence which put one most irresistibly in mind of Bruno's text. For is it not almost in these very words that Bruno concludes the passage in the dedication of the *Eroici furori* in which he explains that he is using the Petrarchan conceits with the meanings of the Canticle? His readers, he says, are not to convert his poetry, 'by virtue of metaphor and a pretext of allegory' into some meaning which pleases their own fancy. The poems are to be understood as he himself wishes them to be understood. Sidney, in the above sonnet, seems to be making exactly the same protest and claim; his lines might indeed stand as a versification of Bruno's words. Placed in the context of the *Eroici furori* dedication they seem to tell us that Sidney, like Bruno, uses the emblematic rather than the allegorical mode of speech in his poetry.

Whilst, therefore, the commentary on the *Eroici furori* poems cannot be a complete substitute for a commentary by Sidney himself on the meanings latent in his sequence, it may be used as an invaluable guide. For there is no doubt whatever that the ***Eroici furori*** and *Astrophel and Stella* come out of the same atmosphere.

The poet Samuel Daniel was very closely connected with Sidney's circle; in fact some of his sonnets appeared, mingled with Sidney's, in the first pirated edition of *Astrophel and Stella.*

Daniel was a pioneer in introducing the Italian emblem literature into England, for his English translation of Paulus Jovius on devices was published in 1585, the same year as the ***Eroici furori.*** An anonymous friend of Daniel's who signs himself 'N. W.' writes an introduction to the work which mentions Bruno and also shows a wide acquaintance with the emblem literature. 'N. W.' is well-versed in the Renaissance theories on the connections of emblems with Egyptian hieroglyphs, he mentions by name a number of well-known emblematists and theoretical exponents of the science of imagery, he congratulates Daniel on his knowledge of Alciati and refers to Mignault's commentary on the latter's emblems. With such an apparatus as this, 'N. W.' would have been in a good position to read and understand the works of Bruno, to whose recent visit to Oxford he alludes in terms which show that both he and Daniel had heard Bruno debating in the Oxford schools.

Daniel, therefore, was both imbued with emblematic learning and in close touch with the Bruno-Sidney atmosphere. He must fully have realized the possible emblematic meanings of the conceits with which his *Delia,* first printed in 1592, abounds.

Here, for instance, is Daniel's version of the stars-eyes:

> Oft do I marvel, whether Delia's eyes,
> Are eyes, or else two radiant stars that
>   shine?
> For how could Nature ever thus devise
> Of earth, on earth, a substance so divine?
> Stars, sure, they are! Whose motions rule
>   desires;
> And calm and tempest follow their aspects:
> Their sweet appearing still such power in-
>   spires,
> That makes the world admire so strange ef-
>   fects.
> Yet whether fixed or wandering stars are
>   they,
> Whose influence rules the Orb of my poor
>   heart?
> Fixed, sure, they are! But wandering make
>   me stray
> In endless errors; whence I cannot part.
> Stars, then, not eyes! Move you, with milder
>   view,
> Your sweet aspect on him that honours you!

The second line states the emblem; two stars in the form of two radiant eyes. The fourth line reminds one of Bruno's remark, quoted by Florio, 'non son femine, non son donne, ma, . . . son di sustanza celeste. Daniel, however, is not using the darts-from-the-eyes form of the stars-eyes emblem, but the form which emphasizes the power of the twin stars to calm storms:

> And calm and tempest follow their aspects.

Many examples might be quoted of Daniel's use of the darts or rays from the eyes conceit. For instance:

> The dart transpiercing were those crystal eyes.

He also twice uses the image of the worn face of the lover:

> Delia herself, and all the world may view
> Best in my face, where cares hath tilled deep fur-
>   rows.

And,

> Read in my face, a volume of despairs!
> The wailing Iliads of my tragic woe:
> Drawn with my blood, and painted with my
>   cares,
> Wrought by her hand that I have honoured so.

There is much emphasis throughout the sequence on the pride and cruelty of Delia, and on the lover's sufferings.

From this brief study of Daniel and his poetry from the emblematic point of view one gains the impression, first, that external circumstances strongly suggest that he had every opportunity of being in this movement, and, secondly, that in his poetry he uses a range of emblem-conceits which is very close indeed to that used in the ***Eroici furori.***

Sir Fulke Greville, Lord Brooke, was Sidney's most intimate friend and biographer, and it was his house which Bruno made the setting for his debate with the Oxford doctors, as described in the ***Cena de le ceneri.*** With Greville, therefore, we are still in the same atmosphere, still in this circle of poets and philosophers grouped round Sidney.

Greville's sonnet sequence was not printed until 1633, when it appeared with the explanation that it had been 'written in his youth and familiar exercise with Sir Philip Sidney.'

It is difficult to find any trace of humanity whatsoever in Greville's 'Caelica' (a rare Latin adjective, meaning, of course, 'heavenly' and derived from *caelum*) or in his 'Cynthia' and 'Myra', the variant names which he sometimes uses in the sequence. Greville's mind moves in a sphere of remote metaphysical abstraction in which the conceits are still used, but used in such a way that their visual, sensual form is, as it were, broken down into philosophical language.

For example, Greville's seventh sonnet is a miniature exposition of mutability—the constant changes of matter into new forms, the passing of time, the movements of the elements. But in the last two lines we reach Myra's eyes and these, we are told, never vary. The sonnet opens with the line 'The world that all contains is ever moving', but this is not an allusion to the Copernican theory, as one might think, for the rest of the poem is built on the old cosmology, with the stars turning on the spheres and the earth standing still. The 'world' of the first line is not the earth but the *caelum,* with its constant ordered movements. Yet although Greville is not a Copernican, the philosophy of mutability which he expounds is very characteristic of Bruno, though of course very far from being peculiar to him:

The World, that all containes, is euer mouing,
The Starres within their spheres for euer turned,
Nature (*the Queene of Change*) to change is lou-
ing,
And Forme to matter new, is still adiourned.

Fortune our *phansie-God,* to varie liketh,
Place is not bound to things within it placed,
The present time vpon time passed striketh,
With *Phoebus* wandring course the earth is
graced.

The Ayre still moues, and by its mouing clea-
reth,
The Fire vp ascends, and planets feedeth,
The Water passeth on, and all lets weareth,
The Earth stands still, yet change of changes
breedeth;

Her plants, which Summer ripes, in Winter fade,
Each creature in vnconstant mother lyeth,
Man made of earth, and for whom earth is made,
Still dying liues, and liuing euer dyeth;
      Onely like fate sweet *Myra* neuer varies,
      Yet in her eyes the doome of all Change
carries.

It seems that what one has here is in effect the familiar conceit of the stars-eyes shining out amidst the tempest. Yet instead of the visual image of the ship tossing at sea to which the appearance of the twin stars brings a sense of calm after storm, or the allied image of the star-like eyes which clear the storm-clouded mind of the lover, we have here the troubled sea of Mutability with which, in the last lines, are contrasted the eyes of Eternity. If this is a correct interpretation, Greville is here using the lyrical statement in conjunction with the philosophical statement in exactly Bruno's manner.

In the sonnet which immediately follows we find allusions to the worn face in the word 'furrows' twice repeated and in the word 'wrinkles'. But the image is so broken up and confused with the leading conceit in the sonnet (which is that of the fire from the heart and the tears from the eyes— the debate of the heart and the eyes—a conceit which we have not here studied but which is very deeply elaborated by Bruno) that we form no clear poetic picture, and instead of flowing with the easy grace of a Sidney or a Daniel, this poem strikes one as difficult:

Selfe-pitties teares, wherein my hope lyes
drown'd,
Sighs from thoughts fire, where my desires lan-
guish,
Despaire by humble loue of beauty crown'd,
Furrowes not worne by time, but wheeles of anguish;
      Dry vp, smile, ioy, make smooth, and see
      Furrowes, despaires, sighes, teares, in beau-
ty be.

Beauty, out of whose clouds my heart teares
rained,
Beauty, whose niggard fire sighs' smoke did
nourish,
Beauty, in whose eclipse despaires remained,
Beauty, whose scorching beames make wrinkles
florish;

Time hath made free of teares, sighs, and
despaire,
      Writing in furrowes deep; *she once was
faire.*

It is in exactly this obscure and broken kind of way that Bruno uses the conceits, and one cannot but think that those interested in Greville's remarkable poetry would find the commentary to the **Eroici furori** a great help.

Greville was a convinced Calvinist and firm believer in predestination and faith without works. One almost fancies that Greville's Calvinism can be detected in his use of the conceits:

And thou O *Laue,* which in these eyes
Hast married *Reason* with *Affection,*
And made them Saints of beauties skyes,
Where ioyes are shadowes of perfection,
Lend me thy wings that I may rise
Vp not by worth but thy election;
      For I haue vow'd in strangest fashion,
      To loue, and neuer seeke compassion.

The wings of Greville's winged heart symbolize, not the worth of his own efforts, but election. It will be remembered that in Bruno's use of the conceit of the winged heart, the wings represented the two powers inherent in the soul, the powers of the intellect and the will—reason and affection. Greville places these in the stars-eyes above him in the sky, towards which he aspires on wings of election.

Greville's sonnet sequence is an early specimen of the 'metaphysical' style in poetry. It should be realized that the emblematic conceit carries within itself the *potentiality* for this metaphysical development, even when its possible metaphysical translation does not appear. For example, Daniel's sonnet to the stars-eyes may have had, in his own mind, an alternative metaphysical form which does not come to the surface of the poem. But in Greville's poem on the ever-moving world, the metaphysical translation becomes audible and visible and fills out the framework of the 'eyes' conceit with philosophical imagery. Metaphysical love poetry uses *simultaneously* those lyrical and philosophical statements, which, in a symbolic system, such as that formulated by Bruno, are thought of as *alternative* ways of saying the same thing.

Michael Drayton prefixed to his sonnet sequence entitled *Ideas Mirrour* a dedicatory poem in which he announces that he is not going to imitate Petrarchist poetry, nor merely borrow from Desportes or form Petrarch as so many other writers do. He underlines this by concluding the poem with a quotation from the 'anti-Petrarchist' sonnet in *Astrophel and Stella:*

Divine Syr Phillip, I avouch thy writ,
I am no Pickpurse of anothers wit.

Here he seems openly to enlist himself under the banner of 'Astrophel' by using the divine Sir Philip's own words of contempt for ordinary imitative Petrarchism.

But when taken at its face value, Drayton's 'anti-Petrarchism' has been even more puzzling to his admirers than that of Sidney. For whilst Sidney still uses the conceits, though professing that he will not do so, he uses them with an air of his own. Whereas Drayton's *Ideas Mirrour* presents the reader with a large repertory of the most conventional conceits reproduced with almost slavish accuracy.

Here, for example, are the 'darts from the eyes':

> Cupid, dumbe Idoll, peevish Saint of love,
>   No more shalt thou nor Saint nor Idoll be,
> No God art thou, a Goddesse shee doth
>   prove,
> Of all thine honour shee hath robbed thee.
>
> Thy Bowe half broke, is peec'd with olde desire,
>   Her Bowe is beauty, with ten thousand
>   strings,
> Of purest gold, tempred with vertues fire:
> The least able to kyll an hoste of Kings.
>
> Thy shafts be spent, and shee (to warre appoint-
> ed)
>   Hydes in those christall quivers of her eyes,
>   More Arrowes with hart-piercing mettel
>   poynted,
>   Then there be starres at midnight in the
>   skyes.
> With these, she steales mens harts for her reliefe,
> Yet happy he thats robd of such a thiefe.

The exactness with which Drayton has elaborated the detailed form of this conceit can be realized by comparing this sonnet with Vaenius' illustration of the same theme. The whole little scene of Cupid reduced to idleness whilst the lady's eyes perform the work of his bow and arrows upon the suffering lover is described by Drayton which makes his sonnet, both in form and style, a perfect counterpart to Vaenius' plate.

Is it possible that the dedication to the *Eroici furori* might provide a clue to Drayton's anti-Petrarchist Petrarchism also? Is *Ideas Mirrour* a translation of the Canticle into Petrarchan emblems?

Drayton began his career as a poet with a volume of spiritual poems called *The Harmony of the Church* (1591) which includes a translation into English verse of the Canticle. Drayton, therefore, had been studying the imagery of the Canticle at about the same time that he was writing his sonnet sequence. Admiring Sidney as he did, it is more than probable that Drayton would have known of the *Eroici furori*, that revealing work which hinted at the existence of Sidney's poems seven years before their publication. And in the dedication of the *Eroici furori* he would have found an explanation by an anti-Petrarchist of the theory of using Petrarchan conceits with meanings corresponding to the allegorical interpretations of the Canticle.

Looking back now on the sonnet just quoted one may almost fancy that the 'anti-Petrarchist' theme is stated in the opposition between Cupid and the Lady. The Lady has vanquished Cupid, whose bow was pieced with old desire, and substituted for his broken bow her bow of Beauty tempered with Virtue. Is this not an emblem of the sublimation of desire?

We know how the love emblems of Vaenius could turn into sacred emblems, and we have pointed out how

Bruno's method differed from that of Vaenius in that the love emblem, to him, is already the sacred emblem. The possibility is worth thinking over very seriously that Drayton may be employing the same technique, representing by the eyes of the lady divine beauty and goodness and by the arrows from the eyes the influences of the divine working upon the soul.

It is interesting to compare Sidney's treatment of this theme with that of Drayton. Sidney, like Drayton, identifies the lady with Beauty and Virtue and suggests the theme of sublimation:

> O eyes! which do the sphere of beauty move;
> Whose beams be joys; whose joys all virtues be;
> Who while they make Love conquer, conquer
> Love.
> The schools where Venus hath learned chastity.

This corresponds to the conquest of Cupid by the Lady in Drayton's sonnet. But whilst the ground-work is the same there is a great difference in the styles of its presentation by the two poets. The visual impression derived from Sidney's use of this conceit consists of very little beyond the two stars in the form of two radiant eyes which are the focus of the lover's aspiration. The dart and ray imagery occurs but is not developed into a very definite picture. In fact, as we have suggested before, Sidney's use of the conceit is 'device-like' in its economy of material. His style is that of a Renaissance *impresa*. But Drayton provides us with the whole drama of Cupid robbed of his bow by the lady, the lady shooting the arrows from her eyes, and the prostrate lover. Sidney's style suggests Ruscelli; Drayton's style suggests Vaenius. Sidney is a Renaissance emblematist; Drayton, a baroque emblematist.

We thus find in the Elizabethan poets the same moment of transition between Renaissance and baroque which was suggested as typical of Bruno's *Eroici furori.* Bruno's style, on the whole, is much nearer to Sidney's than to Drayton's; yet, as we pointed out before, his emblems sometimes anticipate the seventeenth-century manner, and it is interesting to find that the 'winged heart', which we took as an example of such anticipation, is an image which Drayton also uses:

> My Hart imprisoned in a hopeles Ile,
>   Peopled with Armies of pale jealous eyes,
>   The shores beset with thousand secret
> spyes,
>   Must passe by ayre, or else dye in exile.
>
> He framd him wings with feathers of his
> thought,
>   Which by theyr nature learn'd to mount the
> skye,
>   And with the same he practised to flye,
>   Till he himselfe thys Eagles art had taught.
> Thus soring still, not looking once below,
>
>   So neere thyne eyes celestiall sunne aspy-
> red,
>   That with the rayes his wafting pyneons
> fired.
>   Thus was the wanton cause of hys owne
> woe.
> Downe fell he in thy Beauties Ocean drenched,

Yet there he burnes, in fire thats never
    quenched.

With the winged heart emblem, Drayton has combined
the emblem of the eagle soaring so near the sun that it
burns its wings. This is not one which is actually used by
Bruno in the *Eroici furori,* though the butterfly burning
its wings in the flame is used by him with exactly the same
meanings. Drayton's winged heart turns into an eagle in
mid-flight, and burns its wings in the brightness of the
'eyes' which represent the 'celestiall sunne'. Combined
with all these images there is probably an allusion to the
Icarus story.

But the strangest thing is the cage. The cage for Drayton
appears to mean England, in which he is imprisoned and
surrounded by spies and from which his heart can only escape by soaring. This poem appears to reflect Drayton's
determination to escape by an interior mysticism from external circumstances in England which he feels to be unsympathetic. It will be noticed that the wings of his heart
are the innate powers which he learns to use; they are not
the wings of predestination, as in Greville's case. Drayton
is certainly not a Calvinist, and the defence of the pre-
Reformation Catholic tradition which he openly permits
himself in several passages of his *Polyolbion* suggests that
he might have found Bruno's views on this matter congenial. Drayton's sonnet on the winged heart escaping from
the cage, like Bruno's emblem on this theme, anticipates
the Counter Reformation sacred emblem.

When placed in its proper sequence as representing a stage
in the development of emblematic thinking, Bruno's *Eroici furori* is thus seen to be a work of the greatest importance to students of Elizabethan poetry. Through its connections with Sidney, it forms a link between that poetry
and some of the deepest currents of contemporary European thought and feeling; and the relating of Bruno's emblems to the spiritual history of Europe helps to assess the
moment in that history to which the poetic imagery of the
Elizabethans also belongs.

Whitman on Bruno, in an inscription:

As America's mental courage (the thought comes to me
to-day) is so indebted, above all current lands and peoples, to the noble army of Old-World martyrs past, how
incumbent on us that we clear those martyrs' lives and
names, and hold them up for reverent admiration as well
as beacons. And typical of this, standing for it and all
perhaps, Giordano Bruno may well be put, to-day and
to come, in our New World's thankfulest heart and
memory.

Walt Whitman in Daniel G. Brinton's and Thomas
Davidson's Giordano Bruno: Philosopher and Martyr.
Two Addresses, *David McKay, 1890.*

Paul Oskar Kristeller   (essay date 1964)

SOURCE: "Bruno," in *Eight Philosophers of the Italian
Renaissance,* Stanford University Press, 1964, pp. 124-44.

[*A German-born scholar, Kristeller is an acclaimed author
of Italian, German, and English articles and books on Renaissance philosophy. In this excerpt, Kristeller describes
Bruno's background and highlights the philosopher's beliefs
as revealed in several works.*]

[Giordano Bruno's] fame is partly due to the tragedy of
his life and death, but no less deserved by his brilliant gifts
as a thinker and writer. His vision of the world has a distinctly modern quality, and has impressed and influenced
scientists and philosophers throughout the subsequent
centuries. At the same time, his work is still entirely a part
of the Renaissance, not merely in its date and style but in
its premises and problems, whereas such younger contemporaries or successors as Bacon, Galileo, and Descartes
belong to the Renaissance with only a part, and perhaps
not the most significant part, of their thought and work.

Giordano Bruno was born in Nola in southern Italy in
1548, and entered the Dominican order in Naples at the
age of 18. While pursuing theological studies, he also read
extensively in the ancient philosophers, and began to entertain serious doubts about some of the teachings of the
Catholic Church. When he was in Rome in 1576, these
doubts became known to the authorities of his order, and
an indictment for heresy was prepared against him. Before
he could be arrested, Bruno escaped and began a long and
adventurous journey that took him to many parts of Europe. He went first to Noli near Genoa, then to Savona,
Turin, Venice, and Padua, and apparently earned his living by private teaching and tutoring, as he did throughout
most of his later life until his arrest. From Padua he went
to Lyons, and then to Geneva, where he became a Calvinist and met many of the Reformed leaders. Yet soon he
turned against Calvinism and went to Toulouse, where he
obtained a degree in theology and lectured on Aristotle for
two years. Next he went to Paris, where he obtained the
favor of Henry III, held some kind of a lectureship, and
published his first writings in 1582. He then accompanied
the French ambassador, Michel de Castelnaud, Marquis
de Mauvissière, to England, and spent the period from
1583 to 1585 in London. He also held a disputation, and
gave a few lectures, at Oxford, and antagonized the professors both by his manners and by his polemical attacks. Yet
he made friendly contact with Sir Philip Sidney and other
educated Englishmen, and his English period is especially
noteworthy because he published in London, in Italian,
some of his most famous writings.

He returned to Paris with his patron, and held in 1586 in
one of the colleges of the university a violent disputation
against Aristotle, which caused such an uproar that he decided to leave. He went to Marburg and then to Wittenberg, where he lectured for two years at the university on
Aristotle's logic, became a Lutheran, and praised Luther
in his farewell address. He then proceeded to Prague and
to Helmstedt, where he lectured again at the university,
and in 1590 to Frankfurt. His stay in Frankfurt was again
important, since it was in this city, which was then, as

now, a center of the international book trade, that he published his Latin poems (1591), the most important of his published works after his Italian dialogues.

When he was in Frankfurt, he received and accepted an invitation from Giovanni Mocenigo, a Venetian nobleman. After a short stay in Padua, Bruno joined the household of Mocenigo in Venice as his guest and tutor. Shortly afterwards, Mocenigo denounced him to the Inquisition and had him arrested in 1592. Bruno tried to retract, but in January 1593 he was taken to Rome, kept in prison, and subjected to a trial that lasted for many years. After initial hesitations, he firmly refused to recant his philosophical opinions. Finally, in February 1600, he was sentenced to death and burned alive in the Campo di Fiori, where a monument was erected to him during the last century.

Bruno's dreadful end has rightly shocked his contemporaries and posterity. His firm conduct during the trial deserves our highest respect, and goes a long way to balance his human weaknesses, which are all too obvious. The idea that a man should be punished and executed for holding opinions considered wrong by his religious or political authorities is intolerable for any thoughtful person who takes human dignity and liberty seriously, although the deplorable treatment given to Bruno, and the wrong idea underlying it, was by no means peculiar to Bruno's church or to his century, as some historians would have us believe. His death made of Bruno a martyr, not so much of modern science, as was thought for a long time, but rather of his convictions and of philosophical liberty. The records of his trial have not been completely preserved, but several relevant documents have been published, and some very important ones have come to light quite recently, from which the nature and content of the charges made against him have become much clearer than before. It is now quite evident that Bruno's acceptance of the Copernican system constituted but one out of a very large number of accusations, which included a long series of philosophical and theological opinions as well as many specific instances of alleged blasphemy and violations of Church discipline.

Bruno's extant writings are rather numerous and diverse in content. His Italian works, which were all published during his lifetime, include a comedy and several satirical treatises, in addition to his philosophical dialogues, which we shall discuss later. His style is lively and exuberant, and at times quite baroque and obscure. His more numerous Latin writings, some of which were published only in the last century whereas others have come to light quite recently, include several important philosophical poems and treatises, as well as a number of works that reflect his subsidiary interests: mathematics and magic, the art of memory, and the so-called Lullian art.

The art of memory, which grew out of a part of ancient rhetoric, was a subject much cultivated in the Middle Ages and the Renaissance, and there are many treatises dealing with this subject, which scholars have just recently begun to study, and which probably deserve much further exploration. These efforts to devise systems for strengthening a person's memory had a very great practical importance in a period when scholars and men of affairs could not rely as heavily as nowadays on the help of indexes and reference works, and when the ready mastery of knowledge and information was considered a necessary criterion of competence, not only in speeches and disputations but also in many professional activities.

The Lullian art, named after its inventor, the fourteenth-century Catalan philosopher Ramon Lull, was a general scheme of knowledge based on a number of simple terms and propositions, and it was Lull's claim that through appropriate methods of combination this art would lead to the discovery and demonstration of all other knowledge. The method was illustrated by the use of letters, figures, and other symbols, which represented the basic concepts and their combinations. The Lullian art attracted the interest of many thinkers and scholars down to Leibniz, and it is obviously, at least in its claims if not in its achievements, a forerunner of modern symbolic logic. For Bruno, the art of memory and the Lullian art were not merely the subjects of his intellectual curiosity, but also a means of livelihood, for he seems to have instructed his private pupils mainly in these two arts. This side of Bruno's work is less well known, and a detailed study of it has been attempted only in recent years.

Bruno's thought shows many traits of genuine originality, yet at the same time he is indebted to a variety of sources. In spite of his double polemic against the grammarians and the scholastics, he owed much to his humanist education as well as to his Aristotelian and scholastic training. His doctrine of heroic love, which forms the center of his famous *Eroici furori,* is heavily indebted to Ficino, and it has been recently shown that this work belongs to the literary and intellectual tradition of Platonist love treatises, which occupied a rather large place in sixteenth-century thought and literature [John C. Nelson, Renaissance Theory of Love, 1958]. In his metaphysics, Bruno was strongly influenced by Plotinus and Cusanus, whereas his cosmology is based on Lucretius and Copernicus.

Many historians have discovered serious inconsistencies in Bruno's thought, and some scholars have tried to account for them on chronological grounds, assuming that his philosophical thought underwent a certain development. Without excluding such a development, I am inclined to think that from the time of his Italian dialogues his basic position remained unchanged, and that a few ambiguities, oscillations, and logical difficulties are inherent in this very position. At least on one important point that is unclear in Bruno's published writings, a recently discovered document from his last years throws a good deal of light.

Some of Bruno's chief ethical doctrines are contained in his famous *Eroici furori,* a group of dialogues in which the recital and interpretation of a series of poems by Bruno and others, and the explanation of a number of symbolic mottos and devices, occupy a large place, interrupting as well as enlivening the presentation of the chief philosophical ideas. In a free variation upon the common theme of Platonizing love treatises, Bruno opposes heroic love and frenzy to vulgar love. Heroic love has a divine object, and leads the soul in a gradual ascent from the sense world through intelligible objects toward God. The union with God, which is the ultimate and infinite goal of our will and intellect, cannot be attained during the present life. Hence heroic love is for the philosopher a continuous torment. But it derives an inherent nobility and dignity from its ultimate goal, which will be reached after death. It is this emphasis on the suffering which accompanies the unfulfilled heroic love during the present life that distinguishes Bruno's theory from that of most previous writers on the subject, and this may also explain why he chose to call the higher love heroic rather than divine.

A more central aspect of Bruno's thought is expressed in his dialogue *De la causa, principio e uno,* in which some of his basic metaphysical ideas are discussed. He starts from the fundamental notion that God must be conceived as a substance, and His effects as accidents. This is a complete reversal of the traditional Aristotelian notion of substance, according to which the term substance had always been applied to particular sense objects, whereas their permanent or passing attributes had been called accidents. For Bruno, there remains only one substance, namely God, and all particular objects, far from being substances, become accidents, that is, passing manifestations of that single substance. This notion resembles in many ways that of Spinoza, and it has often been asserted that Spinoza owed this basic conception to Bruno, although there seems to be no tangible evidence that Spinoza was familiar with Bruno's thought or writings.

In order to know God, Bruno continues, we must know His image, nature. In pursuing this task, Bruno proceeds to apply to the universe the four causes that in Aristotle and his school had merely served as contributing factors in the attempt to understand particular objects or phenomena. Developing some occasional remarks in Aristotle, Bruno divides the four causes into two groups, one of which he calls causes in the stricter sense of the word, and the other, principles. Form and matter are principles because they are intrinsic to their effect, whereas efficient and final cause are external to their effect. He then identifies the efficient cause of the world with the universal intellect, which is the highest faculty of the world soul. He is drawing here on Plotinian notions, and there is no evidence that he is identifying the world soul or its intellect with God. On the contrary, he explicitly distinguishes this world intellect from the divine intellect, and states that it contains in itself all forms and species of nature, just as our intellect contains in itself all its concepts. Working as an internal artist, this world intellect produces out of matter all material forms, which are images derived from its own internal species. The final cause of the world, on the other hand, is nothing but its own perfection.

The principles, that is, internal constituents, of nature are form and matter. They correspond in name to Aristotle's formal and material cause, but are in fact conceived along Plotinian lines. Bruno asserts that the form coincides to a certain extent with the soul, insofar as every form is produced by a soul. For all things are animated by the world soul, and all matter is everywhere permeated by soul and spirit. Thus it may be said that the world soul is the constituent formal principle of the world, just as matter is its constituent material principle. The world is thus a perpetual spiritual substance that merely appears in different forms.

In this way, form and matter are both perpetual substances and principles, and mutually determine each other, whereas the bodies composed of form and matter are perishable, and must be regarded not as substances but as accidents. Bruno thus seems to conceive of particular things as resulting from a changing interpenetration of two universal principles, and in this suggestive and original view also lies the basic difficulty of his philosophy.

In God, Bruno goes on to say, form and matter, actuality and potentiality, coincide. In what appears to be an important modification of his previous statements, he says that also in the universe there is only one principle, which is both formal and material, and thus the universe, considered in its substance, is only one. This one principle, taken with its two aspects, is said to constitute both all corporeal and all incorporeal beings. Bruno here seems to follow the so-called universal hylemorphism of Avicebron, who, too, composes all incorporeal beings of form and matter. This statement reveals still another basic ambiguity, which Bruno had inherited from Cusanus and other earlier philosophers, and which he never completely overcomes, at least in this work. That is, in speaking about nature and the universe, Bruno seems to think primarily in terms of the physical universe, but at the same time he includes in the universe all incorporeal beings except God. Speaking of matter, he insists that it is not merely negative, but contains in itself all forms, thus taking up a theory of Averroes, and departing from both Aristotle and Plotinus, who had thought of matter as pure potentiality.

Identifying the universe with the substance that comprises both form and matter, Bruno states that the universe is one and infinite, that it is being, true and one, whereas all particular things are mere accidents and subject to destruction. There is no plurality of substances in the world, but merely a plurality of manifestations of a single substance. The plurality of things is only apparent and belongs to the surface grasped by our senses, whereas our mind grasps, beyond this surface, the one substance in which all apparent contrasts coincide. This substance is true and good, it is both matter and form, and in it actuality and potentiality are no longer different from each other. In such formulas the distinction between the universe and God seems to disappear, but in one important passage Bruno differentiates between the physical universe known by the philosophers and the archetypal universe believed in by the theologians.

He thus presents us with an impressive and original vision of reality, but if we compare the various statements contained in the dialogue, a few basic ambiguities remain. Form and matter are clearly universal principles for Bruno, but he treats them sometimes as distinct and sometimes as identical, or rather as two aspects of the same principle. The physical and the metaphysical universe are sometimes identified, and sometimes quite clearly distinguished. Finally, the universe is sometimes treated as an image of God, and as distinct from Him, whereas at times this distinction tends to disappear.

Students of Bruno have tried to cope with these difficulties in a variety of ways. Some have emphasized one set of statements over the other, thus making of Bruno either a

Platonist metaphysician or an outright pantheist. Those who have been willing to admit the ambiguities present in his work have often considered the extreme pantheist position to be his true position, and the dualist statements to be concessions made to popular opinion or potential censors or critics. Others have regarded pantheism as the logical consequence of his position, which he came to adopt gradually, the dualist statements representing a mere residual of his earlier views. This last opinion seems to be the soundest of the ones we have cited. However, I am more inclined to think that Bruno had a vision that was not completely expressible in terms of these antitheses, and that he was quite willing to accept the dilemma, that is, both horns of it, as a paradox and an approximation, without wishing to be pushed into a more extreme position. It is no doubt true that in comparison with his favourite sources, Plotinus and Cusanus, Bruno goes much further in the direction of a pantheistic or immanentistic conception. Yet I doubt very much that he wanted to be an extreme pantheist or naturalist. In one of his latest statements, he tries to show that individual minds are particular manifestations of the universal mind, just as particular bodies are manifestations of universal matter. This statement is a welcome addition to his other writings, in which this particular doctrine is not so clearly stated. It also shows that his position was closer to Cusanus and to the dualistic passages in his dialogues than many interpreters have been willing to admit.

No less interesting and historically significant than Bruno's metaphysics is his conception of the physical universe as we find it developed in his dialogue *De l'infinito, universo e mondi.* In this work, Bruno restates the Copernican system of the universe, and gives it for the first time a philosophical meaning. His chief emphasis is on the infinity of the universe as a whole, as against the innumerable finite worlds that are contained in it. This distinction between the universe and the worlds is borrowed from Lucretius, as is the notion of the infinity of the universe, which is not found in Copernicus at all. We now know that in the sixteenth century the infinity of the physical universe was asserted by Thomas Digges, prior to Bruno, but it is not certain that Bruno was familiar with the writings of this predecessor. We might also compare the view of Patrizi, who assumed an infinite external void surrounding our finite world. For Bruno, there are many such worlds as ours, and the universe outside our world is not a void. Moreover, unlike Patrizi, he conceives our world or solar system according to the system of Copernicus. He further insists that this infinity of the universe cannot be perceived by the senses, but is disclosed by the judgment of reason, thus reverting to Democritus from the sensationalism of the Epicureans and Telesio.

The infinite universe is for Bruno the image of an infinite God. In this context, at least, he clearly distinguishes between God and the universe, and his position may be compared with that of Cusanus. Yet whereas Cusanus reserves true infinity for God alone, Bruno uses the relation between the universe and God as an argument for the infinity of the former. Since God is infinite, also the universe must be infinite, although in a different sense.

As for Patrizi and others, the stars are no longer attached to rigid spheres, but move freely in the infinite space. Yet in accordance with the Neoplatonic tradition, and with a view adopted by most medieval Aristotelians, Bruno assigns the cause for the motion of the stars to their internal principles or souls. The earth is also in motion, and may hence be considered as one of the stars. Only the universe as a whole is at rest, whereas all particular worlds contained in it are in motion. The universe as a whole has no absolute center and no absolute direction; that is, we cannot talk of an upward or a downward direction in an absolute sense. Gravity and lightness have merely a relative meaning with reference to the parts of the universe toward which a given body is moving. This view of Bruno's may be characterized as half-Aristotelian. That is, in his denial of an absolute center, Bruno repeats a formula of Cusanus, interpreting it in a Lucretian sense. In his denial of an absolute direction, he follows the atomists against Aristotle; but in retaining a relative direction, and, above all, in retaining the distinction between gravity and lightness, he is still under the spell of Aristotelian physics.

The individual stars, Bruno argues, are subject to continual change through the influx and efflux of atoms, but persist through some internal or external force. The notion of influx and efflux is again based on atomism, and the notion that the stars are subject to change is another important departure from Aristotelian cosmology, in which the celestial objects, as distinct from the sublunar ones, are considered unchangeable and incorruptible. Yet the internal force seems to be a Neoplatonic rather than an atomistic conception. Bruno knows that the fixed stars are at varying distances from us, and thus discards the traditional notion of a single sphere of fixed stars. He thinks that the entire universe is filled with aether even in the so-called empty spaces between the stars. All stars in the universe are divided into two basic groups, which he calls suns and earths. The prevailing element of the former is fire, of the latter, water. Our earth is like a star, and when seen from the outside, it shines like the other stars. Bruno also assumes that the various worlds outside our own are inhabited. He denies the existence of elementary spheres, thus rejecting another basic conception of traditional Aristotelian cosmology, and calls the notion of a hierarchy of nature a mere product of the imagination.

Bruno's cosmology is quite suggestive, and it anticipates in a number of ways the conception of the universe as it was to be developed by modern physics and astronomy. He is not only the first major philosopher who adopted the Copernican system, but also one of the first thinkers who boldly discarded such time-honored notions as the radical distinction between things celestial and earthly, and the hierarchical view of nature. Being aware of the novelty of his view, he does not spare Aristotle or his followers, whom he pursues with a series of polemical attacks. The fact that Bruno still retains some residuals of Aristotelian physics should not be exaggerated, and it should have been expected in any case. On the other hand, it has been rightly stressed that he was a forerunner, but not a founder, of modern science and philosophy. He was unaware of the role that mathematics and experimental observation were to play in modern science, and did not develop a precise method by which his assertions might have been tested or demonstrated. His merit and his limitation lie in the fact that, through his intuition and vision, he anticipated a number of ideas that resemble those which later centuries were to adopt and to develop on the basis of much more solid evidence. Yet the more we are inclined to extol the role of imagination in the sciences, alongside that of empirical observation and logical deduction, the more we should appreciate the contribution made by such thinkers as Bruno.

The extent of Bruno's influence during the following centuries is hard to estimate. His condemnation and terrible end made it impossible for any Catholic scholar to read or cite him overtly, and even in Protestant countries his works seem to have had a rather limited circulation for a long time. Yet Galileo could have read Bruno long before the latter was condemned, and the resemblance between certain passages in Galileo and Bruno that deal with the place of the earth in the universe is so great that it may not be incidental after all. I am also inclined to see a connection between Bruno and Spinoza, for the conception of the relation between God and particular things as substance and accidents is too similar and too unusual to be a mere coincidence. Aside from many other differences, it was quite natural for Spinoza to replace Bruno's two basic principles, form (or soul) and matter, which have a Neoplatonic, and if you wish an Aristotelian, origin, with the attributes of thought and extension, which are derived from the system of Descartes. I cannot discuss the question whether the theory of monads, as developed in some of Bruno's Latin writings, may have had an influence on Leibniz.

Arthur D. Imerti   (essay date 1964)

SOURCE: An introduction to *The Expulsion of the Triumphant Beast* by Giordano Bruno, translated by Arthur D. Imerti, Rutgers University Press, 1964, pp. 3-68.

[*Imerti is an Italian-American educator, scholar, and author. In this excerpt, Imerti discusses* Lo spaccio de la bestia trionfante, *focussing on aspects of the work that were viewed as heretical by the Roman Catholic Church, and on portions of the work in which Bruno criticizes his society.*]

Bruno's opening words to Sidney in the "Epistola explicatoria" of *Lo spaccio* exhort his readers to be guided by the "intellectual sun," symbolic of reason, "the teacher of the senses, the father of substances, the author of life." The philosopher admonishes: "Cieco chi non vede il sole, stolto chi nol conosce, ingrato chi nol ringrazia. . . ." ("He is blind who does not see the sun, foolish who does not recognize it, ungrateful who is not thankful unto it. . . .")

He who had encountered the opposition of the inquisitorial authorities in Italy, the jeers of his students at Toulouse, and the scepticism of his colleagues at Oxford had no illusions as to the reception his ideas would be given by what he calls the multitude of "foolish, perverse, and wicked" pedants who, "under their severe brows and subdued countenances, their profuse beards and magisterial and grave togas, studiously, to universal harm, contain ignorance no less despicable than haughty, and no less pernicious than the most celebrated ribaldry." The philosopher is deeply confident, however, that *Lo spaccio* will be received with favor by men of the caliber of the erudite, open-minded, and generous Sir Philip Sidney, among whom "works and heroic effects will not be believed to be fruits of no value and vain."

Bruno, dedicating to his friend and benefactor "the numbered and arranged seeds of his moral philosophy," indicates that *Lo spaccio* is not his definitive ethical work, although there are certain truths therein expressed, which he insists must be defended against the assaults of "the wrinkles and the brows of the hypocrites." He affirms that his reason for writing these dialogues is not to disapprove of "that which commonly is esteemed worthy of being approved by all wise and good men," but, rather, to reprove the contrary. He expresses the hope "that there be not anyone of so gross a mind, and so malicious a spirit," that he may conclude that what is written in *Lo spaccio* is said by him in a definitive manner. Determined that no one should say that he is taking "aim at the truth," and hurling stones "against the honest, the useful, the natural, and, consequently, the divine," the philosopher voices the hope that his readers will examine and weigh all the evidence objectively before pronouncing judgment.

Bruno's concept of truth is the source of the most heretical premises contained in *Lo spaccio.* Indeed, the eternal search for truth is the very foundation of the ethical system implicit in the work. Few thinkers have possessed Bruno's fanatical devotion to her; few have been willing to die in her cause. The following passage in *Lo spaccio,* uttered by Saulino, with its ardent allusions to truth, is strongly autobiographical:

> Rather, the more and more she is impugned, the more and more she is resuscitated and grows. Without a defender and protector, she defends herself; and yet she loves the company of a few wise men. She hates the multitude, does not show herself before those who do not seek her for her own sake, and does not wish to be declared to those who do not humbly expose themselves to her, or to all those who fraudulently seek her; and therefore she dwells most high, whither all gaze, and few see.

Bruno equates truth with Divinity itself, declaring that she is "the divinity and the sincerity, goodness and beauty, of things," the unity and goodness which preside over all things. As cause and principle, she is before all things; as substance, she is in all things. Truth, declares the philosopher, is "ideal, natural, and notional"; or, in other terms, "metaphysics, physics, and logic."

The philosopher maintains that truth cannot be crushed by violence, nor can she be corrupted by time; for she is relative to time, and reveals herself as the substance of things in myriad and everchanging forms. She is manifest in all living things, operating through the eternal laws of an immanent God identified with a timeless universe, and although she may appear different in each succeeding generation, she is immutable and immortal. That which in the physical world is revealed to us through our senses, says Bruno, and that which we can comprehend, thanks to our intellect, "is not the highest and first truth, but a certain figure, a certain image, a certain splendor of her."

It is Bruno's belief that if man wishes to ascertain truth, he must approach theology, philosophy, and science without any preconceived attitudes. He, as Brunnhofer points out, is "perhaps the only philosopher who does not claim to have an infalliable method of arriving at the truth [Hermann Brunnhofer, *Giordano Bruno's Weltanschauug and Verhängniss,* 1882]." His impatience with those who lay claim to such "infallible methods" is clearly revealed in the following passage from **De la causa:**

> Because it is a thing fit for an ambitious person, and for a presumptuous, vain, and envious mind, to want to persuade others that there is only one way to investigate and to come to the cognition of nature; and for one to convince himself that that is so, is a thing worthy of a mad man and a man without reason.

The philosopher clung to the belief that there is an element of truth in all doctrines. Thus, in **"De umbris idearum"** he declares:

> We do not abolish the mysteries of the Pythagoreans. We do not belittle the faith of the Platonists and do not despise the ratiocinations of the Peripatetics insofar as these ratiocinations find a real foundation.

An examination of Bruno's sources, and the conclusions the philosopher draws from them, will aid us in identifying and understanding the "certain truths" he wishes to defend; and we shall observe that although as expressed in **Lo spaccio,** they may indeed at times seem fragmentary and indefinitive, the tone in which they are stated leaves little doubt as to their heretical meaning. Thus, the Roman inquisitors could not help but grasp the significance of the heretical religious philosophy that lends the work its controversial nature. Berti observes that although **Lo spaccio** seems to be, on the surface, an indictment of paganism, it is in effect "the proclamation of natural religion and the negation of all positive religions [Domenico Berti, *Vita di Giordano Bruno da Nola,* 1868]."

Probably no man did more to focus the attention of Western thinkers upon pre-Socratic philosophers than did Aristotle himself, their greatest Greek opponent; for in order to refute their doctrines, he was compelled to name many of these thinkers in his *Physics* and *Metaphysics.* It was Bruno's close familiarity with Aristotle's works and his dissatisfaction with the Stagirite that, according to McIntyre, "led him into greater sympathy with the naturephilosophers whom Aristotle decried" [J. Lewis McIntyre, *Giordano Bruno,* 1903]. **Lo spaccio** contains reminiscences of pre-Socratic and Neo-Platonic philosophers whose thinking was considered suspect by the Church. Toward these Bruno maintained the attitude of an eclectic. He does not attempt, as McIntyre points out, "to appreciate their relative value, nor to discover any evolution of thought through the successive systems. From each," continues McIntyre, "he takes that which agrees or appears to agree with his own philosophy, and treats it as an anticipation of, or an authority for, the latter."

Thus, in developing the concept of the Absolute One, Bruno draws upon both Xenophanes, who represents "the static aspect of pantheism," and Heraclitus, who represents the more dynamic concept of pantheism, that is to say, that of a divinity which manifests itself through the finite. To Pythagoras, Bruno owes his concept of the transmigration of souls.

From Anaxagoras, who was the first to introduce the teleological principle in the explanation of the universe, Bruno learned of the relationship existing between Absolute Being and Finite Being. For his doctrine of "motion and change" he is indebted to both Heraclitus and Empedocles.

In the imagery of his language, in his dialectic, in his love of mathematics, in his rational view of life, Bruno shows a close affinity with Plato. His mysticism and his concepts of "substance" and "immanence," on the other hand, seem to stem from Plotinus and other Neo-Platonists.

In **Lo spaccio** Bruno reveals his strong attraction to the mysteries of the Egyptian religion, his curiosity in that cult having been aroused by his reading of the Hermetic writings of Iamblichus and of Lucius Apuleius.

It was not the substance of Ramón Lull's teaching but, rather, his method that attracted Bruno to him; for through this method the Nolan and many other Renaissance thinkers believed that they could acquire universal knowledge.

With his theory of the "coincidence of contraries" and his use of mathematical symbols to explain the Deity, the German cardinal, Nicholas Cusanus, exerted a profound influence upon Bruno. But, as we shall observe, Bruno's conclusions differ fundamentally from those of Cusanus.

Bruno's concept of "substance" is, perhaps, the most heretical premise of **Lo spaccio,** since from it he derives his concept of "immanence," the source of his religion of nature. His religion of nature, in turn, becomes the source of his philosophy of knowledge and of his heretical sociopolitical ideas.

Bruno speaks of an "eternal incorporeal substance" and of an "eternal corporeal substance." Although, according to him, "eternal incorporeal substance" does indeed have "familiarity with bodies," it does not become a "subject of composition," since no part of it can be "changed, formed, or deformed." It is, according to the philosopher, "the divinity, the hero, the demon, the particular god, the intelligence," the "efficient and formative principle," about which the composition of all beings is formed. It is the intrinsic principle and cause of "harmony, complexion and symmetry," and is not an accident derived from these, as taught by Aristotle and Galen, whom Bruno places among "fools under the name of philosophers." In short, it is, according to the philosopher, the "substance which is truly man." Since "eternal incorporeal substance" is rational principle, it is the governor and ruler of the body, and, therefore, superior to and independent of it.

On the other hand, "eternal corporeal substance" emanates from "eternal incorporeal substance." It is not "producible exnihilo, nor reducible ad nihilum, but rarefiable, condensible, formable." But whereas "eternal corporeal substance" remains unchanged, "the complexion is changed, the figure is modified, the being is altered, the fortune is varied."

We shall now turn to Bruno's conception of the doctrine of "motion and change." The opening pronouncement of *Lo spaccio,* uttered by Sophia, is a formulation of this doctrine, evolved by Heraclitus and Empedocles. But whereas the doctrine developed by the pre-Socratic Greek philosophers is, more specifically, of a cosmic nature, in *Lo spaccio* Bruno emphasizes the doctrine's ethical implications. Thus, asserting that there would be no pleasure if "bodies, matter, and entity" did not experience "mutation, variety, and vicissitude," Bruno's Sophia declares:

> The state of venereal ardor torments us, the state of requited lust saddens us; but that which satisfies us is the transit from one state to the other. In no present being do we find pleasure, if the past has not become wearisome to us. Labor does not please except in the beginning, after rest; and unless in the beginning, after labor, there is no pleasure in rest.

In his development of the doctrine of "motion and change" Bruno leans heavily upon the Pythagorean belief in "metempsychosis," a teaching considered heretical by the Catholic Church. For whereas the Church in its Credo unequivocally states its belief in an ultimate return of the soul to its resurrected body, Bruno declares that, guided by the "Fate of Mutation," the soul of man will incur infinite changes of "life and of fortune." He believes that the "High Justice, which presides over all things," will see to it that man is rewarded with a body befitting his conduct in his present state of "metempsychosis." Thus, according to Bruno, a man who has led an "equine or porcine" existence in this life will inherit "equine or porcine" forms in another.

From the consideration of the concept of "motion and change" Bruno is logically led to his interpretation of the doctrine of the "coincidence of contraries," developed by Nicholas Cusanus.

Cusanus maintains that since finite nature is the result of the creative act of an infinite God, those effects which in her seem contradictory to finite minds, do coincide in the mind of God, their creator, who is both the "maximum absolute" and the "minimum absolute."

Bruno believes that "the beginning, the middle, and the end, the birth, the growth, and the perfection of all that we see, come from contraries, through contraries, into contraries, to contraries." He declares that where there is "contrariety, there is action and reaction, there is motion, there is diversity, there is number, there is order, there are degrees, there is succession, there is vicissitude." Every being, then, finds himself "with such a composition, with such accidents and circumstances . . . because of differences which arise from contraries." All contraries are resolved or coincide in one original and prime contrary, "which is the first principle of all the others, which are the proximate efficients of every change and vicissitude." According to the Nolan, that which gives us pleasure and satisfaction is the "mutation from one extreme to the other

through its participants and motion from one contrary to the other through its intermediate points." Consequently, there is a greater attraction between two contraries than between like and like.

Bruno, indicating his indebtedness to Cusanus for his "coincidence of contraries," manifests that he considers it not only an epistemological but also an ethical doctrine. The attraction of contraries becomes for him the very basis of social and political relationships. Therefore, he maintains that there is no appreciation of justice where there is no injustice, no appreciation of harmony where one has not experienced its contrary.

Bruno placed Providence next to Truth in his descending ethical scale. Because she is a companion of Truth, she must be of the essence of Truth; and like the latter, she is both liberty and necessity. She is that attribute which links rational beings with Prudence, inherent in "temporal discourse." She is known as Providence when she "influences and is found in superior principles"; as Prudence when she is "effectuated in us." Prudence is, for Bruno, a reflection of Providence, whom he compares with the sun, "as that body which warms the earth and diffuses light." She abides in universals and particulars, having Dialectic as her "handmaiden" and Acquired Wisdom as her "guide." She instills in human beings the faculty of reason, through which they learn to adapt themselves "to things, to times, and to occasions."

As are Truth and Providence, Sophia, or Wisdom, is of two species. The first is "the superior, supracelestial, and ultramundane," which is "invisible, infigurable, and incomprehensible" and is "above all things, in all things, and between all things"; the second species is "the consecutive, mundane, and inferior," which is "figured in the heaven, illustrated in minds, communicated through words, digested through art, refined through conversation, delineated through writings." Bruno identifies Superior Wisdom with Providence and Truth, which are attributes of the Deity. Earthly, mundane Sophia is not of the essence of Wisdom, but merely partakes of her. Bruno compares earthly Sophia with "an eye which receives light and is illuminated by an external wandering light." She is that indispensable faculty through which man contemplates, comprehends, and explains Truth, "toward which, through various steps and diverse ladders, all aspire, strive, study, and, by rising, force themselves to reach."

Bruno is severe with those who knowingly distort wisdom, calling those who claim to know what they do not know, rash sophists; those who deny knowing what they do know, ungrateful to the "active intellect," "injurious toward truth," and "outrageous" toward wisdom. He condemns all those who do not seek wisdom for her own sake, but would rather sell her "for money or honors or for other kinds of gain." Bruno is scornful of those who desire wisdom in order to win acclaim, or "to detract, and to be able to oppose and stand against the happiness" of those whom they may call "troublesome censors and rigid observers."

For Bruno, Law, the daughter of Sophia, who consists of Divine Law and her derivative, the Law of Nations, is the divine instrument through which "princes reign and kingdoms and republics are maintained." She is the "art of arts and discipline of disciplines," through which men of diverse complexions, customs, inclinations, and wills "must be governed and repressed." Because she is conceived differently by different peoples, she adapts herself to "the complexion and customs of peoples and nations, suppresses audacity through fear, and sees to it that goodness is secure among the wicked."

In his peregrinations through war-torn Europe, Bruno had ample opportunity to observe that the lust for power, which characterized his times, had produced a widespread disregard for law and agreements between and within nations, governed by unprincipled absolute rulers, of which Machiavelli's prince was the prototype. Bruno's condemnation of the faithlessness and hypocrisy of princes is a devastating indictment of his times and a refutation of Machiavelli's political philosophy, as it is expounded in *The Prince.* He declares:

> See to what point the world is reduced, because it has become custom and proverb that in governing faith is not observed. . . . What will the world come to if all republics, kingdoms, dominions, families, and individuals say that one must be a saint with the saint, perverse with the perverse? And will they excuse themselves for being wicked because they have a wicked man as a companion or neighbor?

The immoral environment engendered by these absolute princes, influenced by sycophants of every description, helped to create a faithless, dissolute, irresponsible, and indolent upper class. With penetrating insight and subtle irony, Bruno realistically depicts the dissipation of the sons of the rich, surrounded by a host of servants, as they while away the hours "in the house of Idleness."

Bruno was highly critical of the libidinous conduct of both the married and unmarried women of the upper classes. He deplored the consequences of premarital relations of young women, although he did not consider Virginity something worthy in herself, "because," declares Bruno's Jove, "of herself, she is neither a virtue nor a vice, and does not contain either goodness, dignity, or merit." He did evince great concern, however, for women who unwisely submitted themselves to abortions; and he deemed that it would have been better, had they prevented the waste of that seed which could "give rise to heroes."

The lack of interest shown by wealthy women in their children, whom they often entrusted to dirty and incompetent nursemaids, and their preference, instead, for domestic animals, provoked Bruno's indignation. With cutting irony he satirizes the distorted sense of values characteristic of one of these mothers, who addresses her child thus:

> Oh my son, made in my image, as you show yourself to be a man, would that you also showed yourself to be a rabbit, a she-puppy, a marten, a cat, and a sable. Just as surely as I have committed you into the arms of this servant, of this domestic, of this ignoble nursemaid, of this filthy, dirty, drunken woman, so infecting you with her fetidness (because it is also neces-

sary that you sleep with her), she will easily cause you to die. I, I myself should be she who should carry you in her arms, should nourish you, suckle you, comb you, sing to you, caress you, kiss you, as I do with this gentle animal.

Bruno did not limit himself to satirizing the corruption, despotism, and violence of his times. He proposed as a positive solution the reinstatement of the goddess Law as the moral guide and teacher of nations, who should be especially concerned with "whatever appertains to the communion of men, to civilized behavior." Viewing with alarm the mutual distrust between the governors and the governed, he maintained that the "potent," that is to say those who ruled, should be "sustained by the impotent," or the governed. He insists, however, that "the weak be not oppressed by the stronger."

The state advocated by Bruno must foster "virtues and studies, useful and necessary to the commonwealth"; and its citizens, who most profit from them, should be "exalted and remunerated." Demonstrating a philanthropic concern for the poor, Bruno recommends that they be aided by their wealthy fellow citizens; and in words which might be construed as socialistic, he urges that "the indolent, the avaricious, and the owners of property be scorned and held in contempt."

The citizens of Bruno's state, which should be ruled by laws based on "justice" and "possibility," must not only respect and honor their temporal rulers but also preserve "the fear and the cult of invisible powers."

Despite the fact that out of a sense of gratitude he had extravagant words of praise for such absolute rulers as Henry III of France, Bruno condemns absolutism both in religion and in the state. Advocating the deposition of tyrants and favoring republics, he urges that "just rulers and realms be constituted and strengthened."

Bruno's concept of justice is predicated upon his belief that the state must exert a moral influence upon the lives of its citizens. Therefore, it rests upon the state to see that justice be meted out to all "without rigor," and that it sponsor "Equity, Righteousness," "Gratitude," and "Good Conscience." The state should see to it that individuals be conscious of their own worth, that elders be respected, that equals view one another with equanimity, and that superiors be benign "toward inferiors."

The Roman Republic was for Bruno the symbol of justice, law, and order, that justice, law, and order which he observed in operation in the world of nature. He concurred with Machiavelli in the opinion that Rome attained her leading position among nations, not because she was favored by Fortune, as believed by the ancients, but rather because she practiced virtue. Republican Rome, where the cordial rapport between the state and religion promoted peace and happiness for all its citizens, was for Bruno the ideal state, to be emulated by other peoples. He extolls the Roman people for their "magnanimity, justice, and mercy," qualities which, according to Bruno, made them akin to the gods. Jove's words eloquently express the philosopher's admiration for the Romans:

> because with their magnificent deeds they, more

than the other nations, knew how to conform with and resemble them, by pardoning the subdued, overthrowing the proud, righting wrongs, not forgetting benefits, helping the needy, defending the afflicted, relieving the oppressed, restraining the violent, promoting the meritorious, abasing criminals; and by spreading terror and utmost destruction among the other nations by means of scourges and axes, and honoring the gods with statues and colossi. Whence, consequently, that people appeared more bridled and restrained from vices of an uncivilized and barbarous nature, more excellent and ready to perform generous enterprises than any other people that has ever been seen. And as long as such were their law and religion, their customs and deeds, such were their honor and their happiness.

Bruno's concept of the Deity as pure rational principle, and as both cause and effect, made all positive religions, with their emphasis on the anthropomorphic attributes of God, repugnant to him. Catholicism was no exception, although the universal structure of the Catholic Church, which united peoples of diverse customs and races, so reminiscent of Rome, strongly appealed to the philosopher. Nevertheless, his sly references to monks, monasteries, and relics hint at his disapproval of some of the basic tenets of Catholicism. His ironic allusions to the New Testament, and particularly his satire of Christ, whose life on earth he allegorizes in Orion, and whose "trinitarian" nature, in Chiron the Centaur, are an implied refutation not only of Catholicism but of Christianity itself.

He assailed the Protestants for their confiscation of Catholic schools, universities, hospitals, and other properties, accusing them of being disseminators of that discord and injustice which wreaked so much suffering and destruction upon Europe, at much inconvenience to himself. Referring to Protestant theologians, constantly bickering among themselves, he caustically remarks:

> among ten thousand such pedants there is not one who has not compiled his own catechism, and who, if he has not published it, at least is about to publish that one which approves of no other institution but his own, finding in all the others something to condemn, reprove, and doubt; besides, the majority of them are found in disagreement among themselves, rescinding today what they wrote the day before.

He who had suffered humiliation at the hands of the Calvinists at Geneva acrimoniously impugns their doctrine of predestination and their emphasis on faith, reproaching them for wanting "to reform the deformed laws and religions." The Calvinistic belief in predestination, according to Bruno, induced its adherents "to the contempt of, or at least to little concern for, legislators and laws, by giving them to understand that they propose impossible things, and rule as if in jest." The biting sarcasm with which Bruno refers to the Calvinists and their doctrines, typical of his satirical style, is vividly illustrated in the following passage:

> And so let them depart from those profaned dwellings and not eat of that accursed bread; but

let them go and inhabit those pure and uncontaminated houses and feed upon those victuals that have been destined to them by means of their reformed law, and recently brought forth by these pious individuals—they who hold completed works in such low esteem, and only because of an importune, vile, and foolish imagination consider themselves rules of heaven and children of the gods, and believe more in, and attribute more to, a vain, bovine, and asinine faith than to a useful, real, and magnanimous effect.

Bruno is harsh in his criticism of the Jews, whom he calls the "excrement of Egypt." He maintains that Moses, "who left the court of Pharaoh, learned in all the sciences of the Egyptians," imparted their knowledge to the Jews; and he implies that the evolution of Jewish monotheism, with its emphasis on a personal God, destroyed the concept of the Deity as immanent principle, embodied in the natural religion of the Egyptians.

In his interpretation of the Old Testament Bruno's views clash with both Christian and Jewish teachings. He regards its stories as fables, or metaphorical representations of history, passed on from the Egyptians to the Babylonians and then to the Hebrews. He adduces as evidence of his premise the "metaphor of the raven," which, he declares, was "first found and developed in Egypt and then taken by the Hebrews, through whom this knowledge was transmitted from Babylonia, in the form of a story. . . ."

Bruno is struck by the variations of the Osiris myth in the ancient Mediterranean civilizations, to which he makes a brief allusion. However, he specifically points out analogies between such Greek myths as that of Apollo and the Raven and the biblical Noah and the Raven, between that of Deucalion and Noah, and between that of Cetus and Jonah and the Whale.

The source of the myths shared by the Greeks with the Hebrews, he insists, is not Hebrew but Egyptian. Egypt, indeed, is for Bruno the source of all the myths and fables of the Mediterranean world, all being poetical representations of events dating back to the dawn of Western civilization.

Historically, Egypt represents for Bruno the cradle of Western religion. The Egyptian cult, with its worship of the living effects of nature, seems to come closest to his concept of natural religion. The following quotation from Iamblichus, which in the form of a prophecy laments the disappearance of the natural religion of the Egyptians and the dire effect this loss will have upon humanity, prognosticates a return to the religion of nature; and Bruno's employment of this passage in *Lo spaccio* is most significant:

> Do you not know, oh Asclepius, that Egypt is the image of heaven or, better said, the colony of all things that are governed and practiced in heaven? To speak the truth, our land is the temple of the world. But woe is me! The time will come when Egypt will appear to have been in vain the religious cultivator of divinity, because divinity, remigrating to heaven, will leave Egypt deserted. And this seat of divinity will remain widowed of every religion, having been deprived of the presence of the gods. . . . Oh Egypt, oh

Egypt! Of your religions there will remain only the fables, still incredible to future generations, to whom there will be nothing else that may narrate your pious deeds save the letters sculptured on stones. . . . Shadows will be placed before light, death will be judged to be more useful than life, no one will raise his eyes toward heaven. The religious man will be considered insane, the impious man will be considered prudent, the furious man, strong, the most wicked man, good. And believe me, capital punishment will still be prescribed for him who will apply himself to the religion of the mind. . . . Only pernicious angels will remain, who, mingling with men, will force upon the wretched ones every audacious evil as if it were justice, giving material for wars, rapines, frauds, and all other things contrary to the soul and to natural justice. And this will be the old age and the disorder and irreligion of the world. But do not doubt, Asclepius, for after these things have occurred, the lord and father God, governor of the world, the omnipotent provider, by a deluge of water or of fire, of diseases or of pestilences or of other ministers of his compassionate justice, will doubtlessly then put an end to such a blot, recalling the world to its ancient countenance [*De mysteriis Aegyptiorum,* 1516].

In the words of Isis conveyed by Sophia, Bruno contends that despite the fact that it is true that the Egyptians resorted to some abusive practices in their natural religion, they nevertheless worshiped "the Deity, one and simple and absolute in itself, multiform and omniform in all things"; and therefore, he arrives at the conclusion that their cult was far superior to the anthropomorphic polytheism of the Greeks.

A careful study of *Lo spaccio,* of *De la causa* and of *De l'infinito* would seem to confirm the opinion, held by some scholars, that Bruno was not only a true pantheist but also the direct ancestor of Spinoza. The universe as viewed by both Bruno and Spinoza is governed by an immanent Deity, who is absolute principle; but whereas Spinoza conceives of a static, determined universe, which is merely "the statue of God," Bruno conceives of one containing both necessity and freedom.

Certainly the most heretical aspect of Bruno's philosophy in *Lo spaccio* is his concept of a religion of nature, derived from his doctrine of "immanence."

In developing his concept of "immanence," Bruno establishes the premise that "animals and plants are living effects of Nature," which, he declares, is "nothing else but God in things," or, expressed in other terms, "natura est deus in rebus." Thus, according to Bruno, the universe is an emanation of the Deity within it. Referring to Bruno's universe, Spaventa declares that it is not "the tomb of dead divinity," but rather "the seat of living divinity . . . the true and only life of God." Bruno's Deity, since he is the substance of all things, cannot limit or divorce himself from his infinite universe; for, according to Cassirer, in Bruno's universe, "the one and infinite substance cannot help but reveal itself to itself, in an infinity of effects" [Ernst Cassirer, *Storia della filosofia moderna,* 1952]. Consequently, potency and act coincide in the Deity; and he

is one and the same with the reality that emanates from him.

Bruno believes that Divinity, which is latent in nature, "working and glowing differently in different subjects . . . through diverse physical forms in certain arrangements . . . succeeds in making them participants . . . in her being, in her life and intellect." He alludes to the "ladder of Nature . . . by which Divinity descends even to the lowest things," just as all rational beings "by means of a life, resplendent in natural things," rise "to the life which presides over them."

From Bruno's philosophy of nature is derived his philosophy of knowledge. Since multiform nature in which all opposites coincide is, according to him, the infinite emanation of a Deity who is absolute reason, she (nature) is the teacher of all rational beings. The inference that we may draw from *Lo spaccio* is that the more deeply man penetrates into the laws of nature, by virtue of his intellect, the closer will he come to an understanding of the unity that exists between him and the immanent principle. For in Bruno's doctrine, as Cassirer maintains, the "intellect and all its determinations are a representation and so to speak a symbolic imitation of the same original principle from whose foundation nature has its origin." It is, then, through purely intellectual processes, rather than through a mystical experience, that rational beings can become one with God. Upon this point Gentile observes:

> The knowledge of divinity as championed by Bruno is not ecstasy, or immediate union, although it is indeed union that it has as its end, whereupon the spirit, as he says, "becomes a god upon intellectual contact with that object, deity." It is a rational process, a discourse of the intellect, a true and appropriate philosophy [Giovanni Gentile, *Il pensiero italiano del rinascimento,* 1940].

Bruno scoffs at the classical myth of the Golden Age, so often used as a theme by the writers of the Renaissance; for he, like Hegel, concluded that man living in that legendary period of "peace and plenty" was little more than beast. He firmly believes that man, the "artisan and efficient of God, sacred by his very humanity," could reproduce in society the unity and harmony established in the universe by its immanent, rational principle.

Lo spaccio envisages a society in which the natural religion of the Egyptians, in its purest sense, and the speculative intellect of the Greeks would coincide in a sociopolitical structure patterned after that of the Roman Republic. The source of the state, which Bruno conceives of as "an ethical substance," is God, "the absolute reality, or reality which is the principle of all realities." The state envisaged by the philosopher would be one containing a unity of law and religion, rather than a separation of "the divine from law and civil life." In this state, which in some aspects foreshadows Vico's idealization, natural religion, philosophy, the arts and sciences, would combine to form a religion of reason. Of this ideal state, contemplated by Bruno, Giusso declares:

> In Bruno, as later in Vico, is designed and prophesied, as the perfect state of civilization,

that state in which the arts and the sciences, "since they derive their being from religions and laws, may serve laws and religions" [Lorenzo Giusso, *Scienza e filosofia in Giordano Bruno*, 1955].

Frances A. Yates   (essay date 1964)

SOURCE: "Giordano Bruno: Last Published Work," in *Giordano Bruno and the Hermetic Tradition*, Routledge and Kegan Paul, Ltd., 1964, pp. 325-37.

[*In the following excerpt, Yates examines* De imaginum, signorum et idearum compositione, *contending that in this work, Bruno uses his theory of imagination as a means of attaining the Hermetic goal of becoming "one with the universe."*]

Bruno's stay in Frankfort, where the three Latin poems were printed, falls into two parts. He went there about the middle of 1590, paid a visit to Switzerland during 1591, after which he returned to Frankfort.

A curious character called Hainzell (Johannes Henricius Haincelius), native of Augsburg, had recently acquired an estate at Elgg, near Zurich. This man was interested in alchemy and in various kinds of occultism and magic, and he liberally entertained at Elgg those who had a reputation for proficiency in such arts. Bruno stayed with him for several months, and it was for the strange lord of Elgg that he wrote a work which he himself regarded as very important. This is the *De imaginum, signorum et idearum compositione,* dedicated to Hainzell and published at Frankfort by Wechel in 1591. Bruno probably wrote it at Elgg, or at Zurich where he stayed for a while, and took the manuscript back with him to Frankfort. It was the last book that he published.

It is a magic memory system which has points in common with the **"De umbris idearum,"** published during the first visit to Paris and dedicated to Henri III. That system, as will be remembered, was based on 150 magic or talismanic images; these were the images of the Egyptian decan demons, images of the planets, and other made up images. Around them, on concentric circles, were placed images of animals, plants, stones, etc., the whole world of physical creation, and on the outer circle, all arts and sciences under the images of 150 inventors and great men. The central magic images formed as it were the magical power-station informing the whole system. The system was attributed to "Hermes" and we thought that it related to the experience, described in one of the Hermetic treatises, of the initiate who reflects within his mind the whole universe in the ecstasy in which he becomes one with the Powers.

In the *De imaginum, signorum et idearum compositione* we have a similar idea but in a more elaborate form. The central magical power-station is now represented by twelve "principles". These are the powers or forces of one personality. The contents of the universe, arts and sciences, and so on, are arranged, or rather incoherently jumbled, in a madly elaborate series of rooms, atria, divisions. This arrangement is related to classical mnemonics in

which notions are remembered through images placed in order on places memorised in buildings. But the mnemonic architecture itself has been "magicised" in Bruno's wild scheme, for some of the various plans of memory places in the book are obviously related to the Hermetic "seal" as can be seen by comparing these supposed mnemonic schemes with "seals" in other works. I shall not bewilder the reader by taking him through these magic memory rooms, but the twelve central "principles" or powers on which the whole scheme centres are interesting because they remind us of the gods in the *Spaccio della bestia trionfante.*

The twelve "principles" of the *De imaginum compositione,* some of which have other principles with them, or in the same "field", are as follows: Jupiter, with Juno; Saturn; Mars; Mercury; Minerva; Apollo; Aesculapius, with whom are grouped Circe, Arion, Orpheus, Sol; Luna; Venus; Cupid; Tellus, with Ocean, Neptune, Pluto.

If these twelve principles are set out in a column, and in a parallel column are listed the gods who are the speakers in the *Spaccio,* the gods who hold the council by which the heaven is reformed, the result is as follows:

	The Twelve Principles of G. Bruno's *De imaginum, signorum et idearum compositione,* 1591		The Gods of G. Bruno's *Spaccia della bestia trianfante,* 1585
I	JUPITER	(18 images)	JUPITER
	JUNO		JUNO
II	SATURN	(4 images)	SATURN
III	MARS	(4 images)	MARS
IV	MERCURY	(7 images)	MERCURY
V	MINERVA	(3 images)	MINERVA
VI	APOLLO	(8 images)	APOLLO
VII	AESCULAPIUS	(6 images)	with his magicians
	CIRCE	(1 image)	CIRCE AND MEDEA
	ARION	(1 image)	with his physician
	ORPHEUS	(3 images)	AESCULAPIUS
VIII	SOL	(1 image)	
IX	LUNA	(6 images)	DIANA
X	VENUS	(10 images)	VENUS and CUPID
XI	CUPID	(2 images)	
XII	TELLUS	(3 images)	CERES
	OCEAN	(1 image)	NEPTUNE
	NEPTUNE	(1 image)	THETIS
	PLUTO	(1 image)	MOMUS
			ISIS

As can easily be seen by comparing the two lists, there is a marked similarity between the gods of the *Spaccio* and the "principles" of *De imaginum compositione.* Many, indeed most of them, are the same. There is a general similarity, too, in the fact that both lists contain the seven planetary gods and also other non-planetary principles. Even these non-planetary principles are somewhat similar in both lists; Minerva is in both; if we include with Apollo in the *Spaccio* list, Circe, Medea, Aesculapius who support Apollo in the council, we have something corresponding to the curious Aesculapius group in the *De im-*

aginum compositione; if we remember that Isis can mean the earth or nature, we have something corresponding to the Isis of the *Spaccio* in the Tellus group of the other work.

One naturally thinks, in connection with these "principles", of the twelve Olympian gods whom Manilius associates with the signs of the zodiac, namely Minerva, Venus, Apollo, Mercury Jupiter, Ceres, Vulcan, Mars, Diana, Vesta, Juno, Neptune. It is possible that Bruno has these in mind but is, as usual, adapting and altering a conventional scheme to suit his own purposes. The astrological aspect of Bruno's "principles" is certainly strong, for the seven which correspond to the seven planets (Jupiter, Saturn, Mars, Mercury, Apollo-Sol, Luna, Venus) are actually illustrated by cuts showing the planetary gods riding in their chariots which are taken from an edition of Hyginus.

Not only are the principles of the *De imaginum compositione* of a rather similar character to the gods of the *Spaccio,* but we also have in the former work elaborate lists of epithets applied to each principle, and these epithets are very like those virtues and vices, good and bad qualities, which ascend into, and descend from, the constellations as the heaven is reformed by the central group of gods. For example, the first principle, Jupiter, in the *De imaginum compositione* is preceded by Cause, Principle, Beginning; surrounding him are Fatherhood, Power, Rule; crowning him are Counsel, Truth, Piety, Rectitude, Candour, amiable Cult, Tranquillity, Liberty, Asylum; on the right side of his chariot are Life, incorrupt Innocence, erect Integrity, Clemency, Hilarity, Moderation, Toleration; on its left side are Pride, Display, Ambition, Dementia, Vanity, Contempt for others, Usurpation. With amazing exuberance, Bruno proliferates epithets like these for all the principles, and the above is only a small selection from the Jupiter epithets. Readers of the *Spaccio* will recognise at once that these are of the same type as those in which the reform of the heavens is described in that work. If we were to use the above Jupiter epithets in the *Spaccio* manner, we would say that to such and such a constellation were ascending Candour, amiable Cult, Tranquillity and so on, displacing the descending opposites of Pride, Dementia, Contempt for others, Usurpation and so on. In the *De imaginum compositione,* Bruno does not describe the constellations, nor use the idea of ascent and descent from them of all these brilliantly expressed notions, but it is clear that he is thinking on the same lines as in the *Spaccio* and that the epithets attached to the principles are the raw material for just such a reform as the one described in the *Spaccio.*

In fact, the *De imaginum compositione* gives the clue to the way the epithets are being used in the *Spaccio.* In the above Jupiter example, we can see that the good epithets belong to Jupiter both as a philosophic principle (Cause, Principle, Beginning) and as the planetary god whose characteristics are "jovial" and benevolent, and who is the special planet of rulers. The good Jupiter epithets describe a good, jovial, benevolent type of rule, with Clemency, Hilarity, Moderation, Toleration. The bad Jupiter epithets belong to the bad side of the planet and to the bad ruler; Pride, Ambition, Contempt for Others, Usurpation.

It was from study of the epithets in *De imaginum compositione.* and how these relate to good and bad sides of planetary influences, that I based the statement which I made in the earlier chapter on the *Spaccio* that the reform really represents a victory of good sides of astral influences over bad ones. The way to study the *Spaccio* is to correlate the epithets in it with those in the *De imaginum compositione* which reveals to what planet the epithets belong.

Further, in the *De imaginum compositione* the epithets for Saturn are nearly all bad, things like Squalor, Moroseness, Severity, Rigidity; and so are the epithets for Mars, such as Ferocity, rabid Rigidity, implacable Truculence. Reading round the constellations in the *Spaccio* and noting what bad things are driven down, it becomes evident, when these are compared with Saturn and Mars epithets in the *De imaginum compositione,* that in the celestial reform, Saturn and Mars are downed by the influence of the good planets, Jupiter, Venus, Sol. Lovely indeed are some of the epithets for Venus and Cupid in the *De imaginum compositione*—sweet Unanimity, placid Consent, holy Friendship, innocuous Geniality, Concordance of things, Union—and concepts like these, together with Jovial concepts, will be found in the celestial reform of the *Spaccio* replacing the miseries of Mars and Saturn.

As in the *Spaccio,* the Sun is of central importance in the *De imaginum compositione.* The centre of the list of principles is taken up by a group all of which are solar in character. First, there is Apollo himself, Wealth, Abundance, Fertility, Munificence. Then there is Aesculapius, son of Apollo, with Circe, daughter of the Sun, and Orpheus and Arion. This group is all magical, representing benevolent magic. Aesculapius is acceptable Healing, vigorous Salubrity, among other things. Circe is magic, very powerful she is, and her power can be used benevolently or malevolently. Orpheus and Arion, represent, I think, solar incantations. Finally, in this group, there is Sol himself as Time, Duration, Eternity, Day and Night.

As in the *Spaccio,* the central principles in the *De imaginum compositione* are solar and magical. We are in the presence of the magical reform, which Bruno is going over again in his mind, more or less as he had thought of it years ago in England.

And further, the application of the magical reform to the present-day situation is also perfectly apparent in the way the epithets are used in the *De imaginum compositione,* just as it is in the *Spaccio* where the "pedants" of intolerance are overcome by the Jovial, Solar, and Venereal reform. In the *De imaginum compositione,* the incantations of Orpheus and Arion overcome the miseries of Saturn, which here have obvious reference to bad forms of religion, Lamentation and Wailing, torn out hair, dust and ashes sprinkled on the head, horrible Squalor, mad Tenacity. The evil Mars has reference to religious wars and persecution. And the "grammarian pedants" are represented by the bad side of Mercury, whose splendid good sides are Eloquence, Refining Culture, perverted by grammarian pedantry (actually mentioned here) to Garrulity, Scurrility, sinister Rumour, biting Vituperation.

Of the non-planetary principles of the *De imaginum compositione* list, Minerva is Truth, Candour, Sincerity; whilst the last group with Tellus at their head represent the philosophy of nature. Tellus is Nature, Maternity, Fecundity, Generation (corresponding to the Isis of natural religion among the gods of the *Spaccio*).

Though in the *De imaginum compositione* these remarkable notions are buried beneath the appalling intricacies of a most unattractive, difficult and daunting work apparently about mnemonics, they are in fact the same as those developed with great literary skill and thrilling imagery in the *Spaccio della bestia trionfante.* Bruno is presenting to the eccentric owner of the castle of Elgg the same panacea for the times, the same magical reformation, as he had presented to Philip Sidney in London six years earlier.

Interesting and important though this is, it is still not the most interesting and revealing aspect of the *De imaginum, signorum et idearum compositione.* For the book is really about, as its title states, "the composition of images, signs and ideas", and by this is meant, the composition of magic or talismanic images, signs and ideas, an "idea" being here the equivalent of a talismanic image. To each of the principles, there are attached a number of talismanic or magic images which have been made up, or composed, for a special purpose. This purpose is, or so I believe, to attract into the personality through imaginative concentration on these images, these twelve principles or powers (only the good aspects of them) and so to become a Solar, Jovial and Venereal Magus, the leader of the magical reformation. The number of images attached to each principle varies very greatly. In the list (see above), the number of images with each principle is stated, so that one can see at a glance that whilst Jupiter (with Juno) has eighteen images; Apollo (if one counts with him the Aesculapius group and Sol) has twenty; and Venus and Cupid have twelve; Saturn and Mars have only four each. The personality which has captured powers through these images will thus be mainly Solar, Jovial, and Venereal, with only a little of Martial or Saturnian qualities.

Extraordinary and strange though this may seem, it is not really more strange than the methods taught by Ficino in his *De vita coelitus comparanda.* Ficino's object was to avoid melancholy and the bad influences of Saturn and Mars, by cultivating the good planets, Sol, Jupiter and Venus. He did this by his mild little astral cults which involved the use of talismans, and he intended it as a medical therapy, to cure melancholy in students. Nevertheless it was really more than this; it was, even with Ficino, a kind of religion with a cult which he managed somehow or other to reconcile with his Christian conscience. He did not aim at becoming a Magus or wonder-worker through it. But he did aim at changing the personality, from a melancholy Saturnian one into a happier and more fortunate Jovial-Solar-Venereal type.

Giordano Bruno, as we know from George Abbot, knew Ficino's *De vita coelitus comparanda* by heart and he has developed Ficino's sub-Christian supposedly medical cult

into an inner technique for the formation of a religious Magus. It is really quite a logical development from Ficino; once you start a religion, there is no knowing what it may become. And we have also always to remember to see Bruno in the context of that Christian Hermetism which was such a major force in the sixteenth century and through which many Catholics and Protestants were trying to ease the religious antagonisms. Bruno always goes much further than the Christian Hermetists for he accepts the magical religion of the *Asclepius* as the best religion. Transferred into the inner life, that religion becomes Ficino's talismanic magic used inwardly to form a Magus aiming at being the leader of a magical religious movement.

In composing his images, Bruno has been influenced by astrological talismans, but diversifies these with normal mythological figures, or combines the talismanic with classical figures, or invents strange figures of his own. I can give only a few examples. Here are some of the images of Sol.

> Apollo with a bow and without the quiver, laughing.
> A man with a bow, killing a wolf, above him a crow flying.
> A young and beautiful man with a lute . . .
> An unfamiliar image . . . a bearded and helmeted man riding on a lion, above his helmet a gold crown . . . On the helmet a great cock with a conspicuous crest and ornamented with many colours.

As can be seen here, ordinary classical images are varied with more magical ones, and this kind of mixture is found in all the lists of images. Bruno often introduces the more magical type of image with the remark that this is an "unfamiliar" image. One has a very curious impression of a mixture of the classical with the barbarous in Bruno's images, when one finds strange, dark and violent forms in close juxtaposition to the classical forms. A striking example of this is Orpheus, the first image of whom is the beautiful young man with the lute taming the animals, but his second image is a black king on a black throne before whom a violent sexual scene takes place (there is possibly an alchemical meaning in this).

In composing these images, is Bruno behaving in a highly original way, peculiar to himself? Or is he leaving a door ajar through which we can peer into something which may lie behind much Renaissance imagery? When a man of the Renaissance "composes" an image to be used on his medal, does he compose it in this kind of talismanic way? What is strange about these images of Bruno's is that he would seem to be reversing the process of the early Renaissance by which the more archaic images achieved a classical form. He seems to be deliberately pushing the classical images back towards a more barbarous form. Why? This could be a part of his general "Egyptianism". He wants to gain more magical power from them, or to recover their magical power.

The curious mixture of classical and barbarous or talismanic forms is strangely apparent in this selection from the Venus images:

A girl rising from the foam of the sea, who on reaching dry land wipes off the humour of the sea with her palms.

The Hours place garments on that naked girl and crown her head with flowers.

A less familiar image, A crowned man of august presence most gentle of aspect, riding on a camel, dressed in a garment the colour of all flowers, leading with his right hand a naked girl, moving in a grave and venerable manner. . . . from the west with a benignant zephyr comes an assembly (? *curia*) of omniform beauty.

The first two images here might be something like Botticelli's "Birth of Venus"; the third, with its crowned man on a camel, is talismanic in type, but softened by notions and forms—the garment the colour of all flowers, the benignant zephyr coming in from the west—such as could never find expression in the fixed rigidity of an ordinary talisman.

Was it something after this manner that Ficino himself composed images, in which the basic magical or talismanic power was softened by expansion into Renaissance classical forms? . . . We [have previously] suggested that Botticelli's "Primavera" is basically a talismanic Venus, expanded in just such a way into a richer classical form, and that the whole picture reflects Ficino's astral cult. In Giordano Bruno's Venus images, composed with a definite magical intention, there is perhaps some confirmation of this suggestion.

There is, too, in Ficino's *De vita coelitus comparanda* a precedent for Bruno's practice of reflecting the magic images within, in the imagination and in the magic memory. We saw that in the curious chapter "On making a figure of the universe", that the figure and its images was to be "reflected in the soul". And there also seemed to be a hint that such remembered images unified the multiplicity of individual things, so that a man coming out of his house with such images in his mind saw, not so much the spectacle of individual things, as the figure of the universe and its colours. This was exactly Bruno's aim, in his eternal efforts to find the images, signs, characters in living contact with reality which, when established in memory, would unify the whole contents of the universe.

It is thus possible that—although it comes so late in time—Bruno's *De imaginum, signorum et idearum compositione* may be an important key to the way in which the Renaissance composed images, and also to the way in which it used images.

Bruno's method was still known and being used by Robert Fludd who in the second part of his *Utriusque cosmi . . . historia* of 1619 has a memory system with a celestial basis to which is attached a series of mnemonic places in a theatre—an arrangement like that of the two parts of the *De imaginum compositione* which I think that Fludd must have known. It is interesting that Fludd, too, uses "ideas" not in the usual Platonic sense but as meaning spiritual things, angels, demons, the "effigies of stars" or the "images of gods and goddesses attributed to celestial things".

In the dedication to Hainzell of the *De imaginum composi-* *tione,* Bruno states that the twelve principles are "the effecters, signifiers, enlargers (?) of all things under the ineffable and infigurable optimus maximus". They are thus divine Powers, and the object of the whole system is (I believe) to become identified with such Powers. Once again we are back to a Hermetic notion, the effort of the initiate to become identified with Powers, and so to become divine.

Bruno once more expounds in the first part of the *De imaginum compositione* his theory of the imagination as the chief instrument in religious and magical processes. He had given the theory in the *Explicatio Triginta Sigillorum,* written in England, and gives it most fully of all in the *De magia,* written about 1590 or 1591 (that is at about the same time as the *De imaginum compositione*) and which we used in an earlier chapter. The theory can be interestingly studied in the *De imaginum compositione* where is revealed a curious confusion in Bruno's mind. He cites Aristotle on "to think is to speculate with images". Aristotle's statement is used by Bruno as support for his belief in the primacy of the imagination as the instrument for reaching truth. Later, he quotes Synesius' defence of the imagination in his work on dreams (using Ficino's translation). Synesius is defending imagination because of its use by divine powers to communicate with man in dreams. Bruno seems to fail to realise how totally opposite are the Aristotelian and the Synesian defences of the imagination. Aristotle is thinking of images from sense impressions as the sole basis of thought; Synesius is thinking of divine and miraculous images impressed on the imagination in dreams. Having cited Aristotle on images from sense impressions as the basis of thought, Bruno then goes right to the other extreme of the classical tradition and uses the arguments of a late Hellenistic Neoplatonist in favour of imagination in quite another sense from the Aristotelian, as the most powerful of the inner senses because through it the divine communicates with man.

This confusion belongs to Bruno's transformation of the art of memory from a fairly rational technique using images, theorists on which—amongst them Thomas Aquinas himself—had used the Aristotelian dictum, into a magical and religious technique for training the imagination as the instrument for reaching the divine and obtaining divine powers, linking through the imagination with angels, demons, the effigies of stars and inner "statues" of gods and goddesses in contact with celestial things.

In an extraordinary passage in the *De imaginum compositione,* Bruno mentions the golden calf and the brazen image described in *Genesis* (which he interprets as magic images used by Moses, referring for this astonishing statement to "the doctrine of the Cabalists"), and the clay figures made by Prometheus, as all examples of the power of the simulachrum for drawing down the favour of the gods through occult analogies between inferior and superior things "whence as though linked to images and similitudes they descend and communicate themselves." With the last phrase, we reach the familiar ground of the Egyptian statues, linked with demons, which Bruno has here related to the magic of Moses and Prometheus to produce a truly amazing Hermetic-Cabalist justification for the inner magics in his arts of memory.

Light, says Bruno, is the vehicle in the inner world through which the divine images and intimations are imprinted, and this light is not that through which normal sense impressions reach the eyes, but an inner light joined to a most profound contemplation, of which Moses speaks, calling it "primogenita", and of which Mercurius also speaks in *Pimander*. Here the *Genesis-Pimander* equation, so characteristic of the Hermetic-Cabalist tradition, is applied by Bruno to creation in the inner world.

There are words and passages in the **De imaginum compositione** about the frenzy or *furor* with which the enthusiast hunts after the vestiges of the divine which are very like passages in the **Eroici furori;** and he gives another formulation of his belief that poetry, painting, and philosophy are all one, to which he now adds music. "True philosophy is music, poetry or painting; true painting is poetry, music, and philosophy; true poetry or music is divine sophia and painting."

It is in such contexts as these, which have been little studied by the philosophers who have admired Giordano Bruno, that one should see the philosophy of the infinite universe and the innumerable worlds. Such concepts are not with him primarily philosophical or scientific thinking, but more in the nature of hieroglyphs of the divine, attempts to figure the infigurable, to be imprinted on memory through imaginative effort to become one with the universe, which was the Hermetic aim pursued throughout his life by this intensely religious magician.

> Why, I say, do so few understand and apprehend the internal power? . . . He who in himself sees all things, is all things [**De imaginum compositione**].

M. A. Dynnik   (essay date 1967)

SOURCE: "Man, Sun, and Cosmos in the Philosophy of Giordano Bruno," in *Soviet Studies in Philosophy,* Vol. VI, No. 2, Fall, 1967, pp. 14-21.

[*In this essay, Dynnik examines the merits of Bruno's arguments and conclusions concerning cosmology.*]

Italy was the first country to take the course of elimination of feudal relationships. The Italian Renaissance marked the beginning of the complex and contradictory process whereby the new, capitalist society took form, triumphed, and became firmly established. The epoch of the Renaissance gave birth to centralized national states in what were the most advanced countries of Europe of that time, undermined the intellectual dictatorship of the church, cleared the way for the sciences of nature, and prepared the soil for the appearance of the advanced philosophical teachings of the 17th and 18th centuries.

The Renaissance in Italy found expression in remarkable works of painting and poetry, sculpture and architecture, in brilliant philosophical ideas and discoveries in the natural sciences, in new attitudes and customs filled with the spirit of freedom and independence, in a new morality hos-tile to the hypocritical morality of religion, in a lofty ideal in the arts, and in a vital esthetic of beauty.

Giordano Bruno rightly occupies an honored place among the most outstanding creators of the culture of the Renaissance in Italy, and not only Italy but all of Europe.

Bruno resurrected and developed the ideas and speculations of the great thinkers of antiquity in struggle against medieval scholasticism and theology. He contributed particularly greatly to the renaissance of the naive dialectics of the ancients. Bruno accepted the idea of Heraclitus that the cosmos had not been created by either God or man, that it had always been, is, and will always be a living flame, flaring up and dying down in accordance with law. But the great thinker of the Renaissance did not content himself with this. Whereas in the view of the wise ancient the notion of the eternity of the cosmos and of cosmic motion was merely a guess of genius, in Bruno this idea was a scientific conclusion from the heliocentric system of Copernicus.

On this same scientific foundation of helio-centrism, Bruno developed Democritus' idea of the infinity of the universe and that the number of worlds comprising it are also infinite.

Nor was Bruno foreign to the ancient tradition of the Peripatetics. Taking a stand against the medieval version of Aristotelian philosophy and the Aristotelian-Ptolemaic system of the world, he did much to bring about a rebirth of Aristotle's vital thought, to free it from medieval, scholastic encumbrances and distortions, and to revive and further develop Aristotle's dialectics.

Among the ancient sources that influenced Bruno's world view, Plato's philosophy must be included. Plato's dialectics, as a logical method of dividing and defining concepts with the purpose of seeking the truth, was also taken up and reworked by Bruno in his struggle against the formal dialectics of the scholastics and their method of proving religious dogmas. But Bruno rejected the transcendental world of Plato's ideas, and for Plato's Eros, regarded as a mystical path to the attainment of supersensory reality, he substituted the heroic enthusiasm of the genuine scientist who gained knowledge of the universe despite all religious prejudices.

Bruno experienced the fruitful influence of the philosophy of Ibn Roshd (as did the Paduan Aristotelians). He also shared some of the ideas of Avicenna. Bruno's synthesized preception of the best achievements of philosophical thought of West and East expanded his intellectual horizons and helped him find a profound and well-argued explanation of the phenomena of reality. Bruno's philosophy rested upon the rich traditions of Italian intellectual culture. Among his precursors and contemporaries in Italy, mention must be made of Leonardo da Vinci, Bernardino Telesio, Girolamo Fracastoro, Geronimo Cardano, and Francesco Patrizzi.

The point of departure, internal secret, and final goal of Bruno's world view was the new man—Renaissance man—who saw the rising sun at the end of the night of medievalism and who cast his gaze upon the infinity of the universe. In his dialogue *On Cause, the Principle, and the One,* Bruno gives one of his companions in conversation—his disciple and partisan of the new ideas—the name Heliotrope: "facing the sun." To the new man, the man of the Renaissance, the proponent of science and enlightenment, Bruno contrasted the adherents of the old, the scholastics and pedants, the defenders of blind faith and outdated ideas, the medieval Peripatetics and geocentrists: all those "ludicrous, elegant metaphysicians in cassocks".

Bruno held that to acquire knowledge of the truth and uncover the secrets of nature was the noble task of the new man. In his writings *The Secret of Pegasus* and *The Ass of Silenius,* he employed vivid satirical images to depict the opponents of scientific knowledge. Bruno wished to free the family of philosophy from "low pedants, phrase-mongers, and ignorant frauds." He spoke with bitterness of the fact that the scholastics were the reason why the word "philosopher" had taken on, for the people, the meaning of "do-nothing, pedant, swindler, jester, and charlatan."

Bruno asserted that a new man had been born during the Renaissance, and that that man was free of the old prejudices and confusions: he countered his own free reason to the authority of the church. An apologia for reason was the soul of Bruno's entire philosophy. In this regard he broke decisively with the medieval tradition and the authorities of the church. Anselm of Canterbury said of himself that he did not seek to understand for the sake of believing, but to believe for the sake of understanding. St. Thomas Aquinas, whose teachings were canonized by the Catholic Church, asserted that faith was higher than human reason, as its source was the Divine intellect. "I seek successes in awesome battle with untruth!" exclaims Bruno in his poem **"To Him Who Hates Me."**

Rejecting the authority of the church in the matter of gaining knowledge of the truth, Bruno glorified human reason. "The power of reason and, equally, the vital force of penetration of the human brain will find a means of understanding things and a scale for evaluating them in a field from the borders of which the vast crowd of sophists and ignoramuses turn and flee."

This apologia for reason, this affirmation of the right of man to free thought, is intimately associated in Bruno's philosophy with the restoration of the standing of knowledge acquired through the senses. Bruno, in the wake of da Vinci, recognizes sensations and accumulated experience as the source of theoretical thought. The man of the Renaissance, in the person of Bruno, rejected holy writ as a false source of knowledge and called for an appeal to the evidence of the senses. According to Bruno's theory of knowledge, sense (*sensus*), reason (*ratio*), and intelligence (*intellectus*) comprise the stage of approach to the truth. With the help of his senses, man sees the surface of things (the reflected light of the moon) as through an aperture in a lattice. Reason looks upon things through an open window, while intelligence attains the truth in full (the light of the sun).

The philosophy of Nola, declared Bruno with pride, would bring freedom to the human spirit. In fact the great Italian thinker not only celebrated the reason of man and restored his senses to their proper standing, but laid the foundations for a new morality, rejecting the old, religious morality. Everything changes in the world, said Bruno. That which seemed stable and even eternal grows old and yields place to the new. Man arises from an embryo, a young boy becomes a strong youth, then becomes adult and aged, and becomes a weak old man. Likewise, having been innocent and inexperienced, he becomes capable and experienced, sad and good. Having known nothing he becomes wise, having been given to fury he grows moderate, having lacked self-control he becomes modest, having been light-minded he becomes serious, having been partisan he becomes just. With the passage of time virtues become faults, and faults—virtues. Therefore the new man faces a great moral task—that of cleansing his soul from faults and confusions, of driving out the "triumphant animal": the faults dominant in the world.

Jupiter and the other gods have grown old and have already crossed to the other side of the Acheron. Above the gods there is Necessity, the law of nature, which repeals established laws, statutes, cults, and ceremonies. The new man enters into fierce battle with the "triumphant animal." The rays of the sun destroy faults and confusion both in heaven and in the human soul. Bruno compares truth to the light of the sun. This comparison had particularly deep meaning in the era of struggle for the new, for the heliocentric understanding of the world against the obsolete geocentric system. In one of his poems, Bruno wrote:

> The one, the beginning and the cause,
> From which comes existence, life and motion
> Of which earth, skies and hell are outcome—
> All that extends in distance and breadth and
>   depth.
>
> For senses, reason, intellect—a picture:
> There are no acts, numbers and measurements.
> For that enormous thing, power, striving,
> That eternally towers higher than all peaks.
> Blind trickery, the short span of life, evil fate,
> The dirt of envy, the heat of bestiality in enmity,
> Cruelty and foul wishes
> Attacking ceaselessly, lack the power,
> To pull a shroud over my eyes,
> And hide the beautiful rays of the sun.

However, the "beautiful rays" of the sun were the object not only of Bruno's poetic inspiration, but of his theories of astronomy and his philosophical system. Bruno's service to astronomy is exceptional. Having properly evaluated the revolution in natural science wrought by Copernicus, Bruno consistently defended the great Polish scientist against the ferocious attacks of the scholastics and theologists and promoted in every possible way the dissemination of heliocentric ideas all over Europe. Bruno enriched astronomy with a number of new ideas and insights of genius. He asserted that the sun rotates on its axis but does not remain still, moving in relationship to other stars, and that the earth's atmosphere rotates with the earth. The name of Giordano Bruno has found a firm place in the history of natural science. His brilliant ideas and guesses have been entirely confirmed by the subsequent development of science.

Bruno's critique of the ideas of Osiander, author of the preface to Copernicus' great work, *De revolutionibus orbium coelestium,* is a splendid example of scientific argumentation. As we know, Osiander, in his preface under the title "To the Reader. On the Hypotheses in This Work," distorted the real meaning and scientific significance of the heliocentric theory, and falsely interpreted it as a simple mathematical hypothesis and not as an astronomical theory about real things.

Refuting with outrage this gross distortion of the ideas of Copernicus and disclosing their real content, Bruno called Osiander "an ignorant and presumptuous ass," who was incapable of understanding the revolutionary significance of the heliocentric system and who vainly sought to reconcile it with the Aristotelian-Ptolemaic theory, "as though desiring to apologize for the author and offer him protection, or even setting it as his goal that other asses, finding lettuce and fruits for themselves in this book, would thereby not remain hungry".

Taking a very sharp stand against Osiander in his dialogues, *The Feast Over Dust,* Bruno describes his dispute with Dr. Nundinius, an English scholastic, who upheld the geocentric theory. Nundinius' first argument went: "One must conclude that Copernicus did not hold the view that the earth moves, as that is unacceptable and impossible, but that he ascribed motion to it . . . for convenience of computation." It was precisely in response to this "argument" by Nundinius that Theophilus (Bruno) offered his critical comments on Osiander's preface, asserting, with justice, that in reality Copernicus "fulfilled the function not only of a mathematician, who hypothesizes, but of a physicist, who proves the motion of the earth".

The image of the self-satisfied scholastic and ignoramus—Dr. Nundinius—was a synthesis of the characteristics typical of many opponents of the heliocentric system with whom Bruno had had to dispute.

Nundinius' second argument against heliocentrism consists in the following: "It is improbable that the earth moves, considering that it is the middle and center of the universe, in which it holds the place of a fixed permanent foundation of all motion." Theophilus (Bruno) demonstrates without difficulty that this argument too is utterly untenable, and that Nundinius resembles an individual who rejects, by virtue of faith and habit, all that is new and unfamiliar, and is therefore not capable of independent critical thought. Through detailed examination and refutation of both of these and other arguments of the opponents of the heliocentric system, Bruno validates Copernicus' theory.

In his *Dialogues* Bruno puts forth other representatives of the "asses' science" in the persons of Dr. Torquato ("The Feast Over Dust"), Polinnius (*On Cause, the Principle, and the One*), Burkius (*On Infinity, the Universe, and the Worlds*), Sebasto (*The Secret of Pegasus*), etc. In criticizing the Aristotelian-Ptolemaic system, Bruno does not confine himself solely to analysis of the vulgar arguments

of the scholastics and pedants. He offers critical analysis of the principles of natural science and philosophy underlying geocentrism. From the height of a philosophically synthesized heliocentric system, Bruno subjected to scientific criticism not only medieval Aristotelianism, but Aristotle's actual teachings as well.

The discussion between Philotheus and Albertinus in Bruno's dialogue *On Cause, the Principle, and the One* comprises a brilliant example of scientific argumentation. Analysis of this discussion shows how groundless and false are the widely heard statements to the effect that Bruno offered no systematic presentation of his philosophical views. In reality, behind the creative form of his dialogues there lay hidden a deeply thought-out and brilliantly argued philosophical system that drew general conclusions from the achievements of science of that day. Albertinus is depicted in the dialogues as a serious scholar and proponent of Aristotle's views. Along with other Aristotelians he holds, as does Ibn Roshd, that "it is impossible to know anything that Aristotle did not know". In his debate with Philotheus, Albertinus advances thirty arguments in support of Aristotelian theory, but all these arguments are refuted by Philotheus and his follower Elpinius as a result of circumstantial examination.

Arguing against the first thesis—that space and time are inconceivable outside this world—Philotheus asserts that both time and space exist behind the imaginary circumference and convexity of our universe, inasmuch as other universes exist beyond, in the infinite cosmos. He also refutes a second argument—that a single eternal motive force exists and, consequently, that only "this" one universe exists. Philotheus denies Aristotle's prime mover and affirms the existence of a single, infinite universe.

Philotheus also convincingly refutes a third argument by Albertinus, which seeks to prove the existence of only "this" universe, proceeding from Aristotle's theory of the "places" of moving bodies. Philotheus replies to this that from the standpoint of the infinity of the universe, Aristotle's theory of "places" makes no sense, as the cosmos has neither a middle nor a circumference.

Albertinus' fourth argument resolves to an affirmation of the fact that recognition of a multiplicity of universes leads to an absurdity: the center of one universe will be at a greater distance from the center of another than from its periphery, and this leads to a logical contradiction according to Aristotle's theory of opposites. It took no effort on Philotheus' part to prove this argument also untenable, inasmuch as Aristotle's theory of opposites had become outdated, as had many other propositions of the peripatetic philosophy.

To the nine remaining, analogous arguments of Albertinus, the refutations are presented, at Philotheus' request, by his follower Elpinius. As a result of this discussion, Albertinus recognized Philotheus' reasoning to be persuasive and stated that he was prepared to become his disciple. Thus, Bruno developed, in artistic form, a critique of Aristotelianism and provides a theoretical validation for his world view.

Determination of the real role of the sun in the life of nature and man was, in Bruno's day, a most important achievement not only for natural science but for philosophy. It denoted the triumph of the new world view over the old, of science over religion, of humanism over medieval obscurantism and tyranny. For Bruno, the "Rising Sun" was the best of images for embodying the triumph of reason over confusion.

> All the animate beings hiding from the face of the heavenly luminaries and designated for the eternal chasms, pits, and caves of Pluto, called by the terrible and vengeful summons of Alekto, spread their wings and betake themselves rapidly to their dwellings. But all the animate objects born to see the sun and rejoicing at the end of the hated night, celebrating the favor of heaven and having prepared themselves to take up the so-greatly-desired and long-awaited rays with the centers of the ball-like crystals of their eyes, do obeisance to the East with heart, voice, and hands.

Bruno, having philosophically generalized from the teachings of Copernicus, came to the bold conclusion that the universe is infinite and its worlds innumerable. Reviving the materialist and atheist traditions of the thinkers of antiquity, who had taught the infinity and eternity of the universe and the material unity of nature, and taking as his platform the achievements of the natural science of his day, Bruno developed and validated a new, materialist concept of the cosmos. In accordance with his theory, the universe is one, material, infinite, and eternal. An infinite number of worlds lie beyond the bounds of our solar system. That which is accessible to our view is only a negligible portion of the boundless cosmos. The stars are the suns of other systems of planets. The earth, which theologians hold to be the center of the world, is in fact a speck of dust in the endless expanses of the cosmos. Bruno went beyond Copernicus in his cosmological system, for Copernicus, despite his great discovery, continued to regard the universe as finite and did not raise his thought to the concept of infinity.

Thus, Bruno was the source of the contemporary scientific notion of the world based upon the heliocentric system and recognizing the eternity and infinity of the material world. The great thinker rejected, in argumented fashion, the geocentric system of the world and the medieval theological world view in its entirety.

But Bruno's materialist and atheist ideas were enclosed in a pantheistic envelope. According to Bruno, nature was God contained in things. "The animals and plants are the animate products of nature, while nature itself (as thou must know) is nothing but the embodiment of God (*deus in rebus*)," Bruno [claims in] *The Expulsion of the Triumphant Beast.* Bruno held that nature is capable of giving birth to innumerable forms of life from out of itself. The single material principle underlying all that exists possesses boundless creative force. Bruno's idea of the universal animateness of nature involves this position.

In Bruno's view, the oppositeness of philosophy and religion lies in the fact that the task of philosophy is cognition of the single material substance as cause and principle of all things in nature, while religion refers us to divine sub-

stance. Thus Bruno describes the material substance comprising the subject matter of cognition as the one, the principle, and the cause. As he understands it, the cause is that which acts upon things externally. Such are the efficient cause and the goal. The principle, in Bruno's definition, is that which internally promotes the ordering of things and is preserved in the effects. The single material substance combines in itself the principle and cause of all things. "Just as in art," wrote Bruno,

> there is always retained, despite the infinite (if this were possible) changes of form, the original matter—as, for example, the form of wood is first a tree-trunk, then a log, then boards, then a seat, then little benches, then frames, then cards for wool, etc., but the *wood* always remains the same—so in nature, despite the infinite change in sequence of various forms, the matter is always the same. . . . Do you not see that that which was seed becomes a stalk upon which an ear arises, and from that which was an ear bread arises, and from bread the juices of the stomach, and from it blood, and from it sperm, and from it the embryo, and from it man, and from it a corpse, and from it earth, and from it stone or some other thing, and that one can thus proceed to all the forms in nature . . . ?

> Thus, there necessarily exists one and the same thing that, in itself, is not rock, not earth, not a corpse, not man, not an embryo, not blood and whatever, but which, after having been blood becomes an embryo, acquiring the existence of an embryo; and after it was an embryo acquires the existence of man—becomes man.

It is precisely this single material substance underlying all things in nature that comprises, as Bruno emphasized, the subject matter of philosophy. The divine substance affirmed by religion has proved superfluous for explanation of natural phenomena.

But it is necessary, above all, carefully to analyze how Bruno understood material substance, inasmuch as this concept underlies his entire philosophical system. Material substance, says Bruno, must be differentiated from matter in the concept of the mechanic and the practical physician, i. e., from mercury and silver. In Bruno's words, he himself had previously adhered to Democritus' notion of matter, but later abandoned it. Democritus and the Epicureans, said Bruno, had regarded everything incorporeal as nothing and, counterposing matter as substance to everything incorporeal, had identified it with corporeality. Thus, Bruno approached the wholly correct conclusion that recognition of matter as the primary and non-derivative foundation of all things does not at all mean negation "of everything incorporeal"—i. e., spiritual—but, on the contrary, is a necessary prerequisite for explaining the spiritual.

According to Bruno, Democritus' and the Epicureans' understanding of matter is to be preferred to Aristotle's, but it also must be replaced by a theory taking its origin from the unity of matter and form, of active possibility and passive possibility. The single material substance underlies all natural phenomena, both corporeal and spiritual. Matter, as substance of the cosmos, does not differ from form:

Thus, we have the first principle of the universe, which must also be understood as that within which the material and the formal are no longer distinguished from each other. . . . However, descending the ladder of nature, we discover a dual substance—in one aspect spiritual, in the other corporeal, but in the final analysis both resolve to a single existence and a single root.

Bruno's great service to philosophy was his affirmation that nature has its own creative force and does not stand in need of any "prime mover." Bruno termed the internal productive force of labor the "universal intellect as internal capacity of the soul of the world." Regarding all natural phenomena as animate, Bruno violated, of course, the logical consistency of his system, but by paying that price he gained the opportunity to replace the outdated "prime mover" by the more progressive "internal artist" of nature.

Bruno's theory of the cosmos played a significant role in the development of dialectics. Bruno valued highly the classical dialectics of Heraclitus. He resurrected and worked over the naive dialectics of the ancient Greeks. In nature, Bruno taught, everything is interconnected and in motion, from the finest particle of matter—the atom—to the numberless worlds of the infinite universe. The destruction of one thing, he said, is the origin of another. One form of matter is replaced by another. Many poisons are useful drugs. Love becomes hate, and vice versa. The good becomes the bad, the beautiful—the ugly, and vice versa.

Underlying Bruno's dialectical views was the principle of the coinciding of opposites. Recognizing that the universe is infinite and that its center is everywhere, Bruno came to the conclusion that a minimum comprises a maximum, and that a coincidence of opposites occurs in minima and maxima. The significance of the principle of coincidence of opposites, said Bruno, must be recognized by the physicist, the mathematician, and the philosopher. The maximum and minimum coincide in nature, and reveal a unity of the universe and its finest parts. It is necessary to distinguish three types of minima: in mathematics—a point, in physics—an atom, in philosophy—a monad. The maximum derives from the minimum, the greatest values from the least.

Bruno preferred Heraclitus as a dialectician to Democritus. He held the atomist theory valuable to physics and therefore recognized the atom as the physical minimum. But in the realm of philosophy he regarded acceptance of atoms and emptiness as insufficient, since philosophy had special tasks to perform: the philosopher, in Bruno's words, was in need of a matter that would "glue together" the atoms and empty space. Therefore he regarded as the philosophical minimum not the atom, but the monad that corresponds to the philosophical maximum—the infinite cosmos in the multiplicity and unity of all its forms given rise to by the one: the cause and the principle.

The engendered and the engendering . . . and that from which the engendered arises, all belong to one and the same substance. Thanks to this . . . Heraclitus' maxim to the effect that all things are one, thanks to the variability of all

that they contain, does not seem strange. And inasmuch as all forms are found within it, then consequently all definitions are applicable to it, and thanks to this, contradictory propositions prove to be true.

Thus Heraclitus' theory of the cosmos and of logos as dialectical regularity of the development of things natural was reborn on the basis of the new natural science.

Bruno himself described as follows the tasks posed by his philosophical system: to demonstrate what the sky actually is, and what the planets and other stars are; how certain of the innumerable worlds differ from others; why endless space is not only not impossible but even necessary; how infinite action corresponds to infinite cause; what are true substance, matter, action, and the active cause of everything; how all sense-perceptible and complicated things are composed of identical principles and elements; to render persuasive the theory of the infinite universe; to destroy the notion of the convex and concave surfaces that bound the elements and skies within and without; to ridicule the inventions of deferents and fixed stars; to destroy the idea of the prime mover and ultimate complexity; to destroy the belief that the earth is the single center; to make an end to the faith in the fifth essence; to prove that other stars and worlds are composed precisely as are our star and world; to study the arrangement of infinitely great and extensive worlds, as well as those that are infinitely small; to destroy the claim that there are external motive forces and limits to the skies; to prove that our star resembles others, and that other worlds similar to ours exist; to explain that the motion of all bodies in the world occurs as a consequence of their internal spirit, and by all this to assure advance in the knowledge of nature.

Who can deny that the principal tasks posed by Bruno were successfully resolved by him and that he actually was the pioneer in scientific cognition of the cosmos? Defending his honor as a scientist from the attacks of pedants and sophists, scholastics and theologians, Bruno compared his study of the universe with a flight into the cosmos. He said that he "had found a means to raise himself to the heavens, to run through the sphere of the stars, and to leave behind him the convex surface of the arch of heaven."

> From here I strive upward, full of faith,
> The crystals of the heavens no longer a barrier
>   to me;
> Cutting through them, I raise myself into infinity.
> And yet, like all in other spheres
> I penetrate through the ether's field,
> Below I leave the Milky Way, another world.

The heroic image of a man who flew in space, albeit only in thought, makes the name of Giordano Bruno particularly treasured in the Soviet Union—the land of the first cosmonauts.

Giancarlo Maiorino   (essay date 1977)

SOURCE: "The Breaking of the Circle: Giordano Bruno and the Poetics of Immeasurable Abundance," in *Journal of the History of Ideas,* Vol. XXXVIII, No. 2, April-June, 1977, pp. 317-27.

[*In the following essay, Maiorino discusses Bruno's views on poetry, emphasizing the link between poetic and philosophical thought and the characteristics of both.*]

Since its publication, Torquato Tasso painfully corrected his unorthodox *Gerusalemme liberata* (1575) in compliance with traditional requirements imposed by critical opinion. A few years later, Giordano Bruno declared in his *Eroici furori* (1584-85) that "poetry is not born of rules, except by the merest chance, but that the rules derive from the poetry. For that reason there are as many genres and species of true rules as there are of true poets". Having found its own form, inner expression stimulates originality instead of conformity.

In his humanistic *De vinculis in genere* (1591-92) Bruno dismissed the fifteenth-century emphasis on general norms of beauty, which should be replaced by individual models:

> Because beauty, whether it consists in some kind of proportion or in something incorporeal which shines through physical nature, is manifold and works on countless levels; just as the irregularity of a stone does not fit, coincide, and join with the irregularity of any other stone (but only there where the reliefs and hollows best correspond), in the same way any appearance will not strike just any mind.

Since art has relinquished general contexts, each stone must assert its own beauty. Furthermore, relative standards involve, as Eugenio Battisti remarks, "by relativism in relationships. Each one of us is moved by a particular kind of beauty, according to his own temperament and culture [*Rinascimento e Barocco,* 1960]. Each spectator defines art and becomes its critic. The static and structured world-view of *Umanesimo*—as exemplified in the works of Leon Battista Alberti and Piero della Francesca—assumed that the successful work of art would dominate its public, whereas Bruno and seventeenth-century writers deliberately looked for public consensus. Contact between artist and spectator was sought after, for the reason that, as Battisti points out, "the *Seicento* strongly felt the need for law; since it could not be based on reason, it was founded on consensus [*Rinascimento e Barocco,* 1960]."

Bruno's work is a cry for consensus. With reference to the *Dialoghi italiani,* one can point out the sympathetic relations between the Nolan (Bruno's *drammatis persona*) and Tansillo, the interloculators' acceptance of the Nolan's ideas, the gods' approval of Jove's deliberations and their impact in the streets of Nola and Naples. From an external point of view, one might consider Bruno's search for a consensus on the Copernican theories, and his own, in the *Cena delle ceneri.* Moreover, Bruno's appeals to Sidney, Greville, and Queen Elizabeth were obviously meant to gain their consent. The very nature of the dialogue form facilitated such an attitude, which Bruno reiterated by repeatedly calling on the reader. The sophisticated and exclusive aloofness of Humanistic art involved rational and hidden harmonies, which spectacularly surfaced under the open skies of the late *Cinquecento.* The traditional notions of *decorum,* eloquence, and narrative distance were superseded by a conception of art that deliberately attacked the intellectual and social exclusivism of *Umanesimo* (which the *Controriforma* had already proceeded to modify). As a result, art became more popular, temporal and even sensational, so as to express a unified, exuberant and limitless conception of man and the universe.

In the literary tradition of *Umanesimo,* Bruno presented the new scientific and cultural relativism of the late sixteenth century in a collection of treatises, which played a fundamental role in a culture that was evolving from acceptance of a closed world toward recognition of an infinite universe. Yet, despite the fact that the prominence of Bruno has been acknowledged in the fields of science, philosophy and history of ideas, literary scholarship has remained hesitant and elusive on the subject of his artistic stature. Giorgio Bárberi-Squarotti considers him as *prebarocco,* while Carlo Calcaterra refers to him in the context of the *anti-barocco.* In the realm of aesthetics and art criticism, Eugenio Battisti and Robert Klein see definite baroque positions in Bruno's work, whereas Arnold Hauser defines him as a philosopher of Mannerism. Although this essay declines to label Bruno in any way, it nevertheless draws on such criticism. In addition, the stable world-view of *Umanesimo* will represent a point of comparison in the assessment of Bruno's historical position. In the spirit of the ongoing researches on poetic theories at the end of the *Cinquecento,* it is hoped that the present analysis will contribute to a more articulate understanding of the poetic aspects of such a crucial and complex age.

Having drawn a line between the old and the new, Bruno also discriminates between professional imitators and true poets. In the latter category, Bruno identifies the poet of the myrtle (love poets) and those of the laurel, "who instruct heroic souls through speculative and moral philosophy". Consequently, poetry is conducive to "philosophical studies," which Bruno considers "mothers of the Muses". The structure of the *Eroici furori* articulates both levels of expression, since the work consists of philosophical and critical commentaries on a collection of poems. Furthermore, as Bruno states in the explanatory epistle of the *Spaccio della bestia trionfante,* art gives order and clarity to "moral philosophy according to the internal light that the divine Intellectual Sun has radiated and still radiates within" the artist himself. Bruno reiterates this association in the *Explicatio triginta sigillorum,* in which he states that "the philosophers are poets and painters; the poets, the painters and philosophers." Consistent with the concept of *ut pictura poesis,* the artist defines beauty and truth by means of poetic images that can be interpreted in different contexts. Bruno's exploitation of metaphorical and mythical imagery (phoenix, Acteon, Icarus) also reflect the historical criticism of language, which no longer functioned as a stable carrier of universal truths.

Emphasis on poetic images identifies Bruno's distinction between suggestive and documentative tools. In the *Cena* Bruno separates poetry from history as follows:

> When one is attempting to establish tradition

and give laws, certainly it is necessary to speak at the level of common understanding and to avoid becoming involved with maintaining the unbiased tongue of science. The historian, in handling his material, would be crazy if he expected to introduce an unusual vocabulary. If he were to do this, the reader would be more apt to interpret him as an artist rather than to understand him as a historian. One who desires to give to the general populace laws and guidelines for living is worse, if he uses terms that only he understands or only a few understand.

Such a conceptual and artistic position moves the heroic and myth-making nature of *Umanesimo* beyond history, which usually accommodated mythopoeic constructions. Following Francesco Guicciardini, Bruno expects history to present "events and results," whereas the search for truth belongs to philosophy. Like Bruno, the Humanists separated poetry from history, but they did not extend such a distinction to language (even though they discriminated between high and low levels of style).

Surely, Bruno's unequivocal pronouncements in favor of poetic relativism had to be based on a thorough revision of Aristotelian standards. In fact, Bruno reacted against the codification which the philosopher had undergone in the hands of sixteenth-century critics like Minturno and Giraldi Cinthio, who "do not recognize that these rules [Aristotle's] are there only to show us the kind of epic poet Homer was, and not to serve as modes of instruction to other poets who could in other veins, skills, and frenzies be in their several kinds equal, similar or even greater than Homer". Like Virgil and Lucretius, Homer was "not a poet who depended upon the rules, but he is the cause of the rules". Hence, the standardization of invention represents a later phenomenon, which served the Humanistic translation of the classical lesson into geometric and rational systems. Bruno vindicated artistic originality; in his eyes, the past no longer represented a fixed mirror, but it became a basis for evolution. Having clarified the originality of Homeric poetry, Bruno implicitly recognizes Aristotle as a critic. As a matter of fact, Bruno himself attempts a combination of criticism and invention in the *Eroici furori;* the Nolan becomes a new Homer and a new Aristotle. It is important to notice that Tansillo's criticism is drawn from within the work of art; Bruno did not make Tasso's mistake. As Giorgio Bárberi-Squarotti remarks, the former's position caused the "dissolution of man's faith in the university of the theoretical postulates of art."

Even the Horatian concept of poetry assumes an innovative character in the case of Bruno. His historical vindication of the principle of *utile dulcis* aimed at a return to a comprehensive definition of art. In the first half of the sixteenth century, in fact, the *utile* had often been separated from the *dulcis,* that Castelvetro had proposed as the goal of art (in spite of the pervasive didacticism that was elicited by the spirit of the *Controriforma*). As a result, Bruno criticized the intellectual sterility of Petrarchism, the licentious style and radical criticism of Folengo, Berni, and Aretino, who nevertheless influenced his anti-traditionalism. Variety of poetic expressions was thus committed to the recovery of a stylistic and conceptual

unity that had been dissipated in the meanderings of earlier literature, manneristic or otherwise.

Convinced of the didactic value of poetry, Bruno vehemently confronts the Petrarchists in the Argument of the *Eroici furori:*

> What a tragicomedy! What act, I say, more worthy of pity and laughter can be presented to us upon this world's stage, in this scene of our counsciousness, than of this host of individuals who became melancholy, meditative, unflinching, firm, faithful, lovers, devotees, admirers and slaves of a thing without trustworthiness.

While spiritual love is due to God, its human counterpart belongs to man. The Petrarchists, instead, followed neither nature nor God, since they intellectualized the former and reduced the latter to any unworthy human similitude.

Bruno's independent assessment of Aristotle and Petrarchism is extended to Plato as well. Accordingly, Bruno criticizes those individuals who have become "habitations of the gods or divine spirits, speak and do admirable things for which neither they themselves nor anyone else understand the reason". In the *Ion* Plato clearly stated that poetry is created "in a state of divine insanity," which places definite limitations on artistic ingenuity. Firstly, such a divine inspiration is not brought to life by the poet himself, but it is extended to him by the deity. Since he creates poetry in a state of receptive passivity, the artist also relinquishes the more rational powers of his mind, "for whilst a man retains any portion of the thing called reason, he is utterly incompetent to produce poetry or to vaticinate". Plato reiterates such a conviction in the *Phaedrus:* "Whosoever without the madness of the Muses comes to knock at the doors of poesy, from the conceit that haply by force of art he will become an efficient poet, departs with blasted hopes, and his poetry, the poetry of sense, fades into obscurity before the poetry of madness." Under these conditions, the poet "is excellent in proportion to the extent of his participation in the divine influence, and the degree in which the Muse itself has descended on him". It is in such a state of inspired rapture that the poet becomes a divine mouthpiece. Clearly, Plato emphasizes the poet's communicative—rather than creative—powers.

Bruno, instead, cherishes those individuals who:

> Tansillo—because of a custom or habit of contemplation, and because they are naturally endowed with a lucid and intellectual spirit, when under the impact of an internal stimulus and spontaneous fervor spurred on by the love of divinity, justice, truth and glory, by the fire of desire and inspired purpose, they make keen their senses and in the sulphurous cognitive faculty enkindle a rational flame which raises their vision beyond the ordinary. And these do not go about speaking and acting as mere receptacles and instruments, but as chief inventors and authors.

Although basically critical of Plato's position, Bruno shares with the philosopher the conviction that a frenzied impulse is necessary in order to achieve ultimate revelation and beauty. In both instances, the highest stage of human experience lies beyond reason. However, while detachment from reason conditions any poetic process in the *Ion* and the *Phaedrus,* Bruno's frenzied experience is based on, and supported by, a "rational flame" up to the higher realms of human fulfillment. As in the case of John Donne and St. Ignatius, emotional experiences are controlled by intellectual preparation and self-awareness. As a result, man plays a more active role in the development of the creative process.

Since poetry is intimately related to philosophy, the experience of the heroic frenzy—that is divine beauty and truth—also implies that of art. The experience of poetry is thus defined as a conscious activity that requires a constructive process of internalization. Under these conditions, Bruno's *chief inventor* shares several features with Sidney's notion of the poet as a maker. In light of the fact that the latter's *Defense of Poesie* was finished before Bruno became his personal friend and scholarly admirer, this similarity could indeed be less than accidental. In both instances we find yet another expression—one might think of the Humanistic concept of *virtù* and the system of linear perspective—of the modern artist's attempts to assert his creative genius beyond the boundaries of the classical lesson.

With regard to the creative interaction between fantasy and intellect, it must be pointed out that, for Bruno as well as for Donne, the concept of frenzy, or ecstasy, does not elicit unbridled expressions of emotional raptures, as was the case with the exemplary St. Teresa of Bernini. The mind always controls the heart in the case of Bruno. One must remember that the nature of the *Eroici furori* is that of an expository treatise, which is not particularly conducive to immediate mystical flights. Furthermore, Bruno adds that "these frenzies do not arise from forgetfulness, but from remembrance". As a furor recollected in tranquillity, the heroic frenzy transcends the senses. Giovanni Gentile conclusively remarks that "the knowledge of divinity, as championed by Bruno, is not ecstasy, or immediate union, even though it is union that it has as its end. . . . It is a rational process, a discourse of the intellect [*Il pensiero italiano del Rinascimento,* 1955].

It is apparent that imagination and the senses only provide a first impulse for experiences which belong to the intellect. In the *Eroici furori* the human will, through reason, "governs the affections of the inferior potencies against the surge of their natural violence." In terms of artistic process, fantasy participates in the cycle by leading toward inferior things, whereas the intellect raises the mind heavenward. In the spirit of his reconciliation of contraries, Bruno states that "if it is unjust that the sense outrage the law of reason, it is equally blamable that the reason tyrannize the law of the senses". While the intellect stands for rest and identity, the imagination supports movement and diversity; it is the poet's rational faculty that reconciles the "one and the many, the same and the diverse, motion and position, the inferior with the superior". As a result, Bruno avoids a polarization between the real and the ideal, the perceptual and the intellectual.

Giving poetic expression to his heroic pursuit, Bruno synthesizes his philosophical and artistic outlook in the following sonnet of the *Eroici furori:*

> This phoenix which enkindles itself in the golden sun and bit by bit is consumed, while it is surrounded by splendor, returns a contrary tribute to its star; . . . because that which ascends from it to the sky, becomes tepid smoke and purple fog, which cause the sun's rays to remain hidden from our eyes, and obscure that by which it glows and shines.

> Thus my spirit (which the divine splendor inflames and illumines), while it goes about explaining that which glows so brightly in its thoughts, . . . sends forth verses from its high conceit, only to obscure the shining sun, while I am completely consumed and dissolved by the effort.

> Ah me! This purple and black cloud of smoke darkens by its style what it would exalt, and renders it humble.

Poetic similitudes obscure truth, much as they provisionally make it more accessible. While Raphael and Michelangelo portrayed the divine as a similitude of the human in the *Disputà* and the *Creation of Adam* in the Vatican, Bruno moves beyond the clarity of anthropomorphic equations, since "the divinity can be the object only in similitude, and not a similitude". Whereas the former conception of similitude supports clear and final concordances, its latter version introduces a new cultural and aesthetic relativism. Incapable of reducing divine beauty to human concepts, Bruno states that "the highest and most profound knowledge of divine things is negative and not affirmative". Short of ultimate equations, Bruno promotes verbal speculations which lead to a "similitude the mind can discern by virtue of the intellect".

By stating that the divinity can be perceived in similitude and in negative terms, Bruno drastically modified the whole system of humanistic correspondences. At the same time, however, he gave the artist a new freedom. Since poetry assumes as many shapes as human ingenuity can devise, the experience of the heroic frenzy takes unlimited forms. In the *Eroici furori* Tansillo recommends that we "distinguish between the end which is absolute in truth and essence, and that which is so by similitude, shadow and participation". The principle of relativism is again at work. The prosaic usage of language expresses history and criticism. Metaphorical images suggest the divinity in similitude, but ultimate beauty must be contemplated in silence, since such beauty is without "similitude, analogy, image or species". As the frenzied lover assimilates the divinity into himself, the real and the ideal coalesce; finally, beauty is truth. Contrasts and tensions have been dissolved in the eternal harmony of the Monads.

Inasmuch as "it is neither fitting nor natural that the infinite be understood, or that it present itself as finite, for then it would cease to be infinite," the Nolan's ultimate vision becomes the rare *praxis* of the divine furor, which eludes representational expressions, be it a luminous point (Dante), angelic revelations (Bernini) or the sea (Leopardi). It is thus clear that art becomes a vehicle for a quest that leads to "frenzies" and "philosophical speculations" which resist artistic illusionism. Art offered the Humanist an independent realm in which his provisional experience of reality was organized in patterns of intellectual harmony. In Bruno's poetics of relativism, instead, art becomes a stage in the boundless cycle of human experiences.

The relative and exceptional knowledge of truth and reality leads Bruno to stress process rather than goals. Accordingly, he admits that "cognition can never be perfect to the extent that our intellect has the power to understand the highest object; but only to the extent that our intellect has the power to understand this object. . . . It is enough that all attempt the journey. It is enough that each one do whatever he can". Nevertheless, the poet must face the task of translating such a limitless effort into the confines of a literary form. The aesthetic implications of this frame of mind are apparent and complex. While Humanistic art was as stable and precise as the system of linear perspective which it created, Bruno's artistic guidelines grow, change and expand in accord with the rhythm and mutations of life itself. The principles of selection and limitation are superseded by those of inclusiveness and proliferation.

In the **Dialoghi italiani,** attributes, images, definitions, and levels of narrative multiply themselves to an unprecedented degree. A system of artistic and conceptual frames structures the **Eroici furori.** Its first level of narration is represented by the Nolan's sonnets, which, at the second stage, are commented upon by the interlocutors in philosophical and critical terms. The imaginative nature of the verse is expanded into the expository clarity of a prosaic commentary, in the tradition of Dante's *Vita nuova.* In the process, the narrative extends from the poems to the artist's mind; finally, commentary and invention, exposition and revelation merge together. Like the *ricordo* of Guicciardini and the *essai* of Montaigne, Bruno's dialogue analyzes, dissects, and criticizes the whole intellectual process, "proceeding to the depths of the mind". The literary artifact exemplifies a portrait of the mind.

Following Pico della Mirandola's *Oration on the Dignity of Man,* Bruno considers process and mutability as inherent in man and necessary to nature. This conception also stems from their Hermetic background, which views nature alive and in a state of flux. In the first dialogue of the **Spaccio** Bruno states that "where there is contrariety, there is action and reaction, there is motion, there is diversity . . . there is vicissitude". The attraction of contraries stands as a principle of human and universal relationships, on account of which justice, knowledge—and by extension art and beauty—depend on, and are exalted by, the experience of their opposites. In this spirit, Bruno remarks that "the pain of not having the thing desired is absent, and present is the joy of ever finding the thing sought." Consequently, one ought to produce "an infinite effort". This development from being to becoming from goal to attempts, finds an appropriate illustration in a comparison of two works of sculpture that were produced at both ends of the *Cinquecento:* the ideally aloof David of Michelangelo and the humanly engaged figure of Bernini.

Such a dynamic frame of mind obviously effected the Hu-

manistic system of ideal similitudes. While Michelangelo represented Adam in a godly image of timeless perfection, Bruno subordinated Jove to "the Fate of Mutation" in (**Spaccio,**) Anthropomorphic perfection is superseded by natural growth, according to which the body reaches perfection, but it "cannot eternally nestle among the same temperaments, perpetuating the same threads, and preserving those same arrangements, in one and the same composite". Such a position evidently shatters the humanistic elimination of chance and process in the faultless world of art.

From a literary point of view, process and development lead Bruno to move from simple similarities to complex metaphors, and, finally, to contemplations without "speeches and discourses, but in silence". At one point in the **Eroici furori** the narrative enters the Nolan's mind taking the form of his very thoughts. It seems that human expression is breaking free from the expressive restrictions of literary artistry. In turn, the frenzied ascent has liberated poetry from the traditional notions of imitation and representation. The image of light becomes light itself at the point where "infinite potency and infinite act coincide". Silence supersedes eloquence, to the extent that Bruno can experience the "simplicity of the divine essence". In the case of Bruno, silence implies total vision and complete beauty, which exist beyond the reach of representational means. To a degree, art is subservient to imagination and the senses, whereas intellectual speculations allow the mind to "lose love and affection for every other sensible as well as intelligible object, for joined to that light it becomes that light, and consequently becomes a god". At this stage, the external projections of humanistic art are brought back to the artist himself, as the Nolan confidently states in one of his sonnets:

> My heart is in the place and form of Parnassus,
> which I must ascend for my safety; my muses are
> the thoughts which at every hour reveal to me
> their glorious tale . . .

The beauty of art testifies to the greater magic of the artist-Magus, who can finally ignore the appeal of public acclaim, which Petrarch and Tasso could not resist.

At the level of poetic images and external projections, Bruno compares the changing nature of the gods to their ageless appearance in the artworks. As an illustration, the idealized forms of Giorgione's Venus give way, in the **Spaccio,** to "the wrinkles you have developed, and the furrows dug into your face by the plough of time". Jove adds that the goddess' decay would "make it more and more difficult for the painter, who, if he does not wish to lie, must paint you as you are". Bruno's detailed description of Venus suggests that the literary vehicle can represent life more realistically than painting. This positions seems to negate Bruno's declared endorsement of the concept of *ut pictura poesis.* The contradiction, however, is only apparent. In the first place, Bruno's dynamic world-view would inevitably resist the medium of painting, which physically restricts the expression of time, space, and development. Secondly, Bruno is probably criticizing the static nature of humanistic art. Aiming at a new synthesis of *pictura* and *poesis* beyond Humanistic conventions,

Bruno also seems to search for an expressive vehicle that would combine linguistic mobility with the immediate and suggestive evidence of painting in the new context of a relativistic conception of art. This position represent a significant development from the unilateral discriminations on art that characterize the positions of Leonardo (painting), Alberti (architecture), Michelangelo (sculpture), and Montaigne (literature).

With regard to the relation between universal mutations and the humanistic notion of man as the measure of all things, Bruno points out that human life "is symbolized in the wheel of fortune". Such a traditional cycle is, however, less fatalistic and more individualized than its medieval precedent. Man moves along the wheel in a spirit of initiative rather than resignation. Surely, the individual ceases to be the external and fixed measure of the universe. On the other hand, he becomes a relative center of the cosmos, within which *virtù* and *fortuna* operate in harmony with the eternal vicissitudes of life. Under these conditions, the connection between the individual point and infinite trajectory eventually brings forward, as Bruno states in ***De la causa, principio e uno,*** "the concept of the coincidence of matter and form, potency and act, so that being, logically divided into what is and what it can be, is seen as physically undivided, and one; and this being is at one and the same time infinite, immobile, indivisible, without difference of whole parts, principle and principled."

Faith in the processes of life also reflects Bruno's reevaluation of nature. Since "perfect figures are not found in natural bodies, and they cannot exist either by the power of nature or art". Bruno concludes that the natural "represents its intrinsic principle, which accounts for its own existence". No longer destined to become an artifice, nature is given a form of its own. In the eyes of Bruno, such a recovery of nature compensates for the humanistic dreams that had become obsolete by the end of the *Cinquecento*. This conceptual position established a basis for the proliferation of reality (still life, genre scenes, tableaux of common life) which characterizes seventeenth-century art and literature, from Jacopo Bassano and Caravaggio to Cervantes and Velazquez. At all levels, life exemplifies artistic expressions which the artist can simply present and frame. The humanistic reconstruction of reality is followed by a more strict application of the concept of imitation on the part of Bruno, who replaced the representation of universal forms with the imitation of individual manifestations. Although part of the *Seicento* was to concentrate on the insignificant and even ridiculous particulars of life because it lost faith in higher values, Bruno always believed in the intimate relations between the *infimo* and the *sublime*.

By accepting chance and process, Bruno implicitly recognized value and purpose in all manifestations of life along the entire chain of being. Related to his search for universal consensus, Bruno acknowledges the experience of poets and philosophers as exceptional. Much as the Nolan denounces the illusionism of the nectar of the gods, he also warns his audience against the futility of frenzied pursuits on the part of those who are not ready for them. Although a degree of Humanistic and Hermetic exclusivism still identifies Bruno's attitude, he can indeed state that "it is a law of fate and of nature that each thing work according to the condition of its nature. Why, therefore, in pursuit of coveting the nectar of the gods do you lose that nectar which is proper to you, afflicting yourself perhaps with the vain hope of some other nectar?" Bruno's concern with individual limits and faith in human participation parallels Montaigne's contemporary criticism of theoretical excellence and concern for the human condition.

Frenzied souls and common crowds justified—only to a point, one should say—the commonness and vulgarity that characterize much of Bruno's work. Such devices are deliberately meant to preserve a contact between the higher and the lower aspects of life. The principle of diversity evidently pervades Bruno's ***Dialoghi italiani*** at all levels of human and artistic experience. It is in this spirit that Jove completes his regeneration of mankind by giving instructions concerning an old woman in Fiurulo, who "by the motion of her tongue moving about in her palate, will succeed with the fourth movement in causing the third molar in her right lower jaw to fall out". Likewise, the stories and affairs of the gods are not too far removed from Martinello's undistinguished son and Paolino's breeches. The heavenly assemblage finds a scholarly counterpart in London. Similarly, the dedication of the ***Eroici furori*** celebrates a humanistic *concordia di cor* (Bruno-Greville-Sidney), whereas the dedicatory letter of the ***Candelaio,*** dedicated to Morgana (probably a woman from Nola), is disseminated with obscene overtones. In the ***Cabala del cavallo pegaseo*** Bruno states that "the creation of philosophy without ignorance is madness; ignorance is a necessary means for the acquisition of truth." Within the confines of a rather theoretical projection, ignorance humanizes knowledge and equalizes people. The hero and the villain exemplify aspects and moments of an eternal cycle, as Mercury explains in the ***Spaccio:*** "Everything, then, no matter how minimal, is under infinitely great Providence; all minutiae, no matter how very lowly, in the order of the whole and of the universe, are most important". Considering once again the symbolic figure of David, Bruno, in a manner similar to Bernini's, can see the hero as well as the shepherd.

In spite of his unprecedented acceptance of mutability and relativism, Bruno's poetic conceptions are firmly committed to freedom of inspiration and expression. Satire, irony and invectives are always connected to a world-view in which man and nature breathe in liberty and happiness, certain as they are that the "death of one century brings life to all the others." The concept of alienation, which Hauser considers a major Manneristic trait, does not find support in the Brunian dimensions of spatial infinity and conceptual plenitude. Consistent with the derogatory connotations of the word baroque, the *Seicento* did produce much artistic *praxis* that was alienated from meaningful contexts. Receptive toward neither dissolution nor despair, Bruno's poetics stimulate an ever more challenging sense of fulfillment, in accord with what Ernst Cassirer has defined as a spirit of "immeasurable abundance" [*An Essay on Man*].

Edward A. Gosselin   (essay date 1984)

SOURCE: " 'Doctor' Bruno's Solar Medicine," in *The Sixteenth Century Journal,* Vol. XV, No. 2, Summer, 1984, pp. 209-24.

[*In the following essay, Gosselin analyzes* The Ash Wednesday Supper, *contending that in this work Bruno "bridge[s] the two extremes" of scientific and philosophical solar literature.*]

I. *The Solar Age and the Internal History of Science*

In an article published in 1958, Eugenio Garin discussed the influence of the emperor Julian's *Oratio ad solem* upon the "solar literature" of the Renaissance. Nothing the deeply religious flavor of the texts of such authors as Gemistus Plethon, Marsilio Ficino, Giovanni Pico, and Agostino Steuco, Garin theorized that their platonizing tendencies had led them toward a recuperation, albeit Christian, of the sun worship of Julian [E. Garin, *Studi sul Platonismo medievale,* 1958]. Garin further suggested—and I think entirely correctly this time—that the continuation of the manufacture of "solar literature" into the seventeenth century, that is, from the time of Copernicus to that of Galileo, "could help to underline a double tone, at the same time also ambiguous, of scientific revolution and of religious crisis. . . . Nothwithstanding Galileo's effort, it will be difficult to separate the new scientific vision of the world from a whole complex of religious resonances."

We can readily discern such intertwining themes in two scientific works which were written toward the beginning and toward the end of this era of Renaissance solar literature: Copernicus' *De revolutionibus* and Galileo's *Letter to the Grand Duchess.* At a vital point in his description of the heliocentric model of the universe, Copernicus refers to that part of the *Asclepius* where Hermes calls the Sun a "visible god." And Galileo concludes his *Letter* with a quotation from Julian's *Oratio.*

Whatever we may wish to make of these facts, Copernicus' and Galileo's works are recognizable to us as books of science, with what we would today call scientific intent. Thus do historians of science and intellectual historians now read these works. In addition, both historians of science and intellectual historians would agree that the philosophical and religious writings of Marsilio Ficino and Giovanni Pico della Mirandola are in no way scientific. Yet the texts of all of these men comprise that part of Renaissance literature which Garin calls "solar."

In this article I wish to address the reading of a text which seems curiously to bridge the two extremes of Copernicus and Galileo, on the one hand, and Ficino and Pico, on the other. The text in question is Giordano Bruno's **La Cena de le Ceneri** or, as it is known in English, **The Ash Wednesday Supper.**

The Ash Wednesday Supper is one of the most forceful products of late Renaissance solar literature. Its force comes from its embrace and adaptation of the Copernican achievement as well as from its use of a multi-solar and infinite universe as a means to achieving religious reconciliation in late sixteenth-century Europe. I shall argue that Bruno performs a kind of solar magic in this dialogue and

that the work *must* be read in this way in order to make sense of it. Although I do not wish to enter into a discussion of the question of the relation of Hermetism to the Scientific Revolution, I do want to preface my discourse on **The Ash Wednesday Supper** as solar literature with a brief look at certain internalist, history-of-science views on Bruno's text. Briefly, the internalist's approach endeavors to place Bruno in a kind of positivistic continuum wherein he becomes a fairly important step between Nicholas Oresme and Galileo. While this approach can be defended, for the historian of science to say that any nonscientific or extrascientific reading of the **Supper** is improper cannot be justified.

Many problems arise when the internalist turns to **The Ash Wednesday Supper.** Since this work uses the Copernican theory and adds to it such notions as those of the infinite universe and the plurality of worlds, the reader is tempted, as Professor Emile Namer has suggested should be done, to isolate this work from Bruno's *oeuvre.* This procedure, however, assumes that there was a "true" Bruno and a "cunning" Bruno. The former entrusted his intuitive insights to paper as seldom as possible, though the "modern" reader realizes that it was just these fragmentary insights which bridged the gap between Copernicus and Newton. The latter, "cunning" Bruno knew what kind of superstitious bogus the market would bear, and he opportunistically pandered to this audience. But, as we shall see, **The Ash Wednesday Supper** complements rather than opposes the works written by Bruno at approximately the same time [Emile Namer, *Revue d'Histoire des Sciences et de leurs Applications 29,* 1976].

Yet, this isolating of **The Ash Wednesday Supper** from others of Bruno's writings would seem to lead to edifying results. By ignoring the emblematic nature of Bruno's text and its engravings, a "corrected" and "sanitized" text makes it appear as if Bruno's intentions in the **Supper** were entirely "scientific." Such treatment seems to save Bruno for the internalist historian of science, for it is no longer necessary to think that Bruno was "interested only . . . magical or even political motivations" in **The Ash Wednesday Supper** [R. S. Westman and J. E. McGuire, eds., *Hermeticism and the Scientific Revolution,* 1977].

There is, however, a high price to pay for this too narrow reading of the **Supper.** The rest of the text is truncated and made incomprehensible. If it were true that Bruno was merely following in Oresme's footsteps, why the second dialogue's tale of the Nolan's journey through London; why the constant theme of Unity throughout the **Supper;** why, indeed, the very title of this work, and why the incantation at its end? The internalist approach does not and cannot answer these questions. Yet, surely it is more than an aesthetician's dream that they can be answered and that the text can be read as an integrated whole, not as a cunning medium for a few intuitive insights. It is my contention that an analysis of textual themes will most fruitfully unify the **Supper** and yield Bruno's overall message of the healing powers of the Copernican Sun.

II. *Social and Intellectual Illness*

Since much has already been written about **The Ash**

Wednesday Supper, I need only to summarize some of the most salient points about its general meaning and intent. One of six "Italian dialogues" written by Bruno in England between 1583 and 1585, it is dedicated to the Marquis de Mauvissière, at whose ambassadorial residence Bruno stayed in London. *The Ash Wednesday Supper* telescopes together two events. The first is a description of a "supper" supposedly held at Sir Fulke Greville's home on Ash Wednesday (February 14) 1584. (It is more likely, on the basis of textual evidence and statements Bruno later made to the Inquisition, that the "supper" really took place at Mauvissière's residence.) The subject of this supper was *la Cena,* the Eucharist. The second event is the lecture-debate in which Bruno engaged at Oxford University on the occasion of the visit there of the Polish prince Albert Alasco (June 1583); the subject of that event was supposed to have been the Copernican theory. Bruno, however, created quite a scandal at Oxford not only because of his Italian pronunciation of Latin but also because he apparently "lifted" portions of his remarks from Ficino's famous book on astral magic, *De vita coelitus comparanda.*

We should also bear in mind two facts external to the text: first, that Bruno explicitly said that the "troubles" in religion would only be settled if the dogmatic differences between Protestants and Catholics concerning the Eucharist could be composed, and, second, that Bruno felt that he was in England on a clandestine mission from the French king. It is by remembering that Bruno placed great emphasis on the impasse over the Eucharist and that he thought of himself as Henri III's ambassador without portfolio that we can begin, as we study its thematic structure, to understand the imagery that pervades *The Ash Wednesday Supper* and the role played in it by the Sun.

A major theme of *The Ash Wednesday Supper* is disease and its opposite, health. The Nolan (Bruno) first refers to his two opponents in debate, Doctors Nundinio and Torquato, as "two ghastly harridans, two dreams, two ghosts, two quartan agues." Bruno's prefatory admonition that not one word in the *Supper* will be idle is perhaps not enough to make us attach great importance to the reference to quartan agues. We also know, however, that the medical lore of the time had it that such fevers could be cured by the correct application of communion wafers. Such beliefs were popular and rural, but more sophisticated adherents of the belief could be found among those who were adept in the cabalistic arts. And, of course, the Roman Catholic Mass, just before the communion service, speaks of the Eucharist in terms of spiritual healing, *"Domine, non sum dignus ut intres sub tectum meum, sed tantum dic verbo et sanabitur anima mea."* Drawing upon these ecclesiastical and high- and low-culture traditions, Bruno will, by applying the Eucharist rightly understood, cure the fevers, drive out the bad doctors, and restore health and sanity to England and Europe.

In the first two dialogues of the *Supper* Bruno constantly returns to the theme of disease and health. In addition to calling him a quartan ague, Bruno describes Torquato as a desiccated being from whom not one drop of juice could be extracted by a press. Torquato and Nundinio were Ar-

istotelians at now Protestant Oxford. Speaking of this generalized group of sterile Aristotelians, Teofilo says that the Nolan's opponents are in blindness and the dark. On the other hand, Teofilo asserts that the Nolan and other followers of the "true" solar philosophy are:

> . . . moderate in life, expert in medicine, unique in divination, miraculous in magic, wary of superstition, . . . irreproachable in morality, godlike in every way. All this is proved by the length of their lives [and] their healthier bodies.

Such magi as Bruno "free the human mind" and

> open the cloisters of truth, give eyes to the moles and sight to the blind, loose the tongues of the dumb [so that they can now] express their entangled opinions.

Given the opportunity, then Bruno could even cure the blindness of Nundinio and Torquato.

While the first dialogue offers the reader a picture of diseased intellectuals and their happier alternative—Bruno and all those who enjoy the good health and miraculous powers made available by the solar philosophy—, the second dialogue delineates the social results of the teachings of such Protestant professors as Torquato and Nundinio. Disease, infirmity, and darkness are present throughout this dialogue, which recounts the Nolan's arduous journey from his residence to Sir Fulke Greville's house. Teofilo says that the stars "lay behind a dark, obscure mantle." The pages that follow indicate that this is the dark of social blindness and disease. The social, individual, and physical blight infecting London and its townsmen is evident everywhere: the Nolan's surly and preternaturally decrepit oarsmen with great effort can only move the hollow wreck of a boat a short way before the Nolan and his friends are ungraciously forced to go ashore and make their way through swinish passages and Avernus-like potholes. Worst of all is the boorish and boarish populace they encounter, whose incivility makes of them:

> such a stinkhole that, if they were mightily well repressed . . . , they would send forth such a stink and reek as would darken the name of the whole population, to the extent that England could boast a people which in irreverence, incivility, coarseness, boorishness, savagery and ill-breeding would yield nothing to any other people the earth might nourish on its breast. . . . I set before your eyes [those] who, seeing a foreigner, seem, by God, so many wolves and bears and who, by their grim looks, regard him as a pig would [regard] someone who came to take away his trough.

In characterizing the London mob as "ramming and butting beasts" who, as they lug and push their heavy loads of food and wares, crash into the Nolan and nearly kill him, Bruno seems to allude to the animal and other constellations whose reformation he describes as taking place in the *Spaccio della bestia trionfante (The Expulsion of the Triumphant Beast)*. Perhaps by describing this London mob in their animal forms, Bruno is magically trying to rid them of their baleful power. This interpretation fits well with my discussion of Bruno's powerful conjuration at the end of the *Supper,* which I will give below.

That Bruno is not simply portraying a bestial mob of the sort that could have been found in *any* sixteenth-century city is evidenced by the fact that, later, Bruno explicitly says that the London mob is the epigones of the Oxford doctors and their economy of salvation which frustrates the inclination for "good works." Further indication that Bruno relates the bestiality of the mob to the Protestant dispensation and its "dead" eucharistic Sacrament is given at the end of the second dialogue itself. There Teofilo thanks God that at Greville's supper the "ceremony of the cup" did not take place. Although it did not, Teofilo nevertheless describes it in a marvelous parody of the Protestant communion in both kinds:

> Usually the chalice passes around the table. . . . After the leader of this dance has detached his lips, leaving a layer of grease which could easily be used as glue, another drinks and leaves a bit of meat on the rim, still another drinks and leaves a hair of his beard. . . . Since all of them came together to make themselves into a flesh-eating wolf to eat the lamb or kid or Grunnio Corrocotta, by thus applying each one his mouth to the selfsame tankard, they come to form themselves into one selfsame lech, in token of one community, one brotherhood, one *plague,* one heart, one stomach, one gullet and one mouth [emphasis mine].

We are now once again reminded that the subject of the dialogue is the Supper. And we are now told that the Protestant communion is a plague, that is, a disease.

Having discoursed on the diseases afflicting the university teachers and the English commoners whose rude behavior results from the Protestant doctrine of salvation, which gives no place to the efficacy of good works and thus "quenches the fervor of good actions," Bruno turns to the arguments, in the latter three dialogues, in which we find his physical experiments. It is these that the internalist historian of science relies upon to make of Bruno a link between Oresme and Galileo. Yet, even in these sections—following the dialogues that speak of sickness, the Eucharist, and the solar philosophy—we find him referring again and again to disease. He no longer speaks of quartan fevers and plague but of madness.

Bruno notes the fear with which the Copernican theory was met in some quarters. The prefacer [Osiander] of Copernicus' *De revolutionibus* was afraid, says Bruno through Teofilo, that he and others would be "driven mad" by Copernicus and for this reason had insisted falsely that Copernicus' model had been advanced solely for calculational purposes. Later in the *Supper* Torquato asks the Nolan if he is "sailing to Anticyra," that is, if he is going mad. According to legend one could obtain in Anticyra the "hellebore" which cured madness. In a sense—to Bruno's mind at least—the Nolan was sailing to that fabled place not because *he* was mad but because he was bringing to England the drug which would cure the madness of religious division. This point is implicit in Bruno's statement that it is Torquato who is mad and that he, the

Nolan, is going to "glue together the brains of these mad barbarians."

The "gluing together" of the brains of the Protestant doctors will heal the fevers and madness of Elizabethan society. Or, as the Nolan says in the midst of a seemingly scientific discussion:

> As for those of you who place yourselves under the banner of Aristotle, I advise you not to boast, as if you understood what he penetrates. There is, in fact, the greatest difference between not knowing what he did not know and knowing what he knew, because where that philosopher was ignorant he has for followers not only you [Torquato] but all your ilk, together with the London boatmen and dockers.

The uncouthness and rudeness of the Oxford dons and the London mob are both the consequences of the philosophy of Aristotle as it was vulgarly understood in Protestant England. The reader of *The Ash Wednesday Supper* can only look forward to the amelioration of social and intellectual conditions, the curing of madness and quartan agues, when he reads at the end of the fourth dialogue that Nundinio and Torquato were, as it were, driven out of the dining room by the Nolan's pressing of his Copernican arguments *"ad rem, ad rem."*

III. *Solar Medicine*

The arguments that Bruno pressed *ad rem* have to do with the Sun and its power. As we shall see, the curing of the social and intellectual ills afflicting England is made possible by the eucharistic medicine of the Sun, the "hellebore" that the Nolan was bringing to England.

There is, according to Bruno, a close connection between cosmology and virtue. For this reason, he says, Moses had taught that the earth is motionless at the center of the universe; otherwise his followers, seeing his teaching to be at variance with sensible experience, would no longer have followed the Mosaic Law. But ever since Copernicus had heralded the dawn of a new age, the heretofore necessary exoteric lie was no longer necessary to preserve virtue. Upon Copernicus' astronomy Bruno intended to build a new cosmological dispensation based on the infinite vigor, motion, and thus active good works implicit in his version of heliocentrism.

Accordingly, Bruno transformed Copernicus, self-admittedly understood what Copernicus the "mere mathematician" could not, and spoke of an infinite universe with many living and inhabited worlds, all of which are in motion around their own suns which themselves are in motion. It is unseemly, says Bruno, to think that the earth is at the center of the universe, for it is impossible to conclude that the "totality of innumerable bodies, of which many are known [to be] more splendid and greater [than the earth], look to the earth as the center and basis of their circles and influences. . . ."

The imagery that pervades *The Ash Wednesday Supper* and its physical experiments stresses the theme of Unity. Influenced by Cusanus, Bruno constantly emphasizes the progress from multiplicity to One. Opposites are reconciled. Thus, he describes *The Ash Wednesday Supper* itself as being both "comic and tragic, joyous and choleric, Florentine for its leanness and Bolognese for its fatness." If separated from each other infinitely, stars and planets share their light; the obstacles, the "opaque bodies" which had obstructed the free passage of light between them, become insignificant. At a sufficient distance, a star can illuminate more than a hemisphere; it can illuminate a whole sphere. Polar opposites share the same light and thereby become one.

This healing, antipodal reconciliation is vitally important for Bruno's reunionist schemes. On the celestial level this Brunonian reconciliatory optics supports the idea that the earth is like all the other stars. At one point, in fact, Bruno says that the earth would become as hot as the Sun. In other words, earth and Sun share the same essence. This implies a reconciliation of the most extreme sort, for, according to traditional cosmology, earth was a drossy, mutable body while the Sun was perfect and never-changing.

If the earth and Sun are hot and mobile, then they are both "animals" and have souls. The universe is alive, and we no longer need to look outward for divinity because

> we have the knowledge not to search for divinity removed from us if we have it near; it is within us more than we ourselves are.

Or, speaking on another level, when Torquato asks, "Where is the apogee of the Sun?", the Nolan replies that it is anywhere he wants it to be. To the repeated question the Nolan rephrases his answer to show its true import:

> How many are the sacraments of the Church? [The Sun] is about the twentieth degree of Cancer, and the opposition is about the one-hundred-tenth degree of Capricorn, or above the bell-tower of St. Paul's.

Sacraments, Summer, Winter, England: All these are components of the Nolan's answer to Torquato's question about the apogee of the Sun. Certainly this is not a fitting reply to a supposedly astronomical question. Clearly, Bruno's physical arguments are of a piece with his Cusanan reconciliation of opposites. For Bruno, if the heretofore putatively inert earth moves and is alive, then the universe and each of its parts partake of soul and are alive. If the earth is alive, then the Sacrament, as one of its parts, is no problem, for it, in a similar way, must be alive, mobile, and thus "anywhere you want it to be." It would seem, then, that the eucharistic sacrament need not be defined rigidly. If liberal-minded Protestants and Catholics realize that they all share in divinity and that the Sun's light can shine through even the Eucharist, then the seemingly opaque eucharistic host need no longer impede their interaction.

Bruno's discussion here is to some degree similar to discussions of light's penetration of opaque bodies in his **"De umbris idearum"** ("On the Shadow of Ideas"). This similarity suggests that it might be fruitful, at some future time and in another context, to begin reading *The Ash Wednesday Supper* in the light of this book on Bruno's magic memory system. At this point, I shall only point out that Bruno does not really offer a "doctrine of the Eucharist"; rather, his strategy is to transcend definitions and to allow

the Eucharist to become a noncontroversial object through which, metaphorically, the light of Bruno's solar, nonchristian religion can pass. This is Bruno's eucharistic medicine that will heal the "troubles" in religion and the disease plaguing England.

Bruno therefore looks forward to spiritual calm in the *Supper,* brought about by the dawning Age of the Sun. This calm is indeed the goal of his physics, a fact that is probably best seen in his famous ship experiment. Speaking on an earthly, physical level of the kind of motive attractions found between straw and amber as well as between magnets, Teofilo tells us that a man on the mast of a ship can drop a stone which will fall to the deck directly below, while a man standing on the shore at a point above the ship's mast, not participating in the same system or reference frame, cannot similarly drop a stone to the foot of the mast as the ship passes beneath him. The man atop the mast is successful because he lets the stone fall with an impressed force, a *virtù impressa.* The impressed force of which Teofilo speaks is as much moral and ethical as it is physical. This man atop the mast of this ship which represents spiritual calm, France and Henri III, is a Brunonian solar magus whose solar Sacrament and universe are alive with spiritual force, while the man on the shore, like Nundinio and Torquato, exists in a universe that does not exude divinity, and he consequently has neither the knowledge of the forces of Nature nor the ethical *virtù* of a solar magus.

The efficacy of Bruno's healing "hellebore" is guaranteed, to Bruno's mind, by the Sun itself. The occasion for this dialogue was the Lord's Supper on Ash Wednesday. If, as Bruno would like the reader to think, the Supper was attended by both liberal Catholics and liberal Protestants, then the Supper must have been understood by both sides somewhat heterodoxically. Such heterodoxy supports Bruno's conception of the Sacrament as a metaphorical but vital source for interchange among men and between men and Divinity. On one level Bruno's exposition of the Sacrament through the hieroglyph of Copernican heliocentrism is a metaphor for the proposed Anglo-French union. (Indeed, I am inclined to think that Bruno's very choice of Copernican heliocentrism as a vehicle for expounding his Hermetic "secret" of *la Cène desguisée* was in part due to his awareness that the Dee circle in England—which included the Copernican Thomas Digges—and the Pléiade-Academic movement in Paris both shares an interest in the Copernican theory.) The subject of this dialogue, a sacramental celebration on Ash Wednesday, thereby indicated that a period of spiritual renewal was about to begin: the Lenten season. Again various themes conjoin: Ash Wednesday, sacrifice and self-assessment, renewal, and rebirth of light, all culminating at Easter, that is—on Bruno's nonchristian level—with the coming of Spring. The Sun once more rising above the equator is the bearer of Divinity with which the divinity within men can interact.

Bruno's optimism rests on the life-giving interactions between the divine Sun and the divinity within Nature and Man. Accordingly, the fifth dialogue of the *Supper* describes the Sun's centricity in these vivifying and renewing interactions. For example, Teofilo speaks of the climatic change that he finds, significantly, occurring at his very time:

> . . . and from the fact that France and Italy are gradually becoming warmer, while England is becoming more temperate, we must conclude that in general the characteristics of regions are changing and that the disposition to cold is diminishing toward the Arctic pole.

This change, Teofilo tells his friends, results from the circulation of the Sun. Unlike Copernicus' Sun, Bruno's is in constant motion. The Sun "diffuses and communicates vital forces," and if the Sun

> did not move to the other bodies or the other bodies to it, how could it receive what it does not possess or give what it has?

The Sun, then, is essential for all interaction and change.

The motion of the living earth is also necessary, so that it may imbibe and be nourished by the life-giving forces of the Sun. It is because of the interactions between the two divine animals, Sun and earth, that seas over time become continents and continents seas. As Teofilo sums up:

> . . . in conclusion, every part of the earth comes to have every view of the Sun which every other part has, so that every part eventually participates in every life, every generation, every felicity.

The Sun warms, the earth turns, and changes occur. These changes on the geological level are also antipodal, and things become their opposites. If seas become continents and continents seas, then they are, *sub specie aeternitatis,* the same: One.

The last dialogue of *The Ash Wednesday Supper* is thus a powerful summing up of the themes and "experiments" that have come before, in the context of the Lord's Supper on Ash Wednesday. Now, in the fifth dialogue, the propagators of disease, Nundinio and Torquato, are no longer present, and the events leading up to and including the Supper and debate at Greville's (or Mauvissière's) residence are history. In a sense the reform—metaphorically implicit in the Lenten imagery of *The Ash Wednesday Supper*—has begun. Its arrival is signified by the engine of the Sun, the power-station which accomplishes all change and nourishment. The "engine" is efficacious because of the constant turning and motion of the Sun, earth, and all the other stars. Again, we must ask ourselves, what is the relationship between Bruno's cosmological vision found here in *The Ash Wednesday Supper* and the star images that constantly turn about the Sun and interact in the complex Lullian memory wheels which Bruno describes in **"De umbris idearum?"** However we may eventually answer this question, there is a striking similarity between the Lullian mnemonic art as *perfected* by Bruno in his book on *Shadows* and the Copernican solar system as *perfected* by Bruno in his book on the Ash Wednesday Supper.

Just as the efficacy of the memory system in **"De umbris idearum"** depends on the quasi-Copernican complex of whirling wheels which can store and expose all knowledge, the movement from multiplicity to One and from disease to health in *The Ash Wednesday Supper* is achieved by Bruno through the Sun's circulation and the revolutions of the earth made necessary by the centricity of the Sun in our solar system. Just as Bruno's previous experiments in the *Supper* had *shown* that two stars illuminate each other, so here in the fifth dialogue both Sun and earth are *shown* to turn so that every part of each shares and interacts with the other. If this can happen cosmologically and astronomically, then nothing, to Bruno's mind, prevents the beneficial interaction of the English Protestants, whose Sacrament had been thought to be, like the earth, dead with the French, whose king is that solar lion, the creature of Light, who was praised in *The Ash Wednesday Supper* and to whom **"De umbris idearum"** was dedicated.

IV. *Epilogue*

By way of drawing together the strands and themes that we have been following, I would like to turn back to a certain point in the fourth dialogue of *The Ash Wednesday Supper.* After Frulla and Teofilo have bemoaned the existence of the diseased doctors and of the London mob—the so-called "fruits of England"—, the Nolan and Torquato discuss the apogee of the Sun. As we remember, the Nolan replies with a series of questions: How many sacraments are there? Is it Summer or Winter in England; that is, is the Sun high or low? These strange questions are leading to a confluence of the themes we have discussed and thus are leading up to a very dramatic moment.

Torquato and the Nolan cannot agree about whether Copernicus had put the earth and moon on the same epicycle. Copernicus' book is brought in for all to look at. At the real debate at Oxford Bruno had quoted from Ficino's book on magic, *De vita coelitus comparanda.* This time, in an analogous situation, the Nolan turns to *De revolutionibus.*

The book is opened, and everyone looks at Copernicus' diagram of the heliocentric universe. Although Bruno does not explicitly say it in the *Supper,* we know, he knew, and the guests present at the Supper would have known, what words were printed directly beneath the engraving in the Copernican text:

> In the midst of all this is the Sun. . . . Trimegistus [sic] calls it the visible god.

Clearly, Bruno sees no essential difference between Ficino's book on magic and Copernicus' book on astronomy. They are both mediums for his Hermetic secret.

At this critical juncture of the text, we find telescoped together within a very few pages the diseased "fruits of England," the sacramental cure, the Sun, an allusion to Bruno's discourse on magic at Oxford, and Hermes Trismegistus. The very core of the scientific argument in *The Ash Wednesday Supper* is Hermetic, the quasi-religious revelation of a Sun whose mobility in an animate and mobile universe makes it a powerful image for change. By setting the Sun and earth free or by making the Sun image the center of all "intentions of the will" in a Lullian magic memory wheel (as was found in **"De umbris idearum"**), Bruno's Sun can help to heal, nourish, and redeem a Europe plagued by confessional "troubles."

Perhaps looking forward to a time when his "secret," alluded to in **"De umbris idearum"** and expounded in ***La Cena de le Ceneri,*** will have restored a (nonchristian) unity to Europe, Bruno promises another work on the "fruit of redemption," as ***The Ash Wednesday Supper*** ends. Finally, it is Prudenzio, so often before the butt of criticism and mockery in this work, who ironically is made to deliver the stunning conjuration that sums up Bruno's "medicine": found among the six parts of the conjuration are, for example, the "cure" of the French alliance by the progeny of the Trojan horse; the more traditional cure by Aesculapius of Nundinio and Torquato; and the violent "cures" befitting the "butting and kicking beasts" whom the Nolan had encountered in his journey across London.

Bruno returned to France with Mauvissière in 1585, following an adverse change in the balance of power within France between Henri III and the *Guisards*—a change that nullified Bruno's "mission" to England. From Paris he recommenced his European wanderings. His failed mission to England has therefore left us without the promised ***Purgatorio de l'inferno*** on the "fruit of redemption." Yet, even without it the confluence of themes in the fourth dialogue—preparatory to Bruno's discussion of his solar philosophy in the fifth dialogue—and the magical conjuration at the very end of ***The Ash Wednesday Supper,*** ridding England of its baleful propagators of disease, should be enough to alert us to the fact that what has gone on in the text is more closely related to Hermes the Thrice-Great, to Julian's pagan Sol Invictus, and to Bruno's own work on the magical and Lullian memory system than it is to Oresme's impetus theory and to Galileo's mechanics. More than a practitioner of the astronomical art, Bruno

---

Lindsay on the problems with Bruno's anti-Aristotelian premises:

[I]n the dialogues on Cause, Principle, and Unity, [Bruno] most systematically braces himself to demolish the Aristotelian positions once for all, in all their ramifications, and that . . . means for him the breaking-down of a whole way of life and its substitution by another. ***The Expulsion of the Triumphant Beast*** which soon follows gives the full social programme which is to supplant the social and moral systems linked with Aristotelian logic and geocentric mechanism. But though he wants to bring about a totally new attitude to reality, he is constrained to use the only available tools and terms. Much of his difficulty comes from this fact. He is employing terms based on division to express unity, terms based on abstract logic to express a new sense of dialectical conflict and resolution.

Jack Lindsay in his Introduction to Five Dialogues by Giordano Bruno, Cause, Principle, and Unity, *1962.*

---

is a practitioner of what he will later call the *medicina Lulliana*—the healing art.

Edward A. Gosselin (essay date 1987)

SOURCE: "Fra Giordano Bruno's Catholic Passion," in *Svpplementvm Festivvm: Studies in Honor of Paul Oskar Kristeller,* Center for Medieval and Early Renaissance Studies, 1987, pp. 537-61.

[*In this essay, Gosselin examines the religious aspect of Bruno's work, maintaining that despite his alleged heresy, the philosopher retained some Roman Catholic beliefs at the time of his death.*]

I. *Introduction: The Heretic*

As Giordano Bruno's ashes cooled on February 17, 1600, in the Campo dei Fiori, there was relief that an obstinate heretic had been eliminated. The sentence read (February 8) and the execution carried out, Bruno's words and actions on these occasions seemed to indicate then, and have ever since, that he had had only scorn for his natal faith. Such seemed clear from the philosopher's remark when the sentence was read to him by the inquisitors: "Perhaps you feel more afraid in pronouncing this sentence than I do on hearing it." Such seemed clear also from his scornful turning away from the proffered crucifix as the flames engulfed him. As Gaspar Scioppius, an eyewitness to the execution, said: "When they showed him the image of Christ, as he was on the verge of expiring, he turned his head away and rejected it with a scornful look. . . ." No matter who has written about Bruno since that time, the memory of his condemnation and execution scenes has stood between the Nolan and his subsequent interpreter. "Fu bruciato!" Since February 17, 1600, Bruno's published works and his words at his trial have served only to confirm the terrible judgment carried out on that February morning.

This continuous confirmation of the inquisitorial judgment has prevented complete understanding of Giordano Bruno's ideas and actions as a religious thinker. It would thus be well to read and view Bruno's words anew, trying as much as possible to escape the distorting lens of his condemnation and execution, and thus to view him just before the picture frame froze him forever beyond the pale of Catholic, indeed even Christian, thought and behavioral parameters. I believe that this fresh examination will be useful for several reasons. For one thing, work by Carlo Ginzburg, whatever the final assessment of its methodology may be, has shown that inquisitors did not always easily or accurately comprehend or even taxonomize the responses given them by suspected heretics. This seems especially clear in Bruno's case for, as we shall see below, the inquisitors—as late as September, 1599—had not reached agreement on defining Bruno's heresies. And, indeed, as Hélène Védrine has rightly pointed out, the whole purpose of inquisitorial proceedings was biased, in the first place, and, in the second, was intent upon making the accused "see," "accept," and recant his "errors." We may argue, then, that Bruno's condemnation was *a fortiori* a prejudiced decision and that it could not help but shape all subsequent readings of the Nolan philosopher.

I propose in this paper, then, to survey Bruno's responses to the inquisitors and to try to assess their significance both in the light of related things he had previously written and in that of the problem of the internal consistency of his answers to the questions put to him by his judges. We cannot enter into a detailed accounting of Bruno's quotidial behavior and actions—what he did and said to those around him while he was a monk and while he was not a monk—for the evidence for such a brief does not exist, however lamentable that fact is. Thus we are left with scattered snapshots, as it were, of moments—many of them highly charged—in Giordano Bruno's life, and we must try to infer conclusions about that life from them. In so doing, we will be going through published material that is well known, as no new documents have been uncovered. I am, however, offering a fresh interpretation that is fully allowed by the evidence. By the time we reach the end of this analysis, we will have concluded that Bruno was probably not quite as "unchristian" and "Egyptian" in his religion as Frances Yates averred nor as morally flawed but, *au coeur,* Roman Catholic as Angelo Mercati argued. Fra Giordano rejected much of his Catholicism, but he continued to maintain some feeling for his monastic background and some longing for sacramental ceremonial. He might have been a Nicodemite, but his dislike of the Protestant doctrine of justification prevented, as we shall see, his being a proper Catholic Nicodemite.

II. *The Truth of Words*

The reader might question the sincerity of Bruno's response to the question of whether he had ever said that the miracles of Christ and the Apostles were not real but were done by magical art. The posture and words seem studied. Yet it could also signify genuine shock that such an outrageous thing could have been said about him. One could interpret the above-quoted statement either way. The former interpretation—that he was acting—is more consistent with the normative view of Bruno as a flamboyant individual whose public utterances tended to histrionics and perhaps even intellectual dishonesty. Bruno's shock seems all the more implausible when one recalls Bruno's blasphemous aversion of his eyes from the crucifix in the last moments of his life. But this may be an overhasty conclusion. After all, given the fact that Bruno was finally condemned, as we shall see, despite the inquisitors' difficulty in reaching consensus on his crimes and despite his previous expression of contrition for any errors of thought and action he might have committed, one can well understand that his state of mind on the morning of February 17 would not have induced him to turn toward the crucifix. The evidence against Bruno was in large part drawn from the testimony of his Venetian host-turned-betrayer, Zuan Mocenigo, and from that of his Venetian cellmate, Fra Celestino da Verona. Neither man was unbiased. Mocenigo seems to have felt that Bruno had failed to teach him the art of memory that could have facilitated a brilliant career for the young nobleman, and Celestino may well have betrayed Bruno in a futile attempt to lighten his own sentence. When we survey the extant records of Bruno's trial, we are thus faced with the problem of Bruno's probity in the face of his questioners. The easy assumption is to conclude that Bruno, a brilliant intellectual fencer, ran circles around the inquisitors and generally lied to them. I do not believe that this assumption can be sustained. What seems clear from the testimony as well as from a comparison of the testimony with certain things that Bruno had written in *La Cena de le Ceneri, Lo Spaccio della bestia trionfante,* and *De l'infinito, universo, e mondi,* is that Bruno stayed close to the truth on those matters for which the inquisitors had close-to-hand evidence with which to assess his responses, and that he either stretched the truth of, or obfuscated, issues about which the judges were not likely to have contrary evidence. It was essential for Bruno to stretch the truth in this latter case in order not to reveal his deeper relations with Protestant churches or his Valois-appointed mission to bring about religious reunion. Such matters could not be revealed if Bruno held out any hope that his life be spared and that he be sufficiently reconciled with Rome to allow him active participation in the eucharistic ceremony. Ultimately, as we shall see, while Bruno may not have been orthodox, he saw himself as an apostle of the eucharist.

One of the best instances of Bruno's deliberate obscuring of the truth may be found in his response to a question directly relating to the point just made—whether he had ever written about an Ash Wednesday Supper:

> I once wrote a *book* [my emphasis] titled *The Ash Wednesday Supper.* It is divided into five dialogues which deal with the motion of the earth; and because I engaged in this discussion in England with some physicians at a supper that took place on Ash Wednesday in the French ambassador's residence, I titled these dialogues *The Ash Wednesday Supper,* and dedicated them to the aforementioned ambassador. . . . My intent in the book was only to mock those doctors and their opinions on these matters.

Bruno obviously wanted to avoid giving any religious significance to that Ash Wednesday Supper as he focused the inquisitors' attention on the safer—because then still neutral—ground of the Copernican theory and the comic aspects of the book. On the other hand, despite the care with which Bruno responded to this and other questions put to him, I do not believe we can assume that his responses are entirely devoid of truth value. Somehow it would seem out of character for Bruno to have been able to maintain a façade throughout his eight years of encounters with the inquisitors, notwithstanding the fact that on July 30, 1592 he confessed and begged pardon for all his errors and that, again, in September 1599 torture prompted him momentarily once again to recant, a type of confession that few today would really believe was sincere. On December 21, 1599, Bruno reneged his recantation:

> He said that he ought not and did not wish to recant, that there was no subject about which to recant, and that he did not know about what he should recant.

The modern psychological age might say that Bruno had a death wish. But, more likely, once the pain and memory of torture had abated, he once again realized that the case against him was a slender reed. As far as Bruno's credibility is concerned, credence can, I think, be given to many of his responses by dint of the fact that some were obviously liable to make trouble for him. Thus if he felt compelled to reply honestly concerning some questions, the answers to which threatened his safety, then why should we not assume that he consistently answered as honestly as he could, always trying to be true to his beliefs but yet showing their compatibility with orthodox Roman teaching? The evidence suggests that Bruno in some sense wanted to be reconciled with the Church, although not entirely on the latter's terms.

III. *The Habit, the Tonsure, and* la Cène: *From Naples to Geneva*

Let us turn then to an examination of Bruno's testimony in the context of the chronology of his journey from Naples to Geneva (1576-1579). The confluence of the testimony with the chronology will enable us the better to reach some conclusions about Bruno's religious views and comportment.

Born in Nola in 1548, Filippo Bruno entered the Dominican monastery of San Domenico in Naples on June 15, 1565. After a year, he completed his novitiate and became a Dominican friar, adopting the name "Giordano," in honor of the second leader of the Order. He became a priest in 1572 and sang his first mass at the convent of San Bartolomeo in Campagna. Not much is known of Bruno's activities as a friar over the next few years. By 1576, however, this period of relative calm ended and Bruno came to the attention of his monastic superiors. He had expressed some Arian-sounding ideas and was discovered to have read editions of Erasmus that had been prohibited. In addition, he seems to have taken to heart some of the latter's anti-ritualistic ideas, for Bruno "reformed" his own monastic cell:

> At Naples, I had been brought to account two times: first, for having taken down certain figures and images of the saints, retaining only a crucifix, [and] thus I was thought to despise the images of saints.

There is only fragmentary evidence of Bruno's doings after he had fled Naples, and then Rome, because of the charges of heresy brought against him. He travelled throughout Italy until he crossed the Alps and went to Geneva in 1579. Comments made at his trial indicate that he taught Sacrobosco's *Sphere* in Noli, along with grammar lessons to young boys. He claimed to have published a book, *De' segni de' tempi,* in order to earn money while in Venice; however, its contents are unknown today. Interestingly, at Bruno's request, the Dominican humanist Remigio Fiorentino authorized its publication, a fact that may indicate that the work contained nothing contrary to Catholic teachings. When Bruno finally emerged from Italy, it was after he had once again donned the Dominican habit in Bergamo, having been urged to do so by Dominicans of his acquaintance whom he had met in Padua:

> Leaving Venice, I went to Padua where I met some Dominicans who knew me, [and] they persuaded me to put on the habit again, even should I not wish to return to the Order, as they were of the opinion that it was safer to go with the habit than without it; and with this thought I continued on to Bergamo. [There] I had a [Do-

minican] habit made out of cheap white cloth, and over it I put the scapular that I had kept with me when I left Rome.

Crossing the Alps, Bruno stayed for some time in the Dominican convent in Chambéry and continued to wear his Dominican robes:

> . . . and I continued to wear the habit as I proceeded in the direction of Lyons; and when I was at Chambéry, I lodged at the convent of the Order; and seeing that I was treated soberly, I discussed this with an Italian priest who was there. He said to me: "Be forewarned that you will not find courtesy of any kind in these parts [in convents], and the further you go [toward Lyons and into France] the less you will find."

One interpretation of Bruno's life (shared in certain ways by Yates, Corsano, Védrine and Singer, among others) has it that Bruno was fully formed intellectually and, by implication, religiously, at the time of his flight from Naples. By further adducement, he is thought to have been already an "unchristian," a proponent of the Hermetic "Egyptian" religion, Lullism, and, perhaps, Copernicanism. However, none of the evidence presented here or, as far as I know, extant in the documents completely supports this line of interpretation. Rather, on the eve of Bruno's entrance into Geneva we have a picture of a thirty-one-year-old man, Dominican trained, whose somewhat iconoclastic and Erasmian tendencies had caused him to be alleged a heretic in the Kingdom and again in Rome. Understandably fearful, Bruno ran away and, by that act prompted by fear, he became apostate and thus a heretic.

Bruno is of course not the only monk or brother to have fled the cloister in the sixteenth century. Erasmus and Rabelais also did, to name only two of the most famous—and without the scandal that has hounded Bruno's reputation. Besides, unlike Erasmus and Rabelais, we are beginning to sense that Bruno had not completely broken with and distanced himself from the cloister. It is true that his readoption of the habit could have been purely for safety's sake. But why? How recognizable could Bruno have been as he wandered the streets of Padua and Bergamo? Why could he not have merged in with the other people on the crowded streets of these cities? Might it be the case that, having abandoned the Dominican habit when he fled Rome, he retained the tonsure? Nothing in the trial records or in any other source, as far as I know, speaks one way or the other about this matter. However, Bruno's own account of his arrival in Geneva, immediately after having left Chambéry, may indicate that he in fact did wear a tonsure:

> And [the Marchese of Vico] persuaded me . . . to get rid of my habit, [and] I took off those clothes and had a pair of breeches and other robes made; and the Marchese [and] other Italians gave me [a] sword, hat, cape, and other necessities for dressing myself.

Perhaps Bruno's Genevan friends only wanted him to look the gentleman. But it is likely that, at the same time, they wanted him—whatever his intentions vis-à-vis the Calvinist religion—to hide the tonsure from Calvinist eyes.

It would not be surprising if Bruno had retained the tonsure ever since leaving Rome in 1576, just ahead of the next step of the inquisitorial process. Although he had fled the Inquisition and the Order, he may not have thought of himself as a heretic, no matter how individual his ideas had become or were becoming. Perhaps he kept the tonsure as a sign of private religious commitment. This would explain better why his Dominican friends in Padua advised him to wear the habit—the rest of his body ought to be garbed in line with his tonsure. Being tonsured, he was easily recognizable as a lapsed brother. Since canon law forbade his putting aside the habit, he could have been prosecuted by Italian civil authorities. And certainly, as he continued to wear the Dominican habit even when he entered Geneva, he must have arrived there tonsured as well.

That this maintenance of the tonsure—for I believe that this is what he did, given the evidence that we have seen—and the putting on again of the Dominican robes may well denote more than fear of discovery is supported by the fact that Bruno had kept the Dominican scapular he had worn in San Domenico and Rome. He had carried it with him until he repositioned it over his readopted habit in Bergamo. This behavior betrays more lingering commitment and attachment to the cloister and Church than it would perhaps today for someone who, forsaking his religion entirely, might consign the object to the trash or to a soon-to-be-forgotten spot in a drawer. Bruno had become a wanderer in 1576. Every object he carried along with him must have meant something.

Bruno's residence in Geneva, however, confuses the matter of Bruno's religious feelings, especially since it seems to contradict what the evidence thus far implies: that Bruno retained certain attachments to Catholicism. For it is among the Genevan records that we find *prima facie* evidence that Bruno had entirely forsaken not only the Dominican Order but also the Roman Catholic Church. What else should one make of the fact that in Geneva he abandoned his religious name, "Giordano," and adopted his secular name, "Filippo"? Not only this, but the municipal records found in Spampanato's *Documenti* show that Bruno desired a lifting of the ban that had, to use the Calvinist expression, "fenced him off" from the Lord's Supper in that city.

After his arrival in Geneva, Bruno had created a storm by attacking the Genevan Academy's leading philosopher, Anthoyne de la Faye, claiming that his lectures contained twenty errors. De la Faye brought suit against Bruno and his publisher, Jean Bergeron, and caused them to be imprisoned briefly. Thereafter, we find that on Thursday, 13 August:

> Filippo Bruno appeared in Consistory to acknowledge his fault. . . . He was admonished to follow the true doctrine. He replied that he was prepared to accept censure . . . , [that] he has to acknowledge his fault, and that they had forbidden him the Supper in case he did not wish to confess his fault.

And, on Thursday, 27 August, we learn of:

> Removal of the ban, with warnings. —Filippo Bruno, student, living in this city, appeared in Consistory. He asked that the ban on his taking the Supper be lifted.

One final document, compiled and published in 1650, lists "Filippo Bruno of the Kingdom of Naples" as having been a member of the Italian Protestant church in Geneva.

These shreds of evidence point to Bruno's conversion to Calvinism. He had apparently become a member of the Italian congregation. Later, stung by the furor over and the eucharistic consequences of his published attack on Anthoyne de la Faye, Bruno was above all concerned to be readmitted to the Calvinist Supper. These signs of change are confirmed, it would seem, by his adoption of his secular name. Since the entry of his secular name in the *Livre du Recteur* is an autograph signature, we know that it was not simply the case of a Genevan Calvinist refusing to honor his religious name; yet, registration in the university at most required an acknowledgement of Christian doctrine as it was taught at Geneva, not a confession of faith.

Filippo Bruno the Calvinist? This is quite a different picture from the one we have been sketching thus far. And it is quite a different picture from the one Giordano Bruno painted for his inquisitors:

> [Having left Chambéry, I finally arrived in Geneva.] I went to lodge in an inn; soon thereafter, the Neapolitan Marchese of Vico, resident in that city, asked me who I was and whether I had gone there to settle and to profess the religion of that city. I gave an accounting of myself and the reason why I had left the religious state, [and then] I added that I did not intend to adopt the religion of Geneva, because I did not know what religion it was; and that I desired to stay there in order to be free and secure rather than for any other reason.

Which is the correct version: that contained in the municipal and university records of Geneva, or the one given by Bruno, that he merely wanted security and freedom in Geneva, not a new religion? The answer is that both reasons are correct. Bruno did become a Calvinist congregant for a brief period; and Bruno did want to find a place where he could live securely and without fear of inquisitorial prosecution. Above all, it is not to be wondered that Bruno did not want to confide to the inquisitors during his long trial in Venice and Rome that he had been a Calvinist congregant or a partaker of its communion. This was never admitted openly by Bruno at his trial, but we will be able to understand how he could hunger for both Protestant and Catholic communion when we understand ***The Ash Wednesday Supper.*** For the moment, we should simply realize that, as the rules obtaining at the time of his enrollment in the Academy of Geneva indicate, Bruno did not have to swear a Calvinist confession of faith before he signed his name in the *Livre du Recteur.* Thus, he did not have to commit himself publicly to Calvinist theology even though he seems to have—or at least have wanted to—take the Calvinist Supper.

IV. *Paris, London, and the Eucharist*

I have argued elsewhere that Bruno's long journey from Naples to Paris was intensely educational and that it was only in Paris that Bruno was finally introduced to Ramon Lull, the mystical philosopher who believed in the use of the art of memory to harmonize Muslims with Christians. Paris was where Bruno was introduced to the king who would send him to London to harmonize Anglicans with French Catholics, and where he began to get his first glimmerings of the Copernican Sun that would for Bruno become the sign and the motive engine of the Valois Henrican reform. Sequestered in San Domenico and Naples, Bruno's knowledge of the Reformation and its controversies had probably been indirect and minimal. His only documented exposure was to the scholarly works of Erasmus (which, as I suggested above, either caused or reinforced a sensitive and somewhat reformist religious nature). But, after fleeing Naples and then Rome (out of fear of being prosecuted for having read the prohibited works of Erasmus), his journey northward brought him an ever closer acquaintance with Reformation controversies. Once settled in Geneva, he found a religious community that had been, to some extent, influenced by Erasmian ideas. Certainly Calvinist iconoclasm would have dovetailed with his own modest iconoclastic efforts in his Neapolitan monastic cell. In Geneva, too, he must finally have become aware of a quite different eucharistic feast than that to which he had been accustomed as a priest. This growing awareness was, I believe, the beginning of Bruno's belief that the crucial stumbling block of the Reformation debate, as far as religious reunion was concerned, was the question of Holy Communion, its definition, and its liturgy. In Geneva, Bruno attended public sermons by French and Italian preachers, including homilies on the Pauline Epistles and the Gospels given by Nicolò Balbani. Perhaps thinking that he could find religious peace and communion in Geneva, he joined the Church, but he soon ran afoul of the holy community because of his attacks on de la Faye. (It may be that he already realized, as we will see he did in London, that the Protestant doctrine of justification was anathema to him.) In any case, Bruno did not remain long in Geneva. He betook himself to Toulouse, which was, until the 1590s, a Calvinist town.

In Toulouse, Bruno became affiliated with and taught at the university. Relative religious calm reigned in the city when Bruno arrived, so the usual requirement that professors participate in the Protestant communion was not then enforced. By 1581, Bruno had left Toulouse and gone to Paris. There, he soon became known to court intellectuals and to Henri III himself. The king offered Bruno an ordinary lectureship, but the Nolan declined. Bruno's later remarks to the inquisitors explain why he could accept the teaching position in Toulouse but not in Paris:

> And then, because of the civil wars, I left [Toulouse] and went to Paris where I gave an extraordinary lecture in order to make myself known . . . , but when I was asked to give an ordinary lecture I refused, because full professors in Paris went to mass and other religious services as a matter of course. And I have always

resisted this, knowing that I was excommunicated for having fled the [convent and] Order and for having discarded the habit; while in Toulouse the ordinary lectureship did not require church attendance.

One could read this statement to mean that Bruno refused to attend divine services because of disagreement with and repudiation of both (perhaps all) established religions. This interpretation stretches Bruno's words too far, however. One can more reliably infer that Bruno took his excommunication seriously, especially since—as we shall see—it was in Toulouse and Paris that Bruno was told he could not receive communion until he had received absolution in Rome and that, until such time, he could only pray in church. This reading is more likely, especially when his words here are considered in the light of his other comments about the eucharist.

One senses from Bruno's trial records as well as from *The Ash Wednesday Supper* that he had a special commitment or devotion to the eucharist. In reply to the inquisitors' question, Bruno strenuously averred that he never spoke or wrote against the Roman Catholic doctrine of the eucharist:

> I have never spoken of the sacrifice of the mass, nor of transubstantiation, unless in the manner of the Holy Church; and I have always held and believed, as I now hold and believe, that transubstantiation changes the bread and wine into the body and blood of Christ, really and substantially, as the Church teaches.

This reply is all the more striking when one recalls that Bruno quite calmly admitted that as a philosopher he had difficulty reconciling Christ's humanity with his divinity as well as understanding the hypostatic union of the Three Persons of the Trinity. Indeed, even though Bruno admitted that

> for many years [he] had known and associated with Calvinists, Lutherans, and other sorts of heretics, [he] however did not doubt or argue against the transubstantiation of the sacrament of the Altar.

Bruno's words are carefully chosen, but their artfulness does not, I think, indicate complete falsification. Bruno seems to have valued the eucharist and may privately have held to something that he did not think was completely incompatible with the orthodox doctrine. This inference becomes possible when one reads Bruno's reply to the inquisitors' question concerning his view of the sacrament of penance:

> I know that the sacrament of penance was instituted to purge our sins. . . . It has been about sixteen years since I last went to confession, except for two times: once in Toulouse [where I went to be confessed] by a Jesuit; and another time in Paris [where I tried to be confessed] by another Jesuit. . . . [Saying that my case had not been settled back home], they told me that they could not absolve me for being apostate, and I could not go to divine services [but could pray in church].

It seems, then, that Bruno wanted to return to the Church, at least to be allowed once again to receive the eucharist, and that it had been impossible for the two Jesuits to absolve him for being apostate; only higher (Roman) authorities could do this. We might also note that Bruno does not say that he himself wanted to perform the sacrifice of the mass, but only that he wanted to partake of the communion following that sacrifice. This sets some parameters upon what he meant by reconciliation with Rome.

When one pieces together the various parts of Bruno's testimony, one concludes that the Nolan longed for eucharistic communion, but that this desire was thwarted by his apostasy and by his conscientious understanding of the sacramental consequences of excommunication. We have seen that Bruno desired to partake of Holy Communion in Geneva. We also see that he did not want, according to his words, to go to divine service either in Protestant Toulouse or Catholic Paris.

Bruno's stories here do not seem to coincide with the real record, inasmuch as he denied going to communion in Geneva but yet we have seen him requesting to have the ban on the Supper lifted. Two answers to this contradiction are possible: either he was unable—given the short time he was in Geneva (during part of which he was under the ban)—to have an opportunity to take communion in that community where it was given only four times a year; or, probably more likely, he simply did not want to admit to having taken communion in a non-Catholic land, especially since he had later been told he could not receive it in Catholic lands. Consequently, he consistently denied taking Protestant communion, and said he went to divine services only "out of curiosity," and that

> . . . after the lesson or sermon, when they were about to distribute the bread in the manner of their Supper, I left, . . . nor did I ever take their bread or observe their eucharistic rites.

The evidence is ambiguous. However, whether or not Bruno did participate in the Calvinist liturgy, he ultimately found the Protestant sacrament loathsome. His attacks on Protestant doctrine and practice are based on theological principle and aesthetic judgment.

It is to **The Ash Wednesday Supper** that we must turn for guidance on Bruno's attitudes toward the eucharist and the Protestants. In this work, Bruno exhibits a strong dislike for his English hosts. The **Supper** is replete with disparaging remarks about the English populace, whom Bruno describes as so many kicking and butting beasts, completely devoid of civility and humanity. Their barbarousness results, says Bruno, from the justification-by-faith-alone theology preached in Protestant England. These statements lend credence to Bruno's reply to the inquisitors that

> Faith, hope, and charity [are necessary to salvation]. . . . I have always maintained that good works are necessary for salvation. [And in **De l'infinito, universo, e mondi** I said] "that type of religion which teaches people to trust in salvation without works . . . is more in need of being eradicated from the earth than are serpents, dragons, and other animals pernicious to human nature; because barbarous people become more

barbarous through such confidence, and those who are naturally good become evil. . . ."

Not only did Bruno find England's Protestant religion pernicious to human nature but he also disparaged the Protestant Supper, finding the Communion *sub utraque* repulsive in the extreme.

The second dialogue of **The Ash Wednesday Supper** recounts the Nolan's journey across London as he headed to the home of Sir Fulke Greville (*sic;* in reality, the dinner took place at the residence of the Marquis de Mauvissière, the French ambassador). He had originally been invited for dinner, but no one had come to the French embassy to escort him to Greville's. So, after having gone to visit some Italian friends, he returned to find John Florio, an Italian Protestant residing in England, and Matthew Gwynne waiting to take him to Greville's residence. The dangerous journey along the Strand commenced, and Bruno and his friends encountered swinish passages, Avernus-like potholes, and the murderous "kicking and butting beasts" who worked in the streets and markets of London. Such were the results of the Protestant economy of salvation.

When Bruno's *alter ego,* the Nolan, was finally delivered from this passion and had arrived at Greville's and was seated, Teofilo (Bruno's other *alter ego,* who recounts the story) "thanks God" that the "ceremony of the cup" did not take place. Nonetheless, Teofilo describes it in nauseating detail:

> Usually the goblet or chalice passes from hand to hand all round the table . . . with no order but that dictated by rough politeness and courtesy. After the leader of this dance has detached his lips, leaving a layer of grease which could easily be used as glue, another drinks and leaves you a crumb of bread, another drinks and leaves a bit of meat on the rim, still another drinks and deposits a hair of his bread, and, in this way, with a great mess, no one is so ill-mannered . . . as to omit leaving you some favor of the relics stuck to his moustache. . . . The meaning of all this is that, since all of them come together to make themselves into a flesh- eating wolf to eat as with one body the lamb or kid or Grunnio Corocotta; thus by applying each one his mouth to the selfsame tankard, they come to form themselves into one selfsame leech, in token of one community, one brotherhood, one plague, one heart, one stomach, one gullet and one mouth.

Teofilo goes on to say that this custom did not occur at this feast because it had "remained only at the lowest tables, and has disappeared from these others. . . ."

This passage mocks the Communion *sub utraque.* For Bruno, what began as a sacral meal ends as a travesty of the sacrament, whereby religious brotherhood transforms into illness and alimentary functions. While we realize that many in the sixteenth century welcomed communion in both kinds, it is all too easy to forget that this Protestant liturgical reform could—as in the case of Bruno—have appeared as so much offal to the minds of others who had also been raised and nourished in the Roman faith. It seems unarguable that Bruno's sensitivities concerning eucharistic liturgy tended toward Roman Catholic rather than Protestant. There is also a hint, in the passage just quoted, that the "gentlemen" gathered at the Ash Wednesday Supper (except for Doctors Nundinio and Torquato whom the Nolan debates in the third and fourth dialogues of the *Supper*) tended toward his views (or so he hoped), and that is why the "ceremony of the cup" did not take place. Bruno was obviously appealing in this book to English Protestants who would share his liturgical preferences for a more traditional, i. e., Roman Catholic, ceremonial—although the significance given that ceremonial would transcend narrow confessional understandings.

This interpretation fits well with Bruno's later responses to the inquisitors concerning his beliefs on the eucharist. Bruno was probably telling them the truth, that the Supper took place at Mauvissière's official residence rather than at Greville's. We know that the ambassador accorded Bruno considerable publishing latitude while he lived with him as a visiting foreign gentleman. His residence in the embassy, his publishing enterprise in London, and his letters of introduction to Mauvissière from Henri III all indicate that Bruno operated in London under the aegis of the Most Christian King.

It is not irresponsible, then, to credit Bruno's assertion that the Ash Wednesday Supper took place in the French embassy. However, we have caught Bruno in a deception. He said, in the passage quoted at the head of this section, that he went neither to mass (either inside or outside the embassy) nor to Protestant services. We have also seen him tell the inquisitors that the Ash Wednesday Supper was only a gathering to debate the virtues of Copernicus' assertions about the motion of the earth. But we have just seen that the Ash Wednesday Supper and the book which commemorates it had to do with a sacramental Supper on Ash Wednesday. Why the prevarication? Bruno had to tread very carefully concerning his entire English experience, as he was involved in the middle of a French reunionist scheme. The reputation of Henri III in very orthodox Roman Catholic circles (e. g., among the Leaguers and, to some extent, in Rome) was badly tarnished, so Bruno was wise not to dilate upon his "mission" to England. Yet we can tell that something is awry in this part of his testimony, as he denies even having gone to hear Protestant preachers "just out of curiosity," which he did admit to having done in Geneva. Bruno might not have gone simply because he knew no English. In that case, however, he probably would have given that reason since the harm of wanting to hear Protestant preachers had already been done by his admissions in Geneva. No, he seems carefully to have distanced himself from all religious interests in his testimony about his sojourn in England, a lack of interest that is belied by the six *Dialoghi metafisici e morali* he published there. In a sense, seen in the light of his publications while in England, Bruno's very denial of interest in religion in that country—the only time he is so mute—shouts the opposite meaning to the modern reader of his Italian dialogues and testimony. Bruno, a reformist and apostate Dominican, was the perfect French ploy by which to entice English candidates for conversion to a more moderate, because transcendent,

Catholic understanding of the eucharist than that offered by the Holy See and its political allies, the Spaniards and French Guisards. It made perfect sense, then, to allow Bruno to participate in discussions about some kind of ecumenical celebration of the Lord's Supper on Ash Wednesday, February 14, 1584—the beginning of the Lenten reform and a symbolic day for initiating a reformist and reunionist scheme sponsored by that strange Counter-Reformation figure, Henri III.

To Bruno, the proponent of French Counter-Reformation policy, the transcendent, "Copernican" vision and understanding of the eucharist in no way outwardly contradicted either Roman Catholic or Protestant eucharistic doctrines, nor did it deny the inherent divine nature of the sacrament. Instead, it refocused how one viewed its divine nature. Not interested for this purpose in the issue of Christ's physical presence (though without, as he correctly told the inquisitors, denying transubstantiation), Bruno honed in on the issue—dear to any mystically-inclined soul—of the reciprocal relationship between the Light of Divinity emanating from the central Sun and the spark of divinity inherent in the earth's inhabitants who ceaselessly circle about, to use the Hermetic expression quoted by Copernicus, that "visible God." A kind of Plotinian psychology governed Bruno's views on this matter.

Accordingly, when Bruno was questioned about his views on the eucharist, he was able to say with some degree of truthfulness that his views were Catholic. Whether he had ever actually been a communicant (even though he wanted to be) at a Protestant Supper is unclear; in fact, however, he had been critical of the Protestant rite and of the doctrine of justification in his writings. Thus, Bruno's public views were not necessarily or outwardly incommensurate with Catholic teaching.

V. *Bruno: The Catholic Nicodemite?*

The title of this essay, "Fra Giordano Bruno's Catholic Passion," carries obvious multiple meanings. The record of Bruno's long trial paints a poignant picture of a God-lover fleeing his homeland and cloister for fear of prosecution for reformist ideas. This flight took him throughout Europe, treading paths that had probably once been soaked by the blood of one Christian killed by another in the cause of confessional truth. Bruno's search for security and for spiritual refreshment brought him finally back to Italy where he may have hoped to present his ideas to the pope himself in order that he be reconciled as he had tried to be in Toulouse and Paris and, before that, in another faith in Geneva. Before he could do this, however, Bruno was betrayed and turned over to the Inquisition. His trial makes difficult reading for anyone concerned for human dignity and freedom of ideas. Yet we must always remember that these values were sadly lacking in the late sixteenth century. Nonetheless, the records of Bruno's trial help today to elucidate his views as a religious thinker and actor. Although the ambiguities concerning Bruno will probably never completely vanish, we can now dimly see the shadow (to use a favorite image of his) of a man who hoped to reconcile religious opposites and who hoped also to find a place where he, an "academician of no academy," could find rest. We do know now that the rest he sought had something to do with participation in the ceremonial of the eucharist, if not agreement with a doctrinal definition of its meaning. We also see that, for Bruno, human dignity was bound up with the action and choice of the human free will. We also know that, right up to the return to Italy in 1591, Bruno was able to become a member of the Lutheran community in Wittenberg and yet sign his religious name with a cross, in the manner of a Catholic priest, and, two years later, to live in a Carmelite monastery in Frankfurt. The pattern we have observed for the years between 1576 and 1585 persisted throughout his remaining years of freedom. Bruno could live as a Catholic or as a Protestant.

In a sense, some of the views and sentiments we have seen Bruno embrace are Roman Catholic. He was, as we have seen, more Catholic than Protestant in his sacramental views. But it would be an error, I think, to say, as did Angelo Mercati, that only his "vulgar" and "prideful" nature prevented his return to his original home and beliefs. Mercati has judged Bruno on the basis of *Il Candelaio* and has applied an inappropriate, modern moral judgment on that work that, if applied to Rabelais, for example, would consign him to perdition, too. It is more fruitful, I think, to view Bruno as a kind of Catholic Nicodemite. This is at best only a metaphor and cannot be strained, for Bruno—unlike a true Catholic Nicodemite—was unwilling to accept the Protestant doctrine of justification. Yet there is a similarity, in that both the Nicodemites and Bruno accepted the idea that outward religious form was trivial in comparison with inward belief. Bruno also has similarities to the Familists of the late sixteenth century. He believed in an overarching world harmony that could reconcile conflicting religions. Yet, Bruno did not cite or follow the guiding lights of the Family of Love, Niclaes and Barrefelt. He was, as he said above, an "academician of no academy" both in his philosophy and in his religion, and yet he strangely believed that he might be allowed to rejoin the Order but not live in it. He belonged nowhere and everywhere. Perhaps this is what stirred Henry Cobham, English ambassador to France, to write to Sir Francis Walsingham (as Bruno was about to depart for London): "Doctor Jordano Bruno Nolano . . . intends to pass into England, whose religion I cannot commend."

Hilary Gatti   (essay date 1989)

SOURCE: "The Brunian Setting," in *The Renaissance Drama of Knowledge: Giordano Bruno in England,* Routledge, 1989, pp. 1-34.

[*In the following excerpt, Gatti tracks Bruno's European wanderings, discussing the influential ideas and writings produced by the philosopher during this period of travel.*]

Perhaps no writer more than Giordano Bruno has made such large claims for the extraordinary value of his own work. It is enough to remember the opening of his letter to the Vice-Chancellor of the University of Oxford, written in 1583, where he presents himself as a philosopher whose work is applauded by all noble minds; or the pages of the first dialogue of the *Cena delle Ceneri* in which he praises his own work glowingly between references to Co-

pernicus as the discoverer of a new cosmology and Columbus as the discoverer of a new geography. Eight years later, after a long and often unquiet period in Germany, Bruno dedicates his Latin trilogy containing the final expression of his philosophical vision to Prince Henry Julius of Brunswick. Here he claims, in the first work of the trilogy, the *De triplici minimo,* to have reached through erudition and science an understanding of the primary elements; in the second, the *De monade,* to have penetrated through to the foundations or footsteps of imaginings, opinions, and common assumptions; but it is above all in the third work, the *De immenso,* that his vein of self-assertion is stimulated; for here, he assures his reader, he presents unequivocal, certain, and incontestable demonstrations such as those on the disposition of the worlds in the universe, on the unity of the infinite universe governed by a single principle, and on the manner in which implicitly or explicitly the natural order is revealed. These claims are more circumstantial and clearly defined than those in the letter to the University of Oxford, or in the *Cena;* but they are no less large, and above all they show no mitigation of Bruno's confidence in his own erudition and intellectual powers.

It is easy enough, and has been an almost constant characteristic of Bruno criticism, to declaim against this aspect of his work, dismissing it as eccentric or in strident bad taste. It is more important to understand the intimate motives which led Bruno throughout his life to place himself in such an unusual posture towards his own figure and intellectual enquiry. Undoubtedly the answer is to be found in his sense of the cultural crisis which had developed at the end of the sixteenth century as a consequence of the ferocious tensions in the religious sphere linked to a decadence in the humanistic movement which was beginning to codify in tired and pedantic formulas experiences which had long animated a cultural awakening throughout Europe. In feeling the force of that crisis, Bruno was only one of a number of sensitive European intellects of the final decades of the century. What gives his work its particular power and impetus both within his own times and more generally within the modern world is the nature of his response. For Bruno, placed in front of a newly entrenched and often obscure rigidity on the part of the traditional cultural institutions, both academic and religious, takes upon his own individual intellect the task of repudiating an old and worn-out world order and of opening up new vistas of knowledge and understanding.

His constant reference to his erudition as a primary factor of his intellectual enquiry does not allow accusations of an excessive individualism; for Bruno is always profoundly aware of a centuries-old, internationally wide and immensely rich body of wisdom and knowledge to which the modern intellect must refer and within which it will choose its own essential sources. There is, then, no question with Bruno of disregarding tradition. Rather, his distinctive note is sounded where he claims an unlimited autonomy in operating his cultural choices, and in developing from them his own vision of the truth and order of the universe: it is only to the criterion of a natural principle of truth which lies both within the order of the universe and within the light of reason which illuminates the individual mind that Bruno will declare his adherence:

> He who desires to philosophize will first doubt all things, refusing to assume any position in a debate before having heard the contrasting points of view, and after having well considered the arguments for and against he will judge and take up his position not on the basis of hearsay or according to the opinion of the majority or their age, merits, or prestige, but according to the persuasiveness of an organic doctrine which adheres to reality as well as to a truth which is comprehensible according to the light of reason.

Traditional schools of thought, of whatever origin or kind, tend to require some form of submission to criteria of collective doctrine. The humanist movement had already done much to accentuate the autonomy of the individual intellect with respect to the claims of church, corporation, or civic authority which had had such a dominating influence on the medieval mind. But Bruno's uncompromising position sounds a new and forward-looking note which inevitably brought him to clash with the authorities of his times which had little idea as yet of protecting any rights to protest or dissent. These were primarily the churches as religious authorities, the universities as cultural authorities, and the courts of the Renaissance princes as political authorities. Bruno's story with all of them is one of tension and drama.

The break with the churches was the first stage of his life story in these terms, and had already been completed by the time he reached Paris in 1581. First, in 1576, came his flight from the Monastery of St. Domenic in Naples and then, soon afterwards, from a monastery of the same order in Rome, after enquiries into his religious beliefs had established that he had sympathies with Arian doctrine and consequently that he may not have accepted orthodox belief in the Trinity. In his convent years Bruno is also known to have destroyed his images of the saints leaving only his crucifix intact and to have advised his fellow monks to pay more attention to the early Fathers of the Church: positions which would inevitably be interpreted as moving dangerously near to Protestant doctrine. It may well have been sympathies of this kind which drew Bruno, on his journey north after his escape from Rome, to the Geneva of Calvin. But his stay there in 1579 lasted only a brief space of months; for he was soon arrested for printing a notice objecting to twenty errors contained in the lessons of one of the chief pastors, M. de la Faye. The surviving documents relating to this episode do not specify the nature of these objections but only that Bruno called all the ministers of the Church of Geneva "pedagogues", adding that he had further erred "blasonnant les ministres en plusieurs et diversses facons". By the time he reached London, Bruno's position was one of anti-Christian polemic with both sides of the religious divide.

This position of equidistant refusal of Christian orthodoxies is clearly illustrated in the final image of the Explanatory Epistle prefixed to the *Spaccio della bestia trionfante* ('Expulsion of the triumphant beast'), a text which has recently been at the centre of research into the terms of Bruno's quarrel with Christianity. Here, after describing the rejection of the ancient astrological images which he will carry out in his work envisaging their replacement by moral virtues, Bruno leads his reader to the altar on which he intends to celebrate his own idea of true religion, piety, and faith. This idea corresponds with the substance of his philosophical vision of an infinite, divinely animated universe which becomes the only proper object of contemplation both in the religious and in the philosophical spheres. Such contemplation implies a severe refusal of "iniquous Impiety" and "insane Atheism", which Bruno visualizes as falling down an ignominious precipice on the west side of his heavenly altar. On the east side of the altar are attached the Christian religions of both sorts. The first of these is presented by Bruno as an "iniquous Credulity" linked to "so many forms of madness". These expressions refer to his polemic, which became particularly virulent at that stage of his stay in England, with the Protestant doctrine of salvation by faith alone, with its corresponding rejection of human works as able to save the believer's soul: doctrines which he thought (in not very original terms, for here he is merely repeating, for his own different ends, the main terms of much Catholic abuse of the Protestant movement) were leading to moral hypocrisy and degeneration as well as to cultural laziness and stagnation. The other form of Christianity, the Catholic faith, is rejected by Bruno with equal decision. This he sees (again without great originality, for here he is repeating a widespread Protestant objection to Catholicism) as based on superstition rather than true faith, and as surrounded by what he calls "Cose, coselle e coselline"—*nugae,* small insignificant things—by which he means the various objects and appurtenances, such as images and relics, which play such an important part in Catholic worship. Both forms of Christian religion are then seen as falling together from the east side of Bruno's altar, leaving him free to celebrate what he presents to the reader as the only object of a correctly conceived worship: the Infinite and Universal One as expressed in the Infinite Universe. Bruno believes, with what are clearly Epicurean echoes, that such a form of worship, which is identifiable with philosophical contemplation of the divine principle of order within the infinite universe, will fill the mind with a "voluptuous torrent of joy and delight".

Bruno was not the unrealistic mystic and visionary which he has been made so often to appear. Even after the definition of his own religious position, which is expressed so clearly in this page of the *Spaccio,* he continued to be deeply interested in the various forms of Christianity and their relations with each other, aware as he was that they were not going to fall away in historical terms as easily as in his vision of his ideal altar. But I do not believe that he was primarily interested in a religious reform for its own sake, or that he thought of himself as carrying out a religious mission. Rather he was interested in; and appealed continually in his works for, a movement towards tolerance and religious compromise which would leave the way free for the development of intellectual enquiry into the divine order and harmonies which regulate the universe. It was not his philosophy which modulated continually into a religious message, but his idea of the divinity which governed his conception of the universe as the eternal reflection in terms of multiplicity, movement, and continual process of the infinite One: the scattering into an infinite number of mobile fragments of the single, divine ray of light and truth. The nature of the order governing that multiplicity, in Bruno's opinion, had to be defined by a philosophical enquiry which, in its turn, had to be free to develop according to the impetus of the affections and the light of reason.

It was in these terms that Bruno searched throughout his life for an academic institution within which he could develop his thought and teach it to others. But the universities of the sixteenth century were closely linked to the ecclesiastical authorities of the part of Europe in which they operated, and were unlikely to offer Bruno a comfortable haven. What he was searching for amounts to an early ideal vision of a lay university of European culture rather than to any institution existing at that time. His claim in his letter to the Vice-Chancellor of the University of Oxford that he had been approved and welcomed throughout the principal universities of Europe is far from the truth. In fact, in his journey north, Bruno had taught at Toulouse between 1579 and 1581, but had then been forced to leave because of rising religious tensions between the Catholics and the Huguenots. In Paris he was unable to hold an official position at the Sorbonne where fidelity to the Catholic religion was required, although he became one of the public "royal" lecturers due to the influence of Henry III who was interested in his doctrine of memory and patronized him between 1581 and 1583. His celebrated clash in the summer of 1583 with the Oxford dons over the Copernican question was brief and violent, arising as it did from religious rather than philosophical or, even less, scientific objections. On his return to Paris in 1585, religious tension was far more acute than during his previous visit, with Henry III much weakened by the increasing power and fervour of the Guise faction and the Catholic League which would soon depose him. Henry III's assassination in 1589, followed by the emergence of Henry of Navarre as the new heir to the throne and his conversion to Catholicism in 1593, and finally the achievement of the Edict of Nantes in 1598, which at last conceded liberty of conscience and worship to the French Calvinists, were developments in the history of France which Bruno would only follow from an ever greater distance. The tense and fanatical Paris of 1585—6 was no safe place as yet for a mind like Bruno's, and in the summer of 1586 he left France for Germany. It was Wittemberg which eventually offered him the nearest approach to an academic haven, with a regular teaching post which he covered from 1586 to 1588.

Bruno's arrival in Wittemberg was preceded by a significant interlude at the University of Marburg, where he matriculated on 25 July 1586. He at once petitioned the Rector, Nigidius, a professor of moral philosophy, to be permitted to hold public disputations on philosophy, but this permission was denied him on the grounds of what the Rector, in a personal account of the episode, defined as "weighty reasons". The following scene between Bruno and the Rector, narrated by the latter himself, is often taken as a testimony of Bruno's irascible, southern temperament. But, as the Rector himself seems to have been aware, it is far more telling in its expression of intense dis-

appointment with respect to an ideal academic institution which Bruno was evidently convinced, at this point, he could find in Germany alone:

> he fell into a passion of anger and he insulted me in my house, as though I had acted in this matter against the rights of man and the usages of all the German universities, and against all zeal in learning; and, therefore, he desired not to continue a member of the academy, to which desire we agreed gladly, and his name was cancelled by me on the rolls of the university.

Fortunately the Marburg episode failed to influence Bruno's reception at Wittemberg, where he matriculated on 20 August of the same year. Bruno's arrival at Wittemberg was marked by a stroke of extraordinary good luck and a stroke of equally extraordinary bad luck. His good luck was to find there, in a position of prestige and respect, his fellow countryman Alberigo Gentile, who had probably heard Bruno speak at Oxford where the patronage of Leicester had installed him in a good position and where he would return to be awarded a Chair in 1589. Gentile was a highly respected student of law, who is recognized as having founded the important concept of international law. His influence may perhaps be traced in Bruno's concept of the true law as not only international but universal, as he defines it in the *Spaccio* where the Law, in the reformed universal order, reigns in the heavens beside Prudence and Truth. Gentile had left Italy on account of his Protestant sympathies, and he professed Calvinism during his Oxford years. At Wittemberg he was attached to the English Embassy at the Court of Saxony. It was Gentile's direct influence which obtained for Bruno at Wittemberg a post for teaching the *Organon* of Aristotle and other philosophical subjects. But the stroke of ill luck which marked out Bruno's Wittemberg experience as necessarily brief was not long in making itself felt. The Elector of Saxony, Augustus I, who had favoured religious peace and tolerance, died on 11 February of the year of Bruno's arrival in Wittemberg. His place was taken by his weak and degenerate son Christian who came rapidly under extreme Calvinist influence. The tolerant effects of religious compromise which had been arduously achieved through conventions such as the Treaty of Passau (1552) and the Peace of Augsburg (1555) began to give way within the University of Wittemberg itself; and by 1588 the influence of rigorous Calvinist doctrine was making itself felt. Bruno decided to leave, but not before he had expressed his gratitude to the university in which he was most fully and generously welcomed, in spite of the fact that he taught there doctrines which conceded little to the tastes and canons of the times.

Bruno's public recognition of Wittemberg as a place of culture approaching his ideal of an academic institution was expressed in two separate moments. The first of these was a dedication which he added to his work *De lampade combinatoria Lulliana* published in Wittemberg in 1587. The dedication is addressed to the Senate of the university and it expresses grateful praise for the 'liberty of philosophy' which Bruno found there. Bruno underlines his appearance in Wittemberg as a stranger "not distinguished by any royal commendation, bearing no ensigns of honour". Yet he was never questioned in religion, but allowed to proceed in his own enquiry which he describes as one of "universal philanthropy". In this dedication Bruno further describes Wittemberg as "the Athens of Germany, the daughter of Minerva, and the Queen of German schools". It is the reference to Minerva which he takes up and develops in his *Oratio valedictoria* pronounced to the professors and assembly of the university on 8 March 1588, shortly before his departure from Wittemberg. The oration takes the form of a redefinition of the myth of the golden apple awarded by Paris to Venus on Mount Ida: Bruno's choice goes to Minerva who 'drew me to her, and fettered me'. In the remarkable celebration of Minerva which follows, Bruno mixes elements of classical myth with the language of the psalms and prophetic vision to create an image of wisdom which expresses itself both as the divine unity, inscrutable to man, and as the richness and abundance of universal variety which it is given to man to approach and comprehend through dedicated search and enquiry. The complexity of Minerva's wisdom is expressed through a number of her attributes, foremost among them her helmet. This is crested to signify that we are not to put our trust in strength alone, but to show a courteous and quiet spirit. But above Minerva's crest is a cock with outspread wings which represents the swiftness, vigilance and foresight of the combatant; her keen-edged lance is her intelligence, ready for offence and for defence; while to them who oppose her she shows the Gorgon's head, for her formidable and admirable qualities are such as strike the beholder dumb with awe. Bruno has approached the throne of Minerva which stands on a pillar of clouds:

> On the outer part of the throne I beheld engraven an owl, which is her emblem; for night is not darkness to her, and for her night shines with the light of day, and my countenance is not hidden from her.

The key to this approach to the throne lies in the design on its surface which is the work of Vulcan; for here

> was a wondrous representation of the universe, which is the work of the gods, a plastic picture, and underneath was written, 'He bestowed upon me the knowledge of all living things, so that to me the disposition of the sphere of the earth is laid bare, the powers of the elements, the beginning, the end, and the midst of time, the sway of fate, the changes of custom, the course and lapse of years, the order of the stars, the nature of the animals, the deadly rage of beasts, the powers of the winds, the thoughts of men, the variety of plants, the virtue of roots; for that which is hid from others lies open for ever before me'.

Gradually the sense of Bruno's amalgam of classical myth, the language of prophecy, and mystical vision becomes clear; although, as he had warned his audience at the beginning of the oration, 'fate decrees we shall deal in words with that which is unspeakable'. The question which he poses is whether words, which are the signs and tokens of things, can do more than specify the presence and evidence of objects. He answers his own question when he declares that he is attempting to use words to specify all

three modes of perceiving the sun of intelligence which manifests itself in essence, in substance, and in activity. It is where Bruno considers that manifestation in its incomprehensible essence that he adopts cabbalistic imagery and arcane myths expressing mystical concepts of varying traditions. In the second mode, Wisdom is apparent in substance in the shape and body of all things and takes the name of Minerva: 'it calls upon man with a thousand voices, and in all parts of the earth'. Here all the varieties of language are necessary to express the richness and plenitude of the universal being. In the third mode, Wisdom is implanted within the spirit, in the profound thoughts of mankind. In this expression Wisdom as activity may be seen as having built a house of reason and design in the individual soul from which man can glimpse the image of the first archetypal house which is before the world as well as of the second house, according to the senses and to nature, which is the world.

In Bruno's universe as thus defined time is eternal, and his concept of wisdom looks back to the arcane mysteries which were a form of participation in the divine essence, as well as forward to a more rational and organized enquiry into the order of the universal whole. Bruno's work derives its substance and value from his awareness of the necessity for the individual intellect to hold in harmonious tension these various stages of wisdom: imaginative myth combines with rational discourse; mystical aspiration to absorption into the divine essence is accompanied by a stand in favour of man's historical autonomy and free will; a sense of the magic and occult powers which vivify the universe coexists with an intellect projected towards the rational discovery and revelation of nature's secrets. At this point one wonders how, and in what terms, Bruno will manage to introduce the figure of Luther, who could hardly be left out of a celebration of wisdom pronounced in sixteenth-century Wittemberg; for Bruno has so far defined a complex and coherent philosophical concept of wisdom in terms which include no reference to the Christian faith on which Luther had erected the whole structure of his religious reform.

Bruno's answer to this conundrum is a brilliant one. It ignores any reference to the Lutheran doctrines of justification by faith alone and the refusal of human works which Bruno had opposed so bitterly in his dialogues written in England, but rather it introduces Luther in his heroic stance as the opponent of papal power and authority: 'that vicar of the princes of hell, who by cunning and violence polluted the world', writes Bruno, taking over in mass the familiar terms of Protestant anti-papal polemic. The really significant phrase, however, is that which defines Luther as a 'mighty hero, armed to the teeth with club and sword'. Here Luther is clearly identified with Hercules and thus with the profound significance of the virtue of 'fortezza' (strength) as Bruno had defined it in the *Spaccio.* Although Bruno would remain convinced to the end that Luther's reform was not the right one, it is clear that his welcome in Wittemberg had led him to a revaluation of the reformer's stature as well as of some of the effects, in terms of liberty and tolerance, which his insistence on the divine light which illuminates the individual intellect was leading to. Like Bruno himself, Luther had opposed his own vision of things to the whole weight of an immensely powerful and entrenched prevailing culture. He is accorded the status of a hero in Bruno's scheme of things; and it is even suggested, although in not very precise terms, that the Nolan philosophy, by which Bruno means his own thought, 'is not altogether alien' to the philosophy of contemporary Lutheran Germany. It could be interesting to speculate how far Bruno's reading of Luther, which led to the clear and reasoned refusal of so much of the doctrine of the Reformation in his Italian dialogues written in England, had influenced some of his own way of expressing himself in his most polemical moments. Consider, for example, Luther's angry cry against Erasmus for his defence of the freedom of the will:

> Away, now, with Sceptics and Academics from the company of us Christians; let us have men who will assert, men twice as inflexible as very Stoics! Take the Apostle Paul—how often does he call for that 'full assurance' which is, simply, an assertion of conscience, of the highest degree of certainty and conviction.

Here Bruno is undoubtedly closer to Erasmus's undogmatic humanism on the level of ideas. Yet Bruno's own voice, in his moments of indignation and refusal, often sounds with notes that are reminiscent of Luther's decided and uncompromising tones. It is significant that Bruno concludes his praise of Luther with a reference to what he managed to do 'through the power of the Word'. It is that power which formed Luther's 'Herculean club'; and it is through words (his own words rather than those of the Scriptures) that Bruno too is trying to bring about a cultural reawakening.

Wittemberg listened to that message in spite of the fact that it was very different from what its own reformer had preached. Bruno's farewell to Wittemberg was also a farewell to the academic life of his times which was not yet ready for spirits such as his. He left for Prague, but appears to have ignored the university there; and when later he went to Helmstedt, attracted by the Academia Julia founded by Duke Julius of Brunswick, he took no regular academic post. He appears to have been more interested in seeking the patronage of Emperor Rudolf II at Prague, or of Duke Julius at Brunswick, in the hope, perhaps, that the protection of an enlightened Prince might offer him more security than the academic halls had done.

The third dimension of Bruno's story with the authorities of his times is in fact represented by his relationship with the Princes and their Courts. Here too we have the continually renewed search for an ideal, although in this case the search is less solitary and projects us less into the modern world. Rather it represents a precise moment in the history of political power in Europe linked to the widespread realization, which is such a marked characteristic of the humanist movement in the sixteenth century, that any renovation in the society of the time involved a rethinking of the role of the Prince from whom, wrote Thomas More, all evils and benefits flow as if from a bounteous fountain. More in his *Utopia* proposed a solution well in advance of his times, and certainly uncongenial to his own Tudor monarch Henry VIII, when he saw the necessity of abolishing the hereditary principle and establishing a mecha-

nism of regular elections to positions of power. Machiavelli was equally projected into the modern world where his uncompromising realism left the Prince naked of ambiguous and often imaginary ideal attributes, and offered him instead a manual of instructions in the harsh realities of political virtue. But the solution most widely accepted by the humanists of the period was rather that of Erasmus, which went back through the Middle Ages to Plato's concept of the Philosopher-Prince, developed in a Christian dimension with a primary emphasis on his religious and intellectual education to power. This profound desire to see the Prince absorb into himself the humanist ideal of special forms of wisdom and culture, combining them, in some unspecified, if not miraculous, way, with the active political virtues, seems to have become more widespread and deeply felt as the century progressed. It is clearly linked to the increasing sense of crisis which was beginning to invest the concept of monarchy itself as we see it explored with increasing scepticism in dramatic representations of the weak or incompetent Prince such as Marlowe's *Edward II* or Shakespeare's *Richard II*. It was not the solution which the modern world would adopt, with its progressive emargination of the figure of the monarch and its development of a parliamentary principle. And given that one of the main leads in that direction would so soon be offered by the England of the following century, it remains a curious cultural phenomenon that so meagre a meditation on the parliamentary alternative was developed by the culture of the sixteenth century, in England as elsewhere. Shakespeare, together with his fellow dramatists, remains deeply immersed in a meditation on the figure of the Prince himself. The crisis which was growing around him is clearly felt where the ideal Princes, in the Erasmian sense of the specially wise and cultured princely mind, are deposed or deprived of their rights, as both Hamlet and Prospero are, by more ignorant but wily and unscrupulous rivals. Nevertheless, the solution to the crisis is always proposed in the form of a return of just (at least hypothetically) princely rule, with the arrival of Fortinbras or the return to power of Prospero himself. The extreme limit which Shakespeare achieved, or possibly was able to achieve as a dramatist whose plays were represented at Court, is the doubt and ambiguity which he allows to surround his solution. For it is far from certain that Fortinbras, who leads armies of ignorant soldiers to lose their lives for new territories whose real worth is less than an eggshell, will in fact prove to be the gentle and promising ruler that Hamlet hopefully imagines in his dying speech. As for Prospero, his return to power coincides clearly with his own (or according to another critical tradition, Shakespeare's) setting aside of his magician's cloak with its special forms of secret wisdom and power.

Much Italian and French meditation on the figure of the Prince was based on a far more intense monarchical idealism than is found in the Elizabethan dramatists, who, by the very fact of dramatizing the history of Princes in problematical terms, have been seen as partially subverting their sacred and inviolable authority. The French and Italian tradition, instead, was more concerned with celebrating an ideal of monarchy which was projected towards expanding that authority in terms of empire which looked back to the example of ancient Rome. Bruno has been seen as participating in what was a widespread Italian as well as French reference to the monarchy of France in these terms; for looking back to the figure of Charlemagne, it was possible to see the French kings as inheriting a mission to install a form of Roman-imperialistic rule which would bring back peace and justice to a divided and blood-stained Europe. The tribute to Henry III in the closing pages of the *Spaccio* undoubtedly participates in this tradition, creating of the French king a mythical figure who ascends to the heavens to take the place of the constellation of the Southern Crown, symbolizing with his ascent the opening of the new era of universal peace and tranquillity which Bruno, together with so many of the intellects of his age, ardently desired: 'he loves peace, keeps his loved subjects as far as possible in tranquillity and devotion; he is not pleased by the noise, clashes and fanfares of martial instruments which lead to the blind conquering of unstable tyrannies.'

It is in similar terms that Bruno treats the figure of Elizabeth I, whom he praises above all for the era of peace she had brought to her island kingdom, but also for her culture and intellectual powers which confer on her a status of exceptional authority and standing among the Princes of the time:

> her judgement, wisdom, political virtue, and art of government are next to none who carries a sceptre on earth: in her knowledge of the arts, scientific notions, expertise and practice of all those languages which the educated in Europe are accustomed to speaking, I leave the whole world to judge what rank she holds among her fellow princes.

Bruno treats her in mythological terms as Amphitrite declaring that her rule should ideally extend not just to England but to the world, if not to the universal whole. There is an obvious dose of rhetoric and favour-seeking here, but even so it remains a fact that Bruno's virulent attacks against so many aspects of English life and society never extended to the figure of the Queen even after he had left England and had no further need of her protection. It is a stand which the Inquisitors during his trial would be quick to pick up, accusing him of undue praise of a heretical and excommunicated monarch.

It would appear that Bruno's participation in the cult of the English monarchy in its new imperialistic aspirations was known in the early years of the seventeenth century when the Stuarts, aided by the myth-making art of Rubens and the celebratory masques of Ben Jonson and Inigo Jones, made their dramatic but disastrous attempt to imitate French models of absolute, imperialistic power. For among the Stuart masques, we find the curious work of Carew, *Coelum Britannicum,* in which parts of the *Spaccio,* and in particular the monarchical-imperialistic vision of the closing pages, are used as a source, to be applied, inevitably, to the Stuart rather than to the French monarchy. But it is far from clear that Bruno would have approved of Stuart rule which opposed so many of his desires for religious, political, and cultural tolerance and peace. It was precisely these virtues, which the Stuart kings would so sadly lack, that Bruno extols in the crucially important pages of his dedication to Emperor Rudolf II of the *Articuli centum et sexaginta* published in Prague in 1588.

Bruno's dedication to Rudolf II addresses that monarch as *Divo Rodolpho II Romanorum Imperatori semper Augusto:* a form of address which is not just empty flattery. For Bruno defines human knowledge itself, and the philosopher who pursues it, in terms of a universal brotherhood of intellectual searchers over which Rudolf, in his capacity as Holy Roman Emperor, is seen as presiding. It is in terms of this concept of the universal value which is to be attributed to all true forms of knowledge that Bruno launches into a bitter attack against all those sects and religions which persist in asserting that God has conceded them some particular form of revelation: a conviction which leads them to believe 'that only they dwell in the house of truth (outside which the blind and erring legions wander lost and aimless)'. In his refusal of this concept, Bruno not only urges the necessity of a search for truth based on a spirit of universal love which sees God as the father of all men, 'good and bad, just and unjust', but he makes it clear that he repudiates entirely the whole concept of divine revelation. God has not revealed any sacred truths to any privileged sects, religions, or peoples. He has done something far more valuable and challenging, giving to every man the 'eyes' of sense and intelligence with which to pursue truth on his own account. What derives from this concept is a vision of knowledge as necessarily multiform and conflicting, but at the same time active and assertive: knowledge which, when a man has acquired it through dedicated and rigorous intellectual endeavour, will give him the capacity not only to judge but to 'direct the cause'.

Hermetic elements stressing the autonomy of man within the universal whole amalgamate with what is already a Baconian concept of organized research into the forces regulating the universe which will lead man to an ever greater dominion over the natural world. But above all Bruno is concerned with clarifying here what he sees as the fundamental and necessary condition for such a pursuit of knowledge: a degree of freedom of enquiry which in his time was clearly unrealizable, and which may still be considered as advanced even today. For it is correct to speak of a 'religion of freedom' in Bruno, which goes far beyond an illuministic plea for rational and judicious tolerance and intellectual harmony. Rather, the idea of liberty and autonomy of enquiry becomes the defining characteristic of the truly philosophical spirit: a sign of a fully mature humanity which relegates to the status of beasts (the asses, sheep, etc. of his *Cantus Circaeus*) all those unable or unwilling to carry intellectual enquiry to its greatest possible limits or heights. Although, in the closing passage of his dedication, Bruno admits that the pressures of social cohesion may, in some circumstances, oblige the wise man to hide his wisdom with humility, nevertheless such wisdom must be nourished as the occult sign of God's light which hides within man. When he is occupied with philosophical speculation (which Bruno here formally declares is the sphere of activity to which he has dedicated his life and intellectual powers) the wise man will only agree to listen to those masters who exhort him to open his eyes and not to close them.

Rudolf II had succeeded in the year 1576 to the throne of Maximilian II, the worldly and tolerant emperor who in 1574—5 had given the young Philip Sidney the welcome to his Court remembered in the opening page of his *Defence of Poetry*. Rudolf was a more melancholic figure, something of a recluse with an interest in esoteric studies and enquiries. He had shown rather too keen and ingenuous an interest in the spiritualistic magic of John Dee and his spurious companion Edward Kelley, who had both been entertained at his Court from 1584: Kelley was still there when Bruno arrived from Wittemberg. Bruno clearly hoped that he too would find favour with the eccentric Rudolf II; but he was disappointed. He received only a modest payment for his dedication of the *Articuli centum et sexaginta,* and in August of 1588 he left Prague without having obtained any official post either at the university or the Court. His new journey took him to Helmstedt where he was attracted by the university which had been founded in 1575 by Duke Julius of Brunswick. But Bruno seems to have moved on the outskirts of the Duke's Court rather than the university, in which he held no official position. It was, nevertheless, at the university that he spoke on 1 July 1589, when he pronounced a highly formal and rhetorical *Oratio consolatoria* as part of the funeral rites following Duke Julius's death.

Underneath the elaborate praise Bruno heaps on the dead Duke, it is possible to trace a further meditation on the figure of the Prince, above all in his function of guardian of the intellectual life of his small community. The Duke is pictured as gathered into the heavenly regions from where he looks down on to his academy, guiding it towards new vistas of divine knowledge. It is a concern with this same aspect of the princely role which appears with particular clarity and force in the dedication of his major philosophical work, the so-called Frankfurt Trilogy, [*De triplia minimo, De monade, De immenso*] which Bruno published in that town in 1591, to the son of Duke Julius, the new Duke Henry Julius of Brunswick. This dedication develops a meditation on the figure of the Prince of a different order from that applied to Henry III of France or to Elizabeth I or to Emperor Rudolf II. It is no longer imperial dominion seen as a universal force of cohesion and unity which constitutes the primary element of Bruno's interest here, but rather the aspect of exceptional wisdom and intellectual power which certain Princes are seen as achieving, in part at least due to their divinely consecrated status. Such wisdom gives them particular authority and power within the confines of their kingdom, creating at the same time a special relationship between them and the philosophers among their subjects. This is the concept which lies behind Shakespeare's creation of Prospero, and it appears to constitute an extreme form of meditation on the figure of the Prince. For either he represents an exceptionally potent form of wisdom, with special insight into divine truths, or he has no right to exert his power and dominion over those who dedicate themselves to obtaining similar wisdom through intellectual enquiry.

It is the nature of the relationship which links the figure of the Princely sage to the philosophical enquirer which Bruno is anxious to define in his dedication. Princes who are also sages and seers deserve the name of Trismegisti, which means 'three times great' in virtue of their knowledge, power, and authority: the number three, as Bruno had underlined in the *De monade,* possessing special significance, made up as it is of the first even number added to the first odd number, and so containing within itself potentially all numbers and being. It was among the Trismegisti, the wisest of men, that the ancient Egyptians, Persians, and Romans chose their kings. Constructing his meditation around a complex series of trinities which takes as its starting-point the Trismegistus-Prince and ends with the 'gift' to this Prince of his philosophical trilogy, Bruno sees such Princes as the authorities who decide and defend the laws, religions, and cults to be practised by the community. Such Princes guarantee stability within the state, seen as a necessary condition for philosophical enquiry to proceed and develop. The authority of the Prince, however, cannot extend to an interference with the enquiries of the true philosophers 'who must never suppress the light of reason for fear of those in power, showing themselves insensible to the voice of nature, nor hypocritically hide the truth in order to receive the consent of men of the church'.

Bruno's development of his final meditation on the figure of the Prince in these terms, in a work which is generally considered to contain his most advanced speculations on subjects connected with the development of a new science, is of particular interest if we compare it with Francis Bacon's dedication of *The Advancement of Learning* to James I in 1605. Bacon too was interested in the Prince in so far as he acted, in his special wisdom and power, to guarantee the free advancement of the new scientific philosophy. Bacon's praise of James in these terms echoes so closely Bruno's dedication to the Duke of Brunswick as to make it seem that he is modelling his text on it. For Bacon too uses the term of Trismegistus, applied by the ancient Greeks to the god Hermes, to celebrate the figure of James as sage and seer: 'your Majesty standeth invested of that triplicity which in great veneration was ascribed to the ancient Hermes, the power and fortune of a King, the knowledge and illumination of a Priest, and the learning and universality of a Philosopher'.

Both Bruno and Bacon consider the wisdom of the Trismegistus-Prince in part as a divine gift, and in part as acquired through study and meditation: Bruno praises the Duke of Brunswick as possessing 'all virtue, grace and ornament . . . as innate gifts magnified by a superior, interior Genius'; while Bacon says of James, 'there seemeth to be no less contention between the excellency of your Majesty's gifts of nature and the universality and perfection of your learning'. It is to the Prince who reveals himself in these terms as the example and defender of arcane, semi-divine forms of wisdom and learning, that both men are prepared to offer their works as gifts which, in Bacon's words, constitute 'a fixed memorial, and immortal monument, bearing a character or signature both of the power of a King and the difference and perfection of such a King'.

It was, as we can now see, an impossible ideal which led both men to inevitable disappointment. James I would do almost nothing to further Bacon's project for a new scientific community, which he would be later forced to outline in terms of a Utopia in his *New Atlantis*. As for Bruno, he wrote his dedication after he had left Helmstedt which he would never see again. History would show that the advancement of learning in terms of new and free enquiry into the order of the universe would develop most fully where monarchical absolutism was overcome. But Bruno and Bacon were in many respects in advance of their times, which were still dominated on a political level by the Renaissance Princes and their Courts. This imaginative construction of a figure of the Prince as seer and sage was not so much a question of monarchical faith or political principle as an extreme effort to visualize the form of princely rule which would, they both hoped, offer the maximum guarantee for the development of the new learning. In so far as their image of the Prince as possessing special forms of wisdom projected them clearly into an ideal region outside the process of modern history (recalling a long-lost concept of the Prince as priestly demigod rooted in the dawning centuries of mankind), they can be seen as contributing, even if obliquely, to the critical meditation on the figure and role of the Prince which would eventually culminate in disillusion, leading to the decline of the monarchical principle itself.

The most important event in Bruno's final period of freedom was the publication in Frankfurt of his Latin trilogy containing the dedication to Duke Henry Julius of Brunswick. He supervised the publication himself in spite of the fact that the Senate of the city refused his request, made on 2 July 1590, to lodge with the publisher Wechel. Through Wechel's influence, however, he was allowed to stay in the Carmelite convent where he worked on his publication until February 1591 when he received an order of expulsion from the city. He was thus obliged to leave Frankfurt before the appearance of his final and most ambitious philosophical work which was published during the autumn book fair of that year together with his final work on memory, the ***De imaginum, signorum et idearum compositione.***

It was at this point that Bruno, having received an invitation from the Venetian nobleman Giovanni Mocenigo to stay with him in Venice and teach him the 'secrets of memory', decided to return to Italy. He passed through Zurich where he lectured to private groups of students. At the end of August 1591, he reached Venice; and the last act of his story began.

The decision to return to Italy has been the subject of much and various comment. Apart from the enticement offered by Mocenigo's invitation, there was a historical context of a particular moment of optimism which, as the documents relating to Bruno's trial clarify, he had carefully considered: the accession to the French throne of Henry of Navarre and the rumours of his imminent conversion to Catholicism, which seemed to presage a slackening of the wars of religion; the accession to the papal throne of Clement III who, in 1592, called Francesco Patrizi to Rome and gave him a Chair there in what appeared to be a gesture of goodwill towards the new philosophers. The choice of Venice as a starting-point for the return to Italy clearly related not only to the invitation from Mocenigo

but also to the tolerant religious policy of the independent city-state which had strenuously opposed the efforts of the Catholic church, after the Council of Trent, to exert a much greater control over secular affairs throughout southern Europe. This was a period in which many Protestant visitors to Italy, such as Philip Sidney and his companions in the 1570s, chose to stay only within the Venetian dominions, where they felt safe from religious persecution; while the University at Padua, which was part of Venetian territory, was attracting an ever greater number of celebrated teachers due to the relative freedom of thought and enquiry permitted there. The appointment of Galileo to the Chair of mathematics in 1592 may be considered as symbolic of the standing of the Paduan University at that time; while the final years of the century and the beginning of the new one would see the emergence in Venice itself of the figure of Paolo Sarpi, whose critical *History of the Council of Trent* was to be so deeply admired and studied throughout Protestant Europe. What, then, was so particular about Bruno's position that made his return to Italy end in tragic failure, in spite of the carefully chosen geographical setting and historical moment in which he attempted it?

It is here that opinions diverge. One thesis, which has had several supporters, sees Bruno as planning to initiate in Italy some form of religious 'mission' which, so the thesis goes, with an almost insane recklessness he thought of starting from the very heart of Christianity, that is Rome itself. The Hermetic interpretation of Bruno adopts this thesis, lending it support by pointing out that in Padua, where he went before taking up his final residence in Mocenigo's house in Venice, he dictated to a group of pupils his final works on magic thus defining his 'mission' as a magic-Hermetic one which would inevitably clash with any form of Christian authority. This answer to the problem has recently been rigorously contested and replaced by the thesis that Bruno's real aim in Italy was to obtain an academic position as Patrizi had done, and that he went to Padua attracted by the still vacant Chair of mathematics. This thesis is supported by the recent discovery of two new texts related to his logical-mathematical enquiry which Bruno dictated to private pupils in Padua; thus he was not completely immersed in his magical-Hermetic studies there as had previously been thought. It is a thesis which has the merit of bringing Bruno back from the borders of insanity, and allowing him a greater measure of rational and judicious behaviour. Even so, there is no precise documentary evidence to support the thesis that he was looking for an academic appointment (he had not held one anywhere since his departure from Wittemberg); and if that was the case, it is obvious that he had miscalculated his chances, for after only a brief stay in Padua he went to Venice and took up Mocenigo's invitation. In the end, it is only possible to speculate on the exact reasons which led Bruno to return to Italy; and perhaps there is no need to create hypothetical religious missions or academic programmes to justify them. Bruno had been an exile since his flight from Italy in 1579, and it is natural that he should have wished to return to a country which was not only his by birth, language, and traditions, but which had created and guided the Renaissance culture of which he must be considered still, in many respects, an intimate part. His decision was made in a moment which appeared, in objective historical terms, to be particularly propitious. Furthermore, it is important to understand that the cultural policy of the Counter-Reformation, particularly with respect to the new philosophy, did not become clear at once even to the ecclesiastical authorities themselves. It was only over a long period of discussion and debate, with frequent changes of attitude on both sides, that Bruno's imprisonment, trial, and death at the stake became a symbolic moment in the definition of a rigorously severe policy towards heretical thinking at whatever level. The decision to put Copernicus's *De revolutionibus orbium* on the Index of forbidden books, which was only taken in 1616, has been seen as a direct result of the final outcome of Bruno's trial. According to this interpretation, both events lead directly to the trial and punishment of Galileo, 'grown old', as Milton would write, 'a prisner to the Inquisition, for thinking in Astronomy otherwise than the Franciscan and Dominican licencers thought'. But such severe rigour with respect to the new philosophy and science was only slowly defined, as the hesitations over the case of Copernicus show; and Bruno's trial, rather than the inevitable result of an already rigorously entrenched policy, should properly be seen as one of the main moments through which that policy was gradually defined. The very rigour of his sentence was clearly intended to underline its symbolic character; for Bruno was not only burnt at the stake but carried to his death with his tongue tied to signify the silence imposed on the particularly dangerous and impenitent heretic. Such was the end to the battle with the authorities which Bruno had waged throughout his life in the name of what he called a 'universal philanthropy'. Fortunately history is not made only by the authorities in power. As Milton would write not many years later: 'Many a man lives a burden to the Earth; but a good Booke is the pretious life-blood of a master-spirit, imbalm'd and treasur'd up on purpose to a life beyond life.'

FURTHER READING

Atanasijevic, Ksenija. *The Metaphysical and Geometrical Doctrine of Bruno as Given in His Work* De triplici minimo. Translated by George Vid Tomashevich. St Louis: Warren H. Green, Inc., 1972, 151 p.

Provides detailed analysis of Bruno's *De triplici minimo.*

Bossy, John. *Giordano Bruno and the Embassy Affair.* New Haven: Yale University Press, 1991, 294 p.

Relates in detail Bruno's activities between 1583 and 1586 in London and Paris.

Greenburg, Sidney Thomas. *The Infinite in Giordano Bruno.* 1950. Reprint. New York: Octagon Books, 1978, 203 p.

Provides a "faithful account" and analysis of Bruno's thoughts on the infinite, as well as a translation of *De la causa, pricipio et uno.*

Horowitz, Irving Louis. *The Renaissance Philosophy of Giordano Bruno.* New York: Coleman-Ross Co., 1952, 150 p.

Provides a general introduction to Bruno's philosophy and a detailed study of Bruno's views on the infinite nature of the universe.

Lerner, Lawrence. "Was Giordano Bruno a Scientist?: A Scientist's View." *American Journal of Physics* 41, No. 1 (January 1973): 24-38.

Examines Bruno's cosmological dialogues in order to assess the philosopher's role as a "martyr for modern science."

Massa, Daniel. "Giordano Bruno's Ideas in Seventeenth-Century England." *Journal of the History of Ideas* XXXVIII, No. 2 (April-June 1977): 227-42.

Discusses the influence of Bruno's beliefs and writings on sixteenth century philosophers such as Nicholas Hill and Thomas Hariot.

McIntyre, J. Lewis. *Giordano Bruno.* London: Macmillan and Co., Ltd., 1903, 365 p.

Provides extensive biographical information, as well as detailed discussions of Bruno's philosophy, including analyses of specific works.

Michel, Paul Henri. *The Cosmology of Giordano Bruno.* Translated by R. E. W. Maddison. Paris: Hermann, 1973, 306 p.

Provides an in-depth examination of specific aspects of Bruno's cosmological writings.

Nelson, John Charles. *Renaissance Theory of Love: The Context of Giordano Bruno's* Eroici furori. New York: Columbia University Press, 1958, 280 p.

Explores the relationship between *De gli eroici furori,* "Platonic love treatises," and prose commentaries of sonnets and similar verses.

Paterson, Antoinette Mann. *The Infinite Worlds of Giordano Bruno.* Springfield, Il.: Charles C. Thomas, 1970, 227 p.

Discusses Bruno's beliefs on cosmology, knowledge, and virtue in an effort to establish Bruno's place in "America's heritage."

Singer, Dorothea Waley. "The Cosmology of Giordano Bruno (1548-1600)." *ISIS: An International Review Devoted to the History of Science and Civilization* XXXIII, Pt. 2, No. 88 (June 1941): 187-96.

Analyzes the cosmological arguments of Bruno, comparing his views with those of his predecessors and successors.

Yates, Frances A. "Renaissance Philosophers in Elizabethan England: John Dee and Giordano Bruno." In *History & Imagination: Essays in Honor of H. R. Trevor-Roper,* edited by Hugh Lloyd-Jones, Valerie Pearl, and Blair Warden, pp. 104-14. New York: Holmes & Meier Publications, Inc., 1981.

Compares the separate influences and combined impact of Bruno and philosopher John Dee on Elizabethan Englanders.

William Lilly

1602-1681

English astrologer and autobiographer.

INTRODUCTION

Lilly was the most respected and sought-after of the seventeenth-century English astrologers. He was consulted by a variety of people, from poor farmers to royalty, who solicited his advice on almost every topic imaginable. Lilly's writings frequently sparked political controversy and involved him in legal proceedings on more than one occasion; the exceptional accuracy of his predictions at times caused some of his clients to accuse him of lying or of manipulating events to coincide with his forecasts. However, Lilly defended himself by denying complete responsibility for his prophecies, adopting the credo "non cogunt," that is, "the stars incline, they do not compel." Lilly's astrological writings are now mainly studied for their historical value, and his autobiography, *William Lilly's History of His Life and Times* (1715), continues to attract scholarly interest.

Biographical Information

Most of what is known of Lilly's life comes from his autobiography. He was born in 1602 in Diseworth, a town in which his family had been established for many generations. His father, like his grandfather, was a yeoman, and Lilly mentions that "the free-hold land and houses, formerly purchased by my ancestors, were all sold by my grandfather and father; so that now our family depend wholly upon a college lease." Lilly's mother, aware of her husband's financial failure, became determined that her son would be a scholar, and in 1613 sent young Lilly to Ashby de la Zouch, where he studied Latin, Greek, and theology. When Lilly's mother died in 1619, he was forced to leave school due to his father's poverty. He lived at home for about a year, constantly at odds with his bankrupt father, until he received a letter from a Mr. Gilbert Wright inviting him to come to London to work as a servant. Lilly gladly accepted and worked there for seven years, during which time Wright lost his wife, remarried, and died in 1627; that same year, Lilly married Wright's widow. While Lilly had begun to study astrology in 1632, it was not until after his wife's death in 1633 that he devoted himself completely to his studies. He married again in 1634 and continued to devote most of his time and energy to the study and practice of astrology, at which he was extremely successful and respected. In 1651 he was brought before Parliament and stood trial for his bold predictions, published in *Merlinus Anglicus* (1644-81), which were deemed blasphemous. Lilly was jailed for thirteen days, until (thanks to the influence of several of his extremely powerful friends) it was agreed that he would be released and a committee from Parliament would examine the

questionable material. He married his third wife in 1654, and in 1665 left London for Surrey, where he studied and practiced medicine. In 1674 he became ill, remaining in poor health until his death in 1681.

Major Works

Lilly's almanac, *Merlinus Anglicus*, was first published in 1644 and continued to appear annually for several years. His *An Introduction to Astrology* was denounced by both Presbyterians and Cavaliers upon publication in 1646 for its allegedly heretical content. The next year Lilly published *Christian Astrology*, which firmly established him as a serious astrological scholar, bringing him a great deal of admiration, and attracting a following of clients. In this three-volume set Lilly outlines how to use an astrological chart and explains the characteristics of the zodiac signs and planets, then poses over two hundred sample questions and demonstrates how to answer them using astrology. In 1651 Lilly wrote *Monarchy or No Monarchy in England*, which contained several hieroglyphics. One hieroglyphic—showing three bundles, one exposing an emaciated corpse, with four ominous birds flying over a church in the background—was believed to forecast the 1665 plague in England. Another, depicting men throwing water onto a large bonfire as the Gemini twins (the zodiac sign associated with London) fall into it, was supposed to predict the Great Fire of 1666. Written in 1668, Lilly's autobiography was not published until 1715; the critic C. Lord has praised it as one of the most interesting of its period, "not so much for the information it contains regarding its writer, as for the curious picture it presents of the domestic life of his era."

Critical Reception

From his own era onward, scholars have considered Lilly one of the ablest astrologers of his time. Despite that reputation, however, some modern critics have questioned whether Lilly's prophetical talent was perhaps a product of keen judgement and insight concerning events in the present rather than genuine foresight. They point out that his hieroglyphics prophesying plague and fire, for example, are depictions of two common occurrences in the seventeenth-century, and are not necessarily predictions for specific instances. Regardless of whether or not commentators have agreed about Lilly's ability to foresee the future, they have acknowledged that his writings have provided great insight into the ideals and thought of seventeenth-century society, as well as valuable information about the development of the science of astrology.

PRINCIPAL WORKS

Merlinus Anglicus (almanac) 1644-81
Christian Astrology Modestly Treated in Three Books (treatise) 1647
An Introduction to Astrology (treatise) 1647
Monarchy or No Monarchy in England (prophecies) 1651
William Lilly's History of His Life and Times (autobiography) 1715

CRITICISM

William Lilly (essay date 1647)

SOURCE: "An Epistle to the Student in Astrology," in *An Introduction to Astrology,* G. Bell and Sons, Ltd., 1923, pp. 10-12.

[*In the following excerpt, first published in 1647, Lilly defines some appropriate considerations for the disciple of astrology.*]

My Friend, whoever thou art, that with so much ease shalt receive the benefit of my hard studies, and doest intend to proceed in this heavenly knowledge of the starres; In the first place, consider and admire thy Creator, be thankfull unto him, and be humble, and let no naturall knowledge, how profound or transcendant soever it be, elate thy mind to neglect that Divine Providence, by whose al-seeing order and appointment all things heavenly and earthly have their constant motion: the more thy knowledge is enlarged, the more doe thou magnify the power and wisdome of Almighty God: strive to preserve thyself in his favour; for the more holy thou art, and more neer to God, the purer judgment thou shalt give.

Beware of pride and self-conceit: remember how that long agoe no irrationall creature durst offend man the Macrocosme, but did faithfully serve and obey him; so long as he was master of his own reason and passions, or until he subjected his will to the unreasonable part. But, alas! when iniquity abounded, and man gave the reins to his own affection, and deserted reason, then every beast, creature, and outward harmfull thing, became rebellious to his command. Stand fast (oh, man) to thy God: then consider thy own nobleness; how all created things, both present and to come, were for thy sake created; nay, for thy sake God became man: thou art that creature, who, being conversant with Christ, livest and reignest above the heavens, and sits above all power and authority. How many preeminences, privileges, advantages, hath God bestowed on thee: thou rangest above the heavens by contemplation, conceivest the motion and magnitude of the stars: thou talkest with angels, yea, with God himself: thou hast all creatures within thy dominion, and keepest the devils in subjection. Doe not, then, for shame deface thy nature, or make thyself unworthy of such gifts, or deprive thyself of that great power, glory, and blessednesse, God hath allotted thee, by casting from thee his favour for possession of a few imperfect pleasures.

Having considered thy God, and what thyself art, during thy being God's servant, now receive instruction how in thy practice I would have thee carry thyself. As thou daily conversest with the heavens, so instruct and form thy mind according to the image of Divinity: learn all the ornaments of virtue, be sufficiently instructed therein: be humane, curtius, familiar to all, easie of accesse: afflict not the miserable with terrour of a harsh judgment; direct such to call on God to divert his judgments impending over them: be civil, sober, covet not an estate; give freely to the poor, both money and judgment: let no worldly wealth procure an erronious judgment from thee, or such as may dishonour the art. Be sparing in delivering judgment against the common-wealth thou livest in; avoyd law and controversie: in thy study be *totus in illus,* that thou mayest be *singulus in arte.* Be not extravagant, or desirous to learn every science; be not *aliquid in omnibus;* be faithfull, tenacious, betray no ones secrets. Instruct all men to live well: be a good example thyselfe; love thy own native country; be not dismaid if ill spoken of, *conscientia mille testes.* God suffers no sin unpunished, no lye unrevenged. Pray for the nobility, honour the gentry and yeomanry of England; stand firme to the commands of this parliament; have a reverent opinion of our worthy lawyers, for without their learned paines, and the mutual assistance of some true spirited gentlemen, we might yet be made slaves, but we will not; we now see light as well as many of the clergy. Pray, if it stand with God's will, that monarchy in this kingdom may continue, his Majesty and posterity reigne:

forget not the Scottish nation, their mutual assistance in our necessity, their honourable departure. God preserve the illustrious *Fairfax,* and his whole armye, and let the famous city of London be ever blessed, and all her worthy citizens.

Jurors for the Lord Protector of the Common Wealth of England, Scotland, and Ireland   (essay date 1654)

SOURCE: An indictment filed against Lilly, in *The Last of the Astrologers,* 1715. Reprint by The Folklore Society, 1974, pp. 106-07.

[*The following is the text of the indictment filed against Lilly in 1654, charging him with unlawfully giving judgement on some stolen goods.*]

The Jurors for the Lord Protector of the Common Wealth of *England, Scotland* and *Ireland & c.* upon their Oaths do present, That *William Lilly,* late of the Parish of St. *Clements Danes,* in the County of *Middlesex,* Gent. not having the Fear of God before his Eyes, but being moved and seduced by the Instigation of the Devil, the 10*th* Day of *July,* in the Year of our Lord, 1654, at the Parish aforesaid, in the County aforesaid, wickedly, unlawfully and deceitfully, did take upon him, the said *William Lilly,* by Inchantment, Charm and Sorcery, to tell and declare to one *Anne East,* the Wife of *Alexander East,* where Ten Wastcoats, of the Value of five Pounds, of the Goods and Chattels of the said *Alexander East,* then lately before lost and stolen from the said *Alexander East,* should be found and become; and Two Shillings and Sixpence in Monies, numbered of the Monies of the said *Alexander,* from the said *Anne East,* then and there unlawfully and deceitfully, he, the said *William Lilly,* did take, receive and had to tell and declare to her the said *Anne,* where the said Goods, so lost and stolen as aforesaid, should be found and become; And also that he, the said *William Lilly,* on the said Tenth Day of *July,* in the Year of our Lord, 1654, and divers other Days and Times, as well before as afterwards, at the said Parish aforesaid, in the County aforesaid, unlawfully and deceitfully did take upon him, the said *William Lilly,* by Enchantment, Charm and Sorcery, to tell and declare to divers other Persons, to the said Jurors, yet unknown, where divers Goods, Chattels and Things of the said Persons yet unknown, there lately before lost and stolen from the said Persons yet unknown, shou'd be found and become; and divers Sums of Monies of the said Persons yet unknown, then and there unlawfully and deceitfully, he the said *William Lilly* did take, receive, and had to tell and declare to the said Persons yet unknown, where their Goods, Chattels and Things, so lost and stolen, as aforesaid, should be found and become in Contempt of the Laws of *England,* to the great Damage and Deceit of the said *Alexander* and *Anne,* and of the said other Persons yet unknown, to the evil and pernicious Example of all others in the like Case offending, against the Form of the Statute in this Case and made and provided, and against the publick Peace, *&c.*

Anne East,

Emme Spencer,

Jane Gold,

Katherine Roberts,

Susannah Hulinge.

FINIS.

William Lilly   (essay date 1668)

SOURCE: "How I came to Study Astrology," in *The Last of the Astrologers,* The Folklore Society, 1974, pp. 21-3.

[*In the following excerpt from his autobiography, written in 1668, Lilly outlines how he came to be introduced to astrology.*]

It happened on one *Sunday* 1632, as my self and a Justice of Peace's Clerk were, before Service, discoursing of many Things, he chanced to say, that such a Person was a great Scholar, nay, so learned, that he could make an Almanack, which to me then was strange: One Speech begot another, till, at last, he said, he could bring me acquainted with one *Evans* in *Gun-Powder-Alley,* who had formerly lived in *Staffordshire,* that was an excellent wise Man, and study'd the *Black Art.* The same Week after we went to see Mr. *Evans,* when we came to his House, he having been drunk the Night before, was upon his Bed, if it be lawful to call that a Bed whereon he then lay; he roused up himself, and, after some Complements, he was content to instruct me in Astrology; I attended his best Opportunities for seven or eight Weeks, in which time I could set a Figure perfectly: Books he had not any, except *Haly de judiciis Astrorum,* and *Orriganus* his *Ephemerides;* so that as often as I entered his House, I thought I was in the Wilderness. Now something of the Man: He was by Birth a *Welchman,* a *Master of Arts,* and in Sacred Orders; He had formerly had a Cure of Souls in *Staffordshire,* but now was come to try his Fortunes at *London,* being in a manner enforced to fly for some Offences very scandalous committed by him in these Parts, where he had lately lived; for he gave Judgment upon things lost, the only Shame of Astrology: He was the most *Saturnine* Person my Eyes ever beheld, either before I practised or since; of a middle Stature, broad Forehead, Beetle-brow'd, thick Shoulders, flat Nosed, full Lips, down-look'd, black curling stiff Hair, splayfooted; to give him his Right, he had the most piercing Judgment naturally upon a Figure of Theft, and many other Questions, that I ever met withal; yet for Money he would willingly give contrary Judgments, was much addicted to Debauchery, and then very abusive and quarrelsom, seldom without a black Eye, or one Mischief or other: This is the same *Evans* who made so many *Antimonial* Cups, upon the Sale whereof he principally subsisted; he understood *Latin* very well, the *Greek* tongue not at all: He had some Arts above, and beyond Astrology, for he was well versed in the Nature of Spirits, and had many times used the circular way of invocating, as in the Time of our Familiarity he told me. Two of his Actions I will relate, as to me delivered. There was in *Staffordshire* a young Gentlewoman that had, for her Preferment, marry'd an aged rich Person, who being desirous to purchase some Lands for his Wife's Maintenance; but this young Gentlewoman, his Wife, was desired to buy the

Land in the Name of a Gentleman, her very dear Friend, but for her Use: After the aged Man was dead, the Widow could by no Means procure the Deed of Purchase from her Friend; whereupon she applies her self to *Evans,* who, for a Sum of Money, promises to have her Deed safely delivered into her own Hands; the Sum was Forty Pounds. *Evans* applies himself to the Invocation of the Angel *Salmon,* of the Nature of *Mars,* reads his Litany in the Common-Prayer-Book every Day, at select Hours, wears his Surplice, lives orderly all that Time; at the Fortnight's End *Salmon* appear'd, and having received his Commands what to do, in small Time returns with the very Deed desired, lays it down gently upon a Table where a white Cloth was spread, and then, being dismiss'd, vanish'd. The Deed was, by the Gentleman who formerly kept it, placed among many other of his Evidences in a large wooden Chest, and in a Chamber at one End of the House; but upon *Salmon's* removing and bringing away the Deed, all that Bay of Building was quite blown down, and his own proper Evidences torn all to pieces. The second Story followeth.

Some time before I became acquainted with him, he then living in the Minories, was desired by the Lord *Bothwell* and Sir *Kenelm Digby* to show them a Spirit, he promised so to do; the time came, and they were all in the Body of the Circle, when lo, upon a sudden, after some time of Invocation, *Evans* was taken from out the Room, and carried into the Field near *Battersea* Causway, close to the *Thames.* Next Morning a Country-man going by to his Labour, and espying a Man in black Cloaths, came unto him and awaked him, and asked him how he came there; *Evans* by this understood his Condition, enquired where he was, how far from *London,* and in what Parish he was; which when he understood, he told the Labourer he had been late at *Battersea* the Night before, and by chance was left there by his Friends. Sir *Kenelm Digby* and the Lord *Bothwell* went home without any Harm, came next Day to hear what was become of him; just as they in the Afternoon came into the House, a Messenger came from *Evans* to his Wife, to come to him at *Battersea:* I enquired upon what Account the Spirit carry'd him away, who said he had not, at the time of Invocation, made any Suffumigation, at which the Spirits were vexed. It happen'd that after I discerned what Astrology was, I went weekly into *Little-Britain,* and bought many Books of Astrology, not acquainting *Evans* therewith. Mr. *A. Bedwell,* Minister of *Tottenham-High-Cross* near *London,* who had been many Years Chaplain to Sir *Henry Wotton,* whilst he was Ambassador at *Venice,* and assisted *Pietro Soave Polano,* in composing and writing the Council of *Trent,* was lately dead; and his Library being sold into *Little-Britain,* I bought amongst them my choicest Books of Astrology. The Occasion of our falling out was thus; a Woman demanded the Resolution of a Question, which when he had done, she went her way; I standing by all the while, and observing the Figure, asked him why he gave the Judgment he did, sith the Signification shewed the quite contrary, and gave him my Reasons, which when he had ponder'd, he call'd me Boy, and must he be contradicted by such a Novice! But when his Heat was over, he said, had he not so judged to please the Woman, she would have given him nothing, and he had a Wife and Family to pro-

vide for; upon this we never came together after. Being now very meanly introduced, I apply'd my self to study those Books I had obtain'd, many times twelve, or fifteen, or eighteen Hours Day and Night; I was curious to discover, whether there was any Verity in the Art or not. Astrology in this Time, *viz,* in 1633, was very rare in *London,* few professing it that understood any thing thereof. . . .

George Smalridge   (poem date 1681)

SOURCE: "An Elegy upon the Death of William Lilly the Astrologer," in *The Last of the Astrologers,* The Folklore Society, 1974, pp. 105-06.

[*Below is the epitaph written by Smalridge, then a scholar at Westminster, on the occasion of Lilly's death in 1681.*]

> Our Prophet's gone; no longer may our Ears
> Be charm'd with Musick of th' harmonious
>   Spheres.
> Let Sun and Moon withdraw, leave gloomy
>   Night
> To shew their *Nuncio's* Fate, who gave more
>   Light
> To th' erring World, than all the feeble Rays
> Of Sun or Moon; taught us to know those Days
> Bright *Titan* makes, followed the hasty Sun
> Through all his Circuits, knew th' unconstant
>   Moon,
> And more unconstant Ebbings of the Flood;
> And what is most uncertain, th' factious Brood,
> Flowing in civil Broils, by the Heavens could
>   date
> The Flux and Reflux of our dubious State.
> He saw the Eclipse of Sun, and Change of Moon
> He saw, but seeing would not shun his own:
> Eclips'd he was, that he might shine more
>   bright,
> And only chang'd to give a fuller Light.
> He having view'd the Sky, and glorious Train
> Of gilded Stars, scorn'd longer to remain
> In Earthly Prisons, could he a Village love,
> Whom the Twelve Houses waited for above?
> The grateful Stars a heavenly Mansion gave
> T' his heavenly Soul, nor could he live a Slave
> To Mortal Passions, whose Immortal Mind,
> Whilst here on Earth, was not to Earth confin'd.
> He must be gone, the Stars had so decreed;
> As he of them, so they of him, had need.
> This Message 'twas the Blazing Comet brought;
> I saw the pale-fac'd Star, and seeing thought
> (For we could guess, but only LILLY knew)
> It did some glorious Hero's Fall foreshew:
> A Hero's fall'n, whose Death, more than a War,
> Or Fire, deserv'd a Comet, th' obsequious Star,
> Could be no less than his sad Fate unfold,
> Who had their Risings, and their Settings told.
> Some thought a Plague, and some a Famine
>   near;
> Some Wars from *France,* some Fires at Home
>   did fear:
> Nor did they fear too much, scarce kinder Fate,
> But Plague of Plagues befell th' unhappy State
> When LILLY died. Now Swords may safely come
> From *France* or *Rome,* Fanaticks plot at home.
> Now an unseen, and unexpected Hand,
> By Guidance of ill Stars, may hurt our Land;

Unsafe, because secure, there's none to show
How *England* may avert the fatal Blow.
He's dead, whose Death the weeping Clouds de-
    plore;
I wish we did not owe to him that Show'r.
Which long expected was, and might have still
Expected been, had not our Nations Ill
Drawn from the Heavens a Sympathetick Fear,
England hath cause a second Drought to fear.
We have no second LILLY, who may die,
And by his Death may make the Heavens cry,
Then let your Annals, *Coley,* want this Day,
Think every Year Leap-Year; or if 't must stay,
Cloath it in Black, let a sad Note stand by,
And stigmatize it to Posterity.

E. Walford   (essay date 1884)

SOURCE: "Walford's Antiquarian: Astrology and William Lilly," in *Antiquarian Magazine and Bibliographer,*
Vol. 10, No. 59, 1884, pp. 147-52.

[*In this essay, Walford details the historical background
and significance of astrology, leading up to Lilly.*]

Astrology, which Mr. [G. O.] Fisher defines as "the Science of the Stars," is generally accepted as meaning the art
of foretelling future events from the aspects and conjunctions of the heavenly bodies; and it is tolerably ancient, if
there is truth in the tradition that Adam was the first who
practised it. Josephus tells us that Seth, having learned
from his parent that everything on earth should perish either by fire or water, engraved this knowledge on a column
of stone, which both Josephus and his predecessor Ma-
netho declare to have existed in their own days. Josephus
further states that the art was taught by Enoch and Noah,
who preserved it to the days of Abraham, by whom it was
imparted to the Chaldæans and Egyptians. When Alexander the Great took Babylon, he is said to have found there
astronomical calculations for 1,903 years, that is, reaching
back to within 115 years of the Deluge. Sir Isaac Newton
informs us that, when astronomy had been applied to the
purposes of navigation, and the Egyptians had learned by
it to determine the length of the solar year, an African
prince, with the aid of a priest from Egypt, laid the foundation of astrological science, "basing it not only on the
positions but also on the peculiar appearances of the planets." When the Ethiopians subsequently invaded Egypt,
and the people of that country fled in large numbers to
Babylon, they carried along with them this knowledge,
which they imparted to the Babylonians.

Among the Magi of Persia astrology was cultivated to the
highest degree of perfection, and it is said that an astrologer of that country named Al Hakim, or "the Wise," five
centuries before the Christian era, foretold the birth of the
Messiah and of Mahomet, and the end of the Magian religion. The modern Persians are most devoted followers of
the astral sciences, though they have only one term to denote astronomy and astrology. In China the study of the
stars has been pursued from the earliest times; and the Indians, the Buddhists, and the people of Siam, have always
been devoted to it.

Philostratus tells us that it was practised in Greece as early

as B.C. 1184, and Diodorus Siculus declares that it was introduced into that country by Hercules. Plutarch asserts
that Hesiod was a student of the art; and among its later
students and professors were Thales, Democritus, Pythagoras, Plato, Porphyry, Aristotle, and Proclus. Of Thales
we are told by Aristotle, in the first book of his "Politics,"
a story which may illustrate the above assertion. Being
scoffed at for the profitless character of his philosophy, he
turned his attention to the study of the heavens, when he
found that the next summer was destined to be marked by
an abundant crop of olives. Accordingly, he hired beforehand at a cheap rate all the shops and depositories for the
making of oil, and, having got them into his hands, made
a large fortune when the season for gathering olives came
round. Having thus turned the tables on the scoffers, he
gave away all the money that he had made to the poor.
This was indeed to turn astrological science to a good
practical account. And on this ground Hippocrates, whose
works Galen says are almost inspired, used to say that the
man who despised this art was more of a fool than of a
physician.

Among the Romans, astrology was early known and practised; but Augustus, on coming to the throne, banished its
professors from the imperial city. Tiberius, however, studied it deeply, and prophesied to Galba, the consul, that he
should one day wear the purple. Virgil, Cicero, and Horace all mention astrological practices with more or less of
approval; and Manilius, towards the end of the reign of
Augustus, wrote in praise of it his "Astronomicon," in five
books. Under Nero, Vitellius, and Domitian, the edict of
Augustus was revived, those emperors doubtless considering that it was pleasanter for guilty consciences to live on
in ignorance of "the book of fate." Vespasian, however,
cultivated the art, and foretold the assassination of Domitian; and Suetonius tells us that the year, day, and hour
of that event were predicted by the astrologers. Hadrian
was "profoundly skilled in the occult arts," and in his
reign Claudius Ptolemy wrote in his "Tetrabiplos," or
"Four Books on the Stars," a complete digest of the science. Under Antoninus the study still flourished, and a little later Censorinus wrote his treatise "De Die Natali," a
work of which Vossius speaks in the highest terms of
praise.

Passing to Africa, we find that astrology and magic have
always found a congenial home, and Eastern tales invariably speak of the African tribes as more powerful and
more malevolent in these arts than other nations. The
Ethiopians are said to have obtained, or, at all events, improved their knowledge of the art from the Sheban Queen
of the South, who visited Solomon at his court for the purpose, as we are told, of "listening to his wisdom." The
Arabians, too, cultivated astral science eagerly, and various works on that subject by Arabian writers are even now
in existence. When the Moors passed into Spain, they took
with them the knowledge of the occult sciences; and before
the expulsion of the Moors from that country, Alfonso the
Wise, King of Castile, obtained great fame through his scientific research. "He sent," writes Mr. Fisher, "for Christian and Jewish professors from all parts of Europe to arrange the astronomical tables known by his name; he is
said to have expended 400,000 ducats in arranging and

correcting the observations of Ptolemy; and two cabalistic volumes in cypher yet remaining in the Royal Library at Madrid are believed to have been written by his own hand."

The Venerable Bede and Alcuin, in our Saxon days, pursued the science to some extent; and amongst other followers of it occur the well-known names of Cornelius Agrippa, Jerome Cardan, of Milan; Didacus Placidus de Tito, an Italian monk, author of the "Primum Mobile;" Kepler, Melancthon, Tycho Brahe, and Albrecht von Wallenstein, Duke of Friedland. Coming to our own country, we have among the English astrologers very many of the men of greatest note in the mathematical and philosophic world—Oliver of Malmesbury, Herbert of Lorraine, John of Hexham, Simeon of Durham, Sigidius of St. Albans, Roger Bacon of Oxford, John of Halifax, Michael Scot, Duns Scotus, King Richard II., who is said to have been the author of a MS. on the subject "still in His Majesty's Library at St. James's;" Richard of Wallingford, Abbot of St. Albans; William Rede, afterwards Bishop of Chichester; John Eschenden, John Somer, William of Wyrcester, Lewis Caerlyon, Geoffrey Chaucer, the "good" Duke of Gloucester, and Dr. John Dee, who died in 1572, &c.

In Scotland, the chief astrologer of the sixteenth century was James Bassantin, who is said by Sir James Melvill in his "Memoirs" to have foretold that it would be impossible to reconcile the two queens, Mary and Elizabeth, and that the Scottish queen would meet with "captivity and wreck" at the hands of her English cousin. The Scottish King James was no sooner seated on the throne of England as James I. than every class of occult science received a new stimulus. The King himself wrote a treatise on demonology; and in the time of his son and successor arose the celebrated William Lilly, whose works are still extant, and highly prized. He was "especially great," writes Mr. Fisher, "in the horary branch of astrology; and his prediction of the Great Plague and Fire of London, and his examination on the subject by a committee, are matters of history."

The following account of the proceedings taken by the House of Commons . . . will be especially interesting to my readers, so I give it *in extenso*:—

> "Monday, 22nd October, 1666.—At the committee appointed to enquire after the causes of the late fires:—Ordered, that Mr. Lilly do attend this committee on Friday next, being the 25th of October, 1666, at two of the clock in the afternoon, in the Speaker's chamber, to answer such questions as shall be then and there asked him. Robert Brooke." In remarking on the circumstance he says: "I conceive there was never more civility used unto any than unto myself; and you know there was no small number of parliament men appeared when they heard I was to be there. Sir Robert Brooke spoke this purpose: 'Mr. Lilly, this committee thought fit to summon you to appear before them this day, to know if you can say anything as to the cause of the late fire, or whether there might be any design therein. You are called the rather hither because, in a book of yours long since printed, you hinted some such thing by one of your hieroglyphicks.'

Unto which I replied, 'May it please your honours, after the beheading of the late king, considering that in the three subsequent years the parliament acted nothing which concerned the settlement of the nation's peace, and seeing the generality of the people dissatisfied, the citizens of London discontented, the soldiery prone to mutiny, I was desirous, according to the best knowledge God had given me, to make enquiry by the art I studied what might, from that time, happen unto the parliament and nation in general. At last, having satisfied myself as well as I could, and perfected my judgment therein, I thought it most convenient to signify my intentions and conceptions thereof in forms, shapes, types, hieroglyphicks, &c., without any commentary, that my judgment might be concealed from the vulgar, and made manifest only unto the wise; I herein imitating the examples of many wise philosophers who had done the like. Having found, sir, that the City of London should be sadly afflicted with a great plague, and not long after with an exorbitant fire, I framed these two hieroglyphicks, as represented in the book, which in effect have proved very true.' 'Did you foresee the year?' said one. 'I did not,' said I, 'or was desirous; of that I made no scrutiny.' I proceeded: 'Now, sir, whether there was any design of burning the city, or any employed to that purpose, I must deal ingenuously with you; that, since the fire, I have taken much pains in the search thereof, but cannot or could not give myself any the least satisfaction therein. I concluded that it was the finger of God only; but what instruments he used thereunto I am ignorant.' The committee seemed well pleased with what I spoke, and dismissed me with great civility."

Lilly was consulted by persons of every degree, from the king downwards, and it is very probable that, had Charles I. acted upon the advice which Lilly gave to him, instead of neglecting it, that the course of events then to occur would have been very different, and a great deal of what is now the history of England would never have been occasioned. Lilly, in January, 1649, was present at the trial of King Charles, "who spoke," says he, "excellently well." This remarkable man died on the 9th of June, 1681, "without any show of trouble or pangs." He was buried in the chancel of Walton Church, Surrey, his friend, Sir Elias Ashmole, assisting at the laying him in his grave, which was "on the left side of the communion table." I here give the inscription on his tomb:—

NE OBLIVIONE CONTERETUR URNA

GULIELMI LILLII

ASTROLOGI PERITISSIMI

QUI FATIS CESSIT

QUINTO IDUS JUNII ANNO CHRISTO JULIANO

MDCLXXXI

HOC ILLI POSUIT AMORIS MONUMENTUM

ELIAS ASHMOLE

ARMIGER.

Butler mentions Lilly in his *Hudibras* (1663-78):

A cunning man, hight Sidrophel,
That deals in destiny's dark counsels,
And sage opinions of the moon sells,
To whom all people, far and near,
On deep importances repair.

Do not our great reformers use
This Sidrophel to forebode news?
To write of victories next year,
And castles taken yet i' the air?
Of battles fought at sea, and ships
Sunk two years hence—the great eclipse?
A total overthrow given the king
In Cornwall, horse and foot, next spring?

Samuel Butler, in his Hudibras, *quoted in* The
Continental Monthly, *July 1863.*

C. Lord   (essay date 1893)

SOURCE: "A Seventeenth Century 'Zadkiel'," in *Book-worm*, Vol. 7, Nos. I and II, 1893 and 1894, pp. 265-72, 297-302.

[*Here, Lord summarizes Lilly's life and career, stating that he "may be considered as the last of the 'scientific' astrologers."*]

It is not for the present age, with its belief in hypnotism, mesmerism, and the like, to scoff at the superstition of a previous era; and yet it is strange to remember that little over two centuries ago "astrology" held rank as an actual "science," and was believed in by some of the most enlightened men of the time. *The Life of William Lilly, Student in Astrology, wrote by himself in the 66th year of his age,* is one of the most interesting autobiographies of the seventeenth century, not so much for the information it contains regarding its writer, as for the curious picture it presents of the domestic life of his era.

Lilly may be considered as the last of the "scientific" astrologers. Gypsies and beggarwomen and obscure fortune-tellers of various kinds still undertake to "read your planet" for a consideration, but these miserable professors of the art are not to be ranked with the ancient students of the occult science. An astrologer ruled even the imperious Catherine de Medicis, who gave implicit credence to his vaticinations.

Dr. Dee was favoured by Elizabeth. Men like Sir Kenelm Digby, Elias Ashmole, nay, stranger still, Whitlocke and even Cromwell, were among the friends of Lilly; and amid his many enemies, no one seems to have doubted the truth of his "science." The man himself was certainly no conscious impostor, and modern readers who do not believe in his prophetic gifts will find in his life interesting sketches of many of the celebrities of his era, and much curious historical information.

William Lilly was born in 1602, at Diseworth in Leicestershire. His father was a small landowner in the country. The family were once in fairly prosperous circumstances, but as Lilly remarks, "all the lands purchased by my ancestors had been sold by my father and grandfather," and at the time of the astrologer's birth his parents were reduced to the rank of small farmers. "My mother resolved I should be a scholar . . . seeing my father's backslidings in the world and no hopes by plain husbandry to recruit a decayed estate," and the boy accordingly received the best educational advantages the neighbourhood afforded, going to school with a "Mr. John Brisley, of great abilities for the instruction of youth in the Latin and Greek tongues," who kept an academy at Ashby-de-la-Zouch.

When Lilly had attained his seventeenth year his mother died, but finding that the boy's smattering of knowledge rendered him disinclined to "work, or drive the plough, or do any country labour," both father and son became mutually dissatisfied. "One Mr. Smatty, an attorney," now offered young Lilly a situation in London "where was a gentleman who wanted a youth that could write to attend on him and his wife." The offer was thankfully accepted, and in April, 1620, the country lad came to London. The promised situation proved that of a mere household drudge in the family of a citizen and his wife. "My work was to attend my master when he went abroad, to make clean his shoes, sweep the street, help drive bucks when we washed, fetch water from the Thames, scrape trenchers, &c., all which drudgeries I willingly performed, for I would have been of very mean profession before I returned to the country again."

The lad's cheerful acceptance of his lot brought its reward. His mistress died from a lingering disease within four years of his entrance into her service, and Lilly's devotion to her during her illness won him the favour of both the sufferer and her husband. So great was the invalid's attachment to her attendant that he was the only person whom she would permit to exercise any surgical operations upon her, but we spare our readers the medical details (which Lilly gives at full length), though lovers of "the good old times" might thank fate that they are not called upon to undergo the surgical treatment of the seventeenth century.

After the poor woman's death a bag of charms was found upon her body, and this circumstance appears to have first directed Lilly's attention to astrological "science." He ascertained that these "charms" had been given to his mistress's first husband by the celebrated Dr. Forman, whose name is so familiar in connection with Sir Thomas Overbury's murder. Lilly is as discursive a writer as Philip de Comines, and here breaks off his personal narrative to give an account of the "Life of Dr. Forman," the physician, the astrologer, the suspected poisoner. It is too long to quote here, and the story is sufficiently familiar to most readers of the history of the reign of James I. Lilly lived happily with his master, who "settled on me for my life twenty pounds per annum," presumably in gratitude for his services to his late mistress. In 1625 his master re-married, but only survived his second nuptials a couple of years. His widow was so favourably impressed by Lilly that she virtually proposed to him soon after his master's death, and they were privately married. This union appears to have been a happy one, though the wife was considerably the senior of the pair; and Lilly, now in comfortable circumstances, turned his attention to the fantastic "science" that had so long attracted him. He obtained an introduction to a Mr. Evans, "an excellent wise man who had studied the Black Art" and had been employed by Sir Kenelm Digby and Lord Bothwell to "raise spirits." Under this man, and with the assistance of several other Sidrophels, "one Captain Bubb, who resolved horary questions"; "Jeffry Neve, a student of astrology"; "William Poole, a nibbler at astrology," Lilly seriously studied, with such good effect that he was able "in eight weeks to set a figure (*i.e.,* cast a horoscope) perfectly."

With delightful candour Lilly acknowledges that his tutors were by no means honest even in their pretended "science." He detected his first instructor, Evans, in giving a reply totally at variance with the astrological "resolving of the question," to which the magician coolly replied "that he was bound to answer the woman as it pleased her, otherwise she would have given him nothing, and he had a wife and family to keep."

But the unworthiness of its professors (and some of the astrologers mentioned appear to have been most disreputable characters) did not shake the faith of Lilly in the "glorious science of astrology," and his wife dying in 1633 he devoted himself entirely to his mystical studies.

In 1634 Lilly joined David Ramsey, "his majesty's clockmaker," in an exploration for "a great quantity of treasure which was thought to be concealed in the cloisters of Westminster Abbey," and which the two adepts undertook to discover with the aid of the divining rod, manipulated by an expert named Scott. The Dean of Westminster gave ready permission for the experiments to take place "with this proviso, that if any treasure were discovered his church should have a share." A sudden tempest, however, alarmed the treasure seekers, and Lilly prudently counselled that the explorations should be discontinued, "otherwise I verily believe the demons would have blown down the abbey."

Lilly had now established a reputation of a conjurer or white wizard, and to him came clients akin to those described by Butler (in "Hudibras"), whose Sidrophel is said to be a caricature of our hero. Ladies desiring love potions to win back faithless admirers, persons wishing to recover all kinds of lost property, inquisitive seekers into futurity, all came to have their doubts "resolved," and, according to Lilly's own account, departed well satisfied. Like many other fortune-tellers, Lilly possessed much natural acuteness which he used to supplement the resources of his art. He recovered a compromising document for one patron, not by magical incantations, but by the simple expedient of inviting the holder of the obnoxious paper to dine with him and bring the document for examination, Lilly pretending that he had a grudge against the writer of the paper and would be glad of a weapon against him. After dinner, when the unsuspecting owner of the document had drunk a good deal of wine, Lilly accidentally (?) knocked over the candle, and in the darkness "did convey the paper

into my boot, while they went to re-light the candles." It was some days before the half-tipsy guest discovered that he had lost the most important of his documents, and by that time the paper had "gone into Cumberland, whither I sent it at once with this friendly caveat, 'sin no more'; and so," adds Lilly, with a fine disregard of moral considerations, "this business ended very satisfactorily for my friend and also for myself." Nothing is said regarding the feelings of the man from whom the paper was stolen.

Lilly had now an extensive acquaintance with many influential persons, and their influence often assisted him in working some of his apparent miracles. He was able to protect a royalist friend who had been "abused by the sequestrators," by obtaining a letter of protection from Speaker Lenthall himself, a favour his friend apparently considered as obtained by magical arts, but which Lilly candidly admits he gained through his acquaintance with Whitelocke and Lady Lisle.

In 1644 Lilly first turned author, and indited a book, **Merlinus Anglicus,** which, after some difficulty, he obtained the sanction of the Parliament to print; "for," as he himself remarks, "in it I meddled not with their Dagon."

He continued to publish prophetical works in succession, rousing the jealousy of a brother professor who had been first in the field, and who now attacked the new seer as "a senseless impertinent fellow named William Lilly." Wharton, this rival astrologer, was a Royalist, and on quarrelling with him, Lilly "engaged heart and soul in the cause of the Parliament." Such, however, was the general belief in Lilly's skill, that some of the king's adherents applied to him to advise regarding time of the king's flight from Hampton Court, and the place where the ill-fated monarch would best find refuge; and the astrologer dates the king's after misfortunes to the neglect of the counsel he gave on these subjects.

A prophecy Lilly published in 1645, which appeared to be verified in the battle of Naseby, greatly raised his reputation as a seer. His vaticination was one eminently likely to be fulfilled. "If now we fight, victory stealeth upon us," was the cautious wording; and in most battles "victory" falls to one of the combatants, "we" of course standing for the winning side. In 1645 Lilly's works fell under the ban of some of the stricter members of the Parliamentary party; but thanks to the influence of powerful friends and a specious explanation of some of the suspected passages, the astrologer triumphed over his accusers. In 1646 Lilly began his *magnum opus,* **An Introduction into Astrology,** being, as he says with equal candour and modesty, "touched in conscience; believing that God had not disposed my abilities upon me that I should bury them under a bushel." With this pious purpose he worked for a year, secure in the protection "of the soldiers and the Independent party, who were all for my art; . . . but should the Presbyterian party have prevailed, as they thought of nothing less than to be lords of all, I knew well they would have silenced my pen, and committed the Introduction to everlasting silence."

The famous work was published at length, and attacked by both Cavaliers and Presbyterians. Fairfax, however, graciously received its author, and remarked that "though he understood it not, he hoped the art (of astrology) was lawful, and agreeable to God . . . he doubted not but I feared God, and therefore had a good opinion of me."

Hugh Peters, the famous preacher, was equally favourable; and later on Cromwell extended his powerful protection to the astrologer. In 1650 Lilly, who was a shrewd observer of the "signs of the times," published a prediction "that the Parliament would not long continue, but that a new Government would arise." This prediction was followed by a yet bolder declaration "that the Parliament stood upon a tottering foundation, and that the Commonwealth and soldiery would join together against them." As might be expected, the Long Parliament resented these predictions, and Lilly was summoned before a Committee of the House to answer for the treasonable passages in his book. He had powerful friends; Lenthall, the Speaker, sent for him privately, to inform him what passages "tormented the Presbyterians most highly," that he might be prepared to answer accusations upon them; many members of the Committee were on his side, and Cromwell openly favoured him. Indeed one is tempted to inquire whether Lilly's prophecy of the impending fate of Parliament, so abruptly dissolved by Oliver, had not been "inspired" by the future Protector or his friends. In any case, Cromwell was acute enough to know the value of a soothsayer who was entirely on his side, and had so large an influence with the soldiery and the populace.

The manner in which Lilly justified his book to the Parliamentary Committee is more creditable to his ingenuity than his veracity. After receiving the Speaker's friendly information, he applied to a printer of known Royalist tendencies to print six copies of the *Anglicus with the objectionable passages omitted.* "I told him my design was to deny the book found fault with, and own only these six books; . . . I doubted he would be examined." The Royalist printer had no objection to perjure himself in the cause of a foe to the Parliament. "Hang them" (*i.e.,* the Committee), he readily responded, "they are all rogues; I will swear myself to the devil before they shall gain any advantage of you by my oath." When the attacked work was produced before the Committee, the astrologer boldy denied its authenticity, asserting "it was writ by some malicious Presbyterian to ruin me," and, producing the six copies of the book prepared by his Royalist friend, protested that this, and this edition only, was the genuine one, "the others were counterfeits, and published by my enemies." Lilly was kept in honourable custody for a time while the Committee wrangled over the matter; but thanks to the influence of Sir Arthur Hazelrigg and other powerful friends, he was finally admitted to bail, and the matter slept. In 1655 Lilly's prophecy was fulfilled, and "my old enemies the Parliament men were turned out of doors by Oliver."

A domestic bereavement befell the astrologer in 1654. He lost his second wife, whom he had married some years previously. The widower makes no false pretence of sorrow. "My second wife died for which I shed no tears. She brought me a portion of £500, and she and her poor relations spent over £1,000."

In his curious candour, Lilly sometimes reminds us of the autobiography of Benvenuto Cellini. Eight months after his wife's decease he married a third spouse, "who is totally for my comfort." The events recorded during the next ten years are a strange picture of the career of a seventeenth century astrologer. Lilly is alternately engaged in vulgar disputes with "a half-witted young woman," regarding half-a-crown to be paid for the recovery of some stolen goods; and is consulted by Claypole regarding the best person to appoint as English Ambassador in Sweden. Foreign sovereigns send him gold chains, and poor women pay him small amounts to obtain tidings of absent relatives. Throughout the Protectorate he flourishes, and is courted by men of position and influence. In that superstitious age a "prophetical almanack" maker held a very different rank from that enjoyed by our modern Zadkiels. Cromwell himself could not afford to despise a man whose books were so universally credited. "At one fight in Scotland," writes Lilly, "a soldier stood with my *Anglicus* in his hand and cried, 'Hear what Lilly saith, in this month we are promised victory, so fight it out brave boys.' " Such predictions must often have drawn on their own fulfilment.

Lilly does not disguise that he frequently gained information from mortal rather than from spiritual sources. He confesses that he was for years in correspondence with a "French priest . . . a confessor to one of the Secretaries," by whose means he was supplied with news from France; and doubtless he possessed many similar sources of intelligence. The favour shown by the Protector and his friends suggests the idea that he may have been employed by Oliver as a secret political agent.

At the Restoration, Lilly appears to have been somewhat anxious about his fortunes, but the shrewdness which led him to side with the winning party at the beginning of the civil troubles did not desert him now, and he was as ready to accept King Charles as General Monk himself, and to interpret certain "eminent predictions as clearly foreshadowing his majesty's return." Some enemies attempted to injure him by making public his former services to the Parliamentary cause; but again he found friends and protection, this time in the shape of the son of the gentleman whom he had formerly saved from the persecutions of the sequestrators in 1643. After a short imprisonment at the Gate House (of the miseries of which place Lilly gives a graphic description, adding, "I thought it to be hell") he was released on taking the oath of supremacy, and received a formal pardon. Before his release he was examined regarding that still disputed point of history, the identity of the executioner of Charles I. Lilly had not been present at the execution, although invited to accompany Hugh Peters to the scene; but he stated that he dined with a company of Parliamentarians a few days after the king's death, and that Robert Spavin, secretary to Cromwell, privately informed him that "the man who did the fact was Colonel Joyce . . . for I was in the room when he fitted himself for his work, stood behind him when he did it, and when done went in again with him. There is no man knows this but my master (Cromwell), Commissary Ireton, and myself."

. . . . . .

He nothing common did or mean,
Upon that venerable scene.

Lilly does not appear to have troubled himself greatly about the fate of his quondam associates. He records going to the trial of the regicides, but has no word of pity for them. Perhaps he feared to endanger his own safety by showing any sympathy with members of the Roundhead faction. The *Life of Charles the First,* which Lilly had published in 1651, was certainly so damaging a production that one is surprised that its author obtained his pardon so readily. "Long live the Parliament, . . . God bless the army," is the opening passage of Lilly's biography of the *White King,* and the whole history of Charles's reign is given with this bias. Lilly's *Life of King Charles* reminds the reader of Cowley's *Life of Cromwell,* save that where the royalist poet indulges in irony, Lilly descends to coarse invective. The work was doubtless written to gain the favour of Cromwell, and contains all the accusations, true or false, which were heaped on the unfortunate monarch by his antagonists. Yet even Lilly is forced to do some justice to Charles' higher qualities; and, in his worst attacks, writes of him with a respect lacking in his allusions to James I., whom he describes by the irreverent cognomen of "old Jemmy." His *Life of Charles I.* is interesting, despite its party bias. It contains many sketches of minor historical characters, and a world of quaint anecdotes which "grave historians" would scorn to note. There is a curious story of the ghost of the Duke of Buckingham's father appearing to "an aged gentleman, one Mr. Parker," shortly before the Duke's assassination by Fenton, and how the spectre bade him warn the favourite that "unless he forsake the company of such and such persons he will come to destruction." Mr. Parker prudently considered that if he carried the message to the Duke "men would say he was aged and did dote." But a second visit from the spirit, who now appeared angry, decided him to undertake the required errand. As he expected, the Duke received him with ridicule, but on Mr. Parker's mentioning "some secret" which the ghost had confided to him, Buckingham was greatly startled, and acknowledged "No man knew what you have told me, save my father and I only." But though convinced of Mr. Parker's good faith, the Duke did not obey his counsel: and a few days afterwards the ghost again appeared "very quiet and sorrowful," and thanked Mr. Parker for having delivered his message, adding that he knew his son had slighted it, and he would now only ask that Mr. Parker should go once again and tell the Duke that "a dagger or knife shall end him unless he amend his ways." The ghost vanished with a warning, "Set your house in order, for you, too, shall shortly die." Very unwillingly Mr. Parker delivered this last message, to which the Duke angrily desired him "to trouble him no further with his dreams"; but in another month the deaths of the Duke and of Mr. Parker himself verified the ghost's prediction.

We pass over, as too lengthy to recapitulate, all the attacks on the king's public and private career; all the spiteful gossip which Lilly had probably raked together merely to gratify his Cromwellian allies. Like Andrew Marvell, Lilly is forced to do reluctant justice to the king's dignity and fortitude during the closing scenes of his life,

and ends his history with the remark, "he was not the worst, but the most unfortunate of princes." Like a well-known firm of modern financiers, Lilly appears to have had the strongest aversion to dealing with "unfortunate" persons. Throughout his own life he conscientiously sided with the victorious party, and cannot even write with patience of any unlucky individuals. He censures King Charles for receiving Marie de Medicis (the mother of his consort), on the ground that "wherever this miserable old queen came, there followed immediately after her plague, war, famine, or one misfortune or other. Strange it is, she was fatal to any land she entered into." His "misfortunes" are the crowning accusation against King Charles, and Lilly commends "the far-seeing wisdom" of Queen Anne of Denmark, who discerned "that the Palgrave would be unlucky," and therefore objected to him for a husband for her daughter the "queen of hearts." Lilly is accurate regarding the place of King Charles's burial, naming "King Henry the Eighth's vault" as his final resting place. It is strange, amid all Lilly's attacks on King Charles and his advisers, that he writes with least bitterness regarding the man who is usually blamed as one of the prime movers of the civil troubles—Archbishop Laud. After all his malevolent attacks on the king, Lilly sinks into a vein of respectful sympathy regarding the archbishop. "I ever honoured the man and naturally loved him, though I never had speech or acquaintance with him; . . . let his imperfections be buried in silence."

That this attachment was personal to Laud himself, and arose from no reverence for his office, is evident from Lilly's attack on Bishop Wren for saying "he hoped to see the time when a Master of Arts or a minister, should be as good a man as any gentleman in England"—no very ambitious clerical aspiration, but one Lilly stigmatised as "saucy pride."

How Lilly found such ready pardon for his *Life of King Charles* is not explained, unless by the suggestion that he was too useful a man to quarrel with. He himself was more than willing to attach himself to the royalist side—now it was a successful one. He claims to have prophesied the Restoration sixteen years before it took place, and quotes many enigmatical phrases from his own works, and the prophesies of Merlin, which were certainly capable of interpretation as predicting the accession of Charles II.; and which could also have been translated, with equal facility, to foreshadow any other public event. "Happy for the nation he did come in, and long may he reign over us," exclaims Lilly, after indicating his own prophetic sight.

In 1666 Lilly's too accurate prognostications again brought him into trouble. In 1651 he had published two "Hieroglyphicks," one depicting "coffins, people in winding-sheets, other digging graves," and the other "a great city in flames." When we read the ingenious interpretations Lilly gives (after the events) to all the vague utterances in his almanacks, it is easy to understand that these pictures might be utilised to mean anything. They appear indeed to have attracted little attention till the great Plague of 1665 seemed to verify the first picture. When the

Fire followed in 1666, the committee appointed to inquire into the cause of that conflagration (then generally believed to be the work of an incendiary) bethought them of the prophet; and appear to have suspected that he might be able to throw some light on the origin of the calamity he had foretold. "I was ever timorous of committees," writes Lilly, "being ever by some of them scorned, calumniated, upbraided, and derided." However, he was forced to appear in answer to a citation. Elias Ashmole, the antiquary, to whom Lilly's biography is dedicated, accompanied him to the committee, and used his influence with some of its members "that they should not permit me to be affronted, nor have disgraceful language cast at me."

In answer to questions, the soothsayer declared that he had discovered "by his art" that London should be afflicted with a plague and a fire, but that as regards the exact date of these calamities, "I made no scrutiny, nor was desirous to do so."

As the plague was a steadily recurring visitant (Lilly himself had known two visitations of the disease prior to the one of 1666), and a fire was always a possible calamity in a city of wooden houses, both predictions were likely one day or other to be verified. The astrologer solemnly protested that "whether there was any design in burning the city, or who were employed to that purpose, I know not; I conclude it was only the finger of God, but what instruments He used, I know not." The committee were satisfied, and "dismissed me with great civility."

After this Lilly appears to have withdrawn himself from public notice to a great extent. In 1652 he had purchased a house and some land at Hersham in the parish of Walton-on-Thames, and there he now chiefly resided. He appears to have amused his later years with correspondence and quarrels with brother astrologers, and by the compilation of his "Life." In 1665 he entirely quitted London, and obtained a license to practise as a physician, chiefly devoting himself to gratuitous labours among the poor. "Every Saturday" he rode into Kingston, and when the poor flocked to him "he gave them advice and prescriptions freely, and without money, though from them that were able he took a shilling or half a crown if they offered it, but he demanded nothing." In 1674 his health began to fail. We spare our readers the details of the medical treatment of the era, in spite of which the astrologer lingered for some years, dying at last in 1681 of a palsy following other complaints—and the well-meant efforts of a "skilful surgeon" of the school of Sangrado.

The closing years of Lilly's life had been spent in the practice of much charity and kindness, and his death was lamented by his poorer neighbours. He was interred in the chancel of his parish church, and his friend Elias Ashmole placed "a fair black marble slab," with a Latin inscription, over his grave. His death was commemorated by some Latin and English epitaphs, couched in strains of highest eulogy.

That Lilly himself was a firm believer in his "art" can hardly be doubted; at the same time it is equally certain that he did not disdain to avail himself of sublunary information to help out the advices of his "spirits." The man

was assuredly no conscious impostor, trading on the folly of dupes. In his autobiography we see him depicted as a shrewd and quick-witted man, with a prudent judgment regarding the likely success or failure of future projects, which he appears to have often honestly mistaken for the gift of prophecy. It was rather the keen insight of a man of the world, than the inspiration of a Daniel, which made Lilly foresee the ultimate failure of the royal cause from an early period of the civil struggle, or which taught him that the feeble hands of Richard Cromwell would never long hold the reins of government.

The chief interest in Lilly's autobiography lies in the pictures it gives of the "men and manners" of his era. His calling brought him into contact with all the conjurers and astrologers of the day—he is full of anecdotes of Forman, of Kelly, and of Dr. Dee; of a less well-known seer, one Sarah Skelhorn, who "had the best sight for reading in a crystal that I ever did see." That only persons of good life were qualified to read in the magic mirror of the beryl, or "call upon angelical creatures," is insisted upon by Lilly. He relates how a Suffolk gentleman once enjoyed "the sight and conference with Uriel and Raphael, but lost them by carelessness, so that they would both but rarely appear, and soon be gone, resolving nothing. He would have given £200 for me to have assisted in their recovery, but I am no such man. These glorious creatures, being commanded, do teach the master many things. Neatness in apparel, cleanliness, a strict diet, an upright life, and fervent prayers to God, conduce to assistance of the curious."

Good ears must also be necessary to catch the angelic whispers; as Lilly remarks "the angels speak like the Irish, much in their throats."

Timid persons should not try to call up spirits. There is a story of a man who desired to behold the queen of the fairies; but his heart failed him over the incantation, his hair stood erect, and he begged to be spared the spectacle that he had come to witness. Another weak-minded adept was carried out of the magic circle, and deposited in a ditch some miles from his home, where he was discovered next morning half dead with fright and cold. Lilly relates these and many similar stories with the utmost apparent good faith; and after all, these tales do not make larger claims on our credulity than many of the spiritualistic and "psychical" narratives which are believed in in this enlightened century. Some of the "prophecies" mentioned by Lilly have become historical. That James I. dreamed many years before his death that he heard a Latin verse warning him that "when thy carbuncle falls into the hot fire, thy death is near at hand," and that a carbuncle stone actually did fall out of the king's hat into the flames as he sat over a fire shortly before his decease, has become a well-known tale. That an ancient prophecy foretold disaster to a "White King," and that Charles I. was supposed to have deserved this name by wearing white, not purple, robes at his coronation, is also a familiar story.

Lilly's interpretation of prophetic utterances are indeed so ingenious that it would be difficult to find any that lacked fulfilment. One line in "Merlin's Prophecy," "There shall be merchandise of men, as of an ox or an ass," is explained to stand for the sale of the "wretched Scots in Lancashire after the defeat of 1648. The English merchants bought such of them as were worth anything and sent them to the plantations at Barbadoes." "What price the Scots were sold for I know not; but he that gave but twelve pence apiece for any of that nasty nation gave too much."

The English hatred of the "needy, greedy Scots" so general after the accession of James I., is strongly marked in Lilly's "interpretation"; he never lets slip an opportunity for a fling at "these true harpies, ravening wherever they come."

But it would occupy too much space to dwell further on Lilly's expoundings of prophecy.

We are all familiar with the story of the traditional "self-made man" who comes almost penniless to London to "seek his fortune." So did our astrologer in 1620, to die fifty-one years later in the enjoyment of a "competent estate," having lived in terms of friendship with many of the most celebrated men of his time; been flattered and rewarded by foreign sovereigns and by English statesmen; favoured by the ruling powers at each phase of the Civil struggle; possessed of an extensive reputation—and all by the exercise of an "art" akin to that professed by the gipsy at the country fair, or the tattered sybil who beguiles credulous maid-servants at the back door.

Modern Zadkiels and almanack makers may look back regretfully to an era when their now derided art was the stepping-stone to fame and fortune.

Katherine M. Briggs   (essay date 1974)

SOURCE: An introduction to *The Last of the Astrolgers* by William Lilly, The Folklore Society, 1974, pp. vii-xii.

[*In the following excerpt, Briggs gives a brief biographical overview of Lilly.*]

Every century is a period of change, but the sixteenth and seventeenth centuries in England saw greater revolutions of thought and social structure than any before them since those two crucial periods when the Roman eagles left Britain and when the Normans conquered England. They are only comparable to the changes that the older ones amongst us have witnessed in the present age. If the sixteenth century saw the Tudor succession, the impact of the New Learning, the Reformation, the rise of Bureaucracy and the Middle Classes and the shift from Feudalism to Plutocracy, the seventeenth saw the crystallisation of Parliamentary theory and procedure, the proliferation of sects, the final destruction of the medieval world picture, the rise of Science and Empirical Medicine and the virtual destruction of the sanctions which hedged Monarchy.

It is in this last period that [William] Lilly (1602-81) was born and lived.

Lilly's short account of his Own Life, which reaches a little over a hundred pages in a small octavo volume, touches on so many aspects of the life of his time that it is of value not only to folklorists and students of occult writings, but also to those interested in history, literature, sociology and education. A certain cunning and plausibility is displayed in it. Lilly was, by the time he wrote, a Church Warden and a respected member of society. He was writing soon after the Restoration when loyalty was in fashion, and he could not afford to be candid about little matters of Parliamentary espionage and the like. At the same time he has a certain naïvety, almost candour, which from time to time betrays him. He was a rogue, but he seems really not to have known what a rogue he was. There is an air of triumph about his account of how he juggled matters for his patron William Pennington, who had been accused by a Northern girl of getting her with child. He produced a warrant for her arrest but could not secure her person, but Lilly succeeded in catching her, in throwing discredit on her proffered bail and getting her brought to trial in the North, where she was sentenced to a whipping and a year's imprisonment. Further, Lilly succeeded in discovering the names of the gentry who supported her by the very dubious method of approaching her old father under a false name, making him drunk and stealing away all his papers. By something the same method Lilly stole Pennington's Warrant of Array, given him by Charles II in the second Civil War, from a Mr. Musgrave, who wanted to use it in procuring the sequestration of William Pennington's lands. Of even more social interest was the case brought against Pennington by Isaac Antrobus, a Puritan divine, who was defeated by a counter-accusation brought against him by Lilly on the grounds that he was a notorious drunkard, that he had had illicit intercourse with a woman and her daughter, and that he had christened a cock by the name of Peter. This last would probably be counted a witchcraft practice. Antrobus was adjudged guilty and lost his living. On a later occasion Pennington was in great danger of having the greater part of his wealth sequestrated, but Lilly made interest with Speaker Lenthall, who signed a letter for him which he sent to Pennington to show to the Northern Commissioners. With equal complacency Lilly describes in Chapter XVI how, when an accusation of writing against the government was brought against him by the Presbyterians, he got the printer to falsify his book and swore that the offensive passages had been written in by enemies in order to ruin him. He must have had an engaging personality, for he kept many friends of all opinions, and even his own frank confessions do not seem to have brought him into disrepute.

The account of his own youth well illustrates the continual flux of the society in which he was reared. He belonged to a family with some claims to gentility—his great-uncle, Sir Henry Poole, was one of the Knights of Rhodes—but in the main of yeoman stock with quite an amount of land and property in the small town of Diseworth where he was born. His father, however, had sunk into poverty, and by the time Lilly left home to go to work was lodged in a debtor's prison. In spite of the family difficulties, however, his mother was successful in getting him sent to a local Grammar School at Ashby, where he learnt to speak Latin as well as English, became proficient in making verses and must have made the beginnings of the study of rhetoric, for he was put forward to dispute against visiting divines.

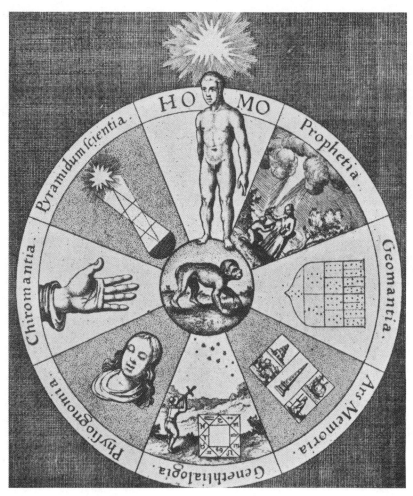

Synoptic diagram of the divinatory arts.

The atmosphere of the town was Puritan, and the most influential man there was Sir Arthur Hildersham, an eminent Puritan divine. Most of Lilly's contemporaries went to the University but his family became too poor to support him, and he was taken home to hang about the farm. After a time he was given a recommendation to a master in London, collected the bare necessities of clothing and a few shillings from some well-wishers and set out to walk up to town with the carrier's cart. In contrast to Lilly's own educational qualifications it is worth nothing that his new master, though Master of the Salter's Company, was unable to read or write. Lilly had no money to pay his indentures and was probably engaged as a menial servant; indeed he gives a list of the various duties he performed, but he must also have helped his master in his business, for he was later made a member of the Salters' Company. One of the most arduous and harrowing duties he had to perform was the nursing of his mistress, who was dying of a cancer in the breast. Lilly gives a painful account of how he cut away her decaying flesh, but he seems to have shown kindness, for he says she would allow no one to nurse her but himself. Lilly had at this time no knowledge of astrology, but he must already have had some interest in magic, for he gives some account of the sigils (engraved seals) and amulets found on his mistress' body after her death. The cutting of these sigils was a large part of the trade of many of the ordinary magicians.

During this time Lilly was evidently gaining his master's confidence for he was left in charge of the house, and presumably what business still remained, when his master left London to escape from the plague. His master soon married again, an elderly but good-natured wife, and when he died Lilly took the first step in building up his fortune by marrying her. This happened in 1627, though the marriage was kept secret for two years. Unless he flatters himself he was a kindly husband to her, and made his friends during her lifetime among elderly and sober men. It was at this time, however, that his interests turned towards astrology, and he draws us the first picture of that shabby, shady gallery of quacks and imposters who make Ben Jonson's Face and Subtle seem comparatively respectable.

He describes his first master in the Art, Evans, with a vigour which is worthy of one of Nash's pamphlets:

> He was the most *Saturnine* Person my Eyes ever beheld, either before I practised or since; of a middle Stature, broad Forehead, Beetle-brow'd, thick Shoulders, flat Nosed, full Lips, down-look'd, black curling stiff Hair, splay-footed; to

give him his Right, he had the most piercing
Judgment naturally upon a Figure of Theft, and
many other Questions, that I ever met withal;
yet for Money he would willingly give contrary
Judgments, was much addicted to Debauchery,
and then very abusive and quarrelsom, seldom
without a black Eye, or one Mischief or other.

We get from Lilly a very good notion of the things most
commonly asked from the magical practitioners. The
commonest of all was the question of thefts, which Lilly
calls "the only shame of astrology". This was probably because it was often a matter of collusion when the magician
had good reason to know where the lost object was. Antimonial cups supposed to nullify poisons were lucrative to
magicians, charms and sigils were used to fend off evil
spirits and to bring luck. People wanted to know fortunate
times to begin enterprises. A knowledge of the future
could be gained by astrology, by the invocation of spirits
or by mediums, called "spectatrices", who often looked in
crystals. Lilly himself on one occasion used a spell to clear
spirits off the ground as a preliminary to digging for treasure. Spirits were supposed to be often set to guard treasures. Lilly's experiment threatened to be dangerous because the spectators did not observe the ritual silence necessary for treasure hunting. Sometimes spirits were used
to purloin documents and other material objects, as the
Angel Salmon did for Evans.

Lilly must have learned mathematics at school, though he
only mentions literature, because he quickly rose to proficiency and began to teach others. One can learn from his
account how much esteemed magical manuscripts were at
the time and how important it was for proficients to acquire a good library. A learned and accomplished astrologer, like Dee, would have a really valuable collection, a
more ignorant and almost illiterate practitioner would
have a printed pamphlet like *Erra Pater,* but original
manuscripts might fall into the hands of ordinary working
men. A large manuscript in the British Museum from Ashmole's collection is marked as bought from a small-coal
man. As Lilly's skill and reputation grew he rose from the
dubious company of such as Evans and Captain Bubb to
Dr. Napper, a cousin of Napier the mathematician, a
pious white magician who worked by the conjuration of
angels and whose knees were horny with praying, until he
associated with true mathematicians like William Ough-
tred and was esteemed by scholars like Ashmole and Aubrey. Ashmole was indeed one of his chief patrons, and it
is to him that the account of his life is addressed.

After his first wife's death in 1633 Lilly studied very sedu-
lously and began to practise both astrology and medicine
about 1640. He became much more generally known,
however, after the publication of his first pamphlets in
1644. By this time the Great Civil War was in full swing.
It was a period of very active propaganda, from the carefully reasoned documents issued by the Parliamentarians
and by the King's supporters to news-sheets, pamphlets,
ballads and prophecies. The official propaganda may be
studied at length in Clarendon's *History of the Great Rebellion.* Much of it is skilfully written and convincing, particularly that written by Hyde himself, but we are more
concerned here with the outpourings of the popular press,

and particularly with the prophecies. Political prophecy
had been a weapon in Civil troubles for many centuries
and was particularly effective in the Wars of the Roses.
The prophecies of Merlin, of Sybilla and of Thomas the
Rhymer were reshaped to meet the occasion. The personages intended were generally cryptically described as animals, sometimes heraldically, sometimes symbolically.
For instance, King Henry IV is indicated as "the Maudri-
gal Mouldiwarp" because of his undermining activities.
Lilly followed the same tradition when he described
Charles II as "the Chicken of the Eagle". His educational
background inclined him to the Puritan side and though
his prophecies were cautiously worded they were generally Pro-Parliament and were enthusiastically read in the
Army. In the Puritan climate of opinion his activities were
sometimes condemned as witchcraft, but Astrology still
ranked as a Science, and though some of his undertakings
might well have been suspect, he always found friends to
protect him and was several times thanked for his services.
The annuity that he was given at one time was avowedly
for these, but it is more likely that they were a spy's wages.
He was consulted by both parties, and had his ears to a
good many keyholes. Madam Whorewood was so rash as
to consult him about the King's escape, and though his advice was not taken over that he is likely to have betrayed
the intention. He admits indeed that the pension of £100
a year was given him for two years because he had the
means of getting perfect intelligence out of France, and in
Chapter XVII he says that he knew all the spies that went
in and out of Oxford while the King was stationed there.
Cromwell, Whitelock, Lenthall, Sir Harbottle Grimston,
Sir Philip Stapleton, Denzil Holles and many other prominent Parliamentarians protected him when he was attacked.

In this little miniature we are able to gain a vivid impression of the cross-currents of opinion and the shifting rival-
ries, the moderate men, the fanatics, the self-servers, the
disputes between the Generals. We see the decay of confidence in the Parliament, the rise of the Army's power and
the desperate counsels that began to prevail. We had a hint
of how Lord Say & Sele, who engineered the start of the
War, began to turn towards the King. There is surely a little disingenuousness in Lilly's disavowal of any knowledge
of the Trial before it actually opened, yet it certainly was
pressed forward quickly, and Fairfax appears to have been
ignorant of the execution until just after it had taken place,
though his lady attended and protested against the Trial.
The time of Cromwell's Protectorate is rather skated over,
for Lilly's personal controversies receive most of his attention, but after Richard Cromwell was set aside public matters again come to the fore, with the return of the Rump,
Lambert's bid for power and the subtle and secret policies
of General Monk. No one was sure of his intentions until
he finally disclosed himself.

After the Restoration Lilly, perhaps naturally, fell under
suspicion. Once he was arrested, but here again he found
friends to speak for him, and before the end of 1660 he had
sued out his pardon, and felt himself secure. In 1666 there
was a nervous time for him when he was questioned about
the origin of the Fire of London, but again he was well
supported. His second wife, whom he made no pretence

of regretting, had died in 1654, and in the same year he had married his third wife, with whom he lived in great contentment. From 1665 the rest of his life was spent in Surrey, in the study and practice of medicine. In 1670 he obtained a licence from the Archbishop of Canterbury to practise Physic. No examination was needed for this except the signatures of two physicians.

He was much esteemed for his charity to the poor of Horsham where he made his last home. He died in 1681, and Elias Ashmole raised a tomb over his grave. A glowing epitaph in Latin and English was composed for him by George Smalridge, afterwards Bishop of Bristol, who had been educated at Ashmole's expense. And so, after all his earlier turns and twists, Lilly passed peacefully away in the odour of sanctity.

Derek Parker   (essay date 1975)

SOURCE: "Some That Have Writ Almanacks," in *Familiar to All: William Lilly and Astrology in the Seventeenth Century,* Jonathan Cape Ltd., 1975, pp. 69-116.

[*Below, Parker assesses Lilly's works, from his first almanacs to his later books.*]

The first of Lilly's own almanacs, the **Merlinus Anglicus** of June 1644, was a relatively slender affair of only twenty-two pages and something like 10,000 words; later that year, his second publication was much more ambitious: **England's Prophetical Merline,** which came out in October, had 126 pages and over 60,000 words. The title-page advertised **Anglicus** as 'The English Merlin revived: or, His prediction upon the affaires of the ENGLISH Commonwealth, and of all or most Kingdomes of Christondome this present Yeare, 1644'.

In a Note to the Reader (written from 'The Three Flower de Luces neere Somerset House', practically on his own doorstep) Lilly contends that the almanac had been printed because it had interested so many people in manuscript form, and had been so widely read and copied. And then, comes an interesting preface 'To Any or Every Man'—a classic astrologers' warning to over-credulous readers:

> It's far from my thoughts that there's any binding or inevitable necessity in what I predict by the radiation of heavenly bodies; the stars have no such unlimited lawes, they are bounded, and give light to us or some small glimpses of the great affaires God intends upon earth, but if we rely on our judgement, without relation to the immediate rule and direction of his eternall providence, alas, how soone of wise men we become errant fooles and Ideots . . .

It has been suggested that the preface was placed at the front of the book at the instigation of the publisher; but it seems very unlikely. Apart from the fact that it adequately represents Lilly's own point of view, there is no evidence to show that any of Lilly's publishers were in the least interested in the matter of his almanacs or books-their sale was what mattered to them. George Wither, author of *The Schollers Purgatory*, sets us right about the stationers and publishers of the 1640s:

> What book soever he may have hope to gain by, he will divulge, though it contain matter against his prince, against the state, or blasphemy against God. All his excuse will be that he knew not it comprehended any such matter. For (give him his right) he scarcely reads over one page of a book in seven year . . .

> He will fawn upon authors at his first acquaintance, and ring them to his hive by the promising sounds of some good advertisement; but as soon as they have prepared the honey to his hand, he drives the bees to seek another stall . . . If his employment be in binding books, so they will hold together but till his workmaster hath sold them, he desireth not they should last a week longer; for by that means a book of a crown is marred in one month which would last a hundred years if it had twopence more workmanship.

Lilly's almanacs were certainly ill-bound, and got such usage from his readers that very few of them have survived outside the great libraries. But they remain more than ephemeral records of what the planets were promising in one year or the other: they reflect the history of astrology, too.

Evidently Lilly had already noticed the increasingly critical attitude taken by some people towards traditional astrology, for he goes on to protest:

> this learning is ancient, and hath had society with Kings; it's now despicable, it hath few favourers, and as few to understand it. I desire to be judged by those that apprehend something in Astrology, and not by the censorious criticall Asse, that beleeves no influence, scarce [of] heaven: It was folly in me to judge of any science I was never acquainted with; hee's as much foole as Phormio that censures my labour, and knowes not what I write of, nor the principles of that Art from which I draw my judgement; I beleeve God rules all by his divine Providence, and that the Stars by his permission are instruments whereby many contingent events may be foreseene as well in the generall accidents of the world as in particular men's fates . . .

Lilly then gives another warning to the credulous, not to expect too much of astrologers:

> The Planets and Stars are ministers not masters: Expect not that all accidents shall precisely happen to a day or a weeke. Do not we first fit the ground, then sow, and after some expiration of time gather and crop? It's impossible for the weaknesse of man at all times to hit the certaine day, or weeke, of many accidents, sometimes we do, or very near, but not constantly . . .

The predictions in the 1644 **Anglicus** are fairly vague; later, Lilly was to become more particular. He starts with a general picture of the year to come (giving, as he was always to do, the astrological reasons for his statements):

> If the rules of Astrology fail me not, or God Almighty cloud not my understanding, and so make me uncapable of judgement, some more than ordinary action and accidents shall this

yeare happen in our Clymate, which is England; and in our neerest adjoyning neighbour countries, which are Scotland, Ireland, France, Denmark, the United (perhaps disjoynted) Provinces, as also in the dominions of his Majesty of Spaine, in Flanders, and Brabant: the Celestiall Scheame it selfe is very strange, all the Angles being fixed, the Moone and Mars in fixed signes, the Sunne, Saturn, Venus and Jupiter being all in the Equinoctiall and Cardinall sign Aries the ascendant of England, as if by this their position they pointed out wee should have action enough, and variety of it, &c., onely Mercury the father of lyes and untruths, and scandalous Pamphlets is in a Common Signe, as if he intended all this whole yeare to vex us with flying reports, continually feares, false alarums, untoward speeches, contradictory newes, lying messengers, and cozening Accomptants, Receivers, Treasures, and the like, &c.

There are a few more particular predictions: 'A proper goodly Noble-man of red or flaxen haire will vex or disturbe the North or North-west or West of *Scotland,* and perhaps some others the South,' he remarks, adding in the margin: 'I heare some such thing hath happened!'

Theft and violence were promised throughout the year; more aborted births than usual; and a conjunction of Saturn and Mars at the end of May which, though it need not mean outbreaks of plague (as some astrologers had promised), 'may produce great weakness in people's sights; the head-ach more than ordinary, and stoppings at the brest, and much slimy fleagme in the throat . . .' There would be a general shortage of money, and 'the Nobility and Gentry shall not be so flush of money as to buy bables and trifles'. One would not have thought that there was much in that first *Anglicus* to dispel doubts about the efficacy of astrology as a means of prediction for the mass of the people, or the country at large. But nevertheless (and by comparison with the other almanacs available) it was an enormous success, and four months later the much more substantial *England's Prophetical Merline* was published.

In the preface Lilly asserted that, long though the book was, it would have been even more substantial 'had I not been as much, during its writing, oppressed with taxes and weekly assessments', and had he not omitted much that might be offensive to the Crown, 'for I love Monarchy, and would not easily displease my Soveraigne'. He also promised 'more misfortunes', for 'truth is truth, and a spade is a spade, if I might freely so call it'.

Before beginning the main body of his text, Lilly again emphasized (for the casual reader) what astrology could, and could not, do. It could not find lost or stolen goods, though many clients demanded that service (and privately got it, though illegally). It could warn a man if the woman he loved was unsuitable; it could advise in matters of health; on the success of voyages; on times when business projects might succeed; on physical danger; and to some extent could predict the results of unwise actions. Lilly could, he said, have warned Charles I that at such-and-such a time 'he should have some scuffling with his subjects'.

Throughout his life Lilly was always repeating these warnings, though in his private practice he often disregarded them. He never stopped attempting to teach the general reader something about his art-and his almanacs contain many more astrological technicalities than anything published since. This makes them somewhat tedious to a twentieth-century reader; but many seventeenth-century readers would have had the smattering of the astrological knowledge necessary to understand them, and since Lilly used current astrological language rather than out-dated jargon, his almanacs were in fact textbooks as well as predictive pocket-books. The warnings he gave in his prefatory notes were a protection against the law: *he* believed he could find stolen articles, and that the law was an ass to say that he should not. The apparent inconsistencies are really quite consistent.

The *Prophetical Merline* proper begins with a long and technical essay on the conjunction of Jupiter and Saturn which took place on February 15th, 1643. Lilly notes the effects of nine previous conjunctions of that sort before proceeding to his conclusions, which are gloomy, and to the effect that he is not surprised that England is in her present unfortunate state. He promises a settlement in 1660, however, by which time all will be well again. (It is doubtful whether in the event he was to consider the Restoration quite the panacea he now had in mind.)

Then comes the ephemeris of a current comet, and reflections on it, listing many difficulties with which it is likely to visit Britain. Then a list of eclipses and lesser conjunctions, with short, snappy comments, some more helpful perhaps than others: January 31st, 1645: 'I fear the plague generally.' February 24th: 'Scarcity of bread and provision.' July 4th: 'Londoner, adventure not too much to sea.' December 26th: 'Arise, O Lord, and help'!

Then comes a didactic section in which Lilly prints, and analyses, several full birth charts. The first is that of 'a Gentleman', which Lilly dissects at length, with the comments of the anonymous subject as footnotes. These are usually favourable, but naturally do not extend to the astrologer's final comment that in 1657, when he would be 73, the subject 'at the fall of the leafe . . . becomes ill, and is oppressed with the wind chollic, but striving to be rid of that, and his Medicines not operating to purpose, it puts the native into a fever, of which, about the 5 of December, according to natural causes, he ought to die.' 'I positively conclude not his death,' Lilly kindly mitigates, 'for that's onely in the hands of God.'

A chart drawn up for the moment at which Lilly received a sample of the urine of John Pym, M.P., who was ill at the time and died shortly afterwards, precedes that for a lawsuit. 'I judged the Querant should overcome his enemy, and so he did,' writes Lilly. 'I said that the judge at the tryall would be angry, and so he was, for the adversaries witnesses knew not what to swear.'

Then there is a chart drawn up in an attempt to discover the characteristics of a thief who had stolen some goods from a client. Lilly did not like that kind of work, he explained, for apart from the fact that nobody seemed to believe that it could be properly done, there could be mistakes and wrongful accusations. In this case, having consulted the chart, he opines that the thief

> was such a one as is signified by Mars, *viz* A fellow of middle stature, strong and well set, broad shoulders, a wrangling searing fellow, of some earthly sordid occupation, that did frequently do drudgeries in the house, of a darke flaxen curling haire, a sun-burnt Complexion, and some materiall cut or gash near the left eye . . . I said further that the fellow had two sweethearts at that time.

The thief, when discovered, answered the description, though the client only recovered half of his stolen goods.

The examples given in the almanac all came from Lilly's private practice, which was obviously in a very healthy state. But his publications for the year were not complete: *A Prophesy of the White King* was still to come, and was to have the greatest success of the three, and to gain considerable fame (or notoriety) for its author. It was as much a political publication as an astrological one. . . .

Early in January of each year (though occasionally publication was delayed) Lilly would publish his *Anglicus* with an ephemeris for the *following* year. The almanac for 1646 began, as usual, with a mildly political comment (mild because Lilly usually reserved his more splenetic attacks for special publications). His preface in the 1646 almanac begins with a plea for the uniting of the country—'for what's he, whose heart bleeds not to see a fruitfull kingdome depopulated and wallowing in its owne blood, only to plead the humour of a few?'

Then comes the ephemeris, showing the position of the planets at noon of each day, the Moon's aspects to each planet, astrological judgments on these positions, and the means to tell what planet 'governs' every hour of every day—an invaluable aid to living one's life, and especially for the gathering of herbs for medical use, which were much more effective if they had been gathered at the right time.

There are again special notes on the progress of the war: Charles will have bad news in May and October, and generally speaking things will go ill for him during the year. (Clarendon, without the aid of astrology, was able to make the same sort of prediction: 'The actions of the last year were attended with so many dismal accidents and events that there were no seeds of hope left to spring up in this ensuing ill year,' he wrote.)

Lilly is not entirely uncritical of Parliament: though he promises the cause general success, he suggests that in January 'our soldiers [will] cry out for money; sure I am that some officers will be removed,' and that there will be some 'crooked and clandestine Councils' in the Parliamentary leadership.

He was not so far out: indeed by January the soldiers were beginning to complain very bitterly about their arrears of pay, which by March amounted to over £300,000. He would have noticed hints of disaffection for that reason during the previous year: at York the troops had mutinied, holding Major-General Poyntz at pistol-point while they shouted 'Money, money, money!' in his face. But Lilly had after all been smart enough (assuming that the Army's predicament was not indeed to be read in the planets) to see that things would reach such a pitch that within the first three months of 1646 infantry regiments would be eighteen weeks in arrears, and cavalry regiments forty-three.

As for the 'crooked Councils' in Parliament, these showed up in the Commons debate of March 29th, when Lilly's enemies the Presbyterians showed their lack of sympathy for the soldiers, and even attempted to have the complainants dealt with as enemies of the State. Lilly of course knew perfectly well who would be most annoyed at his taking the soldiers' side; and that it would do him no harm with Cromwell (supposing the Protector had the time and the inclination to trouble himself about an astrological almanac), since he was extremely incensed by the Presbyterians' attitude. The Presbyterians might try to make trouble for Lilly, but not the kind of trouble which would do very much harm; indeed, the 'success' of this kind of prediction was very good publicity, and the chances of their being able to do him any real harm were small, for 'I had abundance of worthy men in the House of Commons, my assured friends, no lovers of Presbytery, which were then in great esteem and able to protect the art . . . for should the Presbyterians' party have prevailed . . . I knew well that they would have silenced my pen annually.'

For the first time, Lilly began including in the almanac what could be called 'pop astrology'; now, as well as medical aphorisms to assist in the curing of illness, he included profiles of physical types for each Zodiacal sign: Gemini, 'a straight, well-set body, good complecion and colour, and the haire browne, of good speech wit and discourse', for instance.

He was learning all the time from his private clients what they demanded of an almanac or an astrologer. It is clear that during this period Lilly's private practice was building up very satisfactorily. The evidence is rather sparse, but from time to time a note or an incident surfaces which shows that his work was gaining considerable reputation. The attacks made on him are one symptom of his increasing popularity. During 1647, for instance, there was a mild scandal when a clandestine royalist newspaper of which George Wharton (one of Lilly's rivals) was co-editor, published an attack on 'that Jugling Wizard William Lilly, the States Figure-Flinger Generall, a fellow made up of nothing but Mischiefe, Tautologies and Barbarism', who, it was alleged, had helped a Mr. John Howe of Lincoln's Inn to gain the affection of Lady Annabella Scroope (daughter of the Earl of Sunderland, and worth at a conservative estimate £2,500 a year), and then marry her, by 'cheating tricks' and 'abhominable practices'. Howe was a fairly well-known politician, which made it important for Lilly to dispose of the accusation if he was to keep his reputation for honesty.

A reply to the allegations was given in a pamphlet published in February 1647, entitled *The Late Storie of Mr William Lillie,* by an anonymous 'Colonel Th.'. In June or July of 1646, the Colonel says, an unknown man had called on Lilly and paid him ten shillings to discover what sort of woman he would marry (including 'the private moles of her body', presumably so that he would readily—or eventually—recognize her). Lilly had drawn up a chart, and given him the necessary description. Five or six days later, a maid had come on behalf of an anonymous woman, who sent five shillings for a description of the man she should marry. The description was forthcoming and sent off with the maid, and a few days later the woman herself had come and paid a further ten shillings for confirmation.

'But,' writes Colonel Th., evidently answering the particular charge (which is no longer extant), 'as for wishing her to goe to the Spring garden, or appointing her to such or such a walke, and that there she should see the Gentleman should be her husband, or telling her his apparrell, &c . . . these are all malicious and lying suggestions, untruths, and meere forgeries.'

Clearly it had been suggested that for a bribe, Lilly had told the heiress to walk in a particular place at a particular time, and she would see her future husband in such-and-such a dress; and had arranged the whole thing with Mr. Howe. What Lilly claimed was that the unknown man had returned to him saying that he had seen the woman who answered Lilly's description of his wife-to-be, and asked if he should press his suit. Certainly, said Lilly, and charged for the advice. Twice more, the man had returned, and been given the same encouragement. Now, the astrologer was hurt and annoyed (having only received, he says, fifty shillings from the man and fifteen from the woman) at being accused of 'hindering' two noble lords who were also after the heiress, and of telling Lady Annabella that she should 'have none but Master H.'.

But in the event, Lady Annabella confirmed Lilly's version of the affair, and the scandal subsided. 'If Wharton,' the Colonel asserts, 'had smelt of anything but the dung hill, hee would have been ashamed to have related such notorious untruth.' It is not of course impossible that Lilly himself had his head in the Colonel's helmet; indeed, it is likely.

It was during this time that Lilly celebrated his increasing prosperity by having his portrait painted—the only likeness to survive, for all the existing engravings and woodcuts are modelled on it. Lilly stands in front of a piece of drapery, to the right of an open window through which can be seen a somewhat lurid sky, and a piece of anonymous and sickly creeper. But the figure itself is rather impressive: a keen look in the blue-grey eyes, a gingerish moustache and a small tuft below the lower lip; shoulder-length hair above a severely cut collar; and holding a blank birth-chart headed 'Aetatis 45', from which the picture can be dated.

There seems no way of discovering who the artist was; the style is respectably polished as to the portrait, but unremarkable. The picture was given by Lilly to his friend Elias Ashmole only five years or so after it was finished, and survived in his great collection.

One interesting feature of it is that the blank chart also bears the words 'non cogunt', underlining the astrologers' constant assertions that (as the ancient astrological saw has it) 'the stars incline, they do not compel'. No man was

forced by planetary intervention to do, or omit to do, anything. He could always overcome 'his fortune'; the astrologer simply predicted possible trends in his life, and the client himself retained free will. (It is this aspect of astrology which makes it acceptable to the Church; the Roman Catholic view in the 1970s is that astrology is acceptable provided that astrologers do not claim to predict events.)

Apart from working for clients, during the 1640s Lilly was working on a book which was to place him as a serious astrological scholar: his ***Christian Astrology modestly treated in Three Books,*** which came out in 1647. This remains his major published work, and was the textbook from which he taught his pupils.

It is a remarkable work (in all, over 350,000 words long), and anyone requiring evidence that astrology in the seventeenth century was extremely complex and finely organized could do no better than look through it. One thing is abundantly clear: however fond Lilly may have been of turning an honest, or even dubiously honest, penny, he knew his subject well, and treated it with the utmost nicety and care. He also wrote with wit and enthusiasm, and sometimes with some nobility of style. The ***Epistle to the Student In Astrology*** which appeared as a prefatory note has been reprinted since in many specialist astrological textbooks, and remains the astrological equivalent, if you like, of the Hippocratic Oath. . . .

Setting aside the contemporary political cant, it is not an ignoble address. It became well known in the nineteenth century, when 'Zadkiel' reprinted it as the preface to a book which he called *An Introduction to Astrology, by William Lilly.* Published in 1835, it has often been spoken of as a book written entirely by Lilly—an error supported by Lilly's habit of writing, in his autobiography and elsewhere, of 'my *Introduction.*' The first Book of ***Christian Astrology*** is titled ***An Introduction to Astrology,*** and this was in fact what Lilly meant. It is ironical that in the nineteenth and even the twentieth century, Lilly has probably been best known for a book he did not write—a much abbreviated and revised edition of ***Christian Astrology.***

'Zadkiel' must have done well out of his abridgement of Lilly: it was reprinted in 1852, together with a work wholly by 'Zadkiel', and was reproduced again and again from stereotype plates. He put together Books One and Two of ***Christian Astrology,*** often altering, often omitting, sometimes adding material of his own, so that it is difficult to judge, when reading Zadkiel's edition, what is Lilly and what is not.

'Zadkiel' himself was an interesting character; his real name was Richard James Morrison, and he was for many years a naval officer. His *Almanac* became extremely popular in the 1830s. An educated man, he was rather careful to disguise his astrological interests when in polite society, and after his real name was revealed during a libel action in 1863, moved from London to Cheltenham where 'the minds of several people . . . [were] rendered unhappy by astrological predictions'. But his main achievement, as far as we are concerned, was to make Lilly's name once more familiar to English readers—even if under a largely false assumption.

Christian Astrology is the work we must turn to as representative of Lilly's astrological theory at its most comprehensively argued and explained. It is one of the most ambitious textbooks of astrology ever printed in English, the subject 'modestly treated of in three books' (which calls into question Lilly's definition of the word 'modesty').

In Book One, he describes the use of an ephemeris, and the drawing-up of an astrological chart; the 'nature' of the twelve Zodiacal signs, and of the planets. Book Two tells the student how to deal with the questions he may wish to resolve by the use of astrology; and Book Three how to interpret a birth-chart and rectify it by the use of 'Annual Accidents'.

Lilly dedicated his book to his friend Bulstrode Whitelocke, 'to acquaint the present and future times, of your ardent and continuall promoting me and my poore Labours,' and paid generous tribute to Whitelock's constancy not only to the cause of astrology, but the cause of Parliamentary democracy.

Ptolemy, publishing one of the earliest comprehensive astrological textbooks in the second century BC, had pointed out in his prefatory notes that he had presented to the reader nothing new, but simply a compendium of the astrological knowledge passed down in MSS and by word of mouth over the preceding centuries. Similarly, Lilly explains in a Note to the reader that he has consulted a great number of earlier astrological writers (a bibliography at the end of the book lists them), but 'though it was no small trouble unto me, to see the discrepancy of judgement amongst them and the more ancient printed Authors, yet I have with some trouble reconciled their disagreements, and reformed and corrected what might have led the Reader into an errour'.

He excuses the more foolish statements in the ancient authors by simply blaming the translators. And he claims that where he differs from the acknowledged authorities, he does so for the best of reasons: that his own researches have led him to believe otherwise!

Lilly's technical explanations are full and straightforward. A general readability adds to the distinction of ***Christian Astrology.*** Lilly must have been a good teacher: with his customary confidence, he claims that he 'never undertook the instruction of any, whom I have not abundantly satisfied, and made very capable of the Art, in lesse time than any could expect'.

The calculation and erection of an astrological chart is not the simplest of matters, and there are several points at which it is extremely easy to allow a reader to take a wrong turning. Lilly's book is no exception; but he takes pains to write in the very simplest terms: in discussing the drawing-up of a birth-chart, for instance . . . , he writes:

> In the first place you are to draw the figure thus; and to know that those twelve empty spaces are by us called the twelve Houses of Heaven, that square in the middle is to write the day, year, and hour of the day when we set a figure: the first house begins ever upon that line where you see the figure 1 placed, the second house where you

> see the figure of 2 stand, the third house where you see the figure 3 . . .

and so on through the twelve houses. Not much room for misunderstanding.

Lilly then takes the reader through the calculation and setting-up of a chart for a particular time and place, in the clearest detail.

Then comes a discussion of the houses: an astrologer associates each house with a particular aspect of a client's life, or with particular characteristics and events: these are traditional, and some of them were indicated as long ago as 2000 BC. Lilly again lists them very fully and carefully:

> The Sixth House. It concerneth Men and Maid-servants, Gallislaves, Hogges, Sheep, Goats, Hares, Connies, all manner of lesser Cattle, and profit or losse got thereby; Sicknesse, its quality and cause, principal humor offending, curable or not curable, whether the disease be short or long; Day-labourers, Tenants, Farmers, Shepherds, Hogheards, Neatherds, Warriners; and it signifieth Uncles, or the Fathers Brothers and Sisters. It ruleth the inferiour part of the Belly, and intestines even to the Arse . . .

Lilly then deals with the planets separately and at very considerable length. Each planet's astronomical characteristics are summarized, then its astrological significance—the physical and psychological traits it contributes to a man at whose birth it was well (or ill) placed in the sky; the occupations such a man might best try; the sicknesses from which he might suffer; the colours he would like, herbs which would do him good, places he would be happy in; and some characteristics not associated with human beings at all—the planet's effects on the weather and on plants.

Lilly's writing is, as always, extremely readable, witty, and of considerable charm. He has the gift of continually interesting the reader, either by an unexpected epithet, a piece of surprising information, or a casual, almost 'flip' style. One might look at his pages on Venus, for instance, which open as usual with astronomical notes:

> After the *Sunne* succeedeth *Venus;* who is sometimes called *Cytherea, Aphrodite, Phosphoros, Despurgo, Ericina.* She is of a bright, shining colour, and is well known amongst the vulgar by the name of the evening Starre or Hesperus; and that is when she appears after the Sunne is set: common people call her the morning Starre, and the learned Lucifer, when she is seen long before the rising of the Sunne: her meane Motion is 59 min. and 8 seconds: her diurnall motion is sometimes 62 min. a day 64. 65. 66. or 70. 74. 76. minutes; but 82. min. shee never exceedeth; her greatest North or South latitude is nine degr. and two min. in February 1643. she had eight degr. and 36 min. for her North latitude . . .

But then come the astrological details: the qualities the planet can contribute to a horoscope when 'well' or 'ill' dignified'—that is, according to its position in the birth chart. Venus 'well dignified' tends to make a man or woman quiet, not given to Law, Quarrel or Wrangling; not Vitious, Pleasant, Neat and Spruce, loving Mirth in his words and actions, cleanly in Apparel, rather Drinking much than Gluttonous, prone to Venery, oft entangled in Love matters, Zealous in their affections, Musicall, delighting in Baths, and all honest merry Meetings, or Maskes and Stage-Plays, easie of Beliefe, and not given to Labour, or take any Pains. . . .

With Venus 'ill dignified', a man becomes

Riotous, Expensive, wholly given to Loosenesse and Lewd companies of Women, nothing regarding his Reputation, coveting unlawful Beds, Incestuous, an Adulterer, Fantastical, a meer Skip-Jack, of no Faith, no Repute, no Credit; spending his Meanes in Ale-houses, Taverns, and among Scandalous, Loose people; a meer Lazy companion, nothing careful of the things of this life, or any thing Religious; a meer Atheist and natural man.

Physically, Venus could give one 'a lovely Mouth and cherry Lips, the Face pretty fleshy, a rolling wandering Eye, a Body very delightfull, lovely and exceeding well shaped, one desirous of Trimming and making himself neat and compleat both in Cloaths and Body, a love Dimple in his Cheeks, a stedfast Eye, and full of amarous enticements'.

Lilly goes on to suggest suitable employments for people with Venus strong in their charts:

Musicians, Gamesters, Silk-Men, Mercers, Linnen-Drapers, Painters, Jewellers, Players, Lapidaries, Embroiderers, Women-tailors, Wives, Mothers, Virgins, Choristers, Fidlers, Pipers, when joyned with the Moon Ballad-singers, Perfumers . . . all such as sell those Commodities which adorne Women, either in Body (as Cloaths) or in Face (as Complexion-wafers).

Then there are the sicknesses which might be likely to attack such a person: 'principally in the Matrix and members of Generation; in the reines, belly, backe, navill and those parts; the Gonorrea or running of the Reines; French or Spanish Pox; any disease arising by inordinate lust. Prihpism, impotency in generation, Hernias &c. the Diabetes or pissing disease . . .'.

Similar details are given for every planet; then Lilly passes on to short descriptions of the Zodiacal signs. It is interesting that these get only about one-sixth of the space devoted to the planets: a reminder of the inordinate attention given to the signs as opposed to the planets in modern popular astrology; in a book of this kind published in the 1970s, the opposite proportion would be allowed.

Lilly is technical only when he has to be. His technical expositions are of course couched in what has been called 'astrologers' jargon', and it is perhaps fair to point out that astrologers used the language available to them; any lack of clarity is the result of the modern reader not having the basic knowledge many sixteenth- and seventeenth-century readers possessed.

When Lilly says (discussing how to discover 'Whether a Damsel be Virtuous or not') 'Behold the lord of the 7th,

the cusp of the 7th, and the Sun; and if they be in fixed signs and well aspected, you may judge that she is correct', he is making a simple astrological statement. A modern reader, even one who reads his daily horoscope with meticulous attention, will not know what 'the lord of the 7th' is, what 'the 7th' is, what a 'fixed' sign is, or when they are well or ill aspected.

For the astrologer, Book II is perhaps the most fascinating, providing an insight into Lilly's methods of work; to the lay reader it is of negligible interest, however—except inasmuch as it provides insight into Lilly's professional life, the sort of questions his clients brought him, and in some cases into his private life (for he did not hesitate to use personal examples if they were illuminating).

The book consists of a list of questions an astrologer might wish to ask, or might be asked, and Lilly's means of solving them; all in technical astrological language and in great detail. One example will perhaps suffice: 'Whether one absent will returne or not, and when?' Lilly's guide to the discovery of the answer to that question occupies over a thousand words, starting with a consideration of the astrological houses involved:

Consider by what house the absent party is signified, and what Planet is his significator; then see if his significator be in the first house (let his Journey be whither it will), yet if it be a long Journey, and beyond seas, then see if it be in the ninth, or if in the twelfth, if a very long Journey was undertaken; or if he be in the fifth, if a moderate Journey was intended, or in the third, if a short Journey: If he be in any of these houses, or do commit his disposition to any Planet in any of these houses, it signifies the absent will not dye in that Voyage, but returne: if he be in the seventh, he will returne, but not in hast; nay, he will tarry long; and he is at the time of the Question in that country unto which he first went, nor hath he hitherto had any thoughts of returning; howsoever, now he hath: If he be in the fourth, he will stay and abide longer than if he were in the seventh: if his significator be in the third or ninth, and in any aspect with any Planet in the ascendant, the absent is preparing to come home, and is fully resolved thereof; or if he be in the second, in aspect with a Planet in the ninth, he is endeavouring to provide moneys for his Voyage homewards, nor will it be long ere he be at home; but if he be in a Cadent house, and not behold his own ascendant, he neither cares for his returne, or hath any thoughts thereof, nor can he come if so be he would. . . .

And so on. When it is considered that Lilly goes into this sort of detail for no less than 200 questions, the size and comprehensiveness of *Christian Astrology* can be judged. And then, in Book III, he goes on to deal with other technical matters, to give alternative methods of house erection, to print various tables, to consider the houses once more, together with certain questions the answers to which are particularly geared to them ('The Sixth House: of the Infirmities of Bodies, Kinds and Qualities of Diseases, how discoverable from the Planets and Signs . . . of the Tooth-ach, Of the Falling Sicknesse . . . Of violent Falls . . . Of servants and small cattle . . .').

Then (and only then: it is the lay public that has always placed greatest emphasis on 'foretelling the future' in a literal sense) he turns to the possibility of discovering certain trends in the future lives of his clients.

It can hardly be denied that even if Lilly's enormous success as a consultant astrologer depended to a great extent on his own quick wit and the gullibility of his clients, his **Christian Astrology** is a remarkable book, gathering together and rationalizing the extant astrological lore, broadening it by adding his own observations, and presenting it as a scientific body of knowledge.

If one looks at the astronomical and scientific, medical or chemical textbooks of the period, one can only admire Lilly's industry; and his comprehensive knowledge of his subject.

The laudatory verses printed at the front of the book (as the custom was) are negligible: the one friend of Lilly's who at his best was an entertaining amateur poet was Elias Ashmole, and he was ill when the author was collecting the verses from his other acquaintances—from John Booker, so recently his enemy, and the rest. But when Ashmole recovered, and read the book, he sent Lilly a set of verses celebrating it. Too late for printing, even at the end of the book, it conveyed his sincere congratulations:

> I have read your Booke, & though I crawle
> (As th' Sick must doe) behind the press, and all
> That sung your praise in Front; yet in ye rear
> (Rather than not be seen) let me appear;
> And tell the World, it owes much to your Pen
> That has unlockt these cloyster'd secrets, when
> None else would do't; teaching us how to read
> The Minde of Heaven in English, and not dread
> It to be Conjuring; so that by your paines
> No room for that black scandall now
>   remaines . . .

Though that was an over-optimistic view, **Christian Astrology** was certainly the major and the most complete astrological textbook to be written in English during the seventeenth century.

Patrick Curry   (essay date 1989)

SOURCE: "William Lilly and 'Democratic' Astrology," in *Prophecy and Power: Astrology in Early Modern England,* Polity Press, 1989, pp. 28-34.

[In the essay below, Curry discusses Lilly's primary role in establishing judicial astrology in mid-seventeenth-century England.]

Two men in particular acted as the focus for judicial astrology in mid-seventeenth century England: William Lilly (1602-81) and Elias Ashmole (1617-92). From them, the nexus spread out to take in virtually the entire active astrological community. The one who commanded most attention from his contemporaries was Lilly. Born in the Leicestershire village of Diseworth and educated in the local grammar school, he came to London to earn his livelihood at the age of seventeen. In the course of a variety of pursuits, the chance reading of an almanac aroused his interest in astrology. He began to study it in earnest from

the age of thirty, including a spell of tutelage under John Evans, a 'cunning man' residing in Gunpowder Alley. He started to attract clients from about 1635, and [was successful in] his first and subsequent almanacs. . . .

Lilly had the right touch for the time and place. He mixed traditional forms, for example *A Prophecy of the White Kings Dreadfull Dead-man Explaned* (1644), with more astrologically precise judgements on the major issues of the day, such as resolving 'If Presbytery shall stand?' from the detailed interpretation of a horary figure. (His hopeful conclusion was that 'the Commonalty will defraud the expectation of the Clergy, and so strongly oppose them, that the end hereof shall wholly delude the expectation of the Clergy'). His political sympathies, openly displayed, were moderate Parliamentarian; and his (correct) predictions of defeat for the Royalist forces at Naseby (in 1645) and three years later at Colchester, made him as popular among the former as he was hated by the latter. The same year as he was cheering on the besiegers of Colchester, however, he was consulted (probably for a second time) by an emissary of Charles I, Lady Jane Whorwood, on how best to escape from Carisbrook Castle in the Isle of Wight. Ever practical, Lilly supplied both advice and a saw, although to no avail. He seems to have been genuinely horrified by Charles's beheading in 1649.

In that, he may not have been very different from many of his supporters. These came chiefly from the lay Independents and army radicals, and featured men such as Bulstrode Whitelocke (1605-75), a Keeper of the Privy Seal and Commissioner of the Treasury, whose life he regarded Lilly as having saved through the latter's astromedical intervention during a serious illness. In return, Whitelocke more than once saved Lilly from his enemies. These remained numerous, even after Cromwell's triumph, and consisted in the main of Presbyterians. At their instigation, he was examined by Parliamentary committees in 1645 and 1652, and twice briefly imprisoned. Lilly's politics were thus on the radical side, but neither uncritical—he faulted Parliament on more than one occasion—nor extreme. Despite his admiration for the writings of Boehme, he was unsympathetic towards Fifth Monarchists, Levellers, and 'that monstrous people called Ranters'.

In 1652, Lilly withdrew from London to Hersham, in Surrey. He continued producing almanacs, and kept his old 'Corner House on the Strand' for his busy consultation practice. Thomas (whose description of astrology in the consulting room remains unsurpassed) has estimated that Lilly's clients were nearly equally divided between men and women; about one-third may have been female servants, but a high proportion of the remainder were 'gentry or above'. Questions covered all possible aspects of personal life, from children and love-life, to medical problems, to questions of political allegiance. His questioners wanted information or advice, and usually the more precise the better. For this service, Lilly charged a standard rate of about half a crown (12 1/2p) but nothing for the poor, and as much as £40-50 for those members of the aristocracy who could afford it. He also taught astrology for a fee, and for some years received a state pension. All this brought him an income well towards the top end of the contemporary scale (in which he was untypical of most of his colleagues).

Lilly stands out in other ways, too. He was consulted by MPs, members of the aristocracy and some leading radicals. He was generally admitted among judicial astrologers to be their leading representative, and Abraham Whelocke, a professor and Head Librarian at Cambridge University, was accurate in hailing him as the chief 'promoter of these admired studies'. Even his enemies paid him the compliment of complaining that the people 'put more confidence in Lilly than . . . in God'. John Evelyn recalled in 1699 that during an eclipse 'fifty years ago many were so terrified by Lilly that they durst not go out of their houses.' This degree of influence—even more than his record of alarming predictions in matters of State and religion—brought him to the attention of the authorities, both before and after the Restoration. Ironically, in so far as Lilly was identified as the leading representative of his profession, it also helped to undermine the position (and thus eventually, the influence) of his successors.

In his astrology too, Lilly is worth noting as someone whom subsequent developments would render unusual. I am not just referring to his authorship of the first English textbook of astrology, nor to its quality and thoroughness. Lilly's practice relied heavily on horary work (that is, the openly divinatory kind of astrology which is used to answer questions based on a figure of the heavens at the moment the question was asked, or received). There was a strong practical argument in favour of horaries, as distinct from nativities: many people did not know their precise time of birth. Nonetheless, horary practice was criticized by many, including some astrologers, as indefensible on grounds of reason or religion; and it was a favourite target of divines. But Lilly's attitude towards astrology en tout was strangely straightforward and unproblematic: 'the more holy thou art, and the neer to God, the purer Judgement thou shalt give'. Lilly's God thus permitted astrological predictions, of a kind akin to prophecies, vouchsafed to the pure. At the same time, however, He forbade hubris; every extant portrait of Lilly shows him holding a horoscope bearing the words, '*Non cogunt*'—that is, in the words of the old maxim, 'the stars incline but do not compel'. There is no reason to think that this functioned for Lilly and his peers purely as a cynical escape-clause, though doubtless it was that for some; in Lilly's case, his personal (if idiosyncratic) piousness is evident from his writings. But if this attitude to astrology now seems eccentric, it is for two good historical reasons: because it embodies a 'pre-Enlightenment understanding', in which the knowing subject and the objects of knowledge are not seen as cleanly separable; and because it successfully brings off an amalgam of Christianity and popular magic. Generations succeeding and even surrounding Lilly, overtaken by the effects of the Reformation and Counter-Reformation, were persuaded (if that is the word) that these two were fundamentally incompatible.

Lilly seems to have been unaware of, or at least unconcerned by, any such incompatibility. In the early 1640s, he dabbled briefly in overtly magical practices, such as summoning spirits, before giving them up and burning his magic textbooks. But his astrology never lost its divinatory, implicitly magical quality. Indeed, he attributed his more spectacular predictive successes . . . to 'the Secret Key of Astrology, or Prophetical Astrology'. Unlike the leading English astrologers of the next generation, John Gandbury and John Partridge, he neither showed the slightest interest in a 'scientifically' purified astrology, nor agonized over whether his astrology was rational or not. Lilly was really the last great English astrologer who could unselfconsciously advocate astrology as a divinatory craft, and issue his predictions as prophecies.

. . . What is important to note here about Lilly is that his approach was (like that of Culpeper) both magical and demotic, or democratic. As such, it was characteristic of much Interregnum radical thought. And these two strands were indissolubly linked: guidance concerning the microcosm (the Earth) was to be found in the messages of the celestial macrocosm, the coherence of which was guaranteed by relations of sympathy and antipathy; and these messages could be read by anyone with sufficient application to acquire the necessary skills, and the requisite attitude. Hence Lilly's textbook, which attempted to disseminate these essentials. But whether one possessed skill and holiness was ascertainable principally by the success of one's astrological predictions, not by any human authority. Furthermore, Lilly's maxim, '*Non cogunt*', not only left him with room for manoeuvre; it also granted his audience that freedom. It would have been quite inconsistent for him to have adopted a strongly determinist position.

In social terms, Lilly can therefore be seen as a spokesperson not for popular culture—for there was always a high degree of ambivalence in the relations between the latter and radical thought—but for its radicalized and self-conscious elements, whose democratic demands in the mid seventeenth century proved almost as uncomfortable for Cromwell as for the Stuarts (although more completely and successfully rejected, from 1660, by the latter).

FURTHER READING

Josten, C. J., ed. *Elias Ashmole (1617-1692)*. 5 vols. Oxford: at the Clarendon Press, 1966.

    Includes a collection of letters written by Lilly to his friend Ashmole.

McCaffery, Ellen. *Astrology: Its History and Influence in the Western World*. New York: Charles Scribner's Sons, 1942, 408 p.

    Places Lilly within the context of the history of astrology.

Thomas, Keith. *Religion and the Decline of Magic*. New York: Charles Scribner's Sons, 1971, 716 p.

    Chronicles the magical, religious, and scientific beliefs of English society in the sixteenth and seventeenth centuries, noting Lilly's prominence during that time.

Nostradamus

1503-1566

French occultist.

INTRODUCTION

One of the most controversial and widely discussed figures of his era, Nostradamus retains notoriety today as either a prophet, a charlatan, or one of the more misunderstood figures of his age. He has been credited by some with mystically foreseeing the death of Henry II of France, the rise of the sans-culottes, the flight, capture, and execution of Louis XVI and Marie Antoinette, the accession of Napoleon Bonaparte, the rise of Adolf Hitler, and the coming of the Anti-christ in the twenty-first century. These and other prophecies, published in Nostradamus's *Centuries*, have been heatedly defended by believers in post-Biblical prophecy and vigorously debunked by Nostradamus's modern opponents.

Biographical Information

Born in Saint-Rémy, Provence, Michel de Nostradame was the son of a respected physician. He was recognized as a precocious boy and schooled by his grandfathers, who taught him the fundamentals of mathematics, philosophy, rhetoric, Greek, Latin, and Hebrew, as well as the rudiments of astrology. After the boy had mastered all his grandfathers could teach, he was sent to Avignon to study liberal arts, and later to the University of Montpellier for medical training. In 1522, at age nineteen, Nostradame received his bachelor's degree and license to practice medicine; that same year, he demonstrated remarkable success as a healer after the plague broke out in southern France. Leaving Montpellier for a time, he studied alchemy in Narbonne and works of magic and the occult in the library at Avignon. Returning to Montpellier to complete his medical studies, he received his doctorate in 1529, becoming known as Dr. Nostradamus. Three years later he moved to Agen, where he established a medical practice, married, and raised two children, but then lost his wife and children to a plague in 1535. At about the same time, Nostradamus ran afoul of the Inquisition for making disparaging remarks to a workman who was casting a bronze model of the Virgin. He left Agen and wandered about southern France and Italy for several years, treating victims of the recurrent plague. "Throughout his travels," wrote Edgar Leoni, "he seems to have sought contact with all who could in any way add to his medical and pharmaceutical knowledge. There is much reason to believe his round of calls included visits to alchemists, astrologers, cabalists, magicians and the like as well. But in those times . . . the distinction was only blurry." Eventually he settled in the village of Salon in Provence, where he remained the rest of his life, leaving only periodically to work among the sick in plague-stricken areas of France.

MICHEL NOSTRADAMUS.
Médecin,
Né à Sᵗ Remy, en Provence, le 14 Décemb. 1503.
Mort le 2 juillet 1566.

He published an almanac in 1550, issuing a new edition almost every year until his death. In 1554, he became convinced that a time of civil upheaval was ahead for France after a two-headed child and a two-headed horse were born within forty-five days of each other early in the year. In a short time he wrote ten "centuries," each century consisting of one hundred quatrains of mystical poetry containing prophecies for roughly two thousand years, through the year 3797. The centuries were published in 1555 as *Les Prophéties de M. Michel Nostradamus.* (Over time, this work became known as simply *The Centuries.*) Popular reaction was mixed, though the centuries were favorably received by the queen, Catherine de' Medici. After an audience with the queen in Paris, Nostradamus returned to Salon as a popular hero, the Oracle of France, one whose unorthodox beliefs were sanctioned by a royal protector. "Perhaps it is the immense eternity of the great God that has aroused the fervor of Nostradamus," wrote the poet Pierre de Ronsard in 1557. This last period of his life is filled with legends of his success as a possessor of second sight. After a time of suffering from arthritis and dropsy, Nostradamus died at his workbench in 1566.

Major Works

Although he wrote several other works, Nostradamus is best known for his poetically stated prophecies, *The Centuries*. In a prefatory letter to Henry II in the first edition of this work, Nostradamus wrote that his prophecies concern events in Europe, Africa, and Asia. As Leoni has written, "The bulk of the quatrains deal with disasters of various sorts. The disasters include plagues, earthquakes, wars, floods, invasions, murders, droughts, battles and many other themes. Some quatrains cover these in over-all terms; others concern a single person or small group of persons. Some cover a single town, others several towns in several countries." Through the use of arcane geographical references, puns, anagrams, mythological allusions, and other devices, Nostradamus wrote in "a poetic furor, rather than according to the strict rules of poetry." Neither punctuation, rhymes, nor scansion are pronounced in *The Centuries*, though the quatrains are written in basic iambic pentameter.

Critical Reception

Nothing substantial has been written about Nostradamus's almanacs and his few miscellaneous medical treatises. Much, however, has been written about the *Centuries*. Nostradamus's work has been commented upon periodically since the seventeenth century, with critics taking basically one of three views of the writer: true prophet, liar, or muddled mystic. In 1625, Gabriel Naudé wrote that the centuries, "so ambiguous, and so diverse, obscure and enigmatic," lend themselves to prophetic fulfillment by their very nature. As Jean Gimon wrote, in his *Chroniques de Salon* (1882), "The style of the Centuries is so multiform and nebulous that each may, with a little effort and good will, find in them what he seeks. Like airy vapors, they assume, as they unroll, the figures of which the spectator's imagination lends them, and this fact assures this sibylline work of an immense and eternal success with those who are devotees of the marvelous." In the English-speaking world, widespread interest in Nostradamus came into vogue in the late nineteenth century. Numerous books and articles on the subject have been published since then, notably Charles A. Ward's *Oracles of Nostradamus* (1891) and James Laver's *Nostradamus; or, The Future Foretold* (1942). These and other such works are marked by their writers' confident insistence upon Nostradamus's bona fides as a prophet of modern times. Several of these commentators are what Leoni calls "deependers," with one even claiming to be the reincarnation of Nostradamus. There are extreme opinions among the skeptics as well, with one critic charging that Nostradamus was little more than a sot who scrawled his quatrains nightly before passing out in a drunken stupor. The most complete treatment of Nostradamus's life and prophecies for many years has been Leoni's massive *Nostradamus: Life and Literature* (1961), which took a balanced, but fairly skeptical view. Perhaps the most detailed and recent rebuttal, rife with sarcasm, is *The Mask of Nostradamus* (1990), by James Randi. Although Randi, a professional magician and articulate debunker, allows that Nostradamus was "a person of considerable ability who would have succeeded in any age," he demonstrates rational explanations of the prophecies and that many interpretations of Nostradamus's quatrains often contradict each other. With the approach of the twenty-first century and the second millennium of the Common Era, coupled with a decline in Western religious belief, interest in Nostradamus and his prophecies continues to grow.

PRINCIPAL WORKS

Les Prophéties de M. Michel Nostradamus [*The Centuries*] (prophecies)   1555

CRITICISM

Michel Nostradamus   (essay date 1555)

SOURCE: "Préface à mon fils: The Preface of Michael Nostradamus to His Prophecies," in *Oracles of Nostradamus* by Charles A. Ward, Modern Library, 1940, pp. 39-49.

[*In the following excerpt, Nostradamus justifies and explains the intent of his prophecies. As editor Charles A. Ward indicates, this preface, dedicated to his newborn son, was originally published in 1555, and was intended as "a dedication to [Nostradamus's] spiritual sons; that is, to his interpreters and students in all future ages." (Bracketed material within the text was inserted by Ward.)*]

Although for years past I have predicted, a long time in advance, what has afterwards come to pass, and in particular regions attributing the whole accomplishment to divine power and inspiration, also other unfortunate and fortunate occurrences have been pronounced with accelerated promptitude which have since happened in other parts of the world, —for I was willing to maintain silence and to pass over matters that might prove injurious [if published] not only as relates to the present time, but also for the most part of future time, if committed to writing, since kingdoms, sects, and religions will pass through stages so very contrary, and, as regards the present time, diametrically opposed, —that if I were to relate what will happen in the future, governors, sectaries, and ecclesiastics would find it so ill-accordant with [si] their auricular fancy, that they would go near to condemn what future ages will know and perceive to be true. Considering also the sentence of the true Saviour, "*Nolite sanctum dare canibus neque mittatis margaritas vestras ante porcos, ne forte conculcent eas pedibus suis, et conversi dirumpant vos*" [Matt. vii. 6].

This it is which has led me to withhold my tongue from the vulgar, and my pen from paper. But, later on, I thought I would enlarge a little, and declare in dark and abstruse sayings in consideration of [*pour*] the vulgar advent the most urgent of its future causes, as perceived by me, be the revolutionary changes what they may, so only as not to scandalize the auricular frigidity (of my hearers), and write all down under a cloudy figure that shall essentially and above all things be prophetical. Although *"Abscondidisti hœc à sapientibus, et prudentibus, id est, potentibus et regibus, et enucleasti ea exiguis et tenuibus."* ["Thou hast hidden these things from the wise and prudent, i. e. from the powerful and from kings, and hast revealed them to the small and weak." This is Nostradamus's gloss upon Matthew xi. 25.] By the grace of God and the good angels, the Prophets have had committed to them the spirit of vaticination, by which they see things at a distance, and are enabled to forecast future events. For there is nothing that can be accomplished without Him, whose power and goodness are so great to all His creatures as long as they put their trust in Him, much as they may be [exposed] or subject to other influences, [yet] on account of their likeness to the nature of their good guardian angel [or genius] that heat and prophetic power draweth nigh to us, as do the rays of the sun which cast their influence alike upon bodies that are elementary and non-elementary. As for ourselves personally who are but human, we can attain to nothing by our own unaided natural knowledge, nor the bent of our intelligence, in the way of deciphering the recondite secrets of God the Creator. *"Quia non est nostrum noscere tempora, nec momenta"* [Acts i. 7], etc. Although, indeed, now or hereafter some persons may arrive to whom God Almighty may be pleased to reveal by imaginative impression some secrets of the future, as accorded in time past to judicial astrology, when [*que* for *quand*] a certain power and volitional faculty came upon them, as a flame of fire appears. [Nostradamus seems, whenever he alludes to this appearance of flame as preceding vaticination, to have in his mind the descent of tongues of fire at Pentecost (Acts ii. 3). . . . A flame of fire, be it observed, conveys a double symbol: it resembles a tongue in form. Its luminousness and its purifying tendency express the celestial nature of spirit, as contrasted with matter, and also inspiration. So that intrinsically and extrinsically it represents prophetic utterance. Grotius contributes an unusually good note upon this passage, pointing out that as in Genesis (xi. 9), confusion of tongues scattered mankind, so here (Acts ii. 3) the gift of tongues was to bring men again into one brotherhood.] They grew inspired, and were able to judge of all inspiration, human and divine, alike. For the divine works, which are absolutely universal, God will complete; those which are contingent, or medial, the good angels direct; and the third sort come under the evil angels. [This passage is very difficult to bring to a clear sense in translation. . . . It seems to mean that God operates all the great effects in the universe; that, as He is the Maker, so is He the perpetual operator in the world, —its cause and life; but that the guardian angels are good and bad, and are charged with some sort of duty and office, not as affecting the mechanic frame of the world, but in respect of mankind. This is in conformity with the Cabala and Hermetical teaching; but what he precisely means cannot, I think, be quite absolutely stated.]

Perhaps, my son, I speak to thee here a little too occultly. But as to the hidden vaticinations which come to one by the subtle spirit of fire, or sometimes by the understanding disturbed, [it may even be, by] contemplating the remotest

stars, as being intelligences on the watch, even to giving utterance to declarations [that] being taken down in writing declare, without favour, and without any taint of improper loquacity, that all things whatsoever proceed from the divine power of the great eternal Deity from whom all goodness emanates. Further, my son, although I have inserted the name of prophet, I do not desire to assume a title of so high sublimity at the present moment. For he who *"Propheta dicitur hodie, olim vocabatur videns"* ["He who is called prophet now, once was called seer"]; for, strictly speaking, my son, a prophet is one who sees things remote from the knowledge of all mankind. Or, to put the case; to the prophet, by means of the perfect light of prophecy, there lie opened up very manifestly divine things as well as human; which cannot come about, seeing that the effects of future prediction extend to such remote periods. Now, the secrets of God are incomprehensible, and their efficient virtue belongs to a sphere far remote from natural knowledge; for, deriving their immediate origin from the free will, things set in motion causes that of themselves could never attract such attention as could make them recognized, either by human augury, or by any other knowledge of occult power; it is a thing comprised only within the concavity of heaven itself, from the present fact of all eternity, which comes in itself to embrace all time.

Still, by the means of some eternal power, by an epileptic Herculean agitation, the causes by the celestial movement become known. I do not say, my son, in order that you may fully understand me, that the knowledge of this matter cannot yet impress itself upon thy feeble brain, that very remote future causes may not come within the cognizance of a reasonable being; if they are, notwithstanding, purely the creation of the intellectual soul of things present, future things are not by any means too hidden or concealed. But the perfect knowledge of causes cannot be acquired without divine inspiration; since all prophetic inspiration derives its first motive principle from God the Creator, next from good fortune, and then from nature. Wherefore the independent causes being independently produced, or not produced, the presage partially happens, where it was predicted. For the human understanding, being intellectually created, cannot penetrate occult causes, otherwise than by the voice of a genius by means of the thin flame [showing] to what direction future causes incline to develop themselves. And further, my son, I implore you never to apply your understanding on such reveries and vanities as dry up the body and bring perdition to the soul and disturb all the senses. In like manner, I caution you against the seduction of a more than execrable magic, that has been denounced already by the sacred Scriptures, by the divine canons of the Church—although we have to exempt from this judgment Judicial Astrology. By the aid of this it is, and by divine revelation and inspiration, united with deep calculations, we have reduced our prophecies to writing. And, notwithstanding that this occult philosophy was *not* reproved by the Church, I have felt no desire to divulge their unbridled promptings. Although many volumes have come before me, which had laid hidden for many ages. But dreading what might happen in the future, after reading them, I presented them to Vulcan, and as the fire kindled them, the flame, licking the air, shot forth an unaccustomed brightness, clearer than the light is of natural flame, resembling more the explosion of powder, casting a subtle illumination over the house as if the whole were wrapped in sudden conflagration. —So that at last you might not in the future be abused by searching for the perfect transformation, lunar or solar, or incorruptible metals hidden under the earth, or the sea, I reduced them to ashes. —But as to the judgment which perfects itself by means of the celestial judgment, that I am desirous to manifest to you: by that method you may have cognizance of things future, avoiding all fantastic imaginations that may arise, and limiting the particularity of the topics by divine and supernatural inspiration; harmonizing with the celestial figures these topics, and that part of time, which the occult property has relation to, by the potential virtue and faculty divine, in whose presence the three aspects of time are clasped in one by eternity—an evolution that connects in one causes past, present, and future—*"quia omnia sunt nuda et aperta,* etc." ["For all things are naked and open"].

From all which, my son, you can easily comprehend, notwithstanding your tender brain, the things that are to happen can be foretold by nocturnal and celestial lights, which are natural, coupled to a spirit of prophecy, —not that I would assume the name or efficacy of a prophet, but, by revealed inspiration, as a mortal man the senses place me no farther from heaven than the feet are from the earth. *"Possum non errare, falli, decipi"* ["I am able not to err, fail, or be deceived"], (albeit) I am the greatest sinner in this world, and heir to every human affliction. But being surprised sometimes in the ecstatic work, amid prolonged calculation, and engaged in nocturnal studies of sweet odour, I have composed books of prophecies, containing each one hundred astronomic quatrains of forecasts, which I have tried to polish through obscurely, and which are perpetual vaticinations, from now to the year 3797. It is possible that this figure will make some lift up their forehead, at such a vast extent of time, and variety of things to take place under the concave journey of the moon; and this universal treatment of causes, my son, throughout the earth, which, if you reach the natural age of man, you will see in your climate, under the heaven of your proper nativity, as things that have been foreseen.

Although the everlasting God alone knows the eternity of the light proceeding from Himself, I say frankly to all to whom He has decreed in long and melancholy inspiration to reveal His limitless magnitude, which is beyond both mensuration and comprehension, that by means of this occult cause divinely manifested, principally by two chief causes, comprised in the understanding of the inspired one who prophesies. One is that which comes by infusion, which clarifies the supernatural light, in him who predicts by astral process, or forecasts by inspired revelation, which is practically a participation in the divine eternity, by which means the prophet comes to judge of that which his share of divine spirit has given him, by means of communication with God the Creator, and the natural endowment accorded him. It is to know that what is predicted is true, and has had a heavenly origin; that such light and the thin flame is altogether efficacious; that it descends from above, no less than does natural clearness; and natural light renders philosophers quite sure of their principles, so that by means of the principles of a first cause they have penetrated the profoundest abysses and attained the loftiest doctrines.

Walter Besant   (essay date 1874)

SOURCE: "Nostradamus the Astrologer," in *Temple Bar,* Vol. XLI, April 1874, pp. 83-92.

[*Besant was a prolific English novelist, historian, and critic who sought in his fiction to expose and denounce the social evils of late-Victorian England. In the following excerpt, he sarcastically denigrates Nostradamus as a prophet and his admirers for their gullibility.*]

It is sad to read that in his own town [Nostradamus] was always regarded, save by one favourite disciple, as an impostor of the first, and therefore most successful, order. This disciple, Jean de Chavigny, one of those simple and lovable creatures, born for the nourishment of the quack and the humbug, who will believe anything, hovered round the master like Cadijah round Mohammed. He left his native town of Beaune, where the wine is so good, and took up his residence altogether in Salon itself, so as to be always near Nostradamus, abandoning family, estate, occupation, and all. Like another Boswell, he noted the things that fell from the doctor's lips; and after his death, spent twenty-eight years in editing and commentating the *Centuries.* It is delightful to learn that in his society the prophet would unbend from his mystic forereachings into futurity and condescend to predict some of the minor events of life. "We were once," he tells us, in an anecdote of touching simplicity, "walking abroad. I saw two sucking pigs, one black, the other white. 'What will be their fate?' I asked Nostredame. 'We shall eat the black one,' replied he, 'the white will be eaten by a wolf.' In order to elude the prediction, I told the cook to prepare the white pig for dinner. He did so; but as it lay upon the table, a tame wolf belonging to the house, finding no one there, devoured it. Upon which the cook prepared the black pig, and the prophecy of the infallible Nostredame was accomplished." Wonderful indeed! . . .

Honoured as he was, save by his own townsmen, in his life, his real glory begins only after his death. For the *Centuries* are printed and reprinted, commented, furnished with notes, explanations, and illustrations, and even called into the service of history. Nobody, it is true—which is the real drawback to all predictions, ancient and modern—ventured to write from Nostradamus the history of the future; but everybody was prepared to observe, when the things had happened, how wonderfully they fitted in with the words of the prophet. The unbeliever might ask what was the good of a prediction unless you know what it means. He might go further, and decline to investigate past history in order to mark the sagacity of Nostradamus. And if he had the courage of his opinions, he might point out that the disjointed words, the vague phrases, the open-mouthed threats might do for one event quite as well as the other, and therefore the prophet was not, after all, of such amazing wisdom. But unbelievers were scarce, and Nostradamus held his own.

After being the favourite prophet of Catherine de Medicis and her sons, he was studied in turn by Henry the Fourth, by Louis the Thirteenth, and Louis the Fourteenth. He was translated into English and Italian; he was published in twenty editions and more, and even has his believers, one or two, here and there, *rari nantes,* to this very day. And in the name of human credulity, why? There is not from beginning to end, so far at least as I have read—for no mortal man could read all his *Centuries* and survive— one word of sense, precision, or clearness. All is utter, un-redeemed, incredible balderdash and rubbish, written in the most uncouth French, with words of Hebrew, Greek, Latin, and Arabic interspersed; with anagrams such as 'Rapis' for Paris, 'Nersaf' for France, 'Eiouas' for Savoy; the whole designedly meaningless and obscure. And yet I cannot make up my mind that the man was a conscious impostor. It seems to me that, trained in the secrets of as-trology, which followed a uniform method, quite easy to be learned, he did quite honestly occupy himself with the future; that in these *Centuries* he set down in the form which he found easiest the results of his investigations as they worked themselves out. Did you ever see a couple of country girls telling fortunes with a pack of cards? Write down their ejaculations as they deal out the pack, and you will have something like a quatrain of Nostradamus's. Thus:

> A fair-haired man: a letter: and a purse:
> A disappointment: and a wedding ring:
> Cards falling badly: funerals, and a hearse:
> Sorrow: and joy: a lover in the spring.

There, the girls have made me write down unconsciously a quatrain exactly like one of Nostradamus's most spright-ly specimens; only, like most prophets, because people never believe in the advent of good fortune, but are easily impressed with a sense of coming woes and miseries, he deals entirely in the latter:

> The moon at full, upon the palace wall:
> The Lion bruised and beaten in a cage:
> Eyes at midday: claws bare: the servants fall:
> Famine and pestilence: an iron age.

Wretchedly poor stuff! but this is all you will get from Nostradamus. And if no more than this were required to carry on a prophetic trade, one might be quite prepared to set up as a prophet in exactly the same way; only it would be well to know the rules of judicial astrology first, so as to get the formulae right and save the trouble of in-vention.

The *Centuries* being published and the author dead, there remained for future ages the task of fitting them into their proper places. This has been done over and over again, the verses being made to do duty for one king after another, as the ages run on. Of course, you cannot expect the com-mentator to write the history of the next generation. Most singular of all, it is only five or six years since a certain M. Anatole de Pelletier published a volume called *Les Oracles de M. de Nostredame,* in which he too follows the course of history by means of the *Centuries,* showing how, in his opinion, every important event since his death has been

Representation of the Nostradamus home as it probably looked during his lifetime. Drawing by André Cheinet, 1966.

plainly foretold by the astrologer. This sagacious person—a sort of French Doctor Cumming—has, of course, a blind idolatry for his prophet. He worships an infallibility even more certain and perfect than Chavigny discovered. Where we find barbarism he finds an antique grace, effective handling, the rudeness of strength; where we find intentional obscurity he finds the natural obscurity of one whose thoughts are too profound for speech; where we hesitate whether to pronounce the man an impostor or a brain-struck enthusiast, working according to the foolish rules of a mistaken science, he calls upon us to admire the mysterious and divine gift of prophecy. Above all, he quotes what he is pleased to consider direct predictions of the French Revolution. "It is the point," he says, "in history to which his eyes are always turned, his thoughts always recurring; he chisels carefully every detail of this mighty movement" (we shall see how presently); "hither all the forces of his thoughts converge, all the radiation of his intelligence; here is displayed all the lucidity of the mysterious genius which animated him." He afterwards asks us to consider the strange contrasts which the man presented. He is bold in his writing; you see that posterity can neither imprison, fine, nor burn at the stake; they can only admire or laugh. He is timorous towards his contemporaries, and with good reason. He is a good Christian and yet a Pagan; that is, he was wise in his generation. Being a scholar, he was, like all the scholars of his age, a pagan; being a man who valued his personal comfort and safety, he is a Christian in outward observances. Above all—which astonishes M. de Pelletier much more than it does other people—he gave no word of counsel, advice, or guidance to the kings who visited him. We may also add that on his own family accidents he was equally reticent, never having prophesied the death of his earlier children or the violent end of his second son and successor. But these prophets are all alike; while they contemplate the future the baby tumbles into the fire. They can predict a revolution—a thousand years or so is a trifle—but they are all astray in the events of to-morrow, and can no more teach us how to avoid a toothache than they can ward off the blood and slaughter of their own prophecies. *"In alienis,"* said one of these useless gentry, *"mirè oculati, ad nostra caecutire solemus."*

Now for a few quatrains. Observe how history bears out the prediction and how there is no deception. The first predicts the reign of Louis the Fourteenth:

> *Du vieux Charon l'on verra le Phoenix,*
> *Estre premier et dernier des fils,*
> *Reluire en France, &c.*

On this the scholiast, writing in the age of the Grand Monarque, observes that *Charon* is, of course, a clerical error; it should be *Chiren*. This, read properly, is "Henric—Henricus: Henri the Fourth." Now, Louis the Fourteenth being the son of Louis the Thirteenth and the grandson of Henry the Fourth, is, of course, the phoenix who will "reluire en France"; this is without doubt, and ridiculously simple.

I was going to quote another most important quatrain, but I am estopped by the unfortunate fact that it has been by different commentators said to refer to Queen Elizabeth of England, King Charles the First, Charles the Second, and the French Revolution. After studying it very carefully, I conclude that it was so craftily drawn up by the Prophet as to include all four interpretations. This increases our admiration for the astrologer, but tends to lessen our confidence in the commentator.

The same remark cannot be made of the following quatrain, which contains a distinct prophecy about England. It reads thus, and one trembles when one writes it:

> *Sept fois charger verrez gent Britannique*
> *Tainte en sang en deux cents nonante ans.*
> *France? non, point: par appuy Germanique*
> *D'Aries doublé en Pole Bascharian.*

The interpretation is clear to the meanest capacity. Seven times in two hundred and ninety years there shall be a revolution in England. Six of them, the commentator tells us, have already come to pass, viz., in 1649, in 1660, in 1688, in 1689, in 1711 (when there was a change of ministry), and in 1714. The last has yet to come; there is comfort in the thought that it is not due till 1929. We have thus fifty-six years before us to prepare for the event, in which it is only too probable that none of our present leaders will take an active part.

But about the French Revolution, concerning which the prophet has so carefully "chiselled the details." Let us take three or four of the most remarkable. The first points, as any one will remark, to the 22nd of September, 1792:

> *Quand la lictière du tourbillon versée*
> *Et seront faces de leurs manteaux couvers,*
> *La republique par gens nouveaux vexée,*
> *Les blancs et rouges jugeront à l'envers.*

The second clearly predicts the advent of Napolean:

> *Un Empereur naistra près d'Italie,*
> *Qui à l'Empire sera vendu bien cher:*
> *Diront avec quels gens il se ralie,*
> *Qu'on trouvera moins prince que boucher.*

And here is Louis the Sixteenth, drawn to his very eyes:

> *Le trop bon temps, trop de bonté royale,*
> *Fais et deffais, prompt subit, negligence,*
> *Legier croira faux d'espouse loyalle,*
> *Luy mis à mort par la bénévolence.*

And here are the *noyades* of Nantes:

> *Des principaux de cité rebellée*
> *Qui tiendront fort pour liberté ravoir,*
> *Detranchés masle, infelice meslée,*
> *Cris, hurlements à Nantes, piteux voir.*

Out of such stuff as the preceding the reputation of a prophet was made! We can hardly read it with patience. But the wonderful thing is, that even in this present century the name of Nostradamus has weight—that there have been three several serious attempts made in the last seventy years to rehabilitate him—that only six years ago a man was found to publish selections and to revive the stale old story, that during the troubles of the last three years there were whispered abroad rumours that Nostradamus had predicted them all. I could multiply to any extent the selections which I have given. It would be easy to show, in the same way, how Oliver Cromwell, for instance, was so delineated that it was impossible to mistake him. When all is finished there remains nothing but the broad facts that here is a man who pretends to the gift of prophecy, who never once delivers a clear utterance, whose predictions are amazing in their doggerel nonsense, and who yet has believers for three hundred years.

Astrology is dead—true; but the spirit which led to a belief in astrology is not dead. It seems to me that the spirit is alive still and vigorous. What else mean the Spiritualist journals, the séances, the mediums? They too form part of that long chapter of human folly which treats of men's distrust of themselves, their terror of the things which surround them, their eager catching at whatever may clear away the darkness.

C. A. Ward   (essay date 1890)

SOURCE: "Nostradamus," in *The Gentleman's Magazine,* Vol. CCLXIX, No. 1920, December, 1890, pp. 601-14.

[*In the following excerpt from an essay sympathetic to Nostradamus's prophetic skill, Ward examines several of the quatrains. "Our business," he writes, "will be merely to translate these obsolete expressions, to interpret a few of the anagrams and strange allusions, as far as may be, and to apply the sense so sifted out to some of the many historic events foreshadowed."*]

[We will here] set forth a few of the Quatrains of Michael Nostradamus, applying them to the events of which they were anticipatory, and so leave them to make their own impression upon the reader's mind, whilst, if space can be spared, a few words may be devoted to the remarkable man who wrote them. . . .

There is a round thousand of quatrains to pick and choose from: all thrown together purposely in hopeless disorder, and in utter disregard of the chronological sequence of the events. Had the chronological order been preserved to us, doubtless many more of the Quatrains could be rendered intelligible; that clue, however, has for the writer's security been purposely, though silently, withdrawn. Out of so large a number only a very few examples can be selected. We will open with one which is not especially striking: when first read it even seems to be mere jargon, but yet when explained it takes a form and coherency that point clearly to *Henri Quatre* as the subject of it. It would task an ingenious mind to adapt it with equal force to any other historical character existing. It runs:

> *Mandosus tost viendra à son haut règne,*
> *Mettant arrière un peu les Norlaris:*
> *Le rouge blesme, le masle à l'interrègne,*
> *Le jeune crainte, et frayeur Barbaris.*

> *Translation.* —Mendosus shall soon attain to his high dominion, setting back those of Lorraine a little; the pale old Cardinal, the male of the interregnum, the timid youth, and the alarmed barbarian.

This at a first glance resembles unmitigated *blague.* But when you take *mendosus,* full of faults, reading *u* for *v* in

the old fashion, it converts into the anagram of Vendosme, or Vendôme. Again *Norlaris* is the anagrammatic transposition of Lorrains, the patronymic of the Guise family. Michel de Nostredame was a Romanist, and heretics are heavily disparaged by him throughout the whole course of his work. To him, therefore, Henri IV., the heretic Vendôme, furnishing the anagram *mendosus,* or full of faults, would seem to be providentially so named—a man who changed his religion thrice. His mother, Jeanne d'Albert, brought him up as a Protestant. To escape St. Bartholomew's massacre, Aug. 24, 1572, he professed Catholicism. In 1576, that he might head the Calvinist party, he relapsed to Protestantism. But in order to ascend the throne of France it became necessary to proclaim himself Catholic. By this change, and by the Salic law, he excluded the Lorraine princes from the throne of France. He no less shut out the old Cardinal de Bourbon—*le rouge blesme,* the red pale one, or white with age; the Duc de Mayenne, also, who was Lieutenant-General of the kingdom during the interregnum. *Le jeune crainte* stands for the young Duc de Guise; whilst the *Barbaris* seems to be the savage Philip II. of Spain, whose pretension to the crown was derived to him through Elizabeth his wife, the daughter of Henri II. Philip allied himself with the Guises in support of the Catholic League. This explanatory elaboration, referring to merely four lines of the original text, may convey some idea to the reader of the difficulty attending the interpretation of a writer such as Nostradamus. There are stanzas by the hundred like this, so that a busy and sceptical world may be very well excused for dropping the whole volume into oblivion, for ridiculing it as jargon, or if, going farther still, it should condemn it as imposture. Ridicule, abuse and slander have their uses, but they are not arguments. The above should suffice to prove that such lines contain a good deal more than at a first glance meets the eye.

Quatrain 18, century x., will be found to amplify on the same theme, a little less obscurely perhaps. We have not room to enlarge upon Presage 76, but *Henri le Grande* is there called *Le Grande Cape,* or Capet, and his abjuring of Protestantism and assent to the Papal conditions (July 21, 1593,) amid the silence of his enemies, is very intelligibly forecast.

Sixtain vi. relates to the treason of Biron under the anagram of Robin, and is a phenomenal piece of work. It even mentions the name of *Lafin,* who betrays him to the king. But we have no room to indulge curiosity on this point. In century vi., quatrain 70, there occurs a perfectly distinct prophecy touching Henry the Great, as *Le Grand Chyren* (Chyren being the anagram of Henri). It says that he will be chief of the world, and may be rendered thus:

> Chief of the world Henri le Grand shall be,
> More loved in death than life, more honoured
>   he;
> His name and praise shall rise above the skies,
> And men shall call him victor when he dies.

Voltaire says of him in the "Henriade":

> *Il fut de ses sujets le vainqueur et le père.*

That Henri IV. had the Quatrains of Nostradamus presented to him we know as a matter of history. We also know that he aspired to a European monarchy. It might form an interesting subject of inquiry for some historical essayist to handle, how much that line of Nostradamus had to do with suggesting the germ–thought to the king:

Au chef du monde le grand Chyren sera.

But we must pass on, for this is no time to pursue the theme; though it be one surely not unworthy of study to watch prophecy, not only forecasting events, but converting from a vision into a fact of history, from a forecast to a cause.

One more passage we propose to examine of historical detail, but of minor importance, before we open up two or three that relate to epoch-making events. It is desirable to furnish specimens of both kinds, for the minuter details will best illustrate the personal idiosyncrasy of the prophet, whilst the greater topics, which refer to known events, will most interest the world at large as to the possibility, authenticity, and value of prophecy itself.

The punishment of the great Montmorency (October 30, 1632, in the reign of Louis XIII.), shall be the next taken, because it sheds a sudden and as it were accidental light upon a private individual, and discloses a name that history seems only to have inscribed once upon her page, and that once by an off-chance, as one may say.

Le lys Dauffois portera dans Nanci
Jusques en Flandres électeur de l'empire;
Neufve obturée au grand Montmorency
Hors lieux prouvés, délivré à Clerepayne.

The Dauphin shall carry his lily standard into Nancy, just as in Flanders the elector of Trèves shall be carried prisoner of the Spaniards into Brussels. A new prison will be given to the great Montmorency; who will be delivered for execution into the hands of Clerepayne. This man will behead him in a place not devoted to executions.

Obturée is from the Latin *obturare,* to shut up closely. *Prouvés* is to be taken as *approuvés.* Louis XIII., it may be remarked, was the first who bore the title of Dauphin of France—and since the publication, be it observed, in 1566, of Nostradamus's work—he entered Nancy on September 25, 1633, one day later than the entry of his army. In 1635 he crossed into Flanders in aid of the Elector, who had been carried a prisoner into Brussels by the Spaniards on March 26 of that year. Our prophet then reverts to October 30, 1632, when the execution of Montmorency, for rebellion, occurred. He was first *confined* (*obturée*) in the Hôtel de Ville at Toulouse, then just newly built (*neufve*). In the courtyard of this building he was executed by a common soldier of the name of Clerepayne, and not, as was customary, at the spot appointed for public executions, such as was La Grève at Paris, or Tower Hill in London.

It so chances that in two contemporary records the name of Clerepayne is attested: Etienne Joubert is one, and the Chevalier de Jant another. By the researches of M. Motret it has been shown further that the family, by solicitation, obtained two formal concessions from the king in deviation from the official order, which would have named the

place publique or marché for the ceremony. The first concession was that it should be with closed doors, and the other that a soldier should be substituted for the common headsman.

When the reader has familiarised himself with the obsolete language and verbal contortions of this oracular Frenchman, and has quietly realised in his mind the all-but-forgotten historical details above repieced, the solemn scene of great local importance, and of intense though but temporary interest, will come to life before his eyes again, and the vivid historical picture will startle him when compared with the prophetic distich which the event interprets for him. He will become aware strangely that the picture of that event, that has just reshaped itself in his mind two hundred years after its occurrence, must, one hundred years before it occurred, have similarly visited the mental retina of him who could pen the lines. We cannot call it poetry, but it is brimful of imagination, and Tacitus himself grows wordy when set against the brevity of its utterance. It seems from this that to anticipate is, though less common, as human as to look back. It is incredible, yet how can you disbelieve it? There it stood in type in the Royal Library the very day the thing was enacting; it had stood there for eighty long years before, and the same volume stands upon the shelves of the same library to-day. It is not to be understood, but it must be accepted; you may refuse the prophecy, but incredulity incarnate can never change the facts. Adequate explanation will be acceptable, and we invite ingenuity to attempt it. There were more things in the earth and heaven than entered, we know, into Horatio's philosophy; there may also be more things, perhaps, than were ever dreamt of in philosophy itself. . . .

All this wants a book; we feel we cannot do justice to our theme in the space allotted to us. But we will now pass on to a very remarkable quatrain, No. 40 of century x., though we should have liked to place before the reader quatrain 49 of century ix., which contains perhaps the only prophecy of our author that has attained any real publicity in England, viz.:

Sénat de Londres mettront à mort leur Roy.

The number of the quatrain, 49, gives, curiously enough, the year of the occurrence in the 17th century. This may be merely accidental, and is sure to be called so, but if intended where so much is strange it would be nothing specially remarkable. We are not aware that the coincidence has ever attracted comment before, even in France. Every line of this quatrain admits of a fairly clear interpretation in our opinion, and in the *Quarterly Review,* vol. xxvi., the above-quoted line is allowed to be a startling announcement of Charles I.' s death; but the writer, F. Cohen (afterwards Sir F. Palgrave), says that "Oedipus himself could not give the sense of the whole verse." Of course not, if Oedipus be in so great a hurry that he will not give himself time enough to read the riddle that has been clothed under a form more or less obscure, for solid reasons aforethought.

Let us now revert to our specimen, No. 40 of century x.:

Le jeune nay au règne Britannique,

Qu'aura le père mourant recommandé,
Jceluy mort Lonole donra topique,
Et à son fils le règne demandé.

The new-born Prince of the kingdom of Britain,
whose dying father will have recommended him,
this one being dead, Lonole will perorate and
snatch the kingdom from his very son.

James the First of England and Sixth of Scotland was born
June 19, 1566—the year of the publication of the Quatrains—the son of Mary Stuart and Henry, Lord Darnley,
who had commended the child to the Scottish lords before
his assassination by Boswell. In 1603 he mounted the
throne of England, and it was under him that England and
Scotland were first denominated Great Britain. This conveys a great propriety to the words selected by Nostradamus. When this king dies *Lonole* is to seduce England with
artificial rhetoric, and to demand the kingdom, together
with the life of his son, Charles I.

For *Lonole* Garencières reads *Londres,* but the *texte type*
has *Lonole.* It is rather curious that *Lonole* should yield
the anagram *Olleon* . . . as Napoleon does that of . . .
Apollyon. Cromwell and he show numerous points of contact, whether we seek them in history, character, or
prophecy. But a further anagram, still more startling, has
hitherto we believe escaped all the commentators: Ole
Noll in the form of *Old Noll,* has always been the nickname of the Protector, and *Ole Nol* is letter for letter
Lonole. It may stand for Apollyon also, and as such for
"Old Nick" too.

James I. was born June 19, 1566, and thirteen days later,
July 2, 1566, Nostradamus breathed his last. This quatrain, once understood, is one of the clearest and most extraordinary of the forecasts of Nostradamus. Quatrain 80,
of century iii., contains a remarkable announcement of the
overthrow of Charles I., the sacrifice of Strafford, and the
bastard kingship of Cromwell. Century viii., quatrain 76,
points very clearly to Cromwell, and is interesting; but we
must pass it by, together with much more that appears to
have relation to English affairs, including the very clear
prophecy that England is to command the sea for 300
years (century x., 100), a period that ran out two years
since, if we date the commencement of English supremacy
from the defeat of the Spanish Armada, 1588.

We can only treat of three more quatrains, two of which
marvellously point to Louis XVI., and the third to Napoleon as unmistakably. We may here and there glance at
some striking line in passing, if only to indicate the rich
mine that might be worked, did time and space permit.
Pregnant hints abound, such as this (century iii., quatrain
59):

Barbare empire par le tiers usurpé.

What could better foreshadow the assault made upon government and good order in 1789, when the third estate
swallowed up the other two by usurpation? Here is another graphic distich (century i., quatrain 57):

Bouche sanglante dans le sang nagera,
Au sol la face ointe de laict et miel.

The bleeding mouth swims in a tide of blood,

The face anoint drops to the crimson'd turf.

The milk and honey, wine and oil, is clearly allusive to the
oil of *la sainte ampoule,* with which the kings of France
were consecrated and anointed at Reims. But we will confine ourselves to one difficult quatrain (century ix., quatrain 20), and endeavour by means of a close examination
to establish its intelligibility.

De nuict viendra par la forest de Reines
Deux pars, vaultorte, Herne la pierre blanche,
Le moyne noir en gris dedans Varennes,
Esleu Cap. cause tempeste, feu, sang, tranche.

By night shall come through the forest of Reines
Two parts, face about, the Queen a white stone,
The black monk in gray within Varennes.
Chosen Cap. causes tempest, fire, blood, slice.

The bewildered reader may perhaps exclaim, "Surely gibberish can no further go." Well, now, let us see. The Forest
of Reines is on the way to *Varennes*; we place in italics the
two latter syllables, for they appear to constitute a variant
of the same word. *Herne* is the anagram of *Reine* by meta-
plasm of *h* for *i.* The reader will see by referring to the
"Dict. de Trévoux," article "Anagramme," that this is
permissible by the structural rules of the anagram. *Vaul-*
torte is an obsolete word for face-about, as we have translated it. *Deux pars* stands for husband and wife. The queen
is Marie Antoinette. *Le moyne noir en gris* is Louis XVI.;
and the subject of the stanza is obviously the famous flight
of the king and queen from Paris on June 20, 1791, which
terminated in their arrest at Varennes, and their re-entry
as captives into Paris. There are fourteen pages octavo, in
small print, giving details of this tragical journey, in the
Marquis de Bouillés *Mémoires,* full of interesting particulars admirably narrated by that grand and gallant soldier.
Had Bouillé found a Turgot to co-operate with him, instead of the egotistic and irresolute Lafayette, the whole
of the affairs of Europe might have taken a very different
channel. His memoirs disclose him to have been a great
patriot, but scarcely ever is his name now breathed. It is
a book to read if you desire to know the period and to
study the fate of the French king. Prudhomme (*Révol. de*
Paris), if referred to, will establish the singular propriety
of the expression *vaultorte* to describe the king's irresolu-
tion at the divergence of the cross roads—taking, contrary
to previous arrangement, the way to Varennes. Prudhomme further relates at the above passage that the king
was on this occasion attired in gray; he had on an iron-
gray coat (*gris de fer*), and wore a round slouch-hat that
hid the face, so that he would appear a good deal like a
Franciscan (*Le moyne noir en gris*). The queen was dressed
in white, and Madame Campan, in her *Mémoires de Marie*
Antoinette, relates that after the arrest the queen's hair
grew white in a single night, and that she had a lock of this
white hair mounted in a ring for the Princesse de Lambal-
le, inscribed "*blanchis par le malheur.*" She was, like
Niobe, turned to white stone—*la pierre blanche* indeed.
Esleu Cap. involves a propriety most peculiar, which demands a slight insistence, lest it be overlooked. The title
of King of the French, instead of King of France, had been
established since October 16, 1789. But it was not until
Sept. 1, following the above arrest, that the decree was
passed forcing the king to surrender to the will of the peo-

ple and become a constitutional monarch. This he submitted to and signed on Sept. 14, and thus he became *Esleu Cap.* Finally, the word *tranche* is most expressive for the slice, or what is now called the *couperet* of the guillotine. Thus painfully disentangled by us, the gibberish has grown quite fearfully intelligible, and one or two of the words become so singularly select, and so pregnant with meaning, as to suggest pages of history in the condensation of a syllable. Here again we find a dark record flashing upon us with all the certainty of an eyewitness, and we find it to have been unmistakably in type more than 200 years before the realisation took place.

The next we cite is even still more astonishing. After troublesome investigation, it enables us to lift the veil and clear away the multiform obscurities that the indolent have heretofore presumed to be but the empty jargon of a fortune-teller.

> *Le part soluz, mary sera mitré*
> *Retour: conflict passera sur le thuille,*
> *Par cinq cents: un trahyr sera tiltré*
> *Narbon: et Saulce par couteaux avons d'huille.*

> (Century ix., quatrain 34.)

> The husband, alone, afflicted, will be mitred on his return; a conflict will take place at the Tuileries by five hundred men. One traitor will be titled, Narbonne, and (the other) Saulce, grandfather, oilman, will (hand him over) to the soldiery.

This has to be filled in as follows: Louis XVI., now alone, that is to say, without his wife, will suffer the indignity of being crowned with the red cap of Liberty. A revival this was of the Phrygian bonnet or head-gear of the priests of Mithras, hence the word *mitré*. The 500 Marseillais brought from the southern city attack the Tuileries. The titled traitor is the Count de Narbonne, the minister of war. The other name, glimmering suddenly out of the obscurity, as a star through the storm-wrack of a dark night, is that of Saulce (father, son and grandson) the elder, tradesman of Varennes, chandler, grocer, oilman. The elder was *procureur-syndic* of his commune. This man betrayed the king to the populace, so that he was arrested *par couteaux* by the guards. Some read this, *per custodes;* or it may mean *coustiller,* armed with a *coustille,* a short straight cutlass. *Avons* is the old French for grandfather, *avus.*

Madame Campan gives an account of their majesties alighting at this grocery-shop of the Mayor of Varennes, *Saulce,* who could, had he wished it, have saved the king. But this false-weight parody of classic heroism, in reply to the tears of the queen, striking an attitude, ejaculated, "J'aime mon roi, mais je resterai fidèle à ma patrie." For this the assembly voted him, some two months later, 20,000 livres, and, with these two scintillations illuminating him, Saulce quits distinction and the public eye for ever. *Un Brute Francais, qui aime César bien, mais plus encore le sang.*

Thiers, in his account of the attack on the Tuileries, June 20, 1792 (*Révol. France*) draws a pathetic picture of the afflicted king (*mary mitré*) in his sad day-dream and red night-cap. The palace, of which he was no longer master, was evacuated about seven in the evening by the populace peaceably and in good order. Then the king, the queen, his sister, and the children, all met together, shedding a torrent of tears. The king seemed stunned by what had occurred, and now for the first time noticed that the red cap was still upon his head: he seized it and flung it aside with indignation.

Carlyle, in his *French Revolution,* speaks of Barbaroux's "six hundred Marsellese who know how to die," and a few lines lower down he calls them "517 able men." Now Thiers says (*Révol. France*), they arrived on June 30, 1792, and were five hundred men ("*Ils étaient cinq cent.*") We indicate this for the benefit of such as desire to find Nostradamus wrong, and we care nothing for Nostradamus, we only wish to find out what is right. Those who like to examine the conduct of the Count de Narbonne, we refer to Bertrand de Molleville's "Hist. de la Révolution."

We think this quatrain might lie dormant for centuries after realisation—in fact, it practically has done so, since 1792 is little short now of its centenary. It necessarily slept for more than 200 years before the event; for, who could tell anything about the chance rocket *Saulce* before it had risen parabolically and fallen back again? Or who could impart meaning to the *part soluz,* to the mysterious 500, or the titled Narbonne? Six miraculous historical details lay *perdus* till time in two centuries should localise them, and, a hundred years after that, ingenuity should bring them to light. That is a patient way of prophesying, if you think about it. If a knave were at work, his short wisdom would seek a nimbler return than 300 years would give him. "Now or never" is his maxim; a knave knows he is quite a fool at long wisdom.

The thing is so crowded with compressed interest that we have even now omitted a marvellous item: *conflict passera sur le thuille.* When Nostradamus wrote this in 1555, or earlier, the Tuileries site was occupied by extensive tile-kilns, whence the renowned name sprang. Catherine de Médicis began the palace there in 1564. Ten years before the mason had laid the first stone our prophet is writing about it as a place to be stormed by a Marseilles mob two centuries later.

Multiplying pages warn us that we must soon have done, not for want of matter, for that might fill volumes with ample interest, though possibly less intense than what we now pick out; but space will fail us, for a review can only shadow forth a work, not convey one.

Napoleon said he would have a page of history all to himself, and it is true, like a great deal else that he said, though it proceed from the mouth of the greatest falsifier that ever existed. Should anybody think this too plain spoken, let him suspend condemnation until he has read Kléber's letter, Napoleon's counter statement, and Lanfrey's comments on them both. The two first are given in full in the nine-volume edition of the *Mémoires* of Napoleon dictated by himself. Well, he has a page of history all to himself, and a precious figure he cuts in it; yet in historical proportion, as it is meet and right it should be, he has a good many quatrains in Nostradamus "all to himself;" for the reason above named we propose to give but one:

> *De soldat simple parviendra en empire,*
> *De robbe courte parviendra à la longue:*
> *Vaillant aux armes, en église où plus pire,*
> *Vexer les prestres comme l'eau fait l'esponge.*

> From a simple soldier he will rise to empire,
> From a short robe he will attain the long;
> Able in war, he shows to less advantage in
>   Church government,
> He vexes the priesthood like water in a sponge.

The French universally explain this of Napoleon, and it fits him very well. But so analogous are the lives and career of Napoleon and Cromwell that it might be applied to Cromwell, and Garencières does so apply it. Napoleon was plain lieutenant in 1785, consul for life in 1799, emperor from 1804 to 1814. The short robe and long are by Le Pelletier understood to be the consular robe and the imperial. The broader interpretation is perhaps the better: the girt-up military garb of action as contrasted with the long imperial robe, typical of order, leisure and direction. We should observe here that Nostradamus does not say *parviendra à régner, ascenda sur le trône,* but with felicity chooses the very word that will convey the hint required; kingship is over, but an *empire* is begun. He is valiant in arms, but something out of his depth in theology and church government: witness his ridiculous catechism, where schoolboys were taught to love, respect, and obey the emperor—that to serve the emperor was to honour and serve God himself ("il est devenu Point du Seigneur"). Lanfrey remarks here that he makes God useful as gendarme. This is as ridiculous as his ideas were upon literature. He once wrote to Cretel, "de faire faire à Paris des chansons" to rouse enthusiasm, as the *claque* at a theatre would. *Risum teneatis?* When he said to Goëthe, "Vous êtes un homme," how truly might not the poet have rejoined "Vraiment! c'est ce que vous n'êtes pas, Sire." Fancy Burns receiving an order from the Home Office to write "Bannockburn," and send it back by return on a halfpenny post-card. It would not have resulted in "Do or die"—the sole alternative being to die, and not to do it.

But, though far from successful in ecclesiastical direction, he thoroughly vexes the priesthood, penetrating into every hole and corner, as water does into a sponge.

In century i., quatrain 88, we get a wonderful passage. Nostradamus says, *Le divin mal surprendra le grand Prince* a little before his marriage. We take this to mean the Austrian marriage, which was preceded by the divorce of Josephine. His prop and credit, it runs on, shall fall into a sudden weakness and then comes this tremendous sentence:

> *Conseil mourra pour la teste rasée.*

> Counsel shall perish from this shaven poll.

Garencières (who was a doctor, and admitted of our College of Physicians, then in Warwick Lane, or in the original stone house of Knightrider Street before that) could have, of course, no conception of the historical fulfilment, but he renders *le divin mal* as "the falling sickness, called by the Greeks *epilepsia,* and by the Latins *morbus sacer.*"

Nobody else, perhaps, has rendered it "epilepsy," but, thus put, the forecast becomes miraculous. It is a point to rewrite history upon, for history has failed to see this great fact. Herod was smitten, rejoicing to be called a god. Napoleon the same in his concocted catechism.

Napoleon, Cromwell, Mahomet, Caesar, and probably Alexander, were all epileptic. The moral crime, and the blasphemous egotism of this idolator *de mon étoile,* have now convulsed the mighty Leyden jar, or electric battery, of this brain and demon-force that has so mercilessly dealt torpedo shocks to Europe. The Corsican cerebral pap is a weakened centre now; the inner prop is gone; phantasms huger than ever visit the big brain, which itself is readier than ever to entertain them, but with a terribly diminished power of bringing them to any practical evolution. The demigod is turning fast to Byron's "little Pagod," Be these predestinations or not, in the theological sense of the word, here was the sentence of *le divin mal* quietly jotted down in Salon de Craux, and recorded two hundred and fifty years before against the name of the epileptic bandit of Corsica Apollyon—or Napoleon, for those who like the recent form better.

This brings us to the end, not of what has to be said, but

Nostradamus, in full astrological garb.

of the space to say it in, and there is no room left to give the life of our seer, nor to vindicate him from the baseless charges of imposture that, from the issue of his first almanac till now, have from time to time been hurled at him. Whether a vindication be now needed or not, after the little we have here exhibited, is a question. Probably it is, for folly dies hard, but that will be seen later on. We have no theory about this man, we leave it to better hands to supply one. What we do say is: here are facts so far as we can, after no stint of drudgery, either see or arrive at them, and there are thousands more producible as startling as these—very many more, less so, but still inexplicable. These very facts, first of all, we hope to see disputed, or better interpreted, for we feel sure, from the trouble we have taken already, that wider research will only end in establishing our oracle the more by giving data that may help to open up the Quatrains whose sense is latent still.

Henry James Forman   (essay date 1936)

SOURCE: "Europe's Greatest Prophet," in *The Story of Prophecy in the Life of Mankind from Early Times to the Present Day,* Farrar & Rinehart, Incorporated, 1936, pp. 174-93.

[*In the following excerpt, Forman examines several prophecies of Nostradamus, positing possible ancient influences, remarking upon his intentional obscurity, highlighting alleged prophecies that came to pass, and concluding that Nostradamus is the once and future "greatest prophet of modern times."*]

Nostradamus declares that he burned some ancient Egyptian books after having learned their contents by heart. These books, originating in Egypt and in the ancient Persia of the Mages, had come to him by inheritance, from one or the other of his grandfathers. Now, what, ask his latest biographers, Moura and Louvet, did the Hebrews carry away from Egypt in the Exodus? Gold and silver, assuredly, but something besides far more precious.

"They could not have failed to possess themselves of all possible documents from the initiation chambers of the Egyptian temples, all the geometric, cosmographic and algebraic formulae subsequently used in the Torah and in the construction of the Temple of Solomon. Then, one day, the Romans destroyed the Temple of Jerusalem. The Jews were dispersed. Before the Temple was demolished, however, the documents had disappeared. When the Holy of Holies was entered, it was empty."

Those documents have never been found. According to the biographers they were doubtless transmitted from father to son in that Tribe of Issachar, which had always lived close to the Temple and to the Kings of Jerusalem. Also, the builders of the Temple were said to have migrated to Provence. In his preface to a portion of the Centuries addressed to his son (from the second marriage), Caesar, Nostradamus declares that he did not desire to keep those "volumes which had been hidden during long centuries," and that after learning their contents he had burned them. "That flame," he wrote, "was more brilliant than ordinary flame, as though a preternatural lightning flash had

abruptly illumined the house and threw it into a sudden conflagration."

Be that as it may, virtually all his biographers and commentators are at one in attributing supernormal knowledge and wisdom to Nostradamus. A hundred years before Newton he took account of the law of gravitation in his calculations, as also of Kepler's law of the ecliptic, though Kepler was not born until some years after Nostradamus' death. And though he constantly affirmed that he had done nothing marvelous, that he "had received at birth certain astral aspects which predisposed him to this work," that "all came from God," Nostradamus was nevertheless regarded as the greatest prophet of his time, and nightly he sat before the magical brass bowl filled to the brim with water, possibly in a sort of self-hypnosis, listening to his familiar spirit; and nightly he recorded his visions in those Centuries of verses that are still an object of study and speculation.

> *Aprés la terrienne mienne extinction,*
> *Plus fera mon écrit qu'a vivant—*

wrote the prophet:

> After my earthly passing,
> My writ will do more than during life.

The first edition of the **Centuries** was published in March, 1555, by Macé Bonhomme, printer at Lyons. Its success was tremendous. All the court, all the world of fashion at home and abroad could hardly converse of anything else. The polite world regarded him as a prodigy. Poets sent him verses of eulogy and not alone his countrymen, but even many foreigners made long journeys to visit and consult the seer. Salon-en-Craux in Provence became a celebrated town and, though Nostradamus had never invented a mousetrap, the great coaches of the rich and noble wore a path to his door. Nor did all indiscriminately receive his advice or prognostications. To some his answers were strange and perplexingly ambiguous.

In the letter dedicatory to the second edition of the Centuries addressed to King Henry II, "the most humane, most serene," the seer explains that it would be dangerous to be too explicit in his quatrains, "that the danger of the times, O Most Serene Majesty, requires that such hidden events be not manifested save by enigmatic speech; . . . did I so desire, I could fix the time for every quatrain, . . . but that it might to some be disagreeable." Like Shakespeare, who cursed those who would move his bones, Nostradamus ends his sixth Century in Latin thus:

> Let those who read these lines with ripe reflection ponder;
> That the vulgar, ignorant and profane hold off their hands:
> Let all astrologers, imbeciles, barbarians, stand aloof.
> Cursed be he of Heaven who acts in other wise.

"Let those who read these lines with ripe reflection ponder" is all very well. But read his Centuries as we may, and ponder as we will, the words, as one writer puts it, dance in the mind and one hardly knows whether one is hearing things in a dream or in one of those strange made-up languages with more sound than meaning. So great was his desire to conceal his meaning that even the current and common words were twisted about into anagrams, so that Paris became Rapis, France turned into Nersaf and Henric into Chiren.

His quatrains have been described by his most famous and devoted commentator, Le Pelletier, as "a sort of game of Tarot cards in verse, a cabalistic kaleidoscope. His manner brought him closer to the pagan oracles of Egypt, Greece and Italy than to the sober inspiration of the canonical prophets."

Canonical he certainly was not, yet he was profoundly religious. The Church, however, in those days was not to be trifled with, and Nostradamus always maintained a close tie with the Church. Perhaps that profound knowledge of the ideas upon which the Church was based and the human narrowness and zealotry of its officiants was a factor in making him at once bold and timid, obscure and yet, at times, startlingly clear. Some of those lucid prophecies, bearing on Charles I of England and Oliver Cromwell, on Louis XVI and the French Revolution, and on Napoleon, [may be readily] seen. Mostly, however, they are obscure. Every now and then one meets some that are almost lucid, but not quite. For instance, the following is taken to bear upon the American Revolution and the naval help of John Paul Jones:

> The West shall be free of the British Isles,
> The discovered shall pass low, then high,
> Scottish pirates shall on the sea rebel,
> On a rainy and hot night.

Similarly among those said to bear upon Napoleon this stanza is not so clear as some others:

> Of the name that a French King never was,
> There was never a lightning so much feared,
> Italy shall tremble; Spain and the English;
> He shall be much taken by women strangers.

Some there are, however, which remain obscure until one suddenly discerns their meaning:

> When Innocent shall hold the place of Peter,
> The Sicilian Nizaram shall see himself
> In great honors, but after that shall fall
> Into the dirt of Civil War.

"Nothing can be more plain or true," observes a commentator, Garencières, "than this prophecy and those that deny it may also deny light to the sun, but to make it more evident, we will examine it verse for verse. 'When Innocent shall hold the place of Peter,' that is, when one named Innocent shall be Pope, as he was (Innocent X, elected 1644, died 1655).

" 'The Sicilian Nizaram shall see himself in great honors,' that is Mazarin; for Nizaram is the anagram for Mazarin; he was born in Sicily and was then in his greatest splendor.

" 'But shall fall into the dirt of civil war,' as everyone knows he did"—referring to the Civil War of the Fronde, when there were barricades in Paris and the court had to withdraw to Saint-Germain. "And yet," adds Garencières, "when I read this forty years ago, I took it to be ridiculous."

This prophecy was made three quarters of a century before the event.

As to the future beyond our time, there are numerous prophecies contained in the Centuries of Nostradamus, could one but decipher them all. Now and then, however, some appear with marked clarity. Quatrain 72 of **"Century X"** begins with singular explicitness:

> *L'an mil neuf cent nonante neuf sept mois,*
> *Du ciel viendra un grand roi d'effrayeur.*

That is, reckoning the astrological year as beginning in March, in October 1999, a terrible king or leader will assault and invade Paris "du ciel," from the sky. He will come with a host speaking a strange, that is, not a Latin, tongue. They will have not only frightful weapons, but also reindeer! It has been suggested that since the menace of Asiatic invasion of Europe is always present, perhaps the northern Siberian tribes, many of whom still use reindeer, are slowly forming into a new and future menace to Europe. At one point the prophet positively declares that the invader will come from Sclavonia, that is, from Asia. Some now living among us may have opportunity of confirming this prophecy.

Again and again conflagrations and flames are prophesied for Paris. In **"Century VI,"** stanza 98:

> *Instant grande flamme éparse sautera.*

> A driving great flame will leap and scatter everywhere.

In **"Century IV,"** quatrain 82:

> *Puis la grande flamme éteindre ne saura.*

> Then they will be unable to extinguish the great flame.

The fire will come from above (du ciel), which may refer to new methods of civilized warfare, still in the womb of time, or to celestial flames reminiscent of Sodom and Gomorrah.

> *La grande cité sera bien desolée,*
> *Des habitants un seul n'y demourra.*

> The great city will be utterly waste,
> Not one of its dwellers will be left.

So Nostradamus foresees in the 84th quatrain of his Third Century, but that date is still remote. Paris still has fifteen centuries of existence. Its final catastrophe is not due until 3420!

No less than thirty-five prophecies concerning the destruction of Paris have been catalogued and all of these are unanimous in giving conflagration in the course of a war as the cause. No one, observes Piobb, a studious commentator on Nostradamus, gives so many precise details as the French prophet, in both time and space. For with his gift of clairvoyance he combined careful and meticulous calculation. Most prophets being *seers*, that is clairvoyants, inevitably evince the human tendency to exaggerate, to be sensational. It is the calculators, checking their visions with figures, who remain calm. Nostradamus was one of the ablest of the calculators.

The final catastrophe for Europe which will affect the rest of the world, is predicted for the year 7000. In that year is to come the next great deluge since the Biblical one. The Desert of Gobi will once again become a sea and the entire geography of the world will be radically changed.

It is not possible to dwell or even to touch upon all of the predictions of Nostradamus that are entirely or partly comprehensible. For instance,

> *En germanie naistront diverses sectes*
> *S'approchant fort de l'heureux paganisme . . .*

> In Germany will spring up different sects,
> Approaching nearly a careless paganism . . .

may refer to a variety of things including some recent efforts at a revival of pagan Germanic deities. Similarly,

> *Une nouvelle secte de Philosophes*
> *Mesprisant mort, or, honneurs et richesses:*
> *Des monts Germains ne seront limitrophes,*
> *A les ensuyvre appuy et presses.*

> A new sect of Philosophers,
> Despising death, gold, honor and riches,
> They will not be confined to the Mountains of
>   Germany,
> They will have support of followers and press.

This has been construed as referring to Theosophy and Rudolf Steiner's Anthroposophical movement, but it may have reference to events still in the future.

For the Catholic Church the prophet has some gloomy news to bring:

> *Romain pouvoir sera du tout à bas;*
> *Son grand voisin imiter les vestiges;*
> *Occultes haines civiles et débats,*
> *Retarderont aux bouffons leurs folies.*

> Roman power will be completely brought low;
> Italy will imitate the Revolution of France,
> Secret hatreds and civil disagreements
> Will somewhat delay the folly of the fools.

And elsewhere (**"Century X,"** quatrain 65) the prophet sighs:

> Oh, great Rome, thy ruin approaches,
> Not of thy walls, but of thy blood and substance,
> The printed word will work terrible havoc,
> The pointed steel driven home to the hilt.

It may be that Voltaire and the French Encyclopedists, who did so much to shake the Catholic Church, at least in France, would feel that this groaning prophecy on the part of Nostradamus, pronounced more than two centuries before their time, bears directly upon their activities.

He predicts that the blood of clerics will flow like water (**"Century VIII,"** quatrain 98) and that the Holy See will be banished from Rome altogether:

> *Par la puissance des trois Rois temporels,*
> *En autre lieu sera mis le sainct Siège,*
> *Où la substance de l'esprit corporel*
> *Sera remis et receu pour vray siege.*
>   **"Cent. VIII,"** quatrain 99.

> By the power of three realms

The Holy See will be moved elsewhere;
Where the substance of the spirit will be changed
And received for the true seat.

Though the last two verses are obscure, the first two leave no doubt as to the prophet's meaning.

In his letter dedicatory to Henry II, Nostradamus wrote that not only would the Church be persecuted and afflicted, but that the blood of Churchmen would flow "in the streets and temples as flows water after a furious rain. The Holy of Holies will be destroyed by Paganism and the Old as well as the New Testament will be banished and burned."

Eventually a certain great Celtic or French leader, contemporary of the Pastor Angelicus, or the Angelic Pope, will restore the Church to Rome.

> *Le grand Celtique entrera dedans Rome*
> *Menant amas d'exilez et bannis:*
> *Le grand pasteur mettra à mort tout homme*
> *Qui pour le coq estoyent aux Alpes unis.*
>   **"Cent. VI,"** quatrain 28.

> The great Celtic chief will enter Rome
> Leading an army of the exiled and banished
> The great shepherd will put to death every man,
> Who for the sake of the rock (Republic) united
>   in the Alps.

The great shepherd putting men to death does not sound like the Pastor Angelicus, but no one has ever attempted to disguise the obscurity of Nostradamus.

Though a prophet, Nostradamus was not without honor in his little town of Salon. Yet, it was the sixteenth century. A man who dealt with unknown powers, inevitably dealt with dark powers. Peasants, burghers and housewives feared him, notwithstanding that he brought trade and custom to the town. The wrinkled visage, the deep-set eyes, the forked beard, all these inspired dread in the simple folk of rural Provence.

Henry II died as predicted, Francis II was seized with a syncope and ambassadors from the Italian states were whispering about quatrain 39 of **"Century X."**

Francis died; another royal child died; the Spanish ambassador wrote to his King that, so far from being patronized by royalty, the man Nostradamus ought to be punished—as though he had actually caused the deaths! In effect, the reputation of Nostradamus was now at its height, and it was at about this time that the boy King Charles IX paid his visit to the seer and left him as a parting gift the title of Physician and Counselor in Ordinary to His Majesty. . . .

On the evening of July 1, 1556, his friend and pupil, Chavigny, bidding the sick man good night, pronounced the usual formula, "à demain, maître"—until tomorrow, master. But Nostradamus, shaking his head sadly, murmured, "Tomorrow at sunrise I shall no longer be here."

In a quatrain bearing upon his own death he had written:

> *De retour d'ambassade, don du Roy, mis au lieu,*
> *Plus n'en fera, sera allé a Dieu,*
> *Proches parents, amis, frères du sang*

Trouve tout mort, pres du lit et du banc.

Upon returning from a mission, gift of the King,
  back to place,
Nothing more will occur, I shall have gone to
  God;
Near ones, friends, brothers of my blood
Will find me dead, near to the bed and the bench.

He was so found, upon his bench, in the early morning.

For long, his fellow townsmen, who mourned him with tears, believed that he was not dead, but had simply withdrawn from life, to carry on his studies. The curious dared not go too near the portion of the wall in the church which contains his tomb. "Quietem posteri ne invidete" was the inscription he caused to be cut—"Invade not the peace of the dead." His wife, however, added the following epitaph:

> Here repose the bones of the very illustrious Michel Nostradamus, alone, in the judgment of all mortals, worthy of recording with a pen almost divine, in accord with stellar influences, the coming events of the entire world.
>
> He lived sixty-two years, six months and seventeen days. He died at Salon, in the year 1566. Let posterity not disturb his rest.
>
> Anne Ponsart Gemelle, his wife of Salon, wishes her husband true felicity.

Nostradamus has at various times been called, and will not improbably one day again be called, the greatest prophet of modern times.

Lee McCann   (essay date 1941)

SOURCE: In a foreword and "In the Twentieth Century," in *Nostradamus: The Man Who Saw through Time,* Creative Age Press, 1941, pp. xi-xvi, 337-421.

[*In the following excerpt from a book published during the early years of World War II, McCann emphasizes Nostradamus's significance as a prophet of the world's current time of troubles and as a seer of the end of the age. The critic cites prophecies concerning the rise of Africa and Asia as dominant world powers and the subsequent "birth of a new age with a different type of thought and civilization."*]

The rich, actively fulfilled life of the French prophet, Michel de Nostradame, is the story of genius not only in its rarest but its most modern form. His ability foreshadowed a hope, now gaining a first hearing in this our day, that science may, in some not too remote tomorrow, discover principles of mental forces which will permit every man to realize within himself a reflection of the powers of Nostradamus.

Many prophets have crossed the brightly lighted stage of history and paused to utter some astounding bit of prescience. But they are seldom remembered for more than a single episode, some ray of strange illumination that for a moment spotlighted the fate of a throne or a battle. Actually there exist but two written documents of prophecy which have pictured a grandscale continuity of history, and unfolded a tapestry of world futures. One of these is, of course, the mighty word of Scripture. The other is that cryptic romaunt of Europe's fate, the ***Centuries,*** written by Nostradamus, Provençal troubadour of destiny.

No one knows as yet what forces shape a prophet, nor how it is that to "remembrance of things past," he adds "remembrance of the things that are to come." Perhaps the Red Queen knew more about it than most. When Alice asked her why she cried out before, instead of after, she had pricked her finger, her majesty sagely observed that it is a poor rule which doesn't work both ways. Nostradamus would have enjoyed that bit of wit, so like his own, and pertinent to prophecy.

What is "before" and "after"? What is up or down when considered outside the limited, inaccurate criteria of the five senses? The fourth-dimensional vision of Nostradamus, like the Red Queen's cry, transcended the meanings which we give these words. The man who saw through time watched, as through a telescope, the distant stars of future events rise and set, beyond the eye of the present, over a period of four hundred years.

> Heaven from all creatures hide the book of Fate,
> All but the page prescrib'd, their present state.

Pope was within his sceptical rights when he penned that couplet, because the vaticinating exceptions among heaven's creatures have always been so few that for people as a whole his words were true. Another Englishman, the modernist Dean Inge, had however a better perspective. As a churchman he accepted prophecy. As an intelligent modern he said that the phenomenon of prevision was quite possibly part of an evolutionary process which would one day become a developed faculty general to man. Considered in this light, Nostradamus, astounding as are his prophecies, is himself, the man, of even greater fascination than his work, because he attained in its completeness the faculty to which it is at least a possibility that all may eventually aspire. . . .

We are so accustomed to thinking of time as the straight road separated by present experience into its two parts, yesterday and tomorrow. But the scientist is beginning to perceive what the mystic has always known, that time is an unknown country stretching boundlessly in all directions. Nostradamus, in whom awareness of this set him apart from his fellows, was the Marco Polo of time's uncharted land, in which he traveled the future as we travel a continent. From these transcendental voyagings, like Polo, he returned with incredible stories of strange sights. The prophet's rare okapis were a vision of events to come.

Both of these men, whose discoveries were beyond the comprehension of their age, have come late into their own. Archaeology and exploration have verified the narrative of Polo's travels. History, not only since the sixteenth century, but daily, is verifying the time-travels of that other and greater explorer, Nostradamus. He is of yesterday, today, and still a long tomorrow. By virtue of what he was, and of our own hopes, he deserves the distinguished position today which he had in the Renaissance, and serious study in the light of what science is teaching us of the power and forces of the mind.

It is an old and tenaciously held popular idea that interest in and concentration on extra-dimensional qualities of the mind tend inevitably to some form of imbalance which may run the gamut from credulity to insanity. Too often in the past superstition has added to this its dark aura of witchcraft and abnormal rites. Nostradamus was, throughout his life, a striking refutation of such beliefs. His intellectual achievements and emotional balance, his social adaptation and vigorous health show him as the pattern of the well-rounded man. Considering his unique gift, he may be said to have had, besides his genius for prophecy, a veritable genius for normality. Had he never written the **Centuries**, his title to fame would still be clear. The brilliant skill and self-sacrificing devotion which made him the greatest physician in France of his day would alone keep his memory green. Physician, linguist, scholar, diplomat, writer, teacher, *religieux* and prophet, his life touched all phases of Renaissance thought and activity from the hovels of France, where he fought the plague, to the court of the Valois, where he was honored beyond any seer in history.

The Book of Joel, which seems to have made a strong impression upon Nostradamus, contains within its grim forecast the lovely, well-known passage:

> and your sons and your daughters shall prophesy, your old men shall dream dreams, your young men shall see visions.

Nostradamus was the greatest of all who since Biblical ages have given to these words the substance of fulfillment. And perhaps his life was prelusive to the "clear seeing" which may be the glory of the coming age. . . .

Today's news is in the prophecies of the **Centuries.** Russia and England are now fighting on the same side, while war rages in the Orient, just as Nostradamus predicted. Before this book is off the presses, more striking predictions may have seen fulfillment. And perhaps there will be verses, omitted here because their meaning was not yet clear, which will have become clear through the rapid onrush of events. It is difficult to indicate chronological sequence in events of the future, and any interpreter's confusion on this point in unavoidable. Nostradamus may have juggled order to further mask identification and meaning. Also many of the quatrains had to be omitted for lack of space. Those most pertinent to our time, and to the development of the future, are given first consideration here.

The final chapter of the historic cycle of the Nostradamus predictions is naturally the most exciting to us who live in the midst of its predicted alarms and tragic drama and can foresee, in part, some of the fearsome days of the future. Nostradamus has given in the course of the **Centuries** many dates, both actual years and astronomically stated times. He has not given, directly, the date for the emergence of France from her yoke of bondage. But in the opinion of this author he has given it in the number of his verses, one of the cryptic methods which he enjoyed using for his half-concealments. The final edition of his work contained ten Centuries which by right should have totaled a thousand quatrains. There were but nine hundred and forty-four. If one takes these two facts as giving the

elements of a historic date, and adds them, the date is 1944.

This is not to be taken, however, as the date for the crowning of a new king of France, but rather perhaps of his coming to the fore, or raising the royal standard, together with a new attitude in France. In other words, it is the turning point. Several verses indicate that the stabilization of Europe, and the fullness of a new king's power will not come until 1952-3.

The present Pretender to the French throne is Henri, Duc de Guise. He corresponds in the facts of his life to the description given by the prophet of the coming king. The last king of his line, he would be the first to bear the name Henry since the founder of the Bourbon dynasty, Henry of Navarre, and would complete the cycle of the house of Bourbon-Orleans, whose first ruler was born within the lifetime of Nostradamus. . . .

The Rise of the Orient

The author, sometime ago, cited some of the predictions in the following verses to a well-known military commentator. He said that they were not news. That men in his particular work who were always scanning future horizons for long-range prophecies of their own had long accepted the rise of the Orient as a *fait accompli* of the future, and that for this reason the political forecasters gave triple attention to every item that came out of Asia and Africa. Nostradamus in his own day saw the might of the Orient and its menace to Christian Europe, and he knew that cycles return.

VIII—59

> Twice lifted to power, twice overthrown,
> The Orient like the Occident will weaken.
> His adversary after numerous struggles,
> Routed by the sea, in a pinch will fall.

IX—60

> In the conflict with the Barbarian with the black
>   Head-dress
> Bloodshed will make Dalmatia tremble,
> The might of Araby will rear its headland,
> The frogs will shake with fear, Portugal will give
>   help.

The frogs are the French; that is the ancient name from Merovingian times.

VI—85

> The great city of Constaninople will be destroyed by the French;
> The forces of the Turban will be taken captive.
> Help will come by sea from a great leader of Portugal.
> This will happen on the twenty-fifth of May, the day of Saint Urban.

Probably the prophet looks back from this advanced time to what is Portugal today, as this is a small country and may be incorporated in a large one. A modern French commentator, realizing its size, says, naïvely enough, that Portugal will send for the U. S. fleet!

VIII—77

Anti-Christ will be three times annihilated,
Seven and twenty years blood will be shed in
    war.
Dead heretics, captives and exiles there shall be,
Blood, human corpses, crimson waters and hail
    upon the earth.

I—18

Through the negligence and discord of France
An opening will be given to the followers of Mo-
    hammed.
The earth and sea of the north of Italy will be
    bloodsoaked,
The harbor of Marseilles will be filled with ships
    and sails.

III—44

The ancient monarch driven out of power
Will go to fetch his help among those of the Ori-
    ent.
For fear of the cross he will fold his standard.
In Greece he will go by land and sea.

V—112

The sea will not be safe for the monarchy,
Those of self-indulgent life will hold all Africa,
No longer will the hypocrites be in occupation,
And a portion of Asia will change.

Life will be frankly hedonistic in Africa without the mask
of moral hypocrisy.

V—55

In the country of Arabia Felix
There shall be born a puissant leader of the Mo-
    hammedans.
He will trouble Spain and conquer Granada,
And from beyond the sea he shall invade the
    people of the Italian west coast.

VI—80

From Fez the rule shall attain to the countries
    of Europe.
Their cities will be fired and their people pierced
    with a blade,
The chief leader of Asia will bring a great troop
    by land and sea.
He will pursue the royalists, the priests and the
    cross to their death.

III—20

Through the lands watered by the great river
    Bethis
Far within Spain in the kingdom of Granada,
The cross will be driven back by a Mohammed-
    an nation,
    A man of Cordova will betray his country.

I—73

France, through her neglect, will be assailed on
    five fronts,
Tunis and Algiers will be stirred up by the peo-
    ples of Asia,
León, Seville and Barcelona will fall
And they will not have the fleet of Venice to pro-
    tect them.

In the coming invasions of Europe, through the rising of
the Orient, the prophet makes sarcastic reference to the
long years in his own day when the Venetian fleet, unaided, protected Europe against the East while the nations of
Europe quarreled amongst themselves. That situation, he
says, will come again, and this time there won't be the Venetian fleet.

II—96

A burning torch shall appear in the heaven
Above the Rhone from source to mouth.
Famine, sword will afflict, succor will be tardily
    brought.
The Persian will turn to the invasion of Macedo-
    nia.

IX—73

The Monarch of the blue Turban when he has
    entered into Foix
Will rule less than an evolution of Saturn (29
    years).
The King of the white Turban and the high
    courage of Byzantium
Will be manifest near the time of holding when
    Sun, Mars and Mercury are conjoined in
    Aquarius.

This conjunction takes place February 18, 1981.

Presage 35

France shall be greatly saddened by a death,
The mother and tutrice shall be bereft of the
    royal blood.
Government and Lords will be made orphans by
    the Crocodiles,
Strong cities, castles and towns will be taken by
    surprise,
May Almighty God guard them from these
    evils.

The Crocodiles are the people of Africa and tropical Asia
who will overwhelm France, the mother and tutrice, after
the final fall of the Bourbon dynasty.

V—75

The Church of God will be persecuted,
The sacred temples will be despoiled,
The child shall strip the mother of everything,
The Arabs will join the Jews.

V—25

The rule of the Church will succumb by sea
To the Prince of Arabia when Mars, Sun and
    Venus are conjoined in Leo,
Across Persia will come full near a million
    troops,
The true serpent will invade Byzantium and
    Egypt.

The date of this conjunction is August 21, 1987.

The End of the Age

Not only ever since the Christian era, but long before in
the songs and lamentations of the Hebrew prophets, the
end of the great precessional era of the Fishes, Pisces, has
been foretold in a wealth of tragic and saddening detail.

It is not the end of the world, as many people of old times thought, but the end of a grand period, and the birth of a new age with a different type of thought and civilization. Nostradamus prophesied that it would be marked by the downfall of old Europe, and be ushered in with earthquakes and eclipses such as the Bible describes in the scene of the Crucifixion.

Science recognizes that from time to time the earth changes the inclination of its axis. They know this from fossil remains (which, for example, show that Alaska had once a warm climate, and other localities show that similar changes have taken place). But science has no knowledge of what causes this change, nor in what cycle of years its return may be expected. Nor does Nostradamus specify the date for this occurrence, but by implication he links it with the phenomenon of the double eclipse which will take place in 1999.

The two eclipses will occur in the sign Leo, a partial one on July 28th, and a total one on August 11. The event is a very rare astronomical phenomenon. Camille Flammarion wrote of it in detail. All astronomers then living will prepare to observe it with every advanced resource of scientific equipment. Nostradamus, in both his letter to the King and in his verses, has given his picture of what he predicts will affect the entire world. Science is just beginning to have an understanding of terrestrial phenomena, such as floods and earthquakes, coming as the result of celestial phenomena, the doctrine held by astrologers for thousands of years. Science has arrived at some limited conclusions forced by the necessity for better long-range weather forecasting. But the study of earthquakes, floods and volcanoes, made in the light of the gravitational and magnetic strains and stresses of the Sun, Moon and planets, is still in its infancy and as yet almost nothing is known about it. The wise men of old knew these things, and Nostradamus knew them. He needed no telescope for the double eclipse, and he not only saw it, but he saw the train of events that came with it, something no giant telescope can show.

In his letter to the King the prophet has this to say of the last years of the twentieth century:

> Then shall begin the great empire of Antichrist in the invasions of Xerxes and Attila ("one who will revive the King of the Angoumois," and the Oriental invasion) who will come with a countless throng, so that the advent of the Holy Spirit, from the 48th parallel, will make a great change and chase away the abomination of Antichrist that made war on the sovereign Vicar of Christ (the Pope) and against his Church for a time and to the end of time. This will be preceded by an eclipse of the Sun, of denser darkness than has ever been seen since the Creation and up to the passion and crucifixion of Jesus Christ, and from that time until the coming one. There will take place in the month of October a great translation made so that the earth will seem to lose the weight of its natural motion in an abyss of endless darkness. There will be premonitory signs in the spring, and there will be extreme changes, overthrows of kingdoms, and earthquakes. . . .

In the last period all the Christian kingdoms, and those of the infidels, will be shaken for twenty-five years. The wars and battles will be more injurious. Towns, cities, castles, and other buildings will be burned, laid waste, and destroyed, with great blood-shed of vestals, violation of wives and widows, and children at the breast dashed and broken against the walls of the towns. Satan, the prince infernal, will commit so many evils that nearly the whole world will be afflicted and desolated.

After this has endured for a certain length of time, Saturn will almost renew his cycle (twenty-nine years), but God the Creator will bring an age of gold. He will heed the affliction of His people, and He will bind Satan and throw him into the abyss. Then shall begin between God and man a universal peace, and Satan will be bound for a thousand years. Then the cycle will return in grand power, Satan will be once more unbound against the Church.

IV—67

The year that Saturn and Mars are conjunct and combust
The air will be very dry and there will be a long trajection (comet),
Through incendiarism a great locality will be consumed by fire,
There will be little rain, with wind, heat, wars and incursions.

This configuration occurs in April, 1998. It is in that year that Nostradamus predicts the great invasion of France. The path of the solar eclipse, which will be total, passes through northern France and Belgium.

V—54

From the Euxine Sea and great Tartary
There will arise a King who will eventually behold Gaul.
He will traverse Turkey and Germany
And in Byzantium will leave his bloody track.

II—29

The Oriental will go out from his home
To cross the Apennines and look on France.
He will traverse the clouds and the snows of heaven,
And everyone will be struck down with his club.

X—72

In the year 1999 and seven months
From the sky will come a great and terrible King
Who will revive the great King of the Angoumois,
Before and after his coming war will rule at full blast.

The Angoumois were an early Gallic people conquered by the invading Goths. The situation will be similar.

III—84

The Great City will be desolate,
Of her inhabitants not one shall remain to dwell there,

Wall, sex, building and virgin will be violated.
By battle, fire, corruption and cannon the people
    will die.

II—28

The last but one to be called Pope
Will take Diana for his day and his repose,
He will wander afar on account of his distracted
    head,
Seeking to deliver a great people from economic
    oppression.

Diana is the Moon, so that Monday will be the Pope's day of rest. The Moon rules changes, travels and voyagings, and it is involved in mental frenzies and distracted mentalities. In the famous prophecy of Malachi, in his descriptions of the popes yet to come he names third before Petrus Romanus (the last one named) De Medietate Lunae. *De Medietate Lunae* means "relating to the half-Moon, which is the crescent of Diana." Malachi's further description of this pope is: "From the half-moon proceeds this pope sent to Rome by the Divine Doctor, Hail, our well-beloved Pius XII, most holy Mediator, future victim." The present incumbent of the holy See is Pius XII, and more than any previous pope he has "wandered afar." But otherwise the description does not fit, nor does he come in the order given by Malachi. According to the Monk of Padua there will be two popes after the Lunar, and three more before him. Nostradamus names him as the "penultimate" pope. In the times of the Avignon popes and the Great Schism Cardinal Pietro di Luna was one of the false popes. Eustache Deschamps, a famous satiric poet of that time, whose writings were not only familiar to Nostradamus but imitated and quoted by him, wrote a satire called, "Of the Schism in the Church Which is Much Troubled by the Moon" (Luna). Some of Nostradamus' lines are very close to lines in this satire.

III—17

Mount Aventine will be seen flaming in the
    night.
The sky will be suddenly obscured in Flanders.
When the Monarch drives out his nephew,
The people of the Church will commit scandals.

VIII—15

Toward the north great efforts will be made by
    mankind,
Almost all of Europe and the whole world will
    be tormented.
The two eclipses will put men to such pursuit
And will augment life and death among the
    Hungarians.

These two eclipses, one of the Sun and the other of the Moon, both occur in August of 1999, in the sign Leo, traditionally associated.

VIII—16

In the place where the Almighty has built His
    ship (Rome)
The deluge will be so great and so sudden
That there will be no spot of earth for a firm
    foothold.

The wave will cover the Olympus of Fiesole
    (Apennines).

I—69

The great round mountain of the seven hills
    (Rome),
After it has gone through peace, war, famine and
    inundation,
Will tumble far, sending the great country into
    the abyss,
Even its antiquities will be lost and its great
    foundation.

I—56

You will see, early and late, great changes take
    place,
Extremes of horror and prosecutions
As if the Moon were guided by its spirit,
The heavens approach the time of their tilting.

I—84

The Moon obscured in profound darkness,
Her brother (the Sun) will become the color of
    rust,
The great one hidden for a long time in darkness
Will turn the sword in the bloody wound.

I—47

For forty years the rainbow shall not appear.
For forty years all the days shall behold
A barren earth and increasing scarcity,
And great deluges will be perceived.

X—74

At the revolution of the grand number seven
There will appear the hazards of the hecatomb,
Not far from the great Millennial age
The dead shall go out from their tomb.

X—73

Past and present times together
Will be judged by the great Jehovah,
The world in its late stage will be abandoned by
    Him
And sentence will be passed on the disloyal clergy.

VII—41

Those whose bones of hands and feet were shut
    up
In a dwelling long uninhabited by noise
Will be disinherited while they are in the depths
    of their dream
And translated to a house that is salutary and
    calm.

Edgar Leoni   (essay date 1961)

SOURCE: "Background and Rules of the Game," in *Nostradamus: Life and Literature,* Exposition Press, 1961, pp. 102-19.

[*Leoni is the author of* Nostradamus: Life and Literature, *a work containing what is considered the definitive English-language critical edition of Nostradamus's prophecies. (This work was republished in 1982 as* Nostradamus and

His Prophecies.) *He has written of his subject, "Nostradamus provides one of history's classic examples of a 'byword' reputation that persists in clear contradiction to [his having been proven] wrong about practically everything." In the following excerpt, Leoni assesses Nostradamus's prophetic methods and accuracy, concluding that, "At best it can be said of Nostradamus as a prophet that he occasionally had a successful 'vision' of* what *would happen, but never of* when *anything would happen." He also includes an overview of key criticism of Nostradamus through the centuries and probes possible sources of his prophetic inspiration.*]

Summary Criticism Through the Ages

It seems fitting to open this section with some diverse opinions on Nostradamus, coming from friend and foe alike. Between the lot of them, they cover all the principal lines of criticism against the prophet.

The first which we shall look at, coming from [*Les Oracles de Nostredame,* 1867, by] Le Pelletier, one of his principal propagandists, does not differ too greatly from that of many of his scoffers.

> Nostradamus and his works are an enigma. If one looks at them only superficially, one is sur-

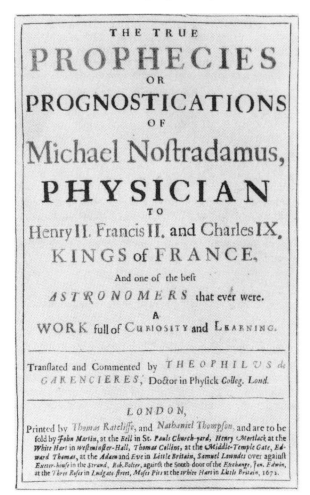

Title page of the 1672 London translation of the Centuries, *translated by Theophilus de Garencières.*

prised and intrigued, dazzled and struck by the reflections of the quatrains, attracted and repelled by the cunning irregularity of the plan: the author seems to be playing with his subject and reader who, for his part, replies in kind and promises himself to laugh at the Centuries and at Nostradamus. . . . All is ambiguous in Nostredame: the man, the thought, the style. The man: at once brave and timid, simple and complicated, playful and sinister, clairvoyant and sham, Christian on the surface and pagan perhaps underneath. . . . The thought is no less ambiguous than the man. Everywhere it takes the amphibological form, so familiar to the pagan oracles, so valuable for concealing himself. . . . Finally, the style is as crafty as the thought. Under the external façades of an elementary rime and a polyglot jargon which does not properly belong to any tongue, the author manifests savage poesy, deep erudition and knowledge of all the tongues used by the learned. . . . In the Centuries there lies no visible plan or method; all seems to be thrown together pell-mell in a universal mass of confusion.

In 1625 Gabriel Naudé wrote of the Centuries [in his *Apologie pour tous les grands personnages . . . soupçonnés de magie*] as follows:

> . . . the Centuries are so ambiguous, and so diverse, obscure and enigmatic, that it is not something to marvel at, if amongst a thousand quatrains, each of which speaks always of five or six different things, and above all of things which happen most ordinarily, one finds sometimes a hemistich which mentions a town in France taken, or the death of a great man in Italy, of a plague in Spain, or of a monster, of a conflagration, of a victory, or of something similar, as if all these things were extraordinary, and as though, if they didn't occur at one period, they couldn't occur at another.

In 1915 an English Jesuit named Father Herbert Thurston wrote in a similar vein in a book called *The War and the Prophets:*

> Undoubtedly the unrivalled success of Nostradamus' oracles is due to the fact that, avoiding all orderly arrangement, either chronological or topographical, and refraining almost entirely from categorical statements, it is impossible ever to say that a particular prognostic has missed the mark, whilst among the multitude of political occurrences vaguely outlined, some quite startling coincidences are sure to be observed in the course of years. In other words, Nostradamus provided an ingenious system of divination in which the misses can never be recorded and only the hits come to the surface. For the reputation of the would-be prophet, such conditions are naturally ideal.

Similar to the view that you just can't call Nostradamus' prophecies lies is the one that holds that one can read anything one wants into them. In 1882 Jean Gimon published a book on the history of Salon which included, inevitably, some mention of its most illustrious citizen. His comment on the prophecies seems to best summarize this school of thought:

> The style of the Centuries is so multiform and nebulous that each may, with a little effort and good will, find in them what he seeks. Like airy vapors, they assume, as they unroll, the figures of which the spectator's imagination lends them, and this fact assures this sibylline work of an immense and eternal success with those who are devotees of the marvelous.

But Pierre Gassendi, the great naturalist, had no hesitation in giving Nostradamus the lie. He wrote as follows:

> It will not be amiss for us, here to reflect upon somewhat of *Michael Nostradamus,* my own Comprovincial, that relates to our present argument; for of those so famous *Centuries of Tetrastichs* composed by him, I have another opportunity to speak. I shall give you only a taste of the Astrology he made use of, and if according to that he failed most shamfully in his predictions, I hope we may well beleeve, that he was not inspired by any divine spirit, or Genius, such as might suggest falshoods to him, or put lies in his mouth.
>
> Being some years since at Salona in company with the worthy person, *Franciscus Bochartius Campinius,* President of the high Court of Justice in *Province,* and that truly noble Man, *John Baptista Suffredus,* Judge of that City; I remember *Suffredus* showed us the Nativity Scheam of *Antonius Suffredus,* his Father, with the judgements thereupon given, under *Nostradamus his own handwriting.* We were much pleased to enquire of him, concerning his Father, whom we knew well, as not dying till his son was almost arrived at Mans estate. The Father, according to that Scheam, was born in the year *MDXLIII:* on the 13th of *January,* 22. minutes after high Noon, the Altitude of the Pole being supposed to be 44 degrees; which is more by the third part of a degree of the Signes inscribed on the Scheam; but the bare Signes, divided into Houses, after the old *Chaldean* way, beginning at *Aries* pertaining to his *Horoscope;* nor was there any mention of the Five wandering Stars, but only of the Sun referred to the second degree of *Aquarius,* and 36 minutes, and of the Moon related to the sixth degree of *Taurus,* without any minute at all. Now the Son *John Suffredus* being not able to give us any account of those accidents, which *Nostradamus* had foretold should befall the Father in his Youth; as that in the 16th year of his age, he should fall into a dangerous *Dysentery or Bloody Flux;* that he should be invaded with an acute and violent fever, in the 17th year of his Life, and in the 20th fall in Love, and relinguish his studies, &c. I shall relate only such, as he could more certainly inform us of. Among other of the Prophets judgements these are most remarkable. *That he should wear his Beard long, and crisped* (but he alwayes shaved his Chin bare) *that in the middle of his age, his Teeth should be rotten* (but he had very white and firm Teeth to his dying day) *that in his old age he should go almost crooked and double* (but he went to the last upright and straight, as any

young man whoever) *that in the 19th year of his Life, he should become exceedingly rich, by inheriting a strangers estate* (but besides what his Father left him, he never had any wealth or estate) *that he should suffer by the treachery of his Brethren,* and again, in the 37th year, *be wounded by his own Mothers son* (but he never had any Brother, nor had his Father more that one Wife) *that he should marry a Forreigner,* (but he married a French woman of Salona) *that in the 27th year, he should be charged with a Bastard Son* (but no Man ever heard of that) *that in the 25th he should be overwhelmed with the Theological Doctrine of some of his Tutors; and that he should be so addicted to Natural Philosophy, and the secrets of Magick, as no man more, as also to Geometry, and Arithmetick, in an extraordinary manner* (when yet it is well known, he never had any particular affection to, or care of any of those Studies, but devoted himself to the knowledge of the Laws, of which *Nostradamus* never dreamt, nor of the Dignity of a Senator, which in that respect was worthily conferred upon him, at Aix, in the 25th year of his age) *that in his old age, he should apply himself to Navigation, and Musick* (but he never delighted much in Musick, nor was ever at Sea in his whole Life) *that he should not pass his 75th year* (but he passed not the 54th; of which *Nostradamus* said not a word). And these things I am the more particular in, to the end that Men may judge, what credit is to be given to such predictions. [From a 1659 translation entitled *The Vanity of Judiciary Astrology: or Divination by the Stars.*]

As the most nearly firsthand evidence of Nostradamus' astrological predictions being tested locally, the above passage represents a rather damning case against our prophet. It has the ring of truth in all respects. The subjects' father appears as one of the witnesses of Nostradamus' will. Old man Suffrens seems to have gone out of his way to give Nostradamus the lie at every turn.

The talented Bishop of Pamiers, Henri de Sponde, seemed to hold an opinion of Nostradamus somewhat similar to that of Gassendi. A noted writer, Sponde, concluded his review of the year 1566 in his *Annals* by providing Nostradamus with a mocking epitaph.

> This year there died that trifler, so famous throughout the world, Michel Nostradamus, who boasted while he lived that he knew and could foretell future events by the influence of the stars, in whose name afterwards many ingenious men have put forth their imaginings. . . .

César Nostradamus, to whom the Preface was dedicated, was never particularly interested in his father's prophecies other than for providing him, by their fame, with great opportunities for social climbing. He refers to them as "obscure verses, in a sybilline style (to avoid their being profaned by the vulgar)."

It is probably Parker who provides Nostradamus with the most pithy tribute:

> All honor, then, to this king of pretenders who has been able to make his bluff good for over three and a half centuries. And the end of his

reign is as yet far in the future. [Unpublished doctoral thesis in Harvard University Archives Room, entitled "Michel Nostradamus— Prophet," 1920.]

Inspiration

A discussion of the inspiration of Nostradamus breaks down into a discussion of each of two major possibilities. The first possibility is that this very learned scholar was so contemptuous of the ignorance of his age that he wrote his prophetic works as a gigantic hoax or satire. Or, as an alternative, he may have been inspired by a desire for fame and wealth, which he certainly did achieve in far greater proportion than he would have had he remained a mere country doctor. Even if this possibility is accepted as the answer, there still remains the big question of the source from which he drew the material for his prophecies.

The second major possibility is that the man sincerely believed that he had seen the future and was writing of it. If this is true, it remains equally important to discover what was the real source of his prophecies. Divine inspiration? Hereditary clairvoyance? Magic? Astrology? All of these things have been attributed to him at one time or another. Each of them he himself has alluded to in different parts of his writings.

Parker is convinced that the first of the two possibilities is the correct one and gives a very thorough explanation of the "inspiration" of Nostradamus the bluffer.

> Nostradamus claims to have been moved to prophecy by divine inspiration but his repeated asseverations fail to prove his statement. Some of his quatrains, which he borrows almost literally from Jamblichus, smack of black magic, but this questionable procedure is no more responsible for his utterances than is his specified pretext, divine inspiration. His actual inspiration is found in a profound scorn for the intelligence of his fellow-men, which he does not hesitate to express in terms that are unquestionable to anyone who is willing to understand his bitter but cleverly expressed sentiments; thus the Centuries take on the form of sharp satire, despite the profound interpretations furnished by the numerous enthusiasts who have essayed to interpret them.

> His method of prophecy is tripartite. Firstly, he takes past events and gives them a figurative garb which renders them unrecognizable, putting them in the future tense. Again, he describes a series of well-chosen probabilities, based on contemporary conditions, and treats them likewise. Thirdly, he makes a series of random shots all of which are unlikely but still possible. The language of all the quatrains has the same tone, and all receive an air of plausibility from the mention of actually existing places, while occasionally a specific date is thrown in for good measure. The disguise is so perfect that it is often impossible to say to which of the three classes a quatrain belongs. Of the first group the most remarkable are his account of the sack of Rome by the Imperial army, and that of the contest over the Hungarian succession after the Battle of Mohacz, both events which happened about thirty

years before the first edition of the Centuries. In the third group is one very striking prediction, "Senat de Londres mettront a mort leur Roy," which, of course, is always interpreted as forecasting the execution of Charles I. Only one actual prophecy appears in the whole work, namely, the end of the Valois dynasty in France and the accession of Henry IV, concerning which the prophet seems to have had a very definite opinion. This opinion was, very likely, based on physical reasons (Nostradamus was physician in ordinary to the king, Henry II) rather than on astrology or divine inspiration.

Such then is the argument of this school of thought. It is a very tempting one, and it further leaves our hero on top with the last laugh. However, it is much too farfetched to be acceptable. Had all his prophecies been written in complete isolation, and discovered only after his death, and had no one known the author, it might be acceptable. But that Nostradamus could have fooled his "disciple" Chavigny, his son, various notables of Salon, the rulers of France and Savoy, several ambassadors and scores of other people with this gigantic "joke" of his is quite ridiculous. Furthermore, the proof of his sincerity lies not only in the Centuries, written indeed to cover a long period of time, but also in the almanacs, written each year for the following year. However, two of the three elements named by Parker do, indeed, show up in various quatrains. They are the element of "retroactive prophecy" and the element of "well-chosen probabilities."

Let us now turn to the probability of Nostradamus' being fundamentally sincere, i. e., really believing he had foreseen future events and was writing of them. Even in this case, the source of his inspiration does not become clear. In various places in his Preface to his son and in his Epistle to Henry II, he refers to having natural powers inherited from his ancestors, to divine inspiration and to adjustment of divine inspiration with astrological computation. Most frequently he refers to the last combination.

He vigorously denounces magic, undoubtedly with his cheek barely able to contain his tongue. Notwithstanding all his protestations, which were for the benefit of a Church which had no objection to prophecy so long as the Dark One was not its source, he was obviously hip-deep in magic. It is fortunate that we know the precise source of all his magical formulas and experiments.

In 1497 that industrious translator and astrologer Marsilio Ficino published in Venice a Latin translation of a classical book on all the magic of the ancient world by Jamblichus, a 4th-century philosopher and Neoplatonist of the Byzantine empire. The book seems to have been quite popular and went through several reprints. One of these was done at Lyons in 1549. There seems little reason to doubt that this was the edition by which Nostradamus was inspired. The two opening quatrains of the Centuries provide his magic formulas for prophesying. They happen to be an almost literal translation from passages of Jamblichus. Buget noted another near-literal translation in the Preface.

We may therefore discard divine inspiration and hereditary powers as mere vainglorious façades. The two principal foundation stones for his prophecies are magic and astrology. From the evidence we have, it would seem that when the spirit moved him, Nostradamus would go up to his secret study, lock himself in, get out all his magic paraphernalia including brass bowl, tripod and laurel branch, and proceed to go through the demon-evoking formulas prescribed by Jamblichus.

What happened next is a matter of opinion and interpretation. The more superstitious might say that he did actually evoke some sort of spirit. The more modern minds will hold that he induced a state of autohypnosis in which his heated imagination could act. The things which he saw while in this state form the basis of his prophecies. It is not at all unlikely that his subconscious drew, *in part,* on past events familiar to him.

This then is what Nostradamus openly referred to as hereditary powers and divine inspiration, what he actually believed to be the revelation of his demon, and what we would now call the product of his subconscious mind. [For more than a score of years, the rabid anti-Nostradamian of Saint-Rémy, Dr. Leroy, has been gathering research for a *magnum opus* to prove that the real inspiration for Nostradamus was the grape, and that he was in effect an "old wino" who scribbled down historical and personal recollections just before he passed out dead drunk. Dr. Leroy has already written and read various academic papers to this effect, and inspired the Nostradamus book of Busquet (1950).]

Once out of his hypnotic state, it was necessary to determine the inter-relationship, temporal and geographic, of various things that he "saw." For this he turned to judicial astrology, which he had long since mastered. Supposing that he had "seen" an event which seemed to indicate a disaster for an Italian seaport, he might then cast horoscopes for Venice, Genoa, et al. If one of these horoscopes reflected an impending calamity, the question was then resolved for him. According to his own claims, through astrology he could fix the temporal relationship between separate events as well, to decide which combination of events should be placed together in individual quatrains. His claim that he could have dated each quatrain, made in the Epistle, is hardly substantiated by the few attempts at actual dates he made. There still remains one to be tested, but on the whole they have served to endanger rather than increase his reputation as a prophet.

The result of this labor so far would be brief notes. The next step was to turn these notes into suitably obscured verses, in the best tradition of oracles if not poets. There is some evidence to indicate that the verses were turned out first in Latin and then translated, almost verbatim, into a language basically French, but with much Latin remaining, not to mention other admixtures. Finally, because there was still some continuity, the verses had to be rearranged. For lack of more exact knowledge, we may assume that each was put on a piece of paper, which was in turn placed in a basket and mixed up with the others. The order in which they were withdrawn was the order of the Centuries. However, this rule, like most, has an exception: there are a few "series" of consecutive quatrains.

The source of Nostradamus' inspiration has been a very controversial issue amongst commentators and critics down through the ages. Many theories have come forth. At best, there can be no final, positive proof as to what was his inspiration. However, the theory we have presented is most in accord with both the facts available and common sense.

The Nature of the Prophecies

In his Preface, Nostradamus states that his prophecies cover events in Europe and parts of Asia and Africa from 1555 to 3797. However, the occurrence of the date 1792 near the end of his prose outline in the Epistle seems to indicate that in his own mind, he did not actually even think he saw beyond the 20th century. There remains, of course, the possibility that 3797 is not A.D. 3797 but 3,797 years after some other event. This, however, seems rather farfetched. In any event, it has always been assumed that 3797 is Nostradamus' nomination for the Last Year, the end of the world.

Quite naturally enough, most of the quatrains which mention place names mention French names. Nostradamus is first, and above all, the Oracle of France. Some of the more reasonable of the commentators have even gone so far as to claim that if no place name is mentioned, the scene is always France. This, however, is a bit too much of a simplification. For instance, a 16th-century writer, prophet or otherwise, who mentions "the Empire" could mean only the Holy Roman Empire, and not a French empire. After France, the scene of most quatrains is Italy. Thereafter, Iberia, England, the Netherlands, Central Europe, the Balkans, North Africa and the Near East share more or less equally. Of Russia, the Middle and Far East and the Americas there is next to nothing. . . .

No one could rightly claim that the meaning of the quatrains is always quite apparent. However, the common view that they either have no meaning at all, or have a meaning so equivocal that they can be applied to almost anything, is far from true. To a large extent, this view has been strengthened by Nostradamus' greatest propagandists who, in an effort to glorify his name, have twisted many prophecies to an application for which they could never have been intended, thus serving only to discredit him.

Thus we find that if Nostradamus mentions a pestilence, some will say he is referring to a religious war. If he mentions Byzantium, some will say he means Paris and others will claim he is referring to the Habsburg Empire. But if we stick to the reasonable view that when he says pestilence he means disease and when he says Byzantium he means Constantinople or Turkey, most of his quatrains will be found generally specific and comprehensible. Although there are indeed some quatrains that are very vague, very general or even meaningless, an overwhelming proportion of them do predict a certain combination of historical events. But alas, not many of the events seem to have occurred since 1555, or are likely to occur any more now.

A rather striking matter in the study of Nostradamus'

prophecies is the variation in his outlook as expressed in the prose outline of the Epistle and his outlook as expressed in the quatrains. We have already mentioned that the prose outline seems to indicate greater and greater glories for Catherine's brood, while some of the quatrains seem to indicate his conviction that Henry of Navarre would found a new dynasty on the ashes of the extinct-to-be Valois dynasty. This deviation provides an excellent example of the relative success of each of these two samples of his prophetic powers.

It seems that in the huge mass of predictions that can be found in the prose outline, there is not a single successful prophecy. The dating of two calamities [1732 as the culmination of upheavals of nature and famine that would practically wipe out the human race; 1792 as the culmination of a long and savage religious persecution] serves to discredit him completely in this work. On the other hand, in the verse quatrains, where he rarely binds himself with any temporal bonds, there occur some successful predictions which, if lucky guesses, are very lucky indeed. This is not to deny that the quatrains also contain some quite clear predictions that were never realized and are never likely to be. Outstanding is the oft-mentioned series involving the new Charlemagne named Henry, of the House of France. Although one cannot say positively that he won't still come, the chances of a French Restoration are now not much better than the chances of the election of a Bolshevik Pope. At best it can be said of Nostradamus as a prophet that he occasionally had a successful "vision" of *what* would happen, but never of *when* anything would happen.

The bulk of the quatrains deal with disasters of various sorts. The disasters include plagues, earthquakes, wars, floods, invasions, murders, droughts, battles and many other themes. Some quatrains cover these in over-all terms; others concern a single person or small group of persons. Some cover a single town, others several towns in several countries. The more intelligent of the commentators have pointed out the helpful method of tying prophecies together by looking for a repetition of the same phrases, or of enigmatic names. By applying this method, we can piece together most of Nostradamus' dream of the career of the new Charlemagne who was never to come, or the theme of the new Arab empire, or that of the removal of the Papacy from Rome. Each of these three examples, it will be noted, involves a repetition of history, which has proven uncoöperative and has not repeated itself in these instances. Of these three examples, only the removal of the Papacy from Rome stands any chance of still being fulfilled.

Undoubtedly the easiest way for an American to comprehend the style of Nostradamus' quatrains is to examine an "americanized" sample. Most of the supposed imitations of Nostradamus by skeptics have nothing whatsoever in common with his quatrains. If we can imagine a Nostradamus otherwise the same living in the United States in the 1950's, a typical quatrain might run like this (with no attempt at poesy):

> Columbian land thou wilt be much changed
> When the Silver House has the young Seminole:

Detroit, Duquesne, Amsterdam, mortal strife,
Pink plot reddened, atomic terror.

The first thing we notice about the verse is that it is tightly packed, full of specific elements, however obscure. An intelligent commentator writing some score years later would be able to point out certain salient facts that might throw light on it. "Columbian land" is of course just a poetic device for America, as in "Hail, Columbia." "The Silver House" is an obscurification of the White House and thus the subject of line 2 is a president. The Seminole Indians live in Florida; therefore, either the President referred to is a native of Florida, or someone actually having Seminole blood is involved.

Fort Duquesne was the ancient name of Pittsburgh. New York was formerly called New Amsterdam. Therefore line 3 concerns bloodshed at three major cities, Detroit, Pittsburgh and New York.

As for line 4, it would be pointed out that the prophet lived in a day when two of the chief subjects were communism and the atomic bomb. These two factors are somehow involved in the last line. Perhaps the meaning is that a project of left-wing liberals would be made use of by deep-dyed "Reds," and that this project would be connected with some atomic weapon.

This would be a sensible interpretation, providing as much information as possible, albeit far from a perfect explanation of what the prophet had in mind.

To match the inane commentators, we would have something like this (with an assurance that all names are purely fictional): The verse refers to Columbus, Ohio. It was fulfilled last year. At about the same time that a hotel that had a ballroom called the Silver Room had a Seminole Indian registered at the hotel, Mr. D. U. Kane (Duquesne), a prominent attorney, got into a fight (mortal strife). His father was from Michigan (Detroit) and his mother's mother came from Belgium, which is next to Holland (Amsterdam). A third event took place the same week: some hoodlums broke up a leftist meeting, and in the terrible confusion that followed, many people thought an atomic bomb had exploded.

Nostradamus' Rules of the Game

Until the 19th century, a proper understanding of the prophecies of Nostradamus required an enormous amount of learning, including mastery of Latin, Greek, Old French, classical and medieval geography and some Provençal. In short, the reader was required to have the same knowledge that Nostradamus had.

But in the last hundred years such vast strides have been taken in the cataloguing of human knowledge in convenient reference books that there now remains very little in the text of the prophecies that has not been clarified, or cannot be clarified. When Le Pelletier wrote his edition during the Second Empire, he already had many tools to work with in compiling his Nostradamian glossary. Today we have many more.

Nostradamus states in several places in his Preface and Epistle that he had deliberately obscured his prophecies and veiled them as heavily as possible. Why he did so is no mystery at all, and any reasonable person will think of many reasons: to avoid offense to the authorities of Church and State, which might have involved his own summary liquidation; to avoid the inconceivably wicked, not to mention confusing, sacrilege of threatening to interfere with the fulfillment of God's Will by disclosing it clearly in advance; and perhaps also because of every prophet's quite human desire to reduce the number of his failures to a minimum by use of mysterious and confusing terminology. The important question is then not *why* but *how* Nostradamus goes about this. These seem to be the principal answers:

1. The innumerable glaring examples of Latin syntax seem to offer satisfactory substantiation for the theory that the quatrains were first written in Latin, perhaps from a rough draft in French. What kind of Latin? We find an example in one quatrain that was left in Latin, the "Incantation Against Inept Critics," found at the end of Century VI. Some commentators call it liturgical Latin, others just Low Latin. Jean Leroux in his Clef (1712) came forth with something much more specific. He was convinced that Nostradamus had read a book called *Progymnasmata in artem oratorium* by Franciscus Sylvius, professor at the University of Paris. This book, printed in 1528, set forth in the greatest detail how to produce the most elegant Latin. Leroux cites chapter and verse of Sylvius' book for ten instances in which his precepts have been followed in this one quatrain alone.

The French translation of this "elegant" Latin is virtually verbatim. This means that Latin syntax, not French syntax, prevails. It means, for instance, that an ablative absolute construction loses its identity as such in uninflected French, and yet requires the translation of an ablative absolute.

By this theory it would seem that the proper sense of the quatrains could best be derived by translating them back, verbatim, into Latin. In his bilingual *Janus* in 1594, Chavigny did indeed give many of the quatrains in Latin, without, however, much more sense being made by them by anyone. Perhaps Chavigny, excellent classics scholar that he was, did not use the proper Latin. Or perhaps the theory is worthy of but limited application. In any case, this theory must be kept in mind, even if its application by no means makes the quatrains much clearer.

2. Although the quatrains are nominally translated into French about 5 per cent of the words are not recognizable as French today. About 2.8 per cent of the vocabulary is merely frenchified Latin (with slight changes in the endings) if not pure Latin. Another 2.1 per cent consists of Old French words. The remaining 0.1 per cent consists of words of Greek or Provençal origin. Le Pelletier mentions Spanish, Italian, Celtic and Hebrew as the source of many words, but there is only one Hebrew word (1096), a sentence in Spanish (1025), and nothing from the other two tongues that could not be derived as well or better from Latin or Old French. Perhaps the biggest source of confusion is in connection with words identical with French words, but which the context shows to have another derivation. Thus the word *pont* means "bridge" in French, but

we find Nostradamus using it to mean "sea," from the Greek *pontos,* or "Papacy" from the Latin *pontifex* (and derivatives). Although *pie* means "magpie" in French, Nostradamus used it as a derivative of the Latin *pius,* "pious."

3. Anagrams were all the rage in Nostradamus' day. It is quite reasonable that he should have made use of them. Thus *Chyren* is put for "Henry" (Henryc-us), *Nersaf* for "France," *Rapis* for "Paris," *noir* for *roy,* "king," and *Mendosus* for "Vendosme" (the actual Bourbon subbranch that came to the throne). In the anagrams latitude is provided by the interchangeability of *y* and *i, u* and *v, s* and *c, i* and *j.* The use of silent *s* instead of a circumflex and similar variations of form in accentation must also be noted. Although the perfect anagram required the use of the same letters, Nostradamus seems to have allowed himself the change of one letter, but never more than one.

Similar to the use of anagrams is the use of enigmas. Prominent amongst these are *Aenobarbe,* which means Bronzebeard but is also the family name of Antichrist Nero, symbol of pagan wickedness; the *Pourceau Mihomme,* which means "pig-half-man"; and various gentlemen named after Roman gods, like Jupiter, Mars and Saturn.

4. Mythological and historical allusions veil several quatrains. One quatrain refers to the story of Bellerophon and Proetus, another to that of Jupiter and Phaeton. In the Epistle someone is called a second Thrasibulus, so we must know that this gentleman was the leader of the popular party at Athens who restored the democracy in 403 B.C. and is therefore the symbol of a radical demagogue.

5. References to many places are veiled by use of their classical names or origin. Thus we find *Port Phocen* for Marseilles, founded by the Phoceans; *Byzantium* for Constantinople or Istanbul; *Agatha* for Agen; *Lutetia* for Paris; *Bastarnia* for Poland; *Hister* for the Danube; *Pannonia* for Hungary; *Lusitania* for Portugal and many, many others.

6. Nostradamus makes ample use of devices variously considered as grammatical, poetical or rhetorical, and derived chiefly from Latin or Greek usage. Chief amongst these are—

> a) ELLIPSIS, the omission of words which are understood. Thus *qui* is used frequently for *ce qui,* "he who."
>
> b) SYNECDOCHE, the part standing for the whole. Thus sword stands for army at times, or Paris may stand for France. A common non-Nostradamian contemporary example is "the Kremlin" for the U.S.S.R. However, this has been carried too far by some interpreters in twisting simple statements into farfetched images.
>
> c) HYPERBATON, the transposition or inversion of the natural order. This is found throughout. The dividing line between it and the previously mentioned use of Latin syntax is rather blurry.
>
> d) APOCOPE, the omission of the last letter or syllable. In Nostradamus, this amounts to ab-

breviation. We find *Carpen* for Carpentras, *Ast* for Asti, *Carcas* for Carcassonne, etc.

e) SYNCOPE, the omission of a letter or syllable from the middle of a word. Thus *donra* is used for *donnera*, *lairra* for *laissera*, *monstra* for *monstrera* and *Tamins* for *Tamisiens* (those of the Thames).

f) APHERESIS, the omission of a letter or syllable from the beginning of a word. Thus, *versé* is used for *renversé*, "overthrown."

g) EPENTHESIS, the insertion of a letter or syllable in the middle. Thus we find *Timbre* for *Tibre*, the Tiber River.

h) PROSTHESIS, the insertion of an extra letter at the beginning of a word. Thus, *Aspire* is put for *Spire*, a city in Bavaria.

i) METATHESIS, the transposition of letters or syllables. Thus *Ucetia* is used for *Uticensia*, Latin name for the town of Uzès.

Within this framework, the majority of the words and phrases make sense, and follow some sort of pattern. Nevertheless, Leroux's view that all the quatrains are actually the epitome of polished literature and contain no barbarities is carrying things a bit too far. There are many instances where an adjective does not agree with a noun it obviously modifies and where a plural verb has a singular subject, or vice versa. In this connection, Parker has made a worth-while comment:

> The obscurity imparted to the Centuries by the willful use of anagrams, apocopation, prosthesis, epenthesis, and other disfigurations of the written word is intensified by the numerous typographical errors which could not fail to creep into the versions printed from manuscript copies. In some cases the misprint was due to the illegibility of the original; in others it was due to the desire of the compositor to rectify what seemed to him incorrect; in the rest it was due to the ordinary mechanical difficulties to which any printing is subject. Moreover, such is the nature of the work that, in the absence of any original manuscript or authentic corrected edition, it is impossible to establish the true reading for many varying passages, for the logical word, or rather, the obvious one, is by no means necessarily the correct one. . . . As a rule, it is seldom that a slight change will make any considerable difference in the meaning, except for fantastic interpretations.

As Nostradamus himself says, the quatrains are composed out of "a poetic furor, rather than according to the strict rules of poetry." No one will argue this point, for as a poet Nostradamus hardly ranks very high. The meter is basically iambic pentameter, with varying "male" and "female" lengths in the alternating pairs of lines. However, there are instances where, notwithstanding all the crabbed twists, the lines don't scan properly.

Punctuation does not seem to have been particularly dear to his heart. What punctuation there is is probably the work of zealous printers, who manifested wide disagreement. Nostradamus' aversion to punctuation is particular-ly distressing in the case of the long-drawn-out Preface, and the even longer Epistle.

James Laver   (essay date 1973)

SOURCE: "Nostradamus and Napoleon I," in *Nostradamus; or, The Future Foretold,* revised edition, George Mann, 1973, pp. 165-89.

[*In the following chapter from a reprint of the 1973 edition of his* Nostradamus; or, The Future Foretold, *Laver interprets sections of the* Centuries *which have been cited by other commentators as concerning the rise, progress, and fall of Napoleon Bonaparte.*]

The French Revolution looms very large in the *Centuries.* It is not perhaps surprising that the career of Napoleon occupies an even larger place. Napoleon was just the kind of fatidic figure to appeal to the Prophet, and indeed a prophet would hardly be worth the name who, concerning himself with French history, should fail to foresee the rise of Bonaparte. But there is foreseeing and foreseeing, and the reader who has followed the argument thus far will feel that he has a right to expect not only a general outline but a wealth of detail concerning the achievements of the Man of Destiny. He will not be disappointed.

Nostradamus begins at the beginning:

> *Un Empereur naistra pres d'Italie,*
> *Qui à l'Empire sera vendu bien cher:*
> *Diront avec quels gens il se ralie,*
> *Qu'on trouvera moins prince que boucher.*

An Emperor will be born near Italy who will cost the Empire dear; when it is seen with what people he allies himself he will be found less like a prince than a butcher. The last line recalls the estimate of Cromwell—*Plus Macelin que Roy,* more like a butcher than a king. There is indeed a curious parallelism in the mind of the Prophet between the two men, as we shall see more clearly when considering another quatrain. The lines quoted above, of course, might refer to one of the Holy Roman Emperors. They *might,* although it is difficult to think of one. They certainly fit Napoleon. And more is to follow:

> *Du plus profond de l'Occident d'Europe,*
> *De pauvres gens un jeune enfant naistra,*
> *Qui par sa langue seduira grande troupe,*
> *Son bruit au regne d'Orient plus croistra.*

In the extreme west of Europe a child will be born of poor parents who will seduce by his speech a great army; his renown will grown greater in the Kingdom of the East. Napoleon was born on August 15th, 1769, in Corsica which is not in the *extreme* west of Europe, although it might seem so by contrast with 'the Kingdom of the East'. The effectiveness of his proclamations to his troops is well known. The reference in the last line is to the campaign in Egypt which so much increased his growing fame.

If this is still not quite satisfactory, we are given a hint of his name:

> *D'un nom farouche tel proferé sera,*
> *Que les trois seurs auront fato le nom:*
> *Puis grand peuple par langue & faict duira,*

*Entrance to Nostradamus's home,
in Salon de Provence.*

Plus que nul autre aura bruit & renom.

The vocable of his name will be as terrible as that which the Three Fates (*les trois saeurs*) received from Destiny (*fato,* from *fatum,* Latin, Destiny). He will lead (*duira* from *duco, ducere*) a great people by his words and his deeds; more than any other he will have fame and renown.

The second part is plain sailing, but why a *nom farouche?* Was the astounding Nostradamus really thinking of that Angel of the Abyss in the Apocalypse, the Destroyer, whom the Jews called Abaddon and the Greeks Apollyon?

Le Pelletier even goes further and suggests $N\eta$—$\alpha\pi o\lambda\lambda\nu\omega\nu$, Verily-the-Exterminator, and to support his claim points out that the η is not arbitrary and is in fact found sculptured on the base of the column in the Place Vendôme:

NEAPOLIO. IMP. AUG.
MONUMENTUM. BELLI. GERMANICI.
ANNO MDCCCV.

Certainly it is just the kind of play upon words in which Nostradamus would have delighted if he could have foreseen—but we are catching ourselves out in an absurdity. Who knows what he could not foresee? He was certainly much preoccupied with the question of the Great Man's name.

> *Du nom qui oncques ne fust au roy gaulois*
> *Jamais ne fut un foudre si craintif.*
> *Tremblant l'Italie, l'Espagne et les Anglois,*

De femme estrange grandement attentif.

Of a name which no King of France had before him never was a thunderbolt so fearful, causing to tremble, Italy, Spain and the English. He will be greatly attentive to a foreign woman.

No ruler of France had borne a new name since Francis I, before Nostradamus was born. Napoleon was the first to do so. The second and third lines explain themselves and the 'foreign woman' can be either the creole Josephine, the Austrian Marie Louise, or the Polish Marie Walewska.

We have seen the tricks which Nostradamus liked to play with names and also his delight in nicknames. He has a nickname for Napoleon; he calls him Teste Raze—Shavenhead, the man whose hair was so short by comparison with that of the Kings of the *Ancien Régime.*

> *De la cité marine & tributaire*
> *La teste raze prendra la satrapie:*
> *Chasser sordide qui puis sera contraire;*
> *Par quatorze ans tiendra la tyrannie.*

The man with short hair will assume power (*la satrapie*) in the marine city, tributary of the enemy. He will chase away the mercenary who afterwards (*puis* for *depuis*) will be against him and he will hold absolute power for fourteen years.

Bonaparte recaptured Toulon from the English in December, 1973; it was his earliest success as a commander and after it his reputation and his power grew steadily. The *sordides* in question may be either these same English (a pre–echo if the phrase be not an absurdity of Napoleon's 'Nation of Shopkeepers') or else the members of the Directory, who were certainly mercenary enough. He held absolute power from the *'Coup d'Etat of 18 Brumaire',* 1799, to his abdication in 1814—fourteen years.

In 1795 the star of Napoleon had risen, but it still glimmered at the horizon. In the year following the recapture of Toulon he set out on that Italian campaign which gave his contemporaries their first taste of his qualities as a general.

> *Terre Italique près des monts tremblera. . . .*

The Italian territory near the mountains (i. e. Lombardy) will tremble. At Milan Bonaparte addressed to his troops one of his first proclamations. The Austrians retired without defending the city and the French entered in triumph.

> *Avant l'assaut l'oraison prononcée,*
> *Milan prins d'Aigle par embusches deceus,*
> *Muraille antique par canons enfoncée,*
> *Par feu et sang à mercy peu receus.*

Before the assault the oration will be pronounced; Milan deceived by ambushes, taken by the Eagle; the ancient wall broken down by cannon in the midst of fire and blood, few will receive mercy.

The second part of the quatrain is thought to refer to Pavia, the inhabitants of which rose against the French. The wall was pierced by a bombardment and the city given over to fire and slaughter.

At Villa-Nova Bonaparte became anxious. The Directoire at home left him without orders and without support. In order to save his army he was compelled to fight at Arcola, joining himself in the hand-to-hand struggle on the bridge. He took Mantua, but treated its defender with generosity. Nostradamus comments:

> *A Cité neufve pensif pour condamner,*
> *L'oisel de proye au ciel se vient offrir,*
> *Après victoire à captif pardonner,*
> *Cremone et Mantoue grands maux aura à souf-*
> *frir.*

At Villa-Nova (the new city) Bonaparte's thought condemns those who have placed him in extremity. The bird of prey offers itself to heaven (by risking its own life). After the victory the captive is pardoned. Cremona and Mantua (i. e. the north of Italy) suffer much in these campaigns.

L'oisel de proye is interesting. In another quatrain Nostradamus calls Bonaparte 'the son of the falcon' (*fils de l'aisnier*). 'Young eagle' seems to have been the idea in his mind, in these days before Bonaparte had reached his full stature.

His boundless ambition, unsatisfied by his Italian conquests, turned its eyes eastward, to Egypt, and the Directoire, partly perhaps to get rid of a general whose growing stature had begun to alarm them, agreed to the fitting out of an expedition against that country. That Nostradamus was aware of the order of these events seems to be shown by the following:

> *Grand Po grand mal pour Gaulois recevra,*
> *Vaine terreur au maritin Lyon,*
> *Peuple infiny par la mer passera*
> *Sans eschapper le quart d'un million.*

The great river Po (i. e. the north of Italy) will receive great harm for (the ambition of) a warrior of Gaul. Vain terror to the maritime Lion. A large number of men will pass by sea, and a quarter of a million of these will never return (will be without escape).

Bonaparte set sail for Egypt with a large army. The second line may mean that his preparations caused vain terror to the English (the maritime Lion) or else that the presence of the British fleet in the Gulf of Lions caused terror to Bonaparte—vain terror because it did not succeed in stopping him.

The first act of the French expedition was to seize Malta, then held by the Knights of Rhodes.

> *Proche de Malthe, Herodde prinse vive,*
> *Et Romain sceptre sera par Coq frappé.*

Near the time (*proche*) when the Roman sceptre shall be smitten by the Cock, Malta will be taken.

By the Treaty of Tolentino (in February of the previous year) the Pope had ceded part of the States of the Church to France. 'Herodde' needs some explanation. Is it a portmanteau word composed of heroes and Rhodes? *'Vive'* would seem to imply that Malta was captured suddenly, or without much bloodshed.

The British, however, were hot on Bonaparte's trail, and

their ships coming from the Adriatic entirely destroyed the French fleet at the Battle of Aboukir.

> *Naufrage à classe près l'onde Hadriatique,*
> *La terre esmeuë sur l'air en terre mis,*
> *Egypt tremble augment Mahometique,*
> *L'Heraut rendre à crier est commis.*

The meaning is not as clear as it might be but the sense seems to be as follows: Shipwreck to the fleet near the Adriatic wave; the earth is convulsed in the air and thrown to earth again; tremble Egypt; the power of Mahomet grows; the herald is sent to demand surrender.

The second line is explained by Elisée du Vignois, who says that 'the disembarked French army was terrified to learn that the admiral's vessel had been blown up and that its fragments strewed the shore.' The herald mentioned in the last line is the one sent to demand the surrender of Acre. This was refused and Bonaparte was compelled to raise the siege.

The ill-success of the expedition was plain to Nostradamus:

> *Si France passes outre mer Lygustique,*
> *Tu te verras en isles et mers enclos,*
> *Mahomet contraire, plus mer Hadriatique,*
> *Chevaux et d'asnes tu rongeras les os.*

France, if you pass the Gulf of Genoa (*Lygusticum mare*) you will find yourself besieged in the islands and on the seas. Mahomet will be against you and even more the Adriatic sea (i. e. the British fleet mentioned in the previous quatrain) and you will be driven to gnaw the bones of horses and asses.

The French, having set out on the Egyptian expedition, found the Turks against them and the British fleet. They were besieged in Malta and at Alexandria and suffered cruelly from hunger.

Still addressing France, Nostradamus warns her never to undertake such an expedition again:

> *De l'entreprinse grande confusion,*
> *Perte de gens thresor innumerable,*
> *Tu n'y dois faire encore extension,*
> *France à mon dire fais que sois recordable.*

From this enterprise will come great confusion with loss of men and countless treasure; you should not attempt such expansion there again. France! see that you remember my words.

It may be objected that there is no proof that this quatrain refers to the expedition to Egypt, but it follows the one above quoted, and seems to be linked with it. It is perhaps worth including as a curiosity. The quatrain concerning the return of Bonaparte is a little more definite:

> *Le chef qu'aura conduit peuple infiny*
> *Loing de son ciel, de moeurs et langue estrange,*
> *Cinq mil en Crete et Thessalie finy,*
> *Le chef fuyant sauvé en marine grange.*

The chief who shall have conducted a large army (*peuple infiny* links the quatrain with II, 94, quoted above: *Peuple infiny par mer passera*) far from the skies of home in a land of strange manners and language, shall have in the end five thousand in Crete and Thessaly. He himself shall be saved by flight in a 'marine grange'.

The final phrase is very clumsy and seems dictated by the rhyme. A marine grange or barn is of course a wooden ship. Bonaparte succeeded in eluding the British fleet and landing in France. His army, reduced to five thousand men, was left in the hands of the Turks, masters of Crete and Thessaly (where there had just been a massacre of the French). The British consented to transport these men back to France.

Such was the famous Expedition to Egypt, and the strange thing is that instead of shattering Bonaparte's reputation for ever it actually seemed to enhance it. During his absence the Directoire had fallen into considerable discredit and he saw that the time had come to seize power for himself. He did so by the *Coup d'Etat of 18 Brumaire* (November 9th, 1799).

We now come to a very odd quatrain. It is written not in French but in Provençal, a language which was probably spoken by Nostradamus in his daily intercourse with the people of Salon.

> Lou grand eyssame se lèvera d'abelhos,
> Que non sauran don te siegen venguddos.
> De nuech l'embousq lou gach dessous las treilhos,
> Ciutad trahido per cinq lengos non nudos.

There will arise a great swarm of bees and no one will know from whence they come. The ambush will be set during the night; the Jay will instal himself in the trellises, and the City will be betrayed by five tongues not naked.

An impenetrable allegory? But let us examine it a little more closely. There will arise a great swarm of bees. If you go to Fontainebleau, or walk through the rooms of Malmaison decorated by Napoleon, you will see it still, that swarm of bees, settled thickly on carpet and wall-hanging and covering even the silk backs of the chairs. Bees were the Napoleonic emblem; they stand also here for the swarm of his relatives which arrived no one knew whence, and settled all over Europe. The ambush is the *coup d'état* of 18 Brumaire, prepared during the previous night. It succeeded, Napoleon took up his quarters in the Tuileries, and, like the jay in the fable who decked himself in the peacock's feathers, was thus invested with some of the splendour of the old Kings of France. *Treilhos* is the anagram of Tholries, a pun on Tuileries. How Nostradamus must have chuckled as he thought that out, and how the modern commentator must wish that he hadn't! The five 'tongues' are the five talkers or politicians who delivered Paris to Napoleon, and they are not naked because they wore their robes as members of the Directory.

Having seized power, as above related, he forced the Great St Bernard pass into Italy and made himself all-powerful there also. Nostradamus comments:

> L'Oriental sortira de son siege,
> Passer les monts Appenons, voir la Gaule,
> Transpercera le ciel, les eaux et neige,
> Et un chacun frappera de sa gaule.

The Man of the East will leave his place (the one assigned to him by the Directory in the hope of getting rid of him, and where he had had to submit to a siege by the English) to pass by Italy (the Apennines) and see France again. He will pierce heaven, the water, and the snows (by crossing the Alps) and will smite everyone with the point of the spear (gaule). By itself the quatrain would be unconvincing, but it serves to fill out the picture which Nostradamus is painting of Bonaparte's progress towards Empire.

> De soldat simple parviendra en empire,
> De robbe courte parviendra à la longue:
> Vaillant aux armes, en Eglise, où plus pyre,
> Vexer les prestres comme l'eau fait l'esponge.

From being just a soldier he attained to the Empire, from the short robe (the Consular robe was short) he attained to the long (the Imperial mantle was long). Valiant in arms, in ecclesiastical matters he was not so successful and he vexed the clergy by alternately elevating them and depressing them (as water swells up a sponge and then leaves it limp and flabby).

Napoleon proclaimed himself Emperor on May 18th, 1804. France was soon to discover his insatiable appetite for conquest:

> Par teste raze viendra bien mal eslire
> Plus que sa charge ne porte passera.
> Si grand fureur et rage fera dire
> Qu'a feu et sang tout sexe tranchera.

In Shaven-head France will come to see that she has made a very bad choice; she will be saddled with a burden (*charge*) beyond her power to carry. He will be animated with such a warlike fury as to make men say that one sex (the whole male population of Europe) would be, by blood and fire, cut off. Comment is needless.

Napoleon himself took a considerable interest in prophecy. He consulted soothsayers in Egypt and some commentators profess to believe that he was acquainted with the 'Prophecy of Olivarius' and the so-called *Prophétie d'Orval*, both of which have been rashly attributed to Nostradamus. They are, in all probability, post-Napoleonic forgeries and we need not here be concerned with them further. But of the prophecies of Nostradamus himself he was certainly aware and if he had not been they would have been brought to his notice by a flattering piece of propaganda issued in Paris in 1806.

This was *Nouvelles Considérations puisées dans la Clairvoyance Instinctive de l'Homme, sur les Oracles, les Sibylles et les Prophéties, et particulièrement sur Nostradamus Par Théodore Bouys, Ancien professeur à l'école centrale du départment de la Nièvre, et avant la révolution, président de l'élection de Nevers.*

The author professed to reveal to his readers the marvels of Magnetism and the instinctive clairvoyance procured by *somnambulisme magnétique*, that instinctive clairvoyance which he declares made known to Nostradamus 'the brilliant destinies of Napoleon the Great, which are to enjoy a long and happy reign, to bring lasting peace to the Continent, to be one day as redoubtable on the sea as he is on land, and to conquer England in order to give to all nations the Freedom of the Seas.'

About an eighth of the work only is devoted to Nostradamus, the rest being concerned with other prophecies, and with considerations on the 'voices' of Joan of Arc and of 'magnetism' in general, but his remarks on the Prophet of Salon gain a certain piquancy by his own strong Bonapartist opinions and the period at which he wrote. His handling is scholarly and not too credulous, and he makes the suggestion (interesting in a schoolmaster of the period) that it is the vice of modern education to prevent the development of certain instinctive faculties which are common enough among less civilized people. He cites the famous quatrain concerning the Flight to Varennes, and adds:

> I owe the explanation of this quatrain, and many others, to an inhabitant of Nevers who has composed a long and interesting commentary on Nostradamus. M. de Vaudeuil, son of the former president of the *parlement* of Toulouse, communicated several to me and I have taken a dozen or more from the old commentators. Without the reading of the work of M. Mxxx which he was good enough to give to his friends, I would never have understood more than five or six quatrains. I would never have thought of opening Nostradamus. All that is found of interest (in my own work) I owe to the private conversations I have had with my compatriot, my old study-companion, who before the revolution had become *promoteur* of the archbishopric of Paris and is now manager and owner of a porcelain factory.

The long and interesting commentary by the mysterious Mxxx, inhabitant of Nevers, seems never to have been published, and research has so far failed to establish his identity, but the passage is of value as showing the interest in Nostradamus at the time, and the fact that contemporaries saw in the events of the French Revolution the fulfilment of some of his prophecies.

After dealing with various quatrains concerning Louis XVI Bouys turns to the 'Predictions of Nostradamus on Napoleon, Emperor of the French, of which some, already accomplished, are a presumption and indeed ought to be an assurance that the remainder will be accomplished also.'

He cites several verses, including:

> *Heureux au règne de France, heureux de vie . . .*

which is now usually referred to Louis XVIII, as it gives him a chance to praise Napoleon for his love of peace (!), and then turns to what is for him the burning question of the moment, the projected invasion of England. Nostradamus had written:

> *Dedans Boulogne voudra laver ses fautes;*
> *Il ne pourra au temple du soleil.*
> *Il volera faisant choses si hautes,*
> *Qu'en hierarchie n'en fut onc un pareil.*

Bouys remarks: 'This quatrain is without doubt one of the most powerful of those written by Nostradamus concerning the Emperor Napoleon. What other prince, in fact, could come to Boulogne to expiate the fault of having been too confident, of having presumed too much on the loyalty of his enemies and their fidelity in the execution of trea-

ties? (The reference is of course to the Peace of Amiens.) What other prince could not succeed in the Temple of the Sun, in Egypt, and yet flies so high that none in all the hierarchy of princes can be considered his equal? Now, he makes formidable preparations at Boulogne and we shall see in the following quatrains that this enterprise will have the greatest success and that the Emperor Napoleon will end by making the conquest of England.' The two quatrains in question are these, and in view of what actually happened, are not without interest:

> *De l'aquilon les efforts seront grands,*
> *Sur l'océan sera la porte ouverte:*
> *Tremblera Londres par voile découverte*
> *Le régne en l'isle sera réintegrant.*
>
> *La forteresse auprès de la Tamise,*
> *Cherra pour lors le roi dedans serré:*
> *Auprès du pont sera vu en chemise,*
> *Un devant mort, puis dans le fort barré.*

We have seen that the first of these, which Bouys quotes incorrectly, reversing the third and fourth lines, can with more likelihood be referred to the expedition of James II to Ireland, aided by the French fleet. The second has never been explained, and may be left to the ingenuity of the reader.

The optimism of the worthy schoolmaster was unjustified, as another quatrain might have told him if he noticed it and had been able to interpret it before the event. It was concerned with nothing less than the Battle of Trafalgar.

> *Entre deux mers dressera promontoire,*
> *Qui puis mourra par le mors du cheval,*
> *Le sien Neptune pliera voile noire,*
> *Par Calpre et classe auprès de Rocheval.*

There is a promontory between two seas; there is one who will die afterwards by the bridle of a horse, and Neptune, for his own, will unfurl the black sail; in the strait of Calpe, when his fleet is near Cape Roche.

Now it would be absurd to pretend that Bouys or any one else could interpret this beforehand. It is none the less extremely curious, for the French admiral Villeneuve was later strangled by the Emperor's Mamelukes whose custom it was to use for such a purpose the bridle of a horse. The other admiral, Neptune's own, the great Nelson himself, fell, as the world knows, in the glorious action and his body was brought back to England, the ship bearing a black sail in sign of mourning. Calpre is the classical Calpe, one of the Pillars of Hercules which we call Gibraltar, and the battle was fought between this and Cape Roche. Trafalgar is itself a promontory between two seas.

Again Nostradamus writes:

> *Après combat et bataille navale,*
> *Le grand Neptune à son plus haut beffroy,*
> *Rouge adversaire de peur viendra pasle,*
> *Mettant le grand Ocean en effroy.*

After the combat and the naval battle, great Neptune (England) will be raised as on a pinnacle. The Red adversary (Napoleon, in the eyes of the Prophet, never ceased to be the revolutionary, the *Rouge*) will grow pale with fear, putting the ocean in a panic. The last line presumably refers to his attempt to institute a blockade against England which, like his naval operations, was a failure.

The fact that we know these things, and know that both Bouys and Napoleon were doomed to disappointment, gives added point to the second half of the Boulogne quatrain. For the Emperor, seeing that the invasion of England was hopeless, wheeled his army about, swept through Europe like a whirlwind and coming up with the two other Emperors, of Austria and Russia, beyond Vienna, won over their combined forces the glorious victory of Austerlitz. 'He will fly so high and do such deeds that in the hierarchy of rulers none will be found his equal.' The abrupt change from failure to triumph staggered Europe and is reflected in the very construction of the prophetic quatrain.

Nostradamus was not a Bonapartist—if the superficial absurdity of the remark may be pardoned—but he regarded Napoleon with a kind of reluctant admiration, rather like that felt by the nineteenth-century French Royalists, and like many of these the Prophet seems to have believed that the Emperor's final misfortunes were a judgement upon him for his treatment of the clergy and, in particular, for his persecution of the Pope.

Nostradamus took considerable interest in the welfare of the Papacy and it is not therefore surprising to find that he devotes several quatrains to its fortunes during the French Revolution and the Empire. In an obscure but extremely interesting quatrain he had written:

> *Istra de mont Gaulfier & Aventin,*
> *Qui par le trou advertira l'armée*
> *Entre deux rocs sera prins le butin,*
> *De SEXT. mansol faillir la renommée.*

Let us take the last two lines first. Between two rocks shall the booty be taken and the renown of *Sext. Mansol* shall fail. Who is *Sext. Mansol? Man. sol.* stands for *manens solus,* the man who lives alone, who has made a vow of celibacy. In other places Nostradamus refers to priests as *les seuls.* Sext. stands for *sextus,* and the priest, *par excellence,* who is also *sextus,* is Pius VI, the *Pastor peregrinus* of the prophecy of Malachy and the only Pontiff to bear that number since the composition of the **Centuries.** By the Treaty of Tolentino of February 19th, 1797, the Pope was deprived of Avignon and of the Romagna and other lands in Italy, the two rocks, as it were, on which his power reposed.

The first two lines of the quatrain are even more curious. The exact construction is difficult to make out, but the words *mont Gaulfier* leap to the attention. For the brothers Montgolfier had invented the air balloon in 1783, and at the Battle of Fleurus in 1794 an attempt was made to use it for military reconnaissance, by suspending, *beneath the hole,* a man in a basket to act as observer (*advertira l'armée*). The result of the battle left Rome (Mount Aventine) open to the Frènch. Whether this interpretation be accepted or not, it seems plain that Nostradamus had 'received' the word Montgolfier (or Mont Gaulfier) two hundred years before the brothers had ever been heard of, and that he had some notion of the construction of their apparatus and some idea of its possibilities in war. Let us return

to the relations between the Papacy and Revolutionary France.

> *Tout à l'entour de la grande cité*
> *Seront soldats logés par champs & villes:*
> *Donner l'assaut Paris Rome incité*
> *Sur le pont lors sera faicte grand pille.*

All around the great city shall soldiers be lodged in fields and towns. Paris being incited to assault Rome, great pillage will be made on the Sovereign Pontiff.

The death of the French general Duphot in a riot gave General Berthier, whose troops surrounded the city, an excuse for an assault on Rome. The Pope was pillaged, being dispossessed of his estates and imprisoned in his palace. He was later taken as a captive to Valence, where he died.

> *Pol mensole mourra trois lieues du Rosne. . . .*

The Great Celibate (*pol.* from the Greek $\pi o \lambda v \delta$, much, *mensole* being the same as *mansol* in the quatrain quoted above) will die three leagues from the Rhone. Valence is in fact on that river which, not far away, at Lyons, is joined by the Saône. Hence Nostradamus writes, with reference to the same event:

> *Romain Pontife garde de t'approcher*
> *De la cité que deux fleuves arrouse.*
> *Ton sang viendra auprès de là cracher,*
> *Toy et les tiens quand fleurira la rose.*

Roman Pontiff, beware of approaching the city (i. e. Lyons) which is bathed by two rivers. You and yours (will be there) when the rose is in bloom.

Pius VI died after violent vomiting on August 29th, 1799. He was accompanied to Valence by thirty-two priests, prisoners like himself, and the reference to the rose may mean that these events took place in the summer. Some commentators see a symbolical meaning, the white lily of legitimacy having given place to the revolutionary red of the rose.

After the death of Pius VI, the cardinals, dispersed by the Revolution, managed, amid many difficulties, to hold a conclave in Venice and elected a new Pope who was known as Pius VII. Meanwhile, Bonaparte had become First Consul.

These events were, in the mind of Nostradamus, closely intertwined.

> *Par l'univers sera faict un monarque*
> *Qu'en paix et vie ne sera longuement,*
> *Lors se prendra la piscature barque,*
> *Sera regie au plus grand detriment.*

A universal monarch will be set up who will not live long in peace; then one will take control of the Fisherman's Boat, and it will be governed to its greatest detriment. The Fisherman's Boat is, of course, the Barque of Peter, the Papacy, the prestige of which suffered by the weakness of the Pope's attitude towards Napoleon. Pius VII came to France for the first time to crown Napoleon Emperor and the second time as his prisoner. The Rapacious Eagle (the *aquila rapax* of the prophecy of Malachy) had him firmly in his claws, and he was only released by the abdication at Fontainebleau. Nostradamus comments:

> *En naviguant captif prins grand Pontife,*
> *Grand après faillir les clercs tumultuez:*
> *Second esleu absent son bien debiffe,*
> *Son favory bastard à mort tué.*

While navigating his Boat the great Pontiff will be taken, and made prisoner. The clergy will be thrown into a tumult. He, the second elected one to be absent from Rome (the first being Pius VI) will dissipate his goods. The illegitimate monarch whom he had favoured by consenting to crown him will be deprived of [political] life.

The States of the Church were incorporated in the Empire in 1809, but the judgement of God was not long to be delayed:

> *Terroir Romain qu'interpretoit Augure,*
> *Par gent Gauloise par trop sera vexée,*
> *Mais nation Celtique craindra l'heure,*
> *Boreas classe trop loing l'avoir poussée.*

The Roman territory governed by him who interprets as Augur (i. e. the successor of the Pontifex Maximus of pagan Rome) will be much troubled by the Gaulish people. But this nation when it has pushed too far (into Russia) shall fear the hour of Boreas, the cold north wind, and its fleet, i. e. the fleet of England (*classe* from the Latin *classis*).

The punishment (to continue this ecclesiastical and apocalyptic interpretation of his history) will be hastened by Napoleon's wickedness in divorcing his first wife, or in terms of the popular legend, Napoleon never had any luck after his abandonment of Josephine.

> *Le divin mal surprendra le grand Prince,*
> *Un peu devant aura femme espousée,*
> *Son appuy et credit à un coup viendra mince,*
> *Conseil mourra pour la teste rasée.*

The punishment of God will fall upon the great Prince; a little before he will have married a wife. The support of his allies and his credit at home will suddenly become very small and Shaven-head will have no good counsel to turn to. If we admit (as we must) that Shaven-head means Napoleon, the quatrain is among the most explicit.

To punish his faithless ally the Emperor Alexander, Napoleon undertook the Campaign of Russia. With an immense army he reached Moscow, the Russians retreating before him. With the old city in flames he was compelled to retreat, and his great plan for a new Roman Empire embracing the whole of Europe (he had just created his infant son King of Rome) crumbled into ruin.

> *Amas s'approche venant d'Esclavonie,*
> *L'Olestant vieux cité ruynera,*
> *Fort désolée verra sa Romanie,*
> *Puis la grande flamme esteindre ne sçaura.*

A great mass of men will be seen coming from the Land of the Slavs (the broken mass of the *Grande Armée* in retreat from Moscow). *L'Olestant,* the Destroyer, will ruin the old city, and he will not know how to put out the great flame. He will see his Roman dream vanish away.

Romanie should not, of course, be confused with Rumania which did not exist at the time. In another quatrain (VIII, 60) Napoleon is referred to as

> *Premier en Gaule, premier en Romanie,*

that is, "first in France and in the lands of Rome". *Olestant* is a harking back to the previous word-play on the Greek root for "destroy". Once more we have a quatrain obscure, and even misleading, when taken by itself, but adding to the cumulative effect.

The ill-success of the *Grande Armée* in Russia showed Europe that Napoleon was not invincible. The nations began to rise against him once more, and the Eagle found itself, as it were, surrounded by other birds of prey ready to devour it.

> *L'aigle poussée entour de pavillons,*
> *Par autres oyseaux d'entour sera chassée. . . .*

The eagle pushed back into his own territory (surrounded by his banners) will be pursued by other birds around, that is by the eagles of Russia, Austria, and Prussia. The sound of military music on her own frontiers will bring France to her senses.

> *Quand bruit des cymbres tube & sonnaillons*
> *Rendront le sens de la dame insensée.*

From the south came Wellington, having fought his way through Spain to be welcomed at Bordeaux as a friend rather than a conqueror.

> *Par la Guyenne infinité d'Anglois*
> *Occuperont par nom Anglaquitaine. . . .*

Across Guyenne an infinite number of English soldiers will occupy the old English province of Aquitaine, thus baptizing it anew (a Nostradamian joke!) with the name of Anglaquitaine.

France is assailed from both sides:

> *Tous ceux de Iler seront dans la Moselle,*
> *Mettant à mort tous ceux de Loyre et Seine,*
> *Le cours marin viendra près d'haute velle,*
> *Quand l'Espagnol ouvrira toute veine.*

Those of the Iller (a tributary of the Danube, that is the Austrians) will advance up the valley of the Moselle, slaying the French (those of the Loire and the Seine). The marine torrent (i. e. the English) will come near the high valley (i. e. will pierce the Pyrenees) when the Spaniard shall open every vein. The last line seems to mean that the reconquest of Spain by Wellington opened the road to France. Some commentators have thought that in the strange phrase "haute velle", the Prophet was groping towards the very name of Wellington, but this supposition is quite unnecessary for the explanation of the quatrain.

> *Les cinq estranges entrez dedans le temple,*
> *Leur sang viendra la terre prophaner,*
> *Aux Tholosains sera bien dur example. . . .*

The Five Strangers (i. e. England, Austria, Prussia, Russia and Spain) will enter the temple (i. e. invade the sacred soil of France). Their blood will profane the earth. Nostradamus seems to have heard far in the future the faint strains of the Marseillaise:

> Qu'un sang impur
> Abreuve nos sillons!

The people of Toulouse will be made a hard example. When the bloody battle of Toulouse was fought by Wellington the war was already over but the combatants did not know it.

Napoleon's desperate situation gave him the opportunity of testing the loyalty of those to whom he had given thrones. One of the bitterest blows was the defection of Murat, King of Naples and the Emperor's brother-in-law. Nostradamus knew all about this too:

> Gaulois qu'empire par guerre occupera,
> Par son beau frere mineur sera trahy;
> Par cheval rude voltigeant trainera,
> Du fait le frere long temps sera hay.

The Gaul who by war will gain an Empire, will be betrayed by his youngest brother-in-law; on horseback this hard-riding cavalier will carry all before him; on account of this (treason) the brother will long be hated.

The phrase: *"son beau frere mineur"* should be noted; Murat was in fact the husband of Napoleon's youngest sister. He was also the most dashing cavalry leader in the whole army. His popularity never recovered from his act of betrayal, and Napoleon refused his proffered help at the Battle of Waterloo.

In the spring of 1814 the Allies advanced on Paris:

> Comme un gryphon viendra le Roy d'Europe,
> Accompagné de ceux d'Aquilon,
> De rouges et blancs conduira grand troupe,
> Et iront contre le Roy de Babylon.

Like a gryphon will come the King of Europe, accompanied by those of the North; he will conduct a great army of the reds and the whites and they will go up against the King of Babylon.

The "King of Europe" means either the King who is recognized by the whole of Europe, or the legitimate King of the noblest throne in Europe. Paris is called Babylon in several quatrains and the King of Babylon is Napoleon. These symbolisms detract from the effect of the quatrain and it would not have been quoted here but for its third line. The great army of "reds" and "whites" are the English and the Austrians whose tunics were respectively red and white.

The rapacious monarch whose power had sprung from the Revolution was now tracked to his lair:

> Avec le noir Rapax et sanguinaire,
> Yssu du peaultre de l'inhumain Neron
> Emmy deux fleuves. . . .

In the **Centuries,** as we have seen, *"noir"* always means *roi* or monarch. The adjective Rapax is interesting. In the prophecy of Malachy, Napoleon, the persecutor of Pius VII, is called *Aquila Rapax,* the greedy eagle. *Peaultre* means rudder, hence government, and "the inhuman Nero" is of course the Revolution already referred to as

acting *"pis que ne fit Neron"*. Emmy deux fleuves, between two streams, means Paris, between Seine and Marne, sometimes called by Nostradamus Babylon or Mesopotamia, which likewise, as its name indicates, lay between two streams, the Euphrates and the Tigris: *"Neufve Babylone, cité libre, assise dans une autre exigue Mesopotamie"*, as he calls the French capital in his Epistle to Henri II. Nostradamus loved these learned circumlocutions.

For a time Napoleon hoped to be able to keep by intrigue the throne he had not been able to preserve by force of arms. The Emperor Alexander was willing to listen but Napoleon had an implacable enemy in Talleyrand:

> De leur senat sacriste fait boiteux,
> Fera scavoir aux ennemis l'affaire.

The senator who is also a priest and lame will reveal the affair to his enemies.

Napoleon went into exile on the Island of Elba, but as every schoolboy knows, the deliberations of the Congress of Vienna, which was to settle the peace of Europe for ever, were interrupted by his unwelcome return. To this world-shattering event the Prophet devoted several quatrains. We shall quote no more than two of them, and unfortunately they are even more than usually marked by that pedantic punning in which Nostradamus took such delight. We must remind ourselves that this learned paronomasia was considered in the sixteenth century to be the very flower of scholarship; and was not thought out of place even on the most serious occasions. In the single phrase which Clément Marot sent to Francis I to console him for the death of his mother there are no less than six puns. The characters of Shakespeare pun when their hearts are breaking—

> Old Gaunt indeed and gaunt in being old.

The indulgence of the reader is asked for the inclusion of quatrains which, in spite of their conceits, are of considerable interest. The impatient sceptic is advised to skip them altogether. The first reads as follows:

> Grand Roy viendra prendre port près de Nisse,
> Le grand empire de la mort si en fera,
> Aux antipolles posera son genisse,
> Par mer la Pille tout esvanouyra.

The Great King will come to port near Nice (city of Niké, Goddess of Victory) but [in spite of that] he will make of his great empire an empire of Death. He will set up his household gods (or his root; some commentators read *genii Lares,* some *genitus*) towards the opposite pole (but probably with a punning reference also to Antibes, which the Ancients called Antipolis, the place "opposite the city" of Nice). The nation above all others given to piracy and pillage (Nostradamus hints elsewhere that this was his opinion of the English) will cause all Napoleon's power to vanish into the sea, by banishing him to St Helena, which being south of the Equator, may be said to lie towards the other pole (*aux antipolles*).

What a farrago! It is like a telegram sent by a miser enamoured of puns and who had had the disadvantage of a classical education. But tiresome as it is, it is not *meaningless.*

Coat of arms of Nostradamus's family.

In fact it has far too much meaning, and it fits the facts of Napoleon's return.

Here is the second quatrain:

> *Au peuple ingrat faictes les remonstrances,*
> *Par lors l'armée se saisira d'Antibe,*
> *Dans l'arc Monech seront les doleances.*
> *Et a Frejus l'un l'autre prendra ribe.*

Remonstrances will be made to the ungrateful People (Louis XVIII issued a proclamation urging fidelity to the new régime which had given them peace; but the only place where the army was faithful to him was Antibes where it seized the town and shut the gates against Napoleon). In the seat of sovereignty there will be lamentation (*arché*, sovereignty and *moné*, dwelling, but with a punning reference to Arké and Monoiké, the ancient names of Hyères and Monaco). And at Fréjus one and the other shall take ship. Louis himself had previously embarked at Fréjus when leaving France; Napoleon embarked there for Elba, and he landed again at Golfe Juan, which is between Fréjus and Antibes, and, of course, near Nice. All these places were well known to Nostradamus himself; during his wanderings in Provence he must have passed through all of them, meditating as he did so on the meaning of their corrupted but still classical names, and seeing in his mind's eye a stout little man in a uniform of a very un-sixteenth-century cut, making a final grasp at a shadowy empire.

And now, leaving aside a dozen quatrains the inclusion of which would have served only to weary and confuse the reader, we come to the Battle of Waterloo.

It is a curious fact that, on those rare occasions when the rebus-verse of Nostradamus rises into poetry, it is inspired by one of the major historical events. he writes:

> *Au mois troisiesme se levant le Soleil,*
> *Sanglier, Leopard, au champ de Mars, pour com-*
> *battre,*
> *Leopard laissé au ciel estend son oeil,*
> *Un Aigle autour du Soleil voit s'esbattre.*

It is such a good stanza that one is tempted to try to translate it into English verse:

> The Hundred Days are past! the hour is nigh,
> Leopard and Boar allied—the fight's begun.
> The Leopard, lonely, lifts an anxious eye—
> An Eagle's wings are blotting out the sun.

Or more literally: At the third month, the sun rising, the Wild Boar and the Leopard are ready to fight on the field of battle. The Leopard, left to himself, lifts his eye to heaven [for help] but sees only a battling eagle against the sun.

The Leopard is, of course, England; the Boar is the brave and headstrong Blücher. But Blücher had been beaten back at Ligny and the junction of the British and Prussians had not taken place when Wellington decided to stand at Waterloo. It was June 18th, 1815, three months, or rather a Hundred Days, after Napoleon's return. All day long his troops battered the English squares while Wellington cast anxious eyes to the horizon hoping for the arrival of his ally to turn the French flank. Up the slope came the flower of Napoleon's army, the Imperial eagles flying. It is astonishing to note that as Wellington faced south he saw them against the sun as Nostradamus had foretold. Then, when the day was nearly over and the British still unbroken, Napoleon saw on his right a cloud of dust. "It is Grouchy", he cried. But it was not Grouchy. It was Blücher.

> *Prest a combattre fera defection,*
> *Chef adversaire obtiendra la victoire,*
> *L'arriere garde fera defension,*
> *Les defaillans mort au blanc territoire.*

He who was ready to fight (Grouchy) will not be present at the battle. The hostile chief (Wellington) will gain the victory. The Imperial Guard, usually kept in reserve in the rear, will make a great defence *(La garde meurt mais ne se rende pas)* and those who fail (that is, the Napoleonic troops) will be either physically or politically dead in a territory which has become once more white, by the restoration of the Bourbons. Paris, says a contemporary, looked as if there had been a fall of snow, there were so many white cockades.

So Napoleon disappeared once more, this time into an exile from which there was no return. And again Nostradamus rises to the occasion.

> *Le grand Empire sera tost translaté*
> *En petit lieu qui bien tost viendra croistre,*
> *Lieu bien infime d'exigue comté*
> *Où au milieu viendra poser son sceptre.*

The commentators here have missed their opportunity. Elisée du Vignois merely remarks: "Napoleon was sent to the Island of Elba, a little country smaller than some counties, the name of which was soon to become celebrated by the treaty which recognized him as its monarch." But Nostradamus saw more clearly than that. He saw the great Empire shrink to a little space (the Island of Elba); he saw it grow again (the Hundred Days), and he saw it shrink once more to nothing but a tiny rock in the middle of the ocean, where at last Napoleon would lay down his sceptre.

So we take leave of Shaven-head, the man with the terrible name of the Destroyer, the Emperor who was born near Italy, the soldier who failed in the Temple of the Sun, the King of Babylon, the fearful Thunderbolt—for all these names does Nostradamus give him. So vanished also the great Swarm of Bees.

David Pitt Francis   (essay date 1984)

SOURCE: "Seer, Scientist, or Biblical Scholar?" in *Nostradamus: Prophecies of Present Times?* The Aquarian Press, 1984, pp. 13-32.

[*In the following excerpt, Pitt Francis engages the question of Nostradamus's legitimacy as a prophet of future events, focusing upon factors that may account for Nostradamus's successful predictions.*]

The Man, and the Enigma

For over four hundred years, with the sole exception of Bible prophecy, no set of predictions has stimulated such an infectious interest as those credited to Nostradamus. They were consulted with religious fervour by some members of the French monarchy, and held in high regard by them until 1781, when they were officially condemned by the Church, by being placed on the *Index Librorum Prohibitorum,* only eight years before the French Revolution. In the nineteenth century, Nostradamus's ten Centuries (sets of a hundred verses each) were denounced as Satanic by Protestant religious fundamentalists, and Nostradamus himself was regarded as something of a witch. The present century has witnessed spasms of revival of interest in his writings, partly because they seemed to provide detailed descriptions of some modern events, such as the atomic bombing of Hiroshima, and partly because of their effect on the course of the Second World War after Hitler had been introduced to them by Frau Goebbels. Hitler's interest is indeed curious. He frowned on the Bible and on Christianity, because of their Jewish origins, yet failed to appreciate that Nostradamus, whose works he seemed to worship, was also a Jew.

Hardly a month passes without the probability that some new event has been pronounced by Nostradamus. For example, quatrain I: 63 foresees a period of relatively safe air travel, followed by 'battles'. Could this be a reference to the advent of air-travel competition, of the kind that forced Sir Freddie Laker into insolvency? If Nostradamus *is* so accurate, then he deserves an answer. . . .

The Centuries

The writings of Nostradamus are virtually unique, because several of his quatrains indisputably relate to events many decades ahead of his own time. In this respect, he differs from the great majority of 'fortune-tellers', who may be able to predict events that are a few years ahead of their predictions but would never pretend to know of events centuries into the future. Most make their predictions about individuals or governments. They must be fulfilled in a single lifetime, and the great majority of personal predictions, from simple premonitions to horoscope readings (using successful data), are fulfilled within an average period of less than thirty years from the time when they are delivered.

There are, of course, some rare exceptions. I have already mentioned the Bible. Some biblical prophecies have very long fulfilment spans. One of the prophecies of Moses in the second millennium BC presented the Jewish nation with a 'thumb-nail' sketch of its history from that period to modern times, including a series of identifiable invasions, its dispersion by the Romans in the first century of our era, and the return to its homeland in the present century. Even if the book of Deuteronomy had been written later than the time of Moses, as some scholars maintain, such a prophecy would still be long-term in its validity. Later Old Testament prophecies in the sixth century BC foretold the destruction of Tyre by Alexander the Great in the fourth century BC in vivid and astonishing detail. A large number of other cases of valid long-term biblical prophecy could be given. Further, the Bible often helped to ignite prophetic foresight in its interpreters, who, though wrong in their interpretations, became valid prophets in their own right when commenting on its prophecies. For example, expositors of the Book of Revelation of John were led by their interpretations to assume, from the early seventeenth century, that the Turkish empire would decline in the nineteenth and twentieth centuries of our era. Well-known writers, such as Joseph Mede and Isaac Newton held these beliefs, and their truth has been confirmed within the past century.

But, other than Nostradamus (and to a *much greater extent* than his writings), the Bible is the only main exception to the theory that most valid prophecies do not have long fulfilment-spans. There are only a handful of other well-researched cases. Buddha, in the sixth century BC, was reputed to have accurately predicted the entry of Buddhism into China in the first century of our era, but there are no manuscripts that survive to prove that the prophecy did not postdate the event, and it was a single prophecy without much detail. In the twelfth century, a Cistercian friend of Bernard of Clairvaux, Malachy of Armagh (1094-1148), predicted the papal succession to the end of the twentieth century, using a series of mottoes, and some of his intuitive flashes were remarkably accurate. But they have little real value in the scientific study of prediction, for it can be reasoned that:

(i) some of the cardinals who are responsible for choosing each successive Pope are aware of Malachy's prophecies;

(ii) it is quite easy for each successor of the papal chair to 'participate' in fulfilling Malachy's prophecies, if he wishes to do so; and

(iii) within a given 'lifetime' it is quite easy to find events that fit each successive 'motto'.

Nostradamus is the great exception to the principle that fulfilment-spans are usually short. No other famous non-biblical prophet produced nearly four thousand lines of closely-packed detail about events centuries beyond his own lifetime. What explanations can be rendered for this remarkable achievement?

His short-term prophecies can be explained, like all other short-term predictions, by simple reference to his own psychic gifts. These are evidenced by the incident that was reputed to have occurred during Nostradamus's visit to Italy in the late 1540s when he addressed a young monk as 'Your Holiness'. The monk, Felice Peretti, within twenty years of Nostradamus's death, became Pope Sextus V. If the story is correct, it is evidence of a 'gift' of personal intuition; but we must be cautious about jumping to a conclusion that these gifts necessarily spring from a knowledge of astrology, the practice of crystal-gazing, or of some other branch of the occult sciences. . . . Nostradamus was as much a scientific astronomer as an astrologer—for his age tended to mix the two sciences—and it would have been difficult for him to have studied the one without also studying the other. Yet he was to some extent, anti-astrological. Not that he tried to debunk astrology—nor would have it been entirely correct for him to have done so, for recent researches suggest a strong correlation between birth-patterns and personal characteristics. But, like the prophets of Israel before him he perceived that astrology was not without its dangers and could lead people into wrong directions, and as most of the astrologers of Nostradamus's times were unreliable, his warnings were even more appropriate.

For example, there are direct warnings, as in VI: 100:

> Let those who read this verse think about it maturely
> and let the profane, unknowing crowd stay away.
> Let astrologers, fools and barbarians keep off
> Whoever does otherwise, let him be priest to the rite!

To couple the astrologers of his day with barbarians and idiots may sound like an insult to those who look today for helpful correlation between birth charts and personal characteristics. But Nostradamus lived at a time when astrology in Christian circles was at its peak and when the distinction between astronomy and astrology had not been clarified. He was not simply trying to be 'biblical' in his apparent condemnation of astrologers; as the last line indicates, he is trying to tell us that there is a truer science of prediction, and that such science is a sacred one.

The distinction between astrologers and 'sacred ones' is clarified in a later stanza (VIII: 71):

> The number of astrologers will become so large
> that they will be driven out, and banned, and their books censored
>
> . . .
>
> None will be assured from the sacred ones

Some of his predictions, assumed to have astrological references, are in fact curious 'puns' on language. The mention of a 'sickle' early in his prophecies may seem like an

astrological reference to Saturn, but perhaps may instead refer to 'd'Estang', while it has been shown that 'Taurer' much later is not 'Taurus', but a variant for 'Tory' or a reference to a local church. . . . There is no doubt of his 'reputation' as an astrologer because he was asked to cast horoscopes for the dowager Catherine, whom he could scarcely refuse. But his knowledge of astrology was incidental to his greater gifts. Were these gifts acquired by using other occult practices?

He condemned many of these with greater zeal than that which he vented on astrology. For example I: 42:

> The fire is extinguished, and the devilish gatherings
> Seek the bones of the demon of Psellus

could be a reference to Psellus, a writer on demonology who lived some centuries earlier, or it would be a corruption of 'Phallus' and indicate the sexual nature of some witchcraft practices of Nostradamus's time. In either case, he is not at all complimentary about the practices, and we cannot imagine his indulging in them.

Alternatively, was he a 'diviner' or a 'scryer'? There is only one apparent reference to divination in the quatrains, where he is also explicitly a participant. It refers to a wand, a flame, a tripod and the sprinkling of hem and feet with water. This is usually taken to mean that there was a bowl of water on the tripod, into which Nostradamus was assumed to gaze in order to obtain his inspiration. The mention of a wand passing between the legs of the tripod is obscure, but at least, the whole thing seems, at first reading, to indicate some practice of magic. The lines (I: 1-2) actually read in translation:

> Sitting solitary at night in secret study
> It is at rest on a tripod of brass
> A scanty flame comes out of the solitude
> and prospers that which should not be believed emptily
> The wand in hand is placed between the branches [tripod's legs]
> He sprinkles fringe and foot with water [literally 'with a wave']
> A voice, be afraid, he trembles, robed!
> Splendour divine—God is near!

Note, firstly, that the lines do not refer to a bowl of water on the brass tripod, but that a flame rests on them. Secondly, as the first line indicates, the lines are not about magical practice, but about *study*. Thirdly, the reference to the scant flame in the third line has a double meaning, for in French the word is *exigue* (= slight or scantly), which is similar to the word *exegete* and its Latin equivalent. The study is to *interpret* something or other. It is not *empty* ('solitude') inspiration (line 3) to assist *empty* (*croire vain*) beliefs, but the study of something that is positively symbolic.

So, the connection with magical practices may be entirely superficial, and even Laver, who suggests that Nostradamus copied the ritual practices of the fourth-century Neoplatonist philosopher Iamblichus, may also have been entirely wrong. If the other quatrains of Nostradamus are to be interpreted symbolically, why should not these two also be symbolic in meaning? 'It', resting on the brass tripod, is clearly the flame. Thus, we can infer that the brass tripod held the only lamp with which Nostradamus 'burned the midnight oil' in study. It caused him to reflect on the Deity—on God. This would have been quite easy, for the figure of a tripod holding a lamp is a close depiction of the Neoplatonist doctrine of the three primal hypostases, the three 'substances' or 'faces' of God—a teaching that later affected the Church as the doctrine of the Trinity. Note that there is no reference in the stanzas to a bowl of water. Indeed, the only reference to water is *l'onde,* which also means a 'wave'. Bodily distractions have to be swept aside (splashed clean) while the 'waves' of inspiration do their work. There is a series of collapsed biblical references, including those to the practice of feetwashing, and the fringes of garments. The whole impact of the two introductory stanzas is that external distractions must be held in check, while inspiration (in interpretation) does its work. In this sense they are innocent of any suggestion of 'black magic' and compare favourably with medieval mystical writings such as *The Cloud of Unknowing* and the writings of the pseudo-Dionysius.

Nostradamus may thus be cleared of being *simply* an astrologer, or *simply* a clairvoyant. He was much more than that; but what *was* he?

The Statistics of the Stanzas

The predictions, published in 1555, are grouped into Centuries (sets of one hundred, four-line stanzas, or 'quatrains'). The first impression that these stanzas give is that they are not arranged in any apparent order. There is no 'time-series' or chronological order of prediction from Nostradamus's time to our own, but each of the ten Centuries contains prophecies relating to each of the periods between the sixteenth century and our own time, and thus each set of a hundred stanzas (Centuries) also contains a small residuum of unfulfilled, or at least unidentifiable, predictions.

Thus, if we take *one* interpretation of the first Century as an example, the proportion of assumed fulfilments is shown below, using several accepted modern interpretations of Nostradamus.

Time Period	Number of Stanzas
1555-1600	18
1601-1700	5
1701-1800	16
1801-1900	20
1901-1983	25
Future twentieth century	4
Unidentifiable	12
Total	100

This table illustrates the apparent jumble, and it is sometimes claimed on behalf of Nostradamus that he deliberately jumbled the historical order of the stanzas so that they would escape easy interpretation. The proportions of fulfilments (with the above date-intervals) in the other Centuries are different, but the order is equally 'random'.

There are a few cases where groups of stanzas in a given Century relate to a single event or set of events. For example, there is a high concentration of stanzas relating to the French monarchy of Henri III's time in the first half of Century III. Also, in the middle of Century VIII, there is a group of apparent predictions of the English monarchy during the Civil War, while Century IX has a seemingly high 'cluster' of predictions relating to the House of Bourbon. Predictions of the French Revolution are also apparently clustered in Centuries I and IX. But these exceptions are only illusory. If a well-known statistical test, known as the *chi*-squared test is applied to the above frequencies to test the relationship to later Centuries they can be proved 'random', not significantly different from later ones, though there are more unidentified stanzas in later Centuries, perhaps because people have thought less about them.

This randomness seems like ammunition for cynics, who sometimes suggest that the prophecies contain so many movements backwards and forwards in history that it is quite easy within four hundred years to identify any number of random events with each of the stanzas. Yet the apparent disorder is probably the greatest clue for the real investigator, for it would have been much too easy for Nostradamus simply to have placed them in historical order. Any number of other arrangements are possible. For example, the 114 suras of the Muslim Qur'an seem to be 'disarrayed' to a casual reader, for the 'creation' narrative appears late, and later events are arranged early on. But this is because the suras are placed in order of size. Nostradamus's predictions appear to be arranged *topically,* some of them showing his scientific insight, and some based on the Bible; and there are whole sequences of stanzas indicating that he 'drew' (whether subconsciously or by interpretation) on his knowledge of the biblical Apocalypse of John.

Nostradamus and Modern Inventions

Let us now explore the 'scientific' and 'biblical' bases of Nostradamus's insight, before trying to provide a number of possible explanations of the apparent accurate fulfilment of many of his prophecies. First, the scientific insight. . . .

One of the earliest of these predictions describes the invention of the submarine, and the firing of a missile from it:

> When the fish that journeys over land and sea
> Is cast on the shore by a great wave—
> its shape, strange, smooth and horrific
> —the enemies soon reach the walls from the sea
> [I:29]

This prediction is not only an example of Nostradamus's knowledge of inventions to come, but also of the principle of 'topical arrangement' suggested in the previous section. It comes only four quatrains later than his prophecy of Pasteur, and though that quatrain may mean something different in context, the 'Pasteur' prophecy *could* mean medicine before its time. He was certainly not the first to conceive of the submarine as a possibility. In fact, over fifty years earlier, the painter Leonardo da Vinci had sketched a drawing of a submarine in one of his notebooks, together with plans of missiles that could be ejected from them. He wrote: 'The evil nature of men is such that they will practice assassination by breaking the hulls of boats and wrecking them. . . .' Nostradamus would have needed no foresight to be able to copy the works or words of Leonardo. His genius lay in arranging this information alongside other prophecies of scientific invention that have also been accurately fulfilled.

For example, the very next stanza predicts death and pillage despite 'palm-branches'.

> Despite the signs of palm-branches,
> —afterward, death and pillage,
> —good counsel arrives too late [1:30]

On first reading this seems like a prophecy of a reversal of peaceful intentions, but it is, in fact, an extraordinary prophecy of nuclear war, in which he not only 'drew' on his knowledge of the direction of modern inventions, but also on his knowledge of biblical prophecy. At some time between the eighth and fourth centuries BC, the Hebrew prophet, Joel, had written: 'I will show wonders in heaven and on earth—blood and fire and pillars [lit. *palm trees*] of smoke'. This was an early biblical prophecy of nuclear war, and used a Hebrew word for 'pillar' (*timorah*) that derives from the word for 'palm-tree' (*tomer*) because the pillars of ancient buildings were often structured to look like palm trees. The word is frequently used in the Old Testament for an artificial palm tree, and aptly describes the spreading shape of a 'cloud' of nuclear 'smoke'. As a Jewish Catholic, Nostradamus acquired a thorough knowledge of Hebrew from his grandfather, Jean.

The prediction, held in isolation, is remarkable enough but its position in the Centuries is even more remarkable. Not only is it a curious piece of *double-entendre,* but it occurs immediately after the submarine prophecy, thus indicating that nuclear power will have originally been discovered with 'peaceful intent'. Yet it associates the submarine with nuclear power (e. g. nuclear warheads) and describes the great havoc that such weapons (as Polaris and its successors) can cause.

Nostradamus and the Revelation of John

Many of Nostradamus's quatrains look like cryptic apocalyptic writings of the style that imitates biblical prophecy, yet recasts its symbols. In Jewish history, such 'apocalypses' were common from the third century BC onwards, and I have shown elsewhere that the Revelation of John was intended to be a Christian 'answer' to such cryptic, apocalyptic writing. Medieval interpreters did not know this, however, and often imagined that the Book of Revelation was simply a sequential political prophecy. Nostradamus would have been aware of their interpretations, some of which were fulfilled, because history sometimes tends to be self-repeating. It may have required an effort on his part to have arranged the 'scientific' stanzas I: 25-30 in a sensible topical order, but it would have required very little effort to have consciously or unconsciously repro-

duced some of the themes from the Apocalypse of John in the very order in which they occurred there. Take, for example, the following sequence, again from Century I.

Revelation of John	*Nostradamus*
1. A warrior with a bow (6:1-2)	1. A reference to "Mars" (I: 15)
2. Bloodshed (6:3-4) associated with the "seventy-sevenfold" ref. to Cain (see Genesis 4:24)	2. Blood to be shed, and a reference to "seventy times" (I: 15)
3. "Archer" symbols (6:1-8)	3. Reference to Sagittarius, the "archer" (I: 16)
4. Plague, famine and death in that order (6:5-9)	4. "Plague, famine and death" (I: 16)
5. Plagued earth (6:7-8)	5. "parched earth" (I: 17)
6. Earth soaked with blood to be avenged (6:9-10)	6. Land and sea soaked with blood (I: 18)
7. "Souls under an altar" (6:9)	7. Snakes around an altar (I: 19)
8. A "great earthquake" (6:12)	8. "Shaking of land and sea" (I: 20)

Does this sequence seem to be unconvincing? It is one of a number of such sequences. Some of the items contain several specific elements of detail that are also in order, as the 'plague, famine and death' of 4; but even if each of the eight elements only contained one item the chances of their being arranged in the same given order would be 1:8! (a mathematical factorical notation) which means 1/40320. But the chance that, in the mass of possible items, the same elements themselves occur in both the Apocalypse and Nostradamus is much greater and it is not the only case of such a sequence. Others occur in later Centuries.

This is not to say that Nostradamus provided the 'best' possible interpretation of John's Revelation. His viewpoint was conditioned by the limitations of the time in which he lived, and history tends to be self-repeating, as far as interpretations of John's Apocalypse are concerned. For example, he used the cipher 'Babylon' of Revelation 17 to mean Paris because, just like ancient Babylon (situated between Tigris and Euphrates), Paris is also situated on two rivers (the Seine and Marne). Such a meaning would never be accepted by modern biblical scholars, but was useful to Nostradamus, because Revelation's predictions are capable of multiple fulfilment in the vast time-continuum of history, and Nostradamus, 'cracked' only one set of meanings of its ciphers—something akin to what is known as the 'historical' school of interpretation, whereby interpreters such as Newton, Mede and Eliott were able to predict some events in the future of France, including the French Revolution.

Some Possible Explanations

The challenge of Nostradamus is an outstanding one on two counts. To a materialist, who believes that the future cannot be predicted successfully, the success of Nostradamus in doing so has to be explained. To the Christian fundamentalist, who may believe that only biblical prophecy accurately anticipates future events, the astonishingly reliable detail of some of the Centuries can present a curious problem. The second part of this chapter attempted to show that Nostradamus was no charlatan but an educated healer, who was, in many respects, ahead of his time. We have seen that Nostradamus was not simply an astrologer, a crystal-gazer, or a black magician. On his own admission he was deeply engrossed in interpreting something. If so, what was he interpreting? Lastly, we have seen that though the Centuries appear to be jumbled, they seem to be arranged in a topical order, reflecting his knowledge of science and of biblical prophecy. If this is so, then scientific foresight and biblical interpretation may be added to the list of part-explanations of his foresight. This being done, we are now in a position to offer some preliminary explanations of his success in forecasting future events.

The *first* of these explanatory factors is *random fulfilment.* Toss a coin, and there is a 0.5 chance of obtaining a desired head or tail. The chance of a 'six' is less (0.16) if a die is cast. If no time limit is specified there is always a greater chance that at some remote time any given combination of events (or cluster of numbers) can occur (or be cast), and this chance increases with the passage of time. If all of Nostradamus's predictions provided only one fulfilment-date and no other, and each fulfilment date had been matched exactly by a fulfilment, the Centuries would be easily vindicated. In some cases, however, the prediction actually failed in its intended fulfilment.

To quote two examples:

1. In Presages CXLI he predicted the details of the events surrounding his death. He would return from an embassy, put away the King's gift and fall on a bench near his bed, where he would be found dead. However, the date of his death was wrongly predicted.

2. In 1:51 he implicitly quoted Roussat's work, and thus predicted a revolution in 1702. The revolution did not come until nearly ninety years afterwards.

So there is a statistical case against Nostradamus, a case that, in a sufficiently long time-span, all its details will be fulfilled, and that when there were references to specific dates these did not see the events that were sometimes intended to fit them.

Secondly, some early fulfilments can be attributed to a *personal gift* of foresight. This gift may be intuitive or logical and varies from one person to another. Some small fulfilment-spans can be anticipated, because of existing conditions. The death of Brezhnev in 1982 could have been foreseen, so could the Falklands crisis. At the time of writing there is a likelihood of a conflict between Venezuela and Guyana over territory around the Esequibo river. Not everyone has the intuitive foresight of a Jeanne Dixon. Some may project trends, as in Alvin Toffler's *Future Shock;* others may construct a model of the future, while yet others may engage in collective 'polls' of opinion about the future. Douglas McGregor, of the Massachussetts Institute of Technology, and Hadley Cantril, of Princeton University, both independently encouraged people in 1936 to make forecasts about near events, including Hitler's war and other matters, and the extent of 'collective' accuracy was astonishing. Later in 1953, Richard Auerbach, a New

York primary school headmaster repeated the experiment, this time using children, by trying to get them to project the world of 1978. Their projections were locked away, and examined in 1978. Again the projections were astonishing.

Astrological studies of correlation between horoscopes and character profiles suggest that astrology has some predictive value. However, in all these cases, the timespan between prediction and fulfilment is a short one (less than a century), and there is no evidence that it could be used successfully to explain much of Nostradamus's apparently long-range perception of the future, though the statistical explanation (see above) enhances accuracy, given that the timespan is not specific.

A *third* set of explanations, as we have seen, involves *prescriptive prophecy.* If a doctor tells a patient that he (the patient) is ill, it may have the effect of making him feel worse than otherwise would be the case. In the same way, an accountant (misusing accounting information) may judge a firm to be nearing bankruptcy. A bank takes the accountant's opinion and refuses credit. Other banks follow suit, and thus an otherwise healthy firm can easily be bankrupted.

A *fourth* explanation is similar, except that the 'subject' of the prophecy voluntarily fulfils it. It is *participative fulfilment.* The popes probably know of the prophecies of Malachy of Armagh mentioned earlier in the chapter, and some may have set about trying to fulfil them. Similarly, Hitler, who believed Nostradamus, attempted in some respects to fulfil Nostradamus's prophecies. . . .

A *fifth* reasonable explanation is *interpretational 'fudge'*— the variety of conflicting and diverse interpretations that hang on a single line. When the Pythoness at Delphi was consulted about the battle between Lydia and Persia she wisely but ambiguously replied that if it occurred a great empire would be overthrown. It was a 'heads I win—tails you lose' prophecy. Both contenders were great empires, and one had to be overthrown. In this context is the obscurity that surrounds much of Nostradamus's crabbed French. For example, an anagram of only six letters may have up to 720 meanings, dependent on the arrangement of the letters, though most arrangements may not have necessary meanings. But there are sufficiently obscure arrangements of anagrams to suggest the most diverse meanings. For example, Lonole is variously interpreted as Oliver Cromwell by James Laver and as London by Erika Cheetham in two equally convincing interpretations of one of Nostradamus's stanzas.

These five explanations exhaust many of the non-specific prophecies—those that seem to have 'worked out' because of chance, preceptiveness, involuntary and voluntary participation on the part of the subject, and the very fact that obscurity of language often enhances the chance of prophetic fulfilment because of the variety of interpretations that such obscurity can produce.

We can also add two more sets of explanations. The first of these is *scientific perceptiveness.* Nostradamus's foresight regarding modern inventions was not unique. This is because we all possess the desire to imagine the impossible, and then set about accomplishing it. I showed earlier that Nostradamus was not alone in anticipating the invention of submarines; Leonardo da Vinci, for example, had done so fifty years before him. Several factors combine to produce scientific predictiveness in people.

The first of these is that design often anticipates discovery by several hundred years. The ancient Greeks were known to have made some progress towards aeronautics; the Egyptians had used Pythagoras's theorem long before Pythagoras propounded it; and other pieces of important data, such as the value of *pi* (to calculate the circumference of a circle) are known to have been discovered independently by different people at different times.

Secondly, inventions are not necessarily accredited to their 'first' inventors, who often live and die in obscurity—thus there is another time-gap between first discovery and popularity.

Thirdly, scientific vision entails 'hit-and-miss' speculation about seemingly impossible inventions—as is clear from much science fiction writing. This very 'scientific vision' itself thus produces expectations, goals and objectives in the minds of people who would like to see them invented.

A fourth factor is that the very expectation of such discoveries carries considerable popularity, and that this, itself, drives people to work, trying to discover how a particular feat (such as radio communication or underwater travel) can be accomplished.

Finally, as with the first factor above, there is no necessary time scale. If people sufficiently believe that a given invention is 'possible', some will carry on working until it is realized. Thus, although I have listed *'scientific perceptiveness'* as a *special explanation* of the accuracy of Nostradamus's predictions, it does combine some of the earlier explanations. Apart from the discovery-popularity 'lag', it combines random speculation with a large element of prescriptive and participative fulfilment. If some 'prophet' can 'dream up' a seemingly impossible feat, and the desire to perform it becomes sufficiently popular, some people will carry on trying to discover how it can be accomplished, until it becomes a reality.

A seventh explanation, or set of explanations, derives from a knowledge of biblical prophecy. This was discussed briefly earlier in this chapter. If the Bible's prophetic claim is correct, and it reflects Divine foresight of human events—as some of the cases quoted earlier, such as the history of Israel and the destruction of Tyre, suggest—then any human 'prophet' can be reliable to the extent that he consciously or unconsciously interprets or recasts biblical prophecy. Some of Nostradamus's predictions, such as his prophecy of the re-creation of the State of Israel, clearly fall into this category, for such an event was foreseen much earlier by Biblical prophets. Even false prophets of a much lower moral calibre, and of much more spurious intentions than Nostradamus, are known to have made 'capital' for themselves, by reinterpreting biblical prophecy. To use a simple illustration, Moses 'warned' Pharaoh that the waters of Egypt would 'become blood' (whatever that meant). The Bible tells us that subsequently: 'the magicians of Egypt did the same by their secret arts'.

It is difficult to imagine that the waters of Egypt 'became blood' twice. It is much more probable that the 'magicians' realized the reliability of Moses' prediction, and simply copied it, claiming it to be their own, and telling a credulous Pharoah that Moses had obtained it from them. Anyone who reads Nostradamus's work will realize that his prophecy of the restoration of Israel is accurate; but it needs a working knowledge of the Bible to give it the credit for having predicted the event nearly 3,000 years earlier.

Finally, there is the *ex eventu* explanation—that some prophecies of Nostradamus may have been written (or 'tampered with') after the events to which they relate occurred. Some biblical scholars are often quick to point out that later books of the Old Testament, such as Daniel, which contains a summary of the histories of Greek dynasties of Egypt and Syria from 330 to 165 BC, may have been written after the event. This is not the place to discuss such a claim, but it is fairly certain that some alterations occurred to the Centuries after Nostradamus's death. The first edition (1555) of the Centuries is incomplete, and only contains the first few centuries. It is also known that there were forgeries later attributed to Nostradamus, such as that relating to Mazarin, Richelieu's successor and that relating to the final supremacy of Louis XIV.

There, then are the eight factors that have helped to make the prophecies of Nostradamus successful predictions of future events. None of these alone is sufficient: all are necessary. Even so, not all of them will necessarily explain the 'genius' that has survived as 'Nostradamus'. . . .

[I believe that, as Nostradamus's career demonstrates] someone with an outdated knowledge of scientific invention and Biblical interpretation *could* (and therefore can!) demonstrate overwhelming powers of foresight. If this was possible in the leisurely unsophisticated times of Nostradamus, how much more possible is it to do so in our own days!

James Randi   (essay date 1990)

SOURCE: "The Ten Quatrains," in *The Mask of Nostradamus,* Charles Scribner's Sons, 1990, pp. 163-218.

[*Known as "The Amazing Randi" and described by* Time *magazine as a "conjurer, showman, crusader, and America's most implacable foe of flummery," Randi is the author of several lively works concerned with exposing metaphysical charlatanism. He has written on Harry Houdini, Uri Geller, and Nostradamus. In the following excerpt, he critically examines several of Nostradamus's best-known quatrains, debunking the claims of "the Nostradamians" throughout.*]

Nostradamus first commanded my attention because of his perennial popularity. As I looked into his life, I became impressed with his ingenuity and his fling at immortality. I recognized his worth as a physician and as a poet, his perseverance and courage. He was a person of considerable ability who would have succeeded in any age.

In this chapter we will examine [several] Nostradamus

quatrains suggested by leading Nostradamians, those most often thrown up by the Believers as positive, irrefutable evidence of prophetic powers. . . .

As a physician, the primary professional skill for which he was trained, the man who was to become known as the single best-known astrologer and prognosticator of all time first published his recipes and a few medical writings of only moderate worth and then in 1550 made his debut as a mystic with the first of his annual astrological almanacs. Copies of his almanacs still survive, the earliest dated 1557.

A physician such as Nostradamus performed a variety of functions. He not only prescribed medicines, but he was his own pharmacist as well. He was expected to know how to compound his own remedies from plant sources—all gathered at the correct phase of the moon—and from varied animal parts as well; the witches of *Macbeth* called for "eye of newt and toe of frog" with some authority. Even today, powdered pearls and cockroaches, black rhinoceros horn and tiger penis form an active part of the traditional pharmacopeia of China.

Nostradamus also advised on cosmetics, beauty aids and deodorants for Renaissance ladies, who as a rule bathed only twice a year and wore the same underclothes for months on end. It may be easily believed that this was a brisk trade.

Those same heavily scented ladies came to him for culinary advice, too. Physicians applied their herbal knowledge to matters of the palate and put together aromatic spices for their clients.

In all likelihood the great popular success that was accorded Nostradamus' prophetic pamphlets encouraged him to begin production of the **Centuries,** the work that was to so impressively survive him. Though he continued his medical practice, eventually becoming, by appointment, physician-in-ordinary to Henry II, Francis II and Charles IX of France, his career as a soothsayer effectively took most of his attention and earned most of his money from that time on.

No book on the seer would be in any way complete without examining the evidence upon which his fame is based. I have selected ten of the prophecies that, in the opinion of the True Believers, present the best evidence for Nostradamus' abilities.

Edgar Leoni quotes an interesting observation that was made by English Jesuit Father Herbert Thurston in 1915. Father Thurston was concerned with the impact that he believed Nostradamus' writings were having on the conduct of World War I, and to minimize the effect on the war effort, he tried to explain just how people were self-deceived when interpreting the quatrains:

> Undoubtedly the unrivalled success of Nostradamus' oracles is due to the fact that, avoiding all orderly arrangement, either chronological or topographical, and refraining almost entirely from categorical statements, it is impossible ever to say that a particular prognostic has missed the mark. . . . Nostradamus provided an ingenious system of divination in which the misses can

never be recorded and only the hits come to the surface. For the reputation of the would-be prophet, such conditions are naturally ideal.

While appreciating his opinion, I must beg to differ somewhat with Father Thurston. *Many* very glaring misses of Nostradamus have been recorded, and prognostications that he made clearly and that were in some cases actually dated are seen to be very wrong.

Mr. Bleiler has pointed out the interesting fact that the form of the Nostradamus quatrains—known as *vers commun*—often reveals discrepancies because of the poor "fit" managed by spurious or altered verses. Both Bleiler and Leoni attribute prodigious wit, poetic quality and sophistication to Nostradamus that I am unable to find. In doing so, they just may be surrendering to the same tendency shown by the interpreters to find meaning where none was intended.

There are a great number of very specialized "rules" applied to handling interpretations of the Nostradamus writings, rules developed by the Nostradamians to allow great latitude in assigning—and creating—correlations between historical fact and prophecy. Probably some of these usages and devices were actually used, but others seem unlikely in the extreme. It is particularly important to note that these gimmicks are invoked when needed, but ignored when not called for. For example, when Nostradamus names the city of Narbonne, a center well known to him and mentioned twelve times in his writings, the interpreters have accepted that he is actually referring to the city in some instances, but they assign another function to the name (proper personal name or rank) when necessary to wring meaning from the verse in which it appears. The French word "noir," meaning "black" in English, is most often presumed to be an almost-anagram (see the rule for creating anagrams up ahead) for the French word "roi" (in English, "king"); in some instances it is simply accepted as "black" because it fits better. The Provençal spelling would have been "roy."

Once they establish—to their satisfaction—that a certain usage or rule makes the prophecy work, the Nostradamians invoke it again and again for any subsequent situation that even remotely resembles the one in which the artifice was established. De Fontbrune clearly expressed the way he did his own research:

> The reader will discover, through the translation of each quatrain, how I have proceeded in order to squeeze the text to the maximum, considering that the only 'key' possible is philological.

The aim is to discover some supposed clever, obscure clue or hint that Nostradamus placed in his verses for future generations of scholars to discover. The fact that the quatrains may have expressed notions about quite ordinary matters in a quite ordinary fashion seems repugnant to these learned folks.

They use the theory they are trying to prove, to prove the theory they are trying to prove. They accept modern usage and spellings ("Nostradamus could see the future, couldn't he?") when those serve the need, but fall back on Latin, Old French, Provençal and Greek when they are needed. *I* cannot accept that Nostradamus knew modern English or French.

Nostradamian Stewart Robb came upon a quatrain which he believes predicts a specific event. The verse says, "Near Saint Memire," but the event he wishes to connect with it didn't happen there. Robb is so convinced his hero has prophetic powers that he actually states

> The rebellion that overthrew him was centered around the Cloister of St. Meri, so Nostradamus either heard the name imperfectly or was anagrammatizing it.

Here are a few of the arbitrary but very useful rules we must be aware of:

(1) Anagrams may be used. An anagram, according to the Oxford English Dictionary, is "A transposition of the letters of a word, name or phrase, whereby a new word or phrase is formed." The Nostradamians, however, allow one, two or more letters to be added, changed, or dropped. Thus, Hadrie can become Henrie, Henry, Harry or a number of other words or names.

(2) Punctuation, we are told, may be inserted where absent, or changed when present, since Nostradamus often failed to use it or to use it correctly.

(3) Symbolic references, using animals, mythical creatures or other words to represent the "intended" thing are said to be quite common in Nostradamus' work. . . .

(4) Quatrains may be used as self-contained units, in sets of two lines, as single lines, in pairs, or any way needed. Parts of quatrains may also be combined.

(5) Names of persons or places, we are told, can be "hidden" in common words. As an example, the French word "Pasteur" ("pastor," in English) can actually mean Louis Pasteur.

(6) Foreign derivations—from *any* language—are embraced. We can easily accept Latin sources, since Nostradamus and other writers of his day used the language. They also delighted in demonstrating their erudition by dropping in classical names and allegorical references as well as obscure foreign words.

(7) Validations for "discoveries" are obtained through *other* "discoveries." This is, quite simply, circular reasoning.

There are five usages of which we may approve:

(1) Synecdoche (Hogue calls it "synedoche"), the use of a part to represent the whole, is applied. An example would be using "Washington" to represent "the United States of America," or "bread" for "food."

(2) The use of ancient, classical names for cities and countries, rather than the then-current names.

(3) The use of "u" for "v," "y" for "i," "i" for "j," etc. These are quite legitimate.

(4) The frequent absence of written accents, because orthography was not well established. In early French the verb "être" was written "estre," the letter "s"—rather than an accent—indicating a vowel inflection.

(5) Ellipsis is allowable, in which obvious words understood to belong in the text are left out.

I will use a classification method of my own for the quatrains. It was admittedly inspired by another similar system in a book on another very doubtful subject. There are six kinds of verses found in Nostradamus:

> Quatrains of the First Kind (Q1K) are those that were made for the safely far future. Since they have all of recorded time in which to be fulfilled, they will very probably come true, or have already come true, within certain limits.
>
> Quatrains of the Second Kind (Q2K) are those that were apt to be fulfilled very soon after they were written. The events were very likely to occur because of historical circumstances then known to Nostradamus.
>
> Quatrains of the Third Kind (Q3K) are those that were absolutely sure to be successful prophecies because they were written *after* the event, sometimes immediately after. They are what Leoni calls "retroactive prophecies."
>
> Quatrains of the Fourth Kind (Q4K) are those that are not handled here at all. Because they are such garbled, mystical nonsense, semantically and logically, they cannot be properly examined.
>
> Quatrains of the Fifth Kind (Q5K) are those that describe quite ordinary events and circumstances in Nostradamus' time, with a bit of a likely story dropped in. They involve matters with which he was familiar, and which would be recognized by his contemporaries. In many cases they are not even attempts at prophecy, being rather editorial commentaries or folk tales.
>
> Quatrains of the Wrong Kind (QWK) are those that were and are simply wrong. Events proved them untrue, either during Nostradamus' lifetime or subsequently.

[Nine] Excellent Examples

I will list the . . . quatrains. They are:

1-35 The Gilded Cage—The Death of Henry II

2-51 The Great Fire of London

9-20 The Flight and Capture of Louis XVI and Marie Antoinette at Varennes

9-34 The Flight and Capture of Louis XVI and the Queen at Varennes and the Attack of the 500 on the Tuileries

9-49 The Execution of Charles I of England

8-1   Napoleon Bonaparte and the Imprisonment of the Popes

2-24 Adolf Hitler I

4-68 Adolf Hitler II

6-74 Life and Death of Elizabeth I

Here, then, are examinations of [several] pieces of the evidence most used to prove that Nostradamus had prophetic ability. These quatrains are constantly dragged out before us as indisputable proof of his powers, so we will explore them in some detail.

THE GILDED CAGE—

THE DEATH OF HENRY II

1-35

Le lyon jeune le vieux surmontera,
En champ bellique par singulier duelle:
Dans caige d'or les yeux luy creuera,
Deux classes vne, puis mourir, mort cruelle.

The young lion will overcome the old one,
On the field of battle in single combat:
He will burst his eyes in a cage of gold,
Two fleets one, then to die, a cruel death.

(I must add this note: The subject of the third line is the "young lion" who will burst the eyes of the "old lion." The usual translation of the strange word "classes" is "wounds," taken from the Greek word "klasis." That derivation is convenient but unlikely, a much better one being the Latin "classis," meaning "fleet" or "army.")

This is, by all standards, the single most famous of the Nostradamus quatrains, one that in his day officially put him at the forefront of all the seers, and continues in that

Commemorative bust of Nostradamus, situated atop a fountain in Salon de Provence.

role even today. Let us examine the historical circumstances of the event that it is said to represent.

In the summer of 1559, the royal court of France held a huge celebration in the streets of Paris to honor a double marriage, one of Henry II's daughter Elizabeth to Philip II of Spain and the other of Henry's sister Marguerite to the Duke of Savoy. In the Rue St. Antoine, a traditional full-scale tournament was staged, with jousting by honored nobles and by the king himself. All was festive until sunset of the last day, the first of July.

Henry had distinguished himself in the jousting, and in these last hours of the celebration, he rode against Gabriel de Lorges, Comte de Montgomery. Having failed to unseat him in the approved manner, the king insisted upon another try. Bound to honor the request, the count gave Henry another chance, but due to his miscalculation, Mongomery's lance shattered as the two met in the course and a splinter entered the helmet of his royal opponent, pierced the skull above his right eye and penetrated his brain. Henry fell, mortally wounded.

For ten days he lingered on in delirium, suffering the best that his physicians could offer him, and at last he died. The kingdom immediately began examining prophecies to discover whether this momentous event had been foreseen by any of the seers. . . .

That Nostradamus . . . expected Henry II to go on living for a long time cannot be doubted. In his introduction to the second section of the ***Centuries*** that comprises books eight to ten, Nostradamus provided a lengthy Epistle to Henry II (dated March 14, 1557), that can induce advanced caries merely from a quick reading. Try this opening on your teeth:

> Ever since my long-clouded face first presented itself before the infinite deity of your majesty, O most Christian and most victorious king, I have remained perpetually dazzled by that sight, not ceasing to honor and worship appropriately that date when I presented myself. . . . I was seized with this singular desire to be transported suddenly from my long-beclouded obscurity to the illuminating presence of the first Monarch of the Universe. . . .

Ad nauseam. . . .

In the Epistle, the prophet predicts great things for Henry, who in actuality was to die immediately after the first probable appearance and circulation of this Epistle in manuscript form, and well before it appeared in print. This obvious and glaring example of a major failure for Nostradamus has been an embarrassment for the Nostradamians ever since, though they have—of necessity—come up with many ingenious excuses to get around it.

The opening words of the Epistle are:

> *A l'invictissime, tres-pvissant, et tres-chrestien Henry Roy de France second; Michel Nostradamus son tres humble, tres-obeissant seruiteur & subject, victoire & felicité.*

To the most invincible, most powerful, and most Christian Henry King of France the second; Michel Nostradamus his most humble, most obedient servant and subject, [wishes] victory and happiness.

Note that the monarch died little more than two years later, a fact that does not speak well for invincibility.

EVIDENCE FROM THE QUATRAIN

The Nostradamians celebrate hugely over the coincidences between Quatrain 1-35 and history, but closer examination of the quatrain itself throws a dark cloud over their bacchanal. Consider the first line:

> The young lion will overcome the old one.

Though Montgomery *was* younger than Henry, the difference was not at all significant, only a few years. Certainly the difference is not one of "young" versus "old." The French kings used the fleur-de-lis in their heraldic devices, and the fighting cock was their animal symbol, not the lion. It would have been very strange to refer to a French king, or any other member of the court, as a "lion." The French, as a matter of record, have never used a lion as a symbol of the monarchy, that use being almost entirely reserved to Britain, Spain, Belgium, Holland and Sri Lanka, along with a few German provinces, though there are no lions in any of these countries, nor have there ever been.

Line two reads:

> On the field of battle in single combat.

It is important to note that the event at which Henry was killed was not a duel nor was he "on the field of battle" at all. It was a formal jousting contest in which serious injury was not expected to take place. It was, in fact, a serious *faux pas* to draw blood at these events.

The third line is full of good symbols:

> [The young lion] will burst [the old lion's] eyes
> in a cage of gold.

James Laver and others assert that Henry's visor was gilded. Still others, to make this line work, claim that it was made of gold. There exists *no evidence whatsoever* that either statement is true, and in fact it is very unlikely to be true. Just take a walk through the remarkable collection of body armor in the Tower of London and you will see that wherever gold appears on the armor, it is in ornamental lines and heraldic devices. No actual piece of armor would *ever* be made of gold, since that metal is soft and of little protective value.

Nowhere is there any indication that Henry II's eyes were "burst." The wound occurred *above* the right eye (remember that Gaurico warned Henry about his *left* eye).

Finally, line four says:

> Two fleets one, then to die, a cruel death.

What the reference to "fleets" is, I do not know, since we know of no union of fleets that satisfies the circumstances. Were I a Nostradamian, I would search around for something like the Greek word previously found, and choose it to make the line work better with the word "wounds." Even then I would be out of luck, since there was but one wound which carried off Henry. I cannot afford that indulgence.

Henry II's end was, indeed, "a cruel death." But these are the *only* few words that connect his demise with this quatrain, and there is an abundance of evidence that denies any connection whatsoever.

Let me leave this suggestion with the reader. It originated from author Louis Schlosser: Move across the English Channel to Britain. Consider the fact that Henry VIII of England, whose symbol was very definitely the lion, at age forty-four, locked up Sir Thomas More (aged fifty-eight) in a very special royal prison (a golden cage?) the Tower of London. This was the result of a protracted battle of wills between the two for control of the religious leadership of England. There were two "classes" in battle here, the Holy Roman Church and the royal insurgency of Henry. Henry won the day, and after a farce of a trial, More was put to a cruel death, decapitation. The event was an affront to Catholic and Protestant alike, and it occurred twenty years before Nostradamus penned 1-35. Just a suggestion, nothing more!

A gentleman named F. Buget, in his *Etude sur Nostradamus et ses Commentateurs* of 1863, concluded about Quatrain 1-35,

> There is not, then, as far as I can see, a single word in this quatrain which is applicable to the unhappy end of this prince [Henry II]. . . .

THE GREAT FIRE OF LONDON

2-51

From Rigaud:

> *Le sang du iuste à Londres fera faulte,*
> *Bruslés par fouldres de vint trois les six:*
> *La dame antique cherra de place haute,*
> *De mesme secte plusieurs seront occis.*

> The blood of the just shall be wanting in London,
> Burnt by thunderbolts of twenty three the Six(es),
> The ancient dame shall fall from [her] high place,
> Of the same sect many shall be killed.

Death, foreign intrigue, wonders of Nature, a mystery woman and suspicious religious overtones are all here in this quatrain, with its vivid imagery which has titillated generations of Nostradamians. It does tell of an historic event, but the verse itself is a Q3K.

In the spurious edition of *Centuries* that Garencières used, the word "Feu" in place of "fouldres" in the second line is wrong. It has been used almost universally by the Nostradamians because it suits their Great Fire of London interpretation better; the original, correct word as shown above, means "thunderbolts." Also, the Rigaud edition of the quatrains says, "de vint [vingt] trois les six," not "vingt & trois," as many other editions do, thus showing an appreciable variation introduced into the text.

Here, the Nostradamians would ask us to believe that their hero was writing about an event that was 111 years in his future: In 1666, London was devastated by a fire that destroyed four–fifths of that city. Garencières, for whom the Great Fire was a very recent event (it occurred only six years before his book was published) was an ardent Monarchist. Ever intent upon adding his own charming mysteries to the muddy brew, he postulated that this fiery disaster was a divinely administered expiation for the 1649 execution of Charles I; the unexplained seventeen years of delay in the retribution seems of no importance to his analysis. He also explained that the last half of line two means, "the number of Houses and Buildings that were burnt," rather than the more popular interpretation by almost everyone else that it means 66, therefore somehow giving them 1666. How that date was obtained by him—or by others, for that matter—is difficult to see. Nonetheless, several of the Nostradamians go on to explain that "La dame antique" refers to St. Paul's Cathedral, which was consumed in the fire, along with many other churches, thus the claimed validation of the line, "Of the same sect many shall be killed."

Problems with History

I consulted many references here and in England, and so far as I have been able to determine, St. Paul's Cathedral was never called "The Old Lady," as many Nostradamians claim. The word "antique" in Old French meant "old" *or* "eccentric." The latter derivation is similar to that of the English word "antic." Usually, in French, "old lady" would be expressed by, "vieille dame." Though the old pre-fire St. Paul's Cathedral was the highest church then known, there is no "high place" from which it could have fallen. Some fans, recognizing this discrepancy, claim that a statue of the Virgin Mary stood atop St. Paul's, and that it was that figure that Nostradamus was referring to as the Old Lady. Not so. My early edition of the *Encyclopaedia Britannica* provides a clear, detailed line illustration of the old pre-fire cathedral that shows it was severe Gothic in style, with a squared roof area and no external statues at all. Another contrived notion falls from its high place. We are left with only the reference to London to tie this quatrain to the Great Fire in that city.

This quatrain is a Q3K. It refers to an actual event which was taking place as Nostradamus was penning his opus, but a very different event, and certainly *not* the Great Fire of London. Here are the historical facts:

(1) In 1554, the ferociously Catholic queen Bloody Mary (I) of England announced a wholesale cleansing of her kingdom, and in January of 1555, she began executing Protestant heretics in London. Their only crime was the variety of their Christianity and their stubborn refusal to abjure it. Many were prominent churchmen, intellectuals and statesmen.

(2) They were burned at the stake with the "merciful" addition of having bags of gunpowder tied between their legs or around their necks to quicken their passage. When they eventually expired, it was with a spectacular explosion. The trial, sentencing and burning of these unfortunates began January 22, 1555, in neat groups of six.

(3) Queen Mary, haggard, totally obsessed with religion, disappointed in love, ill with dropsy and other assorted

diseases repeatedly imagined that she was pregnant by her Spanish husband Philip. The consort was seldom at home and in 1555 left England and Mary for good. She wandered about her palace half-naked while these atrocities were being committed in her name. She died three years later, incoherent and considered quite insane. It was strongly suspected that her exit was hastened.

(4) Over 300 Protestants died this way at that time.

Consider these facts, and compare them line-for-line with Quatrain 2-51 as seen in this much better translation:

> *(1) The blood of the innocent will be an error at London,*
> *(2) Burned by thunderbolts, of twenty-three, the six(es),*
> *(3) The senile lady will lose her high position,*
> *(4) Many more of the same sect will be slain.*

I think my point is plain. Will and Ariel Durant's *Story of Civilization,* from which some of this information was drawn, adds this comment:

> . . . nowhere in contemporary Christendom— not even Spain—were so many men and women burned for their opinions as during [Mary I's reign].

And Nostradamus? The first edition of the *Centuries,* in which this quatrain is printed, is dated May 4, 1555— more than three months *after* the first set of heretics mounted the faggots in London. I believe that the seer was writing of an event which certainly would have made news in France, and—in view of what we now know about his true religious beliefs—about which he was thus expressing his righteous horror.

Some authorities date the 1555 edition of the *Centuries* as March 1, though it is imprinted at the end:

> *Ce present livre a esté achevé*
> *d'imprimer le IIII. iour de may M.DLV.*

(This book was finished printing the fourth day of May 1555.)

The shorter time span—a month or more—would be barely long enough for the news to have reached Nostradamus, even with his informers working out of Paris, but the sentences of the inevitable executions would have been passed some time before the events, since in that day the condemned often spent many months in prison while their wealth was located and acquired by the crown; carefully applied and controlled torture effectively extracted information about concealed assets from the condemned. Thus, either publication date is adequate for the described scenario.

It appears that Nostradamus, in common with other scholars of the day, probably maintained an active "grapevine" with his colleagues. There was a very brisk traffic of couriers hastening along the sea routes and the highways of the continent and Britain, carrying everything from mathematical discoveries to astronomical measurements and observations between interested scholars. This was not a casual, opportunistic process; there were those who made their living as couriers transmitting such information, so much so that a postal system was coming into existence as a result of the demand for this service. Along with that valuable scientific knowledge went current news events, as well, of perhaps equal value. Also, having the approval and support of Catherine, Nostradamus was likely to have her eyes and ears as well, and might hear from Paris much sooner than others not so favored. He would have been in an excellent position to know of quite recent events from faraway places.

THE FLIGHT AND CAPTURE OF LOUIS

XVI AND MARIE ANTOINETTE AT VARENNES

9-20

De nuit viendra par la forest de Reines,
Deux pars vaultorte Herne la pierre blanche,
Le moine noir en gris dedans Varennes
Esleu cap. cause tempeste feu, sang tranche.

By night will come by the forest of Reines,
Two couples, detour, Herne the white stone,
The black monk in gray inside Varennes
Elected cap. causes tempest fire, blood slice.

Le Pelletier and others have decided that this quatrain predicted the same important event of 1791 described ahead in Quatrain 9-34, though the actual historical details of this well-documented incident, which I will now present, are somewhat different from his version.

A Differing Version

A discussion of this quatrain obtained from the *Encyclopedia of Occultism and Parapsychology* gives these rather remarkable interpretations and rationalizations for the words employed by Nostradamus. The *Encyclopedia* tells us that the word "forest" (forêt, in modern French) stands instead for the Latin "fores," meaning "door." The word "pars" means "part" (in Old French, husband or wife), "vaultorte" is a composite of "vaulx" (valley) and "de torte" (tortuous), "Herne" is an anagram for "reine" (Queen), "moine"—they use "moyne"—is Greek for the French "seul" ("alone"), "noir," rather than being the French word for "black," is an anagram for the French word "roi(n)" ("king"), "cap." equals "Capet" (formal name of the king), and "tranche" ("slice") means "knife."

The total meaning they obtain is: Two married people, the king alone, dressed in gray, and the queen, the white precious stone, will leave one night through the door of the queen, take a tortuous road, and enter into Varennes. The election of Capet will cause storm, fire, bloodshed and decapitation.

Most supporting evidence has been taken from the account of one Mme. Campan, lady-in-waiting to the queen, who gave her story in *Les Mémoires de Marie-Antoinette*. She says that during the royal flight, King Louis XVI wore a gray suit, and the queen was dressed in white. She also says that upon their return to Paris at the hands of revolutionaries, the queen's hair had turned white from the ordeal. According to her, the attempted furtive escape of the royal couple was effected from the palace through the special exit door of the queen, a means generally unknown to the public. The route of flight was for some unknown rea-

son altered at the last moment by Louis XVI, to lead from Verdun into Varennes.

Despite the fact that it has been a popular belief for centuries, it is a myth that hair can turn white "overnight," as reported by Mme. Campan, the major source of all this information. In fact, Marie Antoinette's hair was ash-blond, not far from white in the first place. The authenticity of Mme. Campan's account must come under further suspicion when we realize that though she was privy to much information on these matters, she did *not* accompany the king and queen on this aborted journey, as claimed by several of the Nostradamians. In her own personal account, she relates that she was in Paris during that episode, and:

> Therefore I won't be able to give any details of the flight of their majesties other than those I heard from the queen and from the other persons who witnessed her return.

Also, it is not at all probable—in fact, it is highly unlikely—that the queen was dressed in white. The rigors of coach travel in those days, especially over back roads at high speed, would most certainly destroy any appearance of a white costume. Travelers in those days wore dark clothing for such purposes, especially if they were attempting to pass by unnoticed, as this pair certainly should have been. They were fleeing for their lives, against specific injunctions not to do so.

(The above paragraph was written at an early stage of the preparation of this manuscript. Since that time I have conducted a diligent search of historical sources to determine the garb worn by Marie Antoinette. All documents produced from evidence of statements of persons who, unlike Mme. Campan, were eyewitnesses to the flight and/or capture at Varennes state that Marie Antoinette wore a *gray* dress with a black cape. She did not wear white.)

Le Pelletier says that because he had been abandoned by his people, the *"monk"* in *gray* caught in *Varennes* is Louis. Marie Antoinette, the *white stone* (dressed in white, with white hair) left the Tuileries by a secret *door* in her chambers *by night*. The party made a *detour* through Varennes through the *forest* of *Reines*, at the whim of Louis. Louis as an *elected* monarch will cause *fire, blood* and the *slice* of the guillotine.

Let's examine this interpretation. First, the royal party was not one pair or couple, it was three, or just one if we wish to use the designation of a married couple, husband and wife. The numbers just do not agree. The quatrain calls for two couples.

True, Louis was dressed in gray. There was no white stone to be found, certainly not Marie Antoinette, who just does not match the description in any way. The door by which the royal party left—all of them, not just the queen—was all the way at the very opposite end of the palace from the queen's chambers.

True, they left by night. There was no detour made by the royal party, in spite of arguments made by the Nostradamians that Varennes was not on a direct route to Montmédy. That is not true. Leoni even says that, "it is substantially true that the party took a poor route to Montmédy."

Nonsense. Reference to any detailed map of the region shows that the most direct route possibly by coach, without having to pass through the major city of Verdun and risk discovery, is passing through the minor towns named above, exactly as planned for the royal family in great detail, well in advance, by their would-be rescuer, the Swedish count Axel Fersen, who worshiped Marie Antoinette.

Concerning line four: Louis, following his capture, was designated by the National Assembly as a constitutional monarch of France, rather than the absolute monarch he had formerly been. But "cap." as used here might well be the Old French word, "captal," which meant "chief" or "leader." It suits the Nostradamians to have it mean "Capet," the formal name of the king, because that is necessary to give the meaning they seek. Such a use would not have been unknown to Nostradamus, since all French kings, from the year A.D. 987, were known as descendants of Hugh Capet, the first somewhat formal monarch of an area that was roughly France as we now know it.

But Louis XVI was not "elected," as the word "esleu" ("elu") would indicate. He was placed in that lower position by the revolutionaries to incapacitate him without having to do away with him, since he still had the respect of many citizens, and the time had not quite arrived when it could be acceptable for his head to fall to the guillotine.

There was no forest called the Forêt de Reines (which in any case would have been "des Reines,") nor was it the Forêt de la Reine that the royal entourage passed through: it was the famous forest of Argonne. The Forêt de la Reine is more than fifty miles southeast of this particular town of Varennes. And I cannot see why "noir" has to be seen as an anagram for "roi" when it fits so well and so logically into the one line of the four that makes any sense at all.

No, the flight of four royal personages through the Argonne forest is not at all well described by the Nostradamus Quatrain 9-20. A man dressed in gray, a town named Varennes (there are *twenty-six* of them in France!) and a journey by night—the only correspondences that can be agreed upon—are not enough to invoke this important event in the history of France.

We will deal further with this event in the next quatrain we examine.

THE FLIGHT AND CAPTURE OF LOUIS

XVI & THE QUEEN AT VARENNES AND THE

ATTACK OF THE 500 ON THE TUILERIES

9-34

Le part soluz mary sera mittré,
Retour conflict passera sur la thuille:
Par cinq cens un trahyr sera tiltré,
Narbon & Saulce par coutaux avons d'huille.

The single part afflicted will be mitred,
Return conflict will pass over the tile:
By five hundred, treason will be titled,
Narbon and Saulce by knives we have oil.

The premise that Nostradamus was a prophet almost requires that he would be concerned with French history-to-come. In order to support that requirement, believers have searched diligently for anything that seems to indicate events of the French Revolution. Here again, we have the Nostradamians connecting a quatrain with the flight of Louis XVI from Paris.

The above rendition into English is far from satisfactory. The usual translation of, "Par cinq cens" is "By the five hundred." This cannot be, Everett Bleiler points out, because of the required division (caesura) at the end of the fourth syllable, unless Nostradamus was such a bad poet that he could not see the discrepancy in his work. Connecting the "un" and "trahyr" would be impossible by the rules of caesura. It would be equivalent to singing "The Star-Spangled Banner" like this (try it!):

> Say can you see by the,
> Dawn's early light what so,
> Proudly we hail'd at the,
> Twilight's last gleaming whose broad.

Bleiler suggests that the correct reading is "By five-less-one." It's a cute way of saying "four." That may be the case, but I must respectfully reject this conclusion, however, since the literal meaning of "cinq sans un" would be "five *without* one." "Less" would be "moins."

On one point, I will give you some idea of how careful a researcher must be about accepting statements from others. Stewart Robb, one of the leading Nostradamians, tells his readers that in using the word "thuille," which he says refers to the famous palace of Tuileries, Nostradamus shows his powers, since he could not have known of the palace except by prophetic means. Robb says:

> 'Le thuille' means 'the place of the tiles.' When Nostradamus wrote this prophecy, the site of the Tuileries was only an old tile kiln. The palace was not begun till after the prophet's death.

Let us examine that claim, as I had to do before accepting it. Basic history books provide the answers.

A Frenzy of Inspired and Expensive Expansion

In 1528 King Francis I of France, father of Henry II, had begun making extensive alterations to existing buildings in Paris and was creating new architectural wonders. . . .

With the assistance and inspiration of Catherine de Médicis, what is now the modern city of Paris began to take shape. At her order, plans for an extravagant new palace were drawn up by Philibert de l'Orme, the pre-eminent architect of the day. This was to be an extraordinary project of great scope to be built on the site of what was until then only a group of abandoned tile–factories, and it exists today as a monument to the architect's skill and Catherine's good taste. It became known by the name of the site: Tuileries.

Construction was well under way by 1564, and everyone in France was very much aware of it. With his royal patrons so much on his mind, and with his informers, the Seer of Salon could hardly have failed to know of the great project being planned in Paris, and it is no surprise that he worked it into one of his quatrains. Charles IX and the queen mother, Catherine, visited Nostradamus in 1565—

when the palace had already been under construction for a year, and a year before his death. The first *authenticated* edition of the **Centuries** that contained this quatrain *did not appear until 1568,* four years after the building was begun.

It is not impossible that Nostradamus may have been referring to the Tuileries in this quatrain, though I think it is not likely. Though admittedly the detail is not of prime importance in evaluating the verse as prophecy, my point is that Mr. Robb's declaration that Nostradamus could not have known about the palace except through a prophetic vision or his analysis of a particular configuration of the stars and planets is not well derived. He may have simply chosen to accept Charles Ward's declaration that

> the Tuileries . . . [was] not in existence when Nostradamus wrote this in 1555.

The quatrain, as Ward certainly knew, was not even in the 1555 edition. As stated above, it was not in print until 1568.

But that is a small matter, to which I may well have devoted too much time and space. This quatrain has in it a number of seemingly evidential references. The historical facts are that a full year after the royal family had been stopped at Varennes and returned to Paris, a mob broke down the gates to the Tuileries palace and entered to confront Louis XVI and his queen. In a farcical and cruel gesture, he was forced to don the red Phrygian bonnet (a sort of stocking cap) that was a symbol of the Revolution. Marie Antoinette, too, put on an identical cap. It would be comical to suggest that "mitred" refers to that event. The line must indicate that someone will be elevated to the position of bishop, since that is what the verb (miter or mitre) means. To equate it with the tragicomic spectacle of King Louis XVI wearing a silly hat is equally silly. Besides, attempts to explain the "single part afflicted" have failed, since Louis was still very much married, not single nor solitary, though he was certainly "afflicted."

Concerning the translation of line three, Le Pelletier says it means that

> The Marseillais Federates, five hundred of them, will direct the attack of the people, on August 10 of the same year [1792], against the Tuileries Palace.

This is an attempt to incorporate the "cinq cens" ("five hundred") of the quatrain with the storming of the Tuileries, by mentioning that the Marseillais Federates led that attack. The attempt fails miserably, for there were other groups of organized, armed men there as well, numbering in the thousands. Along with them was a huge mob of citizens bradishing every sort of weapon from knives to stones. Those who recorded the event estimated the mob at 20,000.

Unfortunately for the Nostradamians who wish to establish the Five Hundred, there exist in the Archives of France *many* highly dependable firsthand accounts of every event of the Revolution. Those were times when anyone's future could change within hours, and major his-

torical turns in the destiny of France took place with great suddenness.

Those days of turmoil within the Tuileries when the royal family was defending its position under siege were written down in minute detail by the Abbé Gallois, the Royal Sacristan and a close friend of the family. He kept a diary in which actual conversations were recorded. He wrote that when the mob approached the Tuileries in the 1791 assault on that regal residence, and Pierre Louis Roederer, the Prefect of Paris, was begging the royal family to leave the palace and take refuge with the National Assembly, Marie Antoinette objected, "But Monsieur, we have troops." She was referring to the Swiss Guard, who were to be overcome in short order by the enormous mob outside. Replied Roederer, "Madame, all of Paris is marching." The citizens of Paris looted the Tuileries.

A Matter of Names

The name "Narbon" in this quatrain, to the interpreters, seems to fit the Revolutionary picture quite well. Says Le Pelletier:

> Amongst the traitors who contribute powerfully to the ruin of Louis XVI, there will stand out, in the ranks of the nobility, the Count of Narbonne, his Minister of War. . . .

True, Narbonne was a "traitor," among thousands of them. I must point out that his name appears nowhere in the many history books I have consulted, and I must congratulate the Nostradamians for persevering until they found something—anything—to match "Narbon." Anything, that is, except the city of Narbonne, to which Nostradamus often referred. However, that reference does not suit them. And to follow Le Pelletier further in his interpretation, he says:

> . . . amongst the people, a son and grandson of chandler-grocers, named Sauce, procureur-syndic of the commune of Varennes, who will cause him [Louis XVI] to be arrested in this town.

Again, true. And "Sauce" is not far from "Saulce."

I believe it would be difficult for the Nostradamians to explain why, if this quatrain describes the donning of the red bonnet by Louis *and* the flight via Varennes, Nostradamus chose to place the two events, a year apart, in reverse order.

But there is something else which has escaped (perhaps conveniently) the notice of the Nostradamians. Our hero had a strange tendency to group two, three or four towns together in quatrains, usually in very close proximity to one another. This close association of towns is done several places in the **Centuries,** as in 8-22, where "Gorsan" (Coursan), Narbonne, Tucham (Tuchan), and Parpignam (Perpignan) are named, all within a sixty-kilometer pattern. It will occur again when we discuss the famous "Napoleon" Quatrain, 8-1, and in 9-49, the "Charles I" prophecy. Nostradamus' cabalistic/Pythagorean tendencies are showing.

Since we are able to easily find the major city of Narbonne

(formerly Narbo), as just mentioned, in the extreme south of France near the present Spanish border, we might look around a bit. Lo! Just forty kilometers south of Narbonne on the main costal road is the town of Salces, also spelled "Salses."

Well, if Nostradamus was *not* describing Louis's flight, what was he writing about? Historian Louis Schlosser gives a detailed account of the siege of Metz, which occurred in 1553, two years before Nostradamus published. Here are the lines of 9-34, one by one, with historical facts of the Metz siege:

(1) Le part soluz mary sera mittré (The single part afflicted will be mitred). Embattled French ambassador Charles de *Mary*llac, Bishop of Vannes (thus he was already mitred and would soon again be mitred as Bishop of Vienna), was defeated in negotiations with his enemy at Metz.

(2) Retour conflict passera sur la thuille (Return conflict will pass over the tile). The defensive walls around Metz were made of tile, an uncommon material for this purpose. Henry II of France (Nostradamus' king) and Emperor Charles V were the two in conflict at Metz.

(3) Par cinq cens un trahyr sera tiltré (By five hundred, treason will be titled). The day following the failed negotiations with the traitor Marquis de Brandebourg, at Metz, it was recorded that the mayor despatched 500 soldiers to join the mercenaries there.

(4) Narbon & Saulce par coutaux avons d'huille (Narbon and Saulce by knives we have oil). At the siege of Metz, two officers, *D'Albon* and *Saulx,* were in charge of the commissary. A list of their supplies shows: *tiles,* casks of *oil* and pitch, rope and *knives.* The "X" as used in Saulx was often put in place of "s" in Provencal usage. The word "Narbon" is pretty close to "D'Albon," and Nostradamus had used such a gimmick in both quatrains 6-56 and 8-22, wherein both Narbon and Perpignan are mentioned. D'Albon was the besieger of Perpignan, and at the time that Nostradamus wrote this quatrain, he was one of the three commanders of the Catholic army.

Which correspondence seems better?

Everett Bleiler suggests that, as often happens, a correlation with this quatrain might be found in another event of Nostradamus' own day. This is his idea, based upon the possible use of "five-less-one" which he has suggested, and with which I close this examination:

> A stronger explanation is to be found [for quatrain 9-34] in the life of Catherine de Médicis. 'Five less one' is 'quatre,' which is not far [in pronunciation] from [Catherine]. Catherine was involved in a case of simony concerning the Bishopric of Narbonne. A courtier named Saulce befriended Catherine by offering to take his knife and cut off the nose of Diane [de Poitiers], the King's mistress.

An interesting possibility indeed. I refer to the possible correlation, not the drastic rhinoplasty. . . .

THE EXECUTION OF CHARLES I

OF ENGLAND

9-49

Gand & Bruceles marcheront contre Anuers.
Senat de Londres mettront à mort leur roy
Le sel & vin luy seront à l'enuers,
Pour eux auoir le regne en desarroy.

Ghent and Brussels will march against Antwerp,
The senate of London will put to death their king
The salt and wine will be against him,
To have them, the realm in disarray.

The Rigaud copy of the *Centuries* from which I have been taking most of this material, has "Envers," rather than "Anuers," in the first line. I believe this is a typographical error, and I go along with other editions, which show "Anvers." A "u" is often used for a "v." Anvers is the old name for Antwerp.

Nostradamian Charles Ward offers to handle all four lines of this quatrain together. He marvels over the fact that the Treaty of Westphalia in October of 1648 occurred just three months before Charles I of England knelt at the executioner's block in London. He says

> . . . that the conjunction of the two events is extraordinarily definite and remarkable.

The Treaty, says Ward, ended Spain's attempts to establish rights to the Netherlands, and is well described by the words "Ghent and Brussels will march against Antwerp." This is total nonsense. No such action took place.

However, a quick perusal of history books reveals that ninety years previously, when Nostradamus wrote the *Centuries,* there was much activity going on in the area of Ghent, Brussels and Antwerp. In 1555, Emperor Charles V of the Holy Roman Empire (which Voltaire said was none of those three designations) was attempting to consolidate a number of communities that included what is now Belgium, Luxembourg and Holland, and to control a peasantry who were very unhappy with the heavy taxes they paid to Spain, who claimed the area. Charles transferred his power to his son Philip, whose main interest was enforcing the Inquisition.

Nostradamus did well to predict strange events in that area, since it was a confusing time and likely to see armies marching about from city to city. We must recall that our hero was in the habit of naming three French towns or cities in close proximity to one another. Could he have done this here, too? Here we find him naming three cities located close together in an almost perfect equilateral triangle, for whatever reason.

James Laver, pointing out the apparently remarkable prediction when line two of this quatrain is taken alone, reminds us that in 1649 King Charles I was executed at the order of the English parliament. He declares that the prophet would have had to write a million quatrains to come up with that prediction just by chance. Not so. Given all of recorded time for this to occur, with the seer understandably believing that monarchies would continue throughout history, we cannot be surprised if occasionally he got lucky. The thousands of times that he was unlucky must also be counted.

As early as 1625, observer Gabriel Naudé wrote:

> . . . The **Centuries** are so ambiguous, and so diverse, obscure and enigmatic, that it is not something to marvel at, if amongst a thousand quatrains, each of which speaks always of five or six different things . . . one finds sometimes a [line] which mentions [an event] as if all these things were extraordinary, and as though, if they didn't occur at one period, they couldn't occur at another.

But we must also look to events that had already taken place before Nostradamus' time, to see if perhaps the prophet was merely restating history for us, as he sometimes did. Everett Bleiler suggests that this quatrain might be just such an entity. He says,

> Fifteenth century English history, however, can account for the verse fairly well. At about the time that Henry VI died in the Tower, without objection from Parliament, the English were driven out of Guienne, the region from which wine and salt were imported. There was much turmoil in England at the loss of the French territories.

Is this an explanation for Quatrain 9-49? Perhaps. But, given all the colorful metaphors used by Nostradamus, along with the obscurity of his writing, we may be falling into the same trap that the Nostradamians have entered so enthusiastically: We may be looking for a correspondence that is simply not there, in a verse with one line that came true.

NAPOLEON BONAPARTE &

THE IMPRISONMENT

OF THE POPES

8 - 1

PAV, NAY, LORON plus feu qu'à sang sera.
Laude nager, fuir grand aux surrez.
Les agassas entree refusera.
Pampon, Durance les tiendra enserrez.

PAU, NAY, OLORON will be more in fire than
   in blood.
Swimming the Aude, the great one fleeing to the
   mountains.
He refuses the magpies entrance.
Pamplona, the Durance River holds them enclosed.

Lest it be thought that I have gone off into Wonderland with this translation, I should explain some aspects of my version.

(a) Some editions of Nostradamus show "L'Aude" in place of "Laude." The Aude River runs just north of Narbonne near the southeastern edge of the French-Spanish border.

(b) West of that, near the southwestern border, are the three towns Pau, Nay and Oloron. Pau is now a large and prosperous city; Nay and Oloron are minor towns.

(c) The word "surrez" does not show up in French, of whatever vintage, but all through various dictionaries are derivatives suggesting that "surrez" could be "serrez," which denotes a range of jagged or "serrated" mountains. The Spanish word "sierra" refers to a range of mountains. "Serres" shows up in old French as a modifier meaning "hills," and in Nostradamus' time, an accepted practice was to use "z" in place of a final "s."

(d) "Durance" is clearly the Durance River, a prominent tributary which runs just north of Nostradamus' birthplace. It bore that name when he lived there, and it still does.

(e) "Pampon" is most likely a version of the modern name Pamplona, which appears in geographical texts and maps in a great variety of spellings such as: Pamplon, Pampelona, Pampelune and Pampeluna. This city, famous for its annual festival in which overly macho men are pursued in the streets by largely disinterested bulls, was within the kingdom of Navarre in the 16th century.

[It is worth noting, on a map,] the relationship of the four named towns and the Pyrenees range, which marks the border between modern France and Spain.

Here in Quatrain 8-1 we again have the strange device in which Nostradamus names towns or cities located close to one another, and often located in an almost perfect equilateral triangle. Perhaps he consulted maps of his day and merely used this gimmick for his own amusement, or he might have been titilated by the possible prophetic or magical significance of this geometric relationship. I like to imagine that it was one of his little jokes on the readers. . . .

I believe that this quatrain simply expresses Nostradamus' prophecies of: (1) heavy problems in the area of the city of Pau, (2) some prominent person escaping across the Aude River into the mountains, (3) something involving magpies or chattering persons, or possibly pilgrims, (4) something about the city of Pamplona in Spain, and the Durance River offering an impediment to someone. I believe these were intended to be four separate predictions, since they are marked off by periods at the end of each line.

Before leaving this matter of Napoleon-in-Nostradamus, I will give you another example of a place where the Nostradamians have found Bonaparte. Quatrain 8-57 reads:

> *De souldat simple paruiendra en empire,*
> *De robe courte paruiendra à la longue*
> *Vaillant aux armes en eglise ou plus pyre,*
> *Vexer les prestres comme l'eau fait l'esponge.*

> From a simple soldier he will attain to empire,
> From a short robe he will attain to the long
> Valiant in arms, in the church he is the worst,
> Vexing the priests like water does the sponge.

Who is Nostradamus speaking of here? Most of the Nostradamians dearly want it to be Napoleon. Garencières, resident in Britain at the time he wrote and always a royalist, says that he never knew nor heard of any body to whom this Stanza might be better applied, than to the late Usurper Cromwell. . . .

Garencières then gives a number of excellent supporting details for his decision. But the quatrain can apply to Mussolini, Hitler and others just as well. I leave it to my reader to find historical facts on these two that will satisfy the quatrain. They are certainly there to be found.

Wishful thinking aside, Nostradamus did not know Napoleon, nor the other corporal we will next bring up for examination.

ADOLF HITLER I

2-24

Bestes farouches de faim fleuues tranner,
Plus part du champ encontre Hister sera.
En caige de fer le grand fera treisner,
Quand rien enfant de Germain obseruera.

Beasts mad with hunger will swim across rivers,
Most of the army will be against the Lower Danube.
The great one shall be dragged in an iron cage
When the child brother will observe nothing.

In prophecy, it seems that the Antichrist is always imminent. There are different demons for different ages, with Napoleon being replaced by Hitler who in turn is squeezed out by Khomeni, a Khadafy, and so on. To discover a currently prominent devil in Nostradamus is the dearest wish of each devotee of the prophet.

On Roman maps of the area, the lower portion of the Danube River is known as either "Ister" or "Hister." Nostradamus, as we have seen, often used Latin words and names. (In the next quatrain we will discuss, "Hister" is joined with the Rhine River, strengthening our right to believe it to refer, certainly in that verse and very likely in this one, too, to the Lower Danube.)

The Nostradamians sorely need to find an important figure like Adolf Hitler in the prophecies; he just could not have been missed by their hero. Though Nostradamian Stewart Robb recognizes the real meaning of "Hister," he admits the fact then rationalizes it by saying:

> Hister is an old, old name for the Danube, old even when Nostradamus resuscitated it for some good reason of his own. But the passage of the centuries has brought it up to date. It was the obvious word for the prophet to use. It meant the Danube: it also served as an anagram for Hitler. . . . The change of one letter was permissible in anagram writing (see Dictionnaire de Trevoux). What other word could serve better than Hister to specify both the name, and the place of origin of [Hitler]?

I have searched diligently to discover the source of this "change of one letter" rule, and cannot locate the "Dictionnaire de Trevoux," either. *All* of the definitions and discussions of the word "anagram" that I have found omit any mention of this practice. I leave it to my readers to answer Mr. Robb's question as posed above.

The most astonishing fact about Mr. Robb's discussion on

what he calls the "Three Hister Quatrains" is that he admits "Hister" refers to the Lower Danube, but claims it is used here to represent Adolf Hitler, then he proceeds to point out the relationship of the Lower Danube to the Hitler story. He is using "Hister" *both* ways!

As for "de Germain," it is easy to interpret that as meaning "of Germany." Such a usage is reasonable enough, given the strong influence on modern France of English vocabulary, and it can be found in modern French dictionaries. But from the 12th to the 16th century, "de germain" meant "brother" or "near relative" and nothing else. The word "German" came to be used in France only after World War II, to mean an inhabitant of Germany.

Everett Bleiler, as Liberté E. LeVert, suggests that though the Nostradamians have chosen to associate Hitler with this quatrain, it was evident to those of the 1550s that something else was being hinted at. His printing of line four uses "Rin" in place of "rien," thus giving the meaning "child of the Rhine." I believe a better translation of his printing would be "When the child brother will observe the Rhine." However, Mr. Bleiler says:

> For Nostradamus's contemporaries . . . [the verse] embodied clear references to recent advances by the Turks, in which much of the Hungarian plain was lost and Austria was gravely threatened.

Mr. Bleiler goes on to say that

> The 'child of the Rhine' was Charles V, in Flanders, and his brother was Ferdinand, titular King of Hungary.

His analysis is based upon what I believe (because of the Rigaud version which I have consulted) to be a faulted printing of line four, which he translates as, "When a child of the Rhine shall keep watch over his brother."

Bleiler's idea of the Turkish action is quite interesting, though, since in 1529 the Turks had encamped along the Lower Danube and threatened the city of Vienna. Emperor Charles V, the largely absentee ruler of Germany, stopped the Turks at that point. Later, seeing that Henry II, Nostradamus' monarch, had invaded Germany from the west, he tried to regain that territory and failed. His brother, Ferdinand, arranged the Peace of Augsburg in 1555, the year that the *Centuries* (containing this quatrain) was published.

Mr. Bleiler's suggestion, that Quatrain 2-24 is a Q3K, may quite possibly be valid. But where is the Man in the Iron Cage?

ADOLF HITLER II

4-68

En l'an bien proche non esloigné de Venus,
Les deux plus grans de l'Asie & d'Affrique
De Ryn & Hister qu'on dira sont venus,
Crys, pleurs à Malte & costé ligustique.

In the year very near, not far from Venus,
The two greatest of Asia & Africa
From the Rhine & Lower Danube, which will be
  said to have come,

Cries, tears at Malta & the Ligurian coast.

James Laver sees in this quatrain that

> If Mussolini might be called the greatest one in
> Africa and Japan the greatest one in Asia, then
> the second line refers to the Tripartite Pact.
> Both, says the third line, will make themselves
> Hitler's accomplice, and the fourth may be taken
> to refer to the bombing of Malta and the bom-
> bardment of Genoa.

The Tripartite Pact created the Axis powers (Germany, Italy and Japan) in December of 1941. To author Laver, that event was less than a year old when he wrote his analysis. Genoa is the central port city of the Ligurian coast, and was bombarded along with most of the rest of that coast. Hardly any further comment is needed on the lengths to which Laver has reached for this analysis.

I cannot resist the feeling that Nostradamus could not resist the temptation in this quatrain to rhyme "Venus" (the planet or goddess) and "venus," (in French, the plural past participle of the verb "to come"). The "Venus" in line one probably refers to Venice, which is located on the eastern coast of Italy, mirrored by the "Ligurian coast" on the western side. "Hister," as we have seen in the previously discussed quatrain, does not refer to Adolf Hitler, but to the Lower Danube, particularly in view of its association here with the Rhine.

LIFE & DEATH OF ELIZABETH I

6-74

La deschassee au regne tournera,
Ses ennemis trouués des coniurés:
Plus que iamais son temps triomphera,
Trois & septante à mort trop asseurés.

Minimally corrected for modern usage, this becomes:

La dechassée au regne tournera,
Ses ennemis trouvés de conjurés:
Plus que jamais son temps triomphera,
Trois & septante à mort trop assurés.

She who was chased out shall return to the king-
dom,
Her enemies found to be conspirators:
More than ever her time will triumph,
Three and seventy to death much assured.

We must bear in mind that Nostradamus' sovereign was Henry II, archenemy of Elizabeth. Nostradamus was not unaware of the service he could perform for his sovereign by creating discontent in England, which he certainly managed to do with some of his annual almanacs. As taken from Nostradamian Charles Ward's book, line four of Quatrain 6-74 reads:

Trois, et Septante, la mort, trop asseurez.

It appears that Ward made slight alterations from the original here in order to make it not only a reference to Elizabeth, but an accurate prophecy of her future death. He has broken up the last line but explains

> The fourth line is a very singular one. It has no
> punctuation in the edition of 1558; so I intro-

duce a comma between *trois* and *septante*. . . .
Trois stands for 1603. Nostradamus often drops the thousands and hundreds from a date. . . .
The nought in 1603 cannot be given, so that, omitting the figures in the tens, hundreds, and thousands, the *trois* remaining gives the date; so that the line remains 'In the third year (of the seventeenth century) and seventy years old, as-sured death comes.'

This quatrain may well have actually been a direct reference to Elizabeth by Nostradamus, since it seems to describe the conditions of her ascent to the throne. This can be classified as an assured hit by Nostradamus since that event occurred the same year that the quatrain was first published. It is quite clearly a "Q3K."

Obviously, it is the last line that has delighted the Nostradamians. Elizabeth died in 1603, at the age of *seventy*. But that line clearly says "three and seventy." In the original Old French, the word "septante"—seventy—is used. (It would be represented by "soixante-dix" in modern French.) "Seventy-three" would thus be "septante-trois," which would not fit the meter of the verse, so it appears that "trois et septante" was used. But "seventy-three" does not fulfill what the Nostradamians require for a working prophecy. Thus, a comma is inventively inserted into the line. Such manipulation to serve the cause is quite common among the Believers.

To perpetuate their needs, in 1715 the Nostradamus fans liberally retranslated and expanded the quatrain thus:

> (1) The Rejected shall for all that come to the
> Crown;
>
> (2) Her Enemies will be found to have been a
> band of Traitors forsworn against Her.
>
> (3) The Time of her Reign will be more Happy
> and Glorious than any of her Predecessors
>
> (4) In th 3rd Year of the Century, at the Age of
> Seventy She dies, of which I am but too much
> assured.

I find it astonishing how French expands so dramatically to reveal its hidden meanings when merely translated into English!

The gravestone of Nostradamus, set in a church wall in Salon de Provence.

I must mention the very important fact that this same quatrain has been interpreted in radically different ways by other prominent Nostradamians. Consider how many novel ways have been found to make this Nostradamus quatrain work according to expectations:

(1) Garencières, ever the Royalist, says it predicts that Charles II will return to the English throne.

(2) De Fontbrune discovers here the advent of communism in France, which he says will last just three years and seventy days.

(3) Henry C. Roberts tells us he gets a clear picture of liberal Nazis [!?] returning to Germany following World War II.

(4) Vlaicu Ionescu is convinced that it portends that for seventy-three years communism will rule in Russia after being chased there out of France by Napoleon.

(5) Le Pelletier finds here an allegorical reference to events in the French Revolution.

Once more, various interpreters—six of the major figures in the field—believe they have each solved one of the Nostradamus puzzles, and they all have quite different answers. At best, only one can possibly be right, and all appear to be wrong, but their pronouncements have been taken seriously by the Believers.

FURTHER READING

Boswell, Rolfe. *Nostradamus Speaks.* Thomas Y. Crowell, 1941, 381 p.

Offers a detailed interpretation of Nostradamus's so-called Luminary Epistle to Henry II (including remarks about Napoleon, Napoleon III, Adolf Hitler, and the coming of the Antichrist) and the *Centuries.*

Hogue, John. *Nostradamus: The New Revelations.* Lower Lake, Cal.: Element Books, 1994, 256 p.

Traces Nostradamus's prophetic lineage and then interprets the prophecies and their alleged fulfillment from the French Revolution to the modern era. By Hogue's interpretations, Nostradamus foresaw the AIDS epidemic, ecological concerns, and the spiritual directionlessness characteristic of the millennium's approach.

Laver, James. "The Predictions of Nostradamus." *The Spectator* 164, No. 5843 (21 June 1940): 833.

Short summary of Nostradamus's signal predictions, especially in regard to modern history. Laver writes that "there remain enough quatrains to convince any unprejudiced reader that the sixteenth-century Jew had *some* power of seeing into the future, and to those who cling to a rationalistic interpretation of history, Nostradamus must remain an enigma as insoluble as he is disquieting."

Paulson, Michael G. "Nostradamus Saw It First." *The USF Language Quarterly* XXIII, Nos. 3-4 (Spring-Summer 1985): 23-6.

Examines several of Nostradamus's more well-known prophecies. Paulson concludes that because commentators have cited the accuracy rate of the prophecies as anywhere between five and fifty percent, Nostradamus should give pause to those who question his bona fides. "Five or fifty percent accurate, how can we explain this in our modern, scientific age?" he writes. "Did Nostradamus resort to trickery and ruse or did he see it all? It is up to each individual to decide the answer for himself."

Robb, Stewart. *Prophecies of World Events by Nostradamus.* New York: Liveright Publishing, 1961, 144 p.

Discourse upon Nostradamus's major prophecies by a sympathetic author whose stated purpose "is to prove that prophecy is a scientific fact."

Ward, Charles A. *Oracles of Nostradamus.* New York: Modern Library, 1940, 366 p.

Originally published in 1891. This is an orderly explication of Nostradamus's prophecies up to the time of Napoleon III. Ward includes a useful "Life of Nostradamus" and reprints the seer's prefatory epistles to his son and to Henry II.

Renaissance Natural Philosophy

INTRODUCTION

Renaissance natural philosophy was a sixteenth- and seventeenth-century school of thought which rejected the Aristotelian conception of form, matter, and the nature of the soul, among other beliefs. The primary tenet of this philosophy focuses on the relationship between the microcosm and the macrocosm. Philosophers of nature argued, and most people of the time believed, that there exists a direct correspondence between man, the world, and the universe. The universe, according to the cosmology of the time, was infinite and contained an infinite number of solar systems with planets inhabited by conscious, rational beings. Most philosophers of nature, such as Giordano Bruno and Tomasso Campanella, contended that all organic and inorganic objects in the universe, including rocks, trees, animals, humans, stars, and planets, have souls and are united by a greater world-soul. This linkage of all creatures of the world, the microcosm, to those of the universe, the macrocosm, implies that the world of man mirrors that of universal nature. Some natural philosophers, such as Giovanni Pico della Mirandola, focused on the means by which the truth of nature and being could be revealed by observing and examining the symmetries between man, the world, and the universe. These philosophers and others further discussed astrology and magic as methods of understanding the relationship between macrocosm and microcosm. In their writings they also proposed how this knowledge might be practically utilized.

As the belief in the relationship between man and the universe was a widely held one, the belief in and practice of both astrology and magic were similarly common. Throughout the sixteenth and seventeenth centuries, astrology gradually grew from an aspect of the worldview into a distinct system of belief. Astrologers were commonly consulted by rulers such as Henry VIII, Edward VI, and Elizabeth I. Also interested in astrological forecasts were courtiers and intellectuals in England and Europe. Astrologers servicing this elite class made general predictions regarding subjects such as weather, war, and politics. Another branch of astrology included the mapping of the stars and planets as they were situated at the time of a person's birth. This map, known as a nativity, was necessary for an astrologer to predict the right moment for a person to take specific actions in fulfilling his or her destiny. Astrology was made available to society as a whole primarily through almanacs, which predicted astronomical events, marked days of festivals and similar activities, and made prognostications, or forecasts, of notable events of the year. Astrology was also used in the practice of medicine, as different organs and parts of the body were thought to be influenced by planets and signs of the zodiac. Throughout all of these activities, numerous opportunities for astrologers to cheat and deceive people presented themselves, and this made the profession and its practitioners the target of satire in the literature and drama of the time.

The practice of magic, on the other hand, was viewed more seriously by society and by the Roman Catholic Church. Magic, like astrology, was understood to be a means of deciphering the relationship between man and the universe. The practice of natural magic utilized knowledge of occult forces within nature gained through experience, observation, and experiments. As supernatural aid was not involved in natural magic, its practitioners were not harshly judged. However, some forms of magic employed supernatural assistance, such as the aid of spirits and demons, and were practiced only in secrecy. Suspected practitioners of magic were accused of witchcraft and executed. Natural philosophers, such as Marsilio Ficino, Campanella, and Pico della Mirandola, who wrote about the nature of magic and its possibilities, were often imprisoned for their writings, and their works were condemned by the Church.

As the scientific revolution swept through England and Europe in the late seventeenth century, the popularity of the beliefs regarding nature and the universe upheld by Renaissance natural philosophers dwindled. The world and the universe began to be viewed as mechanical in nature. Astrology eventually became less widely practiced. Almanacs, perhaps the most widely utilized form of astrology, began to focus primarily on meteorological predictions and the designation of upcoming holidays and festivals. Magic became a less frequent topic of philosophical discussion. People were no longer executed for witchcraft. The scientific revolution hastened the death of Renaissance natural philosophy and forever changed literature, as the common faith of poets and dramatists in a correspondence between man, his world, and the universe was eliminated. As Marjorie Hope Nicolson has stated in regard to the effect of the "new science" on seventeenth-century poetry, ". . . the animate macrocosm and living microcosm disappeared, and their places were taken by a mechanical clock and men with mechanical hearts."

COSMOLOGY

Alexandre Koyré

SOURCE: "The New Astronomy and the New Metaphysics," in *From the Closed World to the Infinite Universe*, The Johns Hopkins University Press, 1957, pp. 28-57.

[*In the following essay, Koyré examines the development of astronomy and metaphysics by comparing the cosmological beliefs of Copernicus, Digges, Bruno, and Gilbert.*]

Palingenius and Copernicus are practically contemporaries. Indeed, the *Zodiacus vitae* and the *De revolutionibus orbium coelestium* must have been written at about the same time. Yet they have nothing, or nearly nothing, in common. They are as far away from each other as if they were separated by centuries.

As a matter of fact, they are, indeed, separated by centuries, by all those centuries during which Aristotelian cosmology and Ptolemaic astronomy dominated Western thought. Copernicus, of course, makes full use of the mathematical technics elaborated by Ptolemy—one of the greatest achievements of the human mind—and yet, for his inspiration he goes back beyond him, and beyond Aristotle, to the golden age of Pythagoras and of Plato. He quotes Heraclides, Ecphantus and Hiketas, Philolaos and Aristarchus of Samos; and according to Rheticus, his pupil and mouthpiece, it is

> . . . following Plato and the Pythagoreans, the greatest mathematicians of that divine age, that [he] thought that in order to determine the cause of the phenomena, circular motions have to be ascribed to the spherical earth.

I need not insist on the overwhelming scientific and philosophical importance of Copernican astronomy, which, by removing the earth from the center of the world and placing it among the planets, undermined the very foundations of the traditional cosmic world-order with its hierarchical structure and qualitative opposition of the celestial realm of immutable being to the terrestrial or sublunar region of change and decay. Compared to the deep criticism of its metaphysical basis by Nicholas of Cusa, the Copernican revolution may appear rather half-hearted and not very radical. It was, on the other hand, much more effective, at least in the long run; for, as we know, the immediate effect of the Copernican revolution was to spread skepticism and bewilderment of which the famous verses of John Donne give such a striking, though somewhat belated, expression, telling us that the

> . . . new Philosophy calls all in doubt,
> The Element of fire is quite put out;
> The Sun is lost, and th'earth, and no mans wit
> Can well direct him where to looke for it.
> And freely men confesse that this world's spent,
> When in the Planets, and the Firmament
> They seeke so many new; then see that this
> Is crumbled out againe to his Atomies.
> 'Tis all in peeces, all cohaerence gone;
> All just supply, and all Relation.

To tell the truth, the world of Copernicus is by no means devoid of hierarchical features. Thus, if he asserts that it is not the skies which move, but the earth, it is not only because it seems irrational to move a tremendously big body instead of a relatively small one, "that which contains and locates and not that which is contained and located," but also because "the condition of *being at rest* is considered as nobler and more divine than that of *change* and *inconsistency;* the latter therefore, is more suited to the earth than to the universe." And it is on account of its supreme perfection and value—source of light and of life—that the place it occupies in the world is assigned to the sun: the central place which, following the Pythagorean tradition and thus reversing completely the Aristotelian

and mediaeval scale, Copernicus believes to be the best and the most important one.

Thus, though the Copernican world is no more hierarchically structured (at least not fully: it has, so to say, two poles of perfection, the sun and the sphere of the fixed stars, with the planets in between), it is still a well-ordered world. Moreover, it is still a finite one.

This finiteness of the Copernican world may appear illogical. Indeed, the only reason for assuming the existence of the sphere of the fixed stars being their common motion, the negation of that motion should lead immediately to the negation of the very existence of that sphere; moreover, since, in the Copernican world, the fixed stars must be exceedingly big—the smallest being larger than the whole *Orbis magnus*—the sphere of the fixed stars must be rather thick; it seems only reasonable to extend its volume indefinitely "upwards."

It is rather natural to interpret Copernicus this way, that is, as an advocate of the infinity of the world, all the more so as he actually raises the question of the possibility of an indefinite spatial extension beyond the stellar sphere, though refusing to treat that problem as not scientific and turning it over to the philosophers. As a matter of fact, it is in this way that the Copernican doctrine was interpreted by Gianbattista Riccioli, by Huygens, and more recently by Mr. [Grant] McColley.

Though it seems reasonable and natural, I do not believe this interpretation to represent the actual views of Copernicus. Human thought, even that of the greatest geniuses, is never completely consequent and logical. We must not be astonished, therefore, that Copernicus, who believed in the existence of material planetary spheres because he needed them in order to explain the motion of the planets, believed also in that of a sphere of the fixed stars which he no longer needed. Moreover, though its existence did not explain anything, it still had some usefulness: the stellar sphere, which "embraced and contained everything and itself," held the world together and, besides, enabled Copernicus to assign a determined position to the sun.

In any case, Copernicus tells us quite clearly that

> . . . the universe is spherical; partly because this form, being a complete whole, needing no joints, is the most perfect of all; partly because it constitutes the most spacious form which is thus best suited to contain and retain all things; or also because all discrete parts of the world, I mean the sun, the moon and the planets, appear as spheres.

True, he rejects the Aristotelian doctrine according to which "outside the world there is no body, nor place, nor empty space, in fact that nothing at all exists" because it seems to him "really strange that something could be enclosed by nothing" and believes that, if we admitted that "the heavens were infinite and bounded only by their inner concavity," then we should have better reason to assert "that there is nothing outside the heavens, because everything, whatever its size, is within them," in which case, of course, the heavens would have to be motionless: the infinite, indeed, cannot be moved or traversed.

Yet he never tells us that the *visible world,* the world of the fixed stars, is infinite, but only that it is immeasurable (*immensum*), that it is so large that not only the earth compared to the skies is "as a point" (this, by the way, had already been asserted by Ptolemy), but also the whole orb of the earth's annual circuit around the sun; and that we do not and cannot know the limit, the dimension of the world. Moreover, when dealing with the famous objection of Ptolemy according to which "the earth and all earthly things if set in rotation would be dissolved by the action of nature," that is, by the centrifugal forces produced by the very great speed of its revolution, Copernicus replies that this disruptive effect would be so much stronger upon the heavens as their motion is more rapid than that of the earth, and that, "if this argument were true, the extent of the heavens would become infinite." In which case, of course, they would have to stand still, which, though finite, they do.

Thus we have to admit that, even if outside the world there were not nothing but space and even matter, nevertheless the *world* of Copernicus would remain a finite one, encompassed by a material sphere or orb, the sphere of the fixed stars—a sphere that has a centrum, a centrum occupied by the sun. It seems to me that there is no other way of interpreting the teaching of Copernicus. Does he not tell us that

> . . . the first and the supreme of all [spheres] is the sphere of the fixed stars which contains everything and itself and which, therefore, is at rest. Indeed, it is the place of the world to which are referred the motion and the position of all other stars. Some [astronomers] indeed, have thought that, in a certain manner, this sphere is also subjected to change: but in our deduction of the terrestrial motion we have determined another cause why it appears so. [After the sphere of the fixed stars] comes Saturn, which performs its circuit in thirty years. After him, Jupiter, which moves in a duodecennial revolution. Then Mars which circumgirates in two years. The fourth place in this order is occupied by the annual revolution, which, as we have said, contains the Earth with the orb of the Moon as an epicycle. In the fifth place Venus revolves in nine months. Finally, the sixth place is held by Mercury, which goes around in the space of eighty days.

> But in the center of all resides the Sun. Who, indeed, in this most magnificent temple would put the light in another, or in a better place than that one wherefrom it could at the same time illuminate the whole of it? Therefore it is not improperly that some people call it the lamp of the world, others its mind, others its ruler. Trismegistus [calls it] the visible God, Sophocles' Electra, the All-Seeing. Thus, assuredly, as residing in the royal see the Sun governs the surrounding family of the stars.

We have to admit the evidence: the world of Copernicus is finite. Moreover, it seems to be psychologically quite normal that the man who took the first step, that of arresting the motion of the sphere of the fixed stars, hesitated before taking the second, that of dissolving it in boundless space; it was enough for one man to move the earth and to enlarge the world so as to make it immeasurable—*immensum;* to ask him to make it infinite is obviously asking too much.

Great importance has been attributed to the enlargement of the Copernican world as compared to the mediaeval one—its diameter is at least 2000 times greater. Yet, we must not forget, as Professor [A. O.] Lovejoy . . . pointed out, that even the Aristotelian or Ptolemaic world was by no means that snug little thing that we see represented on the miniatures adorning the manuscripts of the Middle Ages and of which Sir Walter Raleigh gave us such an enchanting description. Though rather small by our astronomical standards, and even by those of Copernicus, it was in itself sufficiently big not to be felt as built to man's measure: about 20,000 terrestrial radii, such was the accepted figure, that is, about 125,000,000 miles.

Let us not forget, moreover, that, by comparison with the infinite, the world of Copernicus is by no means greater than that of mediaeval astronomy; they are both as nothing, because *inter finitum et infinitum non est proportio.* We do not approach the infinite universe by increasing the dimensions of our world. We may make it as large as we want: that does *not* bring us any nearer to it.

Notwithstanding this, it remains clear that it is somewhat easier, psychologically if not logically, to pass from a very large, immeasurable and ever-growing world to an infinite one than to make this jump starting with a rather big, but still determinably limited sphere: the world-bubble has to swell before bursting. It is also clear that by his reform, or revolution, of astronomy Copernicus removed one of the most valid scientific objections against the infinity of the universe, based, precisely, upon the empirical, common-sense fact of the motion of the celestial spheres.

The infinite cannot be traversed, argued Aristotle; now the stars turn around, therefore . . . But the stars do not turn around; they stand still, therefore . . . It is thus not surprising that in a rather short time after Copernicus some bold minds made the step that Copernicus refused to make, and asserted that the celestial sphere, that is the sphere of the fixed stars of Copernican astronomy, does not exist, and that the starry heavens, in which the stars are placed at different distances from the earth, "extendeth itself infinitely up."

It has been commonly assumed until recent times that it was Giordano Bruno who, drawing on Lucretius and creatively misunderstanding both him and Nicholas of Cusa, first made this decisive step. Today, after the discovery by Professor Johnson and Dr. Larkey—in 1934—of the *Perfit Description of the Caelestiall Orbes according to the most aunciene doctrine of the Pythagoreans lately revived by Copernicus and by Geometricall Demonstrations approued,* which Thomas Digges, in 1576, added to the *Prognostication euerlasting* of his father Leonard Digges, this honor, at least partially, must be ascribed to him. Indeed, though different interpretations may be given of the text of Thomas Digges—and my own differs somewhat from that of Professor Johnson and Dr. Larkey—it is certain, in any case, that Thomas Digges was the first Copernican to replace his master's conception, that of a closed world, by that of an open one, and that in his *Description,* where he gives a fairly good, though rather free, translation of the cosmological part of the *De revolutionibus orbium coelestium,* he makes some rather striking additions. First, in his description of the orb of Saturn he inserts the clause that this orb is "of all others next vnto that infinite Orbe immouable, garnished with lights innumerable"; then he substitutes for the well-known Copernican diagram of the world another one, in which the stars are placed on the whole page, above as well as below the line by which Copernicus represented the *ultima sphaera mundi.* The text that Thomas Digges adds to his diagram is very curious. In my opinion, it expresses the hesitation and the uncertainty of a mind—a very bold mind—which on the one hand not only accepted the Copernican world-view, but even went beyond it, and which, on the other hand, was still dominated by the religious conception—or image—of a heaven located in space. Thomas Digges begins by telling us that:

> The orbe of the starres fixed infinitely up extendeth hit self in altitude sphericallye, and therefore immouable.

Yet he adds that this orbe is

> the pallace of felicitye garnished with perpetuall shininge glorious lightes innumerable, farr excelling our sonne both in quantity and quanlitye.

And that it is

> the Court of the great God, the habitacle of the elect, and of the coelestiall angelles.

The text accompanying [Digges's diagram of the infinite Copernican universe] develops this idea:

> Heerein can wee never sufficiently admire thys wonderfull and incomprehensible huge frame of goddes woorke proponed to our senses, seinge first the baull of ye earth wherein we moue, to the common sorte seemeth greate, and yet in respecte of the Moones Orbe is very small, but compared with the *Orbis magnus* wherein it is carried, it scarcely retayneth any sensible proportion, so merueillously is that Orbe of Annuall motion greater than this little darke starre wherein we liue. But that *Orbis magnus* beinge as is before declared but as a poynct in respect of the immensity of that immoueable heaven, we may easily consider what little portion of gods frame, our Elementare corruptible worlde is, but neuer sufficiently be able to admire the immensity of the Rest. Especially of that fixed Orbe garnished with lightes innumerable and reachinge vp in *Sphaericall altitude* without ende. Of which lightes Celestiall it is to bee thoughte that we only behoulde sutch as are in the inferioure partes of the same Orbe, and as they are hygher, so seeme they of lesse and lesser quantity, even tyll our syghte beinge not able farder to reache or conceyve, the greatest part rest by reason of their wonderfull distance inuisible vnto vs. And this may well be thought of vs to be the gloriouse court of ye great god, whose vnsercheable works inuisible we may partly by these his visible coniecture, to whose infinit power and maiesty such

an infinit place surmountinge all other both in quantity and quality only is conueniente. But because the world hath so longe a time bin carried with an opinion of the earths stabilitye, as the contrary cannot but be nowe very imperswasible.

Thus, as we see, Thomas Digges puts his stars into a theological heaven; not into an astronomical sky. As a matter of fact, we are not very far from the conception of Palingenius—whom Digges knows and quotes—and, perhaps, nearer to him than to Copernicus. Palingenius, it is true, places his heaven above the stars, whereas Thomas Digges puts them into it. Yet he maintains the separation between our world—the world of the sun and the planets—and the heavenly sphere, the dwelling-place of God, the celestial angels, and the saints. Needless to say, there is no place for Paradise in the astronomical world of Copernicus.

That is the reason why, in spite of the very able defence of the priority rights of Digges made by Professor Johnson in his excellent book, *Astronomical Thought in Renaissance England,* I still believe that it was Bruno who, for the first time, presented to us the sketch, or the outline, of the cosmology that became dominant in the last two centuries, and I cannot but agree with Professor Lovejoy, who in his classical *Great Chain of Being* tells us that,

> Though the elements of the new cosmography had, then, found earlier expression in several quarters, it is Giordano Bruno who must be regarded as the principal representative of the doctrine of the decentralised, infinite and infinitely populous universe; for he not only preached it throughout western Europe with the fervour of an evangelist, but also first gave a thorough statement of the grounds on which it was to gain acceptance from the general public.

Indeed, never before has the essential infinitude of space been asserted in such an outright, definite and conscious manner.

Thus, already in the *La Cena de le Ceneri,* where, by the way, Bruno gives the best discussion, and refutation, of the classical—Aristotelian and Ptolemaic—objections against the motion of the earth that were ever written before Galileo, he proclaims that "the world is infinite and that, therefore, there is no body in it to which it would pertain *simpliciter* to be in the center, or on the center, or on the periphery, or between these two extremes" of the world (which, moreover, do not exist), but only to be among other bodies. As for the world which has its cause and its origin in an infinite cause and an infinite principle, it must be infinitely infinite according to its corporeal necessity and its mode of being. And Bruno adds:

> It is certain that . . . it will never be possible to find an even half-probable reason, why there should be a limit to this corporeal universe, and, consequently, why the stars, which are contained in its space, should be finite in number.

But we find the clearest, and most forceful, presentation of the new gospel of the unity and the infinity of the world in his vernacular dialogues *De l'infinito universo e mondi* and in his Latin poem *De immenso et innumerabilibus.*

There is a single general space, a single vast immensity which we may freely call Void: in it are innumerable globes like this on which we live and grow; this space we declare to be infinite, since neither reason, convenience, sense-perception nor nature assign to it a limit. For there is no reason, nor defect of nature's gifts, either of active or passive power, to hinder the existence of other worlds throughout space, which is identical in natural character with our own space, that is everywhere filled with matter or at least ether.

We have, of course, heard nearly similar things from Nicholas of Cusa. And yet we cannot but recognize the difference of accent. Where Nicholas of Cusa simply states the impossibility of assigning limits to the world, Giordano Bruno asserts, and rejoices in, its infinity: the superior determination and clarity of the pupil compared to his master is striking.

To a body of infinite size there can be ascribed neither center nor boundary. For he who speaketh of emptiness, the void or the infinite ether, ascribeth to it neither weight nor lightness, nor motion, nor upper, nor lower, nor intermediate regions; assuming moreover that there are in this space those countless bodies such as our earth and other earths, our sun and other suns, which all revolve within this infinite space, through finite and determined spaces or around their own centres. Thus we on the earth say that the earth is in the centre; and all the philosophers ancient and modern of whatever sect will proclaim without prejudice to their own principles that here is indeed the centre.

Yet,

Just as we say that we are at the centre of that [universally] equidistant circle, which is the great horizon and the limit of our own encircling ethereal region, so doubtlessly the inhabitants of the moon believe themselves at the centre [of a great horizon] that embraces the earth, the sun and the other stars, and is the boundary of the radii of their own horizon. Thus the earth no more than any other world is at the centre; moreover, no points constitute determined celestial poles for our earth, just as she herself is not a definite and determined pole to any other point of the ether, or of the world-space; and the same is true of all other bodies. From various points of view these may all be regarded either as centres, or as points on the circumference, as poles, or zeniths and so forth. Thus the earth is not in the centre of the Universe; it is central only to our surrounding space.

Professor Lovejoy, in his treatment of Bruno, insists on the importance for the latter of the principle of plenitude, which governs his thought and dominates his metaphysics. Professor Lovejoy is perfectly right, of course: Bruno uses the principle of plenitude in an utterly ruthless manner, rejecting all the restrictions by which mediaeval thinkers tried to limit its applicability and boldly drawing from it all the consequences that it implies. Thus to the old and famous *questio disputata:* why did not God create an infinite world? —a question to which the mediaeval

scholastics gave so good an answer, namely, denying the very possibility of an infinite creature—Bruno simply replies, and he is the first to do it: God did. And even: God could not do otherwise.

Indeed, Bruno's God, the somewhat misunderstood *infinitas complicata* of Nicholas of Cusa, could not but explicate and express himself in an infinite, infinitely rich, and infinitely extended world.

Thus is the excellence of God magnified and the greatness of his kingdom made manifest; he is glorified not in one, but in countless suns; not in a single earth, but in a thousand, I say, in an infinity of worlds.

Thus not in vain the power of the intellect which ever seeketh, yea, and achieveth the addition of space to space, mass to mass, unity to unity, number to number, by the science that dischargeth us from the fetters of a most narrow kingdom and promoteth us to the freedom of a truly august realm, which freeth us from an imagined poverty and straineth to the possession of the myriad riches of so vast a space, of so worthy a field of so many cultivated worlds. This science does not permit that the arch of the horizon that our deluded vision imagineth over the Earth and that by our phantasy is feigned in the spacious ether, shall imprison our spirit under the custody of a Pluto or at the mercy of a Jove. We are spared the thought of so wealthy an owner and subsequently of so miserly, sordid and avaricious a donor.

It has often been pointed out—and rightly, of course—that the destruction of the cosmos, the loss, by the earth, of its central and thus unique (though by no means privileged) situation, led inevitably to the loss, by man, of his unique and privileged position in the theo-cosmic drama of the creation, of which man was, until then, both the central figure and the stake. At the end of the development we find the mute and terrifying world of Pascal's "libertin," the senseless world of modern scientific philosophy. At the end we find nihilism and despair.

Yet this was not so in the beginning. The displacement of the earth from the centrum of the world was not felt to be a demotion. Quite the contrary: it is with satisfaction that Nicholas of Cusa asserts its promotion to the rank of the noble stars; and, as for Giordano Bruno, it is with a burning enthusiasm—that of a prisoner who sees the walls of his jail crumble—that he announces the bursting of the spheres that separated us from the wide open spaces and inexhaustible treasures of the everchanging, eternal and infinite universe. Ever-changing! We are, once more, reminded of Nicholas of Cusa, and, once more, we have to state the difference of their fundamental world views—or world feelings. Nicholas of Cusa *states* that immutability can nowhere be found in the whole universe; Giordano Bruno goes far beyond this mere statement; for him motion and change are signs of perfection and not of a lack of it. An immutable universe would be a dead universe; a living one must be able to move and to change.

There are no ends, boundaries, limits or walls which can defraud or deprive us of the infinite multitude of things. Therefore the earth and the ocean thereof are fecund; therefore the sun's blaze is everlasting, so that eternally fuel is provided for the voracious fires, and moisture replenishes the attenuated seas. For from infinity is born an ever fresh abundance of matter.

Thus Democritus and Epicurus, who maintained that everything throughout infinity suffereth renewal and restoration, understood these matters more truly than those who at all costs maintain a belief in the immutability of the Universe, alleging a constant and unchanging number of particles of identical material that perpetually undergo transformation, one into another.

The importance for Bruno's thought of the principle of plenitude cannot be overvalued. Yet there are in it two other features that seem to me to be of as great an importance as this principle. They are: (a) the use of a principle that a century later Leibniz—who certainly knew Bruno and was influenced by him—was to call *the principle of sufficient reason,* which supplements the principle of plenitude and, in due time, superseded it; and (b) the decisive shift (adumbrated indeed by Nicholas of Cusa) from sensual to intellectual cognition in its relation to thought (intellect). Thus, at the very beginning of his Dialogue on the *Infinite Universe and the Worlds,* Bruno (Philotheo) asserts that sense-perception, as such, is confused and erroneous and cannot be made the basis of scientific and philosophical knowledge. Later on he explains that whereas for sense-perception and imagination infinity is inaccessible and unrepresentable, for the intellect, on the contrary, it is its primary and most certain concept.

> PHILOTHEO—No corporeal sense can perceive the infinite. None of our senses can be expected to furnish this conclusion; for the infinite cannot be the object of sense-perception; therefore he who demandeth to obtain this knowledge through the senses is like unto one who would desire to see with his eyes both substance and essence. And he who would deny the existence of a thing merely because it cannot be apprehended by the senses, nor is visible, would presently be led to the denial of his own substance and being. Wherefore there must be some measure in the demand for evidence from our sense-perception, for this we can accept only in regard to sensible objects, and even there it is not above all suspicion unless it cometh before the court aided by good judgment. It is the part of the intellect to judge yielding due weight to factors absent and separated by distance of time and by space intervals. And in this matter our sense-perception doth suffice us and doth yield us adequate testimony, since it is unable to gainsay us; moreover it advertiseth and confesseth its own feebleness and inadequacy by the impression it giveth us of a finite horizon, an impression moreover which is ever changing. Since then we have experience that sense-perception deceiveth us concerning the surface of this globe on which we live, much more should we hold suspect the impression it giveth us of a limit to the starry sphere.
>
> ELPINO—Of what use are the sense to us? tell me that.

> PHIL.—Solely to stimulate our reason, to accuse, to indicate, to testify in part . . . truth is in but a very small degree derived from the senses as from a frail origin, and doth by no means reside in the senses.
>
> ELP.—Where then?
>
> PHIL.—In the sensible object as in a mirror; in reason, by process of argument and discussion. In the intellect, either through origin or by conclusion. In the mind, in its proper and vital form.

As for the principle of sufficient reason, Bruno applies it in his discussion of space and of the spatially extended universe. Bruno's space, the space of an infinite universe and at the same time the (somewhat misunderstood) infinite "void" of Lucretius, is perfectly homogeneous and similar to itself everywhere: indeed, how could the "void" space be anything but uniform—or *vice versa,* how could the uniform "void" be anything but unlimited and infinite? Accordingly, from Bruno's point of view, the Aristotelian conception of a closed innerworldly space is not only false, it is absurd.

> PHILOTHEO—If the world is finite and if nothing is beyond, I ask you *where* is the world? *Where* is the universe? Aristotle replieth: it is in itself. The convex surface of the primal heaven is universal space, which being the primal container is by nought contained.
>
> FRACASTORO—The world then will be nowhere. Everything will be in nothing.
>
> PHIL.—If thou wilt excuse thyself by asserting that where nought is, and nothing existeth, there can be no question of position in space, nor of beyond, nor outside, yet I shall in no wise be satisfied. For these are mere words and excuses which cannot form part of our thought. For it is wholly impossible that in any sense or fantasy (even though there may be various senses and various fantasies), it is, I say, impossible that I can with any true meaning assert that there existeth such a surface, boundary or limit, beyond which is neither body, nor empty space, even though God be there.

We can pretend, as Aristotle does, that this world encloses all being, and that outside this world there is nothing; *nec plenum nec vacuum.* But nobody can think, or even imagine it. "Outside" the world will be space. And this space, just as ours, will not be "void"; it will be filled with "ether."

Bruno's criticism of Aristotle (like that of Nicholas of Cusa) is, of course, wrong. He does not understand him and substitutes a geometrical "space" for the place-continuum of the Greek philosopher. Thus he repeats the classical objection: what would happen if somebody stretched his hand through the surface of the heaven? And though he gives to this question a nearly correct answer (from the point of view of Aristotle),

> BURCHIO—Certainly I think that one must reply to this fellow that if a person would stretch out his hand beyond the convex sphere of heaven,

the hand would occupy no position in space, nor any place, and in consequence would not exist.

he rejects it on the perfectly fallacious ground that this "inner surface," being a purely mathematical conception, cannot oppose a resistance to the motion of a real body. Furthermore, even if it did, the problem of what is beyond it would remain unanswered:

> PHILOTHEO—Thus, let the surface be what it will, I must always put the question: what is beyond? If the reply is: nothing, then I call that the void, or empty-ness. And such a Void or Emptiness hath no measure nor outer limit, though it hath an inner; and this is harder to imagine than is an infinite or immense universe. For if we insist on a finite universe, we cannot escape the void. And let us now see whether there can be such a space, in which is nought. In this infinite space is placed our universe (whether by chance, by necessity or by providence I do not now consider). I ask now whether this space which indeed containeth the world is better fitted to do so than is another space beyond?

> FRACASTORO—It certainly appeareth to me not so. For where there is nothing there can be no differentiation; where there is no differentiation there is no distruction of quality and perhaps there is even less of quality where there is nought whatsoever.

Thus the space occupied by our world, and the space outside it, will be the same. And if they are the same, it is impossible that "outside" space should be treated by God in any different way from that which is "inside." We are therefore bound to admit that not only space, but also being in space is everywhere constituted in the same way, and that if in our part of the infinite space there is a world, a sun-star surrounded by planets, it is the same everywhere in the universe. Our world is not the universe, but only this *machina,* surrounded by an infinite number of other similar or analogous "worlds"—the worlds of star-suns scattered in the etheric ocean of the sky.

Indeed, if it was, and is, possible for God to create a world in this our space, it is, and it was, just as possible for Him to create it elsewhere. But the uniformity of space—pure receptacle of being—deprives God of any reason to create it here, and not elsewhere. Accordingly, the limitation of God's creative action is unthinkable. In this case, the possibility implies actuality. The infinite world can be; therefore it must be; therefore it is.

> For just as it would be ill that this our space were not filled, that is our world were not to exist, then, since the spaces are indistinguishable, it would be no less ill if the whole of space were not filled. Thus we see that the universe is of indefinite size and the worlds therein without number.

Or, as the Aristotelian adversary of Bruno, Elpino, now converted to his views, formulates it:

> I declare that which I cannot deny, namely, that within infinite space either there may be an infinity of worlds similar to our own; or that this universe may have extended its capacity in order to contain many bodies such as those we name

stars; or again that whether these worlds be similar or dissimilar to one another, it may with no less reason be well that one, than that another should exist. For the existence of one is no less reasonable than that of another; and the existence of many no less so than of one or of the other; and the existence of an infinity of them no less so than the existence of a large number. Wherefore, even as the abolition and non-existence of this world would be an evil, so would it be of innumerable others.

More concretely:

> ELP.—There are then innumerable suns, and an infinite number of earths revolve around these suns, just as the seven we can observe revolve around this sun which is close to us.

> PHIL.—So it is.

> ELP.—Why then do we not see the other bright bodies which are the earths circling around the bright bodies which are suns? For beyond these we can detect no motion whatsoever; and why do all the other mundane bodies appear always (except those known as comets) in the same order and at the same distance?

Elpino's question is rather good. And the answer given to it by Bruno is rather good, too, in spite of an optical error of believing that, in order to be seen, the planets must be formed on the pattern of spherical mirrors and possess a polished, smooth, "watery" surface, for which, moreover, he is not responsible as it was common belief until Galileo:

> PHIL.—The reason is that we discern only the largest suns, immense bodies. But we do not discern the earths because, being much smaller they are invisible to us. Similarly, it is not impossible that other earths revolve around our sun and are invisible to us either on account of greater distance or smaller size, or because they have but little watery surface, or because such watery surface is not turned toward us and opposed to the sun, whereby it would be made visible as a crystal mirror which receiveth luminous rays; whence we perceive that it is not marvellous or contrary to nature that often we hear that the sun has been partially eclipsed though the moon hath not been interpolated between him and our sight. There may be innumerable watery luminous bodies—that is earths consisting in part of water circulating around the sun, besides those visible to us; but the difference in their orbits is indiscernible by us on account of their great distance, wherefore we perceive no difference in the very slow motion discernible of those visible above or beyond Saturn; still less doth there appear any order in the motion of all around the centre, whether we place our earth or our sun as that centre.

The question then arises whether the fixed stars of the heavens are really suns, and centers of worlds comparable to ours.

> ELP.—Therefore you consider that if the stars beyond Saturn are really motionless as they appear, then they are those innumerable suns or

fires more or less visible to us around which travel their own neighbouring earths which are not discernible by us.

One would expect a positive answer. But for once Bruno is prudent:

> PHIL.—Not so for I do not know whether all or whether the majority is without motion, or whether some circle around others, since none hath observed them. Moreover they are not easy to observe, for it is not easy to detect the motion and progress of a remote object, since at a great distance change of position cannot easily be detected, as happeneth when we would observe ships in a high sea. But however that may be, the universe being infinite, there must be ultimately other suns. For it is impossible that heat and light from one single body should be diffused throughout immensity, as was supposed by Epicurus if we may credit what others relate of him. Therefore it followeth that there must be innumerable suns, of which many appear to us as small bodies; but that star will appear smaller which is in fact much larger than that which appeareth much greater.

The infinity of the universe thus seems to be perfectly assured. But what about the old objection that the concept of infinity can be applied only to God, that is, to a purely spiritual, incorporeal Being, an objection which led Nicholas of Cusa—and later Descartes—to avoid calling their worlds "infinite," but only "interminate," or "indefinite"? Bruno replies that he does not deny, of course, the utter difference of the intensive and perfectly simple infinity of God from the extensive and multiple infinity of the world. Compared to God, the world is as a mere point, as a nothing.

> PHIL.—We are then at one concerning the incorporeal infinite; but what preventeth the similar acceptability of the good, corporeal and infinite being? And why should not that infinite which is implicit in the utterly simple and indivisible Prime Origin rather become explicit in his own infinite and boundless image able to contain innumerable worlds, than become explicit within such narrow bounds? So that it appeareth indeed shameful to refuse to credit that this world which seemeth to us so vast may not in the divine regard appear a mere point, even a nullity?

Yet it is just that "nullity" of the world and of all the bodies that constitute it that implies its infinity. There is no reason for God to create one particular kind of beings in preference to another. The principle of sufficient reason reinforces the principle of plenitude. God's creation, in order to be perfect and worthy of the Creator, must therefore contain all that is possible, that is, innumerable individual beings, innumerable earths, innumerable stars and suns—thus we could say that God needs an infinite space in order to place in it this infinite world.

To sum up:

> PHIL.—This indeed is what I had to add; for, having pronounced that the Universe must itself be infinite because of the capacity and aptness of infinite space; on account also of the possibility

and convenience of accepting the existence of innumerable worlds like to our own; it remaineth still to prove it. Now both from the circumstances of this efficient cause which must have produced the Universe such as it is, or rather, must ever produce it such as it is, and also from the conditions of our mode of understanding, we may easily argue that infinite space is similar to this which we see, rather than argue that it is that which we do not see either by example or by similitude, or by proportion, or indeed, by any effort of imagination which doth not finally destroy itself. Now to begin. Why should we, or could we imagine that divine power were otiose? Divine goodness can indeed be communicated to infinite things and can be infinitely diffused; why then should we wish to assert that it would choose to be scarce and to reduce itself to nought—for every finite thing is as nought in relation to the infinite? Why do you desire that centre of divinity which can (if one may so express it) extend indefinitely to an infinite sphere, why do you desire that it should remain grudgingly sterile rather than extend itself as a father, fecund, ornate and beautiful? Why should you prefer that it should be less, or indeed by no means communicated, rather than that it should fulfil the scheme of its glorious power and being? Why should infinite amplitude be frustrated, the possibility of an infinity of worlds be defrauded? Why should be prejudiced the excellency of the divine image which ought rather to glow in an unrestricted mirror, infinite, immense, according to the law of its being? . . . Why wouldst thou that God should in power, in act and in effect (which in him are identical) be determined as the limit of the convexity of a sphere rather than that he should be, as we may say, the undetermined limit of the boundless?

Let us not, adds Bruno, be embarrassed by the old objection that the infinite is neither accessible, nor understandable. It is the opposite that is true: the infinite is necessary, and is even the first thing that naturally *cadit sub intellectus.*

Giordano Bruno, I regret to say, is not a very good philosopher. The blending together of Lucretius and Nicholas of Cusa does not produce a very consistent mixture; and though, as I have already said, his treatment of the traditional objections against the motion of the earth is rather good, the best given to them before Galileo, he is a very poor scientist, he does not understand mathematics, and his conception of the celestial motions is rather strange. My sketch of his cosmology is, indeed, somewhat unilateral and not quite complete. As a matter of fact, Bruno's world-view is vitalistic, magical; his planets are animated beings that move freely through space of their own accord like those of Plato or of Pattrizzi. Bruno's is not a modern mind by any means. Yet his conception is so powerful and so prophetic, so reasonable and so poetic that we cannot but admire it and him. And it has—at least in its formal features—so deeply influenced modern science and modern philosophy, that we cannot but assign to Bruno a very important place in the history of the human mind.

I do not know whether Bruno had a great influence on his

immediate contemporaries, or even whether he influenced them at all. Personally, I doubt it very much. He was, in his teaching, far ahead of his time. Thus his influence seems to me to have been a delayed one. It was only *after* the great telescopic discoveries of Galileo that it was accepted and became a factor, and an important one, of the seventeenth century world-view.

Kepler, as a matter of fact, links Bruno with Gilbert and seems to suggest that it was from the former that the great British scientist received his belief in the infinity of the universe.

This is, of course, quite possible: the thorough criticism of the Aristotelian cosmology may have impressed Gilbert. Yet it would be the only point where the teaching of the Italian philosopher was accepted by him. There is, indeed, not much similarity (besides the animism, common to both) between the "magnetic philosophy" of William Gilbert and the metaphysics of Giordano Bruno. Professor Johnson believes that Gilbert was influenced by Digges, and that, having asserted the indefinite extension of the world "of which the limit is not known, and cannot be known," Gilbert, "to enforce his point, adopted without qualification Digges' idea that the stars were infinite in number, and located at varying and infinite distances from the center of the Universe."

This is quite possible, too. Yet, if he adopted *this* idea of Digges, he completely rejected his predecessor's immersion of the celestial bodies into the theological heavens: he has nothing to tell us about the angels and the saints.

On the other hand, neither Bruno nor Digges succeeded in persuading Gilbert to accept, in its entirety, the astronomical theory of Copernicus of which he seems to have admitted only the least important part, that is, the diurnal motion of the earth, and not the much more important annual one. Gilbert, it is true, does not reject this latter: he simply ignores it, whereas he devotes a number of very eloquent pages to the defence and explanation (on the basis of his magnetic philosophy) of the daily rotation of the earth on its axis and to the refutation of the Aristotelian and Ptolemaic conception of the motion of the celestial sphere, and also to the denial of its very existence.

As to this latter point, we must not forget, however, that the solid orbs of classical—and Copernican—astronomy had, in the meantime, been "destroyed" by Tycho Brahe. Gilbert, therefore, in contradistinction to Copernicus himself, can so much more easily dispense with the perfectly useless sphere of the fixed stars, as he does not have to admit the existence of the potentially useful planetary ones. Thus he tells us:

> But in the first place, it is not likely that the highest heaven and all these visible splendours of the fixed stars are impelled along that most rapid and useless course. Besides, who is the Master who has ever made out that the stars which we call fixed are in one and the same sphere, or has established by any reasoning that there are any real, and, as it were, adamantine spheres? No one has ever proved this as a fact; nor is there a doubt but that just as the planets are at unequal distances from the earth, so are those vast and

multitudinous lights separated from the earth by varying and very remote altitudes; they are not set in any sphaerick frame of firmament (as is feigned), nor in any vaulted body; accordingly the intervals of some are, from their unfathomable distance, matter of opinion rather than of verification; others do much exceed them and are very far remote, and these being located in the heaven at varying distances, either in the thinnest aether, or in that most subtle quintessence, or in the void; how are they to remain in their position during such a mighty swirl of the vast orbe of such uncertain substance . . .

Astronomers have observed 1022 stars; besides these innumerable other stars appear minute to our senses; as regards still others, our sight grows dim, and they are hardly discernible save by the keenest eye; nor is there any possessing the best power of vision that will not, while the moon is below the horizon and the atmosphere is clear, feel that there are many more, indeterminable and vacillating by reason of their faint light, obscured because of the distance.

How immeasurable then must be the space which stretches to those remotest of the fixed stars! How vast and immense the depth of that imaginary sphere! How far removed from the earth must the most widely separated stars be and at a distance transcending all sight, all skill and thought! How monstrous then such a motion would be!

It is evident then that all the heavenly bodies, set as if in a destined place, are there formed unto

---

Arthur O. Lovejoy on Renaissance cosmography:

The truly revolutionary theses in cosmography which gained ground in the sixteenth and came to be pretty generally accepted before the end of the seventeenth century were five in number, none of them entailed by the purely astronomical systems of Copernicus or Kepler. In any study of the history of the modern conception of the world, and in any account of the position of any individual writer, it is essential to keep these distinctions between issues constantly in view. The five more significant innovations were: (1) the assumption that other planets of our solar system are inhabited by living, sentient, and rational creatures; (2) the shattering of the outer walls of the medieval universe, whether these were identified with the outermost crystalline sphere or with a definite "region" of the fixed stars, and the dispersal of these stars through vast, irregular distances; (3) the conception of the fixed stars as suns similar to ours, all or most of them surrounded by planetary systems of their own; (4) the supposition that the planets in these other worlds also have conscious inhabitants; (5) the assertion of the actual infinity of the physical universe in space and of the number of solar systems contained it it.

Arthur O. Lovejoy in The Great Chain of Being: A Study of the History of an Idea, *Harvard University Press, 1936.*

spheres, that they tend to their own centres and that round them there is a confluence of all their parts. And if they have motion that motion will rather be that of each round its own centre, as that of the earth is, or a forward movement of the centre in an orbit as that of the Moon.

But there can be no movement of infinity and of an infinite body, and therefore no diurnal revolution of the *Primum Mobile*.

Marjorie Hope Nicolson

SOURCE: An introduction to *The Breaking of the Circle: Studies in the Effect of the "New Science" upon Seventeenth-Century Poetry,* revised edition, Columbia University Press, 1960, pp. 1-10.

[*In the excerpt that follows, Nicolson argues that full appreciation of English Renaissance literature is dependent upon an understanding of the cosmology of Renaissance poets.*]

Looking back with historical perspective, modern critics draw sharp lines of demarcation between three main epochs in European thought; the classical, the post-Renaissance, and the modern. Each of these had its own way of thinking about man, the world, and the universe. "Greek natural science," writes R. G. Collingwood in *The Idea of Nature,*

> was based on the principle that the world of nature is saturated or permeated by mind. . . . Since the world of nature is a world not only of ceaseless motion and therefore alive, but also a world of orderly or regular motion, they accordingly said that the world of nature is not only alive but intelligent; not only a vast animal with a 'soul' or 'life,' but a rational animal with a 'mind' of its own.

From the time of Thales down through the period we broadly call "the Renaissance," a majority of philosophers taught and most men believed that the world was animate. It lived and flourished as did man, and like man was susceptible of decay, even of death.

During the seventeenth century the old hylozoistic fallacy gave way to the idea of the world as mechanism.

> The Renaissance view of nature began to take shape as antithetical to the Greek view in the work of Copernicus, Telesio, and Bruno. The central point of this antithesis was the denial that the world of nature, the world studied by physical science, is an organism, and the assertion that it is devoid both of intelligence and of life. . . . Instead of being an organism, the natural world is a machine: a machine in the literal and proper sense of the word, an arrangement of bodily parts designed and put together and set going for a definite purpose by an intelligent mind outside itself.

The world-machine was no longer animate, but mechanically responsive to the laws of Nature.

In more modern times, man passed from a conception of

mechanism to one of development. "Modern cosmology, like its predecessors," Mr. Collingwood continues,

> is based on an analogy. What is new about it is that the analogy is a new one. As the Greeks' natural science was based on the analogy between the macrocosm nature and the microcosm man, . . . as Renaissance natural science was based on the analogy between nature as God's handiwork and the machines that are the handiwork of man, . . . so the modern view of nature . . . is based on the analogy between the processes of the natural world as studied by natural scientists and the vicissitudes of human affairs as studied by historians.

Modern cosmology, like all the earlier ones, is based on analogy. But we are aware that it is an analogy. We know that we are attempting to explain the nature of the universe, the world, and man by figures of speech deliberately drawn from historians and natural scientists. We describe our world in similes. Our Elizabethan ancestors thought of their world in metaphors. The world was not simply *like* an animal; it *was* animate. The repetition of pattern, design, function they found in the body of man was not invented by human ingenuity; it actually existed in the three worlds made by God in His image. There was basic correspondence between man's body and the body of the world, between man's soul and the soul of the universe.

Perhaps it was because he lived in an age of mechanism rather than animism that Samuel Johnson frequently misinterpreted the group of writers he called the "metaphysical poets." His criticism is often just, so far as Cowley was concerned. A good deal is not true when applied to Donne and others now included in the "metaphysical" roster. In Johnson's mind, the first fault of these poets lay in what seemed their ostentatious learning.

> As the authors of this race were perhaps more desirous of being admired than understood, they sometimes drew their conceits from recesses of learning not very much frequented by common readers of poetry. . . . The most heterogeneous ideas are yoked by violence together; nature and art are ransacked for illustrations, comparisons, and allusions; their learning instructs, and their subtilty surprises; but the reader commonly thinks his improvement dearly bought, and though he sometimes admires, he is seldom pleased.

Johnson's second critique was basically one with the first. Avid for novelty, these poets "did not much inquire whether their allusions were to things high or low, elegant or gross. . . . Of thoughts so far fetched as to be not only unexpected but unnatural all their books are full." They seemed to Johnson to have racked their brains and exhausted their ingenuity in attempts to find new and startling comparisons. "They looked out not for images but for conceits," he said, and found them "by a voluntary deviation from nature in pursuit of something new and strange."

I should not labor a passage so familiar were it not that Johnson's shadow seems still to dim the eyes of various modern critics, both those who resurrected and almost deified Donne in the 1920s and 1930s and some who, going out with the ebbing tide of enthusiasm, now speak critically of the former idol. "All of us," Cleanth Brooks wrote in *The Well-Wrought Urn,* "are familiar with the censure passed upon Donne and his followers by Dr. Johnson, and a great many of us still retain it as our own, softening only the rigor and thoroughness of its application, but not giving it up as a principle." It was no surprise to many of us who listened to the so-called "recantation" address on Milton that T. S. Eliot should have begun with the words, "Samuel Johnson . . . said. . . ."

The modern critics have often been more subtle than Johnson, and they have used a vocabulary that would have puzzled the Dictionary-Maker, interpreting in terms of "paradox," "irony," "ambiguity," "ambivalence," "tension." They have frequently shown more interest in Donne's "logic" than in his poetry. Although they have analyzed in closer detail such "illustrations, comparisons, and allusions" as those that provoked Johnson to his strictures, many still believe that the essential element of metaphysical poetry lay in a kind of intellectual perverseness, that Donne and his followers deliberately yoked together by violence the most heterogeneous ideas in order to form a *discordia concors.* In effect they seem to say of Donne as Samuel Butler of Hudibras:

> For rhetorick he could not ope
> His mouth, but out there flew a trope.

Although the modern critics more often praised than condemned him for the fact, they insisted that some of Donne's finest figures were "conceits" rather than "images," produced, as Johnson believed, "by a voluntary deviation from nature in pursuit of something new and strange."

To be sure, many of the seventeenth-century poets were learned, though their learning did not seem as ostentatious to their own age as to Johnson's and our own. They were witty poets, too, in all the senses in which their own generation understood wit, and in which Addison both praised and condemend their use of it. But many of the supposed conceits Johnson and they cited were not so novel and strange as they thought. Indeed, the figures were often not conceits but metaphors, drawn from a pattern of the universe which seemed to the poets inevitable, in which the little body of man corresponded exactly to the larger body of the world, and that in turn to the still larger body of the universe, in which "the elements that do man's house compose" were the same elements—earth, water, air, fire—that composed the body of the world and the body of the universe. The pattern of the three interlocking worlds was not invented or discovered by poets, avid for novelty. It was inscribed upon man, world, and universe in which design, plan, and repetition of motif were everywhere apparent. Many of their basic figures of speech which Johnson and some modern critics misunderstood were drawn directly and inevitably from a Nature we have long forgotten.

As critics have either blamed or praised the seventeenth-century poets for the perverseness or brilliance of some supposed "novel" figures that were actually Renaissance commonplaces, so they missed others that were really new when Donne and his contemporaries wrote. Certainly there are comparisons in the poetry of the earlier seventeenth century for which we find no parallels in Chaucer or Spenser or even Shakespeare. The images were new. The poets did not rack their brains or ransack Nature to invent them. They burst around them as bombs around our own atomic age. We can no longer think as our ancestors thought. We can merely try to understand their belief in the three worlds of an animate Nature and sympathetically to appreciate the delight they felt as they found everywhere fresh proof of the design of a "metaphysical" God in the intricate repetitive patterns of man, the world, and the universe, in "correspondence" and "signature," in the "mystical Mathematicks" loved by Sir Thomas Browne that stirred Kepler to rapture when he discovered that Plato's five regular solids afford the clue to the relationship among the planets. Delight in mathematics led Marvell to think of lovers in terms of parallel lines that never meet, Donne to describe them as a pair of compasses, and Milton to use the same symbol when in one of his most reverent scenes in *Paradise Lost* he imagined the creation of the world by the Son of God:

> He took the golden compasses, prepared
> In God's eternal store, to circumscribe
> The Universe and all created things.
> One foot he centered, and the other turned
> Round through the vast profundity obscure,
> And said, "Thus far extend, thus far thy bounds;
> This be thy just circumference, O World"

"Modern cosmology, like its predecessors, is based on an analogy." The cosmology of the Renaissance poets . . . was most often interpreted in terms of the circle—a circle that existed in the perfect spheres of the planets, in the circular globe, in the round head of man. This was not mere analogy to them; it was truth. God had made all things in the universe, the world, and the body of man as near his own symbol, the perfect circle, as their grosser natures would allow. Older theories of history, when they were not degenerative, had been cyclical. Sir Thomas Browne said: "The Lives, not only of Men, but of Commonwealths, and the whole World, run not upon an Helix that still enlargeth, but on a Circle, where, arriving to their Meridian, they decline in obscurity, and fall under the Horizon again."

What once seemed "identicals" have become in our modern world only "similars." Metaphor, based upon accepted truth, inscribed by God in the nature of the universe, has given way to simile. But much more than that, we shall see, is involved in the circle. Why did this metaphor, the most persistent and the most loved metaphor of earlier writers, almost disappear from literature for more than a century? Why, when it returned, did it tend to be "conceit" rather than "image"? The Circle of Perfection, from which man for so long deduced his ethics, his aesthetics, and his metaphysics, was broken during the seventeenth century. Correspondence between macrocosm, geocosm, and microcosm, long accepted as basic to faith, was no longer valid in a new mechanical world and mechanical universe, nor is it valid in the modern world.

During the nineteenth century, when the circle returned to literature, it tended, under the influence of the evolutionary theory and belief in progress, to be not the Circle of Perfection but a spiral, or what Sir Thomas Browne had called "an Helix that still enlargeth." As shades of the prison house have closed around the idea of progress, the circle has suffered still another change. "Things fall apart. The Centre cannot hold," said Yeats, in whose poetry the circle recurs perhaps more than in that of any other English poet. His is no closed circle but a spiral in which the movement is both upward and downward. In our times it would seem that we are approaching the end of a spiral. Yeats's circle was drawn from Vico, as is that of the other modern writer who has most used it in the structure of his work, James Joyce, who said in *Finnegans Wake:* "The Vico road goes round and round to meet where terms begin." There may be variation but there is no progress—repetition, sometimes interruption, even degeneration. We cannot return to a world that died in the seventeenth century, nor feel as men felt when the circle was not a conceit but an image of reality, everywhere inscribed by God in the nature of things.

Even while Donne and his contemporaries were living in a universe of correspondences, other voices were beginning to be heard. "It is incredible," wrote Francis Bacon with his usual prosaic common sense, "what a number of idols have been introduced into philosophy by the reduction of natural operations to a correspondence with human actions, that is, by imagining that nature acts as man does, which is not much better than the heresy of anthropomorphists." To Bacon the Circle of Perfection was a mere fiction, and the inclination of men to find it everywhere on earth and in heaven another indication of the dangerous haziness be found in the "Idols of the Tribe." "The human understanding," he wrote,

> is of its own nature prone to suppose the existence of more order and regularity in the world than it finds. And though there be many things in nature which are singular and unmatched, yet it devises for them conjugates and parallels and relatives which do not exist. Hence the fiction that all celestial bodies move in perfect circles [*Novum Organum*].

As he inveighed against the almost universal tendency of his day to read nonexistent "conjugates and parallels and relatives" into Nature, so he opposed another idea of correspondence that we shall find pervasive in the literature of the earlier seventeenth century: the belief that the "humours" of man's body correspond to the four elements. Here again, as he said, men seemed to "make themselves, as it were, the mirror and rule of nature." And so, indeed, men did.

Baconian common sense was to triumph over mysticism. "Truth," he said, as if setting a motto for his eighteenth-century followers, "is a naked and open daylight." In the full blaze of the Enlightenment the Circle of Perfection disappeared, as Marvell's drop of dew when the sun rose. But Sir Thomas Browne, who felt as poets felt, seems to reply to Bacon: "Light that makes all things seen, makes some things invisible. The greatest mystery of Religion is expressed by adumbration." Much more fully than Bacon, Browne understood an age when man sincerely believed that he was a little world made cunningly, a copy of his

earth, as his earth was a copy of the universe, all three "epitomes" of God. Pondering upon one of his favorite figures, a favorite also of his generation, *Lux est Umbra Dei,* Browne said: "Where there is an obscurity too deep for our Reason,' tis good to sit down with a description, periphrasis, or adumbration" [*Religio Medici*]. If we are to appreciate to its full the literature of the English Renaissance, we too must be willing to sit down with the "description, periphrasis, or adumbration" they used to explain obscurities too deep for Reason. We must come to think as they thought before "The Death of a World," before the animate macrocosm and living microcosm disappeared, and their places were taken by a mechanical clock and men with mechanical hearts. . . .

Hardin Craig

SOURCE: "Derivations and Inferences," in *The Enchanted Glass: The Elizabethan Mind in Literature,* 1936. Reprint by Greenwood Press, Publishers, 1975, pp. 32-60.

[*In the following excerpt, Craig discusses the means by which "cosmological pseudosciences"—astrology and magic—influenced the thinking of Renaissance populations.*]

> For after the articles and principles of religion are placed, and exempted from examination of reason, it is then permitted unto us to make derivations and inferences from and according to the analogy of them.
>
> —Bacon, *The Advancement of Learning*

The subject [of man's role in and reaction to the formal order of the Renaissance] is of course both vague and complicated; but perhaps some idea of the situation can be arrived at by looking at the subject from two major aspects,—first, the aspect of science or the rational aspect, and, secondly, the aspect of religion. With the latter we shall consider certain political and moral effects and tendencies. The former has to do with credulity and scepticism and might be carried, as is customary, into the history of the birth of modern science; the latter has primarily to do with the accepted belief as to the nature and fate of the human soul, which had been placed outside the realm in which reason was allowed to operate. It is no small evidence of the intellectual hardihood of Bacon that he suggests even tentatively that 'it is permitted to make derivations and inferences from and according to the analogy' of the articles and principles of religion, which he has just exempted from reasonable examination. We shall consider the two cosmological pseudosciences of astrology and magic in an attempt to show that these disciplines met with at least partial acceptance, and shall then take up matters in other fields in some sense dependent on the doctrine of the soul. If the soul is conceived of as free, or if it is conceived of as in some sense enthralled, there are consequences in political, social, and individual conduct appropriate to both conditions.

Astronomical phenomena appear obviously and have immediate connexion with cosmological theory. We may therefore find it profitable to begin with astrology. We may ask to what extent astrological influences were be-lieved in by scholars and learned men in England in the sixteenth century. It is a typical question and fortunately very easy to answer. Astrology was the interpretative part of astronomy, was sanctioned by the writings of Ptolemy and by writings attributed to Aristotle, and seems to have held a place in the curriculum of the universities of the Middle Ages and the Renaissance. Astrology was tolerat-ed if not sanctioned by the Church and was, as regards its validity as a science, believed in by all learned men. But there are necessary qualifications of this statement.

Let us begin with the case of one of the most intelligent of the literary men of the sixteenth century, Sir Philip Sid-ney. Fulke Greville, who was himself something of a scep-tic, has the following significant passage in his *Life of the Renowned Sir Philip Sidney:*

> Now though I am not of their faith, who affirme
> wise men can governe the Starres; yet I do
> beleeve no Star-gazers can so well prognosticate
> the good, or ill of all Governments, as the provi-
> dence of men trained up in publique affaires may
> doe. Whereby they differ from Prophets only in
> this; that Prophets by inspiration, and these by
> consequence, judge of things to come.

Among these wise men (those trained up in public affairs) he would reckon Sir Philip Sidney. Greville says that he takes no stock in star-gazers and that in political prophecy he would prefer Sir Philip Sidney's trained observations to astrological prognostications. A good many men no doubt felt as Greville did. He is voicing his own opinions and not those of Sidney, and yet in a general sense Greville probably expresses Sidney's views as well as his own. Sid-ney was indeed a man who, though he was an ardent stu-dent and believed in learned culture, trusted mainly in himself rather than in the stars and preached self-reliance. But, on the other hand, he knew a great deal about astrolo-gy, evidently wished his brother Robert to learn the rudi-ments of the subject, and used astrology very extensively and deftly in his works. The *Diary* of Dr. John Dee [*The Private Diary of Dr. John Dee,* 1842] records two visits by Sidney to Dr. Dee, one of which was immediately before Sidney set out on an expedition. His biographer, Mr. M. W. Wallace, suggests that that particular visit may have been in order to learn the auspices of his journey. If so, it was a customary enough thing to do. *Arcadia* has many seriously intended allusions to horoscopes and astrologi-cal soothsayers; and still further confirmation of Sidney's faith in astrology is to be found in *Astrophel and Stella,* particularly in Sonnet xxvi:

> Though duskie wits doe scorne Astrologie,
>   And fooles can thinke those lampes of purest
>   light,
> Whose number waies greatnes eternitie,
> Promising wondrous wonders to invite,
>   To have for no cause birth-right in the skye.
> But for to spangle the blacke weedes of Night,
> Or for some braue within that Chamber hie,
> They shold still daunce to please a gazers sight.
> For me I nature every deale doe know,
>   And know great causes, great effects procure,
>   And know those bodies high, raigne on the low.
> And if these rules did fall, proofe makes me sure,

> Who oft bewraies my after following case,
> By onely those two starres in *Stellas* face.

The general credence given to astrology will be made still clearer by a consideration of the opinions of Robert Re-corde, who was a humanist of very considerable breadth, a scholar, and the greatest mathematician of his time in England. What would such a man think about the subject of astrology? He has not left us in doubt. *The Castle of Knowledge* (1556) is an excellent work by this man of high standing, whose attitude toward branches of his general subject on which he does not consider himself an authority may be compared to that of many a modern scholar who does not presume to wander from his own specialty, be-cause he respects the specialties of others. Recorde is so modest that he regards astronomy, which he professes, as ancillary to astrology, which he does not profess. On the title-page of his book is engraved a castle-like structure with the queenly figure of Astronomy on top of it; on the left is a female figure holding aloft the *Sphera Fati,* the Sphere of Destiny, whose governor is Knowledge; on the right, another goddess, blindfolded, holds a cord attached to the crank of the *Sphera Fortune,* whose governor is Ig-norance. At the bottom is a piece of poetry:

> Though spiteful Fortune turned her wheele
> To staye the Sphere of Vranye,
> Yet dooth this Sphere resist that wheele,
> And fleeyth all fortunes villanye.
> Though earth do honour Fortunes balle,
> And bytells blynde hyr wheele aduaunce,
> The heavens to fortune are not thralle,
> These Spheres surmount al fortunes chance.

The book is composed of four treatises: (1) an introduction into the Sphere declaring the necessary parts of it, both material and celestial; (2) a treatise on the making of the Sphere, as well 'in sound and massye forme, as also in Ring forme with hoopes'; (3) the uses of the Sphere and other things incident thereto presented for ease in learning without proofs or demonstrations; (4) a treatise on many things that were noted in the earlier parts together with the demonstrations and proofs before omitted. The Pref-ace to the Reader, partly in verse printed as prose, declares that man was given eyes to view the heavens, so that he should not be so vain as not to realize the unimportance of earthly life. Man should study to understand the signs spread out in the heavens, since God wills that nothing should happen suddenly and without warning. Other men besides Noah could have read the signs of the approaching Flood. No great change in the world, no translation of em-pires—scarcely the fall of princes—no dearth and penury, have ever occurred of which God by signs in the heavens 'hath not and doth not premonish men.' This is too well known to require illustration. It belongs however to the judicial part of astronomy and does not, therefore, con-cern the author; yet he will, nevertheless, cite a few cases: There was an eclipse of the Sun before the building of Rome; signs also appeared at the time of the Fall of Rome at the hands of the Goths, and so on. He cites Manilius and Ptolemy to prove that eclipses of Sun and Moon, rain-bows of unusual form, comets, etc., are God's messengers to say that earthly events are accompanied by heavenly signs. His object in writing this book on the Sphere is to render the calculations of those who consult the stars more accurate and easier of accomplishment. He wishes men, not merely to avoid calamity, but to become governors and rulers of the stars. Astronomy is of course important in other matters, particularly in navigation and, as shown by Hippocrates' 'Book of the Air' and Galen's 'Critical Days,' in medicine. Consider, Recorde says, the use of astronomy in sowing grain, in making the calendar, and in computing the seasons. Indeed, astronomy is useful in every art and science, even to grammar, rhetoric, logic, and history. The most important dialogue of *The Castle of Knowledge* between Master and Scholar advances the thesis that marvellous motions in the heavens correspond to strange perturbations on earth. But there is no astrology in the book; it devotes itself to a practical and sane, sometimes a brilliant, exposition of the operative part of astronomy, including several excellent demonstrations of the rotundity of the earth.

And yet contemporary with Robert Recorde, and long before and long after his time, there was a social exercise of the astrological art which such men as he must always have despised. The scorn of the learned for ignorant, and often dishonest, practitioners is beautifully expressed by Gabriel Harvey in his *Marginalia:*

> The A.B.C. of owr vulgar Astrologers, especially such, as ar commonly termed Cunning men or Artsmen . . . Sum call them wissards. Erra Paters prognostication for euer. The Shepherds Kalendar. The Compost of Ptolomeus. Sum fewe add Arcandam: & a pamflet, intituled, The knowledg of things unknowne. I haue heard sum of them name Jon de indagine. Theise be theire great masters: & this in a manner theire whole librarie: with sum old parchment-roules, tables, & instruments. Erra Pater, their Hornebooke. The Shepherds Kalendar, their primer. The Compost of Ptolomeus, their Bible. Arcandam, their newe Testament. The rest, with Albertus secrets, & Aristotles problems Inglished, their great Doctours, & wonderfull Secreta secretorum.

A volume could be written on this list of books. *Erra Pater,* the Esdras prognostications, exists in dozens of manuscripts, English and Latin, often accompanied by a widely circulated traditional series of lunations, prognostications for every day of the moon's age, and was published in English by R. Wyer about 1536. Never a book that a decent scholar would look at, it continued to appear in print at fairly frequent intervals until the middle of the eighteenth century. *The Shepherds Kalendar,* possibly Alexander Barclay's translation of the *Kalendrier des Bergers,* a poetical almanac describing the shepherd's life and work for all the months of the year, was published at Paris in 1503. R. Copland's translation, published first by W. de Worde in 1508, ran through fifteen editions by 1631. *The Compost of Ptholomeus* (published by R. Wyer, 1532?, 1535?, 1540?) is a wretched English translation of what seems to have been a poor French version of the *Centiloquium,* or hundred aphorisms, based on the *Tetrabiblos* of Ptolemy and supposed to give the 'Fruit' of the Ptolemaic teachings as applied to astrological ends. There was an edition of the book as late as 1635(?) and probably other

editions intervening between it and Wyer's publications, it being the sort of cheap and vulgar book that would have been liable to complete loss. The *Arcandam,* described as 'the most excellent booke to fynd the desteny of euery man,' is another work of the same low character. It is one of the translations of William Warde through the French from a Latin original by Richard Roussat. The title-page betrays the book by describing it as *The most excellent, profitable, and pleasaunt book of the famous Doctor and expert Astrologian Arcandam or Aleandrin, to finde the fatal destiny, complexion, and natural inclination of every man and child, by his birth. With an addition of Phisiognomy, very pleasant to reade.* It was published by J. Rowbotham about 1562 and ran through at least seven editions by 1637. This same William Warde gave to the world an English translation of *The Secretes of the Reverende Maister Alexis of Piemont* (1558), a book giving excellent remedies against divers diseases, wounds and other accidents. This was a sort of perennial book. Warde provided second, third, and fourth parts, the fifth, sixth, and seventh being translated by one R. Androse. With the books in Harvey's list, this book, a copy of Vicary's wretched anatomy, and possibly a cheap herbal, a quack could defy the College of Physicians and the Company of Barber-Surgeons. For a complete equipment in superficial learning only the *Pymander* would be needed, and that was to be supplied by the next generation. An idea of the low level of learned culture in the sixteenth century can be gathered from the fact that William Warde was Queen's Professor of Physic at Cambridge. The wide-spread abuse of astrology was found shocking to many men of eminence in the medical profession. Among them it is important to remember John Securis, one of the most learned and careful almanac-makers of the day, who in his *A Detection and Querimonie of the daily enormities and abuses committed in Physick* (1566) attacks quackery from the respectable ground of sincere though erroneous learning. Of the final members of Harvey's list, *Secreta Secretorum* and Aristotle's *Problems,* nothing need be said. The former is one of the most celebrated books of quackery in the world, and the version of the *Problemata,* preserved as *The Problemes of Aristotle with other Philosophers and Phisitions* (published by the Widow Orwin, 1595), is a degenerate specimen of a questionable work. One is moved to add to this pitiful list of works of degraded learning Richard Grafton's *A Litle Treatise conteyning many proper tables and rules* (Tottell, 1571), a vastly popular work and no doubt exceedingly useful to quacks and pretenders to learning; as was also the almanac of Nostradamus, which appeared in English first about 1558.

This ground is familiar, but the reader should remember a distinction probably worth making in connexion with it,—that between the honest, well-informed, and sincere practitioners of a false science and the dishonest, ignorant, and pretentious quacks from whose knavery the profession suffered disgrace. The matter was relative at any given time in the sixteenth century. It was not only relative but changing rapidly. Many works which were adequate expressions of the best learning of say 1550 had become the vulgar knowledge of 1580 and 1590; truer learning had meantime risen to higher planes. Quackery too underwent its changes. It grew more mystical and bombastic; but the ancient cheap stuff, much of which had troubled the Middle Ages, also lived on as it lives now more remotely. Let it not be thought that quackery was then or is now usually insincere; its insincerity was and is a variable factor. Dr. John Dee was a frank thinker and something of a scholar; he was much misled. Dr. Robert Fludd was one of the most learned, most sincere, most bombastic impostors that ever lived. He fooled himself far more than Dr. Dee was fooled by others.

The uses of these books by fanatics and impostors are primarily responsible no doubt for the *odium astrologicum* of which the literature of the time is full. Astrologers were cheats and charlatans. They lived in narrow lanes and dark alleys and dressed themselves like mountebanks. They were often crystal gazers and practitioners of the black art. They interfered in politics, lent their falsity to the causes of slander and prostitution, lived by cheating the foolish poor, and went wrong about the weather year by year and day by day. This attitude toward astrology is freely reflected in literature. It is not that anybody doubted that there might be significance in the behaviour of the stars, but that everybody knew that many astrologers were impostors; and yet the impression one gets from Renaissance literature is not prevailingly adverse to astrology.

There are scornful references in Jonson and other comic writers; specifically, there are John Melton's satire *The Astrologaster* (1620) and later Butler's famous portrait of Sidrophel in *Hudibras*: John Chamber's *Treatise against Iudiciall Astrologie* (1601) and George Carleton's *The Madnesse of Astrologers* (1624), culminating in William Rowland's *Judiciall Astrology Judicially Condemmed* (1652), are not only arguments against astrological beliefs but denunciations of astrologers. There were plenty of books written in favour of the subject, like Sir Christopher Heydon's learned and excellent *A Defence of Judiciall Astrologie* (1603), and so grave and serious are many of the allusions to the starry heavens by the dramatists that they not infrequently suggest religious reverence. Marlowe's heroes are conscious of their stars, as are Chapman's; indeed, the titanic Byron [*Conspiracy of Charles Duke of Byron*] fights against them. Shakespeare's treatment of astrology is respectful and considerate. One recalls the 'pair of star-cross'd lovers' and the 'yoke of inauspicious stars' in *Romeo and Juliet.* Shakespeare knows with Helena [*All's Well That Ends Well*] that 'the fated sky Gives us free scope' and with Cassius that

> The fault, dear Brutus, is not in our stars,
> But in ourselves, that we are underlings.
>   [*Julius Caesar*]

But he shows greater suspension of judgment, more awe, in the passage in which Hamlet speaks of. 'the stamp of one defect,' which is 'nature's livery, or fortune's star,' in the twenty-sixth sonnet, and in Prospero's

>   by my prescience
> I find my zenith doth depend upon
> A most auspicious star, whose influence
> If I now court not but omit, my fortunes
> Will ever after droop.
>
>   [*The Tempest*]

The famous skeptical passage spoken by Edmund in *King Lear* may be intended to exemplify the speaker's rebellious and atheistical character:

> This is the excellent foppery of the world, that, when we are sick in fortune,—often the surfeit of our own behaviour,—we make guilty of our disasters the sun, the moon, and the stars: as if we were villains by necessity; fools by heavenly compulsion; knaves, thieves, and treachers, by spherical predominance; drunkards, liars, and adulterers, by an enforced obedience of planetary influence; and all that we are evil in, by a divine thrusting on: an admirable evasion of whoremaster man, to lay his goatish disposition to the charge of a star!

The opinion of Shakespeare's Edmund the Bastard is not the common one; and, if further confirmation of this statement is needed, consider the eloquent words of Montaigne in the "Apology for Raimond Sebond" on man's indifference and his presumption in his doubts:

> But, poor devil, what is there in him deserving of such a privilege? When we consider the incorruptible life of the heavenly bodies, their beauty, their grandeur, their continual motion by so exact a rule: . . . when we consider the domination and power those bodies have, not only over our lives and the condition of our fortune, . . . but even over our dispositions, our judgement, our will, which they govern, impel and stir at the mercy of their influence, as our reason discovers and tells us: . . . when we see that not only a man, not only a king, but kingdoms, empires, and all this world here below, are moved according to the lightest swing of the heavenly motions: . . . if our virtue, our vices, our talents and our knowledge, if even this dissertation of mine on the power of the stars, this comparison between them and ourselves, comes, as our reason supposes, by their means and their favour; . . . if this little portion of reason we possess has been allotted to us by heaven, how can reason make us the equal of heaven? How can it subject its essence and conditions to our knowledge? All that we see in those bodies fills us with amazement.

We have dwelt upon astrology at length because it offers a crucial instance. It is cosmological, and it had the best chance among the pseudo-sciences to win the sanction of learned men and to escape the numerous prohibitions of the Church, which was naturally jealous of all other agencies that sought to dispense a knowledge of spiritual power or of the will of God. But there are yet to be considered other even more intimate and available means of cosmological interpretation, namely, magical arts and sciences. Of course they are less in evidence in literature than is astrology, but they are not absent or inconsiderable.

Agrippa has things, far reaching in their literary effects, to say about the occult aspects of psychology; for example, on the subject of fascination, which is vitally connected with the all-important literary subjects of love and friendship. The instrument of fascination is the spirit,—a lucid, subtle vapour generated out of the purer blood by the heat of the heart. This spirit sends forth through the eyes rays like to itself. These rays strike into the eyes and possess the breast of him that is stricken; they wound his heart and possess in turn his spirit. References to this principle in the Elizabethan drama and lyric are numberless. Perhaps the most potent eye in literature, if we may believe Biron, is that of Rosaline in *Love's Labour's Lost*:

> A wither'd hermit, five-score winters worn,
> Might shake off fifty, looking in her eye.

Fascination is the art of the witch; witches use for the purpose of fascinating their victims collyries, alligations, and ointments. But these magical influences seem to have been thought operative in many quite legitimate fields. It was known that the blood of doves will produce love fascination, the eyes of wolves fear. Physicians seem to have relied upon it. Montaigne says quite definitely that they did:

> Even the choice of most of their drugs is in some sort mysterious and divine: the left foot of a tortoise, the urine of a lizard, an elephant's dung, a mole's liver, blood drawn from under the right wing of a white pigeon; and for us who have the stone (so scornfully do they take advantage of our misery!), the pulverized droppings of a rat, and other such tomfooleries that are more suggestive of magic and spells than of a serious science. Not to mention their pills, to be taken in uneven numbers, the setting apart of certain days and festivals in the year, of certain hours for gathering the herbs of their ingredients, the grim scowl, the wise and learned looks and demeanour which they put on, and which even Pliny remarked upon with derision.

Souls by their powers of fascination, we are told by Agrippa, may repair dying bodies with other inferior souls; it is even possible, particularly in the condition of melancholy, to induce new spirits into men's bodies, according to the three apprehensions—sense-perception, imagination, and the passions of the mind. These foreign spirits, aided by melancholy (natural melancholy and white choler), might enter an ignorant man, who might presently become a great painter or, if they entered his faculty of reason, he might become a philosopher or an orator; if the divine spirits entered his *intellectus* (or soul of intuition) he might perceive divine secrets and things eternal. It is thus that the Messianic prophecies of the Sybils are to be accounted for. So likewise those near to death or weakened by old age, since they are less hindered by bodily sensation, are capable of divination. Of the doctrine of the induction or transfusion of soul there are plenty of traces in literature, such as the story of the sons of Agape in the third book of the *Faerie Queene* and many references in lyric poetry which may not be wholly figurative; Sidney's sonnet beginning 'My true love hath my heart and I have his' is a case in point. As to the effects of weakened physical powers in increasing the insight of the soul, we have many examples. In *Hamlet* the Ghost of the murdered king says of Gertrude,

> But, look, amazement on thy mother sits:
> O, step between her and her fighting soul:
> Conceit in weakest bodies strongest works:
> Speak to her, Hamlet.

There is no doubt that both the doctrine and its popular appeal appear in *Richard II*. The aged and dying Gaunt, believing that

> the tongues of dying men
> Enforce attention like deep harmony,

says of Richard

> Methinks I am a prophet new inspired
> And thus expiring do foretell of him.

The magical power of the passions of the mind arises from the fact that the spirits (such as those that Lady Macbeth longs to pour into her husband's ear) alter the accidents or accessory qualities of the body and thus the body itself by the moving of the spirits within the person affected. Agrippa's doctrine of the passions or perturbations was that they derive their power, over soul as well as body, by the means of imagination. This is a most interesting psychological doctrine as yet never worked out. Imagination becomes the agent of fascination, the actual destroyer of distance (as in Shakespeare's sonnets), and a misleader of the will within the individual. It can work effects in other bodies besides its own. The machinery which is set in operation is of this sort: in joy the spirits are driven outward, in fear drawn back to the centre, in bashfulness conveyed to the brain. Joy dilates the heart; sadness restricts it. Lovers are so tied together by the commingling of their spirits that one suffers what the other suffers. By the imagination of the mother an infant in the womb may be marked by a sing. Man's mind may be joined with the mind of the celestials and wonderful virtues thereby infused, because when the intellect is intent upon any work the apprehension and power which is in all things are obedient to it. Since the superior binds the inferior, our minds can change, attract, and repel by their excess of passion what they desire to influence if it be inferior in station. Words have a magic power, since speech is the distinguishing gift of man. Adam, whose natural knowledge was perfect, named all things according to their natures. Words are more potent in sentences and when written, for writing is the ultimate expression of mind. Hebrew is nearest the original magic of God's voice and is therefore the greatest of languages. It is thus possible by careful scrutiny and enlightened intelligence to lead the better life by making use of those things which God in His goodness has laid open to our observation.

Agrippa's second book is devoted to magical numbers, to figures and harmonies, particularly the mathematical harmonies supposed to reside in the celestial universe.

In his third book he dwells at length on evil spirits and their orders. His conception of malignant spirits as heathen gods and fallen angels is the traditional one which underlies Heywood's *Hierarchy of the Blessed Angels* and Milton's *Paradise Lost*. It may be that this section, which goes farthest in the direction of evil magic, had much to do with the degeneration which Agrippa's reputation suffered in the later sixteenth century. He made a definite attempt to establish a new order of magic, and in a certain way he succeeded. Agrippa's magic is the characteristic magic of the Renaissance and differs, as he said it did, from that of earlier writers, in general, in its intelligence and in its attempt to establish its orthodoxy. These fea-

Portrait of Paracelsus.

future events, to see and know things done many miles off, and such like as these, by vertue of superior influences, may seem things incredible; Yet read but the ensuing Treatise and thou shalt see the possibility thereof confirmed by reason and example. I speak now to the judicious, for as for others, they neither know, nor believe, nor will know anything but what is vulgar, nay they think, that beyond this there is scarce anything knowable; when as indeed there are profound mysteries in all beings, even from God in the highest heavens to the divels in the lowest hell; yea in very numbers, names, letters, characters, gestures, time, place, and such like, all which this learned Author profoundly discussed.

The doctrines of the demonology of the Renaissance appear and reappear in Elizabethan literature. The long struggle of rationalism against witchcraft was not to be decided for more than a hundred years. It is hard for a modern to conceive imaginatively of a world surrounded and infested with spirits, good and bad. Such spirits must have been controlling agents in all human activities and in all walks of life. It has taken the full force of modernism to break down the belief in spirits. They were abundant in this universe,—the ranked and ordered angels, the unarmed youth of Heaven, the reprobate demons who like a flock of ravenous fowls followed their master to the ruined earth, spirits of fire, air, water, and earth, resident aliens from an almost forgotten paganism, and the ghosts of the departed dead.

> Nor think, though men were none,
> That Heaven would want spectators, God want praise.
> Millions of spiritual creatures walk the Earth
> Unseen, both when we wake, and when we sleep:
> All these with ceaseless praise his works behold,
> Both day and night.
>
> [*Paradise Lost*]

With whatever spiritual hosts the aggregated traditions of human imagination may have peopled all the vast world, the significant fact remains that theology had given to man a soul, and soul is spirit. The life of the soul is the religious life, and in that life resided the deepest interest of the age. So all-important was the subject of religion in every department of Renaissance life that those who seek to know the sources of Elizabethan thought must turn to it. The most fateful questions concerned the soul. Duty, human conduct, was a determinant factor in the soul's fate. Conduct cannot be divorced from responsibility. Was the soul responsible? Was it free? It could not be entirely responsible, entirely free, as long as it was a cog in the grand old cosmological machine. Let us now examine our second major aspect of cosmological thinking—religion—and some of the things determined by it.

tures did not prevent him and Paracelsus and even Cardan from acquiring popularly the reputation of wizardry. There sprang up many tales of the wonders he had wrought by his practise of the black art. His superiority and general plausibility were, however, fully recognized in the great revival of mysticism and cabalism in the seventeenth century. The remarks of his English translator J. F. (1651) in his epistle to the Judicious Reader reveal this:

> To have a bare notion of a Deity, to apprehend some motions of the Celestials, together with the common operations thereof, and to conceive of some Terrest[r]ial productions, is but what is superficiall and vulgar; But this is true, this is sublime, this *Occult Philosophy;* to understand the mysterious influences of the intellectual world upon the Celestial, and of both upon the Terrest[r]ial; and to know how to dispose and fit our selves so, as to be capable of receiving those superior operations, whereby we may be able to operate wonderfull things, which indeed seem impossible, or at least unlawfull, when as indeed they may be affected by a naturall power and without either offence to God, or violation of Religion. To defend Kingdoms, to discover the secret counsels of men, to overcome enemies, to redeem captives, to increase riches, to procure the favor of men, to expell diseases, to preserve health, to prolong life, to renew youth, to foretell

Much of the habit and belief of the old religion lived on undisturbed by the Reformation and carried with it throughout the Renaissance its atmosphere of formal order and permanence. It was the customary thing for large classes of people. Note, for example, the teachings of Robert Allott's popular encyclopædia, *Wits Theater of the Little World* (printed for I. R. for N. L. 1599). Pliny,

Allott says, has described the universal world; Strabo, Pomponius Mela, and Solinus, the particular world, dividing it into heaven and earth. Man belongs to neither of these, but is a little world or microcosm (so called by Aristotle), which corresponds in all details to the great world or macrocosm. God rules in both worlds equally. His organization of powers in the universal world, according to St. Denis, is as follows: (1) above Heaven, the Trinity; (2) In Heaven, the angels; (3) under Heaven, the prelates and ministers of God. From Isidore comes the following outline of the powers of Heaven itself, which, it will be noticed, correspond to the religious faculties of the human heart: *Epiphania,* divided into Seraphim (who excel in zealous love), Cherubim (who excel in knowledge), and Thrones (who excel in justice); *Epiphonomia,* divided into Principalities (who teach the lower states to revere their betters), Powers (who drive away evil spirits), Dominations (who teach men how to behave in spiritual conflicts); *Euphumia,* divided into Virtues (who work miracles), Archangels (who reveal miracles), and Angels (who are messengers and comforters). The avenue by which these powers may enter the human heart is prayer. This scheme is the merest commonplace, but it did not cease to function in men's minds until long after the Renaissance.

As to the nature of the soul, primary subject of religious thought, there is no reason to regard the views of Sir John Davies in *Nosce Teipsum* and other writings as anything less than widely typical. To Davies, as to the Schoolmen, the universe was a duality of God and the world, and man was a duality of soul and body. The first part of *Nosce Teipsum* presents a detailed definition of the soul in positive and negative terms, its functions, and theories as to its origin. The conclusion is that the soul is 'a spirit, and heavenly influence.' An explanation of the relation of the soul to the body, which can hardly be regarded otherwise than as an advanced form of animism, closes the first part. The second part is devoted to answering the most engrossing question of that age (as of almost every other), namely, whether or not the soul is immortal. It is worth noting that the soul, operating through reason, retains in all circumstances her perfect power, which is necessary to her perfect freedom:

> So, though the clouds eclipse the sunne's faire
> light,
> Yet from his face they doe not take one beame;
> So haue our eyes their perfect power of sight,
> Euen when they looke into a troubled streame.
>
> Then these defects in Senses' organs bee,
> Not in the soule or in her working might;
> She cannot lose her perfect power to see,
> Though mists and clouds do choke her window
> light.

Much follows from this principle. For illustration consider the following lines which lay down the doctrine of the idiot. Idiots have as good souls as wise men; the inward senses of idiots are merely indisposed:

> Euen so the Soule to such a body knit,
> Whose inward senses vndisposed be,
> And to receiue the formes of things vnfit;
> Where nothing is brought in, can nothing see.
> This makes the idiot, which hath yet a mind,

> Able to know the truth, and chuse the good;
> If she such figures in the braine did find,
> As might be found, if it in temper stood.

The freedom of the soul, and hence of the will, was doctrinally so important, that even astrology had to admit that the stars incline but not compel. Nothing is more important than a knowledge of the doctrine held at any one time with reference to the immortality of the soul, because the conditions of its immortality often, determine the degree of its freedom. If there is a warfare between reason and the will, it may take one of three forms: (1) the adversaries may be equal (a situation which may be disregarded); (2) reason may be superior, so that we may attain an Aristotelian peace in a life of contemplation; or (3) will may rule, with important results, for the supremacy of will is the fundamental principle of Machiavellianism, Calvinism, Puritanism, and Stoicism. It is obvious that the status of the soul as regards this conflict between will and reason is important in literature, and that Shakespeare, Bacon, and Hooker occupy the second position.

By and large, it is the old, formal, and peaceful religion which is usually to be found in both the learned and the literary works of the age. For example, consider this from Thomas Milles, *The Treasvrie of Avncient and Moderne Times:* Book I, chapter i, furnishes us with a learned discussion of God, with arguments and elucidations drawn from Aristotle, Cicero, Damascene, Chrysostom, Origen, Anselm, Augustine, Dionysius Areopagitica, Justin Martyr, Philemon, and others, and of course from the Holy Scriptures, telling why we know there is a God and only one, what His names are and what they signify, and what is His essence. God in this account is a just, honourable and kindly being. The chapters following deal, in the same manner, with the creation, the orders of the angels, the earthly Paradise, Hell and what its fire is, Man and what is meant by his being created in the image of God, Satan in the serpent's shape with other devils, and death. The chapters are distinguished by their learning and their close logical reasoning, there being, for example, one of the finest possible distinctions drawn between 'Image' and 'Similitude.' It is the soul which is the image or form of God and possesses the three several dignities of God: Understanding, Will, and Memory; whereas similitude refers to the nature and attributes of God: Immortality, Virtue, and Wisdom. The similitude of God is the ruling principle of organized society.

What might be called the political value of the ancient religious system was held on to with some tenacity. Training in religion and piety was the first element in the education of the prince. Bodin in *De la République* has much to say about religion and government. Book I, chapter xiii, tells how a Prince may suppress one religion by favouring another, there being many citizens who follow that which a prince favours. Book IV, chapter ii, declares that it derogates nothing from the majesty of God to seek in the stars indications of changes impending to empires, and later in the book (pp. 535-9) it is said that religion should be once settled and never after called in question, since disputations of religion are dangerous. If the Prince, being well assured of the rightness of his religion, wishes to draw others to it, he should not use force. Men cannot be compelled to believe, and, if forbidden to believe their own way, they may turn atheist, and atheism is worse than superstition. Bodin presents an example of the indirect influence of humanism on religion.

A still more striking case is that of Regius, who confronts and describes a world whose primary aspect, as conceived by science, is endless variety and unceasing change. Regius makes the unity of God's nature the basis of all form, order, decorum, and beauty; therefore, this unity is the basis of all learning, of which religion is the primary type. The inferior world is composed of contrary and conflicting elements; but the principle of unity must exceed the principle of contrariety, or chaos is come again. Heathen philosophers have seen innate powers in the reasonable soul, as if it had been extracted from the Godhead before it came down to earth and forgot its original intelligence by the contagion of the flesh. But Christians reject such fatal necessity and believe that God, according to His pleasure, distributes to different persons different qualities, since the common good and preservation of society cannot endure without many estates, callings, offices, and works. This important philosophy of change and its various reconciliations in religion and elsewhere remains largely unstudied.

The older religious point of view is certainly the persistent one. Charles Butler writes excellently *The Feminine Monarchie, or A Treatise concerning Bees,* which rests squarely upon the idea that religious instruction can be derived from bees. Their government is like the government of an ideal Christian state and God is present with them. Certain bees, he tells us, are known to have built a chapel, with windows, steeple, bells, and altar, for a bit of the Host, which they worshipped with a sweet sound. Bees are models of temperance, justice, and chastity. It is interesting also to find Person in his *Varieties,* a book which bears the closest resemblance to Burton's *Anatomy* of any to be found, declaring that, though the plagues, pestilences and deaths of beasts which follow earth-quakes can be explained philosophically, God's liberty to use these means of forewarning men should not be abridged. The same principle appears in the ingenious traditional argument offered by Huarte, who says take heed that you receive no hurt from leaving out the Pope and his cardinals; for God, knowing the uncertainty of men's reasons, enters into the midst of the congregations of the Church, dispels errors, and reveals a wisdom never attainable by human means alone. One is not to think that the traditional religion was usually less insistent on the punitive activities of a jealous God. The sudden death of the wicked was an act of divine judgment and a thing to be expected. Religious faith was regarded as indispensable to correct conduct, a faith which relied for its efficacy on lurid pictures of impending punishment. Without this bulwark man, because of his degenerate nature, was capable of every form of wickedness, and the denial of religion, or even its minor tenets, was atheism, and atheism was every form of vice. These features are often attributed to Puritanism, but they are almost equally characteristic of all forms of sixteenth-century religion. The very fact of a general belief in the doctrine that every sin must and will be punished here and now, and its other developing dogma to the effect that the

pangs of a guilty conscience are inescapable, cannot but have important bearings in literature.

In England the greatest of religious events was the coming of Calvinism and the Puritanism which followed in its wake. These two established the religion of conscience. It has been so much a matter of custom in the study of English literature to depreciate Calvinism that it is possible the whole question of its literary influences needs re-studying. It was not Scotland and New England only that felt the stress and strain of the great reformer and his followers, but England itself had a bath in Calvinism both thorough and long. When we speak of Puritanism, to be sure, we ordinarily mean the sort of religious beliefs that prevailed longest in Scotland and New England. But Puritanism means much more than this, and we need to reconsider the fine humanistic body of teachings and teachers that entered England largely through a noble and learned group of Huguenots during the last third of the sixteenth century. The influence of this humanistic type of Puritanism was felt by Sidney, Spenser, and certainly by the great mass of the greatest writers and thinkers of the age. The *Institutes* of Calvin, as regards its reflection in literature, needs to be re-studied. It appears in various forms, which reflect various degrees and stages of religious thinking. We know Calvin's general theses, but we do not realize their significance: the knowledge of God is an inward knowledge, innate, which is an Aristotelian principle, to be supplemented by the purely Christian doctrine that God in pity for man's blindness and depravity, in a way which we do not understand but which came to be called election (a Stoical idea), has provided for man's redemption. Fairbairn has said rather shrewdly that Lutheranism saved everything not forbidden by Scripture, whereas Calvinism sacrificed everything not sanctified and justified by Scripture. It therefore tended to free the soul and to rescue it from its cosmological fetters. Calvinism is a primary critical force, and it is perhaps only the minor jealousies of the historians of culture that prevent them from recognizing it as possibly the greatest modernizing agent in the Renaissance world. Calvin's approach was humanistic. He was therefore strong in his educational policy and in his biblical scholarship. He was Stoical in his ethical sympathies and therefore turned attention to the side of polity. Calvinism is sometimes regarded as the source of modern democracy. Like Vives before him, Calvin turned for his ideals of private and domestic morals to that group of Greek and Latin Fathers—tertullian, Ambrose, Augustine, Gregory, and Cyprian—who in their day had striven to save their charges from the contaminations of a degenerate society. The situations were paralle, and Calvin found there what he wanted—namely the Puritan code.

But Calvin and the Calvinists did more than this. They turned to logic. All critics who are effective must do that. They seized upon the philosophy of Aristotle as it had already been developed (and distorted) by the Schoolmen and made of it a most effective disciplinary instrument. In Aristotle's doctrine of form as expressed in the doctrine of the four causes, current Christian Aristotelianism had made the final cause supreme and had identified it with the God of revealed religion. The formal cause was also important as indicating the revealed (and interpreted) mind of God. The material and the efficient causes were on a lower level. What Calvin did was to assume the importance of the final and the formal causes and endow the other two with a power and importance they had never before enjoyed. The thinkers of Puritanism seized upon the efficient cause as their point of argument or restraint, upon the formal cause as a complete justification of the acceptance of the Scriptures as the sole guide to truth, and upon the final cause, or will of God, as the source of perpetual remission of sins and full restoration to eternal life. Thus was the soul, freed from the rather gentle bonds of Scholasticism, shackled again by those of a revivified logic.

One wonders why the logical bases of Puritanism have not been more popularly recognized. There are few religious books written in England or America since the sixteenth century which do not to some degree rest upon this logic of religion. The subject is not dead and cannot die. We have heard it debated in our own day over and over, and we are still in doubt as to whether our own morals and those of society are better protected by removing the occasion and the opportunity for sin and vice, or by trying in some fashion to make ourselves and other men sin-resistant.

The clarity with which the principle was recognized by the Puritans will appear on almost every page of the *Anatomie of Abuses* by the notorious Philip Stubbes; but, because it is rendered clearer in his case by his exaggeration and lack of perspective, one is not to believe that the principle is not almost universal among religious writers. What he has to say about fine clothes will exemplify his method as well as we could wish:

> The apparell in it owne nature is good and the good creature of God (I will not denie) and cannot hurt excepte it be through our owne wickednesse abused. And therefore, woe be [to] them that make the good Creatures of God instrumentes of damnation to themselves, by not using them but abusing them. And yet notwithstanding, it may be said to hurt, or not to hurt, as it is abused or not abused. And whereas they would haue the abuse of apparell (if any be) taken away, and the apparal to remain stil, it is impossible to supplant the one, without the extirpation of the other also. For truly it is sayd, Sublata causa, tollitur effectus. But not, Sublato effectu, tollitur causa. *Take away the cause and the effect fayleth,* but not contrarily, *take away the effect, and the cause fayleth.* The externe efficient cause of pride, is gorgeous attire: [the effect is pride it selfe ingenerate by attire:] but to begin to plucke away the effect, to wit, Pride, and not to take away the cause first, namely sumptuous attire, is as if a man intending to supplant a tree by the rootes, should begin to pull the fruit and branches onely, or to pull downe heaven, should dig in the earth working altogether preposterously, indirectly, and contrarily.

But we need not stop with the narrowness of Philip Stubbes. If we remember that Milton based his argument for freedom of speech on a ground exactly opposite to that of Stubbes, we shall attach a far profounder importance to the question at issue between them. Milton believed that

the efficient cause of sin and of virtue lies, not in external temptation, but within the human heart. Let us quote a familiar passage from *Areopagitica:*

> As therefore the state of man now is; what wisdom can there be to choose, what continence to forbear, without the knowledge of evil? He that can apprehend and consider vice with all her baits and seeming pleasures, and yet abstain, and yet distinguish, and yet prefer that which is truly better, he is the true wayfaring Christian. I cannot praise a fugitive and cloistered virtue unexercised and unbreathed, that never sallies out and seeks her adversary, but slinks out of the race, where that immortal garland is to be run for, not without dust and heat. Assuredly we bring not innocence into the world, we bring impurity much rather; that which purifies us is trial, and trial is by what is contrary. That virtue therefore which is but a youngling in the contemplation of evil, and knows not the utmost that vice promises to her followers, and rejects it, is but a blank virtue, not a pure; her whiteness is but an excremental whiteness; which is the reason why our sage and serious poet Spenser, (whom I dare be known to think a better teacher than Scotus or Aquinas,) describing true temperance under the person of Guion, brings him in with his palmer through the cave of Mammon, and the bower of earthly bliss, that he might see and know, and yet abstain.

From what has been said in this [essay] an idea may be formed as to the main channels through which the ancient cosmology and its laws exerted their influence and as to the varied effects this influence was capable of working in the mind of the Renaissance.

Brian P. Copenhaver and Charles B. Schmitt

SOURCE: "Nature against Authority: Breaking away from the Classics," in *Renaissance Philosophy,* Oxford University Press, Oxford, 1992, pp. 285-328.

[In this excerpt, Copenhaver and Schmitt examine natural philosophy, describing the means by which several Renaissance philosophers exploited and rejected Peripatetic metaphysics.]

In Peripatetic natural philosophy, a physical substance is some particular composite of matter and form. Generation or coming-to-be occurs when matter (*hulê*) gains form (*morphê*), passing-away or corruption when form is lost. If a substance passes from one state to another, as from hot to cold, one term of the change may be seen as a form, the other as its negation or privation; what persists is the material substrate. Hence, matter, form, and privation account for the generation and corruption of substances. Matter without form is entirely indeterminate; it lacks quality and form but has the potency to acquire them. In order to have an identity as some one thing among others, a substance must actually possess distinguishing forms and qualities, said to be educed from the potency of its matter. Some features of a substance—a given colour or weight or shape in an apple, for instance—may not be essential; when they change or disappear, the apple remains the same substance, so they are called accidental forms or qualities. But suppose a human substance loses the feature of rationality. In Aristotelian terms, the person will no longer be human. The individual in question requires rationality in order to count as human; so the human has a substantial form as well as various accidental forms, and that substantial form is rational. Rationality is essential to humanity. But if the form of rationality gives the human substance its being as human, this will be true of all humans, who are members of the same species because they are *rational* animals. Evidently, the substantial or specific form cannot distinguish one human or one apple from others of their species. What makes this apple differ from that one is some definite batch of matter, but matter as a principle of individuation needs forms and qualities; unformed matter, prime matter, is utterly indistinct, so it has no real existence by itself. Only the composite substance, the real apple, actually exists on its own.

Aristotle himself complicated the problem of form when he gave it a leading role in sensation and intellection; these processes occur because disembodied sensible and intelligible forms of the object actually unite with the subject's faculties of mind and sense. How does the form of a substance as *known* differ from the form that *constitutes* the substance? Christian Peripatetics had less trouble with such questions when asked of natural objects—apples and other such things—than when they themselves were involved; the human substance gave more trouble because it had to be immortal. Having defined man's immortal soul as a substantial form and the mortal body as the matter informed by it, they faced such puzzles as the status of the soul after death, before rejoining the resurrected body. A temporarily bodiless form of the body or forms flitting from known to knower were by no means the only chinks in the armour of hylemorphism, but they gave [Pietro] Pomponazzi and others much to worry about. Pomponazzi's approach to the problem caused so much trouble because he took Aristotle's more materialist view of the soul so seriously. More expedient solutions tended to liberate a dematerialized substantial form from the body and to treat it as an autonomous entity. Indeed, by [Giordano] Bruno's time the doctrine of substantial or specific form had become a crux of debate and a focus of explanation in many areas of physics and metaphysics. Physicians, philosophers, theologians, and others depended on hylemorphism as much as we rely on evolution in biology or quantum mechanics in physics, but many of them sensed that the hylemorphic paradigm was crumbling.

Since the high Middle Ages, philosophers had often tried to adapt Peripatetic metaphysics to Christian purposes or to adjust it for various theoretical reasons, but Bruno did more than tinker. In *De la causa* and other works, he dismantled hylemorphism to replace it with a materialist naturalism that preserved certain elements of Aristotle's terminology—the words 'form' and 'matter', for example—but demolished his metaphysics. Bruno's assault on Aristotle was fiercer and showier than other such attacks, but it was part of a larger wave of discontent with a system straining under its own excesses and elaborations after centuries of growth and inbreeding. In the sixteenth cen-

tury and after, even professed Aristotelians from Pomponazzi to Cremonini undermined Peripatetic defenses by reading the Philosopher in rigorously naturalist terms. Others, armed with new information about Stoics, Epicureans, and pre-Socratics, proposed alternatives to part or all of Peripatetic natural philosophy. Many of these challengers were physicians, like Girolamo Fracastoro, who lived until 1553. Best remembered for the poem that gave syphilis its name, Fracastoro was also dedicated to an empirically based medicine. He studied the problem of contagion, often regarded in his time as an occult force, and treated it as one of a larger class of sympathies and antipathies, which he tried to extract from the realm of magic. Referring to the atomism of Lucretius, he explained sympathy as a mechanical attraction resulting from a flow of particles between objects; the *seminaria* or seed-particles that carry contagion are especially fine and hence able to cover great distances and penetrate the bodies they strike. When he made 'spirit' a part of this same mechanism, Fracastoro had in mind a subtle material substance like the Stoic *pneuma,* not a magical ectoplasm.

Less a philosopher in the modern sense than Fracastoro was Philippus Aureolus Theophrastus Bombastus von Hohenheim, known as Paracelsus. His name itself was a defiance. Born in Switzerland in 1493, he wandered all over Europe until his death in 1541, first apprenticed to his physician father, then studying medicine at Ferrara, and perhaps also learning magic from the monk Trithemius. He bloodied his hands as a military surgeon and earned respect for medical practice in Strasbourg and Basle, where two of his more eminent patients were Erasmus and his humanist publisher Johann Froben. Everywhere he went, Paracelsus shattered conventions and exasperated expectations. Early on, he declared his medical independence by burning the books of Galen and Avicenna. His own writings—a jumble of theology, chemistry, medicine, mysticism, folklore, and plain nonsense—resist brief description. Many of their sources are still hidden in the obscurities of Cabala, German folklore, and local traditions long since lost. He wrote mostly in a German dialect, and his Latin was idiosyncratic, to say the least. Some of the most influential and popular works published under his name are spurious. Later Paracelsian thought, which peaked in the seventeenth century, derived almost entirely from Latin texts and mixed the founder's doctrines with accretions and digests from his followers. The original works abhor all except biblical authority, though like other innovators Paracelsus owed more to tradition than he cared to admit.

He was primarily a medical reformer, but he derived his medical theory from a much more ambitious world-view that encompassed all philosophy. Like other philosophers of nature, he rejected the traditional quaternaries of elements, qualities, and humours, and he replaced them with a triad of first principles called mercury, salt, and sulphur. He described mercury as an active and spiritual force, converted chemically to smoke through combustion; physiologically it fixes the body's fluid content. Salt is passive and corporeal, left as ash after combustion and lending form and solidity to physiological change. Sulphur is an intermediate principle; its chemistry makes things combustible, and its role in physiology is to promote growth. When a piece of wood burns, combustion produces mercurial vapours, sulphurous flames, and salty ash. Like Aristotle's elements in relation to the fire, air, water, and earth of daily experience, the Paracelsian *tria prima* were not the same as ordinary mercury, salt, and sulphur. Their properties were much broader and more powerful. Paracelsian matter-theory was certainly novel in the context of normal natural philosophy, but it can be traced to Moslem alchemical theories of the eighth century. Chemistry was central to the Paracelsian world picture, and Paracelsian medicine was really 'iatro-chemistry' or chemical medicine. Paracelsus did not invent iatrochemistry but he promoted it, popularized it, and started it on a vigorous career in the sixteenth and seventeenth centuries. Since health was supposed to depend on a balance of the three principles, Paracelsian medications were chemical combinations of mercury, sulphur, and salt. Besides the three material elements, Paracelsus posited a spiritual 'archeus' which acted as a unifying principle, roughly like the Peripatetic substantial form. Matter, spirit, and soul were fluid rather than discrete properties of reality in a universe where everything was more or less alive. Paracelsus believed in magic, astrology, and personal spiritual beings, but he derived these beliefs as much from personal observation as from the traditions that he wished to abandon.

Another celebrated and rambunctious physician was Girolamo Cardano, who studied medicine at Pavia and Padua to prepare for his doctorate in 1526, after which he practised in Milan before winning his first fame for books on arithmetic and algebra, especially the *Ars Magna* of 1545. Five years later he published his most famous work, *On Subtlety,* a rambling miscellany of natural philosophy which eventually grew to twenty-one books and appeared in many reprints and revisions before and after Cardano's death in 1576. His book *On Variety* of 1557 was a sequel to the successful *De subtilitate,* and his treatises of 1560 *On the One* and *On Nature* extended the anti-Aristotelian implications of that work. About a fifth of Cardano's nearly fifty books deal with philosophical issues, though he is best known today for original work in algebra and probability. Seldom read now but widely cited in its own time and the century following was the *Fifteenth Book of Exoteric Exercises on Subtlety* by Julius Caesar Scaliger, a blast from an admirer of Aristotle bothered by Cardano's prose as well as his originality and sloppiness; Scaliger's title implied that there was enough wrong with *De subtilitate* to have filled fourteen other volumes. At one point, Scaliger thought that his attack had literally killed its victim, but it only helped enlarge his reputation, for better or for worse. *De natura* contains Cardano's strongest critiques of Aristotle, whom he continued to honour, but the first books of *De subtilitate,* which deal with physical principles, present the less pointed material that helped turn his contemporaries against Peripatetic natural philosophy.

De natura confronts Aristotle straightforwardly on a number of topics: privation as an explanation of change, the nature of generation and corruption, the relation of corporeal to incorporeal substance, the existence of prime matter, the number of the elements, and so forth. These challenges are blunted in the more expansive and maddeningly disorganized *De subtilitate.* Although he spends the first paragraphs of the book defining 'subtlety', exactly what Cardano had in mind is hard to say. He seems to have meant that problems are subtle if they are extremely obscure and require the finest sense of discrimination to resolve. He certainly succeeded in demonstrating the first point. After an incredibly involved summary of the whole work, he begins with an orthodox account of matter as what persists when form expires, but then, with no bows to a divine creator, he goes on to describe matter as ungenerated and imperishable. Like Aristotle, he makes form a requirement for the actualization of matter, but he also claims that soul is everywhere because all bodies have a source of motion within them. But what he means by soul or *anima* turns out to be quite mechanical. He names three kinds of universal natural motion. One type of motion begins when nature acts to avoid a vacuum in a change which might otherwise leave *too little matter* for a given form; another starts in order to prevent interpenetration of bodies when change might yield *too much matter* for a particular form; the third occurs when heavy things fall and light things rise, but, having experienced the enormous power of the first two causes of motion in the explosive force of artillery, Cardano is ready almost to ignore the third, which was Aristotle's paradigm of all natural sublunar motion. He counts five natural principles—matter, form, soul, place, and motion—and he makes all of them eternal. No apologies to Aristotle. No worries about the creator. Except to suppose that it was largely unconscious, it is hard to account for Cardano's bravado. He was once detained by the Inquisition, but the charges are unknown.

Bernardino Telesio was just as daring but more deliberate and less prolific. Bacon, who criticized his empiricism as incomplete, honoured him as 'the first of the moderns'. Telesio was born in 1509 in the far south of Italy, in the Calabrian town of Cosenza, to a family powerful in the region. At the age of nine he left for Milan, Rome, and finally Padua, where he began to study Aristotelian philosophy and Galenic medicine around 1530, when debate ran heavy on faults in the scholastic system explored by secular Aristotelians and empiricist physicians. The greatest of the former was Pomponazzi, of the latter Vesalius, who was anatomizing in Padua while Telesio studied there in the 1530s, when important humanist professors were also teaching in the university. Besides Paracelsus and Fracastoro, who published his *De sympathia* in 1546, others who anticipated Telesio in seeking a new basis for natural philosophy included the poet Marcello Palingenio Stellato, whose *Zodiac of Life* of 1535 combined Epicurean with Neoplatonic elements, and Simone Porzio, whose book *On Principles* of 1553 examined physical questions with notable independence of mind. After finishing his degree in 1535, Telesio may have contemplated these developments during a period of withdrawal in a monastery; he sought no university job, but by 1547 his ideas seem to have been in public circulation, and within a few years he was at work on the first version of his treatise *On the Nature of Things According to Their Own Principles,* one of the more incisive titles in Renaissance philosophy and a clear allusion to Lucretius. In 1553 he was back in Cosenza, where he gave much time to the Accademia Cosentina, while travelling frequently to Rome and Naples. Pressed by his followers, he published the original two book version of *De rerum natura* in 1563, having previously tested the soundness of his arguments in conversations with Vincenzo Maggi, a noted Paduan Peripatetic. Another edition followed in 1570; in 1575 Antonio Persio gave public lectures on the Telesian system in Venice, Padua, Bologna, and the south; and in 1586 appeared the definitive expansion to nine books. The author died two years later in Cosenza.

The proem to *De rerum natura* carries a subtitle for the work announcing it as a manifesto for natural philosophy emancipated from Peripatetic rationalism: 'the structure of the world and the nature and magnitude of bodies contained in it are not to be sought from reason, as the ancients did; they must be perceived from sensation and treated as being things themselves.' True to this principle, Telesio laid out the ground-plan of his naturalism in the first two books of his treatise before taking on Aristotle in the third and devoting the rest of the volume to physical, biological, epistemological, and moral implications of his empirical premises. If Aristotle studies being as such in his metaphysics, his physics deals with being in motion, but physical change (*metabolê*) or motion (*kinêsis*) includes transformations not only of quality, quantity, and place but also of substance; hence metaphysical issues became prominent in Peripatetic physics, as indeed they had been in the first two books of the Philosopher's *Physics*. After Galileo and Descartes, motion became a uniquely physical category, and a leading aim of post-Newtonian science has been to account for all change, even its own changes of mind, in terms of matter in motion. Telesio's pre-Galilean perspective was reversed. To make physics autonomous, he had to extricate it from a natural philosophy in which rational principles of form, matter, privation, and passage from potency to act covered change and motion of all kinds. He began with the crude evidence of his senses, all ultimately reducible to touch, and he asserted but never proved that sensation is nature's truest witness. Taken as a whole, the book is a frontal assault on the foundations of Peripatetic philosophy accompanied by a proposal for replacing Aristotelianism with a system more faithful to nature and experience.

First he noted that the sun is a light and bright body that emits heat, while cold comes from the dark, dense earth. Since heat and cold penetrate bodies, and body is impenetrable, these two active principles must be incorporeal, but to exist they need to act upon bodily mass or passive matter, the third basic principle. In Aristotelian terms, they act like material and efficient causes; Telesio distrusted Aristotle's analysis of causation, and he shied away especially from unseen final and formal causes. Invisible, lifeless, and powerless in itself, matter dilates or contracts as heat or cold affect it; otherwise, it can do nothing but fall, which is not really action but absence of action. The heavens and the sun are the region of heat; cold belongs to earthy matter below. Earth and sun are changeless as such, but other bodies pass in and out of being as heat and cold struggle for possession of material mass. From this Heraclitian conflict arises the world's diversity, which Ar-

istotle tried to explain with privation, matter, and form, but Aristotle's account fails at various key points. One failure was to make nature wasteful, a slumbering storehouse of idle forms waiting to be put to work. If all possible forms are really there waiting in matter's potency, what does it mean to say that any form is generated or corrupted? Rejecting metaphysical principles prior to the natural object because he considered them redundant, Telesio insisted that all the object's features are precisely coextensive and simultaneous with its organic development. One of these features is soul or *anima,* in the case of animals a material *spiritus* that grows from the seed and suffuses the whole body except for the bones. Unlike the Peripatetic soul, this *anima* is not the substantial form of the body. If it were, the body would vanish as soon as the soul leaves in death. The ensouled body is an organic or structural rather than a formal unity, like a ship made of many parts all sailing to the same port. One such part is the soul, which the body needs for movement and perception, but not for simple physical integrity.

Human animals like all others require a spiritual soul, but this material faculty cannot explain man's immortality or all his moral and religious instincts, so to account for these data of faith Telesio posited another, immaterial soul, infused by God and left outside the bounds of nature. This implanted soul needs its spiritual counterpart not only to perceive but also to reason. Spirit perceives objects by contact that alters it physically; in effect, perception occurs when spirit feels itself expanded or contracted by heat or cold. Aristotle had claimed that the soul becomes the forms that it perceives, but to avoid the absurdity of formal fire lit in the mind when one sees a flame, Telesio made perception a process of physical contact rather than ontological change; heat simply warms and enlarges the spirit. Yet this transaction is something more than a mechanical impression. The antipathy between cold and heat shows that even these simplest elements sense the hostility between them. When cold reacts against heat's movement toward some bit of matter, response to the aggressive motion requires a perceptive act which is not motion itself. Moreover, the physical apparatus of sensation includes not just discrete perceptions but also their comparison and organization into concepts and patterns of judgment and recollection, all within the ambit of the spiritual soul. Likewise, there is an appetite whose drives are entirely material, directed toward conserving the physical organism and maintaining the spirit in a pleasureably expansive state of warmth and motion. Parallel to sensation and appetite, an immaterial will seeks a divine end, and a rational soul contemplates its immortal destiny. Choices between the objects of these twin faculties give rise to free will. At the same time, however, Telesio proposes to naturalize even the moral basis of human action. Conservation of the spirit in a pleasant and secure state is itself a moral end, whose highest form consists in distinguishing ephemeral from durable pains and pleasures. The philosopher of nature provides a materially grounded ethics suited to the spiritual soul, leaving it to the theologian to deal with the higher immaterial purposes of the rational soul. Telesio left an orderly, coherent system that fails on the crude side of simplicity; its epistemology is untested and its empiricism limited to gross and undisciplined observation. Despite his protestations, Telesio was actually less of an empiricist than the Aristotle of the zoological works, and he seems to have come no closer than such Peripatetic contemporaries as Zabarella to a systematic experimental programme. Neither he nor Zabarella had any conception of the scientific power of mathematics. From a modern point of view, however, it stands to Telesio's credit that he was never charmed by occultism, unlike other philosophers of nature. His sense of empirical science, which included progressive ideas on space, vacuum, and other physical topics, grew out of a disenchanted world-view remarkable for its hard-headed clarity.

Bruno's natural philosophy had different virtues and defects: its extraordinary subtlety often destroys itself in the wildest inconsistency, in swings from monism to pluralism, from unitary substance to atomic discontinuity, from disdain for finite bodies to exaltation of material infinity. Bruno was in his early forties when prison closed his career in 1591. Even during the previous productive decade, his escapades in northern Europe ending in return to Venice and betrayal to the Inquisition can scarcely have enabled him to take a long view of his work, to eliminate contradictions and settle on a cleaner presentation of his thought. Recklessness was so much in Bruno's character that one hesitates to suggest that a 'mature' system was ever in the cards for him; if his achievement was immature, it was also precocious and rich, like that of Shelley or Nietzsche. If one can speak of a 'romantic temperament', Bruno surely had it. Had he mellowed his conduct and softened his tongue, he might not have gone to the stake in 1600, though before he died he attempted to conciliate his inquisitors, who would have been satisfied only with submission, while he kept debating. He recanted and then withdrew his recantation—of what we do not know because the most important records were destroyed. The clerics who jailed him for nine years and then murdered him were surely right to think Bruno a heretic; their worst fears seem to have focused on religious beliefs, to which he was indifferent (when indifference was not an option), rather than the liberty of philosophizing that was his grand and fatal passion. In fact, the final change of heart that led to his grisly execution may have occurred when philosophical issues came to the fore. One cannot say. What horrific credo had he transgressed to make his judges dispense with the usual grotesque mercy of garrotting before they lit the tinder? Bruno burned for philosophy; he was killed for moral, physical, and metaphysical views that terrified and angered the authorities. While pondering our irritations with his changes on such questions, it will be well to recall the price he paid to the hobgoblin of little minds and the demon of clear convictions.

Bruno was a great soul, though it may not have seemed so in 1584 when he first protested at length against Aristotelian physics and metaphysics in *De la causa.* In general, the position of this dialogue is monist, like that of other works that deal with the topic of being, while those on memory and knowledge often preserve the pluralist segregation of things from ideas. The words 'form' and 'matter' survive Bruno's savaging of hylemorphism, but not as independent principles of being. Unlike Aristotle, whose theory of substance was about concrete individuals, Bruno

did not care about individual objects. He saw the particular forms that distinguish one thing from another as ripples in the calm sea of being, mere modes or accidents of universal matter. Nature thrives and breeds transitory forms out of living matter through her own internal force of soul. The single universal form is the world-soul that drives things from within as their principle. Causes that act externally are superficial; a deeper dynamism belongs to principles that move inside. Matter and form unite in the infinite substance that comprehends all. Infinite unitary substance is the opposite of diversity for Bruno and therefore an inversion of Peripatetic substantial form, whose job is to make the object the kind of thing it is. Individual souls in Bruno's system cannot be discrete specific forms because soul is really one; what enlivens a human and a fly are fragments of the same world-soul, which is like a light reflected in a shattered mirror whose splinters are the souls of particular beings. Ultimately, Bruno had little work for form to do, but he gave matter a more dignified role than Christian Peripatetics usually allowed it. Forms come and go as matter endures, ensouled, alive, and divine. Matter is both corporeal and incorporeal, but its bodily manifestations are no more than contractions of a primal matter unlimited by corporeal division. What harm to call such matter divine? God is in things; divinity and the infinite living cosmos are the same, except to timorous theologians who think that abasing nature glorifies God. Albertus, Aquinas, and other eminent scholastics called Avicebron (Ibn Gabirol) and David of Dinant pantheists and materialists because their matter theory infringed the divine prerogative of incorporeality; but Bruno found these thinkers good company.

Like Plotinus, Bruno made matter absolutely indeterminate, but he took this non-feature of matter as proof of its richness. The One is infinite, and so is its material substrate, which is also stable, unitary, eternal, and uncreated; God and the world are the same, so they must be coeval. The unity and stability of being are guaranteed at both extremes of quantity by the coincidence of maximum and minimum. The atomic minimum is a real concrete thing, not a mathematical abstraction. In fact, one of Bruno's flaws was his attitude toward mathematics, which ranged from apathy to animosity with occasional pauses in which he devised a dilettante numerology. Despite his wish to destroy Aristotle's authority in natural philosophy, Bruno kept to a physics at least as qualitative as the Stagirite's. None the less, the minimum yields no experience of quality, so its features must be inferred rationally, by reasons opposed to Peripatetic dogma. In his closed world Aristotle allowed matter to be potentially divisible without limit, but the atoms in Bruno's infinite universe are well-defined minima because they have a least size; they are tiny spheres, indivisible, impenetrable, and homogeneous. Only their arrangement in various structures produces material variety. Some minima—the smallest possible cat, for example—may be organic or structural rather than atomic wholes, and hence corruptible. But an atom is immutable because it is a simple unity, while larger objects made of atoms are transitory aggregates. The atomism of Bruno's earlier works calls on an ordering mind to regulate the shifting swarms of particles, but in the later Latin poem *On the Triple Minimum,* the atom itself becomes a soul, defined either 'privatively' as the smallest part of the continuum (like a letter of the alphabet in an infinite library) or 'negatively' as escaping all limit and definition. The continuum of ordinary matter disaggregates into privative atoms, but infinite soul has no breaks or boundaries; minimal and maximal souls must coincide. Without the world-soul to vitalize it, matter and its atoms would be nothing. Even the negative minimum or monad differs from the Leibnizian entity of the same name, which is created, perceptive, and radically alone—'windowless', in fact—while Bruno's uncreated and insentient monads need the splendour of soul to activate them. Soul's light shines from within, however; no external cause forms the atoms into the shapes that make up the visible world. 'In everything is a share of everything', said Anaxagoras, and Bruno added that everything is God.

Bruno's statue stands in Rome in the Field of Flowers, on the spot where he was burned. Eventually, he became a hero to those who saw him as a martyr for free science and philosophy in their fight against ideological repression; but another view of Bruno hails him chiefly as a progressive in morals and religion, a magical reformer who wanted to save Europe from a decadent Christianity by reviving the Hermetic cult of ancient Egypt. Fortunately, there was enough in Bruno's great soul to please all his friends and annoy all his enemies: the pantheist, the materialist, the libertine free-thinker, and philosophical rogue; the magus, the Lullist, the memory wizard; the atomist, the Copernican, the proponent of infinite worlds, and the advocate of spacious liberty in philosophy. Tommaso Campanella was his immediate heir, another renegade Dominican whom the church imprisoned two years before Bruno died and kept confined for twenty-six more. Born in 1568 in Calabria, Telesio's region, Campanella considered himself a good Catholic, but he was probably a worse danger to the establishment than Bruno, for he had messianic fantasies that incited zany insurrectionist plots which might have done material damage. Having recouped some of its losses after the Reformation, the post-Tridentine church was not amused when the author of the *Monarchy of the Messiah* planned to make the papacy the centre of secular as well as spiritual world government. Today, Campanella's best-remembered book is the *City of the Sun,* a saner utopian design for social reform that gained an immense readership in frequent translations into many languages.

Campanella's first surviving work, *Philosophy Demonstrated by the Senses,* is an immense anti-Peripatetic polemic in defence of Telesio, published in 1591 against a Peripatetic who had attacked the great Calabrian's treatise *On the Nature of Things.* Campanella tried unsuccessfully to meet Telesio before he died, and he chose to build a new philosophy on his country-man's naïve empiricism rather than devise yet another variation on the airy constructs of the Aristotelians. For his independent thinking he was accused of heresy and confined to his convent, the first of many long spells of detention. From the tone and content of his book, one can see why the Thomist Dominicans feared that they had hatched a monster:

> The top Peripatetics, what empty-headed nitwits . . . ! Prime matter is supposed to be nothing really and privation nothing, and yet form gets drawn from the potency of prime matter, which is nothing and does not exist. . . . How great is the ignorance of these people: they want to act like gods, not baulking at producing beings from non-beings, making things out of illusions to trick people.

Campanella denied hylemorphism and replaced it with his own doctrine, sometimes obscured by the old terminology in which he expressed it. The ideas that he rejected were the core of Peripatetic philosophy: that substantial form is a principle of being superior to matter; that form is educed from the potency of matter; that soul is the form of the body; and that the mind knows by abstracting forms from objects. Above all, Campanella insisted that form was known directly through the senses. The Peripatetics had pried form away from sensation, so Campanella anchored it to body. Matter is simply bodily mass, the body or matter of common experience needing no abstract forms to make it real. 'It would be wrong', he argued, 'to say that matter is bodily because of form. . . . Body is body in its own right and . . . the same . . . as matter, quantity, substrate and bodily mass.' We draw our first distinctions among objects from their shape, which we also call 'form', and this leads us by analogy to the concept of internal form. But internal form is a mode or quality of the object, not a being in its own right. Having dispensed with substantial form, Campanella replaced it with Telesio's heat and cold, which cause the particles in a body to take on different arrangements or 'temperaments'. He equated form with temperament and described temperament as the structure of matter heated or cooled. This novel approach first appears in book two of *Philosophia sensibus demonstrata,* where Campanella writes that

> each thing has by nature a consimilar constitutive heat . . . consimilar, I mean, to the heat of a particular star . . . [so that] each thing in the universe can have its own star . . . corresponding to its constitutive heat and leading to procreation and growth, as Hermes, Enoch and Mercurius said . . . , [who] saw such effects and, not knowing how to investigate their causes, attributed them to occult influences and the souls of the stars.

In other words, although the young Campanella believed in astrological causation, he did not believe that celestial causes were *occult.* In effect, he proposed a physical theory of *manifest* forces, heat and cold, to replace the traditional doctrine of occult powers which had long been tied to the hylemorphic metaphysics that he also rejected.

Unlike Telesio, however, who did his best to liberate physics from metaphysics, Campanella was not unfriendly to metaphysics as such. He wanted to change metaphysics, not destroy it. Although his *Eighteen Books of Metaphysics* appeared only in 1638, the year before he died, Campanella had shown interest in writing a metaphysics by 1590 and had produced a version of it by 1602—3. In the published work, he criticized Telesio for attributing too much to the purely natural agency of heat and cold in forming natural bodies, suggesting that these physical powers could act only as instruments of a diviner cause whose various levels he identified as God, the 'primalities', their 'influences', and the world-soul. The distinctive ingredients of Campanella's new metaphysics began to get broad public exposure in the brief *Compendium of Nature* of 1617 and in the 1620 edition of his book *On the Sense in Things and on Magic.* The subtitle of this ebullient volume proclaims its subject as 'occult philosophy, showing the cosmos to be a living, conscious statue of god' and describes the world's 'parts and particles [as] having sensation . . . enough for their conservation'. Most of Campanella's arguments for pansensism remain within the limits of Telesio's physical programme. Since all natural action results from the contrariety of heat and cold, a hot object must somehow be aware that cold is its enemy, otherwise the natural impulse of each active force to inform matter would go uncontested; hostilities would cease, and generation and corruption would end. When Campanella claims that the spirits diffused through nature laugh and weep, however, one may read him simply as expressing a physical antinomy—the common fact of dilation and constriction—poetically. He crossed the line between physics and metaphysics only when he began to describe his complex scheme for God as creator and sustainer of nature:

> God is more within things than the forms themselves, . . . impressing in them the power not only to reach an end but to know how to reach it. . . . All sense is participant in the first wisdom, . . . [and] every form is participant in God. And because god is most powerful, wise, and loving, . . . all beings are composed of Power, Wisdom, and Love, and every being exists because it *can* be, *knows how* to be, and *loves* to be, and when it lacks the power or knowledge or love of being, it dies or changes.

By placing the trinitarian God of power, wisdom, and love—the 'divine Monotriad' of the three primalities—within all things as the ground of their being, Campanella added a metaphysical dimension, an immaterial, god-begotten wisdom, to the physical sense that Telesio had found in nature. Thus, although he admitted in *De sensu* that magic is an 'occult wisdom' and called certain forces and phenomena in nature 'occult', Campanella had not reverted to the hylemorphic occultism rejected in his earlier work, though by this time he had worked out an alternative metaphysics of magic.

The doctrine of primalities and influences runs throughout Campanella's mature work but appears most clearly in the *Metaphysics,* which also describes the role of these Neoplatonic triads in occult causation. Having decided that Telesio's heat and cold needed divine assistance, Campanella described God as directing natural events not by external impulse, as an archer shoots an arrow, but by an internal sense; otherwise things would be *impelled towards* their ends when God intends that they should *seek* them.

> In all things God sowed great influences— Necessity, Fate, and Harmony—as participants in the primalities—Power, Sense, and Love. . . . God uses their actions regulated by the assistance of angels in forming [things] so that they correspond to the divine ideas, no differently than a blacksmith, using fire, iron, anvil, hammer . . . and assistants to hammer and carry, adjusts [the material] to his idea and then forms it into swords, mattocks, stoves, and clocks.

Necessity, Fate and Harmony act metaphysically in physical nature. Taken abstractly, these three great 'influences' seem to correspond to the distinct properties of objects; to the concurrent relations of those properties; and to their functional consequences. They proceed from the primalities, which reflect the triune God, whose ideas they transmit to objects with the aid of angels. God, primalities, influences, ideas, and angels are all metaphysical agents in a process that terminates in a natural object whose form— the product of heat and cold acting as physical instruments of those metaphysical agents—is no less a material structure in Campanella's *Metaphysics* than it was in his youthful Telesian manifesto. However, Campanella's analysis of causation in the *Metaphysics* seems, at first glance, to admit occult activity excluded in the *Philosophia sensibus demonstrata,* where an occult quality is merely a mistake made by astrologers who misunderstand the physical power of heat.

Writing in 1607 to a correspondent who compared his philosophical accomplishments to Giovanni Pico's, Campanella replied that Pico was 'too lofty' a rival for him. 'His philosophy went more above the words of others than into nature', he wrote, 'from which he learned almost nothing, and he condemned the astrologers because he did not look at their experiences. When I was nineteen I condemned them too, but later I saw that within great foolishness they harboured a very lofty wisdom.' In fact, even Campanella's youthful critique of astrology in *Philosophia sensibus demonstrata* concedes much to the stars and planets within the limits of physical action, and his later work makes astral causation compatible with the metaphysics of the primalities. At least two motives lay behind Campanella's growing passion for astrology: first, he found evidence in solar astrology for his messianic and prophetic politics; second, as he once told Galileo, his methodological commitment to an observational natural philosophy constantly convinced him of the truth of astrology. If it seems that even a little empiricism ought to have led Campanella away from astrology and magic, then one should recall his early association with Giambattista Della Porta, around the time when the latter's *Natural Magic* was republished in 1589. Cassirer once described Della Porta's catalogue of unkempt observations as leading 'not to the refutation but to codification of magic'. Because three decades in prison gave him little chance to see the world at first hand, Campanella was in Della Porta's debt for vicarious experience. But he criticized Della Porta's empiricism because it worked 'only to collect facts without finding their causes'. Actually, it was Della Porta's failure to find a 'reason for the sympathy and antipathy in things' that decided Campanella to write *De sensu.* In this work and elsewhere, he felt he had achieved both empirical proof and theoretical understanding of magic and astrology, devoting to the latter not only a separate treatise, *Seven Books on Astrology,* but also considerable attention in his other major works. His confidence in astrological power was so firm that, after many years in prison, he risked reputation and safety by helping Pope Urban VIII to work astrological spells against the doom forecast for him in 1626, and later he tried to forestall his own death in the same way.

Campanella's philosophy is not easy to digest. His work is forbidding in its size alone, not to mention its complexity and its uneven development in a career that kept his books out of circulation for long periods. During part of his imprisonment he enjoyed some freedoms, including access to books, visitors, even students, but at other times his jailers were brutally repressive. The *Philosophia sensibus demonstrata* was never reprinted in his lifetime after the first edition of 1591. The *Metaphysics* appeared only a year before his death. The *Theology* and the *Great Epilogue* were first published in this century. The *Astrology* saw several editions, pirated and authorized, after 1629, and the best-known of his works on magic, the *De sensu*, came out in Frankfurt in 1620, then appeared later in Paris in 1636 and again in 1637. In effect, Campanella became an active citizen of the republic of letters during two periods of frequent publication. Between 1617 and 1623 his books appeared in Frankfurt, where followers saw him as a prophet of religious reform. But from 1629 to 1638 it was French 'Campanellists' who championed his cause. Who were his backers among French intellectuals in the age of Descartes, Gassendi, and Mersenne; what did they really think of him; why did they think about him at all? For one thing, Campanella had shown good taste and good fortune in his choice of enemies: he disliked the right ancients, and the right moderns disliked him. Gabriel Naudé put him among 'the swarm of innovators' who besieged the Peripatetic fortress. Campanella's assault on Peripatetic dogma won him the enmity of the same ecclesiastical establishment that harassed Galileo, thereby gaining him the sympathy that the bolder French *savants* lavished on the great scientist. If some of them saw the flames that consumed Bruno casting a morbid light on Campanella, for others it was the healing shadow of Galileo's tragedy that saved his reputation, especially when his audacious *Apology for Galileo* became known after 1622. The victim and the critic—each was an effective persona for Campanella.

Campanella's *De sensu* was a fashionable book, enough on the lips of the learned to have interested the young Descartes around 1623, but to some of the Christian faithful it was also dangerous. When Father Marin Mersenne sent his first major work to press in 1623—the *Questions on Genesis*—the priest felt such horror at the pansensist *De sensu* that he wanted it burned, more than an academic discourtesy after Giulio Cesare Vanini's execution in Toulouse only four years earlier. But before publication was complete, Mersenne learned of the *Apology for Galileo*, which gave him cause to make kinder if still cautious mention of Campanella's ideas on the plurality of worlds in later additions to his Genesis commentary. He also opened a correspondence with Campanella and offered in 1624 to arrange for publication of the *Metaphysics*. Even so, the kindly Mersenne's attitude toward the irreverent Dominican remained on the whole quite hostile in his early works, where Mersenne linked Campanella with Bruno, Vanini, and other heretics. Mersenne had not yet worked out a philosophical position to replace the Aristo-

telianism that he saw collapsing around him. He distrusted Campanella and other anti-Peripatetics not only because their ideas—especially the world soul so prominent in *De sensu*—threatened his faith but also because he found them credulous. They broke Montaigne's rule that one must establish the fact of an alleged wonder before worrying about its cause. Perhaps Mersenne feared that someone like Campanella would stabilize occultism just when he and his friends were ending its long career as a serious subject of learned discourse.

Jacques Gaffarel, a peripheral member of the circle of learned libertines who corresponded with Mersenne and investigated the elder Pico's Cabala, began to see Campanella in 1628, around the time when he was working astrological magic with the Pope. His visits helped make Campanella (like Galileo) an obligatory stop on the Italian tours of ambitious young Frenchmen. Gaffarel quizzed him about the magical powers that foiled the tortures of his inquisitors. He also let him know about Father Mersenne's unkind suggestion that his book deserved burning. Before Gaffarel's visit, Campanella had probably not seen the Genesis commentary, but from then on he was edgy about Mersenne, who in the mean time had tempered his opposition to Campanella and often asked about him. By 1632, Gassendi and other French intellectuals were in touch with Campanella, and he received visits from Naudé, whom he sent on important publishing errands. These people who became Campanella's cheering section in France were instigators of the scientific revolution and sceptical critics of superstition and dogmatism. It was probably Naudé, scourage of the Rosicrucians and author of the *Apology for All the Great Persons Who Have Been Falsely Suspected of Magic,* whose liking for Campanella gave him this new access to Mersenne's prestigious circle. Jailed again in 1633, released, then cornered again by the Spanish in 1634, Campanella found asylum with the French ambassador in Rome and, on the pope's advice, fled to France in the autumn of that year. In December he arrived in Paris disguised in the habit of Mersenne's own order. Mersenne learned that Campanella was still angry with him, but he hoped for reconciliation and looked forward to a meeting. All went well until some time in the new year, when Campanella was overheard making negative comments on Gassendi's Epicureanism. Finally, he and Mersenne met several times, but their encounters ended Campanella's moment in the sun of the French mind. Mersenne blanched at Campanella's arrogant dismissal of French intellectual achievement, noting that he 'treated him for what he was worth' when Campanella recommended the astrology that Mersenne despised. Granting Campanella 'a good memory and a fertile imagination', he concluded that 'he will teach us nothing in the sciences' even if he was one of Italy's 'two great men'.

Although Louis XIII had received Campanella, at court in February, 1635, within little more than a year he was complaining to his new friends about their slowness to comment on the 1636 edition of *De sensu*. Fervent Campanellists of two years before were not answering Campanella's letters. None the less, the 1637 edition of *De sensu*, augmented by a *Defence*, bore a dedication to Cardinal Richelieu, who arranged for Campanella to cast the horoscope of the Dauphin born on 5 September 1638. As prelude to the reign of the Sun King, the *Horoscopus serenissimi Delphini* made an odd coda to the career of the author of *The City of the Sun.* Campanella's warm reception by king and cardinal did nothing to thaw the hearts of the *savants* who had written him off. His death in 1639 (fated, so he thought, by an eclipse that came a few days later) passed unnoticed in Mersenne's correspondence, but on the last day of that year Mersenne issued another verdict: 'he made no observations, contenting himself with speculation and often fooling himself for want of experience.' A true if incomplete judgement, and certainly less categorical than what Descartes had said to Mersenne in the previous year, breaking his silence on Campanella for the second time. Descartes had admitted to Huygens in 1638 that he remembered reading *De sensu* and other works by Campanella fifteen years earlier, adding that he saw 'so little solidity' in them that he could not recall them and (curiously for such a pioneer) that he found intellectual loners like Campanella more culpable in their mistakes 'than those who fail only in company by following the tracks of many others'. Eight months later, when Mersenne mentioned the newly published *Metaphysics* to Descartes, the great philosopher's reply was even chillier: 'What I have seen previously of Campanella allows me to hope for nothing good from his book. . . . I have no wish to see it.'

Thus was Campanella banished from the history of modern philosophy by its greatest founder. For his own purposes, Descartes may have been right to ignore Campanella, as he dropped almost all the baggage of Renaissance erudition. But the historian can take a longer view. In the larger sense, Campanella's challenge to Aristotle and his promotion of an empiricist naturalism were part of a movement in Renaissance natural philosophy that began with Achillini, Nifo, and Pomponazzi, continued with Cardano, Telesio, and Bruno and bore its richest fruits in the work of Galileo, Mersenne, Gassendi, and Descartes himself. In a narrower sense, Campanella was especially effective in removing the traditional philosophical underpinnings from the branch of pre-Cartesian natural philosophy that interested him most of all—natural magic. More than any of the other *novatores,* including even Bruno, Campanella offered a systematic critique of hylemorphic metaphysics in the special case of natural magic; but, although he tried to substitute a new metaphysics of magic for the old one that he destroyed, the anti-Peripatetic innovators who listened attentively to his polemic against occult qualities and substantial forms would not pay equal respect to the metaphysics of the primalities. Campanella failed where Mersenne had most cause to fear him—in his attempt to tie natural magic to a complete and systematic philosophy. But, despite himself, he succeeded where Mersenne also succeeded. He brought natural magic very near its end as a serious department of natural philosophy. Campanella's pansensism or animism, grounded in an elaborate metaphysics, finally and strongly distinguishes his organic world-view from the victorious mechanical philosophy created by Mersenne, Gassendi, and others who made Campanella an intellectual fashion in the early 1630s. Campanella's place in the history of philosophy stands as much on his metaphysical differences with these *libertins érudits* as on the materialist habits of mind that he shared with them. Although he lived through the fourth decade of the seventeenth century, the Renaissance shaped his philosophical programme, and his remarkable career, in and out of jail, shows how thinkers of the new Cartesian age discarded the heritage of the generations before them.

Rudolf Steiner discusses Giordano Bruno's views on the "world-soul":

Giordano Bruno, upon whom the new Copernican view of Nature forced itself, could grasp Spirit in the world, from which it had been expelled in its old form, in no other manner than as World-Soul. On plunging into Bruno's writings . . . one gets the impression that he thought of things as ensouled, although in varying degree. He has not, in reality, experienced in himself the Spirit, therefore he conceives Spirit after the fashion of the human soul, wherein alone he has encountered it. When he speaks of Spirit, he conceives of it in the following way: "The universal reason is the inmost, most effective and most special capacity, and a potential part of the World-Soul; it is something one and identical, which fills the All, illuminates the universe and instructs Nature how to bring forth her species as they ought to be." In these sentences Spirit . . . is described as a being that is like to the human soul. "Let now a thing be as small and tiny as you please, it yet has within it a portion of spiritual substance, which, when it finds a substratum adapted thereto, reaches out to become a plant, an animal, and organises itself to any body you choose that is ordinarily called ensouled. For Spirit is to be found in all things, and there does not exist even the tiniest little body which does not embrace in itself such a share thereof as causes it to come to life."

Rudolf Steiner in Mystics of the Renaissance, *G. P. Putnam's Sons, 1911.*

ASTROLOGY

Lynn Thorndike

SOURCE: "Astrology to 1650," in *A History of Magic and Experimental Science, Vol. VII,* Columbia University Press, 1958, pp. 89-152.

[*In the following excerpt, Thorndike discusses arguments made for and against astrology in France and Italy during the first half of the seventeenth century.*]

I can see no justification whatever for the attitude which refuses on purely a priori grounds to accept action at a distance . . . Such an attitude bespeaks an unimaginativeness, a mental obtuseness and obstinacy.

—P. W. Bridgman

Attacks upon astrology were numerous in the seventeenth century. . . . On the other hand, . . . the papal bulls against astrology of 1586 and 1631 had only a limited effect, and . . . the subject continued to be taught at the University of Bologna into the seventeenth, and at Salamanca into the eighteenth century. We shall now examine further into its status and the books written for and against it during the first half of the seventeenth century in various regions of Europe. . . . We shall not attempt to cover annual astrological predictions or works elicited by particular comets, eclipses and planetary conjunctions. But even the authors of such judgments might assert that they were free from all superstition. . . .

. . . . .

FRANCE

The conception of macrocosm and microcosm, that man is a little world and corresponds member for member and faculty for faculty with the universe, or, more particularly, with the earth on the one hand and the heavens on the other, is evidently closely connected with the belief that inferiors are ruled by superiors and that man is related to and governed by the stars. It is not merely a fitting foundation for astrology, but really part and parcel of astrology in the broad sense of that word.

All this is well illustrated by one of three philosophic discourses which Jourdain Guibelet, a physician of Evreux, published there in 1603, and which is entitled, *De la comparaison de l'homme avec le monde.* He compares the rational soul with God, human faculties with the Intelligences that move the heavens, the head with the heavens, the heart with the sun, and the liver with the moon. The liver presides over human infancy, as the first age of other animals is under the government of the moon. To Jupiter corresponds the brain; to Venus, the generative organs; to Mercury, the tongue, to Saturn and Mars, the gall and spleen. Guibelet relates the hair to the fixed stars and other parts of the human body to the signs of the zodiac, but he adds that some give the eyes to sun and moon, the ears to Mars and Venus, the nostrils to Jupiter and Saturn, and the mouth to Mercury. Man further comprehends the elements, meteors and minerals, plants and animals. And in the little world as in the great there is republic, aristocracy and monarchy, and cities with all sorts of artisans and instruments to ply each trade. But the world is now in its decrepit old age, and all that heaven and earth engender in their senility is but as mere excrement in comparison with previous periods.

Despite the close connection between human faculties and members and the heavens and stars, which Guibelet made in this first *Discours,* in the second on the principle of human generation the influence of the stars is not mentioned, while in the third on melancholy he declares that the predictions of astrologers seem to him as ill-founded as those of augurs, and that they often turn to magic or demons for assistance. He also now notes that the astrologers assign an excess of melancholic humor to the influence of Mars and Saturn, but that we see many melancholics who are not under those planets, and many persons who are under those planets who are not melancholy.

Thus he tacitly accepts planetary influence on men, although denying the truth of astrological prediction. This apparent discrepancy shows that the house of astrology is being divided against itself, and that, as the seventeenth century opens, a man may condemn prediction, although he accepts doctrines upon which it is based. It further indicates that these doctrines are being disassociated from astrology, although they may seem logically to go with it.

A much more exhaustive and exhausting treatment of the analogy of the microcosm to the macrocosm was turned out by Nicolas Nancelius of Noyon, physician to Leonore Bourbon, abbess of Fontevrault, in 1611. It stretches to thirteen books and 2232 columns in folio, with quotations galore from the classics and church fathers marked by large capital letters across the column and set off by leaving a blank space above and below. It is not worth while to try to pick out his own views, if any, from the mass of citations, quotations and indirect quotations, and most of the text has little or nothing to do with the analogy of microcosm and macrocosm, which merely serves as a springboard for a dive into a sea of quotations and opinions. The subject is said to be treated theologically, physically, medically, historically and mathematically. After a Proemium of forty-eight columns on God, the first book deals with the analogy of man with God, of the soul with the ether, the head with the sky, and "the seven conjugations of nerves" with the planets. Book two has more concerning the spirits of the human body in particular and "the miracles of air and fire." The third book is devoted to the earth and the analogy of parts of the human body with it, while a few columns are devoted to the theme of sleep and waking. Book four proceeds from esophagus to diaphragm, and by Book seven we reach the sexual organs with discussion of various problems of generation, such as whether the eighth month's child will live, and which lead finally to remarks concerning the Gregorian calendar. Book VIII on the arms and hands, in treating of the arts of chiromancy and physiognomy, seems to accept the *Physiognomy* ascribed to Aristotle as a genuine work, yet condemns those arts as false, inane, ridiculous, and full of tricks and impostures. It is absurd to predict one's whole fate from one little part of the body. Nancelius wonders that such grave men as Conciliator, Cardan and Albertus Magnus could waste time over such matters—although he himself devotes considerable space thereto—while he has no use whatever for such writers as Corvo, Tricasso, John of Indagine and Cocles. Later on we find him pointing out the analogy of the humors of the human body with earth's waters and with the four elements, quoting from John of Sacrobosco and Euclid, writing of the origin of fountains and rivers and their marvels, discussing why the sea, especially the Dead Sea, is salt, and such other favorite and time honored questions, as whether the semen comes from the brain or the whole body, whether heart or brain is superior, and whether the world will have an end. He thereby illustrates the narrow range of ideas and problems that then occupied and beset men's minds, even when, like Nancelius, they took plenty of space in which to express themselves.

The Jesuit, Pierre Bourdin (1595–1653) of Moulin, who taught rhetoric for seven, and mathematics for twenty-two

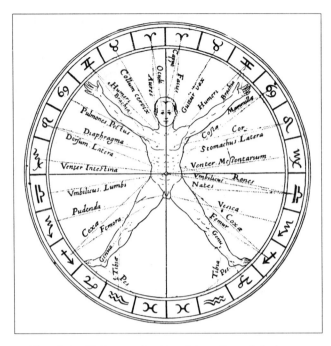

The relationship between the signs of the zodiac and the human body, from Robert Fludd's Utriusque cosmi historia.

years at La Flèche and Paris, besides a number of works in mathematics and related subjects, published together in 1646 a work on the sun as flame and aphorisms on the analogy of microcosm and macrocosm. In the former he not only held that the sun was flame but nourished by vapors from out globe of earth and water, which were impregnated by the influence of the planets. The three chief fluids in the microcosm were chyle, venal blood and arterial blood; in the macrocosm, water, air and fire. The eight founts of fluids in the small world were the mouth, stomach, mesentery, spleen, liver, right sinus of the heart, lungs, and left sinus of the heart. Those of the great world were Saturn, Jupiter, Mars, Venus, Mercury, the moon, our terraqueous globe, and the heart of the world whence the flame of the sum bursts forth like vital spirit from the heart of man. Solar spirits retarded the movement of the superior planets westward. These solar spirits were changed into celestial, which were distributed through the world. Bourdin held that the earth was at rest and did not move about the sun. Vital spirits corresponded to solar; animal, to celestial. Air was the equivalent of the empyrean; and skin, of the firmament. Brain, arms and thighs paralleled the starry spaces; above the diaphragm, corresponded to planetary space; below it, to the moon and earth.

Robert Fludd (1574–1637) in 1617 published the first part on the macrocosm of a work on macrocosm and microcosm. At the close of the Appendix to his *Harmonice mundi* of 1619 Kepler compared the two works as to subjects covered and added qualitative distinctions. Fludd drew from old authorities; Kepler, from the nature of things by observation and experience. Fludd's affinities were with alchemists, Hermetics and Paracelsans; Kepler's, with astronomers and mathematicians. Fludd interpreted harmony in terms of light and darkness; Kepler, in terms of motion. Fludd was arbitrary, mystical and obscure; Kepler, geometrical and natural. Fludd dealt in enigmas, symbols and analogies; Kepler, in demonstrated measurements.

As in the days of the Roman emperors, the attitude of monarchs and governments to astrologers was largely swayed, not by the validity or vanity of the art of astrology, but by the favorableness or unfavorableness of the prediction. Jean Aimes de Chavigny flattered Henri IV by a collection, under the title of *Pleiades,* of seven past predictions which, he insisted, all foretold the happy advent of that monarch. The first, composed by Cataldus, bishop of Trent, over a thousand years ago, was a forecast of future ills of Italy which was brought to light only just before the French invasion by Charles VIII. The second was the vaticination of the Erythraean sibyl; the third, an anonymous tract given to Chavigny twenty years ago by Jaques Gohorry; the fourth, by Lorenzo Bonincontri di San Miniato. Even these first four predictions, according to Chavigny, "make authentic mention of Your Majesty," and at the close of the fourth he has taken occasion to "discourse on some points of your happy birth." The remaining items are the celebrated prediction of Antonio Torquato to Matthias of Hungary in 1480; a translation into French of a previous translation by a German into Latin from Turkish; and a prayer extracted from Hippolytus. Chavigny has annotated them and compared them with the prognostications of Nostradamus. He cites Cyprian Leowitz and prefers his connecting mutations of kingdoms and empires with planetary conjunctions to Bodin's ascribing them to "the force and virtue of numbers." He also cites such astrological authors as Junctinus and Cardan.

But when the physician Senelles predicted from the horoscope of Louis XIII the death of the king in September, 1631, he was accused of lèse-Majesté together with Duval, another royal physician, condemned to the galleys, and his property confiscated.

Similar circumstances and considerations moved Urban VIII, pope from 1623 to 1644, to issue a new bull against astrology. Father Morandi, as a result of astrological calculations and the fact that the pope would be in his sixty-third year or grand climacteric then, came to the conclusion that Urban would die in 1630. He submitted his reckonings to three friends, abbot Luigi Gherardi of Padua, Francesco Lamponi and Father Raffaelo Visconti, for verification or correction. The first two agreed with his conclusion, but Visconti thought that, if the pope did not leave Rome, he would live until 1643 or 1644, and on February 21, 1630 composed *Un discorso sulla vita di Urbana VIII,* which was communicated to many cardinals, prelates and diplomats. But the view of Morandi prevailed and drew various foreign cardinals to Rome in expectation of a conclave to elect Urban's successor. Morandi, despite his reputation for personal piety and high standing in his Order, was imprisoned on July 13, 1630, and died of fever in November, whereupon all the other accused were set at liberty, except that Visconti was rusticated to Viterbo. Urban suspended the process against them on March 15,

1631, but on April first he issued the new bull against astrologers. And on April 22, 1635, for astrological predictions of the pope's death together with incantations, necromancy and sorcery aimed at his life, Giacinto Cantini, nephew of cardinal Felice Cantini, was decapitated, fra Cherubino da Foligno of the Order of Zocolanti and Fra Bernardino, called il Romito, were hanged and afterwards burned in the Campo di Fiori at Rome, while five other friars were condemned to various terms in the galleys.

François de Cauvigny, who was related to Malherbe, published a refutation of judicial astrology in 1614, and the Sorbonne forbade its practice on May 22, 1619. In the same year appeared at Paris *L'incertitude et tromperie des astrologues judiciares* of B. Heurtevyn. After chapters on the dates of creation, of the end of the world, of the deluge, of the birth and death of Jesus, and on religious changes, with the aim to show that astrologers have disagreed or been wrong as to these, comes another series of chapters on incorrect past predictions by them. A long chapter on the failure of astrologers to foresee their own deaths is then followed by a shorter one arguing that the devil is the author of judicial astrology, after which the volume terminates in a series of chapters criticizing the Copernican astronomy and astrological technique. The book is not so well arranged or expressed as this brief summary might seem to suggest, and Heurtevyn matches the incorrect predictions of the astrologers by historical errors and exaggerations of his own, such as the assertion that all the astrologers of Asia, Africa and Europe, and Stoeffler in particular, had predicted a universal flood for 1524, whereas there was such a drought that it withered all the fruit. We shall encounter other instances of misuse of history by opponents of astrology, indicating that they were special pleaders and not strictly accurate or judicial in their attitude.

The *Opuscula* of Julius Caesar Bulenger (1558–1628), a member of the Society of Jesus, printed at Lyons in 1621, include a work on all kinds of divination, of which the main feature is an attack upon astrology. However, he grants that the weather, price of crops, and diseases may be predicted without superstition. He contends that Aristotle did not recognize other influences of the heavens than by their motion and light, but he admits that bodies which are placed under the sky so depend upon the celestial bodies that they cannot long persevere without them. Also he accepts the existence of occult virtues in inferiors, such as the softening of adamant by the blood of a goat, the lion's terror of the cock, Thessalians fascinating by laudation, the animal *catoblephes* killing men from afar by its glance. He further admits that these occult virtues may be produced by the stars. But he regards genitures as fallacious and forbidden, astrological elections as frequently fraudulent, and astrological images as forbidden and magical. The astrologers associate six religions with the relations of Jupiter to the other six planets, but there are actually over a hundred religions. They cannot predict contingent events, and it is ridiculous to say that the stars incline me to play or read or walk or drink at this or that time. But he does not say what does determine his choice in these cases. He makes use of previous authors a great deal: Sixtus ab Hemminga, Augustine and Favorinus, Cicero

and John of Salisbury, Origen, Gregory of Nyssa and Eusebius. He denies that matter is prepared for forms by the heavens alone, or even that critical days are due to the moon. Astrologers could not have learned the forces of the stars from experience. He further attacks various particulars of astrological technique, such as the *monomoeriae* of the Egyptians, *antisica,* conjunctions, and horoscopes for the founding of cities. But there is little logical order, plan or structure to his arrangement and argument. He dismisses astrology as a vain and infidel art, puffed up with lies and day-dreams.

Bulenger was born at Loudun and died at Cahors. He left the Order in 1594 to supervise the education of his brothers and nephews; taught at Paris, Toulouse and Pisa; then re-entered the Order in 1614. He was a doctor of theology and also wrote upon classical antiquities.

Judicial astrology was condemned in French in a little book of 272 pages by Claude Pithoys (1596–1676), printed at Sedan in 1641 and reflecting a Huguenot point-of-view, as Pithoys had declared himself a Protestant in 1632, and taught philosophy at Sedan. The author is described on the title page as a theologian and professor of philosophy and law, and advocate *consultant* at Sedan. He lists a number of -mancies or forms of divination besides astrology, or "astromantie des genethliaques," and regards them all as relics of pagan darkness. He holds that judicial astrology is a magic art, condemned alike by God, canon law, the Fathers and theologians, civil law, philosophy, medicine and astronomy. Kepler and Tycho Brahe are represented as among its foes. It is pernicious to its practitioners, their employers, and the public at large. It attempts the impossible, for the stars cannot act upon the rational soul; the rules and methods of astrology are absurd and ridiculous; the art is not justified by experience, and its predictions are often false. Pithoys distinguishes five kinds of prediction: moral, political, natural, divine, and diabolical. His book was reprinted in 1646.

Another attack upon astrology from an authoritative quarter was made by Claude Saumaise or Salmasius, the great French classical scholar, in his *De annis climactericis et antiqua astrologia diatribae,* a long work published at Leyden in 1648. Gui Patin, in a letter to Spon of May 8, 1648, says that a bookseller in Paris who received twenty copies sold them all within four days. The preface, which occupies most of the preliminary 64 leaves, is devoted to an onslaught upon astrology, which, however, continues to be the object of occasional criticism in the 844 numbered pages of the text proper.

The vanity and unreliability of astrology, Saumaise maintains, are shown by the disagreement between astrological authors, by the fact that the present art differs from the ancient, which is today unknown, and by the gross errors made by Arabic translators from the Greek and by medieval Latin translators from the Arabic. Moreover, the signs of the zodiac are mere creations of human imagination. The Chaldeans recognized only eleven signs, having no Libra, and Scorpio covering sixty degrees. Our zodiac is late and based upon Greek mythology, and much astrological detail is drawn from the fables of the poets. Tartars, Hindus and Chinese have other zodiacs. There probably are other stars, invisible to us, in the vast intervals which separate the named constellations, and so there is nothing solid and true about present celestial configurations. Salmasius also criticizes the division of the signs into decans. He notes that astrology was condemned by the Christian emperors and by many classical authors, and asks why it continues, when other forms of divination have disappeared.

If the stars are inanimate, they can produce only physical effects, not grammarians or rhetoricians or medical men or musicians or smiths or astrologers. How can they indicate future good or evil, when what is good for one man is evil for another? If their influence alters with their changing positions, they are evidently not gods, and Saumaise puts the dilemma: Either the stars are gods, or there is no astrology. Moreover, the telescope has shown us more than seven planets, and if the Copernican system is true, astrology is outlawed along with the Ptolemaic astronomy. Ptolemy makes the absurd statement that the planet Saturn is cold because so far from the sun, and is dry because it so far removed from the vapors which rise from earth, as if such vapors would reach any planet. After questioning whether the nativity should take into consideration the moment of birth or of conception or when the mother first feels the embryo moving, Saumaise asks why not begin to predict anew from each new period of human life, such as childhood, adolescence and youth. Or, if twins have different horoscopes, why should there not be a different nativity for the child who emerges head first, from that whose feet are first to appear?

In the body of the text, Saumaise holds that climacteric years depend upon the horoscope and so stand or fall with it, that sixty-three is not necessarily the grand climacteric, and that even twins have different climacteric years, as they do horoscopes. He argues that the art or science of physiognomy is possible without astrology, and that the tract on astrological medicine according to the position of the moon in the signs should not be ascribed to Hippocrates. He criticizes the use and meaning of technical terms like *hyleg* and *aphetes* at considerable length, and displays a fairly wide acquaintance with medieval Latin and Arabic authors, as well as with classical and more recent writers, upon astrology.

The arguments of Saumaise against astrology were, on the one hand, fresher and more original than were those of most opponents of that art, and, on the other hand, more historical and scholarly, attacking astrology from a factual and linguistic, instead of a primarily rational or religious, standpoint.

Saumaise might attack astrology, but he still believed that there were "marvelous secrets" of chemistry and medicine, and praised his friend, Johann Elichman of Silesia, for his knowledge of them. . . .

The astrological point of view is still prevalent in the large folio history of the maritime world and events by Claude Barthélemy Morisot of Dijon, where the book was printed in 1643 with a dedication to Louis XIII. He affirms that many are called by the stars to a nautical life and naval victories, and that sailors are born rather than made.

Among the Chaldeans Berosus, among the Greeks Eudoxus of Cnidus, Aratus, Aristotle and Empedocles, among the Egyptians Ptolemy, among the Latins Julius Firmicus and Marcus Manilius state that persons born under Pisces or the Dolphin are excellent sailors and divers. The lack of spleen is a great advantage to swimmers and divers. Under Aries are born sailors, towmen, and shipbuilders. Morisot even notes that among the seals of Solomon is a stone with the image of a ship under full sail, carved when the sun was in Leo, with Saturn and Mars to the south. One wearing it becomes a good sailor and fortunate in navigation. He who has Pisces in his horoscope will win naval battles, seek out new worlds, and be a wonderful shipbuilder, pilot, and forecaster of winds and tempests.

Father Octoul, who was a Minime, published *Inventa astronomica* at Avignon in 1643, with diffuse dedicatory epistles to the Virgin and Louis XIV, then a child of five. The brief book is primarily chronological and states that the Church puts the birth of Christ 5199 years and nine months after creation. But it contains some astronomy and astrology: a catalogue of astronomical observations with the Tables of Lansberg, the construction of a *thema caelestis* for the observation of two sun-spots, and a discussion of the restitution of the celestial houses, which is its chief, if not sole, astrological feature.

Jacques Alleaume was a pupil of Vieta and, although a Huguenot, prominent at Paris in mathematical and scientific circles. Snellius in his *Eratosthenes Batavus,* 1617, said that he owed the mechanical division of the circle by compasses to "our most illustrious and ingenious friend, Jacobus Alealmus." Peiresc wrote with admiration of his burning glasses, his machine for shaping parabolic lenses, and other scientific apparatus. He drew up tables of longitudes and in 1624 is spoken of as royal engineer. He was a friend, too, of Paolo Sarpi, to whom he sent a manuscript copy of his work on perspective, which, however, was not printed until 1643, sixteen years after his death in 1627. Yet he also was interested in astrology and translated into French the sixteenth century book of Rantzovius or Rantzau on nativities, which had five Latin editions between 1597 and 1615. Alleaume's French version did not appear until 1657, but this shows that the interest in astrology still continued at that date.

ITALY

Turning now from France to Italy, we first note discussion of climacteric years and critical days. . . .

Codronchi composed a defense of climacteric years in 1609, but deferred publishing it until 1620 in order to get others' criticisms of it first. Meantime at Padua in 1612 appeared the treatise of Ambrose Floridus, on climacteric years and critical days, "in which a marvelous doctrine, taken from sources astrological and philosophical, is revealed; how the whole course of human life, regulated by groups of seven years, is at diverse times seriously disturbed and distorted according to varied conjunctions of the planets." The book is dedicated to cardinal Boniface Cajetan, and closes with the statement that, if anything has been said which does not conform to the edicts of the Holy Roman Catholic Church, "that we completely reject and reprove as false." Floridus abandons any resort to Pythagorean Pythagorean theory of number in favor of a purely astrological explanation. The fifty-fourth year of one's life is very perilous because of the lordship of Mars, and the fifty-sixth year because of the rule of Saturn. Astrologers say that humidity reaches its height in one's twenty-first year, heat at forty-two, dryness at sixty-three, and cold at eighty-four. The last part of old age is governed by Venus whose mild and placid influence preserves men of that age in marvelous wise, so that they rarely die then, but the sixty-sixth year is dangerous for the phlegmatic, the sixty-eighth for the choleric, sixty-ninth for the sanguine, and seventieth for all temperaments. Then decrepitude or the last age of man sets in, which is under the rule of the sun to seventy-seven, and of Mars to eighty-four. After dealing with critical days, which are governed by the moon, Floridus asks what aspects and conjunctions of the planets are more fatal in the whole regimen of human life; why Saturn, when in the terrestrial triplicity, always portends some calamity, especially in one's sixty-third year, the grand climacteric, if in its own house and dignity. And if death comes during that year, one ought to render immortal thanks to God for His kindness in prolonging one's life that far.

In the next year Florido published a brief work on the sea and tides in the form of a dialogue in which a philosopher and a *Philonauticus* were the interlocutors, and the tides were attributed to the influence of the sun as well as to that of the moon. This was likewise the contention of two other treatises, which were bound together with that by Florido in the copy that I consulted. One, by Marcus Antonius de Dominis, archbishop of Spalato, was addressed to Cardinal Barberini and printed at Rome in 1624; the other, in Italian rather than Latin, by Sempronio Lancione, a Roman doctor of philosophy and theology, was addressed to the archbishop of Salzburg and apostolic legate, and printed at Verona in 1629. De Dominis in his treatise speaks favorably of the aspects of the planets.

Giulio Cesare Claudini, who taught the practice of medicine at Bologna from 1578 to 1618, had questioned the astrological explanation of critical days in 1612, but Hyppolitus Obicius, in the appendix to his *Iatroastronomicon* of 1618, held that Claudini had not rightly understood Galen. The work of Claudini, however, was printed again, this time at Basel, in 1620.

The work which Silvaticus published in 1615 against the doctrine of climacteric years strikes one as labored and inferior to that of 1605 on the unicorn, bezoar stone, emerald and pearls. . . . There is excessive citation of Hippocrates, Galen and other ancients, while his list of recent writers on the subject does not include the treatise by Ambrose Floridus of 1612, or even that by de Rossi of Sulmona back in 1585. The most recent book cited by him is that of Federigo Bonaventura on the eighth month's child from the previous century. Sometimes it is adduced in favor of Silvaticus's own contentions. Thus he says that Federicus Bonaventura, a most erudite and learned writer in the fiftieth chapter of *De octimestri partu* ridiculed and confuted those who placed the cause of climacteric years in numbers and boasted that he had found an evident natural cause. In another passage Silvaticus says that he will

not go into the astrological argument for climacteric years because Pico delle Mirandola and many since have condemned it, and Bonaventura has demonstrated more particularly that Mercury is not their cause. But in Bonaventura's work itself we find him defending Galen on critical days against Pico, Fracastoro and others, while the evident natural cause which he had found was the stars. And Silvaticus says towards the close of his treatise: "I say against Bonaventura . . . that, just as critical days do not mark diseases by reason of number as number, as has been demonstrated, so neither have numbers any force in climacteric years."

Baptista Codronchi, whose credulous book on witchcraft and cures therefor had appeared in 1595, finally published his treatise on climacteric years and how to avoid their dangers at Bologna in 1620. It was also printed at Cologne in 1623, and at Ulm in 1651. For several pages he gives lists of the names of men who have died at such ages as 94, 77, 63, 49 and 42. But one reason for his writing the book is his belief that climacteric years are not merely dangerous but may mark a change for the better in one's health. He argues that Hippocrates believed in climacteric years, treats of their causes from astrologers, whose doctrine he defends, and then from philosophers and medical men, and finally answers a celebrated recent writer who had attached them, possibly Silvaticus. The second part of his book then deals with avoidance of their perils. Codronchi included even the patriarchs of the Old Testament among his examples, reckoning their grand climacteric as 910, or seven times 130, instead of 63, which is seven times nine.

Septimius Columbus, a member of the Academy of *Insensati,* in 1625 addressed to Cardinal Francesco Barberini a brief tract on climacteric years. He contended that they were not superstitious, but were supported by both authorities and experience, and by analogy with critical days in disease and with the division of man's life into seven-year periods, marked by teething at seven, puberty at fourteen, and so on. The most reverend bishop (of Volturara), Simon Maiolus, in his work on dog-days had already listed six hundred instances of death in climacteric years. There was considerable difference of opinion as to which climacteric year—49, 63 or 81—was most critical and perilous, but Columbus regarded 63 as the most crucial. He also, although writing as a philosopher and physician rather than astrologer, and suggesting other possible causes for climacteric years, tended to select the stars as the chief cause, the order of the planets reverting every seventh year to Saturn. But the fact of their existence was enough for him.

We turn from the subject of climacteric years to other writings for or against astrology by Italians, and shall treat of those from the same city together.

Ilario Altobelli of Montecchio in Piceno received the doctorate in 1591, was made historian (*chronologus*) of the Franciscan Order in 1617, and died in 1628. He also was interested in astronomy. He wrote on the new star of 1604, in 1610 addressed a letter from Ancona to Galileo on the satellites of Saturn, and in 1615 published a treatise on the occultation of Mars. A letter in Italian by him, in which he opposed the Aristotelian doctrine of comets, was printed at Venice in 1627. In the last year of his life appeared his Tables for dividing the heavens into the twelve signs, and the year following a Demonstration that Regiomontanus's method of directions and determining astrological houses did not agree with that of Ptolemy. The last two works also indicate an interest in astrology, and a prediction from the stars by him in 1607 as to the destiny of the republic of Venice is preserved in a manuscript at Paris, and has already been mentioned in connection with the motion of Mars in our chapter on Kepler. The use of the words *inclinatio* and *conjectura* in its title show a desire to avoid any appearance of attributing fatal necessity to the influence of the stars. At the same time horoscopes or *themata coeli* are given for the foundation of Venice about noon on March 25, 421; for the great conjunction of Saturn and Jupiter at 10.32 P.M., December 19, 1603—which is compared with that of March 2, 411, which preceded the founding of Venice; for the first appearance of the new star at Verona at 5.35 P.M., October 9, 1604; for the solar eclipse at 2.36 P.M., October 12, 1605; and for Leonardo Donato, the present doge of Venice, and it is predicted that he will meet with a violent death either in 1611 at the age of 75 or in 1614 at 78. Four unfavorable astrological directions are also noted between 1607 and 1612, and it is held that two very strong movements, never before made in the heavens since the origin of Venice, are about to threaten its destruction. God is angry at the violation of religion by Venice, but if she amends her ways, she will be renewed like the eagle; "alioquin ad extremum." It is noteworthy that the work is addressed to one of the cardinals.

Father Redento Baranzani was a Barnabite from Vercelli. His *Uranoscopia* was described in the long Latin title as "a new work, necessary, pleasing and useful to natural philosophers, astrologers, medical men and all professors of good arts," and his students seem to have set great store by it. A letter by John Baptista Murator, dated at Annecy on February 20, 1617, states that, because of war, he had left his native place for Annecy, Savoy, where there was a school of the Paulist fathers. But when his teacher in philosophy there, Baranzani, came down with fever, he feared that hope of a path-breaking, methodical work of philosophy, and especially astrology, by the intervention of his genius, was gone. But Baranzani recovered and dictated solely from memory his very rare and out-of-the-way (*peregrinae*) opinions, seldom heard in courses of philosophy, although Murator realizes that the space of only two months cannot attain the heights of his teacher's archetype, and he has had to omit most of the citations. A few pages later is given another letter from Ludovicus des Hayes of Paris, who is also editing the work. And when the second part begins with a new pagination, there is another prefatory letter by both Murator and Hayes, dated at Annecy on March 28, 1617, in which they explain that Baranzani followed a twofold way in saving all the celestial phenomena, following Copernicus in some respects and Aristotle in others. Two years later, Baranzani himself, in his New Opinions in Physics, advises reading his *Uranoscopia* which has been printed again in an enlarged and revised edition at Paris by his dearest disciple of subtle genius, Ludovicus des Hayes.

The book of Baranzani is more astrological than either philosophical or astronomical. An astronomical foundation is laid, but then astrological definitions and rules are given, the substantial influx of the celestial bodies is set forth, and such questions are discussed as whether metals, herbs and plants are produced by the heavens, whether celestial influences are impressed in an instant, how long they last, whether the sky is the cause of some fortuitous events. Furthermore, whether celestial form is nobler and more perfect than any other, whether the heavens are the cause of animals born of putridity, whether there is any occult force from the heavens, whether astrologers can divine human actions and how, whether uncertain knowledge is prohibited by recent canon law? In the second part, with a new pagination and beginning with the empyrean heaven, it is soon asked whether in the primum mobile there are triplicities, houses, exaltations, and other dignities of the planets; and, with regard to the heaven of libration or tenth sphere, whether it is visible, influences sublunars, and what that influence is. Soon the question is raised how to draw up a horoscope, and it is noted that Firmicus, Avenezra, Campanus, Alcabitius and Ptolemy differ as to this. After some discussion of direction, *significator* and *promissor,* pages 66-122 and, after discussion of the planetary spheres, pages 153-176 are devoted to Tables, some of which are astrological, such as the regions subject to each sign of the zodiac, and of diseases under each planet. Then comes what is called "a last question," whether the fixed stars exert more influence than the planets, the superior planets than the inferior, and the moon than any other planet except the sun. But it is followed by one more question, whether all the planets make critical days. Appendix I then deals with climacteric years, and Appendix II inquires whether the sun is the center for Saturn, Jupiter, Mars, Venus and Mercury. Here Tycho's hypothesis is called more improbable, because that of Copernicus is simpler. This is immediately followed by the theory of the planets according to Copernicus and Magini reduced to Tables. A *Prooemiolum* then says:

> While Tychonic Tables are being worked out, Keplerian already happily initiated from the movement of Mars are being perfected, Marianae against Copernicus are awaited, others of Magini with a view to restricting Venus, Mercury and the sun to a single sphere are being prepared, and many others are being composed by the most learned mathematicians of this astrological age, try these (of mine) too, though they may not agree with the proximity of the perigee of Mars to the earth.

There follow tables of the effects of the moon on agriculture, of prognostics from thunder attributed to Bede, of signs of rain, and of fair weather; a golden booklet instructing how to draw up an Almanach and predict crops and sterility, and yet other appendices.

A seventeenth century manuscript at the Vatican contains a defense of judicial astrology by a Ferrante de Septem, which seems to have been composed soon after the opening of the century. Astrology rests upon the assured basis of the influence of the heavens over inferior bodies. "It is certain that the sun by heating, the moon by moistening,

Saturn by chilling, and Mars by drying, are natural causes." Consequently an astrologer may predict as to length of life and the constitution (*complexio*) of the human body. "For those effects neither happen fortuitously nor are dependent upon the air." If they were, persons born in July would be of a hot nature, and those born in January would be very cold. But popes Urban VII and Innocent IX came into the world while the sun was in Leo, yet were very cold by nature, while Sixtus (V) and Clement (VIII), whose horoscopes were in winter while the sun was in Capricorn, were of warm and moist physical constitutions. Astrologers cannot predict purely rational effects and can note only inclination in those mixed events dependent on both soul and body. It appears difficult for them to forecast a violent death or the hour of death, yet Ptolemy treats at length of violent death and was borne out in the cases of Pier Luigi Farnese (natural son of Paul III who was killed on September 10, 1547) and Sebastian, king of Portugal (slain in the battle of Alcazarquivir, August 4, 1578). Many writers, like Pico della Mirandola, Sixtus ab Hemminga, and Benedictus Pererius (1535–1610), do astrologers an injustice by accusing them of what they do not teach or of what they even reject. One should observe astrological conditions in all one's actions. The Bull of Sixtus V against astrology is no deterrent to Ferrante. Ptolemy may seem to predict with certainty events which are dependent upon human free will, but he says to begin with that the stars only incline and do not necessitate. Ferrante's closing words are that not merely is astrology not unworthy of a Christian but that it is fitting for every good and pious man. His defense is followed in our manuscript by astrological figures for such years as 1552 and 1536, or, more recently, 1603 and 1604, 1606 and 1607. These are sometimes accompanied by daily statements of the weather.

An astrological prediction for the year 1618, which was addressed by Gioanni Bartolini to the Cardinal of Santa Susanna, Scipione Cobelluzzi, is preserved in another manuscript at the Vatican. It is written in Italian and calculated for the meridian of Rome according to the observations of Tycho Brahe. The four seasons of the year are taken up in turn, beginning with winter, which is to open on December 22, 1617, at 22.27 and 23 seconds, and with an astrological figure for the moment when each season opens. Prediction is limited to the weather, which is noted for each month, adding changes dependent upon the fixed stars, and to agriculture, crops and vintages, navigation—including days unfavorable for sailing, sickness and medicine, and such astronomical occurrences as eclipses. Bartolini thus keeps roughly within the limitations fixed by the Bull against astrology of Sixtus V in 1586.

Giovanni Autonio Giuffi of Palermo dedicated "these my astrological lucubrations concerning eclipses" in March 1621. They appeared in print at Naples in 1623. The work purports, according to its full title, to discuss what should be considered in the prognostication of eclipses, when they begin to produce their effects, how long they will last, and when their influence will be at its height. How to find the lord or *dispositor* of the eclipse, in what lands and provinces its effects will occur, and in what sort of things, and if it will be good or bad? And what it signifies in each sign

and house, "and some other points worthy of consideration." Ptolemy and Haly are much cited. Each planet is taken up for each sign of the zodiac and what it signifies when lord thereof. Many ills follow, when there is both a solar and a lunar eclipse in one month, especially in those places for which they have especial significance. The work is accompanied by Tables. At its close Giuffi refers to the Bull of Sixtus V against astrology and explains that he is writing only for physicians, sailors and farmers and so is not violating it.

Alexander de Vicentinis, in a treatise on heat and the influence of the heavens, printed at Verona in 1634, "never departing from the principles of Aristotle," was not ready to admit that heat was "of the substance of the heaven." He concluded that motion was the cause of heat and that no one, unless rash and demented, would deny that the heavens by light and especially by motion exerted great influence upon these inferiors. But he held that the heavens influenced only by light and motion, denied the existence of occult qualities, and rejected the details of astrological technique, of which he thought that Pico della Mirandola had sufficiently exposed the vanity. He held that the will was free, the mind divine, education potent, and that hence astrological predictions concerning individuals were undependable. He denied the contention of astrologers that dreams were caused by the stars, and the opinion of Albertus Magnus—and Dante—that a continuous effluvium from a celestial form affected the imagination of the dreamer, and the view that the Intelligences which moved the heavenly spheres were responsible for divining dreams. He seemed to think, however, that some divination from dreams was possible. In his final chapter, devoted to an argument that the fact that different things were produced in different places was not to be ascribed to occult virtue, he noted that Aristotle attributed spontaneous generation to the force of the heavens. But he denies that southerners are timid and short-lived because the planet Saturn rules over them, and northerners bellicose and long-lived because Mars governs them. The southerners are short-lived because the necessities of life are wanting there. "Also Saturn rules in India, and yet there they are long-lived." With which double-faced talk he terminates the treatise.

A prediction for the year, 1607, published by Lodovico Bonhombra at Bologna, takes up the four seasons of the year in turn, then in a closing paragraph states that the inclinations of the stars over this year are subject to answer to prayer by Divine Majesty, also to human prudence, and in all things subject to the Holy Mother Roman Catholic Church. Giovanni Antonio Roffeni of Bologna did not die until 1643 and had issued annual predictions for some thirty years before. Orlandi said that his explanation of meteorological matters extended to the year 1660. In 1614 he had published a work praising true astrology and against its calumniators. He corresponded with Kepler and Galileo, and defended the *Sydereus Nuntius* of the latter against the Bohemian, Martin Hork. Nor did astrological prediction at Bologna cease with Roffeni's death, since nine different *Practicas* for the year 1648 alone were issued there.

Cornelio Ghiradelli of Bologna, a Franciscan and a member of the Academy of *Vespertini,* published *Discorsi Astrologici* from 1617 on for a number of years, also Considerations on the Solar Eclipse of 21 May, 1621, Astrological Observations on the weather in 1622, a weather prediction for the year 1623, and a tract on leap-year of 1624, while a prediction for 1634 is found in the Bibliothèque Nationale, Paris.

Buonaventura Cavalieri, professor of mathematics at Bologna and who was praised by Galileo, together with a Hundred Varied Problems to Illustrate the Use of Logarithms, published a New Practice of Astrology at Bologna in 1639. The license of his ecclesiastical superiors is dated July 31, 1636, and the dedication on April 1, 1637. The book deals especially with astrological directions and was composed for some of his students who, having visited his *Direttorio Uranometrico,* wished to use logarithms in finding directions. There are chapters on finding declinations, right ascensions, *significator* and *promissor* as well as directions.

> The *significator* among astrologers is called that point, place or star in the celestial sphere which carries the lordship and signification of anything. Just as the *promissor* is that which promises any accident when it reaches the site of the *significator.*

Five customary *significatores* are the sun, moon, ascendent, zenith and *Pars fortunae,* adding the governing planet. Promissores may be the planets, their aspects, *termini, antiscii, contra antiscii,* fixed stars, beginnings of houses, and so on.

Alphonsus Pandulphus, bishop of Comacchio, had died in October, 1648, but his Disputations as to the End of the World were not printed until ten years later at Bologna. Since Raphael Aversa is cited in them, they would seem to have been written after 1625. Of these eight disputations, in which the views of philosophers were refuted and evangelical and prophetic doctrine alone received, only that on astrology will concern us, omitting the Pythagorean, Platonic, Aristotelian, Stoic and astronomical discourses which precede it, and the scriptural and theological sections which follow it. In a *Disputatio Prooemialis* Pandulphus lays claim to novelty of matter and treatment, but there is nothing very new in his arguments against astrology. He denies occult qualities to the heavens or that they are the cause of metals. The empyrean heaven does not act upon the inferior world; the heavens influence the intellect only indirectly; and critical days do not depend upon the moon. No change of kingdoms and empires may be inferred from the movement of stars from one sign of the zodiac into another, and astrological houses are rejected.

At Padua, Giacomo Filippo Tomasini (1595–1655?) both praised and practiced astrology. The first work listed under his name by Vedova is on the Revolution of the Year for 1614, 1615 and 1616. In his Eulogies of Illustrious Paduans, first published in 1629, Tomasini praised past devotees of astrology from Peter of Abano on, or affirmed, in the case of opponents like George of Ragusa, who died in 1622 at the age of only forty-three, that their

deaths had been accurately forecast by that art, as has been occasionally noted in our previous volumes. Another instance, not previously noticed, was that of Hieronymus Capivaceus, who taught medicine at Padua from 1552 to 1589. When he was an old man, an astrologer advised him not to undertake any journey, but he persisted in going to Mantua to give medical attendance to its reigning prince. On his return he was suddenly taken ill and died.

The famous Aristotelian philosopher, Casere Cremonini (1550—1631) taught at Padua from 1590 to 1631. There is a manuscript in the library of St. Mark's at Venice dated 1628 of a treatise or lectures on the influence of the heavens by him which opens with the assertion that it is a tenet of Aristotle that sublunars are governed by the heavens. The manuscript is so poorly written, with a number of passages crossed out and marginal summaries or substitutions, that it is difficult reading. But it asserts that the first and last efficient cause is no other than the heavens, by which the elements are constituted, and inquires how motion heats, and especially how the motion of the sun acquires the power of heating by motion. Earlier Jean de Jandun came in for considerable criticism. Other works by Cremonini display a similar attitude as to the influence of the heavens. He maintained the view of Aristotle that they were a fifth substance, distinct from the elements, and that there were movers of the heavens. In a treatise on these Intelligences in a manuscript now at Florence he says that the treatment of separate substances is difficult because they are not perceptible to the senses. After setting forth the Peripatetic doctrine, he adds that the true opinion concerning all separate substances is to be had from the theologians.

Cremonini is said in *Naudaeana* to have lived in a magnificent palace at Padua with a maître d'hotel, valets de chambre and other servants, two coaches and six fine horses. When he died, he left four hundred scholars and two thousand crowns of securities. The Inquisition more than once took exception to the teaching of Cremonini, but he insisted that he was merely setting forth the philosophy of Aristotle, as he was hired to do, and, in the case of objection to his *Apologia* of 1616, that the book had already been approved by the Doge and Senate of Venice, and could not be altered.

The years of the birth and death of Andreas Argolus or Andrea Argoli are given by Zedler as 1570–1651, by Sudhoff as 1568–1657. He was born at Taghacozzo in the Abruzzi, was a student with Magini, and taught Wallenstein and his astrologer Giambattista Zenno at the University of Padua. Perhaps his earliest extant or recorded printed work was Tables of the Primum Mobile with the particular purpose of more easily determining astrological directions. Besides other Tables based upon the hypotheses of Tycho Brahe, Ephemerides for the years, 1631–1700, a dissertation on the comet of 1652–1653, and a *Pandosion sphaericum,* he composed a work on critical days in two books, of which Sudhoff has already given some account, and which we shall further consider here as an example of the continued prevalence of astrology in the seventeenth century. The title, *De diebus criticis etc.,* somewhat obscures the real character and content of the work, which is concerned chiefly with astrology in general and astrological medicine in particular. Having in his early chapters asserted the influence of the stars, Argolus devotes the ninth chapter of the first book to instruction how to predict from one's nativity the coming train of events of the human body. The tenth considers the subjection of the external and internal parts of the body to the planets and signs of the zodiac, and the diseases which are attributed to particular signs and planets. The eleventh chapter maintains that the outcome of illness may be more rationally and evidently investigated by astrological method than by the medical art; the twelfth instructs how to forecast the nature and time of sickness from those superior causes. The thirteenth deals with determination of good or ill health from the revolution of the year, and it is only with chapter 14 that we at last come to critical days of which the discussion continues to chapter 21, where the first book ends. Even then the discussion continues to be primarily astrological, and we are assured that the crises in diseases do not follow a numerical order or proportion, and that a horoscope should be drawn up at the beginning of the illness.

The first six chapter headings of Book II are all astrological: whether the disease is curable, short or long, signs of death, signs of convalescence, relation to the course of the moon, and precepts to be observed in medicine such as that one's nails are to be cut when the moon is waxing in Aries, Taurus, Leo or Libra with Venus or the sun in friendly aspect. After reprinting the *latromathematica* of Hermes Trismegistus to Ammon of Egypt, Argolus regales us with the horoscopes of the nativities and the falling sick of four recent popes, Sixtus V, Clement VIII, Paul V, and Gregory XV. Of the illnes of the last-named, who died in 1623, Argolus says that he was present almost daily with other physicians throughout the entire course of the disease. The new star of 1604 is said to have announced the election of Paul V. Argolus then gives similar data for Henries II, III and IV of France, connects a comet with the horoscope and death in battle on August 4, 1578, of king Sebastian of Portugal, then passes on to Gustavus Adolphus and the nativities of various other princes, cardinals and the like. In the later edition used by Sudhoff, Gregory XIII and Urban VIII (1623–1644) were added to the four popes above mentioned, showing in what light, with what qualifications, and within what limits we should interpret the bulls of Sixtus V in 1586 and Urban VIII in 1631 against astrology. We further see that astrology went on at the University of Padua in the seventeenth century as well as at Bologna and at Salamanca.

The wide currency of the conception, man the microcosm, is further attested by a work of Stephanus Rodericus Castrensis, or Estevan Rodrigues de Castro, of Portugal, first professor of medicine at the University of Pisa, on the Meteors of the Microcosm, in four books, dedicated to the Grand Duke of Tuscany, and printed at Florence in 1621. The idea suggested by this title goes back at least to Severinus, *Idea medicinae philosophicae*, 1571, where it is said that fevers, epilepsy, dropsy, catarrhs, and so forth correspond to meteors in the great world. The representatives of the Inquisition, in their approbation of the work, note that Rodericus revives atomism and regards water as

the principle of things, but only philosophically. The first book, after demonstrating the conformity between the world and man, and that there is a world soul—to which the inquisitors do not seem to have objected, and pointing out the similarity between it and the human soul, attacks Aristotle's arguments for four elements and argues for atoms. The second book inquires whether the origin of the microcosm has been correctly stated by others, considers the human anatomy, asks whether the blood and spirits are alive, and treats of the internal signature of the microcosm. With the third book we at length come to the meteors of the microcosm, and various kinds of fevers are dealt with, which are compared to the fiery impressions in the universe. Asking whether fever is a quality or a substance, Rodericus concludes that all diseases are substances.

The fourth and last book is miscellaneous in content. First it takes up the cure of fevers, then whence *alexipharmaca* or antidotes for poison derive their virtue. Antidotes from gold and pearls are given as well as from animals, plants and minerals in general. "Fires of Vulcan and other fiery meteors" are represented by such diseases as elephantiasis. Epilepsy, apoplexy and paralysis are the lightning and thunderbolts of the microcosm. Menstrual blood is called poisonous. After discussing the nature and causes of winds in the great world, we turn to wind in the microcosm. Sweat is the inundation of the microcosm; catarrh, its rain; and finally we consider its stones.

The same conception appeared again in the *Anatomy of the Microcosm* by J. S. Kozak, printed at Bremen in 1636, in which are chapters on meteors of the macrocosm, and both salutary and morbid meteors of the microcosm. Fortunio Liceto narrowed the comparison to lightning and fevers in particular. Paul Virdung and Genathius had applied it to winds.

Adrian Spigelius or Spiegel (1578–1625) in his anatomical work published posthumously at Venice in 1627, accepted the observation of Falloppia that in the case of deep wounds of the head the brain swelled at the full of the moon and subsided as the moon waned. Furthermore Spigelius held that from this it followed that greater inconveniences would result from a blow on the head when the moon was waning. For then veins were more apt to be severed because of the interval left between the cranium and the hard membrane. Epilepsy was apt to come on at the time of the new moon, because then the humors, denied mixture with humidity, grew sharp and lacerated the brain, especially in the case of melancholy.

Like many, if not most critics of astrology, Antonio Merenda was not an astronomer. A professor of civil law at Pavia, he published his work against astrology in Italian in order to convince those who could not read Latin of what theologians and philosophers had often demonstrated in Latin, the falsity of that art. His argumentation, however, is so quibbling, involved and difficult to follow that it may be doubted whether it would convince any average reader. His attack is directed especially against prediction as to particular individuals, which he stigmatizes as a diabolical art of divination, and contends that no superstitious art is more fitted to forward the aims of the devil than the astrology of Ptolemy. He objects that the influence of the stars at the time of conception or birth is not immutable but subject to change from subsequent celestial influences, and that the astrologers should stick to either the moment of conception or that of birth. He denies that the Bible supports astrology, declares that papal bulls detest it, and that the church fathers were unanimously against it. He repeats Augustine's argument from twins against astrology, and is careful never to cite Aquinas as favoring it. Yet a page which he finally quotes from him turns out to be his usual half-favorable attitude, saving free will but stressing the influence of the stars upon natural inclination. Merenda, on the other hand, had previously represented Aquinas (*Secunda secundae*, quaest. 95, artic. 5) as agreeing with Augustine (*Genesis ad literam*, cap. 17) that the devil, God permitting, interested himself in the predictions of astrologers.

Merenda grants that it is easier to predict the weather or the health of a community than the fortune of an individual. But astrologers do not know all the stars and so cannot foresee even their general influence. They have not yet had sufficient experience of the effects of a great variety of constellations to formulate rules as to these. Ptolemy rejected previous experience and method as too particular and in his *Quadripartitum* laid down general rules largely on the basis of reason and probability. And after him Arabic astrologers were divided into discordant sects. Why should a brief eclipse exert great influence, when daily we are deprived of sunlight all night long, and all day long of that of the moon? Merenda further attacks the doctrine that some one planet is lord of the year.

A birth may be delayed or hastened and so miss its proper and natural constellation. Moreover, few clocks keep exact time, and clocks are found chiefly only in such places as fortresses, monasteries, convents, hospitals and colleges, so that it is difficult to tell the precise moment of birth. Merenda further asks, perhaps sarcastically, why astrologers do not take the nativities of the father, brothers and sisters into consideration as the ancients did. But he above all objects to predictions of violent death, or a rich marriage, or obtaining an office, as violations of freedom of the will. He is much offended that astrologers promise even a cardinalate or the papacy to their clients. Merenda professes originality in his discussion and denies that his method of treatment will be found in other authors, but it has resemblances to that of John Chamber, while he admits that he has not read them all. He closes with a satirical parody, giving nine crafty rules for practical procedure on the part of predicting astrologers.

Urban VIII, who issued a bull against judicial astrology in 1631, appointed Caesar Carena an inquisitor. The latter has a good deal to say concerning astrology in his Treatise on the Office of the Most Holy Inquisition, printed at Cremona in 1636 and 1641, later at Bologna in 1668 and Lyons in 1669. He states that natural astrology, which conjectures what naturally happens from the aspect of the stars, and, if it considers the nativity, infers from it human temperaments and propensities, is licit. So say Suarez and Sanchez. But one should not consider the horoscope of Christ despite d'Ailly's doing so, nor predict concerning the pope and the church, which is forbidden by the papal

bull of Urban VIII of April 1, 1631. An astrologer from the nativity may predict the child's temperament and future infirmities and when they will occur. "This conclusion is certain, nor can there by any doubt about it, because the stars act directly upon the body and its humors," as Aquinas well proved and many others of the Fathers of Coimbra. But actual prediction is an uncertain matter, and Carena does not agree with Hurtado that astrologers can know for certain a time beyond which a person cannot live.

It is licit to construct a *figura coeli* of the beginning of a disease and for the moment of taking to one's bed, of which Maginus treats in his work on the legitimate use of astrology in medicine. But such a figure alone by itself is unreliable, and Campanella in his medical works says that it is insufficient unless it agrees with the horoscope taken at birth. When an astrological direction occurs opposed to the person's temperament, the astrologer is justified in saying that illness threatens. But Carena disapproves of erecting figures for the parents from that of the son, although Cardan, Campanella and Regiomontanus in one of his problems do so. It is more difficult to predict inclinations than physical temperament. One cannot predict, for example, that a person will be a sodomite. And future contingents may have little or no connection with inclinations. Raphael de la Torre holds that predicting human inclinations is not superstitious nor forbidden by the bull of Sixtus V, but Carena insists that prediction of inclinations and of future contingencies are both bad and are forbidden by both papal bulls. The division of the zodiac into astrological houses is uncertain, and astrologers disagree among themselves as to directions and other points, so that there is no sure foundation for judgments, although Carena grants that the planets exert influence not only *per se* but according to their positions in the signs. But one cannot predict future contingent events for individuals, much less political changes. Campanella in his judicial astrology claims to have purged it from all superstition, but actually whatever is superstitious in all astrology is found in that book, which is only a compendium of Cardan's commentary on the *Quadripartitum* of Ptolemy.

Keith Thomas

SOURCE: "Astrology: Its Practice and Extent," in *Religion and the Decline of Magic*, Charles Scribner's Sons, 1971, pp. 283-322.

[*In the following excerpt, Thomas provides a detailed analysis of the practice of astrology, discussing the components of astrological readings and the means by which astrology reached the populace.*]

> I resolve these ensuing astrological questions: the sick whether they shall recover or not; the party absent whether living or dead; how many husbands or children a woman shall have; whether you shall marry the desired party or whom else, whether she has her maidenhead or no, or shall be honest to you after marriage, or her portion well paid; if a man be wise or a fool; whether it be good to put on new clothes, or turn courtier this year or the next; if dreams are for

good or evil; whether a child be the reputed father's or not, or shall be fortunate or otherwise; ships at sea, whether safe or not; whether it be good to remove your dwelling or not; of lawsuits which side shall have the better; and generally all astrological questions whatsoever.

[John Wilson, *The Cheats* (1662)]

Despite refinements in detail, the astrology known to sixteenth- and seventeenth-century Englishmen was recognisably the same subject as that expounded by the Egyptian Ptolemy in his *Tetrabilos* in the second century AD. In the seventeenth century the English astrologers were to popularise the doctrines of their science in a vernacular literature which laid every detail of the subject open to public inspection, but the doctrines they enunciated were essentially traditional. Indeed, several of the English treatises on astrology were little more than translations of earlier Latin writings. Like Christianity, astrology proved strikingly adaptable to the needs of a social environment which was very different from that in which it had originated.

The basic astrological assumptions are not difficult to grasp. For if astronomy is the study of the movements of the heavenly bodies, then astrology is the study of the effects of those movements. The astronomers of the ancient world had been impressed by the regular behaviour of the heavens, in contrast with the flux and mutation of life upon earth. They accordingly assumed a division of the universe whereby the superior, immutable bodies of the celestial world ruled over the terrestrial or sublunary sphere, where all was mortality and change. It was assumed that the stars had special qualities and influences which were transmitted downwards upon the passive earth, and which varied in their effects, according to the changing relationship of the heavenly bodies to each other. Owing to their inadequate techniques of astronomical observation, the early scientists had no conception of the infinite number of existing solar systems nor of the vast distances which separate the visible stars from each other. They were thus led to postulate a single system in which the seven moving stars or planets—Sun, Moon, Saturn, Jupiter, Mars, Venus and Mercury—shifted their position in relation to the earth and each other, against a fixed backcloth of the twelve signs of the zodiac. The nature of the influence exerted by the heavens at any one moment thus depended upon the situation of the various celestial bodies. By drawing a map of the heavens, or horoscope, the astrologer could analyse this situation and assess its implications. By an extension of the same principle, he could, given the necessary astronomical knowledge, construct a horoscope for some future point of time, and thus predict the influence which the heavens would exert on that occasion.

There was nothing esoteric about these general assumptions. At the beginning of the sixteenth century astrological doctrines were part of the educated man's picture of the universe and its workings. It was generally accepted that the four elements constituting the sublunary region— earth, air, fire and water—were kept in their state of ceaseless permutation by the movement of the heavenly bodies.

The various planets transmitted different quantities of the four physiological qualities of heat and cold, dryness and moisture. In the resulting interaction was comprised all physical change. This relationship between earthly events and the movement of the heavens was but one example of the many links and correspondences which were thought to bind the physical universe together. Astrology was thus less a separate discipline than an aspect of a generally accepted world picture. It was necessary for the understanding of physiology and therefore of medicine. It taught of the influence of the stars upon the plants and minerals, and therefore shaped botany and metallurgy. Psychology and ethnography also presupposed a good deal of astrological dogma. During the Renaissance, even more than in the Middle Ages, astrology pervaded all aspects of scientific thought. It was not a coterie doctrine, but an essential aspect of the intellectual framework in which men were educated.

At the beginning of the sixteenth century astrological doctrines were part of the educated man's picture of the universe and its workings. . . . Astrology was . . . less a separate discipline than an aspect of a generally accepted world picture.

—Keith Thomas

Nevertheless, the subject had a life and independent momentum of its own, especially when the prestige of the Ptolemaic picture of the universe began to crumble under the pressure of the astronomical discoveries of the century and a half between Copernicus and Newton. During this period astrology gradually lost its role as a universal symbolism, and ossified into a separate, and ultimately obsolete, system of belief. This change was still in the future when the sixteenth century opened. Although there had been many sceptics about particular details of astrological dogma, especially as regards the possibility of making definite predictions concerning the behaviour of specific human beings, there were not yet any real heretics, so far as the basic principles of the subject were concerned. No one denied the influence of the heavens upon the weather or disputed the relevance of astrology to medicine or agriculture. Before the seventeenth century, total scepticism about astrological doctrine was highly exceptional, whether in England or elsewhere.

During the sixteenth and seventeenth centuries there were four main branches to the practice of judicial astrology (to give it its full title, for the term 'astrology' by itself was often used as synonymous with 'astronomy'). First, there were the *general predictions*, based on the future movements of the heavens, and taking note of such impending events as eclipses of the sun and moon, or the conjunction of the major planets in one sign of the zodiac. These forecasts related to the weather, the state of the crops, mortality and epidemics, politics and war. They indicated the fate of society as a whole, but not that of particular individuals. Secondly, there were *nativities,* maps of the sky at the moment of a person's birth, either made on the spot at the request of the infant's parents, or reconstructed for individuals of mature years who could supply the details of their time of birth. If the date of the birth had been lost, the astrologer could try to work it out by inference from the relationship between the 'accidents', or notable events in his client's life, and the state of the heavens at the time. The horoscope at birth could subsequently be followed up by 'annual revolutions', in which the astrologer calculated the individual's prospects for the coming year.

The details of the client's nativity were also needed before he could avail himself of the astrologer's third main service, that of making *elections,* or choosing the right moment for the right action. By comparing the relationship between the tendencies indicated by the client's horoscope with what was known about the future movement of the heavens, certain times could be identified as more propitious than others for embarking upon any potentially risky undertaking, such as going on a journey or choosing a wife. The election of a proper time was also a desirable procedure for routine operations, like cutting one's hair and nails, or having a bath. Finally, there were *horary questions,* the most controversial part of the astrologer's art, and one which had only been developed after the days of Ptolemy by the Arabs. Its optimistic assumption was that the astrologer could resolve any question put to him by considering the state of the heavens at the exact moment when it was asked—on the principle that "as the nativity is the time of the birth of the body, the horary question is the time of the birth of the mind" [J. Gadbury, *The Doctrine of Nativities,* 1658]. If the question was a medical one the patient might accompany it with a sample of his urine; the astrologer then based his answer upon his interpretation of the sky at the moment when the urine had been voided, or when it had arrived at his consulting-room. But every kind of personal problem could be dealt with as an horary question.

These four spheres of activity—general predictions, nativities, elections and horary questions—formed the sum of the astrologer's art. An individual practitioner might specialise in one rather than another, but he was expected to be a master of them all. He might also possess a certain amount of medical learning. Different signs of the zodiac were thought to rule over different parts of the body, and a proper election of times had to be made for administering medicine, letting blood, or carrying out surgical operations. This was generally recognised by all sixteenth-century physicians. But there had also developed a more idiosyncratic system of astrological medicine which linked every stage of treatment to the disposition of the heavens. By casting a figure for the *decumbiture,* or moment when the patient fell ill, and by resolving a question on sight of his urine, the astrological doctor claimed to be able to diagnose the disease, prescribe the treatment, foretell when the sickness would reach its crisis, and prognosticate its eventual outcome.

Such were the main branches of English (and indeed European) astrology during the sixteenth and seventeenth centuries. Although purporting to be an objective science, the system was highly flexible, since it left room for infinite possibilities of disagreement, both over general principles, and over the interpretation of any particular problem. Every astrological prognosis involved a figure of the heavens, in which the sky was divided up into twelve sections or 'houses', each relating to different aspects of human life. Lack of precision in time-recording made the construction of this figure difficult enough in itself, and there was plenty of scope for mathematical error in the intricate astronomical calculations required. But even when the horoscope had been drawn and agreed upon, the problem of its interpretation remained. The planets were deemed to have colours, sexes, physical qualities, and so forth. But the elaborate mythologies which proliferated along these lines were not always consistent. The planets, moreover, were only one variable in a densely crowded mosaic of fluctuating constituents—elements, humours, qualities, houses and signs of the zodiac. The client's own horoscope might also need to be compared with that of the country in which he lived, or those of the other persons with whom he had dealings. The astrologer thus found himself involved in a welter of combinations and permutations which greatly complicated the task of interpretation. It was generally agreed that to pick his way through them he needed not mere technical skill, but judgment. In other words any interpretation was in the last resort bound to be subjective. Different practitioners might give different answers to the same question, and the more specific the prediction the less likely was it to command unanimous assent.

Astrology was probably the most ambitious attempt ever made to reduce the baffling diversity of human affairs to some sort of intelligible order, but as its vocabulary and techniques swelled to reflect the richness and variability of the material with which it was concerned the problem of reaching a definite answer became increasingly intractable. The more subtle the astrologer's terminology, the greater the number of factors he took into account, the more certainly did the prospect of objective pronouncement elude his grasp. His efforts to sharpen his conceptual tools only meant that he came nearer to reproducing on paper the chaotic diversity which he saw in the world around him.

Such difficulties were only dimly apprehended in England at the beginning of the sixteenth century, when astrological activity seems to have been at a relatively low ebb. In the Middle Ages there had been many prominent English astrological authors, but their numbers fell off sharply during the fifteenth century and did not revive for over a hundred and fifty years. The prognostications in circulation during the early sixteenth century were therefore largely of foreign origin. There was, for example, no English contribution to the large literature produced by the conjunction in 1524 of all seven planets in the watery sign of Pisces, even though rumours of the impending deluge in that year are said to have induced Prior Bolton of St. Bartholomew's, Smithfield, to build himself a house on Harrow Hill and stock it with provisions to withstand the threat of inundation. The lack of English astrological writings during this period reflected the general torpor of English science. Interest revived with the mathematical renaissance pioneered by John Dee and the Digges family during the reign of Elizabeth I, and was more or less sustained until the end of the seventeenth century. If the prestige of astrology is to be measured by the publication of astrological works, then the story is one of a peak reached at around the end of the sixteenth century, followed by a discernible lull in the twenty years before the Civil War, and thereafter an unprecedented torrent of publication, which began with the War, but went on until the end of the seventeenth century.

In terms of popular accessibility, therefore, the crucial period of English astrological publication was the last sixty years of the seventeenth century, and particularly the Interregnum. In the age of Edward VI the bulk of astrological learning was still locked up in the obscurity of a learned language, whereas by the time of Charles II there was no branch of the subject which could not be studied by the English reader. During the Elizabethan period a few original works and foreign translations were published, but the most elaborate native piece of astrological learning, Thomas Allen's commentary on Ptolemy, remained in manuscript. As has already been seen Robert Fludd's voluminous works were written in Latin and published abroad. Only during the Interregnum, that period when so many other *arcana* were exposed to public gaze, did the first vernacular guides to the subject pour off the English presses. The popular writings of William Lilly, Nicholas Culpepper, William Ramesey and John Gadbury were followed after the Restoration by the similar vulgarisations of Richard Saunders, John Partridge, William Salmon and John Case. Designed for a mainly nonlearned audience, they constituted a comprehensive summary of astrological beliefs, issued, ironically, at the very period when the whole system was ceasing to command respect in intellectually more pretentious *milieux*. Ptolemy's astrology was not published in English until 1701.

The availability of English treatises on astrology is thus a poor barometer for the actual prestige of the subject. Despite the lack of a vernacular literature, most Tudor monarchs and their advisers encouraged astrologers and drew upon their advice. Both Henry VII and those engaged in plotting against him maintained relations with the Italian astrologer William Parron. Henry VIII patronised the German, Nicholas Kratzer, prevented his bishops from censuring astrology, and received astrological advice from John Robins, the only contemporary English writer on the subject of any importance. Cardinal Wolsey's interest in astrology was notorious. He was rumoured to have calculated Henry VIII's nativity in order to be able to pander to the King's whims; and he timed the departure of his French embassy in 1527 to coincide with an astrologically propitious moment. The Protector Somerset seems to have been personally sceptical of the predictive powers of astrology, but after his fall the Italian savant, Jerome Cardan, came to England to cast the horoscopes of the young Edward VI and his tutor, John Cheke, a well-known addict. Another leading administrator who shared this interest was the Secretary of State, Sir William Paget, to whom the Basle edition of the Italian astrologer, Guido Bonatus, was dedicated in 1550. His colleague, Sir William Paulet, supported the almanac-maker George Hartgill, while for

Sir Thomas Smith, the ambassador and future Secretary of State, the practice of astrology was no casual interest, but so consuming a passion that he could "scarcely sleep at night from thinking of it" [J. G. Nichols in *Archaeologia*, 1860].

Similar enthusiasm was displayed by the courtiers of Elizabeth I. The Earl of Leicester employed Richard Forster as his astrological physician and commissioned Thomas Allen to set horoscopes. He also offered Allen a bishopric. It was at Leicester's invitation that John Dee chose an astrologically propitious day for the coronation of Elizabeth I. Dee maintained relations with many of the leading nobility of his day and was called in by the Queen to offer his views on the comet of 1577. Burghley made notes on astrological matters, and the Earl of Essex is known to have possessed an elaborate fifteenth-century treatise on astrology and geomancy. Sir Christopher Hatton, Elizabeth's future Lord Chancellor, received the dedication of John Maplet's *The Diall of Destiny* (1581), an astrological text-book. The evidence for Sir Philip Sidney's attitude to astrology is conflicting, but the Earl of Oxford certainly studied the subject. Small wonder that the Puritan Laurence Humphrey complained in 1563 that among the nobility the science of astrology was "ravened, embraced, and devoured of many" [L. Humfrey, *The Nobles: or, of Nobilitye*, 1563]. It was customary for aristocratic families to have horoscopes cast at the birth of their children, and more or less unavoidable for them to have recourse to doctors who used semi-astrological methods.

During the seventeenth century this situation changed only slowly. Many of the leading nobility and politicians retained astrological leanings. The Earl of Arundel employed the almanac-maker, Humphrey Llwyd, as his personal physician. Lord Scrope, President of the Council of the North (1619–28), was a patient of the astrological doctor, Richard Napier. Charles I's Treasurer, Lord Weston, appointed the astrologer, Nicholas Fiske, as tutor to his son. The second Earl of Bristol was himself a highly skilled astrologer. The Marquis of Huntly, executed in 1649, was thought to have been ruined by bad astrological advice. "He believed the stars," wrote Burnet "and they deceived him." Another aristocratic victim of the Civil Wars, the Marquis of Montrose, had as a young man travelled overseas with the Earl of Denbigh; together "they consulted all the astrologers they could hear of."

During the Royalist exile Sir Edward Dering, later a prominent London merchant, had attempted to keep up the spirits of his colleagues by assuring them that the stars were on their side. After the Restoration he became a great patron of contemporary astrologers. Charles II himself took astrological advice upon occasions, as we shall see. Indeed in 1669 Louis XIV thought it worth appointing a French astrologer, the Abbé Pregnani, as a special diplomatic agent to England, after the Duke of Monmouth, one of the Abbé's clients, had told him of the monarch's faith in the art. The venture miscarried after a trip to Newmarket races, where the Abbé unfortunately failed to provide the King with any winners, thus provoking a diplomatic incident which led to his recall. Even after the Revolution of 1688 astrological interests were to be found in high places. Sir John Trenchard, Secretary of State to William III, had his horoscope cast, and confessed on his death-bed that everything the astrologer had predicted for him had come true.

For intellectuals astrology remained a topic of consuming interest. A random list of sympathisers could include such celebrated names as those of Sir Walter Raleigh, Robert Burton, the Anatomist, Lord Herbert of Cherbury, Sir Kenelm Digby and Sir Thomas Browne. Among seventeenth-century scientists, the mathematician Edmund Gunter is known to have cast horoscopes, while belief in the possibilities of astrology, in part or whole, was shared by such notables as Napier of Merchiston, Samuel Hartlib, William Harvey and Henry Oldenburg. As a young man Isaac Newton bought a book on judicial astrology at Stourbridge Fair. Among the papers of John Aubrey is the nativity of Walter Charleton, sometime President of the Royal College of Physicians, set by Lord Brouncker, the first President of the Royal Society. John Dryden remained an astrological devotee throughout his life.

These miscellaneous names testify to the sympathetic attitude in which astrology was held in the sixteenth and seventeenth centuries by many men of rank and intellectual importance. Of course it is not always easy to say just how seriously they took it. Many no doubt had horoscopes cast out of mere amusement or curiosity, whereas others based important decisions on their outcome. But it is certain that until the mid-seventeenth century astrology was no private fad but a form of divination to which many educated people had recourse.

What is more remarkable, however, is that astrological interests were not confined to court circles, or to the entourage of the great, as they had largely been in the Middle Ages, but were widely disseminated throughout the people. For this the invention of printing was chiefly responsible. By its means, astrology was made available to an infinitely wider audience than that enjoyed by the court-based astrologers of the medieval world. The lead in this dissemination was taken by the most widespread form of fugitive literature in early modern England—the almanac.

Strictly speaking, the almanac comprised three quite separate items. There was the Almanac proper, which indicated the astronomical events of the coming year, eclipses, conjunctions and movable feasts. There was the Kalendar, which showed the days of the week and the months, and the fixed Church festivals. Finally, there was the Prognostication, or astrological forecast of the notable events of the year. Usually they were all sold together as one piece, interlarded with the sort of miscellaneous information which diaries still carry today—a list of markets and fairs, a guide to highways and distances by road, a brief chronology of notable historical events since the Creation, medical recipes, legal formulae, hints on gardening. By the mid-seventeenth century they also carried advertisements for books, patent medicines, or teachers of mathematics. These little pocket-books were quite distinct from the broadside sheet almanac, the ancestor of the modern calendar. They contained more information, and were less ephemeral. Contemporaries found them invaluable as diaries, note-books, and vade-mecums generally. As a conse-quence large collections still survive in the Bodleian, British Museum and other large libraries.

The most obvious difference between the pocket almanac and the modern diary is the strong astrological emphasis of the former. The more elaborate almanacs included Ephemerides, or tables showing the daily position of the heavenly bodies throughout the year. With their aid the reader could predict the movement of the planets through the signs of the zodiac, and foresee the various conjunctions and oppositions. Thus armed, he was in a position to set about casting his own horoscopes. In addition he could consult the almanac's diagram of the Anatomical Man indicating the dominion of the different signs of the zodiac over the different parts of the human body. From this he could work out the appropriate time for taking medicine or medical treatment. Above all, there was the prognostication, in which the author of the almanac demonstrated his virtuosity by detailed forecasts of politics, the weather, the state of the crops, and the health of the population in the year to come.

Medieval almanacs had circulated in manuscript, but they seem to have been intended primarily for students and physicians. It was only in the Tudor period that the printed English almanac rose to a position of enormous popular success. During the early sixteenth century various translations of continental prognostications were issued, some of which sold very briskly. But not until 1545 is an Englishman known to have composed his own forecast for publication. He was Andrew Boorde, an ex-Carthusian, and his prognostication was the first of many. Foreign prognostications still circulated, but their place was steadily usurped by domestic products. By 1600 there had been probably over six hundred different almanacs published in England, and they were still on the increase. The number of separate almanacs issued in the seventeenth century has been estimated at more than two thousand, and well over two hundred authors must have been concerned in their publication. The size of a typical edition is unknown. But it is significant that almanacs, like Bibles, were exempt from the limit of twelve to fifteen hundred copies imposed by the Stationers' Company on single editions of other publications. William Lilly's annual almanac and prognostication, *Merlinus Anglicus,* printed 13,500 copies in 1646, 17,000 in 1647, and 18,500 in 1648. By 1659 it was said to be selling nearly 30,000 a year. This particular almanac was unusually popular, but it is clear that the figure of three to four million, which is sometimes suggested as the total production of almanacs in the seventeenth century, is a distinct under-estimate; the ten years after November 1663 alone nearly reached that total. Not even the Bible sold at this rate.

It is easy to see why the almanacs were commercially so successful. They were issued to fit the varying astronomical meridians of different parts of the country, special almanacs being published for particular towns, even relatively small ones like Aylesbury or Saffron Walden. The information they contained was carefully selected according to the type of readership aimed at. Thus there might be legal terms for the Justice of the Peace, advice on land measurement for the surveyor, or nautical hints for the seaman. By the mid-seventeenth century the almanacs even catered for different varieties of political taste. They were also cheap. In the seventeenth century the standard price seems to have been twopence, although more elaborate productions cost more.

Astrological forecasts, however, were by no means an invariable feature of the almanac, and even when included might relate only to the weather. Highly political prognostications, of the kind common during the Civil War, had been relatively infrequent during the previous century. By the 1630s the so-called Prognostication was often merely an additional calendar of secular occurrences during the year. It was only the subsequent breakdown in censorship which made political forecasting commonplace.

Yet even without a prognostication, the almanac provided a guide to daily action. It indicated astrologically favourable days for blood-letting, purging and bathing; and it showed right and wrong times for engaging in most kinds of agricultural operation, planting, sowing, mowing or gelding animals. Armed with his pocket almanac for the year, or perhaps a more durable guide, like Leonard Digges's *Prognostication . . . for ever* (1555, and frequently reissued), the countryman was well equipped to carry out his recurring tasks, while the sick man, whose relatives were responsible for giving him medicine or letting his blood, knew that they were operating according to well-established formulae.

In practice, however, the genuine astrological almanac had to compete for popular favour with some much lower-grade products. Chief among these was the prognostication of *Erra Pater*, allegedly 'a Jew out of Jewry'. ('If one affirm he learned it of a Jew,' ran a contemporary jingle, 'The silly people think it must be true.') *Erra Pater* was in fact derived from the perpetual prognostication of *Esdras*, which had circulated extensively in the Middle Ages. Like Digges's almanac it gave a table forecasting the weather according to the day of the week on which New Year began. It also included a list of unlucky days, "on which if any man or woman be let blood of wound or vein they shall die within twenty-one days following; or who so falleth into sickness on any of these days they shall never 'scape it till dead." (These were not astrological at all, but were a version of the so-called 'Egyptian days', which Englishmen had regarded as unlucky since Anglo-Saxon times.) This crude brochure was reissued at least a dozen times between 1536 and 1640. By the eighteenth century it was being advertised as the work of William Lilly. Henry Peacham wrote of the early Stuart husbandman that "*Erra Pater*, and this year's almanac (if he can read) are the only two books he spends his time in," while Bishop Hall said in his 'Character' of *The Superstitious Man*, that he would never go out "without an *Erra Pater* in his pocket" [H. Peacham, *The Truth of our Times*, 1638].

Closely allied to *Erra Pater* were other crude works of prognostication, vaguely astrological in character, but lacking the rigour of the astrological almanac proper. There was *The Kalender of Shepherdes*, translated from the French in 1503, and reissued at least seventeen times during the ensuing century and a half, despite its distinctly

Roman Catholic character. It offered a guide to the influence of the planets upon the human body and a semi-astrological method of telling fortunes. Its astrological portions were subsequently pirated under the title of *The Compost of Ptolomeus* (1532?), which enjoyed an independent life for at least four editions thereafter. A similar handbook was *Godfridus*, to which was attached *The Husbandman's Practice, or a Prognostication for Ever.* It included a system of long-range weather forecasting, based on the day of the week on which Christmas fell, and a prediction of the fate of persons born on different days of the week or phases of the moon. There were at least twelve editions of this work in the second half of the seventeenth century. These were in addition to *Arcandam*, the *Sphere of Pythagoras*, and other non-astrological handbooks of divination. 'These be their great masters and in this manner their whole library, with some old parchment rolls, tables and instruments,' wrote Gabriel Harvey of the Elizabethan Wizards: "*Erra Pater*, their hornbook; the *Shepherd's Kalendar*, their primer; the *Compost of Ptolomeus*, their Bible; *Arcandam*, their New Testament" [*Gabriel Harvey's Marginalia*, ed. G. C. Moore Smith, 1913]. The astrological almanac was thus but one of a whole genre of publications which told readers how to make predictions about the future, and to choose days which would be particularly favourable for any given course of action. The astrological kind differed from the others only in its intellectual rigour. At the level of popular readership it is doubtful whether the distinction can have been so clear.

The appeal of the almanac was closely related to the belief in the significance of the changing phases of the moon which was extensively held in rural areas and still lingers on today. Most primitive peoples attribute to the moon an influence upon the weather and upon conception and growth, whether of vegetation, animals or human beings. In medieval theory the balance of humours in the human body was believed to fluctuate with the phases of the moon. The moon was thought to control the amount of moisture in the human body, and the brain, as the moistest part of the body, was believed to be particularly subject to its influence. Hence the notion of the insane as 'lunatic' or 'moonstruck'. A child born at full moon, declared an astrologer in 1660, would never be healthy.

Many people accordingly allowed the phases of the moon to determine their timing of various activities. The medieval Church had inveighed against the practice of only celebrating marriages or moving to a new house when the moon was waxing. In the sixteenth and seventeenth centuries the rising moon was still thought of as the time for putting on new clothes or embarking upon some new course of action. Thomas Tusser and other agricultural writers advised farmers to cut crops when the moon was in the wane and to sow when it was on the increase. In the later seventeenth century, hair-cutting and nail-paring were said to be "commonly done according to the increase of the moon." Some of the popular handbooks of prognostication took the principle further by decreeing that specific activities should be timed to coincide with specific days of the month. They laid down appropriate days for blood-letting, purging, going on journeys, buying and selling, even for starting school. Hardly any of their recommendations would have been endorsed by serious astrologers, and they provide a further reminder of the large gulf between would-be scientific astrology on the one hand, and popular beliefs of a vaguely astrological character on the other.

Published astrological forecasts were always in demand. When Thomas Gataker, the Puritan divine, wanted to compose a refutation of one of Lilly's prognostications in 1653, he had great difficulty in finding a copy, so rapidly had it sold out. But readers could be sceptics. Weather forecasts in particular were received with a good deal of scorn; and the almanac met with a stream of satire and burlesque. From the anonymous *A Mery Prognostication* of 1544 to Swift's pitiless mockery of John Partridge in 1708, there was an unbroken barrage of anti-astrological squibs. In 1569 Nicholas Allen in his pamphlet, *The Astronomer's Game,* made effective capital out of a side-by-side comparison of the predictions of three contemporary almanac-makers, and this became a standard method of attack.

But the very frequency with which Elizabethan and Jacobean wits found it necessary to denounce the almanacs and prognostications is in itself testimony to the influence which they exerted, "Who is there," asked one writer in 1612, "that maketh not great account of his almanac to observe both days, times and seasons, to follow his affairs for his best profit and use?" [J. M., *A Christian Almanacke* 1612]. In 1561 Francis Coxe complained of the common people that "scant would they ride or go any journey unless they consulted, either with these blind prophets, or at least with their prophecies." William Perkins declared that men bought almanacs so as to profit by knowing in advance the state of the crops and the price of commodities. A later writer also noticed that "the common people in reading . . . almanacs are . . . are very cautelous in observing them." In 1652 John Gaule observed that it was notorious that the people at large preferred "to look into and commune of their almanacs, before the Bible." In March 1642, on the eve of the Civil War, a responsible observer reported from Westminster that "the best sort even of Parliament men" were much agitated by some passages in John Booker's almanac which forecast "that cruel and bloody counsels shall be put in execution the latter end of this month" [D. Gardiner, *Historic Haven. The Story of Sandwich,* 1954]. Unusually dramatic testimony to the almanac's supposed influence was provided in 1666, when the *London Gazette* revealed that six ex-Parliamentary soldiers involved in a republican plot had chosen the third of September for their attempt, after consulting Lilly's almanac and making an astrological calculation. As late as 1708 Jonathan Swift observed that many country gentlemen spent time "poring in Partridge's almanac to find out the events of the year, at home and abroad; not daring to propose a hunting match till Gadbury or he have fixed the weather."

In addition to the routine prognostication attached to the almanac, there was a fugitive literature devoted to such unusual celestial occurrences as comets, eclipses and conjunctions of the major planets, all of which were thought to portend comparable upheavals upon earth. "There was never any great change in the world," wrote the Tudor mathematician Robert Recorde, "neither translations of empires, neither scarce any fall of famous princes, no dearth and penury, no death and mortality, but God by the signs of heaven did premonish men thereof, to repent and beware betimes." The 'new star' which appeared in the constellation of Cassiopeia in 1572, the comet of 1577, the conjunctions of Jupiter and Saturn in 1583, 1603 and 1623, the solar eclipse of 1652, the comet of 1680—all excited extensive discussion and prognostication. Elizabeth I gained great prestige by manifesting her indifference to the comet of 1577. When her courtiers tried to deter her from looking at the dreaded object, she advanced boldly to the window, declaring *Iacta est alea*—"The dice is thrown" [H. Howard, Earl of Northampton, *A Defensative against the Poyson of Supposed Prophecies* 1620]. James I was reported (after his death) to have summoned Cambridge mathematicians to explain the comet of 1618, and then prophesied both the Thirty Years War, and the fall of the Stuarts.

The reaction which such heavenly portents could produce is well illustrated by 'Black Monday'—the solar eclipse of 29 March 1652. Over a quarter of the publications collected by the bookseller Thomason for the month of March related to the eclipse and its significance. Even the Lord Mayor and Aldermen of London heard a sermon on the subject on the 28th. The alarm among the people was such, recalled John Evelyn, that "hardly any would work, none stir out of their houses, so ridiculously were they abused by knavish and ignorant star-gazers." The rich loaded up their coaches and fled from London, while mountebanks did a thriving trade in cordials which purported to allay the effects of the eclipse. At Dalkeith the poor were said to have thrown away their possessions, "casting themselves on their backs, and their eyes towards heaven and praying most passionately that Christ would let them see the sun again, and save them." One contemporary diarist considered that the ultimate effect of the eclipse was to discredit the prognosticators. No terrible effects followed; indeed it seems to have been a fine day, "so that the astrologers lost their reputation exceedingly." But the forecasts of the astrologers had been political. Lilly predicted the fall of Presbyterianism, the reform of the law and the setting up of a new representative. Culpepper forecast the onset of democracy and the Fifth Monarchy. Other radicals predicted the fall of Rome and the universal end of monarchy. They were probably aiming to counter the original *Black Monday* tract, a veiled piece of Royalist propaganda issued in December 1651. At a popular level the damage had been done by anonymous pamphleteers predicting darkness, sudden death and "great madness, raging and terrifying thousands of the people." In the end the Council of State put out a paper explaining that eclipses were natural events which could have no political effects.

Printed publication was thus one of the main methods by which the astrologers made their impact upon the life and thought of the period. Some almanacs were so popular that they took on a life of their own and continued to appear long after the death of their original founders. The year 1655, for example, saw the publication of almanacs attributed to Allestree, Pond, Dade, Vaux and Wood-house, all of whom were dead. But despite their enormous sales, the almanacs did not usually bring their authors much in the way of remuneration: Sir Thomas Overbury assumed in 1615 that an almanac-maker earned forty shillings a year; and this was probably the normal rate in the seventeenth century. But the almanac enabled the practising astrologer to draw attention to the facilities he had to offer by way of private consultation. For it was private practice which gave the professional astrologer his regular means of subsistence; and it was also the way in which he made his greatest impact upon the lives of other human beings.

By the reign of Elizabeth I astrology had become, as one contemporary put it, 'a very handicraft, so that many lived thereby'. Astrological practice was carried on by men (and in a few cases women) of very different degrees of learning and honesty. Sometimes it was only a sideline to some other occupation. In 1560 William Fulke thought that most astrologers were doctors. Many physicians cast horoscopes in connection with their practice, and some gave astrological advice on non-medical matters as well. Astrological procedures were also advertised by village wizards who purported to be able to set figures for fortune-telling or the recovery of stolen goods. At the other end of the scale there were professionals, with extensive London practices, and high-class virtuosi, who cast horoscopes for themselves or their friends, out of curiosity or intellectual interest.

How long this situation had existed is hard to tell, for the origins of regular astrological practice in England are lost in obscurity. Astrological knowledge seems to have been a rare accomplishment in Anglo-Saxon England (although King Edwin of Northumbria is said to have had an *astrologus* called Pellitus who gave him advice on military matters). It probably only became familiar in court circles with the scientific revival of the twelfth century and the diffusion of Arabic astrological writing. Previously there would have been few men capable of making the observations necessary to set a horoscope. Thereafter it was not uncommon for medieval kings to receive astrological advice or for interest to be aroused by some astrological prognostication. What was much less common was the existence of professional astrologers catering for a wide clientele. Astrology was primarily the concern of Court, nobility and Church. Peter of Blois in the twelfth century thought it worth issuing warnings against astrological consultations, but there is no apparent evidence for the existence in medieval England of anything like the consulting facilities which were available in some contemporary Mediterranean countries.

The first unambiguous testimony to the existence of private astrological practice in England dates from the fifteenth century. A lawsuit of 1505 reveals that the immediate reaction of a carrier, who had money stolen from his pack while lodging at an inn in St. Ives, Huntingdonshire, was to look for an astrologer to help him identify the thief. He failed to find one among the clerks of Cambridge and was forced to go on to London to get a horoscope cast. But he clearly assumed that facilities would be available. (The

astrologer he found was described as a 'necromancer' and it may be that some of the 'necromancers' of the late Middle Ages had also operated by astrological means; it was common for them to be described as 'calculating' the whereabouts of lost goods.) Yet sixteenth-century astrology still retained aristocratic associations. The most famous Elizabethan practitioner, John Dee, was no back-alley quack, but the confidant of the Queen and her ministers, though he also gave advice to humbler persons. As late as 1603, Sir Christopher Heydon, the astrological writer, declared that astrology had not "much conversed at any time with the mean and vulgar sort, but . . . hath been ever most familiar with great personages, princes, kings and emperors." But by this date there was a large, though indeterminate, number of low-level consultants scattered through the country, claiming to operate by astrological methods, and substantially patronised by a popular and unsophisticated clientele.

In practice many of these were indistinguishable from the village wizards. Astrological treatises in English were uncommon before the mid-seventeenth century, so it is doubtful if the learning of earlier would-be astrologers can have amounted to very much. Many, when apprehended by the authorities, proved to be utterly ignorant of the principles of the art which they claimed to practise. Others operated on the basis of a small collection of tattered magical recipes and astrological figures bequeathed by some earlier practitioner. Stephen Trefulacke, for example, who was imprisoned in 1591, proved to be carrying an extensive reference library: two Ephemerides, *Arcandam,* a translation of the *Judgment of Nativities* by the Frenchman, Ogier Ferrier, and a variety of such miscellaneous formulae as

> figures to know how long one shall live and whether they shall obtain the treasures hoped for; figures to know things lost; a book of conjuration for divers things, . . . sundry conjurations of raising spirits and binding them; . . . figures to know whether a man be dead or alive or whether he has another wife; to obtain the love of any woman and other like matters.

This was an imposing if heterogeneous armoury. By contrast, there were cheerful impostors who knew no astrology at all, like John Steward, an exschoolmaster, living at Knaresborough in 1510, and frequently consulted in cases of theft. He readily confessed that he tried to impress clients by pretending to consult a book of astronomy, but that in fact "he could nothing do" although by good luck things did sometimes turn out as he predicted. Astrology was similarly claimed as the basis of his procedures by Thomas Lufkyn, to whom women flocked in Maidstone in 1558, "as it were to a God to know all secrets, past and to come." He was in fact quite innocent of any astrological knowledge, despite his readiness to predict the number of husbands and children his clients would have, and to prophesy death in the coming month for others. Even the notorious 'Doctor' John Lambe, Buckingham's confidant, when examined by the Royal College of Physicians in 1627 proved to be ignorant of the astrological science he professed.

Pretenders of this sort continued to be common, even in

the later seventeenth century, when the dissemination of astrological guides in English made it easy enough for those with only a modest education to take up the art. Elias Ashmole complained in 1652 that astrology was being debased by the existence of "divers illiterate professors" who gave the subject an undeserved bad name; and similar protests continued to be made by many serious practitioners. They had in mind such charlatans as the wandering fortune-teller who caused havoc in a Lincolnshire town in 1695 by informing some of his clients that they were in imminent danger of death, and assuring others that they were undoubtedly bewitched. His equipment comprised some mouldy old almanacs, astrological schemes, and a copy of Wingate's *Arithmetic.*

But apart from the score or so of prominent practitioners who wrote books on the subject and conducted large-scale London practices, there were many provincial figures who were genuinely acquainted with the basic principles of judicial astrology. Edward Banbury, for example, a Glastonbury apothecary, was asked in 1653 to help in a case of stolen goods. He looked in a book, and wrote out a note, for which he charged two shillings. Accused before the quarter sessions of practising magic, he protested that he worked "according to the rules of astrology and not by a diabolical art." He may in fact have been a pupil of William Lilly. Not far away was Jasper Bale of Cheddon Fitzpaine, near Taunton, who also purported to find stolen goods by 'rules of astrology', though with a uniform lack of success. Such people could be found in most parts of England. William Ramesey, physician to Charles II, thought there were astrologers "in every town and country" [W. Ramesey, *Some Physical Considerations of the Matter, Origination, and Severall Species of Wormes,* 1668]. There were after all several hundred almanac-makers in the seventeenth century and many of these were practising astrologers. But there must have been far more practitioners at a humbler level. So often it is only an accident which makes us aware of their existence at all. Edward Ashmore, for example, a Nottingham cordwainer in the 1680s, is only known because he happened to be involved in a Chancery suit, during which his astrological activities were exposed in an effort to discredit him as a witness. The resulting depositions reveal that Ashmore had given hundreds of consultations during the course of his career.

The elite of the astrological profession, however, was to be found in London, and it was the mid-seventeenth century which saw it at the peak of its influence. How far the activities of William Lilly and his associates constituted a genuine astrological revival, how far the Interregnum merely brought into the open what had long been practised underground, is difficult to determine. Lilly himself disparaged the achievements of his predecessors and was happy to see himself as the chief restorer of "this art which was almost lost, not only here but almost all Europe over." Other contemporary testimony supports the view that astrology attained an unprecedented vogue during the Interregnum. Judicial astrology, thought Nathanael Homes in 1652, had been "heeded more of late with us than ever was (to our shame let it be spoken) in any Christian Commonwealth since the Creation." It was, agreed Thomas

Gataker in the following year, "a practice grown of late with us into great esteem." And, looking back from the next century, Daniel Defoe asserted that in the years immediately before the Great Plague of 1665 "the people . . . were more addicted to prophecies and astrological conjurations . . . than ever they were before or since."

Bernard Capp discusses the use of astrology within the medical profession:

[Perhaps] the most important application of astrology lay in the field of medicine. Traditional medical theory and practice depended heavily on astrological assumptions, especially the belief that the four humours of the body corresponded to, and were influenced by, the qualities of the planets and the signs of the zodiac. Different parts of the body were governed by particular signs, explained in most Tudor and Stuart almanacs by an illustration of the 'zodiacal man'. Illness was seen as a disturbance of the humoral balance, to be cured by restoring the equilibrium, which naturally required a close study of the state of the heavens. Most leading Tudor physicians accepted the importance of astrology, whatever their practical knowledge.

Bernard Capp in English Almanacs 1500–1800: Astrology and the Popular Press, *Cornell University Press, 1979.*

Derek Parker

SOURCE: "Astrology and Society," in *Familiar to All: William Lilly and Astrology in the Seventeenth Century,* Jonathan Cape, 1975, pp. 46-68.

[*In this excerpt, Parker discusses the views of Elizabethan society on the nature and uses of astrology.*]

> Were the stars only made to light
> Robbers and Burglarers by night?
> To wait on Drunkards, Thieves, Gold-finders,
> And Lovers solacing behind doors,
> Or giving one another Pledges
> Of matrimony under Hedges?
>   [*Hudibras* (II,II:817)]

It is difficult for a twentieth-century reader to understand the true position of an astrologer in sixteenth- or seventeenth-century society. We are so conditioned to the present popular reputation of astrology—founded on the Sun-sign newspaper columns which originated in the 1920s—that it is the common impression that astrology is too simple a system to have been taken seriously by an intelligent person for any historical period.

This is no place for an analysis of the niceties of that system; it need only be said, briefly, that the astrologers founded their attempts at character delineation and forecasting on much more complex and scientific considerations than the simple one of what astrological sign the Sun occupied when a man or woman was born. Their system entailed the calculation of the precise position of all the planets in all the signs at the moment and for the place of birth; unless he was born in the same room and within four minutes of another person, no single man could have a birth-chart identical with that of any other person ever born.

When the planetary positions had been calculated, the symbols representing the planets were placed in a birth-chart (or 'figure', or 'scheme', as the Elizabethan astrologers called it); and consideration of their relative positions and the angles they made with each other, and would make in the future as they changed position, enabled the astrologer to reach his conclusions. There were other factors to be taken into consideration also: the planets' positions within the Zodiacal signs and houses, for instance; and there was a sufficiently large number of possibilities (the critic would say) to enable the astrologer to produce evidence to support almost any prediction or contention he might make.

All the same, the system was a strict one, based on an empirical collection of information built up over at least four thousand years, with *written* evidence of astrological techniques from 500 BC onwards. There are now many books spelling out in detail the manner of calculation and interpretation of a birth-chart, which differs very little from the manner employed by Ptolemy, Petosiris or Nechepso of Egypt during the three hundred years before the birth of Christ; indeed, the documented history of the technique of astrology is as fascinating as the history of its effect on the social and political life of man. But we need not concern ourselves with it here.

What is important is to understand the climate of opinion about astrology in the sixteenth and seventeenth centuries. . . . It is an area neglected by historians; until Dr. A. L. Rowse's recent examinations of the papers of Simon Forman, an Elizabethan astrologer more or less in [William] Lilly's own class, no serious historian had given much attention to astrology and astrologers—even to John Dee, one of the most truly remarkable men of the Elizabethan age—despite the fact that they had had a very considerable influence on their time.

It is difficult for a non-historian to speak authoritatively of this influence; but there is one source from which any intelligent reader can see quite clearly the average Elizabethan's attitude to the subject—the works of Shakespeare.

One does not need to be warned of the dangers of attributing to Shakespeare the opinions he gives his characters. On the other hand, there are certain conclusions to be drawn from the many astrological allusions in the plays and poems; and from them one can build up a picture of how the Elizabethan man-in-the-street (for Shakespeare, genius though he was, was also that) regarded the influence of the planets on terrestrial affairs.

The first thing to be said is that in general the Elizabethans accepted that influence as natural, and not seriously to be questioned. Shakespeare himself undoubtedly shared that view, and moreover makes it quite clear that it was not the silly view of the modern reader of the astrological columns in the newspapers, or indeed of many unthinking twenti-

eth-century 'believers' in astrology. The position is very different, incidentally, for Lilly's great contemporary Milton, who was obviously totally uninterested in astrology. He only used astrological symbolism very sparingly in his work, though he knew enough about the subject to make an occasional pun, or an occasional semi-technical allusion:

> Among the constellations war were sprung,
> Two planets rushing from aspect malign
> Of fiercest opposition in mid sky . . .
>   [*Paradise Lost,* VI: 313]

In Sonnet 14 (and in the sonnets he was surely speaking from his own heart) Shakespeare wrote:

> Not from the stars do I my judgment pluck,
> And yet methinks I have astronomy;
> But not to tell of good or evil luck,
> Of plagues, of dearths, or seasons' quality;
> Nor can I fortune to brief minutes tell,
> Pointing to each his thunder, rain, and wind
> Or say with princes if it shall go well
> By oft predict that I in heaven find . . .

Although he was aware of the value of astrology ('astronomy' and 'astrology' were often synonyms), the Elizabethan was not given to relying on 'the stars' (by which the planets were meant; the stars of course have nothing to do with astrology) for his decisions, much less to bring him good or bad luck, or to forecast plagues or famines or even the weather—though some work on astrological weather-forecasting had been going on for a thousand years or more. He did not see astrology as a means of 'fortune-telling' which could tell a man when his personal 'weather' would be good, bad or indifferent; nor was he interested in using the science (for so it was regarded) to tell great princes whether they would win battles.

That is what the Elizabethan did *not* feel about astrology. What, then, was it good for? There are various hints. In *Julius Caesar,* for instance, in a passage which has been much misunderstood, Cassius tells Brutus that

> Men at some time are masters of their fates.
> The fault, dear Brutus, is not in our stars,
> But in ourselves, that we are underlings.

That is, there are particular moments of time when men are best able to grasp the opportunities life gives them—are best able to be 'masters of their fates'. They should be careful to note these times (which any competent astrologer could tell them), and taking them at the flood, go on to fortune. In other words, if a man remained an 'underling', it was not because he was forced to do so by the planetary positions, the influence of 'the stars', but because he did not seize the moment when the planetary positions were most propitious for him.

The intelligent Elizabethan believed in such propitious moments, and was often careful to time his important affairs to chime in with them, as Prospero does in *The Tempest,* nothing that the planets at the time of his enemies' wreck are most favourably placed for the accomplishment of his revenge:

> and by my prescience
> I find my zenith doth depend upon

> A most auspicious star, whose influence
> If now I court not, but omit, my fortunes
> Will ever after droop.

The history of this belief is long, going back at least to the time of the rise of Assyria, and even earlier. But that it was, during the sixteenth century, both general and firmly held can scarcely be questioned. Almost any contemporary author will confirm it. Raleigh, for instance, in his *History of the World,* speaks for his contemporaries in a noble passage which clearly shows how rash and foolish he would have considered anyone stupid enough to deny the astrological theory:

> And if we cannot deny but that God hath given virtues to spring and fountain, to cold earth, to plants and stones, minerals, and to the excremental parts of the basest living creatures, why should we rob the beautiful stars of their working powers? For, seeing they are many in number and of eminent beauty and magnitude, we may not think that in the treasury of his wisdom who is infinite, there can be wanting, even for every star, a peculiar virtue and operation; as every herb plant fruit and flower adorning the face of the earth hath the like. For as these were not created to beautify the earth alone and to cover and shadow her dusty face but otherwise for the use of man and beast to feed them and cure them; so were not those uncountable glorious bodies set in the firmaments to no other end than to adorn it but for instruments and organs of his divine providence, so far as it hath pleased his just will to determine?

Shakespeare, similarly, saw that 'men as plants increase / Cheered and checked even by the self-same sky', and his belief found expression again and again in his work, when he wished to comment on the governing forces that inclined men's lives this way or that. And in Sonnet 60, at a moment of pessimism:

> Nativity, once in the main of light,
> Crawls to maturity, wherewith being crowned,
> Crooked eclipses' gainst his glory fight,
> And Time that gave doth now his gift confound.

Time, that is, having given certain propitious planetary attributes at the moment of birth, is later apt to confound them by the planets' progressions.

The fact that there are so many allusions in the plays (apart from glancing references, there are for instance eight specific astrological references in *A Winter's Tale,* six in *I Henry VI,* five in the sonnets, five in *King Lear*) demonstrates not only Shakespeare's recognition of astrology as an everyday influence on life, but the fact that the meanest member of his audience would understand his references. These can even, at times, be moderately technical: when, in *Twelfth Night,* Sir Toby says to Sir Andrew, 'Were we not born under Taurus?' Sir Andrew replies, 'Taurus; that's sides and heart.' 'No, Sir,' replies Toby, 'it is legs and thighs.' And the point of the exchange (lost to modern audiences) is that they are both wrong, and that the Elizabethan audience would recognize the fact. A few lines later on, Sir Andrew underlines the effect by launching into a gobble-de-gook semi-astrological reference: 'In sooth, thou wast in very gracious fooling last night, when thou spok'st of Pigrogromitus, of the Vapians passing the Equinoctial of Quebus.' (Shakespeare was by no means averse to sending up the over-serious astrological apologist, as when Launcelot Gobbo in *The Merchant of Venice* claims that 'it was not for nothing that my nose fell a-bleeding on Black Monday last at six o'clock i' th' morning, falling out that year on Ash Wednesday was four i' th' afternoon'.)

Astrology was a useful dramatic device (a point, again, lost by modern critics). The long speech of Edmund's in *King Lear,* often quoted as 'Shakespeare's attack on astrology', is a case in point. Gloucester, it will be remembered, discovering that Edgar has apparently betrayed him, blames this and other discords in the state on 'these late eclipses in the sun and moon'. When he has left the stage, Edmund, the villain, laughs and launches into the beautifully poised, cynical speech about

> the excellent foppery of the world, that when we are sick in fortune, often the surfeits of our own behaviour, we make guilty of our disasters the sun, the moon, and stars; as if we were villains on necessity; fools by heavenly compulsion; knaves, thieves, and treachers by spherical predominance; drunkards, liars, and adulterers by an enforced obedience of planetary influence; and all that we are evil in, by a divine thrusting on.

'An admirable evasion of whoremaster man,' he continues, 'to lay his goatish disposition on the charge of a star.'

> My father compounded with my mother under the Dragon's Tail, and my nativity was under Ursa Major, so that it follows I am rough and lecherous. Fut! I should have been that I am, had the maidenliest star in the firmament twinkled on my bastardizing . . . Oh, these eclipses do portend these divisions. Fa, sol, la, mi!

The Elizabethan audience will have heard that speech with the increasing realization that Edmund was not to be trusted. How could one rely on the judgment, even the sanity, of a man who argued so against the natural state of things, the self-evident disposition of man under the planets? Instantly, the effect Shakespeare wanted—the establishment of Edmund's perversity—was achieved; and he reinforced it by inserting the high-flown allusions to the Dragon's Tail and Ursa Major, and by having Edmund, within a few lines, demonstrate his duplicity by turning about and taking the opposite view in conversation with Edgar, pretending to mirror Gloucester's attitudes.

Elsewhere in *Lear,* Shakespeare uses astrology respectfully, as when he makes Kent (wondering that Lear should have had three daughters so disparate in character as Goneril, Regan and Cordelia) say:

> It is the stars,
> The stars above us govern our conditions;
> Else one self mate and make could not beget
> Such different issue.

The differing planetary conditions at the time of their birth gave the three daughters their personalities, not the coupling of Lear and his wife.

Time and time again, in play after play, we find serious allusions to astrological forces as *naturally* exerting an influence on man; the Duke in *Measure for Measure,* the repository of all wisdom, tells Claudio, condemned, to 'be absolute for death', for he is merely

> a breath
> Servile to all the skyey influences
> That dost this habitation where thou keep'st
> Hourly afflict.

Yet if man must learn to accept with resignation certain astrological influences, there are others against which he can and must fight. Cassius pointed this out to Brutus, and Helena (a physician's daughter, and all physicians had some astrological training) says in *All's Well that Ends Well:*

> Our remedies oft in ourselves do lie,
> Which we ascribe to heaven. The fated sky
> Gives us free scope; only doth backward pull
> Our slow designs when we ourselves are dull.

Historians have consistently understated the fact that astrology was one of the very few generally recognized universal laws during the Elizabethan age. The astrological theory fitted soundly into the Elizabethan's general conception of the universe, with its great emphasis on *order*—an emphasis which stressed, certainly, the necessity for order within the State, an inflexible social order; but which reached out beyond man's life, or rather through it, to the easily discernible order within the observable universe: the order of the moving planets and the fixed stars, impressive by the fact that it seemed to regulate what otherwise would easily become a chaos, but also because it provided a paradigm by which man could learn about his place in the natural, universal order of things.

Raleigh emphasized this in his *History of the World,* and the idea appears again and again (implicitly as well as explicitly) in other Elizabethan literature. But Shakespeare puts it most memorably in Ulysses' great speech in *Troilus and Cressida:*

> The heavens themselves, the planets, and this
>   centre,
> Observe degree, priority, and place,
> Insisture, course, proportion, season, form,
> Office, and custom, in all line of order:
> And therefore is the glorious planet Sol
> In noble eminence enthron'd and spher'd
> Amidst the other; whose med'cinable eye
> Corrects the ill aspects of planets evil,
> And posts, like the commandment of a king,
> Sans check, to good and bad: but when the planets
> In evil mixture, to disorder wander,
> What plagues and what portents! what mutiny!
> What raging of the sea! shaking of earth!
> Commotion in the winds! frights, changes, horrors,
> Divert and crack, rend and deracinate
> The unity and married calm of states
> Quite from their fixture!

The passage shows more vividly than any other easily accessible quotation the Elizabethan vision of a parallel system of heavenly and earthly order, and more important

from our immediate point of view, of the palpable connection between them.

Astrology had too long been regarded as an immutable law for any but the strongest mind to ignore the fact. It would have taken as much single-minded courage for an Elizabethan positively to deny the planets their effect on man's life as for an early Victorian to deny God his influence.

The educated Elizabethan knew of the continuity of the astrological theory and its effect: of its general use in Babylonia and Egypt, and through the classics of its influence in Greece and, much more extensively, in Rome. In England, within the two hundred years before William Lilly's birth, an interest in the subject had been particular as well as general: Chaucer, whatever his own views on the subject, showed in the *Canterbury Tales* the popular view—the habit of most people of acting in accordance with the positions of the planets, if they knew them. *The Knight's Tale* shows characters acting in careful accordance with the astrological qualities of the separate hours of the day; the Wife of Bath excuses her lust by explaining how it was impressed upon her, or at least encouraged in her, by the positions of the planets at the time of her birth.

During the Renaissance, art and science continually made use of astrology and encouraged its study overtly as well as obliquely. It should be remembered that astronomers were invariably, until after Newton, also astrologers; and that the general desire for more and more accurate horoscopes was at least in part responsible for more accurate astronomical observation. Many astronomers began to suspect that astrological theory could not be as simplistic as unscientific people believed; but very few of them, even after a lifetime's study, concluded that the planets had no effect on terrestrial matters.

Tycho de Brahe, for instance, found himself (like Kepler, some years later) forced to become a court astrologer in order to maintain himself; he cast horoscopes for his patrons and their friends, and evidently did so with his tongue somewhat in his cheek, seeing the work of conventional social astrologers as quackery. But he remained until his death utterly convinced that the planets did influence man's personality and destiny, though the existing astrological techniques failed to reveal how.

England produced no really notable theoretical astrologer during the sixteenth century; but a great many distinguished men practised astrology, some of them to political effect. Perhaps the most notable of these was John Dee, still known popularly as 'Queen Elizabeth's astrologer'. This is perhaps to give the astrological side of his work and personality too much importance, though there is some foundation for such a claim. One cannot, however, underestimate the interest of his character; he was a most remarkable man, and his influence on his contemporaries was enormous. He had befriended Elizabeth while she was still a prisoner at Woodstock, and when she found herself Queen, she engaged him to calculate a propitious date for her coronation. There was a period during her reign when she called on Dee almost every day; for years she asked from time to time for advice on specific events or people, inviting him to cast horoscopes for men she wished to trust or perhaps tended to suspect, to suggest cures for her toothache, to explain the significance of a comet, or to discuss the rumours that she was threatened by witchcraft.

Elizabeth was evidently not temperamentally hostile to astrology: in a letter to Mary Stuart in 1588 she rebuked Mary for her changeability, writing: 'if it were not that I consider that by nature we are composed of earthly elements and governed by heavenly, and that I am not ignorant that our dispositions are caused in part by supernatural signs, which change every day, I could not believe that in so short a time such a change could take place.'

What astrologers tend to forget, in rightly claiming Dee as the foremost prognosticator of his time, is that ironically he was responsible to some degree, and despite himself, for the beginning of the desuetude of astrology. The rumours of sorcery and witchcraft that had first attached themselves to him during his Cambridge days persisted, and were used by his enemies. Shortly after Elizabeth's accession, Bishop Jewell preached a sermon before her which was obviously to some extent directed against Dee and others who showed an interest in witchcraft:

> It may please Your Grace to understand that this kind of people, within these last few years, are marvellously increased within your realm. These eyes have seen most evident and manifest marks of their wickedness. Your Grace's subjects pine away, even unto death, their colour fadeth, their flesh rotted, their speech is benumbed, their senses are bereft. Wherefore your poor subjects' most humble petition unto Your Highness is that the laws touching such malefactors be put into execution.

During Dee's own lifetime he was vehemently attacked by John Foxe, in his widely disseminated *Actes and Monuments*. In the 1563 edition, later ordered to be placed in every cathedral church, and displayed too in many parish churches, Foxe referred to 'Dr. Dee the great Conjurer' as 'a caller of Divils'. Dee complained at this 'damnable sklaunder', and in 1576 issued a plea that Foxe should be refrained from calling him, among other things, 'the Arche Conjurer of England'. The plea evidently succeeded, for all references to him were cut out of the 1576 edition; but the damage was done. From then until our own day, Dee has been widely regarded as a 'magician' and sorcerer, and historians have until very recently dismissed him as 'extremely credulous, extravagantly vain, and a most deluded enthusiast' (to quote *Biographica Britannica*). If the most intelligent of Elizabethan astrologers could be dismissed in that way, what hope was there for the rest? And Dr. Dee was the exception; most of them were far less intelligent than he, and were concerned mainly in acting as consultant psychologists to a wide variety of people—making astrology work for the ordinary man in the street, in the way in which Lilly was to use it. One such, certainly the best known, was Simon Forman, who was born at Quidhampton in 1552.

Left destitute by the death of his father when he was only twelve, Forman determinedly bettered himself, becoming an apprentice to a general dealer in Salisbury, but persuading a schoolboy who lodged with his master to teach him at night what he had been taught during the day. He was 'a person of indefatigable pains', as Lilly said. After some years of schoolmastering, he went to the Hague, where he studied astrology, in which he had been interested for some time. In 1583 he came to London, set up as a consultant astrologer, and remained there until his death in 1611. Among his enthusiasms was the theatre, and he has been chiefly known to historians as the man who left the earliest impressions of Shakespeare's plays by a contemporary member of the audience.

Dr A. L. Rowse's examinations of Forman's papers in the Bodleian Library reveal in some detail the kind of work Forman did (as well as, it is claimed, the identity of Shakespeare's Dark Lady, Emilia Bassano, whose favours were given as freely to the astrologer as to the playwright). Rowse names the Earl of Hertford, Frances Howard Countess of Essex, Vice-Admiral Sir William Monson, Sir Barrington Mullins, and Sir Thomas Shirley as regular clients of Forman; and he was asked a great number of varied questions, more or less important, more or less amusing. Dean Thomas Blague, of Rochester, a chaplain to the Queen, went to him to ask 'whether his wife be enchanted by Dean Wood or no,' while Mrs Blague gave Forman 26s. 8d. to look into the matter of Dean Wood's lovers, and to tell her what would become of them—and promised to pay him another five pounds 'when he [Wood] is a full friend to her'.

Forman was consulted about lawsuits, the sailing and safety of ships, the whereabouts of stolen articles; there seems to have been no question he would not answer. He took advantage of his position to make love to as many of his women clients as possible, and perhaps for this reason—as well as his tendency to get mixed up in various occult experiments—found his business gradually falling off; by the end of the sixteenth century he was practically bankrupt. But, certainly in our view, and perhaps in that of his contemporaries, he redeemed himself during the early 1590s, when he went to work as an amateur physician in the plague-stricken areas of London, even becoming infected himself.

He is sometimes described as a friend of Lilly's. Since the latter was only eight at the time of his death in 1611, this is not very likely; but certainly Lilly knew many stories about Forman, which he tells in his autobiography—one amusing and characteristic enough to quote, not only as evidence of the idiocy to which some astrologers pretended, but once again, of Lilly's racy style of narrative:

> One Coleman, clerk to Sir Thomas Beaumont of Leicestershire, having had some liberal favours both from his lady and her daughters, bragged of it, &c. The Knight brought him into the starchamber, had his servant sentenced to be pilloried, whipped, and afterwards, during life, to be imprisoned. The sentence was executed in London, and was to be in Leicestershire: two keepers were to convey Coleman from the Fleet to Leicester. My mistress [that is, Mrs. Wright, who evidently was a client of Forman's] taking consideration of Coleman and the miseries he was to suffer, went presently to Forman, acquainted

A print by Jan Luyken depicting the torture of a witch in Amsterdam in 1571.

him therewith; who, after consideration, swore Coleman had lain both with mother and daughters; and besides said that the old Lady being afflicted with fits of the mother, called him into her chamber to hold down the fits with his hands; and that he holding his hands about the breast, she said 'Lower, lower,' and put his hands below her belly; and then—He also told my mistress in what posture he lay with the young ladies, &c., and said 'they intend in Leicester to whip him to death; but I assure thee, Margery, he shall never come there; yet they set forward tomorrow,' says he; and so his two keepers did, Coleman's legs being locked with an iron chain under the horse's belly.

In this nature they travelled the first and second day; on the third day the two keepers, seeing their prisoner's civility the two preceding days, did not lock his chain under the horse's belly as formerly, but locked it only to one side. In this posture they rode some miles beyond Northampton, when on a sudden one of the keepers had a necessity to untruss, and so the other and Coleman stood still; by and by the other keeper desired Coleman to hold his horse, for he had occasion also; Coleman immediately took one of

their swords, and ran through two of the horses, killing them stark dead; gets upon the other, with one of their swords; 'Farewell, gentlemen,' quoth he, 'tell my master I have no mind to be whipped in Leicestershire,' and so went his way. The two keepers in all haste went to a gentleman's house near at hand, complaining of their misfortune, and desired of him to pursue their prisoner, which he with much civility granted; but ere the horses could be got ready, the mistress of the house came down and enquired what the matter was, went to the stable, and commanded the horses to be unsaddled, with this sharp speech—'Let the Beaumont and her daughters live honestly, none of my horses shall go forth upon this occasion.'

The kind of astrology practised by Forman (and which was to be practised by Lilly) certainly did no good to what had always been considered a serious study. While Forman claimed to be able to tell Mrs. Wright precisely in what postures Coleman coupled with his mistresses, to give her a charm to prevent her husband committing suicide, to be able to tell some housewife where a stolen jewel was, or when and how he himself would die, more serious theorists stressed that astrology could not be used to predict events; and the astronomers who were reaching out towards new conceptions of the way the universe worked, if they held to the astrological theory at all did so in the belief that it could not be used for the purposes of fortune-telling.

Their scepticism of the popular astrologer, and the ordinary man's tendency to regard him as a magician, somewhat damaged the reputation of astrology. Aubrey, many years, later, wrote of

> those darke times [when] Astrologer, Mathematician, and Conjurer were accounted the same things; and the vulgar did verily believe [Thomas Allen, the mathematician and astrologer] to be a Conjurer. He had a great many Mathematicall Instruments and Glasses in his Chamber, which did also confirme the ignorant in their opinion, and his servitor (to impose on Freshmen and simple people) would tell them that sometimes he should meet the Spirits comeing up his staires like Bees.

But the intelligent man's confidence in the astrologer remained unimpaired, and there was sufficient evidence to bolster it. Aubrey recorded that Allen had calculated the nativity of William Herbert, Earl of Pembroke, and that

> his death was foretold, which happened true at the time praedicted, at his House at Baynard's Castle, in London. He was very well in health; but because of the Fatal Direction which he lay under, he made a great Entertainment (a Supper) for his Friends: ate and dranke plentifully; went to bed, and died in his sleep.

The struggle between the opportunists who saw astrology as a means of earning a good living by playing on the credulous, and the serious theorists, had started some years before, but now became keener because there was more money about, and the very people whom it was easiest to deceive were able to pay more for the deceit. The theorists were fighting a losing battle, as far as publicity was concerned; though their work behind the scenes was much more interesting.

This focused on an attempt to make astrology more natural and scientific in nature, and to provide a bank of information on which astrologers could draw in their attempts to make personal horoscopes more accurate: to put astrological laws, in fact, on an experimental basis. The result was a growing pile of astrological books such as the *Tractatus Astrologicus* of Luce Gaurico, Bishop of Civitate. In several volumes, published in 1552, Gaurico published the horoscopes of a great number of well-known people, living and dead, and drew certain conclusions from them. He included seven popes, twenty-nine cardinals and prelates, thirty-four secular rulers, forty-one men of letters and learning, nine musicians, five artists, and forty-six men who had met violent deaths. The main result of publication, for Gaurico, was that he was attacked for libel, and had to flee his city. But his work was typical of, though more comprehensive than, several works of a similar kind.

Meanwhile astrologers, then as now, prepared and published various papers arguing about such technical matters as the division of astrological houses, or the determi-

nation of the precise moment of birth. Then there were books written in moderately technical terms, but aimed at an intelligent lay public: such as the *Mantice ou discours de la verité de divination par astrologie* published in 1558 by Pontus de Tyard, a friend of Ronsard (who himself accepted the validity of astrology). This is a dialogue in which Le Curieux argues against astrology, Mantice defends it, and the author sums up, concluding that astrologers are inaccurate in their predictions only because past astrological tables did not give the true movements of the planets, and encouraging contemporary astronomers towards greater accuracy. And indeed men like Cyprian Leowitz were tireless in working out true planetary positions and publishing them in ephemerides.

Other astrologers were working out their own theories and elaborating them, dismissing or modifying earlier systems. Joannes Francus Offusius, for instance, found Ptolemaic astrology childish, and giving up a lucrative medical practice and refusing pleasant sinecures offered by various princes, lived in virtual isolation working on his own system, in which he attempted to measure quantitatively the influence of the planets, which he believed they exerted through the four qualities rather than by any occult power. The Sun warmed and dried, the Moon moistened and chilled somewhat, Saturn produced cold and dryness, Mars heat and dryness; Venus gave out moisture and heat, while Mercury dried. Convinced that nature followed a numerical, geometrical order, Offusius worked out a complicated system of calculation by which it could be discovered how much of a planet's particular quality was exuded at any one moment of its orbit. (Hot is to dry as the pyramid to the cube; hot to cold as the pyramid to the octahedron, and so on. A system related, of course, to the Pythagorean theories of relationships between numbers and forms, forms and emotions, linking, say, music to medicine in the same terms.)

Serious work was going on in relation to astrological influences in the field of medicine: in the *Astrological Medicine* of Cornelius Schylander, an Antwerp physician, published in 1570, one is taught diagnosis (without actually having to see the patient!), and how to prognosticate the degree of danger in an illness; and twenty-seven years later, amid a great number of similar works, was published Henri de Monantheuil's *Ludus Iatromathematicus,* in which he proved to his own, and many other doctors', satisfaction that (as Hippocrates had put it two thousand years earlier) 'a physician without a knowledge of astrology has no right to call himself a physician'.

So, though criticism was growing and the climate of belief changing, astrology was still largely respectable; and the astronomers, who eventually were to become most sceptical of all, still held to it, though they were beginning to modify their opinions. Most of them had to cast horoscopes as part of their professional work. Kepler, teaching mathematics and astronomy at Graz, capital of Styria, published an annual almanac of astrological forecasts (for a fee of twenty florins a year).

There was an example of why some astronomers clung to the astrological theory: partly for money—twenty florins was one-twelfth of Kepler's whole annual income!—but partly also because the theory seemed often to work. For instance, in his first almanac, Kepler promised a cold spell and a Turkish invasion. Six months later he wrote to his friend Michael Maestlin:

> By the way, so far the almanac's predictions are proving correct. There is an unheard-of cold in our land. In the Alpine farms people die of the cold. It is reliably reported that when they arrive home and blow their noses, the noses fall off . . . As for the Turks, on January the first they devastated the whole country from Vienna to Neustadt, setting everything on fire and carrying off men and plunder.

Kepler ended his career as Court Astrologer to the Duke of Wallenstein. He called astrology 'the step-daughter of astronomy', and wrote that 'a mind accustomed to mathematical deduction, when confronted with the faulty foundations [of astrology] resists a long, long time, like an obstinate mule, until compelled by beating and curses to put its foot into that dirty puddle.' But, on the other hand, he wrote a series of wholly serious treatises on astrology, and warned his contemporaries that 'while justly rejecting the stargazers' superstitions, they should not throw out the baby with the bathwater.' 'Nothing exists,' he said elsewhere, 'nor happens in the visible sky that is not sensed in some hidden manner by the faculties of Earth and Nature: these faculties of the spirit here on earth are as much affected as the sky itself.' And, conclusively, 'the belief in the effect of the constellations derives in the first place from experience, which is so convincing that it can be denied only by people who have not examined it.'

It was the hope of Kepler and other serious-minded men that the tendency towards levity and quackery which they already discerned in the mid-sixteenth century could be stemmed. Hieronymus Wolf wrote to the astrologer Cyprian Leowitz in 1557 that astrology would never have been the object of so much envy and hatred if it had not been abused and prostituted by unscrupulous or unqualified men. He hoped that Leowitz and his colleague Girolamo Cardan would restore it to its pristine dignity and authority.

But the tide was against them. As popular belief in astrology grew, so intelligent belief in it waned. There were a number of swingeing attacks on astrologers round about the turn of the century: *A Treatise against Judicial Astrology* was published in 1601, for instance, by John Chamber, who objected to the theory on several grounds, notably that no-one could know the *precise* time of a birth (his other objections were properly regarded by astrologers as ignorant; so they are). Thomas Dekker parodied astrology in *The Raven's Almanacke* in 1609; John Cotts attacked medical astrology in 1612; Christopher Davenport and others argued on theological grounds, and indeed there had been a papal bull against astrology in 1586, and there was to be another in 1631. These had no discernible effect.

The tide was slow in turning. European publications during the first half of the seventeenth century were still largely pro-astrology, many of them serious and well argued. Ilario Altobelli, historian of the Franciscan Order, and an eminent astronomer (who was for some time in correspondence with Galileo) published a number of astrological works, as did Fr. Redento Baranzani of Vercelli, Ferrante de Septem, Alexander Vicentinia, Giacomo Filippo Tomasini of Padua, and many other Italians.

In Germany, Spain, France and northern Europe the tendency, similarly, was to uphold and strengthen astrological beliefs. There were attacks, certainly, but these came almost invariably from those who had not studied the subject very closely: one thinks of Newton's alleged response to Halley, when the latter accused him of being silly enough to believe in astrology. 'Sir: I have studied the matter. You have not.' Antonia Merenda, for instance, whose attack (the title itself is long enough to be tedious) was published in 1640, was a professor of civil law at Pavia, and his arguments against astrology are as simplistic and easily refuted as those of St. Augustine, which they resemble.

But in England at all events, such efforts were vain: the financial temptations were too great, and during the years when Lilly was learning and beginning to practise astrology, there were many more quacks than serious astrologers. He gives character sketches of some of them in his autobiography.

There was Alexander Hart, for instance, who lived out at Houndsditch, and 'had been a soldier formerly, a comely old man, of good aspect'. He practised a little medical astrology, but seems mainly to have been concerned to tell young men when they might most profitably play at dice. Lilly says that he went to Hart several times to ask him various questions, and that he failed every time to give a satisfactory answer.

Then there was Captain Bubb,

> a proper handsome man, well spoken, but withal covetous, and of no honesty, as will appear by this story, for which he stood upon the pillory. A certain butcher was robbed, going to a fair, of forty pounds. He goes to Bobb, who for ten pounds in hand paid, would help him to the thief. Appoints the butcher such a night precisely, to watch at such a place, and the thief should come thither—commanded by any means to stop him. The butcher attends according to direction.

> About twelve in the night there comes one riding very fiercely upon a full gallop, whom the butcher knocks down, and seized both upon man and horse. The butcher brings the man and horse to the next town, but then the person whom the butcher attacked was John, the servant of Dr. Bubb; for which the Captain was indicted and suffered upon the pillory, and afterwards ended his days in great disgrace.

Jeffery Neve was scarcely more respectable, and had had an interesting career in local government before setting up as an astrologer. He had been a merchant and alderman at Great Yarmouth, and in 1626 was appointed deputy water-baliff of Dover. He then got into trouble with the local aldermen for abusing his position as commissioner under Henry VIII's Bill to encourage archery: he made a small fortune by rigging the figures of the returns which entitled him to one shilling on every branch cut to make a bow.

He seems to have gone bankrupt; went to Holland to study medicine, graduated M. D. at Frankfurt, and set up in London as a quack astrologer. He put to Lilly a scheme for printing two hundred horoscopes set up to answer various questions, in an effort (modelled perhaps on Gaurico) to show astrology to be a science. But, says Lilly, 'when I had perused the first forty, I corrected thirty of them, would read over no more. I showed him how erroneous they were, desired his emendation of the rest, which he performed not.'

Then there were the downright comics, like William Poole, 'a nibbler at astrology', who had been gardener, drawer of linen, plasterer and bricklayer, and used to brag that he had 'been of seventeen professions'. He was very good company, a likeable fellow (Lilly gave away the bride at his wedding), who seems to have managed to keep out of trouble as far as predictions were concerned, though he was once accused by Sir Thomas Jay, J.P., of being suspiciously implicated in the theft of a silver cup. Perhaps he was, for he packed up and left the district; but hearing some months after that the Justice was dead and buried, he came and enquired where the grave was; and after the discharge of his belly upon the grave, left these two verses upon it, which he swore he made himself:

> Here lieth buried Sir Thomas Jay, Knight,
> Who being dead, I upon his grave did shite.

When he died, in the 1650s, Poole left all his books to Dr. Ardee, another astrologer; and 'one manuscript of my own worth one hundred of Lilly's *Introduction*'; with the note—'Item: if Dr. Ardee give my wife any thing that is mine, I wish the devil may fetch him body and soul.' So the doctor gave all Poole's books to Lilly, who passed them on to the widow.

Dr. Ardee, by the way, informed Lilly (several times) that 'an angel, one time, appeared unto him and offered him a lease of his life for one thousand years. He died about the age of four score years.' Presumably he had rejected the offer. He had been a friend of the Rev. William Bredon, Vicar of Thornton in Buckinghamshire, who was mildly interested in astrology but notoriously addicted to tobacco and drink—or rather to drinking and smoking, for when he had no tobacco, Lilly tells us, 'he would cut the bell-ropes and smoke them'.

And finally there was Nicholas Fiske, a doctor who became a friend of Lilly's soon after Lilly first became interested in astrology. Fiske was a well-educated man, who had been destined for the university, but instead had decided to give his time to privately studying medicine and astrology, both of which he practised in Colchester and later in London. Lilly admits to having learned much of literature from him; though he also accuses him, because he had Scorpio ascending, of being 'secretly envious to those he thought had more parts then himself'. He does not specify whether the 'parts' were intellectual or sexual; both in abundance fit the Scorpio personality.

There, then, was the astrological scene when Lilly came upon it. As far as England was concerned, scholarly and unscholarly attacks on the theory were increasing, and educated men were for the first time in history beginning to be persuaded that the most that could profitably be said of the subject was that it seemed likely that the positions of the planets had some effect upon terrestrial matters, but that astrologers were certainly not in complete command of the means of precisely stating that effect.

But these opinions, like the two papal Bulls, were to have very little effect upon the credulous middle class, which was now composed of men and women with a certain amount of money which they could afford to lay out upon so promising a possibility as knowing the future, forecasting good or evil luck. Jeffery Neve, Alexander Hart and Captain Bubb were the seventeenth century equivalent of the astrologers who, in the 1970s, make a reasonably lucrative living writing astrological columns for the daily press or the monthly magazines.

Lilly evidently always had a sympathetic eye for a rogue, provided he was an interesting, intelligent and amusing rogue. He was also, certainly, credulous in occult matters. He was to engage in a little fortune-telling himself, though always fairly discreetly; and he was always to maintain a much greater degree of wit, and a higher standard of literacy and often of honesty, than his colleagues.

MAGIC

Robert Hunter West

SOURCE: "The Basic Terms and Principal Authors," in *The Invisible World: A Study of Pneumatology in Elizabethan Drama*, University of Georgia Press, 1939, pp. 1-14.

[*In the following excerpt, West discusses pneumatological writings that influenced seventeenth-century beliefs regarding witchcraft, demons, and magic.*]

In The Year 1607, while *Macbeth* was perhaps on the stage in London, the Courts of Assizes of the adjacent county of Essex returned nine indictments for witchcraft, the celebrated occultist Dr. John Dee was still experimenting with his spirit stone, and a daemonologist sat on the throne of England. The learned Ben Jonson owned a manuscript of magical ceremonies, and the yet more learned Francis Bacon had gravely scribbled the margins of a work on how devils deluded old women. It was to be more than a hundred years yet before an academic history of witchcraft, as of a superstition whose time was out, would be written in England, and seventy before the bastions of the witch belief would begin to disintegrate under the pounding of John Webster. The good Sir Thomas Browne, a child of two in 1607, was mature and reputed a wise man when he wrote: "I have ever believed, and do now know, that there are witches. They that doubt of these do not only deny them, but spirits; and are obliquely, and upon consequence, a sort, not of infidels, but atheists."

That Ben Jonson ever seriously performed the rites his manuscript detailed, or that the pious if gullible Dee was guilty of black magic is improbable. That King James, for all his *Daemonologie in Three Books,* was a pedantic monster who stimulated persecution of witches in England has been disproved; and that Shakespeare believed in the spirits he wrote of has been denied. But it cannot be denied that in 1607 Englishmen—even cultivated Englishmen—were seriously aware in a way that we are not of an invisible world about them, and that they spent an appreciable share of their time thinking and writing on spirits and on those affairs of men in which spirits were believed to join. The courtier who in 1606 or 1607 saw *Macbeth* on the stage, or in the same years *The Devil's Charter* or *The Atheist's Tragedy* or *Bussy D'Ambois,* had perhaps a rather detailed understanding of scenes that in themselves are as vague to us now as the sword play in *Hamlet.* It is not likely that King James' courtiers interpreted spirit scenes by childhood impressions from Grimm's fairy tales, as has many a critic in the nineteenth and twentieth centuries. They knew rather more definitely than did editors two hundred years later what such things as *spirits, witches,* and *magicians* were conceived to be. These are terms that have nowadays only figurative or historical signification; but in 1607, as for centuries before and for generations to come, they or their equivalents were part of a universal faith that was, perhaps, as close to the people as technology is to us. There were those who knew little and those who knew much of it; there were those who rejoiced in it and those who fretted against it. But there were few or none whom it did not touch.

A later century was to characterize this faith as *animistic,* for its fundamental article was that behind or within sensible things existed certain supra-sensible living essences which, in the order of God's providence, sometimes wielded the materials of the physical world though distinct and separate from them all. These animating essences, called spirits, were of two kinds: *souls,* which were spirits vitalizing or withdrawn from bodies; and *angels,* otherwise *daemons,* which were spirits unattached, even by history, to vitalized bodies. All unbodied spirits—that is, daemons and souls of the dead—were conceived to inhabit nonspatial realms suitable to their natures, but to apply their powers sometimes also to the corporeal world and even occasionally to be represented by some temporary sensible form. As beings existing in a grade above the elementary, they were believed God's agents for the suspension and redirection or perhaps even the constant control of nature's normal courses, and to them man could address himself by means of magic.

Of magic dealing with spirits Shakespeare's contemporaries made two main divisions: ceremonial magic and witchcraft. Ceremonial magic was, roughly, the manipulation by a proper operator of certain occult and divine properties in things to attract, and perhaps to coerce, unbodied spirits. Of this magic there were—in the intention of the operator, at least—two sorts: white, which tried to identify itself with Christian worship; and black, which frankly made concessions to damned spirits. Distinct from both white and black magic was witchcraft, which was complete abandonment to damned spirits, a deliberate and unreserved worship by bargain of the devil and his demons for worldly ends.

Of these activities and of spirits there were many rationales in Elizabeth's day—some extravagant, some sober, some scoffing. Almost invariably they contained the proposition that to God all things are possible; but tacitly they recognized a qualified actualization in conformity with an eternal plan God had set for Himself to act by. There were no marvels that *a priori* could not occur; this was the ground of credulity. But there was an order to the world; and man's acquaintance with this order through revelation, experience, and reason restricted credulity to the confines of coherent surmise. As regarded unbodied spirits, such surmise touched three broad questions: do they act in the temporal world at all? What is the nature of those that do? What commerce can man have with them?

To these questions Elizabethans made answers of three general kinds: occult, which elaborated the arbitrary powers of spirits in the world and secret means of man's access to them; orthodox, which accepted on authority all spirit wonders not subversive of doctrine; and rationalistic, which tended to find sufficient explanation of every earthly event in a cause of its own category, confined the unbodied spirit to its own sphere.

These interpretations comprised clusters of general ideas that existed in varying focus in the consciousness of men, and which medieval and Renaissance thinkers systematized into bodies of theory which the late seventeenth century was to call *pneumatology.* Ideally, the literature of pneumatology was deliberate rationalization that by checking one datum against another, and all against the more general findings of theology and philosophy, acquired and applied a set of concepts for explaining, testing, and provoking spirit marvels. Actually, of course, the literature of pneumatology was rarely so cool and judicial as the ideal required. Its verdicts, nevertheless, were reasoned and inclusive; it is in their light, perhaps, that the terms and figures of Elizabethan animism take on the full intellectual meaning they could have had for Elizabethans.

It is safe, perhaps, to assume that the Elizabethan plays that use the terms and present the figures of animism draw from common sources with pneumatology—if not from pneumatology itself—and that consequently implicit in the action of such plays, though perhaps not single and consistent, is a pneumatological rationale of one sort or another. Ben Jonson and Francis Bacon, and the judge who sentenced witches, and the courtier who resorted to Dr. Dee or read the *Daemonologie,* and many hundreds besides them, knew the theory of spirits. That they applied it to the action of *Faustus* and *Macbeth* and *The Tempest* there can be hardly a doubt. Nor can there be much doubt that, within degrees proper to works of art, and each in its own way, these plays and others accommodate it.

A critic of Professor Dover Wilson's exposition of the ghost scenes in *Hamlet* has expressed doubt as to whether Shakespeare and his contemporaries were sharply aware of the distinctions Professor Wilson makes between the Protestant dogma on ghosts and the Catholic dogma, and between them both and a rationalistic stand. It may be as well questioned, of course, whether these same Englishmen knew any clear difference between occult, orthodox, and rationalistic views on daemons and on magic. The only affirmative answer possible is that whether the average educated Englishman of the sixteenth century did know the difference or not, he might have, for the distinctions between the three schools of thought were clear in many books available to him and in not a few explicit.

It is true that the sixteenth century was in possession of pneumatological doctrines bewilderingly diverse, and many vague and contradictory; it is true, too, as Professor Wilson's critic asserts, that to the Elizabethan audience of *Hamlet* conflicting hypotheses might be simultaneously present and the play action force no choice. But there is little in the literature of pneumatology to foster doubt that Elizabethans understood not only specific differences in doctrine, but the significance of those differences for a rationale of the whole. That the pneumatological rationale in *Hamlet* is less positive than that in a witch tract affords no certainty that Elizabethans missed it, or that Professor Wilson is straining the text to suit an analysis unimagined by Elizabethans.

The evidence for their clear awareness of the distinctions between occult, orthodox, and rationalistic views on spirits lies chiefly in the special pneumatological treatises of their day. The sixteenth century was flood time of this literature whose particular business it was, in part, to make such distinctions, to label according to sect and trend the myriad doctrines of pneumatology.

Needless to say, the authoritative labels were those applied by the established churches. It is in the orthodox treatises that dogmas, both ancient and contemporary, are explicitly stamped as acceptable, or as superstitious or atheistic. The last two appellations occultists and rationalists were, of course, reluctant to apply to their own beliefs. They preferred to herd with the orthodox in name at least. But of the three general orders of spirit doctrine, however called, few could be ignorant who read such works as Le Loyer's *Treatise of Specters*.

If one may judge from this literature, the theory by means of which the Elizabethan Englishman explained animistic phenomena to himself had its evolutionary source in the doctrines of the ancient and medieval world, and was, further, conspicuously supplied by the very substance of those doctrines. Constant appeal to the past for authority of scripture or of the early church or of classical or scholastic authors is characteristic of the period's polemical and expository writings on spirits. An Elizabethan Englishman might have acquaintance with animistic doctrine in any of its historical stages, and he viewed it not historically as a thing evolutionary and conditioned, but flatly—as a thing whose value was absolute, either index to truth or monument to error. Says *Orthodoxus* gravely in an English dialogue on demonic possession: "Antiquity (how gray-headed soeuer) hath no privilege to errour" [John Deacon and John Walker, *Dialogicall Discourses of Spirits and Devils,* 1601].

It is generally true, perhaps, that despite the importunity of the pagan past almost every serious pneumatological theory in Renaissance Europe had a Christian stamp. But it is equally true that a great body of opinion was so col-ored by the past as to be highly unorthodox in a time when Christian orthodoxy was both various and rigid. The courtier who dabbled in the occult, or the philosopher who was half scientist and half magician, might derive his convictions as directly from Neo-Platonic theurgists as from Scholastics or their Protestant successors. Such men as Cornelius Agrippa in the sixteenth century and Robert Fludd early in the next were seldom hesitant about diluting the doctrines of Christianity with those of antiquity.

Most ancient writers on whom such occultists relied for theory (as distinct from examples) of spirits' work in the world were Platonists. Plato's doctrine of separable form and his hints in the *Timaeus* at a hierarchy of spiritual forces, were philosophic ground to most of those ideas of daemonic mediators between the Supreme and man which were rife in the Mediterranean world and became dazzlingly attractive to the Renaissance scholar. It is true that in Renaissance literature of spirits, references to Plato himself are comparatively rare; but on his easier and more sensational followers, and on mythical seers like Trismegistus who were one with them in manner and general doctrine, there is no end of reliance. Ficino had translated the Hermetic Books and the Orphic Hymns and the somewhat more reliably attributed works of the Neo-Platonic hierophants, Iamblichus and Proclus, and their tenth century Byzantine commentator Michael Psellus. To them Renaissance daemonologists were indebted for the doctrines of theurgy and for the much assailed but persistent classification of daemons according to the elements. Less fanciful Neo-Platonists, such as Plotinus and Porphyry, contributed much, of course, to that general conception of the universe as organic which made sympathetic magic plausible.

Earlier and somewhat less formidable Platonists than the Alexandreans, but also important to daemonology in the sixteenth century, were Plutarch and Apuleius. Plutarch's *Essays,* translated into English in 1603, included much theorizing which Alexandrean Neo-Platonists and after them Christians were to borrow. Particularly important were the essays *De defectu oraculorum* and *De genio Socratis.* Apuleius, also, has a short work on the daemon of Socrates, in which he sets forth "that doctrine of daemonic beings which lies at the heart of ancient religion . . . from Plutarch onwards." Often cited, too, in the Renaissance were passages from Apuleius' *Apology,* in which he says he thinks with Plato that there are between gods and men powers that preside over the miracles of magicians.

Excepting, however, men like Robert Fludd, to whom the esoteric had a special attraction, it is probably true that English animists were more directly supplied by classical literature's fund of illustrations than by its express doctrines. The orthodox cite Apuleius' famous definition of spirits more often to refute him than to use him. But Apuleius and Plutarch had written not only works on the daemon of Socrates, but also the *Lives* and *The Golden Ass*— narrative stored with tales of magic and of spirits. These stories pneumatologists of all persuasions retailed constantly, twisting interpretation to meet their own needs. Equally levied upon, of course, were Hesiod, Lucan,

Pliny, Suetonius, Virgil, and a dozen other literary men of Greece and Rome.

But of course for the sixteenth century the truly universal and irreproachable source of such material was the Bible. Pharoah's magicians, the Witch of Endor, the daemonic possessions in the New Testament—these things, and many like them if less famous, were instances which there was no gainsaying of magic and spirits. The Bible indicated, too—if certain assumptions were made—their explanation: the kingdom of evil whose father was that Adversary that afflicted Job, tempted Adam and Eve as the Serpent, had once been Lucifer, the morning star, flung from heaven. And the Bible gave the law which the sixteenth century so dreadfully interpreted: Thou shalt not suffer a witch to live.

From the accepted books it was but a step to the *Apocrypha* and the story of the demon, Asmodeus, and that of the sons of God who defiled themselves with the daughters of men and begat giants and demons. And beyond this doubtfully scriptural material lay all the marvels of the legend and history of Christianity—Simon Magus, who bargained for the power of the Apostles and was damned; Cyprian, the necromancer who repented and suffered a martyr's death; Theophilus, whom the Virgin released from covenant with Satan. . . .

Each of these tales of magic and spirits required, of course, interpretation in the light of general doctrine. To them all the occultist applied, so far as he dared, the same semi-pagan explanations he put upon similar ethnic fables. The rationalist, on his part, denied what he could, attributed the rest to a special miraculous order of things which God had terminated with Apostolic times. For the orthodox there remained the Patristic and Scholastic close-knit, dogmatic articulation of spirit tales with fundamental doctrine. In the sixteenth century St. Augustine was a basic authority for both Protestants and Catholics, and Aquinas perhaps the most nearly final authority for Catholics. Protestant doctrine varied from Aquinas' only in some special points, not at all on the fundamentals of the reason and method of daemonic action in the world.

Probably the most inclusive, and, at the same time, perhaps the most generally known special expositions of pneumatology in the sixteenth century were the polemics on witchcraft and ghosts. In them are collected for confirmation or refutation, sometimes in quotation, more often in simplified restatement and hasty reference, almost all the pertinent tenets of philosophy and religion, illustrated by the tales and fables of literature and folklore. Frequently enough these treatises, even more contentious than compendious, serve hostile authorities poorly in exposition of their views—and often friendly authorities, especially if abstruse, little better. Many of the polemics, on the other hand, were written by men of great learning and ability. If they seem often to over-simplify their doctrine, it is because their primary aim is to make converts, so that they speak in the most direct terms possible.

Related to the polemical works in subject matter, but severed from them in compositional point of view and not so openly disseminated, were treatises and manuals on magic. These were scholarly or professional in tone rather than argumentative. Suspect as to intention and select in audience, they frequently, for the uninitiate, obscure rather than clarify their matter. They render complex what the polemics simplify, are esoteric as the polemics are democratic.

Most of the special sixteenth century literature on pneumatology falls into three general classes: polemic on spectres; theoretical and practical treatments of ceremonial magic; polemic on witchcraft. Of these the last was the most considerable in bulk and the most inclusive in subject.

The witchcraft controversy, so far as it was a thing peculiar to the sixteenth century, may be said to have opened in 1563 with the publication of *De Praestigiis Daemonum et incantationibus ac veneficiis* by the German physician, Johannes Wier. The book was inspired, apparently, by humanitarian motives, but grounded its argument against persecution of witches upon the theological plea that there were no genuine witches. Devils, it contended, performed of their own wills the crimes attributed to witches and contrived to lay the blame upon friendless women and weak persons and even to induce them to believe and confess themselves guilty. Wier's book had considerable currency. Three editions were published before 1564, and there was a French translation in 1569 that included a sixth book added to the previous five.

The principal work in the field when Wier published was the *Malleus Maleficarum* of the Inquisitors, Sprenger and Institor, which had appeared late in the preceding century and heralded the opening of the witch mania. It was the primary authority of the time on witches and their wickedness and apprehension. To its assistance against Wier and his allies came before the end of the sixteenth century dozens of treatises of varying size and importance written by churchmen and doctors and magistrates, some of whom, as they said, had tried and heard confess hundreds of witches. Nicholas Remy and Henri Boguet were prominent French judges who had been on the bench in scores of witch cases. In the last decade of the century they published works exposing witchcraft; their fellow, Pierre de Lancre, did the same in 1610.

Peter Binsfield, suffragan bishop of Treves, was a churchman who had used plenary powers against witches to half depopulate his diocese. His *De Confessionibus maleficorum* is cited by a later English writer as the work on witchcraft most pleasing to Catholics. A continental Protestant authority was Lambert Daneau, whose *Les Sorcières* was translated into English as *A Dialogue of Witches* in 1575, a year after its French publication.

But perhaps most compendious and influential of orthodox works was *La Demonomanie des Sorciers* by the famous jurist, Jean Bodin. Though his work did not appear until 1580, it replied directly to Wier. It iterates learnedly the orthodox views of dozens of authorities, pagan and Christian, and adds for good measure a few views of Bodin's own which the Sorbonne did not swallow with the best grace. It accuses Wier of being himself a witch.

Bodin was answered from England in 1584 by the Kentish

squire, Reginald Scot, in his famous *Discoverie of Witchcraft.* The discovery that Scot proffered of witchcraft was that it was imposture. Skillfully using his and England's Protestantism—he says that he writes against the massmonger as well as the witchmonger—to shield himself and his doctrine, he attacks belief in witchcraft and magic at its root by denying altogether the participation of unbodied spirits in the sensible world. To his sixteen books and an appended *Discourse of Devils and Spirits,* King James of Scotland replied briefly in 1597, calling Scot a Sadducee and Wier a witch and setting forth a severely simplified doctrine of demons.

Besides James and Scot there were many less celebrated British writers on witchcraft. Their works, like that of James, are, on the whole, marked by a certain insularity. Though within the general European tradition and expounding a demonology closely related and often indebted to that of the continent, they seem soberer, more homely, than the contemporary French, Teutonic, and Italian authors. Most of them were ministers. George Gifford, an Essex preacher, issued two works, in 1587 and 1593, in which he assumed Wier's position with some modifications. In general opposed was the eminent Cambridge theologian and preacher, William Perkins, whose sermon, *A Discourse of the Damned Art of Witchcraft,* was published posthumously in 1608. It is, perhaps, the clearest and most cogently reasoned of all the English treatises. John Cotta, a physician, also of Cambridge, exerted himself in his *Tryall of Witchcraft* published in 1616, to improve the methods for the identification of witches in order that diseased persons might not be mistakenly prosecuted.

It was impossible to write extensively on witchcraft without touching on the kindred subject of ceremonial magic, and almost all the eristics did treat of it. The most considerable work on magic of every sort was the *Disquisitionum Magicarum* of the Jesuit, Martin Delrio. It pushes with a creeping dialectical treatment through a multitudinous array of questions on all kinds of spirit dealing. Delrio and his allies had reason to treat ceremonial magic the more fully because such magic—unlike witchcraft, which was an occupation of the ignorant and the destitute—had a literature of its own, advancing claims and contentions that required answer. This literature was of two not very clearly distinguished sorts: treatises more or less academic, expounding the theory of magic; manuals, not at all academic, detailing the *modus operandi* of magic.

Of the first sort the most celebrated written within the sixteenth century and the most excoriated by the witchmongers was the *De Occulta Philosophia* of the German savant, Henry Cornelius Agrippa von Nettesheim. It was written about 1510, but the second and third of its three books were not published until 1533, although pirated and distorted versions had apparently circulated for some years before this date. It treated of Natural, Mathematical, and Ceremonial magic, of which it made out the last to be the highest and, in its operations, inclusive of the other two. Agrippa recanted and late in life wrote *De Incertitudine et Vanitate Scientiarum et Artium,* published

1532 at Cologne, in which he anathematized magic in a fairly orthodox fashion.

Not so odious as Agrippa to the witchmongers—Bodin refers to him as the greatest philosopher of his age—was Agrippa's stormy contemporary, Paracelsus, who devised and in many treatises expounded, original theories of magic and of spirits. Sometimes accepted, more often denounced, was Agrippa's preceptor, the Abbott Trithemius of Spanheim, who dabbled in all sorts of occult matters and wrote a work on magic called the *Steganographie.* Another preceptor of Agrippa, the great German humanist, Reuchlin, presented an elevated theory of magic as connected with the mystical system of the Jewish Cabala.

All the works on magic of these celebrated men were produced in the early part of the sixteenth century, but persisted as authoritative throughout the century and well into the next. With them belong some of the even earlier works of the Italian mystic, Pico della Mirandola.

Falsely attributed to Agrippa and to others of his notable stamp were the handbooks of practical magic of which many, some new, some survivals, were abroad in the sixteenth century. After Agrippa's death appeared a *Fourth Book of Occult Philosophy* fathered on him despite the objection of his pupil, Wier. It gave instructions for the commanding of good and evil spirits. Like it, but much more circumstantial in its treatment, was the *Heptameron or Magical Elements* ascribed to the fourteenth century pedant, Peter of Abano. Probably forged early in the sixteenth century, it was translated into English in 1600. Also forged, frankly black magic—that is, devil art—was the *Grimoire of Honorius,* "the Constitution of Pope Honorius the Great wherein may be found the Arcane conjurations which must be used against the spirits of darkness." Related to these works were those of the cycle of Solomon, collections of enchantments which, it was claimed, were translated from the Hebrew form in which the wise Solomon had found them efficacious. Chief monuments of this cycle were *Clavicula Salomonis,* the Key of Solomon the King, probably collected in the fourteenth and fifteenth centuries, and the *Lemegeton* or Lesser Key of Solomon. The Solomonic cycle was held to be a part of the "practical" Cabala, wonder working receipts deducible from the esoteric theory of the Cabala.

None of these works on magic directly gainsaid Christian doctrine; most tried to appeal to it as the foundation of their efficacy; yet there was hardly a one but was implicitly inimical to Christianity in its fundamental assumptions.

Not so extensive as the special literature on witchcraft and magic was that on ghosts. It was comprised chiefly in two books: the *De Spectris, lemuribus et magnis atque insolitis fragoribus* of Ludvig Lavater, Protestant minister of Tigurine in Switzerland; and the four *Livres des Spectres* of Pierre Le Loyer, a French advocate. Lavater's work appeared in 1570 and an Englishman, R. H., translated it in 1572. Le Loyer published his work in 1586 and the first book was translated into English in 1605 at which time there was also a revised edition of the French. An ally and perhaps a collaborator of Le Loyer's was the Capuchin,

Noel Taillepied, who published in 1588 a relatively brief treatise: *Psichologie ou traité de l'apparition des esprits.*

The works on ghosts were more severely denominational than those on witchcraft; for Protestant and Catholic theologians were largely in agreement on witchcraft, but definitely divided on ghosts. Lavater, asserting the Protestant position, denied that the souls of the dead ever returned to the world; they were gone, he said, to either eternal bliss or eternal punishment. Le Loyer and Taillepied reaffirmed the Catholic position that ghosts were sometimes sent to warn or to plead with men or otherwise to minister God's will.

Although the special polemic on this subject was comparatively slight—its slightness was perhaps owing in part to the fact that ghost doctrine was not the occasion of a persecution mania—the question was extensively argued as an incidental point in dogma concerning purgatory and other major tenets. Calvin, and Lavater's father-in-law, Bullinger, and many other Protestant theologians made pronouncements on the ghost question. Most of the witch-mongers, both Protestant and Catholic, have digressions on it.

A minor and subsidiary pneumatological controversy which, particularly in England, had a literature of its own was on demonic possession and exorcism. The English church inclined to deny the reality of possession since Biblical times and to condemn ministers who undertook to exorcise persons apparently possessed. In this it joined issue with both Catholics and Puritans. The position of the English church was a most uncertain one, however, for the activity of devils against men it did not deny; therefore some ministers—notably one John Darrel, a Puritan—were undertaking with seeming success to cast out devils. Darrel's pretensions were officially attacked for the Church of England by two preachers, John Deacon and John Walker, who collaborated on two long and weighty works of ten dialogues each, intended to prove Darrel an impostor and to present a proper conception of demonic assaults. Deacon and Walker entered the controversy to the assistance of Samuel Harsnett, who had written in a lighter vein than theirs against Darrel. Harsnett later took part in a similar quarrel against the Jesuit exorcist, Weston.

It is impossible now, of course, to estimate accurately the acquaintance of the populace of Elizabethan England with the special literature of pneumatology, nor does it matter particularly for purposes of this study whether such acquaintance was widespread and thorough or local and slight. That the more general tenets of spirit doctrine were common property is certain; that at least a few educated persons knew some or all of the controversial and esoteric works that refined and integrated the general ideas is equally certain. To such persons the terms and figures of animistic material in the drama might suggest concepts more complete than those of the groundling. To re-establish such concepts now is to relate the spirit episodes of the plays to a definite, if special, phase of that world to which they most naturally refer, the Elizabethan world.

Lynn Thorndike on natural magic:

Natural magic is the working of marvelous effects, which may seem preternatural, by a knowledge of occult forces in nature without resort to supernatural assistance. It was therefore regarded, unless employed for evil purposes, as permissible, whereas diabolical magic, worked by demon aid, was illicit. Natural magic was also distinguished from natural science, as being more mysterious and less explicable in universal, regular and mathematical terms. Indeed, since demons were often thought to work their magic simply by superior insight into the secrets of nature based on long experience, the connection between natural and diabolical magic was somewhat closer than that between natural magic and classified and generally accepted natural science.

As organized and systematic human scientific experimentation and research on a large scale gradually overhauled the superior but undisciplined intelligence and the long but empirical experience of the demons, the need and urge to avail oneself of their assistance has kept diminishing. On the other hand, the frontiers of natural science have been gradually extended over that wild borderland, which was once the domain of natural magic. Forests of occult virtues have been cleared; swamps of erroneous notions have been reclaimed; the old savages that inhabited them have been civilized, and the imaginary gnomes, satyrs and specters that once haunted them have ceased to exist.

Lynn Thorndike in A History of Magic and Experimental Science, Vol. VII, *Columbia University Press, 1958.*

Hiram Haydn

SOURCE: "The Science of the Counter-Renaissance," in *The Counter-Renaissance,* Charles Scribner's Sons, 1950, pp. 176-276.

[*In this excerpt, Haydn provides an overview of the three realms of magic and discusses the characteristics of the "magician-scientist" of the Counter-Renaissance.*]

The dissatisfaction of men like Agrippa and Montaigne with Scholastic science led them to positions of extreme skepticism about the existence of any ascertainable natural laws. But this is not to say that they denied the existence of these laws. They maintained rather that the knowledge of them was proper to God but not to man—that man could not, with his reason, attain to any considerable understanding of them.

This distinction is not simply a formal or dialectical one. The scientific and philosophical skepticism of the Counter-Renaissance was profoundly anti-intellectualistic. But it did not mean the complete loss of "that faith in the ultimate rationality of the universe" upon which "the very possibility of science is dependent. . . ." Even Montaigne, the arch-heretic, makes the distinction between reason and human reason, in his version of Tertullian's *credo quia impossibile.* For he hopes

> to induce Christians to believe, when they chance to meet with any incredible thing, that it is so much the more according to reason, by how much more it is against human reason.

Hence it is the impotence of man's intellect to find out the truths of nature which the leaders of the Counter-Renaissance proclaim, rather than the absence of any such truths. Hypothesis, logic, the syllogism, deductive reasoning—all the favorite instruments of Scholastic science—lead only to *the invention of an imaginary nature.* As a result, the "scientists" of the Counter-Renaissance seek other methods to the understanding of nature—methods for which the Scholastic tools are useless.

Two methods emerge as basic—those of magic and of "pure" empiricism. The first adopts a passive theory of knowledge in the interests of an aggressively individualistic motive; the second employs an aggressively active empiricism in the service of a humanitarian ideal. For the magicians seek to learn the secrets of nature largely through illumination, revelation and initiation into a body of ancient esoteric knowledge—while the radical empiricists of the Counter-Renaissance concentrate upon the investigation of the particular *facts* of nature. The first group, holding that nature is full of the *symbols* of God, believes that it may be understood only through esoteric lore and experiment, the formulas and equations and hieroglyphs of the Pythagoreans and the Cabala, alchemy and astrology—through the correct interpretation of a body of long-established secret knowledge. The second, holding equally that a synthetic knowledge of the *laws* of nature is impossible, is concerned with discovering particular natural facts which may be of practical utility.

Again, while both have *power* as their goal, they do not interpret "power" in the same way. The magicians, believing nature to be full of miracles and mysteries, hope to be able to learn how to control these by a proper manipulation of natural sympathies and antipathies, and thus to exercise an almost godlike individualistic power. The empiricists, believing nature to be full of things useful to the practical living of life, desire to make these available to mankind, for its greater comfort, health and prosperity. Both attitudes, it is obvious, are remote from the goal of medieval scientists—a knowledge of the truths of God—and from that of the orthodox Renaissance humanists, who (showing a greater interest in the arts and humanities than in natural science) found the value of all learning in its contribution to the virtuous life.

At first glance, the methods and goals of the magicians and the empiricists seem extremely different. Yet curiously enough, many of those practicing primarily in the tradition of one of these two groups also dabble in the other—or occupy an ambiguous position, partaking of each attitude, midway between the two. Paracelsus, Jerome Cardan and John Dee illustrate this ambiguity beautifully. Each seems half bombastic charlatan, half genuine scientist—at least to a twentieth-century observer.

However, the close relationship of the magic and the empiricism of the Counter-Renaissance is not so paradoxical as it superficially seems. In the first place, medieval empiricists like Roger Bacon and Albertus Magnus had never distinguished clearly between empirical science and the practical natural magic they endorsed, and one or another kind of experimentation is integral to various occult traditions. Moreover, Lynn Thorndike's assertion that "the sixteenth century in general was not an age of scientific specialization but marked by a somewhat amateurish literary interest," [*A History of Magic and Experimental Science,* Vol. V, 1941], is *in general* true, and particularly of many of the Counter-Renaissance scientists. Hence one should expect to find superstition and real scientific insight in the same men.

Moreover, the magicians and empiricists are at one on many points. Both groups are in revolt against the logician-physicists of Scholasticism; both are seeking anti-intellectualistic approaches to nature. Each endorses a "return to nature"—to use Francis Bacon's words, an "Interpretation" rather than an "Anticipation" of nature. Each, in a different sense, advocates a return to first principles—the one to an ancient body of revealed knowledge, the other to the direct observation of nature. Each is attempting a simplification of approach—the one in its reduction of the acquisition of knowledge to the learning of an established lore, the other in its reliance upon observation and the storing away of facts. Each takes part in the endorsement of the value of the humble peculiar to the Counter-Renaissance: the magicians in their protestations of humility as being merely God's chosen vessels of truth; the empiricists in their insistence upon the significance of the brute fact and their encouragement (and reception into their own number) of unlearned artisans; both in their refusal to consider *matter* as essentially undignified or bad. Finally, each group, interestingly enough, has certain affinities with the Reformation: the magicians in their emphasis upon faith and revelation, the empiricists in theirs upon a practical science, with utility as its goal.

Yet all these similarities of purpose point to an alliance, rather than to a complete identification; and it is possible in many individual cases to distinguish sharply between the practitioners of experimental magic and those of empirical science. The former, on the whole, live in a world which may best be called that of theosophy, since "theosophy shares theology's belief in the supernatural and philosophy's faith in nature"; the latter in the material world of a "neutralized" nature.

Again, both groups contribute to the decentralization process of the Counter-Renaissance: to its rejection of law and reason, and its nominalistic espousal of the particular rather than the universal—but in different ways. For the magician-scientists believe that science "rests upon an inner revelation, which is superior to sensible experience and reasoning"—thus at least roughly approximating that part of Ockham's epistemology which affirms the power of intuitive *supra-sensible* knowledge to make direct contact with a particular reality. On the other hand, the empiricist-scientists rest their knowledge solely upon observation and experiment, thereby endorsing Ockham's insistence upon the validity of intuitive *sensible* knowledge—

"for experience brings us into contact with the singular. . . ."

Hence each of these two groups, denying the validity of the abstract intellectual concept, and thus the place of reason in science, makes impossible the *study* of the *universal,* and so the understanding of the *laws* of nature. It is this common attitude which at once denies to both the status of true science, as we understand it today, and makes of them two further and allied phenomena in the decentralizing course of the Counter-Renaissance. But a clear understanding of the differences, similarities, and even overlappings of the two groups will be facilitated by an examination of their particular representatives. . . .

The occult traditions of the Counter-Renaissance are highly eclectic. Mystical Pythagoreanism, astrology, alchemy, and Neoplatonic, Cabalistic and Hermetic love meet and mingle in the doctrines of many individual figures. Yet there is a surprising unity in the outlooks, the methods, the definitions and the avowed purposes of these various esoteric factions, and for the purposes of this [essay] their detailed doctrinal differences may be largely ignored.

At any rate, this unity of outlook and method results in a general conviction that magic which, according to Agrippa, constitutes "the whole knowledge of nature, the perfection of all true philosophy," is composed of three realms: Divine Magic; dealing with "the mysteries of God," which is the chief domain of the Cabala; Celestial Magic, dealing with the celestial bodies and their influence upon the sublunary world, hence the concern of astrology and the Pythagorean science of numbers; and Natural Magic, dealing with the hidden virtues of natural objects, which is therefore the province of alchemy, magical medicine, and that "philosophy of nature" which treats the symbolic significances of sublunary phenomena.

THE THREE WORLDS OF THE CABALA
OR
THE THREE KINDS OF MAGIC

1. INTELLECTUAL or THEOLOGICAL WORLD or DIVINE MAGIC deals with "the mysteries of God." Includes: Ceremonial matters, necromancy, divination, sacred names, the "spiritual" lore: heroes, demons, demi-gods.

Chief sources:

The higher mysteries of the Cabala and the Orphic-Pythagorean-Neoplatonic line of "a certain devout philosophy," including the Hermetic *corpus.*

2. CELESTIAL or MATHEMATICAL WORLD deals with "the quantity of bodies in their three dimensions and the motion of celestial bodies," and the "influences of the stars into these lower elements." Includes: Some kinds of astrology; the science of numbers and letters; "astronomy"; arithmetic.

Chief sources:

The Pythagorean-Neoplatonic mathematics and

some branches of the Cabala and eclectic astrology (including Hermes).

3. NATURAL or ELEMENTAL WORLD or NATURAL MAGIC deals with "the occult virtues in natural objects" and "the transmutation of metals." Includes: Natural magic, or "the philosophy of nature"; alchemy.

Chief sources:

The "ancient wisdom" of Zoroaster, etc. and the Hermetic *corpus* and Albertus, Bacon, Lully and the alchemical tradition.

If this diagram is compared with one which a student of Pico has recently made of the Florentine's cosmology, as exemplified in the *Heptaplus,* it becomes evident to what extent esoteric dogma could penetrate—or, at least, did parallel—Renaissance "Christian" expositions of *Genesis.*

PICO, HEPTAPLUS

GOD
INTELLIGENCE
HEAVENS . . . .
ELEMENTS . . . .

MAN, as microcosm, is
parallel to whole
macrocosm.
A favorite esoteric concept.

THE ECLECTIC INITIATE TRADITIONS

INTELLECTUAL OR THEOLOGICAL WORLD—
DIVINE MAGIC
CELESTIAL OR MATHEMATICAL WORLD
NATURAL OR ELEMENTAL WORLD—NATURAL
MAGIC

There are, to be sure, quite definite medieval influences perceptible in the occultism and magic of the Counter-Renaissance. Cusanus' Pythagorizing interests, Lully's "Ars Magna," and the more practical and empirical natural magic of Roger Bacon and Albertus Magnus were all familiar to the sixteenth-century magicians. Yet Denis Saurat points out that, to the Renaissance, occultism meant chiefly the Cabala and Hermetic books; and unquestionably the publication of the *Zohar* (1559-60), with the research Pico and Reuchlin expended upon it, and Ficino's new Latin translation of Hermes' *Asclepius* (1469) and *Pimander* (1471), accelerated a general interest in these esoteric traditions [Denis Saurat, *Literature and Occult Tradition,* 1930]. Moreover, the Neoplatonic revival centering in the Florentine Academy had an extensive influence upon the course of sixteenth-century occultism.

For Neoplatonism had frequently tended to esotericism and eclecticism. The Syrian Neoplatonism of Iamblichus and Proclus (fourth and fifth centuries A.D.) was strongly mystical, drawing its inspiration from Pythagoras, the religious mysteries of the Orient and Egypt, and other initiate traditions, as well as from Plato and Plotinus. Indeed, to Proclus the practice of magic was the essence of religion. And these tendencies had marked the marked the course of Neoplatonism ever since. To mention only a few of the barnacles which adhered to it through the centuries (some almost from its inception)—it had come to have definite associations with Orphic theology, with Neopythagoreanism, and with the Cabala.

Many of these interests are apparent in Ficino's "certain devout philosophy," although they do not dominate his thought. But with Pico, we come to a veritable renascence of magic and esotericism. We have already observed how, in his office of reconciler of theology and philosophy, he contributed to the effort of the Renaissance Christian humanists to balance reason and faith. But Pico is not to be confined to a single tradition—or, rather, in his conviction that there is but *a single tradition of truth,* he necessarily will appear in a study of various, even (to others) conflicting traditions. And his attitude toward philosophic truth establishes that of succeeding Renaissance magician-scientists:

> For Pico, the criterion of philosophic truth consists in its constancy, in its uniformity and sameness. He understands philosophy as *philosophia perennis—as the revelation of an enduring Truth, in its main features immutable . . . . He is convinced that what is true requires no "discovery," no finding out through any personal inquiry of the individual; rather has it existed from time immemorial.* What is characteristic for Pico is hence not the way in which he *increased* the store of philosophic truth, but the way in which he made it manifest.

Ernest Cassirer not long ago advanced the thesis that Pico's most distinctive category of thought is that of symbolic thought. He saw Pico, although primarily a speculative thinker, as coming more and more—under the growing influence of mysticism—to believe "that our thinking and conceiving, in so far as it is directed toward the Divine, can never be an adequate expression, but only an image and metaphor." Thus Pico affirms that "the deepest secrets of Being can be treated in the language of numbers and figures—" which amounts to an endorsement of the Cabalistic approach to Divine and to Celestial Magic.

For by "numbers" he does not mean scientific mathematics and astronomy; he does not believe that there is any road leading "to a scientific mathematics and to an exact knowledge of nature." On the contrary, he asserts outright, "Nihil magis nocivum theologo quam frequens et assidua in mathematicis Euclidis exercitatio." The only kind of mathematics which he recognizes with approval is the sort also to be found in Reuchlin's *De arte cabalistica* and *De verbo mirifico*—magical mathematics.

Pico displays a similar enthusiasm for Natural Magic—not, to be sure, the alchemical version of Paracelsus, but a "natural philosophy" which treats of the hidden virtues of natural objects as the symbols of God. Thus he tends to deviate from the most usual Neoplatonic solutions, from Plotinus down, of the problem of "the Many and the One"—of the emanating God and the transcendent God. Professor Cassirer explains,

> Pico is no longer trying to exhibit the Many as the *effect* of the One, or to deduce them as such from their cause, with the aid of rational concepts. He sees the Many rather as *expressions,* as *images,* as *symbols* of the One.

In Pico's own highly figurative language:

> Then Bacchus, leader of the Muses, showing forth to us philosophers in his mysteries, that is in the visible symbols of nature, the invisible things of God, shall satisfy us from the abundance of the house of God, in all of which we shall, like Moses, be found faithful.

Clearly, then, Pico desires to compass the *secrets* and *mysteries* of nature. Magic abounds, he declares in his oration *Of the Dignity of Man,*

> in the loftiest mysteries, embraces the deepest contemplation of the most secret things, and at last the affinity of all nature.

The glory is God's and nature's; the magician does not exhibit the power of his own mind so much as he reveals the miracles which God has sown in nature. For magic,

> in calling forth into the light as if from their hiding-places the powers scattered and sown in the world by the loving kindness of God, does not so much work wonders as diligently serve a wonder-working nature. . . . [It,] making use of the suitable and peculiar inducements . . . for *each single thing* [my italics], brings forth into the open the miracles concealed in the recesses of the world, in the depths of nature, and in the storehouses and mysteries of God, just as if nature herself were their maker; and, as the farmer weds his elms to vines, even so does the *magus* wed earth and heaven, that is, he weds lower things to the endowments of higher things.

Pico is here referring to the Neoplatonic principle of magic

> that the world is a hierarchy of divine forces, a system of agencies forming an ascending and descending scale, in which the higher agencies command and the lower ones obey.

Pico, to be sure, does not inform us why the magus should want to "wed earth to heaven," except with the safe and pious explanation that

> nothing moves one to religion and to the worship of God more than the diligent contemplation of the wonders of God; if we thoroughly examine them by this natural magic which is my subject, we shall be compelled to sing, more ardently inspired to the worship and love of the Creator: "The heaven and all the earth are full of the majesty of thy glory."

Yet he hastens to add, "And this is enough about magic"—quite appropriately, for surely the desire of the magician to be united with the "higher agencies" whom "the lower ones obey" is motivated by his hope "to govern nature and to change it according to his wishes."

There was no doubt in Pico's nephew's mind that his uncle's motive was not simply "The worship and love of the Creator":

> Ful of pryde & desirous of glorie and mannes praise (for yet was he not kindled in the love of god) he went to Rome, and there (coveting to make a show of his conning, and litel consider-

ing how great envie he should raise against him-self) ix.C. questions he purposed, of diverse and sondry maters: as well in logike and Philosophie as divinitee, with great studie piked and sought out, as wel of the Laten auctours as the grekes: and partly set out of the secret misteries of the Hebrewes, Caldees & Arabies: and many things drawen out of the olde obscure Philosophie of Pythagoras, Trismegistus, and Orpheus, & many other thynges strange: and to all folks (except right few speciall excellent men) before that day: not unknowen only: but also unherd.

Nor did his propositions meet with much favor from the Church. . . .

Finally, Pico, with his overt statement that his *Magica Theoremata* include an interpretation of the "mysterious poems of Orpheus," and his contention that Pythagoras had founded his secret doctrine of numbers upon the model of Orphic theology, could hardly have been un-aware that "the aim of Orphism and the mysteries [was] to make gods" of men.

Thus we find illustrated in Pico all the basic characteristics of the magician-scientist of the Counter-Renaissance: his concern with the secrets or mysteries of nature; his emphasis upon the roles of revelation and initiation and interpretation in the process, rather than upon "personal inquiry"; and despite his denial of the importance of his own intellectual contribution (Pico explains, "I have wished to give assurance by this contest of mine, not so much that I know a great deal, as that I know things of which many are ignorant"), the individualistic goal of power and glory.

To be sure, this last question is wrapped up in the larger one of the distinction between "lawful" and "black" magic. Pico makes a particular and redundant point of emphasizing this difference, declaring that

> Magic has two forms, one of which depends entirely on the work and authority of devils, a thing to be abhorred, so help me the God of truth, and a monstrous thing. The other, when it is rightly pursued, is nothing else than the utter perfection of natural philosophy. . . . The former is the most deceitful of arts, the latter is a higher and more holy philosophy. The former is vain and empty, the latter, sure, trustworthy, and sound.

And we have no reason, on the face of his performance, to doubt his sincerity. Yet similar protestations are forthcoming from Paracelsus, Agrippa, John Dee, and all those other fascinating figures of the sixteenth century who are constantly embroiled in controversies over their practice of the "black art," often fleeing from the authorities and an outraged population, frequently accused of being in league with Satan—and consistently protesting their innocence.

The whole somewhat complicated problem narrows down to these alternatives: the practitioner of "lawful" magic is celebrating the majesty of God through "the diligent contemplation of the wonders of God"; while the "black" magician, sold "to the enemies of God," turns his back on God and exercises his art in pursuit of personal power. Yet

for individual cases, the problem remains unresolved. Who is to judge of the legality of the practices of a particular magician? Everyone, and therefore no one.

Consider Paracelsus. He rejects the "philosophical wisdom of the Greeks as being *a mere speculation* [my italics], utterly distinct and separate from other true arts and sciences." He attacks Thomas Aquinas—with charges of blasphemy (sic) against the "secret fire of the philosophers"—and all the rest who ignore the inner light "that is much superior to bestial reason."

> For man is assuredly born in ignorance, so that he cannot know or understand anything of himself, but only that which he receives from God, and understands from nature.

But he himself has been chosen by God for a vessel of revelation:

> From the middle of this age the Monarchy of all the Arts has been at length derived and conferred on me, Theophrastus Paracelsus, Prince of Philosophy and of Medicine. For this purpose I have been chosen by God to extinguish and blot out all the phantasies of elaborate and false works, of delusive and presumptuous words, be they the words of Aristotle, Galen, Avicenna, Mesva, or the dogmas of any among their followers.

"Not," he goes on shortly thereafter, with the "humility" of the magical tradition,

> that I praise myself: Nature praises me. Of her I am born; her I follow. She knows me, and I know her. The light which is in her I have beheld in her.

Yet this man, this self-acknowledged chosen of God and of Nature, is the "devil's disciple" to the majority of his age. And whomever he worships, he is obviously drunk with the sense of power.

However, from Raymond Lully down, the occult philosophers and magical scientists had all cherished the legend of the "Philosopher's Stone"—had envisioned the discovery of a single formula which would "reduce man's search for knowledge to a principle of unity leading to mastery of Nature" [D. B. Durand, "Nicole Oresme and the Medieval Origins of Modern Science," *Speculum,* Vol. XVI, No. 2, 1941]. It is thus unquestionably a dream of power which motivates them. And this dream finds frequent expression like the following words of Trithemius, Agrippa's teacher and friend:

> Study generates knowledge; knowledge bears love; love, likeness; likeness, communion; communion, virtue; virtue, dignity; dignity, power; and *power performs the miracle. This is the unique path to the goal of magic perception, divine as well as natural.*

Beyond this we cannot go. For it is only in a play or a story that a man permits the naïve lay world to see with what forces he is trafficking. Yet it is certainly pertinent that Marlowe's Doctor Faustus, who dips his pen into his own blood to assure us that he is really in league with Lucifer, and who travels the world with Mephistopheles, is a true son of the magician-scientists of the Counter-Renaissance. He endorses and utilizes their methods and their materials, and his imagination is fired by the same vision of god-like power. Finally, if one may believe current rumor that Marlowe's association with Ralegh, Northumberland and Hariot would give him an opportunity to watch magic and occult practices at first hand, here is important testimony to the uniformity of the magic and occultism practiced by the "seers" of the Counter-Renaissance, with that of black magic.

Faustus reveals the new spirit of the Counter-Renaissance at the outset of Marlowe's play, in his rejection of each of the Scholastic studies. He pins upon "Logicke" the definition given it by Peter Ramus, in defiance of Aristotle: "Bene disserere est finis logices." He associates medicine with alchemy. He employs the new belittling techniques of the scientific and legalistic skeptics to

> . . . the institute
> And universall body of the law.

And he sardonically applies the Reformation's doctrine of original sin and predestination to the medieval "the wages of sin is death," to argue a fatalistic necessity for universal sin and everlasting death.

Thus, he depreciates the major disciplines of the Scholastic learning through the agency of those new forces of the Counter-Renaissance which were weakening and disrupting each: Aristotle's logic, through Ramus'; Galen's medicine, through Paracelsus'; Justinian's *Institutes* through arguments like those of Agrippa; theology ("Divinitie" and "Jerome's Bible") through Calvinism. In other words, Faustus establishes himself as a child of the Counter-Renaissance before he ever mentions the word "magic."

But "'tis Magicke, Magicke that hath ravisht" him; he has already made it clear that he has the magician's itch. After reviewing "Logicke," he demands

> Affoords this Art *no greater myracle?* [my italics]

He turns to medicine with the exultant injunction to himself,

> Be a physitian *Faustus, heape up golde,*
> And be eternizde *for some wondrous cure* [my italics]

And after professing contempt for the traditional "end of physicke" as "our bodies health," he asks,

> Wouldst thou make man to live eternally?
> Or being dead, raise them to life againe?

(both dreams of the alchemical physicians in connection with their search for the Philosopher's Stone), and concludes

> *Then* this profession were to be esteemed [my italics].

The law he finds "too servile and illiberall for me"; divinity he rejects because of its denial of free will.

What he wants is a knowledge of the mysteries, secrets and miracles of "nature's treasury," and he wants it for the

power it will give him. "Yet art thou still but *Faustus,* and a man," he cries after reviewing his past exploits as a physician. It is magic alone that can provide this godlike power, and he finds that

> These Metaphysickes of Magicians,
> And Negromanticke bookes are heavenly:
> Lines, circles, sceanes, letters and characters. . . .

He exclaims,

> O what a world of profit and delight,
> Of power, of honor, of omnipotence
> Is promised to the studious Artizan?

and is jubilantly convinced that

> his dominion that exceedes in this,
> Stretcheth as farre as doth the minde of man.
> A sound Magician is a mighty god:
> Heere *Faustus* trie thy braines to gain a deitie.

These last lines do not imply that he expects to master the "science" of magic through his own intellectual efforts. Instead (and observe the use of "*sound* magician") they refer to the work involved in learning the revealed body of knowledge. Moreover, the very next lines indicate that he is aware of the need of an interpreter to guide him to an understanding of this body of revealed truth. Sending Wagner for Valdes and Cornelius, he tells himself,

> Their conference will be a greater help to me,
> Than all my labours, plodde I nere so fast.

With the arrival of Valdes and Cornelius, he announces that he

> Will be as cunning as *Agrippa* was,
> Whose shadows made *all Europe* honor him.

And the ensuing conversation follows the traditional lines of the magic of the Counter-Renaissance. Valdes declares,

> *Faustus,*
> These bookes, thy wit and our experience
> Shall make all nations to canonize us,
> As Indian Moores obey their Spanish lords,
> *So shall the subjects of every element*
> *Be alwaies serviceable to us three.*

Cornelius outlines the needs of the magician:

> He that is grounded in Astrologie,
> Inricht with tongues, well seene in minerals,
> Hath all the principles Magicke doth require,

and these three requirements—astrology; the use of languages, to read the Cabalistic and other occult literature, and to understand and pronounce "sacred names"; and alchemy—correspond very neatly to the generally approved three realms of magic: the Celestial, Divine and Natural, respectively.

But Faustus himself later gives an even more exact rendition of the three worlds of the Cabala, or the three divisions of magic, when he asks Mephistopheles for three books: first, one

> Wherein I might beholde al spels and incantations, that I

might raise up spirits when I please;

secondly, one containing

> al characters and planets of the heavens, that I
>   might know
> their motions and dispositions;

and thirdly, one

> wherin I might see al plants, hearbes and trees
>   that grow
> upon the earth.

These three correspond with scholarly exactitude to the three worlds of the Cabala and the three kinds of magic. . . .

The conversation with Valdes and Cornelius contains other references and allusions which are related to a consideration of the magical science of the Counter-Renaissance. Faustus is eager to behold "some demonstrations magicall," and Valdes requests him to bring

> wise Bacons and Albanus workes,
> The Hebrew Psalter, and new Testament.

This combination of the Jewish and Christian Cabala with the practical natural magic of Roger Bacon and Albertus Magnus, as requisites for the practice of what we soon discover to be black magic, suggest that, to Marlowe, there is no real distinction between "legitimate" and "illegitimate" magic.

An etching by Rembrandt of Dr. Faustus.

Finally, Cornelius states,

> *Valdes,* first let him know the words of art,
> And then all other ceremonies learnd,
> *Faustus* may trie his cunning by himselfe,

thereby asserting plainly once more the dependence of the "cunning" of the magician upon the set procedure of a revealed body of knowledge.

There are other passages in the play which suggest further similarities between Faustus' experience with magic and the professional accounts of the sixteenth century, but those quoted should suffice to establish the relation beyond doubt. Like the magician-scientists of the Counter-Renaissance, Faustus seeks to investigate the secrets and mysteries of nature, which are contained in the threefold world of the Cabala; like them, he practices a magic which is a revealed body of knowledge, and to which he is introduced by "masters" or initiate interpreter-guides; like them, he seeks to control Nature and plans to change its course through a union with its "higher agencies."

And so, like them, his dream is one of unlimited power. The discrepancy between his aspirations and the actual use he makes of his magical skill has often been noted. That a man with the intoxicating vision of extending his sway "as farre" as "the minde of man" might reach, and even to the condition of a "deitie," should entertain himself with the horseplay of the scenes with the Pope, the antlered Knight, and the Horse-courser, and with the stage manipulator's tricks of producing Alexander and his paramour, or a "dish of ripe grapes" in winter, is indeed ridiculous. But even a casual student of Marlowe knows that these incongruities run every-where through the ore of his rich and extravagant but often naïve genius. *Faustus* is no exception; here, as elsewhere, most of the meaty passages which show his awareness of the intellectual currents of his time are packed into the early part of the play; it is as though he wearies of the ideas he is treating after an enthusiastic beginning, and usually he regains his intellectual and aesthetic interest and power only near the end of the play. In *Doctor Faustus* the serious interest in magic drops off sharply after the first six hundred lines; indeed, most of it is crowded into the first two hundred. But as long as Marlowe is actually concerned with this aspect of his subject, the play provides the most vivid imaginative treatment of the whole field in the literature of the sixteenth century—a treatment, moreover, as authentically faithful as it is lively.

K. M. Briggs

SOURCE: "Tricksters and Quacks," in *Pale Hecate's Team: An Examination of the Beliefs on Witchcraft and Magic among Shakespeare's Contemporaries and His Immediate Successors,* The Humanities Press, 1962, pp. 131-50.

[In the following essay, Briggs examines the satire of magic and its practitioners in seventeenth-century dramas.]

The dramatists of the seventeenth century found good material in the practitioners of magic, the exorcists, astrologers and pretenders to the art of alchemy that abounded in those troubled days. From medieval times we find records of superstitious practices, and alchemy in particular enjoyed more serious repute in medieval and Tudor England than it did in the seventeenth century. The ferment of beliefs after the Reformation, the various strands of thought and the spread of scientific inquiry brought many things to the surface that had been quietly out of sight for centuries. We can ascertain from the diaries of some of the fashionable magicians how well-grounded the satires were. Some of the Chancery cases are also illuminating. In *The Anatomy of Puck* I have cited the autobiographical writings of Forman, Dee and Lilly as evidence of fairy trickery. Dee was an honest, if credulous, man, but the same cannot be said of his assistant, Kelly, who was exposed to all the temptations that beset a medium, and seems to have yielded to most of them. He undoubtedly made unscrupulous use of Dee's credulity, and he was even accused of an attempt at necromancy in the churchyard at Walton-le-Dale.

> This diabolicall questioning of the dead, for the knowledge of future accidents, was put in practice by the foresaid *Kelley;* who, vpon a certaine night, in the Parke of Walton in le dale, in the county of Lancaster, with one *Paul Waring,* (his fellow companion in such deeds of darknesse) inuocated some of the infernall regiment, to know certaine passages in the life, as also what might be known by the deuils foresight, of the manner and time of the death of a noble young Gentleman, as then in his wardship. The blacke ceremonies of that night being ended, *Kelley* demanded of one of the Gentleman's seruants, what corse was the last buried in Law-Church-yard, a Church thereunto adioyning, who told him of a poore man that was buried there but the same day. Hee and the said *Waring,* intreated this foresaid seruant, to go with them to the grave of the man so lately interred, which hee did; and withall did helpe them to digge up the carcase of the poore caitiffe, whom by their incantations, they made him (or rather some euill spirit through his Organs,) to speake, who deliuered strange predictions concerning the said Gentleman.

[J. Weever, *Ancient Funerall Monuments,* 1631]

Dee and Kelly travelled about Europe together for some years with their two wives. Finally Dee returned to England and died there in poverty, and Kelly remained in Germany to enjoy a short time of reputation and prosperity. After that he fell into disgrace with the Emperor, and the story went that he died after breaking his leg in an attempt to escape from Prague.

These two were probably the last English Alchemists to enjoy any considerable credit. The researches of the true alchemists did much for Science, but already in Chaucer's time the quacks among them were beginning to be suspect, and in King Henry VIII's reign Thomas Norton exposed the false alchemist in his *Ordinal:*

> The fals man walketh from Towne to Towne,
> For the most parte in a three-bare-Gowne;
> Ever searching with diligent awaite

> To winn his praye with some fals deceit
> Of swearing and leasing; such will not cease,
> To say how they can Silver plate increase.
> And ever they rayle with perjury;
> Saying how they can Multiplie
> Gold and silver, and in such wise
> With promise thei please the Covetise,
> And Causeth his minde to be on him sett,
> Then Falsehood and Covetise be well mett.
> But afterwards within a little while
> The Multiplier doth him beguile
> With his faire promise, and with his fals othes,
> The Covetise is brought to threed-bare clothes.

If we may judge from Norton and from such indications as William Stapleton's letter England at that time was seething with greedy attempts to make or find treasure. Norton's *Ordinal* was written to protect the ignorant from unskilled and fraudulent practitioners.

> And merveile not Lords, ne ye freinds all,
> Why so noble a *Scyence,* as all Men this Arte
>   call,
> Is here set out in *English* blunt and rude,
> For this is soe made to teach a Multitude
> Of rude people which delen with this Werkes,
> Ten Thousand *Laymen* against ten able *Clerks:*
> Whereby yearely greate Riches in this *Londe*
> Is lewdly lost, as Wisemen understonde;
> And manie men of Everie degree
> Yearely be brought to great Povertee.
> Cease *Laymen,* cease, be not in follie ever;
> Lewdnes to leave is better late than never.

By the seventeenth century the vogue for Alchemy had somewhat declined, though Ben Jonson's *Alchemist* shows that some dupes and pretenders were still to be found. The Astrologers were still high in popular credit, however, and William Lilly may be taken as a prime example of them. He enjoyed considerable reputation in his lifetime both as an astrologer and a man of learning; but he seems, even from his own account, to have been almost as shady a character as Kelly himself. In the Civil War and Commonwealth times his predictions were favourable to the Parliamentarians, and for this reason, or possibly because he may have acted as their secret agent, he was granted an annuity by the Parliament. His contemporary, Booker, was also Roundhead, and the Royalists tried to counter the influence of these two almanack makers by employing George Naworth, or Wharton, but he seems never to have been so popular as Booker or Lilly. Butler satirized Lilly in *Hudibras* under the name of Sidrophel.

> Do not our great *Reformers* use
> This *Sidrophel* to foreboad *News?*
> To write of *Victories* next year,
> And *Castles* taken yet i' th' *Air;*
> Of *Battels* fought at *Sea,* and Ships
> Sunk, two years hence, the last *Eclips?*
> A Total O'erthrow giv'n the *King*
> In *Cornwal, Horse* and *Foot,* next Spring?
> And has he not point-blank foretold
> Whats'er the close *Committee* would?
> Made *Mars* and *Saturn* for the *Cause,*
> The *Moon* for fundamental *Laws?*
> The *Ram,* and *Bull,* and *Goat* declare
> Against the Book of *Common Pray'r?*
> The *Scorpion* take the *Protestation*

An engraving of Dr. John Dee and Edward Kelly raising the dead in a cemetery.

And *Bear* engage for *Reformation?*
Made all the *Royal Stars* recant,
Compound, and take the *Covenant?*

A few lines later on Butler scoffs at the learning on which
Lilly prided himself.

> He had been long t'wards *Mathematicks,*
> *Opticks, Philosophy* and *Staticks,*
> *Magick, Horoscopy, Astrology,*
> And was *old Dog* at *Physiology;*
> But as a Dog that turns the spit,
> Bestirs himself, and plies his feet,
> To climb the *Wheel;* but all in vain,
> His own weight brings him down again:
> And still he's in the self-same place,
> Where at his setting out he was.
> So in the *Circle* of the *Arts*
> Did he advance his nat'ral Parts;
> Till falling back still, for retreat,
> He fell to *Juggle, Cant,* and *Cheat* . . .
> H'had read *Dee's* Prefaces before
> The *Dev'l,* and *Euclids* o'er and o'er.
> And all th'*Intregues,* 'twixt him and *Kelly,*
> *Lescus* and th'*Emperor* (would) tell ye.
> But with the *Moon* was more familiar
> Than e'er the *Almanack well willer.*
> Her secrets understood so clear,
> That some believ'd he had been there.

Lilly, though he had been poorly bred, was proud of his
schooling and his early bent towards knowledge. In his autobiography he tells of it in some detail, though his early
bent seems to have been towards the classics.

> For the two last Years of my being at School, I
> was in the highest Form in the School, and chief-
> est of that Form; I could then speak *Latin* as
> well as *English;* could make *Extempore* Verses
> upon any Theme; all Kinds of Verses, Hexame-
> ter, Pentameter, Phaleuciacks, Iambicks, Sapph-
> icks, etc. so that if any Scholars from remote
> Schools came to dispute, I was Ringleader to dis-
> pute with them; I could cap Verses, etc. If any
> Minister came to examine us, I was brought
> forth against him, nor would I argue with him
> unless in the *Latin* Tongue, which I found few
> of them could well speak without breaking *Pri-
> scian's* Head; which if once they did, I would
> complain to my Master, *None bene intelligit
> Linguam Latinam, nec prorsus loquitur.* In the
> Derivation of Words I found most of them de-
> fective, nor indeed were any of them good
> Grammarians.

Then, as later, Lilly's quick wit seems to have served him
well, but he sounds an intolerable prig at this time, and indeed he was reared in the strictest Puritanism; but his poverty led him to take service in London, where he fell into
dubious company, and at last took up Astrology and
Magic. He tells us how he was first introduced to this
study.

> It happened on one *Sunday* 1632, as my self and
> a Justice of Peace's Clerk were, before Service,
> discoursing of many Things, he chanced to say,
> that such a Person was a great Scholar, nay, so
> learned, that he could make an Almanack,
> which to me then was strange: One Speech begot

another, till, at last, he said, he could bring me
acquainted with one *Evans* in Gun-Powder-
Alley, who had formerly lived in *Staffordshire,*
that was an excellent wise Man, and study'd the
Black Art. The same week after we went to see
Mr. *Evans;* when we came to his House, he having been drunk the Night before, was upon his
Bed, if it be lawful to call that a Bed whereon he
then lay; he roused up himself, and, after some
Complements, he was content to instruct me in
Astrology; I attended his best Opportunities for
seven or eight Weeks, in which time I could set
a Figure perfectly.

Lilly did not confine himself to Astrology, he seems to
have covered much the same ground as Subtle did, except
that he was more prosperous, having made a match with
his master's widow, and that by his time Alchemy had
gone out of fashion. Otherwise Subtle is a good portrait
of him, hardly caricatured. Jonson's alchemist was visited
by Sir Epicure Mammon, a covetous and grandiose
knight, and by the representatives of a sect of Puritans,
both seeking the Philosopher's Stone; by a gamester who
wanted a familiar spirit to direct his play—this request
had been made to magicians from medieval times; —by a
druggist, asking directions about a propitious aspect for
his new shop and appropriate conjurations to inscribe
above the counters; by a boy who wanted to become a du-
ellist—this was a hit at Roaring Boys who are so often
mentioned in contemporary drama—by a maid who
wished to know if she would ever take precedence over her
mistress; by a sailor's wife asking her husband's whereabouts, and by a widow to know her future fortunes in
marriage. He cozens Sir Epicure Mammon by tempting
him with a woman, and then pretending that the necessary
chastity had been violated, and the spells undone.

> SUBTLE. How! What sight is here!
> Close deeds of darknesse, and that shunne the
> light!
> Bring him againe. Who is he? What, my sonne!
> O, I haue liu'd too long!
>
> MAMMON. Nay good, deare father,
> There was no vnchast purpose.
> SUBTLE. Not? and flee me,
> When I come in?
>
> MAMMON. That was my error.
>
> SUBTLE. Error?
> Guilt, guilt, my sonne. Giue it the right name.
> No maruaile,
> If I found check in our *great worke* within,
> When such affaires as these were managing!
>
> MAMMON. Why, haue you so?
>
> SUBTLE. It has stood still this halfe houre:
> And all the rest of our *lesse workes* gone back.
> Where is the instrument of wickednesse,
> My lewd false drudge?
>
> MAMMON. Nay, good sir, blame not him.
> Beleeue me,' twas against his will, or knowledge.
> I saw her by chance.
>
> SUBTLE. Will you commit more sinne
> T'excuse a varlet?

MAMMON. By my hope,' tis true, sir.

SUBTLE. Nay, then I wonder lesse, if you, for
whom
The blessing was prepar'd, would so tempt he-
auen:
And loose your fortunes.

MAMMON. Why sir?

SUBTLE. This 'll retard
The *worke,* a month at least.

MAMMON. Why, if it doe,
What remedie? but thinke it not, good father:
Our purposes were honest.

SUBTLE. As they were
So the reward will proue (*a great crack and noise
within.*)
How now! Aye me.
God, and all Saints be good to vs. (*re-enter
FACE.*)
What's that?

FACE. O, sir, we are defeated! all the *workes,*
Are flowne *in fumo:* every glasse is burst.
Fornace, and all rent downe! as if a bolt
Of thunder had beene driuen through the house.
Retorts, Receiuers, Pellicanes, Bolt-heads,
All strooke in shiuers (SUBTLE *falls downe as in
a swoune.*)

[*The Alchemist. Works of Ben Jonson,*
1937, Vol. V, act IV, sc. v]

Lilly, like Subtle, lays stress on the necessity of pure living for success with spirits, indeed this was a commonplace with magicians; and the questions his customers asked were of much the same kind. They came for his help in finding hidden treasure, and for the recovery of thefts; husbands and wives consulted him as to which should die first; they asked for success in love, to know lucky days for bargains or enterprises, the whereabouts of their friends and the cure of sickness. People were cured of epilepsy, skin diseases and the haunting of spirits by amulets, questions were resolved either by astrology or by crystal-gazing with the help of a medium, and spirits, more or less amenable according to the purity and psychic power of the conjurer, were raised at the request of the more influential patrons. The many surviving magical manuscripts show us how seriously this was taken. Some of them dealt with angels, some with devils, some with unspecified spirits or elementals; sometimes, as when a bone or piece of body was taken, we have a modified form of Kelly's necromancy; sometimes only churchyard mould was used. There were many charms for driving spirits from the ground where treasure was hid. All these seem to have survived alchemical practices. One of the latest poetic references to the trickster alchemists is to be found in Cartwright's Poems, and perhaps it is already a literary allusion.

Come! I will undeceive thee, they that tread
Those vain Aëriall waies,
Are like young Heyrs and Alchymists misled
To waste their Wealth and Daies,
For searching thus to be for ever Rich
They only find a Med'cine for the itch.

There may be a reference here to the ritual purity enjoined on Sir Epicure.

Shirley, in his borrowing from *The Alchemist* makes fun of another superstition. The fool, Pazzorello, wishes to be made shot-free, like the soldier mentioned by Aubrey; and Flavia is disguised not as a fairy but a witch.

DIDIMO. That is she.

PAZZORELLO. That old hag?

DIDIMO. Good words; she has come two hundred mile to-day upon a distaff, salute her, she expects it.

PAZZORELLO. Would you have me kiss the devil?

DIDIMO. Do, as I say. —
This is the gentleman, my loving aunt,
For whom I do beseech your powerful spells.

FLAVIA. To make him slick (stick) and shot free?

DIDIMO. Right, dear aunt,
He is a precious friend of mine, and one
That will be ready servant to your pleasures,
At midnight, or what hour you please to call him.

PAZZORELLO. Thou wouldst not have me lie with the old witch?
What a generation of hobgoblins should we have together!

DIDIMO. Nor, for this benefit, shall you find him (not) only
Obedient to yourself, but very dutiful
To any devil you have.

FLAVIA. He is welcome, child.

PAZZORELLO. What a saltpetre breath she has!

FLAVIA. Where is Mephistophilus?

PAZZORELLO. No more devils, if you love me.

FLAVIA. I must have some to search him.

This is, of course, the prelude to removing his money and jewels; and he then receives even rougher treatment than Dapper.

FLAVIA. *Now rub his temples, forehead eke,*
Give his nose a gentle tweak,

Strike off paleness, and bestow
On either cheek a lusty blow;
Take him by the hair, and pull it:
Now his head's free from sword and bullet.

PAZZORELLO. What will they do with the rest of my body? (*aside*)

FLAVIA. *Grasp his neck till he groan twice.*

PAZZORELLO. Oh, oh!

FLAVIA. *Enough, now let the young man rise.*
Thus on his shoulder I dispense
My wand to keep all bullets thence; . . .
Farewell to both! For now must I
On my winged gennet flie.—

Suckle and Hoppo, fetch long strides
By your mistress as she rides. (Exit FLAVIA.)

PAZZORELLO. Whither is she gone now?

DIDIMO. Home to a witches' upsitting; she's there by this time.

PAZZORELLO. Where?

DIDIMO. In Lapland; she will cross the sea in an egg-shell, and upon land hath a thousand ways to convey herself in a minute; I did but whistle, and she came to me.

PAZZORELLO. She knows your whistle belike.

[*The Young Admiral. The Dramatic Works and Poems of James Shirley,* 1833, Vol. III, Act IV, sc. i]

Flavia was well-read in witch plays, all her devils came from them. But, derivative though the scene may be, it attaches itself, as *The Alchemist* does, to a real contemporary superstition. *The Alchemist* is, however, the more realistic of the two, and is enriched by half the trickeries exposed in the Jacobean pamphlets, and richest of all in its alchemical talk. John Read, in his *Alchemist in Life, Literature and Art,* while admitting the accuracy of the jargon, does not believe that Subtle ever did any practical alchemy. It is clear, however, from the opening quarrel that he was an alchemist, though a cheating one. Face says:

When all your *alchemy,* and your *algebra,*
Your *mineralls, vegetalls,* and *animalls,*
Your coniuring, cosning, and your dosen of
    trades,
Could not relieue your corps, with so much lin-
    nen
Would make you tinder, but to see a fire;
I ga' you count'nance, credit for your coales,
Your stills, your glasses, your *materialls;*
Built you a fornace, drew you customers,
Aduanc'd all your black arts; lent you, beside,
A house to practise in.—

A little later he says, describing Subtle's trickeries:

Haue all thy tricks
Of cosning with a hollow cole, dust, scrapings,
Searching for things lost, with a sive, and
    sheeres,
Erecting figures, in your rowes of houses,
And taking in of shaddowes, with a glasse,
Told in red letters: And a face, cut for thee,
Worse than GAMALIEL RATSEY'S.

Evidently Subtle sometimes used a coal, or, as Surly later suggested, a hollow rod stopped with mercury, with silver or gold in it, which, when burnt away, left the metal exposed, and so led on his patrons with the hope of success. It was a famous trick of the quack alchemists. From this account Subtle had many strings to his bow; from the sieve and shears, which was almost amateur magic, to astrology and crystal gazing; but his chief occupation was in alchemy, and he had taught Face as he boasted, a handsome smattering of the jargon, which they displayed in the alchemical catechism recited before Ananias.

The Wise-woman of Hogsdon, in Heywood's play of that name, had no such skill, but depended solely on the information given by the credulity of her customers. It is a satire on the perennial willingness of human beings to help in cheating themselves in supernatural matters. Anyone who has ever played at fortune-telling can vouch for the accuracy of this part of Heywood's representation. If he is to be equally depended upon in his account of the Wise Woman's elaborate arrangements for forwarding illicit love affairs and disposing of unwanted babies, it is plain that there was some reason for the severity of the witch persecutions. It is surprising that so modest and respectable a girl as the first Luce should have been so well acquainted with her. The best description of her activities is given in her initiation of the Second Luce, who, disguised as a boy, has taken service with her.

LUCE. But Mistris, what meane all these womens pictures, hang'd here in your withdrawing roome?

WISEWO. Ile tell thee, Boy; marry thou must be secret. When any Citizens, or young Gentlemen come hither, under a colour to know their Fortunes, they looke upon these pictures, and which of them they best like, she is ready with a wet finger: here they have all the furniture belonging to a privat-chamber, bedde, bed-fellow and all; but mum, thou knowest my meaning, Iacke.

LUCE. But I see comming and going, Maids, or such as goe for Maids, some of them, as if they were ready to lie downe, sometimes two or three delivered in one night; then suddenly leave their Brats behind them, and conveigh themselves into the Citie againe: what becomes of their Children?

WISEWO. Those be Kitchin-maids, and Chamber-maids, and some-times good men's Daughters; who having catcht a clap, and growing near their time, get leave to see their friends in the Countrey, for a weeke or so: then hither they come, and for a matter of money, here they are delivered. I have a Midwife or two belonging to the house, and one *Sir Boniface,* a Deacon, that makes a shift to christen the Infants; we have poore, honest and secret Neighbours, that stand for common Gossips. But dost thou not know this?

LUCE. Yes, now I doe: but what after becomes of the poore Infants?

WISEWO. Why, in the night we send them abroad, and lay one at this man's doore, and another at that, such as are able to keep them; and what after becomes of them, we inquire not. And this is another string to my Bowe.

LUCE. Most strange, that woman's brain should
    apprehend
Such lawlesse, indirect and horrid meanes
For covetous gaine! How many unknowne
    Trades
Women and men are free of, which they never
Had Charter for? but Mistris, are you so
Cunning as you make your selfe: you can
Neither write nor reade, what doe you with
    those

Bookes you so often turn over?

WISEWO. Why tell the leaves; for to be ignorant, and seeme ignorant, what greater folly?

LUCE. Beleeve me, this is a cunning Woman; neither hath shee her name for nothing, who out of her ignorance can foole so many that thinke themselves wise. But wherefore have you built this little Closet close to the doore, where sitting, you may heare every word spoken, by all such as aske for you.

WISEWO. True, and therefore I built it: if any knock, you must to the doore and question them, to find what they come about, if to this purpose or to that. Now they ignorantly telling thee their errand, which I sitting in my Closet, overheare, presently come forth, and tell them the cause of their comming, with every word that hath past betwixt you in private: which they admiring, and thinking it to be miraculous, by their report I become thus famous.

> [Thomas Heywood, *The Wise Woman of Hogsdon,* 1638, Act III, sc. ii]

Like Lilly the Wise Woman gives a list of her predecessors and contemporaries:

> You have heard of Mother *Nottingham,* who for her time, was prettily well skill'd in casting of Waters: and after her, Mother *Bombye;* and then there is one *Hatfield* in Pepper-Alley, hee doth prettie well for a thing that's lost. There's another in *Cole-harbour,* that's skill'd in the Planets. Mother *Sturton* in *Goulden-Lane* is for Forespeaking; Mother *Phillips* of the *Banke-side,* for the weaknesse of the backe: and then there's a very reverent Matron on *Clerkenwell-Green,* good at many things: Mistris *Mary* on the *Banke-side* is for recting a Figure: and one (what doe you call her) in *Westminster,* that practiseth the Booke and the Key, and the Sive and the Sheares: and all doe well, according to their talent. For my self, let the world speake.

This, though it contains some of the traditional witches, is evidently meant to be a catalogue of shabby and disreputable practitioners of the type of Lilly's first master Evans; though Evans was more learned than the Wise Woman. Lilly gives us a lively account of him:

> He was by Birth a *Welchman,* a *Master of Arts,* and in Sacred Orders; he had formerly had a Cure of Souls in *Staffordshire,* but was now come to try his Fortunes at *London,* being in a manner enforced to fly for some Offences very scandalous committed by him in these Parts, where he had lately lived; for he gave Judgment upon things lost, the only Shame of Astrology: He was the most *Saturnine* Person my Eyes ever beheld, either before I practised or since; of a middle Stature, broad Forehead, Beetle-brow'd, thick Shoulders, flat Nosed, full Lips, downlook'd, black curling stiff Hair, splay-footed; to give him his Right, he had the most piercing Judgment naturally upon a Figure of Theft, and many other Questions, that I ever met withal; yet for Money he would willingly give contrary Judgments, was much addicted to Debauchery,

and then very abusive and quarrelsome, seldom without a black Eye, or one Mischief or other. This is the same *Evans* who made so many *Antimonial* Cups, upon the Sale whereof he principally subsisted; he understood *Latin* very well, the *Greek* Tongue not at all: He had some Arts above, and beyond Astrology, for he was well versed in the Nature of Spirits, and had many times used the circular way of invocating.

The Wise Woman pretended to the art of astrology, but disavowed the dangerous traffic with spirits:

> BOYSTER. Can'st conjure?
>
> WISE WOMAN. That's a foule word! But I can tell you your Fortune, as they say; I have some little skill in Palmistry, but never had to doe with the devill.

It was a traffic too near witchcraft for her to claim it; and in the same way Subtle only gives the fly familiar under a promise of secrecy. Lilly and Evans, however, managed it with impunity, by claiming to have to do with angels.

The Wise Woman had her pretensions to learning; for she says: "In, in: Ile but read a little of *Ptolomie* and Erra Pater; and when I have cast a Figure, Ile come to you presently." The second Luce, however, who is Heywood's mouthpiece in this, entirely disbelieves in her skill, though she is not sceptical about occult arts in properly skilled hands.

> Tis strange the Ignorant should be thus fool'd.
> What can this Witch, this Wizard, or old Trot,
> Doe by Inchantment, or by Magicke spell?
> Such as professe that Art should be deepe Schollers.
> What reading can this simple Woman have?
> 'Tis palpable grosse foolery.

The Alchemist and *The Wise Woman of Hogsdon* are two plays which treat of this type of quackery at the greatest length, but references to it are so common throughout the dramatists as to lead one to suppose that the abuse was a rampant one. Massinger in *The City Madam,* has an astrologer, Stargaze, something after Lilly's type, but rather more domesticated. He is Lady Frugal's tame astrologer.

> You shall first know him, then admire him
> For a man of many parts, and those parts rare
>   ones.
> He's every thing, indeed; parcel physician,
> And as such proscribes my diet, and fortels
> My dreams when I eat potatoes; parcel poet,
> And sings encomiums to my virtues sweetly;
> My antecedent, or my gentleman-usher,
> And as the stars move, with that due proportion
> He walks before me: but an absolute master
> In the calculation of nativities:
> Guided by that ne'er-erring science call'd,
> Judicial Astrology.
>
> [*The City Madam. The Plays of Philip Massinger,* ed. F. Cunningham, Act II, sc. ii]

Fletcher's references to magicians and astrologers are a good example of his general attitude towards the supernatural. He uses it much as a nineteenth-century author would have done, for decoration. From his own poem

Upon an Honest Man's Fortune we know him to have dis-believed in astrology, and his fairly frequent allusions to it are generally of trickery or delusion.

In *Thierry and Theoderet* the wicked doctor, Lecure, dis-guises himself as an astrologer, and by a false prophecy tries to procure the death of the queen. Vecchio in *The Chances,* is as much an impostor, though an amiable one. His manipulation brings about the happy ending, but it seems he had previously made profit out of fraud.

> Those your Grace saw,
> Which you thought spirits, were my Neighbours
>   Children
> Whom I instruct in Grammar here, and Musick;
> Their shapes, the Peoples fond opinions,
> Believing I can conjure, and oft repairing
> To know of things stoln from 'em, I keep about
>   me,
> And always have in readiness, by conjecture
> Out of their own confessions, I oft tell 'em
> Things that by chance have fallen out so.

> [John Fletcher, *The Chances. The Works of
> Beaumont and Fletcher,* Vol. IV, Act V, sc.
>   iii]

Both these are alterations of the material used. The histor-ical foundation of *Thierry and Theoderet* provided proba-bly by de Serres, is very slight, with no mention of this par-ticular incident, and Fletcher has changed the end of *La Senora Cornelia,* from which the plot of *The Chances* was taken. The mock conjurer, Vecchio, replaces a priest, who was in the habit of showing his guests curiosities, but with no hint of magic. This is characteristic of Fletcher. Wher-ever possible he gave a supernatural, or mock supernatu-ral, turn to his plots, but with no appearance of belief be-hind it; his use of the subject was purely decorative.

In Day's *Law Tricks* Polymetus is a quick astrologer, and in Randolph's *Jealous Lovers* Demetrius is disguised as an astrologer, and Ballio professes to be able to confer invin-cibility in love:

> I'll teach you in one fortnight by Astrologie
> To make each Burgesse in all Thebes—your
>   Cuckold,

and the Epilogue is couched in astrological language: "I find by the horoscope, and the elevation of the bright Al-deboran a Sextile opposition; and that th'Almutes is in-clining to the enemies house."

One of Randolph's poems is full of references to magi-cians, contemporary and legendary, as well as to astrolo-gers in general, to Merlin, Friar Bacon and Friar Bungay, Dr. Lambe, and Dame Eleanor Davies, the queer, crazed wife of Sir John Davies, whose predictions frightened Henrietta Maria and annoyed King Charles.

> Is *Frier Bacon* nothing but a name?
> Or is all Witchcraft brain'd with Doctor *Lamb?*
> Does none the learned *Bungies* soul inherit?
> Has Madam *Davers,* dispossest her spirit?
> Or will the Welshmen give me leave to say
> There is no faith in *Merlin?* none, though they
> Dare swear each letter Creed, and pawn their
>   blood

> He prophecied an age before the flood
> Of holy *Dee,* which was as some have said
> Ten generations ere the Ark was made.
> All your predictions but impostures are,
> And you but prophecy of things that were.
> And you Coelestiall juglers that pretend
> You are acquainted with the stars, and send
> Your spies to search what's done in every
>   sphear,
> Keeping your State-intelligences there;
> Your art is all deceit, for now I see
> Against the Rules of deep Astrology,
> Girls may be got when *Mars* his power doth
>   vaunt,
> And boyes when *Venus* is Predominant.

There are similar references in Master's poem *On Lute Strings Cat-Eaten,* which is . . . full of folklore references, and . . . much less known than it deserves to be. . . . Davenant refers to Booker and Allestree, a pair of popular almanack makers. These almanacks and rehashing of old prophecies flooded the press at this time, and were eagerly read by the unlearned, even among the puritans. They sur-vive to the present day, though Old Moore has outlived Merlin in popularity.

Another type of quack was the pretended exorcist, like Dr. Pinch the Conjurer in *The Comedy of Errors.* It was against these that Samuel Harsnett wrote his two books, *A Discovery of the Fraudulent Practises of John Darrell* (1599) and *A Declaration of Egregious Popish Impostures* (1603). Sometimes these exorcists worked, like Dr. Pinch, on an unwilling patient, sometimes on an hysterical sub-ject who began by inventing experiences and would after-wards gladly have escaped from treatment, like Sara Wil-liams and her sister Fid; sometimes, as in the cases of Grace Sowerbutts and William Perry, they trained an ac-complice to feign possession so that they might show their skill. In the *Declaration of Popish Impostures* Harsnett worked on a cold trail, for the case was some years old, and his chief source of evidence was an hysterical girl, very apt to say what gave most satisfaction to her hearer. It is probable that the priests who assembled at Sir George Peckham's house, at Lord Vaux's or at the Earl of Lin-coln's were honestly doing their best for their patients, however mistaken their methods. The same does not seem to be true of the other cases, though some of these, too, may have been the dupes of their patients. For there were those who feigned possession on their own account, either to satisfy their malice or for gain. Among these were the beggars, after the type of Mad Tom, the disguise assumed by Edgar in *King Lear.* These Bedlam Men, real or pre-tended madmen who were supposed to be possessed, and who roved about the country begging, must have added a very real terror to quiet places. The Abram Cove, as he was called, was often treated in the cant literature of the times. One of the fullest descriptions of him is in Dekker's *O Per Se O.*

> The abram Cove is a lusty strong rogue, who
> walketh with a slade about his quarroms (a sheet
> about his body) trining (hanging) to his hams,
> bandolierwise, for all the world as cutpurses and
> thieves wear their sheets to the gallows, in which
> their trulls are to bury them. . . . These, walk-

ing up and down the country, are more terrible to women and children, than the name of Raw-head and Bloody-bones, Robin Goodfellow, or any other hobgoblin. . . .

And to colour their villainy the better, every one of these abrams hath a several gesture in playing his part. Some make an horrid noise, hollowly sounding; some whoop, some hollow, some show only a kind of wild distracted ugly look, uttering a simple kind of maunding, with these addition of words: 'Well and wisely'. . . .

The second begins: 'Now dame, well and wisely, what will you give poor Tom now? One pound of your sheep's feathers to make poor Tom a blanket? Or one cutting of your sow side, no bigger than my arm? or one piece of your salt meat to make poor Tom a sharing horn? or one cross of your small silver towards the buying a pair of shoes—well and wisely.

There was a certain fashion for writing songs about these men at the beginning of the seventeenth century, which passed into folklore in such songs as the Somersetshire "Bedlam." The whole subject of madness was of great interest to the writers of that time, and a sub-product of it was an unusual number of nonsense verses, almost after a surrealistic style.

A very early play to deal with pretended exorcism was *The Buggbears,* one of the few manuscripts which escaped the destructive hand of Warburton's cook. It was translated from *La Spiritata* of Grazzini (1561) by one John Jeffrey, not otherwise known as an author. The editor, Warwick Bond, on the evidence of the orthography and metrical style, put it as early as 1566—60. If it was written as early as that the Author had not been long in assimilating Weyer's *De Praestigiis Daemonum,* which was first published in 1563. It almost seems as if Reginald Scot must have owed something to the list of spirits given by the mock conjurer. The trickster in this play was not a professional, the plot is about a trick, with pretended hauntings and exorcisms, played by some young men and servants on their covetous elders. It is the first of the sceptical plays.

Very near to the exorcists were the witch-finders, of which Matthew Hopkins made himself the type. The general hatred in which he was held gave rise to a story that he was swum himself at the last and proved to be a witch. One can only hope that the tale was true, though others said that he retired on the profits of his trade. Henry King, in a neat embroidery on the text "The sin of rebellion is as witchcraft" begins with a reference to Hopkins.

> We need not here on skillfull *Hopkins* call,
> The States allowed *Witch-finder General,*
> For (though Rebellion wants no Cad nor Elfe,
> But is a perfect Witchcraft in it self)
> We could with little help of art reveal
> Those learn'd Magitians with whom you deal:
> We all Your Juggles both for Time and Place
> From *Darby*-house to *Westminster* can Trace,
> The Circle where the factious Jangle meet
> To Trample Law and Gospel under feet;
> In which, like Bells rung backward, they pro-
>   claim

> The Kingdom by their Wild-fire set on flame,
> And, quite Perverting their First Rules, invent
> What mischief may be done by Parliament.
> Ye know your holy Flamens, and can tell
> What Spirits Vote within the Oracle:
> Have found the Spells and Incantations too
> By whose assistance You such Wonders do.

This contains references to a good many sides of the witch-craft belief, but the fullest verse comment on Hopkins and his methods comes from Butler.

> Has not this present *Parliament*
> A *Legar* to the Devil sent,
> Fully empower'd to Treat about
> Finding revolted *Witches* out:
> And has not he, within a year,
> Hang'd threescore of them in one *Shire?*
> Some only for not being *drown'd.*
> And some for sitting above ground,
> Whole *days* and *nights* upon their *breeches,*
> And feeling pain, were hang'd for *Witches.*
> And some for putting *Knavish* tricks
> Upon *Green-Geese,* and *Turkey Chicks,*
> Or *Pigs,* that suddenly deceast,
> Of griefe unnat'ral, as he guest;
> Who after prov'd himself a *Witch.*
> And made a Rod for his own *breech.*

[S. Butler, Hudibras]

Rudolf Steiner on Paracelsus and the microcosm and macrocosm:

Man is the universe in his own particular way; he regards his oneness with the universe as a duality: he is the very same that the universe is; but he is the universe as a repetition, as a single being. This is the contrast which Paracelsus feels as the Microcosm (Man) and the Macrocosm (Universe). Man, for him, is the universe in miniature. That which makes man regard his relationship to the world in this way, that is his spirit. This spirit appears as if bound to a single being, to a single organism: and this organism belongs, by the very nature of its whole being, to the mighty stream of the universe. It is one member, one link in that whole, having its very existence only in relation with all the other links or members thereof. But spirit appears as an out-come of this single, separated organism, and sees itself at the outset as bound up only with that organism. It tears loose this organism from the mother earth out of which it has grown. So, for Paracelsus, a deep-seated connection between man and the universe lies hidden in the basic foundations of being, a connection which is hidden through the presence of "spirit." That spirit which leads us to higher insight by making knowledge possible, and leads on this knowledge to a new birth on a higher level—this has, as its first result for us men, to veil from us our own oneness with the whole.

Rudolf Steiner in Mystics of the Renaissance, *G. P. Putnam's Sons, 1911.*

Beyond these obvious quacks there were a certain number of old women who blackmailed their neighbours by claiming powers which they knew to be imaginary, but the most part of them believed themselves to be witches, and from the beginning to the middle of the century these claims became increasingly dangerous.

Brian P. Copenhaver

SOURCE: "Natural Magic, Hermetism, and Occultism in Early Modern Science," in *Reappraisals of the Scientific Revolution,* edited by David C. Lindberg and Robert S. Westman, Cambridge University Press, 1990, pp. 261-302.

[*In the following essay, Copenhaver discusses the concepts of magic and hermeticism within the context of the scientific revolution.*]

*Hermes Trismegistus and early modern science:
The "Yates thesis"*

A quarter of a century ago, in 1964, Dame Frances Yates published *Giordano Bruno and the Hermetic Tradition.* In the first half of this book, Yates described the ancient sources of her hermetic tradition and their rediscovery and interpretation by such eminent Renaissance thinkers as Marsilio Ficino and Pico della Mirandola. In the second half of her extraordinarily influential work, she depicted the controversial Bruno not as a martyr for the progress of science but as a magus, whose program of religious and cultural reform, rooted in hermetic texts mistakenly dated to remotest Egyptian antiquity, was retrograde rather than progressive. Yates sharply opposed Bruno's Copernicanism, which she associated with animism, magic, and an essentially pictorial world view, to the heliocentrism of such persons as Kepler and Galileo, whom she connected with "genuine science" and the study of nature through quantitative analysis. Yates had strong views on the seventeenth century as a watershed between a murky magical past and a future clarified by the advance of science: "No one will deny that the seventeenth century represents that momentous hour in the history of man in which his feet first began to tread securely in the paths which have since led him unerringly onwards to that mastery over nature in modern science which has been the astonishing achievement of modern European man." "With the history of genuine science," she added, "this book has nothing whatever to do," but in the history of science she detected a failure, "a gap." "The history of science can explain and follow the various stages leading to the emergence of modern science in the seventeenth century," she contended, "but it does not explain *why* this happened at this time."

Yates then proposed that, since "an intellectual movement" originates in "a movement of will," *one* source of the movement called the Scientific Revolution might be that new attitude toward the relation between will and the world that she detected in Renaissance reactions to the *Hermetica.* "Whence and how had this new direction [in science] arisen?" she asked. "One answer . . . is 'Hermes Trismegistus.' " She explained that the name Hermes

Trismegistus meant a great many things to her: magic; esoteric numerology; ontological and methodological monism; Ficino's Neoplatonism and Pico's Cabala; Bruno's emblematic heliocentrism; but above all the chronological errors that legitimized the *Hermetica* for Renaissance Christians. She maintained that the same Christian scholars who read in the *Hermetica* a directive to "operate" magically on the world also extended that mandate toward scientific analysis and its technological operations. In John Dee, "a genuine mathematician," she found her best exemplar of the magus whose will reached not only beyond the world but also toward it, and in Isaac Newton she saw a beneficiary of Bruno's hermetic heliocentrism. "Drained of its animism," she claimed, ". . . Bruno's universe would turn into something like the universe of Isaac Newton."

All this Dame Frances wrote in the last chapter of *Giordano Bruno,* which contains the germ of what later became known as the "Yates thesis" on the relation between "hermeticism" and the rise of modern science. In this essay I shall explore some problems with this thesis, whose author always understood it, I believe, more as a stimulus for the research of other historians than as her own definitive response to central historical questions. My own inquiries, in large measure inspired by Dame Frances's example, have convinced me that she was right to see magic, astrology, Cabala, and related belief systems as proper objects of study for the history of science but that her conclusions and speculations on these topics, especially in light of their very great influence, deserve the debate they have provoked and still require correction. Before proposing a few corrections in an essay whose scope cannot match the broader implications, both substantive and methodological, of her work, let me review what Yates and others wrote about Hermes and science after the publication of *Giordano Bruno.*

In 1966, J. E. McGuire and P. M. Rattansi published their widely read article "Newton and the 'Pipes of Pan.' " McGuire and Rattand analyzed draft revisions of the *Principia* in which Newton claimed that Thales, Pythagoras, Democritus, and other ancient sages had anticipated him in professing a theory of universal gravitation, as well as other ideas central to his world system. Newton constructed an elaborate "ancient theology" (*prisca sapientia*) as the historiographic foundation of his new science. He saw himself as restorer of an ancient wisdom known to deepest antiquity but lost in later ages of decadence. Among the wise men who once understood the true nature of the world, Newton mentioned Mercurius and Orpheus, favorites of the Renaissance hermetists, but it was a nonhermetic strain of ancient wisdom that most attracted him—a genealogy for Greek atomism that traced this notoriously materialist philosophy back to Moses and the sacred tale of Genesis. The role of this Mosaic atomism in Newton's reasoning, it should be noted, was genealogical or doxographic, not material; fathering atomism on the author of the Pentateuch sanctified a reputedly impious theory of matter for a readership that still venerated biblical antiquity, but the legitimizing association was no source of new scientific insight.

Yates cited McGuire and Rattansi in 1968 in "The Hermetic Tradition in Renaissance Science," where she proposed the emergence of a "Rosicrucian" phase in the hermetic tradition. She described Rosicrucianism as a Paracelsian current in hermetism that was more given to scientific curiosity than the older, aesthetic hermetism that she ascribed to Ficino and his imitators. She also remarked that the word "Rosicrucian" resembled the word "baroque" in referring vaguely to a broad style or sensibility rather than precisely naming a discrete social or cultural phenomenon. Through Rosicrucianism, the hermetic tradition became an antecedent of modern science; in fact, seventeenth-century science could be seen as a mathematical and mechanical manifestation of the same impulses expressed in magical and animist philosophies of nature in the preceding century. Common to both was a "new turning toward the world and operating on the world . . . , the Hermetic attitude." The Newton who heard the pipes of Pan, she hypothesized, may also have listened to the voice of Hermes.

Yates made her last important statement on the hermetic tradition and the new science in *The Rosicrucian Enlightenment* of 1972. She noted how Elias Ashmole, charter member of the Royal Society, had written of the hermetic John Dee and the Rosicrucian Michael Maier in his *Theatrum chemicum* and how Newton, a later member of the Royal Society, owned and read not only Ashmole's alchemical collection but also the same Rosicrucian material to which Ashmole had referred. Despite her earlier disclaimers of any concrete social realization of the Rosicrucian sensibility, on the basis of such bibliographic and organizational commonalities she speculated "that behind the great exoteric movement typified by Newton's achievements in . . . mathematics and physics, there was also an esoteric movement, connected with the exoteric movement through . . . the importance . . . it attached to number, but developing this through another approach to nature . . . through alchemy. . . . The two approaches could have met through Rosicrucian alchemy. . . . Traces of the Rosicrucian outlook could be detected," she concluded, ". . . even in Isaac Newton."

Historians have discussed Yates's views widely. Learned journals have filled with rebuttals of her ideas and with refutations of those rebuttals. Whatever the final consensus on the Yates thesis, there can be no doubt that the learned and imaginative woman who created it led the world of learning in giving the subject of postmedieval occultism a new legitimacy and a new celebrity as a topic of historical discourse. Even though Yates did not make scientific ideas her leading concern, her views became controversial among historians of science. Her notoriety was overdetermined. Because those of her works that are immediately relevant to the history of science were mostly published between 1964 and 1972, in a period full of experiments with irrationalism in politics and culture, she unwittingly contributed to broader historiographic and philosophical debates on "internal" and "external," "rational" and "irrational" schemes of causation and change in the history of science. The polemics that she sparked fueled interest in the writings of other scholars who worked on topics that, like hers, had previously seemed

marginal, insignificant—not the "done" thing. It is hard to imagine—before Yates—the History of Science Society awarding its most prestigious prize to a book on the period of the Scientific Revolution largely concerned with alchemy. Without the enormous impact of her work, it is hard to account for the publication, by a great university press, of a survey as much unlike Marie Boas's *Scientific Renaissance, 1450–1630* (1962) as Allen Debus's *Man and Nature in the Renaissance* (1978), which treats essentially the same period. "Hermeticism," which rates fourteen entries in Debus's index, is not to be found in Boas's.

Not all historians of the Scientific Revolution have been convinced of either the truth or the significance of the Yates thesis. One evidence of the uneven reception of her views is the absence, in recent Newtonian scholarship, of a positive, or even a very strong, reaction to Yates's speculations on Newton as heir of Hermes. Among synthetic works of the last few years, I. B. Cohen's *Newtonian Revolution* alludes only briefly to Newton's belief that the Pythagoreans knew the inverse-square law. In *Never at Rest,* R. S. Westfall, who has written elsewhere on the importance of hermetism, finds no hermetic (in Yates's sense) or Rosicrucian motivations in Newton's science. By Westfall's account, the "Hermes" and "hermetic writers" whom Newton knew were alchemical authorities. Westfall's argument that Newton's alchemical studies contributed significantly to his matter-theory and physics is an important confirmation of the relevance, for the history of science, of an *occultist* tradition of alchemical, astrological, and magical beliefs but scarcely of Yates's conception of a *hermetic* tradition as wellspring of modern science. Westfall also reports that a corrupted "gentile theology" professing an atomist physics was a regular historiographic point of reference for Newton, but he records no role for Hermes Trismegistus in this ancient theology. Gale Christianson's recent study of Newton also treats Yates's Hermes as, at best, an incidental contributor to Newton's intellectual biography: Newton's interest in the *prisca sapientia* reflected "his preoccupation with the great alchemical masters from Hermes Trismegistus to Michael Maier," but Newton also learned from the Cambridge Platonists about a Mosaic, nonhermetic succession of natural-philosophical ideas that lent support to his world system. In these most current versions of Newton's story, so crucial to the Scientific Revolution and so regularly mentioned by Yates, Hermes is not a principal player.

Historical understanding of hermetic influence in early modern science is problematic in many respects, not all of them arising directly from Yates's own writing. In what follows, I shall deal briefly with only a few such problems. I shall attempt, first, to distinguish a stronger *doxographic role* for ancient theologians such as Hermes in validating claims about the natural world from their weaker *theoretical role* in supplying new and convincing explanations of natural phenomena; second, to show how early modern readers found a credible *theory* of natural magic in authoritative and nonhermetic sources from antiquity and the Middle Ages; third, to describe a tradition of *empirical* belief about natural objects whose magical effects were thought to confirm magical theory; and, finally, to argue for a more precise use, in the history of science, of "magic," "hermetic," "occultist," and related terms.

I shall not try to cover all the bases marked out by those who have debated the Yates thesis, much less to answer or even ask all the more important questions about magic and occultism that ought to interest students of early modern science. Despite their reputations for gullibility and mysticism, how did the Italian "philosophers of nature"— Girolamo Cardano, Bernardino Telesio, Francesco Patrizi, Giambattista Della Porta, Giordano Bruno, Tommaso Campanella—weaken the metaphysical foundations of magical belief? How much common ground was shared by two traditions that seemed especially hostile to many of the heroes of the Scientific Revolution: that is, the occultist tradition, from Marsilio Ficino through Tommaso Campanella; and the Peripatetic tradition, from Pietro Pomponazzi through Cesare Cremonini? Did Francis Bacon's polemic against traditional natural philosophy do more to strengthen, or to weaken, occultism? Did Galileo's laconic abandonment of the Aristotelian doctrine of qualities encourage such later thinkers as Robert Boyle and John Locke to construct a systematic critique of occult qualities? Why did Marin Mersenne, René Descartes, and Pierre Gassendi take up different positions against the bases of magical belief in school philosophy? When Leibniz criticized Newton's idea of force as an occult quality, what did this criticism imply to contemporaries? Did occultist teachings on *spiritus (pneuma)* help breed the aethers, effluvia, fluids, and spirits that thrived even among corpuscular and mechanical philosophers? Can one distinguish alchemy from chemistry in the seventeenth century? What did alchemy contribute to early modern theories of matter? By what date had astrology become incredible to European intellectuals? Did the acceptance of the Copernican world view diminish the reputation of astrology? When did physicians cease to regard astrology, demonology, and witchcraft as medical issues? What did the adjectives "natural," "supernatural," and "miraculous" mean to natural philosophers of Newton's day? Did the organization and institutionalization of early modern science, from the Accademia del cimento to the Royal Society, encourage or discourage belief in magic? These are only a few of the larger questions that suggest how relevant occultism is to the history of early modern science. By taking up different, but related, lines of inquiry, I hope to contribute something to a clarification of terms and purposes that may stimulate others to search out fuller answers.

Discovery and doxography

In 1499 Polydore Vergil, an Italian scholar who spent most of his life in England, published his *De inventoribus rerum.* This history, the first comprehensive account of discoveries written since classical times, has been called a precursor of later histories of technology and science. The reader who notes that the organization of the first book of Polydore's history roughly reflects the curricula of medieval schools and universities may be struck by the last three of its twenty-four chapters, those on magic and divination; they occupy more than one-tenth of the space in Book 1, whose earlier chapters discuss discoveries in various areas of theology, religion, philosophy, language, liter-

ature, medicine, mathematics, and natural philosophy. What of Polydore's three chapters on magic and divination? Do they, like his writings on geometry, astronomy, and medicine, also qualify him as an ancestor of Pierre Duhem and George Sarton?

Polydore, who agreed with Pliny the Elder that magic emerged from a mixture of medicine, religion, and astrology, would have considered himself a historian of science, if by "science" we mean a systematic effort to explain the world of nature in natural terms. But he was no magus, and no admirer of magic. He repeated Pliny's claim that magic was "the falsest of arts," and in all three of his chapters on magical arts he condemns their practitioners as frauds. Of the inventors of magic he spoke with less conviction. He knew that Pliny had traced its origins to ancient Persia, but neither he nor Pliny had any clear idea of the identity or chronology of the first magicians whom Pliny names. The most familiar was Zoroaster, who probably lived between 1400 and 1000 B.C. By placing Zoroaster five or six millennia before the Trojan War, however, Pliny magnified the antiquity of the magic he despised. He also fortified its authority by linking it with the philosopher Democritus of Abdera. According to one tradition known to Pliny, a Persian magus accompanied Xerxes on his Greek expedition, and another story told that Democritus's teachers were magi left to his father in gratitude by Xerxes. This is probably the origin of the strange tale, reported by Pliny and repeated by Polydore, that the materialist and unmystical Abderite shared with the shadowy Persians primary responsibility for introducing magic to Greece. Democritus, Pythagoras, Empedocles, and Plato all—as Pliny and Polydore tell it—went to the barbarian East for a magical *prisca sapientia* that began with Zoroaster. It is as remarkable that Hermes Trismegistus is not named by Polydore and his ancient sources when they recite the pedigree of magical wisdom as that these same texts give so prominent a place to Democritus the atomist.

The main inspirations of Polydore's *De inventoribus* were ancient literary and historical sources. He rarely cited a philosophical text, depending instead on the *Lives and Opinions of Eminent Philosophers* by Diogenes Laertius (third century A.D.), and he seems not to have been influenced by the great Platonic philosopher of the fifteenth century, Marsilio Ficino, who published his Latin translation of the first fourteen treatises of the Hermetic corpus in 1471. Ficino also wrote the most influential work on magic of the early modern period, *De vita coelitus comparanda,* the third book of his *De vita libri tres,* published in 1489 and republished in more than thirty editions by the middle of the seventeenth century. In the epistolary preface to *De vita,* Ficino cites Pythagoras, Democritus, Plotinus, and Apollonius of Tyana as "ancient philosophers" whose teachings were important for understanding his magic. More than half a dozen times in the text of this work he also mentions Zoroaster, the magi who followed him, and the *Chaldaean Oracles* attributed to him. Gemistus Pletho, a Byzantine contemporary of Ficino's who popularized the notion that Zoroaster had written the *Oracula,* was emphatic in regarding the Persian sage as the fountainhead of ancient wisdom. But Ficino, motivated by his own dramatic "discovery" of the *Hermetica* in 1462, sometimes began his genealogy of *prisca sapientia* with Hermes. Yet in the *De vita,* his longest and most important analysis of magic, Ficino mentions his *Hermetica* only in two chapters out of twenty-six, neither of them particularly kind to the thrice-great Hermes.

For the origins of ancient magic the best evidence was the material from Pliny and Diogenes Laertius that pointed to Zoroaster as source and to Democritus as propagator. The celebrity of these texts would have made it difficult for Ficino to substitute Hermes for Zoroaster as inventor of magic; moreover, it was not in his interest to do so. Ficino's original claim that the ancient wisdom came from Hermes appeared in his translation of the *Hermetica,* where he called Hermes "the first author of theology." And in later writings, even when he puts Zoroaster in first position, Ficino remains interested primarily in an ancient gentile theology, not in an ancient magic. This is not to say that he had no concern for the magical content of the *Hermetica* or for the antiquity of magic. His syncretic convictions about the unity of wisdom are another facet of his belief in its antiquity. All the streams of true knowledge, including magical knowledge, converge as they approach their beginning. But the *Hermetica,* the charter documents of ancient wisdom that he had resurrected, are essentially expressions of piety and theology. They have relatively little to say about magic. This is clear whether one reads the texts themselves or the commentaries (argumenta) by Ficino and Lefèvre d'Etaples that accompany them in Ficino's translation.

The physical and cosmological material in the hermetic treatises that Ficino translated is slighter even than their philosophical content, which is derivative, eclectic, and loose in its organization. But the *Hermetica* were of great moment to a man of Ficino's eirenic disposition because they supported such central Christian doctrines as the divine creation of man, the immortality of his soul, his fall through sin, and his eventual salvation. The pagan wisdom that Ficino admired in these texts was sanctified by its similarity to divine revelation, and the Christian dogma that guided his life could be ennobled by association with learned and literate antiquity. For the author of a *Platonic Theology,* so much the better if the teachings of Hermes helped him trace the path between the author of Genesis and the author of the *Timaeus.*

Hellenistic Jews and Christians had also recognized the necessity of associating themselves with the Greco-Roman culture that surrounded them. To this end, Jewish and Christian apologists and historians had adapted an important strategy of Greek historiography to their own needs. Greek "heurematographers" ("discovery writers," from *heurema,* "discovery"), authors of a genre of which no complete text survives, had encountered the problem of contradictory claims for priority of discovery among gods and heroes of localities separated by accidents of geography and dialect. They were also aware that the civilizations of Egypt and Mesopotamia were older than their own, and so they sometimes settled their arguments by ascribing discoveries to the East. Two characteristics of inventors named in this lost body of ancient historical writing became crucial to its Christian users: that they were

very old; and that they were not Greek. This apologetic ethnography and chronology allowed the church fathers to ascribe many discoveries to heroes of the Old Testament, especially Moses, and hence to bracket whatever seemed valuable in the classical tradition—Plato's philosophy, for example—between the new covenant and the old. Likewise, because of their ages and nationalities, non-Greek sages like the Persian Zoroaster and the Egyptian Hermes proved almost as important for church fathers as biblical figures. Because the fathers found heurematography useful in their polemics, its influence survived the Middle Ages until it could be more fully exploited by Polydore Vergil, who, like his Christian predecessors, tried to find a Jewish or oriental inventor for almost everything, including magic.

Doxography, the record of the succession of opinions in Greek philosophy, was another variety of ancient historiography that proved helpful to the fathers in their effort to legitimize Christian thought by linking it to a tradition holier and more venerable than the Greek. This was especially true of doxographical works "on the successions (*peri diadochon*) of philosophers" that originated around 200 B.C. and eventually influenced the *Lives* of Diogenes Laertius. The method of the doxographers, which sets philosophical opinions not only in their biographical contexts but also in the larger framework of world history, appealed to the humanist taste for history, in particular to their impulse to equate value with antiquity. In order to understand any human activity, humanists were inclined to seek its genesis, and because they admired the ancients so intensely and imitated them so zealously, they were also inclined to identify the older with the better. These humanist dispositions help explain the popularity of Polydore's *De inventoribus,* which saw thirty Latin editions in his lifetime and more than one hundred editions, in eight languages, by the early eighteenth century. They also help account for the power of the idea of a *prisca sapientia* in early modern thinking about the past. It is in the context of this search for genetic explanations and intellectual genealogies that the belief in a tradition of ancient pagan learning had its greatest influence. Likewise, the mythical Hermes Trismegistus was most important not so much for the content of what he taught as for the age and provenance of the alien wisdom that he represented. The material in the hermetic treatises became credible and legitimate not because they solved new problems or offered striking explanations but because they referred otherwise commonplace ideas to a sanctifying past. Thus, Ficino's *Hermetica* could be a source of doxographic authority even for magic and natural philosophy, fields to which their material contributions were slight. As Martin Nillson said of the influence of Zoroaster and Hermes in antiquity, "These names were letters of recommendation for the works that bore them." The hermetic signature gave prestige to the few and ordinary magical ideas contained in the writings ascribed to Hermes.

Magical theory

To appreciate the conceptual insignificance of the texts attached to these names for natural magic and natural philosophy, it is important to understand how certain other texts did in fact provide a different and indispensable kind of intellectual support for the renaissance of ancient magic in the early modern period. What was so compelling about this nondoxographic evidence? Why did Ficino, a premier intellectual figure of his age, believe so strongly in the reality and value of magic that he risked publishing his defense of it just at the moment when his contemporary, Pico della Mirandola, had fallen into disgrace with the church for professing similar doctrines? Three categories of ideas bolstered Ficino's convictions.

First, there is the *doxographic* or *genealogical* material described in the preceding section of this [essay]. Though Ficino's treatment of magic in *De vita* does not depend heavily on hermetic authority, of which he was so acutely aware, it is full of references to mythical and historical figures, who are usually ancient, often exotic, and sometimes related to one another in intellectual succession, as in the following discussion of astronomical images:

> Trismegistus says that the Egyptians used to make [moving images] from particular materials of the world and insert the souls of demons into them. . . . The magi, followers of Zoroaster, used a sort of golden globe marked with characters of the heavenly bodies to evoke a spirit from Hecate. . . . I omit their chants . . . , [which] Psellus the Platonist disapproves and derides. Their astrologers think that the Hebrews reared in Egypt learned to make a golden calf to catch the favor of Venus and the Moon. . . . Porphyry . . . testifies that images are efficacious . . . , [and] Iamblichus affirms that not only celestial but also demonic and divine powers and effects can be received in materials naturally conforming to superior entities. . . . Proclus and Synesius say exactly the same.

This passage confirms belief in astrological images not just by piling authority on authority but also by setting the succession of Platonists among the chosen people and gentile sages who preceded them. Without understanding the attitudes to the genealogy of authority discussed earlier, a modern reader will not feel the effect of Ficino's reasoning about the lineage of his ideas.

Ficino used *theoretical* as well as doxographic arguments in *De vita,* though he did not find his theory of magic in the *Hermetica.* Since *De vita* is an excursus from his long commentary on Plotinus, it comes as no surprise that Ficino took much of the philosophic support for his analysis of magic from the Neoplatonists—Plotinus, Porphyry, Iamblichus, Synesius, and Proclus. One of the last philosophers of the ancient world, Proclus wrote one of the few surviving texts that provides substantial theoretical understanding of the magic of late antiquity. Ficino translated it under the title *De sacrificio* (On Sacrifice) and used it to support one of the key arguments in *De vita,* that a natural magic is possible because natural connections among terrestrial, celestial, and higher entities can be awakened by the magus who understands how to manipulate them. This claim was useful to any Christian magus who wished to avoid the charge of using magic for commerce with demons. It is also of interest to the historian of science, for it shows how the magic of Proclus and Ficino depended

on or, better, was identical with, certain notions about the structure of the natural world. In *De sacrificio* Proclus describes a hierarchical taxonomy of entities that make up the universe and a set of rules governing relations of cause and effect among them. The lion, the cock, and the sun, for example, all belong to one category. The sun is obviously higher than the two earthly animals, but the magus also knows that the cock is higher than the lion, because birds are creatures of the air. He knows, moreover, that both are solar animals: The cock crows at sunrise; the constellation Leo is a solar sign. Hence, the solar powers of the cock can be used magically to counteract the lower, but cognate, powers of the lion. These ideas may seem idiosyncratic and baseless, but they were neither. The cock's power over the lion was attested in a literary tradition already ancient in Proclus's time and fated to endure for centuries after. The physical and metaphysical theories explaining the relation between these magical objects and others are apparent in other works of Proclus, especially the *Elements of Theology.* Proclus, whose contributions to philosophy, mathematics, and science are well known, was no fatuous theosophist. His theory of magic was a serious philosophical undertaking.

So was the *De vita* of Ficino, who consulted a wide range of philosophical, medical, and scientific authorities in order to construct his theory of magic. Since *De vita libri tres* was a medical treatise (its first two books were on health and longevity, the third on astrological medicine), its author knew the works of Galen, who was primarily responsible for the lasting effect of the idea of occult qualities in medicine and philosophy. When Galen had to explain the action of a food or a drug on the body, he preferred explanations based on the perceptible or manifest properties (hot, cold, dry, wet) of the four elements (fire, earth, air, water), but some substances ingested by the body (certain foods, drugs, and poisons) or applied to it (certain amulets) would not yield to such explanations. In these difficult cases, Galen resorted to explanations based on *idiotetes arretoi,* or "indescribable properties," which later came to be called *proprietates occultae,* or "hidden properties," in Latin. Galen taught that "manifest properties," those evident to the senses, could be understood rationally because they fit into the prevailing post-Aristotelian theory of matter, but he regarded experience of occult properties as merely empirical and irrational because it fell outside the system. The purgative action of rhubarb or the antiepileptic properties of a peony amulet were undeniable facts of the physician's experience, but they did not fit the categories available in Galen's matter-theory. If he could not match rhubarb's powers with its manifest properties, an alternative was to attach them to the plant as a whole; thus, Galen spoke of such powers as coming from the "whole substance" of an object.

Avicenna, Albertus Magnus, Thomas Aquinas, and other thinkers well known to Ficino elaborated this relation between the ideas of occult quality and whole substance into an important feature of medieval and early modern medicine and natural philosophy. The key to these later developments was the Peripatetic concept of *substantial form.* The term does not occur in Aristotle, who nonetheless prepared the way for its emergence in late antiquity and its fuller development in the Middle Ages. Two fundamental dichotomies in Peripatetic metaphysics are *substance/accident* and *form/matter*. The *matter* of a particular object makes it an individual: this emerald rather than that one; its *form* makes it an object of a given kind: an emerald rather than a ruby. The hylemorphic union of matter (*hule*) and form (*morphe*) constitutes an entity whose being is independent, a *substance,* this particular emerald, but the gem's special shade of green has no existence apart from the emerald; it is an *accident.* The *substantial form* of the emerald gives the stone its existence as such, making it a member of the *species* of emeralds. This is why substantial form and *specific form* are sometimes synonymous. But *accidental form*—the shape of the gem, its weight, its color, the smoothness of its surface—can change while its substantial or specific being remains unaffected. Accidental forms are perceptible; they can be analyzed in terms of the manifest properties associated with the elements. Substantial form in itself, as opposed to its effects, remains hidden from the senses. Thus, just as Galen had called the action of the whole substance "indescribable," medieval authorities who traced this action to the powers of specific or substantial form called it *occultus,* or "hidden."

Medieval thinkers believed that physical change could transform one substance into another. What happened to the substantial form of the old substance? Where did the substantial form of the new substance come from? The theory of elements and qualities complicated these questions, because an element like water was also considered a substance endowed with substantial form. If the elements and qualities of an old substance altered to engender a new one, it would be necessary to account not only for the substantial form of the substance compounded of the elements but also for the substantial forms of the elements themselves. One result of the complex debate on these questions was that some medieval thinkers traced the origin of new substantial forms to the heavenly bodies. If it was difficult to find terrestrial solutions for all the problems of Peripatetic matter-theory and metaphysics, then a celestial remedy was always at hand, especially for Christian thinkers accustomed to looking heavenward for answers to their questions.

Ficino's *De vita* was a treatise in iatromathematics or astrological medicine. As a physician, he wanted to take therapeutic advantage of natural powers hidden in the stars and planets, but as a Christian and a priest he worried about the orthodoxy of his position. Was the medical astrology that he wished to practice physically efficacious? Was it also legitimately Christian? The two questions were inseparable for Ficino, and they were most worrisome in the case of amulets and talismans, for the wearing of decorated or undecorated objects for curative purposes raised the specters of idolatry and superstition. In fact, it was Ficino's wish not to cross the fine line between a conceivably legitimate natural magic and a clearly sinful demonic magic that caused him to write ambiguously of the hermetic *Asclepius* in the longest passage of *De vita* devoted to the *Hermetica.* The "god-making" texts of the *Asclepius* described the invocation of spirits in order to animate magical statues, which resemble talismans in all respects

but size. Aquinas had followed Augustine in condemning the demonic statues of Hermes, but he did not agree with him that all such objects—talismans and amulets, for example—were absolutely prohibited. The more flexible attitude of Aquinas was crucial for Ficino, and it depended on the ideas of substantial form and occult quality.

Aquinas and Ficino, much like Galen, could agree that the curative power of an undecorated amulet is *both* occult *and* nondemonic or natural because it comes from an imperceptible substantial form—not from manifest qualities of the natural object nor from the personal agency of a spiritual being. Moreover, since Aquinas had admitted that their substantial forms arose in the heavens, Ficino also had good precedent for treating such objects as sources of astrological power. But suppose the magus wished to decorate an object with astrological signs in order to enhance its kinship to the heavens. Aquinas ruled that if such talismanic signs could be regarded only as a message, then, because messages must be sent and received by intelligent agents, it must be that such signs are directed to nonterrestrial persons; thus they become dangerous occasions of sin against religion. Some talismanic signs, however, might not be messages. If a magus carves a likeness of the constellation Leo on a ruby, the gem becomes a member of the same species of objects that includes the constellation and the animal lion. The carving does not change the substantial form of the stone, which remains a ruby, but it does make the stone a member of a new species; so Thomas said that such carvings or figures were "like specific forms." Unlike words or letters, which could be construed only as messages, these figures could operate in the absence of any exchange of information between minds; hence, they acted naturally, in the same sense that the whole substance or substantial form of any material object was a natural feature of its being. The activity of all these entities was occult because it arose from imperceptible sources, but it was also natural activity, if by "natural" we mean "nondemonic."

The physical and metaphysical theory of substantial forms and occult qualities allowed Ficino to explain the efficacy of his iatromathematics by referring to familiar and well-respected doctrines of medieval philosophy and science whose influence continued well into the early modern period; Robert Boyle and John Locke, for example, found these teachings worthy of extensive rebuttal. The hierarchical cosmologies of the Neoplatonists served Ficino in the same way and would also be remembered after him, especially by the Cambridge Platonists of the seventeenth century. The systematic teachings of Plotinus, Proclus, Galen, and Avicenna were of much greater theoretical influence in Ficino's astral magic than the eclectic *Hermetica,* and the ideas that Ficino found in Aquinas were even more significant, not only because they were clearer and fuller than earlier philosophical material (e. g., Proclus) that was often fragmentary and opaque, but also because they were authoritatively Christian ideas. In Ficino's humanist philosophy, the force of personal authority and the force of philosophical theory became indistinguishable, just as the power of literary tradition and the power of empirical evidence worked synergistically in the same current of argument.

Empirical magic

In much the same sense that we might cite empirical data of X-ray crystallography to substantiate theory in molecular biology, Ficino had *empirical* as well as doxographic and theoretical reasons for his belief in magic. Ficino made claims that can be called empirical about animals, plants, and minerals not because he derived them from his own sense experience nor because he checked them against his own observations; usually he did neither. Such claims qualify as empirical only insofar as they referred to a class of physical objects thought to exist in the world and to have characteristics taken to validate or instantiate various theoretical propositions. Ficino's source for these claims was almost always an indirect, literary report of an (allegedly) direct observation. The point is that his theoretical convictions about magic were not merely theoretical or wholly a priori; they were also the products of induction - attached, at some distance, to someone's experience of the world, however attenuated or distorted. For example, in explaining his theory about the relation between occult qualities and celestial forces, Ficino asks the reader of *De vita,*

> Who does not know that the occult virtues of things, which are called "specific" by physicians, come not from an elementary nature but from a celestial one? Therefore, . . . rays [from the heavens] can impress on images wondrous and occult powers . . . [which] arise much more quickly than in various mixtures of elements and elementary qualities. . . . Is it not said that certain families among the Illyrians and the Triballi kill people by looking at them, when they are angry, and that certain women in Scythia do the same? And catoblepas and regulus snakes destroy people by shooting rays from their eyes. The marine torpedo also suddenly benumbs the hand that touches it, even at a distance through a rod, and by contact alone the little echinus fish is said to retard a great ship. The phalangia in Apulia transform and quickly benumb the spirits and the mind with a secret (*occultus*) bite of some sort. How does a rabid dog have its effect, even if no bite appears?

> . . . Will you then deny that celestial bodies can perform wonders with the rays of their eyes that gaze on us?

Ficino wishes to attribute extraordinary, occult powers to the rays (*radii*) of stars and planets. He begins by alluding to an element of the larger theoretical framework of his natural magic: that all occult powers come from the heavens and are thus stronger than the manifest qualities of earthly elements. Next he provides a list of toxic terrestrial phenomena that are all mysterious because their mechanisms are unknown and their effects are rapid. If earthbound objects act so quickly and so marvelously, he concludes, no one can doubt that heavenly bodies work even greater wonders. The theoretical proposition is that occult, celestial forces are very powerful causes of terrestrial effects; the evidence is a set of empirical claims about natural, earthly objects.

An odd list of natural objects. Illyrians, Scythians, Triballi, and other peoples of southeastern Europe had a reputation for the evil eye among the Romans, who liked to locate their witches in faraway places, but to Ficino these can have been no more than names. The "catoblepas," or "downlooker," a beast that took its name from a head supposedly too heavy to hold up, may be a confused memory of the African gnu. The "regulus," or "basilisk," may be a distant and fabulous cousin of the spitting cobra (*Hemachatus hemachatus*), which aims its venom at its victim's eyes. The notorious "phalangium" may belong to the genus of spiders called *Lathrodectus,* and the "torpedo" is certainly the electric ray of the Mediterranean, *Torpedo narce.* The Latin word *echinus* refers to a hedgehog or a sea urchin or a plant, but when Ficino speaks of it he really has in mind the Greek *echeneis,* or "ship-holder," an imaginative amalgam of several marine species. What did Ficino know about these strange people and exotic animals? What (beyond their allegedly magical properties) do they have in common?

Direct experience of spider bites and rabid dogs were certainly within Ficino's means. Anyone who traveled to the Italian seacoast or shopped at a fish market might have seen an electric ray. But many of these magical objects, which are the evidence for Ficino's theory of magic, were beyond the range of his observation, either because they did not exist or because they lived only in remote places. As textual rather than natural objects, however, most of them could be found in the *Natural History* of Pliny the Elder, who in turn depended chiefly on an older genre of writings about "natural and mystical powers" inaugurated by Bolos Democritus of Mendes. Pliny, who wrote his great encyclopedia in the first century A.D., confused this Egyptian of the third century B.C. with the atomist philosopher of the fifth century B.C. Despite the stories connecting the Greek Democritus with the Persian magi, he seems to have been far removed from the mentality that produced the fragments of crude folk magic attributed to Bolos Democritus. The latter's surviving recipes, most of them preserved by Pliny, are the remains of catalogs of cures based on sympathies, antipathies, and other magical powers of natural objects. Of the considerable literature on magic and alchemy inspired by Bolos Democritus, one of the few survivors is the *Kyranides,* a compendium of magical medicine whose earliest elements can be traced to the third century A.D. and that advertised itself as a divine gift from Hermes Trismegistus. When the names Hermes and Thoth appear in medieval works on magic, some of them known to Ficino, they most frequently allude either to the *Kyranides* and similar works or to other hermetic texts on astrology or alchemy that survived into the Middle Ages. Thus, when Ficino listed magical objects from Pliny's collection, he was unwittingly and indirectly referring to an obscurer hermetic textual tradition, which, unlike the "philosophical" *Hermetica* that he had translated, contributed materially to his own defense of natural magic.

It is important to recognize that this "popular" hermetism, despite its present fragmentary condition, aided the transmission of a coherent tradition of medical and natural-historical information about magical objects from antiquity through the Middle Ages and into the early modern period. Thus, Ficino's choice of evidence to support his theory of magic was not autonomous or whimsical; it was constrained by a tradition. The same magical objects—the cock and the lion, the torpedo and the echeneis, the basilisk, the magnet, the heliotrope, and many more—come up again and again in Western magical literature through the eighteenth century, just as in modern biology textbooks the same examples appear over and over. The medium for both of these traditions is literary, but in the older tradition there was for a long time no systematic requirement that what was claimed in a text should correspond to what could be perceived in the world. Without any regular empirical check on the tradition of magical objects, its literary manifestation came not merely to represent the evidence but actually to constitute the evidence.

Studies of the cock in ancient literature, for example, have shown that its magical dominance over the lion was already canonical by the time Proclus referred to it in *De sacrificio.* As far as I know, no one has attempted to examine the *fortuna* of these or any other magical objects from their emergence in antiquity to their decline in the early modern period. In order to illustrate the role of this tradition in early modern thinking about natural magic, I shall attempt a brief sketch of the long history of Ficino's two magical fish, the torpedo and the echeneis.

The torpedo is a real, identifiable species whose stunning effects were correctly observed in antiquity, yet, in the absence of any notion of electricity, the ray's powers resisted explanation. One behavior reported for the echeneis, that it stuck to ships, applies to the modern remora, the marine lamprey, and to other varieties, and it is easy to imagine how such reports might have become associated with otherwise unexplained cases of stalled ships. But the crucial fact was textual: In the beginning of Book 32 of his *Natural History,* which deals with the medical and magical properties of marine life, Pliny described the electric ray and the ship-holder as the two outstanding examples of natural objects possessing occult powers. Many other ancient authorities before and after Pliny—especially Aristotle, Plutarch, Athenaeus, Aelian, and Oppian—debated, amplified, and confirmed the magical reputation of the two fish. Even literary writers uninterested in natural philosophy used them as stock examples of magical objects. Later generations found it especially memorable that Galen recognized the "unnameable properties" of the torpedo, whose medical significance had already surpassed that of the echeneis in late antiquity. Medieval authors accepted both fish as instances of occult power and also saw them as proofs that miracles had been wrought by a mighty and providential God. Meanwhile, any attachment between the fabled ship-stopper and an actual, identifiable fish completely eroded in the Middle Ages. Even the lexical identity of Pliny's echeneis disappeared in the confusion of texts that failed to distinguish it from his *echinus,* or sea urchin.

Ficino's contemporary, Ermolao Barbaro, solved this textual problem in his critical and editorial work on Pliny, but his philological achievement did nothing to dissolve the bond that kept the echeneis twinned to the torpedo; through much of the seventeenth century they remained an exemplary pair of magical objects. Natural historians

from Pierre Belon and Guillaume Rondelet through Ulisse Aldrovandi and Jan Jonston knew what the torpedo was but not how it numbed its prey. By repeatedly confirming the fact of its effect, they also confirmed the time-honored resort to occult qualities as explanation of the effect. And since their humanist natural history was so loaded with philological baggage, these reformers of biology also recertified the intellectual value of the Greco-Roman sources that nourished belief in magic. Because the reformers depended so much on ancient books, and so little on contemporary experience, the best they could do with the echeneis was to reveal the bewilderment of the classical authors. Their most striking use of personal experience was actually to reinforce older tales of ship stopping with current examples. Physicians, theologians; philosophers, and many other writers joined the natural historians in commenting on the two fish, almost always as a pair. Those who did not use occult qualities to explain their effects proposed explanations that were sometimes ingenious but never convincing enough to displace occult qualities. This was true through the middle of the seventeenth century, when alternative explanations were often cast in terms of the fashionable corpuscular and mechanical paradigms.

The echeneis lost its magic when it gained a biological identity—primarily because of maritime voyages of discovery, exploration, and trade that allowed regular observation of the remora, a fish that stuck to ships but obviously did not stop them. By the early eighteenth century, the remora's arresting but unmagical behavior was so well known, and it was so regularly identified as the echeneis of antiquity, that the fish lost its status as a magical object and its link to the torpedo. The same improvements in habits of observation that disconfirmed ship stopping reconfirmed the still mysterious powers of the torpedo. Because the prevailing corpuscular and mechanical modes of explanation failed to disenchant the torpedo, the notion of "torporific virtue" remained an idea worth belittling, as late as 1765, in the *Encyclopédie,* nearly a century after Lorenzo Redi and Stefano Lorenzini had moved understanding of the ray's gross anatomy very nearly to modern standards and nearly a century after Molière had made a joke of "dormitive virtue." Taxonomy and anatomy were to prevail in the Linnaean natural history of the eighteenth century, and the great ichthyologist of the period, Peter Artedi, wished to banish *proprietates,* occult or other, from natural history; yet the ray's effect remained a puzzle and a focus of attention and, potentially, a buttress to the decaying edifice of magical belief. In the 1760s, Edward Bancroft and others, having concluded that the effect of the famous South American eel was in fact electrical, guessed that the same might be true of the torpedo. In a series of simple experiments, John Walsh confirmed Bancroft's conjecture and ended the ray's career as a magical object in 1773—except insofar as eighteenth-century conceptions of "electrical fluid" resembled the *spiritus* and *pneumata* long counted among the arcana of the magus.

This brief tale of two fishes raises questions about the stories of other magical objects. How many of them remained, like the torpedo and the echeneis, credible instances of magical power through much of what we call the Scientific Revolution? The fate of these two magical objects, in any event, shows that lists of such phenomena in early modern texts should not be assumed to be idiosyncratic or capricious; that, on the contrary, such objects are often cited as instances of magical power on the basis of an authoritative tradition whose elements played a role like that of empirical data in the confirmation of modern scientific theories; that the longevity of this tradition was great, and that its end was complex, in that not all its elements lost their credibility at the same time or for the same reasons; that the intensifying and refining of scientific observation in the early modern period could reinforce, as well as diminish, the reputation of magical objects; and, finally, that there was no single feature of the Scientific Revolution (much less the mechanical and corpuscular episodes of that revolution) that convinced educated Europeans to end their fascination with magical objects.

The terminology of natural magic, occultism, and hermetism

Thus, during the centuries of the Scientific Revolution, an *empirical* occultism emerged from an ancient literary tradition, enjoyed an expansion of its textual content and an enlargement of its reputation until the early seventeenth century, and remained an important source of natural-historical information through the middle of that century. Proponents of natural magic believed that this *empirical* occultism confirmed a *theoretical* occultism rooted in authoritative concepts of speculative and natural philosophy drawn from works of leading intellectual figures, Christian writers included. A third source of confirmation for belief in natural magic, the magic most of interest to the history of science, was *doxographic,* and it represented not so much a succession of ideas as a succession of names, attached, often vaguely, to ideas. The vagueness of this doxography is a special problem for the history of natural magic in the Scientific Revolution.

Some distinctions of terminology may be helpful. In ordinary modern English, "magic" is a vague term. Like "occultism," it can refer to a set of beliefs and practices historically and materially distinguishable from one another but customarily treated as a group, because from the point of view of orthodox religion or philosophy or, more recently, science, they have seemed illegitimate, erroneous, somehow marginal. The set includes astrology, demonology, divination, witchcraft, Cabala, alchemy, and others, all of which are of historical interest, but not all alike for the history of science. For early modern science, in particular, the most important kind of occultism was what Ficino and his contemporaries called "natural magic." This is how Ficino described it:

> Using natural objects, natural magic captures the beneficial powers of the heavenly bodies to bring good health. This means of action must surely be conceded to those who use their talents lawfully, just as it is in medicine and farming. . . . One practices agriculture, another mundiculture. . . . Just as the farmer tempers his field to the weather to give sustenance to man, so this wise man, this priest, for the sake of man's safety tempers the lower objects of the cosmos [*mundus*] to the higher. . . . [Natural

magic] puts natural materials in a correct relationship with natural causes.

Writing in a medical context, Ficino focused on medical magic, but his definition applies broadly. Just as the farmer and the physician use their expert knowledge to manipulate natural objects for desired physical effects, so the magus uses arcane knowledge of the contents of microcosm and macrocosm to achieve wondrous, but natural, results. Part of the special knowledge required for natural magic may be expressed as a set of theoretical principles, of which these are especially important:

> 1. Occult—as opposed to manifest—powers and forces can and must be used to explain certain natural phenomena.
>
> 2. On a cosmic scale, causality is a vector, moving from above to below, from without to within, and thus lending credence to astrology.
>
> 3. Fine material substances or gross spiritual substances—*spiritus* or *pneumata*—can and must be used to explain coherence and continuity of action among natural phenomena.
>
> 4. The prevailing explanatory context for natural phenomena is organic rather than mechanical.

These principles, which were seriously debated through the middle of the seventeenth century and beyond, had been developed by thinkers of the stature of Plato, Aristotle, Galen, Ptolemy, Plotinus, Avicenna, and Aquinas. There is no doubt that they are generally compatible with the *Hermetica* translated by Ficino. Moreover, a few passages of the philosophical *Hermetica* explicitly support various points of occultist theory, particularly the notion of astrological causality. But principles of natural magic were low on the hermetic agenda, and, more important, no idea of natural magic susceptible to rigorous and detailed historical analysis can be said to be "hermetic," as opposed to "Peripatetic" or "Stoic" or "Galenic" or "Neoplatonic." This is not because there are no such ideas (see the sketch of the history of occult qualities above) but because there is no coherent and distinctly hermetic theory of natural magic.

The adjective "hermetic" is an old one. Iamblichus used it in discussing the dubious ancestry of works that circulated under the name of Hermes in his day. Much later, in his debate with Robert Fludd, Johann Kepler used the expression "Hermetic manner" (*mos Hermeticus*) to characterize what he objected to in Fludd's way of thinking. Seventeenth-century writers frequently used "hermetic" to mean "alchemical" and thus, by extension, to refer to the occultist beliefs and practices with which alchemy was associated. By the middle of the next century, Jakob Brucker, the great historian of philosophy, connected Hermes, Orpheus, and Zoroaster with what he called "the Pythagorean—Platonic—Cabbalist philosophy" of suppositious syncretism, showing that the associations of "hermetic" had drifted far from the texts that Ficino had made famous. Frances Yates, who made "hermetic" and its cognates important and controversial for modern historians of science, sometimes used this term as if it meant the same thing as "magical" or "occultist" broadly understood. Other historians have done the same, but the history of natural magic in its relation to science would be well served by greater terminological precision and a shift of emphasis.

Kepler can guide us here. In the "Appendix" to the fifth book of his *Harmonices mundi,* published in 1619, he took issue with notions of cosmic harmony professed by Fludd in the first sections of his enormous *Utriusque cosmi historia,* which had appeared in 1617 and 1618. Kepler's remarks were only the first round in a long series of polemics that ultimately matched Fludd against Mersenne, Gassendi, and lesser prophets of the new science, but they give insight into a new and pejorative meaning that the term "hermetic" had acquired by Kepler's time. Fludd, who cites the philosophical *Hermetica* at every turn, had spoken on the subject of cosmic music just at the moment when Kepler was about to make his own declaration in *Harmonies of the Cosmos,* so Kepler wished ardently to distinguish his views from Fludd's:

> In [Fludd's] work there are many pictures; in mine, mathematical diagrams keyed with letters. You may also note that he takes great delight in the shadowy mysteries of things, while I strive to bring these same things, wrapped in obscurity, into the light of understanding. The one habit belongs to Chemists, Hermetists, Paracelsians; the other is the specialty of Mathematicians. . . . What he adopts from the ancients, I draw out from nature and build it up from its very elements; he makes confused and incorrect use of what he takes, because of variations of opinion in the traditions, but I proceed in natural order so that everything is corrected according to the laws of nature, and this avoids confusion. In fact, I never attend to opinions established by the ancients except where no confusion follows: Thus, where I expressly refute the ancients . . . , he unwaveringly follows them. . . . When he introduces music into the cosmos, there is this very great difference between us: first, the harmonies he aims to teach are mere symbols . . . , poetic or rhetorical rather than philosophical or mathematical. This is the spirit of his whole book, as the title, *Macrocosm and Microcosm,* makes clear. . . . Following the celebrated axiom of Hermes, he makes *things above similar* or analogous *to things below.* But in order for this analogy to apply everywhere he must often drag things in by the hair so that they will apply on both sides. My view on analogies . . . is clear; they are apt to run on into infinity.

In effect, Kepler has provided a table of opposites that establishes a pejorative sense for "hermetic" as opposed to "philosophical" or "mathematical," the terms Kepler chose to describe the character of the new science he helped found. He contrasted Fludd's pictures to his diagrams; Fludd's poetic symbols to his mathematical notation; Fludd's mysteries to his clarity; Fludd's arguments based on authority and entangled in tradition to his explanations drawn from nature and ordered by nature's laws; Fludd's profligate application of analogy to his much stricter view of the uses of analogy in mathematics. These

were the features of what Kepler called Fludd's "Hermetic manner" or "Hermetic philosophy" in Kepler's *Apologia* of 1622, the work in which he answered Fludd's 1621 rejoinder to his original comments on *Utriusque cosmi historia.* The *Apology* told Fludd that Kepler held "in contempt whatever mathematics you do in a Hermetic manner, not out of hatred for Hermetic matters themselves, . . . but because I have never learned to grasp mathematics except by mathematical demonstrations nor to see into the inner sanctum of your Hermes, which is always completely dark to mathematical eyes." Kepler found Fludd's methods alien and utterly useless to his own inquiries into nature.

Robert Westman has argued persuasively that the antipathy between the hermetic-poetical Fludd and the mathematical-philosophical Kepler was largely a disagreement over the status of pictorial signs and written signs in their relations with things. Everyone remembers Kepler's famous picture of planetary polyhedra, but this geometrical image was for Kepler only a symbol of real, immaterial, invisible relations among the planets. Where Kepler used pictures as adjuncts to arguments expressed in words and numbers, as tokens convenient to the human sensory apparatus and symbolic of intelligible realities, Fludd made pictures essential in his books, not ancillary, and hoped to explain the cosmos through pictures by recreating it poetically. Kepler explained and theorized through linguistic analysis, Fludd through pictorial mimesis. Fludd's wish to mimic the Creator by making his own book of the world elevated his pictures beyond mere *representation* or description. Like some of the magical textual objects of empirical occultism, Fludd's pictures *presented* a reality that was autonomous, in that it was independent of reference to any other physical object.

Fludd's theologically audacious project of explaining by the direct, creative act of picturing, rather than by an indirect act of analysis, recalls the mystical tradition in Christianity, which favored an immediate, intuitive relation with God over scholastic ratiocination or sacerdotal ceremony. Fludd unquestionably belonged to a hermetic tradition, however one wishes to define it, but his poetic-intuitive epistemology and psychology also place him in the line of Jacob Boehme, Oswald Croll, Valentin Weigel, Paracelsus, and, ultimately, Johann Tauler, Meister Eckhardt, and the *Theologia Germanica.* Weigel's thought illuminates the kinship between Fludd's hermetism and this German spiritualism. Like Paracelsus, who taught that man gained true knowledge of nature only when human *experientia* became the *scientia* innate in natural objects, Weigel claimed that to know an object was to become that object. Thus possessed of an epistemology that resembled Paracelsian teaching in its religious motivations as much as in its conclusions, Weigel went on to borrow other ideas from Paracelsus: not only the microcosm—macrocosm theory that set the cosmological stage for his epistemology, but also the alchemical and astrological terminology in which he and Boehme cast the drama of human spiritual development. By the middle of the seventeenth century, Weigel, Croll, and Boehme were much in vogue in English translation; their original works had begun to appear in the first decades of the century, when Fludd and Kepler began their polemics. Henry More and other English critics used the word "theosophy" to refer specifically to Boehme's ideas (his collected works of 1730 were titled *Theosophia revelata*) but also more broadly to those of Fludd, Paracelsus, and Agrippa. This German spiritualism, or theosophy, fortified by Paracelsian notions of alchemy, cosmology, and matter-theory and amplified by Fludd's special commitments to pictorialism and hermetism, is likely what Kepler had in mind when he condemned Fludd in the following terms: "You say that *certain understanding of the world is given not to worldly but to theosophical wisdom.* A *theosophist* you certainly are; others are cosmosophists. You are wise in invisible quantities, uncountable numbers, a spiritual Sun, self-straying planets discernible only to the mind." This reading of Kepler's pejorative use of the term "theosophy" may also prove helpful to modern scholars in distinguishing the theosophical hermetism of Robert Fludd from the natural magic of Marsilio Ficino, which was not strongly hermetic. Ficino, whose philosophical, literary, and medical skills earned the respect of peers in all fields, developed a natural magic that looked back to the normative natural philosophies of antiquity and the Middle Ages. By contrast, given the filiation of the Weigels and "Behmenists" of the early modern period with the adherents of the Theosophical Society or the followers of a Madame Blavatsky of more recent times, one may say, without taint of Whiggery, that Fludd's theosophical hermetism, which was at odds with prominent natural philosophies of his own day, looked forward to occultist movements culturally more marginal than anything Ficino proposed. By the eighteenth century, the rationalist *Encyclopédie* classified as "theosophists" not only Paracelsus, Weigel, and Fludd but also Croll, Heinrich Khunrath, and John Baptista Van Helmont, concluding that they were "men of ardent imagination who corrupted theology, obscured philosophy and abused their chemical knowledge."

If Kepler's description of Fludd's thinking as both "theosophical" and "hermetic" helped establish a pejorative use of those terms in natural philosophy, the status of "hermetic" as a synonym for "alchemical" is less clear. The name Hermes had long been associated with alchemical texts like the *Emerald Tablet.* Some of these alchemical *Hermetica* were read by seventeenth-century "chemical philosophers," who made good use of the legitimacy given the alchemical Hermes by association with Ficino's philosophical *Hermetica*—although not everyone conceded the relationship. As early as 1533, Symphorien Champier, a physician and a follower of Ficino, had argued that the alchemical Hermes was not Ficino's philosophical author but a fabrication of the Moslems and "a stranger to true philosophy." In the next century, although Croll and other Paracelsians still spoke admiringly of "that holy man Hermes," Croll's enemy Andreas Libavius scorned the hermetic tradition as a fount of obscurantism, enthusiasm, and charlatanry. Libavius also saw it as a threat to the humanist Aristotelian philosophy and pedagogy upon which he had based his efforts to construct an autonomous disciplinary and didactic base for chemistry. Although Libavius saw hermetic Egypt as the homeland of an *"impostoria chymia,"* (fake chemistry), Michael Maier—who shared a publisher and an illustrator with Fludd—used his

own books of emblems to make early modern alchemy a distinctly hermetic art by interpreting the whole Renaissance misunderstanding of Egypt, its gods, and its hieroglyphics as an allegory on the alchemical work.

In this context, it is important to recall the relation between Westman's account of Fludd's pictorialism and C. G. Jung's views on the purpose of the alchemical work. According to Jung, alchemy was more therapy than technology. In order to manipulate them symbolically, the alchemist projected the contents of the unconscious—Jung's archetypes—onto matter, whose transformations could be treated physically and described verbally as surrogates of less accessible processes in the psyche. The special therapeutic motivation of alchemy demanded just such an efflorescence of the pictorial imagination as appeared in Maier's emblems; the alchemist's therapeutic aims and their consequences were as unlike Kepler's analytic ambitions and achievements as anything in Fludd. Contemplating Maier's alchemy or Fludd's theosophy, one can only suggest that modern scholars deal cautiously with such subtle and refractory materials, especially in deciding what it means to apply the same label, "hermetic," to these authors and to Ficino.

Allen Debus, in a section of the first chapter of his *Chemical Philosophy* entitled "The Hermetic Revival and the Study of Nature," finds a bond between François Rabelais and the Paracelsian Peter Severinus in their common urge "to discard their books and seek the truth of nature directly through observation. . . . The ultimate source for both authors," he maintains, "is the Hermetic . . . *Asclepius.*" The text that Debus cites from Rabelais's *Pantagruel* is part of Gargantua's famous letter to his son. Although it is full of praises for books, printing, libraries, erudition, classical studies—in short, the whole humanist program—Debus reads it as an expression of anti-livresque empiricism on the part of Rabelais. Passing over the view of some critics that the letter is a parody—not a representation of Rabelais's attitude—we may ask how Rabelais's commonplace recitation qualifies as hermetic. Gargantua advised his son

> that there is no sea, river or spring whose fish you shouldn't know; all the birds of the air, all the trees, bushes and shrubs of the forest; all the plants of the earth; all the metals hidden in the belly of the abyss; the stones of all the Orient and the South - let none of this be unknown to you. Then carefully reread the books of the Greek, Arab and Roman physicians, without slighting the Talmudists and Cabalists, and by frequent anatomies gain complete familiarity with the other world that is man. And several hours each day begin reading Holy Scripture, first of all the New Testament and the Epistles of the apostles in Greek, and then in Hebrew the Old Testament.

The text of the *Asclepius,* alleged to be "the ultimate source" of these thoughts, is as follows:

> As a prophet, I will tell you that after us there will remain none of that simple regard for philosophy found only in the continuing reflection and holy reverence by which one must recognize

divinity. Many make philosophy obscure in the multiplicity of their reasoning by combining it through ingenious argument with various branches of study that are not comprehensible— arithmetic, music, and geometry. Pure philosophy that depends only on reverence for god should attend to these other [teachings] only to wonder at the recurrence of the stars, how their measure stays constant in prescribed stations and in the orbit of their turning; it should learn the dimensions, qualities, and quantities of the land, the depths of the sea, the power of fire, and the nature and effects of all such things, in order to commend, worship, and wonder at the skill and mind of god. . . . The men who will come after us, deceived by the ingenuity of sophists, will be estranged from the true, pure, and holy philosophy. To adore the divinity with simple mind and soul, to honor his works and also to give thanks to the will of god . . . , this is a philosophy unprofaned by relentlessly curious thinking. And this is the treatment of these things.

Wonder, piety, simplicity, contemplation, the danger of curiosity, the incomprehensibility of mathematics—these are surely not the ingredients of a hermetic manifesto for the progress of science. In characterizing the "hostility to the sciences" that he finds in this passage of the *Asclepius,* A. J. Festugière cites the famous words of Tertullian on the remoteness of learned Athens from pious Jerusalem: "After Jesus Christ, all curiosity ceases, all inquiry after the Gospel. Believe, and want nothing more." According to Debus, the *Asclepius* advocates a "Christianized search for God's truth in nature that was to appeal to Renaissance philosophers," but if this text resembles anything Christian, it is the Christianity of patristic writers like Tertullian and Augustine, who feared the world of nature, along with the flesh and the devil, and grudgingly permitted study of nature only as a propaedeutic to piety. It was not the Christianity of John Ray, who saw God's wisdom manifest in his works and believed that the deepest study of nature was a holy calling. Nor, obviously, was it the Christianity of the world-affirming Rabelais, whose Gargantua moved easily from the book of nature to the books of Scripture and whose mind was as far from this ascetic text as his language. This passage of the *Asclepius* cannot even be called uniquely or distinctively "hermetic," except in the textual—and trivial—sense, for *both* the world-affirming *and* the world-denying messages broadcast in the various Platonizing religions and pious philosophies of late antiquity were heard by the authors of the hermetic corpus, who produced a medley of discordant views on the moral qualities of nature. For example, the tenth treatise tells us that the cosmos is not good because it is made of matter; the ninth maintains that to speak of an evil cosmos is blasphemous—despite the fact that the earth is evil. However, even the cosmic piety of the ninth tract leads not to a scientific cosmology but, at best, to an accommodation of cosmology with theology, at the expense of the former as an independent intellectual enterprise. The status of the study of material objects was low even for the "optimist" tracts, because of the pervasive influence in them of the contempt for matter that was widespread in Middle Platonism. Even the ninth treatise is a far cry from the

"hermetic theme" that Debus sees in Peter Severinus. After the customary Paracelsian (but un-Rabelaisian) exhortation to book burning, Severinus advises his readers to build their knowledge entirely upon immediate sense experience of human, natural, and artificial objects. If this emphasis on sense experience is truly and distinctively a hermetic theme in Severinus, how does it accord with the hermetism of the ninth *logos,* which justifies sensation only by making it a kind of intellection and calls the earth "the native land of evil"?

In an essay on Isaac Newton, Richard Westfall has suggested that hermetism was important to seventeenth-century science as a position opposed to the mechanical paradigm. While there is no doubt that Hermes remained an authoritative figure for many who contributed to the debates of the Scientific Revolution, it is less certain that our modern conceptions of hermetism have yet become clear and stable enough to guide us reliably through the thickets of seventeenth-century controversy. Westfall's hermetist, for example, saw nature as active, organic, and psychic (or ensouled); he asserts that this vitalist and animist conception of nature also encouraged belief in sympathies and spirits. Eugenio Garin has criticized Westfall's effort to find such "a general meaning" for hermetism, because it fails to appreciate the special historical circumstances of hermetism in Newton's time, as compared to Ficino's or Thomas Bradwardine's, and because it gives no distinctive meaning to the word. By Westfall's account, for example, Henry More would qualify as a hermetist. Yet Isaac Casaubon's redating of the *Hermetica* had convinced More that the Egyptian Hermes was a fraud, and More's doxography of natural philosophy in the *Conjectura cabbalistica* paid Hermes no honor. That Newton's biographer has concerned himself with intellectual-historical realities previously ignored or scorned by historians shows how much the history of science has matured, but this "general" understanding of hermetism can lead only to more confusion.

In my view, the term "hermetic" should be used primarily to name a set of texts: either the philosophical *Hermetica* published by Ficino and Lodovico Lazarelli—which, we should note, have little to say about magic or science—or popular *Hermetica,* such as the *Kyranides,* which were sources of empirical occultism. How else *might* "hermetic" be used? We might use it to refer to the ideas expressed in the texts just mentioned: As we have noted, however, these ideas are not only generally incoherent but, as far as the philosophical texts are concerned, especially uninteresting for natural philosophy. Again, the word might be used to describe a body of ideas—or the people who held them—without precise reference to either set of texts. Kepler's *mos Hermeticus* is evidence of such a usage, which seems to have developed further between his time and Brucker's; but historians should understand how diffuse the adjective becomes in these contexts. Perhaps by bearing in mind the theosophical and alchemical applications that I have described, scholars can prevent this slippery word from evading our comprehension entirely. The assumption that "hermetic" implies "magical" and the reverse is especially to be avoided. During the Scientific Revolution much debate about magic made no reference to the

Hermetica; by the same token, for a Fludd or a Francesco Giorgi the theological appeal of the hermetic writings could operate quite independently of any interest in magic. As a substitute for "hermetic," I suggest that the term "occultist" will serve to refer generally to magic, astrology, demonology, and divination. The term "occultism" and its cognates admittedly are problematic, in the same way that the term "humanism" is problematic. "Occultism" is a nineteenth-century invention, obscured by the special attitudes of that period and by subsequent semantic overlay; hence, it is colored both by nineteenth-century positivism and by twentieth-century occultist fads. But there is precedent for this broad use of "occultist," and unlike "hermetic," which should be freed for more exact employment, it implies no particular textual or doxographic content.

Future debate on hermetism in the history of science should focus on four problems: first, on discovering precisely how natural philosophers and others used the word "hermetic" in the early modern period; second, on deepening our understanding of the meaning of the word in alchemy and the new theosophy; third, on evaluating the significance of the hermetic doxographic tradition as compared to other doxographies bearing on science, especially the tradition that legitimized atomism by associating it with Moses, Pythagoras, and Democritus; and fourth, on determining the contribution of the popular *Hermetica* to the development of a body of empirical evidence for occultism. Except as they may be interested in topics such as these, scholars who wish to explore the relation between occultism and early modern science can turn their attention from the "Yates thesis," if they understand this thesis to claim that a distinctly hermetic tradition based on the philosophical *Hermetica* was of central importance in the history of early modern science. Even as a doxography, and especially after Casaubon's redating of the philosophical Hermetica to late antiquity, hermetism was probably less important than Mosaic atomism. In my opinion, however, historians of science ought to pursue the broader implications of the work of Frances Yates, especially her catholic and imaginative desire to explore areas of thought and culture hitherto considered insignificant or inappropriate to serious historical discourse. The decline of natural magic as a normal and legitimate concern of Western natural philosophy, for example, was one of the most important features of the Scientific Revolution. The complexity of that revolution will be better appreciated when research is based on more precise use of terms such as "natural magic" and "hermetism."

FURTHER READING

Cosmology

Dick, Steven J. "The Heliocentric Theory, Scripture, and the Plurality of Earths." In *Plurality of Worlds: The Origins of the Extraterrestrial Life Debate from Democritus to Kant.* Cambridge: Cambridge University Press, 1982, 246 p.
> Discusses the influence of philosophers Giordano Bruno and Tommaso Campanella and astronomer Johannes Kepler on Renaissance beliefs regarding the nature of the world and the universe.

Johnson, Francis R. *Astronomical Thought in Renaissance England: A Study of the English Scientific Writings from 1500 to 1645.* Baltimore: Johns Hopkins Press, 1937, 357 p.
> Discusses the writings of Copernicus, Thomas Digges, and Tycho Brahe in an analysis of the development of cosmological beliefs.

Astrology

Allen, Don Cameron. *The Star-Crossed Renaissance: The Quarrel about Astrology and Its Influence in England.* Durham, N.C.: Duke University Press, 1941, 280 p.
> Discusses the influence of the astrological beliefs of Marsilio Ficino, Giovanni Pico della Mirandola, and Giovanni Pontano on Elizabethan England, and examines Elizabethans' arguments and reactions to the astrological doctrine of their time.

Curry, Patrick. *Prophecy and Power: Astrology in Early Modern England.* Cambridge: Polity Press, 1989, 238 p.
> Provides a detailed analysis of the development of astrology through the Interregnum and after the Restoration, from its heyday to its demise.

Garin, Eugenio. *Astrology in the Renaissance.* Translated by Carolyn Jackson and June Allen. London: Routledge & Kegan Paul, 1983, 145 p.
> Discusses the historical aspects of astrology, as well as the relationship between astrology, magic, neoplatonism, and hermeticism.

Halbronn, Jacques E. "The Revealing Process of Translation and Criticism in the History of Astrology." In *Astrology, Science and Society: Historical Essays,* edited by Patrick Curry, pp. 197-218. Suffolk, England: The Boydell Press, 1987.
> Analyzes the influence of French astrological and anti-astrological writings in England.

Heninger, S. K., Jr. *A Handbook of Renaissance Meteorology.* Durham, N.C.: Duke University Press, 1960, 269 p.
> Discusses astrological meteorology and the use of meteorological imagery by Edmund Spenser, Christopher Marlowe, Ben Jonson, George Chapman, John Donne, and William Shakespeare.

Parr, Johnstone. *Tamburlaine's Malady and Other Essays on Astrology in Elizabethan Drama.* University, Ala.: University of Alabama Press, 1953, 158 p.
> Discusses allusions to astrology in a number of Elizabethan dramas using information from Renaissance and Elizabethan astrological textbooks.

Magic

Merkel, Ingrid, and Debus, Allen G., eds. *Hermeticism and the Renaissance: Intellectual History and the Occult in Early Modern Europe.* London: Associated University Presses, 1988, 438 p.
> Provides a brief history of hermeticism and discusses it within the context of magic, philosophy, science, literature, and art.

Vickers, Brian, ed. *Occult and Scientific Mentalities in the Renaissance.* Cambridge: Cambridge University Press, 1984, 408 p.
> Analyzes the extent to which magic and science influenced each other during the Renaissance.

Walder, D. P. *Spiritual and Demonic Magic: From Ficino to Campanella.* London: Warburg Institute of the University of London, 1958, 244 p.

    Analyzes the forms and practices of spiritual and demonic magic as discussed by such philosophers as Marsilio Ficino, Gemistus Pletho, Lodovico Lazarello, and Tommaso Campanella.

Webster, Charles. *From Paracelsus to Newton: Magic and the Making of Modern Science.* Cambridge: Cambridge University Press, 1982, 107 p.

    Discusses the relationship between prophecy, spiritual magic, demonic magic, and science.

Yeats, W. B. "Per Amica Silentia Lunae: Anima Mundi." In *Essays,* pp. 507-35. New York: Macmillan Co., 1924.

    Discusses spiritual magic and the nature of the soul.

Henry Vaughan

1621-1695

Welsh-born English poet.

INTRODUCTION

Vaughan is among the foremost of the seventeenth-century religious poets of the Commonwealth era, occupying a high position in the literature of his time along with John Donne and George Herbert. While his early poetry places him among the "Sons of Ben," imitators of Ben Jonson, his poetry from the late 1640s and 1650s, published in two editions of *Silex Scintillans* (1650 and 1655) places him in the School of Donne and the religious poets of the period. His transition from the influence of the Jacobean neoclassical poets to the Metaphysicals was one manifestation of his reaction to the English Civil War, which concluded with the Church of England outlawed and low-church Protestantism in ascendancy. Vaughan kept faith with Anglicanism largely through *Silex Scintillans*, his sympathetic poetic response to Herbert's poetic expression of Christian belief, *The Temple* (1633). Vaughan's reputation rests squarely upon *Silex Scintillans*, in which appear his best-known works, including "The Retreat," "The World," which begins with the often-quoted lines, "I saw Eternity the other night / Like a great *Ring* of pure and endless light," and the poem called by one scholar "the crown of Vaughan's poetry," "They are all gone into the world of light!"

Biographical Information

Vaughan was the elder of twin sons born to Thomas and Denise Vaughan of Newton-by-Usk, Brecknockshire, in South Wales. (His brother, Thomas, grew up to become a poet in his own right, as well as a mystic and alchemist.) He was raised on a small estate in the parish of Llanssantffread, within sight of the mountains, valleys, and the river Usk, which figure strongly in his poetry. Most biographers posit that he matriculated at Oxford with his brother Thomas in 1638, but that he left in 1640 without taking a degree, journeying to London to study law at the Inns of Court. Vaughan's law studies were interrupted by the outbreak of the Civil War in 1642. It is unclear whether he participated in the war as a combatant, but it is clear that the war's aftermath, especially the suppression of the Anglican church, had a profound impact on his poetry. In 1650, the year after Charles I was executed, Vaughan published the first edition of his *Silex Scintillans*, which marked the beginning of his most active period as a writer. In addition to poetry, Vaughan published a prose devotional work, *The Mount of Olives* (1652), and translated several short works by Plutarch, Maximus Tirius, Johannes Nierembergius, Eucherius of Lyons, and Paulinus of Bordeaux on such topics as morality, humility, temperance, patience, and the meaning of life and death. In the

mid 1650s, at age thirty-five, Vaughan turned from poetry to a career of practicing medicine. After beginning his medical practice he published nothing for the next twenty years, until the appearance of *Thalia Rediviva*. He adopted the life of a Welsh country gentleman and gave himself the title "the silurist" (after the ancient Silures, who had once inhabited his native South Wales). Having twice married, and having fathered several children by both wives, Vaughan spent his last years embroiled in a series of legal actions taken by his children in which he defended himself against charges of favoritism in the dispersal of family property. Vaughan finally resolved the matter the year before his death in 1695.

Major Works

Vaughan's first volume, *Poems, with the tenth Satyre of Juvenal Englished*, appeared in 1646, attracting scant but respectful notice. Another collection of secular poetry, *Olor Iscanus*, was completed within a year of the appearance of *Poems* but not published until 1651. The work included a brief prefatory remark by Thomas Vaughan intimating that but for his influence the poems would have been destroyed by their author. During this period, it is believed that Vaughan's anxiety and grief associated with the anti-royalists' triumph in the Civil War and the death of a younger brother contributed to a profound religious experience that turned him to the writing of poetry on Christian themes. His poetry, which had to this point followed the neoclassical emphasis upon form and objective contemplation of the inanimate, became personal and contemplative within a Christian-humanist framework. The first volume of *Silex Scintillans* was considered far superior in power to the poet's earlier work. The second, enlarged edition of *Silex Scintillans*, though not considered an overall improvement, does include the acclaimed "They are all gone into the world of light!" The next few years saw Vaughan publishing much of a Christian humanist nature, notably the devotions included in *The Mount of Olives* and the new poetry collection *Flores Solitudinis* (1654). Vaughan's final publication, *Thalia Rediviva*, includes juvenilia and odd pieces written both before and (it is believed) after *Silex Scintillans*. The work also contains poems by Thomas Vaughan and several prefatory encomnia in verse.

Critical Reception

Vaughan's poetry was neglected by critics until it came to the attention of the Romantics near the end of the eighteenth century. Wordsworth acquired a copy of *Silex Scintillans*, and it is believed by many that Vaughan's "The Retreat" directly influenced his "Ode: Intimations of Immortality," with both poems being bittersweet, personal ruminations upon the divine source of childhood innocence. This question of influence is the source of much critical discussion, with recent scholarship noting that though direct influence cannot be proved, it is certain that Vaughan's poetry and its metaphysical concerns were certainly "in the air" among Wordsworth's circle. Several editions of Vaughan's works were published during the nineteenth century, culminating in Alexander B. Grosart's four-volume omnibus collection in 1871. This edition was succeeded by L. C. Martin's collected edition of 1914, which roughly coincided with a rise in critical and popular interest in the poetry of John Donne and the Metaphysicals, due largely to H. J. C. Grierson's editions of their works. Martin's edition spurred much critical and biographical activity, eliciting comment and seminal studies by T. S. Eliot, E. L. Marilla, Frank Kermode, E. C. Pettet, and F. E. Hutchinson, author of the definitive biography. Kermode articulated one point of critical debate that endures: the question of Vaughan's alleged religious transformation before the publication of *Silex Scintillans*. Kermode contends that the poet's conversion "was rather a poetic than a religious experience," holding that Vaughan's poems should be appraised "as poetry rather than as prayer." Kermode has been answered by other scholars, notably H. J. Oliver. Another point, debated by many critics, is the question of whether Vaughan's accomplishment evidences sustained poetic power or, rather, mere flashes of occasional but undeniable brilliance. On these and other issues have many full-length studies of Vaughan's works been published since 1960.

PRINCIPAL WORKS

Poems, with the Tenth Satyre of Iuvenal Englished (poetry) 1646
Silex Scintillans; or, Sacred Poems and Priuate Eiaculations (poetry) 1650; revised edition, 1655
Olor Iscanus (discourses) 1651
The Mount of Olives; or, Solitary Devotions (discourse and devotions) 1652
Flores Solitudinis (discourses and devotions) 1654
Thalia Rediviva (poetry) 1678
The Works of Henry Vaughan. 2 vols. (poetry, discourses, and devotions) 1916

Orinda   (poem date 1651)

SOURCE: "To Mr. Henry Vaughan the Silurist: Upon These and His Former Poems," in *The Works in Verse and Prose Complete of Henry Vaughan, Silurist,* Vol. II, edited by Rev. Alexander B. Grosart, Blackburn, 1871, pp. 187-89.

[*Katherine Philips, who wrote under the pseudonym Orinda, was a seventeenth-century English poet whose work was highly regarded during her lifetime and by John Keats during the nineteenth century. She was hailed as "the match-*

less Orinda" by her contemporaries. In the following set of iambic pentameter couplets, which preface Olor Iscanus *(1651), Orinda eloquently celebrates Vaughan's accomplishment as a poet.*]

Had I ador'd the multitude, and thence
Got an antipathy to wit and sence,
And hugg'd that fate, in hope the world
    would grant
'Twas good affection to be ignorant:
Yet the least ray of thy bright fancy seen,
I had converted, or excuseless been.
For each birth of thy Muse to after-times
Shall expiate for all this Age's crimes.
First shines thy **"Amoret,"** twice crown'd by
    thee:
Once by thy love, next by thy poetrie;
Where thou the best of unions dost dispense,
Truth cloth'd in wit, and Love in innocence.
So that the muddie lover may learn here,
No fountains can be sweet, that are not clear.
There Juvenal, by thee reviv'd declares
How flat man's joys are, and how mean his
    cares;
And wisely doth upbraid the World, that they
Should such a value for their ruine pay.
        But when thy sacred Muse diverts her quill
The landskip to design of Sion's Hill,
As nothing else was worthy her, or thee,
So we admire almost t' idolatrie.
What savage breast would not be rap'd to find
Such jewels in such cabinets enshrin'd?
Thou fill'd with joys—too great to see or
    count:—
Descend'st from thence, like Moses from the
    Mount,
And with a candid, yet unquestion'd awe
Restor'st the Golden Age, when verse was Law.
Instructing us, thou so secur'st thy fame,
That nothing can disturb it but my name.
Nay I have hopes that standing so near thine
Twill loose its dross, and by degrees refine.
Live! till the disabusèd world consent
All truths of use, of strength or ornament,
Are with such harmony by thee display'd
As the whole world was first by number made;
And from the charming rigour thy Muse brings
Learn, there's no pleasure but in serious things!

Nathaniel Williams   (poem date 1678)

SOURCE: "To the Ingenious Author of *Thalia Rediviva,*" in *The Works in Verse and Prose Complete of Henry Vaughan, Silurist,* Vol. II, edited by Rev. Alexander B. Grosart, Blackburn, 1871, pp. 190-92.

[*Williams was a friend and admirer of Vaughan. In the following poem, which prefaces* Thalia Rediviva *(1678), he praises Vaughan as one blessed by the poetic Muse to lead readers into the path of Virtue. (Williams's "an immortal offering" concludes an allusion to Vaughan's translation of Claudian's "Phoenix" in* Thalia Rediviva.*)*]

ODE. I.

Where reverend bards of old have sate
    And sung the pleasant enterludes of Fate,

Thou takest the hereditary shade
Which Nature's homely art had made,
And thence thou gav'st thy Muse her swing, and
she
Advances to the galaxie;
There with the sparkling COWLEY she above
Does hand in hand in grateful measures move.
We groveling mortals gaze below,
And long in vain to know
Her wondrous paths, her wondrous flight:
In vaine, alas! we grope,
In vain we use our earthly telescope,
We'r blinded by an intermedial night:
Thine eagle-Muse can only face
The fiery coursers in their race,
While with unequal paces we do try
To bear her train aloft, and keep her company.

II.

The loud harmonious Mantuan
Once charm'd the world; and here's the Uscan
swan
In his declining years does chime,
And challenge the last remaines of Time.
Ages run on, and soon give o're,
They have their graves as well as we;
Time swallows all that's past and more,
Yet Time is swallow'd in eternity:
This is the only profit poets see.
There thy triumphant Muse shall ride in state
And lead in chains devouring Fate;
Claudian's bright phoenix she shall bring
Thee an immortal offering;
Nor shall my humble tributary Muse
Her homage and attendance too refuse;
She thrusts her self among the crowd
And joyning in th' applause she strives to clap
aloud.

III.

Tell me no more that Nature is severe
Thou great philosopher!
Lo! she has laid her vast exchequer here.
Tell me no more that she has sent
So much already, she is spent;
Here is a vast America behind
Which none but the great Silurist could find.
Nature her last edition was the best,
As big as rich as all the rest:
So will we here admit
Another world of wit.
No rude or savage fancy here shall stay
The travailing reader in his way,
But every coast is clear: go were he will
Vertu's the road THALIA leads him still
Long may she live, and wreath thy sacred head
For this her happy resurrection from the dead.

Rev. H. F. Lyte   (essay date 1847)

SOURCE: "Biographical Sketch of Henry Vaughan," in *The Sacred Poems and Private Ejaculations of Henry Vaughan,* edited by Rev. H. F. Lyte, Little, Brown, and Company, 1854, pp. 1-30.

[*Lyte was an English clergyman and minor poet who published* The Sacred Poems and Private Ejaculations of Henry Vaughan *along with the following assessment of Vaughan's achievement shortly before his death in 1847.*]

The mind and heart of [Vaughan] are abundantly exhibited in his writings, which are full of individuality; and, while we would deprecate pledging ourselves to every sentiment they contain, we feel that they claim for him unvarying respect, and commend themselves to us as the genuine overflowings of a sincere and humble spirit. We feel, while reading them, that we have to do with a truly good and earnest man. His poems display much originality of thought, and frequently likewise much felicity of expression. The former is, indeed, at times condensed into obscurity, and the latter defaced with quaintness. But Vaughan never degenerates into a smooth versifier of commonplaces. One, indeed, of his great faults as a poet, is the attempt to crowd too much of matter into his sentences, so that they read roughly and inharmoniously, the words almost elbowing each other out of the lines. His rhymes, too, are frequently defective; and he delights in making the sense of one line run over into the line following. This, when not overdone, is doubtless a beauty in versification, and redeems it from that monotony which so offends in the poets of Queen Anne's time. Yet even this may be pushed to excess, and become by its uniformity liable itself to the imputation of monotony. Take, for instance, the very beautiful lines of Vaughan entitled **"Rules and Lessons,"** the first five stanzas of which strikingly exemplify the fault here specified; and it was perhaps their consequent harshness that induced Bernard Barton to transpose them, not infelicitously, into a different stanza. A more favourable specimen of line flowing into line is the following morning address to a **"Bird:"** —

Hither thou com'st. The busie wind all night
Blew through thy lodging; where thy own warm
wing
Thy pillow was; and many a sullen storm,
For which coarse man seems much the fitter
born,
Rained on thy bed,
And harmless head;
And now, as fresh and cheerful as the light,
Thy little heart in early hymns doth sing!

This will be felt to be very tender and beautiful, notwithstanding the imperfect rhyme in the fourth line; and the volume now republished is full of like passages. Indeed, it may with truth be said of Vaughan, that his faults are in a great measure those of the age he lived in, and the master he imitated, while his beauties are all his own. That he will ever become a thoroughly popular poet is scarcely to be expected in this age. But among those who can prize poetic thought, even when clad in a dress somewhat quaint and antiquated, who love to commune with a heart overflowing with religious ardour, and who do not value this the less because it has been lighted at the earlier and purer fires of Christianity, and has caught a portion of their youthful glow, poems like [those] of Henry Vaughan's will not want their readers, nor will such readers be unthankful to have our author and his works introduced to their acquaintance.

George MacDonald   (essay date 1868)

SOURCE: "A Mount of Vision—Henry Vaughan," in *England's Antiphon,* Macmillan & Co. Publishers, 1868, pp. 251-79.

[*A Scottish man of letters, MacDonald was a key figure in shaping the fantastic and mythopoeic literature of the nineteenth and twentieth centuries. Such novels as* Phantastes *(1858) and* The Princess and the Goblin *(1872) are considered classics of fantasy literature. These works have influenced C. S. Lewis, Charles Williams, T. S. Eliot, J. R. R. Tolkien, and other seekers of divine truth, adventure, and escape from mortal limitations. During his long, prolific career, MacDonald also wrote in several other genres, achieving particular success with his novels of British country life. In the following excerpt from his* England's Antiphon *(1868), he offers an overview of Vaughan's career, focusing upon the mystical, the naturalistic, and the child-centered elements in the poetry, and comparing Vaughan's work to that of George Herbert and William Wordsworth.*]

Henry Vaughan belongs to the mystical school, but his poetry rules his theories. You find no more of the mystic than the poet can easily govern; in fact, scarcely more than is necessary to the highest poetry. He develops his mysticism upwards, with relation to his higher nature alone: it blossoms into poetry. His twin-brother Thomas developed his mysticism down-wards in the direction of the material sciences—a true effort still, but one in which the danger of ceasing to be true increases with increasing ratio the further it is carried. . . .

Henry Vaughan was then nearly thirty years younger than George Herbert, whom he consciously and intentionally imitates. His art is not comparable to that of Herbert: hence Herbert remains the master; for it is not the thought that makes the poet; it is the utterance of that thought in worthy presence of speech. He is careless and somewhat rugged. If he can get his thought dressed, and thus made visible, he does not mind the dress fitting awkwardly, or even being a little out at elbows. And yet he has grander lines and phrases than any in Herbert. He has occasionally a daring success that strikes one with astonishment. In a word, he says more splendid things than Herbert, though he writes inferior poems. His thought is profound and just; the harmonies in his soul are true; its artistic and musical ear is defective. His movements are sometimes grand, sometimes awkward. Herbert is always gracious—I use the word as meaning much more than *graceful.*

Let any one who is well acquainted with Wordsworth's grand ode—that on the "Intimations of Immortality"—turn his mind to a comparison between that and [**"The Retreat"**]: he will find the resemblance remarkable. Whether **"The Retreat"** suggested the form of the "Ode" is not of much consequence, for the "Ode" is the outcome at once and essence of all Wordsworth's theories; and whatever he may have drawn from **"The Retreat"** is glorified in the "Ode." Still it is interesting to compare them. Vaughan believes with Wordsworth and some other great men that this is not our first stage of existence; that we are haunted by dim memories of a former state. This belief is not necessary, however, to sympathy with the poem, for whether the present be our first life or no, we have come from God, and bring from him conscience and a thousand godlike gifts. —"Happy those early days," Vaughan begins: "There was a time," begins Wordsworth, "when the earth seemed apparelled in celestial light." "Before I understood this place," continues Vaughan: "Blank misgivings of a creature moving about in worlds not realized," says Wordsworth. "A white celestial thought," says Vaughan: "Heaven lies about us in our infancy," says Wordsworth. "A mile or two off, I could see his face," says Vaughan: "Trailing clouds of glory do we come," says Wordsworth. "On some gilded cloud or flower, my gazing soul would dwell an hour," says Vaughan: "The hour of splendour in the grass, of glory in the flower," says Wordsworth.

Wordsworth's poem is the profounder in its philosophy, as well as far the grander and lovelier in its poetry; but in the moral relation, Vaughan's poem is the more definite of the two, and gives us in its close, poor as that is compared with the rest of it, just what we feel is wanting in Wordsworth's—the hope of return to the bliss of childhood. We may be comforted for what we lose by what we gain; but that is not a recompense large enough to be divine: we want both. Vaughan will be a child again. For the movements of man's life are in spirals: we go back whence we came, ever returning on our former traces, only upon a higher level, on the next upward coil of the spiral, so that it is a going back and a going forward ever and both at once. Life is, as it were, a constant repentance, or thinking of it again: the childhood of the kingdom takes the place of the childhood of the brain, but comprises all that was lovely in the former delight. The heavenly children will subdue kingdoms, work righteousness, wax valiant in fight, rout the armies of the aliens, merry of heart as when in the nursery of this world they fought their fancied frigates, and defended their toy-battlements. . . .

Many a true thought comes out by the help of a fancy or half-playful exercise of the thinking power. There is a good deal of such fancy in [**"The Night"**], but in the end it rises to the height of the purest and best mysticism. We must not forget that the deepest man can utter, will be but the type or symbol of a something deeper yet, of which he can perceive only a doubtful glimmer. . . .

[**"The Night"**] is glorious; and its lesson of quiet and retirement we need more than ever in these hurried days upon which we have fallen. If men would but be still enough in themselves to hear, through all the noises of the busy light, the voice that is ever talking on in the dusky chambers of their hearts! . . . I think this poem *grander* than any of George Herbert's. I use the word with intended precision. [Consider also **"The Dawning,"**] the end of which is not so good, poetically considered, as the magnificent beginning, but which contains striking lines throughout. . . .

I do not think [Vaughan's] description of the dawn has ever been surpassed. The verse "All expect some sudden matter," is wondrously fine. The water "dead and in a grave," because stagnant, is a true fancy; and the "ac-

The Breconshire Beacons, mountains visible from Vaughan's childhood home in the parish of Llansantffraed.

quainted elsewhere" of the running stream, is a masterly phrase. I need not point out the symbolism of the poem.

I do not know a writer, Wordsworth not excepted, who reveals more delight in the visions of Nature than Henry Vaughan. He is a true forerunner of Wordsworth, inasmuch as the latter sets forth with only greater profundity and more art than he, the relations between Nature and Human Nature; while, on the other hand, he is the forerunner as well of some one that must yet do what Wordsworth has left almost unattempted, namely—set forth the sympathy of Nature with the aspirations of the spirit that is born of God, born again, I mean, in the recognition of the child's relation to the Father. Both Herbert and Vaughan have thus read Nature, the latter turning many leaves which few besides have turned. In this he has struck upon a deeper and richer lode than even Wordsworth, although he has not wrought it with half his skill. In any history of the development of the love of the present age for Nature, Vaughan, although I fear his influence would be found to have been small as yet, must be represented as the Phosphor of coming dawn. Beside him, Thomson is cold, artistic, and gray: although larger in scope, he is not to be compared with him in sympathetic sight. It is this insight that makes Vaughan a mystic. He can see one thing everywhere, and all things the same—yet each with a thousand sides that radiate crossing lights, even as the airy particles around us. For him everything is the expression of, and points back to, some fact in the Divine Thought. Along the line of every ray he looks towards its radiating centre—the heart of the Maker.

Rev. Alexander B. Grosart   (essay date 1871)

SOURCE: "Essay on the Life and Writings of Henry Vaughan, Silurist," in *The Works in Verse and Prose Complete of Henry Vaughan, Silurist,* Vol. II, edited by Rev. Alexander B. Grosart, Blackburn, 1871, pp. ix-ci.

[*Grosart was a nineteenth-century English clergyman and editor of numerous collections of works by British authors from the period 1400 to 1800. He published editions of the works of Richard Crashaw, Samuel Daniel, Sir Philip Sidney, and several other literary figures. In the following excerpt from his prefatory essay in volume two of Vaughan's collected works, Grosart compares Vaughan's accomplishment favorably to that of George Herbert.*]

Comparisons have been instituted between Vaughan and GEORGE HERBERT of the most uncritical and baseless kind. I must frankly avow that it is a wonder to me how a mind of the insight and acumen of DR. GEORGE MACDONALD in *Antiphon*—where he has written so many wise and beautiful things about him—came to adjudge the Poet of *The Temple* a higher place *qua* Poet than the Silurist. With all my reverence and love for critic and subject, I must regard the verdict as a freak of judgment resting on some early (tacit) association. It is the very *fantastique* of criticism, as I take it, either in substance or workmanship to exalt good George Herbert above either Vaughan or RICHARD CRASHAW. His was a lovely soul, and in his verse there is the very spicery of a sweet, gentle, innocent piety: but after all it is fragrance rather than form, flower-scent not flower-beauty. I do not find in all GEORGE HER-BERT has written one scintillation of that interblending of Imagination and Fact that stamps a man as a Maker: his foot never crossed that spirit-region wherein Fancy (in its deepest sense) sculptures her grand conceptions and whence there come from the very blows of the worker, bursts of music. So that I must regard the Silurist's gener-ous praise of Herbert as true to his feeling but untrue and misleading to his genius. It is the mere tradition of criti-cism to class **Silex Scintillans** with *The Temple*. From the inevitableness of common themes and common experience and common beliefs, there are occasional reminiscences of the latter in the former: but with these slight exceptions, HENRY VAUGHAN indubitably is a Poet of an incompara-bly loftier and original caste. There are things in Vaughan's poetry that Herbert never could have dared to reach: and indeed Dr. MacDonald has glimpses of this, though he does not give it that preponderance that belongs to it.

I limit VAUGHAN's debt to HERBERT almost wholly to spiritual quickening and the gift of gracious feeling: more than that is profoundly exaggerate, and I must absolutely affirm with ARCHBISHOP TRENCH: "As a divine Vaughan may be inferior, but as a poet he is certainly superior, to Herbert, who never wrote anything so purely poetical as "**The Retreat**". I regret that his Grace should have added: "Still Vaughan would never probably have written as he has, if Herbert, whom he gratefully owns as his Master, had not shown him the way". Vaughan has nowhere called Herbert his Master *as a Poet* and their poetry is fun-damentally distinct, to every one who will ponder their ways of looking at precisely the same things. That spiritu-ally Herbert had the most potential influence on Vaughan is certain. His Epistle and Preface to **Silex Scintillans** gratefully proclaim it: and in his Prose Writings the im-press of *The Temple* is plain. He works into the **Mount of Olives** stanzas from Herbert, and but that they were famil-iar to us, from the way they are introduced we might have regarded them as his own. Then unconsciously I believe, his thoughts clothed themselves in his prose with Her-bert's words. For example we read in the **Mount of Olives** the following, "Let sensual natures judge as they please, but for my part, I shall hold it no paradoxe to affirme, there are no pleasures in this world. *Some coloured griefes of blushing woes there are, which look as clear as if they were true complexions; but it is a very sad and a tryed truth, that they are but painted*". This is plainly fetched from Herbert's "Rose":

> Press me not to take more pleasure
> In this world of sugar'd lies,
> And to use a larger measure
> Than my strict yet welcome size.
> *First, there is no pleasure here:*
> *Colour'd griefs indeed there are,*
> *Blushing woes that look as clear,*
> *As if they could beauty spare.*

I can't say I was sorry to trace the sentiment to another than Vaughan himself: its second-hand derivation allows me to think its touch of misanthropy was not spontaneous. A small whimper of this sort has nothing of the terrible pathos of the old "*Vanitas Vanitatum*": and in this still ra-

diant Earth is a blunder if not worse, though meant for spiritual-mindedness. Summarily I deny that HENRY VAUGHAN was an imitator of GEORGE HERBERT. In the latter's "Decay", a frequent thought with the Silurist is found but it is one of the blessed common-places of the Bible, to wit, the familiarity of the Divine presence in the Earth under the elder dispensation. Herbert's "Peace", has tones that resound sweetly in Vaughan's **"Peace"** but again there is nothing peculiar to either or rather both had evidently before them the grand old hymn "O mother dear Jerusalem". One is at a loss to know where WILLMOTT found 'imitation' in "**Beyond the Veil**" 's final stanza,

> Either disperse those mists which blot and fill
> My perspective as they pass,
> Or else remove me hence unto that Hill
> Where I shall need no glass:

of Herbert's "Grace", as thus,

> O come! for Thou dost know the way
> Or if to me Thou wilt not move,
> Remove me where I need not say—
> Drop from above.

The thing is rediculous. I notice only another point, viz., the alleged superior art of HERBERT. Says Dr. MACDON-ALD "His [Vaughan's] art is not comparable to that of Herbert: hence Herbert remains the master; for it is not the thought that makes the poet; it is the utterance of that thought in worthy presence of speech. He is careless, and somewhat rugged. If he can get his thought dressed, and thus made visible, he does not mind the dress fitting awk-wardly, or even being a little out at elbows. And yet he has grander lines and phrases than any in Herbert. He has oc-casionally a daring success that strikes one with astonish-ment. In a word, he says more splendid things than Her-bert, though he writes inferior poems. His thought is pro-found and just; the harmonies in his soul are true; its artis-tic and musical ear is defective. His movements are some-times grand, sometimes awkward. Herbert is always gra-cious—I use the word as meaning much more than *grace-ful*." The appreciation of Vaughan by Dr. MacDonald is so wholehearted, and elsewhere so nobly stated that it pains me to say so: but the negligence of HERBERT's versi-fication, the incongruity of many of his images, the triviali-ty of his conceits, the meanness of his symbols, and the ab-sence of that grandeur which is patent in Vaughan, have been so long admitted as blots that I am at a stand to know by what *glamour* they have been passed by such a Critic. I will not deny that there are what seem discordant notes or tones in Vaughan, even occasional inadequacy in the wording for the thinking or feeling; but to liken the march of his splendid Poetry for one instant with the tinkling pie-ties of *The Temple* or to weigh graciousness of sentiment against grandeur of thought, is I apprehend superlatively uncritical and esthetically false. Moreover I demur to "ut-terance of the thought in worthy presence of speech" being *the* criterion of the Poet. By that standard you will make DENHAM and POPE earlier and Campbell and Sam-uel Rogers later *the* poets of their century or in our day you will put WILLIAM MORRIS above ROBERT BROW-NING. Besides, one must get his spirit 'keyed' (to use Vaughan's word) to the music and rhythm of a master-poet before you say of him that he is 'awkward'. There are odd and puzzling rhymes in Vaughan: but twenty-fold more such in Herbert. . . .

Correctness, immaculate measure and 'smoothness' without 'the thoughts that breathe' will never make a man more than a Versifier. The thought not the form decides the question: perfection of both is only to be found once in centuries. Vaughan's thought is always true, his feelings fine and his utterance melodious. Herbert's thought is often thin and his feelings oftener valetudinarian, and his wording common-place. It is his pervading goodness and sanctity that have so transfigured his Verse: and his Life as told by ISAAC WALTON is so charmingly sweet, tender, loveable that one has an accusing sense in saying one syllable derogatory. Nevertheless, the truth must be spoken as meeting the preposterous claim for him of higher *poetic* power than Vaughan's.

Then in another aspect, I believe that the Silurist with all his spontaneity, as of a Nightingale, spent more time in fining and refining his verse than might be supposed. . . .

It would seem clear, therefore, that while the art was concealed, there was art in our Worthy's workmanship on his verse, as well on its rhythm as rhyme. There are occasional alliterations long-drawn out, and the thought of one line passed on into another, as tune melting into tune, that betoken studied intention so to present what he had to sing. His use of monosyllables or what may be and ordinarily are such so as to compel the Reader to make them dissyllables, and similarly with others, produces a fine effect, as of a stone splitting a stream and making a sweeter and tender music thereby. Altogether with every abatement in respect of defective rhymes by our standard that were not defective at the period, through their pronounciation, and accordingly are found in the highest Masters, and conceding that the thought is sometimes so thick-coming and weighty as to give a shadow of obscurity (or call it *chiaroscuro*) or at least ellipsis at a first reading, I must regard HENRY VAUGHAN as more than the equal of GEORGE HERBERT even in form. In the deeper elements, in the electric flash that does'nt so much tell of Wordsworth's supernal light, as of the fire of genius kindled by the Great Giver alone, and which no mere piety or mere culture can ever send forth—the penetrative seizure of the innermost subtleties of feeling and prisoning them in human speech, such as later was the imperial gift of Shelley—the vision of the mysteries of the Universe, veiled and curtained, fold on fold, to ordinary mortal eyes—the sudden surprise of grand thoughts uttered with the simpleness of a child and as though nothing remarkable, and really to the utterer un-remarkable—the calm footstep and the uplifted eye in the most interior regions of Wonder-land—the transfiguring radiance cast on lowliest things so as to lift the "meanest flower that blows" into fellowship with man—the recognition of the manifold symbolisms of Nature in opposition to mere conceits of analogy put into Nature—the bird-like bursts of *abandonment* of verbal music that no Thalberg-fingers can simulate—comparison of the "sweet Singer" of *The Temple* with the poet of *Silex Scintillans* is to my mind an outrage by every canon of critical estimate. I rejoice that it has been given to me worthily to reproduce for the first time the complete Words of a genius

so idiosyncratic, so certain to win capable Readers the more he is studied; and my satisfaction is the truer, in that with all his morbid modesty and depreciation of himself, HENRY VAUGHAN again and again reveals his consciousness of being a Poet concerning whom Posterity should inquire, one whose gift it was to confer immortality. May his beloved USCA, lucent and beautiful to-day as in his day, abide in ever-enduring association with his name: or, adapting MATTHEW ARNOLD's exquisite tribute to WORDSWORTH, I would address WELSHMEN (if they be not too degenerate in poetic sympathy to enter into it,) thus:

> Keep fresh the grass upon his grave,
> O Usca! with thy living wave,
> Sing him thy best! for few or none,
> Hear thy voice right, now he is gone.

George Saintsbury   (essay date 1890)

SOURCE: "Caroline Poetry," in *A History of Elizabethan Literature,* second edition, 1890. Reprint by The Macmillan Company., 1924, pp. 354-93.

[*Saintsbury was a late-nineteenth and early-twentieth-century English literary historian and critic. Hugely prolific, he composed histories of English and European literature as well as numerous critical works on individual authors, styles, and periods. In the following excerpt from the second (1890) edition of his* History of Elizabethan Literature *(reprinted several times during its publishing history), Saintsbury briefly dismisses Vaughan as a poet lacking sustained poetic skill, depth, and originality.*]

Henry Vaughan was born in 1622, published *Poems* in 1646 (for some of which he afterwards expressed a not wholly necessary repentance), *Olor Iscanus* (from Isca Silurum) in 1651, and *Silex Scintillans,* his best-known book, in 1650 and 1656. He also published verses much later, and did not die till 1693, being the latest lived of any man who has a claim to appear in this book, but his aftergrowths were not happy. To say that Vaughan is a poet of one poem would not be true. But the universally known

> They are all gone into the world of light

is so very much better than anything else that he has done that it would be hardly fair to quote anything else, unless we could quote a great deal. Like Herbert, and in pretty obvious imitation of him, he set himself to bend the prevailing fancy for quips and quaintnesses into sacred uses, to see that the Devil should not have all the best conceits. But he is not so uniformly successful, though he has greater depth and greater originality of thought.

[In a footnote, Saintsbury adds: "Since this chapter was in type, some persons whose judgment I respect have expressed to me surprise and regret that I have not given a higher and larger place to Henry Vaughan. A higher I cannot give, because I think him, despite the extreme beauty of his thought and (more rarely) of his expression, a most imperfect poet; nor a larger, because that would involve a critical arguing out of the matter, which would be unsuitable to the plan and scale of this book. Had he oftener written as he wrote in the famous poem referred to in the text, or as in the magnificent opening of 'The World'—

> I saw Eternity the other night,
> *Like a great ring of pure and endless light,*
>   All calm as it was bright,

there would be much more to say of him. But he is not master of the expression suitable to his noble and precious thought except in the briefest bursts—bursts compared to which even Crashaw's are sustained and methodical. His admirers claim for **'The Retreat'** the germ of Wordsworth's great ode, but if any one will compare the two he will hardly complain that Vaughan has too little space here."]

Louise Imogen Guiney (essay date 1894)

SOURCE: "Henry Vaughan," in *A Little English Gallery*, Harper and Brothers, 1894, pp. 55-118.

[*Guiney was an American poet, literary essayist, and Vaughan scholar who edited and published an edition of* The Mount of Olives *in 1902. In 1895 she began corresponding with a fellow admirer of Vaughan, Gwenllian Morgan, and together they made plans to publish an edition of Vaughan's poetry, with biographical essays by the editors. This work was not completed during the lifetime of either woman; but after their deaths, the notes they had compiled in preparation were used by F. E. Hutchinson in his definitive* Henry Vaughan: A Life and Interpretation *(1947). In the following excerpt from an essay originally published in the* Atlantic Monthly *in 1894, Guiney offers high praise for Vaughan as an essentially orthodox Christian poet, comparable in accomplishment to Edmund Spenser.*]

It is a saw of Dr. Johnson's that it is impossible for theology to clothe itself in attractive numbers; but then Dr. Johnson was ignorant of Vaughan. It is not in human nature to refuse to cherish the "holy, happy, healthy Heaven" which he has left us (in a graded alliteration which smacks of the physician rather than of the "gloomy sectarian"), his very social "angels talking to a man," and his bright saints, hovering and smiling nigh, who

> are indeed our pillar-fires
>   Seen as we go;
> They are the city's shining spires
>   We travel to.

Who can resist the earnestness and candor with which, in a few sessions, he wrote down the white passion of the last fifty years of his life? No English poet, unless it be Spenser, has a piety so simple and manly, so colored with mild thought, so free from emotional consciousness. The elect given over to continual polemics do not count Henry Vaughan as one of themselves. His double purpose is to make life pleasant to others and to praise God; and he considers that he is accomplishing it when he pens a compliment to the valley grass, or, like Coleridge, caresses in some affectionate strophes the much-abused little ass. All this liberal sweetness and charity heighten Vaughan's poetic quality, as they deepen the impression of his practical Christianity. The nimbus is about his laic songs. When he talks of moss and rocks, it is as if they were incorporated

into the ritual. He has the genius of prayer, and may be recognized by "those graces which walk in a veil and a silence." He is full of distinction, and of a sort of golden idiosyncrasy. Vaughan's true "note" is—Vaughan. To read him is like coming alone to a village church-yard with trees, where the west is dying, in hues of lilac and rose, behind the low ivied Norman tower. The south windows are open, the young choir are within, and the organist, with many a hushed unconventional interlude of his own, is rehearsing with them the psalm of "pleasures for evermore."

Francis Thompson (essay date 1897)

SOURCE: "Henry Vaughan," in *The Real Robert Louis Stevenson, and Other Critical Essays by Francis Thompson,* edited by Rev. Terence L. Connolly, University Publishers Incorporated, 1959, pp. 87-9.

[*Thompson was one of the most important poets of the Catholic Revival in nineteenth-century English literature. Often compared to the seventeenth-century metaphysical poets, especially Richard Crashaw, he is best known for his poem "The Hound of Heaven" (1893), which displays his characteristic themes of spiritual struggle, redemption, and transcendent love. Like other writers of the fin de siècle period, Thompson wrote poetry and prose noted for rich verbal effects and a devotion to the values of aestheticism. In the following excerpt from a review (originally published in the* Athenaeum *in 1897) of E. K. Chambers's* Poems of Henry Vaughan, *he discusses Vaughan's derivitiveness as a poet, noting the inadequacy of comparisons with Wordsworth and Herbert.*]

The poems on which [Vaughan's] fame must rest, **Silex Scintillans,** appear to have gone through two editions in five years, and then completely to have collapsed. There is no certain trace of any further edition from the seventeenth century until nearly half through the nineteenth century. We doubt whether any poems of like merit can show a like extraordinary eclipse—an eclipse so long and total that it might well seem final. Yet the neglected volume had become operative before its republication, and on no less a poet than Wordsworth. It is now proved that Wordsworth had amongst his books a copy of **Silex Scintillans**; and the influence of Vaughan's mystical philosophy is clearly visible on Wordsworth's, the influence of Vaughan's poetry evident in many a Wordsworthian passage, particularly in the famous "Intimations of Immortality." Indeed, not only does this contain reminiscences of individual passages in Vaughan, but the whole germ of the great ode is manifestly a certain poem of Vaughan's—the beautiful and most Wordsworth-like **"Retreat."** The extent to which Vaughan followed Herbert has caused them to be compared. Poem for poem, Vaughan comes ill out of the comparison. Herbert has more of level excellence, is nearer to an artist—though both seem far enough from artists to our modern criticism. There is a more than Wordsworthian waste of dreariness in Vaughan—recompensed, as in Wordsworth, by a flash, a line, a passage, here and there. Very few, too few, are the poems which stand forth as wholes. But when he *is* touched by that parsimonious inspiration, it is not in Herbert, it is not in Crashaw, it is not in anything of the sixteenth or seventeenth century, that we can find his likeness. His lines then have so instantaneous a magic, make such wonderfulness of everyday words, are so one with the brain of nature, that they cannot be paralleled before the advent of Wordsworth himself. . . .

He is full, too, of strange gleams of poetic intuition into things not yet quite known to science. In one poem he makes solemn use of the idea, not unfamiliar to modern mystical writers, that all man's acts are invisibly photographed on the inanimate things around him: —

> I—alas!
> Was shown one day in a strange glass
> That busy commerce kept between
> God and His creatures, though unseen.
> They hear, see, speak,
> And into loud discoveries break,
> As loud as blood. . . .
>   Hence sand and dust
> Are shak'd for witnesses, and stones,
> Which some think dead, shall all at once
> With one attesting voice detect
> The secret sins we least suspect.
> For know, wild men, that when you err,
> Each thing turns scribe and register. . . .

Like Wordsworth, he "wakens a sort of soul in sense," can give to plain speech mystery and depth which take us by surprise. Felicity starts on us as from an ambush.

Paul Elmer More   (essay date 1916)

SOURCE: "Henry Vaughan," in *The Demon of the Absolute*, Princeton University Press, 1928, pp. 143-64.

[*More was an American critic who, along with Irving Babbitt, formulated the doctrines of New Humanism in early twentieth-century American thought. The New Humanists were strict moralists who adhered to traditional conservative values in reaction to an age of scientific and artistic self-expression. In regard to literature, they believed a work's implicit reflection of support for the classic ethical norms to be of as much importance as its aesthetic qualities. In the following excerpt from an essay originally published in the* Nation *in 1916, More celebrates Vaughan's achievement as a poet of bittersweet spiritual longing in a fallen world.*]

There are poets who, by virtue of some affinity of spirit with our own, appeal to us with an intimacy that takes our judgement captive; we go to them in secret, so to speak, and love them beyond the warrant of our critical discernment. Such a poet Henry Vaughan has long been to me, and in undertaking to make an essay on his works . . . I am fully aware of the risk inherent in the attempt to give a sort of public validity to what ought to be, in Vaughan's own language, "a sweet privacy in a right soul."

The task would be easier if we knew more of the man's life. Yet if there are few events to record, his career is typical of many who pursued the hidden way in that much distracted age.

To understand him, as to understand the other religious poets of the age, we must never forget the dark background of malice, confusion, calumny, and violent change out of which their songs arose. Most of these singers were of the party of Vaughan; they were bound to feel that the victorious iconoclasm of the Puritans was sweeping from them ruthlessly all the comfortable traditions which stayed the inherent restlessness of man's soul, all the symbols which had trained the imagination to take its due share in the act of worship. These things lay heavily upon Vaughan's mind. He was not, in that part of his work which counts, a poet of cheer; neither indeed was Milton on his side, nor any other of those who reflected the turmoil and double defeat of the times.

This dejection we who again look upon a world filled with the alarms of war and the hatred of man for man, and ache for deliverance from "the tedious reign of our calamity"— this darkness of spirit we can comprehend; and I confess that, much as I have always loved Vaughan, the pathos of his cry for civil peace touches me now in a peculiar manner. But there was another source of darkness in Vaughan's mind for which we, with our modern training, are not so ready to feel sympathy—I mean the shade of life itself, the sorrow and discontent that are caused by no accidental evils of an age but are inherent in the very conditions of mortal existence. In these latter years we have been caught in a kind of conspiracy of silence on this matter, until, as it sometimes seems, we have become cowards to the truth. Our modern books are filled with complaints against society and government as these are organized, and against the failure of institutions and the inadequacy of traditional beliefs, but it is really astonishing how seldom any writer dares to touch on the crude imperfections and cruel necessities that always have been, and must always be, the law of life; to speak with any frankness of these bitter facts is frowned upon as disloyalty to the popular dogma of progress and perfectibility, or as ignorance of those implications of cosmic evolution which command us to be credulous only of good. How then shall we feel ourselves at home with those moralists who took a sort of savage delight in spreading before our eyes the blacker side of man's natural feebleness and perversity? Yet we quite misunderstand such a poet as Vaughan, if we turn from him as from one essentially gloomy and depressing. The joy in him still overrides the gloom, the joy that came to him, as it can only come to a man then or at any time, from lifting his eyes out of these shades and flickering lights to the radiance of another sun, and to the possession of a peace that is not of earth:

> I saw Eternity the other night,
> Like a great ring of pure and endless light,
>   All calm, as it was bright;
> And round beneath it, Time in hours, days, years,
>   Driven by the spheres,
> Like a vast shadow moved; in which the world
>   And all her train were hurl'd.

Such is the great note of Vaughan and of his contemporaries in their moments of inspiration, purer and higher in Vaughan than in any other, though not so powerfully sustained as in Milton; and it is the occasional occurrence of this note that makes the religious poetry of the period, despite its mass of fumbling attempts, something unique in English literature. Faint echoes or distorted repetitions of it you will catch in Whittier and Newman and Francis Thompson and other poets of the nineteenth century; but the glorious courage and assurance, the pure joy, the full flight against the sun, you will meet nowhere in England since the Revolution, with the new politics, brought in the grey reign of naturalism.

It is not to be supposed that Vaughan rose often to this height, nor, indeed, do we who have long prized him in private rest our affection on the few poems in which he shows himself a master of his craft. As with most of the writers of the day, there is much of the careless amateur in his method: he lacked self-criticism, failed to distinguish between what was commonplace and what was exquisite in his perceptions, and even in his moments of inspiration left the labour of expression too much to chance; as a whole his achievement is sadly at loose ends. But he never forgot or misrepresented himself, and it is his constant betrayal of a rare personality, his adjustments to life, the sincere variation of his moods, his faithful expectation of the coming of the light, that draw us back to his books again and again and lend a peculiar interest to poems which we should find it hard to recommend to unwilling ears. It is the man Vaughan, who dwelt by the river Usk and himself walked in the valley with God, we seek always, not the artist; and if we admit readily that this is not the attitude we take towards those who have achieved an invulnerable position, yet we love him none the less. Naturally this quality of his work cannot be exhibited in a specimen or two; nevertheless, so far as this may be done, I would point to the artless charm of such a poem as **"The Bee,"** and particularly to such lines in it as these:

> Hail crystal fountains and fresh shades!
> Where no proud look invades,
> No busy worldling hunts away
> The sad retirer all the day!
> Hail, happy, harmless solitude!
> Our sanctuary from the rude
> And scornful world; the calm recess
> Of faith, and hope, and holiness!
> Here something still like Eden looks;
> Honey in woods, juleps in brooks;
> And flowers, whose rich unrifled sweets
> With a chaste kiss the cool dew greets.
> When the toils of the day are done,
> And the tired world sets with the sun,
> Here flying winds and flowing wells
> Are the wise watchful hermit's bells;
> Their busy murmurs all the night
> To praise or prayer do invite,
> And with an awful sound arrest
> And piously employ the breast.
>   When in the east the dawn doth blush,
> Here cool, fresh spirits the air brush;
> Herbs straight get up, flowers peep and spread,
> Trees whisper praise, and bow the head;
> Birds, from the shades of night release,
> Look round about, then quit the nest,
> And with united gladness sing
> The glory of the morning's King.
> The hermit hears, and with meek voice
> Offers his own up, and their joys;
> Then prays that all the world may be
> Blest with as sweet an unity.

If such a passage makes no appeal to you, why, then it doesn't; but one can perhaps hint at certain qualities in it which endear the writer to some of us. In the first place we feel here the reality of the divine immanence in nature which everywhere speaks in Vaughan's verse, and which curiously enough, paradoxically you may say, comes to poignant expression only in those who deplore the natural world as fallen from Grace and given over to the powers of evil. It is he who believes in a paradise lost, actual or symbolical—

> He sighed for Eden, and would often say,
>   Ah, what-bright days were those!
> Nor was heaven cold unto him; for each day
>   The valley or the mountain
> Afforded visits, and still paradise lay
>   In some green shade or fountain.
> Angels lay lieger here; each bush and cell,
>   Each oak and highway, knew them:
> Walk but the fields, or sit down at some well,
>   And he was sure to view them—

it is he who sees that about the world the "curtains are close-drawn," who will also, by some strange legerdemain of the human heart, draw away the veil from your eyes and show you the truth of the everlasting mythology:

> My God, when I walk in those groves,
>   And leaves, Thy spirit still doth fan,
> I see in each shade that there roves
>   An angel talking with a man.
>
> Under a juniper some house,
>   Or the cool myrtle's canopy;
> Others beneath an oak's green boughs,
>   Or at some fountain's bubbling eye.

But to return to the lines of **"The Bee"** which we have taken as typical of the retired life, we may note in them something more specific than the feeling of a man who, by submission to the divine will, re-creates for himself a lost paradise; they direct us to a peculiarity of the imagination, a habit of mind, which Vaughan shared indeed with the other poets of his day, but possessed to a degree that marks a real distinction. Simcox, in his introduction to the selection in Ward's *English Poets,* calls attention to the prominence of the dawn, "the awe of the freshness of morning among the Welsh mountains," in Vaughan's reflexions on nature. The observation is just; but it was not so much the beauty of the morning in itself that seems to have impressed the poet as its contrast with the hours of darkness past. I am sure that Vaughan, something of a valetudinarian we know, was often sleepless, and sometimes in these wakeful seasons felt the presence of the stars as a "host of spies" stealing out from heaven, and was entranced by the palpable nearness of the spirit world in the silence and abstraction of visible things:

> Dear night! this world's defeat;
> The stop to busy fools; care's check and curb;
> The day of spirits; my soul's calm retreat
>   Which none disturb!
> Christ's progress, and His prayer time;
>   The hours to which high Heaven doth chime.
>
> God's silent, searching flight;

When my Lord's head is filled with dew, and all
His locks are wet with the clear drops of night;
     His still, soft call;
  His knocking-time; the soul's dumb watch,
  When spirits their fair kindred
catch. . . .

   There is in God—some say—
  A deep, but dazzling darkness. . . .

At other times Vaughan seems to have been oppressed by the thought of the suspension of life through these hours, as if Nature nightly retired into a tomb, from which she could be aroused only by the miraculous voice of her Creator. Out of these nocturnal meditations, being an early riser, he went forth to view the dawn, already quickened in spirit, as he would say, by the celestial dews, or ready to join the "hymning circulations" at the spectacle of the earth's perpetual rebirth. In such a mood he could scarcely walk abroad without looking for the promised coming of his Lord:

   Or shall these early fragrant hours
     Unlock Thy bowers?
   And with their blush of light descry
   Thy locks crown'd with eternity?

It is hard for me to leave these things: there is so much more that I could say from my long reading of Vaughan—how, for example, his characteristic ideas of nature are associated together like a golden chain, link with link, so that the sight of a withered flower would remind him of the morning freshness, and this thought would lift his eyes to the hills of his valley from which the dew was supposed to fall, and beyond these to the light that appeared to stream from the mountain of God:

   Come, sapless blossom, creep not still on earth,
     Forgetting thy first birth.
   'Tis not from dust; or if so, why dost thou
     Thus call and thirst for dew? . . .

   Who placed thee here, did something then infuse
     Which now can tell thee news.
   There is beyond the stars an hill of myrrh,
     From which some drops fall here. . . .

I fear that this will seem but a straggling set of rhymes to anyone whose judgement is not already bribed in their favour. As for myself, I cannot quote them without a vivid recollection of a certain "white day" when, walking alone on the bank of the Usk, I myself saw such a sapless flower in a dry spot, and for the rest of my way went piecing together what I could recall of Vaughan's lines.

It is thus we of the brotherhood find our pleasure in these poems, not because of their perfection as works of art, but because of a certain transparent honesty in them which enables us to enter into the privacy of a singularly beautiful spirit. Again, not a dominating spirit: Vaughan was not one of the stalwarts of the age, not a Milton, not even a Falkland, but one who shrank almost pathetically from contention and the noise of tongues. But neither was there anything to reprobate in his flight from the world, unless we think that all men are called to fight in the hour of desperation. There was nothing, or at least very little, of Crashaw's morbid substitution of religious emotion for the plain duties of life; no taint of self-indulgence in voluptuous sensation or relaxing revery. Nature was a retreat for him, but he found there the visible presence of a God who had not laid aside His commands and prohibitions; the impulse to compose came to him chiefly, we think, in the fresh breath of morning, when he set out from home on his errands to the sick and suffering. And if his verse lacks finish, it has yet the substance of poetry which was the birthright of that age. Sometimes it has more than that. Suddenly, as if by a divine accident, he will reach a strain—a single line, or group of lines, it may be—which startles the reader, as the ear is caught by a few notes of piercing melody breaking through a monotonous chant. In the midst of rather commonplace reflexions he will unexpectedly gather up the meaning of life in a sharp pregnant image, such as this:

         But now
  I find myself the less the more I grow.
         The world
  Is full of voices; man is call'd, and hurl'd
    By each; he answers all,
    Knows every note and call—

or this:

  Man is the shuttle, to whose winding quest
    And passage through these looms
  God order'd motion, but ordain'd no rest—

or this:

  Where frail visibles rule the mind,
  And present things find men most kind;
  Where obscure cares the mean defeat,
  And splendid vice destroys the great—

or this:

  And how of death we make
    A mere mistake.

Or he will celebrate the sweet influences of a holy life:

  Stars are of mighty use; the night
    Is dark, and long;
  The road foul; and where one goes right,
    Six may go wrong—

or in slower measure will praise the gift of Sir Thomas Bodley to Oxford, and express in memorable language the gratitude of all readers for the preservation of good books:

  And in this age, as sad almost as thine,
  Thy stately consolatiöns are mine.

These are not the accidents that come to a little man; and occasionally Vaughan's performance is even greater. Once or twice he will sustain this elevation from the beginning to the end, producing a thing as exquisitely perfect as **"The Retreat,"** which certainly helped Wordsworth in the composition of his famous ode, and, strange juxtaposition, may have been in the mind of James Thomson (B. V.) when he wrote one of the most haunting cantos of *The City of Dreadful Night;* or rising to the bold flight of those stanzas, unnamed, than which there is nothing purer and deeplier felt, nothing truer to the strangely mingled exaltation and humility of sound religion, nothing more superb, in the sacred literature of our English speaking people:

They are all gone into the world of light!
   And I alone sit lingering here;
Their very memory is fair and bright,
   And my sad thoughts doth clear.

It glows and glitters in my cloudy breast,
   Like stars upon some gloomy grove,
Or those faint beams in which this hill is drest
    After the Sun's remove.

I see them walking in an Air of Glory,
   Whose light doth trample on my days—
My days, which are at best but dull and hoary,
    Mere glimmering and decays.

O holy hope! and high humility!
   High as the Heavens above!
These are your walks, and you have show'd
   them me
    To kindle my cold love.

Dear, beauteous death, the Jewel of the Just;
   Shining no where but in the dark!
What mysteries do lie beyond thy dust,
    Could man outlook that mark.

He that hath found some fledged bird's nest,
   may know
   At first sight if the bird be flown;
But what fair well, or grove he sings in now,
    That is to him unknown.

And yet, as Angels in some brighter dreams
   Call to the soul when man doth sleep,
So some strange thoughts transcend our wonted
   themes,
    And into glory peep.

If a star were confined into a tomb,
   Her captive flames must needs burn there;
But when the hand that lockt her up gives room,
    She'll shine through all the sphere.

O Father of eternal life, and all
   Created glories under thee!
Resume thy spirit from this world of thrall
    Into true liberty!

Either disperse these mists, which blot and fill
   My pérspective still as they pass;
Or else remove me hence unto that hill,
    Where I shall need no glass.

Edmund Blunden (essay date 1927)

SOURCE: "On the Poems of Henry Vaughan," in *On the Poems of Henry Vaughan: Characteristics and Intimations,* Richard Cobden-Sanderson, 1927, pp. 7-49.

[*Blunden was associated with the Georgians, an early twentieth-century group of English poets who reacted against the prevalent contemporary mood of disillusionment and the rise of artistic modernism by seeking to return to the pastoral, nineteenth-century poetic traditions associated with William Wordsworth. In this regard, much of Blunden's poetry reflects his love of the sights, sounds, and ways of rural England. As a literary critic and essayist, he often wrote of the lesser-known figures of the Romantic era and of the pleasures of English country life. In the following excerpt, he praises Vaughan's metaphysical nature poetry in*

superlative terms, judging Vaughan superior to George Herbert in poetic accomplishment. Upon publication, Blunden's essay drew critical scorn from T. S. Eliot.]

Wherever the question of the survival of the best in poetry without the assistance of biographers and popularisers is being debated, the instance of Henry Vaughan should not be left out. His present fame is one of the best practical arguments for the belief that the good thing is strong enough to pass through all the obstacles and shadows of a period into a permanent and conspicuous renown.

> Through night at first it will rejoice,
>   And travel into day,
> Pursuing, with a still small voice,
>   That light that leads the way.

Campion, Traherne, Christopher Smart, Blake, Clare—these all reveal at a glance the mysterious silent evolution of poetic fame, and Vaughan is with them, illustrating perhaps more vividly than the others the same strangely beautiful theme, the seed growing secretly. . . .

[In] ***Silex Scintillans*** and what few subsequent "pious thoughts and ejaculations" Vaughan gives us, we see the poet more and more in his garden, perhaps not only contemplating, but also supplying his "dispensatorie" with herbs and flowers. There is no great obstacle to imagining that his rides and walks into the lonelier parts of the district, bearing physic and piety for his patients, brought him into closer intimacy with nature and landscape, of which also we discern a deeper and more varied spirit in his latter pages. The Vaughan landscape is inimitable. Its clouds are so fleecy, its winds so eager to address and arouse man, its sunbeams so vital, its pasturing life so unalarmed and unalterable, that it needs no signature. Probably the inhabitants of his native vale could recognise the geography of it—"that drowsie Lake", the water-fall "where often I have sate", the *"clear heights"* which beacon it above the storm, "this restless, vocal *Spring*", are all from the life. And his birds and flowers too must be still familiar by the Usk, unless the raven has left his ancient rock. Rocks and caves are permitted to lend a terrible (and allegorical) aspect to this landscape now and then; "mists and shadows hatch" from the low grounds, and in one of his master-pieces there is a famous gloomy grove.

But what are these? —mere proofs of his conquering radiance and calm. Vaughan's year has no winter; "the frosts are past." If storms come over, the rainbow enchants them; rain that falls there is "warm summer rain" as sweet as honey. The shadows are seldom more sinister than lily-shades. The mountain-top is twinkling with blossom. Over all, through all, light beams and smiles and purifies: "and, I pray, are not *light* and *life* compatriots?" It is original light which inspires him, and hence he is not among the exceeding admirers of the moon, but to the sun and stars he makes his tireless response, from "fresh, spicie mornings" to "calme, golden Evenings" and through nights in which even "one twinkling ray shot o'er some cloud" is often a joy. The happy brilliance springing from poem after poem is no other than the white radiance of Eternity, and if one would attempt some account of Vaughan's starry, fountained, infinite dream, one might fairly say that he has a Shelleian quickness and farness about him.

With that are ever compacted and connoted a simple humanity and common charity, Vaughan's daily self plodding along the flinty track. His kind watchfulness must have worked inestimable good among the cottages. We see his nature perfectly in such a detail (unobserved by himself) as his frequent introduction of a ruined dwelling to symbolize his own unworthiness. He was no stranger to

> a ruined peece
>   Not worth thy Eyes;
> And scarce a room, but wind and rain
>   Beat through, and stain
> The seats, and Cells within.

In his **"Rules and Lessons"** his wholesome affection for the small calls and wants of life is displayed without reserve, and we seem to be accompanying him on his round, from enemy to fried, from cottage to inn, and home to lamplit reflection. Our love for him, warmed by this picture of humility in action, is even increased by those poems in which he speaks with nature familiarly and reverently—**"The Bird"**, **"Cock-crowing"**, **"The Book"**, **"The Ass"**, **"Palm-Sunday"**. Harmlessness, unquestioning reliance on Providence, a simple cleanness and well-being—these things delight him, and the consciousness that there is a sense in a bird or a bee which man has almost lost adds a mystical quality to this Franciscan companionship.

In the union of the temporal with the immortal, this world and the world beyond, Vaughan obtains an early hold upon his reader, and is able to suggest strange and celestial concords by the simplest references to daily experience here. Simplicity is a perfection arising from so complicated an interflow of gifts and decisions that criticism seldom endeavours to analyse it. I shall not. I know, and passionately and amazedly rejoice in, the greatness of the poet who can produce "the Platonic reminiscence" in semblance of a child sweetheart, that has not yet

>   walked above
> A mile or two from his first love.

Such a flower of ages is not a stroke of luck in Vaughan, but again and again he shows us how easy it is to call up spirits. His tears insist in heaven, and

> As rain here at our windows beats,
>   Chide in thine Ears;

he is sure that the Second Coming will be in the hour of dawn, because that is the natural time:

> Stars now vanish without number,
> Sleepie Planets set and slumber,
> The pursie Clouds disband and scatter,
> All expect some sudden matter;
> Not one beam triumphs, but from far
>   That morning-star.

As we read, the star seems about to break forth into the personal annunciation of God. Who but this Vaughan writes so often of the present deity—and even whimsically, from his rare festivity, complains

> If thou steal in amidst the mirth
> And kindly tell me, *I am Earth,*
>   I shut thee out, and let that slip;

Such Musick spoils good fellowship?

or have we among our delimited, penetrative and scientifically equipped poetic enquirers any that finds greater significance in a day's march than Vaughan in **"The Shower"**:

> Waters above! Eternal springs!
> The dew that silvers the Dove's wings!

This man going about the countryside alone, who laments the age when man had speech with angels, but who seems to us to have come very close to the mystery so described, can have had little desire to publish his poems at all, and probably that is the reason why his *ars poetica* is not so great as his inspiration and exaltation. His verse is chiefly the intimate record of his spiritual life. It never aimed for the laurels of reputation. We receive it therefore with all its imperfections, driftings of argument, weakenings of phrase, disjunctions of rhythm, and often a decline from some sublime opening to pedestrian insipidity. Admiration for Herbert's adroit cats'-cradles of versification sometimes caused Vaughan to imitate with unhappy results, as in the clockwork versicles at the end of *"The Search"*. In metre Vaughan had one vital gift and no more: for iambic verse, and particularly for the eight-syllable couplet. This measure, of which he is a master, conveys the majority of his finest ideas. Its quick yet strong flow apparently suited with the rate of his deciphering mood into language, distilling language into poetic elixir. So long as he is employing octosyllables his thought advances vigorously and clearly, and is strengthened by apt modifications of accent and sound. Nothing could be more expressive than (in their contexts) the shortened line describing his realization that stones are not dead matter:

> They héar, sée, spéak.

that in **"Childe-hood"** suddenly questioning,

> Wh'y should mén lóve
> A wolf more than a Lamb or Dove?

There are several of these powerful abruptnesses in **"Abel's blood"**:

> Sad, purple well! whose bubling eye
> Did first against a Murth'rer cry;
> Whose streams still vocal still complain
>   Of bloody *Cain*——

What a vehemence is in that ending!

In respect of vocabulary and general use of language Vaughan anticipates the theory of Wordsworth, selecting from the language of the ordinary man, and having the air of one addressing us not through a book but rather by word of mouth. This is in keeping with his poetical creed (such a phrase, though convenient, scarcely has to do with Vaughan), with his philosophy of life altogether,

> The creature's Jubilee; God's parle with dust;
> Heaven here; Man on those hills of Myrrh
>   and flowers;

he will not need high-sounding expressions, but discover the gleam in ordinary ones. His achievements are almost always spoken in the idiom of good conversation, as,

> If thou canst get but thither,
>   There growes the flowre of peace,
> The Rose that cannot wither,
>   Thy fortresse, and thy ease,

and

> I see them walking in an Air of glory,
>   Whose light doth trample on my days;
> My days, which are at best but dull and hoary,
>   Meer glimering and decays.

If he goes beyond this diction, it is in such a page where his especial hint or illustration is derived from a scientific or technical source, and so requires a special term; occasionally he uses a Latinism, as "voices" in the sense of "opinions"; and where intensity requires a flash of audacity he will often seize a noun and make it a verb; so Christ *"heavened* their walks," or was not too proud to *"inn"* with man; so the dew of regeneration *"Blouds* and *Spirits* all my Earth."

It has been common to couple the name of Vaughan with that of Herbert, his admired example, and certainly the list of verbal transferences from *The Temple* to the rougher edifice of **Silex Scintillans** is a long one. But despite those marks of an early fascination and initiation, despite Vaughan's repeated tributes to "Mr. *George Herbert* of blessed memory; See his incomparable prophetick Poems, and particularly these, *Church-musick, Church-rents, and schisms, The Church militant,*" still time begins to distinguish between the master's ingenuity and the pupil's genius. Herbert seems to be usually concerned with putting things quaintly; his piety is running an obstacle race; no doubt God is the prize, but our attention is too much occupied with the feats and acrobatics on the course. Moreover, the object of his journey is God according to vestry arrangements; a noble ideal, far finer than the blurred unvision of many of us, but narrow in comparison with Vaughan's solar, personal, firmamental, flower-whispering, rainbow-browed, ubiquitous, magnetic Love. The elaborateness of Herbert's poetry cannot help him across the space between his sectarian purity and trust and that conjunction of all thoughts, all passions, all delights, that consciousness of the innumerable affinities of created and creator, of an advance of the entire fabric towards one serene and supreme discovery. "O knowing, glorious Spirit!" So one would perhaps borrow from Vaughan's verses a phrase to do justice to his memory; but the certainty instantly supervenes that no such attribution could please him, and that he was content to leave his body "above the voiceful windlings of a river" with [an] unselfish sole epilogue on its sheltering stone. . . .

T. S. Eliot (essay date 1927)

SOURCE: "The Silurist," in *The Dial,* Chicago, Vol. LXXXIII, No. 9, September, 1927, pp. 259-63.

[*Perhaps the most influential poet and critic to write in the English language during the first half of the twentieth century, Eliot is closely identified with many of the qualities denoted by the term Modernism: experimentation, formal complexity, artistic and intellectual eclecticism, and a classicist's view of the artist working at an emotional distance from his or her creation. He introduced a number of terms and concepts that strongly affected critical thought in his lifetime, among them the idea that poets must be conscious of the living tradition of literature in order for their work to have artistic and spiritual validity. In general, Eliot upheld values of traditionalism and discipline, and in 1928 he annexed Christian theology to his overall conservative world view. Of his criticism, he stated: "It is a by-product of my private poetry-workshop: or a prolongation of the thinking that went into the formation of my verse." In the following excerpt from a review of Edmund Blunden's* On the Poems of Henry Vaughan: Characteristics and Intimations *(1927), Eliot comments about various aspects of Vaughan's poetic accomplishment, taking issue throughout with Blunden's inflated view of it.*]

There is apt to prevail a critical misconception about any poet who is also suspected of being a mystic. The question whether a poet is a mystic is not, for literary criticism, a question at all. The question is, how far are the poetry and the mysticism one thing? Poetry is mystical when it intends to convey, and succeeds in conveying, to the reader (at the same time that it is real poetry) the statement of a perfectly definite experience which we call the mystical experience. And if it is real poetry it will convey this experience in some degree to every reader who genuinely feels it as poetry. Instead of being obscure, it will be pellucid. I do not care to deny that good poetry can be at the same time a sort of cryptogram of a mysticism only visible to the initiate; only, in that case, the poetry and the mysticism will be two different things. Some readers have professed to discover in Vaughan the traces of an hermetic philosophy of profound depths. It may be there; if so, it belongs not to literature but to cryptography. The mystical element in Vaughan which belongs to his poetry is there for any one to see; it is "mysticism" only by a not uncommon extension of the term. A genuine mystical *statement* is to be found in the last canto of the *Paradiso;* this is primarily great poetry. An equally genuine mysticism is expressed in the verses of St John of the Cross; this is not a statement, but a riddling expression; it belongs to great mysticism, but not to great poetry. Vaughan is neither a great mystic nor a very great poet; but he has a peculiar kind of feeling which Mr Blunden is qualified to appreciate.

Vaughan is in some ways the most modern—that is to say, the most nineteenth-century—of the so-called metaphysical poets of the seventeenth century. He has much more in common with the age to which Mr Blunden belongs than Donne, or Crashaw, or Herbert, or Benlowes. A poem to which Mr Blunden seems particularly attached is **"The Retreat,"** the poem of Vaughan which has become famous as the precursor of the "Ode on Intimations of Immortality" of Wordsworth. The comparison is of course (it is a tradition of criticism, not an invention of Mr Blunden's) unfair to Vaughan and to Wordsworth also. The two poems have little in common; Wordsworth's "Ode" is a superb piece of verbiage, and Vaughan's poem is a simple and sincere statement of feeling. But Mr Blunden's praise of this poem, and praise of this sort of poetry which is reminiscent of childhood and its imagined radiance, is significant of the weakness of both Vaughan and Blunden.

Lamb's dream in prose, 'The Child Angel,' appears to have turned upon a reminiscence of Vaughan. . . . There is a general strange correspondence between the essay and the poem; yet not so strange, for what was Elia by his own confession but a man in love with his childhood?

And so forth; but it does not occur to Mr Blunden that this love of one's own childhood, a passion which he appears to share with Lamb and Vaughan, is anything but a token of greatness. We all know the mood; and we can all, if we choose to relax to that extent, indulge in the luxury of reminiscence of childhood; but if we are at all mature and conscious, we refuse to indulge this weakness to the point of writing and poetizing about it; we know that it is something to be buried and done with, though the corpse will from time to time find its way up to the surface. About Charles Lamb I know little, and care less; but this reminiscent humour of Vaughan, upon which Mr Blunden has pounced so delightedly, has always seemed to me one of the reasons for his inferiority to the best of his contemporaries. It is not a common weakness at that time; it is rather prophetic; and it can be recognized and diagnosed by any one who has read Rousseau's *Confessions.* "The very word *young,*" Mr Blunden tells us complacently, "is henceforward charged with a yearning pathos in his mind"; and that yearning pathos, we might add, is exactly the material out of which poetry is not made. Vaughan's apparent love of the country and country life, presently connected by Mr Blunden with his yearning pathos of childhood, comes also to assume a neurasthenic complexion; and the fact that Vaughan was a stout Royalist, with some experience of civil scuffling, and a stout Anglican, does not atone for it. Even Vaughan's religion is a little suspect; Mr Blunden apologizes for such severity as Vaughan displays in the matter of feasts and revels; and Vaughan's Anglicanism is far from the cheerfulness and democracy of Laud, and rather near to a sombre Welsh non-conformity.

Vaughan is in some ways more nineteenth century than most of his contemporaries. On the other hand, Vaughan does belong to his own time. He employs the *conceit,* though with a difference, and the conceit is not merely a negligible affectation of seventeenth-century poets; it represents a particular way of thinking and feel-century poets; it represents a particular way of thinking and feeling: Vaughan is related to poets who have little in common with Mr Blunden. And it is impossible to understand or place or value any poet of this time without saturating oneself in all of the poets of this time. Thus Mr Blunden appears to understand Vaughan so long as he confines himself to Vaughan; but the one comparison that he draws is by no means fortunate. He admits, what is certain, that Vaughan owed much to the work of George Herbert; but he considers that Herbert is inferior to Vaughan. . . . No poet, of all that age, ever brought his quaintness more exactly to the verge of pure simplicity than George Herbert; and no poet of that passionately religious time wrote such fine devotional verse. . . . To appreciate Herbert's sensibility we have to penetrate the thought and emotion of the time; we should know Andrewes and Hooker. In short, the emotion of Herbert is clear, definite, mature, and sustained; whereas the emotion of Vaughan is vague, adoles-

cent, fitful, and retrogressive. This judgement is excessively harsh; but it is only as much as to say that Mr Blunden, like some persons of vague thinking and mild feeling, yearns towards a swooning ecstasy of pantheistic confusion. Vaughan is a true poet; and he wrote fine lines that no one else has written; but his best qualities are those which he shares with other and greater poets of his time, rather than those which he shares with Mr Blunden.

J. B. Leishman   (essay date 1934)

SOURCE: "Henry Vaughan," in *The Metaphysical Poets: Donne, Herbert, Vaughan, Traherne,* 1934. Reprint by Russell & Russell, 1963, pp. 145-87.

[*An English educator and translator, Leishman was the author of* The Metaphysical Poets *(1934) and* Themes and Variations in Shakespeare's Sonnets *(1961). In the following excerpt from a reprint edition of the former, he surveys Vaughan's poetry and highlights several key thematic characteristics.*]

About 1643 [Vaughan] he began to practise as a physician at Brecknock, and in 1646 he published his first volume of poems, with the title *Poems, with the tenth Satyre of Iuvenal Englished.* There is little that is distinctively 'metaphysical' in the style of these poems—most of them are in the sprightly manner of the popular Cambridge poet, Thomas Randolph, and other members of the Tribe of Ben; although there are two poems ["**To Amoret gone from him**" and "**To Amoret, of the difference twixt him, and other Lovers, and what true Love is**"] which seem to have been inspired by Donne's "Valediction: forbidding mourning," especially by the following stanzas of that poem:

> Dull sublunary lovers love
> (Whose soule is sense) cannot admit
> Absence, because it doth remove
> Those things which elemented it.
>
> But we by a love, so much refin'd,
> That our selves know not what it is,
> Inter-assured of the mind,
> Care lesse, eyes, lips, and hands to misse . . .

Another poem in this volume must come as a surprise to those who only know Vaughan as the author of *Silex Scintillans.* It is called "**A Rhapsodie. Occasionally written upon a meeting with some of his friends at the Globe Taverne.**" The following description of London at night is admirable, and reminiscent of Donne in his realistic vein:

> Should we goe now awandring, we should
>   meet
> With Catchpoles, whores, & Carts in ev'ry
>   street:
> Now when each narrow lane, each nooke &
>   Cave,
> Signe-posts, & shop-doors, pimp for ev'ry knave,
> When riotous sinfull plush, and tell-tale spurs
> Walk Fleet street, & the Strand, when the soft
>   stirs
> Of bawdy, ruffled Silks, turne night to day;
> And the lowd whip, and Coach scolds all the
>   way;

When lust of all sorts, and each itchie bloud
From the Tower-wharfe to Cymbelyne, and
     Lud,
Hunts for a Mate, and the tyr'd footman reeles
'Twixt chaire-men, torches, & the hackny
     wheeles.

And he concludes with a rollicking catch:

Lets laugh now, and the prest grape drinke,
Till the drowsie Day-Starre winke;
And in our merry, mad mirth run
Faster, and further then the Sun;
And let none his Cup forsake,
Till that Starre againe doth wake;
So we men below shall move
     Equally with the gods above. . . .

Vaughan does not seem to have remained long at Breck-nock, but to have removed to his native Newton St. Bridget, where he spent the rest of his life; for the dedication of his next volume of poems, *Olor Iscanus,* is dated 'Newton by Usk this 17, of Decemb. 1647'. The history of this volume is somewhat obscure; the dedication to Lord Kildare Digby bears the date 1647, but it was not published until 1651, apparently by Vaughan's brother Thomas, and without the author's consent, for in an address by 'The Publisher to the Reader' we are told that 'the Author had long agoe condemn'd these Poems to Obscuritie, and the Consumption of that Further Fate, which attends it'. In the interval between composition and publication there must have occurred that strange and sudden conversion to which we must soon refer. In style and spirit this volume is akin to its predecessor. The author is in complete sympathy with contemporary literature: there are commendatory verses on Mrs. Katherine Philips ('the Matchless Orinda'), on Davenant's *Gondibert,* and on the plays of Fletcher and Cartwright—'wit in Cartwright at her Zenith was'. There is also a very pleasant, witty poem *"To his retired friend, an invitation to Brecknock",* in which he describes the miserable condition of Brecknock, whose walls had been pulled down by its inhabitants to prevent the town from being occupied. . . . Another poem, *"Upon a Cloke lent him by Mr. J. Ridsley",* suggests that Vaughan took some part in the fighting. He implies that he was on of the garrison who left Beeston Castle on its surrender to the Parliamentary forces in 1645, and he wishes that he had had the cloak, which seems to have been of very ample dimensions, from the beginning of his military career:

O that thou hadst it when this Jugling fate
Of Souldierie first seiz'd me! at what rate
Would I have bought it then, what was there but
I would have giv'n for the *Compendious hutt?*

The profound spiritual revolution which Vaughan underwent about this time is revealed by the publication in 1650 of **Silex Scintillans.** The work was reissued in 1655 with a second part, containing additional poems, and a preface, in which Vaughan expresses profound dissatisfaction with contemporary literature and with his own earlier performances. His attitude to the wits, whom, as we have seen, he had imitated and commended, has completely changed. 'That this Kingdom hath abounded with those ingenious persons, which in the late notion are termed *Wits,* is too

well known. Many of them having cast away all their fair portion of time, in no better employments, then a deliberate search, or excogitation of *idle words,* and a most vain, insatiable desire to be reputed *Poets.*' He keenly regrets his own efforts in this kind: 'And here, because I would prevent a just *censure* by my free *confession,* I must remember, that I my self have for many years together, languished of this very *sickness;* and it is no long time since I have recovered.' He has suppressed his 'greatest follies', and although he thinks those which escaped were fairly harmless, he declares that his guilt in writing them 'can never be expiated without *special sorrows'.* 'The true remedy', he concludes,

lies wholly in their bosoms, who are the gifted persons, by a wise exchange of *vain* and *vitious subjects,* for *divine Themes* and *Celestial praise. . . .* The first, that with any effectual success attempted a *diversion* of this foul and overflowing *stream,* was the blessed man, Mr. George Herbert, whose holy *life* and *verse* gained many pious Converts, (of whom I am the least)... He that desires to excel in this kinde of *Hagiography,* or holy writing, must strive (by all means) for *perfection* and true *holyness,* that a *door may be opened to him in heaven,* Rev. 4.1. and then he will be able to write (with *Hierotheus* and holy Herbert) A true Hymn.

How can we explain this sudden and complete change of outlook? Some allusions in **Silex Scintillans,** especially the beautiful poem **"Silence, and stealth of days,"** seem to connect it with the death of that brother who is also referred to by Thomas Vaughan at the conclusion of his *Anthroposophia Theomagica,* where, apologizing for the defects of his book, he says that it was 'compos'd in *Haste,* and in my *Dayes of Mourning,* on the *sad Occurence* of a *Brother's Death'.* The book was published in 1650, but the Latin dedication is dated 'Oxonii 48'.

Then too, there came a time when Vaughan was no longer able to dismiss the confusion and troubles of the Civil War in the same light-hearted and contemptuous way as at the conclusion of his **"Invitation to Brecknock."** As with others of his contemporaries, they led him to turn his thoughts heavenward and suggested to him that 'the fashion of this world passeth away'. In the **Mount of Olives,** a volume of devotions, published in 1652, and of which the dedication bears the date October 1651, he declares:

We could not have lived in an age of more instruction, had we been left to our own choice. We have seen such vicissitudes and examples of humane frailty, as the former world (had they happened in those ages) would have judged prodigies. We have seen Princes brought to their graves by a new way, and the highest order of humane honours trampled upon by the lowest. We have seene Judgment beginning at Gods Church, and (what hath beene never heard of, since it was redeem'd and established by his blessed Son,) we have seen his Ministers cast out of the Sanctuary, & barbarous persons without *light* or *perfection,* usurping holy offices. A day, an hour, a minute (saith *Causabone*) is sufficient to over-turn and extirpate the most settled Governments, which seemed to have been founded and rooted in Adamant. Suddenly do the high things of this world come to an end, and their delectable things passe away, for when they seem to be in their *flowers* and full strength, they perish to astonishment; And sure the ruine of the most goodly peeces seems to tell, that the dissolution of the whole is not far off.

We [may notice] similar reflections in Donne's *Anniversaries* and in Reynolds's *Mythomystes*.

Whether the feelings and reflections aroused by his brother's death and by the spectacle of the Civil War actually caused Vaughan's conversion or were themselves largely directed by that fact it is impossible to say. The connexion between great spiritual experiences and particular events, even when much detailed knowledge is available, must always remain obscure; for, after all, the spirit bloweth where it listeth.

It is probable that sickness visited him about this time, for the **Flores Solitudinis,** a volume of translations from various devotional works, published in 1654, though the preface 'To the Reader' bears the date April 17, 1652, carries the subtitle 'Collected in his Sicknesse and Retirement'. In his dedication to Sir Charles Egerton he says:

> The incertainty of life, and a peevish, inconstant state of health would not suffer me to stay for greater performances, or a better season;

and in his address to the reader he says:

> It may be thy spirit is such a popular, phantastick *flye,* as loves to gad in the *shine* of this world; if so, this *light* I live by in the *shade,* is too great for thee. I send it abroad to bee a companion of those wise *Hermits,* who have withdrawne from the present generation, to confirme them in their solitude, and to make that rigid *necessity* their pleasant *Choyse.*

We have now been able to form some picture of the author of **Silex Scintillans.** Illuminated by some profound spiritual experience, saddened by death, sickness, and the misery and confusion of the world around him, he has resolved to spend the rest of his days in his native village on the banks of his beloved Usk, devoting his practical energies to the relief of sickness, and his thoughts to the contemplation of the mercies and mysteries of God—listening for those divine intimations which he cannot hear amid the noises of the busy world, but which come to him in solitude, especially among the sights and sounds of nature, where, as in the days of his childhood—that childhood when he seemed nearest to God and immortality, —he is able to detect

> some shadows of eternity.

Let us consider some of the characteristics of his poems. They are full of the imagery of light and darkness. To him the world is no abiding home, but a place of pilgrimage and trial, in general a somewhat dark and unfamiliar place except when illuminated by flashes of divine love, reminding man of the place from whence he has come and to which he is journeying. In one of the meditations in the **Mount of Olives** he says:

When thou art to go from home, remember that thou art to come forth into the *World,* and to Converse with an Enemy; And what else is the World but a Wildernesse? A darksome, intricate wood full of *Ambushes* and dangers; A Forrest where spiritual hunters, principalities and powers spread their nets, and compasse it about.

And again:

> Let sensual *natures* judge as they please, but for my part, I shall hold it no *Paradoxe* to affirme, *there are no pleasures in this world.* Some *coloured griefes* and *blushing woes* there are, which look so clear as if they were *true complexions;* but it is a very sad and a tryed truth that they are but *painted.* To draw then to an end, let us looke alwayes upon this *Day-Lilie* of life, as if the *Sun* were already set.

Over and over again in these meditations his favourite text and image of the light shining in darkness appears. In his prayer '*When thou dost awake*' he exclaims:

> O God the Father! who saidst in the beginning, *Let there be light,* and it was so; *Inlighten my Eyes that I never sleepe* in death: lest at any time my Enemy should say, *I have prevailed against him.*
>
> O God the Sonne! light of light; the most true and perfect light, from whom this light of the Sun, and the day had their beginning; thou, that art the light shining in darknesse, Inlightning every one that cometh into this world, expell from me all Clouds of Ignorance, and give me true understanding, that in thee, and by thee I may know the *Father;* whom to know is to live, and to serve is to reigne.

And in the course of his '**Meditation before the receiving of the holy Communion'** he exclaims:

> O light of light, the all-seeing light that shineth in darknesse, and the darknesse comprehendeth it not, what will become of me, when I shall appear before thy glorious and searching Eye!

Elsewhere:

> It is an observation of some *spirits,* that *the night is the mother of thoughts.* And I shall adde, that those thoughts are *Stars,* the *Scintillations* and *lightnings* of the soul strugling with *darknesse.*

'The Contemplation of *death*', he declares,

> is an obscure, melancholy *walk,* an Expatiation in *shadows & solitude,* but it leads unto *life,* & he that sets forth at *midnight,* will sooner meet the *Sunne,* then he that sleeps it out betwixt his curtains.

Finally, at the conclusion of his preface to **Flores Solitudinis** he says:

> All that may bee objected is, that I write unto thee out of a land of darkness, out of that unfortunate region, where the Inhabitants sit in the shadow of death: where destruction passeth for propagation, and a thick black night for the glorious day-spring. If this discourage thee, be

pleased to remember, that there are bright starrs under the most palpable clouds, and light is never so beautifull as in the presence of darknes.

His poems, as I have said, are full of this imagery. At the conclusion of **"Resurrection and Immortality"** the soul says to the body:

> So shalt thou then with me
>   (Both wing'd and free,)
> Rove in that mighty, and eternall light
>   Where no rude shade, or night
> Shall dare approach us; we shall there no more
>   Watch stars, or pore
> Through melancholly clouds, and say
>   Would it were Day!
> One everlasting Saboth there shall runne
> Without Succession, and without a Sunne. . . .

Then there is that poem ["As time one day by me did pass"] where he describes how in time's book he saw, amid many disordered lives, the fair white page of his brother's. The verses convey a marvellous impression of *lux in tenebris.* Vaughan resembles Donne in his power of creating emotional atmosphere, although his reverie, his intense contemplation, burning like a steady flame, is quite unlike Donne's feverish intellectual activity. Above all, there is **"The Night,"** one of the most exquisitely tender and sensitive of all religious poems, suggested by St. John's phrase about Nicodemus, 'The same came unto him by night'. Notice the speaking tone of the verses, their 'still, soft call'. One of Donne's innovations was to make the rhythm of lyric poetry approach more nearly to that of impassioned colloquial speech, and Vaughan nobly carried on the tradition. Finally, there is that truly remarkable poem **"The World."** Vaughan quotes at its conclusion I John, ii. 16-17.

> All that is in the world, the lust of the flesh, the lust of the Eys, and the pride of life, is not of the father, but is of the world.

> And the world passeth away, and the lusts thereof, but he that doth the will of God abideth for ever.

It is possible, however, that Vaughan had also in mind a famous passage in the *Timaeus* (37d), where Plato describes how God or the Demiurge created time:

> He conceived the idea of making a moving image of eternity, and accordingly when he ordered the heavens he made an image of eternity, in such fashion that while eternity itself remained unmoved, the image thereof had a motion according to number; and this image we call time.

It is interesting to observe how naturally the thought and language of the *Timaeus* combine with Vaughan's mystical Christianity. And it is the truest and highest kind of mysticism, not cloudy and obscure, but concrete and clear, where conceptions have the intensity and vividness of perceptions. Here is a poet thinking through the senses, exercising in a wonderful way that power which Carew recognized in Donne, when he said that Donne could

> the deepe knowledge of darke truths so teach,

As sense might judge, what phansie could not reach. . . .

About most of these poems there is something brooding and meditative; they seem to have been composed at night; they suggest one sitting in darkness and celebrating the divine illumination that has visited him there; but Vaughan has also written some exquisite morning hymns, penetrated with a radiant and lyric joy. No poet, not even Shelley, has written more beautifully of light, or better expressed the sacramental significance of dawn.

Let us now proceed to the consideration of another characteristic feeling or idea in Vaughan's poetry. As we have seen, he has, like many of his contemporaries, a strong conviction that the world has grown old and out of joint and that it has travelled far away from God. This conviction often leads him to meditate on the youth of the world, on the days when angels mingled with men, and heaven and earth seemed nearer together. This is the theme of the poem **"Corruption"**. . . .

It is interesting to note that in each of the two following poems the phrase 'white days' occurs. In **"The Search,"** an allegorical description of the search for divine truth, we have the lines:

> Tyr'd here, I come to *Sychar;* thence
> To *Jacobs wel,* bequeathed since
> Unto his sonnes, (where often they
> In those calme, golden Evenings lay
> Watring their flocks, and having spent
> Those white dayes, drove home to the Tent
> Their *well-fleec'd* traine;)

And in **"Isaacs Marriage,"** noticing the fact that Isaac prayed for his bride, instead of using oaths and compliments, he exclaims:

>   . . . happy those
> White dayes, that durst no impious mirth expose!

And of course there is the famous line in **"The Retreate"** where he regrets the

> white, Celestiall thought
> of his childhood. . . .

In these poems, then, Vaughan muses on the early days of the world and of Christianity in much the same way as Spenser and other poets had mused on the traditional legend of a Golden Age and on the days of Chivalry. The difference is that, while the ideal with which Spenser unfavourably contrasted his own age was formed from the romances and the classic poets, Vaughan's was formed from Scripture. But these reflections on the world's decay also suggested to Vaughan another line of meditation which, I think, is to be found in the works of only one other of his contemporaries, Thomas Traherne. He returned, not only to the early days of the world, but to his own early days, to the days of his childhood, in which, so it seemed to him, his soul, not yet corrupted by the ways of the world or dulled by the lethargy of custom, had looked upon the Creation as God intended all men to look upon it, as a wonderful and glorious thing, the garment of God. This idea is expressed in the most amous of all his poems, **"The Retreate** [and in **"Childe-hood"**]. . . . Only in these two poems does Vaughan reveal to us that he had made the new and thrilling discovery of the divinity of childhood—that discovery which forms the basis of all the thinking of his contemporary Traherne. To be able to look upon the world as something wonderfully fresh and beautiful and fascinating, to feel that it all belongs to you and yet to have no desire to call anything in it your own, but to be content to possess it by loving it and understanding it, and thus to create in your own mind a second creation more glorious than the first, because you have given it a voice to praise God and have thus helped him to realize his design in the first creation—this, declares Traherne, is the secret of childhood, and we must recapture it if we are to attain true felicity. 'Certainly Adam in Paradise had not more sweet and curious apprehensions of the world, than I when I was a child', he exclaims; and this is how he describes them:

> The corn was orient and immortal wheat, which never should be reaped, nor was ever sown. I thought it had stood from everlasting to everlasting. The dust and stones of the street were as precious as gold: the gates were at first the end of the world. The green trees when I saw them first through one of the gates transported and ravished me; their sweetness and unusual beauty made my heart to leap, and almost mad with ecstasy, they were such strange and wonderful things. The Men! O what venerable and reverend creatures did the aged seem! Immortal Cherubims! And young men glittering and sparkling Angels, and maids strange seraphic pieces of life and beauty! Boys and girls tumbling in the street, and playing, were moving jewels. I knew not that they were born or should die: But all things abided eternally as they were in their proper places. Eternity was manifest in the Light of the Day, and something infinite behind everything appeared: which talked with my expectation and moved my desire. The city seemed to stand in Eden, or to be built in Heaven. The streets were mine, the temple was mine, the people were mine, their clothes and gold and silver were mine, as much as their sparkling eyes, fair skins and ruddy faces. The skies were mine, and so were the sun and moon and stars, and all the World was mine; and I the only spectator and enjoyer of it. I knew no churlish proprieties, nor bounds, nor divisions: but all proprieties and divisions were mine: all treasures and the possessors of them. So that with much ado I was corrupted, and made to learn the dirty devices of this world. Which now I unlearn, and become, as it were, a little child again that I may enter into the Kingdom of God. . . .

Let us now pass on to another characteristic of Vaughan's poetry. We often find in Vaughan, as we sometimes find in Herbert, an antithesis between nature and man, between the calm, orderly, and obedient behaviour of nature, and the restlessness, self-will, and disobedience of man. Vaughan, like his brother Thomas and many of his contemporaries, believed that the world was the manifestation of a divine spirit, was penetrated by that spirit, but that while animals and plants and inanimate things always in-

stinctively, naturally, inevitably obeyed the laws and motions of that spirit, man alone, having the power of choice or free will, was able to resist these motions and laws; and accordingly he often exhorts man to do voluntarily and reasonably what the rest of the creation do naturally and instinctively—like Wordsworth, though with a difference, he bids him learn from nature. . . .

In a poem to which he has prefixed a paraphrase of a text from Romans viii. 19, **'Etenim res Creatae exerto Capite observantes expectant revelationem Filiorum Dei'**, Vaughan moralizes on this theme. . . . [Under] the inspiration of St. Paul, Vaughan suggests that the obedience of the creatures is not dictated merely by natural instincts and laws and by the influence of the stars, but also by some obscure and latent will to Good. . . . And in the poem **"Man"** he reflects on what seems to him the contrast between the steadfastness of nature and the restlessness of man in a way that is reminiscent of Herbert's "Pulley". . . . Finally, in his last volume of verse, *Thalia Rediviva* (1678), he has a delightful poem called **"The Bee"** in which he calls up a picture of the hermit living alone with nature and joining in creation's hymn. . . .

But not only does Vaughan insist on this contrast between the orderliness and obedience of nature and the caprice and self-will of man; he would also have us regard Nature as a system of divine hieroglyphs, revealing to the loving and careful observer something of the will and power of God; he would have us recognize in natural laws real and not merely casual analogies with spiritual laws. This way of regarding nature was in a sense very old. From the earliest times, influenced doubtless by the magnificent poetry of the Psalms, the Church had taught that knowledge of God was to be sought not only in the Bible, the *Liber Revelationis,* but also in Nature, the *Liber Creaturarum.* Nevertheless, its appeals to Nature had generally been trite and conventional: the old Bestiaries, where the lion appears as the symbol of strength, the fox of cunning, &c., are a good example of its method. Moreover, those who pushed their inquiries into the secrets of nature too far were regarded with suspicion and often treated as sorcerers or magicians. . . .

Men like Cornelius Agrippa and his humble disciple Thomas Vaughan approached chemistry with a kind of mystical enthusiasm: they pursued it, not for the sake of any material or practical end, but because it seemed to enable them in some small measure to repeat the processes of creation. Indeed, they called it 'natural magic'.

This tendency of thought had been greatly stimulated by the *Heptaplus* of Pico della Mirandula, a work in which that ardent humanist tried to fortify and recommend his conviction that all human doctrine and belief was part of one original revelation of God to man by proposing a sevenfold method of interpreting the Mosaic account of the creation—an attempt that was closely imitated, a hundred years later, by Henry More in his *Conjectura Cabbalistica.* 'In explaining the harmony between Plato and Moses', says Pater, in his delightful essay,

> Pico lays hold on every sort of figure and analogy, on the double meaning of words, the symbols of the Jewish ritual, the secondary meanings of

obscure stories in the later Greek mythologists. Everywhere there is an unbroken system of correspondences. Every object in the terrestrial world is an analogue, a symbol or counterpart, of some higher reality in the starry heavens, and this again of some law of the angelic life in the world beyond the stars. There is the element of fire in the material world; the sun is the fire of heaven; and in the super-celestial world there is the fire of the seraphic intelligence. 'But behold how they differ! The elementary fire burns, the heavenly fire vivifies, the supercelestial fire loves.' In this way, every natural object, every combination of natural forces, every accident in the lives of men, is filled with higher meanings. Omens, prophecies, supernatural coincidences, accompany Pico himself all through life. There are oracles in every tree and mountain-top, and a significance in every accidental combination of the events of life.

In order to understand Vaughan and many of his contemporaries it is most important to recognize that this attitude to the study of nature, this belief in the method of analogy, was still very common. . . .

In **"The Constellation"** he seems to insist that what we should call the scientific study of nature is mere idle curiosity, and that the true method is the analogical. He says to the stars:

> Silence, and light, and watchfulnes with you
>   Attend and wind the Clue,
> No sleep, nor sloth assailes you, but poor man
>   Still either sleeps, or slips his span. . . .
>
> Perhaps some nights hee'l watch with you, and peep
>   When it were best to sleep,
> Dares know Effects, and Judge them long before,
>   When th'herb he treads knows much, much more.
>
> But seeks he your *Obedience, Order, Light,*
>   Your calm and wel-train'd flight,
> Where, though the glory differ in each star,
>   Yet is there peace still, and no war?

In the life of nature he is continually finding intimations and confirmations of spiritual truths. . . .

Finally, there is that exquisite poem **"The Water-fall"**. The water seems to pause on the brink of the fall, and seems afraid, just as the soul is afraid when it approaches death. Nevertheless, the soul, like the water, will

> rise to a longer course more bright and brave.

Read the first stanza carefully. There is more loving natural description in Vaughan than in any other seventeenth-century poet, except, perhaps, Marvell; but then Marvell rarely ventures beyond his garden.

> With what deep murmurs through times silent stealth
> Doth thy transparent, cool and watry wealth
>   Here flowing fall,
>   And chide, and call,
> As if his liquid, loose Retinue staid

> Lingring, and were of this steep place afraid,
>   The common pass
>   Where, clear as glass,
>   All must descend
>   Not to an end:
> But quicknd by this deep and rocky grave,
> Rise to a longer course more bright and brave.

L. C. Martin   (essay date 1938)

SOURCE: "Henry Vaughan and the Theme of Infancy," in *Seventeenth Century Studies Presented to Sir Herbert Grierson,* Oxford at the Clarendon Press, 1938, pp. 243-55.

[*Martin was an English scholar who edited the definitive edition of Vaughan's canon, the two-volume* Works of Henry Vaughan *(1916). In the following excerpt from an essay contributed to a distinguished* Festschrift, *he explores the sources of the theme of pre-natal existence in Vaughan's poetry and the influence of that theme upon Wordsworth. He concludes that though the evidence for Vaughan's direct influence upon Wordsworth is inconclusive, Vaughan inherited a rich tradition of literature supporting the theme of children having come into the world in innocence, having but recently enjoyed fellowship with God, and that this same tradition was familiar to Wordsworth and his immediate predecessors.*]

As the poetry of Henry Vaughan gained standing in the nineteenth century its correspondences with that of Wordsworth were frequently pointed out. Both, it was noticed, were poets of nature in the sense that they not only admired its phenomena but recommended a communing with it which would have beneficial effects of a moral or spiritual order; and both were poets of childhood, which they represent as a time when the soul, fresh from its Source and unspotted by the world, has at least some clearer spiritual perceptions than the grown man can compass or comprehend. There is the important difference that whereas Vaughan longs

> to travell back
> And tread again that ancient track,

Wordsworth would make the most of the capacities and appreciations proper to the years which bring the philosophic mind; but they agree that with the passing of childhood a paradise is lost that can never be wholly found again.

When, therefore, it was alleged that Wordsworth owned a copy of **Silex Scintillans** it could easily seem to follow that he had been influenced by its writer and even that the existence of the 'Immortality Ode' had depended upon the example of **'The Retreate'**. The evidence was supplied by Archbishop Trench in a note in *A Household Book of English Poetry:* 'A correspondent, with date July 13, 1869, has written to me, "I have a copy of the first edition of the **Silex,** incomplete and very much damp-stained, which I bought in a lot with several other books at the poet Wordsworth's sale" '; to which Grosart added a statement, not founded on fact, that **Silex Scintillans** is entered in the sale-catalogue of Wordsworth's books. The volume may, of course, have been one of a group listed without titles or other description.

It has recently been observed by Miss Helen N. McMaster in her essay 'Vaughan and Wordsworth', *Review of English Studies,* July 1935 that the grounds for associating the two poets in this way are not very satisfactory, that there is no mention of Vaughan in the whole body of Wordsworth's writings, and that even if the volume in question was in Wordsworth's library it has yet to be proved that he took any influence from it. So far as the 'Immortality Ode' is concerned there were other channels through which its main doctrine could have reached him, if indeed any definite 'sources' are to be alleged. Wordsworth himself remarked that 'a pre-existent state has entered into the popular creeds of many nations; and, among all persons acquainted with classic literature, is known as an ingredient in Platonic philosophy'. And although it is quite possible that **'The Retreate'** and other poems by Vaughan may have consciously or unconsciously affected Wordsworth's imagination, the question of origins still deserves further investigation with a view to showing in what conditions of thought and sentiment Vaughan himself may have been moved towards the speculative attitude which **'The Retreate'** implies. It is indeed a question of conditions rather than of 'influences', although these are categories which cannot always be kept distinct. The theories of pre-existence which had often been held since the time of Plato are part of these conditions. We have, however, to consider, not a simple expression of the Platonic theory or myth, but a fusion of it with the widespread sentiment which attributes a special innocency and insight to children. The occurrence in literature of this fusion is relatively rare, and when it occurs it is not to be accounted for merely by showing that it has occurred before, but by considering also what factors in the writer's nature and experience might cause any antecedent or contemporary thought of a similar kind to appeal to him.

A study of Henry Vaughan's works reveals him as one who, for reasons which a modern psychologist might try to discover, was particularly interested in images of freshness, purity, and primal vigour, and his attitude to infancy may be seen as one more instance of the tendency which attracted him to the primrose and the lily, to whiteness among the colours, and to spring and the dawn among times and seasons. Or it may be regarded as the transference to the individual plane of thoughts concerning the childhood of the race and the degeneration of 'civilized' man from a Golden Age typified otherwise in Vaughan's poetry by the original sinlessness of Adam, by the artless fidelities of the Jewish patriarchs, or by the uncorrupted condition of the early Christian community.

In what degree his numerous reflections of this kind were brought about or intensified in him by the political events of the mid-century and by personal troubles partly connected with those events it would be hard to estimate; but from his references it is clear that the Civil War and especially the harsh measures adopted by the Puritan revolutionaries did much to induce in him a state of depression favourable, as Wordsworth was to show in circumstances partly analogous, to nostalgic exaltations of nature and childhood. 'We could not', Vaughan writes in **The Mount of Olives** (1652),

have lived in an age of more instruction, had we been left to our own choice. We have seen such vicissitudes and examples of humane frailty, as the former world (had they happened in those ages) would have judged prodigies. We have seen Princes brought to their graves by a new way, and the highest order of humane honours trampled upon by the lowest. We have seene Judgement beginning at Gods Church, and (what hath beene never heard of, since it was re-deem'd and established by his blessed Son,) we have seen his Ministers cast out of the Sanctuary, & barbarous persons without light or perfection, usurping holy offices. . . . Suddenly do the high things of this world come to an end, and their delectable things passe away. . . . And surely the ruine of the most goodly peeces seems to tell, that the dissolution of the whole is not far off.

A quarter of a century had passed since George Hakewill had in 1627 first published his *Apologie or Declaration of the Power and Providence of God in the Government of the World,* maintaining that the world had still as many potentialities for good as at any time in the past and attacking 'the weake grounds which the contrary opinion of the Worlds decay is founded vpon'. Henry Vaughan, however, was evidently still of those who in spite of Hakewill accepted the doctrine of world or universal degeneration. This doctrine and the melancholy attending it had gained force from recent astronomical discoveries in the light of which the most ancient heavens could no longer seem so fresh and strong, so pure and incorruptible, as the traditions would have them seem to be. The stellar system was now, it appeared, demonstrably unexempt from processes of change and decay. Vaughan apparently never accepted this subversive astronomy; he needed the stars as an image of orderliness and willing obedience to law contrasting with the instability and frowardness of man. With his deep sense of human decadence he needed also, for his imaginative solace, the concept of human nature in earlier unspoilt phases; and could easily pass from this to the idealization of childhood. It is not a far cry from the beginning of Boethius's *Metrum 5* as translated by Vaughan in **Olor Iscanus:**

> Happy that first white age! when wee
> Lived by the Earths meere Charitie,

to the beginning of **'The Retreate:**

> Happy those early dayes! when I
> Shin'd in my Angell-infancy.

'Those early days' had been spent in the impressive mountainous regions of South Wales; and after studying at Oxford and having some experience of London and the Civil War Vaughan went to live again, and to practise as a doctor, in his native place. This he did at about the age at which after the French Revolution Wordsworth went to settle in the Lake District, and with a mind similarly disillusioned regarding the ways of sophisticated man. In each case the poet's 'retreat' to childhood appears to be bound up with his return, in fact and in imagination, to the nature by which his childhood had been surrounded.

These are circumstances which may well have affected the

poet's attitude towards the theme of infancy, but they do not explain his development of it, the terms and images which he employs; in particular they do not explain the doctrine hinted in **'The Retreate'**, of a sinless pre-existent state, which the child in some sort remembers and in some degree inherits. It may be said that it was an easy step for the poet thus to rationalize his sentiment, but the answer to this might be that Wordsworth has made it easy for us to think so. In point of fact it was a step that apparently had not been taken before by an English poet. Correspondences, however, may be found for the doctrine, not only in the literature of past ages but in that of Vaughan's own time; and since they appear in works of which some at least were readily accessible and likely to be attractive to him on general grounds, it is of some moment to take account of them as aids to the recognition of the background, the intellectual atmosphere, in which his poetry took its shape.

The inquiry leads into the by-ways rather than the main tracks of speculative literature. Vaughan's attitude in **'The Retreate'** may seem to be related to the Platonic αναμνησι and so in some degree it is, but the relationship is not very close; indeed Vaughan, who respects the child's emotional and quasisensuous intuitions, who had *felt*

> through all this fleshly dress
> Bright shootes of everlastingnesse,

contradicts the Platonic teaching that αναμνησι is the hard-won result of processes, ratiocinative in essence, whose higher functions are possible only to an adult intelligence; and Vaughan's conception of the grown man's descent from a childhood more closely in touch with divine things does not merely repeat the notion of the soul's descent into its fleshly tenement. What it adds to that notion is something which Hellenic thought, untouched by alien speculation, was perhaps not very likely to add or to encourage.

There is, however, one striking anticipation in the Neo-Platonic writings attributed to 'Hermes Trismegistus', still in seventeenth-century England a name for some to conjure by; it occurs in Libellus X of the *Hermetica,* where the sage adjures his disciple thus:

> Look at the soul of a child, my son, a soul that has not yet come to accept its separation from its source; for its body is still small, and has not yet grown to its full bulk. How beautiful throughout is such a soul as that! It is not yet fouled by the bodily passions; it is still hardly detached from the soul of the Kosmos. But when the body has increased in bulk, and has drawn the soul down into its material mass, it generates oblivion; and so the soul separates itself from the Beautiful and Good, and no longer partakes of that; and through this oblivion the soul becomes evil. . . .

It may appear strange that the concept of a Golden Age in the life of the individual, before or after birth, should not have attracted the poets who preceded Vaughan more often than it appears to have done. It represents certainly a somewhat precarious idealization of the childish state,

but it is neither unintelligible nor baseless, in spite of the rude refutations which children themselves can so readily seem to supply. There are traces of it in Roman culture and literature, and Christian poets in particular might have been expected to make much of the symbolism in which the child becomes a type of the Kingdom of Heaven, and of which Luther makes some interesting applications. It may be supposed that what chiefly stood in the way was the doctrine of original sin. Christians who harboured ideas resembling the Jewish notions alluded to above would risk the charge that they were straying from the paths of orthodox belief in the direction of the Pelagian heresy. But Pelagianism was one of the many heretical tendencies, new and old, which enliven the history of religious thought in the seventeenth century. It was an essential part of 'Anabaptist' teaching that children who die unbaptized would nevertheless be saved, and a similar heterodoxy was recommended by Jeremy Taylor in his *Unum Necessarium* (1655), where the doctrine of original sin loses some of its harshness and is interpreted in its bearings upon childhood in a way that Henry Vaughan was likely to find agreeable:

> But it is hard upon such mean accounts to reckon all children to be born enemies of God . . . full of sin and vile corruption, when the Holy Scriptures propound children as imitable for their pretty innocence and sweetness, and declare them rather heirs of heaven than hell. 'In malice be children': and, 'unless we become like to children, we shall not enter the kingdom of heaven'; and 'their angels behold the face of their Father which is in heaven'. . . . These are better words than are usually given them; and signify, that they are beloved of God, not hated, designed for heaven, and born to it, though brought thither by Christ, and by the Spirit of Christ, not born for hell: that was 'prepared for the devil and his angels', not for innocent babes. This does not call them naturally wicked, but rather naturally innocent, and is a better account than is commonly given them by imputation of Adam's sin.

It is indeed a better account than was commonly given them. Milton is nearer to orthodoxy when he writes in *Areopagitica:*

> Assuredly we bring not innocence into the world, we bring impurity much rather: that which purifies us is triall, and triall is by what is contrary. That vertue therefore which is but a youngling in the contemplation of evil, and knows not the utmost that vice promises to her followers, and rejects it, is but a blank vertue, not a pure.

There are, however, other signs that the 'climate of thought' in the seventeenth century was becoming favourable to the inspiration of **'The Retreate'** and the poems of similar drift in **Silex Scintillans** and **Thalia Rediviva.** Probably Henry Vaughan was not himself aware of all the precedents which the literature of his time had furnished; but the sort of imaginative fuel which lay to his hand and which in those poems he kindled into life is represented in any allusions and adherences to the Platonic theory of pre-existence, any contrastings of childish innocence with adult depravity, and, above all, any suggestions that the youthful superiority is connected with a pre-existent state. . . .

Owen Felltham's *Resolves* (c. 1623) have the special importance that they were well known to Henry Vaughan, who often quoted from them although never with acknowledgement. Vaughan derived from Felltham one of the most striking phrases in **'The Retreate'**, 'Bright shootes of everlastingnesse', Felltham having written of the soul that 'The *Conscience,* the *Caracter* of a *God* stampt in it, and the apprehension of *Eternitie,* doe all proue it a shoot of everlastingness'. Vaughan may well also have dwelt upon the following passages, the first of which testifies to the prevalence of Neo-Platonic theory:

> 'Tis the *bodies contagion,* which makes the *Soule* leprous. In the opinion that we all hold, at the first infusing 'tis *spotlesse* and *immaculate.*

And

> How blacke a *heart* is that, which can giue a *stabbe,* for the *innocent smiles* of an *Infant?* Surely *Innocence* is of that purity, that it hath more of the *God* in it, than any other *qualitie;* it intimates a freedom from *generall Vice.*

The intellectual relations between Henry Vaughan and his twin brother Thomas, minister and 'chymist', were closer still. Their writings show that they explored some of the same imaginative fields, although Thomas was less controlled in his thought and more obscure in his utterance. In the turbid stream of his speculations many currents met, themselves already of diverse origins, Neo-Platonic and Jewish, Hermetic and Kabalistic, western theosophy and oriental magic. But he clearly belonged to the class of mystical investigator represented before him by Paracelsus and Cornelius Agrippa, the type which is drawn to the study of 'Nature', *naturans* and *naturata,* its essence and its processes, with a view to the mastery of its physical secrets but ultimately to establishing contact with a supersensible Reality and acquiring some of its spiritual power, to an alchemy of the soul rather than of metals. . . .

Thomas Vaughan refers in one place to 'Jacob Behmen *his most excellent and profound* Discourse of the Three Principles', and it is very likely that his indebtedness to the mystic of Görlitz went farther than this single reference would suggest. Boehme, whose works were much translated into English during the fifth and sixth decades of the seventeenth century, is another who recommends seekers after divine truth to cultivate the childlike spirit:

> Our whole Religion is but a child-like worke; namely, that we wholly forsake and disclaime our owne knowing, willing, running, disputing . . . and persevere in the way which bringeth us againe to our owne native Countrey.

> Loving Sir, it is a simple *childlike way* that leadeth to the highest wisedome, the World knowes it *not.*

Moreover, Boehme in his *XL Questions* (translated 1647)

introduces a doctrine of reminiscency in connexion with the theme of childish innocence:

> Little Children are our Schoolmasters till evill stirre in them, and so they embrace the *Turba Magna,* but they bring their sport from the Mothers wombe, which [sc. the sport] is a Remnant of Paradise: but all the rest is gone till we receive it againe.

When we receive it again 'we shall lead a life like children, who rejoyce and are very merry in their Sports'. And if Henry Vaughan had needed any authority for the phrase 'Angell infancy' he could have found it in Boehme's *Aurora* (translated 1656), where the question 'To whom now shall I liken the Angels?' is answered:

> I will liken them to *little* children, which walk in the fields in *May,* among the *flowers,* and pluck them, and make curious Garlands, and Poseys, carrying them in their hands rejoycing. . . .

During the century which separates Vaughan and Traherne from William Blake English poets showed little interest in the theories concerning childhood which attracted these predecessors. Even Blake, who recognized the visionary powers of children, attaches to those powers no definite lore of preexistency and reminiscence. Mr. Garrod has argued that although 'the ultimate source of the doctrine of reminiscence is, of course, Plato and the Neo-Platonists', the immediate source upon which Wordsworth drew in the 'Immortality Ode' was 'not Plato, but Coleridge'. It then becomes tempting to ask what near or remote authority, if any, Coleridge himself may have found for a doctrine which, in Wordsworth's presentation of it, is not very much like Plato's.

> Oft o'er my brain does that strong fancy roll
> Which makes the present (while the flash doth last)
> Seem a mere semblance of some unknown past,
> Mixed with such feelings, as perplex the soul
> Self-questioned in her sleep; and some have said
> We lived, ere yet this robe of flesh we wore.

Thus Coleridge began the sonnet written in 1796 on hearing of the birth of his son, Hartley; and in connexion with it he referred to Plato and to Fénelon. 'Almost all the followers of Fénelon', he wrote to Poole, 'believe that men are degraded intelligences, who had all once lived together in a paradisiacal or perhaps heavenly state.' It will be noticed that although there may be significance in the fact that the occasion for this sonnet was the birth of a child, Coleridge does not here or elsewhere claim that the reminiscent faculty is stronger in childhood than in later life. Coleridge was, however, widely versed in mystical literature. In the *Biographia* (ch. ix), besides acknowledging a great debt to Plato and his followers, he alludes with special reverence to Boehme and other Christian illuminati; and whether Wordsworth knew Vaughan's poetry or not it seems possible that the 'Immortality Ode' derives in part, and chiefly through Coleridge, from the same traditions of thought and sentiment which lay behind the conception of **'The Retreate'**.

F. E. Hutchinson   (essay date 1947)

SOURCE: "The Prose Treatises," in *Henry Vaughan: A Life and Interpretation,* Oxford at the Clarendon Press, 1947, pp. 127-40.

[*Hutchinson was an English academic and scholar who wrote what is recognized as the most complete biographical and critical treatment of Vaughan to date. His* Henry Vaughan: A Life and Interpretation *was composed using research materials—notebooks, files, genealogies, copies of legal documents, magazine articles, and correspondence—assembled by Gwenllian Morgan and Louise Guiney, both of whom died before their own proposed biography of Vaughan could be written. In the following excerpt from his chapter "The Prose Treatises," Hutchinson examines the translation, devotions, and treatises which appear in* Olor Iscanus, The Mount of Olives, *and* Flores Solitudinus. *His purpose for doing so stems from the belief that the mind of Vaughan becomes "clearer to us if we take stock of the books which he was reading, translating, and writing in the years when he was engaged upon his sacred poems."*]

The mind of the author of *Silex Scintillans* will become clearer to us if we take stock of the books which he was reading, translating, and writing in the years when he was engaged upon his sacred poems. Of his bookish habits we learn from his poems **'On Sir Thomas Bodley's Library'** and **'To his Books'**. Books were his 'consolations' in 'sad times', and they survived to keep him company when other companions were lost to him:

> Burning and shining *Thoughts;* man's posthume
> *day:*
> The *track* of fled souls, and their *Milkie-way.*
> The dead *alive* and *busie,* the still *voice*
> Of inlarg'd Spirits, kind heav'ns white *Decoys.*

Before his conversion we are made aware of his interest in contemporary poetry and of his considerable intimacy with the Latin classics. From 1648 to 1655, except for some allusions to contemporary poetry in *Olor Iscanus,* there is a marked diversion of his literary interest to works of piety, primitive, medieval, and of his own day. Together they show a remarkable width of reading for one who was still in the early thirties. One wonders, too, how he had access in a remote Welsh village to books of some rarity. Either he must have bought freely in London or he was lent books by some older friend like Thomas Powell. **'Man in Darkness'**, one of Vaughan's few original prose works, is very full of quotations and references for so short a treatise. Besides the classical authors, the Fathers are cited—Chrysostom, Cyprian, Ambrose, Gregory the Great, Jerome, Anselm. There are also citations from writers so little known as Marcellus Empiricus, a physician of the fifth Christian century, and Alanus de Insulis. Vaughan quotes repeatedly from treatises of Petrarch and Drexelius, though he does not name the latter. . . .

Even clearer light on the way in which Vaughan's mind was working in these years may be obtained from considering the books which he elected to translate. The choice was almost certainly his own, as it is hard to suppose that any publisher proposed to him works so little likely to find purchasers. They did not, in fact, sell well, as no second editions were called for. Vaughan's translations were not publishers' hack-work, but works which the translator believed to be for the edification of such readers as he could find. There were in all nine translated treatises which he printed in these years—four short pieces in *Olor Iscanus,* a short piece attributed to St. Anselm in *The Mount of Olives,* three more in *Flores Solitudinis,* and the only long one, Nolle's Treatise on *Hermetical Physick,* printed separately a little before the enlarged *Silex Scintillans.*

The four brief discourses which fill out *Olor Iscanus* to make it a volume of any size are perhaps the least significant of Vaughan's mind. The two discourses of Plutarch and the one by Maximus of Tyre, a Greek sophist of the second Christian century, he translated from the Latin versions in a posthumous edition of 1613 by Dr. John Reynolds, President of Corpus Christi College, Oxford. The first discourse, **'Of the Benefit we may get from our Enemies'**, may have appealed to him as the treatment of a practical question in troubled times, though Plutarch probably had private rather than public enemies in mind. 'To forbeare revenge upon an Enemie, when wee opportunely may, is the highest glory in all humanity'—this is a sentiment which the times needed. Vaughan was well aware that the sufferings and deprivations caused to himself and his friends by the Civil War and the subsequent Puritan régime were likely enough to stir feelings of revenge and, at times also, to excite hopes of a war of retaliation. However much such feelings may have rankled in the breasts of his associates, Vaughan strove to repress them in himself. Many of his sacred poems show how he shrank from any idea of a renewal of civil war:

> Give me humility and peace,
> Contented thoughts, innoxious ease,
> A sweet, revengeless, quiet minde,
> And to my greatest haters kinde.

With his intense feeling about 'this iron age' 'exil'd Religion', it was only his sense of the duty of maintaining a Christian temper that could be proof against what Plutarch called 'obtrectation, malevolence, with an Implacable and endles resentment of Injuries'.

The second discourse of Plutarch, **'Of the Diseases of the Mind and the Body'**, and the companion piece of the **'Platonick Philosopher'**, Maximus Tirius, with the same title, may show Vaughan's growing interest in medicine, though there is little in them about physical treatment. Plutarch's is a pleasant little essay, maintaining that diseases of the mind, because unperceived by the patient, are more dangerous than those of the body which force themselves on the patient's attention and oblige him to have resort to the physician. Maximus Tirius also finds the diseases of the mind more pernicious: 'The disease of the body hath never yet occasion'd wars, but that of the mind hath occasion'd many'. The sufferer from bodily ills is made 'desirous of health' and therefore 'fitter for cure', but the mind, once infected and bewitched, 'will not somuch as heare of health'.

Olor Iscanus ends with Vaughan's translation from a Latin version of **'The Praise and Happinesse of the Countrie-Life; Written Originally in *Spanish* by *Don Antonio de Guevara,* **Bishop of Carthagena, and Counsellour of

Estate to Charls the Fifth Emperour of Germany'. The bishop's gentle moralizing is obvious enough and presents a romantic and unreal picture of rural innocence, but it may have attracted the Silurist who had early turned his back on the attractions of the town and elected to spend the rest of life in his native village. In his poem 'Retirement' he professes to understand why Abraham left to Lot 'the Cities of the plain' which were 'the Thrones of Ill', and for himself 'Did love to be a Country liver'.

To the original prose writings which form the first two sections of **The Mount of Olives** Vaughan added, as a companion piece to his own **'Man in Darkness'**, for the comfort of the reader 'after thou hast past through that Golgotha', a discourse of the blessed state of the saints in the New Jerusalem, entitled **'Man in Glory'**. The Latin original had been printed for the first time in 1639 in Paris, 'where', says Vaughan, 'it took so well, that it was presently translated into French'. Its Jesuit editor took it to be a work of St. Anselm, transcribed by Eadmer, a canon regular of Canterbury, Anselm's chaplain and biographer. 'Some brokages and disorderly parcels of it' were already to be found in the *De Similitudine,* also attributed to Anselm. Neither work is now believed to be Anselm's, and **'Man in Glory'** will not add to his credit or to Vaughan's judgement in choosing it. It includes a terrible passage in which the writer attempts to describe the eternal pains of hell. The most original passage is that in which it is represented that no one need fear shame when his secret sins are made known in heaven, as the sins and failings of St. Peter and 'that blessed Convert *Mary Magdalen'* are already known there and only redound to the glory of God. The saints 'will have no such thoughts of thee, as thou at present dost suspect', for 'when they see that God hath freely and fully forgiven thee, they will not so much as have a thought of abhorring, or judging thee in the smallest matter', but rather 'have in greater admiration the infinite mercy of God both towards thee, and towards themselves'. A strange attraction of heaven is that the blessed will be rendered 'equall for swiftnesse to the very Angels'; their 'velocity' is likened to 'the beams of the Sunne, which as soone as ever the body of that Planet appears above the earth in the East, passe in a moment to the utmost West'. It is a little surprising that these rather childish fancies should please Vaughan or that he should expect them to please readers in his generation. He prefixes a poem of his own on St. Anselm, which probably has a hidden allusion to the execution of Laud; Anselm had fled from the persecution of William II, but, were he to return and see the present plight of the Church, he would declare that, in comparison with the persecution to-day, *'Rufus was a Saint'*. Such a judgement does more credit to Vaughan's heart than to his head.

Of more significance in illustrating Vaughan's mind at this time are the 'rare and elegant pieces' which make up his next book, **Flores Solitudinis.** In the dedication to his wife's uncle, Sir Charles Egerton, he tells him that these pieces 'Collected in his Sicknesse and Retirement' will lead him 'from the *noyse* and *pompe* of this world into a silent and solitary *Hermitage'.* And in the preface, dated 17 April 1652, he tells the reader that he sends the book abroad 'to bee a companion of those wise *Hermits,* who

have withdrawne from the present generation, to confirme them in their solitude, and to make that rigid *necessity* their pleasant *Choyse'.* It is evident that Vaughan, in his continued ill health and in his abhorrence of the regning powers, was well content to escape into his 'private grove' where he could pursue his meditations undisturbed. Such poems as **'The Retreate', 'The Dawning',** and **'Rules and Lessons'** in the first part of **Silex Scintillans** show how he had come to value retirement and solitude like an eremite. For him, when he was almost despairing of outward things, 'the contempt of the world', which he tells Egerton is the theme of his book, is not difficult, but congenial.

All the contents of **Flores Solitudinis** are of Jesuit origin. Johannes Eusebius Nierembergius, in spite of his German name, was a Spanish Jesuit, who was born and died at Madrid. For the Epistle of Eucherius and the Life of Paulinus Vaughan was indebted to Jesuit editors. In his obscurity he could afford to ignore the prejudices of the day, find his spiritual nourishment where he would, and commend it to the few who read his books.

Nieremberg's *De Arte Voluntatis* (1631), from which Vaughan selected two long sections for translation, was a work intended to give the pith (*medulla*) of Platonic, Stoic, and Christian ethic, and is therefore more plentifully illustrated from pagan writers—Plato and the Platonists, Seneca and Epictetus—than from Christian. The section, **'Of Temperance and Patience',** may well have appealed to Vaughan with its emphasis upon indifference to worldly possessions and upon the patience that is needed to endure troublous times, and, after his manner, he interpolates many allusions to his own times. The discourse, if sometimes ponderous, has its occasional brilliant passages, as when virtue is likened to music or when it is said of the Creator:

> God made not man by a *Fiat,* as he did the rest of the Creatures, but fell to work himself, and like the *Potter* that first tempers, then fashions the Clay, he made him by makeing, not by speaking.

It is just as the sculptor at the north portal of Chartres Cathedral has represented the creation of man. Again, the comparison of man's life to an actor's is familiar, but Nieremberg handles the theme well, and Vaughan translates him well:

> The *World* is a meer *Stage;* the *Master* of the *Revels* is *God;* the *Actors* are *Men;* the Ornaments and flourishes of the *Scenes* are honour, power and pomp; the transitory and painted *Streams* of Mortality, which passe along with the *current* of time, and like *flowers,* do but onely appeare, when they stay longest. . . .

> The *Actors* care not how the *Scenes* varie: they know, that when the *Play* is ended, the *Conquerour* must put off his *Crown* in the same *Ward-robe* where the *Fool* puts off his *Cap.* . . .

> The *stageplayer* is not commended, because he *acts* the *part* of a *Prince,* but because hee *acts* it well, and like a *Prince.* It is more commendable to *act* a foole, a begger, or a mourner to the life; then to *act* a King, or a Philosopher foolishly.

Vaughan's second choice from Nieremberg's book is an eloquent meditation on the theme, *Memento mori,* 'a very humane and elegant *Philosophy,* which taught men to season, and redeeme all the daies of their lives, with the memory of the one day of their death'. At the time when Vaughan was translating this discourse he was hardly expecting his long sickness to issue otherwise than in death. But for this fact its pietism might seem exaggerated: '*Philosophie,* or humane Knowledge is nothing else but a Contemplation of death; . . . for the fruit of Philosophy is Virtue, and Virtue is nothing else but an imitation of death, or the Art of dying well, by beginning to dye while we are alive.' Even this sentiment had been already expressed in **Silex Scintillans:**

> Thy Accounts thus made, spend in the grave one
> houre
> Before thy time; Be not a stranger there
> Where thou may'st sleep whole ages; Lifes poor
> flowr
> Lasts not a night sometimes. Bad spirits fear
> This Conversation; But the good man lyes
> Intombed many days before he dyes.

The third item in **Flores Solitudinis** is 'The World Contemned, in a Parenetical Epistle written by the Reverend Father Eucherius, Bishop of *Lyons,* to his kinsman Valerianus'. Eucherius is a conspicuous example of *contemptus mundi.* As Vaughan states in his preface, Eucherius shows to his kinsman 'the *vanity,* and the *iniquity* of *riches* and *honours',* which Vaughan calls 'the two grand inticements of *popular spirits'.* With a characteristic glance at the times, Vaughan adds that 'the Age we live in hath made all his *Arguments, Demonstrations'.* Eucherius was persuaded that his age was witnessing the 'convulsions of the dying world'; 'for certain it cannot last very long'. Vaughan enlarges upon his original, and in the same volume, in his preface to the *Life of Paulinus,* he expresses his own belief that the end of this world 'truely draws near, if it be not *at the door'.* Eucherius turned his back on the worldly distinction which had begun to open before him, entered the recently established abbey of Lerins in A.D. 432, and twelve years later was obliged to yield to the public opinion which demanded that he should be bishop of Lyons.

In his Epistle to Valerianus Eucherius instanced Paulinus, 'the great Ornament and light of France', as one of those who had given up great place to enter the religious life, and Héribert Rosweyde, the Jesuit editor of Eucherius, appended a Life of Paulinus, 'collected out of his own Works and ancient records of him' by another Jesuit writer, Francesco Sacchini. It was, therefore, natural for Vaughan, who translated the Epistle of Eucherius from Rosweyde's edition, to add a Life of Paulinus under the title, **'Primitive Holiness, Set forth in the Life of blessed Paulinus. Collected out of his own Works, and other Primitive Authors by *Henry Vaughan,* Silurist.'** This description might be taken by the reader to mean that Vaughan compiled his Life from the Works of Paulinus 'and other Primitive Authors', but the words only reproduce what is found in Sacchini's title of his *Vita Paulini,* 'Ex scriptis eius, & veterum de eo Elogiis concinnata.' The larger part of Vaughan's **'Primitive Holiness'** is a free translation and adaptation of the *Vita Paulini,* so that it is very much more his work than the translations hitherto discussed.

A further reason for Vaughan's choosing to write this Life is that Paulinus not only turned to the religious life but also devoted himself to the composition of sacred poetry. What Dr. Raby says of Paulinus is hardly less true of Vaughan himself:

> But for his conversion, he would have employed his poetical gifts upon trifling subjects and rhetorical themes; now that he had devoted himself to religion, he used his talent to express those ideas and emotions which had really mastered his life. In short, he became a true poet.

Paulinus was born in or near Bordeaux, where his father had an estate, besides other patrimonies in Italy 'more becomming a Prince then a private man'. He was educated by Ausonius; this in itself would interest Vaughan, who, in the opening poem of **Olor Iscanus,** alludes to Ausonius's famous poem on the Moselle, and, later in that book, gives an English version of his idyll, 'Cupido cruci affixus'. When Paulinus embraced the Christian faith under the influence of Ambrose at the age of 38 and decided to relinquish his high position in the imperial service, Ausonius sought to dissuade him from 'changing thy Ivorie-chair for a dark Cell', and hinted that his wife Therasia, with her ardent Spanish temperament, was a 'Tanaquil, the Imperatrix of her Husband'. Paulinus replied in a poem, which Vaughan translates, 'I am not he, whom you knew then'; serious thoughts now engage his soul, and he must 'leave false honours, and that share Which fell to mee of this fraile world'. After his wife's death Paulinus became bishop of Nola in 410 and laboured there till his death in 431.

Vaughan is much freer in telling the life of Paulinus than in translating Nieremberg and Eucherius, and the narrative is attractively written. The poems introduced from the *Carmina* of Paulinus and from other writers give him an opportunity of exercising his gift of verse-translation. He is also freer than ever to make topical allusions. He accompanies a passage from the *Vita Paulini* about the evil of bringing 'unseason'd persons into the Ministry' with his own comment: 'Wee need no examples: Wee have lived to see all this our selves.' When he tells of Hadrian's desecration of Bethlehem and Calvary, he proceeds:

> Some men amongst us have done the like: Two *Seasons* in the year were consecrated by the *Church* to the memory of our *Saviour:* The *Feast* of his *Nativity* and *Circumcision,* and the *Feast* of his *Passion* and *Resurrection.* These two they have utterly taken away: endeavouring (in my opinion) to extinguish the *memory* of his *Incarnation* and *Passion,* and to race his blessed name out of those *bright columnes of light,* which the *Scripture* calls *daies.* They will not allow him two daies in the year, who made the dayes and the nights.

Vaughan's comparison of Puritan prohibitions with the Emperor's iconoclasm shows grievous lack of proportion, but it reveals the depth of his feeling.

Two prose works remain to be discussed that are wholly his own composition: **'Solitary Devotions'** and **'Man in Darkness, or A Discourse of Death',** which are the first two items in *The Mount of Olives.* He must have been engaged upon this book very soon after he had published the first part of **Silex Scintillans,** as his dedication to Sir Charles Egerton is dated 'this first of October. 1651', and the book was entered at Stationers' Hall on the following 16 December. His purpose in publishing 'these weake productions' is made clear in the dedication and preface as well as in the text of the book. In this time of spiritual destitution, as he regards it, when the parish churches are 'now vilified and shut up' and when 'Thy Service and thy Sabbaths, thy own sacred Institutions and the pledges of thy love are denied unto us', he would encourage his readers to maintain the private exercise of their religion in regular prayer and meditation, lest the good seed 'wither away in these times of persecution and triall'. His choice of the title and sub-title of the book answers to this emphasis upon the value of 'Solitary Devotions':

> The *Sonne* of *God* himselfe (when *he* was *here,)*
> had no place to put his head in; And his *Servants*
> must not think the *present measure* too hard,
> seeing their *Master* himself took up his *nights-*
> *lodging* in the cold *Mount of Olives.*

That a young layman of thirty years of age should publish a book of devotions is remarkable, but there were precedents for the spiritual life of the Church being promoted by the writings of laymen: for instance, Sir Richard Baker printed several volumes of *Meditations* on the Lord's Prayer and the Psalms, and, among Welshmen, Rowland Vaughan of Caer Gai translated into Welsh Bishop Bayly's *Practice of Piety* (1630) and other devotional books.

Vaughan's **'Solitary Devotions'** are original, though he draws freely from the Bible and the Book of Common Prayer. They come from one who accepts whole-heartedly the theology and religious practices of an Anglican churchman. There is the full orthodox belief in the Divinity of Christ 'very God, and very man', the Trinity, the Redemption, and the Atonement; 'the great design and end of thine Incarnation was to save sinners.' He loves the observance of the Church feasts and 'that more strict and holy season, called Lent', for 'Such was in our Church . . . and such still are the preparation-dayes before this glorious Sabbath in all true Churches'. It is noticeable that nearly half of the **'Devotions'** is concerned with preparation for receiving the Holy Communion and with prayers to use privately at 'this glorious Sacrament', 'this soveraigne Sacrament', 'this great and solemne Feast, this Feast of mercy and miracles'. The ample provision of devotions at the Sacrament suggests that Vaughan, like John Evelyn, contrived to receive it from time to time at the hands of priests who continued to minister after their eviction and after the prohibition of the Prayer Book. Vaughan's explicit and devoted churchmanship, so fully evinced in **The Mount of Olives,** makes it clear that his celebration of the great Christian doctrines and of the Church's year in **Silex Scintillans** is no mere imitation of George Herbert but expresses his own mind, while it is also true that, with an elevation above Herbert's, he as-

cends in his greater poems to the remote spaces of eternity. It is characteristic of the author of **Silex Scintillans** that he should also in **The Mount of Olives** dwell so often on the thought of the departed and the eternal order.

There are many echoes in **The Mount of Olives** of the poems in the first part, and anticipations of those yet to be published in the second part, of **Silex Scintillans.** In the opening paragraph of **The Mount of Olives** he bids the reader 'be up before the Sun-rising'; 'When all the world is asleep, thou shouldst watch.' The same counsel is offered in stanzas of great beauty in **'Rules and Lessons'** and appears again in **'The Dawning'** and **'The Night'.** It corresponds with Vaughan's own spiritual experience of the value of solitude in the night and before the world is astir. It is the same voice that speaks to us in the meditations and prayers as in the meditative poems; we understand the poems all the better for being familiar with **The Mount of Olives.**

'Man in Darkness', 'a short and plaine Discourse of Death', pursues a theme which was congenial to that age. A fine example of this kind of writing is *Contemplatio Mortis et Immortalitatis,* put out anonymously in 1631 by Henry Montagu, Earl of Manchester, and better known in its later editions as *Manchester al Mondo.* Of greater and more enduring fame is Jeremy Taylor's *The Rule and Exercises of Holy Dying,* published a few months before **The Mount of Olives,** while its author was serving as chaplain to Richard Vaughan, Earl of Carbery, at Golden Grove in Carmarthenshire. The tone of **'Man in Darkness'** is devout and humble, sombre, and even macabre, as in a passage on hell which he takes from Drexelius. He translates long passages from Petrarch's *De Contemptu Mundi* and *De Otio Religiosorum.* Other patristic and medieval writers are quoted, and it is characteristic of Vaughan's mind at this time for him to appeal to primitive Christianity: 'let us but have recourse to the ages that are past, let us ask the *Fathers.'* The little treatise as a whole has a medieval cast, ascetic and severely orthodox. Like the medieval writers, he accepts many edifying but pre-scientific notions—the hyena's tears, the torpedo-fish which kills the fisherman with its eye (he had already used this illustration in **'The Charnel-house'**), and the turtle-dove that 'hath no gall'. He cites as 'a *Symboll* of the resurrection' Cornelius Agrippa's professed discovery of indications of life in the severed members of creatures when cast 'into a pot of seething water'. The phrase, 'a *deaths-head* crownd with *roses',* is verbally repeated in his poem **'Joy'.** But if there is an unmistakable sternness in the theme, there is also considerable beauty in the writing. Flowers move him by their loveliness as well as by their fragility: 'let us looke always upon this *Day-Lilie* of life, as if the *Sun* were already *set.'* His delight in the singing of birds, a natural music 'to which all *arted strains* are but *discord',* is more than once expressed, and any mention of the stars makes him eloquent:

> When thou also seest those *various, numberles,*
> *and beautiful luminaries* of the night to move on
> in their *watches,* and some of them to *vanish* and
> *set,* while all the rest do *follow after,* consider
> that *thou* art carried on with *them* in the *same*
> *motion,* and that there is no hope of subsisting

for thee, but in *him who never moves, and never sets.*

His allusion to Christ's passing the night in prayer 'when the birds of the aire lay warme in their nests' reminds us of his poem **'The Bird'**, in which the bird pillows its head in its 'own warm wing' through the stormy night. The ass on Palm Sunday 'made infinitely happy by so glorious a rider' anticipates the thought in his poem **'The Ass'.**

Vaughan's prose, whether original or in translating, has a quiet beauty and an epigrammatic force: 'Vanity is oftentimes a bubble that swims upon the face of Virtue'; 'Death is the *Inne* where we take up, that we may with more chearfullnesse set forwards, and be enabled to overtake, and to keep company with eternity'; 'Mutuall Consolations are a double banquet, they are the Churches *Eulogiae,* which we both give and take.' A longer passage will better illustrate the fineness of the thought and its concise expression:

> Charity is a relique of Paradise, and pitty is a strong argument that we are all descended from one man: He that carries this rare Jewell about him, will every where meete with some kindred. He is quickly acquainted with distressed persons, and their first sight warmes his blood. I could believe, that the word *stranger* is a notion received from the posterity of *Cain,* who killed *Abel.*

As in his poems, Vaughan makes much use of alliteration: 'All is gone, all is dust, deformity, and desolation'; and less often he uses assonance: 'Keep me . . . from the hours and the powers of darknesse.' Like Sir Thomas Browne, he takes pleasure in unusual words of Latin origin: ejulation, presension, velitation, manuduction (instruction), relucencies, contristation, delirations of philosophers, revertency, the great Archiplast, luctual, lusorie, uberous, extrarious, irremisse, dejicient, assimilant, concrescent, salutiferous. The use of such words seldom leaves the reader in any doubt of their meaning, and the strangeness adds a touch of distinction. Vaughan is another example of a poet who can write graceful and effective prose.

E. L. Marilla   (essay date 1948)

SOURCE: "The Secular and Religious Poetry of Henry Vaughan," in *Modern Language Quarterly,* Vol. 9, No. 3, December, 1948, pp. 394-411.

[*Marilla was a prominent American scholar of English Renaissance poetry and the poetry of John Milton. He edited* The Secular Poems of Henry Vaughan *(1958). In the following excerpt, Marilla examines poems from the two editions of* Silex Scintillans *as well as* Poems *and* Olor Iscanus. *His purpose is threefold: to demonstrate that Vaughan's secular verse is characterized by craftmanship that is distinctly similar to and nearly as skillful as that of the religious poetry, that (contrary to the claims of other critics) the secular poems are indicative of Vaughan's immanent maturity as a poet, and that Vaughan's entire poetic canon deserves to be reevaluated.*]

It is obvious that Henry Vaughan's rescue from long oblivion by nineteenth-century clerical editors was inspired more by evangelical interest than by artistic perception. Devout men like John Mitford, R. A. Willmott. Richard Cattermole, H. F. Lyte, A. B. Grosart, keenly aware of the need of spiritual reassurance for an era disturbed by the teachings of the New Science, labored diligently to enlist the testimony of Vaughan's religious utterances. These men shared the common aversion of their time to the metaphysical style, but the piety of Vaughan's religious verse overcame their objection to his literary manner. Naturally, then, they did not appreciate his secular verse, especially since this was much in the metaphysical tradition. Eager for corroborative evidence, these and other admirers of the religious poetry found biographical and bibliographical "support" for their assumption that the secular poems represented false starts of poetic inspiration that later found expression in an entirely different vein. Thanks to their well-meant diligence, by the end of the nineteenth century Vaughan's status was that of an important religious poet whose "early" secular verse—the basis of his limited literary reputation during his own time—received little critical attention. . . .

The purpose of the present study is actually threefold: first, to show that the secular verse is characterized by craftsmanship that is distinctly similar to and but little less skillful than that of the religious poetry; second, to point out even more obvious, though hitherto unrecognized, parallels between the secular and religious verse that contradict the prevailing theory that the secular poems represent immature interests and manifest little promise of Vaughan's achievement as a religious poet; third, to illustrate, at the same time, the need of a reëvaluation of his poetic work as a whole. This purpose can be achieved, I believe, through brief examination of specimens from *Silex Scintillans* (1650), *Poems* (1646), *Olor Iscanus* (1651), and *Silex Scintillans* (1655).

We may begin with a short poem (without title) from the 1650 *Silex Scintillans.*

> Come, come, what doe I here?
>   Since he is gone
> Each day is grown a dozen year,
>   And each houre, one;
>   Come, come!
> Cut off the sum,
> By these soil'd tears!
> (Which only thou
> Know'st to be true,)
> Dayes are my feares.   10
>
>   2.
>
> Ther's not a wind can stir,
>   Or beam passe by,
> But strait I think (though far,)
>   Thy hand is nigh;
>   Come, come!
> Strike these lips dumb:
> This restles breath
> That soiles thy name,
> Will ne'r be tame
> Untill in death.   20
>
>   3.
>
> Perhaps some think a tombe

No house of store,
But a dark, and seal'd up wombe,
Which ne'r breeds more.
Come, come!
Such thoughts benum;
But I would be
With him I weep
A bed, and sleep
To wake in thee.   30

This poem shows a subtle thematic development. It opens with dramatic abruptness, and the first quatrain stimulates interest through suggestion and suspense. From this quatrain one might infer that the poet is here moodily chiding himself for needlessly increasing his grief by remaining in the vicinity of a recently deceased friend or relative. We must read to the end of the stanza before it becomes apparent that, instead, he is pleading for death as an escape from a world made intolerable by his bereavement. The poet, however, does not imply that his life has been suddenly blighted by this one sorrow. Considered in its context, the statement that "Each day is grown a dozen year, And each houre, one" reveals that the stanza is the expression of one whose life had previously become a trial and who is now prostrate from a recent addition to his burden. The concluding lines of this stanza more perceptibly direct the appeal to the Deity and foreshadow clearer definition of the poet's attitude in the next.

The first four lines of the second stanza emphasize the poet's eagerness for death, and the subsequent couplet further intensifies the mood. The suggestion here that the appeal for death is inspired as much by Christian hope as by despair anticipates the final commitment in the last stanza. The first six lines of this reflect a conception of the tomb as a habitation of the body until an ultimate Resurrection. In this new context the poet's desire for immediate death as expressed in the next two lines appears logical, and the attitude that inspired the poem becomes completely defined and justified in the concluding couplet.

Contrary to the implication of previous criticism, the poem is more than a vigorous expression of religious faith. Quite obviously, its primary purpose is to project a mood of bereavement, and any evaluation of the poem that tends to overlook its objective (and, hence, its effective structure) is unreliable. And it deserves mention here that the strict classical regard for structural unity (as well as reliance upon dramatic effect) as exemplified in this poem is an important feature of Vaughan's method in his secular and religious poetry alike.

The method that characterizes the poem from *Silex Scintillans* is essentially the same as that employed in the following from *Poems,* Vaughan's first production:

To His Friend
Being in Love.

Aske Lover, ere thou dyest; let one poor breath
Steale from thy lips, to tell her of thy Death;
Doating Idolater! can silence bring
Thy Saint propitious? or will *Cupid* fling
One arrow for thy palenes? leave to trye
This silent Courtship of a sickly eye;
Witty to tyranny: She too well knowes

This but the incense of thy private vowes,
That breaks forth at thine eyes, and doth betray
The sacrifice thy wounded heart would pay; 10
Aske her, foole, aske her, if words cannot move,
The language of thy teares may make her love:
    Flow nimbly from me then; and when you fall
On her breasts warmer snow, O may you all,
By some strange Fate fixt there, distinctly lye
The much lov'd Volume of my Tragedy.
    Where if you win her not, may this be read,
    The cold that freez'd you so, did strike me dead.

Despite its title, this poem is a soliloquy, and here also is a progressive thematic development. The composition, like that just considered, opens abruptly, and suspense is created immediately. True, we recognize in the opening couplet a literary convention of the time and infer that the poem represents an expression of a desperate lover. But the couplet itself reveals neither what it is that the "Lover" is to "Aske" nor why he has gone far enough. From the next four lines one could infer that the speaker is diffidently considering whether he should openly declare his affection for a lady whom he has hitherto silently adored. The mood is intensified in the next four lines, and emphasis and unity are achieved through renewal of the initial entreaty in the subsequent couplet, which concludes the argument. And it is in this last couplet of the first paragraph that the real issue is revealed. Here we learn that the speaker, far from worshipping in silence, has despaired of the efficacy of mere words, and is debating whether he should confess with the convincing humility of tears the full measure of his love for the unresponsive lady. It is not by accident, of course, that the debate ends at the point where the issue becomes clearly defined.

The sudden change of tone in the next paragraph is dramatically correct. Here the problem is resolved, and the mood is that of resolute decision. The overt and intense expression in this paragraph of the attitude that has been gradually revealed in the preceding verses provides emphasis, and strengthens the total effect of the poem. At the same time, this open manifestation of humility builds for the surprise ending, which, accordingly, has the dramatic force of an unexpected retaliation. But notwithstanding its element of surprise, this concluding couplet is closely integrated in the composition and, in fact, defines the attitude that inspired the poem.

A significant detail of the composition is its concrete imagery. This contributes much to the vigor of the expression and, hence, to its tone of spontaneity, which distinguishes the poem from much of the love verse of the time. To claim that this poem manifests unusual artistic skill, however, would be a mistake; but it is no less a mistake, certainly, to consider it inept and of no literary value.

In view of the similarity of method in the previous selections from *Silex Scintillans* and *Poems,* it is not surprising to find much the same kind of craftsmanship in the following specimen from the latter work:

To Amoret gone from him.

Fancy, and I, last Evening walkt,
And, *Amoret,* of thee we talkt;

The West just then had stolne the Sun,
And his last blushes were begun:
We sate, and markt how every thing
Did mourne his absence; How the Spring
That smil'd, and curl'd about his beames,
Whilst he was here, now check'd her streames:
The wanton Eddies of her face
Were taught lesse noise, and smoother grace;
And in a slow, sad channell went,
Whisp'ring the banks their discontent:
The carelesse ranks of flowers that spread
Their perfum'd bosomes to his head,
And with an open, free Embrace,
Did entertaine his beamy face;
Like absent friends point to the West,
And on that weake reflection feast.
If Creatures then that have no sence,
But the loose tye of influence,
(Though fate, and time each day remove
Those things that element their love)
At such vast distance can agree,
    Why, *Amoret,* why should not wee.

This poem has appeared in more than one modern anthology as a single selection from Vaughan's secular verse, and it is almost certain that the melancholy tone and sensuous imagery of the composition have been its chief attraction. Apparently, however, no one has recognized that its nature imagery is an integral element in a carefully devised synthesis.

Here again is a progressive development of theme. The dramatic opening couplet introduces an atmosphere of solitude, but reveals only that the poet is reflecting on his relationship with Amoret. The next eight couplets depict a nature scene which may at first seem to be a mere ornamental setting for the poet's solitary meditations. Despite evident modern appreciation of the imagery, this scene is in itself notable chiefly for its conventionality. Its imagery and concept, however, have a fundamental structural importance. In the context, the "blushes" of the personified "Sun" in the first of these eight couplets suggests romantic love. Hence, the mourning of "every thing" in the next symbolizes the grief of separated lovers. This concept is reënforced by the particularized behavior of the "Spring" in the next few lines, and is further intensified through additional concrete suggestion of romantic love in the description of the "flowers," receiving emphasis in the paradox of line 18.

It is obvious enough that the poet's own mood is mirrored in the scene envisaged here, but the passage is more closely integrated in the poem than may be immediately apparent. The concept of the affection of the spring and flowers for the sun is not a mere superimposed fantasy; it is based upon the philosophic idea (prevalent in metaphysical writers) that the Divine Spirit is immanent in all forms of being, and that, accordingly, romantic love is a manifestation of a cosmic affinity. The imagery of the nature scene is a visualization of this affinity as operating among natural objects and is intended as "rational" reënforcement of the plea that emerges in the remaining verses (the periodic syntax of which suspends the ultimate conclusion till the last line). Thus considered, the poem turns out to be a carefully unified expression of a lover's disconsolate mood.

There is also an important relationship between the poet's method in the selection from *Silex Scintillans* and that in the following composition from *Poems:*

**To Amoret, of the difference 'twixt him, and
other Lovers,
and what true Love is.**

Marke, when the Evenings cooler wings
    Fanne the afflicted ayre, how the faint
Sunne,
        Leaving undone,
        What he begunne,
Those spurious flames suckt up from slime, and
earth
        To their first, low birth,
        Resignes, and brings.

They shoot their tinsill beames, and vanities,
    Thredding with those false fires their way;
        But as you stay 10
        And see them stray,
You loose the flaming track, and subt'ly they
        Languish away,
        And cheate your Eyes.

Just so base, Sublunarie Lovers hearts
    Fed on loose prophane desires,
        May for an Eye,
        Or face comply:
But those removed, they will as soone depart,
        And shew their Art, 20
        And painted fires.

Whil'st I by pow'rfull Love, so much refin'd,
    That my absent soule the same is,
        Careless to misse,
        A glaunce, or kisse,
Can with those Elements of lust and sence,
        Freely dispence,
        And court the mind.

Thus to the North the Loadstones move,
    And thus to them th' enamour'd steel as-
pires: 30
        Thus, *Amoret,*
        I doe affect;
And thus by winged beames, and mutuall fire,
        Spirits and Stars conspire,
        And this is Love.

In this poem there is, again, a gradual thematic development, which reaches a conclusion in the last line. The first stanza envisages an instance of the sun's failure to sustain its elevating force upon lifted spirals of mist, and attributes this failure to the inevitable fanning of "the Evenings cooler wings." In the second stanza this phenomenon is projected in the casual observer's view and becomes the familiar fanlike design sometimes seen under the lowering sun (and commonly known as the sun's drawing of water). Here it is an attractive deception, but by its close analogy with the process described in the preceding stanza it is an inevitable deception. The line-by-line parallel in imagery continues through the third stanza, where the "prophane desires" are analogous to the "spurious flames" and "false fires" of the preceding stanzas, and the "Eye or face" is a parallel of the "Sunne" in the first. Now in the poet's "scientific" view as reflected in the first stanza, the "flames" are caught up involuntarily by the attraction of the sun, and the gradual weakening of that attraction is due to their impurity. Hence, by the close analogy that extends through the third stanza this becomes a "logical" argument that the beautiful woman (in this case, Amoret) is always endangered by her charms, since these, however chaste, naturally attract "Sublunarie" lovers whose affection, convincing though it may appear, is by its very nature transitory.

The basic concept of the poem becomes apparent in the last two stanzas. The first of these declares that the speaker's affection, unlike that of "prophane" lovers, is a constant spiritual affinity, and the second, in keeping with the method of the previous argument, "scientifically" establishes the assertion. The newly discovered principle of magnetism comported well with the widely current idea of the all-pervasiveness of the Divine Spirit (even in the stones), and we can deny the appropriateness of this concluding metaphysical conceit, it seems to me, only through failure to understand the poem. The figure of the magnet here is not only philosophical reënforcement of the speaker's assertion in the preceding stanza, but is actually the foundation of the antithesis that constitutes the argument of the poem.

In its total effect *"To Amoret, of the difference"* is perhaps the least successful poem in the volume, but the opinion that its weakness resides in inept metaphysical conceits is not only incorrect, but, as we shall see, also illogical. Its effect is impaired, in the first place, by the over-explicit "philosophic" argument, and, besides, as a love poem it suffers from the detached mood that results from the predominance of the intellectual factor.

It is impossible, I submit, to reconcile the evidence of these specimens with the persistent assumption that Vaughan's secular poems represent naïve experiments with a method for which he had no aptitude and which he later, as a religious poet, abandoned. Plainly enough, essentially the same method is employed in all four selections, and it is no less obvious that the secular pieces exemplify skill in craftsmanship that strongly foreshadows the artistic quality of the poem from *Silex Scintillans.*

Examination of additional specimens will further illustrate the similarity in method between the secular and religious poetry and will show also even more obvious parallels. As a matter of fact, *"To Amoret, of the difference"* is related in more than one way to the following poem from the 1650 *Silex Scintillans:*

The Showre.

'Twas so, I saw thy birth: That drowsie Lake
From her faint bosome breath'd thee, the disease
Of her sick waters, and Infectious Ease.
    But, now at Even
    Too grosse for heaven,
Thou fall'st in teares, and weep'st for thy mistake.

2.

Ah! it is so with me; oft have I prest
Heaven with a lazie breath, but fruitles this
Peirc'd not; Love only can with quick accesse
    Unlock the way,   10

    When all else stray
The smoke, and Exhalations of the brest.

3.

Yet, if as thou doest melt, and with thy traine
Of drops make soft the Earth, my eyes could weep
O're my hard heart, that's bound up, and asleep,
    Perhaps at last
    (Some such showres past,)
My God would give a Sun-shine after raine.

Important parallels between the two poems can hardly escape even casual observation. Quite obviously, the nucleus of **"The Showre"** is a metaphysical conceit based on the same natural phenomenon used in the first figure of the secular poem, and the same Paracelsian and Aristotelian theories underlying the imagery of that conceit are similarly fundamental in this poem. In structural pattern the poems are notably similar, and in tone, as well as in specific details of imagery, **"The Showre"** is distinctly reminiscent of the first two stanzas of *"To Amoret, of the difference,"* and even verbal echoes occur. Moreover, the two poems are particularly alike in method of organization in that both rely heavily upon parallel and antithesis as integrating devices.

The opening stanza of **"The Showre"** serves as a framework for a progressive development of theme. In the parallel in concept between the first three lines of this stanza and the corresponding lines of the next, the "lazie breath" of the second is analogous to the "sick waters" of the first; hence, the reference to the straying "Exhalations" in the concluding lines of the second is an acknowledgment that these issued from an evil heart. But this same reference implies that "Love" could have given "quick accesse." The concept of the latter lines, however, is antithetical to that of the corresponding lines of the first stanza, and in the contrast between the behavior of the "lazie breath" and that of the "sick waters" lies the suggestion that the "Exhalations" were ineffectual, not because they were impure, but because they did not humbly confess their unworthiness. The first three lines of the last stanza therefore imply that the way to grace is through the penitence of tears, and the concluding lines reveal that the poem is an orthodox Christian's confession of insufficient humility and a prayer for increased awareness of human depravity as a means to salvation.

No more than passing notice of the following stanzas from **"Disorder *and* frailty"** (*Silex Scintillans,* 1650) is necessary to show that this poem, too, is related to *"To Amoret, of the difference"* not only by its pattern, but also by an underlying parallel in imagery:

2.

I threaten heaven, and from my Cell
Of Clay, and frailty break, and bud
Touch'd by thy fire, and breath; Thy bloud
Too, is my Dew, and springing wel.
    But while I grow
And stretch to thee, ayming at all
    Thy stars, and spangled hall,
    Each fly doth tast
    Poyson, and blast

My yielding leaves; sometimes a showr
Beats them quite off, and in an hour
    Not one poor shoot
    But the bare root
Hid under ground survives the fall.
        Alas, frail weed!

3.

Thus like some sleeping Exhalation
(Which wak'd by heat, and beams, makes up
Unto that Comforter, the Sun,
And soars, and shines; But e'r we sup
    And walk two steps
Cool'd by the damps of night, descends,
    And, whence it sprung, there ends,)
        Doth my weak fire
        Pine, and retire,
And (after my hight of flames,)
In sickly Expirations tames
        Leaving me dead
        On my first bed
Untill thy Sun again ascends.
        Poor, falling Star!

The neglect of the following poem from **Olor Iscanus** betrays an important oversight in the traditional conception of Vaughan's poetic development and literary achievement.

The Charnel-house.

Blesse me! what damps are here? how stiffe an
    aire?
Kelder of mists, a second *Fiats* care,
Frontspeece o' th' grave and darkness, a Display
Of ruin'd man, and the disease of day;
Leane, bloudless shamble, where I can descrie
Fragments of men, Rags of Anatomie;
Corruptions ward-robe, the transplantive bed
Of mankind, and th' Exchequer of the dead.
How thou arrests my sense? how with the sight
My *Winter'd* bloud growes stiffe to all
    delight?   10
Torpedo to the Eye! whose least glance can
Freeze our wild lusts, and rescue head-long man;
Eloquent silence! able to Immure
An *Atheists* thoughts, and blast an *Epicure.*
Were I? *Lucian,* Nature in this dresse
Would make me wish a Saviour, and Confesse.
    Where are you shoreless thoughts, vast ten-
    ter'd hope,
Ambitious dreams, *Aymes* of Endless scope,
Whose stretch'd Excesse runs on a string too
    high
And on the rack of self-extension dye?   20
Chameleons of state, Aire-monging band,
Whose breath (like Gun-powder) blowes up a
    land,
Come see your dissolution, and weigh
What a loath'd nothing you shall be one day,
As th' Elements by Circulation passe
From one to th' other, and that which first was
Is so again, so 'tis with you; The grave
And Nature but Complott, what the one gave
The other takes; Think then, that in this bed
There sleep the Reliques of as proud a
    head   30
As stern and subtill as your own, that hath

Perform'd, or forc'd as much, whose tempest-
    wrath
Hath levell'd Kings with slaves, and wisely then
Calme these high furies, and descend to men;
Thus *Cyrus* tam'd the *Macedon,* a tombe
Checkt him, who thought the world too straight
    a Room.
    Have I obey'd the *Powers* of a face,
A beauty able to undoe the Race
Of easie man? I look but here, and strait
I am Inform'd, the lovely Counterfeit   40
Was but a smoother Clay. That famish'd slave
Begger'd by wealth, who starves that he may
    save.
Brings hither but his sheet; Nay, th' *Ostrich-man*
That feeds on *steele* and *bullet,* he that can
Outswear his *Lordship,* and reply as tough
To a kind word, as if his tongue were *Buffe,*
Is *Chap*-faln here, wormes without wit, or fear
Defie him now, death hath disarm'd the *Bear.*
Thus could I run o'r all the pitteous score
Of erring men, and having done meet
    more,   50
Their shuffled *Wills,* abortive, vain *Intents,*
Phantastick *humours,* perillous *Ascents,*
False, empty *honours,* traiterous *delights.*
And whatsoe'r a blind Conceit Invites;
But these and more which the weak vermins
    swell,
Are Couch'd in this Accumulative Cell
Which I could scatter; But the grudging Sun
Calls home his beams, and warns me to be gone,
Day leaves me in a double night, and I
Must bid farewell to my sad library.   60
Yet with these notes. Henceforth with thought
    of thee
I'le season all succeeding Jollitie,
Yet damn not mirth, nor think too much is fit,
Excesse hath no *Religion,* nor *Wit,*
But should wild bloud swell to a lawless strain
One Check from thee shall *Channel* it again.

The first line dramatically suggests that the speaker has just entered the charnel house, and the initial paragraph reflects his growing repulsion. The poet's sole purpose in this paragraph is to convey a mood, and it is debatable whether anywhere else he more successfully achieves his aim. The concrete imagery is, of course, an important factor in the effectiveness of these lines, and the elliptical style contributes much to the appropriate acrid tone. In fact, the entire poem would serve admirably as an example of effective accommodation of imagery and sound to sense.

Poetic interest in the chastening message of the charnel house was, of course, conventional, but here the concept itself is not the poet's primary concern. The opening emphasis upon the irony of man's temporal aspirations introduces a theme of the poet's own that is forcefully developed in the subsequent divisions of the poem. The first four couplets of the second paragraph focus the admonitory implication of the charnel house upon the Parliamentarians, the poet's prospering political enemies. In the next two couplets this reminder that the ambitious "*Chameleons* of state" must sometime pay their debt to nature is reënforced by a metaphysical conceit (reflecting the Aristotelian theory of the Generation of the Elements), and the remaining lines of this section further emphasize the argument with parallel and example.

The poet quite probably was aware that the third paragraph might lead casual readers among his contemporaries to regard the poem as a "harmless" experiment with a familiar idea; but, in fact, throughout this last paragraph the admonishing theme, sufficiently focused in the preceding section, is continued and vigorously intensified. Here we find a relevant view of death as the Nemesis of *all* worldly power. This oblique reproof of what the poet considered a tragic case of arrogance and presumption begins with specific instances of the triumph of the charnel house. But more than ordinary rhetorical importance is involved in these examples. True, the allusion to the defeat of the charms of feminine beauty is safely general in its implication, as is also the pronouncement upon the conventionally disparaged miser's wealth. But last in what is obviously an ascending series comes notice of the annihilation of the arrogant *"Ostrich-man,"* who clearly enough represents a Parliamentarian from a Royalist's point of view. With this additional glance at the enemies of the traditional religious and political order—whose ambition the typical Royalist like Vaughan regarded as defiance of divine law—the poet reënforces his thrust with a hurried résumé of the host of "erring men" who, for all their irrational ambition and arrogance, could not escape "this Accumulative Cell" and are now, the whole innumerable throng, mere dust that the poet himself "could scatter." This passage, though strenuously emphasizing the underlying thesis of the poem, tends, nevertheless, to become a digression, and the author's usual regard for structural unity is to be observed in the return to subtle but pointed denunciation, in the remaining lines of the poem, of the political and religious ideals of the reactionaries.

In the poem below (from **Silex Scintillans,** 1650) we detect further evidence that previous commentators have overlooked obvious and fundamental relationships between Vaughan's secular and religious verse.

The Check.

Peace, peace! I blush to hear thee; when thou art
     A dusty story
A speechless heap, and in the midst my heart
     In the same livery drest
     Lyes tame as all the rest;
When six years thence digg'd up, some youthfull
     Eie
     Seeks there for Symmetry
But finding none, shal leave thee to the wind,
     Or the next foot to Crush,
     Scatt'ring thy kind   10
     And humble dust, tell then dear flesh
     Where is thy glory?

2.

As he that in the midst of day Expects
     The hideous night,
Sleeps not, but shaking off sloth, and neglects,
     Works with the Sun, and sets
     Paying the day its debts;
That (for Repose, and darknes bound,) he might
     Rest from the fears i' th' night;

So should we too. All things teach us to
     die   20
     And point us out the way
     While we passe by
     And mind it not; play not away
     Thy glimpse of light.

3.

View thy fore-runners: Creatures giv'n to be
     Thy youths Companions,
Take their leave, and die; Birds, beasts, each tree
     All that have growth, or breath
     Have one large language, *Death.*
O then play not! but strive to him, who
     Can   30
     Make these sad shades pure Sun,
Turning their mists to beams, their damps to
     day,
     Whose pow'r doth so excell
     As to make Clay
     A spirit, and true glory dwell
     In dust, and stones.

4.

Heark, how he doth Invite thee! with what voice
     Of Love, and sorrow
He begs, and Calls; *O that in these thy days*
     Thou knew'st but thy own good!   40
     Shall not the Crys of bloud,
Of Gods own bloud awake thee? He bids beware
     Of drunknes, surfeits, Care,
But thou sleep'st on; wher's now thy protestation,
     Thy Lines, thy Love? Away,
     Redeem the day,
     The day that gives no observation,
     Perhaps to morrow.

The pattern of this composition resembles that of three poems previously considered, including **"To Amoret, of the difference,"** and it is worth noting that the device of periodic syntax employed in the first stanza of that secular poem appears again in the opening stanza of this. But a much closer relationship exists between **"The Check"** and **"The Charnel-house."** It seems significant, to begin with, that the title of the religious poem echoes the last couplet of the other, and an interesting parallel in concept and method of development is quite perceptible. **"The Check"** opens with a dramatic expression of disgust at the pretensions of mortality, and the first stanza derides man's worldly interests by focusing, let us note, upon his inevitable "dissolution" in the "humble dust" of the charnel house. The second stanza, like the third paragraph of **"The Charnel-house,"** emphasizes the universality of death and thus reënforces the implied admonition to the worldly minded. The parallel with the secular poem continues in the third stanza, which, in the interest of unity and intensity, focuses again on the scene of physical disintegration. The first four lines of this stanza emphasize the concept introduced in the first stanza, and the remaining lines repeat and amplify the exhortation of the second—and contain verbal echoes of **"The Charnel-house."** The implication of the first two stanzas becomes explicit in the third, where the "one large language, *Death,*" and "dust, and stones" are regarded as a benevolent though sorrowful agency (the "sad library" of **"The Charnel-house,"** line 60) through which the Deity counsels man to seek haven in the spiritual life. And in this development we recognize the emergence of the basic theme, which receives dramatically appropriate emphasis in the concluding stanza.

"The Charnel-house" is plainly the more subtle of the two poems, and there might be some justifiable difference of opinion concerning their relative merit. More important is the fact that any estimate (however favorable) of **"The Check"** which ignores the relationship between its structure and its aim represents no less an injustice to the poet than does similar failure to interpret properly **"The Charnel-house"** and to consider its method of achieving its purpose.

We must include, finally, brief notice of the following from the 1655 *Silex Scintillans:*

The Garland.

Thou, who dost flow and flourish here below,
To whom a falling star and nine dayes glory,
Or some frail beauty makes the bravest shew,
Hark, and make use of this ensuing story.

    When first my youthfull, sinfull age
      Grew master of my wayes,
Appointing errour for my Page,
      And darknesse for my dayes;
I flung away, and with full crie
      Of wild affections, rid   10
In post for pleasures, bent to trie
      All gamesters that would bid,
I played with fire, did counsell spurn,
      Made life my common stake;

    But never thought that fire would
      burn,
      Or that a sould could ake.
Glorious deceptions, gilded mists,
      False joyes, phantastick flights,
Peeces of sackcloth with silk-lists,
      These were my prime
        delights.   20
I sought choice bowres, haunted the
      spring,
      Cull'd flowres and made me po-
        sies:
Gave my fond humours their full
      wing,
      And crown'd my head with
        Roses.
But at the height of this Careire
      I met with a dead man,
Who noting well my vain Abear,
      Thus unto me began:
Desist fond fool, be not undone,
      What thou hast cut to day   30
Will fade at night, and with this Sun
      Quite vanish and decay.

Flowres gather'd in this world, die here; if thou
Wouldst have a wreath that fades not, let them
    grow,

And grow for thee; who spares them here, shall
    find
A Garland, where comes neither rain, nor wind.

By its somber admonition to those preoccupied with the transitory awards of this life, the opening stanza recalls both **"The Check"** and **"The Charnel-house,"** and the third line is a clear echo of lines 37-41 of the latter poem. The first ten lines of the "ensuing story" project (in dramatically appropriate lilting rhythm) the reckless attitude of the youthful "fool." The undertone of penitence, however, becomes distinct in the last two of these and anticipates the restrospective denunciation of his folly in the next four lines. And both in manner and imagery these are almost identical with lines 49-53 of **"The Charnel-house,"** and even contain distinct verbal echoes of that passage. The next four lines depict the mounting recklessness of the youth's course and thus lend dramatic effect to the conclusion of the "story." In this conclusion it is revealed that the speaker's early consuming interest in transitory values was checked by the precepts of "a dead man"—that is, by the lesson of the charnel house. The corollary of this ominous though benevolent counsel of the "dead man" (again, the message of the "sad library") becomes in the last stanza explicitly the theme of the poem.

Twentieth-century criticism has contributed much to an understanding of the poet's personality and has variously provided insight necessary to a broad perspective, but we cannot deny the evidence that proper interpretation and estimate of Vaughan's secular and religious poetry have not yet been achieved. I believe that the present study adequately illustrates the error of the prevailing theory that the secular verse reflects no important stage in the poet's artistic development. This assumption of previous criticism is sufficiently indicted, I submit, in that it not only denies the quite demonstrable fact that the poet's method in the secular verse is basically the same as that in ***Silex Scintillans,*** but also overlooks a further relationship no less obvious and significant than prominent parallels in imagery, concept, theme, and even attitude. Nor can we dismiss the implication of the corollary that critical opinion on the religious poetry reflects oversight of the same relevant details. But more important still is the positive evidence set down here that in two ways Vaughan suffers the injustice of deficient critical attention. We cannot avoid, on the one hand, the ironic conclusion that, although modern criticism has persistently deplored the previous neglect of the poet for more than a century, he is still denied the measure of prestige which careful evaluation of his secular verse will award. It is no less evident, on the other, that notwithstanding his acceptance today as an important sacred poet, the actual merit of his religious poetry yet awaits proper acknowledgment. Indeed not the least strange anomaly in the history of Vaughan's literary reputation is the fact that, despite his rapid increase in stature during the past five decades, his real artistic importance has not yet been recognized. When a true evaluation of his poetic work is accomplished. Vaughan's reputation will be far less dependent upon extra-literary interest. His prestige will then have better insurance than mere accident during eras like our own when readers cease to share the evangelical enthusiasm of the poet's nineteenth-century clerical editors.

Frank Kermode (essay date 1950)

SOURCE: "The Private Imagery of Henry Vaughan," in *The Review of English Studies,* Vol. 1, No. 3, July, 1950, pp. 206-25.

[*Kermode is an English critic whose career combines modern critical methods with expert traditional scholarship, particularly in his work on Shakespeare. He characterizes all human knowledge as poetic, or fictive: constructed by humans and affected by the perceptual and emotional limitations of human consciousness. Because perceptions of life and the world change, so does human knowledge and the meaning attached to things and events. Thus, there is no single fixed reality over time. Similarly, true or "classic" literature, to Kermode, is a constantly reinterpreted living text, "complex and indeterminate enough to allow us our necessary pluralities." In the following excerpt, he examines Vaughan's uses of devotional themes in his poetry and prose to suggest that the poet's conversion, widely discussed among critics, "was rather a poetic than a religious experience, and to appraise some of the poems as poetry rather than as prayer."*]

Although research has increased the materials available to the critic of Vaughan, certain aspects of his poetry are still obscured by exegetical fallacies which take their origin from unwarranted assumptions about the poet's conversion and his manner of using devotional themes. The object of this essay is to suggest that the conversion was rather a poetic than a religious experience, and to appraise some of the poems as poetry rather than as prayer.

Vaughan was a bookish poet; by this I mean that not only was his poetry often imitative, but that his most authentic and individual inspirations were frequently rooted in words and rhythms, and in imagery conventionalized by earlier use, rather than in visual impressions. The conventional description of Vaughan as a 'nature-mystic' is therefore pointless. Like the reluctance to draw the obvious conclusion from Vaughan's use of Herbert, Felltham, Cartwright, Randolph, and his brother Thomas, it is a feature of the romantic conspiracy to redeem the poet from a period cursed with obsolete learning. Vaughan has in common with Donne the habit of making his poems, whatever their true cause, meditations on an idea which may be trivial or which may be obscure, but which can rarely be described as a genuine *aperçu* of his own. But Vaughan differs from the earlier poet in that the range of his fancy is much narrower. By far the most important source of his poetry is the poetry of Herbert, for not only does he borrow theme and vocabulary from Herbert, but very often he owes the germ of a poem to this master, in whom we can study Vaughan's idea, either as a phrase or as a rhythm.

There is a fine example of this dependence in Vaughan's poem 'The Morning-Watch':

> O Joyes! Infinite sweetnes! with what flowres,
> And shoots of glory, my soul breakes, and buds!

The germ of this poem is Herbert's 'The Holy Scriptures' and also his second 'Prayer'. Vaughan's opening lines took shape from a meditation on Herbert's—'Oh Book! infinite sweetnesse! let my heart Suck ev'ry letter . . . .' For a few words the language, and for a few more, the rhythm, of Vaughan's poem runs parallel to Herbert's. Then the idea is totally altered and becomes Vaughan's own, stamped as his by *shoots of glory,* even before he has broken away from Herbert's rhythmic pattern. He turns, characteristically, from the Book to the Book of Nature. A passage in short lines follows, which is supplied with notions from Vaughan's main reservoir of philosophical imagery, a hermeticism modified to the point where it is scarcely distinguishable from a less doctrinaire microcosmism. But this passage is a bridge to the second idea borrowed from Herbert, which is the main support of the poem. 'O how it *Blouds* And *Spirits* all my Earth!' is a transmutation, in the curiously abnormal language of a poet striving for individuality, of the close of Herbert's poem 'Prayer': 'Church-bels beyond the starres heard, *the souls blood . . .*'. Vaughan then takes up another line from the same poem: 'A kinde of tune, which all things heare and fear.' The musical idea expressed in both these lines gives rise to the central passage in Vaughan's poem:

> all is hurl'd
> In sacred *hymnes,* and *Order,* The great *Chime*
> And *Symphony* of nature.

The sequel indicates that this idea must come home to the second of Herbert's lines: 'Prayer is The world in tune.' Vaughan has here developed a favourite idea, that of the *Musica Mundana;* in **'Affliction'** he again employs it and again, as Professor Martin has pointed out, the immediate source of the idea is in Herbert. It is not difficult to see that the vast lore of the universal musical correspondences would particularly appeal to Vaughan, committed as he was to a belief in the validity of the specialized microcosmism of hermeticism. In much the same way he saw the potential value of magnetism for poetic imagery. Nevertheless, in both these poems he depends on Herbert for the initial impulse to use the musical metaphor, although he develops it in his own way.

The peculiarity of this mode of imitation indicates, in a somewhat negative way, the authenticity of Vaughan's genius; he owes nothing to Herbert for doctrine or for prose meaning. An original poem has grown out of the sympathetic rhythm of a line from 'The Holy Scriptures' and the artificially disject analogues of 'Prayer'. Having made these his own, Vaughan, persisting in the brusquely opposed long and short lines forced upon him by the nature of the poem's origin, develops the poetic image in his own way, proceeding not from prayer to the universal harmony, but from that harmony to Herbert's 'Prayer', with a verbal reminiscence; thenceforward the poem concerns itself with prayer in language which is once more drawn from other sources than Herbert. It would be difficult to find an example more certain than this of a poem which begins as a rhythm only, and reaches verbal actuality with the aid of ideas of identifiable and bookish origin; yet its dignity and autonomy may be tried upon the pulses.

There is nothing in Vaughan which differentiates him more clearly from Herbert than this curious faculty of adapting words and rhythms to a new and remote idea. It does not, of course, operate constantly; in **'The World',** for instance, he develops a given idea much in the manner of his predecessors. But whereas the general misreading of that poem proceeds from the critical error of refusing to treat Vaughan's poetry as poetry so long as it may be treated as prayer, the common complaint that Vaughan is only too often a matter of brilliant moments, 'gleams and fractions'—that he is often disorderly and frequently for long passages unmemorable—has some substance. Only occasionally does the necessary fusion of the alien matter and the personal meditative continuum occur. When it does not, there is left only the shabbiness of plagiarism, the doubtful fascination of ideas unassimilated to poetry expressed in loose and uninteresting verse. Of Vaughan's debt to Herbert, Canon Hutchinson rightly said that 'There is no example in English literature of one poet borrowing so extensively from another'. The imitation of Herbert is sometimes mechanical, as one would expect in these circumstances; but when, as in **'The Morning-Watch'**, it provides the poet with a characteristic theme, tenuous, independent of metaphysical ratiocination, in a word assimilable to the quietly bizarre qualities of his personality, the result is unique. Wanting such a catalyst, his talent is frequently unpurged and discursive. His poems are systems developed from some central literary point. This is true of his use of occult writings, as well as of his debt to English writers.

Vaughan uses the language of the Hermetica, and of the pseudo-Dionysius, not only in **Silex Scintillans** but also in little-read poems written before his supposed conversion, and the use of such language does not, of course, guarantee the value of the poem, though the 'mystical' element in the poet depends upon it. W. O. Clough, indeed, has argued that 'Vaughan uses the Hermetic language . . . when he is less a poet, not more'. But his use of the terminology is so extensive that this is a very arbitrary determinant. The truth is that he is a poet when he uses the language in a poet's way, which is not the way of the philosopher or the mystic. But this question is evidently involved with his status as a mystical author. I believe there is much that might usefully be said on this point, but I must defer it to some other occasion. For the present it is enough to say that perfection of the life and perfection of the work are often, as by Yeats and the Japanese dramatists, and also by Brémond, held to be antinomies; though this is not to say that literature may not conduce to prayer and the contemplative life.

The distinction is relevant to the study of Vaughan, who must have occupied a place in the devotions of many. Very often he uses language which has previously been used by mystical writers, who are always dependent upon symbol and allegory in their attempts to describe the incommunicable; obviously there is nothing to prevent any non-mystic from adopting their terminology. Vaughan, for example, employs the Dionysian concept of the Divine Dark.

> The Divine Dark is naught else but that inaccessible light wherein the Lord is said to dwell. Although it is invisible because of its dazzling splendour and unsearchable because of the abundance of its supernatural brightness, nevertheless, whosoever deserves to see and know

God rests therein; and by the very fact that he neither sees nor knows, is truly *in* that which surpasses all truth and all knowledge.

This idea, much developed by the mystics, was in Vaughan's mind when he wrote:

> There is in God (some say)
> A deep but dazzling darkness, as men here
> Say it is late and dusky because they
>   See not all clear;
>   O for that night! where I in him
>   Might live invisible and dim.

Vaughan is at least not attempting to claim the authority of such a vision. He is working out a conceit which involves the glorification of night—I shall say more of this later—and he is using the theme of the Divine Dark for this purpose, much as another poet might use ideas from scholastic philosophy or Galenist medicine, though in Vaughan the concept acquires a special value from the pattern of ideas, discernible in his poetry, in which it is located. At the moment it is with this purely poetic phenomenon that we are concerned, and it is important not to be misled by the significances of certain of Vaughan's words when used in the context of mystical writing.

Miss Helen White, in her excellent study *The Metaphysical Poets* (1936), is careful to draw a distinction between poet and mystic, but is wrong, I think, in her view that there are poems which are both poetry and mysticism. It is very doubtful that Vaughan's poetry is any more closely related to his religious experience than Sidney's *Astrophel and Stella* is to his amorous experience. Like Sidney, Vaughan uses a specialized language which is neither original nor to be taken at its face-value; it is, as it were, a cheque drawn on the bank of Hermes Trismegistus. Vaughan's poem **'The World'** has been much admired for what seem to be quite the wrong reasons. It has sometimes been printed as if it were only seven lines long; those lines are taken to be a genuine description of what, without irreverence, may be described as a mystical peep. Vaughan certainly employs imagery which is used by the mystics. The *circle* is a frequently recurring image of this sort, and so is the Dionysian 'ray of darkness'. The circle, or ring, may, as W. O. Clough suggests, combine the function of Hermetic symbol and of the Milky Way and a number of other things. (It will be remembered that Herbert uses the galaxy as a type of prayer.) Vaughan may have borrowed the idea from Felltham, or from Hermes himself. What is certain is that he uses the idea in several other poems, including **'Vanity of Spirit'**, **'Ascension-Hymn'**, and **'The Queer'**. What is more, he uses it in one of the poems which certainly antedate any conversion, **'To Amoret Walking in a Starry Evening'**. In *The Mount of Olives* Vaughan gives a prose equivalent for his poem in **'A Meditation at the setting of the Sun, or the Souls Elevation to the true light'**.

> The path of the Just (O my God) is as the shining light, that shineth more and more unto a perfect day of eternity, *Prov. 4*. But the wicked neither know, nor understand, they walk in darkness, and from the inward darknesse of their minds passe at last into the outward, eternal darknesse.

The matter of the poem is devotional; the imagery constantly in use, and derivative. The famous opening lines establish the terms of the rhetorical formula in which the extended conceit is to be worked out. No one is inclined to take literally Vaughan's statement that

> I (Alas!)
> Was shown one day in a strange glass
> That busie commerce kept between
> God and his Creatures, though unseen.

Yet this is a very similar observation. Vaughan simply does not supply the form of words proper to the announcement of such a theme. If he had been as straightforward in this matter as Donne, there would be no difficulty.

> Let mans Soule be a Spheare, and then, in this,
> The intelligence that moves, devotion is.

This is a statement of the same order as Vaughan's at the opening of **'The World'**; so, for that matter, is 'If all the sky were paper'.

Eternity as a ring is an old notion; Vaughan equates it with the region of the fixed stars, where the blessed dwell—a world out of time, beneath which the corrupt world of nature spins. He ends the poem by expressing the relationship between this ring and God in language which can be paralleled in Suso and Ruysbroeck. The inhabitants of the shadow world, some of whom may soar into the bright ring, are described with a pleasant conventionality; the Lover, doting on the wrong Treasure, the Politician, the Miser, the Epicure who 'plac'd heav'n in sense', all those who flout the truth by prizing the ungodly above the godly; and the few who, by contemplation of the superior orders of existence, transport their souls to a knowledge of the true God, as by

> . . . the scale of nature set
> From center to circumference, whereon
> In contemplation of created things
> By steps we may ascend to God.

This poem is, indeed, an admirable example of that species of poetic architecture which is notoriously more common in Herbert than in Vaughan. Vaughan is here imitating Herbert, though less obviously than in the poem analysed above. The rapid ballad-like setting of the scene is an old trick of Herbert's which Vaughan imitates in many poems—'And do they so?', 'Peace, peace, it is not so', and many others. Characteristically he establishes his pattern with imagery drawn from the mystics. Miss White is the only critic I know who has pointed out that the poem is a planned whole, and not a simple case of inspiration and collapse; but even she appears to miss the point, implying that in spite of all, the opening lines have a truly mystic splendour, while the rest is no more than pleasant.

Vaughan attempted in his verse to emulate Boehme and his own brother, who used the same vocabulary for certain purposes which may safely be described as non-poetic. This is not to say that Vaughan had not a professional interest in the subject; he adds to his translation of Nollius a justification of Hermeticism as scientific, and would have shared his brother's attitude to More's sneer that the Doctrine of Signatures was 'fansifull' and 'Poeticall'. 'True Philosophy', he wrote in an interpolated comment, 'is nothing else but a Physicall practise or triall, communicat-

ing daily to industrious and learned operators, most usefull and various conclusions and medicines.' It would appear that Vaughan was somewhat concerned to justify studies in the hermetic tradition in a manner which was, for good or ill, becoming fashionable; the philosophy had to be shown to be capable of dealing with what were regarded as facts, and with the realities of matter and human experience. But as a poet he was nearly always too wise to allow himself expressions whose force depended upon a technical signification outside the poem.

Miss Holmes discusses the manner in which the vocabulary of Hermeticism is converted for the purposes of Christian allegory, and Canon Hutchinson suggests that Vaughan 'passed the Hermetic ideas and terms so integrally into the common language of Christian tradition that they do not disconcert the reader. . . . The poet has assimilated the Hermetic ideas until they harmonise with general Christian thought'. I think these views are substantially correct.

I have already pointed out that the use of Hermetic language is not confined to the religious verse. In the early poem **'To Amoret, Walking in a Starry Evening'**, he uses the familiar idea of sympathetic relationships existing between stars and sublunary organisms. In **'To Amoret gone from him,'** he writes of 'the loose tye of influence' binding 'Creatures . . . that have no sence'. Similarly, in poems belonging to the pre-devotional period, but published in ***Thalia Rediviva*** (1678), there is fairly elaborate use of the Hermetic vocabulary pressed into amorous service. The translations of Boethius, printed early and late, also bear the marks of the special terminology. It affects the prose collection of devotions, ***The Mount of Olives;*** without previous knowledge of Vaughan, such a phrase as 'Ray thy selfe into my soule . . .' would pass unnoticed. The Night of Dionysius, and the synteresis of the mystics are similarly used in contexts which carry no suggestion of mystical theology. There is no lack of evidence that Vaughan had, early and late, the knack of using the hermetic terminology in this denatured manner. It is scarcely necessary to say that Suso and Boehme used it very differently, as did Vaughan himself in more technical contexts, for example in the ***Hermetical Physick.*** He believed the tradition had a contribution to make to truth, and this belief no doubt gives his poetic use of it a force which helps to differentiate it from the merely conceited; so does the extraordinarily high incidence of this special imagery in his poetry, which gives it as a whole an unmetaphysical tone by comparison with the drag-net fancies of some contemporaries. But it is nevertheless very far from mysticism.

In an age when it was becoming increasingly difficult to write in the manner of Donne, for the reason (among others) that the same wide fields of reference were no longer valid for imagery, Vaughan found and extensively worked this new territory. One of the habits which make him recognizably of his time is this way of converting to the purposes of his poetic argument material which is not germane to it. The *cause* of his poem may be devotional or amorous; the language of hermeticism, which, with constant use, acquires a range of tone personal to the poet, is indiscriminately employed. The object of the poet is hardly ever to make the hermetic or Dionysian idea the central one; it is always illustrative, lighting and enriching the tenuous, often Herbert-inspired, argument of the poem. Sometimes this is obvious enough from the mélange of imagery and faintly specialized language from hermetic and other sources which are found together in the same poem; a good example of this is **'The Lampe'**, which is an emblematic poem of the Herbert type, with just this personal colouring from the vocabulary which Vaughan in this curious and very literary fashion made his own.

There are occasions when, by its prevalence, this special vocabulary causes obscurity. **'Cockcrowing'** is an example of this, though its lyric argument is simple enough. The cock, by virtue of its eager annunciation of daylight, becomes an emblem of that spark in the soul which has an affinity with the light of the deity. The moralization is conventional. If the cock can watch for the light, how should not man, made in God's image, and bearing within him the remnant at least of natural law and goodness—synteresis, or as applied to particular cases, conscience—pray in the dark? The formerly easy commerce between the soul, with its 'seed' of light, and the source of light—easy in the absence of sin—has been forfeited; but grace can tear the veil which obscures the light. This is a crude paraphrase, but it reveals the logic of the poem. The hermetic element which obscures it is at times very close to traditional theology, and at times to the interests of more orthodox science. The reference to magnetism, for example, which is repeated in the following poem, **'The Starre'**, proceeds naturally enough from the hermetic interest in 'tyes' and 'influences'. The idea of an unbroken mystical communion existing, according to the Hermetics, between nature—an *unfallen* nature, presumably, such as M. Saurat argues to have passed from Cabbalistic sources into Renaissance currency—gives rise to a 'mystical' (in the sense of sacramental) significance in the relationship of star to herb, star to stone, and 'the tye of bodies' generally. Magnetism is, then, simply a physical index of these sympathies, which are constantly mentioned by Vaughan, e. g. in **'Rules and Lessons'**, **'The Constellation'**, **'Christs Nativity'**, and in the untitled poems **'And do they so?'** and **'I walked the other day. . . .'** A similar use is made of the idea in the early poem **'In Amicum Faeneratorem'**. But it could have been made by a poet with no special interest in hermetic literature, as a useful devotional image; indeed Quarles twice uses magnetic imagery in his *Emblemes*, where many of Vaughan's most characteristic ideas are foreshadowed. Nor would the invocations 'Father of lights!' and 'O thou immortal light and heat!' seem far out of the way if found in isolation in some other poet, though it might be remarked that this is language borrowed from mystical writing; there are parallels, for example, in Richard Rolle. But it is known that there are also parallels in Thomas Vaughan, who can justly be described as an exponent not of *mystik* so much as of *mystizismus*.

The concept of synteresis is common in Vaughan. It occurs in **'The Check'**, **'The Favour'**, **'Resurrection and Immortality'** (a poem which may have its roots in the Hermetica) in **'The World Contemned'**, **'The Mount of Olives'**, **Mans Fall and Recovery'**, where it is clearly an aspect of natural and not mystical theology, as it is here also, in

spite of the misleading context, and in **'The Sap'**, where, in a Herbertian cryptoemblematic setting, it is related to the Redemption. It provides a good example of the difficulty in Vaughan of drawing the line between specialized language used in a manner akin to that for which it was evolved and the same language, with the personal colouring it acquires from constant use in varying contexts by the same poet, or with the generally acceptable non-mystical meanings the vocabulary has acquired in *general* use. How imperceptibly the characteristic language sometimes merges into the general devotional theme may be seen in **'The Incarnation and Passion'**.

> To put on Clouds instead of light,
> And cloath the morning-starre with dust,
> Was a translation of such height
> As, but in thee, was ne'r exprest. . . .

The first line here could be taken as an alternative mode of expressing the idea of the second, the perennial conceit of the

> maker pent up in a grave,
> Life lockt in death, heav'n in a shell;

but we know that there is in that line, since Vaughan wrote it, a second significance; an implication that the Incarnation meant that God forfeited his own light and assumed the human veil, which is pierced only by 'gleams and fractions'. There is a slight, but substantial, ambiguity. That Vaughan was conscious of it is suggested by his ability, in what are perhaps very early poems, but nevertheless the product of a normal maturity, to exercise his image-making talent in a perfectly conventional way. **'The Eagle'**, for example, uses much Donne-like imagery in a rather impersonal way:

> Sometimes he frights the starrie *Swan,* and now
> *Orion's* fearful *Hare* and then the Crow.
> Then with the *Orbe* it self he moves, to see
> Which is more swift, th' *Intelligence* or *He.*

Yet even here, it is fair to add, the celestial heaven has, unobtrusively, 'pure and peaceful air'—a foretaste of **'The World'**. Another example of this kind of poetry is **'In Zodiacum Marcelli Palingenii'**, and **'The Importunate Fortune'**, in spite of its almost certain connexion with the Hermetica, has a quite conventional empyrean-flight and plays with the idea of the *fortunatus*, which really belongs to earlier poetry. Vaughan is from the beginning a poet with his roots in poetry rather than in religious experience; his interest in theological and philosophical thought is governed by the limitations imposed upon such thought by its poetic conventionalization, and it follows both that the germs of his poems are to be found within that pale, and that his own use of what we may call extra-poetic speculation will generally be to conventionalize it in the same way before he employs it.

'Cockcrowing' and certain other poems do seem to contain elements of speculative thought which have not undergone this process. Some of them become less obtrusive with the realization that the cock is after all emblematic, and that his divine powers are not, in terms of the poem, ends in themselves. But there remains in suspension an unresolved extra-poetic element. (I believe that this no longer exists if the work of the poet is studied as a whole; an unresolved idea may acquire a positive poetic value on repetition in intelligibly related contexts, as Mr. T. S. Eliot's poetry shows.) Vaughan has been careful in some ways; he rarely, for example, allows the hermetic language to carry any alchemical overtone; but in this poem his *seed* is something the reader might strain at if he has not already swallowed the hermetical camel of related poems, or seen the private value accorded the expression by its use in **'Disorder and Frailty'**—a poem which is in many respects a useful 'key' to what I have called the private continuum of Vaughan's mind.

> Let not perverse
> And foolish thoughts adde to my Bil
> Of forward sins, and Kil
> That seed, which thou
> In me didst sow,
> But dress, and water with thy grace
> Together with the seed, the place;
> And for his sake
> Who died to stake
> His life for mine, tune to thy will
> My heart, my verse.

Here, once more under the aegis of Herbert, the expression reveals its exact relationship to the rest of Vaughan's devotional material. Whatever its significance in alchemy or hermetics, it is here a conceited summary of the residual light-veil-cloud constellation which we have seen expressed so many times before. It is equally clear in **'Repentance'**:

> Lord, since thou didst in this vile Clay
> That sacred Ray
> Thy spirit *plant,* quickning the whole
> With that one grains Infused wealth,
> My forward flesh creept on, and subtly stole
> Both growth and power; checking the health
> And heat of thine. . . .

But the constellation has more stars than this. In examining this single expression we stumble upon one of the most unusual and least understood features of Vaughan's poetry, the particular values he gives to the concept of sin by the idiosyncrasy of his literary habit. In his treatment of the Fall Vaughan is very close to his brother. 'I look on this life as the Progress of an Essence Royall: The Soul but quits her *court* to see the *countrey*', writes Thomas. Release from the veil-body meant the restoration of life and light. 'Ignorance gave this *release* the name of Death, but properly it is the *Soules Birth.*' In Henry Vaughan these ideas certainly have an unorthodox tone, though they have implications which will not be quite unfamiliar to the student of Spenser; whatever their origin (Mr. Wardle and Professor Martin have suggested that it may be hermetic) they strongly colour his poetry whenever childhood, sin, prayer, and death are its theme. Miss Holmes writes very interestingly on various occult interpretations of the Fall which were current in Vaughan's time, and with which he is likely to have been familiar. But at best he took only a hint from somewhere; the idea becomes precisely his own, and it is used to give a new and personal force to meditations which have their origin in much more commonplace reflections.

The poetry of the period contains a curious genre of which the distinctive characteristic is the exploitation in garden-poetry of a pastoral-allegorical vein. Marvell offers the most conspicuous examples of the genre in his Mower poems, 'To Little T. C.', 'The Nymph Complaining', and in 'The Garden' itself. The lesser poets with whom Marvell is associated also dabble in the convention, and the allegorical node is clearly exposed in Beaumont's 'The Garden', and in Shirley's poem of the same title. A second biblical garden is associated with the theme—the garden of the *Song of Solomon,* the relevant lines of which are quoted by Vaughan at the end of 'Regeneration', in which poem he employs the imagery of the *Canticles* in a manner resembling that of St. John of the Cross. The garden was, therefore, a poetic symbol of a more or less general significance, which was a good deal more complicated in its suggestiveness than might be supposed. It stands for unfallen and asexual life (this may have added to Milton's difficulties in his treatment of prelapsarian sexuality) and it is also associated with the idea of a blessed locality in which the breath of inspiration may be felt; an idea derived from a love-poem which was constantly interpreted as relating allegorically to the mystical life. It is from an Eden conceived as a garden in which man, like the rest of the creation, is in constant mystical intercourse with God, that Vaughan's simple soul sets out. Eden is used in this sense in the poem **'Corruption'**. In that poem the unfallen and fallen states are contrasted. In his early days, like Adam, man

> saw Heaven o'r his head, and knew from whence
> He came (condemned) hither.

As he moved away from Paradise, he retained, for a time, his pristine powers. But he quarrelled with nature (compare Marvell, 'The Mower on Gardens') which he had ruined by his fall. Nevertheless, there were still occasions when his surroundings could seem paradisal. Now, it appears, even his sighs for the lost Eden are a thing of the past; the soul (says Vaughan with a return to this dominant image) is veiled in a thick cloud, to be pierced only by the grace of God.

'The Retreat' is a poem on almost the same subject. Its connexion with the earlier translation from Boethius, *Felix prior aetas qua paucis homines contenti,* indicates, in a manner reinforced by its similarities with 'Corruption', that the 'I' represents the speaker as the type of Man, and one infers that in his personal fall from grace he is merely repeating in little the general history of mankind. There was, historically speaking, a 'white age' in which mankind was in the position of the child who has not yet begun to obscure the element of natural law implanted in him at birth by God—the seed. (It was not necessarily Pelagian to hold such a doctrine.) At a short distance from this personal Eden, man can still 'spy some shadows of eternity' in a flower, because he has not begun the process of attempting, through sin, entirely to ruin this original gift of God, and to obscure the natural light. Before the veil is drawn by sin he continues to feel

> Through all this fleshly dress
> Bright *shootes* of everlastingnesse.

The desire of the penitent soul is to return to this Eden of perfect luxuriance—the fantastic gardens of Marvell and Milton become, in Vaughan's poem, 'That shady City of Palme trees'. But this is impossible; all that the poet can wish for is to achieve at death a condition of primitive simplicity, unveiled and paradisal. The parallel to '**Corruption**' which Professor Martin quotes from Thomas Vaughan in the note in his edition is a parallel also to '**The Retreat**'. 'He was excluded from a *glorious Paradyse,* and confin'd to a *base world,* whose *sickly infected Elements* conspiring with his *own* Nature, did assist and hasten that *Death,* which already began to reign in his *Body. . . .*' All poetry conventionalizes the philosophic material; there may be occult elements in these poems, but they are all reduced to poetry.

In '**Mans Fall and Recovery**' there is ample confirmation of the use of 'I' to signify 'Man' in general. Here the theme is much the same as that of the other two poems; the 'Everlasting hills' are Eden, which Man has left to live under Clouds, where his divine element (here represented by a flower) droops and sleeps. He is now a slave to passion, and has lost the true light (with a suggestion that the fixed stars are its symbol) retaining only the ineradicable conscience. After two thousand years came the old Law, which by its dominantly prohibitive nature exacerbated rather than controlled his state of sin; until the Incarnation gave him in its place a law of love by faith in which he can be justified. The poem ends with an elaborate and somewhat frigid conceit of a kind not often found in Vaughan but it is nevertheless a good example of the nature of the convention I am seeking to illustrate.

With the untitled poem which begins '**They are all gone into the world of light!**' it is possible to see what happens to this poetic habit of mind when it is applied to the idea of death. The illuminating memory of the dead suggests starlight in darkness; since these memories are within the poet's breast, they seem to be a substitute for the light which once inhabited it, but which has been clouded; the effect again relates them to stars, which are elsewhere used as symbols of the divine light. The dead are then spoken of as if they were stars; the luminaries of the incorruptible heaven which 'trample on' the corrupted world in which he lives under his veil. He expresses gratitude for this indication of the issue of death, suggesting that this indication of the destiny of the dead is equivalent to an angelic visitation in a dream, giving unnatural signs of a glorious hereafter. The element of divinity in man has been confined to a tomb; when God himself releases that element it will once more be seen for what it is. With this idea, Vaughan resumes the star image.

> If a star were confin'd into a Tomb
> Her captive flames must need burn there;
> But when the hand that lockt her up, gives
>   room,
> She'l shine through all the sphaere.

This enables him not only to make his usual equivalence between the synteresis and light, but also to continue the idea of the dead as stars. He ends the poem with a stanza which lapses into more commonplace language, asking God to take up his spirit from a 'world of thrall' into the heavenly world of liberty; followed by a stanza which

characteristically reverts to his favourite cloud-complex, asking that the mists which obscure his 'perspective' should be dispelled, or that he should be removed to the paradisal hill where these mists do not exist. The final version in this poem of the star image is closely paralleled in the '**Ascension-Hymn**', a poem which reiterates the theme of '**Corruption**'. The soul must put off corruptibility; it is, however—to paraphrase 'Regeneration'—possible, by grace and merit, to 'die' in this way before one's death.

> And yet some
> That know to die
> Before death come,
> Walk to the skie
> Even in this life; but all such can
> Leave behinde them the old Man.

This suggests the whole complex of ideas concerning the union of the veiled and the true light which is represented by the stars; and introduces the idea of the soul as a star clad in mortality.

> If a star
> Should leave the Sphaere,
> She must first mar
> Her flaming wear,
> And after fall, for in her dress
> Of glory, she cannot transgress.

From this point there is a natural progression to the Eden-idea; in his *prior aetas* man could shine 'naked, innocent and bright'; he soiled this brightness, and so remained until the Redemption, which gave him the power to 'ascend', presumably to the stars. The whole Eden-corruption-death-star idea is very complex but essentially poetic; it is never worked out like a theorem, but is constantly insinuating itself into, and taking control of, commonplace devotional themes. It is almost certainly affected by advanced contemporary interpretations of the Fall as a psychological as well as an historical phenomenon; it may have pure hermetic elements; it may owe something to Cornelius Agrippa or to Nieremberg and the others discussed by Miss Holmes; but it has become Vaughan's own, and it would be less confusing to call it an image than to call it an idea.

Once the *poetic* nature of this idea-cluster has been grasped, it will be seen RV'S that it is the very basis of Vaughan's best work, the force which gives relevance to the mass of unassimilated thought which I have called the personal continuum—that which takes on new and suggestive configurations whenever the need to write is sharpened by some irritant, a phrase from Herbert, an aspect of devotion, whether liturgical or meditative. 'The Night' shows how darkness is associated with this leading idea. It has its origin in the story of Nicodemus, who went to Jesus by night. In doing so he came to resemble a plant (the continuity of the plant's intercourse with the light being unbroken). This resemblance is somewhat obscurely stated in the third stanza, but clearly in the fourth. The poem then becomes: eulogy of night, wherein the willing soul can, like the plants and unlike the Jews, commune with the symbolic starlight; it is 'the day of Spirits'. This theme is developed with a number of Herbertian analogues.

Gods silent, searching flight:
When my Lords head is fill'd with dew, and all
His locks are wet with the clear drops of night;
His still, soft call;
His knocking time; The souls dumb watch,
When Spirits their fair kinred catch.

The second and third lines here provide an extraordinary example of the way in which Vaughan could fuse into his dominant image material from another source. This quotation from the *Canticles,* which superficially aligns him with certain mystical writers, is assimilated to the characteristic starlight symbol; 'the clear drops of night' are stars. The significance of the lines depends primarily upon Vaughan's own idea-cluster, though they are enriched by the mystical connotations of the passage in its original context. The conceit is very daring; the sky is God's hair, and the stars are the drops of night dew sprinkled upon it.

Vaughan continues with a lament that his life cannot resemble this peaceful beauty, for the light of the sun returns, by which contemplation is impossible. He ends with an explicit reference to the Dionysian darkness, carefully establishing the distance between this quasi-technical notion and his own image by the qualifying clause, '(some say)'. **'The Night'** is not a poem about the Dionysian darkness, but a meditation or night-thought of which the logical prose content is to be found in ***The Mount of Olives,*** where Vaughan cites an Italian proverb which says that night is the mother of thoughts, continuing:

> And I shall add, that those thoughts are *Stars,* the *Scintillations* and *lightnings* of the soul struggling with darknesse. This *Antipathy* in her is *radical,* for being descended from the *house of light,* she hates a contrary *principle,* and being at that time a prisoner in some measure to an enemy, she becomes pensive, and full of thoughts. Two great extremes there are, which she equally abhors, *Darkness* and *Death.* . . . The Contemplation of *death* is an obscure, melancholy *walk* an *Expiation* in *shadows & solitude,* but it leads unto *life,* & he that sets out at *midnight,* will sooner meet the *Sunne,* than he that sleeps it out betwixt his curtains. . . .

But the full meaning of the poem does not yield itself to the reader who is unable to supply the context of this night-idea; a context in which it is associated with the theme of paradisal origins, corruption, and the interrupted communion, and the symbolic starlight. Like **'The Lampe'** and **'Regeneration'**, this poem could be described as a blend of Herbertian, Biblical, and hermetic ideas; but it is far truer to say that although the original impulse may have been Biblical, the imagery of the poem belongs to a highly personal synthesis of Vaughan's own making.

Vaughan's use of the night as a devotional symbol is therefore by no means commonplace. Without doubt it is affected by these words of Dionysius:

> . . . by . . . unceasing and absolute renunciation of thyself and all things, thou shalt in pureness cast all things aside, and be released from all, and so shalt be led upwards to the Ray of that Divine Darkness which exceedeth all existence.

But, as the idea occurs in Vaughan it simply cannot be equated with any extra-poetic statement; it exists in terms of the image-convention which he himself has devised, and grows naturally out of its *données.* The same may be said for his use of the idea of the dead as stars. This is very explicit in the untitled poem beginning **'Joy of my Life!'**, where he addresses some dead friend and exclaims upon the way in which the friend's influence continues to guide him.

Stars are of mighty use: The night
Is dark, and long;
The Rode foul, and where one goes right,
Six may go wrong.
One twinkling ray
Shot o'r some cloud,
May clear much way
And guide a croud.

. . . .

They are (indeed,) our Pillar-fires
Seen as we go,
They are that Cities shining spires
We travel too;
A swordlike gleame
Kept man for sin
First *Out;* This beame
Will guide him *In.*

Even in this comparatively simple example Vaughan suggests the whole private context with the conceit of a sword-guarded Eden in this last stanza. The logic is superficially obvious; the star-ray, which is guiding man towards salvation, suggests the flash of the archangelic swords at the gates of Eden. But in the alogical context of the poetic image, the interest resides in the fact that the end-product of the process I have been describing inevitably suggests its origins; the idea of the dead as stars, in the course of its expounding, draws into its context the idea of the lost psychological paradise. Although Vaughan was probably familiar with the Greek star-heroes it is unnecessary to pursue the question of his indebtedness to such classical notions. The whole poetic organism has acquired autonomy, and is to be understood in its own terms.

It may be too much to suggest that only when Vaughan is in some way (almost always by a literary stimulus) induced to allow this poetic organism to be modified by some external force which alters its environment does he produce a poem wholly characteristic and convincing, though sometimes tenuous in argument—a consequence of the material and method. There are times when the notion of the sympathetic communion of nature with heaven becomes indistinguishable from a simpler microcosmism, or from more commonplace exercises on the theme of 'the book of nature' such as may be found in many contemporary poets, including Donne, Beaumont, and Habington. There are poems like **'Religion',** which, though it looks back along the road from Paradise, treats its subject in terms of a metaphor drawn from the popular cosmology of the time, enriched with a reference to the miracle at Cana, and based on a line from the *Canticles.* This complexity is characteristic enough, but it has no evident relationship to the process I am postulating. Vaughan, as we have seen, also makes effective use of the concept of world-harmony, though this is only distantly related to his dominant images. To claim that this pattern can be discerned in all his poetry which is worth reading would be to force the issue; it is enough to say that it is dominant, and that a recognition of this fact is essential to a true understanding of the poet.

Part of the intention of this paper was to vindicate Vaughan as a poet pure and simple. He is in no sense at all a mystic; he makes a poet's use of the mystic's language. He has almost entirely converted it to his own purposes, and he has profoundly altered the value of its various terms by organizing them into a pattern which has its effect upon their individual significations.

There is, among students of Vaughan, some doubt as to the nature and date of Vaughan's conversion. The evidence for it is indeed very slight, and there is, on the evidence of his poetry, no case for it sufficiently substantial to warrant further search. What cannot be too strongly stated is the absolute uselessness of attempts to discuss the poetry as if its value were determined by his religious life, and of seeking in the poetry evidence, to be interpreted in philosophical or theological terms, of a religious experience or a series of such experiences. Vaughan was a poet of predominantly literary inspiration, who, for a few years, achieved a remarkable mental condition in which much thought, reading, and conversation coalesced to form a unique corpus of homogeneous poetic material, available whenever some external stimulus called it into creative action for the development of any suitable theme in poetry. Therein lies the singularity of *Silex Scintillans;* the elements of the great image-pattern were already present in earlier years, but they were disjunct and powerless. Something happened, something to do with poetry, and not with prayer; a trumpet sounded and the bones lived. The return to disjection, the moment that ended this imaginative cohesion, was, more directly than any event in the external world, the signal for Vaughan's poetic death; and it can no more be explained than the force which brought him to birth as a poet, or the grim truth that many other creative artists have, like Vaughan, survived by a generation their potent, delicate gift.

Joan Bennett (essay date 1953)

SOURCE: "Henry Vaughan, 1622-1695," in *Four Metaphysical Poets: Donne, Herbert, Vaughan, Crashaw,* second edition, Cambridge at the University Press, 1957, pp. 71-89.

[*Bennett was an English educator who wrote studies on the works of Virginia Woolf (1945) and George Eliot (1948). She is also the author of* Four Metaphysical Poets: Donne, Herbert, Vaughan, Crashaw *(1934; revised 1953). In the following excerpt from that work, she offers a thematic overview of Vaughan's poetry, comparing it with that of Herbert.*]

Vaughan was fascinated by the phrases of other poets. This is not unusual in a young poet; but the habit of bor-

rowing continued with Vaughan to the end. At first his borrowings strike no roots, they are picked blossoms that have caught his fancy, later they are young shoots that bloom anew in his poems. In his two collections of secular poems, *Poems, with the Tenth Satire of Juvenal Englished* (1646) and *Olor Iscanus* (1651), the most obvious debts are to Donne and Habington, though he is attracted also by the Elizabethan use of mythological names and their Petrarchan attitude to the mistress. He seldom strikes a personal note; one suspects he is not sure of what he wants to say. His poems seem to fall apart, an elaborate image is followed by a lame conclusion. He is more interested in poetry than in his poem. In *Silex Scintillans* (1650), Herbert's influence is predominant. He rehandles Herbert's themes, borrows his phrases, copies his metrical effects, repeats his titles and yet now the poem is his own. Whatever he takes from Herbert he transmutes because his way of apprehending is different. The influence of Herbert's teaching, and probably other influences as well, operated a 'conversion' in Vaughan and he became a religious poet; but his religious experience was unlike Donne's or Herbert's and required for its expression different imagery and different rhythms.

Vaughan's indebtedness in his early volumes needs no elaborating. Mr L. C. Martin, in his excellent edition (Clarendon Press, 1914), notes the various parallels. The fact that Vaughan borrows phrases, images or whole lines from his contemporaries is unimportant; it was the custom of the time. Donne's phrases are remodelled or even merely repeated in the poems of Carew, of Habington, of Suckling, of Godolphin and it is not surprising that Vaughan too made use of them, sometimes taking them direct from Donne himself, sometimes preferring the version of an imitator. But there are two peculiarities in these early poems. The first is that Vaughan never appears to be interested in his subject. He plays lovingly with an image and delays its application which is finally huddled into a last stanza. The other is that he prefers to draw his images from the countryside even when his model was Donne, who seldom looked in that direction. The result is often that his own experience, which finds an outlet in the image, has no inevitable connection with the situation to which he applies it with a logic more painstaking than convincing.

> **'To *Amoret*, of the difference 'twixt him, and other Lovers, and what true Love is'.**
>
> Marke, when the Evenings cooler wings
>   Fanne the afflicted ayre, how the faint Sunne,
>   Leaving undone,
>   What he begunne,
> Those spurious flames suckt up from slime, and earth
>   To their first, low birth,
>   Resignes, and brings.
>
> They shoot their tinsill beams, and vanities,
>   Thredding with those false fires their way;
>   But as you stay
>   And see them stray,
> You loose the flaming track, and subt'ly they
>   Languish away,
>   And cheate your Eyes.
> Just so base, Sublunarie Lovers hearts

> Fed on loose prophane desires,
> May for an Eye,
> Or face comply:
> But those removed, they will as soone depart,
> And shew their Art
> And painted fires.
>
> Whilst I by pow'rfull Love, so much refin'd
> That my absent soule the same is
> Carelesse to misse,
> A glaunce, or kisse,
> Can with those Elements of lust and sence,
> Freely dispence,
> And court the mind.
>
> Thus to the North the Loadstones move,
> And thus to them th'enamour'd steel aspires:
> Thus, *Amoret,*
> I doe affect;
> And thus by winged beames, and mutuall fire,
> Spirits and Stars conspire,
> And this is LOVE.

In the first two stanzas he is describing an effect of the evening light which he himself has noted: he has no literary model, he is interested, and he dwells on more detail than he can make use of for his parallel. There is no convincing relation between the behaviour of light at sunset and of 'base, Sublunarie Lovers hearts'; they remain two separate observations arbitrarily linked together. He fares no better in the last stanza, into which he crowds two more images, the already hackneyed loadstone, and the image beloved by Donne of the stars in their spheres governed by an 'intelligence' or spirit. The total impression left by Vaughan's poem is that the metaphysical conceit was, at this time, a fashion he accepted rather than the outcome of his own habit of mind. He had not, like Donne, the kind of mind that is immediately aware of logical situations recurring in diverse kinds of experience; nor had he as yet, what he was to discover later, a conception of the universe as a whole, which would lead him to perceive a relation between its various parts. There are signs in these early poems of the direction in which Vaughan would look for such a conception. His poetry becomes sensitive and individual when it describes nature, as it does nowhere else. He dwells with loving particularity on scenes he has noted, and especially on changes of light. A modern reader, wise after the event, can recognize the poet of **The Dawning, The Morningwatch, Midnight, The Search** and the many more in which sunrise, sunset and starlight are significant, when he reads such a poem as **To Amoret gone from Him** with its sensitive, although half fanciful, description of the way in which the life fades out of a country scene at sunset. . . . His secular poems, lacking as they do any individual outlook, only come to life when they reflect his responsiveness to the world about him. He looks even at nature partly through the eyes of other poets, but his own awareness and interest percolate through their phrases and fancies, even when he is writing complimentary verses, for instance: **To the best, and most accomplish'd Couple**—

> Fresh as the *houres* may all your pleasures be,
> And healthfull as *Eternitie!*
> Sweet as the flowers *first breath,* and Close
> As th'*unseen spreadings* of the Rose,

> When he unfolds his Curtained head,
> And makes his bosome the *Suns bed,*

which, with its feeling for the secret, luxurious beauty of the rose, recalls Blake's "Sick Rose", and Shelley's rose in "The Sensitive Plant"''

> Which unveiled the depth of her glowing breast
> Till, fold after fold, to the fainting air
> The soul of her beauty and love lay bare.

What was needed to make Vaughan a poet who stands out from the contemporary galaxy of good versifiers, was some central experience to which to relate his awareness of nature. His poems became entities when he recognized the phenomena of nature as relevant to his interpretation of the world.

The main importance of Herbert's influence is that it helped him to this end. Vaughan's preface to the second edition of **Silex Scintillans** (1655) suggests that, whatever influences combined to make him a religious *man,* Herbert was largely instrumental in making him a religious *poet.* Vaughan here dissociates himself from 'those ingenious persons, which in the late notion are termed *Wits',* namely, those poets whom in his first two volumes he had, almost slavishly, imitated 'and here' he adds 'because I would prevent a just *censure* by my free *confession,* I must remember, that I my self have, for many years together, languished of this very *sickness;* and it is no long time since I have recovered. But (blessed be God for it!) I have by his saving assistance suppress my *greatest follies,* and those which escaped from me, are (I think) as innoxious, as most of that *vein* use to be; besides, they are interlin'd with many virtuous, and some pious mixtures.' Something had happened to make him turn away with contempt from the amorous verse he had so lately practised and he now claimed a new allegiance to 'that blessed man *Mr George Herbert,* whose holy *life* and *verse* gained many pious *Converts* (of whom I am the least) and gave the first check to a most flourishing and admired wit of his time'.

Under Herbert's influence Vaughan discovered what he really wanted to say. He was passionately concerned, like Herbert himself, with the relation between God and the individual soul, and this concern increased and gave significance to his observations in the external world. When Vaughan began to explore his religious belief he found that it centred in his conception of nature. From being merely an ornament or an illustration his perceptiveness became the core of his poetry. Vaughan emerged from his contact with Herbert a metaphysical poet, not because Herbert was a metaphysical poet and he an imitative one, but because he now achieved a sense of direction and became capable of correlating his experiences. When he constructed his poems to *Amoret* on the metaphysical plan, he was only an imitator. His arguments were ingenious elaborations of 'occult resemblances'. But in true metaphysical poetry the intellectual parallel, or the recondite image, expresses awareness of a world in which the separate and apparently unrelated parts strangely echo one another. They are suddenly seen in the poetry as facets of a single whole. So it is when Donne cries out to his weeping mistress:

O more than Moone,
Draw not up seas to drowne me in thy spheare,

or when, in "The Extasie", he describes the relation between the self and the body:

Wee are
The intelligences, they the spheare.
We owe them thankes, because they thus,
Did us, to us, at first convay,
Yeelded their forces, sense, to us,
Nor are drosse to us, but allay.

Successful metaphysical imagery demands and repays close scrutiny. The meaning of the image tends to expand as we contemplate it, for instance in Donne's image of the moon his mistress is 'more than Moone' because she is more fair, more dear; because she draws the poet to her as the moon the tides; because she draws up tears as the moon will draw up the seas on which he is about to voyage; and her tears are salt like the seas and like the seas they may destroy him. All this and more is compressed within the image. In false metaphysical poetry the relation contemplated depends upon a one-sided and superficial resemblance. Of such a kind is the predominant difference between Vaughan's secular poetry and *Silex Scintillans.* He contemplates the same things, sunset and starlight, birds and flowers; but, whereas before he looked round for a subject they could adorn and contented himself with a partial relevance, they now appear in the poetry as the terms in which he is thinking; their relation to the subject is therefore intricate and rich. The lingering light of evening, for instance, so laboriously linked with the thought of his absent mistress in **To Amoret gone from him,** is now identified with the effect upon his mind of the memory of the dead, the relation seems as inevitable as it is rich in implications:

They are all gone into the world of light!
   And I alone sit lingring here;
Their very memory is fair and bright,
   And my sad thoughts doth clear.

It glows and glitters in my cloudy brest
   Like stars upon some gloomy grove,
Or those faint beams in which this hill is drest,
   After the Sun's remove.

Herbert had little to teach Vaughan about the relation between God and the created world. He himself contemplated God in the gospel story and in the forms and ceremonies of the church. He seldom looked at the countryside; poems in which it figures are rare. There is the savour of first-hand enjoyment in **Easter:**

I got me flowers to straw thy way;
I got me boughs off many a tree:
But thou wast up by break of day,
And brought'st thy sweets along with thee.

And in 'The Flower' he recognizes the kinship between the return of spring and the rhythmical recurrences of God's grace:

How fresh, O Lord, how sweet and clean
   Are thy returns! ev'n as the flowers in spring;
To which, besides their own demean,
   The late-past frosts tributes of pleasure bring.

Grief melts away
Like snow in May
As if there were no such cold thing.

In "Easter-wings" the song and flight of the lark have been perceived as symbols. But these are exceptions in Herbert's work, whereas for Vaughan, after his 'conversion',

all the vast expence
In the Creation shed, and slav'd to sence
Makes up but lectures for his eie, and ear.

Nature for Vaughan is a revelation of the fulfilment of God's will. Herbert had envied her constancy; in his poem "Employment" (II) he exclaims,

Oh that I were an Orenge-tree,
   That busie plant!
Then should I ever laden be,
   And never want
Some fruit for him that dressed me.

The 'Orenge tree' which bears fruit and blossom at the same time was an apt illustration for his purpose. Vaughan looked nearer home and discerned in his immediate surroundings similar grounds for envy.

I would I were a stone, or tree,
   Or flowre by pedigree,
Or some poor high-way herb, or Spring
   To flow, or bird to sing!
Then should I (tyed to one sure state,)
   All day expect my date;
But I am sadly loose, and stray
   A giddy blast each way;
   O let me not thus range!
   Thou canst not change.

Again, in **Rules and Lessons,** a poem profoundly influenced by Herbert as regards rhythm and structure, when he speaks of his favourite theme Vaughan is the loving observer of small sights and sounds, he bids man

Walk with thy fellow-creatures: note the *hush*
And *whispers* amongst them. There's not a
   Spring
Or *Leafe* but hath his *Morning-hymn;* each *Bus*
And *Oak* doth know I AM; canst thou not sing?

In **Christs Nativity,** bird song and starlight remind him of the difference between man and the rest of the creation:

I would I were some *Bird,* or Star,
Flutt'ring in woods, or lifted far
   Above this *Inne*
   And Rode of sin!
Then either Star, or *Bird,* should be
Shining, or singing still to thee.

In **Distraction,** starlight, rainbows and the radiance of pearls are envied because, though they spend their light, it does not diminish:

Hadst thou
Made me a starre, a pearle, or a rain-bow,
   The beames I then had shot
   My light had lessend not,
   But now
I find my selfe the lesse, the more I grow;

Like Wordsworth, Vaughan is tempted to look back to his

childhood with regret, because to both poets it seemed that children, like stars or flowers, fulfil the law of their being unconsciously and inevitably. The thought expressed in Vaughan's **Retreat** is, as has often been pointed out, similar in some respects to the thought in Wordsworth's "Intimations of Immortality"; this is due to an essential similarity in the outlook of the two poets. Both believe in the creation as the expression of a single mind, they turn to nature, not only to envy and admire, but to discover. Nature is God's book; Wordsworth turns her pages to find the prescriptions of that 'Stern Daughter of the voice of God' whom men call Duty:

> Stern Lawgiver! yet thou dost wear
> The Godhead's most benignant grace;
> Nor know we anything so fair
> As is the smile upon thy face:
> Flowers laugh before thee on their beds
> And fragrance in thy footing treads;
> Thou dost preserve the stars from wrong;
> And the most ancient heavens, through
>   Thee are fresh and strong.

In the same spirit Vaughan contemplates the ordered motions of the stars:

> Fair, order'd lights (whose motion without noise
>   Resembles those true Joys
> Whose spring is on that hil where you do grow
>   And we here tast sometimes below,)
>
> With what exact obedience do you move
>   Now beneath, and now above,
>
> And in your vast progressions overlook
>   The darkest night, and closest nook!
>
> Some nights I see you in the gladsome East,
>   Some others neer the West,
> And when I cannot see, yet do you shine
>   And beat about your endles line.
>
> Silence, and light, and watchfulnes with you
>   Attend and wind the Clue,
> No sleep, nor sloth assailes you, but poor man
>   Still either sleeps, or slips his span.

Both poets expect to find in nature the secret of that

>   something far more deeply interfused
> Whose dwelling is the light of setting suns
> And the round ocean, and the living air,
> And the blue sky, and in the mind of man:
> A motion and a spirit, that impels
> All thinking things, all objects of all thought,
> And rolls through all things.

Several of Vaughan's contemporaries observed and enjoyed the world about them (Herrick for instance, and Marvell, and Milton); but Vaughan's nature poetry is different from theirs; he thinks of nature as a source of revelation and could have said with Sir Thomas Browne:

> There are two Books from whence I collect my Divinity; besides that written one of God, another of his servant Nature, that universal and publick Manuscript, that lies expans'd unto the Eyes of all: those that never saw him in the one, have discovered him in the other.

Even for Traherne, who, among the poets of the century,

approaches nearest to Vaughan's attitude, nature is rather a playground than an instructress; she is a delightful gift from God, rather than his interpreter:

>   O hevenly Joy!
> O Great and Sacred Blessedness
>   Which I possess!
>   So great a Joy
> Who did into my Arms convey?
>
>   From God abov
> Being sent, the gift doth me enflame
>   To prais his Name;
>   The Stars do mov,
> The Sun doth shine, to show his Lov.

For Vaughan and later for Wordsworth nature shows not so much the love of God as his mind and meaning. Wordsworth tells us,

> As if awakened, summoned, roused, constrained,
> I looked for universal things; perused
> The common countenance of earth and sky:

and Vaughan prays,

> O thou! whose spirit did at first inflame
>   And warm the dead,
> And by a sacred Incubation fed
>   With life this frame
> Which once had neither being, forme, nor name,
>   Grant I may so
>   Thy steps track here below,
>
> That in these Masques and shadows I may see
>   Thy sacred way, . . .

Vaughan observes and often closely imitates the workmanship of Herbert in *Silex Scintillans,* but this attitude to the created world constantly affects his choice and use of imagery. In a poem called **Affliction,** for instance, there is every indication that he has been studying Herbert's poetry, particularly the four poems with this same title, as well as Herbert's "Deniall." The theme is similar to that of Herbert's "Affliction" (I). Both poets are contemplating the suffering with which God purges his elect. The opening lines are in that staccato speech accent, which Herbert adapted from Donne:

> Peace, peace; It is not so. Thou doest miscall
>   Thy Physick; Pils that change
> Thy sick Accessions into setled health,
> This is the great *Elixir* that turns gall
> To wine and sweetness; Poverty to wealth,
>   And brings man home, when he doth range.

The device, used by Herbert in "Deniall" and elsewhere, of making an imperfect rhyme scheme reflect an inharmonious mood, is here adapted by Vaughan. He stresses the irregularities of his metrical pattern until the end, when it is regularized to represent the return of peace. But the difference between Vaughan's poem and any of Herbert's is far more essential than the resemblance. Whereas Herbert may chance to draw a simile from nature, attaching no more importance to it than that it affords the resemblance he requires:

> We are the trees whom shaking fastens more;

or

Dissolve the knot
As the sunne scatters by his light
All the rebellions of the night;

Vaughan sees in such parallels a revelation of unity between the pattern of the world and the ordering of men's souls:

Did not he, who ordain'd the day,
　　Ordain night too?
And in the greater world display
What in the lesser he would do?
All flesh is Clay, thou know'st; and but that God
　　Doth use his rod,
And by a fruitfull Change of frosts, and showres
　　Cherish, and bind thy *powr's,*
Thou wouldst to weeds, and thistles quite disperse,
And be more wild than is thy verse.

　　　　. . . . .

Were all the year one constant Sun-shine, wee
　　Should have no flowres,
All would be drought, and leanness; not a tree
　　Would make us bowres;

　　　　. . . . .

Thus doth God *Key* disorder'd man
　　(Which none else can,)
Tuning his brest to rise, or fall;
And by a sacred, needfull art
Like strings, stretch ev'ry part
　Making the whole most Musicall.

Vaughan lays stress upon the repetition in the microcosm of the pattern of the macrocosm.

The Morning-watch, perhaps the most perfect whole among all Vaughan's poems (for he is often fragmentary), seems to have developed out of a chance phrase of Herbert's. Herbert's poem, "Prayer" (I), is a rapid succession of similes; among other things prayer is likened to

A kinde of tune which all things heare and fear.

Here is the poem which this line apparently suggested to Vaughan.

The Morning-watch

O Joyes! Infinite sweetness! with what flowres,
And shoots of glory, my soul breakes, and buds!
　　All the long houres
　　Of night, and Rest
　　Through the still shrouds
　　Of sleep, and Clouds,
This Dew fell on my Breast;
　　O how it *Blouds*
And *Spirits* all my Earth! heark! In what Rings,
And *Hymning Circulations* the quick world
　　Awakes, and sings;
　　The rising winds,
　　And falling springs,
　　Birds, beasts, all things
Adore him in their kinds.
　　Thus all is hurl'd
In sacred *Hymnes,* and *Order,* The great *Chime*
And *Symphony* of nature. Prayer is

The world in tune,
A spirit-voyce,
And vocall joyes
Whose Echo is heav'ns blisse.
　　O let me climbe
When I lye down! The Pious soul by night
Is like a clouded starre, whose beames though sed
　　To shed their light
　　Under some Cloud
　　Yet are above
　　And shine, and move
Beyond that mistie shorwd.
　　So in my Bed
That Curtain'd grave, though sleep, like ashes, hide
My lamp, and life, both shall in thee abide.

This is a very different way of recasting another poet's phrase, from that exemplified in the **Lines to Amoret.** The lines borrowed from Donne lost their original vigour and gained nothing new from Vaughan's poem. But Herbert's chance phrase is transformed into the focal point of an apprehension of the world, which Herbert had not developed and perhaps not thought of. His influence on Vaughan cannot be overstated in so far as it directed him to the contemplation from which his poetry was to spring; but it can be misstated if the wrong kind of importance is attached to the verbal resemblances. Herbert may have made Vaughan a poet, but he did not make him in his own image. Vaughan is weak where Herbert is strong, and strong where he is weak. He lacks form, order, economy, he seldom knows where to stop; whereas the perfection of form is characteristic of Herbert's poetry. On the other hand Vaughan has a gift of song which Herbert often lacks. He can convey the ecstasy of joy or grief or worship by the movement of the verse, and he has a stronger instinct than Herbert for the magic of words and phrases. A selection of the best from Herbert would be a selection of poems, a selection of the best from Vaughan would include some single stanzas, lines, or even half lines.

Among these would be several that were suggested to him by Herbert. 'Prayer is the world in tune' would need to be set in its context to convey all the meaning Vaughan perceived in it. Other phrases can be enjoyed in isolation. A phrase which to Herbert was only an essential part of the structure of a poem, was sometimes picked out by Vaughan and lovingly worked on till it satisfied his ear. Herbert had written, in a poem called "The Familie,"

Joyes oft are there, and griefs as oft as joyes;
　　　　But griefs without a noise;
Yet speak they louder then distemper'd fears.
　　What is so shrill as silent tears?

Vaughan, in *Olor Iscanus* (1651), in "An Epitaph upon the Lady Elizabeth," made his first attempt to incorporate Herbert's phrase:

Thy portion here was *griefe,* thy years
Distilld no other rain, but tears,
Tears without noise, but (understood)
As lowd, and shrill as any bloud;

It was not very successful and the words still haunted him.

In *Silex Scintillans,* in a poem called "Admission," he found their final form:

> How shril are silent teares? . . .

It is the first half of a line of a poem which does not fulfil its promise; but the history of the line shows an interest in the choice and arrangement of words to produce an emotional impact. The magic of the phrase is Vaughan's, though it owes something to Herbert which is of vital importance. Vaughan learnt from Herbert the value of under-emphasis. He learnt to lead his reader on with commonplace words in a prose order until, all unprepared, he is brought up short by some startlingly poignant phrase. Instead of being first lifted out of the rut of triviality by the poet's emphasis and solemnity, he is shown the problems of life, death, time and eternity within the orbit of his daily experience. To speak familiarly of ultimate things is the prerogative of the metaphysical poets. Their habit of connecting the temporal and the eternal made it possible for them. It is not with any intention of avoiding the trivial that Vaughan most frequently expresses himself in terms of light and stars and running water; these were the stuff of his daily experience. He assimilated and adapted the manner of Herbert, which Herbert in turn had learnt from Donne. Without ceremony, as it were casually, these poets plunge us into the problems that baffle thought; so Donne,

> What if this present were the worlds last night?

or Herbert,

> Lord, how can man preach thy eternal word?

and Vaughan, in the same tradition, gives us,

> I saw Eternity the other night
> Like a great *Ring* of pure and endless light,
>   All calm, as it was bright,
> And round beneath it, Time in hours, days, years
>   Driv'n by the spheres
> Like a vast shadow mov'd, In which the world
> And all her train were hurl'd; . . .

Here is no imitation, but Vaughan has been able to assimilate the influence of Donne, just as Herbert, with his different outlook and temperament, had assimilated it. The problem of time haunted Vaughan. Few poets have phrased more beautifully the experience of time-bound man striving to apprehend eternity; or of the bewildering variation in the rate at which time passes:

> Silence, and stealth of dayes! 'Tis now
>   Since thou art gone,
> Twelve hundred houres. . . .

is the opening of a poem about the death of his brother. For Vaughan, as for Donne, the 'houres, dayes, weeks are but the rags of time',

>   Heav'n
> Is a plain watch and without figures winds
> All ages up; who drew this Circle even
> He fills it; Dayes, and hours are *Blinds.*

Donne's influence over this school of poetry was very great; but each of his followers who deserves separate attention contributed something of his own to the tradition.

Vaughan brought a new range of experience within the compass of this style. No one else among Donne's followers watched the earth, sky, and water, the birds and flowers with the same emotion, nor with the same delicacy of observation. Vaughan lacked Donne's vigorous and varied awareness of human character and affairs; he lacked Herbert's sobriety and exquisite sense of form, his undeviating control of powerful feeling; but often his poetry has a radiance and a movement which neither of these attempts. Vaughan, who resembles Wordsworth in his nature mysticism, sometimes resembles Shelley in the ecstatic outpouring of his numbers. He is more lyrical than his masters. Perhaps he is less restrained by intellectual perplexity. He could immerse himself in rapturous contemplation of dawn or sunset. Neither Donne nor Herbert could have written "The Dawning:" but Vaughan would not have written it as he did had he not learnt from them and assimilated the metaphysical influence. It is a song of rapture, but with an intellectual ground base. . . . From first to last Vaughan laid himself open to the influence of other poets, but he emerged with a way of perceiving and of expressing his perceptions which bore his own hallmark.

H. J. Oliver   (essay date 1954)

SOURCE: "The Mysticism of Henry Vaughan: A Reply," in *The Journal of English and Germanic Philology,* Vol. LIII, No. 3, July, 1954, pp. 352-60.

[*In the following excerpt, Oliver takes issue with Frank Kermode's 1950 essay on Vaughan, contending that "Vaughan makes a mystic's use of the poet's language." (Kermode had held that Vaughan "is from the beginning a poet with his roots in poetry rather than in religious experience. . . .")*]

In an article published in *The Review of English Studies* in 1950 Mr. Frank Kermode has stated in its extreme form a belief that has been held by an increasing number of scholars in the last few years and has argued that Henry Vaughan "is in no sense at all a mystic; he makes a poet's use of the mystic's language":

> Vaughan is from the beginning a poet with his roots in poetry rather than in religious experience, his interest in theological and philosophical thought is governed by the limitations imposed upon such thought by its poetic conventionalization, and it follows both that the germs of his poems are to be found within that pale, and that his own use of what we may call extrapoetic speculation will generally be to conventionalize it in the same way before he employs it.

It is, however, still possible to hold the traditional view—that, briefly, Vaughan makes a mystic's use of the poet's language; and I should like to state that case again and so to answer Mr. Kermode, but not point by point. One thing that becomes clear in the process is how very slight the differences between the two views sometimes are in detail: a mere difference of emphasis can lead to opposite conclusions.

Between, possibly, December 1647 (the alleged date of the

dedication to **Olor Iscanus**) and 1650 (the date of the first publication of **Silex Scintillans**), something happened to Vaughan that persuaded him to withhold the publication of the volume of secular verse as it originally was, to publish instead his religious poems, and then to publish the original volume (in 1651) only in an emasculated version. His own account is given in the 1654 preface to the second edition of **Silex Scintillans,** in which he takes up the question of the corruption of secular verse:

> . . . I my self have for many years together, languished of this very *sickness;* and it is no long time since I have recovered. But (blessed be God for it!) I have by his saving assistance supprest my *greatest follies,* and those which escaped from me, are (I think) as innoxious, as most of that *vein* use to be; besides, they are interlined with many virtuous, and some pious mixtures.

This statement alone makes it extremely difficult to agree with Mr. Kermode's conclusion that "Something happened, and something to do with poetry and not with prayer," particularly as Vaughan goes on to complain (almost as if he had anticipated the objection) that those who imitated Herbert failed precisely because "they aimed more at *verse,* then perfection."

Granting the importance to the poet of the death of his younger brother, William, in 1648; granting the extended study of the Bible and of George Herbert; granting, too, that Vaughan suffered an extended illness, it is possible to argue that all these were only subsidiary to the coming to the poet of his first mystical experience, in the strictest sense, the experience described by Emily Bronte, and by Wordsworth in *The Prelude:*

> the light of sense
> Goes out, but with a flash that has revealed
> The invisible world (VI.600-02).

The records of mysticism do not seem to me to support the commonly held belief that mysticism generally begins with vague feelings, transitory experiences; nor is there any evidence for Osmond's view [in *The Mystical Poets of the English Church,* 1919] that Vaughan had passed through the regular stages of "mortification, detachment, and meditation, to a state of inward calm and lucidity." But Miss White [in *The Metaphysical Poets,* 1936] is undoubtedly correct in saying that to Vaughan the experience of God came first, the identification or explanation of the experience later. Vaughan is wrongly pictured, I believe, as unduly intellectual; Mrs. Bennett's "Perhaps he is less restrained by intellectual perplexity" than Donne or Herbert [from her *Four Metaphysical Poets,* 1934] is a most curious understatement. For to Vaughan, as he expressly says in the preface to **The Mount of Olives,** the usual analytic approaches to problems of Devotion are "but so many fruitlesse curiosities of Schoole-Divinity."

St. Augustine, it may be remembered, was a mystic before he was a Christian. Similarly, Vaughan would perceive that his mystical experience "could be fitted into the context of his very real and sincere Christian belief" [according to Miss White]—which it probably did not occur to him to question. Mysticism was naturally (though not inevitably) thus fused with a religious creed until modern ways of thought suggested alternative explanations. But with Vaughan the mysticism fused equally well with Platonism or, of course, Neo-Platonism.

There is evidence of this in the fact that Vaughan has not a personal view of God. Osmond points out that to Herbert "Jesus is 'My Master:' Vaughan prefers to call Him 'My dear, bright Lord, my Morning Star.' " Where Vaughan does speak to God as to a person, it is precisely where he is imitating Herbert: and the mode of address is quickly dropped again.

What this means is that Mr. Kermode is correct in so far as he suggests that there is something unusual about Vaughan's mysticism, as Mr. T. S. Eliot was correct in suggesting that there is something odd about his Anglicanism. But what is odd is simply that the mysticism is explained *in terms of* an Anglican creed. Any other creed, one may feel, would have done as well: it does not follow that Vaughan's religion is superficial, and indeed **The Mount of Olives** proves the contrary.

It may be significant that one feature of Christianity that particularly appeals to Vaughan is the guidance it gives him in the ordering of his daily life. There is no need to marvel that Emily, alone of the Bronte sisters, did not mind housework; for it is precisely because of the mystic's conviction of the relative unimportance of everything except his communion with God, that he willingly accepts routine. And so Vaughan finds that the Christian way of life helps him and helps him as mystic; particularly he cherishes the methods of devotion and particularly the Sacrament; and it is the deprivation of this that he deplores, when South Wales is left almost without clergymen during the Commonwealth, in his "Prayer in time of persecution and Heresie."

This coalescing of mysticism with something like the orthodox Christian's feeling for his God has the effect of making Vaughan less dissatisfied with his lot: which is why he lacks the passion of Emily Bronte's cries for renewal of the experience. But he is certain, too, that his knowledge of God is closer than is the usual Christian's and will not be fully understood. Here, surely, is the explanation of the paragraph in the Preface to **Silex Scintillans** in which Vaughan speaks of the *remoteness* of some of his verses—a passage which, I feel sure, Mr. Kermode would have difficulty in explaining.

> In the *perusal* of it, you will (peradventure) observe some *passages,* whose *history* or *reason* may seem something *remote:* but were they brought *nearer,* and plainly exposed to your view, (though that (perhaps) might quiet your *Curiosity)* yet would it not conduce much to your greater *advantage.* And therefore I must desire you to accept of them in that latitude, which is already alowed them.

Is not this distinction between the poet and his fellows also the point of the introductory verses to the 1655 edition?

> Vain Wits and eyes
> Leave, and be wise:
> Abuse not, shun not holy fire,
> But with true tears wash off your mire.
> Tears and these flames will soon grow kinde,

And mix an eye-salve for the blinde.
Tears cleanse and supple without fail,
And fire will purge your callous veyl.
Then comes the light! which when you spy,
And see your nakedness thereby,
Praise him, who dealt his gifts so free
In tears to you, in fire to me.

There is, then, far more than mere holiness involved in Vaughan's love of God, which is, as he says, rare:

Sure, *holyness* the *Magnet* is,
And *Love* the *Lure,* that woos thee down;
Which makes the high transcendent bliss
Of knowing thee, so rarely known.

"Fire" and "light," it is clear, are Vaughan's symbols—the traditional mystic symbols, I agree—for his communion with God; and the "veil" which comes between men and God is his recognition of his inability to maintain the experience. The veil Vaughan, as a Christian, identifies with the body, or sometimes original sin. thereby differing from, say, Emily Bronte again or Mr. Charles Morgan. What he shares with other mystics is the "roving extesie" of the quest; and there seems to be a similar conviction that night and early morning (see the beautiful **"The Dawning"**) are the times most likely to bring success. Vaughan shares also the mystic's refusal to be frightened of death, the final union; but again Christianity prevents him from saying he actually longs for death. As a result he limits his subject matter even more than do most mystics: and the number of things about which Vaughan can write is remarkably small. (The point will be appreciated if it is remembered how much of Emily Bronte's poetry is taken up with the expression of her longing for renewal or death; or how largely the subject figures—to the novel's disadvantage—in *Sparkenbroke.*)

Vaughan does, of course, share Emily Bronte's feeling for nature, contemplation of which is for her a means towards the desired end. His interest. however, is of a different kind: it derives from his conviction that birds and animals, and even flowers and plants, themselves partake of the divine essence. They do not "range"; or, in Mr. Leishman's phrase, they "do naturally and instinctively" what man must make an effort to do (although I question Mr. Leishman's gloss of this, as obeying "the laws and motions" of God).

The crucial poem is **"And do they so?"**

Etenim res creata exerto Capite observantes expectant revelationem Filiorum Dei.

And do they so? have they a Sense
Of ought but Influence?
Can they their heads lift, and expect,
And grone too? why th'Elect
Can do no more: my volumes sed
They were all dull, and dead,
They judg'd them senslesse, and their state
Wholly Inanimate.
Go, go; Seal up thy looks,
And burn thy books.

2.

I would I were a stone, or tree,

Or flowre by pedigree,
Or some poor high-way herb, or Spring
To flow, or bird to sing!
Then should I (tyed to one sure state,)
All day expect my date;
But I am sadly loose, and stray
A giddy blast each way;
A let me not thus range!
Thou canst not change,

3.

Sometimes I sit with thee, and tarry
An hour, or so, then vary.
Thy other Creatures in this Scene
Thee only aym, and mean;
Some rise to seek thee, and with heads
Erect peep from their beds;
Others, whose birth is in the tomb,
And cannot quit the womb,
Sigh there, and grone for thee,
Their liberty.

4.

O let not me do less! shall they
Watch, while I sleep, or play?
Shall I thy mercies still abuse
With fancies, friends, or newes?
O brook it not! thy bloud is mine,
And my soul should be thine;
O brook it not! why wilt thou stop
After whole showres one drop?
Sure, thou wilt joy to see
Thy sheep with thee.

Here, perhaps, the Hermetic philosophy becomes relevant, and a knowledge of it as expounded by Miss Holmes [in *Henry Vaughan and the Hermetic Philosophy,* 1942] and Mr. Walters [in "Henry Vaughan and the Alchemists," *Review of English Studies* XXIII, 1947] helps in an understanding of Vaughan. But I think the Hermetic philosophy is itself only a mode of expression to him. Mr. Kermode makes the point that "there is fairly elaborate use of the Hermetic vocabulary pressed into amorous service" in verses written presumably before Vaughan's conversion. Exactly. What follows is not that the "conversion" is insincere but that the belief in the Hermetic philosophy possibly is. Or to be more precise, the Hermetic doctrine of the three levels, terrestrial, celestial and intellectual, one forming an analogue of the other, gives Vaughan his imagery, as Science, "the new philosophy," gave Donne his or the philosophy of Plotinus gave St. Augustine his. There is, of course, reason for saying that Vaughan did believe in the Hermetic philosophy, but a seventeenth-century poet will use for purposes of imagery a doctrine in which he does not necessarily believe; as Cowley said, the poet "professes too much the use of *Fables* (though without the malice of deceiving) to have his testimony taken even against himself." And nobody has argued that Donne, simply because he used the same imagery for love poetry and for divine, was not a devout Christian, that his conversion was not sincere.

Vaughan, then, in Mr. Walters' phrase, is constantly expressing "spiritual processes in alchemical terms" (and, I should add, philosophical and theological terms). It may also be suggested that the very expression of his experience in such imagery itself suggests further qualities of the experience—in which sense, if at all, Vaughan is a metaphysical poet.

Just as Vaughan's use of the Hermetic philosophy has been misunderstood, there has been misconception, it seems to me, of his alleged "philosophy" of childhood. Vaughan, I venture to say, had no philosophy of childhood; the Platonic doctrine of reminiscence simply provides him with an analogue to his belief that the child (like the bird) is capable of the selfless absorption that the adult attains only rarely—and that is why Vaughan would fain return. (**"The Retreat"** and **"Childehood."**) It does not worry Vaughan that there is some slight discrepancy here even within his religious texts; the Synoptic Gospels would give him warrant, if he needed it, for his idea of the essential purity of childhood, but he also quotes with approval from *Ecclesiastes* "Childhood and Youth are Vanity." To a philosopher, the conflict might well have been disturbing.

It is, then, possible to insist on the view of Vaughan as a mystic and perhaps even to believe still that it was the unexpected dawning of the Invisible, to use Emily Bronte's famous words, that caused the change to **Silex Scintillans** in 1650 and 1655, with the original and translated prose devotions, **The Mount of Olives** 1652 and **Flores Solitudinis** 1654. And then, except for **Thalia Rediviva** in 1678, and that consisting almost entirely of the poems rejected from **Olor Iscanus,** Vaughan, having exhausted his small stock of material, sinks into silence. Particularly when one is, because of creed, restrained from expressing constantly one's dissatisfaction with the chain of one's fleshly existence—

> O dreadful is the check—intense the agony—
> When the ear begins to hear, and the eye begins
>   to see;
> When the pulse begins to throb—the brain to
>   think again—
> The soul to feel the flesh, and the flesh to feel the
>   chain—

the logical outcome of mysticism *is* silence.

It remains to suggest that Vaughan's poetic faults and virtues are precisely those which are natural to a mystic.

His verse has a marked limitation of subject, already commented on and not surprising from one who writes "Let sensual *natures* judge as they please, but for my part, I shall hold it no *Paradoxe* to affirme, *there are no pleasures in this world*" and "I protest piously unto thee, and without *Scepticisme,* that there is no such thing in this world, as *misfortune*" (man merely misconstrues the ways of Providence).

Accordingly he repeats himself again and again. particularly as he has no great power of developing thought. A poem like **"The Water-fall"** is exceptional, or **"The Book,"** where the continuity is provided, as it were, by the subject itself (Vaughan thinks in turn of each of its parts, its history, known to God), or **"To the Holy Bible,"** where something like autobiography gives the poem progressiveness. Generally Vaughan is a static poet; and even a famous poem like **"The Bird"** is not properly sustained.

Nearly always Vaughan returns to God or to himself, notably in **"Cock- Crowing"** where the bird and the Hermetic philosophy merely provide the starting point and we come back, significantly, to the Veil. **"The Timber"** is another example.

This is why Vaughan is generally good only in short bursts. There are exceptional poems, of course, like **"Thou that knowst for whom I mourn"** where an idea is carried brilliantly through sixty-four lines, or **"Silence and Stealth of dayes."** But generally, as Mrs. Bennett has put it, Vaughan "lacks form, order, economy; he seldom knows where to stop . . . a selection of the best from Vaughan would include some single stanzas, lines, or even half lines." One may add that most of these would be opening lines: "They are all gone into the world of light," "I saw Eternity the other night," and so on. I also note a significant tendency towards shorter lyrics in the **"Pious Thoughts and Ejaculations"** of *Thalia Rediviva.*

Vaughan's vocabulary is also very limited. He uses contless times "fair," "bright," "light," "ray," "faint," "veil." "dew," and the all-important "white" (with the connotations of the Welsh "gwyn," as Professor Rhys long ago suggested). The more homely "nap," "yell," and "spittle" probably derive from Herbert. (I do not think it has been pointed out that Vaughan is remarkably found of monosyllables in his verse—a deliberate simplicity, since his prose is often polysyllabic in awkward ways.)

Similarly, perhaps because it comes naturally to one not inclined to sustained thought, Vaughan makes extensive use of the simple contrast and paradox. Lines like "I have outlived my life," "though life be dead," and "a deep but dazling darkness" are frequent; and whole poems, such as **"The Incarnation, and Passion,"** are built up in this way. Argument by simple analogy is also common:

> If a mere blast so fill the Sail,
> Shall not the breath of God prevail?

and direct question and exclamation are constantly used:

> Ah! what time wilt thou come? when shall that
>   crie
> *The Bridegroom's coming! fill the sky?*

or

> Oh for that Night! Where I in Him
> Might be invisible and dim!

Yet there is seldom more than one such challenging statement or exclamation in any one poem.

Nor is there great metrical variation within Vaughan's poetry. It may be significant that he writes verses in Praise of Mr. ML's "reduction of the Psalms into Method"; he is noticeably not very successful with the couplet or with the longer poetic measures that are fittest for discourse and nearest prose. He is best with the short singing measures and particularly with alternating long and short lines.

We have long since passed the time at which it was proper to say [as has Osmond] that "Vaughan's main importance in English Literature rests upon his influence on Wordsworth" and Mr. Kermode does well to insist that the emphasis must be on the poetry itself. But it is in the more than competent yet uneven, craftsmanship of a writer not intellectually profound but profoundly moved, by his special experience of God, that there lies the best explanation of the poetic achievement of Vaughan.

E. C. Pettet   (essay date 1960)

SOURCE: "The Unity and Continuity of *Silex Scintillans,*" in *Of Paradise and Light: A Study of Vaughan's 'Silex Scintillans,'* Cambridge at the University Press, 1960, pp. 196-207.

[*Pettet is an English scholar who has written at length on the accomplishments of Shakespeare, Vaughan, and John Keats. In the following chapter from his study* Of Paradise and Light, *he compares the two editions of* Silex Scintillans *(which he calls Part I and Part II) to demonstrate their thematic "unity and continuity" as reflections of the poet's spiritual beliefs. Pettet concludes, "Part II is both a continuation from Part I and distinct from it, though we must not exaggerate the differences."*]

Though it consists of one hundred and twenty-nine mainly short poems and is divided into two Parts that were separated by five years in publication, *Silex Scintillans,* like *The Temple,* Shakespeare's Sonnets, *Fleurs du Mal* (and we might add Hopkins' *Poems*) is essentially a poetic *work,* not a collection of miscellaneous lyrics: it makes an impact, perhaps its profoundest impact, as a whole. As Blunden truly says: 'There are many threads and clues which connect the poems of Vaughan and make it more profitable to read his work as a whole than in separate examples.'

One obvious reason for this unity of *Silex Scintillans* is the continuous and predominant devotional nature of the poems; another the fact that they clearly fall into a small number of groups—those on Biblical subjects and personages, on Christ, on the central articles of the Christian faith, on the various Church days and festivals, and on Vaughan's own spiritual progress. Though this last group is an extensive one, it is made up of variations on a limited number of themes, while the elegies and pietistic pieces are most closely related to these devotional groups, often overlapping them. Further, all the poems are bound together by an abundance of imagery drawn from Nature, by frequent Herbert and Scriptural echoes and quotations, and by the continual hermetic allusions and terminology.

Besides these general groupings, there are also six poems in Part I that have their complement in Part II and at least half a dozen sequences of closely interrelated poems. The volume begins with such a sequence in the three pieces **'Death, Resurrection and Immortality,'** and **'Day of Judgment.'** Two other instances of marked continuity are to be seen in **'The Ass,' 'The Hidden' 'Treasure,'** and **'Childhood,'** poems intimately connected by their themes of humility, submission, and renunciation of intellectual inquiry and knowledge, and in the six poems on death and resurrection towards the end of Part II, **'The Throne,' 'Death,' 'The Feast,' 'The Obsequies,' 'The Waterfall,'** and **'Quickness'.**

Another link between the poems is the fairly frequent repetition of identical (or near identical) phrases and turns of expression. Admittedly, most of these iterations are slight in effect and may long pass unnoticed by the reader. But one or two of them stand out quite prominently, like the 'homing' idea, which, after its appearance in **'Affliction'**—

> And brings man home when he doth range

—occurs five times in the next thirteen poems.

Throughout both Parts of **Silex Scintillans** repetitions or cross-echoes of whole lines and passages are also quite common. For instance, there is an obvious resemblance between two lines in 'And do they so?' (a poem in Part I)—

> Can they their heads lift, and expect,
> And groan too?

—and two lines in **'Palm Sunday'** (which occurs in Part II):

> Trees, flowers, and herbs; birds, beasts, and
>   stones,
> That since man fell, expect with groans
> To see the Lamb. . . .

(Here, of course, the similarity arises from a common echo of Rom. 8. 19 and 22-3.) A more sustained example of such reminiscence is to be found in **'Corruption,'** where Vaughan's picture of the childhood of man—

> He shin'd a little, and by those weak rays
>   Had some glimpse of his birth.
> He saw heaven o'er his head, and knew from
>   whence
>   He came, condemned, hither;
> And, as first love draws strongest, so from hence
>   His mind sure progress'd thither

—immediately recalls his description in **'The Retreat'** of his own first years:

> Happy those early days, when I
> Shin'd in my angel-infancy. . . .
> When yet I had not walk'd above
> A mile or two from my first love,
> And looking back—at that short space—
> Could see a glimpse of His bright face.

Occasionally, too, some odd line has the effect of evoking in a flash an entire poem. How immediately, for example, the close of **'The Star,'** unmistakable Vaughan in every word—

>   as herbs unseen
> Put on their youth and green

—calls up his elegy 'I walk'd the other day'; and how beautifully and suggestively epitomised is **'The Star'** itself by these two lines from **'Love-Sick'**:

> That Thou wert pleas'd to shed Thy grace so far
> As to make man all pure love, flesh a star!

But perhaps the most striking of all such cross-references is a passage in **'Providence'**:

>   Poor birds this doctrine sing,
>   And herbs which on dry hills do spring,

> Or in the howling wilderness
>   Do know Thy dewy morning hours,
>   And watch all night for mists or showers,
> Then drink and praise Thy bounteousness.

Here the 'poor birds' and their 'doctrine' at once recall the poem **'The Bird,'** which also deals with the theme of Providence; while the thought of these lines, with some very slight reminiscence of phrase, runs close to that of stanzas two and three in the earlier poem.

However, the most continuous and fundamental link between the poems of *Silex Scintillans,* giving the work a greater unity than *The Temple,* is their common and highly individualised imagery—the very large number of repeated single images, the recurrent image-clusters, and the distinctive 'world' within, and to some extent behind, the poems, turning perpetually to its elemental rhythm of light and darkness, daybreak and night. Outstanding as this kind of cohesion is, it requires no further stressing here, for it has already been sufficiently discussed. But perhaps two further relevant points may be briefly made. First, because there is this unmistakable Vaughan world and because it is so richly epitomised in his masterpieces, these poems act in an exceptional way as nodal points for the whole work. They are filamented, so to speak, to a large number of inferior pieces—the scattered rough sketches for the concentrated finished picture. Secondly, those fragmentary lines and half lines of surprising exceptional beauty that so often light up Vaughan's mediocre poems (this is of course one of the main features of his work) are not merely redeeming 'fine phrases' in the usual sense of that term, admirable epithets, metaphors, etc.: they often have the effect, which contributes to the unity of *Silex Scintillans,* of instantly transporting us into the centre of his imaginative world.

It must be admitted that these repetitions of theme, phrasing, and to some extent of imagery expose the limitations of Vaughan's poetry. To put the criticism simply, he is a writer of narrow, though intensely cultivated, experience who does sometimes rather repeat himself. But, paradoxically, these limitations of the poet are a source of strength to his book, for his repetitions (which rarely approach monotony and never poverty, a different matter) certainly help to make his collection of lyrics a unified whole. Had he been more widely ranging and inventive, *Silex Scintillans* would obviously have been richer and more varied in appeal; but, almost as certainly, it would have lost much of its coherence as a work.

Much the same could probably be said of *A Shropshire Lad,* written by a poet far more limited than Vaughan. Many nineteenth- and twentieth-century collections of lyrics contain poems that are greatly superior to anything Housman ever wrote. For instance, nothing in *A Shropshire Lad* approaches 'Poem in October' or 'Fern Hill' in Dylan Thomas's volume *Deaths and Entrances;* yet it can hardly be denied that *A Shropshire Lad* strikes us as a unified whole in a way that *Deaths and Entrances*—or, for that matter, Thomas's *Collected Poems*—do not. And this total effect in a volume of lyrical poems is a real aesthetic sensation that does count for something.

While *Silex Scintillans* has thus a considerable degree of

unity, its two Parts are clearly distinct in tone; and it is obvious that the five years separating their publication mark a discernible stage in Vaughan's spiritual development.

Reading Part I, which is appropriately introduced by a key poem on regeneration, we have a strong impression of a struggle for assured faith and salvation, of spiritual unquiet, conflict, and often of deep anguish. There are certainly intervals of joy and serenity, captured in such poems as **'The Morning-Watch'** and **'Peace';** but these moments are rare. The main, and characteristic, themes are death, the spiritual quest (and its complement, apathy, back-sliding, and distraction), the desperate need for repentance, and the value of affliction. There is also considerable emphasis on the Fall of man, and, parallel with this, an extreme stress on the poet's own sinfulness, worthlessness, and vileness:

> In all this round of life and death
> Nothing's more vile than is my breath;
> Profaneness on my tongue doth rest,
> Defects and darkness in my breast;
> Pollutions all my body wed,
> And even my soul to Thee is dead.
>   **'Repentance'**

Typical and indicative titles, not to be matched in Part II, are: **'The Search,' 'Distraction,' 'The Storm,' 'The Relapse,' 'The Mutiny,' 'Misery.'**

Unquestionably we should be distorting Part II if we forced it into a sharp and continuous antithesis with Part I. Just as the first Part has its moments of joy, so the second, in such poems as **'Love-Sick,', 'Begging,'** and **'Anguish,'** rings at times with the old note of self-condemnation and a deeply troubled spirit. Nevertheless, the characteristic themes of the first volume are less prominent in the second, and in so far as they remain they are often handled in a very different way. For instance, the subject of death (as we may see by comparing the two poems of that name, one in each Part) is treated much more in a spirit of calm assurance than in the agitation of one hungry for reassurance: turning away from mortality, physical corruption, and from resurrection as a doctrine, Vaughan's attention is more steadily settled on the bliss of the life hereafter; he yearns for heaven rather than hopes for it. That is why 'They are all gone into the world of light', characterised by such lines as

> Dear, beauteous Death! the jewel of the just,

belongs to Part II as it never could to Part I.

But there is a positive change between the two Parts even more striking than the negative. The opening lines of Part II,

> Lord Jesus! with what sweetness and delights,
> Sure, holy hopes, high joys, and quick'ning
>   flights,
> Dost Thou feed Thine!

—indeed the whole of this first poem—truly intimates the prevailing mood of the volume. As we read on, we feel that the prayer in the penultimate poem of Part I—

> Show me Thy peace,

> Thy mercy, love, and ease

—has been largely answered. Though Vaughan is still at times wrung with pangs of remorse for his old sinful ways—

> Yet joy itself will make a right soul grieve
> To think he should be so long vainly
> led;
> **'The Timber'**

—in a number of poems we now feel that his spiritual night—to say nothing of his earlier unregenerate days—is more of a recollection than a present actuality. He has found God for certain:

> But I am sure Thou dost now come
> Oft to a narrow, homely room,
> Where Thou too hast but the least part;
> My God, I mean my sinful heart;
> **'The Dwelling-Place'**

and with the finding of God, this sense of His presence, he has discovered true joy and a serener, more balanced attitude:

> Thou hast
> Another mirth, a mirth, though overcast
> With clouds and rain, yet full as calm and fine
> As those clear heights which above tempests
> shine.
> **"Joy"**

This new attitude is admirably reflected in **'The Bird,'** a poem which—though of course without any warrant from Vaughan—we might read as an allegory of his own spiritual history:

> Many a sullen storm
> For which coarse man seems much the fitter
> born,
> Rain'd on thy bed
> And harmless head.
>
> And now as fresh and cheerful as the light
> Thy little heart in early hymns doth sing
> Unto that Providence, Whose unseen arm
> Curb'd them, and cloth'd thee well and warm.

Mingled with this joy, assurance, and serenity in Part II there is still an intense note of spiritual distress. But Vaughan's anguish now is not so much for his shortcomings and sinfulness as for the frustration of this 'false' mortal existence to one 'love-sick' for home and the true life. Further, though he has found God, he suffers, as never before, the pangs of separation from Him, the intermittency of the vision, and the sense of obscuring veils hung between himself and the Divine Light. This is the lament we hear continually in Part II, in lines like:

> O Thy bright looks! Thy glance of love
> Shown, and but shown, me from above!
> Rare looks! that can dispense such joy
> As without wooing wins the coy,
> And makes him mourn, and pine, and die,
> Like a starv'd eaglet, for Thine eye.
> **'The Favour'**

There are also two smaller changes to be noticed in Part II. The first, already apparent in some of the last poems

of Part I like **'The World,' 'The Constellation,'** and **'Man,'** is a slight shift away from preoccupation with his own spiritual condition to that of mankind in general—a shift that can be seen, for instance, if we compare the two opening poems of each volume. Certainly in **'Regeneration'** Vaughan has an eye for the state of mankind, as in **'Ascension-Day'** he is much concerned about the reality and significance of Christ's rising for himself. But for all his ecstatic self-projection into the event he is describing, his **'Ascension-Day'** is, as a whole, a more objective poem than **'Regeneration.'**

Secondly, the poems in Part II are distinguished by a more evident spirit of humility and submissiveness. In particular—as we may see from the sequence **'The Ass,' 'The Hidden Treasure,'** and **'Childhood'**—Vaughan has abandoned the 'search' in so far as it involves intellectual probing, speculation, and argument—even, one may sometimes suspect, among the congenial ideas of hermetic philosophy. He is prepared to rest on faith instead of reason:

> Grant I may soft and lowly be,
> And mind those things I cannot see;
> Tie me to faith, though above reason;
> Who question Power, they speak treason:
> Let me, Thy ass, be only wise
> To carry, not search, mysteries.
> Who carries Thee, is by Thee led;
> Who argues, follows his own head.
> **"The Ass"**

A few random quotations might be used to prove anything; but the representative nature of those just given can be demonstrated to a certain extent by comparing some of the parallel poems of Parts I and II.

Consider, for example, the two **'Day of Judgment'** poems. The first, the utterance of a man newly awakened, or reawakened, to the prospect of spiritual damnation, is a violent, agitated piece of writing in which the main stress is on destruction and on the terror of 'Too late':

> Repentance there is out of date,
> And so is Mercy too.

With this appalling prospect in front of him Vaughan cries out for the penitential scourge of affliction. In the second poem, on the other hand—a lyric fairly summarised by its opening line,

> O day of life, of light, of love!

—all that troubled, almost frantic note has died away. Sin, and even the Judgment itself, is but lightly touched on; filled now with the thought of resurrection and 'all things new' instead of destruction, of the Divine love and mercy instead of punishment, Vaughan yearns for the day that he had once dreaded:

> O come! arise! shine! do not stay,
> Dearly lov'd day!
> The fields are long since white, and I
> With earnest groans for freedom cry.

In place of the flame, thunder, and blast of the first poem, we have an imagery dominated by light; and while Vaughan is still not prepared to entertain a conception of illimitable Divine mercy, he thinks of punishment falling on the Puritans for their 'forgeries' and 'impious wit' rather than on sinners like himself, 'all filth and obscene'.

Another revealing pair of poems is **'The Constellation'** (Part I) and **'The Star'** (Part II). In the first Vaughan uses the stars to paint, by way of contrast, a depressing picture of the state of man—his disobedience, distraction, spiritual sloth and blindness, his lusts, his errors leading to bloodshed, and his persecution of the true Church. The stars—and heaven—are very far away:

> Fair order'd lights—whose motion without
>   noise
>   Resembles those true joys
> Whose spring is on that hill, where you do grow,
>   And   we   here   taste   sometimes
>   below. . . .

In the Part II counterpart of this poem the stars, no longer remote but bound to earth in magnetic sympathy, intimate the hope of union between God and the soul. Joy and beauty, Vaughan now suggests, are possible even in this mortal life; and where in the previous poem his emphasis had been on the spiritual blindness of man—

> He gropes beneath here, and with restless care,
>   First makes, then hugs a snare;
> Adores dead dust, sets heart on corn and grass,
>   But seldom doth make heav'n his glass

—now, much more optimistically, he stresses man's spiritual potentialities:

> For where desire, celestial, pure desire,
> Hath taken root, and grows, and doth not tire,
>   There God a commerce states, and sheds
>   His secret on their heads.

There is one detail common to both poems that significantly underlines their difference. In the first Vaughan takes up a word much in use in Commonwealth days—'commission'—and, thinking of the Roundheads, gives it a pessimistic, ironic twist:

> But here, commission'd by a black self-will,
>   The sons the father kill.

The same word recurs in **'The Star,'** but it is disinfected now of all bitterness and harmonises with a fundamental optimistic faith instead of denying it:

> Yet, seeing all things that subsist and be,
> Have their commissions from Divinity. . . .

On the other hand, it would be unsound to generalise too widely from these contrasting pairs of poems. For one thing, while the two **'Day of Judgment'** poems are almost antithetical, there is also another poem on the same theme in Part I, **'The Dawning,'** that comes very close in spirit to the **'Day of Judgment'** of Part II. Again, among the remaining pairs of parallel poems (excluding the two on Death), it is only the pair dealing with the Bible that reflects anything of that general spiritual development of Vaughan that we have described. Where in his earlier sonnet, **'Holy Scriptures,'** he had been preoccupied with his 'hard heart', praising the Bible as a means to his personal salvation, in his second poem he sees his worst sinfulness in retrospect; and he now believes that his salvation has

been largely achieved, thanks in a great measure to the Scriptures:

> Fruition, union, glory, life,
> Thou didst lead to, and still all strife.
> Living, thou wert my soul's sure ease,
> And dying mak'st me go in peace.

However, there is little notable difference to be observed between **'The Holy Communion'** and **'The Feast,'** while **'The Retreat'** and **'Childhood'** both express the same Christian—not Wordsworthian—attitude to infancy. If anything, **'Childhood'** is a sadder, not to say more pessimistic, poem than **'The Retreat,'** for while the early, happy days of innocence, purity, and vision seem further away, unattainable even in imagination, Vaughan is now also much more conscious of the vanity of adult experience.

But, as we have already said, such notes as these in Part II do not seriously affect the general picture of Vaughan's spiritual development, which could never have followed a simple, continuous, geometric line. Part II is both a continuation from Part I and distinct from it, though we must not exaggerate the differences.

Cleanth Brooks   (essay date 1962)

SOURCE: "Henry Vaughan: Quietism and Mysticism," in *Essays in Honor of Esmond Linworth Marilla*, edited by Thomas Austin Kirby and William John Olive, Louisiana State University Press, 1970, pp. 3-26.

[*Brooks was the most prominent of the New Critics, an influential movement in American criticism which also included Allen Tate and John Crowe Ransom, and which paralleled a critical movement in England led by I. A. Richards, T. S. Eliot, and William Empson. Although the various New Critics did not subscribe to a single set of principles, all believed that a work of literature had to be examined as an object in itself through the close analysis of symbol, image, and metaphor. For the New Critics, literary works were not manifestations of ethics, sociology, or psychology, and could not be evaluated in the general terms of any nonliterary discipline. For Brooks, metaphor was the primary element of literary art, and the effect of that metaphor of primary importance. His most characteristic essays are detailed studies of metaphoric structure, particularly in poetry. In the following excerpt from the text of a lecture first given in a somewhat expanded form in 1962, Brooks offers an insightful reading of "The Retreate," "Night," and several of Vaughan's other poems, finding that though "in his celebration of childhood and innocence, [Vaughan] seems at many points to look forward to the poetry of the nineteenth century, in some of his nature poetry, and in his meditative quality, he is in fact very much closer to Donne and Herbert than he is to the Romantic poets of the Age of Wordsworth."*]

Henry Vaughan did not begin as a religious poet. His rather uneven secular verse reflects the themes and manners of the day, but it lacks conviction. The disaster of the English Civil Wars and the death of his beloved younger brother William, in 1648, moved him toward a more serious frame of mind. In 1650, he published ***Silex Scintillans,*** which is to be translated as "the sparkling flintstone"—that is, sparks of fire struck from the smitten flint. In 1655, in the second and enlarged edition of this book, Vaughan repudiates his earlier and less serious poetry, and in doing so, goes on to pay a deep personal tribute to George Herbert. He writes in his preface that "The first, that with any effectual success attempted a *diversion* of this foul and overflowing *stream* [of vain poetry], was the blessed man, Mr. *George Herbert,* whose holy *life* and *verse* gained many pious *converts,* (of whom I am the least). . . ." A few lines later in the preface he expresses the hope that he may be able to write, like "holy *Herbert,*" a *"true Hymn."*

As one might expect from these references, Vaughan's debt to Herbert turns out to be heavy, but that is not a matter on which I need to dwell here. For derivative as much of Vaughan is—from Herbert and from others—his best poems strike an authentic and original note. In such poems, matter that we can show him to have appropriated from Herbert, for instance, is quite transformed. Vaughan's poetry has its own distinctive character.

I should like, at this point, to mention one or two other general characteristics of Vaughan's poetry. He is a Platonist, but more specifically, he is a student of the Hermetic tradition. Vaughan's twin brother, Thomas, was deep in Hermetical lore and scholars have argued for the influence of such lore, descending, say, from Cornelius Agrippa and Paracelsus, on specific poems by Vaughan.

One other feature that tends to distinguish Vaughan from the other metaphysical poets is his mysticism. Donne and Herbert and Crashaw are not mystics. They deal with the mysteries of the Christian religion, to be sure, but they do not have visions—not even Donne's celebrated dream of his wife's appearing to him with their dead child in her arms, a dream which turned out to be ture, amounts to that. Donne, Herbert, and Crashaw are sensitive men, of great imaginative power, and deeply versed in Christian symbolism. But I do not think that it can be said of any of them that they wrote mystical poetry. In this matter I think that Vaughan differs with them, though this does not necessarily make him either a better or a worse poet.

I am aware that some have denied that Vaughan is a mystic. T. S. Eliot, I believe, questioned that view of him in an article published in 1927. But other writers, including recent students of his poetry, continue to call him a mystic. Mr. S. L. Bethell writes: "[Vaughan's] religious insight is intuitional, not ratiocinative. . . .

    I saw Eternity the other night,

he asserts, with the almost casual effrontery of a true mystic." Much depends upon what we are to understand by the term. I think that it is conceded by all that Vaughan probably never experienced the higher stages of mystical life, including the "dark night" of the soul or the final state of feeling oneself granted the Beatific Vision. But nearly all would also agree that Vaughan's poetry is a poetry of mystical moments and intuitions of a transcendental world. A recent book on Vaughan [E. C. Pettet's *Of Paradise and Light* (1960)] makes the point that his "poetry

often evokes a strange otherworldliness that marks it off from all the other religious verse of his age." I concur in this view, and it is in something like this sense that I refer to Vaughan's mysticism.

It is possible to argue that Vaughan's tendencies toward Platonism and neo-Platonism and Hermeticism and mysticism all point away from orthodoxy and may indeed be taken as signs of the disintegration of the orthodox tradition. Perhaps they are, but there is no doubt in my own mind that Vaughan remains a Christian; that he is, in the main doctrines at least, quite orthodox, and that his Christianity is a deeply felt and finally rather simple-minded Christianity. It seems to me a narrower and less sophisticated Christianity than that of Andrew Marvell. But my chief concern here is not to try to "place" Vaughan in the intellectual currents of the century or to assign to him a special niche in the framework of the theological and philosophical ideas of the age. My primary concern is with his poetry, and it is to the poems that I now mean to turn.

A good place to begin a reading of Vaughan is with his poem simply entitled **"Man."**

Man

> Weighing the stedfastness and state
> Of some mean things which here below reside,
> Where birds like watchful Clocks the noiseless date
>   And Intercourse of times divide,
> Where Bees at night get home and hive, and flowrs
>   Early, as wel as late,
> Rise with the Sun, and set in the same bowrs;
>   I would (said I) my God would give
> The staidness of these things to man! for these
> To his divine appointments ever cleave,
>   And no new business breaks their peace;
> The birds nor sow, nor reap, yet sup and dine,
>   The flowres without clothes live,
> Yet *Solomon* was never drest so fine.
>
>   Man hath stil either toyes, or Care,
> He hath no root, nor to one place is ty'd,
> But ever restless and Irregular
>   About this Earth doth run and ride,
> He knows he hath a home, but scarce knows where,
>   He says it is so far
> That he hath quite forgot how to go there.
>
>   He knocks at all doors, strays and roams,
> Nay hath not so much wit as some stones have
> Which in the darkest nights point to their homes,
>   By some hid sense their Maker gave;
> Man is the shuttle, to whose winding quest
>   And passage through these looms
> God order'd motion, but ordain'd no rest.

The first stanza of this poem, by the way, provides a kind of link with Andrew Marvell. You will remember the way in which Marvell's "Garden" ends with the floral sundial in the garden, the numerals of which are worked out in beds of flowers, where "th' industrious Bee" / Computes its time as well as we." In Vaughan's poem, nature too computes its time as well as we, but as in Marvell's poem, time as it affects the creatures of nature is not the harried and feverish time that man knows. Contemplating nature, Vaughan reflects that "birds like watchful Clocks the noiseless date / And Intercourse of times divide," and he observes how the bees know their seasons, when to return to "home and hive," and when to get up.

Noticing how well ordered nature is, the speaker of his poem wishes that God would give "The staidness of these things to man!" His yearning for the "staidness of things" is beautifully stated. As he puts it, "these / To his divine appointments ever cleave, / And no new business breaks their peace. . . ." Observe that the poet does not say that these creatures ever cleave to their appointments. If the appointments were theirs, presumably they would be as restless and confused as man is. But the creatures cleave to His divine appointments-appointments made by God himself. So placed in this divine ordering of affairs, "The birds, nor sow, nor reap, yet sup and dine, / The flowres without clothes live, / Yet *Solomon* was never drest so fine."

The reader may feel that "flowres without clothes live" is a kind of botched re-rendering of "Consider the lilies of the field, how they grow; they toil not, neither do they spin: And yet I say unto you, That even Solomon in all his glory was not arrayed like one of these." Yet I would urge that Vaughan's rendition is, in his own context, quite perfect. He is contrasting the divine order of nature with man's hurried and futile busyness, and his recasting the passage from the King James version into humdrum, even colloquial, idiom is, in the context of his poem, quite right.

One further comment on this passage in which the poet yearns to substitute for his state of restlessness as a human being the divine order of nature. It is a note that is struck in Marvell and Herbert, and of course it will sound later in English poetry. There is, for example, the wonderful gloss to Coleridge's *Rime of the Ancient Mariner* in which the Mariner, alone on the cursed ship, becalmed on a rotting sea, looks up in his agony to the moving heavens: "In his loneliness and fixedness he yearneth towards the journeying Moon, and the stars that still sojourn, yet still move onward; and everywhere the blue sky belongs to them, and is their appointed rest, and their native country and their own natural homes, which they enter unannounced, as lords that are certainly expected and yet there is a silent joy at their arrival." Coleridge places this magnificence in a context quite other than Vaughan's, and with the eye of the observer fixed upon the great lights of the heavens. Vaughan's speaker watches the divine appointments as worked out in terms of humbler things. Yet the situation is essentially the same. One is inclined to say that something like this is the perennial commentary upon nature that the Christian poet will always be constrained to make.

Vaughan's speaker now turns from his moment of contemplation to consider the state of man. Man hath, he says, "either toyes, or Care"—that is, either frivolous pleasures or the concerns of business. Unlike the flower, he "hath no root, nor to one place is ty'd." He "About this Earth doth run and ride, / He knows he hath a home, but scarce knows where. . . ." The contrast in this second in-

stance would point back to the birds or perhaps to the homing bees of the first stanza. Here is man, then, filled with a chronic homesickness, yet unable to find his way home. And so we come to the closing stanza:

> He knocks at all doors, strays and roams,
> Nay hath not so much wit as some stones have
> Which in the darkest nights point to their
>   homes,
> By some hid sense their Maker gave. . . .

Here of course Vaughan has in mind the medieval notion that even the mineral kingdom had its affections and revulsions. He is thinking particularly of the lodestone, which because of its magnetic power points to the north. The line "Which in the darkest nights point to their *homes*" [italics mine], however, presents some difficulties. In pointing north does the lodestone point to its true home? Is Vaughan alluding here to some Hermetical document that supports this view? Or is the line simply a highly compressed way of saying that even in darkness the lodestone can orient itself whereas man, even by broad daylight, cannot do as much? More probably, the last.

The poem comes to an end with a magnificent (if unoriginal) figure taken from the weaver's art. "Man is the shuttle, to whose winding quest / And passage through these looms / God order'd motion, but ordain'd no rest." The editors and commentators point quite rightly to Herbert's poem "The Pulley," as the source of this concluding line, and doubtless they are right. The influence of George Herbert's poetry is everywhere to be found in Vaughan. But the stanza is not in any disparaging sense derivative, and the image of the restless shuttle constantly flickering back and forth through the threads of the warp provides a powerful conclusion for the poem.

I would like to stress once more the attitude toward nature adopted by this poet. Like Herbert and like Marvell, Vaughan loves nature, and in some sense yearns toward its order and stability and unthinking, undoubting, unagonizing serenity. These poets of the seventeenth century find in nature evidence of God's workmanship—this is particularly true of Vaughan—and they find in the quieter and more harmonious moments of nature hints of the divine world which lies on beyond nature. But for all the charm that nature exerts upon these poets, they never for a moment entertain the notion that they may solve their problems simply by falling back upon nature or subsiding into nature. This modern-romantic view will make itself felt only at a later period. In fact, for the metaphysical poet, the highest compliment paid to man is that, though he is tied to the world of nature and yearns toward it, he is actually barred out from it, and must sojourn beyond it if he is to fulfill his own true nature. If being alienated from nature is in some sense to be thought of as a curse upon man, it also constitutes his greatest commendation: man cannot be simply a good and healthy innocent animal. He is destined for higher things and a different kind of life and must finally arrive at something much higher than the world of nature—or else must fall far below it.

After this digression, it is high time to turn back to others of Vaughan's poems. Let us look at **"The Dwelling-place."**

The Dwelling-place

What happy, secret fountain,
Fair shade, or mountain,
Whose undiscover'd virgin glory
Boasts it this day, though not in story,
Was then thy dwelling? did some cloud
Fix'd to a Tent, descend and shrowd
My distrest Lord? or did a star
Becken'd by thee, though high and far,
In sparkling smiles haste gladly down
To lodge light, and increase her own?
My dear, dear God! I do not know
What lodged thee then, nor where, nor how;
But I am sure, thou dost now come
Oft to a narrow, homely room,
Where thou too hast but the least part,
My God, I mean *my sinful heart.*

Vaughan appends to the poem a reference to the Gospel according to St. John (1:38-39). In these verses, two of the disciples of John the Baptist follow Jesus and when He asks them what they are looking for, they say, "Rabbi . . . where dwellest thou?" Jesus says to them: "Come and see. They came and saw where he dwelt, and abode with him that day: for it was about the tenth hour." The Gospel does not tell us, however, where Jesus was dwelling at that time, and it is this lack of information that allows the poet to spin out the conjectures that constitute his poem.

Where did Jesus abide at this time, the poet asks? "What happy, secret fountain, / Fair shade, or mountain, / Whose undiscover'd virgin glory / Boasts it this day, though not in story, / Was then thy dwelling?" The particular earthly spot that Jesus occupied could never, down to this day, the poet feels, have forgotten that it had once so glorious a guest, and boasts the fact still, "though not in story," Vaughan adds, since neither the Scriptures nor any legend preserves its name.

The poet further speculates as to whether, seeing that Jesus is the Lord of creation, some cloud did not descend to furnish a kind of tent for him, or whether some star "Becken'd by thee, though high and far, / In sparkling smiles [hastened] gladly down / To lodge light and increase her own?"

I wish that Mr. L. C. Martin, Vaughan's editor, had given us a note on the phrase "lodge light." I am not sure that I understand it. Presumably some star, answering the beckoning finger of Christ, hurried down to provide, not a lodging place for him but to serve in his lodging place as a kind of taper—that is, to "lodge" or "provide" a receptacle for light. In any case, the last part of the line "and increase her own" is an obvious allusion to the fact that the star in the presence of the sun of righteousness, would receive more light *from* Him than it could furnish *to* Him.

But with line 11, the poet suspends his conjectures, admitting that he does not know "What lodged thee then, nor where, nor how. . . ." What he is sure of is that nowadays Christ often comes to a poorer, more narrow, and more homely room than any that ever lodged Him on the occasion of which St. John wrote; for now in the new dispensation He comes to the poet's own sinful heart, a place

where the poet remorsefully acknowledges "thou too hast but the least part. . . ."

Obviously this poem of Vaughan echoes George Herbert's "Decay." The third stanza of that poem reads as follows:

But now thou dost thy self immure and close
In some one corner of a feeble heart;
Where yet both Sinne and Satan, thy old foes
Do pinch and straiten thee, and use much art
To gain thy thirds and little part.

The derivation of Vaughan's poem—or at least of this part of it—is thus obvious, but how different the two poems are in tone!

If in **"The Dwelling-place,"** as in so many other poems by Vaughan, the world of natural objects shines with a special light and the poet handles those objects with a kind of joy, still he never regards nature of itself divine. The poem entitled **"Quickness"** will furnish support for this remark.

Quickness

False life! a foil and no more, when
　　　Wilt thou be gone?
Thou foul deception of all men
That would not have the true come on.

Thou art a Moon-like toil; a blinde
　　　Self-posing state;
A dark contest of waves and winde;
A meer tempestuous debate.

Life is a fix'd, discerning light,
　　　A knowing Joy;
No chance, or fit; but ever bright,
And calm and full, yet doth not cloy.

'Tis such a blissful thing, that still
　　　Doth vivifie,
And shine and smile, and hath the skill
To please without Eternity.

Thou art a toylsom Mole, or less,
　　　A moving mist;
But life is, what none can express,
A quickness, which my God hath kist.

True, what comes in for reprehension in this poem is not nature but "false life." Still, one can notice a very different feeling for the various objects of nature as they are presented in this poem. False life, according to the poet, is a blind "self-posing state." "Pose" is here used in the old sense of "question," and "self-posing" would be self-questioning—that is, this life in its blindness does not know what it is. But this abstract statement is worked out in a number of concrete images drawn largely from the sea. False life is a "Moon-like toil," a labor which gets nowhere, an action like the tides that come in over the beach and then go out again, only to repeat themselves endlessly. This toil is moon-like not only because the moon is the very symbol of change, but because the moon actually controls the changing tides. False life is also, the poet says, "A dark contest of waves and winde." Vaughan does not go on to say, quoting Shakespeare, that it amounts to "sound and fury, signifying nothing," but this, of course, is the meaning of Vaughan's own figure, and that figure is neatly capped with the last line of the stanza, a line which is partially statement, partially a continuation of the wind-wave figure: false life is "A meer tempestuous debate."

All of this is said, of course, of that life which men in their blindness—Vaughan uses the term "foul deception"—take to be true life. But true life—Vaughan at the beginning of stanza three is content to call it simply "life"—is not moving, but fixed; it is discerning, and not "self-posing," that is, self-questioning. On the contrary, it is a "knowing Joy." True life is conscious of itself and knows itself as joy. True life does not alter with the waxing and waning which we associate with mortal change, but is "calm and full." And yet it does not, like most static and motionless things as we know them in this world, "cloy." Its calm does not mean stagnation and insipidity.

With the last stanza the poet addresses false life once more: "Thou art," he says, "a toylsom Mole, or less/A moving mist." Again, the images connect false life with motion and with blindness—either with things lacking sight like moles or with things which shroud the sight of others, like "moving mist[s]." But life itself is inexpressible-though the poet makes one more effort to express it by terming it *A quickness, which my God hath kist.* The word "quickness"—which furnishes the title of the poem, of course, is here very rich. "Quick" originally meant "living"—in the Apostle's Creed the "quick and the dead" are, of course, the living and the dead. But very early the term took on shadings of its modern meaning-for an obvious test of life is the presence of movement, and so to be quick came to mean speedy in movement. (In the King James version the adverb *quickly* regularly means "rapidly.")

Throughout Vaughan's poem, as we have already seen, false life has been associated with movement, with the moon-like toil and the moving mist, and true life has been identified with that which is fixed, calm, and full—that which, being perfect, cannot suffer alteration and change. One is tempted to say that in this poem the word "quickness" as mere movement becomes associated with "false life" since movement without God's sanction and blessing is self-confounding. "Quickness" indeed becomes "life" only when kissed by the Almighty.

One of Vaughan's most celebrated poems is **"The Retreate."**

The Retreate

Happy those early dayes! when I
Shin'd in my Angell-infancy.
Before I understood this place
Appointed for my second race,
Or taught my soul to fancy ought
But a white, Celestiall thought,
When yet I had not walkt above
A mile, or two, from my first love,
And looking back (at that short space,)
Could see a glimpse of his bright-face;
When on some *gilded Cloud,* or *flowre*
My gazing soul would dwell an houre,
And in those weaker glories spy
Some shadows of eternity;
Before I taught my tongue to wound

My Conscience with a sinfull sound,
Or had the black art to dispence
A sev'rall sinne to ev'ry sence,
But felt through all this fleshly dresse
Bright *shooes* of everlastingnesse.
    O how I long to travell back
And tread again that ancient track!
That I might once more reach that plaine,
Where first I left my glorious traine,
From whence th'Inlightned spirit sees
That shady City of Palme trees;
But (ah!) my soul with too much stay
Is drunk, and staggers in the way.
Some men a forward motion love,
But I by backward steps would move,
And when this dust falls to the urn
In that state I came return.

When Vaughan, after almost complete neglect throughout the eighteenth century, was revived in the nineteenth, one of the things which first struck his readers was his resemblance to Wordsworth, and particularly the resemblance between his **"Retreate"** and Wordsworth's great "Intimations Ode." The question of whether Wordsworth knew **"The Retreate"** and whether his own poem was influenced by it are matters that have been debated now for a good many years. My own opinion, for what it is worth, is that it is very unlikely that Wordsworth knew **"The Retreate,"** or at least that he could have known it early enough for it to have influenced the "Intimations Ode." The resemblances between the poems can more plausibly be accounted for by supposing that the two poets drew upon the same general traditional sources.

Yet Vaughan's poem will probably remind most modern readers of Wordsworth's "Ode," and I think that the resemblances and the differences to be noted can be useful in putting Vaughan's poem in clearer perspective. For one thing, the theme of the soul's preexistence is for Wordsworth primarily a metaphor. You will remember that Wordsworth, in one of his notes on the "Ode," repudiates any literal belief in the soul's pre-existence. But Vaughan, so far as one can tell, did believe in it quite literally. Thus, the beginning of the poem constitutes one of the clearest instances of Vaughan's making use of Hermetic lore. Compare with the opening lines of **"The Retreate"** the following passage from *The Hermetica* (Libellus 10 15 b.): "Look at the soul of the child, my son, the soul that has not come to accept his separation from its source; for its body is still small, and has not yet grown to its full bulk. How beautiful throughout is such a soul as that! It is not yet fouled by the bodily passions; it is still hardly detached from the soul of the Kosmos. But when the body has increased in bulk, and has drawn the soul down into its material mass, it generates oblivion; and so the soul separates itself from the Beautiful and Good, and no longer partakes of that; and through this oblivion the soul becomes evil."

The Hermetic material, however, is used here by Vaughan in a completely Christian context. For he is also remembering St. Mark (10: 14-15), where Jesus says: "Suffer the little children to come unto me, and forbid them not: for of such is the kingdom of God. Verily I say unto you, whosoever shall not receive the kingdom of God as a little child, he shall not enter therein." The phrase "my second race" in line 4 perhaps requires a note. For one, who, like Vaughan, believes in the pre-existence of the soul, the first race has to do with the soul's course before it is born into a human body; the second race is that of its earthly existence; and its third race will be its life in eternity after death.

Marvell in his "Garden" gives us a "green Thought in a green Shade." Vaughan, just as characteristically, presents us in line 6 with a "white, Celestiall thought." In line 8, "my first love" is a phrase which is taken from the book of *Revelation* (2:4). The church at Ephesus is commended for its works and its labor and its patience, but it is also chidden in the following words: "I have somewhat against thee, because thou has left thy first love."

Lines 11 through 20 are perhaps the best-known lines that Vaughan ever wrote. Here he expresses a genuine love of nature, but he loves it because he can read into it some reflection of the eternity from which his soul has come and glories it remembers: "When on some *gilded Cloud, or flowre* / My gazing soul would dwell an houre, / And in those weaker glories spy / Some shadows of eternity. . . ." But as the soul of the child moves further and further from its dayspring in the east, and more and more miles from its first love, it becomes stained with sin. Now, soiled and degraded, it yearns for that state of innocence in which it would still feel "through all this fleshly dresse / Bright *shootes* of everlastingnesse."

The soul is homesick for its original state and is anxious to return to it. If some men love a forward motion, the man who speaks in this poem would prefer to move by backward steps, "And when this dust falls to the urn /In that state I came return." The "shady City of Palme trees" (line 26) is, as Mr. Pettet tells us, Jericho. But in order to understand what is going on here, we need to be reminded of the context from which the phrase is taken. Chapter 34 of the Book of Deuteronomy has to do with Moses's going up into the mountain of Pisgah over against Jericho and the Lord's showing him from this vantage point the Promised Land, to the borders of which he has led his people, but into which he himself will not be allowed to enter. In **"The Retreat"** Vaughan's speaker is a kind of Moses in reverse. He early had his sight of the promised land, and is now going away from it, not approaching it. Moving away from it, he has gone out into the wilderness, having left behind his glorious train. Now he would fain return to have sight of "That shady City of Palme trees" once more.

In a sense, **"The Retreate"** is a rather slight poem, and I can imagine some moderns grumbling at it because for them it will represent certain morbidly regressive tendencies. But one ought to distinguish the child-like harmony and integrity for which the poet yearns and mere childishness, which is something else. In any case, the longing to return to childhood is not an obsessive theme for Vaughan. Few of his poems voice it, and in this rather slight and simple poem, the theme receives no questionable elaboration. The poem says what it wants to say with tact and a sense of proportion.

"The Retreate" is not nearly so ambitious a poem as Wordsworth's "Intimations Ode." It does not even deal with the same problem. Wordsworth's more elaborate poem has to do with a situation that we feel is peculiarly modern: the difficulty of maintaining some kind of continuity between the vision that the poet experienced as a child and his present state as an adult. The veteran sojourner in this life seems to have lost something infinitely precious, something which plainly he cannot hope to recapture but which nevertheless he refuses to dismiss as having been simply a childish illusion. Wordsworth's problem is complicated by the fact that the world about which he writes has been so thoroughly drained of sacramental sanctity that his first problem is how to vindicate that sense of sanctity and holiness (or something comparable to it) in the face of the analytic Cartesian and Newtonian rationalism that has succeeded it. I have had my say about Wordsworth's poem elsewhere and shall not discuss it further here except to reiterate that some knowledge of Wordsworth's "Ode" can do much to throw into sharp relief the contrasting "situation" of our poet of the latter seventeenth century.

Vaughan's poem shows the advantages held by the poet whose sense of the transcendent God has not been seriously disturbed and whose problems as a man tend to be the usual moral problems of how to combat one's vanity, sloth, and pride, and whose problems as a poet tend to be the usual rhetorical problems of how to make vivid and significant that which is too often smudged and dulled by custom. These are sufficiently formidable problems for a religious poet, but they are problems of a different order from those that beset Wordsworth.

Vaughan's masterpiece, in my opinion, is his poem entitled **"The Night."**

The Night

Through that pure *Virgin-shrine*,
That sacred vail drawn o'r thy glorious noon
That men might look and live as Glo-worms shine,
    And face the Moon:
    Wise *Nicodemus* saw such light
    As made him know his God by night.

Most blest believer he!
Who in that land of darkness and blinde eyes
Thy long expected healing wings could see,
    When thou didst rise,
    And what can never more be done,
    Did at mid-night speak with the Sun!

O who will tell me, where
He found thee at that dead and silent hour!
What hallow'd solitary ground did bear
    So rare a flower,
    Within whose sacred leafs did lie
    The fulness of the Deity.

No mercy-seat of gold,
No dead and dusty *Cherub*, nor carv'd stone,
But his own living works did my Lord hold
    And lodge alone;
    Where *trees* and *herbs* did watch and peep
    And wonder, while the *Jews* did sleep.

Dear night! this worlds defeat;

The stop to busie fools; cares check and curb;
The day of Spirits; my souls calm retreat
    Which none disturb!
  Christs progress, and his prayer time;
    The hours to which high Heaven doth chime.

Gods silent, searching flight:
When my Lords head is fill'd with dew, and all
His locks are wet with the clear drops of night;
    His still, soft call;
  His knocking time; The souls dumb watch.
  When Spirits their fair kinred catch.

Were all my loud, evil days
Calm and unhaunted as is thy dark Tent,
Whose peace but by some *Angels* wing or voice
    Is seldom rent;
  Then I in Heaven all the long year
  Would keep, and never wander here.

But living where the Sun
Doth all things wake, and where all mix and tyre
Themselves and others, I consent and run
    To ev'ry myre,
  And by this worlds ill-guiding light,
  Erre more then I can do by night.

There is in God (some say)
A deep, but dazzling darkness; As men here
Say it is late and dusky, because they
    See not all clear;
  O for that night! where I in him
  Might live invisible and dim.

Like **"The Dwelling-place"** this poem begins with a speculation set in motion by a passage in the Gospel according to St. John. In Chapter 3, verse 2, we are told that Nicodemus "came to Jesus by night, and said unto him, Rabbi, we know that thou art a teacher, from God: for no man can do these miracles that thou doest, except God be with him." Characteristically, however, what caught Vaughan's eye was the first part of the verse, "came to Jesus by night," and Vaughan confines his poetic speculations to that circumstance. Why was the night an appropriate time for Nicodemus to meet his Master, and why is it now an appropriate time for the soul to find its way to God?

As thoroughly as any other person of his time, Vaughan was aware that Christ is the sun of righteousness and that God is light. It is by a kind of sanctified perversity, therefore, that he tries to find in night, not a negation of God but a special and appropriate means for apprehending God's divine light. In taking on human flesh, God has drawn a sacred veil over his "glorious noon." But it is a veil: it only dims the light, it does not obliterate it. The epithet **"Virginshrine"** is a reference, of course, to the fact that the flesh that constitutes the veil of the shrine came from the Virgin Mary.

The third line of the stanza is difficult and I don't think that any of the commentators have given us much help. Mr. E. C. Pettet argues that the glowworms "shine because they 'face' the moon: when the moon has gone, their light is dead. In the same way men, worms also in their insignificance, 'live' only when they look upon their 'glorious noon' and sun of Christ." This, in my opinion, is far-

fetched and does not answer to the purpose. I think it more plausible to say that the glowworms by daylight cannot be seen and thus cannot be said to shine at all. If men's looking and living are somehow equated with the glowworm's shining (see 1. 3), then it makes sense to say that men, confronted by a lesser light, can live and shine just as glowworms can continue to shine and yet "face" the moon. So interpreted, lines 3 and 4 then follow on and develop the basic simile about Christ's glorious noon being veiled for man's benefit. This is precisely the meaning which Petter rejects, writing that "the sense that man can only look on the Divine light when it is mercifully shrouded . . . cannot be the intended meaning" of the glowworm simile.

Lines 5 and 6 of the first stanza make the point that even "Through that pure *Virgin-Shrine*" Nicodemus was able to see such light "As made him know his God by night." The divine light, rendered supportable because veiled, even so reveals itself to the blessed believer as divine. The implication of the second stanza is that since Nicodemus had recognized his Savior despite the fact that he lived in a "land of darkness and blinde eyes," the darkness of night constituted no hindrance at all to his recognition.

"Thy long expected healing wings could see" is a quotation from the Book of Malachi (4:2): "But unto you that fear my name shall the Sun of righteousness arise with healing in his wings." The second stanza concludes with the paradox which Crashaw uses in his "Nativity Hymn," and which was a favorite with all the metaphysical poets: One of the miracles of the Incarnation is that Nicodemus could "at mid-night speak with the Sun!"

Stanza 3 continues the kind of speculation with which Vaughan occupies himself in **"The Dwelling-place."** He wonders what was the particular spot in which Nicodemus found his Lord—what hallowed bit of ground could bear "So rare a flower." Evidently the poet is sure that it was not in the Temple or indeed in a building of any sort that Nicodemus encountered Christ, for in the fourth stanza we find Vaughan developing the idea that it was proper that the Lord should "lodge alone" among "his own living works," the trees and the herbs, which watched him with wonder "while the Jews did sleep." The poet emphasizes the contrast between the night scene in some kind of grove or garden and that inside the synagogue, with its "mercy-seat of gold" and its "dead and dusty *Cherub* . . . [of] carv'd stone."

Mr. Petter warns us not to interpret this stanza as an "expression of the modern belief that God may be worshipped as truly in the countryside as in church. Deep as Vaughan's regard for Nature was, it never betrayed him into this heresy." I dare say that the point is well taken, and perhaps the warning is necessary; on the other hand, there is no gainsaying the slighting quality of the reference to the "dead and dusty *Cherub!*" A cherub's angelic flesh ought to be all luminosity and ethereality, completely instinct with vibrant life. But such angelic flesh reduced to carved stone, arrested and static, and now covered with a graying film of dust—all this amounts to a contradiction in terms. Vaughan has put brilliantly the contrast between the shrine provided by the Virgin, the living human flesh that encloses the divine Lord, and the shrine of all too solid wood and stone which, if it is in some sense the work of the Lord, is surely not one of his "living" works.

Stanza 5, through a series of bold epithets, turns the night into the day of spirits. It is the day of spirits because it is the time for meditation and prayer. The night is so because it is the world's defeat—Vaughan is evidently thinking of some such context as the world, the flesh, and the devil—and because it is the "stop to busie fools," whose practical business, when measured by the standards of truth, turns out to be simply a kind of foolishness.

In Stanza 6 the visitation of God is set forth vividly and beautifully. The poet has incorporated a verse from the book of Revelation (3:20): "Behold, I stand at the door, and knock: if any man hear my voice, and open the door, I will come in to him, and will sup with him, and he with me." With this passage is combined a reminiscence of the *Song of Songs* (5:2): "I sleep, but my heart waketh: it is the voice of my beloved that knocketh, saying, Open to me, my sister, my love, my dove, my undefiled: for my head is filled with dew, and my locks with the drops of the night."

The last line of the stanza—"When Spirits their fair kin-red catch"—is very interesting, though the editors and commentators, so far as I know, have failed to gloss it. The line may have in it some echo of Vaughan's Hermetical learning. But whether it has or not, the line does add an important note to the poem. Man's soul is of heaven. The celestial spirits are its kindred. It is in the night season, if the soul will watch prayerfully and silently—I am alluding here to Vaughan's phrase, "The souls dumb watch"—it may "catch" its celestial kindred. The word "catch" as used here is richly suggestive: doesit mean catch hold of them, or merely catch sight of them? Perhaps it does not matter.

Such an interpretation of this last line of Stanza 6 would seem to be corroborated by the stanza that follows. Vaughan here imagines the night as a great tent, the canopy of which is seldom torn—"rent" is his word—except by some angel's wing or angel's voice. The suggestion here is that of spirits from heaven who at this time may pierce to earth through the sheltering tent of night. How faint and delicate would be the sound of tearing when the fabric of night, the most diaphonous silken fabric that one can imagine, is "rent" by an angel's wing!

The poet goes on to say that if all of his "loud" and "evil" days were as calm as this dark tent, then he would remain "in Heaven all the long year." For the night season, as Vaughan interprets it here, is a kind of heaven. What breaks the silence of night—loudness is here equated with evil—and what dissipates night's sheltering tent, is the sun. The sun-lit world is inimical to spirituality; yet it is the world dominated by the sun that the poet is forced to inhabit, where, as he puts it, "the Sun / Doth all things wake." It is also a world where "all mix and tyre / Themselves and others. . . ." The poet's phrasing here is obscure and the editors and commentators are not of much help. Martin gives nothing. Pettet conjectures that "Mix' may carry the notion that all created things are mortal be-

cause they are impure mixtures of the elements," but surely this interpretation is wide of the mark. The basic idea is the paradox that the mortal world as lighted up by the sun is an obscure world where the poet goes astray far more than he ever could by night. It is tempting, therefore, to say that "where all mix" means where all objects blur out and lose their firm outlines, mingling themselves with each other, and that "tire" means cloak themselves and other objects with disguises. In a world so confused by the sun's "ill-guiding light," it is difficult not to go astray. "Tire" in the sense of "attire" is certainly a possible meaning, duly vouched for by the *Oxford English Dictionary*. But I submit this interpretation with proper hesitation. The meaning of the lines may simply be "where all things lose their firm outlines (mix) and wear out themselves and others."

Vaughan achieves a fine climax in his last stanza by importing the idea of darkness into the nature of God himself. "There is in God (some say) / A deep, but dazling darkness." We have a pretty good idea who the "some" are who say this. Dionysius the Areopagite writes that "The divine light is an inaccessible darkness which God is said to inhabit, . . . invisible, because of the outpouring effusion of supernatural light." Vaughan may have known this passage at first hand or perhaps he got at it through his brother's "Lumen de lumine," in which Thomas Vaughan writes, "That which is above all degree of intelligence is a certain infinite, inaccessible fire or light. Dionysius calls it Divine Darkness, because it is invisible and incomprehensible."

Vaughan has been quite right to make his reference indefinite—even if the only consideration be the tone of the poem. Vaughan does not venture to say with first-hand knowledge that God's divine light is a deep but dazzling darkness. He merely reports that some say that it is, with the implication that he could easily believe it to be true, for confronted with the divine light, men's eyes would be dazzled, and they would report that they saw only darkness. But if there is such a darkness in God, he would ask nothing better than to be swallowed up in it.

The closing lines, by the way, seem to echo the third line of the poem, in which God has veiled his glorious noon in order that "men might look and live as Glo-worms shine, / And face the moon." It is in something of that spirit that the speaker now would be content to live "invisible and dim." The last line, by the way, is used by T.S. Eliot in his poem "Mr. Eliot's Sunday Morning Service": "Under the penitential gates /Sustained by staring Seraphim / Where the souls of the devout / Burn invisible and dim."

Henry Vaughan is at his best a very powerful poet, one thoroughly worthy of holding a place among his peers, the other great devotional poets of the century. Though in his celebration of childhood and innocence, he seems at many points to look forward to the poetry of the nineteenth century, in some of his nature poetry, and in his meditative quality, he is in fact very much closer to Donne and Herbert than he is to the Romantic poets of the Age of Wordsworth. The late S. L. Bethell puts the matter very accurately, I think. He writes that "Vaughan had the supreme advantage of being a poet in the metaphysical tradition—and one who had served a pretty arduous apprenticeship in secular verse. The type of poetry favoured by the metaphysicals provided an excellent medium for the expression of mystical states and devotional aspirations. After the attitudinizing Petrarchans, Donne had encouraged honesty: there is quitei a modern 'toughness' about the metaphysicals, and they seem to have enjoyed being occasionally shocking. But, also, they were gentlemen: they knew their manners and practised a restraint which presented a combination of dignity and ease . . . . In such company devotional poets were discouraged from exhibiting the mealymouthed piety and sentimental extravagance which are the tribe's besetting sins."

In this passage, as we see, Bethell moves from some specific comments on Vaughan to a general account of metaphysical devotional poetry, and in that account I think that he also provides an accurate and useful summary. He says with reference to the metaphysicals: "Imagery could be drawn from the most recondite or the most commonplace sources: there was no need for it to be beautiful—only effective. Colloquial speech and everyday imagery are particularly important to the religious poet, whose problem is to convey the reality and immediacy of an experience which has not taken place in the material world. . . . The metaphysical manner makes religious experience quite uncomfortably real. . . ."

This is well said. It is because of this sense of reality in spiritual experience that we value the metaphysical poets. If I may be allowed to utter a paradox somewhat in the metaphysical manner, their poetry is *comforting* to the earnest Christian precisely because it is at times *uncomfortably* real. It is a poetry that carries conviction.

R. A. Durr   (essay date 1962)

SOURCE: "Appendix C: Poetry and Mysticism," in *On the Mystical Poetry of Henry Vaughan,* Cambridge, Mass.: Harvard University Press, 1962, pp. 123-38.

[*In the following excerpt, Durr illuminates the nature of the mystic experience and its relationship to reality, and offers high praise of Vaughan as one of the few individuals in human history who have possessed the faculties and genius to formulate the mystical vision of Reality "in words of poetic effect."*]

When it happens that a man breaks through—is brought through—the narrow confines of his conventional nature, his ego, or "outer man," when perhaps suddenly, in the twinkling of an eye, the gates of his perception hitherto set to admit only such data as wear the badge of "a priori" definition open toward their full dimension, "then comes the light!" Then he enters the land of the living, Reality flows in, and he sees that "things," *Natura naturata,* are the products of man's abstracting intellect, and that Nature, the manifold universe, is the single and glorious signature of the Divine Life that informs it. Thereafter his life is in the country of the Real, and what he seeks to depict through his use of the language of symbolism is always that numinous region, Reality unnamed and unnameable. To be sure, he looks at the same tree we do, but for him

it is realized, and so transfigured, for he sees the light of eternity shining through and composing its very life. Our tree is unreal only insofar as it is a delimitation and frustration of "tree's" real being and glory, "sicuti est." But for the seer, as for Whitman, "a leaf of grass is no less than the journey-work of the stars." Things become, in their *istigheit,* as Eckhart would say, surcharged with "meanings" not other than, but transcendent of, their materiality, or, more exactly, their finitude. For him, as for Thomas Traherne, "Eternity was manifest in the Light of Day, and something infinite behind everything appeared . . ."

No art can reproduce the experience of life itself; it is never in that sense real. But Vaughan's poetry *is* able to give us an experience, of the kind we call esthetic, correspondent to what he underwent: it has a power, a life of its own, born of those illimitable and nearly intangible interrelationships of image, diction, tone, rhythm, and so forth, to the effect of which we assign the name of poetry.

Both St. Teresa in her prose and verse and Vaughan in his poetry are concerned with a unique and profound human event, but while the saint has drawn us a helpful map, often lovely in line and color, of the place she had been, the poet has shown us, even though in a glass darkly, something *of,* as well as something *like,* that region itself. St. Teresa's prose refers always to the event outside itself; Vaughan's poetry, though it, too, has reference to that event in life, is in itself an event, not identical with, but symbolical of, the actual experience, partaking "of the reality which it renders intelligible." We must settle for something like Susanne Langer's "symbolic transformation of experience," for while a clear perception of the nature of the transformation—*how* the effect of poetry is different from the experience it is about—may not readily be had, still we now understand that a symbol is more than a sign, its relation to the experience it represents more than analogous (insofar as "analogy" denotes only a set of resemblances between the attributes of things fundamentally disparate). By choosing that term we acknowledge that Vaughan's poetry is itself an experience, an act, and not merely a system of counters for an experience. We assert that our interest is in Vaughan's mystical poetry—not simply in his mysticism nor yet again only in his artistry. We cannot know the dancer from the dance.

But the poet and the mystic do have something in common that is of the essence. It is not—as with Vaughan, for example—that the poet necessarily writes out of a transcendent experience, though much great poetry does so emanate. It is rather that the poet (taking the term in its broader application to all creative artists) and the mystic are they who break through, or are brought through, the crusts of convention, the veils of maya—all that vast configuration of assumptions, artifacts, and categories, that we mean by culture; break through and by the excellence they own face existence with an open mind. They are the ones who know the thing itself; they build, sometimes by first destroying, our human world and find our meaning in the *prima materia* of experienced Reality. They are turned to immediate Reality; we are turned to them. That is why the true poet and the genuine mystic speak with authority, and not as the scribes. They do not need to concern themselves with what this or that important person has affirmed; they turn themselves to what they have known and speak from that. We depend on them not as we have come to depend upon the technician, for our ease and convenience, but for the life that is not fed by bread alone.

What I have said above sounds hyperbolic, but I am not attempting a thorough analysis of the relation between poetry and mysticism, an analysis that would call for many qualifications, explanations, and developments—and at great length. I want only to intimate more fully what would otherwise have existed in this essay as assumption. Yet it is necessary to enter into at least one qualification here, for what I have said so far pertains more nearly and fully to the great geniuses of the religious life than to the poets, though in its broadest sense it does pertain to them. The mystic's vision is ultimate; he has known Reality; the poet's may be ultimate, and then the lines of demarcation between them are more difficult to draw (though obviously one has to do with the poet's superior powers of communication). But more often the poet has not penetrated to the very essence of being and knowing. His vision is normally tangential and fugitive in comparison, but it is a genuine vision: he has the strength and genius to see with his own eyes and proclaim the truth of what he sees. But . . . most fundamentally important and valuable, as I see it, is the truth the religious genius whom we call a mystic has discovered; for what he knows is not partial and peripheral and subject to change; it is not one man's opinion or "view of life"; it is all there is to know, and all we need to know. When a vision of this kind combines with large powers of expression the highest poetry results.

To me, Henry Vaughan was one of the very rare men in human history who, having been graced with intuitions of Reality, possessed both the genius and the training that enabled him to formulate his vision in words of poetic effect.

Louis L. Martz   (essay date 1963)

SOURCE: "Henry Vaughan: The Caves of Memory," in *The Paradise Within: Studies in Vaughan, Traherne, and Milton,* Yale University Press, 1964, pp. 1-31.

[*Martz is an American educator and prominent scholar of English and American poetry. In the following excerpt from an essay originally published in* PMLA *in 1963, he examines Vaughan's poetry in the first edition of* Silex Scintillans *finding it to reflect the Augustinian concept of interior "illumination."*]

Modes of Communion

In the year 1649 Richard Crashaw died in exile at Loreto, a little more than six months after his master King Charles died on the scaffold at Whitehall. An era had ended for English political and religious institutions, and also for English religious poetry. With Crashaw's death the power of liturgical and eucharistic symbols died away in English poetry of the seventeenth century: the symbols earlier celebrated by Southwell, Alabaster, Donne, and Herbert. These poets had their doctrinal differences, and I do not

wish to minimize those differences; but they had something more in common: a devotion to the mysteries of the Passion and to a liturgy that served to celebrate those mysteries. All five of these poets entered into holy orders; all five would have agreed with George Herbert's vision of "The Agonie":

> Who knows not Love, let him assay
> And taste that juice, which on the crosse a pike
> Did set again abroach; then let him say
>   If ever he did taste the like.
> Love is that liquour sweet and most divine,
> Which my God feels as bloud; but I, as wine.

In 1650 Andrew Marvell wrote his famous "Horatian Ode" in honor of the man who

> Could by industrious Valour climbe
> To ruine the great Work of Time,
>   And cast the Kingdome old
>   Into another Mold.

And in the same year appeared the first edition of Henry Vaughan's *Silex Scintillans,* a volume that, along with Milton's miscellaneous *Poems* of 1645, marks the emergence of the layman as a central force in religious poetry of the period. Vaughan's volume, though written by a staunch Royalist and Anglican, nevertheless stands as a sign of a profound mutation in human affairs. Without neglecting the highly individual qualities of Vaughan's vision, I should like here to consider his volume of 1650 as the symbol of a vital transformation in the religious outlook of the age.

It is important to look closely at *Silex Scintillans,* 1650. For Vaughan's enlarged volume of 1655, with its second part and its greatly expanded opening matter, presents a modified outlook, a less consistent fabric, and a weaker body of poetry, despite the fact that seven or eight of Vaughan's finest poems did not appear until the 1655 edition. The common charges against Vaughan's poetry— that his poems often begin with a flash of power, but then dwindle off into tedious rumination, that he works by fits and starts, that he cannot sustain a whole poem—these charges find their chief support in Book II of *Silex,* which reveals many signs of a failing inspiration. There is a greater reliance on the ordinary topics of piety, especially in the many labored poems based on Biblical texts; there is a marked decline in the frequency of Herbertian echoes, and a corresponding rise in the use of conventional couplet-rhetoric, after the manner of the Sons of Ben Jonson: a school to which Vaughan showed his allegiance in his undistinguished volume of secular poems in 1646. At the same time the crabbed and contentious Preface of 1655 strikes a tone quite out of line with the dominant mode of the poems in the 1650 volume, here bound up as the first "book" of what has now become a religious miscellany. But the volume of 1650 is a whole, like Herbert's *Temple;* and indeed there are many signs that the volume was deliberately designed as a sequel, a counterpart, and a tribute to Herbert's book.

Vaughan's subtitle is exactly the same as Herbert's: "Sacred Poems and Private Ejaculations"; but the main title represents a vast difference, enforced, in the 1650 volume alone, by the engraved title page presenting the emblem

Engraved title page of Silex Scintillans (1650). *Depicted here, God's wrath enflames and softens the stonelike human heart.*

of the Flashing Flint—the stony heart weeping, bleeding and flaming from the hand of God that strikes direct from the clouds, steel against flint. Furthermore, a careful look at this flinty heart will reveal something that I never noticed until my friend Evelyn Hutchinson, examining this title page with his scientific eye, asked, "Do you see a human face peering forth from within the heart?" It is certainly so: a man within can be clearly seen through an opening in the heart's wall. And facing this we have, again in the 1650 volume only, an intimate confession in the form of a Latin poem, explaining the emblem. Perhaps a literal version of this cryptic Latin will show how essential this poem and this emblem are for an understanding of the 1650 volume as a whole:

> *The Author's Emblem (concerning himself)*
> You have often touched me, I confess, without a wound, and your *Voice,* without a voice, has often sought to counsel me; your diviner breath has encompassed me with its calm motion, and in vain has cautioned me with its sacred murmur. I was deaf and dumb: a *Flint:* You (how great care you take of your own!) try to revive another way, you change the Remedy; and now

angered you say that *Love* has no power, and you prepare to conquer force with *Force,* you come closer, you break through the *Rocky* barrier of my heart, and it is made *Flesh* that was before a *Stone.* Behold me torn asunder! and at last the *Fragments* burning toward your skies, and the cheeks streaming with tears out of the *Adamant.* Thus once upon a time you made the *Rocks* flow and the *Crags* gush, oh ever provident of your people! How marvellous toward me is your hand! In *Dying,* I have been born again; and in the midst of my *shattered means* I am now *richer.* . . .

At once, after this story of a sudden, violent illumination, comes the short and simple poem headed, like the opening poem of Herbert's *Temple,* "The Dedication"; it contains a number of verbal echoes of Herbert, and the whole manner of the poem represents a perfect distillation of Herbert's intimate mode of colloquy:

> Some drops of thy all-quickning bloud
> Fell on my heart, these made it bud
> And put forth thus, though, Lord, before
> The ground was curs'd, and void of store.

These three elements, then: engraved title page, Latin confession, and Herbertian Dedication form the utterly adequate preface to **Silex Scintillans,** 1650. They introduce a volume that will have two dominating themes: first, the record and results of the experience of sudden illumination; and second, a tribute to the poetry of George Herbert, which, it seems, played an important part in cultivating Vaughan's peculiar experience. Thus, toward the middle of Vaughan's volume, after hundreds of unmistakable echoes of Herbert in title, phrasing, theme, and stanza-form, Vaughan at last openly acknowledges his debt by accepting the invitation of Herbert's poem "Obedience," where Herbert offers his poetry as a written deed conveying himself to God, with this conclusion:

> He that will passe his land,
> As I have mine, may set his hand
> And heart unto this Deed, when he hath read;
> And make the purchase spread
> To both our goods, if he to it will stand.
>
> How happie were my part,
> If some kinde man would thrust his heart
> Into these lines; till in heav'ns Court of Rolls
> They were by winged souls
> Entred for both, farre above their desert!

Vaughan, in **"The Match,"** answers in Herbert's own mode of familiar address:

> Dear friend! whose holy, ever-living lines
> Have done much good
> To many, and have checkt my blood,
> My fierce, wild blood that still heaves, and inclines,
> But is still tam'd
> By those bright fires which thee inflam'd;
> Here I joyn hands, and thrust my stubborn heart
> Into thy Deed. . . .

As we look back, this joining of hands and hearts between Vaughan and Herbert is almost equally evident in the opening poem of the volume proper: **"Regeneration."** Here the allegorical mode of the painful quest, the imagery of struggling upward toward a "pinacle" where disappointment lies, the sudden cry mysteriously heard upon this hill, and even some aspects of the stanza-form—all these things show a poem that begins by playing variations on Herbert's poem "The Pilgrimage," which leads the speaker through "the wilde of Passion" toward the hill suggesting Calvary:

> When I had gain'd the brow and
>   top,
> A lake of brackish waters on the ground
>   Was all I found.
>
> With that abash'd and struck with many a sting
>   Of swarming fears,
> I fell, and cry'd, Alas my King!
>   Can both the way and end be tears?
> Yet taking heart I rose, and then perceiv'd
>   I was deceiv'd:
>
> My hill was further: so I flung away,
>   Yet heard a crie
> Just as I went, *None goes that way*
> *And lives:* If that be all, said I,
> After so foul a journey death is fair,
>   And but a chair.

But Vaughan's pilgrimage has quite a different theme: in the fourth stanza the Herbertian echoes fade out, as Vaughan's pilgrim is called away into an interior region of the soul, here imaged with the combination of natural and Biblical landscape that often marks Vaughan at his best:

> With that, some cryed, *Away;* straight I
>   Obey'd, and led
> Full East, a faire, fresh field could spy
>   Some call'd it, *Jacobs Bed;*
> A Virgin-soile, which no
>   Rude feet ere trod,
> Where (since he stept there,) only go
>   Prophets, and friends of God.

The allusion to Jacob's vision and journey toward the East (Genesis 28:10-22; 29:1) is only the first of many such allusions by Vaughan to the "early days" of the Old Testament; here the scene begins an allegorical account of the mysterious workings of grace; the pilgrim enters into a state of interior illumination, where he is prepared to apprehend the presence of God and to hear the voice of the Lord. In the remaining six stanzas the setting mysteriously changes to another landscape, a springtime scene, where a grove contains a garden with a fountain; the state of grace is imaged by combining the natural imagery of spring with subtle echoes of the most famous of all springsongs: the Song of Solomon. The key to these stanzas is given by Vaughan himself in a verse from the Canticle appended to the poem: "Arise O North, and come thou Southwind, and blow upon my garden, that the spices thereof may flow out." It is the Garden of the Soul: one of the great central symbols in the Christian literature of meditation and contemplation. For Vaughan's poem here

we need to recall especially the four verses of the Canticle (4:12-15) that immediately precede Vaughan's citation:

> A garden inclosed is my sister, my spouse; a
>   spring shut up, a fountain sealed.
> Thy plants are an orchard of pomegranates, with
>   pleasant fruits; camphire, with spikenard,
> Spikenard and saffron; calamus and cinnamon,
>   with all trees of frankincense; myrrh and
>   aloes, with all the chief spices:
> A fountain of gardens, a well of living waters,
>   and streams from Lebanon.

So in Vaughan's spiritual landscape "The aire was all in spice," while

> Only a little Fountain lent
>   Some use for Eares,
> And on the dumbe shades language spent
>   The Musick of her teares;
> I drew her neere, and found
>   The Cisterne full
> Of divers stones, some bright, and round
>   Others ill-shap'd, and dull.
>
> The first (pray marke,) as quick as light
>   Danc'd through the floud,
> But, th'last more heavy then the night
>   Nail'd to the Center stood;

Vaughan is developing his favorite image-cluster of light and darkness through symbols that suggest one of his favorite Biblical passages: the third chapter of St. John's gospel, where Nicodemus hears the words of Jesus by night:

> Except a man be born of water and of the Spirit,
> he cannot enter into the kingdom of God.
>
> That which is born of the flesh is flesh; and that
> which is born of the Spirit is spirit.

So in Vaughan's allegory, the spiritual part of man is here reborn, made bright and "quick" as light; while the fleshly part remains dull and heavy, nailed to the earth. Much the same significance is found in the following scene, where in a bank of flowers, representing his own interior state, the speaker finds

> Some fast asleepe, others broad-eyed
>   And taking in the Ray. . . .

And finally, all the images and themes of this poem coalesce with a three- fold allusion to the "winds" of grace: the "rushing mighty wind" of Pentecost (Acts 2:2), the winds that are prayed for in Vaughan's quotation from the Canticle, and the wind described in the words of Jesus to Nicodemus: "The wind bloweth where it listeth, and thou hearest the sound thereof, but canst not tell whence it cometh, and whither it goeth: so is every one that is born of the Spirit." And so the poem concludes:

> Here musing long, I heard
>   A rushing wind
> Which still increas'd, but whence it stirr'd
>   No where I could not find;
>
> I turn'd me round, and to each shade
>   Dispatch'd an Eye,
> To see, if any leafe had made

Least motion, or Reply,
But while I listning sought
My mind to ease
By knowing, where 'twas, or where not,
It whisper'd; *Where I please.*

Lord, then said I, *On me one breath,*
And let me dye before my death!

So the poem, like dozens of others by Vaughan, begins with echoes of George Herbert, whose simplicity of language and intimacy of tone pervade the whole poem and the whole volume of 1650; but, like all of Vaughan's better poems, **"Regeneration"** moves away from Herbert to convey its own unique experience through its own rich combination of materials, in which we may discern three dominant fields of reference: the Bible, external Nature, and the interior motions of the Self. There is in **"Regeneration"** not a single reference that could be called eucharistic. Yet Herbert opens the central body of his poems with an emblematic Altar, typographically displayed upon the page, and he follows this with the long eucharistic meditation entitled **"The Sacrifice,"** where he develops the meaning of the Passion through a variation on the ancient Reproaches of Christ, spoken from the Cross as part of the Good Friday service. Nothing could speak more eloquently of the vast difference between these two poets.

In accordance with his central symbols, at the outset of his *Temple* Herbert gives seventy-seven stanzas of epigrammatic advice on how to lead a good life, under the title, "The Churchporch"; these stanzas form a preparation for the mental communion that constitutes the heart of Herbert's central body of poetry, "The Church," as he makes plain by these lines on the threshold:

Thou, whom the former precepts have
Sprinkled and taught, how to behave
Thy self in church; approach, and taste
The churches mysticall repast.

Now Henry Vaughan also has a group of stanzas in this epigrammatic form, under the title **"Rules and Lessons";** they come exactly in the center of the 1650 volume, as though the advice there given formed the center of the volume's devotional life. But Vaughan's advice bears no relation to any ecclesiastical symbolism: it is as though the earthly church had vanished, and man were left to work alone with God. Vaughan's rules and lessons for the devout life lay down, in twenty-four stanzas, certain ways of individual communion with God in every hour of the day, from early morning, through the worldly work of midday, and on through night, until the next day's awakening: one couplet gives the essence of the rules:

A sweet *self-privacy* in a right soul
Out-runs the Earth, and lines the utmost pole.

Man's duty is to cultivate the inner self, using as aids the two "books" that we have seen in **"Regeneration"**: the Book of Nature, and the Book of Scripture, as Vaughan suggests in his advice for morning devotions:

Walk with thy fellow-creatures: note the *hush*
And *whispers* amongst them. There's not a
Spring,

Or *Leafe* but hath his *Morning-hymn;* Each
Bush
And *Oak* doth know *I AM;* canst thou not sing?
O leave thy Cares, and follies! go this way
And thou art sure to prosper all the day.

Serve God before the world; let him not go
Until thou hast a blessing, then resigne
The whole unto him; and remember who
Prevail'd by *wrestling* ere the *Sun* did *shine.*
Poure *Oyle* upon the *stones,* weep for thy sin,
Then journey on, and have an eie to heav'n.

Note the rich and curious complex of the Biblical and the natural: the allusion to the bush from which Moses heard the voice of God; the extended reference to the time when Jacob wrestled with the mysterious stranger "until the breaking of the day," when he won the stranger's blessing, and knew at last that he had "seen God face to face" (Genesis 32:24-30); and the shorter allusion to the familiar scene of Jacob's vision, after which "Jacob rose up early in the morning, and took the stone that he had put for his pillows, and set it up for a pillar, and poured oil upon the top of it" (Genesis 28:18).

The Bible, Nature, and the Self thus come together in a living harmony, as in Vaughan's **"Religion"** (a poem that, typically, seems to take its rise from Herbert's poem "Decay"):

My God, when I walke in those groves,
And leaves thy spirit doth still fan,
I see in each shade that there growes
An Angell talking with a man.

Under a *Juniper,* some house,
Or the coole *Mirtles* canopie,
Others beneath an *Oakes* greene boughs,
Or at some *fountaines* bubling Eye;

Here *Jacob* dreames, and wrestles; there
Elias by a Raven is fed,
Another time by th' Angell, where
He brings him water with his bread;

In *Abr'hams* Tent the winged guests
(O how familiar then was heaven!)
Eate, drinke, discourse, sit downe, and rest
Untill the Coole, and shady *Even.* . . . .

One must read several stanzas before it becomes clear that the "leaves" here are essentially the leaves of the Bible, where the self can learn to live intimately with God; but at the same time the vivid apprehension of natural life here may suggest that nature itself is still inspired by the divine presence.

The fact that Vaughan so often, in his best poems, seeks out these individual ways of communion with God does not mean that he chooses to neglect or ignore traditional devotions to the Eucharist. On the contrary, he is acutely aware of the importance of the eucharistic allusions in Herbert's *Temple,* for he makes frequent efforts to follow Herbert's central mode of mental communion. But he does not often succeed, as we may see in four sizable poems in the 1650 volume that are devoted to eucharistic celebration. His poem **"The Passion"** is an extended effort to meditate upon the traditional themes, but the poem is wooden, labored, and forced in its effect. One may perhaps trace a cause of this failure to the fact that Vaughan does not visualize the Passion "as if he were present," in the ancient tradition of such meditations; instead, he puts the whole occasion in the past. He does not memorialize the Passion as a present reality. In another poem, **"Dressing,"** he performs a preparation for "Thy mysticall *Communion,*" but the poem is so worried by contemporary doctrinal quarrels that it ends with a bitter attack on Puritan views, and not with any devotional presence. Another poem, entitled **"The Holy Communion,"** begins by echoing the first two lines of George Herbert's eucharistic poem, "The Banquet": "Welcome sweet, and sacred feast; welcome life!" but Vaughan's poem immediately veers away from the feast to ponder the action of grace within the self, and the operation of God's creative power over the entire universe.

Vaughan's one and only success in this kind of poetic celebration comes significantly in his poem **"The Sap,"** where he approaches the Eucharist indirectly, through a tale told to himself by his inmost self:

> Come sapless Blossom, creep not stil on Earth
>   Forgetting thy first birth;
> 'Tis not from dust, or if so, why dost thou
>   Thus cal and thirst for dew?
> It tends not thither, if it doth, why then
>   This growth and stretch for heav'n? . . .
> Who plac'd thee here, did something then Infuse
>   Which now can tel thee news.
> There is beyond the Stars an hil of myrrh
>   From which some drops fal here,
> On it the Prince of *Salem* sits, who deals
>   To thee thy secret meals . . .
> Yet liv'd he here sometimes, and bore for thee
>   A world of miserie . . .
> But going hence, and knowing wel what woes
>   Might his friends discompose,
> To shew what strange love he had to our good
>   He gave his sacred bloud
> By wil our sap, and Cordial; now in this
>   Lies such a heav'n of bliss,
> That, who but truly tasts it, no decay
>   Can touch him any way. . . .

The whole poem, as several readers have pointed out, bears some resemblance to Herbert's poem "Peace," but the contrasts are more significant. In Herbert's poem the seeker after peace comes upon a "rev'rend good old man" who tells him the story of "a Prince of old" who "At Salem dwelt"—alluding to Christ under the figure of Melchizedek, who "brought forth bread and wine" (Genesis 14:18; Hebrews 7). Herbert's poem presents an allegory of the apostolic succession: the "good old man" offers the bread of life derived from the "twelve stalks of wheat" that sprang out of Christ's grave:

> Take of this grain, which in my garden grows,
>   And grows for you;
> Make bread of it: and that repose
>   And peace, which ev'ry where
> With so much earnestnesse you do pursue,
>   Is onely there.

But Vaughan does not end his poem with such an echo of the ecclesiastical ritual; instead he closes with what ap-

pears to be yet another tribute to the poems of George Herbert, as he seems to echo here at least four of Herbert's eucharistic poems.

> Then humbly take
> This balm for souls that ake,
> And one who drank it thus, assures that you
>   Shal find a Joy so true,
> Such perfect Ease, and such a lively sense
>   Of grace against all sins,
> That you'l Confess the Comfort such, as even
>   Brings to, and comes from Heaven.

But this comfort remains, in Vaughan's poetry, a promise and a hope: his central channels of communion lie elsewhere, channels with a long and venerable history.

The Augustinian Quest

Perhaps the discussion of Vaughan's characteristic triad, the Bible, Nature, and the Self, has already suggested the three "books" cultivated by the medieval Augustinians, and especially by St. Bonaventure: the Book of Scripture, the Book of Nature, and the Book of the Soul. The three books are, essentially, one: the revelation given in the Bible shows man how to read, first nature, and then his own soul. That is to say, in Augustinian terms: man, enlightened by Biblical revelation, can grasp the Vestiges, the "traces," of God in external nature; and from this knowledge he can then turn inward to find the Image of God within himself. It is an Image defaced by sin, but with its essential powers restored by the sacrifice of Christ. Man is not simply fallen: he is fallen and redeemed. It is man's responsibility, with the omnipresent help of grace, to clear and renew this Image, until it may become a true Similitude. But the renewal can never be wholly accomplished in this life: thus, as in **"Regeneration,"** the poems that relate Vaughan's journey of the mind toward God end with a cry for help, a prayer for some momentary glimpse of perfection, as in his **"Vanity of Spirit,"** where he performs a journey like that in Bonaventure's *Itinerarium,* first searching through all Nature, and then finding at last within himself

> A peece of much antiquity,
> With Hyerogliphicks quite dismembred,
> And broken letters scarce remembred.
> I tooke them up, and (much Joy'd,) went about
> T' unite those peeces, hoping to find out
>   The mystery; but this neer done,
>   That little light I had was gone:
>   It griev'd me much. At last, said I,
> *Since in these veyls my Ecclips'd Eye*
> *May not approach thee, (for at night*
> *Who can have commerce with the light?)*
> *I'le disapparell, and to buy*
> *But one half glaunce, most gladly dye.*

In this effort to piece together broken letters scarce remembered, by the aid of an interior light, Vaughan displays the essential action of that kind of meditation which may be termed Augustinian. Its finest explanation is still the one most easily available: it lies in the great climactic section of Augustine's *Confessions,* the chapters of the tenth book (6-27) where he marvels at and meditates upon the power of Memory. If we read and reread these chapters, we may come to feel them acting more and more as a commentary upon the poems of *Silex Scintillans,* 1650; and we may come to understand more clearly the ways in which Vaughan's finest poetry draws its strength from the great central tradition of Platonic Christianity.

The process of Augustinian meditation begins, as Vaughan's volume of 1650 begins, with an effort to apprehend the meaning of an experience of sudden illumination: *percussisti cor meum verbo tuo, et amavi te*—"Thou hast strucken my heart with thy word, and therupon I loved thee. . . . What now do I love, whenas I love thee?"

> not the beauty of any *corporall thing,* not the order of times; not the brightnesse of the *light,* which is so gladsome to our eyes: not the pleasant *melodies* of songs of all kinds; not the fragrant smell of flowers, and oyntments, and spices: not *Manna* and honey, nor any *fayre limbs* that are so acceptable to fleshly embracements.
>
> I love none of these things, whenas I love my God: and yet I love a certaine kinde of *light,* and a kind of *voyce,* and a kinde of *fragrancy,* and a kinde of *meat,* and a kind of *embracement.* Whenas I love my God; who is both the *light,* and the voyce, and the sweet *smell,* and the *meate,* and the *embracement* of my inner man: where that *light* shineth unto my soule, which no place can receive; that *voyce* soundeth, which time deprives me not of; and that fragrancy *smelleth,* which no wind scatters . . .
>
> This is it which I love, when as I love my God.

Here is the spiritual landscape of the redeemed soul, described by Vaughan in his **"Regeneration,"** glimpsed throughout his volume in the many fresh images from nature that he uses to relate the experience, and summed up once again near the close of the volume, in the poem **"Mount of Olives."** This title represents a traditional symbol of the soul's retirement to prayer and meditation, here to recall, like Augustine, a moment which gave his life its meaning:

> When first I saw true beauty, and thy Joys
> Active as light, and calm without all noise
> Shin'd on my soul, I felt through all my powr's
> Such a rich air of sweets, as Evening showrs
> Fand by a gentle gale Convey and breath
> On some parch'd bank, crown'd with a flowrie
>   wreath;
> Odors, and Myrrh, and balm in one rich floud
> O'r-ran my heart, and spirited my bloud . . .
> I am so warm'd now by this glance on me,
> That, midst all storms I feel a Ray of thee;
> So have I known some beauteous *Paisage* rise
> In suddain flowres and arbours to my Eies,
> And in the depth and dead of winter bring
> To my Cold thoughts a lively sense of spring.

With the memory of such an experience within him, the Augustinian seeker turns to question external nature, as in the *Confessions:*

> I askt the *Earth,* and that answered me, *I am not it;* and whatsoever are in it, made the same confession. I asked the *Sea* and the *deepes,* and the *creeping things,* and they answered me, *We are*

> *not thy God, seeke above us.* . . . I asked the heavens, the Sunne and Moone, and Starres, Nor (say they) are wee the *God* whom thou seekest.

All creatures give for Augustine the same answer: "they cryed out with a loud voyce, *He made us.*" It is the questioning of nature that runs throughout Vaughan's poetry, where "Each *tree, herb, flowre* / Are shadows of his *wisedome,* and his Pow'r." Thus in **"The Tempest"** Vaughan prays that man "would hear / The world read to him!" and declares:

> all the vast expence
> In the Creation shed, and slav'd to sence
> Makes up but lectures for his eie, and ear.

(lectures in the old medieval sense, readings of the book, with commentary and elucidation:)

> Sure, mighty love foreseeing the discent
>   Of this poor Creature, by a gracious art
>   Hid in these low things snares to gain his
> heart,
> And layd surprizes in each Element.
>
> All things here shew him heaven; *Waters* that
> fall
>   Chide, and fly up; *Mists* of corruptest fome
>   Quit their first beds & mount; trees, herbs,
> flowres, all
> Strive upwards stil, and point him the way
> home.

And the way home lies through an interior ascent, climbing upward and inward through the deepest regions of the human soul:

> I beg'd here long, and gron'd to know
> Who gave the Clouds so brave a bow,
> Who bent the spheres, and circled in
> Corruption with this glorious Ring,
> What is his name, and how I might
> Descry some part of his great light.
> I summon'd nature: peirc'd through all her
>   store,
> Broke up some seales, which none had touch'd
>   before,
> Her wombe, her bosome, and her head
> Where all her secrets lay a bed
> I rifled quite, and having past
> Through all the Creatures, came at last
> To search my selfe, where I did find
> Traces, and sounds of a strange kind.
>   (**"Vanity of Spirit"**)

So Augustine turns to search within himself and comes "into these fields and spacious palaces of my *Memory,* where the treasures of innumerable *formes* brought into it from these things that have beene perceived by the *sences,* be hoarded up."

> And yet doe not the things themselves enter the *Memory;* only the *Images* of the things perceived by the *Sences,* are ready there at hand, when ever the *Thoughts* will recall them. . . .
>
> For there have I in a readinesse, the heaven, the earth, the sea, and what-ever I can thinke upon in them. . . . There also meete I with my *selfe,*

I recall my *selfe,* what, where, or when I have done a thing; and how I was affected when I did it. There be all what ever I remember, eyther upon mine owne experience, or others credit. Out of the same store doe I my selfe compare these and these likelyhoods of things; eyther of such as I have made experience of, or of such as I have barely beleeved upon experience of some things that bee passed: and by these do I compare actions to *come,* their *events* and *hopes:* and upon all these againe doe I meditate, as if they were now present. . . .

Great is this force of *memory,* excessive great, O my *God:* a large and an infinite roomthynes [*penetrale:* inner room], who can plummet the bottome of it? yet is this a *faculty* of mine, and belongs unto my nature: nor can I my self comprehend all that I am.

Yet things even more wonderful lie beyond, as he probes ever and ever more deeply into the recesses of the memory. "Here also bee all these precepts of those *liberall Sciences* as yet unforgotten; coucht as it were further off in a more inward place." These things could not have been conveyed within by the senses; how was it then that he came to accept these precepts as true?

unless because they were already in my memory; though so farre off yet, and crowded so farre backeward as it were into certaine secret caves, that had they not beene drawne out by the advice of some other person, I had never perchance beene able so much as to have thought of them?

Here the hint of the presence of something like innate ideas in the deep caves of the soul leads directly to a long account of what might be called the dramatic action of Augustinian meditation. It is an action significantly different from the method of meditation later set forth by Ignatius Loyola and his followers; for that later method shows the effects of medieval scholasticism, with its powerful emphasis upon the analytic understanding, and upon the Thomist principle that human knowledge is derived from sensory experience. Ignatian meditation is thus a precise, tightly articulated method, moving from the images that comprise the composition of place into the threefold sequence of the powers of the soul, memory, understanding, and will, and from there into the affections and resolutions of the aroused will. But in Augustinian meditation there is no such precise method; there is, rather, an intuitive groping back into regions of the soul that lie beyond sensory memories. The three powers of the soul are all used, but with an effect of simultaneous action, for with Augustine the aroused will is using the understanding to explore the memory, with the aim of apprehending more clearly and loving more fervently the ultimate source of the will's arousal.

Wherefore we find, that to learne these things whose *Images* we *sucke* not *in* by our Sences, but perceive *within* by themselves, without Images, as they are; is nothing else, but by *meditating* to *gather together,* and by diligent *marking,* to take notice of those same *notions* which the *memory* did before contayne more scatteringly and confusedly . . .

But these things are evasive and elusive; unless we engage in a continual act of re-collection, "they become so drowned againe, and so give us the slip, as it were, backe into such remote and privy lodgings, that I must be put againe unto new paines of mediation, for recovery of them to their former perfection . . . they must be *rallied* and drawne together againe, that they may bee knowne; that is to say, they must as it were be *collected* and *gathered together* from their dispersions: whence the word *cogitation* is derived."

The seventeenth-century translator has been frequently rendering the word *cogitare* by the word *meditate,* thus providing his own account of Augustinian meditation: to draw together these things scattered in the memory. It would seem that poetry composed under the impulse of this kind of meditation would differ considerably in its structure from any poetry written under the impulse of the Ignatian mode of meditation—such as Donne's Holy Sonnets. The poetry of Augustinian meditation would perhaps tend to display an order akin to that which Pascal saw in the writings of Augustine: "Cet ordre consiste principalement à la digression sur chaque point qu'on rapporte à la fin, pour la montrer toujours." That *Pensée* may at least suggest the poetry of Vaughan, where the order often consists chiefly in what appear to be digressions, but are really exploratory sallies or *excursus* in the manner indicated by the following passage of the *Confessions:*

Great is this power of Memory; a thing, O my God, to bee amazed at, a very profound and infinite multiplicity: and this thing is the minde, and this thing am I. . . . Behold, in those innumerable fields, and dennes, and caves of my memory, innumerably full of innumerable kinds of things, brought in, first, eyther by the *Images,* as all *bodies* are: secondly, or by the *presence* of the *things* themselves, as the *Arts* are: thirdly, or by certaine *notions* or *impressions,* as the *Affections* of the mind are . . . Thorow all these doe I runne and tumble [*discurro et volito*]; *myning* into them on this side, and on that side, so farre as ever I am able, but can finde no bottome. So great is the force of memory, so great is the force of this life of man, even whilest hee is mortall.

Thus in many of Vaughan's best poems, as in **"Regeneration,"** the characteristic movement is a "mining" of associations, a roving search over a certain field of imagery, a sinking inward upon the mind's resources, until all the evocative ramifications of the memory have been explored; and then the poem ends rather abruptly, with a cry for divine help, or some generalizing moral conclusion. The movement is seen at its best in **"Corruption,"** where the mind lingers over the memories of the "early days" of Genesis:

Sure, It was so. Man in those early days
    Was not all stone, and Earth,
He shin'd a little, and by those weak Rays
    Had some glimpse of his birth.
He saw Heaven o'r his head, and knew from
    whence
    He came (condemned,) hither,
And, as first Love draws strongest, so from
    hence

His mind sure progress'd thither.

Under the impulse of this love, Vaughan's mind progresses backward to recover the memory of Paradise:

> He sigh'd for *Eden,* and would often say
> *Ah! what bright days were those?*
> Nor was Heav'n cold unto him; for each day
> The vally, or the Mountain
> Afforded visits, and still *Paradise* lay
> In some green shade, or fountain.
> Angels lay *Leiger* here; Each Bush, and Cel,
> Each Oke, and high-way knew them,
> Walk but the fields, or sit down at some *wel,*
> And he was sure to view them.

Deep within all such associations lies that essential memory toward which Augustine's digressive and "tumbling" meditations have been subtly and inevitably leading: the memory of a "happy life," a "blessed life," *beata vita.* . . .

It is the central image of **Silex Scintillans:** the flash, the spark, the glance, the beam, the ray, the glimmering of light that comes from the memory of an ancient birthright of blessedness—*utrum singillatim omnes, an in illo homine, qui primus peccavit:* whether it be a memory of each man's individual life, or whether it be a memory of Adam's original happy life—that memory remains, yet un-put-out in men. The image is notable in the poem **"Silence, and stealth of dayes,"** where this Augustinian motif is used in recalling the memory of a loved one who has died (evidently Vaughan's brother):

> As he that in some Caves thick damp
> Lockt from the light,
> Fixeth a solitary lamp,
> To brave the night
> And walking from his Sun, when past
> That glim'ring Ray
> Cuts through the heavy mists in haste
> Back to his day,
> So o'r fled minutes I retreat
> Unto that hour
> Which shew'd thee last, but did defeat
> Thy light, and pow'r,
> I search, and rack my soul to see
> Those beams again. . . .

The "Sun" here is the "solitary lamp" within the cave of the speaker's soul: the memory of his loved one is the light within that serves as an interior sun. Sometimes, carried toward the things of the outer world, the speaker tends to walk away from that "glim'ring Ray," but, remembering that he has forgotten, he walks, he walks, in Augustine's way, back toward the memory of light. The beams of this loved one's soul, he comes to realize, now shine in heaven, and he cannot track them there; yet something bright remains within, as he concludes:

> Yet I have one *Pearle* by whose light
> All things I see,
> And in the heart of Earth, and night
> Find Heaven, and thee.

It is the indestructible Image of God, apprehending the presence of God in the memory: "Sure I am, that in it thou dwellest: even for this reason, that I have preserved the memory of thee, since the time that I first learnt thee: and for that I finde thee in my memory, whensoever I call thee to remembrance" (*Confessions*).

So the memory of that inner presence runs throughout Vaughan's volume of 1650, as Vaughan struggles backward on his ancient journey of return toward the memory of blessedness. Sometimes the journey backward takes the form of **"The Retreate"** toward the days of the individual's childhood. . . .

The poem presents the essence of the *Phaedo,* as qualified and developed by Christian Platonism. Indeed, the *Phaedo* gives the closing image of the drunken man, in an important passage that suggests the kernel of this poem:

> And were we not saying long ago [asks Socrates] that the soul when using the body as an instrument of perception, that is to say, when using the sense of sight or hearing or some other sense . . . were we not saying that the soul too is then dragged by the body into the region of the changeable, and wanders and is confused; the world spins round her, and she is like a drunkard, when she touches change? . . .

> But when returning into herself she reflects, then she passes into the other world, the region of purity, and eternity, and immortality, and unchangeableness, which are her kindred. . . .

In Vaughan, as in Augustine's *Confessions,* there is of course only the most guarded and glancing use of the Platonic doctrine of reminiscence: any hint of the soul's pre-existence is used by Vaughan as a metaphor of innocence; and the whole poem is toward the close clearly transmuted into orthodox Christianity. The poet superimposes upon the Platonic suggestions the concept of the "Inlightned spirit" which catches a vision of the promised land, as did Moses when he "went up from the plains of Moab unto the mountain of Nebo . . . And the Lord shewed him all the land of Gilead . . . and all the land of Judah, unto the utmost sea, And the south, and the plain of the valley of Jericho, the city of palm trees . . ." (Deuteronomy 34:1–3).

So the "early days" of the individual's childhood become one with the "early days" of the human race, as related in the Old Testament; and both together form powerful symbols of the memory of a happy life that lives, however glimmeringly, within the soul that has, through regeneration, come into yet a third state of childhood: the state of the "children of God" set forth in the eighth chapter of Romans.

Such is the paradise within, compounded of the Bible, of Nature, and of the Self, which lies at the heart of Vaughan's **Silex Scintillans,** 1650: a vision that results from the constant effort to remember the beauty of the sudden illumination described in his opening Latin confession. That Latin poem and its emblem of the Flashing Flint, with its image of the man within, are once more brought to mind by the well-known passage that concludes Augustine's sequence of meditations on the force of memory:

> Too late beganne I to love thee, O thou beauty both so ancient and so fresh, yea too too late

came I to love thee. For behold, thou wert *within* mee, and I *out* of my selfe, where I made search for thee; deformed I, wooing these beautifull pieces of thy workmanship. . . . Thou *calledst,* and criedst unto mee, yea thou even brakest open my *deafenesse.* Thou discoveredst thy beames, and *shynedst* out unto mee, and didst chase away my blindnesse. Thou didst most *fragrantly blow* upon me, and I drew in my *breath* and panted after thee. I *tasted* thee, and now doe *hunger* and *thirst after thee.* Thou didst *touch* mee, and I even *burne* againe to enioy thy peace.

James D. Simmonds   (essay date 1972)

SOURCE: "Love Poetry," in *Masques of God: Form and Theme in the Poetry of Henry Vaughan,* University of Pittsburgh Press, 1972, pp. 65-84.

[*An Australian-born American scholar of English literature, Simmonds is also the editor of* Milton Studies, *a playwright, and the author of an important study of Vaughan's accomplishment,* Masques of God: Form and Theme in the Poetry of Henry Vaughan *(1972). In this work, he declines to follow "the usual custom of treating the secular and sacred verse as separate categories; rather, he examines Vaughan's poetic, intellectual, and religious development and their "essentially organic, continuous, and natural" flow. In the following chapter from this work, Simmonds explores Vaughan's love poetry.*]

Most of Vaughan's love poems are grouped in two distinct sequences, addressed to "Amoret" and "Etesia" respectively. Each brief story of courtship begins in the traditional way with love at first sight, but each develops toward a different resolution. The sequences reflect in their thematic emphases two distinct modes of the Renaissance love lyric. Like Spenser's *Shepheardes Calender* and the sequences of Petrarch and Sidney, the Etesia poems record the torments of an idealizing passion denied possession of its object. Though they begin in this vein, the Amoret poems, like Spenser's *Amoretti and Epithalamion,* record the satisfying growth of a sustaining, mutual love which is completed and symbolized by marriage. The Etesia poems descend from the medieval fusion of Platonic idealism with erotic passion in adulterous courtly romance; the Amoret poems are products of the Protestant, middle-class effort, beginning in the sixteenth century, to escape the social, moral, and psychological dilemmas of the medieval tradition by romanticizing a mutual affection of "true plaine hearts" which culminates in married union. In *The Allegory of Love,* C. S. Lewis made the classic case for Spenser, especially in the central books of *The Faerie Queene,* as the author of "the final defeat of courtly love by the romantic conception of marriage," as "the greatest among the founders of that romantic conception of marriage which is the basis of all our love literature fom Shakespeare to Meredith." But Grierson's earlier presentation of Donne as a rebel against Petrarchan conventions and a pioneer in the expression of natural passion had already accustomed critics to seeing a predominant influence from Donne in seventeenth-century treatments of love as an innocent, happy union. It happens that a few of the less successful poems to Amoret on this theme fol-

low Donne in imagery, phrasing, and technique, and this has prompted some critics to dismiss the whole sequence as a series of weak, insignificant experiments in the Donne manner. Worse still, the more derivative of the Amoret poems have been taken as representative of Vaughan's achievement as a love poet, the poems to Etesia being seldom noticed and almost never anthologized. I agree with S. L. Bethell that the Etesia poems are more often successful than those to Amoret, although, in his words, the latter have "a gracious tenderness about them and a combination of pretty delicacy and sober strength which gives some indication of greatness to come." Worst of all, the Amoret poems have often been spoken of as though they were the summit of Vaughan's accomplishment as a secular poet. For example, Helen Gardner speaks of "the conversion which turned the tepid wooer of Amoret into a poet who brings us 'authentic tidings of invisible things'." Thus Vaughan's secular poetry as a whole, and not just the love poetry, comes to be popularly regarded as trivial and uninteresting.

The ideal form of love, according to Vaughan, is a reciprocal love between two persons whose souls are in harmony with divine law; their passionate union is therefore innocent, natural, and happy. It is symbolized by the coupling of roses and is closely associated with nature's self-perpetuating fertility and the plenitude of nature's beauty. Treating love as an aspect of nature's innocence and creativity, presenting love, virtue, and natural fertility as components of an ideal order which is, in a sense, permanent, Vaughan is far from Donne. He is close to the pastoral tradition, to the Shakespeare of the sonnets on "increase," and to the Spenser of the *Epithalamion,* the Garden of Adonis episode in book III of *The Faerie Queene,* and the Mount Acidale episode in book VI. The poem *"To I. Morgan.. . upon his sudden Journey and succeeding Marriage"* is typical of Vaughan's ideal of love:

> So two sweet *Rose-buds* from their *Virgin-beds*
> First peep and blush, then kiss and couple heads;
> Till yearly blessings so increase their store
> Those two can number two and twenty more,
> And the fair *Bank* (by heav'ns free bounty Crown'd)
> With choice of *Sweets* and *Beauties* doth abound;
> Till time, which *Familys* like *Flowers* far spreads;
> Gives them for *Garlands* to the best of heads.

Earlier in the poem love is seen as an elixir, a philosopher's stone which contains the essence of nature's creativity and can transfigure dull matter into a thing of precious beauty. The lover, impregnated with divine *"Love* and *Wisdom,"* is likened to the sun, whose analogous *"Light* and *Heat"* work on "senseless *Stones"* to convey "Fire into *Rubies,* into *Chrystalls* day." Human procreation is analogous to this alchemical transmutation of base matter; the lover recreates and perpetuates the "bright Blessings" which have been generated in him by a higher power:

> you, like one ordain'd to shine, take in
> Both *Light* and *Heat:* can *Love* and *Wisdom* spin
> Into one thred, and with that firmly tye

The same bright Blessings on posterity;
Which so intail'd, like *Jewels* of the Crown,
Shall with your *Name* descend still to your own.

The sense of a continual interchange between the natural and spiritual orders is intensified if we may read the "best of heads," to which Time eventually gives the offspring as garlands, as referring to the Son of God, head of the mystical body of the Church. By this reading, the conceit is close to some more explicit lines in the penultimate stanza of Spenser's *Epithalamion,* when he prays to the "high heavens"

> That we may raise a large posterity,
> Which from the earth, which they may long possesse,
> With lasting happinesse,
> Up to your haughty pallaces may mount,
> And for the guerdon of theyr glorious merit
> May heavenly tabernacles there inherit,
> Of blessed Saints for to increase the count.

Similarly, in the poem **"To the best, and most accomplish'd Couple—,"** the end of love is seen as the prolongation of nature's beauty through "that mysterie / Your selves in your Posteritie"; and the physical union of the lovers is presented in its ideal form through the metaphorical union of a rose with the sun:

> Fresh as the *houres* may all your pleasures be,
>   And healthfull as *Eternitie!*
>   Sweet as the flowres *first breath,* and Close
>   As th'*unseen spreadings* of the Rose,
>   When he unfolds his Curtain'd head,
>   And makes his bosome the *Suns* bed.

In **"To the River *Isca,"*** through the hypothetical form of an invocation and prayer, Vaughan presents us with a composite symbol of nature as an ideal order. As symbol, the valley of the river Usk is *"The Land redeem'd from all disorders";* completely alien to it are

>   those *lowd, anxious Cares*
> For *dead* and *dying things* (the Common *Wares*
> And *showes* of time.)

Redeemed from all disorders, it is redeemed from time, change, and death, and from lust as well. Its qualities are *"Freedome, safety, Joy and blisse / United* in one loving *kisse."* The river itself is the central symbol of love's fertilizing, transfiguring power, generating all forms of natural beauty and dispelling everything harsh, ugly, or violent. From this valley the *"wilie, winding Snake"* is banished, as are *"sullen heats"* and offensive flames; the symbol of human love is the innocent, natural union of roses. All the rich, spicy odors of nature are concentrated here, deceit and lust are unknown, and innocent love is celebrated joyfully with *"Garlands,* and *Songs,* and *Roundelayes."* This is Vaughan's version of the ancient figure of the enclosed garden of love. Rooted perhaps equally in classical pastoral and the *Song of Solomon,* its best-known Renaissance forms are the Garden of Adonis in *The Faerie Queene* and the Garden of Eden in book IV of *Paradise Lost:*

> May thy gentle *Swains* (like *flowres*)
> Sweetly spend their *Youthfull hours,*
> And thy *beauteous Nymphs* (like *Doves*)

Be *kind* and *faithfull* to their *Loves;*

. . . .

> In all thy *Journey* to the *Main*
> No *nitrous Clay,* nor *Brimstone-vein*
> Mixe with thy *streams,* but may they passe
> Fresh as the *aire,* and cleer as *Glasse,*
> And where the *wandring Chrystal* treads
> *Roses* shall *kisse,* and *Couple* heads.
> The *factour-wind* from far shall bring
> The *Odours* of the *Scatter'd* Spring,
> And *loaden* with the rich *Arreare,*
> *Spend* it in *Spicie whispers* there.

Spenser's Amoret was raised up "In all the lore of love, and goodly womanhead" in the "thickest covert" of a wood where "all plentie, and all pleasure flowes." Vaughan's Amoret is discovered by him wandering in the "coole, leavie House" of the Priory Grove, whose "sacred shades" are now consecrated as the garden symbol of their union:

> Henceforth no melancholy flight,
> No sad wing, or hoarse bird of Night,
> Disturbe this Aire, no fatall throate
> Of Raven, or Owle, awake the Note
> Of our laid Eccho, no voice dwell
> Within these leaves, but *Philomel.*
> The poisonous Ivie here no more
> His false twists on the Oke shall score,
> Only the Woodbine here may twine,
> As th' Embleme of her Love, and mine.

The poet's imagined transfiguration of the grove into a symbol of an ideal natural order expresses the power of love to transfigure a fallen world. As in the Usk poem, the description of the ideal qualities of the garden by exclusion of their contraries makes us fully aware of all the destructive forces of nature which threaten its beauty and peace. Thus we perceive the stability and contentment of the love which the garden symbolizes, not as a given, but as something won out of opposition to the forces of the fallen world which impinge upon and threaten to impair its harmony. The force which the language exerts to exclude these contrary qualities expresses the psychological force which is needed to transcend them and assert the supremacy of love. The image of the grove eventually clothed "in an aged Gray" is an image of the lovers' future selves. Like the grove, they must yield to "the consuming yeares," and the irrefragability of their union is secured, not in time, but only through their immortality. In imagination, the grove, transplanted, becomes "A fresh Grove in th' Elysian Land," the scene of a renewal of the lovers' "first Innocence, and Love." The earthly paradise of the grove, subject to time, is only a fragile antitype of the heavenly paradise, where "in thy shades, as now, so then, / Wee'le kisse, and smile, and walke agen." By contrast, in **"To my Ingenuous Friend, *R. W.,"*** Vaughan imagines an Elysium without love and without women, an Elysium where "learned Ghosts" admire one another's poetry and the souls of "murther'd" lovers seek dolefully to appease the torments of "th' inconstant, cruell sex."

In *The Faerie Queene,* the antithesis of the Garden of Adonis is the Bower of Bliss. The beautiful plenitude of the natural, innocent garden is replaced by an artificial ersatz, and the free exchange of passion between lovers is distorted into a lust to possess or to use the other. An aspect of the distortion is that, in a sense, the body of the beloved comes to be seen as itself a garden to be plundered of its beauty. The essential egotism and impersonality of the attitude is clearly evident in Donne's Elegy XIX:

> O my America! my new-found-land,
> My kingdome, safeliest when with one man
> man'd,
> My Myne of precious stones, My Emperie,
> How blest am I in this discovering thee!

Vaughan creates such an antithesis of the garden of love in the poem *"In Amicum foeneratorem,"* as the speaker mocks the usurer by offering in repayment of his debts an imaginary kingdom of erotic fantasies. Typically, predatory metaphors invite the usurer to imagine limitless feminine beauties, depersonalized by metaphors of coral, gold, and timber, as mere agents of his pleasure:

> Wee'l suck the *Corall* of their lips, and feed
> Upon their spicie breath, a meale at need,
> Rove in their *Amber-tresses,* and unfold
> That glist'ring grove, the Curled wood of gold,
> Then peep for babies, a new Puppet-play,
> And riddle what their *pratling Eyes* would say.

The speciousness of this counterfeit coin is neatly pinpointed by the word "Puppet-play"; the speaker completes the game by playing mock pander for the "waggish *Nymphs*": "But here thou must remember to dispurse, / For without money all this is a Curse."

Similarly, in **"FIDA: *Or The Country-beauty*,"** the woman's body, so carefully inventoried, is merely the cynosure of an obsessive gaze. The catalogue of her "charming *Sweets*"—hair, eyes, cheeks, lips, teeth, tongue, skin, neck, breasts—is summarized by the word "piece": "A piece so full of *Sweets* and *bliss.*" She is the moral equivalent of a cookie jar or a candy-store window, all the more desirable for being labeled "Do Not Touch." Her "prudent Rigor" adds the spice of challenge to the fascination engendered by her physical attributes: "A face, that hath no Lovers slain, / Wants forces, and is near disdain." Addressed *"to* Lysimachus," the poem implies a dramatic situation: the speaker has been sceptical of Lysimachus's reports of the wondrous beauty of his mistress, but one look at her has infatuated him equally, and now he can do nothing but confirm his friend's account. The speaker's "stupid" infatuation is reflected in the exuberant agility with which he compiles similitudes to prove that she is the paragon of animals. The organization of the poem is simple, loose, and free: the speaker merely begins at the top of her head and proceeds anatomically with breathless speed, eagerly skipping from detail to detail as sensations crowd upon him. Vaughan always handles octosyllabic couplets with dexterity; here, by often varying the basic measure with lines of nine syllables, he creates an effect of spontaneous improvisation which is further heightened by numerous feminine rhymes and an occasional near-rhyme. The chief difference between this poem and others of its kind, such as Carew's "The Complement," is that Vaughan does not descend below the waist. This restraint, together with the poem's liveliness and lightness in

rhythms and sound effects, makes it a fine example of the Cavaliers' ideal of delicate grace:

> Her *Hair* lay'd out in curious *Setts*
> And *Twists,* doth shew like silken *Nets,*
> Where (since he play'd at *Hitt* or *Miss:*)
> The God of *Love* her pris'ner is,
> And fluttering with his skittish Wings
> Puts all her locks in Curls and Rings.

The poems to Etesia and Amoret are less concerned with the woman's attributes and more with her effect upon the lover and with his relationship to her. The central image in the Fida poem is the image of the woman's body as a pastoral paradise—"a rich and flowry *Plain.*" The woman in the Etesia and Amoret poems is usually expressed by images of the sun or a star, and the relationship between her and the lover is most often defined in terms of stellar or planetary influence. The central topic in each sequence is the relation of love to freedom of the will. The thematic contrast between them may be explained by examination of the different ways this topic is worked out.

The Etesia poems define the lover's plight in terms of astrological determinism, expressing by these means the traditional Christian-Platonic idea of the power of passion to enslave the whole personality. The clearest, though not the best, example is *"To Etesia looking from her Casement at the full Moon."* The speaker declares his lifelong subjection to the capricious influence of the moon, his natal star. Though his "constant mind" is "fix'd" in its affections, his fortunes are "humorous as wind." His life is full of *"Sorrows"* and "sad *Eclipses"* because it is his fate to pursue with constancy objects that are fickle and unstable. He is trying to overthrow the "Laws of Fate" and gain his freedom by reasoning himself out of vain passions when he suddenly falls in love with Etesia. The implication at the end of the poem is that Etesia has supplanted the moon as the capricious manipulator of his fortunes. Similar language of compulsion is characteristic of *"To Etesia (for* Timander,) *the first Sight."* It is her natal star that "Made me the *Subject:* you the *Queen"*; now that "sparkling *Planet"* works on him from her eyes with "nearer force, and more acute"; her eyes "controul" him, he "must adore" her. Undone with one bright glance, his loss of liberty is sudden and complete. Of course she can predominate in this way only because she is a miracle of nature, formed "that we might see / Perfection, not Variety." Passionate enslavement to perfection is pleasant pain.

We have seen that in some poems Vaughan presents reciprocated love as an aspect of an ideal natural order and that in others he presents the woman as an ideal natural object for man's possession or use. In some of these poems to Etesia the balance is tipped the other way, and the woman is presented as part of an ideal, supranatural order from which the man is separated by a vast moral gulf. His terrestrial passions have no counterpart in her world and he inevitably becomes the sport and plaything of his own desires. He is frustrated not so much by her indifference to his desires—the celebrated cruelty of the courtly mistress—as by their incompatability with the exalted conception he has of her. Seeking to justify his passions in terms of the Platonic theory of love as a desire for the beautiful and the good, he finds himself on the horns of a dilemma. The logical consequence of that theory, strictly followed, is that the highest form of love is an act of pure contemplation, an entirely intellectual act devoid of passional elements. This consequence is presented in *"The importunate Fortune,"* where the soul's ascent to comprehension of "the Deitie" is accomplished through a purgation of all earthly faculties:

> First my dull Clay I give unto the *Earth,*
> Our common Mother, which gives all their
>   birth.
> My growing Faculties I send as soon
> Whence first I took them, to the humid *Moon.*
> All Subtilties and every cunning Art
> To witty *Mercury* I do impart.
> Those fond Affections which made me a slave
> To handsome Faces, *Venus* thou shalt have.
>
> . . . .
>
>   Get up my disintangled Soul, thy fire
> Is now refin'd & nothing left to tire,
> Or clog thy wings. Now my auspicious flight
> Hath brought me to the *Empyrean* light.
> I am a sep'rate *Essence,* and can see
> The *Emanations* of the Deitie.

The lover of Etesia might solve his problem, in accordance with the ethical implications of lady-service in medieval romance, by a similar purgation of base affections. He would then be capable of the act of pure contemplation which is alone consistent with the exalted conception of her expressed in *"The Character, to Etesia."* At least he could then meet her on her own level, from which they both might "descend / T'affections, and to faculties." But it is the dilemma of the Platonizing lover to desire the best of both worlds and to be satisfied with neither. Desire and admiration fuse at the level of worship rather than of love, and the verse assumes the incantatory grandeur of a ritual act:

> Thou art the dark worlds Morning-star,
> Seen only, and seen but from far;
> Where like Astronomers we gaze
> Upon the glories of thy face,
> But no acquaintance more can have,
> Though all our lives we watch and Crave.
> Thou art a world thy self alone,
> Yea three great worlds refin'd to one.
> Which shews all those, and in thine Eyes
> The shining *East,* and *Paradise.*

The chief difference between Vaughan's audacity here and Donne's audacity in such poems as "The Canonization" and "The Sunne Rising" is that Donne makes such claims as this for both lover and mistress, whereas Vaughan exalts only the woman. As S. L. Bethell remarks, the poem expresses "a virtual adoration of the lady as not merely representing but really participating in the divine glory." The morning star is to the sun what the Son of God is to God the Father; this is the language that Vaughan would use later in his sacred poems to express a love with nothing earthly for its object. She is the cynosure of the universe and its epitome, the source of the dark world's light and happiness, the origin and end of its creative energy:

> Thy Soul (a *Spark* of the first *Fire,*)
> Is like the *Sun,* the worlds desire;
> And with a nobler influence
> Works upon all, that claim to sense.

According to the Christian concept of the *imago Dei* and the Neoplatonic theory of creative emanation, every natural creature participated, to some degree, in the divine glory; every soul was a spark of the divine fire. But few were like the morning star or capable of nobler influence than the sun. The hyperboles at the center of the poem are prepared for by the opening conceits; echoing the fantastic errands of Donne's "Goe, and catche a falling starre," they declare the impossibility of making an adequate "character" of Etesia with even the most prodigious of natural materials. She is ultimately beyond even the extraordinary dispensation of nature to which phoenixes and rivers of milk belong: "Such objects and so fresh would be / But dull Resemblances of thee." Her place is with the Platonic Ideas or Forms of the most superlative things of the natural world, as a contemporary comment acknowledges:

> Nor does thy other softer Magick move
> Us less thy fam'd *Etesia* to love;
> Where such a *Character* thou giv'st that shame
> Nor envy dare approach the Vestal Dame:
> So at bright Prime *Idea's* none repine,
> They safely in th' *Eternal Poet* shine.

The paradox for the Platonizing lover is that passion dare approach "bright Prime *Idea's*" no more than envy and shame. But her charms nevertheless "seize" his heart and "oblige" him to admire her. He barely stops on this side idolatry:

> O thou art such, that I could be
> A lover to Idolatry!
> I could, and should from heav'n stray,
> But that thy life shews mine the way,
> And leave a while the *Diety,*
> To serve his *Image* here in thee.

The idea that spiritual love of the angelic mistress prepared the soul for the love of God was the solution of the problem for Dante and Petrarch. But the speaker in this poem has given vent to a dual passion, based as much on what she has in common with the "Rich *odours* . . . and *Sweetnesses*" of earth's flowers as on her morning-star qualities. The conclusion does not reconcile these diverse elements; it is an attempt to escape from the problem by ignoring one side of the speaker's nature. Only by self-delusion does he escape the ambiguities of the self-imposed dilemma with which courtly sonneteers had prevaricated in similar fashion many times before.

The character of Etesia changes with the fourth poem in the series, *"To Etesia parted from him, and looking back."* No longer the remote, capricious, untouchable paragon of the early poems, she reciprocates his passion or, at the least, responds with human kindness. She remains unattainable, and he remains in torment, because of an ordinary, irreducible situation: an apparently enforced separation. The poem dramatizes the way this situation transfigures all, converting even the manna of her kindness to gall:

> Strange *Art* of Love! that can make sound,

And yet exasperates the wound;
That *look* she lent to ease my heart,
Hath pierc't it, and improv'd the smart.

These lines catch the very moment when she is parted from him and looking back. Their paradoxical healing-wounding motif runs through the whole poem, creating, with some lesser oxymora, an intense statement of the strangeness, the mystery, of love's contrarieties. Only gradually does the speaker come to the final recognition that the contradictions which make up his misery are inherent in the experience of love under these particular circumstances. For a while he questions whether the woman is not willfully cruel:

Hath she no *Quiver,* but my Heart?
Must all her Arrows hit that part?
Beauties like Heav'n, their Gifts should deal
Not to destroy us, but to heal.

The conclusion of the poem, implicitly absolving the woman, answers these questions by confirming the first stanza's impassioned recognition that the strangeness of his experience is due to the very nature of love:

O Subtile Love! thy Peace is War;
It wounds and kills without a scar:
It works unknown to any sense,
Like the Decrees of Providence,
And with strange silence shoots me through;
The *Fire* of Love doth fall like *Snow.*

This treatment of love had been standard for centuries; Vaughan brings it to life by dramatizing it as a personal experience. S. L. Bethell's remark that the fifth line is marked by "the emotive use of language to convey experience qualitatively rather than by objective definition" might be extended to the poem as a whole.

Between this poem and the more successful **"Etesia absent,"** which ends the series, are placed two poems which further develop the situation of the parting itself. The description of her "charming grief" in the Latin "In Etesiam lachrymantem" tends to humanize her still more and to intensify the impression that she accepts as reluctantly as he the "ill fortune" of their parting. The inferior **"To Etesia *going beyond Sea"*** bids her "Go, if you must!" but detains her long enough for him to swear to keep the regular schedule of pining lovers. The tone of **"Etesia absent"**—a poem that is decidedly superior to the much anthologized **"To Amoret gone from him"**—stems mainly from the serious use of philosophic, religious, and scientific concepts. The poem's basic proposition, tersely compressed in the opening invocation, is "the common Renaissance conception that divine love was immanent throughout the cosmos and was, basically, the force effecting universal order and harmony." The recession of human love through the woman's absence is presented as an alienation from this universal principle and, therefore, as a spiritual death far more dreadful than the death of the body:

Love, the Worlds Life! what a sad death
Thy absence is? to lose our breath
At once and dye, is but to live
Inlarg'd, without the scant reprieve
Of *Pulse* and *Air:* whose dull *returns*

And narrow *Circles* the Soul mourns.

Vaughan's paradoxical development of the basic idea makes the poem a tissue of oxymora. What we ordinarily think of as death merely frees the soul from its physical privations to enjoy an enlarged kind of life. By contrast, the "sad death" which the lover lives in the absence of his beloved is a severe privation, a lapse of his soul from joyful participation in the animating spirit of the universe, the very source of life. Real death is redeemed by the Resurrection; for the lover's living death there is no redemption except the woman's return. The antithetical structure of thought in the poem's opening statement is underscored by the stark antitheses between words denoting life and love and the far more numerous expressions denoting death, loss, and privation. Beneath this antithesis is an implied analogy between the soul mourning the death-in-life of its physical imprisonment and the lover mourning the death-in-life occasioned by his beloved's absence. This may be more than analogy, and hence more than hyperbole: according to the poem's basic conception of universal love, the aim of the lover seeking reunion is essentially cognate with that of the soul seeking fulfillment.

The opening conceits establish a basic definition of the lover's predicament; the remaining lines amplify the basic definition by developing these antitheses and analogies still further. The frustration of the lover's quest for a more vital life is dramatized in a series of violent antitheses:

But to be dead alive, and still
To wish, but never have our will:
To be possess'd, and yet to miss;
To wed a true but absent bliss:
Are lingring tortures, and their smart
Dissects and racks and grinds the Heart!

The discrepancy between the goal of desire and the lover's actual condition is insistently underscored by the connectives: *and still, but never, and yet, but.* The analogous structure of the conflicting clauses further points up the antithesis. The periodic structure of the sentence holds back the most forceful images of the lover's condition while short, sharply conflicting clauses build up tension, finally releasing their energy in "Are lingring tortures, and their smart / Dissects and racks and grinds the Heart!" An effect of rhythmically swinging blows is created by the mechanical repetition of "and" and by the fall of the heavy stresses on the harsh, violent verbs and on the lover's "Heart."

In the poem's beginning the living and dead states of the soul are dichotomized and static, reflecting the idea that the lovers' separation brings death by dichotomizing a living whole. At the conclusion, the lover anticipates a desperately slow movement toward an eventual reunion, presented as a return to life through analogy with the reunion of soul and body at the Resurrection. The clogged, dragging movement of the lines reflects the massive inertia of "Times long *train,"* through which the lover looks in vain. Time takes on the sense of an almost physical obstacle and weight, shutting out life and light and entombing the lover in a dark torpor of spirit:

As Soul and Body in that state
Which unto us seems separate,

Cannot be said to live, until
Reunion; which dayes fulfill
And slow-pac'd seasons: So in vain
Through hours and minutes (Times long *train,*)
I look for thee, and from thy sight,
As from my Soul, for life and light.
For till thine Eyes shine so on me,
Mine are fast-clos'd and will not see.

In the first five poems of the 1646 volume the mistress is presented as an irresistible, heartless beauty who aggrandizes herself at the expense of her admirers' brokenhearted deaths. The song beginning *"**Amyntas** goe, thou art undone"* is typical:

This Cruell thou hast done, and thus,
    That Face hath many servants slaine.
Though th' end be not to ruine us,
    But to seeke glory by our paine.

Here we are close to the first year's cycle of Spenser's *Amoretti* and to thousands of conventional love lyrics. But with **"To Amoret, Walking in a Starry Evening"** we get a different mood. As in the early poems to Etesia, the woman is associated with the stars and the sun; but the relation between her and the lover is not defined simply in terms of stellar influence on a passive terrestrial creature. Instead it is presented as a "sympathie" between "two conspiring minds." And whereas in **"The Character, to Etesia"** she was a distant star upon which he could gaze only like an astronomer, here "no distance" can disrupt their unity. Similarly, **"To Amoret gone from him"** argues by analogy with the sympathy between flowers and the sun that the lovers also "At such vast distance can agree." **"A Song to *Amoret*"** and **"*To* Amoret, *of the difference* . . ."** boast of the lover's worthiness to be beloved by insisting on the purity of his soul and the spiritual foundation of his affections. The latter poem defines true love by analogy with the "mutuall fire" of "Spirits and Stars." In **"To Amoret Weeping"** the speaker tries to allay her distress over the mediocrity of their shared estate by boasting at length of the power of his soul to transcend misfortunes and by urging her to recognize their mutual love as more precious than gold. In these poems the speaker muses, reflects, deliberates, confidently reasons with the woman, remonstrates with her, and cajoles her—all from a position of either equality or superiority. Love is presented as not merely compatible with spiritual freedom but as in large measure the very foundation of that freedom.

The equanimity of the lover in these poems is reflected in the equable temperament of the verse. This is a poetry of cool, deliberate statement and reasoned argument rather than of passionate ardors and hyperbolical enthusiasms. The imagery is not as profuse as in the Etesia poems, the studied development of a single image being sometimes sufficient for a whole poem. But an awkwardness in the development of thought and in the handling of the complex stanzaic patterns too often produces a heavy, turgid effect. **"To Amoret gone from him"** succeeds better than most, perhaps because Vaughan is more comfortable with the octosyllabic couplet. But the **"Song to *Amoret*"** is for me the most satisfying of these poems apart from **"To Amoret Weeping."** . . . The neat, precise symmetry of the song's quatrains makes it the perfect vehicle for the speaker's

emotional repose. He holds in suspension until the last stanza his sober statement of sincere, unshakeable affection while he imperturbably hypothesizes the character of "Some fresher youth" who, if the speaker were dead, might try "To warme thee with new fires." His strategy is simple: he grants to his hypothetical supplanter all that can be granted of virtue and wealth and then puts in the opposite scale the simplest of things: "So rich a heart as mine."

Fortune and beauty thou mightst finde,
    And greater men then I:
But my true resolved minde,
    They never shall come nigh.

For I not for an houre did love,
    Or for a day desire,
But with my soule had from above,
    This endles holy fire.

As in **"To Amoret Weeping,"** Vaughan counterbalances the weighty values of the world—fortune, beauty, greatness—with a simple, lightly touched affirmation of love. The declaration that such a constant, sincere, and pure devotion will not coincide with worldly glory could not be more lightly yet firmly and effectively made. It brings to a point the evaluation of this hypothetical suitor which the language of the poem has been making all along:

Were he as faithfull as the Sunne,
    That's wedded to the Sphere;
His bloud as chaste, and temp'rate runne,
    As Aprils mildest teare;

Or were he rich, and with his heapes,
    And spacious share of Earth,
Could make divine affection cheape,
    And court his golden birth . . .

The effect of the anticlimactic "spacious share of *Earth*" (my italics) and of the derogatory "heapes" is obvious; the rest of the stanza insinuates that he is vainly proud of his wealth and arrogantly insensitive to the superiority of "divine affection." He is pictured as one who expects to be loved because of his money. At first glance, the other stanza just quoted seems very much like the speaker's own protestation at the end of the poem. This is the standard rhetoric of the wooer; but here it is slightly exaggerated, the claim to constancy and temperance being twice buttressed with hyperbolical similitudes. The rhetoric is further made to parody itself by the way it is introduced:

If I were dead, and in my place,
    Some fresher youth *design'd*
To warme thee with new fires . . . (my italics)

The word "Arts" insinuates hypocrisy more directly; and finally there is the mocking summation in the phrase "the mighty Amorist."

For all these Arts I'de not believe,
    (No though he should be thine)
The mighty Amorist could give
    So rich a heart as mine.

In these subtleties, as well as in its smooth, balanced progression, the poem foreshadows the accomplishment of "They are all gone into the world of light!" It seems to me quite as attractive as the best-known songs of Carew and Lovelace.

Kenneth Friedenreich (essay date 1978)

SOURCE: "Important Characteristics of Vaughan's Style," in *Henry Vaughan,* Twayne Publishers, 1978, pp. 31-45.

[*Friedenreich was an American educator who published essays on various English poets and dramatists, including Christopher Marlowe, John Milton, William Shakespeare, among others. In the following excerpt from his monograph on Vaughan, he examines key characteristics of Vaughan's style, paying particular attention to the influence of the poet's Welsh heritage, the Bible, and Hermetic philosophy.*]

As mentioned above, Henry Vaughan is regarded as a Metaphysical poet. He is considered an heir to the "school" of Donne and Herbert on the strength of his best-known work, *Silex Scintillans.* The hallmarks of Metaphysical writers are their personal intensity, intellectual awareness, and their habit for minute analysis of experiences, feelings, ideas, perceptions. Their verse—in contrast to that of the Cavaliers with whom Vaughan served his poetic apprenticeship—is marked by stanzaic and metrical irregularity, by colloquial diction, and by imagery drawn from both common and uncommon sources. Frequently, Metaphysical writers use images and allusions in startling juxtapositions.

The most "metaphysical" traits of Vaughan's *Silex Scintillans* are its images and allusions. The imagery is sensuous and intense and luminous. Frequently the images fall into clusters—like clouds/mists, white/green, spirit/retreat, morning/bright—whose patterns are varied, repeated, or reversed. Vaughan's allusiveness may make the modern reader think his work is obscure or difficult. The following sections, however, identify the main sources from which Vaughan shapes his poetic language, principally in *Silex Scintillans,* but also in his other works. Taken together they reflect the inquisitive quality of his mind and his perceptions of the worlds—hidden and revealed—around him.

Finally, a word of caution: in his valuable essay, "The Private Imagery of Henry Vaughan," Frank Kermode points out that it is wrong to take a poet's use of imagery drawn from particular sources as proofs of doctrine or, literally, as statements of belief. Rather, Kermode rightly says, Vaughan employs images to enrich the meaning of his poetry. The sources of the imagery may be interesting, but it is Vaughan's characteristic handling of them in his work which ought to command most of the reader's attention.

I *Welsh Language and Poetry*

Hutchinson's biography contains an entire chapter on the survival of Welsh language and techniques of Welsh poetry in Vaughan's work. He points out the likelihood that the twin sons of Thomas Vaughan, Gentleman, were raised bilingually in Welsh and English. Examples in Vaughan's work of the influence of Welsh language are not uncommon.

The Welsh language does not have a *z*-sound, for instance. On evidence of Vaughan's rhyme-words, Hutchinson concludes that the poet pronounced *s* and *z* alike as *ss*. The survival of Welsh influence can be seen in this couplet from a poem in *Thalia Rediviva,* "The Revival":

> The lofty groves in express Joyes
> Reply unto the *Turtles* voice. (ll. 11-12)

From Welsh poetry Vaughan may have developed his fondness for assonance and alliteration. The final lines from the opening stanza of **"Regeneration"** in *Silex Scintillans* provide a striking example of assonance:

> Yet was *it* frost w*ith*in,
>   And surl*y* w*i*nds
> Blasted m*y i*nfant buds, and s*i*nne
> L*i*ke Clouds eccl*i*ps'd m*y* m*i*nd.

The unity of sounds extends beyond the short and long *i*-vowel to the repetition of consonants as well, particularly with *n,* and the alliteration of "Blasted . . . buds" in line seven and "my mind" in line eight. Lines from Vaughan's elegy on the death of Hall, published in *Olor Iscanus* further reveal his penchant for alliteration:

> *M*ore than a blot unto thy *M*artyrdo*m*e
> Which *s*corn*s* such wretched *s*uffrage*s,* and
>   *s*tands. . . .

Of greater interest are transformations of techniques found in Welsh poetry into English verse. The Welsh term for white is *gwyn;* yet it also means "fair," "happy," and "blessed." Similarly, the Welsh term for Paradise is *gwynfyd,* literally "white world." In **"Dressing,"** Vaughan begins, "O thou that lovest a pure *whitend* soul!" The Welsh connotation doubly stresses "blessedness"; for a "pure soul" is, one assumes, blessed already. Whiteness intensifies its happy state. The effect is the same in the opening lines of **"Tears":** "O when my God, my glory brings, / His *white* and *holy* train . . ." (italics added). The meanings are enriched by knowledge of Vaughan's "Welshness."

This carry-over into English is also found in his secular poetry. Its witty and playful dimensions are revealed in the first stanza of **"The Character, to Etesia"** in *Thalia Rediviva.* The speaker, seeking the proper means by which to inspire his muse to praise Etesia, settles soon on the quality of her own being and person:

> Now for an untouch'd, spotless *white*
> For blackest things on paper write;
> *Etesia* at thine own Expence
> Give me the *Robes* of innocence.

The Welsh connotations of *gwyn* by extension include the quality of the lady's "innocence"; her "spotless white" complexion is also a reflection of her inner character, and together the combination of her visible and invisible virtues inspire the poet.

Vaughan transforms from Welsh poetry to English the technique of the *dyfalu,* the layering of one comparison upon another. Consider the many ways that Vaughan describes the descent of light in the first stanza of **"The Starre"** in *Silex Scintillans:*

> What ever 'tis, whose beauty here below

> Attracts thee thus & makes thee stream & flow,
> And winde and curle, and wink and smile,
> Shifting thy gate and guile:

The movements of starlight are compared successively to streaming, flowing, winding, curling, winking, and smiling. The *dyfalu* is further compounded by Vaughan's repetition of "&/and" in these lines.

These phenomena taken by Vaughan from Welsh language and verse—both of which interested him throughout his life—should not discourage a modern reader into believing that knowledge of Welsh language is a prerequisite to understanding Vaughan's poetry. Instead these survivals suggest his ability to incorporate or transform for poetic effect certain characteristics of the Welsh heritage of which he was so conscious and proud.

II *The Bible*

No doubt Vaughan derived comfort, instruction, and inspiration from the Bible. He was able to fashion the Word of God, however, into the personal utterance of his own verse. One readily can see looking at **Silex Scintillans** that Vaughan often bases individual lyrics on specific passages from the bible. Likewise, he borrows images directly from the Bible, or alludes to them. Thus, in **"The Retreate,"** the mention of "that shady City of Palme trees" at line twenty-six is taken from a description of Jericho found in Deuteronomy 34:3-4, where Moses saw to the south from the summit of Mount Nebo "the plain and valley of Jericho, the city of palm trees, unto Zoar." The context of the allusion, however, makes it especially fitting for Vaughan's purposes. The passage from the Bible tells us that Moses is about to die. He can only see the Promised Land from the summit of Nebo. In **"The Retreate,"** Vaughan declares his desire to return to the realm of his "Angell-infancy," which is heaven. The Promised Land is, in turn, a metaphor for Heaven. Thus the allusion suggests that Vaughan feels longing for and a sense of separation from what he most desires, as he imagines Moses must have felt looking into Israel, but being unable to reach it.

In a similar way, the concluding four lines of Vaughan's epitaph upon the Princess Elizabeth in **Olor Iscanus** echo Scripture in order to make a very topical point:

> These were the Comforts she had here,
> As by an unseen hand 'tis cleer,
> Which now she reads, and smiling wears
> A Crown with him, who wipes off tears.

The opening thirty-four lines of the verse describe how the young daughter of the martyred Charles I suffered patiently through the upheavals of the civil wars that brought about the death of her father. These are the "Comforts" to which the poet ironically refers. The final line apparently paraphrases Revelations 7:17, "and God shall wipe away all tears from their eyes." The allusion not only shows that the quiet endurance of the princess is rewarded by God, but also indicates that the age in which she lived anticipates the upheavals of the Apocalypse. In drawing such a parallel by his Biblical paraphrase, Vaughan joins many of his contemporaries in the attitude that the civil and religious wars were perhaps the beginning of the end of the world.

Vaughan particularly draws on the concept of spiritual espousal which is celebrated so sensuously in The Song of Songs; moreover, he translates its rich landscape to his own sense of time and place. The lines quoted above from **"The Revival,"** which mark the voice of the dove and the disappearance of winter, are based on the Song of Solomon 2:11-12:

> For, lo, the winter is past,
> the rain is over and gone;
> The flowers appear on the earth;
> the time of the singing of birds is come,
> and the voice of the turtle is heard in our land.

Vaughan transfigures it:

> Hark! how his *winds* have chang'd their *note,*
> And with warm *whispers* call thee out.
> The *frosts* are past, the *storms* are gone:
> And backward *life* at last comes on.
> The lofty *groves* in express Joyes
> Reply unto the *Turtles* voice,
> And here in *dust* and *dirt,* O here
> The *Lillies* of his love appear!

The coming of spring symbolizes the awakening of the speaker's love of God; the reference to "lillies" in line fourteen is inspired by another passage in the Song of Songs where the maiden expresses her joyful anticipation of her union with the bridegroom: "I am my beloved's, and my beloved is mine: / he feedeth among the lillies" (6:3). The two allusions are charged with excitement of union and awareness of renewal. Vaughan incorporates the sensations described in Scripture for his own contemplation of the rebirth of the year at springtime.

Vaughan's allusions to and paraphrases of Scripture often extend the implications of passages he finds there. In **"The Retreate"** and in **"The Revival"** the Biblical allusions emphasize larger themes of the poems. However, in **"The Dawning,"** the allusions to Scripture prompt fresh speculation and response to what the cited passage only begins to suggest. It reveals Vaughan at his most original, borrowing from Scripture not solely to enrich meaning, but as a starting point for personal interpretation of what the passages mean to him:

> Ah! what time wilt thou come? when shall the
>   crie
>   The *Bridegroome's Comming!* fil the sky?
>   Shall it in the Evening run
> When our words and works are done?
>   Or wil thy all-surprizing light
>   Break at midnight?
> When either sleep, or some dark pleasure
> Possesseth mad man without measure;
> Or shal these early, fragrant hours
>   Unlock thy bowres?
> And with their blush of light descry
> Thy locks crown'd with eternitie;
> Indeed it is the only time
> That with thy glory doth best chime,
> All now are stirring, ev'ry field
>   Ful hymns doth yield,
> The whole Creation shakes off night,
> And for thy shadow looks the light,
> Stars now vanish without number,
> Sleepie Planets set, and slumber,

The pursie Clouds disband and scatter,
All expect some sudden matter,
Not one beam triumphs, but from far
    That morning-star; . . .

The quoted lines represent exactly one-half of the poem. The question that is asked in the opening of **"The Dawning"** comes from the parable of the foolish and wise virgins in Matthew 25:1-13. Vaughan read there that "at midnight there was a cry, 'Behold the bridegroom. Come out to meet him.' " The final verse of the parable is a forceful call: "Watch, therefore, for you know neither the day or the hour." In *Silex Scintillans* particularly, the idea of watchful waiting occurs frequently. **"The Dawning"** is one of the lyrics in which this idea is developed. Musing on the call of the parable, Vaughan asks at what time the bridegroom will call for him. That is, in terms of the spiritual espousal whose Old Testament type is found in the Song of Solomon, at what moment will he be united with God?

The mounting intensity and anticipation build inevitably in the first half of the poem to reveal the day of God's final judgment. The force of the description of the Last Day is realized through Vaughan's keen sense of the beauty of the dawn of *any* day. God's plan for man not only is revealed in his Word, Scripture, but in his "second book," Nature. The actual description of the day—an ordinary day—is beautiful, but its beauty suggests to the speaker the glory of the final day. Thus Biblical allusions are subsumed in the fabric of Vaughan's description of a very natural event, which he captures in the emergent glory of the early morning sun.

In answering the question inspired by the parable, Vaughan rejects the idea that God will come in the evening, when man has finished his allotment of "words and works." Nor will he come at midnight—thus contradicting the parable source—because his spouse, the speaker, will be either asleep (unaware) or worse, unprepared, when "some dark pleasure / Possesseth mad man without measure." The nature of the questions themselves may seem naive, but they suggest man's essentially limited perspective in knowing God's exact ways. The best man can know is taken from what God's Word and his World reveal in the way of a promise. Vaughan discovers the promise in the beautiful dawn he describes: nature stirs, the fields yield up hymns, and the "whole Creation shakes off night." Metaphorically the dawn of the Last Day will shake off night forever, and the powers of darkness. As the inexorable movement of the light of the morning sun waxes, Vaughan imagines that he is witnessing the dawn of the final day. His mood is one of awe, wonder, surprise, anticipation. Vaughan's description of the actual sunrise, where the stars and planets fade away and the clouds vanish, apparently recalls a passage from Revelations 6:13-14:

> And the stars of heaven fell unto earth, even as a fig tree casteth her untimely figs, when she is shaken of a mighty wind. And the heaven departed as a scroll when it is rolled together. . . .

The echo of the passage in Vaughan is at best faint; but it serves to strengthen the connection between the actual and the imaginary, the prophecies of Scripture and the revealed promise observed in nature. One senses the power of the Second Coming in the gradual realization of the speaker that the dawn he sees *could be* the last day. Absorbed totally in a moment where the actual and transcendent coexist, the speaker offers a prayer, which forms the poem's second half.

He asks to be made ready for Judgment Day and for the ability to make himself ready. He acknowledges that his ultimate understanding of the divine plan is beyond his limited mortal perception. No matter how much nature reveals, God still holds a mystery. Thus the celebration of the dawn is also a lesson in humility. The speaker, having wondered what time of day the bridegroom would come, realizes that it is most important that he be prepared,

> So when that day, and hour shal come
> In which thy self wil be the Sun,
> Thou'lt find me drest and on my way,
> Watching for the Break of thy great day.

The poet's observations cause him to relearn the parable of the wise and foolish virgins, to render the Scriptural passage in terms of his own time, place, and experience. His question about the appropriate time of day leads him to confirm the promise of the parable through observing nature. In turn, however, he realizes that part of the injunction to watch for the bridegroom is also a charge that he be as ready, as good, as possible. **"The Dawning"** shows Vaughan forging an entirely new comprehension that moves far beyond the literal use of Biblical allusion.

III *Hermetic Philosophy*

In *Thalia Rediviva,* Vaughan includes a poem on the theme of the penury of poets called *"The importunate Fortune, written to Doctor* **Powel** *of Cantre."* It rationalizes his lack of worldly wealth. Because he is poor, the speaker says, he is free to contemplate higher things and can cleanse his soul from worldly dross:

> First my dull Clay I give unto the *Earth,*
> Our common Mother, which gives all their
>   birth.
> My growing Faculties I send as soon
> Whence first I took them, to the humid *Moon.*
> All Subtilties and every cunning Art
> To witty *Mercury* I do impart.
> Those found Affections which made me a slave
> To handsome Faces, *Venus* thou shalt have.
> And saucy Pride (if there was ought in me,)
> *Sol,* I return it to thy Royalty.
> My daring Rashness and Presumptions be
> To *Mars* himself an equal Legacy.
> My ill-plac'd Avarice (sure 'tis but small;)
> *Jove,* to Thy Flames I do bequeath it all.
> And my false *Magic,* which I did believe,
> And mystic Lyes to *Saturn* do I give.
> My dark Imaginations rest you there,
> This is your grave and Superstitious Sphaere.
>   Get up my disintangled Soul, thy fire
> Is now refin'd & nothing left to tire,
> Or clog thy wings. Now my auspicious flight
> Hath brought me to the *Empyrean* light.

Readers familiar with the "Elizabethan World Picture" will see that Vaughan's progression is faithful to the model: the earth is in the center, surrounded by concentric spheres whose outermost member touches the edge of heaven. The first sphere is that of the moon, the next of Mercury, the next Venus, and so on. The progress is set forth in couplets until at last the soul is free of the vices attendant on mortal existence. The refined soul is able to contemplate "The *Emanations* of the Deity."

While Vaughan thus follows the model employed by poets since ancient times—the Ptolomeic cosmos—he nonetheless qualifies the ascent from sphere to sphere by drawing on a passage from Libellus which gives to each planet certain aspects of human behavioral psychology:

> And thereupon . . . the man mounts upward through the structure of the heavens. And to the first zone he gives up the force which works increase. .. and decrease; to the second zone, the machinations of evil cunning; to the third zone, the lust whereby men are deceived; to the fourth zone domineering arrogance; to the fifth zone unholy daring rash audacity; to the sixth zone, evil strivings after wealth; and to the seventh zone, the false-hood which lies in wait to work harm.

The source from which Vaughan drew the passage by Libellus comes from a body of literature called the *Corpus Hermetica,* and to it the poet frequently is indebted for imagery, The Hermetic writings appeared in Greek during the early Christian era under the name Hermes Trismegistus, literally, "thrice-great Hermes." Much of the writing deals with the occult sciences, embracing astrology and alchemy. While a portion of the *Hermetica* was known to medieval writers, the full body of the writings did not reappear until the early Renaissance. The first complete edition was published in 1554. While it was thought that these writings formed a kind of "missing link" to ancient Egyptian culture, Isaac Casaubon proved in the early seventeenth century that the work actually came from the first century after Christ.

Hermetic philosophy is a complex subject; it embraces theology and philosophy in addition to alchemical and astrological speculation. One of the best introductions to it can be found in Wayne C. Schumaker's *The Occult Sciences in the Renaissance.* We are indebted to his research for the following list of basic Hermetic beliefs: 1. God created Man to contemplate the order of the universe. Man's understanding of the universe is not based on empirical evidence obtained through the senses, but through Mind— *Novs.*

2. Knowledge is obtained through Mind; knowledge of God comes through contemplation where the senses are suspended.

3. God is the source of the sensible world contemplated by Man; because God made all things they are good and part of His totality. Thus, metonymically, anything that is part of God, "is" God. His presence can be found in all the objects of creation.

4. God creates—and has created the world—so He might be seen. By analogy, the world is visible in order that it may be seen.

5. Man has a unique position in the universe; he is capable of adoring God on the one hand through Mind; but his

material being can pull him downwards to animality. He is capable of becoming godlike, perceiving things not through the eyes (sensory) but through intellectual energy (the power of Mind).

6. Each individual soul is departed from the total soul *miâs wvmns.* All souls undergo a series of changes ranging from the lowest level (aquatic) to the highest (planets or stars). A virtuous human soul will ascend, lifted by virtue. A vicious human soul will descend, weighed down by ignorance.

7. By means of death, God has provided for the purification of nature and the deficiation of the soul.

8. The highest state of temporal existence is palingenesis or regeneration, as described in the *Corpus Hermetica* XIII. Rebirth is not the result of good works "but by a piety which consists of an intense concentration of the mind on God and by a suspension of sensory observation which makes the initiate accessible to something not entirely different from Christian grace."

To what degree does Vaughan owe a debt to this body of ideas? He did, as mentioned in Chapter One, translate two "Hermetical" books following the publication of the bulk of his poetry and was surely familiar with the work of his brother Thomas. E. C. Pettet rightly points out characteristic words which Vaughan employs that have "Hermetic" meanings—beam, balsam, commerce, essence, exhalation, glance, grain, hatch, influence, invisible, key, magnetism, ray, refine, seed, sympathy, tie, veil, vital. And critics have often noted the similarity between the opening lines of "Cock-Crowing," and lines from Thomas Vaughan's *Anima Magica Abscondita.* Sometimes Vaughan does engage in a wholesale borrowing from a Hermetic source, as in the passage quoted above. Its presence individualizes Vaughan's treatment of a stock poetic theme—the penury of poets—and ought not to be interpreted by modern readers as a statement of his exclusive belief in Hermetic doctrines.

Perhaps Vaughan's debt to Hermetic ideas is of a more general nature. The secular poem to Powell still reflects Vaughan's interest in the ascent of the soul that is a subject of his devout poems. The otherworldly direction of Hermetic thought harmonizes with Vaughan's personal movement from city poet to country poet and his contemplation of nature as a means of apprehending divinity. This impulse however reflects the movement of mid-seventeenth century poetry towards retirement. Hermeticism complements it; Vaughan's use of Hermetic ideas or images distinguishes his work within the broader traditions of pastoral and retirement verse. Knowing Hermetic implications enriches the poetic meanings, but they are not the meanings of the poems per se. Aware of the Hermetic belief that the objects of God are imbued with his spirit leads Vaughan to declare in the poem based on Romans 8:19:

> I would I were a stone, or tree,
>   Or flowre by pedigree,
> Or some poor high-way herb, or Spring
>   To flow, or bird to sing!
> Then should I (tyed to one sure state,)
>   All day expect my date;

But I am sadly loose, and stray
   A giddy blast each way;
   O let me not thus range!

Elsewhere he says of the human condition in **"Man"** that "he knocks at all doors, strays and roams, / Nay hath not so much wit as some stones have / Which in the darkest nights point to their homes."

Both examples are informed by the Hermetic belief in the animation of God's entire creation, from herbs to streams to stones that possess magnetic properties that permit them to "point to their homes." Both passages display the unique position of man's place in the universe as Vaughan sees it. As a rational creature, he must tend heavenwards by his own volition. He must make a choice that the lesser orders of creatures need not make. Their animus is automatically fixed. Thus in one sense man is greater than all of the other creatures, possessing the awareness to aspire towards God. In another sense, however, he is subject to failure of awareness which the other creatures are not; and in this sense man is less fortunate, which moves the poet to wish that he were created other than human, "a stone, or tree / Or flowre by pedigree." The Hermetic background helps to enhance the meaning of the two passages and the feeling that the speaker in each lyric is painfully aware of his separation from God. His very nature, his *man*hood, makes him conscious of his estrangement from his creator. However, the Hermetic background is not necessary as a gloss to these passages; their meanings are explicit in any case.

Schumaker has written that "a small scholarly industry (not . . . always adequately informed) has grown up about the alleged Hermeticism of Henry and Thomas Vaughan . . ." He goes on to generalize that outside of a small circle of thinkers and writers who flourished at Cambridge, "theological Hermeticism was never a powerful intellectual force in England." Bearing this observation in mind, we might conclude this chapter by asserting that the characteristics of Vaughan's style identified here— Welsh language, the Bible, and Hermetic philosophy— suggest approaches to Vaughan's writing by illuminating his technique. They may lead toward and enrich interpretations of individual works but should not be considered ends in themselves. We might consider the famous opening of Vaughan's **"The World,"** "I saw Eternity the other night / Like a great *Ring* of pure and endless light" and follow Maren-Sofie Røstvig's belief that the speaker's perspective is Hermetic. Her reason for this interpretation is indicated by the idea that the universe appears as "a great *Ring* of pure and endless light." According to Røstvig, Vaughan follows Libellus and traces the ascent of the soul through the seven spheres to the eighth, the realm of pure spirit. It is the same ascent described by Vaughan in the poem to Powell discussed above. According to Røstvig, the Hermetic metaphor overcomes the claim made by many other critics that **"The World"** falls flat after its magnificent opening because it gives the poem a sense of overall unity and focus.

However, in a much earlier poem, **"To Amoret, Walking in a Starry Evening,"** Vaughan used a similar striking image of the universe as he suggests that he and his love were intended for each other by "some predestin'd sympathie":

   We might suspect in the vast Ring,
     Amidst these golden glories,
       And fierie stories;
   Whether the Sunne had been the King,
     And guide of Day,
   Or your brighter eye should sway; . . .

Vaughan establishes an analogy in the opening stanza between the first, or primal light of the universe, and the face of his beloved, both of which set patterns of design for the future. The "glorious Eye / In the first birth of light" fills the heavens with stars. Likewise, Amoret's eye, which rivals the first light for brilliance and power, fills the speaker with "sympathie" for her. The "Ring" of heavenly lights implicitly suggests the perfection of two lovers "which no accident, or sight, / Did thus unite." Would the image of the ring in this poem suggest a parallel to Hermetic lore? Does knowledge of Libellus add anything to the meaning of the poem? We must cautiously answer "no" to both questions. The poem's meaning is evident without knowing about Libellus. And yet, elsewhere in Vaughan's output, a similar metaphor for the universe is taken literally as a Hermetic allusion in order to provide a very detailed reading of **"The World."**

Surely a poet's choice of metaphorical language need not remain perpetually constant; but in Vaughan's case, because his imagination is kaleidoscopic, the reader should be cautious before extending the significance of a particular image, metaphor, or allusion towards some rigid theological or philosophical interpretation of an entire work. Thus, the "Ring" in the poem to Amoret and the "Ring" in **"The World"** are part of Vaughan's poetic vocabulary; it is a vocabulary that embraces Vaughan's Welsh heritage, the Bible, and Hermeticism. Rather than restrict our responses to his work, Vaughan's personal poetic language should suggest that the relationship between his sacred and secular writing is dynamic, full of reverberations and interactions.

Vaughan shares with some of his Metaphysical predecessors, particularly Donne, the ability to juxtapose symbols in order to link one idea or emotion with others. Primal light and Amoret's eye provide one such example—the juxtaposed images at once suggest the tranquility one might feel in a meadow on a sparkling summer night and the deep stirrings of affection for another person. There are leaps—and links between time and space in **"To Amoret"** and in **"The World"** which are characteristic of Vaughan, between the here and now and times and places past and to come. The people whom Vaughan castigates in **"The World"** are seen against the backdrop of eternity; the speaker's love for Amoret is not only immediate and intense, but is the result of a grand design born at the beginning of time. Vaughan's imagination seems far more flexible than he is given credit for; to take the characteristics of Vaughan's style for the works themselves is a mistake. That is the point Kermode makes in his essay on Vaughan's imagery.

Critics have had to take these characteristics into account and have argued for their relative significance in interpreting Vaughan's work. Yet no commentator failed to deal at some point with the larger question of Vaughan's view of or response to nature. Nature provides a context in which Vaughan's individualistic treatment of Welsh language, Scripture, and Hermetic philosophy may be seen. All four together help to bring us closer to an appreciation and understanding of his works.

Noel Kennedy Thomas   (essay date 1986)

SOURCE: "Our Sad Captivity," in *Henry Vaughan: Poet of Revelation,* Churchman Publishing, 1986, pp. 1951.

[*An English literary scholar, Thomas was Head of the Department of English at Westhill College, affiliated with the University of Birmingham, for over a quarter century. His areas of specialization include seventeenth-century literature, twentieth-century drama, religious poetry of all periods, and Shakespeare's works. In the following chapter from his book on Vaughan, Thomas argues "that it is impossible to understand Vaughan's spiritual vision without recognising the enormous impact which the Civil War had upon him and upon his native Breconshire. In the midst of the persecution and bitterness Vaughan pleads passionately for the sanity, peace and the righteousness of 'the antient way'."*]

Henry Vaughan grew up to manhood in the Breconshire of the sixteen thirties, the years of the gathering storm. Religious and political dissent were growing rapidly and the seeds of Parliament's quarrel with the king were sown in the developing conflicts of these years. And throughout this period the steady growth of Puritan ideas and congregations was sharpening the issues which would divide the country only a few years later.

Vaughan's years in London, probably from 1640 to 1642, must have left an abiding impression upon his mind. On October 22nd, 1640, an excited crowd broke into the Court of High Commission, and made its work impossible. The following month the Long Parliament impeached Strafford, and he was later committed to the Tower. In April of 1641, the Parliament passed the Bill of Attainder against Strafford, and on May 10th, after scenes of great agitation and violence, the King was forced to agree to Strafford's execution.

It would have been absolutely impossible for Vaughan to have been unaware of the seriousness of what was happening, and very difficult indeed for him not to have taken sides. Coming, as he did, from a strong Anglican and Royalist tradition, he must have been appalled by what he saw, and there seems no reason to doubt Hutchinson's view that Vaughan's 'detestation of "the populacy"', which is constantly found in his secular and even in his religious verse, dated from these events of 1641.'

It is significant that the longest poem in his first collection, *Poems, with the Tenth Satyre of Iuvenal Englished,* has an unmistakeable attack upon the Parliamentarians for their behaviour, and especially for the murder of Strafford. 'A Rhapsodie', written after a meeting with friends in the Globe Taverne, uses Roman history to veil, albeit very thinly, his sense of outrage. Vaughan proposes three

toasts. The first celebrates Caligula's affront to the Senate of Rome by making his horse a Senator. Vaughan uses the Roman Senate to express his anger at the actions of Parliament. In the second toast Vaughan again indicts the Parliament and uses the figure of Caesar to symbolize King Charles I's attempts to arrest five members of Parliament in January, 1641:

> Now crown the second bowle, rich as his
>   worth,
> I'le drinke it to; he! that like fire broke forth
> Into the Senates face, crost Rubicon,
> And the States pillars, with their Lawes thereon:
> And made the dull gray beards, & furr'd gowns
>   fly
> Into *Brundusium* to consult, and lye:

The analogy is not historically very accurate, but that is far less important than the fact that Vaughan feels so passionately about the behaviour of the Parliamentarians that he enters into the details of the long and bitter conflict as it was unfolding in 1641. In the final toast, to 'brave *Sylla*', Vaughan clearly commemorates the death of Strafford. Once again the historical parallel is a very rough one, but it at least makes the point that Sulla, like Strafford, was the upholder of the Patrician class, and thus a target for the rage of the people:

> This to brave *Sylla!* why should it be sed,
> We drinke more to the living, then the ded?
> Flatt'rers, and fooles doe use it: Let us laugh
> At our owne honest mirth; for they that quaffe
> To honour others, doe like those that sent
> Their gold and plate to strangers to be spent:

If Vaughan showed this degree of involvement in public affairs, and personal passion in the Royalist cause, so early in his career, it is inconceivable that the anguished years which followed, and especially his own part in the Civil War, did not affect him very deeply. Indeed, two of the finest poems in *Olor Iscanus* reveal great compassion for those who have been killed in the battles of the Civil War. **'An Elegie on the death of Mr. R. W. . . .'** is a most moving lament not only for the man but for the terrible times through which he had lived. And his tribute is touched not only by a deeply felt personal emotion but by a bitter attack on the hypocrisy of the Puritans who have, in Vaughan's view, confused the good of the people with their own selfish aims:

> He knew no *fear* but of his *God;* yet durst
> No injurie, nor (as some have) e'r purs't
> The sweat and tears of others, yet would be
> More forward in a royall gallantrie
> Than all those vast pretenders, which of late
> Swell'd in the ruines of their King and State.
> He weav'd not *Self-ends,* and the *Publick* good
> Into one piece, nor with the peoples bloud
> Fill'd his own veins;

Clearly this is not the poetry of a man unaffected by the sorrows of his age. On the contrary, it shows strong and direct emotional involvement. The second, **'An Elegie on the death of Mr. R. Hall, slain at Pontefract, 1648'**, shows the same personal sincerity and passionate involvement in the tragedy of the period. In addition it underlines Vaughan's distress at the damage being done to the true

Church of England. R. Hall was very probably a clergyman and Vaughan feels justified in referring to his death as **'Martyrdome'.** There is, moreover, a considerable political sharpness to this lament, and Vaughan's ending reminds us, not for the last time in his poetry, that it is those who have died in the cause of King and true Church who are the 'Saints' and not the self-styled 'Saints' of Cromwell's militia:

> Since then (thus flown) thou art so much refin'd,
> That we can only reach thee with the mind,
>   will not in this *dark* and *narrow glasse,*
> Let thy scant *shadow* for *Perfections* passe,
> But leave thee to be read more high, more
>   queint,
> In thy own bloud a *Souldier* and a *Saint.*

When one turns to Vaughan's major work, **Silex Scintillans,** it becomes apparent that far from avoiding the tragic events of the Civil War, some of his finest poetry was written as a direct response to the difficulties and problems which a new political regime had thrust upon him, his family and his friends. Indeed, his own inner religious conflicts must be seen in the immediate context of a wider struggle against the Puritan Commissioners and their agents, of whom he did not approve and whose work he plainly considered to be a work of darkness, not of light. They were 'Commission'd by a black self-wil'. It is therefore a double captivity of which he speaks in **Silex Scintillans.** There are at least nine poems in the first part, and thirteen in the second part, in which political material is used quite substantially and openly in the argument. But there are many others where the occasional mention or inference betrays Vaughan's constant concern with the situation as it existed not only in the country as a whole but especially in his own native Breconshire.

It is therefore essential to examine in some detail what was happening in Vaughan's own county in the years immediately following the collapse of the King's military hopes in Midsummer, 1646, and especially the ferment in the Church, and the Second Civil War in 1648. Some of the poems from the first part of **Silex Scintillans,** which he was writing during 1648 and 1649, must be looked at in that context. Before he wrote the poems which are included in the second part of the work the new Puritan regime had introduced the Act of Propagation of 1650. So controversial was this piece of legislation that it caused a furore of protest throughout the Principality and it was particularly disliked and contested in Breconshire. It is very important to take detailed note of the act and its main consequences before examining some of the political aspects of **Silex Scintillans, Part Two.**

The first relevant factor is the condition of Breconshire when he returned to it from military service either towards the end of 1645 or in the first part of 1646. The crucial changes which began to occur in that year were both political and ecclesiastical, but it would appear that the religious discontent which ensued was the principal focus of popular attention:

> Already Brecknockshire had had an opportunity to appreciate that the growing power of Parliament meant the extension to the county of those arrangements for the reformation of religion which had been initiated in other parts of the kingdom. The two powerful Parliamentary committees known as the Committee for Scandalous Ministers and the Committee of Plundered Ministers were reviewing with a critical eye the work done by ministers of religion. Those who were deemed inefficient were being replaced by men who gave promise of preaching the Word of God more conscientiously. By 1649 Brecknockshire had seen this process at work. Seven clergymen had been ejected up to that year. They were Rowland Gwyn of Llangorse, Thomas Lewis of Llanfeygan, Josias Morgan of Vaynor, Thomas Powell of Cantreff, Rowland Watkins of Llanfrynach, Thomas Davis of Hay and Matthew Herbert of Llangattock, who had been six years tutor to Henry Vaughan the Silurist. [R. Tudor Jones, 'Religion in Post-Restoration Brecknockshire, 1660-1688', *Brycheiniog,* VIII]

There are two points of note here. The first is that five of the seven ministers must have been known to the Vaughan family as these churches are within a few miles of Llansantffraed. With one of them, Matthew Herbert, there was of course a closer connection, and it would be remarkable, also, if they did not know the incumbent at Hay, though it is rather further away than the others. It is very significant that such a high proportion of churchmen who were thrown out of their livings came from such a small part of this large county in which Vaughan himself lived. Secondly, it is clear that these ejections had been thoroughly discussed in Puritan circles for more than a year. The local churches round Vaughan's home must therefore have been fully aware of the impending catastrophe throughout 1648, as Vaughan was beginning work on the first part of **Silex Scintillans.**

This was by no means all. In August, 1647, Sir William Lewis of Llangorse, who sat in Parliament for Petersfield (Hants.), was one of eleven Presbyterians who were forced to withdraw from the House of Commons because they wished the army to be disbanded. But in fact Sir William, a very close neighbour of the Vaughans, was quite openly accused of protecting delinquents and of letting them off payment of fines. Vaughan's own immediate locality was therefore seen to be directly connected with the worst discontent and potential revolt.

The actual revolt, when it came in 1648, spread quickly through South Wales and developed into what is often termed the Second Civil War. Whether Vaughan had any direct part in it is not known; what is certain is that nobody in Breconshire could have been unaware of what was happening:

> Royalists were only too ready to exploit the revolt. In Brecon an attempt was made to garrison the town. But Colonel Thomas Horton who had been sent to prevent the troubles from spreading dispersed the Royalist sympathisers and arrested their leaders. [F. Rees, 'Breconshire during the Civil War', *Brycheiniog,* (1962).]

By May 8th the revolt had been suppressed and the Puritan grip on the county inevitably tightened, with all the leaders either imprisoned or under threat. Only two months later Vaughan's brother, William, died and if we take the phrase 'dearest and nearest relatives' in *The Mount of Olives* to refer to him, then it would certainly appear likely that his death is in some way connected with the violence of the Civil War. 1648 was therefore a most distressing year in every sense. The only possible hope was that while the King lived there might be some chance, however small, of a rapprochement between the two bitterly divided camps. The execution of the King in January of the following year ended this hope and sealed the despair which had been mounting relentlessly ever since the end of the Civil War.

In view of all these events it is not in the least surprising that one of the major themes of the first part of *Silex Scintillans* is that of deliverance from bondage. The last six stanzas of **'Religion'**, the fourth poem in the book, proclaim this note strongly. Vaughan is centrally concerned here with the desperate need of an entire people for the Water of Life. True religion comes, like the water which sustains the bodies of men, from a secret, deep place, but in its long passage to the surface it has become tainted. As in so many of the poems in *Silex Scintillans* Vaughan deliberately combines different Biblical passages in the thought and imagery. Here, quite apart from general allusions to the Psalms and Christ on the sea, there are two main sources. Christ's journey into Samaria is purposely combined with His attendance at the wedding feast in Cana of Galilee. Although he closes the poem with a very strong couplet based on the latter story, the central implied text is surely from the story of Christ and the woman of Samaria:

> Jesus answered and said unto her, Whosoever drinketh of this water shall thirst again:
>
> But whosoever drinketh of the water that I shall give him shall never thirst; but the water that I shall give him shall be in him a well of water springing up into everlasting life.

The underlying question is clear. What is the source of the corruption? It is important to recognize that Vaughan does not name man's own individual preference for sin, as Donne and Herbert had so often done, and as he himself did in many poems. Here is no individual aberration; it is nothing less than the spoiling of true religion by a whole corrupt regime. It is a picture of a people so starved of real spirituality that they mistake poison for the Water of Life. And only God, in Christ, as absolute Deliverer, can remedy this situation:

> So poison'd, breaks forth in some Clime,
> And at first sight doth many please,
> But drunk, is puddle, or meere slime
> And 'stead of Phisick, a disease;
>
> Just such a tainted sink we have
> Like that *Samaritans* dead *Well*,
> Nor must we for the Kernell crave
> Because most voices like the *shell*.
>
> Heale then these waters, Lord; or bring thy flock,
> Since these are troubled, to the springing rock,
> Looke downe great Master of the feast; O shine,

And turn once more our *Water* into *Wine!*

It is a cry repeated with less obvious power perhaps but more poignancy three poems later in the very aptly titled poem **'The British Church'**. The first line is interesting in that it could refer either to the King or Christ. The King was of course Head not only of the State but the Church too and the 'head' in the third line may well extend this reference to the King. If the King is indeed combined with Christ in a double meaning it would certainly add sharpness to the lament. But the central appeal of the poem is certainly addressed to Christ, for deliverance from a rude and ignorant military tyranny which is deriding even the central symbol of the Church's faith, the sacrificial offering of Christ Himself. There is no doubt that Vaughan uses this Puritan sacrilege as a general symbol of the destruction of the Church in the name of a new, and in his judgement, completely bogus religion:

> Ah! he is fled!
> And while these here their *mists*, and *shadows* hatch,
> My glorious head
> Doth on those hills of Mirrhe, and Incense watch.
> Haste, hast my dear,
> The Souldiers here,
> Cast in their lots again,
> That seamlesse coat
> The Jews touch'd not,
> These dare divide, and stain.

As in **'Religion'** Vaughan's imagery is a combination of Biblical sources, in this instance the 'roe' and 'myrrh' of the *Song of Solomon* and the various gospel accounts of the Crucifixion. The meaning is clear. These Christian men and women have been slaughtered and the property of the Church destroyed or stolen. Nothing but the direct intervention of the Deliverer can save the people and their Church:

> Write in thy bookes
> My ravish'd looks
> Slain flock, and pillag'd fleeces,
> And hast thee so
> As a young Roe
> Upon the mounts of spices.

But Vaughan by no means confines himself to a general cry for deliverance from Puritan oppression. There are several poems in which he attacks specific Puritan abuses of the Church, its doctrine and its practice. In the reorganization of the Church, which we have already briefly discussed, it was inevitable that many Ministers, fearing the loss of their livings, collaborated with the authorities. Breconshire was certainly no exception. But staunch Royalists and Anglicans were bound to accuse them of responding to bribery. There is no doubt, either, that the Ministers who were ejected up to 1649 levelled the charge of corruption at the men who were to succeed them. This accusation would certainly seem to be present in several stanzas of **'Rules *and* Lessons'**:

> Through all thy *Actions, Counsels,* and *Discourse,*
> Let *Mildness,* and *Religion* guide thee out,
> If truth be thine, what needs a brutish force?

But what's not *good,* and *just* ne'r go about.
  Wrong not thy Conscience for a rotten
stick,
  That gain is dreadful, which makes spirits
sick.

To God, thy Countrie, and thy friend be true,
If *Priest,* and *People* change, keep thou thy
ground.
Who sels Religion, is a *Judas Jew,*
And, oathes once broke, the soul cannot be
sound.
  The perjurer's a devil let loose: what can
  Tie up his hands, that dares mock God, and
man?

There were many local as well as national examples of 'brutish force' as Vaughan was writing. It is worth noting that Jenkin Jones of Llandetty, only a few miles from Vaughan's home, was both a fervent Puritan preacher and a most aggressive military commander, frequently cited by his opponents as a man who used physical threats and intimidation in order to change people's religious attitudes. 'Rotten stick' re-enforces the image of violence used in the service of untruth. His pointed accusation 'who sels Religion', in the context of *'Priest,* and *People* change', must be seen as a direct comment on the alleged inducements offered to ministers who were prepared to sympathize with the new order, and a number of ministers in Breconshire were certainly said to have done so. But in doing so they had violated their sacred oath of allegiance to the one true Church whose Head on Earth was the King. Hence 'oathes once broke', they had effectively sold their souls by this act of perjury.

Equally serious in Vaughan's view was the direct interference with the essential worship of the Church in celebration and sacrament. In **'Christ's Nativity'**, he is deeply aware of the damage being done to the Church, and the Christian souls it is supposed to protect, by the Puritan prohibition on the formal observation of the principal Christian Feasts, in this case the Nativity. The form of the poem is interesting. In a five stanza lyric of great beauty he uses first formal pastoral imagery and then more personal nature images to express the glory of the Saviour's birth and his own incapacity to respond to it as he should. There is only one reference to the responsibility of man in general:

  Man is their high-priest, and should rise
  To offer up the sacrifice.

The implication is that man does not respond as he should.

In the second part, consisting of only eighteen lines, he develops this idea but changes the mood of the poem by making a direct thrust against the political masters who are deliberately preventing the response which every man should make:

  And shall we then no voices lift?
    Are mercy, and salvation
  Not worth our thanks? Is life a gift
    Of no more acceptation?
  Shal he that did come down from thence,
    And here for us was slain,
  Shal he be now cast off? no sense

  Of all his woes remain?
  Can neither Love, nor suff'rings bind?
    Are we all stone, and Earth?
  Neither his bloudy passions mind,
    Nor one day blesse his birth?
  Alas, my God! Thy birth now here
  Must not be numbred in the year.

By including 'suff'rings' and 'bloudy passions' he not only reminds his readers that the Nativity and the Passion are inextricably linked in the worship of the Church, but he also points to the fact that Good Friday has been banned as a day of formal observation.

The structure of **'Christ's Nativity'** is worthy of note because it gives us the overall pattern which he uses in most of the religious poems in which he is also making political attacks. God's love for man is shown in the birth of Christ. This is the formal statement in the first part of the poem and it is applied to the sin and therefore the necessity for grace in his own life. The particular sin and stubbornness of the men who claim to represent the new order is thus set quite firmly against the operation of the Divine Love. Vaughan is extremely careful not to indulge in political argument, weighing one course of action against another in terms of human strategy. He always attempts to show the extreme weakness and wickedness of the Puritan attitude to life by contrasting it sharply with Biblical truth and, where necessary, the established practice of the Church.

In **'Dressing'** he attacks the Puritans for their violation of the Holy Communion. The prayer of longing for the Divine Presence, with which the poem opens, takes its main image from the *Song of Solomon* but its fervour and passion is more reminiscent of the *Book of Revelation,* which Vaughan used so often. However, the pattern is familiar in that God's sacred gift of the 'mysticall Communion' speaks to him, and should speak to man in general, of the essential character of God:

  Whatever thou dost bid, let faith make good,
  Bread for thy body, and Wine for the blood.
    Give him (with pitty) love,
    Two flowres that grew with thee above;
    Love that shal not admit
    Anger for one short fit,
  And pitty of such a divine extent
  That may thy members, more than mine, resent.

The central argument is that it should be impossible for man to refuse such pity and love. But as in **'Christ's Nativity'** Vaughan shows that some men do refuse. They know so little of God's goodness towards them that they insult His very Presence and his sacrificial offering by sitting down while they accept it:

  Give me, my God! thy grace,
    The beams, and brightness of thy face,
    That never like a beast
    I take thy sacred feast,
  Or the dread mysteries of thy blest bloud
  Use, with like Custome, as my Kitchin food.
    Some sit to thee, and eat
    Thy body as their Common meat,
    O let not me do so!

At the end of the poem Vaughan implies that the Puritans

have in fact lost all their reverence for God. His use of 'Saints' in the last line makes this absolutely clear; they were the self-styled saints who knew nothing of the Sainthood of God.

> Then kneel my soul, and body; kneel, and bow;
> If *Saints,* and *Angels* fal down, much more thou.

There are two poems towards the end of the first part of *Silex Scintillans* in which Vaughan is concerned rather less with the alleged vandalism and hypocrisy of Puritan Church policy and more with the grievous condition of the entire nation. The first is **'The World'**. . . . But the political implications of the second stanza raise two interesting points. The first is that although Vaughan gives a complete and very powerful picture of the affairs of state, as distinct from Church dogma or administration, his 'darksome States-man' and all the problems which flow from his mismanagement, are seen under an aspect of eternity. Though Vaughan repeatedly condemns the Puritan regime for its interference with religious life it is important to recognize that he largely separates Church and State in his thinking. His statesman is judged, and found wanting, by the light of Divine truth as revealed in the *First Epistle of John,* which he takes as his text, and also the *Book of Revelation* which inspires so much of the poem's thought and imagery. This statesman has chosen the darkness of death and destruction, rather than the light:

> The darksome States-man hung with weights
>   and woe
> Like a thick midnight-fog mov'd there so slow
>   He did nor stay, nor go:
> Condemning thoughts (like sad Ecclipses) scowl
>   Upon his soul,
> And Clouds of crying witnesses without
>   Pursued him with one shout.
> Yet dig'd the Mole, and lest his ways be found
>   Workt under ground,
> Where he did Clutch his prey, but one did see
>   That policie,
> Churches and altars fed him, Perjuries
>   Were gnats and flies,
> It rain'd about him bloud and tears, but he
>   Drank them as free.

The second question this stanza raises is whether Vaughan had any particular Puritan politician in mind. It is very tempting, of course, to identify the main figure with Cromwell, and there are certainly considerable similarities. But I would agree with Hutchinson that there is no real evidence for this view. It would, in any case, be not only against the mood and spirit of the poem as a whole but at variance with Vaughan's practice of drawing a composite picture in order to illustrate a broad theme. This is his method throughout *Silex Scintillans,* with only one or two exceptions, and it is certainly the method he adopts here. The politician's inability to solve the nation's problems, his tendency to condemn and be negative, and his marked deviousness are general indications of what Vaughan believed about the nation's government at the time he was writing. Notwithstanding the pointed accusation that 'Churches and altars fed him' the point and force of this example of the world's decay and corruption is in its gen-

eral reference and not in its identification with any particular person of the period.

'The Constellation' is the other poem which is directly concerned with the condition of the state as a whole. It is very similar to **'The World'** in that it seeks to place the greed and envy of the world, and more especially the sheer corruption and hypocrisy of Puritan politics, very firmly under the judgement of an Eternal Law. Indeed, this is even more pronounced in **'The Constellation'** because of the description of man's restlessness and insecurity in a Universe of peace, calm and order. There seems no doubt that the Hermetic philosophy inspired some of the imagery and ideas here. The contrast is immediate and intensely dramatic, one of the most striking he ever achieved:

> Some nights I see you in the gladsome East,
>   Some others neer the West,
> And when I cannot see, yet do you shine
>   And beat about your endless line.
>
> Silence, and light, and watchfulnes with you
>   Attend and wind the Clue,
> No sleep, nor sloth assailes you, but poor man
>   Still either sleeps, or slips his span.

The move away from man in general to man under a vicious political regime is equally swift and Vaughan's picture is stark and particularized. In this it differs from **'The World'** and most of his other poems in *Silex Scintillans:*

> But here Commission'd by a black self-wil
>   The sons the fathers kil,
> The Children Chase the mother, and would heal
>   The wounds they give, by crying, zeale.
>
> Then Cast her bloud, and tears upon thy book
>   Where they for fashion look,
> And like that Lamb which had the Dragons
>   voice
>   Seem mild, but are known by their noise.

There is no doubt whatever that the King is 'the father' and the Church 'the mother'. But what is just as striking is the violence and terror which he depicts quite openly. After these two specific references he launches an attack which, as in **'The World'**, goes well beyond the area of organized religion. In both poems it is the entire corruption of the State which he takes as his theme, though he returns to the condition of the Church as an instrument of God's peace in the final stanza of **'The Constellation'**:

> Give to thy spouse her perfect, and pure dress,
>   *Beauty* and *holiness,*
> And so repair these Rents, that men may see
>   And say, *Where God is, all agree.*

These two poems very near the end of the first part of *Silex Scintillans* would seem to signal a much more fortright attack on the Puritan regime than one sees earlier in his work. Vaughan was probably still shocked by the execution of the King. Furthermore the first batch of evictions of Church Ministers had by now been announced so his own locality would be reeling from a double blow. At least one thing was clear. All hope of a reconciliation between Parliamentarians and Royalists was now gone for some years. The general impact of this changed situation, coupled with his own anger and despair, certainly appears to have had its effect towards the end of his first volume. As he prepared these poems for publication and began work on others, the situation in Breconshire became even worse with the *Act for the Better Propagation and Preaching of the Gospel in Wales,* which was passed in February, 1650.

The evictions of 1649, to which reference has already been made, were in some respects a prelude to the Act of Propagation. What had been achieved by this change in ministers, and the consequent reorganization of their churches, would now, through the formal act, be possible on a much wider front and have a much more permanent basis. One needs, therefore, to note the main provisions of the Act and its chief propagandists before looking at the effects it had on Vaughan's own area.

> This Act, which was to be in force for three years, vested the control of the established Church in Wales in a body of 71 Commissioners. They were given authority to hear complaints against any Minister and if the allegations were substantiated by the sworn evidence of witnesses and not disproved by the defendants, the Commissioners or any five of them had power to eject the offending minister and to allow up to one-fifth of the value of the living for the upkeep of his wife and children. Another body of 25 Approvers were named to examine the qualifications of men who were prepared to minister in the church, whether in the parishes or as itinerant preachers or as schoolmasters. [R. Tudor Jones, op. cit.]

It was unfortunate for the Anglican churches of Vaughan's own locality that two of the Approvers, men of extreme Puritan convictions and fiery temper, had an intimate knowledge of the churches near his home. One of them, Jenkin Jones of Llandetty, has already been mentioned. He was extremely active in the Tal-y-bont area, near to his home in Llandetty. The Act was carried out to the letter in all the churches he personally knew. The second Approver who would have been known to the Vaughan family was Vavasor Powell of Knucklas, who had been in trouble with the authorities for preaching extreme sermons as early as 1640, and was particularly active in the area which lay between Vaughan's home and the Olchon Valley. These two men of great power and undoubted courage were certainly detested by Anglicans and Royalists in the area and provoked great hostility by their claim that the Act of Propagation gave them virtually divine dispensation to order the life of the local churches as God had directly told them.

When the list of evictions was published as a consequence of the 1650 Act it was obvious that the churches in Vaughan's locality had suffered very badly:

> Richard Habberley, rector of Llys-wen, was charged with being a 'Common swearer, malignant and scandalous'. Illegal induction was the charge against both Griffith Hattley, vicar of Aberysgir, and Andrew Watkins, vicar of Penderyn, but John Perrot, rector of Cathedine, lost his living for being a common swearer and a drunkard and for helping the King in the war. Samuel Prytherch, rector of Llanhamlach, was ejected for drunkenness, fornication, lying and

quarrelling and James Thomas, vicar of Llanwrthwl, for drunkenness, swearing and simony. Thomas Vaughan, vicar of Llansantffraed and brother of Henry Vaughan the Silurist, was described as a common swearer, no preacher and in arms against the Parliament. [R. Tudor Jones, op. cit.]

Of the twenty-five Ministers named, no fewer than thirteen had their churches within six miles of Vaughan's home, and every one of the churches within immediate walking distance of Llansantffraed are included. When these are coupled with the evictions of the previous year it can be seen that there must have been a wholesale disruption of religious practice in his locality. In addition the universal banning of the Book of Common Prayer, nonobservance of Feast Days and suspension of Holy Communion imposed an almost intolerable strain on the loyalty of Anglicans. There must also have been acute personal distress at the discomfiture of so many clergymen who were well known in the area.

It is fortunate that the parish register of one Breconshire church has been preserved intact from this period. It is, of course, only one example and may well be an extreme case. Nevertheless it is important because the attitudes of strong Anglicans and Royalists in the county were very much shaped by what they heard of cases like this. The register is of Llanafan Fawr:

> After this time (sc. 1650) there was a generall cessation of officiating in Church either for Baptisme Marriadge or Buriall. The then Vicar William Wms Mr of Arts being ejected by the Act of Propagation of —49 & none officiated unless some curates did it in private houses or buried upon their perill in 1649 one Evan Bowen a mason by his trade & a souldier at ye Garrison of Red Castle by his profession being an illiterate man that could neither reade write or speake English was by the Commissioners made vicar of the parish who also did not at all officiate, nor could he tell how to Doe it. All that while the Church & Chapells belonging to Lanavanfawr, were without prayer or preaching or officiating unless in some of them some itinerants came once in a month or quarter or year in some not at all during that time or as yet in 1659 . . .

There is one further factor relevant to Vaughan's work in the second part of *Silex Scintillans.* 1651 saw the beginning of a well organized movement of protest against the Act of Propagation. This affected South Wales as a whole but there were many signatures from Breconshire among the fifteen thousand on the Petition of Protest. This was presented to Parliament in March, 1652 and had been the subject of many meetings during which there was fierce denunciation of the Commissioners and the Approvers. Both Jenkin Jones and Vavasor Powell hit out angrily at their accusers and argued that their opponents' case was based on wild rumour and downright falsehood. The years in which Vaughan was completing his work were therefore filled with attack and counter-attack, protest, recrimination and bitter dispute, involving Church and community life which he must have known intimately.

There are some marked differences between the poems in

Part One and those in Part Two. First, there are far more references to the Church politics of the age, and the tone of his comments is on the whole more bitter. One would expect no less in view of the marked deterioration in the situation. Second, his arguments against the violence of the Civil War, and against Puritanism in general, are developed more elaborately and at greater length. Finally, there is some attempt, particularly towards the end of the book, to gather together the many lines of his thought and reach a judgement upon which he can base his hopes and fears for the years that lie ahead.

The urgent note of Deliverance which we have noted in the first part of his work becomes even stronger in the second. It is sounded in the passage with which he chose to preface both parts of the work when he published it in 1655. It is therefore intended as a keynote to the work as a whole:

> O Lord, the hope of Israel, all they that forsake thee shall be ashamed; and they that depart from thee, shall be written in the earth, because they have forsaken the Lord, the fountain of living waters.

Vaughan does not use any one psalm but a skilful pastiche of various psalms to point his desperate need for release from his own slavery to sin, and also the wider captivity which the Puritan forces have imposed upon the land. But if Deliverance from the bondage of an alien religion is still his great cry he is more aware now that Judgement by God must be an integral part of that Deliverance.

There are several important poems in this second part of his work which link these two themes. The first is **'The Jews'** in which he employs the general history of the Jewish people to show the folly and blindness of those who have turned away from God, refused to admit the love of Christ and have finally been judged by God. And the judgement is that they are to be shamed by the Gentiles so that all men may see what happens to those who will not respond to the promises of the Almighty:

> You were the *eldest* childe, and when
> Your stony hearts despised love,
> The *youngest,* ev'n the Gentiles then
> Were chear'd, your jealousie to move.
>
> Thus, Righteous Father! doest thou deal
> With Brutish men; Thy gifts go round
> By turns, and timely, and so heal
> The lost Son by the newly found.

The change from the past to the present tense is unmistakable and the message is clear. The general comparison of the stubbornness of the Jews and the insensitivity and even downright wickedness of the Puritans cannot be escaped. But the poem is much more biting than that. Within the framework of his general comparison Vaughan has projected a powerful prophetic vision both of the deliverance of God and His Judgement. He uses the celebrated vision from the fourth chapter of the prophet Zechariah, but he simplifies the symbolism to some extent, using only the Angels and the Olive, not the gold candlestick and bowl. The effect is intended to be the same as in the vision of Zechariah, however. The deliverance, though long de-

layed, will come, angels will talk with men, Peace will renew the land and its people. All this is in the future, yet the promise of God is as sure as the branching of the Olive:

> When the fair year
> Of your deliverer comes,
> And that long frost which now benums
> Your hearts shall thaw; when Angels here
> Shall yet to man appear,
> And familiarly confer
> Beneath the Oke and Juniper:
> When the bright *Dove*
> Which now these many, many Springs
> Hath kept above,
> Shall with spread wings
> Descend, and living waters flow
> To make drie dust, and dead trees grow;
>
> O then that I
> Might live, and see the Olive bear
> Her proper branches! which now lie
> Scattered each where,
> And without root and sap decay
> Cast by the husband-man away.

This poem is therefore not only a vision of peace and righteousness, but also a prophecy of Judgement. It is perhaps the symbol of the husband-man which finally gives it full penetration and power. The fulfilment of Zechariah's vision is worked out in the life of a corrupt society. The husbandmen of *St. Matthew's Gospel* deliberately sought to deny the master what was rightfully his. They misused the estate and killed the master's servants and even the master's son but the end is swift and certain because the master 'will miserably destroy those wicked men, and will let out his vineyard unto other husbandmen, which shall render him the fruits in their seasons.' This is one of Vaughan's sharpest attacks on his Puritan masters, and also one of his most powerful poems. It also shows how shortsighted it is to attempt a separation of the political and the spiritual in his work. The force and clarity of his spiritual vision here springs from the bitter adversity of religious and political repression, and his emphasis on the Judgement of God arises from the conviction that before there is any lasting peace God must deal with the wickedness of the oppressors, and the righteous husband-men must at last become the custodians of God's estate.

There is no evidence whatever that Vaughan's appeal for judgement of the Puritan oppressors is diminished in the latter part of his work in *Silex Scintillans,* Part Two. It is true that he appears to become sickened by the blood that has been shed and he does recognize towards the end of his work that there must be reconciliation. Both these trends will be discussed later, but they in no way lessen his desire for God's justice upon the enemies of truth. In a remarkably fierce attack in **'The day of Judgement'**, one of the last poems in the collection and the second he wrote on this general theme, he catalogues the crimes of the new Puritan order. It is difficult to avoid the conclusion that he has in mind here the various malpractices which were alleged to have been committed under the umbrella of the Act of Propagation. He is in fact saying no more than was said in the Petition to Parliament of 1652, which has already been discussed. What is interesting, however, is that Vaughan believes the wickedness to have been so great that mercy, though it belongs to God, might be inappropriate. Perhaps there is only judgement left:

> Nor moan I onely (though profuse)
> Thy Creatures bondage and abuse;
> But what is highest sin and shame,
> The vile despight done to thy name;
> The forgeries, which impious wit
> And power force on Holy Writ,
> With all detestable designs
> That may dishonor those pure lines.
> O God! though mercy be in thee
> The greatest attribute we see,
> And the most needful for our sins;
> Yet, when thy mercy nothing wins
> But meer disdain, let not man say
> *Thy arm doth sleep;* but write this day
> Thy judging one: Descend, descend!
> Make all things new! and without end!

There are two further points which arise from this passage. The first is that Vaughan does not separate personal sinning from political errors and misjudgements which lead to sin. The latter may be more deliberate and devilish than the former but he passes immediately from the one to the other. The crimes of a whole government are still manifestations of sin; political behaviour is after all an integral part of life. Secondly he ends the poem very characteristically with a call for newness of life. Nothing but the direct and full revelation of God's truth will save the nation from its sin and bitterness. The very great emphasis on the need for Divine Revelation throughout the whole of *Silex Scintillans* arises at least partly from his experience of the Puritan captivity.

There is evidence that the conflict between the demands of Vaughan's inner spiritual life and the public clamour of the world outside is much sharper in the second part of *Silex Scintillans* than it was in the earlier poems. Whereas in **'The World'** and **'The Constellation'** there is a degree of detachment and objectivity in the portrayal of the conflict, in two poems placed near the beginning of Part Two there are clear signs that he is having to defend his isolation, perhaps even for his own reassurance. These are **'White Sunday'** and **'The Proffer'**.

'White Sunday' is the third and final poem in a sequence exploring Ascension-Tide, which opens his second collection. Once again there appear to be clear echoes of the very recent hated legislation and its immediate consequences. The claim by the Puritan preachers, such as Jones and Powell, that only they could interpret God's commands to the people, not only upset but seriously demoralized Anglican congregations. Had the old Church gone for ever? Was this new dispensation what they must now believe? Moreover these same men proclaimed in their sermons that no days were special to them. Once saved, God's light shone on them from that moment through life and all eternity. The vehemence of Vaughan's cry against this blasphemy, coupled with the suggestion that at least he will protest while he still can, intensifies the sense of isolation conveyed in the lines:

> Can these new lights be like to those,
> These lights of Serpents like the Dove?
> Thou hadst no *gall,* ev'n for thy foes,

And thy two wings were *Grief* and *Love.*
> Though then some boast that fire each day,
> And on Christs coat pin all their shreds;
> Not sparing openly to say,
> His candle shines upon their heads:

> Yet while some rays of that great light
> Shine here below within thy Book,
> They never shall so blinde my sight
> But I will know which way to look.

This feeling of extreme isolation deepens as the poem continues and the whole tragedy of the situation, sealed by the execution of the King and now brought home to ordinary people by the purge of the Church in 1649 and 1650, is conveyed with swiftness and power.

> Again, if worst and worst implies
> A State, that no redress admits,
> Then from thy Cross unto these days
> The *rule* without *Exception* fits.

'The Proffer' is an even starker poem than **'White Sunday'** and the inner spiritual conflict is more intense. The spiritual quest he has undertaken seems threatened by worldly people who want to take all the goodness of his redeemed soul away. The sense of isolation which he portrayed in **'White Sunday'** is considerably intensified, and the picture he gives us is of a soul under siege. His attackers want to destroy everything he has gained on his spiritual quest. Although he is passionate in defending the glories and joys that he has won with such difficulty there is a note of real desperation here:

> Think you these longing eyes,
> Though sick and spent,
> And almost famish'd, ever will consent
> To leave those skies,
> That glass of souls and spirits, where well drest
> They shine in white (like stars) and rest.

The 'poys'nous, subtile fowls' who flock round him with their inducements are by no means all members of the Puritan regime. The conflict is not only with political forces but apparently with all those agencies which would dissipate his spiritual energy. But it is fairly easy to read into this poem all manner of mystical ideas for which there is little hard evidence. Durr takes this to very far lengths [in *On the Mystical Poetry of Henry Vaughan* (1962)]. What is very definitely in the poem is a castigation of the Puritans who have corrupted the souls of so many, and are now trying to corrupt him. [In his *Henry Vaughan: A Life and Interpretation* (1947)] Hutchinson argues convincingly that it seems very likely Vaughan was offered some inducement under the Commonwealth, and that the middle sections of the poem constitute his answer. It would not have been surprising if he had been approached to serve in some capacity. It is perfectly obvious from the history of Breconshire immediately following the Act of Propagation that the leading Puritans realized how isolated they were. They needed men to carry on the administration of the county; Vaughan's cousin, Charles Walbeoffe held office under them, though he was constantly in trouble for trying to temper their doctrine. Indeed, Vaughan's moving elegy, **'To the Pious Memory of C. W. Esquire'**, testifies to his courage in a period of great adversity.

The remarkable quality of 'The Proffer' is the sheer passion of the conflict. The contrast between the feebleness of his decaying life and the glory of eternity is rendered with a power and clarity which he rarely surpassed in all his work:

> Shall my short hour, my inch,
>   My one poor sand,
> And crum of life, now ready to disband
>   Revolt and flinch,
> And having born the burthen all the day,
>   Now cast at night my Crown away?
>
>   No, No; I am not he,
>   Go seek elsewhere.
> I skill not your fine tinsel, and false hair,
>   Your Sorcery
> And smooth seducements: I'le not stuff my story
>   With your Commonwealth and glory.

'The Proffer' is arguably the most sombre poem he ever wrote, and his most scathing attack on the Commonwealth reveals an intensity and bitterness of mood which is a clear reflection both of the depression in Breconshire following the Act of Propagation and his own feeling of desolation and loneliness. Vaughan seems, in effect, to have reached a point of virtually complete exile, whether voluntary or not, from the political evil and social rottenness of the world about him.

The great prophetic notes of Deliverance and Judgement, begun in the first part of Vaughan's work, are carried right through the Second Part of **Silex Scintillans** and there they become deeper personal statements than earlier. There is another theme which becomes much more important in this second part, and that is his treatment of violence as an instrument of political policy. There is, in particular, a very significant group of poems placed in the latter half of the collection. In these he is tormented by the deaths which have been caused by the wilful shedding of blood.

The first in sequence is **'The Men of War'**, based upon the text in Luke's gospel:

> And Herod with his men of war set him at nought, and mocked and arrayed him in a gorgeous robe, and sent him again to Pilate.

In fact Vaughan interprets the text broadly and takes it as a general base upon which to build his own defence against the violence of his age. There are three striking features of the poem which need comment. The first is his implication that the men who have so recently led a whole nation into bondage have in fact imprisoned themselves. This is the first time in **Silex Scintillans** that he has attacked the Puritans with the full moral weapons of Christian love and peace. The real text of the poem is therefore in the first few lines:

> *If any have an ear*
> *Saith holy John, then let him hear.*
> *He that into Captivity*
> *Leads others, shall a Captive be.*
> *Who with the sword doth others kill,*
> *A sword shall his blood likewise spill.*
> *Here is the patience of the Saints,*
> *And the true faith, which never faints.*

The second interesting feature is his quite open acknowledgement of the deep conflict between his desire to achieve power by force and the Christian commandment to use in his life the patience and love which alone can bring him his 'crown'. There seems no doubt that, whatever his views of Puritanism and the hypocrisy of its followers, he had been tempted to stifle his real views and feelings and accept an offer they either had made him or would make him.

> Were not thy word (dear Lord!) my light,
> How would I run to endless night,
> And persecuting thee and thine,
> Enact for *Saints* my self and mine.
> But now enlighten'd thus by thee,
> I dare not think such villainy;
> Nor for a temporal self-end
> Successful wickedness commend.

His deliberate use of 'Saints' here would seem to indicate who his tempters are, and later in the poem he prays for patience to 'slight the *Lure*', which appears to have been an inducement from the Puritan 'saints' of his own home area.

The final point of interest is how powerfully he turns on himself, using the blood of the martyrs and finally the blood of Christ to show the moral depravity of the men of war who spill blood and finally drown in their own sin. It is a depravity so powerful that it threatened to engulf him. Only the blood of Christ makes it possible for him one day to enter the sainthood of God:

> That when *thy Throne is set,* and all
> These *Conquerors* before it fall,
> I may be found (preserv'd by thee)
> Amongst that chosen company,
> Who by no blood (here) overcame
> But the blood of the *blessed Lamb.*

It seems clear from this poem that Vaughan could see no end to the shedding of blood if revenge became, as it certainly had become for some of his friends, a way of life and reason for being. Despite the extraordinary tensions and conflicts the poem reveals, Vaughan's final underlying message is that the bloodshed has to end if the nation wishes to return finally to sanity and peace under God.

'Abels blood', placed five poems later in the collection, reveals both the sadness and the passion for peace contained in **'The Men of War'**, but there is no further hint of any offer which the Puritans had made to him. It is more stark and dramatic than the earlier poem and the obsession with the shedding of blood is even greater. Starting with a brief but telling picture from *Genesis,* Vaughan emphasizes the sheer vileness of the taking of life. For him the most striking feature of the story is that Abel's voice is still heard crying to his Maker. The implication is that the soul of the murdered man has no final peace or rest:

> Sad, purple well! whose bubling eye
> Did first against a Murth'rer cry;
> Whose streams still vocal, still complain
>   Of bloody *Cain,*
> And now at evening are as red
> As in the morning when first shed.

What follows is interesting in two respects. First, the way in which Vaughan constructs a complex and powerful web of images on the parallel of water and blood, translating his general argument into a particular indictment of the bloody crimes committed in the Civil War and after. It is perhaps the most frightening picture in all his poetry. Those who have died would seem to have found no peace in death, nor can they ever find peace until God, as righteous Judge, has avenged their deaths. So the souls of the righteous slain move, as if in Purgatory, restless and unfulfilled, and Vaughan's specific use of 'altar' would seem to symbolize that cause for which they died. The new men of religion, guilty of so many murders, have abolished the altar from their worship, mocking God's Sanctuary just as they have mocked God's great commandment. This is also one of the many occasions in **Silex Scintillans** in which Vaughan cleverly adapts a Biblical passage to his own direct purpose and uses it to emphasize a deep and burning grievance which shows plainly all his bitterness against the Parliamentarians and the terrible wrongs of the Puritans. The passage upon which lines 20-22 of his poem are based is taken from one of Vaughan's favourite books, *Revelation:*

> And when he had opened the fifth seal, I saw under the altar the souls of them that were slain for the word of God, and for the testimony which they held:

> And they cried with a loud voice, saying, How long, O Lord, how long and true, dost thou not judge and avenge our blood on them that dwell on the earth.

It is an exceptionally vivid and dramatic use of the Bible to underline his theme.

> What thunders shall those men arraign
> Who cannot count those they have slain,
> Who bath not in a shallow flood,
> But in a deep, wide sea of blood?
> A sea, whose lowd waves cannot sleep,
> But *Deep* still calleth unto *deep:*
> Whose urgent *sound* like unto that
> *Of many waters,* beateth at
> The everlasting doors above,
> Where souls behind the altar move,
> And with one strong, incessant cry
> Inquire *How long?* of the most high.

The second interesting feature is that in the passage which immediately follows he makes a direct reference to himself, thanking God for having kept him from 'bloody men' when he was in 'thick death and night!' It is the only direct mention in **Silex Scintillans** of his own immediate involvement in the violence of the Civil War. But in the passage which closes the poem he prays passionately for those who have been slain. One wonders whether his reference to 'That proudly spilt and despis'd blood' is not a specific reminder of the King's death. There may also be an intentional comparison between the King and Christ in the final couplet, which would point even more forcibly his savage denunciation of the Puritan oppressors, and his prayer that the souls of all the martyrs shall find peace:

> I, may that flood,
> That proudly spilt and despis'd blood,

> Speechless and calm, as Infants sleep!
> Or if it watch, forgive and weep
> For those that spilt it! May no cries
> From the low earth to high Heaven rise,
> But what (like his, whose blood peace brings)
> Shall (when they rise) *speak better things,*
> Then *Abels* doth! may *Abel* be
> Still single heard, while these agree
> With his milde blood in voice and will,
> *Who* pray'd for those that did him kill!

'Abels blood' is a poem of quite extraordinary power and beauty, which completely contradicts the assertion that Vaughan's finest poetry has nothing to do with the political tumult of his time.

In the very next poem of the collection, **'Righteousness'**, Vaughan again deals with the shedding of blood. The righteous man has 'The clean, pure hand, which never medled pitch?' and in the sixth stanza he gives a composite picture reflecting once more the agony and bitterness of the Civil War and the troubled violent years since:

> Who spills no blood, nor spreds
>   Thorns in the beds
> Of the distrest, hasting their overthrow;
>   Making the time they had
>   Bitter and sad
> Like *Chronic* pains, which surely kill, though
> slow

There were certainly numerous cases in Breconshire, as elsewhere, of harassment of men who had the wrong political and religious colours, but Vaughan's picture here might well include the death of William two years after the end of the Civil War, to which reference has already been made. Certainly 'Chronic' would seem to indicate long and slow torment.

Vaughan's persistent conflict between the desire for revenge and the need to reach true peace of spirit may well be said to reach a climax in **'Jacobs Pillow, and Pillar'**, in which he devotes a substantial part of his poem to an exploration of the vicarious suffering of Christ. Once again he is forced to place this example of Christ in the context of his own age and now he seems to reach a resolution of his conflict. It is only the heart which knows and practises God's peace which can resist the advance of evil and wait in patience until God brings about complete deliverance.

> . . . . And when slain by the crowd
> (Under that stately and mysterious cloud
> Which his death scatter'd) he foretold the place,
> And form to serve him in, should be true grace
> And the meek heart, not in a Mount, nor at
> *Jerusalem,* with blood of beasts, and fat.
> A heart is that dread place, that awful Cell,
> That secret Ark, where the milde Dove doth
>   dwell
> When the proud waters rage: when Heathens
>   rule
> By Gods permission, and man turns a Mule.
> This little *Goshen,* in the midst of night,
> And *Satans* seat, in all her Coasts hath light,

Is there, by the end of his work in **Silex Scintillans,** any substantial change in his attitude towards the Puritan rulers, their supporters, propagandists and preachers? There is certainly no alteration whatever in his view that their purposes are wrongly conceived and that Puritanism in his own part of the world had been as disastrous in practice as the theory and dogma would have led him to believe. Although there are fewer detailed references to the abuse of the Church in the last half of Part Two than there are in the rest of his work, there is no clear evidence that he has changed his viewpoint. He condemns both the method and substance of the new regime right to the end. Indeed his attack on their beliefs and the consequences of those beliefs is both sharper and deeper towards the end of his work than at the beginning. But there is also, towards the end of the collection, a realization that there must be a new initiative if the worst of the rancour and bitterness is to be cleared away. The emphasis on the need for peace in 'Jacobs Pillow, and Pillar' reveals only one aspect of this shift of emphasis. Several of the last poems stress the Christian qualities of mercy, forgiveness and fresh hope. In 'The Feast' he rejoices in a newness of life and thanks God for 'This healing peace'. In both 'Tears' and 'The Throne' he prays for true humility of life and a quiet obedience to the will of God. Coming after the blood-guilt poems in sequence, these late poems re-enforce the impression that he was utterly weary of the violence of past years.

Finally, in 'L'Envoy' which closes his book and is therefore of particular importance, there is absolutely no doubt that he wants the great process of healing to begin quickly. But he is still insistent that this cannot mean peace on any terms. The men who have done wrong must face the judgement of God, but once that has happened there must be a general movement towards real peace. It may well be that two general factors influenced Vaughan's work as he reached a conclusion. First, the undoubted success of the campaign to amend the Act of Propagation. The impassioned protest against the bill and the inability of Jenkin Jones and others to suppress the protestors undoubtedly made for a resurgence of confidence among many Anglicans and supporters of the old order. The Act was not renewed in 1653, so the protestors could claim victory. The other factor of importance may have been the ending of the hated Long Parliament in 1653 and the beginning of the Protectorate. There was some ground for hope that the coming years would be more stable and at least put an end to the worst of the petty tyranny.

In 'L'Envoy', therefore, Vaughan is able to pass fairly quickly and naturally from Judgement, to Mercy and Reconciliation:

> Frustrate those cancerous, close arts
> Which cause solution in all parts,
> And strike them dumb, who for meer words
> Wound thy beloved, more then swords.
> Dear Lord, do this! and then let grace
> Descend, and hallow all the place.
> Incline each hard heart to do good,
> And cement us with thy sons blood,
> That like true sheep, all in one fold
> We may be fed, and one minde hold.

This final poem is an excellent example of the way in which the sorrows and losses of the Civil War, and its deeply troubled aftermath, have deepened and intensified Vaughan's own spiritual awareness. 'L'Envoy' is a complete answer to those critics who have attempted to separate the political and public aspects of his poetry from his personal quest for the certainty and sublimity of God's truth, and so depict him as a man who retreats into an inner Kingdom. This is to misunderstand the entire basis of his poetry. There are certainly occasions when he longs for an escape from the particular troubles and dangers of his times; it would be very strange if he had not done so. There are also moments when he allows his detestation of the Puritans to overwhelm his judgement so that he tends to become purely propagandist, but these moments are rare. The quality of most of the poems which treat the political and religious issues of his period is very high, and there is a depth and consistency in both the imagery and thought of the best of them which is very impressive. Poems such as 'Religion', 'The Constellation', 'The Proffer', 'The Jews', 'The Men of War', 'Abels blood', 'Jacobs Pillow, and Pillar' and 'L'Envoy' should be included in any selection of the finest poetry he wrote. They would give a much more balanced view of Vaughan's work in *Silex Scintillans* than anthologies usually do. They would also help to explain, at least in part, the anguish of 'the captivity' which substantially affects his distinctive vision of life.

> Therefore write in their hearts thy law,
> And let these long, sharp judgements aw
> Their very thoughts, that by their clear
> And holy lives, mercy may here
> Sit regent yet, and blessings flow
> As fast, as persecutions now.
> So shall we know in war and peace
> Thy service to be our sole ease,
> With prostrate souls adoring thee,
> Who turn'd our sad captivity!

Siegfried Sassoon's "At the Grave of Henry Vaughan":

> Above the voiceful windings of a river
> An old green slab of simply graven stone
> Shuns notice, overshadowed by a yew.
> Here Vaughan lies dead, whose name flows on
>   for ever
> Through pastures of the spirit washed with dew
> And starlit with eternities unknown.
> Here sleeps the Silurist; the loved physician;
> The face that left no portraiture behind;
> The skull that housed white angels and had vision
>   sion
> Of daybreak through the gateways of the mind.
>   Here faith and mercy, wisdom and humility
>   (Whose influence shall prevail for evermore)
>   Shine. And this lowly grave tells Heaven's
>   tranquillity.
>   And here stand I, a suppliant at the door.

Siegfried Sassoon, "At the Grave of Henry Vaughan," in The Heart's Journey, *Harper and Brothers, 1929.*

Arthur L. Clements   (essay date 1990)

SOURCE: "Henry Vaughan: 'I saw Eternity the other night'," in *Poetry of Contemplation: John Donne, George Herbert, Henry Vaughan, and the Modern Period*, State University of New York Press, 1990, pp. 129-72.

[*In the following excerpt from an essay originally published in a different form in* Studia Mystica *in 1987, Clements seeks "to clarify the question of mysticism in Vaughan's poetry and to illustrate the kind of study of individual poems necessary for determining the nature and extent of Vaughan's mysticism."*]

As with Donne's and Herbert's poetry, critical opinion concerning meditation and contemplation in Henry Vaughan's poetry is strongly divided. First, there are those critics, most notably Louis Martz, who argue ably and knowledgeably that Vaughan is a meditative poet; secondly, those, like Helen White, Itrat Husain, R. A. Durr, Cleanth Brooks, H. J. Oliver, and Anthony Low, who adduce considerable scholarship to establish Vaughan not primarily as a meditative but as a mystical poet; and, thirdly, those, such as E. L. Marilla, James Simmonds, Frank Kermode, and Jonathan Post, who with seemingly equal skill contend that he is not at all a mystic or who at least reject the primacy of mysticism.

One reason for the critical division regarding Vaughan's mysticism simply involves the matter of which poems a critic focuses upon. Some of Vaughan's poems, like **"Peace,"** are conventionally religious and pious; some, like **"The Search,"** are mainly meditative; but others, usually Vaughan's most distinguished and highly regarded poems, have profound and powerful mystical elements in them, sometimes alongside the pious and meditative elements. Hence critics may well be divided and hence the answer to the question is Vaughan a mystical poet (which some critics answer yes and others no) is yes and no—depending on which Vaughan one has in mind, which of his poems one is referring to, whether one believes a few or many poems must be mystical before designating a poet mystical, and, especially, how one understands the meaning of "mysticism." Some critics, for example, apparently take "mysticism" in diminished, trivial, or vague senses, as a visionary exaltation or "sudden visitation" (Marilla) or a kind of "otherworldliness" (Brooks). Another critic argues that Vaughan's poetic subjects are devotional or meditative but that "he is in no sense at all a mystic" (Kermode), as if these terms were mutually exclusive rather than interconnected and conducive one to the other. Still another scholar seems to associate "mystical vision" with "emotional rapture, ecstasy, or excitement of one kind or another" (Simmonds).

As with Donne's and Herbert's poetry, critical confusion concerning mysticism in Vaughan's poetry also arises from the failure carefully to distinguish the stages of the spiritual life, the differences between meditation and contemplation, and the different kinds of mystical Visions. In an effort to clarify the question of mysticism in Vaughan's poetry and to illustrate the kind of study of individual poems necessary for determining the nature and extent of Vaughan's mysticism, section II of this chapter will first,

through a detailed analysis, observe some of the meditative, contemplative, and biblical elements in a familiar and famous poem of Vaughan's, **"The Night,"** a poem much discussed by critics and variously regarded as Metaphysical, Hermetic, meditative, or mystical; section III will then discuss **"The Night"** and its mystical elements in the illuminating context of ancient-medieval-Renaissance contemplative tradition (with special focus on St. John of the Cross) and of the stages and common characteristics of mysticism; and section IV, touching upon the important matter of sequences, will discuss the archetype of death and rebirth and the Visions of Dame Kind and of God in a number of Vaughan's other poems. Finally, . . . section V will offer some comparisons of Donne, Herbert, and Vaughan.

II

My view, in essence, is that **"The Night"** is a paradoxical prayer in which Vaughan draws mainly on the Bible as source; its structure is that of a modified meditation; it is pervaded by a number of the distinctive characteristics of mysticism; it indicates the realization of the mystical stages of Illumination and the Dark Night of the Soul; and its intention and goal are infused contemplation or mystical Union in a Vision of God. **"The Night"** is a mystical poem, let me emphasize, not because it may contain allusions to Dionysius or St. John, as it does to the Bible, but because it exhibits unmistakable signs of mystical consciousness and experience.

Vaughan's reference to John 2:3, heading **"The Night,"** should read John 3:2. The Fourth Gospel is, according to Dean Inge, the charter of Christian mysticism, and Jesus' conversation with Nicodemus in chapter 3 is among those Johannine passages most valued by mystics. John 3:2 tells of the Pharisee, Nicodemus, a ruler of the Jews, who "came to Jesus by night, and said unto him, Rabbi, we know that thou art a teacher come from God: for no man can do these miracles that thou doest, except God be with him." Jesus answers in paradox, the language of mystical religion, that "Except a man be born again . . . of water and of the spirit, he cannot enter into the Kingdom of God" (John 3:3, 5). This paradox of rebirth, then, is the essential text for Vaughan's poem. Employing the image of the night, it is extended throughout the poem: just as Nicodemus "did at midnight speak with the Sun" so Vaughan prays for the mystical experience whereby he might be reborn and "enter into the Kingdom of God," "where I in him," the "deep, but dazling darkness," "Might live invisible and dim."

Of course, not all paradox is mystical, but mystical consciousness and experience, in plain contradiction of the laws of logic, are radically and distinctively paradoxical. . . . W. T. Stace includes paradoxicality among the common characteristics of both extrovertive and introvertive mystical experiences (*Mysticism and Philosophy*), and he also lists and discusses some of the major paradoxes of mysticism. These paradoxes are not the merely verbal and witty kinds but those having to do with the discovery of hidden affinities or identities between disparate phenomena and with the consequent compelling deduction that some aspects of reality are inconsistent with certain logical patterns of human thinking and therefore that some thinking has to be modified, made more imaginative and realistic. The fundamental and most important mystical paradox, as we observed in Chapter One, is that of the dual and contradictory nature of human beings, who have, as it were, two selves: an ego or false self and a true Self, this latter being identical with divinity (or, at the least, made in the divine image): "I in him / Might live invisible and dim." Many biblical passages are metaphors for the essential transformation or experience of giving up the illusional, egoistic life to realize the life of the true Self. As noted, this central paradox of gain through loss, of life through death, embodies the traditional distinction between the outward and the inward man, between the first Adam who is a living soul and the last Adam who is a quickening spirit (1. Cor. 15:45). And, as also observed, traveling the *via mystica* is the highest act of self-knowledge: it is to make that spiritual journey, often begun in prayer, whereby one is transformed from egohood to selfhood; it is to be trans-humanized, in Dante's phrase, from man into a god.

Significantly, stanzas 5 and 6 of **"The Night"** specifically concern meditation and contemplation, or prayer, as the preparation for the desired "infused contemplation" of stanza 9. Adopting Martz's outline of the meditative structure, we find that **"The Night,"** like Donne's "The Exstasie," falls into three distinguishable parts: composition, analysis, and colloquy; these parts correspond to the acts of memory, understanding, and will. Although there are actually no hard and fast lines, we might profitably view the stanzas of the poem as corresponding to the above division in this manner: stanzas 1 and 2, the composition, set the scene in discussing Nicodemus' finding of God during a time of literal and spiritual darkness; stanzas 3 to 6, the analysis, raise the question how one is to know God during the present age, which is also a time of spiritual darkness, and give the partial and temporary answer that during literal darkness, the night, one may come closer to God through prayer and love; stanzas 7 to 9, the colloquy, consider the inevitable coming of daylight with its evils and conclude therefore with the wish for mystical union with the "deep, but dazling darkness," such union being the full and final permanent answer.

> Through that pure *Virgin-shrine,*
> That sacred vail drawn o'r thy glorious noon
> That men might look and live as Glo-worms shine,
> 　　　And face the Moon:
> Wise *Nicodemus* saw such light
> As made him know his God by night.
>
> Most blest believer he!
> Who in that land of darkness and blinde eyes
> Thy long expected healing wings could see,
> 　　　When thou didst rise,
> And what can never more be done,
> Did at mid-night speak with the Sun!

Although the phrase "that pure *Virgin-shrine*" may refer to the mother of Christ, the Virgin Mary, who was conceived immaculately and with whom "the Moon" is traditionally associated, it refers primarily to the stainless temple of Christ's mortal body; for, ultimately, both "pure *Virgin-shrine*" and "sacred vail" mean the flesh which is

the veil that dims the divine glory of Christ in order that men, Nicodemus here in particular, might see the veiled Son whose unveiled light, "thy glorious noon," would be too bright for ordinary men. The conventional, poetic Son-Sun pun is involved in the complex analogical metaphor of stanza 1: as the moon dimly reflects the sun, so the mortal Christ (who was given flesh by a woman traditionally associated with the moon) is a dimmed divinity; moreover, as glowworms may shine only in the relatively dim light of the moon, so mortal men may see only a dimmed divinity, a veiled or fleshly son, for they cannot gaze with the naked physical eye upon the unveiled, divine brightness of the Son (Exodus 33:20). Paradoxically, then, divinity is veiled in order that it may be revealed.

That Vaughan drew heavily on biblical sources becomes more and more evident on examination. The main source of Vaughan's symbol of the veil is, as M. M. Mahood observes, the Bible, "where St. Paul had already achieved a fusion between different symbolistic uses of the word *'veil'.* For the Apostle, Isaiah's prophecy, 'And he will destroy in this mountaine the face of the covering cast over all people, and the vail that is spread over all nations,' [Isa. 25:7] was fulfilled when the rent veil of the Temple disclosed 'a new and living way, which he hath consecrated for us, through the vail, that is to say, his flesh' [Hebrews 10:20]." Vaughan uses the word *veil* variously to stand for *"the Old Law, time, the body,* and *the limits of the physical world:* four barriers between the soul and God which were penetrated in [the Incarnation and] the first Resurrection and which are to be destroyed at the last" (263, 264). Although the "vail" as Christ's body is the dominant meaning, some of these other meanings of *veil* may be implicit in line 2. Moreover, because all created things point to the creator and are symbols by which he may be partially known, the night itself is also a "vail." Thus line 6 is profoundly rich: Nicodemus knew "his god by night," that is, during the literal night time, in the flesh, and perhaps through created things, though Nicodemus' distinction of course is that he knew his God directly as Jesus Christ. Part of the great accomplishment of **"The Night"** resides in the ways that Vaughan, largely though not entirely through biblical allusion, confers a rich multisignificance upon words like *vail, night, darkness,* and *light.*

Several verses in *John* underlie stanza 2. To the skeptical Jews, Jesus says "I am the light of the world: he that followeth me shall not walk in darkness, but shall have the light of life" (John 8:12). The first chapter of *John* is of course full of comment relevant to these lines: "And the light shineth in darkness; and the darkness comprehended it not. . . . He was in the world, and the world was made by him, and the world knew him not. He came unto his own, and his own received him not" (John 1:5, 10, 11). And finally, "this is the condemnation, that light is come into the world, and men loved darkness rather than light, because their deeds were evil" (John 3:19). The "land of darkness and blinde eyes" is Israel in the time of Christ; the darkness here is evil, the sin and ignorance of the nonbelievers, who are blind to God, though He stood veiled in flesh before their eyes. Nicodemus is the exceptional man; before the Pharisees in the temple he defends Christ (John 7:50ff). Lines 9 and 10 have their source in Malachi

4:2. "But unto you that fear my name shall the Sun of righteousness arise with healing in his wings;" and in **The Mount of Olives** Vaughan writes: "Thou Sun of righteousness with healing under thy wings arise in my heart. In the poem, "Sun" is of course a play on the "Son" who is Christ; thus the ambiguous "rise," which inevitably implies the resurrection of Christ, is more forcefully felt. Though it is not essential, possibly Vaughan also assumes that Nicodemus was among the disciples to whom Christ appeared after His resurrection (John 20:19ff.). It is more certain, however, that "mid-night" in line 12 and therefore "by night" in line 6 are used both literally and figuratively to mean the night as the dark part of the diurnal cycle and the night or darkness as an era or period of sin and ignorance in Israel.

The transition to the personalized stanza 3, which begins the analysis, is more smoothly felt when one considers that seventeenth century England, like the Israel of Christ's time, was a land of religious as well as political strife, as Vaughan well knew.

> O who will tell me, where
> He found thee at that dead and silent hour!
> What hallow'd solitary ground did bear
> So rare a flower,
> Within whose sacred leafs did lie
> The fulness of the Deity.
>
> No mercy-seat of gold,
> No dead and dusty *Cherub,* nor carv'd stone,
> But his own living works did my Lord hold
> And lodge alone;
> Where *trees* and *herbs* did watch and peep
> And wonder, while the *Jews* did sleep.
>
> Dear night! this worlds defeat;
> The stop to busie fools; cares check and curb;
> The day of Spirits; my souls calm retreat
> Which none disturb!
>
> *Christs* progress, and his prayer time;
> The hours to which high Heaven doth chime.
> Gods silent, searching flight:
> When my Lords head is fill'd with dew, and all
> His locks are wet with the clear drops of night;
> His still, soft call;
> His knocking time; The souls dumb watch,
> When Spirits their fair kindred catch.

The analysis starts with a sense of the absence of God, specifically with the realization that men and particularly the I-narrator can no longer speak with Christ in Israel at night nor, for that matter, anywhere on earth, day or night—not, that is, in the literal sense as Nicodemus did. But stanzas 3 and 4 not only carry over the literal neutral significance and the figurative pejorative significance of "night," but also continue to suggest and begin to explore an honorific significance which attaches to "night," this last meaning being most explicitly developed in stanzas 5 and 6. Stanza 3, which is dominated by important garden and flower imagery, an imagery associated with one of the three major contemplative metaphors (see Durr, 29-78), begins with Vaughan's wish that he might repeat Nicode-

mus' experience of finding God "by night." This stanza's first two lines could carry all three meanings of "by night" just discussed: during the literal night time, in the flesh, and through created things. Because the first two meanings of "night" are no longer available as ways of finding Christ, the next few stanzas, as we shall see, propose still another way, that of prayer at night. The paradox of Light veiled in a land of darkness is in stanza 3 restated in terms of flower imagery and symbolism: the flower presents only its outer appearance, but hidden within is the total divinity; paradoxically, it took root in a sunless garden, the land of Israel. This suggests that the calcified heart may yet be regenerated. Subsequent stanzas develop this suggestion and continue the garden imagery in mystically significant terms.

Understood as "the golden covering placed upon the Ark of the Covenant and regarded as the resting-place of God" (O.E.D.), "mercy-seat" alludes to Exodus 25:17ff.: "And thou shalt make a mercy seat of pure gold . . . And thou shalt make two cherubins of gold . . . in the two ends of the mercy seat . . . and thou shalt put the mercy seat above upon the ark; and in the ark thou shalt put the testimony that I shall give thee." Christ's coming replaces or supplements the old law, as is symbolized by the rending of the temple veil. "But Christ being come an high priest of good things to come, by a greater and more perfect tabernacle [his body and blood], not made with hands, that is to say, not of this building" (Hebrews 9:11). Thus, we read lines 19-22 as: it was not the mercy seat, not mere dead stone but his own living works which did hold the Lord and lodge him alone. "Living works" may refer to Christ's deeds, his miracles, and to his true followers, both of which or whom testify to his divinity, and indeed may refer to the human body and blood born of the Virgin Mary. But given the context of stanzas 3 and 4 and especially the dominant garden and flower imagery, it is clear that "living works" particularly refers to the physical creation (theologically understood to be created by the Second Person) and specifically to watching, wakeful, plant nature, the "*trees* and *herbs*" which are alive to Christ, while "the *Jews,*" human nature with a heart of stone, in the night indifferently close their eyes to Him. Stanza 4, especially its last two lines, is also reminiscent of the garden of Gethsemane (Matthew 26:39ff.), where Christ's followers slept after he had asked them to watch and pray with him. Vaughan often writes of plant nature being in sympathy with and testifying to God; a plant's growing and striving upward makes it an apt and natural symbol for such sympathy and testimony. Throughout his poetry he frequently uses "a stone" as the symbol of the unregenerate heart. The ultimate source for the central image of **Silex Scintillans,** the flint and stone (heart-shaped in the 1650 title page) which must be struck before it can emit a fire, is, again, the Old Testament; and, notably, Ezekiel 36 addresses sinful Israel, promising to cleanse and deliver it "into your own land," the promised Edenic Garden: "A new heart also will I give you, and a new spirit will I put within you: and I will take away the stony heart out of your flesh and I will give you an heart of flesh" (36:26). Thus stanza 4 suggests, as subsequent stanzas bear out, that in order to hold and lodge the Lord, the stony heart must be refined and regenerated; the heart must become pure as a flower, like the "trees and herbs" alert to Christ, watered by the dew of his blood. (Concerning Christ in the Garden of Gethsemane, Luke 22:44 reads: "and his sweat was as it were great drops of blood falling down to the ground.") The way of the flowers which held commerce with Christ at night is, so to speak, the way still available for men to speak with the Son. How do men's heart's become pure, living, and watchful as flowers, watered by dew? The next stanzas show that the night, the time of meditation and contemplation, or prayer, can make the heart another Virgin-shrine for Christ to enter.

In many of Vaughan's poems, "night" and "darkness" have disvalues (or, at best, less positive values than "light" and "day") and symbolize sin, error, ignorance, the flesh, the old law, ceremonies, and so on, as in **"The World," "Rules and Lessons," "Ascension Day," "Faith,"** and **"Repentence,"** among many poems. In other poems it is the stars as guiding lights that are valued, not the night, as for example in **"Midnight," "Joy of my life,"** and **"The Constellation."** Of the few poems in which "night" or "darkness" has multiple and contradictory values, **"The Night"** is Vaughan's clearest expression. Like Herbert, but unlike Traherne, Vaughan is a poet who seldom travels the *via negativa* to contemplative union.

In the appositive lines 25-36, which bear structural similarity to Herbert's sonnet "Prayer," Vaughan now develops the positive values of night, which till now have mainly been only implicit. If sleep in the metaphorical sense of indifferently closing one's eyes and heart to Christ has disvalue, then sleep at night in the literal sense of physical inactivity has the value of preventing the "busie fools," nonbelievers and unregenerate hearts from committing further evil. "The day of Spirits" is a rich figure: first, night traditionally is a spiritual time of various kinds; second, as the body is inactive at night, the spirit may be active; third, as the poem has shown, night acts as a veil to spiritual reality, paradoxically giving man access to that reality by dimming it; fourth, because of the preceding reasons, it is a time of renewed innocence, as "my souls calm retreat" suggests. This last phrase also suggests, as subsequent lines make explicit, the inner pilgrimage, the soul's night journey through a land of darkness, in which the soul is alienated from God, to Light and reconciliation or union with God. To line 29 Vaughan gives these textual references: "And in the morning, rising up a great while before day, he went out, and departed into a solitary place, and there prayed" (Mark 1:35); "And in the day time he was teaching in the temple; and at night he went out, and abode in the mount that is called the mount of Olives." (Luke 21:37). The line, then, echoes back to the preceding stanza. With the word *progress* being used in its now rare sense, "Christs progress" is a journey at night to and of prayer.

Biblical allusion continues in the next stanza to enrich the poem. In line 31, the metaphor of "flight," a term of Falconry meaning the "pursuit of game, etc., by a hawk" (O.E.D.), would seem to be a reasonable alternative to the "fisher-of-men" metaphor of the Gospels. God pursues men at night and through the night. Lines 32-33 are adopted by Vaughan from The Song of Solomon 5:2: "I

sleep but my heart waketh: *it is* the voice of my beloved that knocketh, *saying,* Open to me, my sister, my love, my dove, my undefiled: for my head is filled with dew, and my locks with the drops of the night." With regard to "His knocking time," Revelation 3:20 reads "Behold, I stand at the door, and knock: if any man hear my voice, and open the door, I will come in to him, and will sup with him, and he with me." The Gospel of John, which Vaughan cited at the beginning of his poem, also contains a verse relevant to these lines: "Jesus answered [to the question how will he manifest himself] and said unto him, If a man love me, he will keep my words: and my Father will love him, and he will come unto him, and make our abode with him" (John 14:23).

It is not by random choice that lines 25-36 are structurally similar to Herbert's "Prayer"; for the content of these lines is prayer. Working within the traditions of meditation and contemplation, Vaughan, variously influenced by Herbert, uses the structure of "Prayer" for that part of his poem's content pertaining directly to prayer, a word closely associated with meditation and contemplation. Such a practice indicates a highly conscious and deliberate craftsmanship, and, for the reader, the integration of structure and content yields an added pleasure. In stanzas 5 and 6, Vaughan employs a poetic device, apposition (many terms with a single referent), that is precisely suited to the subject of mystical Union, the many in the one. Without main finite verbs and therefore in a sense timeless and beyond the sequential, reasoning intellect, stanzas 5 and 6 modify the conventional analysis of meditative structure and mark the transition between meditation and contemplation, an essential point to be developed along with the significance of the rich biblical allusions, in section III's fuller discussion of these most important stanzas.

> Were all my loud, evil days
> Calm and unhaunted as is thy dark Tent,
> Whose peace but by some *Angels* wing or voice
>   Is seldom rent;
>   Then I in Heaven all the long year
>   Would keep, and never wander here.
>
>   But living where the Sun
> Doth all things wake, and where all mix and tyre
> Themselves and others, I consent and run
>   To ev'ry myre,
>   And by this worlds ill-guiding light,
>   Erre more then I can do by night.
>
>   There is in God (some say)
> A deep, but dazling darkness; As men here
> Say it is late and dusky, because they
>   See not all clear;
>   O for that night! where I in him
>   Might live invisible and dim.

These stanzas (which at least begin as a colloquy; note line 38) logically and emotionally extend the preceding stanzas. Night must pass into day, and night's meditation and contemplation must end. Stanzas 7 and 8 develop the idea of the day as evil and by contrast praise the night. The poem has paradoxically reversed the significance of light and dark imagery by subtle equivocation, by gradually shifting the denotations and connotations of light or day and night or dark. By the last stanza, the poem in this progressive manner earns maximum value for night as an aspect of divinity.

"Thy dark Tent" is of course the night which houses Christ. But there is a further subtlety involved here too. "Tent" also means "tabernacle," and in Jewish history the tabernacle was "the curtained tent, containing the Ark of the Covenant and other sacred appointments, which served as the portable sanctuary of the Israelites during their wandering in the wilderness and afterwards till the building of the temple" (O.E.D.). Numbers 10:15 reads "And on the day that the tabernacle was reared up the cloud covered the tabernacle, *namely,* the tent of the testimony. . . ." We have seen (stanza 4) that no mercy-seat or carved stone or tabernacle held and lodged Christ. It is rather the night in its various meanings which is his dwelling-place, his tabernacle or tent—the night which, encouraging prayer, can purify and enliven the heart in order that Christ may enter. Lines 39 and 40 refer to various angelic events which are recorded in the Bible and which are accordingly evoked by the lines. The word "wander" in line 42 involves the major contemplative metaphor of the quest as well as wandering as *straying,* losing the Way: "I . . . would . . . never wander here" because the quest would be over. Union would be achieved if all the days were like the nights.

However, stanza 8 says this is not the case, for "I" live where the Sun and not the Son wakes all things, and so paradoxically "I" wander more "by this worlds ill-guiding light . . . then I can do by night." That the "Sun" in line 43 (as opposed to the multi-significant "Sun" of line 12) refers only to the sun of the phenomenal world is a clear instance of Vaughan's reversing of the significance of light and dark in particular preparation for the final paradox of stanza 9.

Since "night" in the sense of stanzas 5 and 6, night as the time of meditation leading to contemplation, cannot continue perpetually but must give way to the day of stanzas 7 and 8 and its evils, Vaughan prays in stanza 9 for that permanent night of the "deep but dazling darkness"—i. e. for the mystic experience of the Divine Darkness or Negative Divinity, an idea pervasive in Christian mysticism. Various commentators have suggested that the source for lines 49-50 may be Dionysius the Areopagite's *Mystic Theology.* "The Divine dark is nought else but that inaccessible light wherein the Lord is said to dwell. Although it is invisible because of its dazzling splendours and unsearchable because of the abundance of its supernatural brightness, nevertheless, whosoever deserves to see and know God rests therein, and, by the very fact that he neither sees nor knows, is truly in that which surpasses all truth and all knowledge." Dionysius the Areopagite, like Gregory of Nyssa, Augustine, and others, preached the method of negation, which consists in denying all predicates of God, because the Godhead is beyond the pale of the rational intellect and predicating conceptualization. Interpreting the trumpets that Moses heard on his first ascent of Mount Sinai, Gregory describes in his *Life of Moses* a kind of Platonic ascent from contemplation of the universe, a Vision of Dame Kind, to contemplation of the invisible and incomprehensible divine darkness, a Vi-

sion of God: "When the hearing of the heart has been purified, then will a man hear this sound—that is, the contemplation of the universe from which we derive our knowledge of the divine omnipotence—and by this he is led in spirit to penetrate to the realm where God exists. This realm the Scriptures call a dark cloud (*gnophos*). And by this is meant the invisibility and incomprehensibility of God. It is in this darkness that he sees the tabernacle not made by human hands." Other mystics who follow the example of Gregory or Dionysius might be included in Vaughan's parenthetical "some say"; the phrase indicates that Vaughan himself did not achieve, at least as far as this poem is concerned, the final stage of mystical union but that he is with appropriate humility referring to the experience of other mystics, while earnestly desiring union for himself.

This desire for union is the essence of mysticism, as of religion generally, and Vaughan's distinction, as every mystic's distinction, is that he attains to such union or an aspect of it (even if only initially, incompletely, and temporarily at earlier stages of spiritual progress, such as Illumination) *in this life,* and need not wait entirely until the afterlife.

III

As previously remarked, we might well find both meditative and contemplative elements in a single poem. In fact, in one form or another, *lectio divina,* meditation, prayer, and contemplation all appear in **"The Night."** And where we find clear evidence of, say, the stage of Illumination, rather than just Purgation, we may be confident that the poem or certain parts of it are contemplative rather than just meditative. While **"The Night"** clearly indicates that the speaker had not attained final Union at that point, it also unmistakably reveals, I believe, that he had realized not only Illumination, a remarkable realization in itself, but also the Dark Night of the Soul if this term is fully and correctly understood in the Renaissance formulation given by the great contemplative St. John of the Cross.

Even more so than Dionysius the Areopagite or St. Gregory of Nyssa, St. John of the Cross is regarded by some scholars as "the leader of the 'apophatic' theologians, the teachers of the 'dark' knowledge of God [according to Thomas Merton]. He completes and fulfills the tradition of the greatest contemplatives among the Greek Fathers." In the *Ascent of Mount Carmel* and *Dark Night of the Soul,* companion volumes which outline the scale of perfection in one of its most influential Renaissance forms, St. John actually distinguishes several dark nights. First, there is the night of the sense and the night of the spirit. In St. John's words: "This night, which, as we say, is contemplation, produces in spiritual persons two kinds of darkness or purgation, corresponding to the two parts of man's nature—namely, the sensual and the spiritual. And thus the one night or purgation will be sensual . . . and the other is a night or purgation which is spiritual, wherein the soul is . . . made ready for the union of love with God. The night of sense is common and comes to many. . . . The night of the spirit is the portion of very few, and these are they that are already practiced and proficient. . . ." Secondly, St. John distinguishes active and passive modes, also called the active and passive nights. His earlier work treats the active night of sense and spirit and *Dark Night of the Soul* treats the passive night of sense and spirit. "Active" refers to the soul's own purging of itself, and "passive" pertains to the soul's being purged by God. In other words, in the active night the mystical aspirant may purify himself with the ordinary help of grace in order to prepare his senses and spirit for union with God. In the passive night, with more abundant grace than before, while the individual soul is passive, God does the purifying of the senses and spirit for the same ultimate purpose of union. This passive night also obtains in Vaughan's poem, as I shall shortly demonstrate. What does not obtain in the poem for the speaker is the final vision of God as "dark night to the soul," God as the "dazling darkness" that is incomprehensible to man's reasoning intellect.

Since purification is an ongoing process, different stages may be simultaneously present. "In a sense [writes Evelyn Underwood] the whole of the mystical experience in this life consists in a series of purifications, whereby the Finite slowly approaches the nature of its Infinite Source." As Christ's sermon on the mount tells us, blessed are the pure in heart, for they shall see God. "For cleanness of heart is nothing less than the love and grace of God" (*Dark Night*). As previously noted, purification leads to vision and enlightenment, but these latter in themselves are and help to provide a further purification leading to still deeper vision and enlightenment. At the risk of oversimplifying, it may be said that contemplative life consists of increasing purification and enlightenment, or the *nada y todo* of St. John: everything that is not divine is to be negated or purified away so that with intensifying illuminations the mystic may eventually be wholly united with the divine All.

For St. John of the Cross [according to E. W. Trueman Dicken] the traditional *via mystica* (Purgation, Illumination, Union) "provides the basic framework of his whole teaching on spiritual progress." Because purification is an ongoing process, the following comparative table helpfully amplifies and refines the traditional threefold way in a manner which distinguishes between different degrees of purification:

> Active Night of the Senses Purgation
> Passive Night of the Senses Transition to Illumination
>
> Active Night of the Spirit Illumination
> Passive Night of the Spirit Transition to Union

The stage of Union is just beyond the passive night of the spirit. Understanding St. John's commentary within this traditional framework should help to provide clearer insight into the mystical aspects of **"The Night."**

In general, stanzas 5 through 9 of the poem suggest the speaker realized Illumination, as well as Purgation, and indicate that he dwelled in the nights of the senses and spirit. As observed, **"The Night"** is a modified meditative poem. Stanzas 5 and 6, similar in structure to Herbert's "Prayer," reveal that there must have been many "illuminations" enjoyed by Vaughan or the speaker and suggest that Vaughan or the speaker progressed to the dark nights of the senses and spirit. With Christ no longer on earth,

prayer at night is the way now for man "at mid-night [to] speak with the Sun!" " 'What is prayer?' asks Meister Eckhart, and answers in the words of Dionysius the Areopagite: 'The mind's ascent to God, that is what prayer means' " (cited in Durr, *On the Mystical Poetry*). These appositive stanzas, stylistically implying the many in the one and marking the transition from multiplicity to unity, have no independent finite verbs (verbs appear only in subordinate modifying clauses) and are thus in a sense eternal or timeless, existing in the eternal now-moment: "The hours to which high Heaven doth chime." Anthony Low's critical comment on these stanzas is insightful: "The poem moves insensibly from the historical-material world of the meditating imagination into a spiritual world of mystical contemplation. . . . The tense also changes. Up to this point, the past perfect of completed action was used, and Vaughan even asserted that the experience of Nicodemus, meeting with God at midnight, cannot be repeated. The poem now belies that assertion. What Vaughan describes seems like something presently happening. Grammatically, the two stanzas are an extended apostrophe to Night that have no tense because they lack a main verb. They are in the timeless rather than the simple present. . . ."

A passage from St. John of the Cross is also in various ways illuminating of stanzas 5 and 6: "in this state of contemplation, which the soul enters when it forsakes meditation for the state of the proficient, it is God Who is now working in the soul; He binds its interior faculties, and allows it not to cling to the understanding, nor to have delight in the will, nor to reason with the memory. . . . God now begins to communicate Himself to it, no longer through sense, as he did aforetime, by means of reflections which joined and sundered its knowledge, but by pure spirit, into which consecutive reflections enter not; but He communicates Himself to it by an act of simple contemplation . . ." (*Dark Night*).

The night as the dark part of the diurnal cycle effectively shuts off the sense of sight, the dominant mode of perception among the five senses, accounting for the great majority of all our perceptual data. But stanzas 5 and 6 (and 7 as well) also emphasize the turning off to the outside world of the sense of hearing, humans' second most important sense, thereby providing silence and stillness. To be quiet and receptive seems a necessary condition for contemplative communication or communion with divinity. "It is in the stillness, in the silence, that the word of God is to be heard [says Meister Eckhart]. There is no better avenue of approach to this Word than through stillness, through silence." In Vaughan's quiet night, "God now begins to communicate Himself to [the soul] no longer through sense": "Gods silent, searching flight . . . His still, soft call . . . The souls dumb watch." These phrases plainly reveal that the soul is passive and God active, that in the nights (in the sense of dark periods of the day) referred to in these stanzas Vaughan expresses his passing through the passive night: "it is God Who is now working in the soul." And God communicates himself "by pure spirit into which consecutive reflections enter not . . . by an act of simple contemplation." The night is "The day of Spirits . . . When Spirits their fair kindred catch."

Engraved title page of Olor Iscanus *(1651).*

Beyond the senses and the temporal, reasoning intellect (with its "consecutive reflections") and marking the mind's ascent to God, the mode and meaning of the appositive stanzas modify the conventional analysis of meditative structure and move the poem from meditation to contemplation, from the lower stages of mystical or pre-mystical activity to the higher mystical stage of Illumination and then, subsequently, to the passive night of the spirit. In time, on different nocturnal occasions, Vaughan or the speaker apparently experienced the night as Purgation and as a night of the senses and spirit. Because Vaughan or the speaker is or was in a night of the senses, he experiences the illuminations of stanzas 5 and 6 and he moves toward the night of the spirit, as also indicated elsewhere in the poem. During the period of "the aridities of this night of sense," God draws "forth the soul from the life of sense into that of the spirit—that is, from meditation to contemplation. . . . The way in which they are to conduct themselves in the night of sense is to devote themselves not at all to reasoning and meditation . . . but to allow the soul to remain in peace and quietness . . . and persevere in prayer without making any effort" (*Dark Night*). These timeless stanzas 5 and 6 portray the night in which the soul finds "the most serene and loving con-

templation and spiritual sweetness without the labor of meditation" (*Dark Night*). In their timelessness, they apparently refer to many nights of Illumination and various past dark nights, which may have occurred on numerous separate, timeless nocturnal occasions but which are by the poet inductively collapsed into a detailed, generalized description of "Dear night," profoundly rendering its meaning as if it were nevertheless a single night. One imagines that the night of these stanzas may very well include among its many occasions the one referred to in those brilliant opening lines of **"The World"**:

> I saw Eternity the other night
> Like a great Ring of pure and endless light,
>   All calm, as it was bright.

The vital difference between meditation and contemplation is precisely the vital difference between the rational intellect and Love (there is not a better word unless one uses Greek terms like the Platonic *noesis* or the biblical *pneuma*). Just as the absence of main verbs stylistically and structurally signal that the meditating mind has no place in the eternal now-moment, so the relevance of the previously noted biblical passages on love reveal that stanzas 5 and 6 are in the mode of contemplation. Like Dante's Virgil, the meditating intellect may help guide one through the Inferno and up Mount Purgatory, but it is Love that leads into the Garden of Eden and Paradise. Just as Stanley Stewart, in his study of the imagery of the Song of Songs, has demonstrated with respect to Vaughan's **"Regeneration"** and Marvell's "The Garden," the full context of **"The Night,"** so rich in biblical allusions, also includes the Song of Songs with its themes and imagery of love, timelessness, and the garden. In his commentary on his own *Spiritual Canticle,* which is also a commentary on Solomon's Song, St. John of the Cross holds, as did Origen and Gregory of Nyssa in their Commentaries on the Song of Songs, that the true subject of the biblical Song is the wonder of the mystical state. The interpretation by Origen and St. Gregory of the Canticles, rich in garden imagery, as representing the union of love between God and the soul has generally been accepted by all subsequent mystical theologians.

The imagery of the garden in which Christ was wont to pray at night runs through and unites stanzas 3, 4, 5, and 6 of Vaughan's poem. The night is the time of prayer; Christ prayed in the garden at night. "God's silent, searching flight" is his night prayers, by which he seeks out humankind. Lines 32-33, adopted from The Song of Songs, with its references to love, echo the flower imagery of stanza 3: Christ is a rare and sacred flower, his head "filled with dew." The symbol of dew in Vaughan's poetry is invariably to be interpreted as having a healing and saving power. Dew is a symbol of regeneration, the symbol of God's grace and Christ's blood. (Expecially because of the reference to the mount of Olives in Luke 21:37, noted by Vaughan, lines 29-33 also suggest Christ in Gethsemane, its dark night of agonizing purification and "bloody sweat.") In *I Sleep and My Heart Wakes,* a title of course taken from the same passage in the Song of Songs that Vaughan alludes to, the English mystic and poet Richard Rolle distinguishes three degrees of love by which man comes to be united to God. One particular passage in

Rolle's discussion of the second degree, which involves the love of Jesus Christ and "meditating upon His Passion," seems especially pertinent to the middle stanzas of **"The Night":** "and when your heart is completely disposed to the service of God, and when all worldly thoughts are expelled from it, then you will wish to steal away and be alone to think of Christ and to spend much time in prayer" (*The Mediaeval Mystics of England*). This is similar to St. John's third sign of positive attraction for solitary contemplative prayer, the most important of the three signs for indicating that the soul is ready to leave behind meditation and to dwell in passive contemplation.

We have also seen the relevance of The Song of Songs 5:2 and Revelation 3:20 to "His knocking time." "As we read in Mrs. Sutcliff's *Meditations of Man's Mortalitie* (1634), the only cure for the sickness of the Spouse, expressed in the complaint in the Song of Songs, is the Second Coming, described by St. John in the Apocalypse [writes Stanley Steward in *The Enclosed Garden*]. . . . There was a sense, then, in which the Song of Songs was understood as an apocalyptic prayer." The marriage metaphor obtains in the poem largely through biblical allusion. This metaphor, fundamental and vital in the writing also of St. John of the Cross, is one of the three basic contemplative figures in Vaughan's poetry, as R. A. Durr has shown, figures which symbolically transform archetypal mystical experience and embody the theme of regeneration or rebirth. The heart is the Bridegroom's, the Lord's chamber; but the heart ordinarily is calcified, is like the "carv'd stone," and the Bridegroom must stand outside and knock. Two things are working in "busy commerce" for the desired union of man with God. One is, metaphorically, God's "prayer," that is, his suffering, crucifixion, resurrection, the grace of his redeeming dew or blood. The Lord knocks, but the heart must be prepared and answer if there is to be mystical union. The prayer of man is the other force working for union. Night stops the busy day; it permits, indeed, it *is* "the souls dumb watch," its silent prayer. By the Lord's knocking and "the souls dumb watch," apocalyptic Union in this life, or at least temporary Illuminations, may be achieved, "Spirits [may] their fair kindred catch." ("Kindred," of course, means "relationship by blood, sometimes by marriage.") Man's love and prayer and Christ's love and "prayer," or redeeming dew, soften the heart, open the door, and permit the Bridegroom to enter. Mythically understood, such apocalyptic entering is both sacramental marriage and rebirth. "Except a man be born again . . . of water [dew] and *of* the Spirit, he cannot enter into the Kingdom of God" (John 3:3, 5). Love and prayer or contemplation at night, then, are the way for man "at mid-night [to] speak with the Sun!"

In her chapter on "The Dark Night of the Soul," Evelyn Underhill points out that in its movement toward transcendent reality "the self experiences a series of oscillations between 'states of pleasure' and 'states of pain'. . . oscillations between a joyous and a painful consciousness seem to occur most often at the beginning of a new period of the Mystic Way. . . . Mystics call such oscillations the 'Game of Love' in which God plays, as it were, 'hide and seek' with the questing soul." The centrally important

stanzas 5 and 6 suggest that Vaughan or the speaker enjoyed through love and prayer timeless illuminations and that he had passed through nights of sense and passive nights. But the quiet night (as the dark part of the day) of contemplative prayer and love ends with daylight and swings over to "loud, evil days." Stanzas 7 through 9 especially show clearly the oscillation from Illumination to St. John's passive night of the spirit or, in a modern formulation, to "The Dark Night of the Soul" exactly as Underhill describes that Night.

Stanzas 7 through 9 are a modified colloquy in that they begin with the speaker addressing God (as signaled by the second person "thy" in line 38) but then by the last stanza move on to regarding God in the third person (as signalled especially, though not only, by "him" in the penultimate line). This shift from second to third person reveals and underscores the fact, fully developed in stanza 9, that, although the poet or speaker after the illuminations of stanzas 5 and 6 feels close enough to God for direct address in the following stanza, he still does not yet enjoy Union. His address to God in stanza 7 subjunctively observes that "Were all my loud, evil days / Calm and unhaunted as in thy dark Tent," then he would in effect enjoy permanent Union "here" in this life: "Then I in Heaven all the long year / Would keep, and never wander here." Like the nontemporal stanzas 5 and 6, these lines express the peculiar non-temporal and perhaps also non-spatial characteristics of mystical experience, as noted by Stace (*Mysticism and Philosophy*) and other distinguished commentators on mysticism. That is, more precisely, he would paradoxically be both in and out of ordinary space and time, enjoying Heaven eternally while still here on earth, though never again wandering, "all the long year."

A major aspect of the poem, however, is exactly that the speaker does not at this point dwell in permanent Union but rather suffers a Dark Night of the Soul. Such Union "is the 'perfection' toward which the beginner aspires when he undertakes the active mortification ('night') of the senses, and which the progressive approaches in the 'passive nights' of the senses and of the spirit. Neither beginners nor progressives have attained this 'Divine Union.' It is the reward of the 'perfect.' Yet progressives are already contemplatives, which is to say, in Saint John of the Cross's language, mystics" (Merton). The fact that the speaker so fervently wishes for the unitive dwelling in the "deep, but dazling darkness" is in itself a likely sign that he has passed through the various stages following Purgation and preceding Union, but there is abundant other evidence for such passage, for his being a "progressive" or mystic. The sense of the present absence of God pervades much of the whole poem. The sense of sin appears particularly in lines 37 and 45 to 48. The former peace, joy, and blessedness, all characteristics of mystical experience (Stace, *Mysticism and Philosophy*) and indicated by stanzas 5 and 6, are revealed as lost in stanzas 7 and 8, which along with stanza 3, especially mark the grief and suffering. And all of this that Vaughan or the speaker feels—the absence of God, the sense of sin, the loss of former peace and joy and blessedness, the grief and suffering, the apparent relapse to a lower spiritual level—are "types of darkness," "forms" or characteristics of the Dark Night of the Soul (Underhill, *Mysticism*). The Dark Night of the Soul "is the completion of that ordering of disordered loves, that transvaluation of values, which the Way of Purgation began" (Underhill). It is the full and final humbling of the false self so that the true self may eventually be exalted in full and final Union; it is that total self-simplification and emptying which leads paradoxically to a fullness of effulgent beatitude. In St. John's words, "although this happy night brings darkness to the spirit, it does so only to give it light in everything; . . . although it humbles it and makes it miserable, it does so only to exalt it and to raise it up; and although it impoverishes and empties it of all natural affection and attachment, it does so only that it may enable it to stretch forward, divinely, and thus to have fruition and experience of all things. . . . In this way, being empty, it is able indeed to be poor in spirit and freed from the old man, in order to live that new and blessed life which is attained by means of this night, and which is the state of union with God." This night is St. John's passive night of the spirit; and **"The Night"** manifests this advanced degree of mystic consciousness.

The last stanza, which has elicited much comment, has puzzled critics unfamiliar with mystical tradition. John Pollock, for example, thinks that the final line contains an inconsistency which reveals Vaughan's "divided consciousness." "The last line is not, however, simply a straightforward cry for mystical union with God, for Vaughan—to put the matter bluntly—is contradicting himself: to be dim is not to be invisible. This contradiction suggests that Vaughan actually has drawn back from an ultimate commitment to invisibility, that is to the total renunciation of self that invisibility implies. It is as if his mind were divided against itself, for at the very moment he asks to be taken into the Divine Nothingness, part of him hesitates and so he totters on the brink, afraid to lose himself entirely."

Such a view of the poem thoroughly violates its whole progress, meaning, and integrity. Of course, "to be dim is not to be invisible," but Vaughan is not contradicting himself, nor is he drawing back from a full commitment. Here is a clear instance of serious confusion owing to the critical failure to understand mystical tradition and Vaughan's place in it, specifically to understand "the essential paradoxicality of the mystical consciousness" and to realize that "the paradox of the dissolution of individuality, in which dissolution the 'I' both disappears and persists, is reported in all ages and cultures by countless independent witnesses" (Stace, *Mysticism and Philosophy*). In other words, in accord with the central paradox of rebirth or of life through death, Vaughan or the speaker prays for the ego or false self to be annihilated, made "invisible," and for the regenerated true Self to be exalted and united to God, whose "dazzling" nature makes that Self appear "dim." His is not a divided consciousness but rather one deeply desirous of Union with the Highest Consciousness or with what Stace in the same book designates the "Unitary Consciousness." Like Dionysius, Vaughan unhesitatingly says "Unto this Darkness which is beyond Light, we pray that we may come" (*Divine Names and the Mystical Theology*). A modified meditation employing the meditative structure, the poem has steadily moved us toward

contemplation and the ultimate object of contemplation, the "deep, but dazling darkness." The alliteration in this phrase serves to emphasize the paradoxical nature of God and to focus attention on the climatic word, "dim," which also involves that paradox. (It should also be noted that contemplation of the Dionysian "Divine Dark" is traditionally referred to as "dim contemplation," as in St. John's *Dark Night of the Soul*.) While the first four lines of the last stanza emphasize the negative, mysterious nature of God, the concluding couplet intensely sums up, in terms of the marriage metaphor, Vaughan's prayer for union with God, "that night," in which his false individuality would be abolished, dissolved (the point of "invisible") and in which by losing his life he would gain it (a large part of the point of "dim"), so that his true "individuality" would be realized. That is, the poem takes us back full circle to the first stanza: the speaker, like Nicodemus, wishes "to know his God by night," to become Christlike, to be exactly the dimmed divinity that Christ is at the beginning of the poem. And in this highly accomplished way, Vaughan brilliantly brings together the two main streams of Christo-mysticism and God-mysticism, the originating founts of which are the Johannine and Pauline writings and the Christian Neoplatonism of Dionysius. As we read in a favorite mystical text, "ye shall know that I am in my Father, and ye in me, and I in you" (John 14:20).

IV

The three kinds of contemplation that appear in varying degrees in **"The Night"** were typically described by medieval and Renaissance mystics in the terms used by St. Edmund Rich, a Dionysian theologian whose *The Mirror of Holy Church* achieved wide circulation in both Latin and English. "The first is contemplation of created beings, the second of the Scriptures, the third of God Himself and His nature. Contemplation is nothing else than looking at God: and His creatures can look at Him in this way" (in *The Medieval Mystics of England*). The first two forms of contemplation are an acquired contemplation—of created beings and of the Scriptures. The Scriptures included the Bible and the Fathers, and Vaughan practically treats Herbert as if he were a Church Father, alluding to his work only a little less frequently than to the Bible. The third kind of contemplation, of God Himself and His nature, is an infused contemplation, often leading inwardly along the *via negativa,* as in **"The Night,"** and often referred to as "the Book of the Soul," so that there are "three books." A single poem may of course refer to several kinds of both meditation and contemplation. **"The Night,"** as we have seen, touches upon and hints of past contemplative experiences of created things that many other poems dwell upon more explicitly and fully. Whereas **"The Night"** primarily presents Vaughan's desire for a Vision of God through the *via negativa,* in many of his other poems, as we shall be discussing, Vaughan reads the book of nature and the book of Scriptures and looks both outside of and within himself to find God.

Although it was a medieval and Renaissance commonplace to regard nature as a book, Vaughan's poems portray his contemplation of created things as so special, distinctive, and charged with numinous significance that these portraits, while they are common or frequent in his work, are never commonplace. Nor should such contemplation be confused with abstract, discursive reasoning from the existence of a creation to a Creator, in the manner of scholastic rational argument. Rather, many of Vaughan's poems concern the unmediated sights or actual direct experience of divinity in created things. For all of the important pervasive presence of Herbert in Vaughan's work, this kind of contemplation distinguishes Vaughan's poetry and moves him away from both Herbert and Donne and closer to his later contemporary, Traherne. Like Herbert, Vaughan places a series of eschatological poems near the end of *Silex Scintillans* (Part II). Unlike Herbert, who follows his eschatological poems and concludes "The Church" with the eucharistic and unitive "Love" (III), Vaughan concludes his book with **"The Book"** and **"To the Holy Bible"** (preceding his **"L'Envoy"**). Biblical allusion and meditation on or contemplation of the Scriptures of course figure prominently in both Herbert and Vaughan. But, although they are significant in Vaughan, eucharistic imagery and themes do not in his work have the central and pervasive importance that they do in "The Church." Vaughan's poems on the contemplation of created things make the difference. Vaughan is led to mystical experience more by book (one or the other) than by Eucharist. His **"To the Holy Bible"** contains a catalog of some distinctive contemplative characteristics, including "union." Remarking upon the commonplace of seeing the world of nature as a book, Alan Rudrum rightly observes about **"The Book"** that "Vaughan's originality is to see the world of nature in a book" (*Henry Vaughan: The Complete Poems*). With the mystic's passion for seeing things as interrelated and unified, Vaughan describes how various created, natural objects go into the making of a book, no doubt the Good Book (but possibly also *Silex Scintillans?*), suggesting that God's books are interconnected. **"The Book"** Concludes:

> O knowing, glorious spirit! when
> Thou shalt restore trees, beasts and men,
> When thou shalt make all new again,
> Destroying onely death and pain,
> Give him amongst thy works a place
> Who in them lov'd and sought thy face!

Coming in a crucial position near the end of *Silex Scintillans,* **"The Book"** summarizes and emphasizes with all the weight of Vaughan's book what many of Vaughan's poems individually reveal: Vaughan loved, searched for and sometimes found God not only in Scriptures and inwardly in the Book of the Soul but also outwardly in nature, "amongst thy works," for now we see through a glass darkly, but then, when the veil of custom, convention, and selfish solicitude drops away, shall we see face to face, in the extrovertive Vision of Dame Kind, to use W. H. Auden's phrase. Auden describes this Vision in the following manner: "The basic experience is an overwhelming conviction that the objects confronting [the mystic] have a numinous significance and importance, that the existence of everything he is aware of is holy. And the basic emotion is one of innocent joy, though this joy can include, of course, a reverent dread. . . . So long as the vi-

sion lasts the self is 'noughted,' for its attention is completely absorbed in what it contemplates; it makes no judgment and desires nothing, except to continue in communion with what Gerald Manley Hopkins called the inscape of things."

To the familiar idea that, as Gregory of Nyssa expressed it, all things are in the divinity, and the divinity is in all things, we should equally stress the idea of God's transcendence. An important factor of the mystical experience is, Thomas Merton reminds us, the mystic's paradoxical "discovery of God in His immanence and His transcendence. Everything that the soul experiences flows from this central mystery that God is in all things and in the soul, and that He is nevertheless infinitely above the soul and above all things." On balance, Vaughan's poems suggest that Vaughan more fully experienced God's immanence than God's transcendence, that he more frequently and deeply enjoyed the Vision of Dame Kind than he did the Vision of God. Perhaps that is another reason why in **"The Night,"** Vaughan, led on by past illuminative visions, so ardently expresses the desire for a unitive Vision of God. That powerful desire for what remains just beyond realization finds vivid expression in the opening lines of **"Childe-hood,"** the poem immediately preceding **"The Night"**:

> I cannot reach it; and my striving eye
> Dazles at it, as at eternity.

Referring to the biblical idea of being born again and becoming like unto a child to enter the kingdom of heaven, the central mystical paradox of regeneration, Vaughan writes "he / Must live twice, that would God's face see;" and he concludes **"Childe-hood"** by returning to the metaphor of light which opened the poem and then pleading "O for thy Center and mid-day! / For sure that is the *narrow way.*"

The final couplet of the much discussed and highly acclaimed **"Regeneration,"** the first poem of *Silex Scintillans,* which sets in motion and governs the sequence that follows, expresses Vaughan's desire for the mystic death of the first Adam for the sake of rebirth in God:

> Lord, then said I, *On me one breath,*
> And let me dye before my death.

This figurative or spiritual dying which is to precede his actual, literal physical death is the self-noughting which Auden and contemplatives speak of and which precedes or accompanies that spiritual rebirth or regeneration that is the heart of mystical experience. Unlike Donne, who in his divine poems tends to take "death" in its literal sense, as we observed in our discussion of "Hymn to God my God, in my sicknesse," Vaughan sometimes intends the word in its literal and sometimes in its figurative senses. The first two stanzas of "Ascension Hymn," near the beginning of Part II (1655) of *Silex Scintillans* plainly refer to both kinds of death:

> Dust and clay
> Mans antient wear!
> Here you must stay,
> but I elsewhere;
> Souls sojourn here, but may not rest;

Who will ascend, must be undrest.

> And yet some
> That know to die
> Before death come,
> Walk to the skie
> Even in this life; but all such can
> Leave behinde them the old Man.

The dying "Before death . . . Even in this life" clearly refers to mystical death, the death of the first Adam: "but all such can / Leave behinde them the old Man."

The poem **"Regeneration,"** as Stanley Stewart remarks, "represents the three stages—purgative, illuminative, and unitive—of the mystical life" (*The Enclosed Garden*), and, especially, through its last lines, it alerts the reader to the special meaning of death in many of the poems that follow it. Vaughan not only concludes *Silex Scintillans* with a series of eschatological poems, as Herbert concludes "The Church," but so much is death and rebirth or resurrection his primary theme that he also places the closely related eschatological poems **"Death," "Resurrection and Immortality,"** and **"Day of Judgment"** after **"Regeneration."** In the first stanza of the next poem, **"Religion,"** expecially in groves, and leaves, Vaughan in effect locates the setting, or places of self-discovery, of many of his poems: either in the natural world, "groves," or the "leaves" of the Bible or other holy writings, such as Herbert's. The following meditative poem describes **"The Search"** for the essential self: "all night have I / Spent in a roving Extasie / to find my Saviour." Not at all having the sense it does for Donne, "Extasie" here means a mental wandering or following of the life of Christ from birth through resurrection and apocalypse at various biblically-mentioned places. By the end of the poem, the speaker, who has never actually left his cell or his meditations, "heard one singing," and so learns to "leave thy gadding thoughts" and to "Search well another world," not "The skimme and shell of things" but the inner world and the inward man, as the concluding verse from Acts 17:27-28 indicates: "That they should seek the Lord, if happily they might feel after him, and finde him, though he be not far off from every one of us, for in him we live, and move, and have our being."

Again, in contemplative tradition there are two worlds: the perfect, natural world, including creatures and objects, and created by God and by God in the redeemed person; and the fallen world fabricated by man's conceptualizing ego, an artificial, prideful, and illusory world. The seeming contradiction (in Vaughan and in general) of condemning and enjoying the world is thus resolved by the realization that one must give up the vain, illusory, time-bound world of getting and spending, in which we lay waste our God-given powers, for the sake of (not, as in Donne's resolution, the microcosm of the lovers in a Vision of Eros, but) the natural macrocosm eternally charged with God's grandeur and quickened by Christ playing in ten thousand places or re-created by the last Adam in the redeemed person's imaginative, loving consciousness during a Vision of Dame Kind. These two worlds are conveniently and briefly referred to as the inner and outer worlds of nature, or

the world of Eternity and the world of Time, as in Vaughan's famous poem **"The World."**

Many of Vaughan's poems search well both the world of the inner self and the inner world of nature, which worlds, seemingly two, are one, in that the special unitive relationship between the seeming two is what is most real, and in that Vaughan finds the single reality of divinity, or "my Saviour," at and as the heart of Nature and the inner self. Like **"The Night,"** a large number of Vaughan's poems have both meditative and contemplative elements in them, one typical pattern being for a poem to begin in meditation and end in, or at least move toward, contemplation. This pattern finds one kind of expression in the actual movement of the speaker from indoors to outdoors, as in **"Vanity of Spirit":**

> Quite spent with thoughts I left my Cell, and lay
> Where a shrill spring tun'd to the early day.
>   I beg'd here long, and gron'd to know
>   Who gave the Clouds so brave a bow,
>   Who bent the spheres, and circled in
>   Corruption with this glorious Ring,
>   What is his name, and how I might
>   Descry some part of his great light.
> I summon'd nature: peirc'd through all her store,
> Broke up some seales, which none had touch'd
>   before,   10
>   Her wombe, her bosome, and her head
>   Where all her secrets lay a bed
>   I rifled quite, and having past
>   Through all the Creatures, came at last
>   To search my selfe, where I did find
>   Traces, and sounds of a strange kind.
> Here of this mightly spring, I found some drills,
> With Ecchoes beaten from th' eternall hills;
>   Weake beames, and fires flash'd to my sight,
>   Like a young East, or Moone-shine
>   night,   20
>   Which shew'd me in a nook cast by
> A peece of much antiquity,
>   With Hyerogliphicks quite dismembred,
>   And broken letters scarce remembred.
> I tooke them up, and (much Joy'd) went about
> T'unite those peeces, hoping to find out
>   The mystery; but this neer done,
>   That little light I had was gone:
>   It griev'd me much. At last, said I,
> *Since in these veyls my Ecclips'd Eye*   30
> *May not approach thee, (for at night*
> *Who can have commerce with the light?)*
> *I'le disapparell, and to buy*
> *But one half gluance, most gladly dye.*

Leaving behind his cell and his discursive, meditative thoughts, the speaker goes outdoors to a spring, signifying an actual source of water and symbolizing, as in Traherne, pneuma or the essential self, in search of his Saviour, here the Creator. Whereas the typical setting for Donne (at least in the Songs and Sonnets) is the bedroom and for Herbert the church, the setting for Vaughan is often outdoors in nature. Even poems set indoors frequently contain images of nature, particularly what Durr has designated as the major metaphor of the seed and flower. Vaughan is a "nature" poet in the sense that he summons and searches nature to find his God, as Donne and Herbert do not. The vain world (of **"Corruption"**) is "circled . . . with this glorious Ring," imagery echoed in the opening lines of **"The World,"** which distinguish between the worlds of time and eternity. Both positive and negative aspects obtain, as Thomas Merton observes, in "the contemplation of God in nature, which the Greek Fathers called *theoria physica.* On the one hand, *theoria physica* is a positive recognition of God as He is manifested in the essences (*logoi*) of all things. It is not a speculative science of nature but rather a habit of religious awareness which endows the soul with a kind of intuitive perception of God as He is reflected in His creation. . . . The negative aspect of *theoria physica* is an equally instinctive realization of the vanity and illusion of all things as soon as they are considered apart from their right order and reference to God their Creator. Saint Gregory of Nyssa's commentary on *Ecclesiastes,* from which we have quoted, is a tract on the 'contemplation of nature' in its twofold aspect. . . ." Vaughan's editors cite the pertinent text from Ecclesiastes 1:14: "I have seen all the works that are done under the sun; and, behold, all *is* vanity and vexation of spirit."

Like **"The Night,"** **"Vanity of Spirit"** apparently concerns just one occasion but appears to summarize or concentrate into that one occasion many different actual occasions of summoning and searching nature. While other poems present even more certain evidence of successful searchings, lines 9-14 suggest that the quest for finding the Creator in the creation and in creatures fruitfully reveals some secrets. Interestingly, Vaughan's "nature," Dame Kind, is pictured, much as Plato's *Timaeus* pictures the unity of the whole cosmos, as one living creature: "Her wombe, her bosome, and her head . . . ," a point to be returned to later. Moving up the chain of being (see also, for example **"I walkt the other day," "The Sap," "The Tempest,"** and **"Man"**), "having past / Through all the Creatures," the speaker "came at last / To search my selfe." The search of the created being which is "my selfe" for signs of the Creator reveals something more: "Traces, and sounds of a strange kind." The language of the second half of the poem suggests Neoplatonic emanationism. Teaching that all things are emanations from God, an inevitable overflow of infinite actuality, Plotinus employed not only the metaphor of the sun which radiates light without loss to itself but also the metaphor of the spring from which the stream flows without exhausting its source. The speaker has a Platonic insight into his own nature as partaking of the divine nature, the way small streams emanate from a mighty spring or echoes resound from eternal hills. Reminiscent of **"The Night,"** he finds a dimmed sun within, "Like a young East." The experience is incomplete, broken off, temporary but nevertheless very joyful, a partially successful Vision of Dame Kind continuing on to a partial but illuminative Vision of God within, and the whole experience leads him to wish for that figurative and/or literal death that will give him fuller and more unified vision.

The very next poem, **"The Retreat,"** which word implies a withdrawal from the vain world as well as backward motion, recalls such greater vision from early childhood:

> When on some *gilded Cloud,* or *flowre*
> My gazing soul would dwell an houre,
> And in those weaker glories spy
> Some shadows of eternity;
> Before I taught my tongue to wound
> My Conscience with a sinfull sound,
> Or had the black art to dispence
> A sev'rall sinne to ev'ry sence,
> But felt through all this fleshy dresse
> Bright *shootes* of everlastingnesse.

The theme of childhood is not as primary or pervasive in Vaughan or Herbert as it is in Traherne but it does on occasion, as here, give a varied expression to the overriding archetype of rebirth and to a (past) Vision of Dame Kind. Like Traherne, Vaughan paradoxically regards language, one of man's highest abilities and that which most distinguishes him as a civilized human creature, as a means by which man falls from those felicitous early days. Yet still more paradoxically, by language and intellect, by reading Scripture and by meditating through language on things, man may be led back *toward* eternity and ultimately be truly and fully civilized. Virgil, who stands for reason and language, among other things, can lead Dante through Hell and up Mount Purgatory but not into Eden nor into Paradise. For these last journeys, intuition and revelation, St. Bernard and Beatrice (or, as we shall say in the last chapter, Imagination and Love, the work of poetry) provide guidance. The psyche, the center of the meditating intellect and discursive language, is to a degree instrumental in its own regeneration. What it most critically learns is its own incapacity to effect salvation. He who would save his life shall lose it; he who loses his life, gives up the egoistic struggle, wholly admits, that is, his total dependence on God and discovers God's nearness, attains to wisdom and lives in the mode of eternity.

Whereas **"The Retreat"** concerns the individual's progress in terms of the theme of childhood, **"Corruption"** treats mankind's progress in terms of the myth of the Fall, both theme and myth being vehicles for the archetype of death and rebirth and figures for each other:

> Sure, It was so. Man in those early days
>   Was not all stone, and Earth,
> He shin'd a little, and by those weak Rays
>   Had some glimpse of his birth.
>
>   . . . .
>
> He sigh'd for *Eden,* and would often say
>   *Ah! What bright days were those?*   20
> Nor was Heav'n cold unto him; for each day
>   The vally, or the Mountain
> Afforded visits, and still *Paradise* lay
>   In some green shade, or fountain.
> Angels lay *Leiger* here; Each Bush, and Cel,
>   Each Oke, and high-way knew them,
> Walk but the fields, or sit down at some *wel,*
>   And he was sure to view them.
> Almighty *Love!* where art thou now? mad man
>   Sits down, and freezeth on,   30
>
>   . . . .
>
> All's in deep sleep, and night; Thick darkness lyes
>   And hatcheth o'r thy people;

But hark! what trumpets that? what Angel cries
Arise! Thrust in thy sickle.   40

As the child of **"The Retreate"** "Shin'd in my Angell-infancy," so also early man in **"Corruption"** "shin'd a little," "shined" being a word (as it is in "Batter my heart") especially associated with Christ. The spiritual progress of the individual recapitulates that of the human race and vice versa, so that both journey individually and historically from innocence through fallen experience to redemption, as the structure of each poem suggests. Both find paradise or some hint of eternity in the natural world. Both gradually lose sight of divinity and of their own divine origin and nature. And both yearn for or proceed toward, explicitly or implicitly, spiritual rebirth. In **"Corruption,"** filled with biblical allusion and all three major metaphors of regeneration, the seed evidently has been growing secretly and is now ripe for harvest, as the poem concludes with a sudden reversal. Several biblical verses, which express the archetype of death and rebirth in terms of the metaphor of reaping or harvesting, participate in the poem's ending: "So is the Kingdom of God, as if a man should cast seed into the ground: And should sleep, and rise day and night, and the seed should spring and grow up, he knoweth not how . . . he putteth in the sickle, because the harvest is come" (Mark 4:26-27, 29); "Thrust in thy sickle, and reap: for the time is come for thee to reap; for the harvest of the earth is ripe" (Rev. 12:15; see also Joel 3:13).

Appropriately following this poem that recounts the basic biblical myth extending from Creation and the Fall to Redemption and Apocalypse is **"H. Scriptures,"** which in its third stanza alludes to "The Altar" and to "Judgement," poems at the beginning and the end of Herbert's "The Church." **"Unprofitablenes"** follows **"H. Scriptures"** and echoes phrases and motifs from a number of Herbert's poems, including "The Flower," with which it shares the themes of spiritual reversal and writing poetry:

> How rich, O Lord! how fresh thy visits are!
> 'Twas but Just now my bleak leaves hopeles
>   hung   10
>
>   . . . .
>
> I smell a dew like *Myrrh,* and all the day
> Wear in my bosome a full Sun; such store
>   Hath one beame from thy Eys.
> But, ah, my God! what fruit hast thou of this?
>   What one poor leaf did ever I yet fall
>   To wait upon thy wreath?

The "leaves" are those of the flower which symbolizes the self. They are also associated, here at least by juxtaposition with the preceding **"H. Scriptures,"** with biblical leaves and verses. And "one poor leaf " seems to suggest a poem, particularly since a few leaves off lies the self-reflecting **"Idle Verse."** Both **"Idle Verse"** and **"Unprofitablenes"** contain implicit resolves to turn from matters of lesser to greater import, from profane or secular to divine concerns in both spiritual and poetic matters. The word "dew" is a familiar symbol of grace and of Christ's presence, and the frequent seventeenth-century pun on Sun-Son no doubt obtains, so that the lines reveal that through God's graces the eternal generation or rebirth of the Son of God

takes place in the hearts of the devout suppliant. "The true and definitely mystical life does and must open," Evelyn Underhill reminds us, "with that most actual, though indescribable phenomenon, the coming forth into consciousness of man's deeper, spiritual self, which . . . mystical writers of all ages have agreed to call Regeneration or Rebirth" (*Mysticism*). Given all this and the fact, too, that myrrh was among the gifts presented by the wise men upon Jesus' birth, it is appropriate that the next poem is **"Christs Nativity,"** which encourages the "glad heart" to awake and sing, and which, given the recurrent fluctuations of the mystic life, again prays for spiritual renewal:

> And let once more by mystick birth
> The Lord of life be borne in Earth.

The context of the lines and the second of the poem, including the line "Are we all stone, and Earth," ("Man in those early days," **"Corruption"** begins, "Was not all stone, and Earth"), make it very clear that the prayer is for the birth of Christ also within the individual ("in Earth").

Preceding **"Unprofitablenes"** by fifteen leaves, **"The Morning-watch,"** like that poem and some of Herbert's poetry (and using some of the same imagery), opens with one of the many self-renewals found in Vaughan's poetry. As did Herbert, Vaughan repeatedly experiences the alternations between illuminations and dark nights of the soul, which are the mark of the mystic. Both Herbert and Vaughan use the image of the flower to symbolize the re-awakened soul. But unlike Herbert, Vaughan sees nature as more than symbol. **"The Morning-watch"** concerns not only the renewal of the self but also the renewal of nature, and in Vaughan the two are closely related or at one. After all, divinity graces, animates, and pervades the self and all creation. As in the poem beginning "And do they so?" Vaughan sees all of nature filled with a kind of intelligence, a sense, and a desire for God.

The Morning-watch

> O Joyes! Infinite sweetnes! with what flowres
> And shoots of glory, my soul breakes, and buds!
>   All the long houres
>   Of night, and Rest
>   Through the still shrouds
>   Of sleep, and Clouds,
>   This Dew fell on my Breast;
>   O how it *Blouds,*
> And *Spirits* all my Earth! heark! In what Rings,
> And *Hymning Circulations* the quick world   10
>   Awakes, and sings;
>   The rising winds,
>   And falling springs,
>   Birds, beasts, all things
>   Adore him in their kinds.
>   Thus all is hurl'd
> In sacred *Hymnes,* and *Order,* The great *Chime*
> And *Symphony* of nature. Prayer is
>   The world in tune,
>   A spirit-voyce,   20
>   And vocall joyes
>   Whose *Eccho* is heav'ns blisse.
>   O let me climbe
> When I lye down! The Pious soul by night

Is like a clouded starre, whose beames though
sed
  To shed their light
  Under some Cloud
  Yet are above,
  And shine, and move
Beyond that mistie shrowd.   30
  So in my Bed
That Curtain'd grave, though sleep, like ashes,
hide
My lamp, and life, both shall in thee abide.

Mario Di Cesare rightly notes that *Bloods, Spirits,* and *Circulations* combine the "old notion of blood creating 'spirits' (highly rarefied substance linking soul and body) and Harvey's new theory of circulation of the blood," and he cites Joan Bennett: "The blood begotten vital spirits and the circular movement of the blood represent the revitalizing of the poet and the rest of the created world at dawn" (*George Herbert and the Seventeenth-Century Religious Poets*). We must also consider more fully, as related to yet beyond this significance, two important concepts: the larger doctrine of circulation and the relationship of self to world.

The doctrine of circulation perhaps stems, as so much else does, from Plato, who in his *Timaeus* introduces the theory that the four elements pass into one another "in an unbroken circle of birth." This idea finds expression in numerous writers, from the ancients Homer, Cleanthes, Cicero, Seneca, and Pliny, to contemporaries of Vaughan, such as the hermetist Robert Fludd, John Milton, who was not a mystic, and Thomas Traherne, who was a mystic. In the later Christian writers it is naturally given a peculiarly Christian significance. In *Paradise Lost* (which of course Vaughan could not have read before publication of *Silex Scintillans*), when Raphael sits down with Adam and Eve to their Edenic feast, which some commentators have taken as a prefiguration of the Eucharistic feast, the Angel explains that "whatever was created, needs / to be sustain'd and fed" and later adds that "one Almighty is, from whom / All things proceed, and up to him return." In his poetry and prose, Traherne gives the doctrine the particular Christian contemplative significance that we find clearly (though somewhat less fully) in Vaughan's work. Traherne's sequence of six poems from "The Circulation" to "Another" present the doctrine of Circulation in the mystic terms of its relation to the Godhead and to contemplative vision. "All Things to Circulations owe / Themselves; by which alone / They do exist" (*Poems and Thanksgivings,*). All things are empty and as nothing unless God fills them. "All things do first receive, that give." Throughout this sequence, eating and food metaphors, many with eucharistic connotations, are used to signify that the whole physical-spiritual world is to be regarded as a universal communion feast. All things in the universe are not isolated fragments but interdependent parts of the whole, sustaining one another. All things flow from God and return to Him, Who is the fountain, means, and end. Actually seeing or experiencing all of this requires divine or imaginative vision and is or results in the extrovertive Vision of Dame Kind, seeing the world, as noted in our earlier discussion, with the redeemed heart through the senses. By this contemplative vision, when Christ in us

sees, God's infinite gifts are infinitely regarded, loved, and returned. And that all things are circulatory both signalizes and symbolizes the perfection of God's created and ordered world, versus the vanity and illusion of all things considered apart from their right order and reference to God.

Between the Platonic or pagan expression of the doctrine of circulation and Vaughan's work are all the Christian contemplatives who help to give the doctrine the precise significance it has in Vaughan. That significance is succinctly expressed for us by St. Augustine, who writes, "of him, and by him, and in him are all things," in close paraphrase of Romans 11:36. The development of the doctrine from Plato through the contemplatives to Traherne (though again, of course, Vaughan could not have read Traherne before *Silex Scintillans*) should help illuminate Vaughan's work, here particularly, **"The Morning-watch"** and closely related poems. As in **"The Night,"** night in this poem is a period of "Rest," peace, stillness, silence, the death ("Through the still shrouds / of sleep") of the false self and the rebirth of the true self by means of "This Dew [that] fell on my Breast," dew again being the traditional symbol of transforming grace and Christ's presence. The line "O how it *Blouds,* / And *Spirits* all my Earth," a curious and emphatic use of substantives as verbs, suggests that the self is vitalized, animated, inspired, brought fully to life by "This Dew," which like the Old Testament manna also symbolizes eucharistic food. As in **"Corruption"** and **"Christs Nativity"**, "Earth" represents the first Adam, of the earth, red clay. "The first man is of the earth, earthy" (1 Cor. 15:47). But "Earth" is also earth, the earth referred to at the beginning of Genesis. That is, the language of these lines, particularly lines 7 to 11, subtly reveals the relationship of the self to the whole of creation to be distinguishable yet indivisible, to be essentially at one, because it is Christ or Wisdom playing in all these places. On a first reading it might seem that Vaughan turns in the middle of line 9 from the self to God's creation, "the quick world," the world of nature. (He does. And he does not.) This interpretation of turning is supported by lines 12 to 15, which refer to "The rising winds, / And falling springs, / Birds, beasts, all things" that "Adore him in their kinds," in their natures, in their true nature. But surely, on a second look, "the quick world" may also be seen to refer to "my Earth" which has been *blooded, spirited,* or quickened by the dew, quickened by "the last Adam . . . a quickening spirit" (1 Cor. 15:45), especially because "the quick world / Awakes, and sings" as does the poet's "glad heart," which is encouraged in **"Christs Nativity"** to "Awake . . . and Sing." Every day is Christ's Nativity whenever "by mystick birth / The Lord of life [is] borne in Earth." The "Earth" of **"The Morning-watch"** is the first Adam and it is the earth, God's creation, the world of nature, and both have been Christ-quickened. The language of this poem (and other Vaughan poems) and the seeming transition in line 9 from the poet's self to the larger creation rhetorically and poetically suggest that the two are somehow one. They are one in the sense that though distinguishable they yet both in some very real sense are false or dead until they are God-quickened and then they awake and sing, realizing the mystical body of Christ, in the single "great Chime / And

Symphony of nature." Then "God is in man and God is in everything" and "There is no doer but he," in the sense explained in **"The Holy Communion"**:

> Welcome sweet, and sacred feast; welcome life!
>   Dead I was, and deep in trouble;
> But grace, and blessings came with thee so rife,
> That they have quicken'd even drie stubble;
>   Thus soules their bodies animate,
>   And thus, at first, when things were rude,
>   Dark, void, and Crude
> They, by thy Word, their beauty had, and date;
>   All were by thee,
>   And stil must be,   10
>   Nothing that is, or lives,
>   But hath his Quicknings, and reprieves
>   As thy hand opes, or shuts;
>   Healings, and Cuts,
>   Darkness, and day-light, life, and death
>   Are but meer leaves turn'd by thy
>   breath. . . .

In the poem **"Quickness"** (a favored word, which in its various grammatical forms appears repeatedly in Vaughan's work), Vaughan distinguishes between false life and true life and concludes with the characteristic alleged ineffability of the mystic that "life is, what none can express, / *A quickness, which my God hath kist.*" To paraphrase another Welsh poet, the divine force that through the green fuse quickens the flower also quickens the poet's green self. It follows that, as Julian writes, "God's will is that we should greatly value all his works," a sentence which accurately reflects Vaughan's attitude toward all creation, and that "The fullness of joy is to see God in all things," a sentence which characterizes Vaughan's most passionate desire and on occasion, as in **"The Morning-watch,"** its fulfillment. This sense of oneness or, more specifically, the sense of a divine presence in all things, which finds expression in other seventeenth- century writers, including Jakob Boehme and Thomas Traherne, is frequently expressed in images of circularity, as in Vaughan's "In what Rings / and *Hymning Circulations* the quick world / Awakes, and sings." We recall also the "glorious Ring" of **"Vanity of Spirit."** Similarly, **"The World"** famously begins:

> I saw Eternity the other night
> Like a great *Ring* of pure and endless light,
>   All calm, as it was bright,
> And round beneath it, Time in hours, days,
>   years
>   Driv'n by the spheres
> Like a vast shadow mov'd, In which the world
>   And all her train were hurl'd.

The poem then considers "The doting Lover," "The darksome States-man," "The fearful miser," "The down-right Epicure," and "some who all this while did weep and sing, . . . soar'd up into the *Ring.*" Just as there are two selves or lives, false and true, outward and inward, so there are two worlds, Eternity and Time, the God-quickened and ordered world and the world of vanity and illusion. Those who soared up into the Ring are at one with the Ring, like Dante's doxology of all Paradise, becoming the mystical bride or body of Christ (see Rev. 19 and 21). The others are of and in the world of Time. As

Boehme, who considered man "the little spark of light," writes in *The Way To Christ,* "so is man created according to the outward humanity, he is the time, and in the time, and the time is the outward world, and it is also the outward man. The inward man is eternity and the spiritual time and world." While the title, **"The World,"** and much of the poem might initially encourage readers to take the glorious first line, "I saw Eternity the other night," as a reference only to the Vision of Dame Kind, the concluding lines confirm through the major metaphor of spiritual marriage that it refers as well to the Vision of God, the other important vision in Vaughan's work:

> But as I did their madnes so discusse
>   One whisper'd thus,
> *This Ring the Bride-groome did for none provide*
> *But for his bride.*

One kind of vision may lead to another, and, as observed, Vaughan's poetry repeatedly expresses such a pattern. In "I walkt the other day," a poem variously like **"The Morning-watch"** and **"Vanity of Spirit,"** the speaker again leaves his cell to walk outdoors in a field "to spend my hour" meditating upon "A gallant flowre," such meditation often preceding contemplative vision. Like St. John of the Cross, who also took long walks into the country, Vaughan evidently loved nature in ways which make him, like St. John, akin to St. Francis of Assisi. And while Vaughan is not Blake or Wordsworth, earlier critics perceived important parallels, including so-called nature mysticism, between him and English Romantic Poets. "I walkt the other day" plainly indicates that attentively looking at nature may provide moral instruction and reveal divinity:

> 6.
>
> And yet, how few believe such doctrine springs
>   From a poor root
> Which all the Winter sleeps here under foot
>   And hath no wings
> To raise it to the truth and light of things,   40
>   But is stil trod
>   By ev'ry wandring clod.
>
> 7.
>
> O thou! whose spirit did at first inflame
>   And warm the dead,
> And by a sacred Incubation fed
>   With life this frame
> Which once had neither being, forme, nor name,
>   Grant I may so
>   Thy steps track here below,
>
> 8.
>
> That in these Masques and shadows I may
>   see   50
>   Thy sacred way,
> And by those hid ascents climb to that day
>   Which breaks from thee
> Who art in all things, though invisibly;
>   Shew me thy peace,
>   Thy mercy, love, and ease,

9.

And from this Care, where dreams and sorrows
  raign
    Lead me above
Where Light, Joy, Leisure, and true Comforts
  move
      Without all pain,   60
There, hid in thee, shew me his life again
    At whose dumbe urn
    Thus all the year I mourn.

Alan Rudrum rightly notes that in "Masques and shadows" "there may be . . . a significant pun, involving the notion of mask: concealment and masque; stage representation . . . The idea is that the natural world both reveals and conceals God" (*Henry Vaughan.*) The run-on last three stanzas, the protracted quality of which in itself suggests timelessness, lead the speaker from moral instruction (stanza 6), arising from meditation on things (here specifically the flower and its "poor root") to a prayer for a contemplative Vision of Dame Kind, such vision permitting him again to climb from the chain of created being to God, "Who art in all things, though invisibly"; leaving behind the vain world of anxious thought and sorrow, he will be led above to heaven ("Light, Joy, Leisure" interestingly echo Herbert's "Heaven"), where in the final Vision of God he will see too, hid in God, "his life again," his brother (and the flower, and Christ), "For ye are dead and your life is hid with Christ in God" (Col. 3:3).

V

As we have just seen, Vaughan is the only one of the three contemplative poets studied thus far [the other two being Donne and Herbert] who reads the book of nature, whose poetry contains abundant signs and characteristics of the Vision of Dame Kind. "I walkt the other day" and other poems indicate that Vaughan finds in the creation Christ playing in ten thousand places. But in the passionate desire for union all three poets do seek the Word in the book of Scriptures, and that book has for them the meaning that it had, according to Andrew Louth, for the early Church Father Origen:

> Understanding Scripture is not for Origen simply an academic exercise but a religious experience. The meaning found in the Scripture is received from the Word, and the experience of discovering the meaning of Scripture is often expressed in 'mystical' language; he speaks of a 'sudden awakening,' of inspiration, and of illumination. . . . In this engagement with Scripture, Origen enters more and more deeply into communion with God—and leads others into this communion.

So too in differing degrees and ways through their poetry Donne, Herbert, and Vaughan seek, are led, and lead others into this communion, such is the power of the Word. Vaughan's poetry is itself also testimony, as is his 1655 Preface to **Silex Scintillans,** that meditative and contemplative poetry, particularly Herbert's poetry, may, like the Scriptures, lead the self and others to a foretaste of heaven. "Holy writing" has transformative powers. After remark-

ing in his Preface that Herbert's "holy *life* and *verse* gained many pious *Converts,* (of whom I am the least)," Vaughan goes on to suggest the vital connection between the poet's experience and his text:

> It is true indeed, that to give up our thoughts to pious *Themes and Contemplations* (if it be done for pieties sake) is a great *step* towards *perfection;* because it will *refine,* and *dispose* to devotion and sanctity. And further, it will *procure* for us (so easily communicable is that *loving spirit*) some small *prelibation* of those heavenly *refreshments,* which descend but seldom, and then very sparingly, upon *men* of an ordinary or indifferent *holyness;* but he that desires to excel in this kinde of *Hagiography,* or holy writing, must strive (by all means) for *perfection* and true *holyness,* that a *door may be opened to him in heaven,* Rev. 4. I. and then he will be able to write (with *Hierotheus* and holy *Herbert*) A true *Hymn.*

Vaughan makes plain what Herbert also believed: only to the extent that the writer realizes the Word will he or she be able to write true Hymns, for the life of the Spirit and the life of poetry, inspiration from the gods, are profoundly interrelated. Whereas reading the book of nature leads to the extrovertive Vision of Dame Kind and reading the book of the Soul or Self leads to the introvertive Vision of God, reading the book of Scriptures (or any book of holy writing) may conduce to either extrovertive or introvertive contemplative experiences. In the extrovertive visions, one discovers Christ playing in the places of nature or in the beloved or in other humans; in the introvertive vision, one inwardly discovers one's own Godlike, Christlike nature. Whatever book one reads, it is the Word that is finally apprehended. In this sense and in the sense that ultimately Christ is the only effective writer, speaker, doer, contemplation of God is possible only *per Christum.* The Incarnation is a constantly renewed fact of experience.

Reading the Scriptures may become, as St. Edmund Rich and others point out, a form of contemplation. To the four Visions previously discussed, we might well add a fifth, the Vision of Art, insofar as reading any holy writing (or experiencing non-verbal art work) becomes a religious experience, a matter of entering (as for Origen) "more and more deeply into communion with God." Just as the natural creation and creatures are created by God (or, more exactly, by Christ or the Word as the Second Person, for the First Person), so is all art created by Christ in us (the deific powers of the Imagination. Especially in the modern era, "we say God and the imagination are one," as Wallace Stevens writes.) One may thus experience the presence of divinity in its creations through the Vision of Art as well as through the other Visions. The end or purpose of holy writing is contemplative experience, the realization of one's divine identity. One writes (or Christ, as the only *effective* doer, writes) to bring one's fallen self (and others) to God. Needless to say, this journey is usually a long and arduous one, but then, one should add, the longest way round is paradoxically the shortest way home. Like the other Visions, the Vision of Art, poetry of contemplation, has transformative powers, which will be discussed further in the next chapter, on the modern period.

The central mystical paradox of death and rebirth, the myth of the fall and redemption, is found in all three poets' religious poetry in different degrees. All three poets seek the Vision of God, but actually attain to different stages. Donne's divine poetry seems not to advance beyond Purgation; it is meditative rather than contemplative, premystical rather than precisely mystical. The stages of Illumination and the Dark Night of the Soul appear in Vaughan's religious poetry, as in Herbert's, which is the most spiritually advanced. The sequence of "The Church," exhibiting the contemplative passion for complex unity and interconnections, is a various alternating record of many spriritual conflicts, griefs, and joys, moving in an essentially eucharistic ascent from meditation to contemplation, integrated by the theme of submission to God's will, which helps to effect the transformation of psyche to pneuma, and ending in "Love" (III), a description of the self's perfection in union with Christ, the two Adams or "I"'s becoming one. As a lyric sequence, Herbert's "The Church," with its many purgations, illuminations, dark nights, and final union, is the most fully realized poetic expression of a complex *via mystica* in the English language.

Although there are some hints in a few of Vaughan's love poems, such as **"To Amoret, Walking in a Starry Evening"** and the derivative **"To Amoret, of the difference 'twixt him, and other Lovers,"** the evidence (the characteristics of contemplative experience) is much too insufficient, so that one must conclude that Vaughan's secular poetry, unlike Donne's, reveals no Vision of Eros. . . .

The mystical theology of many Church Fathers shows a mutual interacting of the mystical and ecclesiastical. And while Donne, Herbert, and Vaughan, like most devout souls, may pursue contemplative ends in predominantly solitary ways, in that love and vision which unites the self to God and to others the contemplative life and the active life eventually come together. The contemplative life may be both essential prelude to and an integral part of the active life. J. Daniélou comments that "the mystical graces have an apostolic purpose. They are all in a sense charismatic graces. To this apostolic aspect of the mystical life there corresponds inversely the mystical aspect of the apostolic life. By that I mean that it is above all in attaining personal sanctity that the soul becomes a source of grace for others. Thus sanctification, far from separating her from the others, is on the contrary that which enables her to serve them. The image which Gregory [of Nyssa] gives us is that of a soul wholly turned towards God, who only draws others to herself for the sake of him."

There is a Buddhist parable that is pertinent. Three monks, who have searched long and hard for Nirvana, finally find it, eagerly climb over its walls and then luxuriate in paradisal delights. Suddenly, one of them gets up, runs back to the wall and starts to climb back over it. Puzzled, the other two shout at him, "But why are you going?" He answers, "I'm going to tell the others where Nirvana is." Some may end their quest in contemplation; some may follow contemplation with an active life in one form or another. The significance of Donne, Herbert, and Vaughan for the twentieth century, an age literally much more apocalyptic than their own, an age that more than ever needs to learn to live in peaceable and sociable union, is that their contemplative poetry may, like all holy writing, tell us something about where Heaven is and how to get there in this life.

Finally, for all of Herbert's great influence on Vaughan and the many vital similarities between them, including Vaughan's sharing with Herbert the mystic wisdom that weal and woe are equally God's love, as a poem like Vaughan's **"Affliction"** shows, Vaughan is in some important ways a poet much like Traherne. (It is significant that before Traherne's poetry was properly identified by Bertram Dobell, it was thought to be by Vaughan.) Until the nineteenth century, the poetic expressions of the Vision of Dame Kind by Vaughan and Traherne were unsurpassed in English. The real heirs to the seventeenth-century Metaphysical poets are some of the English Romantics and American Transcendentalists in the sense that some of these latter poets continue the extrovertive Visions of the former, especially the Visions of Dame Kind of Vaughan and Traherne. That Traherne could not have been known to the nineteenth-century writers suggests that such Visions are far more a matter of profound experience rather than literary convention. The discovery of God or a numinous presence in nature by Vaughan, Traherne and later poets was perhaps importantly fostered in part (but only in part) by the Renaissance exaltation of man and the Renaissance's directing of attention and knowledge toward nature, whether in the astronomer's study of stars and planets, the explorer's discovery and exploration of the New World, the physician's study of human anatomy, or the botanist's cataloging of plants and flowers; and so on. Although obviously different enough from the nineteenth-century English Romantic poets and American Transcendentalists and certain . . . twentieth-century poets, Vaughan and Traherne are very like some of these writers insofar as they all see God in nature or, as Wordsworth and Blake put it, see "every common sight apparelled in celestial light" and "everything as it is, infinite." While Donne, Herbert, Vaughan and Traherne all seek and variously find an introvertive Vision of God (some more, some less), only Vaughan and Traherne truly experience the extrovertive Vision of Dame Kind, a point which significantly helps to account for similarities of subject and style in the two later poets. The two commonplaces that during the sixteenth century men took possession of the book of God and that during the seventeenth century (while the earlier possession continued) they began to decode the book of nature both may help to account, I believe, for important differences between the two earlier and the two later seventeenth-century poets. That the rise of science in the seventeenth and subsequent centuries and the scientific study of nature may be linked to the increasing so-called nature mysticism is a [characteristic of] . . . the modern period, a period when science has become significantly different from what it was in the time of Newton and Blake.

Further Reading

Alvarez, A. "The Poetry of Religious Experience: II. Henry Vaughan." In his *The School of Donne*, pp. 91-98. New York: Pantheon Books, 1961.

Examines Vaughan as a crafter of original "poetry of experience with devotional themes": poetry which "rises from a single, intense moment of perception and concerns the poet's reaction to the object, rather than the object itself."

Calhoun, Thomas O. *Henry Vaughan: The Achievement of "Silex Scintillans"*. Newark: University of Delaware Press, 1981, 265 p.

Examines Vaughan's accomplishment in *Silex Scintillans*, concluding that the "shocks, disjunctions, momentary victory, and extended disappointment" reflected in the constituent poems indicate Vaughan's acceptance not of order in the world, but orders: a splintered but coherent vision of Creation and Providential activity within it.

Clough, Wilson O. "Henry Vaughan and the Hermetic Philosophy." *PMLA* XLIX, No. 3 (September 1933): 1108-30.

Examination of Vaughan's Hermeticism, concluding that Vaughan was "a poet, assimilating and subordinating his borrowings from the Hermetist, if such there were, for the purposes of a song that soars beyond the circle of initiates and gathers the volume of a universal note," which is expressed in the opening stanza of "The World."

Garner, Ross. *Henry Vaughan: Experience and the Tradition*. Chicago: University of Chicago Press, 1959, 176 p.

Close reexamination of Vaughan's poetic canon.

Holmes, Elizabeth. *Henry Vaughan and the Hermetic Philosophy*. New York: Russell & Russell, 1967, 62 p.

Short study "of Henry Vaughan's connection with the Hermetic or 'occult' philosophy which his brother Thomas embraced and practised, and so of the poet's relations with his brother and possibly with others of the Hermetic manner of belief, notably Jacob Boehme, but also Cornelius Agrippa, Paracelsus, and others of obscurer name." This essay was originally published in 1932.

Judson, Alexander C. "Cornelius Agrippa and Henry Vaughan." *Modern Language Notes* XLI, No. 3 (March 1926): 178-81.

Essay which initiated scholarly interest in the possible influence of Hermetic belief upon Vaughan and his poetry. Considering Vaughan's poem "The Ass," Judson posits that Agrippa was "the probable source of Vaughan's quaint use of the term ass as a synonym for the simple-minded Christian who is ready to accept the mysteries of religion without questioning," and that Agrippa's influence may well have extended further in Vaughan's belief system.

Lewalski, Barbara K. "Typology and Poetry: A Consideration of Herbert, Vaughan, and Marvell." In *Illustrious Evidence: Approaches to English Literature of the Early Seventeenth Century*, edited by Earl Miner, pp. 41-69. Berkeley and Los Angeles: University of California Press, 1975.

Examines, in editor Miner's words, "what is important in the religious thought of Vaughan's poetry," showing how Vaughan uses certain Protestant emphases and concerns, in comparison to such usage in the works of George Herbert and Andrew Marvell. In particular, Miner writes, "Vaughan gives us a consistent use of the Old Testament to provide types for his own experience, making himself, rather than the chief Person in the New Testament, the antitype. What defines the nature of such figuralism is, we are shown, the particular types chosen and their combination with such religious concerns as eschatology."

Peers, Edgar Allison. "Henry Vaughan: Flint Flashing Fire." In his *Behind That Wall: An Introduction to Some Classics of the Interior Life*, pp. 157-68. 1948. Reprint. Freeport, N.Y.: Books for Libraries Press, 1969.

Appreciative essay focusing on Vaughan's value as a Christian poet and focusing upon *Silex Scintillans*, which Peers translates as "the flint flashing fire." "That name fits all he wrote," writes the critic, "prose as well as verse, exactly. So much of it is dull and unattractive, like the dingy brown flint-stone. But every now and then you get flashes of pure poetry—and of pure love."

Quiller-Couch, Sir Arthur. "Herbert and Vaughan." In his *Studies in Literature*, pp. 118-45. New York: G. P. Putnam's Sons, 1918.

Text of a lecture which begins with a lengthy discourse on the nature of mysticism and concludes (pp. 138-45) by comparing Vaughan favorably with Herbert, elaborating upon the paradoxical thesis that "The first and most obvious remark upon Vaughan is that his genius was largely imitative; the next and almost as obvious, that it was curiously original."

Rudrum, Alan, ed. *Essential Articles for the Study of Henry Vaughan*. Hamden, Conn.: Archon Books, 1987, 332 p.

Selection of 21 key essays on Vaughan's works. Contributors include Don Cameron Allen, L. C. Martin, Louis Martz, and James D. Simmonds, among others.

Seelig, Sharon Cadman. "The Shadow of Time: Vaughan." In her *The Shadow of Eternity: Belief and Structure in Herbert, Vaughan and Traherne*, pp. 44-102. Lexington: University of Kentucky Press, 1981.

Close reading of Vaughan's poems, focusing upon the spiritual elements of Vaughan's belief reflected in them. Seelig notes a progression from the early poems, in which Vaughan expresses his yearning to see God, to his later poems, in which the poet, through the imagery of night, expresses his desire to obey God.

Smith, A. J. "Henry Vaughan's Ceremony of Innocence." *Essays and Studies* 26 (1973): 35-52.

Reads *Silex Scintillans* as a work which must be seen "in the first place—if only in the first place—as a whole," a struggle to make sense of the shattering experiences of loss and change which affected "a very few years of the poet's life, so that he may build anew." Smith understands Vaughan's "otherworldliness" as entailing belief in spiritual regeneration in the face of "a world disintegrating about him and his sense that this could not be true reality."

Summers, Joseph H. "A Foreign and a Provincial Gentleman: Richard Crashaw and Henry Vaughan." In his *The Heirs of Donne and Jonson*, pp. 102-29. New York and London: Oxford University Press, 1970.

A balanced overview of Vaughan's poetic career. Summers acknowledges passages of brilliance in Vaughan's poetry, but also notes, "It is difficult to imagine that an English poet who had attended Westminster School or had been resident longer or nearer to the universities and the Court and London would have settled for so many oddly unrhymed lines, lines so twisted to achieve their rhymes, such imperfect rhymes, such awkward shifts in stanzaic and rhetorical constructions, so many sudden (and sometimes even bathetic) poetic descents."

Trickett, Rachel. "Henry Vaughan and the Poetry of Vision." *Essays and Studies* 34 (1981): 88-104.

Examines Vaughan's poetry as belonging not to the landscape of the mind, but of the poet's own response to a particular locale and climate; in the case of Vaughan, the Usk valley, where he spent most of his life. "And though he is in no sense so great a poet as Wordsworth," writes Trickett, "he can properly be compared with him for this reason as much as for his interest in the state of childhood, innocence and pre-existence, among the topics they share."

Underwood, Horace H. "Time and Space in the Poetry of Henry Vaughan." *Studies in Philology* LXIX, No. 2 (April 1972): 231-41.

Examines the concepts of time and eternity in Vaughan's poetry in conjunction with the poet's thought about space as a concept dominated by the idea of humanity's rising to God "and an image of vertical movement linking the world to heaven." Underwood writes, "In [Vaughan's] poetry the world and heaven, time and eternity are combined in a complex metaphorical system where mention of any element evokes the entire system and the symbolized spiritual exile from and longing for God."

Wall, John N. "Henry Vaughan." In his *Transformations of the Word: Spenser, Herbert, Vaughan*, pp. 273-365. Athens and London: University of Georgia Press, 1988.

Study which argues that the poems of Vaughan are best seen in the context of the "Church of God," which was for him the Church of England. Wall's thesis is that through his writings Vaughan set out to promote the social agenda of the Anglican Church, "both its assurance-

giving worship and its transformation-promoting goal of realizing the true Christian commonwealth in England."

Wardle, Ralph M. "Thomas Vaughan's Influence upon the Poetry of Henry Vaughan." *PMLA* LI, No. 4 (December 1936): 1936-52.

Discourses upon the premise that "Henry owed his knowledge of Hermetica to his brother. The metaphysical approach which Thomas used is reflected in the mystical handling of Hermetic principles which typifies Henry's attitude toward the philosophy" as evidenced in his poetry.

Wells, H. W. *The Tercentenary of Henry Vaughan*. 1922. Reprint. Folcroft, Pa.: Folcroft Press, 1969, 16 p.

Appreciative thematic overview of Vaughan's life and accomplishment. "The mirth and peace of children, the faith of friends, patience, kindness, all joys that are calm and smooth and bright, the freedom of the soul, a knowledge of man's wretchedness, nature's beauty and her sternness, and through mankind and nature, the love of God—in these Vaughan lived," writes Wells, adding, "His three greatest loves, the love of art, the love of nature and the love of Christ, are ensphered in his poetry as one."

Williamson, George. "Structure in Vaughan's Poetry." In his *Milton & Others*, 2nd ed., pp. 165-79. Chicago: University of Chicago Press, 1970.

Examines and illustrates the way "Vaughan's poems are often built on fundamental antitheses explored by the wit that Samuel Butler called the 'expressing of Sense by Contradiction and Riddle'." In addition, as Williams demonstrates, "Not only religious ideas and paradoxes but both the union and opposition of nature and the supernatural entered into the structure of [Vaughan's] poems and left their stamp upon his language."

Willy, Margaret. "Henry Vaughan." In her *Three Metaphysical Poets*, pp. 19-31. London: British Council, 1961.

A trenchant survey of Vaughan's poetic canon which concludes by closely examining the nature of the poet's beliefs concerning the spiritual nature of humanity and his belief in the sanctity of childhood.

Additional coverage of Vaughan's life and career is contained in the following source published by Gale Research: *Dictionary of Literary Biography*, Vol. 131.

Literature
Criticism from
1400 to 1800

Cumulative Indexes

How to Use This Index

The main references

Calvino, Italo
1923-1985.....CLC 5, 8, 11, 22, 33, 39,
73; SSC 3

list all author entries in the following Gale Literary Criticism series:

BLC = Black Literature Criticism
CLC = Contemporary Literary Criticism
CLR = Children's Literature Review
CMLC = Classical and Medieval Literature Criticism
DA = DISCovering Authors
DC = Drama Criticism
HLC = Hispanic Literature Criticism
LC = Literature Criticism from 1400 to 1800
NCLC = Nineteenth-Century Literature Criticism
PC = Poetry Criticism
SSC = Short Story Criticism
TCLC = Twentieth-Century Literary Criticism
WLC = World Literature Criticism, 1500 to the Present

The cross-references

See also CANR 23; CA 85-88;
obituary CA 116

list all author entries in the following Gale biographical and literary sources:

AAYA = Authors & Artists for Young Adults
AITN = Authors in the News
BEST = Bestsellers
BW = Black Writers
CA = Contemporary Authors
CAAS = Contemporary Authors Autobiography Series
CABS = Contemporary Authors Bibliographical Series
CANR = Contemporary Authors New Revision Series
CAP = Contemporary Authors Permanent Series
CDALB = Concise Dictionary of American Literary Biography
CDBLB = Concise Dictionary of British Literary Biography
DLB = Dictionary of Literary Biography
DLBD = Dictionary of Literary Biography Documentary Series
DLBY = Dictionary of Literary Biography Yearbook
HW = Hispanic Writers
JRDA = Junior DISCovering Authors
MAICYA = Major Authors and Illustrators for Children and Young Adults
MTCW = Major 20th-Century Writers
NNAL = Native North American Literature
SAAS = Something about the Author Autobiography Series
SATA = Something about the Author
YABC = Yesterday's Authors of Books for Children

Literary Criticism Series
Cumulative Author Index

Abasiyanik, Sait Faik   1906-1954
See Sait Faik
See also CA 123

Abbey, Edward   1927-1989 . . . . . . **CLC 36, 59**
See also CA 45-48; 128; CANR 2, 41

Abbott, Lee K(ittredge)   1947- . . . . . . **CLC 48**
See also CA 124; DLB 130

Abe, Kobo   1924-1993 . . . . . **CLC 8, 22, 53, 81**
See also CA 65-68; 140; CANR 24; MTCW

Abelard, Peter   c. 1079-c. 1142 . . . **CMLC 11**
See also DLB 115

Abell, Kjeld   1901-1961 . . . . **CLC 15**
See also CA 111

Abish, Walter   1931- . . . . **CLC 22**
See also CA 101; CANR 37; DLB 130

Abrahams, Peter (Henry)   1919- . . . . . **CLC 4**
See also BW 1; CA 57-60; CANR 26;
DLB 117; MTCW

Abrams, M(eyer) H(oward)   1912- . . . **CLC 24**
See also CA 57-60; CANR 13, 33; DLB 67

Abse, Dannie   1923- . . . . **CLC 7, 29**
See also CA 53-56; CAAS 1; CANR 4;
DLB 27

Achebe, (Albert) Chinua(lumogu)
1930- . . . . . **CLC 1, 3, 5, 7, 11, 26, 51, 75;**
BLC; DA; WLC
See also BW 2; CA 1-4R; CANR 6, 26;
CLR 20; DLB 117; MAICYA; MTCW;
SATA 38, 40

Acker, Kathy   1948- . . . . **CLC 45**
See also CA 117; 122

Ackroyd, Peter   1949- . . . . **CLC 34, 52**
See also CA 123; 127

Acorn, Milton   1923- . . . . **CLC 15**
See also CA 103; DLB 53

Adamov, Arthur   1908-1970 . . . . . . **CLC 4, 25**
See also CA 17-18; 25-28R; CAP 2; MTCW

Adams, Alice (Boyd)   1926- . . . **CLC 6, 13, 46**
See also CA 81-84; CANR 26; DLBY 86;
MTCW

Adams, Andy   1859-1935 . . . . **TCLC 56**
See also YABC 1

Adams, Douglas (Noel)   1952- . . . **CLC 27, 60**
See also AAYA 4; BEST 89:3; CA 106;
CANR 34; DLBY 83; JRDA

Adams, Francis   1862-1893 . . . . . . **NCLC 33**

Adams, Henry (Brooks)
1838-1918 . . . . **TCLC 4, 52; DA**
See also CA 104; 133; DLB 12, 47

Adams, Richard (George)
1920- . . . . **CLC 4, 5, 18**
See also AITN 1, 2; CA 49-52; CANR 3,
35; CLR 20; JRDA; MAICYA; MTCW;
SATA 7, 69

Adamson, Joy(-Friederike Victoria)
1910-1980 . . . . **CLC 17**
See also CA 69-72; 93-96; CANR 22;
MTCW; SATA 11, 22

Adcock, Fleur   1934- . . . . **CLC 41**
See also CA 25-28R; CANR 11, 34;
DLB 40

Addams, Charles (Samuel)
1912-1988 . . . . **CLC 30**
See also CA 61-64; 126; CANR 12

Addison, Joseph   1672-1719 . . . . **LC 18**
See also CDBLB 1660-1789; DLB 101

Adler, C(arole) S(chwerdtfeger)
1932- . . . . **CLC 35**
See also AAYA 4; CA 89-92; CANR 19,
40; JRDA; MAICYA; SAAS 15;
SATA 26, 63

Adler, Renata   1938- . . . . **CLC 8, 31**
See also CA 49-52; CANR 5, 22; MTCW

Ady, Endre   1877-1919 . . . . **TCLC 11**
See also CA 107

Aeschylus
525B.C.-456B.C. . . . . **CMLC 11; DA**

Afton, Effie
See Harper, Frances Ellen Watkins

Agapida, Fray Antonio
See Irving, Washington

Agee, James (Rufus)
1909-1955 . . . . **TCLC 1, 19**
See also AITN 1; CA 108;
CDALB 1941-1968; DLB 2, 26

Aghill, Gordon
See Silverberg, Robert

Agnon, S(hmuel) Y(osef Halevi)
1888-1970 . . . . **CLC 4, 8, 14**
See also CA 17-18; 25-28R; CAP 2; MTCW

Agrippa von Nettesheim, Henry Cornelius
1486-1535 . . . . **LC 27**

Aherne, Owen
See Cassill, R(onald) V(erlin)

Ai   1947- . . . . **CLC 4, 14, 69**
See also CA 85-88; CAAS 13; DLB 120

Aickman, Robert (Fordyce)
1914-1981 . . . . **CLC 57**
See also CA 5-8R; CANR 3

Aiken, Conrad (Potter)
1889-1973 . . . **CLC 1, 3, 5, 10, 52; SSC 9**
See also CA 5-8R; 45-48; CANR 4;
CDALB 1929-1941; DLB 9, 45, 102;
MTCW; SATA 3, 30

Aiken, Joan (Delano)   1924- . . . . **CLC 35**
See also AAYA 1; CA 9-12R; CANR 4, 23,
34; CLR 1, 19; JRDA; MAICYA;
MTCW; SAAS 1; SATA 2, 30, 73

Ainsworth, William Harrison
1805-1882 . . . . **NCLC 13**
See also DLB 21; SATA 24

Aitmatov, Chingiz (Torekulovich)
1928- . . . . **CLC 71**
See also CA 103; CANR 38; MTCW;
SATA 56

Akers, Floyd
See Baum, L(yman) Frank

Akhmadulina, Bella Akhatovna
1937- . . . . **CLC 53**
See also CA 65-68

Akhmatova, Anna
1888-1966 . . . . **CLC 11, 25, 64; PC 2**
See also CA 19-20; 25-28R; CANR 35;
CAP 1; MTCW

Aksakov, Sergei Timofeyvich
1791-1859 . . . . **NCLC 2**

Aksenov, Vassily . . . . **CLC 22**
See also Aksyonov, Vassily (Pavlovich)

Aksyonov, Vassily (Pavlovich)
1932- . . . . **CLC 37**
See also Aksenov, Vassily
See also CA 53-56; CANR 12

Akutagawa Ryunosuke
1892-1927 . . . . **TCLC 16**
See also CA 117

Alain   1868-1951 . . . . **TCLC 41**

Alain-Fournier . . . . **TCLC 6**
See also Fournier, Henri Alban
See also DLB 65

Alarcon, Pedro Antonio de
1833-1891 . . . . **NCLC 1**

Alas (y Urena), Leopoldo (Enrique Garcia)
1852-1901 . . . . **TCLC 29**
See also CA 113; 131; HW

Albee, Edward (Franklin III)
1928- . . . . . . **CLC 1, 2, 3, 5, 9, 11, 13, 25,**
53; DA; WLC
See also AITN 1; CA 5-8R; CABS 3;
CANR 8; CDALB 1941-1968; DLB 7;
MTCW

Alberti, Rafael   1902- . . . . **CLC 7**
See also CA 85-88; DLB 108

Alcala-Galiano, Juan Valera y
See Valera y Alcala-Galiano, Juan

Alcott, Amos Bronson   1799-1888 . . **NCLC 1**
See also DLB 1

Alcott, Louisa May
1832-1888 . . . . **NCLC 6; DA; WLC**
See also CDALB 1865-1917; CLR 1;
DLB 1, 42, 79; JRDA; MAICYA;
YABC 1

Aldanov, M. A.
See Aldanov, Mark (Alexandrovich)

Aldanov, Mark (Alexandrovich)
1886(?)-1957 . . . . **TCLC 23**
See also CA 118

Aldington, Richard   1892-1962 . . . . . . **CLC 49**
See also CA 85-88; CANR 45; DLB 20, 36,
100

Anthony, Piers 1934- . . . . **CLC 35**
See also AAYA 11; CA 21-24R; CANR 28;
DLB 8; MTCW

Antoine, Marc
See Proust, (Valentin-Louis-George-Eugene-)
Marcel

Antoninus, Brother
See Everson, William (Oliver)

Antonioni, Michelangelo 1912- . . . . . **CLC 20**
See also CA 73-76; CANR 45

Antschel, Paul 1920-1970
See Celan, Paul
See also CA 85-88; CANR 33; MTCW

Anwar, Chairil 1922-1949 . . . . **TCLC 22**
See also CA 121

Apollinaire, Guillaume . . **TCLC 3, 8, 51; PC 7**
See also Kostrowitzki, Wilhelm Apollinaris
de

Appelfeld, Aharon 1932- . . . . **CLC 23, 47**
See also CA 112; 133

Apple, Max (Isaac) 1941- . . . . **CLC 9, 33**
See also CA 81-84; CANR 19; DLB 130

Appleman, Philip (Dean) 1926- . . . . . **CLC 51**
See also CA 13-16R; CAAS 18; CANR 6,
29

Appleton, Lawrence
See Lovecraft, H(oward) P(hillips)

Apteryx
See Eliot, T(homas) S(tearns)

Apuleius, (Lucius Madaurensis)
125(?)-175(?) . . . . **CMLC 1**

Aquin, Hubert 1929-1977 . . . . **CLC 15**
See also CA 105; DLB 53

Aragon, Louis 1897-1982 . . . . **CLC 3, 22**
See also CA 69-72; 108; CANR 28;
DLB 72; MTCW

Arany, Janos 1817-1882 . . . . **NCLC 34**

Arbuthnot, John 1667-1735 . . . . **LC 1**
See also DLB 101

Archer, Herbert Winslow
See Mencken, H(enry) L(ouis)

Archer, Jeffrey (Howard) 1940- . . . . **CLC 28**
See also BEST 89:3; CA 77-80; CANR 22

Archer, Jules 1915- . . . . **CLC 12**
See also CA 9-12R; CANR 6; SAAS 5;
SATA 4

Archer, Lee
See Ellison, Harlan

Arden, John 1930- . . . . **CLC 6, 13, 15**
See also CA 13-16R; CAAS 4; CANR 31;
DLB 13; MTCW

Arenas, Reinaldo
1943-1990 . . . . **CLC 41; HLC**
See also CA 124; 128; 133; HW

Arendt, Hannah 1906-1975 . . . . **CLC 66**
See also CA 17-20R; 61-64; CANR 26;
MTCW

Aretino, Pietro 1492-1556 . . . . **LC 12**

Arghezi, Tudor . . . . **CLC 80**
See also Theodorescu, Ion N.

Arguedas, Jose Maria
1911-1969 . . . . **CLC 10, 18**
See also CA 89-92; DLB 113; HW

Argueta, Manlio 1936- . . . . **CLC 31**
See also CA 131; HW

Ariosto, Ludovico 1474-1533 . . . . **LC 6**

Aristides
See Epstein, Joseph

Aristophanes
450B.C.-385B.C. . . . . **CMLC 4; DA; DC 2**

Arlt, Roberto (Godofredo Christophersen)
1900-1942 . . . . **TCLC 29; HLC**
See also CA 123; 131; HW

Armah, Ayi Kwei 1939- . . . . **CLC 5, 33; BLC**
See also BW 1; CA 61-64; CANR 21;
DLB 117; MTCW

Armatrading, Joan 1950- . . . . **CLC 17**
See also CA 114

Arnette, Robert
See Silverberg, Robert

**Arnim, Achim von (Ludwig Joachim von
Arnim)** 1781-1831 . . . . **NCLC 5**
See also DLB 90

Arnim, Bettina von 1785-1859 . . . . **NCLC 38**
See also DLB 90

Arnold, Matthew
1822-1888 . . . . . **NCLC 6, 29; DA; PC 5;
WLC**
See also CDBLB 1832-1890; DLB 32, 57

Arnold, Thomas 1795-1842 . . . . . . **NCLC 18**
See also DLB 55

Arnow, Harriette (Louisa) Simpson
1908-1986 . . . . **CLC 2, 7, 18**
See also CA 9-12R; 118; CANR 14; DLB 6;
MTCW; SATA 42, 47

Arp, Hans
See Arp, Jean

Arp, Jean 1887-1966 . . . . **CLC 5**
See also CA 81-84; 25-28R; CANR 42

Arrabal
See Arrabal, Fernando

Arrabal, Fernando 1932- . . . **CLC 2, 9, 18, 58**
See also CA 9-12R; CANR 15

Arrick, Fran . . . . **CLC 30**

Artaud, Antonin 1896-1948 . . . . . **TCLC 3, 36**
See also CA 104

Arthur, Ruth M(abel) 1905-1979 . . . . **CLC 12**
See also CA 9-12R; 85-88; CANR 4;
SATA 7, 26

Artsybashev, Mikhail (Petrovich)
1878-1927 . . . . **TCLC 31**

Arundel, Honor (Morfydd)
1919-1973 . . . . **CLC 17**
See also CA 21-22; 41-44R; CAP 2;
CLR 35; SATA 4, 24

Asch, Sholem 1880-1957 . . . . **TCLC 3**
See also CA 105

Ash, Shalom
See Asch, Sholem

Ashbery, John (Lawrence)
1927- . . . . . . **CLC 2, 3, 4, 6, 9, 13, 15, 25,
41, 77**
See also CA 5-8R; CANR 9, 37; DLB 5;
DLBY 81; MTCW

Ashdown, Clifford
See Freeman, R(ichard) Austin

Ashe, Gordon
See Creasey, John

Ashton-Warner, Sylvia (Constance)
1908-1984 . . . . **CLC 19**
See also CA 69-72; 112; CANR 29; MTCW

Asimov, Isaac
1920-1992 . . . . . **CLC 1, 3, 9, 19, 26, 76**
See also BEST 90:2; CA 1-4R; 137;
CANR 2, 19, 36; CLR 12; DLB 8;
DLBY 92; JRDA; MAICYA; MTCW;
SATA 1, 26, 74

Astley, Thea (Beatrice May)
1925- . . . . **CLC 41**
See also CA 65-68; CANR 11, 43

Aston, James
See White, T(erence) H(anbury)

Asturias, Miguel Angel
1899-1974 . . . . **CLC 3, 8, 13; HLC**
See also CA 25-28; 49-52; CANR 32;
CAP 2; DLB 113; HW; MTCW

Atares, Carlos Saura
See Saura (Atares), Carlos

Atheling, William
See Pound, Ezra (Weston Loomis)

Atheling, William, Jr.
See Blish, James (Benjamin)

Atherton, Gertrude (Franklin Horn)
1857-1948 . . . . **TCLC 2**
See also CA 104; DLB 9, 78

Atherton, Lucius
See Masters, Edgar Lee

Atkins, Jack
See Harris, Mark

Atticus
See Fleming, Ian (Lancaster)

Atwood, Margaret (Eleanor)
1939- . . . . . **CLC 2, 3, 4, 8, 13, 15, 25, 44,
84; DA; PC 8; SSC 2; WLC**
See also AAYA 12; BEST 89:2; CA 49-52;
CANR 3, 24, 33; DLB 53; MTCW;
SATA 50

Aubigny, Pierre d'
See Mencken, H(enry) L(ouis)

Aubin, Penelope 1685-1731(?) . . . . **LC 9**
See also DLB 39

Auchincloss, Louis (Stanton)
1917- . . . . **CLC 4, 6, 9, 18, 45**
See also CA 1-4R; CANR 6, 29; DLB 2;
DLBY 80; MTCW

Auden, W(ystan) H(ugh)
1907-1973 . . . . . . **CLC 1, 2, 3, 4, 6, 9, 11,
14, 43; DA; PC 1; WLC**
See also CA 9-12R; 45-48; CANR 5;
CDBLB 1914-1945; DLB 10, 20; MTCW

Audiberti, Jacques 1900-1965 . . . . . . **CLC 38**
See also CA 25-28R

Audubon, John James
1785-1851 . . . . **NCLC 47**

Auel, Jean M(arie) 1936- . . . . **CLC 31**
See also AAYA 7; BEST 90:4; CA 103;
CANR 21

Auerbach, Erich 1892-1957 . . . . **TCLC 43**
See also CA 118

Augier, Emile 1820-1889 . . . . **NCLC 31**

August, John
See De Voto, Bernard (Augustine)

Augustine, St. 354-430 . . . . **CMLC 6**

Aurelius
See Bourne, Randolph S(illiman)

Austen, Jane
1775-1817 . . . . **NCLC 1, 13, 19, 33; DA;**
WLC
See also CDBLB 1789-1832; DLB 116

Auster, Paul 1947- . . . . **CLC 47**
See also CA 69-72; CANR 23

Austin, Frank
See Faust, Frederick (Schiller)

Austin, Mary (Hunter)
1868-1934 . . . . **TCLC 25**
See also CA 109; DLB 9, 78

Autran Dourado, Waldomiro
See Dourado, (Waldomiro Freitas) Autran

Averroes 1126-1198 . . . . **CMLC 7**
See also DLB 115

Avison, Margaret 1918- . . . . **CLC 2, 4**
See also CA 17-20R; DLB 53; MTCW

Axton, David
See Koontz, Dean R(ay)

Ayckbourn, Alan
1939- . . . . **CLC 5, 8, 18, 33, 74**
See also CA 21-24R; CANR 31; DLB 13;
MTCW

Aydy, Catherine
See Tennant, Emma (Christina)

Ayme, Marcel (Andre) 1902-1967 . . . **CLC 11**
See also CA 89-92; CLR 25; DLB 72

Ayrton, Michael 1921-1975 . . . . **CLC 7**
See also CA 5-8R; 61-64; CANR 9, 21

Azorin . . . . **CLC 11**
See also Martinez Ruiz, Jose

Azuela, Mariano
1873-1952 . . . . **TCLC 3; HLC**
See also CA 104; 131; HW; MTCW

Baastad, Babbis Friis
See Friis-Baastad, Babbis Ellinor

Bab
See Gilbert, W(illiam) S(chwenck)

Babbis, Eleanor
See Friis-Baastad, Babbis Ellinor

Babel, Isaak (Emmanuilovich)
1894-1941(?) . . . . . . **TCLC 2, 13; SSC 16**
See also CA 104

Babits, Mihaly 1883-1941 . . . . **TCLC 14**
See also CA 114

Babur 1483-1530 . . . . **LC 18**

Bacchelli, Riccardo 1891-1985 . . . . . **CLC 19**
See also CA 29-32R; 117

Bach, Richard (David) 1936- . . . . **CLC 14**
See also AITN 1; BEST 89:2; CA 9-12R;
CANR 18; MTCW; SATA 13

Bachman, Richard
See King, Stephen (Edwin)

Bachmann, Ingeborg 1926-1973 . . . . . **CLC 69**
See also CA 93-96; 45-48; DLB 85

Bacon, Francis 1561-1626 . . . . **LC 18**
See also CDBLB Before 1660

Bacon, Roger 1214(?)-1292 . . . . . . **CMLC 14**
See also DLB 115

Bacovia, George . . . . **TCLC 24**
See also Vasiliu, Gheorghe

Badanes, Jerome 1937- . . . . **CLC 59**

Bagehot, Walter 1826-1877 . . . . . . **NCLC 10**
See also DLB 55

Bagnold, Enid 1889-1981 . . . . **CLC 25**
See also CA 5-8R; 103; CANR 5, 40;
DLB 13; MAICYA; SATA 1, 25

Bagrjana, Elisaveta
See Belcheva, Elisaveta

Bagryana, Elisaveta
See Belcheva, Elisaveta

Bailey, Paul 1937- . . . . **CLC 45**
See also CA 21-24R; CANR 16; DLB 14

Baillie, Joanna 1762-1851 . . . . **NCLC 2**
See also DLB 93

Bainbridge, Beryl (Margaret)
1933- . . . . **CLC 4, 5, 8, 10, 14, 18, 22, 62**
See also CA 21-24R; CANR 24; DLB 14;
MTCW

Baker, Elliott 1922- . . . . **CLC 8**
See also CA 45-48; CANR 2

Baker, Nicholson 1957- . . . . **CLC 61**
See also CA 135

Baker, Ray Stannard 1870-1946 . . . **TCLC 47**
See also CA 118

Baker, Russell (Wayne) 1925- . . . . . . **CLC 31**
See also BEST 89:4; CA 57-60; CANR 11,
41; MTCW

Bakhtin, M.
See Bakhtin, Mikhail Mikhailovich

Bakhtin, M. M.
See Bakhtin, Mikhail Mikhailovich

Bakhtin, Mikhail
See Bakhtin, Mikhail Mikhailovich

Bakhtin, Mikhail Mikhailovich
1895-1975 . . . . **CLC 83**
See also CA 128; 113

Bakshi, Ralph 1938(?)- . . . . **CLC 26**
See also CA 112; 138

Bakunin, Mikhail (Alexandrovich)
1814-1876 . . . . **NCLC 25**

Baldwin, James (Arthur)
1924-1987 . . . . . . **CLC 1, 2, 3, 4, 5, 8, 13,**
15, 17, 42, 50, 67; BLC; DA; DC 1;
SSC 10; WLC
See also AAYA 4; BW 1; CA 1-4R; 124;
CABS 1; CANR 3, 24;
CDALB 1941-1968; DLB 2, 7, 33;
DLBY 87; MTCW; SATA 9, 54

Ballard, J(ames) G(raham)
1930- . . . . **CLC 3, 6, 14, 36; SSC 1**
See also AAYA 3; CA 5-8R; CANR 15, 39;
DLB 14; MTCW

Balmont, Konstantin (Dmitriyevich)
1867-1943 . . . . **TCLC 11**
See also CA 109

Balzac, Honore de
1799-1850 . . . . **NCLC 5, 35; DA; SSC 5;**
WLC
See also DLB 119

Bambara, Toni Cade
1939- . . . . **CLC 19; BLC; DA**
See also AAYA 5; BW 2; CA 29-32R;
CANR 24; DLB 38; MTCW

Bamdad, A.
See Shamlu, Ahmad

Banat, D. R.
See Bradbury, Ray (Douglas)

Bancroft, Laura
See Baum, L(yman) Frank

Banim, John 1798-1842 . . . . **NCLC 13**
See also DLB 116

Banim, Michael 1796-1874 . . . . . . **NCLC 13**

Banks, Iain
See Banks, Iain M(enzies)

Banks, Iain M(enzies) 1954- . . . . **CLC 34**
See also CA 123; 128

Banks, Lynne Reid . . . . **CLC 23**
See also Reid Banks, Lynne
See also AAYA 6

Banks, Russell 1940- . . . . **CLC 37, 72**
See also CA 65-68; CAAS 15; CANR 19;
DLB 130

Banville, John 1945- . . . . **CLC 46**
See also CA 117; 128; DLB 14

Banville, Theodore (Faullain) de
1832-1891 . . . . **NCLC 9**

Baraka, Amiri
1934- . . . . **CLC 1, 2, 3, 5, 10, 14, 33;**
BLC; DA; PC 4
See also Jones, LeRoi
See also BW 2; CA 21-24R; CABS 3;
CANR 27, 38; CDALB 1941-1968;
DLB 5, 7, 16, 38; DLBD 8; MTCW

Barbellion, W. N. P. . . . . **TCLC 24**
See also Cummings, Bruce F(rederick)

Barbera, Jack (Vincent) 1945- . . . . . . **CLC 44**
See also CA 110; CANR 45

Barbey d'Aurevilly, Jules Amedee
1808-1889 . . . . **NCLC 1; SSC 17**
See also DLB 119

Barbusse, Henri 1873-1935 . . . . **TCLC 5**
See also CA 105; DLB 65

Barclay, Bill
See Moorcock, Michael (John)

Barclay, William Ewert
See Moorcock, Michael (John)

Barea, Arturo 1897-1957 . . . . **TCLC 14**
See also CA 111

Barfoot, Joan 1946- . . . . **CLC 18**
See also CA 105

Baring, Maurice 1874-1945 . . . . **TCLC 8**
See also CA 105; DLB 34

Barker, Clive 1952- . . . . **CLC 52**
See also AAYA 10; BEST 90:3; CA 121;
129; MTCW

Barker, George Granville
1913-1991 . . . . **CLC 8, 48**
See also CA 9-12R; 135; CANR 7, 38;
DLB 20; MTCW

Barker, Harley Granville
See Granville-Barker, Harley
See also DLB 10

Barker, Howard 1946- . . . . CLC 37
See also CA 102; DLB 13

Barker, Pat 1943- . . . . CLC 32
See also CA 117; 122

Barlow, Joel 1754-1812 . . . . NCLC 23
See also DLB 37

Barnard, Mary (Ethel) 1909- . . . . CLC 48
See also CA 21-22; CAP 2

Barnes, Djuna
1892-1982 . . . CLC 3, 4, 8, 11, 29; SSC 3
See also CA 9-12R; 107; CANR 16; DLB 4,
9, 45; MTCW

Barnes, Julian 1946- . . . . CLC 42
See also CA 102; CANR 19; DLBY 93

Barnes, Peter 1931- . . . . CLC 5, 56
See also CA 65-68; CAAS 12; CANR 33,
34; DLB 13; MTCW

Baroja (y Nessi), Pio
1872-1956 . . . . TCLC 8; HLC
See also CA 104

Baron, David
See Pinter, Harold

Baron Corvo
See Rolfe, Frederick (William Serafino
Austin Lewis Mary)

Barondess, Sue K(aufman)
1926-1977 . . . . CLC 8
See also Kaufman, Sue
See also CA 1-4R; 69-72; CANR 1

Baron de Teive
See Pessoa, Fernando (Antonio Nogueira)

Barres, Maurice 1862-1923 . . . . TCLC 47
See also DLB 123

Barreto, Afonso Henrique de Lima
See Lima Barreto, Afonso Henrique de

Barrett, (Roger) Syd 1946- . . . . CLC 35

Barrett, William (Christopher)
1913-1992 . . . . CLC 27
See also CA 13-16R; 139; CANR 11

Barrie, J(ames) M(atthew)
1860-1937 . . . . TCLC 2
See also CA 104; 136; CDBLB 1890-1914;
CLR 16; DLB 10, 141; MAICYA;
YABC 1

Barrington, Michael
See Moorcock, Michael (John)

Barrol, Grady
See Bograd, Larry

Barry, Mike
See Malzberg, Barry N(athaniel)

Barry, Philip 1896-1949 . . . . TCLC 11
See also CA 109; DLB 7

Bart, Andre Schwarz
See Schwarz-Bart, Andre

Barth, John (Simmons)
1930- . . . . . . CLC 1, 2, 3, 5, 7, 9, 10, 14,
27, 51; SSC 10
See also AITN 1, 2; CA 1-4R; CABS 1;
CANR 5, 23; DLB 2; MTCW

Barthelme, Donald
1931-1989 . . . . . CLC 1, 2, 3, 5, 6, 8, 13,
23, 46, 59; SSC 2
See also CA 21-24R; 129; CANR 20;
DLB 2; DLBY 80, 89; MTCW; SATA 7,
62

Barthelme, Frederick 1943- . . . . CLC 36
See also CA 114; 122; DLBY 85

Barthes, Roland (Gerard)
1915-1980 . . . . CLC 24, 83
See also CA 130; 97-100; MTCW

Barzun, Jacques (Martin) 1907- . . . . CLC 51
See also CA 61-64; CANR 22

Bashevis, Isaac
See Singer, Isaac Bashevis

Bashkirtseff, Marie 1859-1884 . . . NCLC 27

Basho
See Matsuo Basho

Bass, Kingsley B., Jr.
See Bullins, Ed

Bass, Rick 1958- . . . . CLC 79
See also CA 126

Bassani, Giorgio 1916- . . . . CLC 9
See also CA 65-68; CANR 33; DLB 128;
MTCW

Bastos, Augusto (Antonio) Roa
See Roa Bastos, Augusto (Antonio)

Bataille, Georges 1897-1962 . . . . CLC 29
See also CA 101; 89-92

Bates, H(erbert) E(rnest)
1905-1974 . . . . CLC 46; SSC 10
See also CA 93-96; 45-48; CANR 34;
MTCW

Bauchart
See Camus, Albert

Baudelaire, Charles
1821-1867 . . . . . NCLC 6, 29; DA; PC 1;
WLC

Baudrillard, Jean 1929- . . . . CLC 60

Baum, L(yman) Frank 1856-1919 . . . TCLC 7
See also CA 108; 133; CLR 15; DLB 22;
JRDA; MAICYA; MTCW; SATA 18

Baum, Louis F.
See Baum, L(yman) Frank

Baumbach, Jonathan 1933- . . . . . . CLC 6, 23
See also CA 13-16R; CAAS 5; CANR 12;
DLBY 80; MTCW

Bausch, Richard (Carl) 1945- . . . . . . CLC 51
See also CA 101; CAAS 14; CANR 43;
DLB 130

Baxter, Charles 1947- . . . . CLC 45, 78
See also CA 57-60; CANR 40; DLB 130

Baxter, George Owen
See Faust, Frederick (Schiller)

Baxter, James K(eir) 1926-1972 . . . . CLC 14
See also CA 77-80

Baxter, John
See Hunt, E(verette) Howard, Jr.

Bayer, Sylvia
See Glassco, John

Baynton, Barbara 1857-1929 . . . . . . TCLC 57

Beagle, Peter S(oyer) 1939- . . . . CLC 7
See also CA 9-12R; CANR 4; DLBY 80;
SATA 60

Bean, Normal
See Burroughs, Edgar Rice

Beard, Charles A(ustin)
1874-1948 . . . . TCLC 15
See also CA 115; DLB 17; SATA 18

Beardsley, Aubrey 1872-1898 . . . . . NCLC 6

Beattie, Ann
1947- . . . . CLC 8, 13, 18, 40, 63; SSC 11
See also BEST 90:2; CA 81-84; DLBY 82;
MTCW

Beattie, James 1735-1803 . . . . NCLC 25
See also DLB 109

Beauchamp, Kathleen Mansfield 1888-1923
See Mansfield, Katherine
See also CA 104; 134; DA

Beaumarchais, Pierre-Augustin Caron de
1732-1799 . . . . DC 4

**Beauvoir, Simone (Lucie Ernestine Marie
Bertrand) de**
1908-1986 . . . . CLC 1, 2, 4, 8, 14, 31, 44,
50, 71; DA; WLC
See also CA 9-12R; 118; CANR 28;
DLB 72; DLBY 86; MTCW

Becker, Jurek 1937- . . . . CLC 7, 19
See also CA 85-88; DLB 75

Becker, Walter 1950- . . . . CLC 26

Beckett, Samuel (Barclay)
1906-1989 . . . . . . CLC 1, 2, 3, 4, 6, 9, 10,
11, 14, 18, 29, 57, 59, 83; DA; SSC 16;
WLC
See also CA 5-8R; 130; CANR 33;
CDBLB 1945-1960; DLB 13, 15;
DLBY 90; MTCW

Beckford, William 1760-1844 . . . . NCLC 16
See also DLB 39

Beckman, Gunnel 1910- . . . . CLC 26
See also CA 33-36R; CANR 15; CLR 25;
MAICYA; SAAS 9; SATA 6

Becque, Henri 1837-1899 . . . . NCLC 3

Beddoes, Thomas Lovell
1803-1849 . . . . NCLC 3
See also DLB 96

Bedford, Donald F.
See Fearing, Kenneth (Flexner)

Beecher, Catharine Esther
1800-1878 . . . . NCLC 30
See also DLB 1

Beecher, John 1904-1980 . . . . CLC 6
See also AITN 1; CA 5-8R; 105; CANR 8

Beer, Johann 1655-1700 . . . . LC 5

Beer, Patricia 1924- . . . . CLC 58
See also CA 61-64; CANR 13; DLB 40

Beerbohm, Henry Maximilian
1872-1956 . . . . TCLC 1, 24
See also CA 104; DLB 34, 100

Beerbohm, Max
See Beerbohm, Henry Maximilian

Begiebing, Robert J(ohn) 1946- . . . . . CLC 70
See also CA 122; CANR 40

Behan, Brendan
1923-1964 . . . . CLC 1, 8, 11, 15, 79
See also CA 73-76; CANR 33;
CDBLB 1945-1960; DLB 13; MTCW

Behn, Aphra
1640(?)-1689 . . . . LC 1; DA; DC 4; WLC
See also DLB 39, 80, 131

Behrman, S(amuel) N(athaniel)
1893-1973 . . . . CLC 40
See also CA 13-16; 45-48; CAP 1; DLB 7,
44

Belasco, David 1853-1931 . . . . **TCLC 3**
See also CA 104; DLB 7

Belcheva, Elisaveta 1893- . . . . **CLC 10**

Beldone, Phil "Cheech"
See Ellison, Harlan

Beleno
See Azuela, Mariano

Belinski, Vissarion Grigoryevich
1811-1848 . . . . **NCLC 5**

Belitt, Ben 1911- . . . . **CLC 22**
See also CA 13-16R; CAAS 4; CANR 7;
DLB 5

Bell, James Madison
1826-1902 . . . . **TCLC 43; BLC**
See also BW 1; CA 122; 124; DLB 50

Bell, Madison (Smartt) 1957- . . . . . . **CLC 41**
See also CA 111; CANR 28

Bell, Marvin (Hartley) 1937- . . . . . **CLC 8, 31**
See also CA 21-24R; CAAS 14; DLB 5;
MTCW

Bell, W. L. D.
See Mencken, H(enry) L(ouis)

Bellamy, Atwood C.
See Mencken, H(enry) L(ouis)

Bellamy, Edward 1850-1898 . . . . . . **NCLC 4**
See also DLB 12

Bellin, Edward J.
See Kuttner, Henry

Belloc, (Joseph) Hilaire (Pierre)
1870-1953 . . . . **TCLC 7, 18**
See also CA 106; DLB 19, 100, 141;
YABC 1

Belloc, Joseph Peter Rene Hilaire
See Belloc, (Joseph) Hilaire (Pierre)

Belloc, Joseph Pierre Hilaire
See Belloc, (Joseph) Hilaire (Pierre)

Belloc, M. A.
See Lowndes, Marie Adelaide (Belloc)

Bellow, Saul
1915- . . . . . . **CLC 1, 2, 3, 6, 8, 10, 13, 15,
25, 33, 34, 63, 79; DA; SSC 14; WLC**
See also AITN 2; BEST 89:3; CA 5-8R;
CABS 1; CANR 29; CDALB 1941-1968;
DLB 2, 28; DLBD 3; DLBY 82; MTCW

Bely, Andrey . . . . **TCLC 7**
See also Bugayev, Boris Nikolayevich

Benary, Margot
See Benary-Isbert, Margot

Benary-Isbert, Margot 1889-1979 . . . **CLC 12**
See also CA 5-8R; 89-92; CANR 4;
CLR 12; MAICYA; SATA 2, 21

Benavente (y Martinez), Jacinto
1866-1954 . . . . **TCLC 3**
See also CA 106; 131; HW; MTCW

Benchley, Peter (Bradford)
1940- . . . . **CLC 4, 8**
See also AITN 2; CA 17-20R; CANR 12,
35; MTCW; SATA 3

Benchley, Robert (Charles)
1889-1945 . . . . **TCLC 1, 55**
See also CA 105; DLB 11

Benedikt, Michael 1935- . . . . **CLC 4, 14**
See also CA 13-16R; CANR 7; DLB 5

Benet, Juan 1927- . . . . **CLC 28**
See also CA 143

Benet, Stephen Vincent
1898-1943 . . . . **TCLC 7; SSC 10**
See also CA 104; DLB 4, 48, 102; YABC 1

Benet, William Rose 1886-1950 . . . **TCLC 28**
See also CA 118; DLB 45

Benford, Gregory (Albert) 1941- . . . . **CLC 52**
See also CA 69-72; CANR 12, 24;
DLBY 82

Bengtsson, Frans (Gunnar)
1894-1954 . . . . **TCLC 48**

Benjamin, David
See Slavitt, David R(ytman)

Benjamin, Lois
See Gould, Lois

Benjamin, Walter 1892-1940 . . . . . **TCLC 39**

Benn, Gottfried 1886-1956 . . . . **TCLC 3**
See also CA 106; DLB 56

Bennett, Alan 1934- . . . . **CLC 45, 77**
See also CA 103; CANR 35; MTCW

Bennett, (Enoch) Arnold
1867-1931 . . . . **TCLC 5, 20**
See also CA 106; CDBLB 1890-1914;
DLB 10, 34, 98

Bennett, Elizabeth
See Mitchell, Margaret (Munnerlyn)

Bennett, George Harold 1930-
See Bennett, Hal
See also BW 1; CA 97-100

Bennett, Hal . . . . **CLC 5**
See also Bennett, George Harold
See also DLB 33

Bennett, Jay 1912- . . . . **CLC 35**
See also AAYA 10; CA 69-72; CANR 11,
42; JRDA; SAAS 4; SATA 27, 41

Bennett, Louise (Simone)
1919- . . . . **CLC 28; BLC**
See also BW 2; DLB 117

Benson, E(dward) F(rederic)
1867-1940 . . . . **TCLC 27**
See also CA 114; DLB 135

Benson, Jackson J. 1930- . . . . **CLC 34**
See also CA 25-28R; DLB 111

Benson, Sally 1900-1972 . . . . **CLC 17**
See also CA 19-20; 37-40R; CAP 1;
SATA 1, 27, 35

Benson, Stella 1892-1933 . . . . **TCLC 17**
See also CA 117; DLB 36

Bentham, Jeremy 1748-1832 . . . . . **NCLC 38**
See also DLB 107

Bentley, E(dmund) C(lerihew)
1875-1956 . . . . **TCLC 12**
See also CA 108; DLB 70

Bentley, Eric (Russell) 1916- . . . . . . **CLC 24**
See also CA 5-8R; CANR 6

Beranger, Pierre Jean de
1780-1857 . . . . **NCLC 34**

Berger, Colonel
See Malraux, (Georges-)Andre

Berger, John (Peter) 1926- . . . . . . **CLC 2, 19**
See also CA 81-84; DLB 14

Berger, Melvin H. 1927- . . . . **CLC 12**
See also CA 5-8R; CANR 4; CLR 32;
SAAS 2; SATA 5

Berger, Thomas (Louis)
1924- . . . . **CLC 3, 5, 8, 11, 18, 38**
See also CA 1-4R; CANR 5, 28; DLB 2;
DLBY 80; MTCW

Bergman, (Ernst) Ingmar
1918- . . . . **CLC 16, 72**
See also CA 81-84; CANR 33

Bergson, Henri 1859-1941 . . . . **TCLC 32**

Bergstein, Eleanor 1938- . . . . **CLC 4**
See also CA 53-56; CANR 5

Berkoff, Steven 1937- . . . . **CLC 56**
See also CA 104

Bermant, Chaim (Icyk) 1929- . . . . . . **CLC 40**
See also CA 57-60; CANR 6, 31

Bern, Victoria
See Fisher, M(ary) F(rances) K(ennedy)

Bernanos, (Paul Louis) Georges
1888-1948 . . . . **TCLC 3**
See also CA 104; 130; DLB 72

Bernard, April 1956- . . . . **CLC 59**
See also CA 131

Berne, Victoria
See Fisher, M(ary) F(rances) K(ennedy)

Bernhard, Thomas
1931-1989 . . . . **CLC 3, 32, 61**
See also CA 85-88; 127; CANR 32;
DLB 85, 124; MTCW

Berriault, Gina 1926- . . . . **CLC 54**
See also CA 116; 129; DLB 130

Berrigan, Daniel 1921- . . . . **CLC 4**
See also CA 33-36R; CAAS 1; CANR 11,
43; DLB 5

Berrigan, Edmund Joseph Michael, Jr.
1934-1983
See Berrigan, Ted
See also CA 61-64; 110; CANR 14

Berrigan, Ted . . . . **CLC 37**
See also Berrigan, Edmund Joseph Michael,
Jr.
See also DLB 5

Berry, Charles Edward Anderson 1931-
See Berry, Chuck
See also CA 115

Berry, Chuck . . . . **CLC 17**
See also Berry, Charles Edward Anderson

Berry, Jonas
See Ashbery, John (Lawrence)

Berry, Wendell (Erdman)
1934- . . . . **CLC 4, 6, 8, 27, 46**
See also AITN 1; CA 73-76; DLB 5, 6

Berryman, John
1914-1972 . . . . . . **CLC 1, 2, 3, 4, 6, 8, 10,
13, 25, 62**
See also CA 13-16; 33-36R; CABS 1;
CANR 35; CAP 1; CDALB 1941-1968;
DLB 48; MTCW

Bertolucci, Bernardo 1940- . . . . **CLC 16**
See also CA 106

Bertrand, Aloysius 1807-1841 . . . . **NCLC 31**

Bertran de Born c. 1140-1215 . . . . . **CMLC 5**

Besant, Annie (Wood) 1847-1933 . . . **TCLC 9**
See also CA 105

Bessie, Alvah 1904-1985 . . . . **CLC 23**
See also CA 5-8R; 116; CANR 2; DLB 26

Bethlen, T. D.
See Silverberg, Robert

Beti, Mongo . . . . **CLC 27; BLC**
See also Biyidi, Alexandre

Betjeman, John
    1906-1984 . . . . **CLC 2, 6, 10, 34, 43**
See also CA 9-12R; 112;
    CDBLB 1945-1960; DLB 20; DLBY 84;
    MTCW

Bettelheim, Bruno 1903-1990 . . . . . . **CLC 79**
See also CA 81-84; 131; CANR 23; MTCW

Betti, Ugo 1892-1953 . . . . **TCLC 5**
See also CA 104

Betts, Doris (Waugh) 1932- . . . . **CLC 3, 6, 28**
See also CA 13-16R; CANR 9; DLBY 82

Bevan, Alistair
See Roberts, Keith (John Kingston)

Bialik, Chaim Nachman
    1873-1934 . . . . **TCLC 25**

Bickerstaff, Isaac
See Swift, Jonathan

Bidart, Frank 1939- . . . . **CLC 33**
See also CA 140

Bienek, Horst 1930- . . . . **CLC 7, 11**
See also CA 73-76; DLB 75

Bierce, Ambrose (Gwinett)
    1842-1914(?) . . . . **TCLC 1, 7, 44; DA;
                                        SSC 9; WLC**
See also CA 104; 139; CDALB 1865-1917;
    DLB 11, 12, 23, 71, 74

Billings, Josh
See Shaw, Henry Wheeler

Billington, (Lady) Rachel (Mary)
    1942- . . . . **CLC 43**
See also AITN 2; CA 33-36R; CANR 44

Binyon, T(imothy) J(ohn) 1936- . . . . **CLC 34**
See also CA 111; CANR 28

Bioy Casares, Adolfo
    1914- . . . . **CLC 4, 8, 13; HLC; SSC 17**
See also CA 29-32R; CANR 19, 43;
    DLB 113; HW; MTCW

Bird, C.
See Ellison, Harlan

Bird, Cordwainer
See Ellison, Harlan

Bird, Robert Montgomery
    1806-1854 . . . . **NCLC 1**

Birney, (Alfred) Earle
    1904- . . . . **CLC 1, 4, 6, 11**
See also CA 1-4R; CANR 5, 20; DLB 88;
    MTCW

Bishop, Elizabeth
    1911-1979 . . . . . . **CLC 1, 4, 9, 13, 15, 32;
                                        DA; PC 3**
See also CA 5-8R; 89-92; CABS 2;
    CANR 26; CDALB 1968-1988; DLB 5;
    MTCW; SATA 24

Bishop, John 1935- . . . . **CLC 10**
See also CA 105

Bissett, Bill 1939- . . . . **CLC 18**
See also CA 69-72; CAAS 19; CANR 15;
    DLB 53; MTCW

Bitov, Andrei (Georgievich) 1937- . . . **CLC 57**
See also CA 142

Biyidi, Alexandre 1932-
See Beti, Mongo
See also BW 1; CA 114; 124; MTCW

Bjarme, Brynjolf
See Ibsen, Henrik (Johan)

Bjornson, Bjornstjerne (Martinius)
    1832-1910 . . . . **TCLC 7, 37**
See also CA 104

Black, Robert
See Holdstock, Robert P.

Blackburn, Paul 1926-1971 . . . . . . **CLC 9, 43**
See also CA 81-84; 33-36R; CANR 34;
    DLB 16; DLBY 81

Black Elk 1863-1950 . . . . **TCLC 33**
See also CA 144

Black Hobart
See Sanders, (James) Ed(ward)

Blacklin, Malcolm
See Chambers, Aidan

Blackmore, R(ichard) D(oddridge)
    1825-1900 . . . . **TCLC 27**
See also CA 120; DLB 18

Blackmur, R(ichard) P(almer)
    1904-1965 . . . . **CLC 2, 24**
See also CA 11-12; 25-28R; CAP 1; DLB 63

Black Tarantula, The
See Acker, Kathy

Blackwood, Algernon (Henry)
    1869-1951 . . . . **TCLC 5**
See also CA 105

Blackwood, Caroline 1931- . . . . . . **CLC 6, 9**
See also CA 85-88; CANR 32; DLB 14;
    MTCW

Blade, Alexander
See Hamilton, Edmond; Silverberg, Robert

Blaga, Lucian 1895-1961 . . . . **CLC 75**

Blair, Eric (Arthur) 1903-1950
See Orwell, George
See also CA 104; 132; DA; MTCW;
    SATA 29

Blais, Marie-Claire
    1939- . . . . **CLC 2, 4, 6, 13, 22**
See also CA 21-24R; CAAS 4; CANR 38;
    DLB 53; MTCW

Blaise, Clark 1940- . . . . **CLC 29**
See also AITN 2; CA 53-56; CAAS 3;
    CANR 5; DLB 53

Blake, Nicholas
See Day Lewis, C(ecil)
See also DLB 77

Blake, William
    1757-1827 . . . . . **NCLC 13, 37; DA; WLC**
See also CDBLB 1789-1832; DLB 93;
    MAICYA; SATA 30

Blasco Ibanez, Vicente
    1867-1928 . . . . **TCLC 12**
See also CA 110; 131; HW; MTCW

Blatty, William Peter 1928- . . . . **CLC 2**
See also CA 5-8R; CANR 9

Bleeck, Oliver
See Thomas, Ross (Elmore)

Blessing, Lee 1949- . . . . **CLC 54**

Blish, James (Benjamin)
    1921-1975 . . . . **CLC 14**
See also CA 1-4R; 57-60; CANR 3; DLB 8;
    MTCW; SATA 66

Bliss, Reginald
See Wells, H(erbert) G(eorge)

Blixen, Karen (Christentze Dinesen)
    1885-1962
See Dinesen, Isak
See also CA 25-28; CANR 22; CAP 2;
    MTCW; SATA 44

Bloch, Robert (Albert) 1917- . . . . **CLC 33**
See also CA 5-8R; CANR 5; DLB 44;
    SATA 12

Blok, Alexander (Alexandrovich)
    1880-1921 . . . . **TCLC 5**
See also CA 104

Blom, Jan
See Breytenbach, Breyten

Bloom, Harold 1930- . . . . **CLC 24**
See also CA 13-16R; CANR 39; DLB 67

Bloomfield, Aurelius
See Bourne, Randolph S(illiman)

Blount, Roy (Alton), Jr. 1941- . . . . . **CLC 38**
See also CA 53-56; CANR 10, 28; MTCW

Bloy, Leon 1846-1917 . . . . **TCLC 22**
See also CA 121; DLB 123

Blume, Judy (Sussman) 1938- . . . **CLC 12, 30**
See also AAYA 3; CA 29-32R; CANR 13,
    37; CLR 2, 15; DLB 52; JRDA;
    MAICYA; MTCW; SATA 2, 31, 79

Blunden, Edmund (Charles)
    1896-1974 . . . . **CLC 2, 56**
See also CA 17-18; 45-48; CAP 2; DLB 20,
    100; MTCW

Bly, Robert (Elwood)
    1926- . . . . **CLC 1, 2, 5, 10, 15, 38**
See also CA 5-8R; CANR 41; DLB 5;
    MTCW

Boas, Franz 1858-1942 . . . . **TCLC 56**
See also CA 115

Bobette
See Simenon, Georges (Jacques Christian)

Boccaccio, Giovanni
    1313-1375 . . . . **CMLC 13; SSC 10**

Bochco, Steven 1943- . . . . **CLC 35**
See also AAYA 11; CA 124; 138

Bodenheim, Maxwell 1892-1954 . . . **TCLC 44**
See also CA 110; DLB 9, 45

Bodker, Cecil 1927- . . . . **CLC 21**
See also CA 73-76; CANR 13, 44; CLR 23;
    MAICYA; SATA 14

Boell, Heinrich (Theodor)
    1917-1985 . . . . **CLC 2, 3, 6, 9, 11, 15, 27,
                                        32, 72; DA; WLC**
See also CA 21-24R; 116; CANR 24;
    DLB 69; DLBY 85; MTCW

Boerne, Alfred
See Doeblin, Alfred

Bogan, Louise 1897-1970 . . . . . **CLC 4, 39, 46**
See also CA 73-76; 25-28R; CANR 33;
    DLB 45; MTCW

Brathwaite, Edward (Kamau)
1930- .... **CLC 11**
See also BW 2; CA 25-28R; CANR 11, 26;
DLB 125

Brautigan, Richard (Gary)
1935-1984 .... **CLC 1, 3, 5, 9, 12, 34, 42**
See also CA 53-56; 113; CANR 34; DLB 2,
5; DLBY 80, 84; MTCW; SATA 56

Braverman, Kate 1950- .... **CLC 67**
See also CA 89-92

Brecht, Bertolt
1898-1956 ...... **TCLC 1, 6, 13, 35; DA;**
DC 3; WLC
See also CA 104; 133; DLB 56, 124; MTCW

Brecht, Eugen Berthold Friedrich
See Brecht, Bertolt

Bremer, Fredrika 1801-1865 ..... **NCLC 11**

Brennan, Christopher John
1870-1932 .... **TCLC 17**
See also CA 117

Brennan, Maeve 1917- .... **CLC 5**
See also CA 81-84

Brentano, Clemens (Maria)
1778-1842 .... **NCLC 1**

Brent of Bin Bin
See Franklin, (Stella Maraia Sarah) Miles

Brenton, Howard 1942- .... **CLC 31**
See also CA 69-72; CANR 33; DLB 13;
MTCW

Breslin, James 1930-
See Breslin, Jimmy
See also CA 73-76; CANR 31; MTCW

Breslin, Jimmy .... **CLC 4, 43**
See also Breslin, James
See also AITN 1

Bresson, Robert 1907- .... **CLC 16**
See also CA 110

Breton, Andre 1896-1966... **CLC 2, 9, 15, 54**
See also CA 19-20; 25-28R; CANR 40;
CAP 2; DLB 65; MTCW

Breytenbach, Breyten 1939(?)- .. **CLC 23, 37**
See also CA 113; 129

Bridgers, Sue Ellen 1942- .... **CLC 26**
See also AAYA 8; CA 65-68; CANR 11,
36; CLR 18; DLB 52; JRDA; MAICYA;
SAAS 1; SATA 22

Bridges, Robert (Seymour)
1844-1930 .... **TCLC 1**
See also CA 104; CDBLB 1890-1914;
DLB 19, 98

Bridie, James .... **TCLC 3**
See also Mavor, Osborne Henry
See also DLB 10

Brin, David 1950- .... **CLC 34**
See also CA 102; CANR 24; SATA 65

Brink, Andre (Philippus)
1935- .... **CLC 18, 36**
See also CA 104; CANR 39; MTCW

Brinsmead, H(esba) F(ay) 1922- .... **CLC 21**
See also CA 21-24R; CANR 10; MAICYA;
SAAS 5; SATA 18, 78

Brittain, Vera (Mary)
1893(?)-1970 .... **CLC 23**
See also CA 13-16; 25-28R; CAP 1; MTCW

Broch, Hermann 1886-1951 ...... **TCLC 20**
See also CA 117; DLB 85, 124

Brock, Rose
See Hansen, Joseph

Brodkey, Harold 1930- .... **CLC 56**
See also CA 111; DLB 130

Brodsky, Iosif Alexandrovich 1940-
See Brodsky, Joseph
See also AITN 1; CA 41-44R; CANR 37;
MTCW

Brodsky, Joseph .. **CLC 4, 6, 13, 36, 50; PC 9**
See also Brodsky, Iosif Alexandrovich

Brodsky, Michael Mark 1948- ..... **CLC 19**
See also CA 102; CANR 18, 41

Bromell, Henry 1947- .... **CLC 5**
See also CA 53-56; CANR 9

Bromfield, Louis (Brucker)
1896-1956 .... **TCLC 11**
See also CA 107; DLB 4, 9, 86

Broner, E(sther) M(asserman)
1930- .... **CLC 19**
See also CA 17-20R; CANR 8, 25; DLB 28

Bronk, William 1918- .... **CLC 10**
See also CA 89-92; CANR 23

Bronstein, Lev Davidovich
See Trotsky, Leon

Bronte, Anne 1820-1849......... **NCLC 4**
See also DLB 21

Bronte, Charlotte
1816-1855 ... **NCLC 3, 8, 33; DA; WLC**
See also CDBLB 1832-1890; DLB 21

Bronte, (Jane) Emily
1818-1848 .... **NCLC 16, 35; DA; PC 8;**
WLC
See also CDBLB 1832-1890; DLB 21, 32

Brooke, Frances 1724-1789 .... **LC 6**
See also DLB 39, 99

Brooke, Henry 1703(?)-1783 .... **LC 1**
See also DLB 39

Brooke, Rupert (Chawner)
1887-1915 .... **TCLC 2, 7; DA; WLC**
See also CA 104; 132; CDBLB 1914-1945;
DLB 19; MTCW

Brooke-Haven, P.
See Wodehouse, P(elham) G(renville)

Brooke-Rose, Christine 1926- ...... **CLC 40**
See also CA 13-16R; DLB 14

Brookner, Anita 1928- ...... **CLC 32, 34, 51**
See also CA 114; 120; CANR 37; DLBY 87;
MTCW

Brooks, Cleanth 1906-1994 .... **CLC 24**
See also CA 17-20R; 145; CANR 33, 35;
DLB 63; MTCW

Brooks, George
See Baum, L(yman) Frank

Brooks, Gwendolyn
1917- ...... **CLC 1, 2, 4, 5, 15, 49; BLC;**
DA; PC 7; WLC
See also AITN 1; BW 2; CA 1-4R;
CANR 1, 27; CDALB 1941-1968;
CLR 27; DLB 5, 76; MTCW; SATA 6

Brooks, Mel .... **CLC 12**
See also Kaminsky, Melvin
See also DLB 26

Brooks, Peter 1938- .... **CLC 34**
See also CA 45-48; CANR 1

Brooks, Van Wyck 1886-1963 ...... **CLC 29**
See also CA 1-4R; CANR 6; DLB 45, 63,
103

Brophy, Brigid (Antonia)
1929- .... **CLC 6, 11, 29**
See also CA 5-8R; CAAS 4; CANR 25;
DLB 14; MTCW

Brosman, Catharine Savage 1934-.... **CLC 9**
See also CA 61-64; CANR 21

Brother Antoninus
See Everson, William (Oliver)

Broughton, T(homas) Alan 1936- ... **CLC 19**
See also CA 45-48; CANR 2, 23

Broumas, Olga 1949- .... **CLC 10, 73**
See also CA 85-88; CANR 20

Brown, Charles Brockden
1771-1810 .... **NCLC 22**
See also CDALB 1640-1865; DLB 37, 59,
73

Brown, Christy 1932-1981 .... **CLC 63**
See also CA 105; 104; DLB 14

Brown, Claude 1937- .... **CLC 30; BLC**
See also AAYA 7; BW 1; CA 73-76

Brown, Dee (Alexander) 1908- .. **CLC 18, 47**
See also CA 13-16R; CAAS 6; CANR 11,
45; DLBY 80; MTCW; SATA 5

Brown, George
See Wertmueller, Lina

Brown, George Douglas
1869-1902 .... **TCLC 28**

Brown, George Mackay 1921-.... **CLC 5, 48**
See also CA 21-24R; CAAS 6; CANR 12,
37; DLB 14, 27, 139; MTCW; SATA 35

Brown, (William) Larry 1951-...... **CLC 73**
See also CA 130; 134

Brown, Moses
See Barrett, William (Christopher)

Brown, Rita Mae 1944- ..... **CLC 18, 43, 79**
See also CA 45-48; CANR 2, 11, 35;
MTCW

Brown, Roderick (Langmere) Haig-
See Haig-Brown, Roderick (Langmere)

Brown, Rosellen 1939- .... **CLC 32**
See also CA 77-80; CAAS 10; CANR 14, 44

Brown, Sterling Allen
1901-1989 .... **CLC 1, 23, 59; BLC**
See also BW 1; CA 85-88; 127; CANR 26;
DLB 48, 51, 63; MTCW

Brown, Will
See Ainsworth, William Harrison

Brown, William Wells
1813-1884 .... **NCLC 2; BLC; DC 1**
See also DLB 3, 50

Browne, (Clyde) Jackson 1948(?)-... **CLC 21**
See also CA 120

Browning, Elizabeth Barrett
1806-1861 ..... **NCLC 1, 16; DA; PC 6;**
WLC
See also CDBLB 1832-1890; DLB 32

Browning, Robert
1812-1889 . . . . **NCLC 19; DA; PC 2**
See also CDBLB 1832-1890; DLB 32;
YABC 1

Browning, Tod 1882-1962 . . . . **CLC 16**
See also CA 141; 117

Bruccoli, Matthew J(oseph) 1931- . . **CLC 34**
See also CA 9-12R; CANR 7; DLB 103

Bruce, Lenny . . . . **CLC 21**
See also Schneider, Leonard Alfred

Bruin, John
See Brutus, Dennis

Brulard, Henri
See Stendhal

Brulls, Christian
See Simenon, Georges (Jacques Christian)

Brunner, John (Kilian Houston)
1934- . . . . **CLC 8, 10**
See also CA 1-4R; CAAS 8; CANR 2, 37;
MTCW

Bruno, Giordano 1548-1600 . . . . **LC 27**

Brutus, Dennis 1924- . . . . **CLC 43; BLC**
See also BW 2; CA 49-52; CAAS 14;
CANR 2, 27, 42; DLB 117

Bryan, C(ourtlandt) D(ixon) B(arnes)
1936- . . . . **CLC 29**
See also CA 73-76; CANR 13

Bryan, Michael
See Moore, Brian

Bryant, William Cullen
1794-1878 . . . . **NCLC 6, 46; DA**
See also CDALB 1640-1865; DLB 3, 43, 59

Bryusov, Valery Yakovlevich
1873-1924 . . . . **TCLC 10**
See also CA 107

Buchan, John 1875-1940 . . . . **TCLC 41**
See also CA 108; 145; DLB 34, 70; YABC 2

Buchanan, George 1506-1582 . . . . **LC 4**

Buchheim, Lothar-Guenther 1918- . . . **CLC 6**
See also CA 85-88

Buchner, (Karl) Georg
1813-1837 . . . . **NCLC 26**

Buchwald, Art(hur) 1925- . . . . **CLC 33**
See also AITN 1; CA 5-8R; CANR 21;
MTCW; SATA 10

Buck, Pearl S(ydenstricker)
1892-1973 . . . . **CLC 7, 11, 18; DA**
See also AITN 1; CA 1-4R; 41-44R;
CANR 1, 34; DLB 9, 102; MTCW;
SATA 1, 25

Buckler, Ernest 1908-1984 . . . . **CLC 13**
See also CA 11-12; 114; CAP 1; DLB 68;
SATA 47

Buckley, Vincent (Thomas)
1925-1988 . . . . **CLC 57**
See also CA 101

Buckley, William F(rank), Jr.
1925- . . . . **CLC 7, 18, 37**
See also AITN 1; CA 1-4R; CANR 1, 24;
DLB 137; DLBY 80; MTCW

Buechner, (Carl) Frederick
1926- . . . . **CLC 2, 4, 6, 9**
See also CA 13-16R; CANR 11, 39;
DLBY 80; MTCW

Buell, John (Edward) 1927- . . . . **CLC 10**
See also CA 1-4R; DLB 53

Buero Vallejo, Antonio 1916- . . . **CLC 15, 46**
See also CA 106; CANR 24; HW; MTCW

Bufalino, Gesualdo 1920(?)- . . . . **CLC 74**

Bugayev, Boris Nikolayevich 1880-1934
See Bely, Andrey
See also CA 104

Bukowski, Charles
1920-1994 . . . . **CLC 2, 5, 9, 41, 82**
See also CA 17-20R; 144; CANR 40;
DLB 5, 130; MTCW

Bulgakov, Mikhail (Afanas'evich)
1891-1940 . . . . **TCLC 2, 16**
See also CA 105

Bulgya, Alexander Alexandrovich
1901-1956 . . . . **TCLC 53**
See also Fadeyev, Alexander
See also CA 117

Bullins, Ed 1935- . . . . **CLC 1, 5, 7; BLC**
See also BW 2; CA 49-52; CAAS 16;
CANR 24; DLB 7, 38; MTCW

Bulwer-Lytton, Edward (George Earle Lytton)
1803-1873 . . . . **NCLC 1, 45**
See also DLB 21

Bunin, Ivan Alexeyevich
1870-1953 . . . . **TCLC 6; SSC 5**
See also CA 104

Bunting, Basil 1900-1985 . . . . **CLC 10, 39, 47**
See also CA 53-56; 115; CANR 7; DLB 20

Bunuel, Luis 1900-1983 . . **CLC 16, 80; HLC**
See also CA 101; 110; CANR 32; HW

Bunyan, John 1628-1688 . . **LC 4; DA; WLC**
See also CDBLB 1660-1789; DLB 39

Burford, Eleanor
See Hibbert, Eleanor Alice Burford

Burgess, Anthony
. **CLC 1, 2, 4, 5, 8, 10, 13, 15, 22, 40, 62, 81**
See also Wilson, John (Anthony) Burgess
See also AITN 1; CDBLB 1960 to Present;
DLB 14

Burke, Edmund
1729(?)-1797 . . . . **LC 7; DA; WLC**
See also DLB 104

Burke, Kenneth (Duva)
1897-1993 . . . . **CLC 2, 24**
See also CA 5-8R; 143; CANR 39; DLB 45,
63; MTCW

Burke, Leda
See Garnett, David

Burke, Ralph
See Silverberg, Robert

Burney, Fanny 1752-1840 . . . . **NCLC 12**
See also DLB 39

Burns, Robert
1759-1796 . . . . . . **LC 3; DA; PC 6; WLC**
See also CDBLB 1789-1832; DLB 109

Burns, Tex
See L'Amour, Louis (Dearborn)

Burnshaw, Stanley 1906- . . . . . **CLC 3, 13, 44**
See also CA 9-12R; DLB 48

Burr, Anne 1937- . . . . **CLC 6**
See also CA 25-28R

Burroughs, Edgar Rice
1875-1950 . . . . **TCLC 2, 32**
See also AAYA 11; CA 104; 132; DLB 8;
MTCW; SATA 41

Burroughs, William S(eward)
1914- . . . . **CLC 1, 2, 5, 15, 22, 42, 75;
DA; WLC**
See also AITN 2; CA 9-12R; CANR 20;
DLB 2, 8, 16; DLBY 81; MTCW

Burton, Richard F. 1821-1890 . . . . **NCLC 42**
See also DLB 55

Busch, Frederick 1941- . . . **CLC 7, 10, 18, 47**
See also CA 33-36R; CAAS 1; CANR 45;
DLB 6

Bush, Ronald 1946- . . . . **CLC 34**
See also CA 136

Bustos, F(rancisco)
See Borges, Jorge Luis

Bustos Domecq, H(onorio)
See Bioy Casares, Adolfo; Borges, Jorge
Luis

Butler, Octavia E(stelle) 1947- . . . . . **CLC 38**
See also BW 2; CA 73-76; CANR 12, 24,
38; DLB 33; MTCW

Butler, Robert Olen (Jr.) 1945- . . . . . **CLC 81**
See also CA 112

Butler, Samuel 1612-1680 . . . . **LC 16**
See also DLB 101, 126

Butler, Samuel
1835-1902 . . . . . . **TCLC 1, 33; DA; WLC**
See also CA 143; CDBLB 1890-1914;
DLB 18, 57

Butler, Walter C.
See Faust, Frederick (Schiller)

Butor, Michel (Marie Francois)
1926- . . . . **CLC 1, 3, 8, 11, 15**
See also CA 9-12R; CANR 33; DLB 83;
MTCW

Buzo, Alexander (John) 1944- . . . . . . **CLC 61**
See also CA 97-100; CANR 17, 39

Buzzati, Dino 1906-1972 . . . . **CLC 36**
See also CA 33-36R

Byars, Betsy (Cromer) 1928- . . . . **CLC 35**
See also CA 33-36R; CANR 18, 36; CLR 1,
16; DLB 52; JRDA; MAICYA; MTCW;
SAAS 1; SATA 4, 46

Byatt, A(ntonia) S(usan Drabble)
1936- . . . . **CLC 19, 65**
See also CA 13-16R; CANR 13, 33;
DLB 14; MTCW

Byrne, David 1952- . . . . **CLC 26**
See also CA 127

Byrne, John Keyes 1926-
See Leonard, Hugh
See also CA 102

Byron, George Gordon (Noel)
1788-1824 . . . . . . **NCLC 2, 12; DA; WLC**
See also CDBLB 1789-1832; DLB 96, 110

C. 3. 3.
See Wilde, Oscar (Fingal O'Flahertie Wills)

Caballero, Fernan 1796-1877 . . . . . **NCLC 10**

Cabell, James Branch 1879-1958 . . . **TCLC 6**
See also CA 105; DLB 9, 78

Cable, George Washington
1844-1925 . . . . **TCLC 4; SSC 4**
See also CA 104; DLB 12, 74

Cabral de Melo Neto, Joao 1920- . . . **CLC 76**

Cabrera Infante, G(uillermo)
1929- . . . . **CLC 5, 25, 45; HLC**
See also CA 85-88; CANR 29; DLB 113;
HW; MTCW

Cade, Toni
See Bambara, Toni Cade

Cadmus and Harmonia
See Buchan, John

Caedmon fl. 658-680 . . . . **CMLC 7**

Caeiro, Alberto
See Pessoa, Fernando (Antonio Nogueira)

Cage, John (Milton, Jr.) 1912- . . . . . **CLC 41**
See also CA 13-16R; CANR 9

Cain, G.
See Cabrera Infante, G(uillermo)

Cain, Guillermo
See Cabrera Infante, G(uillermo)

Cain, James M(allahan)
1892-1977 . . . . **CLC 3, 11, 28**
See also AITN 1; CA 17-20R; 73-76;
CANR 8, 34; MTCW

Caine, Mark
See Raphael, Frederic (Michael)

Calasso, Roberto 1941- . . . . **CLC 81**
See also CA 143

Calderon de la Barca, Pedro
1600-1681 . . . . **LC 23; DC 3**

Caldwell, Erskine (Preston)
1903-1987 . . . . **CLC 1, 8, 14, 50, 60**
See also AITN 1; CA 1-4R; 121; CAAS 1;
CANR 2, 33; DLB 9, 86; MTCW

Caldwell, (Janet Miriam) Taylor (Holland)
1900-1985 . . . . **CLC 2, 28, 39**
See also CA 5-8R; 116; CANR 5

Calhoun, John Caldwell
1782-1850 . . . . **NCLC 15**
See also DLB 3

Calisher, Hortense
1911- . . . . **CLC 2, 4, 8, 38; SSC 15**
See also CA 1-4R; CANR 1, 22; DLB 2;
MTCW

Callaghan, Morley Edward
1903-1990 . . . . **CLC 3, 14, 41, 65**
See also CA 9-12R; 132; CANR 33;
DLB 68; MTCW

Calvino, Italo
1923-1985 . . . . . **CLC 5, 8, 11, 22, 33, 39,
73; SSC 3**
See also CA 85-88; 116; CANR 23; MTCW

Cameron, Carey 1952- . . . . **CLC 59**
See also CA 135

Cameron, Peter 1959- . . . . **CLC 44**
See also CA 125

Campana, Dino 1885-1932 . . . . **TCLC 20**
See also CA 117; DLB 114

Campbell, John W(ood, Jr.)
1910-1971 . . . . **CLC 32**
See also CA 21-22; 29-32R; CANR 34;
CAP 2; DLB 8; MTCW

Campbell, Joseph 1904-1987 . . . . . . **CLC 69**
See also AAYA 3; BEST 89:2; CA 1-4R;
124; CANR 3, 28; MTCW

Campbell, Maria 1940- . . . . **CLC 85**
See also CA 102; NNAL

Campbell, (John) Ramsey 1946- . . . . **CLC 42**
See also CA 57-60; CANR 7

Campbell, (Ignatius) Roy (Dunnachie)
1901-1957 . . . . **TCLC 5**
See also CA 104; DLB 20

Campbell, Thomas 1777-1844 . . . . **NCLC 19**
See also DLB 93; 144

Campbell, Wilfred . . . . **TCLC 9**
See also Campbell, William

Campbell, William 1858(?)-1918
See Campbell, Wilfred
See also CA 106; DLB 92

Campos, Alvaro de
See Pessoa, Fernando (Antonio Nogueira)

Camus, Albert
1913-1960 . . . . **CLC 1, 2, 4, 9, 11, 14, 32,
63, 69; DA; DC 2; SSC 9; WLC**
See also CA 89-92; DLB 72; MTCW

Canby, Vincent 1924- . . . . **CLC 13**
See also CA 81-84

Cancale
See Desnos, Robert

Canetti, Elias 1905- . . . . . . **CLC 3, 14, 25, 75**
See also CA 21-24R; CANR 23; DLB 85,
124; MTCW

Canin, Ethan 1960- . . . . **CLC 55**
See also CA 131; 135

Cannon, Curt
See Hunter, Evan

Cape, Judith
See Page, P(atricia) K(athleen)

Capek, Karel
1890-1938 . . . . . **TCLC 6, 37; DA; DC 1;
WLC**
See also CA 104; 140

Capote, Truman
1924-1984 . . . . . . **CLC 1, 3, 8, 13, 19, 34,
38, 58; DA; SSC 2; WLC**
See also CA 5-8R; 113; CANR 18;
CDALB 1941-1968; DLB 2; DLBY 80,
84; MTCW

Capra, Frank 1897-1991 . . . . **CLC 16**
See also CA 61-64; 135

Caputo, Philip 1941- . . . . **CLC 32**
See also CA 73-76; CANR 40

Card, Orson Scott 1951- . . . . **CLC 44, 47, 50**
See also AAYA 11; CA 102; CANR 27;
MTCW

Cardenal (Martinez), Ernesto
1925- . . . . **CLC 31; HLC**
See also CA 49-52; CANR 2, 32; HW;
MTCW

Carducci, Giosue 1835-1907 . . . . . . **TCLC 32**

Carew, Thomas 1595(?)-1640 . . . . **LC 13**
See also DLB 126

Carey, Ernestine Gilbreth 1908- . . . . **CLC 17**
See also CA 5-8R; SATA 2

Carey, Peter 1943- . . . . **CLC 40, 55**
See also CA 123; 127; MTCW

Carleton, William 1794-1869 . . . . . . **NCLC 3**

Carlisle, Henry (Coffin) 1926- . . . . . **CLC 33**
See also CA 13-16R; CANR 15

Carlsen, Chris
See Holdstock, Robert P.

Carlson, Ron(ald F.) 1947- . . . . **CLC 54**
See also CA 105; CANR 27

Carlyle, Thomas 1795-1881 . . **NCLC 22; DA**
See also CDBLB 1789-1832; DLB 55; 144

Carman, (William) Bliss
1861-1929 . . . . **TCLC 7**
See also CA 104; DLB 92

Carnegie, Dale 1888-1955 . . . . **TCLC 53**

Carossa, Hans 1878-1956 . . . . **TCLC 48**
See also DLB 66

Carpenter, Don(ald Richard)
1931- . . . . **CLC 41**
See also CA 45-48; CANR 1

Carpentier (y Valmont), Alejo
1904-1980 . . . . **CLC 8, 11, 38; HLC**
See also CA 65-68; 97-100; CANR 11;
DLB 113; HW

Carr, Emily 1871-1945 . . . . **TCLC 32**
See also DLB 68

Carr, John Dickson 1906-1977 . . . . . . **CLC 3**
See also CA 49-52; 69-72; CANR 3, 33;
MTCW

Carr, Philippa
See Hibbert, Eleanor Alice Burford

Carr, Virginia Spencer 1929- . . . . **CLC 34**
See also CA 61-64; DLB 111

Carrier, Roch 1937- . . . . **CLC 13, 78**
See also CA 130; DLB 53

Carroll, James P. 1943(?)- . . . . **CLC 38**
See also CA 81-84

Carroll, Jim 1951- . . . . **CLC 35**
See also CA 45-48; CANR 42

Carroll, Lewis . . . . **NCLC 2; WLC**
See also Dodgson, Charles Lutwidge
See also CDBLB 1832-1890; CLR 2, 18;
DLB 18; JRDA

Carroll, Paul Vincent 1900-1968 . . . . **CLC 10**
See also CA 9-12R; 25-28R; DLB 10

Carruth, Hayden
1921- . . . . . . **CLC 4, 7, 10, 18, 84; PC 10**
See also CA 9-12R; CANR 4, 38; DLB 5;
MTCW; SATA 47

Carson, Rachel Louise 1907-1964 . . . **CLC 71**
See also CA 77-80; CANR 35; MTCW;
SATA 23

Carter, Angela (Olive)
1940-1992 . . . . . . **CLC 5, 41, 76; SSC 13**
See also CA 53-56; 136; CANR 12, 36;
DLB 14; MTCW; SATA 66;
SATA-Obit 70

Carter, Nick
See Smith, Martin Cruz

Carver, Raymond
1938-1988 . . . **CLC 22, 36, 53, 55; SSC 8**
See also CA 33-36R; 126; CANR 17, 34;
DLB 130; DLBY 84, 88; MTCW

Chaviaras, Strates 1935-
See Haviaras, Stratis
See also CA 105

Chayefsky, Paddy .... **CLC 23**
See also Chayefsky, Sidney
See also DLB 7, 44; DLBY 81

Chayefsky, Sidney 1923-1981
See Chayefsky, Paddy
See also CA 9-12R; 104; CANR 18

Chedid, Andree 1920- .... **CLC 47**
See also CA 145

Cheever, John
1912-1982 ...... **CLC 3, 7, 8, 11, 15, 25,**
64; DA; SSC 1; WLC
See also CA 5-8R; 106; CABS 1; CANR 5,
27; CDALB 1941-1968; DLB 2, 102;
DLBY 80, 82; MTCW

Cheever, Susan 1943- .... **CLC 18, 48**
See also CA 103; CANR 27; DLBY 82

Chekhonte, Antosha
See Chekhov, Anton (Pavlovich)

Chekhov, Anton (Pavlovich)
1860-1904 ..... **TCLC 3, 10, 31, 55; DA;**
SSC 2; WLC
See also CA 104; 124

Chernyshevsky, Nikolay Gavrilovich
1828-1889 .... **NCLC 1**

Cherry, Carolyn Janice 1942-
See Cherryh, C. J.
See also CA 65-68; CANR 10

Cherryh, C. J. .... **CLC 35**
See also Cherry, Carolyn Janice
See also DLBY 80

Chesnutt, Charles W(addell)
1858-1932 .... **TCLC 5, 39; BLC; SSC 7**
See also BW 1; CA 106; 125; DLB 12, 50,
78; MTCW

Chester, Alfred 1929(?)-1971 ...... **CLC 49**
See also CA 33-36R; DLB 130

Chesterton, G(ilbert) K(eith)
1874-1936 .... **TCLC 1, 6; SSC 1**
See also CA 104; 132; CDBLB 1914-1945;
DLB 10, 19, 34, 70, 98; MTCW;
SATA 27

Chiang Pin-chin 1904-1986
See Ding Ling
See also CA 118

Ch'ien Chung-shu 1910- .... **CLC 22**
See also CA 130; MTCW

Child, L. Maria
See Child, Lydia Maria

Child, Lydia Maria 1802-1880 .... **NCLC 6**
See also DLB 1, 74; SATA 67

Child, Mrs.
See Child, Lydia Maria

Child, Philip 1898-1978 .... **CLC 19, 68**
See also CA 13-14; CAP 1; SATA 47

Childress, Alice
1920- .... **CLC 12, 15; BLC; DC 4**
See also AAYA 8; BW 2; CA 45-48;
CANR 3, 27; CLR 14; DLB 7, 38; JRDA;
MAICYA; MTCW; SATA 7, 48

Chislett, (Margaret) Anne 1943- .... **CLC 34**

Chitty, Thomas Willes 1926- ...... **CLC 11**
See also Hinde, Thomas
See also CA 5-8R

Chomette, Rene Lucien 1898-1981
See Clair, Rene
See also CA 103

Chopin, Kate .... **TCLC 5, 14; DA; SSC 8**
See also Chopin, Katherine
See also CDALB 1865-1917; DLB 12, 78

Chopin, Katherine 1851-1904
See Chopin, Kate
See also CA 104; 122

Chretien de Troyes
c. 12th cent. - .... **CMLC 10**

Christie
See Ichikawa, Kon

Christie, Agatha (Mary Clarissa)
1890-1976 ...... **CLC 1, 6, 8, 12, 39, 48**
See also AAYA 9; AITN 1, 2; CA 17-20R;
61-64; CANR 10, 37; CDBLB 1914-1945;
DLB 13, 77; MTCW; SATA 36

Christie, (Ann) Philippa
See Pearce, Philippa
See also CA 5-8R; CANR 4

Christine de Pizan 1365(?)-1431(?) .... **LC 9**

Chubb, Elmer
See Masters, Edgar Lee

Chulkov, Mikhail Dmitrievich
1743-1792 .... **LC 2**

Churchill, Caryl 1938- .... **CLC 31, 55**
See also CA 102; CANR 22; DLB 13;
MTCW

Churchill, Charles 1731-1764 .... **LC 3**
See also DLB 109

Chute, Carolyn 1947- .... **CLC 39**
See also CA 123

Ciardi, John (Anthony)
1916-1986 .... **CLC 10, 40, 44**
See also CA 5-8R; 118; CAAS 2; CANR 5,
33; CLR 19; DLB 5; DLBY 86;
MAICYA; MTCW; SATA 1, 46, 65

Cicero, Marcus Tullius
106B.C.-43B.C. .... **CMLC 3**

Cimino, Michael 1943- .... **CLC 16**
See also CA 105

Cioran, E(mil) M. 1911- .... **CLC 64**
See also CA 25-28R

Cisneros, Sandra 1954- ...... **CLC 69; HLC**
See also AAYA 9; CA 131; DLB 122; HW

Clair, Rene .... **CLC 20**
See also Chomette, Rene Lucien

Clampitt, Amy 1920- .... **CLC 32**
See also CA 110; CANR 29; DLB 105

Clancy, Thomas L., Jr. 1947-
See Clancy, Tom
See also CA 125; 131; MTCW

Clancy, Tom .... **CLC 45**
See also Clancy, Thomas L., Jr.
See also AAYA 9; BEST 89:1, 90:1

Clare, John 1793-1864 .... **NCLC 9**
See also DLB 55, 96

Clarin
See Alas (y Urena), Leopoldo (Enrique
Garcia)

Clark, Al C.
See Goines, Donald

Clark, (Robert) Brian 1932- .... **CLC 29**
See also CA 41-44R

Clark, Curt
See Westlake, Donald E(dwin)

Clark, Eleanor 1913- .... **CLC 5, 19**
See also CA 9-12R; CANR 41; DLB 6

Clark, J. P.
See Clark, John Pepper
See also DLB 117

Clark, John Pepper 1935- .... **CLC 38; BLC**
See also Clark, J. P.
See also BW 1; CA 65-68; CANR 16

Clark, M. R.
See Clark, Mavis Thorpe

Clark, Mavis Thorpe 1909- .... **CLC 12**
See also CA 57-60; CANR 8, 37; CLR 30;
MAICYA; SAAS 5; SATA 8, 74

Clark, Walter Van Tilburg
1909-1971 .... **CLC 28**
See also CA 9-12R; 33-36R; DLB 9;
SATA 8

Clarke, Arthur C(harles)
1917- ...... **CLC 1, 4, 13, 18, 35; SSC 3**
See also AAYA 4; CA 1-4R; CANR 2, 28;
JRDA; MAICYA; MTCW; SATA 13, 70

Clarke, Austin 1896-1974 .... **CLC 6, 9**
See also CA 29-32; 49-52; CAP 2; DLB 10,
20

Clarke, Austin C(hesterfield)
1934- .... **CLC 8, 53; BLC**
See also BW 1; CA 25-28R; CAAS 16;
CANR 14, 32; DLB 53, 125

Clarke, Gillian 1937- .... **CLC 61**
See also CA 106; DLB 40

Clarke, Marcus (Andrew Hislop)
1846-1881 .... **NCLC 19**

Clarke, Shirley 1925- .... **CLC 16**

Clash, The
See Headon, (Nicky) Topper; Jones, Mick;
Simonon, Paul; Strummer, Joe

Claudel, Paul (Louis Charles Marie)
1868-1955 .... **TCLC 2, 10**
See also CA 104

Clavell, James (duMaresq)
1925- .... **CLC 6, 25**
See also CA 25-28R; CANR 26; MTCW

Cleaver, (Leroy) Eldridge
1935- .... **CLC 30; BLC**
See also BW 1; CA 21-24R; CANR 16

Cleese, John (Marwood) 1939- ..... **CLC 21**
See also Monty Python
See also CA 112; 116; CANR 35; MTCW

Cleishbotham, Jebediah
See Scott, Walter

Cleland, John 1710-1789 .... **LC 2**
See also DLB 39

Clemens, Samuel Langhorne 1835-1910
See Twain, Mark
See also CA 104; 135; CDALB 1865-1917;
DA; DLB 11, 12, 23, 64, 74; JRDA;
MAICYA; YABC 2

Cleophil
See Congreve, William

Corbiere, Tristan 1845-1875 . . . . . **NCLC 43**

Corcoran, Barbara 1911- . . . . **CLC 17**
See also CA 21-24R; CAAS 2; CANR 11,
28; DLB 52; JRDA; SATA 3, 77

Cordelier, Maurice
See Giraudoux, (Hippolyte) Jean

Corelli, Marie 1855-1924 . . . . **TCLC 51**
See also Mackay, Mary
See also DLB 34

Corman, Cid . . . . **CLC 9**
See also Corman, Sidney
See also CAAS 2; DLB 5

Corman, Sidney 1924-
See Corman, Cid
See also CA 85-88; CANR 44

Cormier, Robert (Edmund)
1925- . . . . **CLC 12, 30; DA**
See also AAYA 3; CA 1-4R; CANR 5, 23;
CDALB 1968-1988; CLR 12; DLB 52;
JRDA; MAICYA; MTCW; SATA 10, 45

Corn, Alfred (DeWitt III) 1943- . . . . **CLC 33**
See also CA 104; CANR 44; DLB 120;
DLBY 80

Cornwell, David (John Moore)
1931- . . . . **CLC 9, 15**
See also le Carre, John
See also CA 5-8R; CANR 13, 33; MTCW

Corso, (Nunzio) Gregory 1930- . . . **CLC 1, 11**
See also CA 5-8R; CANR 41; DLB 5, 16;
MTCW

Cortazar, Julio
1914-1984 . . . . . . **CLC 2, 3, 5, 10, 13, 15,
33, 34; HLC; SSC 7**
See also CA 21-24R; CANR 12, 32;
DLB 113; HW; MTCW

Corwin, Cecil
See Kornbluth, C(yril) M.

Cosic, Dobrica 1921- . . . . **CLC 14**
See also CA 122; 138

Costain, Thomas B(ertram)
1885-1965 . . . . **CLC 30**
See also CA 5-8R; 25-28R; DLB 9

Costantini, Humberto
1924(?)-1987 . . . . **CLC 49**
See also CA 131; 122; HW

Costello, Elvis 1955- . . . . **CLC 21**

Cotter, Joseph Seamon Sr.
1861-1949 . . . . **TCLC 28; BLC**
See also BW 1; CA 124; DLB 50

Couch, Arthur Thomas Quiller
See Quiller-Couch, Arthur Thomas

Coulton, James
See Hansen, Joseph

Couperus, Louis (Marie Anne)
1863-1923 . . . . **TCLC 15**
See also CA 115

Coupland, Douglas 1961- . . . . **CLC 85**
See also CA 142

Court, Wesli
See Turco, Lewis (Putnam)

Courtenay, Bryce 1933- . . . . **CLC 59**
See also CA 138

Courtney, Robert
See Ellison, Harlan

Cousteau, Jacques-Yves 1910- . . . . . . **CLC 30**
See also CA 65-68; CANR 15; MTCW;
SATA 38

Coward, Noel (Peirce)
1899-1973 . . . . **CLC 1, 9, 29, 51**
See also AITN 1; CA 17-18; 41-44R;
CANR 35; CAP 2; CDBLB 1914-1945;
DLB 10; MTCW

Cowley, Malcolm 1898-1989 . . . . **CLC 39**
See also CA 5-8R; 128; CANR 3; DLB 4,
48; DLBY 81, 89; MTCW

Cowper, William 1731-1800 . . . . . . **NCLC 8**
See also DLB 104, 109

Cox, William Trevor 1928- . . . **CLC 9, 14, 71**
See also Trevor, William
See also CA 9-12R; CANR 4, 37; DLB 14;
MTCW

Cozzens, James Gould
1903-1978 . . . . **CLC 1, 4, 11**
See also CA 9-12R; 81-84; CANR 19;
CDALB 1941-1968; DLB 9; DLBD 2;
DLBY 84; MTCW

Crabbe, George 1754-1832 . . . . **NCLC 26**
See also DLB 93

Craig, A. A.
See Anderson, Poul (William)

Craik, Dinah Maria (Mulock)
1826-1887 . . . . **NCLC 38**
See also DLB 35; MAICYA; SATA 34

Cram, Ralph Adams 1863-1942 . . . . **TCLC 45**

Crane, (Harold) Hart
1899-1932 . . . . **TCLC 2, 5; DA; PC 3;
WLC**
See also CA 104; 127; CDALB 1917-1929;
DLB 4, 48; MTCW

Crane, R(onald) S(almon)
1886-1967 . . . . **CLC 27**
See also CA 85-88; DLB 63

Crane, Stephen (Townley)
1871-1900 . . . . **TCLC 11, 17, 32; DA;
SSC 7; WLC**
See also CA 109; 140; CDALB 1865-1917;
DLB 12, 54, 78; YABC 2

Crase, Douglas 1944- . . . . **CLC 58**
See also CA 106

Crashaw, Richard 1612(?)-1649 . . . . . . **LC 24**
See also DLB 126

Craven, Margaret 1901-1980 . . . . **CLC 17**
See also CA 103

Crawford, F(rancis) Marion
1854-1909 . . . . **TCLC 10**
See also CA 107; DLB 71

Crawford, Isabella Valancy
1850-1887 . . . . **NCLC 12**
See also DLB 92

Crayon, Geoffrey
See Irving, Washington

Creasey, John 1908-1973 . . . . **CLC 11**
See also CA 5-8R; 41-44R; CANR 8;
DLB 77; MTCW

Crebillon, Claude Prosper Jolyot de (fils)
1707-1777 . . . . **LC 1**

Credo
See Creasey, John

Creeley, Robert (White)
1926- . . . . . **CLC 1, 2, 4, 8, 11, 15, 36, 78**
See also CA 1-4R; CAAS 10; CANR 23, 43;
DLB 5, 16; MTCW

Crews, Harry (Eugene)
1935- . . . . **CLC 6, 23, 49**
See also AITN 1; CA 25-28R; CANR 20;
DLB 6, 143; MTCW

Crichton, (John) Michael
1942- . . . . **CLC 2, 6, 54**
See also AAYA 10; AITN 2; CA 25-28R;
CANR 13, 40; DLBY 81; JRDA;
MTCW; SATA 9

Crispin, Edmund . . . . **CLC 22**
See also Montgomery, (Robert) Bruce
See also DLB 87

Cristofer, Michael 1945(?)- . . . . **CLC 28**
See also CA 110; DLB 7

Croce, Benedetto 1866-1952 . . . . . . **TCLC 37**
See also CA 120

Crockett, David 1786-1836 . . . . **NCLC 8**
See also DLB 3, 11

Crockett, Davy
See Crockett, David

Crofts, Freeman Wills
1879-1957 . . . . **TCLC 55**
See also CA 115; DLB 77

Croker, John Wilson 1780-1857 . . **NCLC 10**
See also DLB 110

Crommelynck, Fernand 1885-1970 . . **CLC 75**
See also CA 89-92

Cronin, A(rchibald) J(oseph)
1896-1981 . . . . **CLC 32**
See also CA 1-4R; 102; CANR 5; SATA 25,
47

Cross, Amanda
See Heilbrun, Carolyn G(old)

Crothers, Rachel 1878(?)-1958. . . . . **TCLC 19**
See also CA 113; DLB 7

Croves, Hal
See Traven, B.

Crowfield, Christopher
See Stowe, Harriet (Elizabeth) Beecher

Crowley, Aleister. . . . . **TCLC 7**
See also Crowley, Edward Alexander

Crowley, Edward Alexander 1875-1947
See Crowley, Aleister
See also CA 104

Crowley, John 1942- . . . . **CLC 57**
See also CA 61-64; CANR 43; DLBY 82;
SATA 65

Crud
See Crumb, R(obert)

Crumarums
See Crumb, R(obert)

Crumb, R(obert) 1943- . . . . **CLC 17**
See also CA 106

Crumbum
See Crumb, R(obert)

Crumski
See Crumb, R(obert)

Crum the Bum
See Crumb, R(obert)

Dickinson, Emily (Elizabeth)
1830-1886 .. NCLC 21; DA; PC 1; WLC
See also CDALB 1865-1917; DLB 1;
SATA 29

Dickinson, Peter (Malcolm)
1927- .... CLC 12, 35
See also AAYA 9; CA 41-44R; CANR 31;
CLR 29; DLB 87; JRDA; MAICYA;
SATA 5, 62

Dickson, Carr
See Carr, John Dickson

Dickson, Carter
See Carr, John Dickson

Diderot, Denis 1713-1784 .... LC 26

Didion, Joan 1934- ..... CLC 1, 3, 8, 14, 32
See also AITN 1; CA 5-8R; CANR 14;
CDALB 1968-1988; DLB 2; DLBY 81,
86; MTCW

Dietrich, Robert
See Hunt, E(verette) Howard, Jr.

Dillard, Annie 1945- .... CLC 9, 60
See also AAYA 6; CA 49-52; CANR 3, 43;
DLBY 80; MTCW; SATA 10

Dillard, R(ichard) H(enry) W(ilde)
1937- .... CLC 5
See also CA 21-24R; CAAS 7; CANR 10;
DLB 5

Dillon, Eilis 1920- .... CLC 17
See also CA 9-12R; CAAS 3; CANR 4, 38;
CLR 26; MAICYA; SATA 2, 74

Dimont, Penelope
See Mortimer, Penelope (Ruth)

Dinesen, Isak .... CLC 10, 29; SSC 7
See also Blixen, Karen (Christentze
Dinesen)

Ding Ling .... CLC 68
See also Chiang Pin-chin

Disch, Thomas M(ichael) 1940- ... CLC 7, 36
See also CA 21-24R; CAAS 4; CANR 17,
36; CLR 18; DLB 8; MAICYA; MTCW;
SAAS 15; SATA 54

Disch, Tom
See Disch, Thomas M(ichael)

d'Isly, Georges
See Simenon, Georges (Jacques Christian)

Disraeli, Benjamin 1804-1881 .. NCLC 2, 39
See also DLB 21, 55

Ditcum, Steve
See Crumb, R(obert)

Dixon, Paige
See Corcoran, Barbara

Dixon, Stephen 1936- ..... CLC 52; SSC 16
See also CA 89-92; CANR 17, 40; DLB 130

Dobell, Sydney Thompson
1824-1874 .... NCLC 43
See also DLB 32

Doblin, Alfred .... TCLC 13
See also Doeblin, Alfred

Dobrolyubov, Nikolai Alexandrovich
1836-1861 .... NCLC 5

Dobyns, Stephen 1941- .... CLC 37
See also CA 45-48; CANR 2, 18

Doctorow, E(dgar) L(aurence)
1931- .... CLC 6, 11, 15, 18, 37, 44, 65
See also AITN 2; BEST 89:3; CA 45-48;
CANR 2, 33; CDALB 1968-1988; DLB 2,
28; DLBY 80; MTCW

Dodgson, Charles Lutwidge 1832-1898
See Carroll, Lewis
See also CLR 2; DA; MAICYA; YABC 2

Dodson, Owen (Vincent)
1914-1983 .... CLC 79; BLC
See also BW 1; CA 65-68; 110; CANR 24;
DLB 76

Doeblin, Alfred 1878-1957 .... TCLC 13
See also Doblin, Alfred
See also CA 110; 141; DLB 66

Doerr, Harriet 1910- .... CLC 34
See also CA 117; 122

Domecq, H(onorio) Bustos
See Bioy Casares, Adolfo; Borges, Jorge
Luis

Domini, Rey
See Lorde, Audre (Geraldine)

Dominique
See Proust, (Valentin-Louis-George-Eugene-)
Marcel

Don, A
See Stephen, Leslie

Donaldson, Stephen R. 1947- .... CLC 46
See also CA 89-92; CANR 13

Donleavy, J(ames) P(atrick)
1926- .... CLC 1, 4, 6, 10, 45
See also AITN 2; CA 9-12R; CANR 24;
DLB 6; MTCW

Donne, John
1572-1631 .... LC 10, 24; DA; PC 1
See also CDBLB Before 1660; DLB 121

Donnell, David 1939(?)- .... CLC 34

Donoso (Yanez), Jose
1924- .... CLC 4, 8, 11, 32; HLC
See also CA 81-84; CANR 32; DLB 113;
HW; MTCW

Donovan, John 1928-1992 .... CLC 35
See also CA 97-100; 137; CLR 3;
MAICYA; SATA 29

Don Roberto
See Cunninghame Graham, R(obert)
B(ontine)

Doolittle, Hilda
1886-1961 ..... CLC 3, 8, 14, 31, 34, 73;
DA; PC 5; WLC
See also H. D.
See also CA 97-100; CANR 35; DLB 4, 45;
MTCW

Dorfman, Ariel 1942- .... CLC 48, 77; HLC
See also CA 124; 130; HW

Dorn, Edward (Merton) 1929- ... CLC 10, 18
See also CA 93-96; CANR 42; DLB 5

Dorsan, Luc
See Simenon, Georges (Jacques Christian)

Dorsange, Jean
See Simenon, Georges (Jacques Christian)

Dos Passos, John (Roderigo)
1896-1970 ...... CLC 1, 4, 8, 11, 15, 25,
34, 82; DA; WLC
See also CA 1-4R; 29-32R; CANR 3;
CDALB 1929-1941; DLB 4, 9; DLBD 1;
MTCW

Dossage, Jean
See Simenon, Georges (Jacques Christian)

Dostoevsky, Fedor Mikhailovich
1821-1881 ...... NCLC 2, 7, 21, 33, 43;
DA; SSC 2; WLC

Doughty, Charles M(ontagu)
1843-1926 .... TCLC 27
See also CA 115; DLB 19, 57

Douglas, Ellen .... CLC 73
See also Haxton, Josephine Ayres;
Williamson, Ellen Douglas

Douglas, Gavin 1475(?)-1522 .... LC 20

Douglas, Keith 1920-1944 .... TCLC 40
See also DLB 27

Douglas, Leonard
See Bradbury, Ray (Douglas)

Douglas, Michael
See Crichton, (John) Michael

Douglass, Frederick
1817(?)-1895 .... NCLC 7; BLC; DA;
WLC
See also CDALB 1640-1865; DLB 1, 43, 50,
79; SATA 29

Dourado, (Waldomiro Freitas) Autran
1926- .... CLC 23, 60
See also CA 25-28R; CANR 34

Dourado, Waldomiro Autran
See Dourado, (Waldomiro Freitas) Autran

Dove, Rita (Frances)
1952- .... CLC 50, 81; PC 6
See also BW 2; CA 109; CAAS 19;
CANR 27, 42; DLB 120

Dowell, Coleman 1925-1985........ CLC 60
See also CA 25-28R; 117; CANR 10;
DLB 130

Dowson, Ernest Christopher
1867-1900 .... TCLC 4
See also CA 105; DLB 19, 135

Doyle, A. Conan
See Doyle, Arthur Conan

Doyle, Arthur Conan
1859-1930 .... TCLC 7; DA; SSC 12;
WLC
See also CA 104; 122; CDBLB 1890-1914;
DLB 18, 70; MTCW; SATA 24

Doyle, Conan
See Doyle, Arthur Conan

Doyle, John
See Graves, Robert (von Ranke)

Doyle, Roddy 1958(?)- .... CLC 81
See also CA 143

Doyle, Sir A. Conan
See Doyle, Arthur Conan

Doyle, Sir Arthur Conan
See Doyle, Arthur Conan

Dr. A
See Asimov, Isaac; Silverstein, Alvin

Drabble, Margaret
　1939- . . . . **CLC 2, 3, 5, 8, 10, 22, 53**
　See also CA 13-16R; CANR 18, 35;
　CDBLB 1960 to Present; DLB 14;
　MTCW; SATA 48

Drapier, M. B.
　See Swift, Jonathan

Drayham, James
　See Mencken, H(enry) L(ouis)

Drayton, Michael　1563-1631 . . . . **LC 8**

Dreadstone, Carl
　See Campbell, (John) Ramsey

Dreiser, Theodore (Herman Albert)
　1871-1945 . . . . **TCLC 10, 18, 35; DA;**
　　　　　　　　　　　　　　　　　　　WLC
　See also CA 106; 132; CDALB 1865-1917;
　DLB 9, 12, 102, 137; DLBD 1; MTCW

Drexler, Rosalyn　1926- . . . . **CLC 2, 6**
　See also CA 81-84

Dreyer, Carl Theodor　1889-1968 . . . . **CLC 16**
　See also CA 116

Drieu la Rochelle, Pierre(-Eugene)
　1893-1945 . . . . **TCLC 21**
　See also CA 117; DLB 72

Drinkwater, John　1882-1937 . . . . . **TCLC 57**
　See also CA 109; DLB 10, 19

Drop Shot
　See Cable, George Washington

Droste-Hulshoff, Annette Freiin von
　1797-1848 . . . . **NCLC 3**
　See also DLB 133

Drummond, Walter
　See Silverberg, Robert

Drummond, William Henry
　1854-1907 . . . . **TCLC 25**
　See also DLB 92

Drummond de Andrade, Carlos
　1902-1987 . . . . **CLC 18**
　See also Andrade, Carlos Drummond de
　See also CA 132; 123

Drury, Allen (Stuart)　1918- . . . . **CLC 37**
　See also CA 57-60; CANR 18

Dryden, John
　1631-1700 . . . **LC 3, 21; DA; DC 3; WLC**
　See also CDBLB 1660-1789; DLB 80, 101,
　131

Duberman, Martin　1930- . . . . **CLC 8**
　See also CA 1-4R; CANR 2

Dubie, Norman (Evans)　1945- . . . . . . **CLC 36**
　See also CA 69-72; CANR 12; DLB 120

Du Bois, W(illiam) E(dward) B(urghardt)
　1868-1963 . . . . . . **CLC 1, 2, 13, 64; BLC;**
　　　　　　　　　　　　　　　　　DA; WLC
　See also BW 1; CA 85-88; CANR 34;
　CDALB 1865-1917; DLB 47, 50, 91;
　MTCW; SATA 42

Dubus, Andre　1936- . . . **CLC 13, 36; SSC 15**
　See also CA 21-24R; CANR 17; DLB 130

Duca Minimo
　See D'Annunzio, Gabriele

Ducharme, Rejean　1941- . . . . **CLC 74**
　See also DLB 60

Duclos, Charles Pinot　1704-1772 . . . . . **LC 1**

Dudek, Louis　1918- . . . . **CLC 11, 19**
　See also CA 45-48; CAAS 14; CANR 1;
　DLB 88

Duerrenmatt, Friedrich
　1921-1990 . . . . . **CLC 1, 4, 8, 11, 15, 43**
　See also CA 17-20R; CANR 33; DLB 69,
　124; MTCW

Duffy, Bruce　(?)- . . . . **CLC 50**

Duffy, Maureen　1933- . . . . **CLC 37**
　See also CA 25-28R; CANR 33; DLB 14;
　MTCW

Dugan, Alan　1923- . . . . **CLC 2, 6**
　See also CA 81-84; DLB 5

du Gard, Roger Martin
　See Martin du Gard, Roger

Duhamel, Georges　1884-1966 . . . . **CLC 8**
　See also CA 81-84; 25-28R; CANR 35;
　DLB 65; MTCW

Dujardin, Edouard (Emile Louis)
　1861-1949 . . . . **TCLC 13**
　See also CA 109; DLB 123

Dumas, Alexandre (Davy de la Pailleterie)
　1802-1870 . . . . **NCLC 11; DA; WLC**
　See also DLB 119; SATA 18

Dumas, Alexandre
　1824-1895 . . . . **NCLC 9; DC 1**

Dumas, Claudine
　See Malzberg, Barry N(athaniel)

Dumas, Henry L.　1934-1968 . . . . . **CLC 6, 62**
　See also BW 1; CA 85-88; DLB 41

du Maurier, Daphne
　1907-1989 . . . . **CLC 6, 11, 59**
　See also CA 5-8R; 128; CANR 6; MTCW;
　SATA 27, 60

Dunbar, Paul Laurence
　1872-1906 . . . . . . **TCLC 2, 12; BLC; DA;**
　　　　　　　　　　　　　　PC 5; SSC 8; WLC
　See also BW 1; CA 104; 124;
　CDALB 1865-1917; DLB 50, 54, 78;
　SATA 34

Dunbar, William　1460(?)-1530(?) . . . . **LC 20**

Duncan, Lois　1934- . . . . **CLC 26**
　See also AAYA 4; CA 1-4R; CANR 2, 23,
　36; CLR 29; JRDA; MAICYA; SAAS 2;
　SATA 1, 36, 75

Duncan, Robert (Edward)
　1919-1988 . . . . **CLC 1, 2, 4, 7, 15, 41, 55;**
　　　　　　　　　　　　　　　　　　　　PC 2
　See also CA 9-12R; 124; CANR 28; DLB 5,
　16; MTCW

Dunlap, William　1766-1839 . . . . **NCLC 2**
　See also DLB 30, 37, 59

Dunn, Douglas (Eaglesham)
　1942- . . . . **CLC 6, 40**
　See also CA 45-48; CANR 2, 33; DLB 40;
　MTCW

Dunn, Katherine (Karen)　1945- . . . . . **CLC 71**
　See also CA 33-36R

Dunn, Stephen　1939- . . . . **CLC 36**
　See also CA 33-36R; CANR 12; DLB 105

Dunne, Finley Peter　1867-1936 . . . . **TCLC 28**
　See also CA 108; DLB 11, 23

Dunne, John Gregory　1932- . . . . **CLC 28**
　See also CA 25-28R; CANR 14; DLBY 80

Dunsany, Edward John Moreton Drax
　Plunkett　1878-1957
　See Dunsany, Lord
　See also CA 104; DLB 10

Dunsany, Lord . . . . **TCLC 2**
　See also Dunsany, Edward John Moreton
　Drax Plunkett
　See also DLB 77

du Perry, Jean
　See Simenon, Georges (Jacques Christian)

Durang, Christopher (Ferdinand)
　1949- . . . . **CLC 27, 38**
　See also CA 105

Duras, Marguerite
　1914- . . . . . . **CLC 3, 6, 11, 20, 34, 40, 68**
　See also CA 25-28R; DLB 83; MTCW

Durban, (Rosa) Pam　1947- . . . . **CLC 39**
　See also CA 123

Durcan, Paul　1944- . . . . **CLC 43, 70**
　See also CA 134

Durkheim, Emile　1858-1917 . . . . . . **TCLC 55**

Durrell, Lawrence (George)
　1912-1990 . . . . **CLC 1, 4, 6, 8, 13, 27, 41**
　See also CA 9-12R; 132; CANR 40;
　CDBLB 1945-1960; DLB 15, 27;
　DLBY 90; MTCW

Durrenmatt, Friedrich
　See Duerrenmatt, Friedrich

Dutt, Toru　1856-1877 . . . . **NCLC 29**

Dwight, Timothy　1752-1817 . . . . . . **NCLC 13**
　See also DLB 37

Dworkin, Andrea　1946- . . . . **CLC 43**
　See also CA 77-80; CANR 16, 39; MTCW

Dwyer, Deanna
　See Koontz, Dean R(ay)

Dwyer, K. R.
　See Koontz, Dean R(ay)

Dylan, Bob　1941- . . . . . . **CLC 3, 4, 6, 12, 77**
　See also CA 41-44R; DLB 16

Eagleton, Terence (Francis)　1943-
　See Eagleton, Terry
　See also CA 57-60; CANR 7, 23; MTCW

Eagleton, Terry . . . . **CLC 63**
　See also Eagleton, Terence (Francis)

Early, Jack
　See Scoppettone, Sandra

East, Michael
　See West, Morris L(anglo)

Eastaway, Edward
　See Thomas, (Philip) Edward

Eastlake, William (Derry)　1917- . . . . . **CLC 8**
　See also CA 5-8R; CAAS 1; CANR 5;
　DLB 6

Eastman, Charles A(lexander)
　1858-1939 . . . . **TCLC 55**
　See also YABC 1

Eberhart, Richard (Ghormley)
　1904- . . . . **CLC 3, 11, 19, 56**
　See also CA 1-4R; CANR 2;
　CDALB 1941-1968; DLB 48; MTCW

Eberstadt, Fernanda　1960- . . . . **CLC 39**
　See also CA 136

Endo, Shusaku 1923- ..... **CLC 7, 14, 19, 54**
　　See also CA 29-32R; CANR 21; MTCW

Engel, Marian 1933-1985 .... **CLC 36**
　　See also CA 25-28R; CANR 12; DLB 53

Engelhardt, Frederick
　　See Hubbard, L(afayette) Ron(ald)

Enright, D(ennis) J(oseph)
　　1920- .... **CLC 4, 8, 31**
　　See also CA 1-4R; CANR 1, 42; DLB 27;
　　SATA 25

Enzensberger, Hans Magnus
　　1929- .... **CLC 43**
　　See also CA 116; 119

Ephron, Nora 1941- ...... **CLC 17, 31**
　　See also AITN 2; CA 65-68; CANR 12, 39

Epsilon
　　See Betjeman, John

Epstein, Daniel Mark 1948- .... **CLC 7**
　　See also CA 49-52; CANR 2

Epstein, Jacob 1956- .... **CLC 19**
　　See also CA 114

Epstein, Joseph 1937-............. **CLC 39**
　　See also CA 112; 119

Epstein, Leslie 1938- .... **CLC 27**
　　See also CA 73-76; CAAS 12; CANR 23

Equiano, Olaudah
　　1745(?)-1797 .... **LC 16; BLC**
　　See also DLB 37, 50

Erasmus, Desiderius 1469(?)-1536.... **LC 16**

Erdman, Paul E(mil) 1932- .... **CLC 25**
　　See also AITN 1; CA 61-64; CANR 13, 43

Erdrich, Louise 1954-.......... **CLC 39, 54**
　　See also AAYA 10; BEST 89:1; CA 114;
　　CANR 41; MTCW

Erenburg, Ilya (Grigoryevich)
　　See Ehrenburg, Ilya (Grigoryevich)

Erickson, Stephen Michael 1950-
　　See Erickson, Steve
　　See also CA 129

Erickson, Steve .... **CLC 64**
　　See also Erickson, Stephen Michael

Ericson, Walter
　　See Fast, Howard (Melvin)

Eriksson, Buntel
　　See Bergman, (Ernst) Ingmar

Eschenbach, Wolfram von
　　See Wolfram von Eschenbach

Eseki, Bruno
　　See Mphahlele, Ezekiel

Esenin, Sergei (Alexandrovich)
　　1895-1925 .... **TCLC 4**
　　See also CA 104

Eshleman, Clayton 1935-........... **CLC 7**
　　See also CA 33-36R; CAAS 6; DLB 5

Espriella, Don Manuel Alvarez
　　See Southey, Robert

Espriu, Salvador 1913-1985........ **CLC 9**
　　See also CA 115; DLB 134

Espronceda, Jose de 1808-1842... **NCLC 39**

Esse, James
　　See Stephens, James

Esterbrook, Tom
　　See Hubbard, L(afayette) Ron(ald)

Estleman, Loren D. 1952- .... **CLC 48**
　　See also CA 85-88; CANR 27; MTCW

Eugenides, Jeffrey 1960(?)- .... **CLC 81**
　　See also CA 144

Euripides c. 485B.C.-406B.C. .... **DC 4**
　　See also DA

Evan, Evin
　　See Faust, Frederick (Schiller)

Evans, Evan
　　See Faust, Frederick (Schiller)

Evans, Marian
　　See Eliot, George

Evans, Mary Ann
　　See Eliot, George

Evarts, Esther
　　See Benson, Sally

Everett, Percival L. 1956- .... **CLC 57**
　　See also BW 2; CA 129

Everson, R(onald) G(ilmour)
　　1903- .... **CLC 27**
　　See also CA 17-20R; DLB 88

Everson, William (Oliver)
　　1912-1994 .... **CLC 1, 5, 14**
　　See also CA 9-12R; 145; CANR 20; DLB 5,
　　16; MTCW

Evtushenko, Evgenii Aleksandrovich
　　See Yevtushenko, Yevgeny (Alexandrovich)

Ewart, Gavin (Buchanan)
　　1916- .... **CLC 13, 46**
　　See also CA 89-92; CANR 17; DLB 40;
　　MTCW

Ewers, Hanns Heinz 1871-1943 ... **TCLC 12**
　　See also CA 109

Ewing, Frederick R.
　　See Sturgeon, Theodore (Hamilton)

Exley, Frederick (Earl)
　　1929-1992 .... **CLC 6, 11**
　　See also AITN 2; CA 81-84; 138; DLB 143;
　　DLBY 81

Eynhardt, Guillermo
　　See Quiroga, Horacio (Sylvestre)

Ezekiel, Nissim 1924-............. **CLC 61**
　　See also CA 61-64

Ezekiel, Tish O'Dowd 1943- .... **CLC 34**
　　See also CA 129

Fadeyev, A.
　　See Bulgya, Alexander Alexandrovich

Fadeyev, Alexander............... **TCLC 53**
　　See also Bulgya, Alexander Alexandrovich

Fagen, Donald 1948-............. **CLC 26**

Fainzilberg, Ilya Arnoldovich 1897-1937
　　See Ilf, Ilya
　　See also CA 120

Fair, Ronald L. 1932-............. **CLC 18**
　　See also BW 1; CA 69-72; CANR 25;
　　DLB 33

Fairbairns, Zoe (Ann) 1948- .... **CLC 32**
　　See also CA 103; CANR 21

Falco, Gian
　　See Papini, Giovanni

Falconer, James
　　See Kirkup, James

Falconer, Kenneth
　　See Kornbluth, C(yril) M.

Falkland, Samuel
　　See Heijermans, Herman

Fallaci, Oriana 1930-............. **CLC 11**
　　See also CA 77-80; CANR 15; MTCW

Faludy, George 1913-............. **CLC 42**
　　See also CA 21-24R

Faludy, Gyoergy
　　See Faludy, George

Fanon, Frantz 1925-1961..... **CLC 74; BLC**
　　See also BW 1; CA 116; 89-92

Fanshawe, Ann 1625-1680 .... **LC 11**

Fante, John (Thomas) 1911-1983 ... **CLC 60**
　　See also CA 69-72; 109; CANR 23;
　　DLB 130; DLBY 83

Farah, Nuruddin 1945-........ **CLC 53; BLC**
　　See also BW 2; CA 106; DLB 125

Fargue, Leon-Paul 1876(?)-1947 ... **TCLC 11**
　　See also CA 109

Farigoule, Louis
　　See Romains, Jules

Farina, Richard 1936(?)-1966 .... **CLC 9**
　　See also CA 81-84; 25-28R

Farley, Walter (Lorimer)
　　1915-1989 .... **CLC 17**
　　See also CA 17-20R; CANR 8, 29; DLB 22;
　　JRDA; MAICYA; SATA 2, 43

Farmer, Philip Jose 1918-....... **CLC 1, 19**
　　See also CA 1-4R; CANR 4, 35; DLB 8;
　　MTCW

Farquhar, George 1677-1707....... **LC 21**
　　See also DLB 84

Farrell, J(ames) G(ordon)
　　1935-1979 .... **CLC 6**
　　See also CA 73-76; 89-92; CANR 36;
　　DLB 14; MTCW

Farrell, James T(homas)
　　1904-1979 .... **CLC 1, 4, 8, 11, 66**
　　See also CA 5-8R; 89-92; CANR 9; DLB 4,
　　9, 86; DLBD 2; MTCW

Farren, Richard J.
　　See Betjeman, John

Farren, Richard M.
　　See Betjeman, John

Fassbinder, Rainer Werner
　　1946-1982 .... **CLC 20**
　　See also CA 93-96; 106; CANR 31

Fast, Howard (Melvin) 1914- ...... **CLC 23**
　　See also CA 1-4R; CAAS 18; CANR 1, 33;
　　DLB 9; SATA 7

Faulcon, Robert
　　See Holdstock, Robert P.

Faulkner, William (Cuthbert)
　　1897-1962 ..... **CLC 1, 3, 6, 8, 9, 11, 14,**
　　18, 28, 52, 68; DA; SSC 1; WLC
　　See also AAYA 7; CA 81-84; CANR 33;
　　CDALB 1929-1941; DLB 9, 11, 44, 102;
　　DLBD 2; DLBY 86; MTCW

Fauset, Jessie Redmon
　　1884(?)-1961 .... **CLC 19, 54; BLC**
　　See also BW 1; CA 109; DLB 51

Forche, Carolyn (Louise)
　　1950- . . . . **CLC 25, 83; PC 10**
　　See also CA 109; 117; DLB 5

Ford, Elbur
　　See Hibbert, Eleanor Alice Burford

Ford, Ford Madox
　　1873-1939 . . . . **TCLC 1, 15, 39, 57**
　　See also CA 104; 132; CDBLB 1914-1945;
　　DLB 34, 98; MTCW

Ford, John　1895-1973. . . . . **CLC 16**
　　See also CA 45-48

Ford, Richard　1944- . . . . **CLC 46**
　　See also CA 69-72; CANR 11

Ford, Webster
　　See Masters, Edgar Lee

Foreman, Richard　1937-. . . . . **CLC 50**
　　See also CA 65-68; CANR 32

Forester, C(ecil) S(cott)
　　1899-1966 . . . . **CLC 35**
　　See also CA 73-76; 25-28R; SATA 13

Forez
　　See Mauriac, Francois (Charles)

Forman, James Douglas　1932-. . . . . . **CLC 21**
　　See also CA 9-12R; CANR 4, 19, 42;
　　JRDA; MAICYA; SATA 8, 70

Fornes, Maria Irene　1930-. . . . . . **CLC 39, 61**
　　See also CA 25-28R; CANR 28; DLB 7;
　　HW; MTCW

Forrest, Leon　1937- . . . . **CLC 4**
　　See also BW 2; CA 89-92; CAAS 7;
　　CANR 25; DLB 33

Forster, E(dward) M(organ)
　　1879-1970 . . . . . **CLC 1, 2, 3, 4, 9, 10, 13,**
　　　　　　　　　　　　　　15, 22, 45, 77; DA; WLC
　　See also AAYA 2; CA 13-14; 25-28R;
　　CANR 45; CAP 1; CDBLB 1914-1945;
　　DLB 34, 98; DLBD 10; MTCW;
　　SATA 57

Forster, John　1812-1876 . . . . **NCLC 11**
　　See also DLB 144

Forsyth, Frederick　1938- . . . . . . **CLC 2, 5, 36**
　　See also BEST 89:4; CA 85-88; CANR 38;
　　DLB 87; MTCW

Forten, Charlotte L. . . . . **TCLC 16; BLC**
　　See also Grimke, Charlotte L(ottie) Forten
　　See also DLB 50

Foscolo, Ugo　1778-1827. . . . . **NCLC 8**

Fosse, Bob . . . . **CLC 20**
　　See also Fosse, Robert Louis

Fosse, Robert Louis　1927-1987
　　See Fosse, Bob
　　See also CA 110; 123

Foster, Stephen Collins
　　1826-1864 . . . . **NCLC 26**

Foucault, Michel
　　1926-1984 . . . . **CLC 31, 34, 69**
　　See also CA 105; 113; CANR 34; MTCW

Fouque, Friedrich (Heinrich Karl) de la Motte
　　1777-1843 . . . . **NCLC 2**
　　See also DLB 90

Fournier, Henri Alban　1886-1914
　　See Alain-Fournier
　　See also CA 104

Fournier, Pierre　1916- . . . . **CLC 11**
　　See Gascar, Pierre
　　See also CA 89-92; CANR 16, 40

Fowles, John
　　1926- . . . . **CLC 1, 2, 3, 4, 6, 9, 10, 15, 33**
　　See also CA 5-8R; CANR 25; CDBLB 1960
　　to Present; DLB 14, 139; MTCW;
　　SATA 22

Fox, Paula　1923-. . . . . **CLC 2, 8**
　　See also AAYA 3; CA 73-76; CANR 20,
　　36; CLR 1; DLB 52; JRDA; MAICYA;
　　MTCW; SATA 17, 60

Fox, William Price (Jr.)　1926- . . . . . **CLC 22**
　　See also CA 17-20R; CAAS 19; CANR 11;
　　DLB 2; DLBY 81

Foxe, John　1516(?)-1587 . . . . **LC 14**

Frame, Janet . . . . **CLC 2, 3, 6, 22, 66**
　　See also Clutha, Janet Paterson Frame

France, Anatole. . . . . **TCLC 9**
　　See also Thibault, Jacques Anatole Francois
　　See also DLB 123

Francis, Claude　19(?)- . . . . **CLC 50**

Francis, Dick　1920- . . . . **CLC 2, 22, 42**
　　See also AAYA 5; BEST 89:3; CA 5-8R;
　　CANR 9, 42; CDBLB 1960 to Present;
　　DLB 87; MTCW

Francis, Robert (Churchill)
　　1901-1987 . . . . **CLC 15**
　　See also CA 1-4R; 123; CANR 1

Frank, Anne(lies Marie)
　　1929-1945 . . . . **TCLC 17; DA; WLC**
　　See also AAYA 12; CA 113; 133; MTCW;
　　SATA 42

Frank, Elizabeth　1945-. . . . . **CLC 39**
　　See also CA 121; 126

Franklin, Benjamin
　　See Hasek, Jaroslav (Matej Frantisek)

Franklin, Benjamin　1706-1790. . . **LC 25; DA**
　　See also CDALB 1640-1865; DLB 24, 43,
　　73

Franklin, (Stella Maraia Sarah) Miles
　　1879-1954 . . . . **TCLC 7**
　　See also CA 104

Fraser, (Lady) Antonia (Pakenham)
　　1932- . . . . **CLC 32**
　　See also CA 85-88; CANR 44; MTCW;
　　SATA 32

Fraser, George MacDonald　1925-. . . . **CLC 7**
　　See also CA 45-48; CANR 2

Fraser, Sylvia　1935-. . . . . **CLC 64**
　　See also CA 45-48; CANR 1, 16

Frayn, Michael　1933-. . . . . . **CLC 3, 7, 31, 47**
　　See also CA 5-8R; CANR 30; DLB 13, 14;
　　MTCW

Fraze, Candida (Merrill)　1945- . . . . . **CLC 50**
　　See also CA 126

Frazer, J(ames) G(eorge)
　　1854-1941 . . . . **TCLC 32**
　　See also CA 118

Frazer, Robert Caine
　　See Creasey, John

Frazer, Sir James George
　　See Frazer, J(ames) G(eorge)

Frazier, Ian　1951-. . . . . **CLC 46**
　　See also CA 130

Frederic, Harold　1856-1898. . . . . . **NCLC 10**
　　See also DLB 12, 23

Frederick, John
　　See Faust, Frederick (Schiller)

Frederick the Great　1712-1786 . . . . . . **LC 14**

Fredro, Aleksander　1793-1876. . . . . **NCLC 8**

Freeling, Nicolas　1927- . . . . **CLC 38**
　　See also CA 49-52; CAAS 12; CANR 1, 17;
　　DLB 87

Freeman, Douglas Southall
　　1886-1953 . . . . **TCLC 11**
　　See also CA 109; DLB 17

Freeman, Judith　1946-. . . . . **CLC 55**

Freeman, Mary Eleanor Wilkins
　　1852-1930 . . . . **TCLC 9; SSC 1**
　　See also CA 106; DLB 12, 78

Freeman, R(ichard) Austin
　　1862-1943 . . . . **TCLC 21**
　　See also CA 113; DLB 70

French, Marilyn　1929-. . . . . . **CLC 10, 18, 60**
　　See also CA 69-72; CANR 3, 31; MTCW

French, Paul
　　See Asimov, Isaac

Freneau, Philip Morin　1752-1832. . **NCLC 1**
　　See also DLB 37, 43

Freud, Sigmund　1856-1939 . . . . **TCLC 52**
　　See also CA 115; 133; MTCW

Friedan, Betty (Naomi)　1921-. . . . . . **CLC 74**
　　See also CA 65-68; CANR 18, 45; MTCW

Friedman, B(ernard) H(arper)
　　1926- . . . . **CLC 7**
　　See also CA 1-4R; CANR 3

Friedman, Bruce Jay　1930- . . . . **CLC 3, 5, 56**
　　See also CA 9-12R; CANR 25; DLB 2, 28

Friel, Brian　1929-. . . . . **CLC 5, 42, 59**
　　See also CA 21-24R; CANR 33; DLB 13;
　　MTCW

Friis-Baastad, Babbis Ellinor
　　1921-1970 . . . . **CLC 12**
　　See also CA 17-20R; 134; SATA 7

Frisch, Max (Rudolf)
　　1911-1991 . . . . . **CLC 3, 9, 14, 18, 32, 44**
　　See also CA 85-88; 134; CANR 32;
　　DLB 69, 124; MTCW

Fromentin, Eugene (Samuel Auguste)
　　1820-1876 . . . . **NCLC 10**
　　See also DLB 123

Frost, Frederick
　　See Faust, Frederick (Schiller)

Frost, Robert (Lee)
　　1874-1963 . . . . **CLC 1, 3, 4, 9, 10, 13, 15,**
　　　　　　　　　　　　26, 34, 44; DA; PC 1; WLC
　　See also CA 89-92; CANR 33;
　　CDALB 1917-1929; DLB 54; DLBD 7;
　　MTCW; SATA 14

Froude, James Anthony
　　1818-1894 . . . . **NCLC 43**
　　See also DLB 18, 57, 144

Froy, Herald
　　See Waterhouse, Keith (Spencer)

Fry, Christopher　1907-. . . . . . . **CLC 2, 10, 14**
　　See also CA 17-20R; CANR 9, 30; DLB 13;
　　MTCW; SATA 66

Frye, (Herman) Northrop
1912-1991 . . . . **CLC 24, 70**
See also CA 5-8R; 133; CANR 8, 37;
DLB 67, 68; MTCW

Fuchs, Daniel 1909-1993 . . . . **CLC 8, 22**
See also CA 81-84; 142; CAAS 5;
CANR 40; DLB 9, 26, 28; DLBY 93

Fuchs, Daniel 1934- . . . . **CLC 34**
See also CA 37-40R; CANR 14

Fuentes, Carlos
1928- . . . . . . **CLC 3, 8, 10, 13, 22, 41, 60;**
DA; HLC; WLC
See also AAYA 4; AITN 2; CA 69-72;
CANR 10, 32; DLB 113; HW; MTCW

Fuentes, Gregorio Lopez y
See Lopez y Fuentes, Gregorio

Fugard, (Harold) Athol
1932- . . . . **CLC 5, 9, 14, 25, 40, 80; DC 3**
See also CA 85-88; CANR 32; MTCW

Fugard, Sheila 1932- . . . . **CLC 48**
See also CA 125

Fuller, Charles (H., Jr.)
1939- . . . . **CLC 25; BLC; DC 1**
See also BW 2; CA 108; 112; DLB 38;
MTCW

Fuller, John (Leopold) 1937- . . . . **CLC 62**
See also CA 21-24R; CANR 9, 44; DLB 40

Fuller, Margaret . . . . **NCLC 5**
See also Ossoli, Sarah Margaret (Fuller
marchesa d')

Fuller, Roy (Broadbent)
1912-1991 . . . . **CLC 4, 28**
See also CA 5-8R; 135; CAAS 10; DLB 15,
20

Fulton, Alice 1952- . . . . **CLC 52**
See also CA 116

Furphy, Joseph 1843-1912 . . . . **TCLC 25**

Fussell, Paul 1924- . . . . **CLC 74**
See also BEST 90:1; CA 17-20R; CANR 8,
21, 35; MTCW

Futabatei, Shimei 1864-1909 . . . . . . **TCLC 44**

Futrelle, Jacques 1875-1912 . . . . . . **TCLC 19**
See also CA 113

Gaboriau, Emile 1835-1873 . . . . . . **NCLC 14**

Gadda, Carlo Emilio 1893-1973 . . . . **CLC 11**
See also CA 89-92

Gaddis, William
1922- . . . . **CLC 1, 3, 6, 8, 10, 19, 43**
See also CA 17-20R; CANR 21; DLB 2;
MTCW

Gaines, Ernest J(ames)
1933- . . . . **CLC 3, 11, 18; BLC**
See also AITN 1; BW 2; CA 9-12R;
CANR 6, 24, 42; CDALB 1968-1988;
DLB 2, 33; DLBY 80; MTCW

Gaitskill, Mary 1954- . . . . **CLC 69**
See also CA 128

Galdos, Benito Perez
See Perez Galdos, Benito

Gale, Zona 1874-1938 . . . . **TCLC 7**
See also CA 105; DLB 9, 78

Galeano, Eduardo (Hughes) 1940- . . **CLC 72**
See also CA 29-32R; CANR 13, 32; HW

Galiano, Juan Valera y Alcala
See Valera y Alcala-Galiano, Juan

Gallagher, Tess 1943- . . . . **CLC 18, 63; PC 9**
See also CA 106; DLB 120

Gallant, Mavis
1922- . . . . **CLC 7, 18, 38; SSC 5**
See also CA 69-72; CANR 29; DLB 53;
MTCW

Gallant, Roy A(rthur) 1924- . . . . **CLC 17**
See also CA 5-8R; CANR 4, 29; CLR 30;
MAICYA; SATA 4, 68

Gallico, Paul (William) 1897-1976 . . . **CLC 2**
See also AITN 1; CA 5-8R; 69-72;
CANR 23; DLB 9; MAICYA; SATA 13

Gallup, Ralph
See Whitemore, Hugh (John)

Galsworthy, John
1867-1933 . . . . **TCLC 1, 45; DA; WLC 2**
See also CA 104; 141; CDBLB 1890-1914;
DLB 10, 34, 98

Galt, John 1779-1839 . . . . **NCLC 1**
See also DLB 99, 116

Galvin, James 1951- . . . . **CLC 38**
See also CA 108; CANR 26

Gamboa, Federico 1864-1939 . . . . . . **TCLC 36**

Gann, Ernest Kellogg 1910-1991 . . . . **CLC 23**
See also AITN 1; CA 1-4R; 136; CANR 1

Garcia, Cristina 1958- . . . . **CLC 76**
See also CA 141

Garcia Lorca, Federico
1898-1936 . . . . **TCLC 1, 7, 49; DA;**
DC 2; HLC; PC 3; WLC
See also CA 104; 131; DLB 108; HW;
MTCW

Garcia Marquez, Gabriel (Jose)
1928- . . . . **CLC 2, 3, 8, 10, 15, 27, 47, 55,**
68; DA; HLC; SSC 8; WLC
See also AAYA 3; BEST 89:1, 90:4;
CA 33-36R; CANR 10, 28; DLB 113;
HW; MTCW

Gard, Janice
See Latham, Jean Lee

Gard, Roger Martin du
See Martin du Gard, Roger

Gardam, Jane 1928- . . . . **CLC 43**
See also CA 49-52; CANR 2, 18, 33;
CLR 12; DLB 14; MAICYA; MTCW;
SAAS 9; SATA 28, 39, 76

Gardner, Herb . . . . **CLC 44**

Gardner, John (Champlin), Jr.
1933-1982 . . . . . **CLC 2, 3, 5, 7, 8, 10, 18,**
28, 34; SSC 7
See also AITN 1; CA 65-68; 107;
CANR 33; DLB 2; DLBY 82; MTCW;
SATA 31, 40

Gardner, John (Edmund) 1926- . . . . . **CLC 30**
See also CA 103; CANR 15; MTCW

Gardner, Noel
See Kuttner, Henry

Gardons, S. S.
See Snodgrass, W(illiam) D(e Witt)

Garfield, Leon 1921- . . . . **CLC 12**
See also AAYA 8; CA 17-20R; CANR 38,
41; CLR 21; JRDA; MAICYA; SATA 1,
32, 76

Garland, (Hannibal) Hamlin
1860-1940 . . . . **TCLC 3**
See also CA 104; DLB 12, 71, 78

Garneau, (Hector de) Saint-Denys
1912-1943 . . . . **TCLC 13**
See also CA 111; DLB 88

Garner, Alan 1934- . . . . **CLC 17**
See also CA 73-76; CANR 15; CLR 20;
MAICYA; MTCW; SATA 18, 69

Garner, Hugh 1913-1979 . . . . **CLC 13**
See also CA 69-72; CANR 31; DLB 68

Garnett, David 1892-1981 . . . . **CLC 3**
See also CA 5-8R; 103; CANR 17; DLB 34

Garos, Stephanie
See Katz, Steve

Garrett, George (Palmer)
1929- . . . . **CLC 3, 11, 51**
See also CA 1-4R; CAAS 5; CANR 1, 42;
DLB 2, 5, 130; DLBY 83

Garrick, David 1717-1779 . . . . **LC 15**
See also DLB 84

Garrigue, Jean 1914-1972 . . . . **CLC 2, 8**
See also CA 5-8R; 37-40R; CANR 20

Garrison, Frederick
See Sinclair, Upton (Beall)

Garth, Will
See Hamilton, Edmond; Kuttner, Henry

Garvey, Marcus (Moziah, Jr.)
1887-1940 . . . . **TCLC 41; BLC**
See also BW 1; CA 120; 124

Gary, Romain . . . . **CLC 25**
See also Kacew, Romain
See also DLB 83

Gascar, Pierre . . . . **CLC 11**
See also Fournier, Pierre

Gascoyne, David (Emery) 1916- . . . . **CLC 45**
See also CA 65-68; CANR 10, 28; DLB 20;
MTCW

Gaskell, Elizabeth Cleghorn
1810-1865 . . . . **NCLC 5**
See also CDBLB 1832-1890; DLB 21, 144

Gass, William H(oward)
1924- . . . **CLC 1, 2, 8, 11, 15, 39; SSC 12**
See also CA 17-20R; CANR 30; DLB 2;
MTCW

Gasset, Jose Ortega y
See Ortega y Gasset, Jose

Gates, Henry Louis, Jr. 1950- . . . . . . **CLC 65**
See also BW 2; CA 109; CANR 25; DLB 67

Gautier, Theophile 1811-1872 . . . . . **NCLC 1**
See also DLB 119

Gawsworth, John
See Bates, H(erbert) E(rnest)

Gaye, Marvin (Penze) 1939-1984 . . . **CLC 26**
See also CA 112

Gebler, Carlo (Ernest) 1954- . . . . **CLC 39**
See also CA 119; 133

Gee, Maggie (Mary) 1948- . . . . **CLC 57**
See also CA 130

Gee, Maurice (Gough) 1931- . . . . **CLC 29**
See also CA 97-100; SATA 46

Gelbart, Larry (Simon) 1923- . . . **CLC 21, 61**
See also CA 73-76; CANR 45

Gelber, Jack 1932- . . . . **CLC 1, 6, 14, 79**
See also CA 1-4R; CANR 2; DLB 7

Gellhorn, Martha (Ellis) 1908- . . **CLC 14, 60**
See also CA 77-80; CANR 44; DLBY 82

Genet, Jean
1910-1986 . . . **CLC 1, 2, 5, 10, 14, 44, 46**
See also CA 13-16R; CANR 18; DLB 72;
DLBY 86; MTCW

Gent, Peter 1942- . . . . **CLC 29**
See also AITN 1; CA 89-92; DLBY 82

Gentlewoman in New England, A
See Bradstreet, Anne

Gentlewoman in Those Parts, A
See Bradstreet, Anne

George, Jean Craighead 1919- . . . . . . **CLC 35**
See also AAYA 8; CA 5-8R; CANR 25;
CLR 1; DLB 52; JRDA; MAICYA;
SATA 2, 68

George, Stefan (Anton)
1868-1933 . . . . **TCLC 2, 14**
See also CA 104

Georges, Georges Martin
See Simenon, Georges (Jacques Christian)

Gerhardi, William Alexander
See Gerhardie, William Alexander

Gerhardie, William Alexander
1895-1977 . . . . **CLC 5**
See also CA 25-28R; 73-76; CANR 18;
DLB 36

Gerstler, Amy 1956- . . . . **CLC 70**

Gertler, T. . . . . **CLC 34**
See also CA 116; 121

Ghalib 1797-1869 . . . . **NCLC 39**

Ghelderode, Michel de
1898-1962 . . . . **CLC 6, 11**
See also CA 85-88; CANR 40

Ghiselin, Brewster 1903- . . . . **CLC 23**
See also CA 13-16R; CAAS 10; CANR 13

Ghose, Zulfikar 1935- . . . . **CLC 42**
See also CA 65-68

Ghosh, Amitav 1956- . . . . **CLC 44**

Giacosa, Giuseppe 1847-1906 . . . . . . **TCLC 7**
See also CA 104

Gibb, Lee
See Waterhouse, Keith (Spencer)

Gibbon, Lewis Grassic . . . . **TCLC 4**
See also Mitchell, James Leslie

Gibbons, Kaye 1960- . . . . **CLC 50**

Gibran, Kahlil
1883-1931 . . . . **TCLC 1, 9; PC 9**
See also CA 104

Gibson, William 1914- . . . . **CLC 23; DA**
See also CA 9-12R; CANR 9, 42; DLB 7;
SATA 66

Gibson, William (Ford) 1948- . . . **CLC 39, 63**
See also AAYA 12; CA 126; 133

Gide, Andre (Paul Guillaume)
1869-1951 . . . . **TCLC 5, 12, 36; DA;
SSC 13; WLC**
See also CA 104; 124; DLB 65; MTCW

Gifford, Barry (Colby) 1946- . . . . . . **CLC 34**
See also CA 65-68; CANR 9, 30, 40

Gilbert, W(illiam) S(chwenck)
1836-1911 . . . . **TCLC 3**
See also CA 104; SATA 36

Gilbreth, Frank B., Jr. 1911- . . . . **CLC 17**
See also CA 9-12R; SATA 2

Gilchrist, Ellen 1935- . . **CLC 34, 48; SSC 14**
See also CA 113; 116; CANR 41; DLB 130;
MTCW

Giles, Molly 1942- . . . . **CLC 39**
See also CA 126

Gill, Patrick
See Creasey, John

Gilliam, Terry (Vance) 1940- . . . . **CLC 21**
See also Monty Python
See also CA 108; 113; CANR 35

Gillian, Jerry
See Gilliam, Terry (Vance)

Gilliatt, Penelope (Ann Douglass)
1932-1993 . . . . **CLC 2, 10, 13, 53**
See also AITN 2; CA 13-16R; 141; DLB 14

Gilman, Charlotte (Anna) Perkins (Stetson)
1860-1935 . . . . **TCLC 9, 37; SSC 13**
See also CA 106

Gilmour, David 1949- . . . . **CLC 35**
See also CA 138

Gilpin, William 1724-1804 . . . . . . **NCLC 30**

Gilray, J. D.
See Mencken, H(enry) L(ouis)

Gilroy, Frank D(aniel) 1925- . . . . **CLC 2**
See also CA 81-84; CANR 32; DLB 7

Ginsberg, Allen
1926- . . . . . . **CLC 1, 2, 3, 4, 6, 13, 36, 69;
DA; PC 4; WLC 3**
See also AITN 1; CA 1-4R; CANR 2, 41;
CDALB 1941-1968; DLB 5, 16; MTCW

Ginzburg, Natalia
1916-1991 . . . . **CLC 5, 11, 54, 70**
See also CA 85-88; 135; CANR 33; MTCW

Giono, Jean 1895-1970 . . . . **CLC 4, 11**
See also CA 45-48; 29-32R; CANR 2, 35;
DLB 72; MTCW

Giovanni, Nikki
1943- . . . . . . **CLC 2, 4, 19, 64; BLC; DA**
See also AITN 1; BW 2; CA 29-32R;
CAAS 6; CANR 18, 41; CLR 6; DLB 5,
41; MAICYA; MTCW; SATA 24

Giovene, Andrea 1904- . . . . **CLC 7**
See also CA 85-88

Gippius, Zinaida (Nikolayevna) 1869-1945
See Hippius, Zinaida
See also CA 106

Giraudoux, (Hippolyte) Jean
1882-1944 . . . . **TCLC 2, 7**
See also CA 104; DLB 65

Gironella, Jose Maria 1917- . . . . **CLC 11**
See also CA 101

Gissing, George (Robert)
1857-1903 . . . . **TCLC 3, 24, 47**
See also CA 105; DLB 18, 135

Giurlani, Aldo
See Palazzeschi, Aldo

Gladkov, Fyodor (Vasilyevich)
1883-1958 . . . . **TCLC 27**

Glanville, Brian (Lester) 1931- . . . . . . **CLC 6**
See also CA 5-8R; CAAS 9; CANR 3;
DLB 15, 139; SATA 42

Glasgow, Ellen (Anderson Gholson)
1873(?)-1945 . . . . **TCLC 2, 7**
See also CA 104; DLB 9, 12

Glaspell, Susan (Keating)
1882(?)-1948 . . . . **TCLC 55**
See also CA 110; DLB 7, 9, 78; YABC 2

Glassco, John 1909-1981 . . . . **CLC 9**
See also CA 13-16R; 102; CANR 15;
DLB 68

Glasscock, Amnesia
See Steinbeck, John (Ernst)

Glasser, Ronald J. 1940(?)- . . . . **CLC 37**

Glassman, Joyce
See Johnson, Joyce

Glendinning, Victoria 1937- . . . . **CLC 50**
See also CA 120; 127

Glissant, Edouard 1928- . . . . **CLC 10, 68**

Gloag, Julian 1930- . . . . **CLC 40**
See also AITN 1; CA 65-68; CANR 10

Glowacki, Aleksander
See Prus, Boleslaw

Glueck, Louise (Elisabeth)
1943- . . . . **CLC 7, 22, 44, 81**
See also CA 33-36R; CANR 40; DLB 5

Gobineau, Joseph Arthur (Comte) de
1816-1882 . . . . **NCLC 17**
See also DLB 123

Godard, Jean-Luc 1930- . . . . **CLC 20**
See also CA 93-96

Godden, (Margaret) Rumer 1907- . . . **CLC 53**
See also AAYA 6; CA 5-8R; CANR 4, 27,
36; CLR 20; MAICYA; SAAS 12;
SATA 3, 36

Godoy Alcayaga, Lucila 1889-1957
See Mistral, Gabriela
See also BW 2; CA 104; 131; HW; MTCW

Godwin, Gail (Kathleen)
1937- . . . . **CLC 5, 8, 22, 31, 69**
See also CA 29-32R; CANR 15, 43; DLB 6;
MTCW

Godwin, William 1756-1836 . . . . . . **NCLC 14**
See also CDBLB 1789-1832; DLB 39, 104,
142

Goethe, Johann Wolfgang von
1749-1832 . . . . **NCLC 4, 22, 34; DA;
PC 5; WLC 3**
See also DLB 94

Gogarty, Oliver St. John
1878-1957 . . . . **TCLC 15**
See also CA 109; DLB 15, 19

Gogol, Nikolai (Vasilyevich)
1809-1852 . . . . **NCLC 5, 15, 31; DA;
DC 1; SSC 4; WLC**

Goines, Donald
1937(?)-1974 . . . . **CLC 80; BLC**
See also AITN 1; BW 1; CA 124; 114;
DLB 33

Gold, Herbert 1924- . . . . **CLC 4, 7, 14, 42**
See also CA 9-12R; CANR 17, 45; DLB 2;
DLBY 81

Goldbarth, Albert 1948- . . . . **CLC 5, 38**
See also CA 53-56; CANR 6, 40; DLB 120

Goldberg, Anatol 1910-1982 ...... **CLC 34**
See also CA 131; 117

Goldemberg, Isaac 1945- .... **CLC 52**
See also CA 69-72; CAAS 12; CANR 11,
32; HW

Golding, William (Gerald)
1911-1993 .... **CLC 1, 2, 3, 8, 10, 17, 27,
58, 81; DA; WLC**
See also AAYA 5; CA 5-8R; 141;
CANR 13, 33; CDBLB 1945-1960;
DLB 15, 100; MTCW

Goldman, Emma 1869-1940 ...... **TCLC 13**
See also CA 110

Goldman, Francisco 1955- .... **CLC 76**

Goldman, William (W.) 1931- ... **CLC 1, 48**
See also CA 9-12R; CANR 29; DLB 44

Goldmann, Lucien 1913-1970 ...... **CLC 24**
See also CA 25-28; CAP 2

Goldoni, Carlo 1707-1793 .... **LC 4**

Goldsberry, Steven 1949- .... **CLC 34**
See also CA 131

Goldsmith, Oliver
1728-1774 .... **LC 2; DA; WLC**
See also CDBLB 1660-1789; DLB 39, 89,
104, 109, 142; SATA 26

Goldsmith, Peter
See Priestley, J(ohn) B(oynton)

Gombrowicz, Witold
1904-1969 .... **CLC 4, 7, 11, 49**
See also CA 19-20; 25-28R; CAP 2

Gomez de la Serna, Ramon
1888-1963 .... **CLC 9**
See also CA 116; HW

Goncharov, Ivan Alexandrovich
1812-1891 .... **NCLC 1**

Goncourt, Edmond (Louis Antoine Huot) de
1822-1896 .... **NCLC 7**
See also DLB 123

Goncourt, Jules (Alfred Huot) de
1830-1870 .... **NCLC 7**
See also DLB 123

Gontier, Fernande 19(?)- .... **CLC 50**

Goodman, Paul 1911-1972 .... **CLC 1, 2, 4, 7**
See also CA 19-20; 37-40R; CANR 34;
CAP 2; DLB 130; MTCW

Gordimer, Nadine
1923- .... **CLC 3, 5, 7, 10, 18, 33, 51, 70;
DA; SSC 17**
See also CA 5-8R; CANR 3, 28; MTCW

Gordon, Adam Lindsay
1833-1870 .... **NCLC 21**

Gordon, Caroline
1895-1981 ... **CLC 6, 13, 29, 83; SSC 15**
See also CA 11-12; 103; CANR 36; CAP 1;
DLB 4, 9, 102; DLBY 81; MTCW

Gordon, Charles William 1860-1937
See Connor, Ralph
See also CA 109

Gordon, Mary (Catherine)
1949- .... **CLC 13, 22**
See also CA 102; CANR 44; DLB 6;
DLBY 81; MTCW

Gordon, Sol 1923- .... **CLC 26**
See also CA 53-56; CANR 4; SATA 11

Gordone, Charles 1925- .... **CLC 1, 4**
See also BW 1; CA 93-96; DLB 7; MTCW

Gorenko, Anna Andreevna
See Akhmatova, Anna

Gorky, Maxim .... **TCLC 8; WLC**
See also Peshkov, Alexei Maximovich

Goryan, Sirak
See Saroyan, William

Gosse, Edmund (William)
1849-1928 .... **TCLC 28**
See also CA 117; DLB 57, 144

Gotlieb, Phyllis Fay (Bloom)
1926- .... **CLC 18**
See also CA 13-16R; CANR 7; DLB 88

Gottesman, S. D.
See Kornbluth, C(yril) M.; Pohl, Frederik

Gottfried von Strassburg
fl. c. 1210- .... **CMLC 10**
See also DLB 138

Gould, Lois .... **CLC 4, 10**
See also CA 77-80; CANR 29; MTCW

Gourmont, Remy de 1858-1915 .... **TCLC 17**
See also CA 109

Govier, Katherine 1948- .... **CLC 51**
See also CA 101; CANR 18, 40

Goyen, (Charles) William
1915-1983 .... **CLC 5, 8, 14, 40**
See also AITN 2; CA 5-8R; 110; CANR 6;
DLB 2; DLBY 83

Goytisolo, Juan
1931- .... **CLC 5, 10, 23; HLC**
See also CA 85-88; CANR 32; HW; MTCW

Gozzano, Guido 1883-1916 .... **PC 10**
See also DLB 114

Gozzi, (Conte) Carlo 1720-1806 .. **NCLC 23**

Grabbe, Christian Dietrich
1801-1836 .... **NCLC 2**
See also DLB 133

Grace, Patricia 1937- .... **CLC 56**

Gracian y Morales, Baltasar
1601-1658 .... **LC 15**

Gracq, Julien .... **CLC 11, 48**
See also Poirier, Louis
See also DLB 83

Grade, Chaim 1910-1982 .... **CLC 10**
See also CA 93-96; 107

Graduate of Oxford, A
See Ruskin, John

Graham, John
See Phillips, David Graham

Graham, Jorie 1951- .... **CLC 48**
See also CA 111; DLB 120

Graham, R(obert) B(ontine) Cunninghame
See Cunninghame Graham, R(obert)
B(ontine)
See also DLB 98, 135

Graham, Robert
See Haldeman, Joe (William)

Graham, Tom
See Lewis, (Harry) Sinclair

Graham, W(illiam) S(ydney)
1918-1986 .... **CLC 29**
See also CA 73-76; 118; DLB 20

Graham, Winston (Mawdsley)
1910- .... **CLC 23**
See also CA 49-52; CANR 2, 22, 45;
DLB 77

Grant, Skeeter
See Spiegelman, Art

Granville-Barker, Harley
1877-1946 .... **TCLC 2**
See also Barker, Harley Granville
See also CA 104

Grass, Guenter (Wilhelm)
1927- ..... **CLC 1, 2, 4, 6, 11, 15, 22, 32,
49; DA; WLC**
See also CA 13-16R; CANR 20; DLB 75,
124; MTCW

Gratton, Thomas
See Hulme, T(homas) E(rnest)

Grau, Shirley Ann
1929- .... **CLC 4, 9; SSC 15**
See also CA 89-92; CANR 22; DLB 2;
MTCW

Gravel, Fern
See Hall, James Norman

Graver, Elizabeth 1964- .... **CLC 70**
See also CA 135

Graves, Richard Perceval 1945- .... **CLC 44**
See also CA 65-68; CANR 9, 26

Graves, Robert (von Ranke)
1895-1985 ...... **CLC 1, 2, 6, 11, 39, 44,
45; PC 6**
See also CA 5-8R; 117; CANR 5, 36;
CDBLB 1914-1945; DLB 20, 100;
DLBY 85; MTCW; SATA 45

Gray, Alasdair 1934- .... **CLC 41**
See also CA 126; MTCW

Gray, Amlin 1946- .... **CLC 29**
See also CA 138

Gray, Francine du Plessix 1930- .... **CLC 22**
See also BEST 90:3; CA 61-64; CAAS 2;
CANR 11, 33; MTCW

Gray, John (Henry) 1866-1934 .... **TCLC 19**
See also CA 119

Gray, Simon (James Holliday)
1936- .... **CLC 9, 14, 36**
See also AITN 1; CA 21-24R; CAAS 3;
CANR 32; DLB 13; MTCW

Gray, Spalding 1941- .... **CLC 49**
See also CA 128

Gray, Thomas
1716-1771 ...... **LC 4; DA; PC 2; WLC**
See also CDBLB 1660-1789; DLB 109

Grayson, David
See Baker, Ray Stannard

Grayson, Richard (A.) 1951- .... **CLC 38**
See also CA 85-88; CANR 14, 31

Greeley, Andrew M(oran) 1928- .... **CLC 28**
See also CA 5-8R; CAAS 7; CANR 7, 43;
MTCW

Green, Brian
See Card, Orson Scott

Green, Hannah
See Greenberg, Joanne (Goldenberg)

Green, Hannah .... **CLC 3**
See also CA 73-76

Green, Henry. . . . . CLC 2, 13
See also Yorke, Henry Vincent
See also DLB 15

Green, Julian (Hartridge) 1900-
See Green, Julien
See also CA 21-24R; CANR 33; DLB 4, 72;
MTCW

Green, Julien . . . . CLC 3, 11, 77
See also Green, Julian (Hartridge)

Green, Paul (Eliot) 1894-1981. . . . . . CLC 25
See also AITN 1; CA 5-8R; 103; CANR 3;
DLB 7, 9; DLBY 81

Greenberg, Ivan 1908-1973
See Rahv, Philip
See also CA 85-88

Greenberg, Joanne (Goldenberg)
1932- . . . . CLC 7, 30
See also AAYA 12; CA 5-8R; CANR 14,
32; SATA 25

Greenberg, Richard 1959(?)- . . . . CLC 57
See also CA 138

Greene, Bette 1934- . . . . CLC 30
See also AAYA 7; CA 53-56; CANR 4;
CLR 2; JRDA; MAICYA; SAAS 16;
SATA 8

Greene, Gael . . . . CLC 8
See also CA 13-16R; CANR 10

Greene, Graham
1904-1991 . . . . CLC 1, 3, 6, 9, 14, 18, 27,
37, 70, 72; DA; WLC
See also AITN 2; CA 13-16R; 133;
CANR 35; CDBLB 1945-1960; DLB 13,
15, 77, 100; DLBY 91; MTCW; SATA 20

Greer, Richard
See Silverberg, Robert

Greer, Richard
See Silverberg, Robert

Gregor, Arthur 1923- . . . . CLC 9
See also CA 25-28R; CAAS 10; CANR 11;
SATA 36

Gregor, Lee
See Pohl, Frederik

Gregory, Isabella Augusta (Persse)
1852-1932 . . . . TCLC 1
See also CA 104; DLB 10

Gregory, J. Dennis
See Williams, John A(lfred)

Grendon, Stephen
See Derleth, August (William)

Grenville, Kate 1950- . . . . CLC 61
See also CA 118

Grenville, Pelham
See Wodehouse, P(elham) G(renville)

Greve, Felix Paul (Berthold Friedrich)
1879-1948
See Grove, Frederick Philip
See also CA 104; 141

Grey, Zane 1872-1939 . . . . TCLC 6
See also CA 104; 132; DLB 9; MTCW

Grieg, (Johan) Nordahl (Brun)
1902-1943 . . . . TCLC 10
See also CA 107

Grieve, C(hristopher) M(urray)
1892-1978 . . . . CLC 11, 19
See also MacDiarmid, Hugh
See also CA 5-8R; 85-88; CANR 33;
MTCW

Griffin, Gerald 1803-1840 . . . . NCLC 7

Griffin, John Howard 1920-1980. . . . CLC 68
See also AITN 1; CA 1-4R; 101; CANR 2

Griffin, Peter 1942- . . . . CLC 39
See also CA 136

Griffiths, Trevor 1935- . . . . CLC 13, 52
See also CA 97-100; CANR 45; DLB 13

Grigson, Geoffrey (Edward Harvey)
1905-1985 . . . . CLC 7, 39
See also CA 25-28R; 118; CANR 20, 33;
DLB 27; MTCW

Grillparzer, Franz 1791-1872. . . . . . NCLC 1
See also DLB 133

Grimble, Reverend Charles James
See Eliot, T(homas) S(tearns)

Grimke, Charlotte L(ottie) Forten
1837(?)-1914
See Forten, Charlotte L.
See also BW 1; CA 117; 124

Grimm, Jacob Ludwig Karl
1785-1863 . . . . NCLC 3
See also DLB 90; MAICYA; SATA 22

Grimm, Wilhelm Karl 1786-1859 . . NCLC 3
See also DLB 90; MAICYA; SATA 22

Grimmelshausen, Johann Jakob Christoffel
von 1621-1676 . . . . LC 6

Grindel, Eugene 1895-1952
See Eluard, Paul
See also CA 104

Grisham, John 1955(?)- . . . . CLC 84
See also CA 138

Grossman, David 1954- . . . . CLC 67
See also CA 138

Grossman, Vasily (Semenovich)
1905-1964 . . . . CLC 41
See also CA 124; 130; MTCW

Grove, Frederick Philip . . . . TCLC 4
See also Greve, Felix Paul (Berthold
Friedrich)
See also DLB 92

Grubb
See Crumb, R(obert)

Grumbach, Doris (Isaac)
1918- . . . . CLC 13, 22, 64
See also CA 5-8R; CAAS 2; CANR 9, 42

Grundtvig, Nicolai Frederik Severin
1783-1872 . . . . NCLC 1

Grunge
See Crumb, R(obert)

Grunwald, Lisa 1959- . . . . CLC 44
See also CA 120

Guare, John 1938- . . . . CLC 8, 14, 29, 67
See also CA 73-76; CANR 21; DLB 7;
MTCW

Gudjonsson, Halldor Kiljan 1902-
See Laxness, Halldor
See also CA 103

Guenter, Erich
See Eich, Guenter

Guest, Barbara 1920- . . . . CLC 34
See also CA 25-28R; CANR 11, 44; DLB 5

Guest, Judith (Ann) 1936- . . . . CLC 8, 30
See also AAYA 7; CA 77-80; CANR 15;
MTCW

Guild, Nicholas M. 1944-. . . . . CLC 33
See also CA 93-96

Guillemin, Jacques
See Sartre, Jean-Paul

Guillen, Jorge 1893-1984. . . . . CLC 11
See also CA 89-92; 112; DLB 108; HW

Guillen (y Batista), Nicolas (Cristobal)
1902-1989 . . . . . CLC 48, 79; BLC; HLC
See also BW 2; CA 116; 125; 129; HW

Guillevic, (Eugene) 1907-. . . . . CLC 33
See also CA 93-96

Guillois
See Desnos, Robert

Guiney, Louise Imogen
1861-1920 . . . . TCLC 41
See also DLB 54

Guiraldes, Ricardo (Guillermo)
1886-1927 . . . . TCLC 39
See also CA 131; HW; MTCW

Gunn, Bill . . . . CLC 5
See also Gunn, William Harrison
See also DLB 38

Gunn, Thom(son William)
1929-. . . . . CLC 3, 6, 18, 32, 81
See also CA 17-20R; CANR 9, 33;
CDBLB 1960 to Present; DLB 27;
MTCW

Gunn, William Harrison 1934(?)-1989
See Gunn, Bill
See also AITN 1; BW 1; CA 13-16R; 128;
CANR 12, 25

Gunnars, Kristjana 1948-. . . . . CLC 69
See also CA 113; DLB 60

Gurganus, Allan 1947-. . . . . CLC 70
See also BEST 90:1; CA 135

Gurney, A(lbert) R(amsdell), Jr.
1930- . . . . CLC 32, 50, 54
See also CA 77-80; CANR 32

Gurney, Ivor (Bertie) 1890-1937. . . TCLC 33

Gurney, Peter
See Gurney, A(lbert) R(amsdell), Jr.

Guro, Elena 1877-1913. . . . . TCLC 56

Gustafson, Ralph (Barker) 1909-. . . . CLC 36
See also CA 21-24R; CANR 8, 45; DLB 88

Gut, Gom
See Simenon, Georges (Jacques Christian)

Guthrie, A(lfred) B(ertram), Jr.
1901-1991 . . . . CLC 23
See also CA 57-60; 134; CANR 24; DLB 6;
SATA 62; SATA-Obit 67

Guthrie, Isobel
See Grieve, C(hristopher) M(urray)

Guthrie, Woodrow Wilson 1912-1967
See Guthrie, Woody
See also CA 113; 93-96

Guthrie, Woody. . . . . CLC 35
See also Guthrie, Woodrow Wilson

Guy, Rosa (Cuthbert) 1928-........ **CLC 26**
See also AAYA 4; BW 2; CA 17-20R;
CANR 14, 34; CLR 13; DLB 33; JRDA;
MAICYA; SATA 14, 62

Gwendolyn
See Bennett, (Enoch) Arnold

H. D. .... **CLC 3, 8, 14, 31, 34, 73; PC 5**
See also Doolittle, Hilda

H. de V.
See Buchan, John

Haavikko, Paavo Juhani
1931- .... **CLC 18, 34**
See also CA 106

Habbema, Koos
See Heijermans, Herman

Hacker, Marilyn 1942- .... **CLC 5, 9, 23, 72**
See also CA 77-80; DLB 120

Haggard, H(enry) Rider
1856-1925 .... **TCLC 11**
See also CA 108; DLB 70; SATA 16

Haig, Fenil
See Ford, Ford Madox

Haig-Brown, Roderick (Langmere)
1908-1976 .... **CLC 21**
See also CA 5-8R; 69-72; CANR 4, 38;
CLR 31; DLB 88; MAICYA; SATA 12

Hailey, Arthur 1920- .... **CLC 5**
See also AITN 2; BEST 90:3; CA 1-4R;
CANR 2, 36; DLB 88; DLBY 82; MTCW

Hailey, Elizabeth Forsythe 1938-... **CLC 40**
See also CA 93-96; CAAS 1; CANR 15

Haines, John (Meade) 1924-....... **CLC 58**
See also CA 17-20R; CANR 13, 34; DLB 5

Haldeman, Joe (William) 1943-..... **CLC 61**
See also CA 53-56; CANR 6; DLB 8

Haley, Alex(ander Murray Palmer)
1921-1992 .... **CLC 8, 12, 76; BLC; DA**
See also BW 2; CA 77-80; 136; DLB 38;
MTCW

Haliburton, Thomas Chandler
1796-1865 .... **NCLC 15**
See also DLB 11, 99

Hall, Donald (Andrew, Jr.)
1928- .... **CLC 1, 13, 37, 59**
See also CA 5-8R; CAAS 7; CANR 2, 44;
DLB 5; SATA 23

Hall, Frederic Sauser
See Sauser-Hall, Frederic

Hall, James
See Kuttner, Henry

Hall, James Norman 1887-1951 ... **TCLC 23**
See also CA 123; SATA 21

Hall, (Marguerite) Radclyffe
1886(?)-1943 .... **TCLC 12**
See also CA 110

Hall, Rodney 1935- .... **CLC 51**
See also CA 109

Halleck, Fitz-Greene 1790-1867 .. **NCLC 47**
See also DLB 3

Halliday, Michael
See Creasey, John

Halpern, Daniel 1945- .... **CLC 14**
See also CA 33-36R

Hamburger, Michael (Peter Leopold)
1924- .... **CLC 5, 14**
See also CA 5-8R; CAAS 4; CANR 2;
DLB 27

Hamill, Pete 1935-.............. **CLC 10**
See also CA 25-28R; CANR 18

Hamilton, Clive
See Lewis, C(live) S(taples)

Hamilton, Edmond 1904-1977...... **CLC 1**
See also CA 1-4R; CANR 3; DLB 8

Hamilton, Eugene (Jacob) Lee
See Lee-Hamilton, Eugene (Jacob)

Hamilton, Franklin
See Silverberg, Robert

Hamilton, Gail
See Corcoran, Barbara

Hamilton, Mollie
See Kaye, M(ary) M(argaret)

Hamilton, (Anthony Walter) Patrick
1904-1962 .... **CLC 51**
See also CA 113; DLB 10

Hamilton, Virginia 1936-.......... **CLC 26**
See also AAYA 2; BW 2; CA 25-28R;
CANR 20, 37; CLR 1, 11; DLB 33, 52;
JRDA; MAICYA; MTCW; SATA 4, 56,
79

Hammett, (Samuel) Dashiell
1894-1961 .... **CLC 3, 5, 10, 19, 47;
SSC 17**
See also AITN 1; CA 81-84; CANR 42;
CDALB 1929-1941; DLBD 6; MTCW

Hammon, Jupiter
1711(?)-1800(?) .... **NCLC 5; BLC**
See also DLB 31, 50

Hammond, Keith
See Kuttner, Henry

Hamner, Earl (Henry), Jr. 1923- ... **CLC 12**
See also AITN 2; CA 73-76; DLB 6

Hampton, Christopher (James)
1946- .... **CLC 4**
See also CA 25-28R; DLB 13; MTCW

Hamsun, Knut .... **TCLC 2, 14, 49**
See also Pedersen, Knut

Handke, Peter 1942- .. **CLC 5, 8, 10, 15, 38**
See also CA 77-80; CANR 33; DLB 85,
124; MTCW

Hanley, James 1901-1985 ... **CLC 3, 5, 8, 13**
See also CA 73-76; 117; CANR 36; MTCW

Hannah, Barry 1942-.......... **CLC 23, 38**
See also CA 108; 110; CANR 43; DLB 6;
MTCW

Hannon, Ezra
See Hunter, Evan

Hansberry, Lorraine (Vivian)
1930-1965 ...... **CLC 17, 62; BLC; DA;
DC 2**
See also BW 1; CA 109; 25-28R; CABS 3;
CDALB 1941-1968; DLB 7, 38; MTCW

Hansen, Joseph 1923-............. **CLC 38**
See also CA 29-32R; CAAS 17; CANR 16,
44

Hansen, Martin A. 1909-1955..... **TCLC 32**

Hanson, Kenneth O(stlin) 1922-.... **CLC 13**
See also CA 53-56; CANR 7

Hardwick, Elizabeth 1916- .... **CLC 13**
See also CA 5-8R; CANR 3, 32; DLB 6;
MTCW

Hardy, Thomas
1840-1928 ...... **TCLC 4, 10, 18, 32, 48,
53; DA; PC 8; SSC 2; WLC**
See also CA 104; 123; CDBLB 1890-1914;
DLB 18, 19, 135; MTCW

Hare, David 1947- .... **CLC 29, 58**
See also CA 97-100; CANR 39; DLB 13;
MTCW

Harford, Henry
See Hudson, W(illiam) H(enry)

Hargrave, Leonie
See Disch, Thomas M(ichael)

Harjo, Joy 1951- .... **CLC 83**
See also CA 114; CANR 35; DLB 120

Harlan, Louis R(udolph) 1922-..... **CLC 34**
See also CA 21-24R; CANR 25

Harling, Robert 1951(?)- .... **CLC 53**

Harmon, William (Ruth) 1938-..... **CLC 38**
See also CA 33-36R; CANR 14, 32, 35;
SATA 65

Harper, F. E. W.
See Harper, Frances Ellen Watkins

Harper, Frances E. W.
See Harper, Frances Ellen Watkins

Harper, Frances E. Watkins
See Harper, Frances Ellen Watkins

Harper, Frances Ellen
See Harper, Frances Ellen Watkins

Harper, Frances Ellen Watkins
1825-1911 .... **TCLC 14; BLC**
See also BW 1; CA 111; 125; DLB 50

Harper, Michael S(teven) 1938- .. **CLC 7, 22**
See also BW 1; CA 33-36R; CANR 24;
DLB 41

Harper, Mrs. F. E. W.
See Harper, Frances Ellen Watkins

Harris, Christie (Lucy) Irwin
1907- .... **CLC 12**
See also CA 5-8R; CANR 6; DLB 88;
JRDA; MAICYA; SAAS 10; SATA 6, 74

Harris, Frank 1856(?)-1931....... **TCLC 24**
See also CA 109

Harris, George Washington
1814-1869 .... **NCLC 23**
See also DLB 3, 11

Harris, Joel Chandler 1848-1908 ... **TCLC 2**
See also CA 104; 137; DLB 11, 23, 42, 78,
91; MAICYA; YABC 1

Harris, John (Wyndham Parkes Lucas)
Beynon 1903-1969
See Wyndham, John
See also CA 102; 89-92

Harris, MacDonald................ **CLC 9**
See also Heiney, Donald (William)

Harris, Mark 1922- .... **CLC 19**
See also CA 5-8R; CAAS 3; CANR 2;
DLB 2; DLBY 80

Harris, (Theodore) Wilson 1921-.... **CLC 25**
See also BW 2; CA 65-68; CAAS 16;
CANR 11, 27; DLB 117; MTCW

Harrison, Elizabeth Cavanna   1909-
See Cavanna, Betty
See also CA 9-12R; CANR 6, 27

Harrison, Harry (Max)   1925- . . . . . . CLC 42
See also CA 1-4R; CANR 5, 21; DLB 8;
SATA 4

Harrison, James (Thomas)
1937- . . . . CLC 6, 14, 33, 66
See also CA 13-16R; CANR 8; DLBY 82

Harrison, Jim
See Harrison, James (Thomas)

Harrison, Kathryn   1961- . . . . CLC 70
See also CA 144

Harrison, Tony   1937- . . . . CLC 43
See also CA 65-68; CANR 44; DLB 40;
MTCW

Harriss, Will(ard Irvin)   1922- . . . . . . CLC 34
See also CA 111

Harson, Sley
See Ellison, Harlan

Hart, Ellis
See Ellison, Harlan

Hart, Josephine   1942(?)- . . . . CLC 70
See also CA 138

Hart, Moss   1904-1961 . . . . CLC 66
See also CA 109; 89-92; DLB 7

Harte, (Francis) Bret(t)
1836(?)-1902 . . . . TCLC 1, 25; DA;
SSC 8; WLC
See also CA 104; 140; CDALB 1865-1917;
DLB 12, 64, 74, 79; SATA 26

Hartley, L(eslie) P(oles)
1895-1972 . . . . CLC 2, 22
See also CA 45-48; 37-40R; CANR 33;
DLB 15, 139; MTCW

Hartman, Geoffrey H.   1929- . . . . CLC 27
See also CA 117; 125; DLB 67

Haruf, Kent   19(?)- . . . . CLC 34

Harwood, Ronald   1934- . . . . CLC 32
See also CA 1-4R; CANR 4; DLB 13

Hasek, Jaroslav (Matej Frantisek)
1883-1923 . . . . TCLC 4
See also CA 104; 129; MTCW

Hass, Robert   1941- . . . . CLC 18, 39
See also CA 111; CANR 30; DLB 105

Hastings, Hudson
See Kuttner, Henry

Hastings, Selina. . . . . CLC 44

Hatteras, Amelia
See Mencken, H(enry) L(ouis)

Hatteras, Owen. . . . . TCLC 18
See also Mencken, H(enry) L(ouis); Nathan,
George Jean

Hauptmann, Gerhart (Johann Robert)
1862-1946 . . . . TCLC 4
See also CA 104; DLB 66, 118

Havel, Vaclav   1936- . . . . CLC 25, 58, 65
See also CA 104; CANR 36; MTCW

Haviaras, Stratis. . . . . CLC 33
See also Chaviaras, Strates

Hawes, Stephen   1475(?)-1523(?) . . . . . LC 17

Hawkes, John (Clendennin Burne, Jr.)
1925- . . . . . . CLC 1, 2, 3, 4, 7, 9, 14, 15,
27, 49
See also CA 1-4R; CANR 2; DLB 2, 7;
DLBY 80; MTCW

Hawking, S. W.
See Hawking, Stephen W(illiam)

Hawking, Stephen W(illiam)
1942- . . . . CLC 63
See also BEST 89:1; CA 126; 129

Hawthorne, Julian   1846-1934 . . . . . TCLC 25

Hawthorne, Nathaniel
1804-1864 . . . . . . NCLC 39; DA; SSC 3;
WLC
See also CDALB 1640-1865; DLB 1, 74;
YABC 2

Haxton, Josephine Ayres   1921-
See Douglas, Ellen
See also CA 115; CANR 41

Hayaseca y Eizaguirre, Jorge
See Echegaray (y Eizaguirre), Jose (Maria
Waldo)

Hayashi Fumiko   1904-1951 . . . . . . TCLC 27

Haycraft, Anna
See Ellis, Alice Thomas
See also CA 122

Hayden, Robert E(arl)
1913-1980 . . . . . . CLC 5, 9, 14, 37; BLC;
DA; PC 6
See also BW 1; CA 69-72; 97-100; CABS 2;
CANR 24; CDALB 1941-1968; DLB 5,
76; MTCW; SATA 19, 26

Hayford, J(oseph) E(phraim) Casely
See Casely-Hayford, J(oseph) E(phraim)

Hayman, Ronald   1932- . . . . CLC 44
See also CA 25-28R; CANR 18

Haywood, Eliza (Fowler)
1693(?)-1756 . . . . LC 1

Hazlitt, William   1778-1830 . . . . . NCLC 29
See also DLB 110

Hazzard, Shirley   1931- . . . . CLC 18
See also CA 9-12R; CANR 4; DLBY 82;
MTCW

Head, Bessie   1937-1986 . . . CLC 25, 67; BLC
See also BW 2; CA 29-32R; 119; CANR 25;
DLB 117; MTCW

Headon, (Nicky) Topper   1956(?)- . . . CLC 30

Heaney, Seamus (Justin)
1939- . . . . CLC 5, 7, 14, 25, 37, 74
See also CA 85-88; CANR 25;
CDBLB 1960 to Present; DLB 40;
MTCW

Hearn, (Patricio) Lafcadio (Tessima Carlos)
1850-1904 . . . . TCLC 9
See also CA 105; DLB 12, 78

Hearne, Vicki   1946- . . . . CLC 56
See also CA 139

Hearon, Shelby   1931- . . . . CLC 63
See also AITN 2; CA 25-28R; CANR 18

Heat-Moon, William Least. . . . . CLC 29
See also Trogdon, William (Lewis)
See also AAYA 9

Hebbel, Friedrich   1813-1863 . . . . . NCLC 43
See also DLB 129

Hebert, Anne   1916- . . . . CLC 4, 13, 29
See also CA 85-88; DLB 68; MTCW

Hecht, Anthony (Evan)
1923- . . . . CLC 8, 13, 19
See also CA 9-12R; CANR 6; DLB 5

Hecht, Ben   1894-1964 . . . . CLC 8
See also CA 85-88; DLB 7, 9, 25, 26, 28, 86

Hedayat, Sadeq   1903-1951. . . . . . . TCLC 21
See also CA 120

Hegel, Georg Wilhelm Friedrich
1770-1831 . . . . NCLC 46
See also DLB 90

Heidegger, Martin   1889-1976 . . . . . . CLC 24
See also CA 81-84; 65-68; CANR 34;
MTCW

Heidenstam, (Carl Gustaf) Verner von
1859-1940 . . . . TCLC 5
See also CA 104

Heifner, Jack   1946- . . . . CLC 11
See also CA 105

Heijermans, Herman   1864-1924 . . . TCLC 24
See also CA 123

Heilbrun, Carolyn G(old)   1926-. . . . . CLC 25
See also CA 45-48; CANR 1, 28

Heine, Heinrich   1797-1856 . . . . NCLC 4
See also DLB 90

Heinemann, Larry (Curtiss)   1944-. . CLC 50
See also CA 110; CANR 31; DLBD 9

Heiney, Donald (William)   1921-1993
See Harris, MacDonald
See also CA 1-4R; 142; CANR 3

Heinlein, Robert A(nson)
1907-1988 . . . . . . CLC 1, 3, 8, 14, 26, 55
See also CA 1-4R; 125; CANR 1, 20;
DLB 8; JRDA; MAICYA; MTCW;
SATA 9, 56, 69

Helforth, John
See Doolittle, Hilda

Hellenhofferu, Vojtech Kapristian z
See Hasek, Jaroslav (Matej Frantisek)

Heller, Joseph
1923- . . . . . CLC 1, 3, 5, 8, 11, 36, 63; DA;
WLC
See also AITN 1; CA 5-8R; CABS 1;
CANR 8, 42; DLB 2, 28; DLBY 80;
MTCW

Hellman, Lillian (Florence)
1906-1984 . . . . . . CLC 2, 4, 8, 14, 18, 34,
44, 52; DC 1
See also AITN 1, 2; CA 13-16R; 112;
CANR 33; DLB 7; DLBY 84; MTCW

Helprin, Mark   1947- . . . . . CLC 7, 10, 22, 32
See also CA 81-84; DLBY 85; MTCW

Helvetius, Claude-Adrien
1715-1771 . . . . LC 26

Helyar, Jane Penelope Josephine   1933-
See Poole, Josephine
See also CA 21-24R; CANR 10, 26

Hemans, Felicia   1793-1835 . . . . . . NCLC 29
See also DLB 96

Hemingway, Ernest (Miller)
1899-1961 .... **CLC 1, 3, 6, 8, 10, 13, 19, 30, 34, 39, 41, 44, 50, 61, 80; DA; SSC 1; WLC**
See also CA 77-80; CANR 34;
CDALB 1917-1929; DLB 4, 9, 102;
DLBD 1; DLBY 81, 87; MTCW

Hempel, Amy 1951- .... **CLC 39**
See also CA 118; 137

Henderson, F. C.
See Mencken, H(enry) L(ouis)

Henderson, Sylvia
See Ashton-Warner, Sylvia (Constance)

Henley, Beth .... **CLC 23**
See also Henley, Elizabeth Becker
See also CABS 3; DLBY 86

Henley, Elizabeth Becker 1952-
See Henley, Beth
See also CA 107; CANR 32; MTCW

Henley, William Ernest
1849-1903 .... **TCLC 8**
See also CA 105; DLB 19

Hennissart, Martha
See Lathen, Emma
See also CA 85-88

Henry, O. .... **TCLC 1, 19; SSC 5; WLC**
See also Porter, William Sydney

Henry, Patrick 1736- .... **LC 25**
See also CA 145

Henryson, Robert 1430(?)-1506(?). ... **LC 20**

Henry VIII 1491-1547 .... **LC 10**

Henschke, Alfred
See Klabund

Hentoff, Nat(han Irving) 1925- ..... **CLC 26**
See also AAYA 4; CA 1-4R; CAAS 6;
CANR 5, 25; CLR 1; JRDA; MAICYA;
SATA 27, 42, 69

Heppenstall, (John) Rayner
1911-1981 .... **CLC 10**
See also CA 1-4R; 103; CANR 29

Herbert, Frank (Patrick)
1920-1986 ...... **CLC 12, 23, 35, 44, 85**
See also CA 53-56; 118; CANR 5, 43;
DLB 8; MTCW; SATA 9, 37, 47

Herbert, George 1593-1633 .... **LC 24; PC 4**
See also CDBLB Before 1660; DLB 126

Herbert, Zbigniew 1924- .... **CLC 9, 43**
See also CA 89-92; CANR 36; MTCW

Herbst, Josephine (Frey)
1897-1969 .... **CLC 34**
See also CA 5-8R; 25-28R; DLB 9

Hergesheimer, Joseph
1880-1954 .... **TCLC 11**
See also CA 109; DLB 102, 9

Herlihy, James Leo 1927-1993 ..... **CLC 6**
See also CA 1-4R; 143; CANR 2

Hermogenes fl. c. 175- .... **CMLC 6**

Hernandez, Jose 1834-1886 ...... **NCLC 17**

Herrick, Robert
1591-1674 .... **LC 13; DA; PC 9**
See also DLB 126

Herring, Guilles
See Somerville, Edith

Herriot, James 1916- .... **CLC 12**
See also Wight, James Alfred
See also AAYA 1; CANR 40

Herrmann, Dorothy 1941- .... **CLC 44**
See also CA 107

Herrmann, Taffy
See Herrmann, Dorothy

Hersey, John (Richard)
1914-1993 ...... **CLC 1, 2, 7, 9, 40, 81**
See also CA 17-20R; 140; CANR 33;
DLB 6; MTCW; SATA 25;
SATA-Obit 76

Herzen, Aleksandr Ivanovich
1812-1870 .... **NCLC 10**

Herzl, Theodor 1860-1904 .... **TCLC 36**

Herzog, Werner 1942- .... **CLC 16**
See also CA 89-92

Hesiod c. 8th cent. B.C.- .... **CMLC 5**

Hesse, Hermann
1877-1962 .... **CLC 1, 2, 3, 6, 11, 17, 25, 69; DA; SSC 9; WLC**
See also CA 17-18; CAP 2; DLB 66;
MTCW; SATA 50

Hewes, Cady
See De Voto, Bernard (Augustine)

Heyen, William 1940- .... **CLC 13, 18**
See also CA 33-36R; CAAS 9; DLB 5

Heyerdahl, Thor 1914- .... **CLC 26**
See also CA 5-8R; CANR 5, 22; MTCW;
SATA 2, 52

Heym, Georg (Theodor Franz Arthur)
1887-1912 .... **TCLC 9**
See also CA 106

Heym, Stefan 1913- .... **CLC 41**
See also CA 9-12R; CANR 4; DLB 69

Heyse, Paul (Johann Ludwig von)
1830-1914 .... **TCLC 8**
See also CA 104; DLB 129

Hibbert, Eleanor Alice Burford
1906-1993 .... **CLC 7**
See also BEST 90:4; CA 17-20R; 140;
CANR 9, 28; SATA 2; SATA-Obit 74

Higgins, George V(incent)
1939- .... **CLC 4, 7, 10, 18**
See also CA 77-80; CAAS 5; CANR 17;
DLB 2; DLBY 81; MTCW

Higginson, Thomas Wentworth
1823-1911 .... **TCLC 36**
See also DLB 1, 64

Highet, Helen
See MacInnes, Helen (Clark)

Highsmith, (Mary) Patricia
1921- .... **CLC 2, 4, 14, 42**
See also CA 1-4R; CANR 1, 20; MTCW

Highwater, Jamake (Mamake)
1942(?)- .... **CLC 12**
See also AAYA 7; CA 65-68; CAAS 7;
CANR 10, 34; CLR 17; DLB 52;
DLBY 85; JRDA; MAICYA; SATA 30,
32, 69

Hijuelos, Oscar 1951- ...... **CLC 65; HLC**
See also BEST 90:1; CA 123; HW

Hikmet, Nazim 1902(?)-1963 ...... **CLC 40**
See also CA 141; 93-96

Hildesheimer, Wolfgang
1916-1991 .... **CLC 49**
See also CA 101; 135; DLB 69, 124

Hill, Geoffrey (William)
1932- .... **CLC 5, 8, 18, 45**
See also CA 81-84; CANR 21;
CDBLB 1960 to Present; DLB 40;
MTCW

Hill, George Roy 1921- .... **CLC 26**
See also CA 110; 122

Hill, John
See Koontz, Dean R(ay)

Hill, Susan (Elizabeth) 1942- .... **CLC 4**
See also CA 33-36R; CANR 29; DLB 14,
139; MTCW

Hillerman, Tony 1925- .... **CLC 62**
See also AAYA 6; BEST 89:1; CA 29-32R;
CANR 21, 42; SATA 6

Hillesum, Etty 1914-1943 .... **TCLC 49**
See also CA 137

Hilliard, Noel (Harvey) 1929- ...... **CLC 15**
See also CA 9-12R; CANR 7

Hillis, Rick 1956- .... **CLC 66**
See also CA 134

Hilton, James 1900-1954 .... **TCLC 21**
See also CA 108; DLB 34, 77; SATA 34

Himes, Chester (Bomar)
1909-1984 .... **CLC 2, 4, 7, 18, 58; BLC**
See also BW 2; CA 25-28R; 114; CANR 22;
DLB 2, 76, 143; MTCW

Hinde, Thomas .... **CLC 6, 11**
See also Chitty, Thomas Willes

Hindin, Nathan
See Bloch, Robert (Albert)

Hine, (William) Daryl 1936- .... **CLC 15**
See also CA 1-4R; CAAS 15; CANR 1, 20;
DLB 60

Hinkson, Katharine Tynan
See Tynan, Katharine

Hinton, S(usan) E(loise)
1950- .... **CLC 30; DA**
See also AAYA 2; CA 81-84; CANR 32;
CLR 3, 23; JRDA; MAICYA; MTCW;
SATA 19, 58

Hippius, Zinaida .... **TCLC 9**
See also Gippius, Zinaida (Nikolayevna)

Hiraoka, Kimitake 1925-1970
See Mishima, Yukio
See also CA 97-100; 29-32R; MTCW

Hirsch, E(ric) D(onald), Jr. 1928- ... **CLC 79**
See also CA 25-28R; CANR 27; DLB 67;
MTCW

Hirsch, Edward 1950- .... **CLC 31, 50**
See also CA 104; CANR 20, 42; DLB 120

Hitchcock, Alfred (Joseph)
1899-1980 .... **CLC 16**
See also CA 97-100; SATA 24, 27

Hitler, Adolf 1889-1945 .... **TCLC 53**
See also CA 117

Hoagland, Edward 1932- .... **CLC 28**
See also CA 1-4R; CANR 2, 31; DLB 6;
SATA 51

Hoban, Russell (Conwell) 1925- .. **CLC 7, 25**
See also CA 5-8R; CANR 23, 37; CLR 3;
DLB 52; MAICYA; MTCW; SATA 1,
40, 78

Hobbs, Perry
See Blackmur, R(ichard) P(almer)

Hobson, Laura Z(ametkin)
1900-1986 .... **CLC 7, 25**
See also CA 17-20R; 118; DLB 28;
SATA 52

Hochhuth, Rolf 1931- .... **CLC 4, 11, 18**
See also CA 5-8R; CANR 33; DLB 124;
MTCW

Hochman, Sandra 1936- .... **CLC 3, 8**
See also CA 5-8R; DLB 5

Hochwaelder, Fritz 1911-1986 ...... **CLC 36**
See also CA 29-32R; 120; CANR 42;
MTCW

Hochwalder, Fritz
See Hochwaelder, Fritz

Hocking, Mary (Eunice) 1921- ..... **CLC 13**
See also CA 101; CANR 18, 40

Hodgins, Jack 1938- .... **CLC 23**
See also CA 93-96; DLB 60

Hodgson, William Hope
1877(?)-1918 .... **TCLC 13**
See also CA 111; DLB 70

Hoffman, Alice 1952- .... **CLC 51**
See also CA 77-80; CANR 34; MTCW

Hoffman, Daniel (Gerard)
1923- .... **CLC 6, 13, 23**
See also CA 1-4R; CANR 4; DLB 5

Hoffman, Stanley 1944- .... **CLC 5**
See also CA 77-80

Hoffman, William M(oses) 1939- ... **CLC 40**
See also CA 57-60; CANR 11

Hoffmann, E(rnst) T(heodor) A(madeus)
1776-1822 .... **NCLC 2; SSC 13**
See also DLB 90; SATA 27

Hofmann, Gert 1931- .... **CLC 54**
See also CA 128

Hofmannsthal, Hugo von
1874-1929 .... **TCLC 11; DC 4**
See also CA 106; DLB 81, 118

Hogan, Linda 1947- .... **CLC 73**
See also CA 120; CANR 45

Hogarth, Charles
See Creasey, John

Hogg, James 1770-1835 .... **NCLC 4**
See also DLB 93, 116

Holbach, Paul Henri Thiry Baron
1723-1789 .... **LC 14**

Holberg, Ludvig 1684-1754 .... **LC 6**

Holden, Ursula 1921- .... **CLC 18**
See also CA 101; CAAS 8; CANR 22

Holderlin, (Johann Christian) Friedrich
1770-1843 .... **NCLC 16; PC 4**

Holdstock, Robert
See Holdstock, Robert P.

Holdstock, Robert P. 1948- .... **CLC 39**
See also CA 131

Holland, Isabelle 1920- .... **CLC 21**
See also AAYA 11; CA 21-24R; CANR 10,
25; JRDA; MAICYA; SATA 8, 70

Holland, Marcus
See Caldwell, (Janet Miriam) Taylor
(Holland)

Hollander, John 1929- ...... **CLC 2, 5, 8, 14**
See also CA 1-4R; CANR 1; DLB 5;
SATA 13

Hollander, Paul
See Silverberg, Robert

Holleran, Andrew 1943(?)- .... **CLC 38**
See also CA 144

Hollinghurst, Alan 1954- .... **CLC 55**
See also CA 114

Hollis, Jim
See Summers, Hollis (Spurgeon, Jr.)

Holmes, John
See Souster, (Holmes) Raymond

Holmes, John Clellon 1926-1988 .... **CLC 56**
See also CA 9-12R; 125; CANR 4; DLB 16

Holmes, Oliver Wendell
1809-1894 .... **NCLC 14**
See also CDALB 1640-1865; DLB 1;
SATA 34

Holmes, Raymond
See Souster, (Holmes) Raymond

Holt, Victoria
See Hibbert, Eleanor Alice Burford

Holub, Miroslav 1923- .... **CLC 4**
See also CA 21-24R; CANR 10

Homer c. 8th cent. B.C.- ..... **CMLC 1; DA**

Honig, Edwin 1919- .... **CLC 33**
See also CA 5-8R; CAAS 8; CANR 4, 45;
DLB 5

Hood, Hugh (John Blagdon)
1928- .... **CLC 15, 28**
See also CA 49-52; CAAS 17; CANR 1, 33;
DLB 53

Hood, Thomas 1799-1845 .... **NCLC 16**
See also DLB 96

Hooker, (Peter) Jeremy 1941- ...... **CLC 43**
See also CA 77-80; CANR 22; DLB 40

Hope, A(lec) D(erwent) 1907- .... **CLC 3, 51**
See also CA 21-24R; CANR 33; MTCW

Hope, Brian
See Creasey, John

Hope, Christopher (David Tully)
1944- .... **CLC 52**
See also CA 106; SATA 62

Hopkins, Gerard Manley
1844-1889 .... **NCLC 17; DA; WLC**
See also CDBLB 1890-1914; DLB 35, 57

Hopkins, John (Richard) 1931- ...... **CLC 4**
See also CA 85-88

Hopkins, Pauline Elizabeth
1859-1930 .... **TCLC 28; BLC**
See also BW 2; CA 141; DLB 50

Hopkinson, Francis 1737-1791 ...... **LC 25**
See also DLB 31

Hopley-Woolrich, Cornell George 1903-1968
See Woolrich, Cornell
See also CA 13-14; CAP 1

Horatio
See Proust, (Valentin-Louis-George-Eugene-)
Marcel

Horgan, Paul 1903- .... **CLC 9, 53**
See also CA 13-16R; CANR 9, 35;
DLB 102; DLBY 85; MTCW; SATA 13

Horn, Peter
See Kuttner, Henry

Hornem, Horace Esq.
See Byron, George Gordon (Noel)

Horovitz, Israel 1939- .... **CLC 56**
See also CA 33-36R; DLB 7

Horvath, Odon von
See Horvath, Oedoen von
See also DLB 85, 124

Horvath, Oedoen von 1901-1938 ... **TCLC 45**
See also Horvath, Odon von
See also CA 118

Horwitz, Julius 1920-1986 .... **CLC 14**
See also CA 9-12R; 119; CANR 12

Hospital, Janette Turner 1942- ..... **CLC 42**
See also CA 108

Hostos, E. M. de
See Hostos (y Bonilla), Eugenio Maria de

Hostos, Eugenio M. de
See Hostos (y Bonilla), Eugenio Maria de

Hostos, Eugenio Maria
See Hostos (y Bonilla), Eugenio Maria de

Hostos (y Bonilla), Eugenio Maria de
1839-1903 .... **TCLC 24**
See also CA 123; 131; HW

Houdini
See Lovecraft, H(oward) P(hillips)

Hougan, Carolyn 1943- .... **CLC 34**
See also CA 139

Household, Geoffrey (Edward West)
1900-1988 .... **CLC 11**
See also CA 77-80; 126; DLB 87; SATA 14,
59

Housman, A(lfred) E(dward)
1859-1936 ...... **TCLC 1, 10; DA; PC 2**
See also CA 104; 125; DLB 19; MTCW

Housman, Laurence 1865-1959 ..... **TCLC 7**
See also CA 106; DLB 10; SATA 25

Howard, Elizabeth Jane 1923- ... **CLC 7, 29**
See also CA 5-8R; CANR 8

Howard, Maureen 1930- ..... **CLC 5, 14, 46**
See also CA 53-56; CANR 31; DLBY 83;
MTCW

Howard, Richard 1929- ...... **CLC 7, 10, 47**
See also AITN 1; CA 85-88; CANR 25;
DLB 5

Howard, Robert Ervin 1906-1936 ... **TCLC 8**
See also CA 105

Howard, Warren F.
See Pohl, Frederik

Howe, Fanny 1940- .... **CLC 47**
See also CA 117; SATA 52

Howe, Irving 1920-1993 .... **CLC 85**
See also CA 9-12R; 141; CANR 21;
DLB 67; MTCW

Howe, Julia Ward 1819-1910 ..... **TCLC 21**
See also CA 117; DLB 1

Howe, Susan 1937- .... **CLC 72**
See also DLB 120

Howe, Tina 1937- .... **CLC 48**
See also CA 109

Irving, John (Winslow)
1942- .... **CLC 13, 23, 38**
See also AAYA 8; BEST 89:3; CA 25-28R;
CANR 28; DLB 6; DLBY 82; MTCW

Irving, Washington
1783-1859 .... **NCLC 2, 19; DA; SSC 2;**
WLC
See also CDALB 1640-1865; DLB 3, 11, 30,
59, 73, 74; YABC 2

Irwin, P. K.
See Page, P(atricia) K(athleen)

Isaacs, Susan 1943- .... **CLC 32**
See also BEST 89:1; CA 89-92; CANR 20,
41; MTCW

Isherwood, Christopher (William Bradshaw)
1904-1986 .... **CLC 1, 9, 11, 14, 44**
See also CA 13-16R; 117; CANR 35;
DLB 15; DLBY 86; MTCW

Ishiguro, Kazuo 1954- ...... **CLC 27, 56, 59**
See also BEST 90:2; CA 120; MTCW

Ishikawa Takuboku
1886(?)-1912 .... **TCLC 15; PC 10**
See also CA 113

Iskander, Fazil 1929- .... **CLC 47**
See also CA 102

Ivan IV 1530-1584 .... **LC 17**

Ivanov, Vyacheslav Ivanovich
1866-1949 .... **TCLC 33**
See also CA 122

Ivask, Ivar Vidrik 1927-1992...... **CLC 14**
See also CA 37-40R; 139; CANR 24

Jackson, Daniel
See Wingrove, David (John)

Jackson, Jesse 1908-1983 .... **CLC 12**
See also BW 1; CA 25-28R; 109; CANR 27;
CLR 28; MAICYA; SATA 2, 29, 48

Jackson, Laura (Riding) 1901-1991
See Riding, Laura
See also CA 65-68; 135; CANR 28; DLB 48

Jackson, Sam
See Trumbo, Dalton

Jackson, Sara
See Wingrove, David (John)

Jackson, Shirley
1919-1965 ..... **CLC 11, 60; DA; SSC 9;**
WLC
See also AAYA 9; CA 1-4R; 25-28R;
CANR 4; CDALB 1941-1968; DLB 6;
SATA 2

Jacob, (Cyprien-)Max 1876-1944 ... **TCLC 6**
See also CA 104

Jacobs, Jim 1942-................ **CLC 12**
See also CA 97-100

Jacobs, W(illiam) W(ymark)
1863-1943 .... **TCLC 22**
See also CA 121; DLB 135

Jacobsen, Jens Peter 1847-1885 .. **NCLC 34**

Jacobsen, Josephine 1908-......... **CLC 48**
See also CA 33-36R; CAAS 18; CANR 23

Jacobson, Dan 1929- .... **CLC 4, 14**
See also CA 1-4R; CANR 2, 25; DLB 14;
MTCW

Jacqueline
See Carpentier (y Valmont), Alejo

Jagger, Mick 1944-............. **CLC 17**

Jakes, John (William) 1932-....... **CLC 29**
See also BEST 89:4; CA 57-60; CANR 10,
43; DLBY 83; MTCW; SATA 62

James, Andrew
See Kirkup, James

James, C(yril) L(ionel) R(obert)
1901-1989 .... **CLC 33**
See also BW 2; CA 117; 125; 128; DLB 125;
MTCW

James, Daniel (Lewis) 1911-1988
See Santiago, Danny
See also CA 125

James, Dynely
See Mayne, William (James Carter)

James, Henry
1843-1916 ...... **TCLC 2, 11, 24, 40, 47;**
DA; SSC 8; WLC
See also CA 104; 132; CDALB 1865-1917;
DLB 12, 71, 74; MTCW

James, M. R.
See James, Montague (Rhodes)

James, Montague (Rhodes)
1862-1936 .... **TCLC 6; SSC 16**
See also CA 104

James, P. D. .... **CLC 18, 46**
See also White, Phyllis Dorothy James
See also BEST 90:2; CDBLB 1960 to
Present; DLB 87

James, Philip
See Moorcock, Michael (John)

James, William 1842-1910..... **TCLC 15, 32**
See also CA 109

James I 1394-1437 .... **LC 20**

Jameson, Anna 1794-1860 .... **NCLC 43**
See also DLB 99

Jami, Nur al-Din 'Abd al-Rahman
1414-1492 .... **LC 9**

Jandl, Ernst 1925- .... **CLC 34**

Janowitz, Tama 1957- .... **CLC 43**
See also CA 106

Jarrell, Randall
1914-1965 ...... **CLC 1, 2, 6, 9, 13, 49**
See also CA 5-8R; 25-28R; CABS 2;
CANR 6, 34; CDALB 1941-1968; CLR 6;
DLB 48, 52; MAICYA; MTCW; SATA 7

Jarry, Alfred 1873-1907....... **TCLC 2, 14**
See also CA 104

Jarvis, E. K.
See Bloch, Robert (Albert); Ellison, Harlan;
Silverberg, Robert

Jeake, Samuel, Jr.
See Aiken, Conrad (Potter)

Jean Paul 1763-1825 .... **NCLC 7**

Jefferies, (John) Richard
1848-1887 .... **NCLC 47**
See also DLB 98, 141; SATA 16

Jeffers, (John) Robinson
1887-1962 .... **CLC 2, 3, 11, 15, 54; DA;**
WLC
See also CA 85-88; CANR 35;
CDALB 1917-1929; DLB 45; MTCW

Jefferson, Janet
See Mencken, H(enry) L(ouis)

Jefferson, Thomas 1743-1826 .... **NCLC 11**
See also CDALB 1640-1865; DLB 31

Jeffrey, Francis 1773-1850....... **NCLC 33**
See also DLB 107

Jelakowitch, Ivan
See Heijermans, Herman

Jellicoe, (Patricia) Ann 1927-...... **CLC 27**
See also CA 85-88; DLB 13

Jen, Gish .... **CLC 70**
See also Jen, Lillian

Jen, Lillian 1956(?)-
See Jen, Gish
See also CA 135

Jenkins, (John) Robin 1912-....... **CLC 52**
See also CA 1-4R; CANR 1; DLB 14

Jennings, Elizabeth (Joan)
1926- .... **CLC 5, 14**
See also CA 61-64; CAAS 5; CANR 8, 39;
DLB 27; MTCW; SATA 66

Jennings, Waylon 1937-........... **CLC 21**

Jensen, Johannes V. 1873-1950.... **TCLC 41**

Jensen, Laura (Linnea) 1948- ...... **CLC 37**
See also CA 103

Jerome, Jerome K(lapka)
1859-1927 .... **TCLC 23**
See also CA 119; DLB 10, 34, 135

Jerrold, Douglas William
1803-1857 .... **NCLC 2**

Jewett, (Theodora) Sarah Orne
1849-1909 .... **TCLC 1, 22; SSC 6**
See also CA 108; 127; DLB 12, 74;
SATA 15

Jewsbury, Geraldine (Endsor)
1812-1880 .... **NCLC 22**
See also DLB 21

Jhabvala, Ruth Prawer
1927- .... **CLC 4, 8, 29**
See also CA 1-4R; CANR 2, 29; DLB 139;
MTCW

Jiles, Paulette 1943-.......... **CLC 13, 58**
See also CA 101

Jimenez (Mantecon), Juan Ramon
1881-1958 .... **TCLC 4; HLC; PC 7**
See also CA 104; 131; DLB 134; HW;
MTCW

Jimenez, Ramon
See Jimenez (Mantecon), Juan Ramon

Jimenez Mantecon, Juan
See Jimenez (Mantecon), Juan Ramon

Joel, Billy .... **CLC 26**
See also Joel, William Martin

Joel, William Martin 1949-
See Joel, Billy
See also CA 108

John of the Cross, St. 1542-1591 .... **LC 18**

Johnson, B(ryan) S(tanley William)
1933-1973 .... **CLC 6, 9**
See also CA 9-12R; 53-56; CANR 9;
DLB 14, 40

Johnson, Benj. F. of Boo
See Riley, James Whitcomb

Johnson, Benjamin F. of Boo
See Riley, James Whitcomb

Kastel, Warren
See Silverberg, Robert

Kataev, Evgeny Petrovich   1903-1942
See Petrov, Evgeny
See also CA 120

Kataphusin
See Ruskin, John

Katz, Steve   1935-. . . . . **CLC 47**
See also CA 25-28R; CAAS 14; CANR 12;
DLBY 83

Kauffman, Janet   1945-. . . . . **CLC 42**
See also CA 117; CANR 43; DLBY 86

Kaufman, Bob (Garnell)
1925-1986 . . . . **CLC 49**
See also BW 1; CA 41-44R; 118; CANR 22;
DLB 16, 41

Kaufman, George S.   1889-1961 . . . . . **CLC 38**
See also CA 108; 93-96; DLB 7

Kaufman, Sue . . . . **CLC 3, 8**
See also Barondess, Sue K(aufman)

Kavafis, Konstantinos Petrou   1863-1933
See Cavafy, C(onstantine) P(eter)
See also CA 104

Kavan, Anna   1901-1968 . . . . . . **CLC 5, 13, 82**
See also CA 5-8R; CANR 6; MTCW

Kavanagh, Dan
See Barnes, Julian

Kavanagh, Patrick (Joseph)
1904-1967 . . . . **CLC 22**
See also CA 123; 25-28R; DLB 15, 20;
MTCW

Kawabata, Yasunari
1899-1972 . . . . . **CLC 2, 5, 9, 18; SSC 17**
See also CA 93-96; 33-36R

Kaye, M(ary) M(argaret)   1909-. . . . . **CLC 28**
See also CA 89-92; CANR 24; MTCW;
SATA 62

Kaye, Mollie
See Kaye, M(ary) M(argaret)

Kaye-Smith, Sheila   1887-1956. . . . . **TCLC 20**
See also CA 118; DLB 36

Kaymor, Patrice Maguilene
See Senghor, Leopold Sedar

Kazan, Elia   1909-. . . . . **CLC 6, 16, 63**
See also CA 21-24R; CANR 32

Kazantzakis, Nikos
1883(?)-1957 . . . . **TCLC 2, 5, 33**
See also CA 105; 132; MTCW

Kazin, Alfred   1915- . . . . **CLC 34, 38**
See also CA 1-4R; CAAS 7; CANR 1, 45;
DLB 67

Keane, Mary Nesta (Skrine)   1904-
See Keane, Molly
See also CA 108; 114

Keane, Molly. . . . . **CLC 31**
See also Keane, Mary Nesta (Skrine)

Keates, Jonathan   19(?)- . . . . **CLC 34**

Keaton, Buster   1895-1966 . . . . **CLC 20**

Keats, John
1795-1821 . . . **NCLC 8; DA; PC 1; WLC**
See also CDBLB 1789-1832; DLB 96, 110

Keene, Donald   1922- . . . . **CLC 34**
See also CA 1-4R; CANR 5

Keillor, Garrison . . . . **CLC 40**
See also Keillor, Gary (Edward)
See also AAYA 2; BEST 89:3; DLBY 87;
SATA 58

Keillor, Gary (Edward)   1942-
See Keillor, Garrison
See also CA 111; 117; CANR 36; MTCW

Keith, Michael
See Hubbard, L(afayette) Ron(ald)

Keller, Gottfried   1819-1890 . . . . . . **NCLC 2**
See also DLB 129

Kellerman, Jonathan   1949- . . . . **CLC 44**
See also BEST 90:1; CA 106; CANR 29

Kelley, William Melvin   1937-. . . . . . **CLC 22**
See also BW 1; CA 77-80; CANR 27;
DLB 33

Kellogg, Marjorie   1922-. . . . . **CLC 2**
See also CA 81-84

Kellow, Kathleen
See Hibbert, Eleanor Alice Burford

Kelly, M(ilton) T(erry)   1947-. . . . . . **CLC 55**
See also CA 97-100; CANR 19, 43

Kelman, James   1946-. . . . . **CLC 58**

Kemal, Yashar   1923- . . . . **CLC 14, 29**
See also CA 89-92; CANR 44

Kemble, Fanny   1809-1893 . . . . **NCLC 18**
See also DLB 32

Kemelman, Harry   1908-. . . . . **CLC 2**
See also AITN 1; CA 9-12R; CANR 6;
DLB 28

Kempe, Margery   1373(?)-1440(?) . . . . . **LC 6**

Kempis, Thomas a   1380-1471 . . . . . . **LC 11**

Kendall, Henry   1839-1882. . . . . . . **NCLC 12**

Keneally, Thomas (Michael)
1935- . . . . . . **CLC 5, 8, 10, 14, 19, 27, 43**
See also CA 85-88; CANR 10; MTCW

Kennedy, Adrienne (Lita)
1931- . . . . **CLC 66; BLC**
See also BW 2; CA 103; CABS 3;
CANR 26; DLB 38

Kennedy, John Pendleton
1795-1870 . . . . **NCLC 2**
See also DLB 3

Kennedy, Joseph Charles   1929-
See Kennedy, X. J.
See also CA 1-4R; CANR 4, 30, 40;
SATA 14

Kennedy, William   1928-. . . **CLC 6, 28, 34, 53**
See also AAYA 1; CA 85-88; CANR 14,
31; DLB 143; DLBY 85; MTCW;
SATA 57

Kennedy, X. J.. . . . . **CLC 8, 42**
See also Kennedy, Joseph Charles
See also CAAS 9; CLR 27; DLB 5

Kent, Kelvin
See Kuttner, Henry

Kenton, Maxwell
See Southern, Terry

Kenyon, Robert O.
See Kuttner, Henry

Kerouac, Jack . . . . . **CLC 1, 2, 3, 5, 14, 29, 61**
See also Kerouac, Jean-Louis Lebris de
See also CDALB 1941-1968; DLB 2, 16;
DLBD 3

Kerouac, Jean-Louis Lebris de   1922-1969
See Kerouac, Jack
See also AITN 1; CA 5-8R; 25-28R;
CANR 26; DA; MTCW; WLC

Kerr, Jean   1923-. . . . . **CLC 22**
See also CA 5-8R; CANR 7

Kerr, M. E. . . . . **CLC 12, 35**
See also Meaker, Marijane (Agnes)
See also AAYA 2; CLR 29; SAAS 1

Kerr, Robert . . . . **CLC 55**

Kerrigan, (Thomas) Anthony
1918-. . . . . **CLC 4, 6**
See also CA 49-52; CAAS 11; CANR 4

Kerry, Lois
See Duncan, Lois

Kesey, Ken (Elton)
1935- . . . . . **CLC 1, 3, 6, 11, 46, 64; DA;
WLC**
See also CA 1-4R; CANR 22, 38;
CDALB 1968-1988; DLB 2, 16; MTCW;
SATA 66

Kesselring, Joseph (Otto)
1902-1967 . . . . **CLC 45**

Kessler, Jascha (Frederick)   1929-. . . . **CLC 4**
See also CA 17-20R; CANR 8

Kettelkamp, Larry (Dale)   1933- . . . . **CLC 12**
See also CA 29-32R; CANR 16; SAAS 3;
SATA 2

Keyber, Conny
See Fielding, Henry

Keyes, Daniel   1927-. . . . . **CLC 80; DA**
See also CA 17-20R; CANR 10, 26;
SATA 37

Khanshendel, Chiron
See Rose, Wendy

Khayyam, Omar
1048-1131 . . . . **CMLC 11; PC 8**

Kherdian, David   1931-. . . . . **CLC 6, 9**
See also CA 21-24R; CAAS 2; CANR 39;
CLR 24; JRDA; MAICYA; SATA 16, 74

Khlebnikov, Velimir . . . . **TCLC 20**
See also Khlebnikov, Viktor Vladimirovich

Khlebnikov, Viktor Vladimirovich   1885-1922
See Khlebnikov, Velimir
See also CA 117

Khodasevich, Vladislav (Felitsianovich)
1886-1939 . . . . **TCLC 15**
See also CA 115

Kielland, Alexander Lange
1849-1906 . . . . **TCLC 5**
See also CA 104

Kiely, Benedict   1919-. . . . . **CLC 23, 43**
See also CA 1-4R; CANR 2; DLB 15

Kienzle, William X(avier)   1928- . . . . **CLC 25**
See also CA 93-96; CAAS 1; CANR 9, 31;
MTCW

Kierkegaard, Soren   1813-1855. . . . **NCLC 34**

Killens, John Oliver   1916-1987. . . . . **CLC 10**
See also BW 2; CA 77-80; 123; CAAS 2;
CANR 26; DLB 33

Killigrew, Anne   1660-1685. . . . . **LC 4**
See also DLB 131

Kim
See Simenon, Georges (Jacques Christian)

Kincaid, Jamaica 1949- . . . **CLC 43, 68; BLC**
See also BW 2; CA 125

King, Francis (Henry) 1923- . . . . . **CLC 8, 53**
See also CA 1-4R; CANR 1, 33; DLB 15,
139; MTCW

King, Martin Luther, Jr.
1929-1968 . . . . **CLC 83; BLC; DA**
See also BW 2; CA 25-28; CANR 27, 44;
CAP 2; MTCW; SATA 14

King, Stephen (Edwin)
1947- . . . . . . **CLC 12, 26, 37, 61; SSC 17**
See also AAYA 1; BEST 90:1; CA 61-64;
CANR 1, 30; DLB 143; DLBY 80;
JRDA; MTCW; SATA 9, 55

King, Steve
See King, Stephen (Edwin)

Kingman, Lee . . . . **CLC 17**
See also Natti, (Mary) Lee
See also SAAS 3; SATA 1, 67

Kingsley, Charles 1819-1875 . . . . . **NCLC 35**
See also DLB 21, 32; YABC 2

Kingsley, Sidney 1906- . . . . **CLC 44**
See also CA 85-88; DLB 7

Kingsolver, Barbara 1955- . . . . . . **CLC 55, 81**
See also CA 129; 134

Kingston, Maxine (Ting Ting) Hong
1940- . . . . **CLC 12, 19, 58**
See also AAYA 8; CA 69-72; CANR 13,
38; DLBY 80; MTCW; SATA 53

Kinnell, Galway
1927- . . . . **CLC 1, 2, 3, 5, 13, 29**
See also CA 9-12R; CANR 10, 34; DLB 5;
DLBY 87; MTCW

Kinsella, Thomas 1928- . . . . **CLC 4, 19**
See also CA 17-20R; CANR 15; DLB 27;
MTCW

Kinsella, W(illiam) P(atrick)
1935- . . . . **CLC 27, 43**
See also AAYA 7; CA 97-100; CAAS 7;
CANR 21, 35; MTCW

Kipling, (Joseph) Rudyard
1865-1936 . . . . . . **TCLC 8, 17; DA; PC 3;
SSC 5; WLC**
See also CA 105; 120; CANR 33;
CDBLB 1890-1914; DLB 19, 34, 141;
MAICYA; MTCW; YABC 2

Kirkup, James 1918- . . . . **CLC 1**
See also CA 1-4R; CAAS 4; CANR 2;
DLB 27; SATA 12

Kirkwood, James 1930(?)-1989 . . . . . . **CLC 9**
See also AITN 2; CA 1-4R; 128; CANR 6,
40

Kis, Danilo 1935-1989 . . . . **CLC 57**
See also CA 109; 118; 129; MTCW

Kivi, Aleksis 1834-1872 . . . . **NCLC 30**

Kizer, Carolyn (Ashley)
1925- . . . . **CLC 15, 39, 80**
See also CA 65-68; CAAS 5; CANR 24;
DLB 5

Klabund 1890-1928 . . . . **TCLC 44**
See also DLB 66

Klappert, Peter 1942- . . . . **CLC 57**
See also CA 33-36R; DLB 5

Klein, A(braham) M(oses)
1909-1972 . . . . **CLC 19**
See also CA 101; 37-40R; DLB 68

Klein, Norma 1938-1989 . . . . **CLC 30**
See also AAYA 2; CA 41-44R; 128;
CANR 15, 37; CLR 2, 19; JRDA;
MAICYA; SAAS 1; SATA 7, 57

Klein, T(heodore) E(ibon) D(onald)
1947- . . . . **CLC 34**
See also CA 119; CANR 44

Kleist, Heinrich von
1777-1811 . . . . **NCLC 2, 37**
See also DLB 90

Klima, Ivan 1931- . . . . **CLC 56**
See also CA 25-28R; CANR 17

Klimentov, Andrei Platonovich 1899-1951
See Platonov, Andrei
See also CA 108

Klinger, Friedrich Maximilian von
1752-1831 . . . . **NCLC 1**
See also DLB 94

Klopstock, Friedrich Gottlieb
1724-1803 . . . . **NCLC 11**
See also DLB 97

Knebel, Fletcher 1911-1993 . . . . **CLC 14**
See also AITN 1; CA 1-4R; 140; CAAS 3;
CANR 1, 36; SATA 36; SATA-Obit 75

Knickerbocker, Diedrich
See Irving, Washington

Knight, Etheridge
1931-1991 . . . . **CLC 40; BLC**
See also BW 1; CA 21-24R; 133; CANR 23;
DLB 41

Knight, Sarah Kemble 1666-1727 . . . . . **LC 7**
See also DLB 24

Knister, Raymond 1899-1932 . . . . . . **TCLC 56**
See also DLB 68

Knowles, John
1926- . . . . **CLC 1, 4, 10, 26; DA**
See also AAYA 10; CA 17-20R; CANR 40;
CDALB 1968-1988; DLB 6; MTCW;
SATA 8

Knox, Calvin M.
See Silverberg, Robert

Knye, Cassandra
See Disch, Thomas M(ichael)

Koch, C(hristopher) J(ohn) 1932- . . . **CLC 42**
See also CA 127

Koch, Christopher
See Koch, C(hristopher) J(ohn)

Koch, Kenneth 1925- . . . . **CLC 5, 8, 44**
See also CA 1-4R; CANR 6, 36; DLB 5;
SATA 65

Kochanowski, Jan 1530-1584 . . . . **LC 10**

Kock, Charles Paul de
1794-1871 . . . . **NCLC 16**

Koda Shigeyuki 1867-1947
See Rohan, Koda
See also CA 121

Koestler, Arthur
1905-1983 . . . . **CLC 1, 3, 6, 8, 15, 33**
See also CA 1-4R; 109; CANR 1, 33;
CDBLB 1945-1960; DLBY 83; MTCW

Kogawa, Joy Nozomi 1935- . . . . **CLC 78**
See also CA 101; CANR 19

Kohout, Pavel 1928- . . . . **CLC 13**
See also CA 45-48; CANR 3

Koizumi, Yakumo
See Hearn, (Patricio) Lafcadio (Tessima
Carlos)

Kolmar, Gertrud 1894-1943 . . . . . . **TCLC 40**

Konrad, George
See Konrad, Gyoergy

Konrad, Gyoergy 1933- . . . . . . **CLC 4, 10, 73**
See also CA 85-88

Konwicki, Tadeusz 1926- . . . . . **CLC 8, 28, 54**
See also CA 101; CAAS 9; CANR 39;
MTCW

Koontz, Dean R(ay) 1945- . . . . **CLC 78**
See also AAYA 9; BEST 89:3, 90:2;
CA 108; CANR 19, 36; MTCW

Kopit, Arthur (Lee) 1937- . . . . **CLC 1, 18, 33**
See also AITN 1; CA 81-84; CABS 3;
DLB 7; MTCW

Kops, Bernard 1926- . . . . **CLC 4**
See also CA 5-8R; DLB 13

Kornbluth, C(yril) M. 1923-1958 . . . . **TCLC 8**
See also CA 105; DLB 8

Korolenko, V. G.
See Korolenko, Vladimir Galaktionovich

Korolenko, Vladimir
See Korolenko, Vladimir Galaktionovich

Korolenko, Vladimir G.
See Korolenko, Vladimir Galaktionovich

Korolenko, Vladimir Galaktionovich
1853-1921 . . . . **TCLC 22**
See also CA 121

Kosinski, Jerzy (Nikodem)
1933-1991 . . . . **CLC 1, 2, 3, 6, 10, 15, 53,
70**
See also CA 17-20R; 134; CANR 9; DLB 2;
DLBY 82; MTCW

Kostelanetz, Richard (Cory) 1940- . . **CLC 28**
See also CA 13-16R; CAAS 8; CANR 38

Kostrowitzki, Wilhelm Apollinaris de
1880-1918
See Apollinaire, Guillaume
See also CA 104

Kotlowitz, Robert 1924- . . . . **CLC 4**
See also CA 33-36R; CANR 36

Kotzebue, August (Friedrich Ferdinand) von
1761-1819 . . . . **NCLC 25**
See also DLB 94

Kotzwinkle, William 1938- . . . **CLC 5, 14, 35**
See also CA 45-48; CANR 3, 44; CLR 6;
MAICYA; SATA 24, 70

Kozol, Jonathan 1936- . . . . **CLC 17**
See also CA 61-64; CANR 16, 45

Kozoll, Michael 1940(?)- . . . . **CLC 35**

Kramer, Kathryn 19(?)- . . . . **CLC 34**

Kramer, Larry 1935- . . . . **CLC 42**
See also CA 124; 126

Krasicki, Ignacy 1735-1801 . . . . **NCLC 8**

Krasinski, Zygmunt 1812-1859 . . . . **NCLC 4**

Kraus, Karl 1874-1936 . . . . **TCLC 5**
See also CA 104; DLB 118

Kreve (Mickevicius), Vincas
1882-1954 . . . . **TCLC 27**

Kristeva, Julia 1941- . . . . **CLC 77**

Kristofferson, Kris 1936- . . . . **CLC 26**
See also CA 104

Krizanc, John 1956- . . . . **CLC 57**

Krleza, Miroslav 1893-1981 . . . . **CLC 8**
See also CA 97-100; 105

Kroetsch, Robert 1927- . . . . . . **CLC 5, 23, 57**
See also CA 17-20R; CANR 8, 38; DLB 53;
MTCW

Kroetz, Franz
See Kroetz, Franz Xaver

Kroetz, Franz Xaver 1946- . . . . **CLC 41**
See also CA 130

Kroker, Arthur 1945- . . . . **CLC 77**

Kropotkin, Peter (Aleksieevich)
1842-1921 . . . . **TCLC 36**
See also CA 119

Krotkov, Yuri 1917- . . . . **CLC 19**
See also CA 102

Krumb
See Crumb, R(obert)

Krumgold, Joseph (Quincy)
1908-1980 . . . . **CLC 12**
See also CA 9-12R; 101; CANR 7;
MAICYA; SATA 1, 23, 48

Krumwitz
See Crumb, R(obert)

Krutch, Joseph Wood 1893-1970 . . . . **CLC 24**
See also CA 1-4R; 25-28R; CANR 4;
DLB 63

Krutzch, Gus
See Eliot, T(homas) S(tearns)

Krylov, Ivan Andreevich
1768(?)-1844 . . . . **NCLC 1**

Kubin, Alfred 1877-1959 . . . . **TCLC 23**
See also CA 112; DLB 81

Kubrick, Stanley 1928- . . . . **CLC 16**
See also CA 81-84; CANR 33; DLB 26

Kumin, Maxine (Winokur)
1925- . . . . **CLC 5, 13, 28**
See also AITN 2; CA 1-4R; CAAS 8;
CANR 1, 21; DLB 5; MTCW; SATA 12

Kundera, Milan
1929- . . . . **CLC 4, 9, 19, 32, 68**
See also AAYA 2; CA 85-88; CANR 19;
MTCW

Kunene, Mazisi (Raymond) 1930- . . . **CLC 85**
See also BW 1; CA 125; DLB 117

Kunitz, Stanley (Jasspon)
1905- . . . . **CLC 6, 11, 14**
See also CA 41-44R; CANR 26; DLB 48;
MTCW

Kunze, Reiner 1933- . . . . **CLC 10**
See also CA 93-96; DLB 75

Kuprin, Aleksandr Ivanovich
1870-1938 . . . . **TCLC 5**
See also CA 104

Kureishi, Hanif 1954(?)- . . . . **CLC 64**
See also CA 139

Kurosawa, Akira 1910- . . . . **CLC 16**
See also AAYA 11; CA 101

Kushner, Tony 1957(?)- . . . . **CLC 81**
See also CA 144

Kuttner, Henry 1915-1958 . . . . **TCLC 10**
See also CA 107; DLB 8

Kuzma, Greg 1944- . . . . **CLC 7**
See also CA 33-36R

Kuzmin, Mikhail 1872(?)-1936 . . . . **TCLC 40**

Kyd, Thomas 1558-1594 . . . . **LC 22; DC 3**
See also DLB 62

Kyprianos, Iossif
See Samarakis, Antonis

La Bruyere, Jean de 1645-1696 . . . . . . **LC 17**

Lacan, Jacques (Marie Emile)
1901-1981 . . . . **CLC 75**
See also CA 121; 104

Laclos, Pierre Ambroise Francois Choderlos
de 1741-1803 . . . . **NCLC 4**

La Colere, Francois
See Aragon, Louis

Lacolere, Francois
See Aragon, Louis

La Deshabilleuse
See Simenon, Georges (Jacques Christian)

Lady Gregory
See Gregory, Isabella Augusta (Persse)

Lady of Quality, A
See Bagnold, Enid

La Fayette, Marie (Madelaine Pioche de la
Vergne Comtes 1634-1693 . . . . . . **LC 2**

Lafayette, Rene
See Hubbard, L(afayette) Ron(ald)

Laforgue, Jules 1860-1887 . . . . **NCLC 5**

Lagerkvist, Paer (Fabian)
1891-1974 . . . . **CLC 7, 10, 13, 54**
See also Lagerkvist, Par
See also CA 85-88; 49-52; MTCW

Lagerkvist, Par
See Lagerkvist, Paer (Fabian)
See also SSC 12

Lagerloef, Selma (Ottiliana Lovisa)
1858-1940 . . . . **TCLC 4, 36**
See also Lagerlof, Selma (Ottiliana Lovisa)
See also CA 108; SATA 15

Lagerlof, Selma (Ottiliana Lovisa)
See Lagerloef, Selma (Ottiliana Lovisa)
See also CLR 7; SATA 15

La Guma, (Justin) Alex(ander)
1925-1985 . . . . **CLC 19**
See also BW 1; CA 49-52; 118; CANR 25;
DLB 117; MTCW

Laidlaw, A. K.
See Grieve, C(hristopher) M(urray)

Lainez, Manuel Mujica
See Mujica Lainez, Manuel
See also HW

Lamartine, Alphonse (Marie Louis Prat) de
1790-1869 . . . . **NCLC 11**

Lamb, Charles
1775-1834 . . . . **NCLC 10; DA; WLC**
See also CDBLB 1789-1832; DLB 93, 107;
SATA 17

Lamb, Lady Caroline 1785-1828 . . **NCLC 38**
See also DLB 116

Lamming, George (William)
1927- . . . . **CLC 2, 4, 66; BLC**
See also BW 2; CA 85-88; CANR 26;
DLB 125; MTCW

L'Amour, Louis (Dearborn)
1908-1988 . . . . **CLC 25, 55**
See also AITN 2; BEST 89:2; CA 1-4R;
125; CANR 3, 25, 40; DLBY 80; MTCW

Lampedusa, Giuseppe (Tomasi) di . . . **TCLC 13**
See also Tomasi di Lampedusa, Giuseppe

Lampman, Archibald 1861-1899 . . **NCLC 25**
See also DLB 92

Lancaster, Bruce 1896-1963 . . . . **CLC 36**
See also CA 9-10; CAP 1; SATA 9

Landau, Mark Alexandrovich
See Aldanov, Mark (Alexandrovich)

Landau-Aldanov, Mark Alexandrovich
See Aldanov, Mark (Alexandrovich)

Landis, John 1950- . . . . **CLC 26**
See also CA 112; 122

Landolfi, Tommaso 1908-1979 . . . **CLC 11, 49**
See also CA 127; 117

Landon, Letitia Elizabeth
1802-1838 . . . . **NCLC 15**
See also DLB 96

Landor, Walter Savage
1775-1864 . . . . **NCLC 14**
See also DLB 93, 107

Landwirth, Heinz 1927-
See Lind, Jakov
See also CA 9-12R; CANR 7

Lane, Patrick 1939- . . . . **CLC 25**
See also CA 97-100; DLB 53

Lang, Andrew 1844-1912 . . . . **TCLC 16**
See also CA 114; 137; DLB 98, 141;
MAICYA; SATA 16

Lang, Fritz 1890-1976 . . . . **CLC 20**
See also CA 77-80; 69-72; CANR 30

Lange, John
See Crichton, (John) Michael

Langer, Elinor 1939- . . . . **CLC 34**
See also CA 121

Langland, William
1330(?)-1400(?) . . . . **LC 19; DA**

Langstaff, Launcelot
See Irving, Washington

Lanier, Sidney 1842-1881 . . . . **NCLC 6**
See also DLB 64; MAICYA; SATA 18

Lanyer, Aemilia 1569-1645 . . . . **LC 10**

Lao Tzu . . . . **CMLC 7**

Lapine, James (Elliot) 1949- . . . . **CLC 39**
See also CA 123; 130

Larbaud, Valery (Nicolas)
1881-1957 . . . . **TCLC 9**
See also CA 106

Lardner, Ring
See Lardner, Ring(gold) W(ilmer)

Lardner, Ring W., Jr.
See Lardner, Ring(gold) W(ilmer)

Lardner, Ring(gold) W(ilmer)
1885-1933 . . . . **TCLC 2, 14**
See also CA 104; 131; CDALB 1917-1929;
DLB 11, 25, 86; MTCW

Laredo, Betty
See Codrescu, Andrei

Larkin, Maia
See Wojciechowska, Maia (Teresa)

Larkin, Philip (Arthur)
1922-1985 .... **CLC 3, 5, 8, 9, 13, 18, 33,**
39, 64
See also CA 5-8R; 117; CANR 24;
CDBLB 1960 to Present; DLB 27;
MTCW

Larra (y Sanchez de Castro), Mariano Jose de
1809-1837 .... **NCLC 17**

Larsen, Eric 1941- .... **CLC 55**
See also CA 132

Larsen, Nella 1891-1964 ..... **CLC 37; BLC**
See also BW 1; CA 125; DLB 51

Larson, Charles R(aymond) 1938-... **CLC 31**
See also CA 53-56; CANR 4

Lasker-Schueler, Else 1869-1945 .. **TCLC 57**
See also DLB 66, 124

Latham, Jean Lee 1902-.......... **CLC 12**
See also AITN 1; CA 5-8R; CANR 7;
MAICYA; SATA 2, 68

Latham, Mavis
See Clark, Mavis Thorpe

Lathen, Emma .... **CLC 2**
See also Hennissart, Martha; Latsis, Mary
J(ane)

Lathrop, Francis
See Leiber, Fritz (Reuter, Jr.)

Latsis, Mary J(ane)
See Lathen, Emma
See also CA 85-88

Lattimore, Richmond (Alexander)
1906-1984 .... **CLC 3**
See also CA 1-4R; 112; CANR 1

Laughlin, James 1914-........... **CLC 49**
See also CA 21-24R; CANR 9; DLB 48

Laurence, (Jean) Margaret (Wemyss)
1926-1987 .. **CLC 3, 6, 13, 50, 62; SSC 7**
See also CA 5-8R; 121; CANR 33; DLB 53;
MTCW; SATA 50

Laurent, Antoine 1952- .... **CLC 50**

Lauscher, Hermann
See Hesse, Hermann

Lautreamont, Comte de
1846-1870 .... **NCLC 12; SSC 14**

Laverty, Donald
See Blish, James (Benjamin)

Lavin, Mary 1912-...... **CLC 4, 18; SSC 4**
See also CA 9-12R; CANR 33; DLB 15;
MTCW

Lavond, Paul Dennis
See Kornbluth, C(yril) M.; Pohl, Frederik

Lawler, Raymond Evenor 1922-.... **CLC 58**
See also CA 103

Lawrence, D(avid) H(erbert Richards)
1885-1930 .... **TCLC 2, 9, 16, 33, 48;**
DA; SSC 4; WLC
See also CA 104; 121; CDBLB 1914-1945;
DLB 10, 19, 36, 98; MTCW

Lawrence, T(homas) E(dward)
1888-1935 .... **TCLC 18**
See also Dale, Colin
See also CA 115

Lawrence of Arabia
See Lawrence, T(homas) E(dward)

Lawson, Henry (Archibald Hertzberg)
1867-1922 .... **TCLC 27**
See also CA 120

Lawton, Dennis
See Faust, Frederick (Schiller)

Laxness, Halldor .... **CLC 25**
See also Gudjonsson, Halldor Kiljan

Layamon fl. c. 1200-............ **CMLC 10**

Laye, Camara 1928-1980 ... **CLC 4, 38; BLC**
See also BW 1; CA 85-88; 97-100;
CANR 25; MTCW

Layton, Irving (Peter) 1912-..... **CLC 2, 15**
See also CA 1-4R; CANR 2, 33, 43;
DLB 88; MTCW

Lazarus, Emma 1849-1887....... **NCLC 8**

Lazarus, Felix
See Cable, George Washington

Lazarus, Henry
See Slavitt, David R(ytman)

Lea, Joan
See Neufeld, John (Arthur)

Leacock, Stephen (Butler)
1869-1944 .... **TCLC 2**
See also CA 104; 141; DLB 92

Lear, Edward 1812-1888 .... **NCLC 3**
See also CLR 1; DLB 32; MAICYA;
SATA 18

Lear, Norman (Milton) 1922- ...... **CLC 12**
See also CA 73-76

Leavis, F(rank) R(aymond)
1895-1978 .... **CLC 24**
See also CA 21-24R; 77-80; CANR 44;
MTCW

Leavitt, David 1961-........... **CLC 34**
See also CA 116; 122; DLB 130

Leblanc, Maurice (Marie Emile)
1864-1941 .... **TCLC 49**
See also CA 110

Lebowitz, Fran(ces Ann)
1951(?)- .... **CLC 11, 36**
See also CA 81-84; CANR 14; MTCW

Lebrecht, Peter
See Tieck, (Johann) Ludwig

le Carre, John .... **CLC 3, 5, 9, 15, 28**
See also Cornwell, David (John Moore)
See also BEST 89:4; CDBLB 1960 to
Present; DLB 87

Le Clezio, J(ean) M(arie) G(ustave)
1940- .... **CLC 31**
See also CA 116; 128; DLB 83

Leconte de Lisle, Charles-Marie-Rene
1818-1894 .... **NCLC 29**

Le Coq, Monsieur
See Simenon, Georges (Jacques Christian)

Leduc, Violette 1907-1972........ **CLC 22**
See also CA 13-14; 33-36R; CAP 1

Ledwidge, Francis 1887(?)-1917 ... **TCLC 23**
See also CA 123; DLB 20

Lee, Andrea 1953- .... **CLC 36; BLC**
See also BW 1; CA 125

Lee, Andrew
See Auchincloss, Louis (Stanton)

Lee, Don L. .... **CLC 2**
See also Madhubuti, Haki R.

Lee, George W(ashington)
1894-1976 .... **CLC 52; BLC**
See also BW 1; CA 125; DLB 51

Lee, (Nelle) Harper
1926- .... **CLC 12, 60; DA; WLC**
See also CA 13-16R; CDALB 1941-1968;
DLB 6; MTCW; SATA 11

Lee, Julian
See Latham, Jean Lee

Lee, Larry
See Lee, Lawrence

Lee, Lawrence 1941-1990......... **CLC 34**
See also CA 131; CANR 43

Lee, Manfred B(ennington)
1905-1971 .... **CLC 11**
See also Queen, Ellery
See also CA 1-4R; 29-32R; CANR 2;
DLB 137

Lee, Stan 1922-................. **CLC 17**
See also AAYA 5; CA 108; 111

Lee, Tanith 1947-............... **CLC 46**
See also CA 37-40R; SATA 8

Lee, Vernon .... **TCLC 5**
See also Paget, Violet
See also DLB 57

Lee, William
See Burroughs, William S(eward)

Lee, Willy
See Burroughs, William S(eward)

Lee-Hamilton, Eugene (Jacob)
1845-1907 .... **TCLC 22**
See also CA 117

Leet, Judith 1935- .... **CLC 11**

Le Fanu, Joseph Sheridan
1814-1873 .... **NCLC 9; SSC 14**
See also DLB 21, 70

Leffland, Ella 1931- .... **CLC 19**
See also CA 29-32R; CANR 35; DLBY 84;
SATA 65

Leger, Alexis
See Leger, (Marie-Rene Auguste) Alexis
Saint-Leger

Leger, (Marie-Rene Auguste) Alexis
Saint-Leger 1887-1975........ **CLC 11**
See also Perse, St.-John
See also CA 13-16R; 61-64; CANR 43;
MTCW

Leger, Saintleger
See Leger, (Marie-Rene Auguste) Alexis
Saint-Leger

Le Guin, Ursula K(roeber)
1929- .... **CLC 8, 13, 22, 45, 71; SSC 12**
See also AAYA 9; AITN 1; CA 21-24R;
CANR 9, 32; CDALB 1968-1988; CLR 3,
28; DLB 8, 52; JRDA; MAICYA;
MTCW; SATA 4, 52

Lehmann, Rosamond (Nina)
1901-1990 .... **CLC 5**
See also CA 77-80; 131; CANR 8; DLB 15

Lucas, Craig 1951- . . . . CLC **64**
See also CA 137

Lucas, George 1944- . . . . CLC **16**
See also AAYA 1; CA 77-80; CANR 30;
SATA 56

Lucas, Hans
See Godard, Jean-Luc

Lucas, Victoria
See Plath, Sylvia

Ludlam, Charles 1943-1987 . . . . . CLC **46, 50**
See also CA 85-88; 122

Ludlum, Robert 1927- . . . . CLC **22, 43**
See also AAYA 10; BEST 89:1, 90:3;
CA 33-36R; CANR 25, 41; DLBY 82;
MTCW

Ludwig, Ken . . . . CLC **60**

Ludwig, Otto 1813-1865 . . . . NCLC **4**
See also DLB 129

Lugones, Leopoldo 1874-1938 . . . . . TCLC **15**
See also CA 116; 131; HW

Lu Hsun 1881-1936 . . . . TCLC **3**

Lukacs, George . . . . CLC **24**
See also Lukacs, Gyorgy (Szegeny von)

Lukacs, Gyorgy (Szegeny von) 1885-1971
See Lukacs, George
See also CA 101; 29-32R

Luke, Peter (Ambrose Cyprian)
1919- . . . . CLC **38**
See also CA 81-84; DLB 13

Lunar, Dennis
See Mungo, Raymond

Lurie, Alison 1926- . . . . CLC **4, 5, 18, 39**
See also CA 1-4R; CANR 2, 17; DLB 2;
MTCW; SATA 46

Lustig, Arnost 1926- . . . . CLC **56**
See also AAYA 3; CA 69-72; SATA 56

Luther, Martin 1483-1546 . . . . LC **9**

Luzi, Mario 1914- . . . . CLC **13**
See also CA 61-64; CANR 9; DLB 128

Lynch, B. Suarez
See Bioy Casares, Adolfo; Borges, Jorge
Luis

Lynch, David (K.) 1946- . . . . CLC **66**
See also CA 124; 129

Lynch, James
See Andreyev, Leonid (Nikolaevich)

Lynch Davis, B.
See Bioy Casares, Adolfo; Borges, Jorge
Luis

Lyndsay, Sir David 1490-1555 . . . . . . LC **20**

Lynn, Kenneth S(chuyler) 1923- . . . . CLC **50**
See also CA 1-4R; CANR 3, 27

Lynx
See West, Rebecca

Lyons, Marcus
See Blish, James (Benjamin)

Lyre, Pinchbeck
See Sassoon, Siegfried (Lorraine)

Lytle, Andrew (Nelson) 1902- . . . . . . CLC **22**
See also CA 9-12R; DLB 6

Lyttelton, George 1709-1773 . . . . LC **10**

Maas, Peter 1929- . . . . CLC **29**
See also CA 93-96

Macaulay, Rose 1881-1958 . . . . . TCLC **7, 44**
See also CA 104; DLB 36

Macaulay, Thomas Babington
1800-1859 . . . . NCLC **42**
See also CDBLB 1832-1890; DLB 32, 55

MacBeth, George (Mann)
1932-1992 . . . . CLC **2, 5, 9**
See also CA 25-28R; 136; DLB 40; MTCW;
SATA 4; SATA-Obit 70

MacCaig, Norman (Alexander)
1910- . . . . CLC **36**
See also CA 9-12R; CANR 3, 34; DLB 27

MacCarthy, (Sir Charles Otto) Desmond
1877-1952 . . . . TCLC **36**

MacDiarmid, Hugh
. . . . CLC **2, 4, 11, 19, 63; PC 9**
See also Grieve, C(hristopher) M(urray)
See also CDBLB 1945-1960; DLB 20

MacDonald, Anson
See Heinlein, Robert A(nson)

Macdonald, Cynthia 1928- . . . . . . CLC **13, 19**
See also CA 49-52; CANR 4, 44; DLB 105

MacDonald, George 1824-1905 . . . . . TCLC **9**
See also CA 106; 137; DLB 18; MAICYA;
SATA 33

Macdonald, John
See Millar, Kenneth

MacDonald, John D(ann)
1916-1986 . . . . CLC **3, 27, 44**
See also CA 1-4R; 121; CANR 1, 19;
DLB 8; DLBY 86; MTCW

Macdonald, John Ross
See Millar, Kenneth

Macdonald, Ross . . . . . CLC **1, 2, 3, 14, 34, 41**
See also Millar, Kenneth
See also DLBD 6

MacDougal, John
See Blish, James (Benjamin)

MacEwen, Gwendolyn (Margaret)
1941-1987 . . . . CLC **13, 55**
See also CA 9-12R; 124; CANR 7, 22;
DLB 53; SATA 50, 55

Macha, Karel Hynek 1810-1846 . . NCLC **46**

Machado (y Ruiz), Antonio
1875-1939 . . . . TCLC **3**
See also CA 104; DLB 108

Machado de Assis, Joaquim Maria
1839-1908 . . . . TCLC **10; BLC**
See also CA 107

Machen, Arthur . . . . TCLC **4**
See also Jones, Arthur Llewellyn
See also DLB 36

Machiavelli, Niccolo 1469-1527 . . LC **8; DA**

MacInnes, Colin 1914-1976 . . . . . . CLC **4, 23**
See also CA 69-72; 65-68; CANR 21;
DLB 14; MTCW

MacInnes, Helen (Clark)
1907-1985 . . . . CLC **27, 39**
See also CA 1-4R; 117; CANR 1, 28;
DLB 87; MTCW; SATA 22, 44

Mackay, Mary 1855-1924
See Corelli, Marie
See also CA 118

Mackenzie, Compton (Edward Montague)
1883-1972 . . . . CLC **18**
See also CA 21-22; 37-40R; CAP 2;
DLB 34, 100

Mackenzie, Henry 1745-1831 . . . . NCLC **41**
See also DLB 39

Mackintosh, Elizabeth 1896(?)-1952
See Tey, Josephine
See also CA 110

MacLaren, James
See Grieve, C(hristopher) M(urray)

Mac Laverty, Bernard 1942- . . . . CLC **31**
See also CA 116; 118; CANR 43

MacLean, Alistair (Stuart)
1922-1987 . . . . CLC **3, 13, 50, 63**
See also CA 57-60; 121; CANR 28; MTCW;
SATA 23, 50

Maclean, Norman (Fitzroy)
1902-1990 . . . . CLC **78; SSC 13**
See also CA 102; 132

MacLeish, Archibald
1892-1982 . . . . CLC **3, 8, 14, 68**
See also CA 9-12R; 106; CANR 33; DLB 4,
7, 45; DLBY 82; MTCW

MacLennan, (John) Hugh
1907-1990 . . . . CLC **2, 14**
See also CA 5-8R; 142; CANR 33; DLB 68;
MTCW

MacLeod, Alistair 1936- . . . . CLC **56**
See also CA 123; DLB 60

MacNeice, (Frederick) Louis
1907-1963 . . . . CLC **1, 4, 10, 53**
See also CA 85-88; DLB 10, 20; MTCW

MacNeill, Dand
See Fraser, George MacDonald

Macpherson, (Jean) Jay 1931- . . . . . . CLC **14**
See also CA 5-8R; DLB 53

MacShane, Frank 1927- . . . . CLC **39**
See also CA 9-12R; CANR 3, 33; DLB 111

Macumber, Mari
See Sandoz, Mari(e Susette)

Madach, Imre 1823-1864 . . . . NCLC **19**

Madden, (Jerry) David 1933- . . . . CLC **5, 15**
See also CA 1-4R; CAAS 3; CANR 4, 45;
DLB 6; MTCW

Maddern, Al(an)
See Ellison, Harlan

Madhubuti, Haki R.
1942- . . . . CLC **6, 73; BLC; PC 5**
See also Lee, Don L.
See also BW 2; CA 73-76; CANR 24;
DLB 5, 41; DLBD 8

Maepenn, Hugh
See Kuttner, Henry

Maepenn, K. H.
See Kuttner, Henry

Maeterlinck, Maurice 1862-1949 . . . TCLC **3**
See also CA 104; 136; SATA 66

Maginn, William 1794-1842 . . . . . . NCLC **8**
See also DLB 110

Mahapatra, Jayanta 1928- . . . . CLC **33**
See also CA 73-76; CAAS 9; CANR 15, 33

Marsden, James
  See Creasey, John

Marsh, (Edith) Ngaio
  1899-1982 . . . . CLC 7, 53
  See also CA 9-12R; CANR 6; DLB 77;
  MTCW

Marshall, Garry 1934- . . . . CLC 17
  See also AAYA 3; CA 111; SATA 60

Marshall, Paule
  1929- . . . . CLC 27, 72; BLC; SSC 3
  See also BW 2; CA 77-80; CANR 25;
  DLB 33; MTCW

Marsten, Richard
  See Hunter, Evan

Martha, Henry
  See Harris, Mark

Martial 40-104 . . . . PC 10

Martin, Ken
  See Hubbard, L(afayette) Ron(ald)

Martin, Richard
  See Creasey, John

Martin, Steve 1945- . . . . CLC 30
  See also CA 97-100; CANR 30; MTCW

Martin, Violet Florence
  1862-1915 . . . . TCLC 51

Martin, Webber
  See Silverberg, Robert

Martindale, Patrick Victor
  See White, Patrick (Victor Martindale)

Martin du Gard, Roger
  1881-1958 . . . . TCLC 24
  See also CA 118; DLB 65

Martineau, Harriet 1802-1876. . . . NCLC 26
  See also DLB 21, 55; YABC 2

Martines, Julia
  See O'Faolain, Julia

Martinez, Jacinto Benavente y
  See Benavente (y Martinez), Jacinto

Martinez Ruiz, Jose 1873-1967
  See Azorin; Ruiz, Jose Martinez
  See also CA 93-96; HW

Martinez Sierra, Gregorio
  1881-1947 . . . . TCLC 6
  See also CA 115

Martinez Sierra, Maria (de la O'LeJarraga)
  1874-1974 . . . . TCLC 6
  See also CA 115

Martinsen, Martin
  See Follett, Ken(neth Martin)

Martinson, Harry (Edmund)
  1904-1978 . . . . CLC 14
  See also CA 77-80; CANR 34

Marut, Ret
  See Traven, B.

Marut, Robert
  See Traven, B.

Marvell, Andrew
  1621-1678 . . . . . LC 4; DA; PC 10; WLC
  See also CDBLB 1660-1789; DLB 131

Marx, Karl (Heinrich)
  1818-1883 . . . . NCLC 17
  See also DLB 129

Masaoka Shiki. . . . . TCLC 18
  See also Masaoka Tsunenori

Masaoka Tsunenori 1867-1902
  See Masaoka Shiki
  See also CA 117

Masefield, John (Edward)
  1878-1967 . . . . CLC 11, 47
  See also CA 19-20; 25-28R; CANR 33;
  CAP 2; CDBLB 1890-1914; DLB 10;
  MTCW; SATA 19

Maso, Carole 19(?)- . . . . CLC 44

Mason, Bobbie Ann
  1940- . . . . CLC 28, 43, 82; SSC 4
  See also AAYA 5; CA 53-56; CANR 11,
  31; DLBY 87; MTCW

Mason, Ernst
  See Pohl, Frederik

Mason, Lee W.
  See Malzberg, Barry N(athaniel)

Mason, Nick 1945- . . . . CLC 35

Mason, Tally
  See Derleth, August (William)

Mass, William
  See Gibson, William

Masters, Edgar Lee
  1868-1950 . . . . . . TCLC 2, 25; DA; PC 1
  See also CA 104; 133; CDALB 1865-1917;
  DLB 54; MTCW

Masters, Hilary 1928- . . . . CLC 48
  See also CA 25-28R; CANR 13

Mastrosimone, William 19(?)- . . . . . . CLC 36

Mathe, Albert
  See Camus, Albert

Matheson, Richard Burton 1926- . . . CLC 37
  See also CA 97-100; DLB 8, 44

Mathews, Harry 1930- . . . . CLC 6, 52
  See also CA 21-24R; CAAS 6; CANR 18,
  40

Mathews, John Joseph 1894-1979. . . CLC 84
  See also CA 19-20; 142; CANR 45; CAP 2

Mathias, Roland (Glyn) 1915- . . . . . . CLC 45
  See also CA 97-100; CANR 19, 41; DLB 27

Matsuo Basho 1644-1694. . . . . PC 3

Mattheson, Rodney
  See Creasey, John

Matthews, Greg 1949- . . . . CLC 45
  See also CA 135

Matthews, William 1942- . . . . CLC 40
  See also CA 29-32R; CAAS 18; CANR 12;
  DLB 5

Matthias, John (Edward) 1941- . . . . . . CLC 9
  See also CA 33-36R

Matthiessen, Peter
  1927- . . . . CLC 5, 7, 11, 32, 64
  See also AAYA 6; BEST 90:4; CA 9-12R;
  CANR 21; DLB 6; MTCW; SATA 27

Maturin, Charles Robert
  1780(?)-1824 . . . . NCLC 6

Matute (Ausejo), Ana Maria
  1925- . . . . CLC 11
  See also CA 89-92; MTCW

Maugham, W. S.
  See Maugham, W(illiam) Somerset

Maugham, W(illiam) Somerset
  1874-1965 . . . . . . CLC 1, 11, 15, 67; DA;
  SSC 8; WLC
  See also CA 5-8R; 25-28R; CANR 40;
  CDBLB 1914-1945; DLB 10, 36, 77, 100;
  MTCW; SATA 54

Maugham, William Somerset
  See Maugham, W(illiam) Somerset

Maupassant, (Henri Rene Albert) Guy de
  1850-1893 . . . . NCLC 1, 42; DA; SSC 1;
  WLC
  See also DLB 123

Maurhut, Richard
  See Traven, B.

Mauriac, Claude 1914- . . . . CLC 9
  See also CA 89-92; DLB 83

Mauriac, Francois (Charles)
  1885-1970 . . . . CLC 4, 9, 56
  See also CA 25-28; CAP 2; DLB 65;
  MTCW

Mavor, Osborne Henry 1888-1951
  See Bridie, James
  See also CA 104

Maxwell, William (Keepers, Jr.)
  1908- . . . . CLC 19
  See also CA 93-96; DLBY 80

May, Elaine 1932- . . . . CLC 16
  See also CA 124; 142; DLB 44

Mayakovski, Vladimir (Vladimirovich)
  1893-1930 . . . . TCLC 4, 18
  See also CA 104

Mayhew, Henry 1812-1887 . . . . . . NCLC 31
  See also DLB 18, 55

Maynard, Joyce 1953- . . . . CLC 23
  See also CA 111; 129

Mayne, William (James Carter)
  1928- . . . . CLC 12
  See also CA 9-12R; CANR 37; CLR 25;
  JRDA; MAICYA; SAAS 11; SATA 6, 68

Mayo, Jim
  See L'Amour, Louis (Dearborn)

Maysles, Albert 1926- . . . . CLC 16
  See also CA 29-32R

Maysles, David 1932- . . . . CLC 16

Mazer, Norma Fox 1931- . . . . CLC 26
  See also AAYA 5; CA 69-72; CANR 12,
  32; CLR 23; JRDA; MAICYA; SAAS 1;
  SATA 24, 67

Mazzini, Guiseppe 1805-1872 . . . . NCLC 34

McAuley, James Phillip
  1917-1976 . . . . CLC 45
  See also CA 97-100

McBain, Ed
  See Hunter, Evan

McBrien, William Augustine
  1930- . . . . CLC 44
  See also CA 107

McCaffrey, Anne (Inez) 1926- . . . . . . CLC 17
  See also AAYA 6; AITN 2; BEST 89:2;
  CA 25-28R; CANR 15, 35; DLB 8;
  JRDA; MAICYA; MTCW; SAAS 11;
  SATA 8, 70

McCann, Arthur
  See Campbell, John W(ood, Jr.)

Merritt, E. B.
See Waddington, Miriam

Merton, Thomas
1915-1968 .. **CLC 1, 3, 11, 34, 83; PC 10**
See also CA 5-8R; 25-28R; CANR 22;
DLB 48; DLBY 81; MTCW

Merwin, W(illiam) S(tanley)
1927- ...... **CLC 1, 2, 3, 5, 8, 13, 18, 45**
See also CA 13-16R; CANR 15; DLB 5;
MTCW

Metcalf, John 1938-.............. **CLC 37**
See also CA 113; DLB 60

Metcalf, Suzanne
See Baum, L(yman) Frank

Mew, Charlotte (Mary)
1870-1928 .... **TCLC 8**
See also CA 105; DLB 19, 135

Mewshaw, Michael 1943-.......... **CLC 9**
See also CA 53-56; CANR 7; DLBY 80

Meyer, June
See Jordan, June

Meyer, Lynn
See Slavitt, David R(ytman)

Meyer-Meyrink, Gustav 1868-1932
See Meyrink, Gustav
See also CA 117

Meyers, Jeffrey 1939- .... **CLC 39**
See also CA 73-76; DLB 111

Meynell, Alice (Christina Gertrude Thompson)
1847-1922 .... **TCLC 6**
See also CA 104; DLB 19, 98

Meyrink, Gustav .... **TCLC 21**
See also Meyer-Meyrink, Gustav
See also DLB 81

Michaels, Leonard
1933- .... **CLC 6, 25; SSC 16**
See also CA 61-64; CANR 21; DLB 130;
MTCW

Michaux, Henri 1899-1984 ...... **CLC 8, 19**
See also CA 85-88; 114

Michelangelo 1475-1564............ **LC 12**

Michelet, Jules 1798-1874....... **NCLC 31**

Michener, James A(lbert)
1907(?)-.......... **CLC 1, 5, 11, 29, 60**
See also AITN 1; BEST 90:1; CA 5-8R;
CANR 21, 45; DLB 6; MTCW

Mickiewicz, Adam 1798-1855 ..... **NCLC 3**

Middleton, Christopher 1926-...... **CLC 13**
See also CA 13-16R; CANR 29; DLB 40

Middleton, Richard (Barham)
1882-1911 .... **TCLC 56**

Middleton, Stanley 1919-........ **CLC 7, 38**
See also CA 25-28R; CANR 21; DLB 14

Migueis, Jose Rodrigues 1901-..... **CLC 10**

Mikszath, Kalman 1847-1910 ..... **TCLC 31**

Miles, Josephine
1911-1985 .... **CLC 1, 2, 14, 34, 39**
See also CA 1-4R; 116; CANR 2; DLB 48

Militant
See Sandburg, Carl (August)

Mill, John Stuart 1806-1873 ..... **NCLC 11**
See also CDBLB 1832-1890; DLB 55

Millar, Kenneth 1915-1983 .... **CLC 14**
See also Macdonald, Ross
See also CA 9-12R; 110; CANR 16; DLB 2;
DLBD 6; DLBY 83; MTCW

Millay, E. Vincent
See Millay, Edna St. Vincent

Millay, Edna St. Vincent
1892-1950 ...... **TCLC 4, 49; DA; PC 6**
See also CA 104; 130; CDALB 1917-1929;
DLB 45; MTCW

Miller, Arthur
1915- .... **CLC 1, 2, 6, 10, 15, 26, 47, 78;
DA; DC 1; WLC**
See also AITN 1; CA 1-4R; CABS 3;
CANR 2, 30; CDALB 1941-1968; DLB 7;
MTCW

Miller, Henry (Valentine)
1891-1980 .... **CLC 1, 2, 4, 9, 14, 43, 84;
DA; WLC**
See also CA 9-12R; 97-100; CANR 33;
CDALB 1929-1941; DLB 4, 9; DLBY 80;
MTCW

Miller, Jason 1939(?)- .... **CLC 2**
See also AITN 1; CA 73-76; DLB 7

Miller, Sue 1943- .... **CLC 44**
See also BEST 90:3; CA 139; DLB 143

Miller, Walter M(ichael, Jr.)
1923- .... **CLC 4, 30**
See also CA 85-88; DLB 8

Millett, Kate 1934-.............. **CLC 67**
See also AITN 1; CA 73-76; CANR 32;
MTCW

Millhauser, Steven 1943-....... **CLC 21, 54**
See also CA 110; 111; DLB 2

Millin, Sarah Gertrude 1889-1968 .. **CLC 49**
See also CA 102; 93-96

Milne, A(lan) A(lexander)
1882-1956 .... **TCLC 6**
See also CA 104; 133; CLR 1, 26; DLB 10,
77, 100; MAICYA; MTCW; YABC 1

Milner, Ron(ald) 1938-....... **CLC 56; BLC**
See also AITN 1; BW 1; CA 73-76;
CANR 24; DLB 38; MTCW

Milosz, Czeslaw
1911- ... **CLC 5, 11, 22, 31, 56, 82; PC 8**
See also CA 81-84; CANR 23; MTCW

Milton, John 1608-1674... **LC 9; DA; WLC**
See also CDBLB 1660-1789; DLB 131

Minehaha, Cornelius
See Wedekind, (Benjamin) Frank(lin)

Miner, Valerie 1947- .... **CLC 40**
See also CA 97-100

Minimo, Duca
See D'Annunzio, Gabriele

Minot, Susan 1956- .... **CLC 44**
See also CA 134

Minus, Ed 1938-................. **CLC 39**

Miranda, Javier
See Bioy Casares, Adolfo

Mirbeau, Octave 1848-1917...... **TCLC 55**
See also DLB 123

Miro (Ferrer), Gabriel (Francisco Victor)
1879-1930 .... **TCLC 5**
See also CA 104

Mishima, Yukio
.... **CLC 2, 4, 6, 9, 27; DC 1; SSC 4**
See also Hiraoka, Kimitake

Mistral, Frederic 1830-1914 ...... **TCLC 51**
See also CA 122

Mistral, Gabriela........... **TCLC 2; HLC**
See also Godoy Alcayaga, Lucila

Mistry, Rohinton 1952-........... **CLC 71**
See also CA 141

Mitchell, Clyde
See Ellison, Harlan; Silverberg, Robert

Mitchell, James Leslie 1901-1935
See Gibbon, Lewis Grassic
See also CA 104; DLB 15

Mitchell, Joni 1943-.............. **CLC 12**
See also CA 112

Mitchell, Margaret (Munnerlyn)
1900-1949 .... **TCLC 11**
See also CA 109; 125; DLB 9; MTCW

Mitchell, Peggy
See Mitchell, Margaret (Munnerlyn)

Mitchell, S(ilas) Weir 1829-1914 .. **TCLC 36**

Mitchell, W(illiam) O(rmond)
1914- .... **CLC 25**
See also CA 77-80; CANR 15, 43; DLB 88

Mitford, Mary Russell 1787-1855.. **NCLC 4**
See also DLB 110, 116

Mitford, Nancy 1904-1973........ **CLC 44**
See also CA 9-12R

Miyamoto, Yuriko 1899-1951 ..... **TCLC 37**

Mo, Timothy (Peter) 1950(?)-...... **CLC 46**
See also CA 117; MTCW

Modarressi, Taghi (M.) 1931-...... **CLC 44**
See also CA 121; 134

Modiano, Patrick (Jean) 1945-..... **CLC 18**
See also CA 85-88; CANR 17, 40; DLB 83

Moerck, Paal
See Roelvaag, O(le) E(dvart)

Mofolo, Thomas (Mokopu)
1875(?)-1948 .... **TCLC 22; BLC**
See also CA 121

Mohr, Nicholasa 1935-...... **CLC 12; HLC**
See also AAYA 8; CA 49-52; CANR 1, 32;
CLR 22; HW; JRDA; SAAS 8; SATA 8

Mojtabai, A(nn) G(race)
1938-............... **CLC 5, 9, 15, 29**
See also CA 85-88

Moliere 1622-1673 .... **LC 10; DA; WLC**

Molin, Charles
See Mayne, William (James Carter)

Molnar, Ferenc 1878-1952....... **TCLC 20**
See also CA 109

Momaday, N(avarre) Scott
1934-........... **CLC 2, 19, 85; DA**
See also AAYA 11; CA 25-28R; CANR 14,
34; DLB 143; MTCW; NNAL; SATA 30,
48

Monette, Paul 1945-.............. **CLC 82**
See also CA 139

Monroe, Harriet 1860-1936....... **TCLC 12**
See also CA 109; DLB 54, 91

Monroe, Lyle
See Heinlein, Robert A(nson)

Montagu, Elizabeth 1917- . . . . NCLC 7
See also CA 9-12R

Montagu, Mary (Pierrepont) Wortley
1689-1762 . . . . LC 9
See also DLB 95, 101

Montagu, W. H.
See Coleridge, Samuel Taylor

Montague, John (Patrick)
1929- . . . . CLC 13, 46
See also CA 9-12R; CANR 9; DLB 40;
MTCW

Montaigne, Michel (Eyquem) de
1533-1592 . . . . LC 8; DA; WLC

Montale, Eugenio 1896-1981 . . . CLC 7, 9, 18
See also CA 17-20R; 104; CANR 30;
DLB 114; MTCW

Montesquieu, Charles-Louis de Secondat
1689-1755 . . . . LC 7

Montgomery, (Robert) Bruce 1921-1978
See Crispin, Edmund
See also CA 104

Montgomery, L(ucy) M(aud)
1874-1942 . . . . TCLC 51
See also AAYA 12; CA 108; 137; CLR 8;
DLB 92; JRDA; MAICYA; YABC 1

Montgomery, Marion H., Jr. 1925- . . CLC 7
See also AITN 1; CA 1-4R; CANR 3;
DLB 6

Montgomery, Max
See Davenport, Guy (Mattison, Jr.)

Montherlant, Henry (Milon) de
1896-1972 . . . . CLC 8, 19
See also CA 85-88; 37-40R; DLB 72;
MTCW

Monty Python
See Chapman, Graham; Cleese, John
(Marwood); Gilliam, Terry (Vance); Idle,
Eric; Jones, Terence Graham Parry; Palin,
Michael (Edward)
See also AAYA 7

Moodie, Susanna (Strickland)
1803-1885 . . . . NCLC 14
See also DLB 99

Mooney, Edward 1951-
See Mooney, Ted
See also CA 130

Mooney, Ted . . . . CLC 25
See also Mooney, Edward

Moorcock, Michael (John)
1939- . . . . CLC 5, 27, 58
See also CA 45-48; CAAS 5; CANR 2, 17,
38; DLB 14; MTCW

Moore, Brian
1921- . . . . CLC 1, 3, 5, 7, 8, 19, 32
See also CA 1-4R; CANR 1, 25, 42; MTCW

Moore, Edward
See Muir, Edwin

Moore, George Augustus
1852-1933 . . . . TCLC 7
See also CA 104; DLB 10, 18, 57, 135

Moore, Lorrie . . . . CLC 39, 45, 68
See also Moore, Marie Lorena

Moore, Marianne (Craig)
1887-1972 . . . . CLC 1, 2, 4, 8, 10, 13, 19,
47; DA; PC 4
See also CA 1-4R; 33-36R; CANR 3;
CDALB 1929-1941; DLB 45; DLBD 7;
MTCW; SATA 20

Moore, Marie Lorena 1957-
See Moore, Lorrie
See also CA 116; CANR 39

Moore, Thomas 1779-1852 . . . . NCLC 6
See also DLB 96, 144

Morand, Paul 1888-1976 . . . . CLC 41
See also CA 69-72; DLB 65

Morante, Elsa 1918-1985 . . . . CLC 8, 47
See also CA 85-88; 117; CANR 35; MTCW

Moravia, Alberto . . . . . . CLC 2, 7, 11, 27, 46
See also Pincherle, Alberto

More, Hannah 1745-1833 . . . . NCLC 27
See also DLB 107, 109, 116

More, Henry 1614-1687 . . . . LC 9
See also DLB 126

More, Sir Thomas 1478-1535 . . . . . . LC 10

Moreas, Jean . . . . TCLC 18
See also Papadiamantopoulos, Johannes

Morgan, Berry 1919- . . . . CLC 6
See also CA 49-52; DLB 6

Morgan, Claire
See Highsmith, (Mary) Patricia

Morgan, Edwin (George) 1920- . . . . . CLC 31
See also CA 5-8R; CANR 3, 43; DLB 27

Morgan, (George) Frederick
1922- . . . . CLC 23
See also CA 17-20R; CANR 21

Morgan, Harriet
See Mencken, H(enry) L(ouis)

Morgan, Jane
See Cooper, James Fenimore

Morgan, Janet 1945- . . . . CLC 39
See also CA 65-68

Morgan, Lady 1776(?)-1859 . . . . . . NCLC 29
See also DLB 116

Morgan, Robin 1941- . . . . CLC 2
See also CA 69-72; CANR 29; MTCW

Morgan, Scott
See Kuttner, Henry

Morgan, Seth 1949(?)-1990 . . . . CLC 65
See also CA 132

Morgenstern, Christian
1871-1914 . . . . TCLC 8
See also CA 105

Morgenstern, S.
See Goldman, William (W.)

Moricz, Zsigmond 1879-1942 . . . . . TCLC 33

Morike, Eduard (Friedrich)
1804-1875 . . . . NCLC 10
See also DLB 133

Mori Ogai . . . . TCLC 14
See also Mori Rintaro

Mori Rintaro 1862-1922
See Mori Ogai
See also CA 110

Moritz, Karl Philipp 1756-1793 . . . . . . LC 2
See also DLB 94

Morland, Peter Henry
See Faust, Frederick (Schiller)

Morren, Theophil
See Hofmannsthal, Hugo von

Morris, Bill 1952- . . . . CLC 76

Morris, Julian
See West, Morris L(anglo)

Morris, Steveland Judkins 1950(?)-
See Wonder, Stevie
See also CA 111

Morris, William 1834-1896 . . . . NCLC 4
See also CDBLB 1832-1890; DLB 18, 35, 57

Morris, Wright 1910- . . . CLC 1, 3, 7, 18, 37
See also CA 9-12R; CANR 21; DLB 2;
DLBY 81; MTCW

Morrison, Chloe Anthony Wofford
See Morrison, Toni

Morrison, James Douglas 1943-1971
See Morrison, Jim
See also CA 73-76; CANR 40

Morrison, Jim . . . . CLC 17
See also Morrison, James Douglas

Morrison, Toni
1931- . . CLC 4, 10, 22, 55, 81; BLC; DA
See also AAYA 1; BW 2; CA 29-32R;
CANR 27, 42; CDALB 1968-1988;
DLB 6, 33, 143; DLBY 81; MTCW;
SATA 57

Morrison, Van 1945- . . . . CLC 21
See also CA 116

Mortimer, John (Clifford)
1923- . . . . CLC 28, 43
See also CA 13-16R; CANR 21;
CDBLB 1960 to Present; DLB 13;
MTCW

Mortimer, Penelope (Ruth) 1918- . . . . CLC 5
See also CA 57-60; CANR 45

Morton, Anthony
See Creasey, John

Mosher, Howard Frank 1943- . . . . . . CLC 62
See also CA 139

Mosley, Nicholas 1923- . . . . CLC 43, 70
See also CA 69-72; CANR 41; DLB 14

Moss, Howard
1922-1987 . . . . CLC 7, 14, 45, 50
See also CA 1-4R; 123; CANR 1, 44;
DLB 5

Mossgiel, Rab
See Burns, Robert

Motion, Andrew 1952- . . . . CLC 47
See also DLB 40

Motley, Willard (Francis)
1909-1965 . . . . CLC 18
See also BW 1; CA 117; 106; DLB 76, 143

Motoori, Norinaga 1730-1801 . . . . NCLC 45

Mott, Michael (Charles Alston)
1930- . . . . CLC 15, 34
See also CA 5-8R; CAAS 7; CANR 7, 29

Mowat, Farley (McGill) 1921- . . . . . CLC 26
See also AAYA 1; CA 1-4R; CANR 4, 24,
42; CLR 20; DLB 68; JRDA; MAICYA;
MTCW; SATA 3, 55

Moyers, Bill 1934- . . . . CLC 74
See also AITN 2; CA 61-64; CANR 31

Mphahlele, Es'kia
See Mphahlele, Ezekiel
See also DLB 125

Mphahlele, Ezekiel 1919-..... **CLC 25; BLC**
See also Mphahlele, Es'kia
See also BW 2; CA 81-84; CANR 26

Mqhayi, S(amuel) E(dward) K(rune Loliwe)
1875-1945 .... **TCLC 25; BLC**

Mr. Martin
See Burroughs, William S(eward)

Mrozek, Slawomir 1930-........ **CLC 3, 13**
See also CA 13-16R; CAAS 10; CANR 29;
MTCW

Mrs. Belloc-Lowndes
See Lowndes, Marie Adelaide (Belloc)

Mtwa, Percy (?)-................. **CLC 47**

Mueller, Lisel 1924-.......... **CLC 13, 51**
See also CA 93-96; DLB 105

Muir, Edwin 1887-1959.......**TCLC 2**
See also CA 104; DLB 20, 100

Muir, John 1838-1914 .... **TCLC 28**

Mujica Lainez, Manuel
1910-1984 .... **CLC 31**
See also Lainez, Manuel Mujica
See also CA 81-84; 112; CANR 32; HW

Mukherjee, Bharati 1940-........ **CLC 53**
See also BEST 89:2; CA 107; CANR 45;
DLB 60; MTCW

Muldoon, Paul 1951-.......... **CLC 32, 72**
See also CA 113; 129; DLB 40

Mulisch, Harry 1927-............ **CLC 42**
See also CA 9-12R; CANR 6, 26

Mull, Martin 1943-.............. **CLC 17**
See also CA 105

Mulock, Dinah Maria
See Craik, Dinah Maria (Mulock)

Munford, Robert 1737(?)-1783 .... **LC 5**
See also DLB 31

Mungo, Raymond 1946-.......... **CLC 72**
See also CA 49-52; CANR 2

Munro, Alice
1931- .... **CLC 6, 10, 19, 50; SSC 3**
See also AITN 2; CA 33-36R; CANR 33;
DLB 53; MTCW; SATA 29

Munro, H(ector) H(ugh) 1870-1916
See Saki
See also CA 104; 130; CDBLB 1890-1914;
DA; DLB 34; MTCW; WLC

Murasaki, Lady................. **CMLC 1**

Murdoch, (Jean) Iris
1919- ...... **CLC 1, 2, 3, 4, 6, 8, 11, 15,**
22, 31, 51
See also CA 13-16R; CANR 8, 43;
CDBLB 1960 to Present; DLB 14;
MTCW

Murnau, Friedrich Wilhelm
See Plumpe, Friedrich Wilhelm

Murphy, Richard 1927-.......... **CLC 41**
See also CA 29-32R; DLB 40

Murphy, Sylvia 1937-............. **CLC 34**
See also CA 121

Murphy, Thomas (Bernard) 1935-... **CLC 51**
See also CA 101

Murray, Albert L. 1916- .... **CLC 73**
See also BW 2; CA 49-52; CANR 26;
DLB 38

Murray, Les(lie) A(llan) 1938- ..... **CLC 40**
See also CA 21-24R; CANR 11, 27

Murry, J. Middleton
See Murry, John Middleton

Murry, John Middleton
1889-1957 .... **TCLC 16**
See also CA 118

Musgrave, Susan 1951- .... **CLC 13, 54**
See also CA 69-72; CANR 45

Musil, Robert (Edler von)
1880-1942 .... **TCLC 12**
See also CA 109; DLB 81, 124

Musset, (Louis Charles) Alfred de
1810-1857 .... **NCLC 7**

My Brother's Brother
See Chekhov, Anton (Pavlovich)

Myers, Walter Dean 1937- ... **CLC 35; BLC**
See also AAYA 4; BW 2; CA 33-36R;
CANR 20, 42; CLR 4, 16, 35; DLB 33;
JRDA; MAICYA; SAAS 2; SATA 27, 41,
71

Myers, Walter M.
See Myers, Walter Dean

Myles, Symon
See Follett, Ken(neth Martin)

Nabokov, Vladimir (Vladimirovich)
1899-1977 ..... **CLC 1, 2, 3, 6, 8, 11, 15,**
23, 44, 46, 64; DA; SSC 11; WLC
See also CA 5-8R; 69-72; CANR 20;
CDALB 1941-1968; DLB 2; DLBD 3;
DLBY 80, 91; MTCW

Nagai Kafu..................... **TCLC 51**
See also Nagai Sokichi

Nagai Sokichi 1879-1959
See Nagai Kafu
See also CA 117

Nagy, Laszlo 1925-1978............ **CLC 7**
See also CA 129; 112

Naipaul, Shiva(dhar Srinivasa)
1945-1985 .... **CLC 32, 39**
See also CA 110; 112; 116; CANR 33;
DLBY 85; MTCW

Naipaul, V(idiadhar) S(urajprasad)
1932-.......... **CLC 4, 7, 9, 13, 18, 37**
See also CA 1-4R; CANR 1, 33;
CDBLB 1960 to Present; DLB 125;
DLBY 85; MTCW

Nakos, Lilika 1899(?)-............ **CLC 29**

Narayan, R(asipuram) K(rishnaswami)
1906-............... **CLC 7, 28, 47**
See also CA 81-84; CANR 33; MTCW;
SATA 62

Nash, (Frediric) Ogden 1902-1971 .. **CLC 23**
See also CA 13-14; 29-32R; CANR 34;
CAP 1; DLB 11; MAICYA; MTCW;
SATA 2, 46

Nathan, Daniel
See Dannay, Frederic

Nathan, George Jean 1882-1958 ... **TCLC 18**
See also Hatteras, Owen
See also CA 114; DLB 137

Natsume, Kinnosuke 1867-1916
See Natsume, Soseki
See also CA 104

Natsume, Soseki .... **TCLC 2, 10**
See also Natsume, Kinnosuke

Natti, (Mary) Lee 1919-
See Kingman, Lee
See also CA 5-8R; CANR 2

Naylor, Gloria
1950-.......... **CLC 28, 52; BLC; DA**
See also AAYA 6; BW 2; CA 107;
CANR 27; MTCW

Neihardt, John Gneisenau
1881-1973 .... **CLC 32**
See also CA 13-14; CAP 1; DLB 9, 54

Nekrasov, Nikolai Alekseevich
1821-1878 .... **NCLC 11**

Nelligan, Emile 1879-1941....... **TCLC 14**
See also CA 114; DLB 92

Nelson, Willie 1933-.............. **CLC 17**
See also CA 107

Nemerov, Howard (Stanley)
1920-1991 .... **CLC 2, 6, 9, 36**
See also CA 1-4R; 134; CABS 2; CANR 1,
27; DLB 6; DLBY 83; MTCW

Neruda, Pablo
1904-1973 ..... **CLC 1, 2, 5, 7, 9, 28, 62;**
DA; HLC; PC 4; WLC
See also CA 19-20; 45-48; CAP 2; HW;
MTCW

Nerval, Gerard de 1808-1855...... **NCLC 1**

Nervo, (Jose) Amado (Ruiz de)
1870-1919 .... **TCLC 11**
See also CA 109; 131; HW

Nessi, Pio Baroja y
See Baroja (y Nessi), Pio

Nestroy, Johann 1801-1862...... **NCLC 42**
See also DLB 133

Neufeld, John (Arthur) 1938- ...... **CLC 17**
See also AAYA 11; CA 25-28R; CANR 11,
37; MAICYA; SAAS 3; SATA 6

Neville, Emily Cheney 1919-....... **CLC 12**
See also CA 5-8R; CANR 3, 37; JRDA;
MAICYA; SAAS 2; SATA 1

Newbound, Bernard Slade 1930-
See Slade, Bernard
See also CA 81-84

Newby, P(ercy) H(oward)
1918-..................... **CLC 2, 13**
See also CA 5-8R; CANR 32; DLB 15;
MTCW

Newlove, Donald 1928- .... **CLC 6**
See also CA 29-32R; CANR 25

Newlove, John (Herbert) 1938-..... **CLC 14**
See also CA 21-24R; CANR 9, 25

Newman, Charles 1938-.......... **CLC 2, 8**
See also CA 21-24R

Newman, Edwin (Harold) 1919- .... **CLC 14**
See also AITN 1; CA 69-72; CANR 5

Newman, John Henry
1801-1890 .... **NCLC 38**
See also DLB 18, 32, 55

Newton, Suzanne 1936-........... **CLC 35**
See also CA 41-44R; CANR 14; JRDA;
SATA 5, 77

O'Donovan, Michael John
1903-1966 . . . . CLC 14
See also O'Connor, Frank
See also CA 93-96

Oe, Kenzaburo 1935- . . . . CLC 10, 36
See also CA 97-100; CANR 36; MTCW

O'Faolain, Julia 1932- . . . . CLC 6, 19, 47
See also CA 81-84; CAAS 2; CANR 12;
DLB 14; MTCW

O'Faolain, Sean
1900-1991 . . . . CLC 1, 7, 14, 32, 70;
SSC 13
See also CA 61-64; 134; CANR 12;
DLB 15; MTCW

O'Flaherty, Liam
1896-1984 . . . . CLC 5, 34; SSC 6
See also CA 101; 113; CANR 35; DLB 36;
DLBY 84; MTCW

Ogilvy, Gavin
See Barrie, J(ames) M(atthew)

O'Grady, Standish James
1846-1928 . . . . TCLC 5
See also CA 104

O'Grady, Timothy 1951- . . . . CLC 59
See also CA 138

O'Hara, Frank
1926-1966 . . . . CLC 2, 5, 13, 78
See also CA 9-12R; 25-28R; CANR 33;
DLB 5, 16; MTCW

O'Hara, John (Henry)
1905-1970 . . . . CLC 1, 2, 3, 6, 11, 42;
SSC 15
See also CA 5-8R; 25-28R; CANR 31;
CDALB 1929-1941; DLB 9, 86; DLBD 2;
MTCW

O Hehir, Diana 1922- . . . . CLC 41
See also CA 93-96

Okigbo, Christopher (Ifenayichukwu)
1932-1967 . . . . . CLC 25, 84; BLC; PC 7
See also BW 1; CA 77-80; DLB 125;
MTCW

Olds, Sharon 1942- . . . . CLC 32, 39, 85
See also CA 101; CANR 18, 41; DLB 120

Oldstyle, Jonathan
See Irving, Washington

Olesha, Yuri (Karlovich)
1899-1960 . . . . CLC 8
See also CA 85-88

Oliphant, Laurence
1829(?)-1888 . . . . NCLC 47
See also DLB 18

Oliphant, Margaret (Oliphant Wilson)
1828-1897 . . . . NCLC 11
See also DLB 18

Oliver, Mary 1935- . . . . CLC 19, 34
See also CA 21-24R; CANR 9, 43; DLB 5

Olivier, Laurence (Kerr)
1907-1989 . . . . CLC 20
See also CA 111; 129

Olsen, Tillie
1913- . . . . CLC 4, 13; DA; SSC 11
See also CA 1-4R; CANR 1, 43; DLB 28;
DLBY 80; MTCW

Olson, Charles (John)
1910-1970 . . . . . CLC 1, 2, 5, 6, 9, 11, 29
See also CA 13-16; 25-28R; CABS 2;
CANR 35; CAP 1; DLB 5, 16; MTCW

Olson, Toby 1937- . . . . CLC 28
See also CA 65-68; CANR 9, 31

Olyesha, Yuri
See Olesha, Yuri (Karlovich)

Ondaatje, (Philip) Michael
1943- . . . . CLC 14, 29, 51, 76
See also CA 77-80; CANR 42; DLB 60

Oneal, Elizabeth 1934-
See Oneal, Zibby
See also CA 106; CANR 28; MAICYA;
SATA 30

Oneal, Zibby . . . . CLC 30
See also Oneal, Elizabeth
See also AAYA 5; CLR 13; JRDA

O'Neill, Eugene (Gladstone)
1888-1953 . . . . . . TCLC 1, 6, 27, 49; DA;
WLC
See also AITN 1; CA 110; 132;
CDALB 1929-1941; DLB 7; MTCW

Onetti, Juan Carlos 1909-1994 . . . CLC 7, 10
See also CA 85-88; 145; CANR 32;
DLB 113; HW; MTCW

O Nuallain, Brian 1911-1966
See O'Brien, Flann
See also CA 21-22; 25-28R; CAP 2

Oppen, George 1908-1984 . . . . CLC 7, 13, 34
See also CA 13-16R; 113; CANR 8; DLB 5

Oppenheim, E(dward) Phillips
1866-1946 . . . . TCLC 45
See also CA 111; DLB 70

Orlovitz, Gil 1918-1973 . . . . CLC 22
See also CA 77-80; 45-48; DLB 2, 5

Orris
See Ingelow, Jean

Ortega y Gasset, Jose
1883-1955 . . . . TCLC 9; HLC
See also CA 106; 130; HW; MTCW

Ortiz, Simon J(oseph) 1941- . . . . CLC 45
See also CA 134; DLB 120

Orton, Joe . . . . CLC 4, 13, 43; DC 3
See also Orton, John Kingsley
See also CDBLB 1960 to Present; DLB 13

Orton, John Kingsley 1933-1967
See Orton, Joe
See also CA 85-88; CANR 35; MTCW

Orwell, George
. . . . TCLC 2, 6, 15, 31, 51; WLC
See also Blair, Eric (Arthur)
See also CDBLB 1945-1960; DLB 15, 98

Osborne, David
See Silverberg, Robert

Osborne, George
See Silverberg, Robert

Osborne, John (James)
1929- . . . . CLC 1, 2, 5, 11, 45; DA; WLC
See also CA 13-16R; CANR 21;
CDBLB 1945-1960; DLB 13; MTCW

Osborne, Lawrence 1958- . . . . CLC 50

Oshima, Nagisa 1932- . . . . CLC 20
See also CA 116; 121

Oskison, John Milton
1874-1947 . . . . TCLC 35
See also CA 144

Ossoli, Sarah Margaret (Fuller marchesa d')
1810-1850
See Fuller, Margaret
See also SATA 25

Ostrovsky, Alexander
1823-1886 . . . . NCLC 30

Otero, Blas de 1916-1979 . . . . CLC 11
See also CA 89-92; DLB 134

Otto, Whitney 1955- . . . . CLC 70
See also CA 140

Ouida . . . . TCLC 43
See also De La Ramee, (Marie) Louise
See also DLB 18

Ousmane, Sembene 1923- . . . . CLC 66; BLC
See also BW 1; CA 117; 125; MTCW

Ovid 43B.C.-18(?) . . . . CMLC 7; PC 2

Owen, Hugh
See Faust, Frederick (Schiller)

Owen, Wilfred (Edward Salter)
1893-1918 . . . . . . TCLC 5, 27; DA; WLC
See also CA 104; 141; CDBLB 1914-1945;
DLB 20

Owens, Rochelle 1936- . . . . CLC 8
See also CA 17-20R; CAAS 2; CANR 39

Oz, Amos 1939- . . . CLC 5, 8, 11, 27, 33, 54
See also CA 53-56; CANR 27; MTCW

Ozick, Cynthia
1928- . . . . CLC 3, 7, 28, 62; SSC 15
See also BEST 90:1; CA 17-20R; CANR 23;
DLB 28; DLBY 82; MTCW

Ozu, Yasujiro 1903-1963 . . . . CLC 16
See also CA 112

Pacheco, C.
See Pessoa, Fernando (Antonio Nogueira)

Pa Chin . . . . CLC 18
See also Li Fei-kan

Pack, Robert 1929- . . . . CLC 13
See also CA 1-4R; CANR 3, 44; DLB 5

Padgett, Lewis
See Kuttner, Henry

Padilla (Lorenzo), Heberto 1932- . . . CLC 38
See also AITN 1; CA 123; 131; HW

Page, Jimmy 1944- . . . . CLC 12

Page, Louise 1955- . . . . CLC 40
See also CA 140

Page, P(atricia) K(athleen)
1916- . . . . CLC 7, 18
See also CA 53-56; CANR 4, 22; DLB 68;
MTCW

Paget, Violet 1856-1935
See Lee, Vernon
See also CA 104

Paget-Lowe, Henry
See Lovecraft, H(oward) P(hillips)

Paglia, Camille (Anna) 1947- . . . . CLC 68
See also CA 140

Paige, Richard
See Koontz, Dean R(ay)

Pakenham, Antonia
See Fraser, (Lady) Antonia (Pakenham)

Police, The
See Copeland, Stewart (Armstrong);
Summers, Andrew James; Sumner,
Gordon Matthew

Pollitt, Katha 1949- .... **CLC 28**
See also CA 120; 122; MTCW

Pollock, (Mary) Sharon 1936-...... **CLC 50**
See also CA 141; DLB 60

Pomerance, Bernard 1940-........ **CLC 13**
See also CA 101

Ponge, Francis (Jean Gaston Alfred)
1899-1988 .... **CLC 6, 18**
See also CA 85-88; 126; CANR 40

Pontoppidan, Henrik 1857-1943 ... **TCLC 29**

Poole, Josephine .... **CLC 17**
See also Helyar, Jane Penelope Josephine
See also SAAS 2; SATA 5

Popa, Vasko 1922- .... **CLC 19**
See also CA 112

Pope, Alexander
1688-1744 .... **LC 3; DA; WLC**
See also CDBLB 1660-1789; DLB 95, 101

Porter, Connie (Rose) 1959(?)- ..... **CLC 70**
See also BW 2; CA 142

Porter, Gene(va Grace) Stratton
1863(?)-1924 .... **TCLC 21**
See also CA 112

Porter, Katherine Anne
1890-1980 ...... **CLC 1, 3, 7, 10, 13, 15,
27; DA; SSC 4**
See also AITN 2; CA 1-4R; 101; CANR 1;
DLB 4, 9, 102; DLBY 80; MTCW;
SATA 23, 39

Porter, Peter (Neville Frederick)
1929- .... **CLC 5, 13, 33**
See also CA 85-88; DLB 40

Porter, William Sydney 1862-1910
See Henry, O.
See also CA 104; 131; CDALB 1865-1917;
DA; DLB 12, 78, 79; MTCW; YABC 2

Portillo (y Pacheco), Jose Lopez
See Lopez Portillo (y Pacheco), Jose

Post, Melville Davisson
1869-1930 .... **TCLC 39**
See also CA 110

Potok, Chaim 1929- .... **CLC 2, 7, 14, 26**
See also AITN 1, 2; CA 17-20R; CANR 19,
35; DLB 28; MTCW; SATA 33

Potter, Beatrice
See Webb, (Martha) Beatrice (Potter)
See also MAICYA

Potter, Dennis (Christopher George)
1935-1994 .... **CLC 58**
See also CA 107; 145; CANR 33; MTCW

Pound, Ezra (Weston Loomis)
1885-1972 ...... **CLC 1, 2, 3, 4, 5, 7, 10,
13, 18, 34, 48, 50; DA; PC 4; WLC**
See also CA 5-8R; 37-40R; CANR 40;
CDALB 1917-1929; DLB 4, 45, 63;
MTCW

Povod, Reinaldo 1959- .... **CLC 44**
See also CA 136

Powell, Anthony (Dymoke)
1905- .... **CLC 1, 3, 7, 9, 10, 31**
See also CA 1-4R; CANR 1, 32;
CDBLB 1945-1960; DLB 15; MTCW

Powell, Dawn 1897-1965 .... **CLC 66**
See also CA 5-8R

Powell, Padgett 1952-............ **CLC 34**
See also CA 126

Powers, J(ames) F(arl)
1917- .... **CLC 1, 4, 8, 57; SSC 4**
See also CA 1-4R; CANR 2; DLB 130;
MTCW

Powers, John J(ames) 1945-
See Powers, John R.
See also CA 69-72

Powers, John R. .... **CLC 66**
See also Powers, John J(ames)

Pownall, David 1938-............ **CLC 10**
See also CA 89-92; CAAS 18; DLB 14

Powys, John Cowper
1872-1963 .... **CLC 7, 9, 15, 46**
See also CA 85-88; DLB 15; MTCW

Powys, T(heodore) F(rancis)
1875-1953 .... **TCLC 9**
See also CA 106; DLB 36

Prager, Emily 1952-............. **CLC 56**

Pratt, E(dwin) J(ohn)
1883(?)-1964 .... **CLC 19**
See also CA 141; 93-96; DLB 92

Premchand .... **TCLC 21**
See also Srivastava, Dhanpat Rai

Preussler, Otfried 1923-......... **CLC 17**
See also CA 77-80; SATA 24

Prevert, Jacques (Henri Marie)
1900-1977 .... **CLC 15**
See also CA 77-80; 69-72; CANR 29;
MTCW; SATA 30

Prevost, Abbe (Antoine Francois)
1697-1763 .... **LC 1**

Price, (Edward) Reynolds
1933- .... **CLC 3, 6, 13, 43, 50, 63**
See also CA 1-4R; CANR 1, 37; DLB 2

Price, Richard 1949- .... **CLC 6, 12**
See also CA 49-52; CANR 3; DLBY 81

Prichard, Katharine Susannah
1883-1969 .... **CLC 46**
See also CA 11-12; CANR 33; CAP 1;
MTCW; SATA 66

Priestley, J(ohn) B(oynton)
1894-1984 .... **CLC 2, 5, 9, 34**
See also CA 9-12R; 113; CANR 33;
CDBLB 1914-1945; DLB 10, 34, 77, 100,
139; DLBY 84; MTCW

Prince 1958(?)-.................. **CLC 35**

Prince, F(rank) T(empleton) 1912-.. **CLC 22**
See also CA 101; CANR 43; DLB 20

Prince Kropotkin
See Kropotkin, Peter (Aleksieevich)

Prior, Matthew 1664-1721.......... **LC 4**
See also DLB 95

Pritchard, William H(arrison)
1932- .... **CLC 34**
See also CA 65-68; CANR 23; DLB 111

Pritchett, V(ictor) S(awdon)
1900- .... **CLC 5, 13, 15, 41; SSC 14**
See also CA 61-64; CANR 31; DLB 15,
139; MTCW

Private 19022
See Manning, Frederic

Probst, Mark 1925- .... **CLC 59**
See also CA 130

Prokosch, Frederic 1908-1989.... **CLC 4, 48**
See also CA 73-76; 128; DLB 48

Prophet, The
See Dreiser, Theodore (Herman Albert)

Prose, Francine 1947-............ **CLC 45**
See also CA 109; 112

Proudhon
See Cunha, Euclides (Rodrigues Pimenta) da

Proulx, E. Annie 1935- .... **CLC 81**

**Proust, (Valentin-Louis-George-Eugene-)
Marcel**
1871-1922 ... **TCLC 7, 13, 33; DA; WLC**
See also CA 104; 120; DLB 65; MTCW

Prowler, Harley
See Masters, Edgar Lee

Prus, Boleslaw 1845-1912 .... **TCLC 48**

Pryor, Richard (Franklin Lenox Thomas)
1940- .... **CLC 26**
See also CA 122

Przybyszewski, Stanislaw
1868-1927 .... **TCLC 36**
See also DLB 66

Pteleon
See Grieve, C(hristopher) M(urray)

Puckett, Lute
See Masters, Edgar Lee

Puig, Manuel
1932-1990 ... **CLC 3, 5, 10, 28, 65; HLC**
See also CA 45-48; CANR 2, 32; DLB 113;
HW; MTCW

Purdy, Al(fred Wellington)
1918- .... **CLC 3, 6, 14, 50**
See also CA 81-84; CAAS 17; CANR 42;
DLB 88

Purdy, James (Amos)
1923- .... **CLC 2, 4, 10, 28, 52**
See also CA 33-36R; CAAS 1; CANR 19;
DLB 2; MTCW

Pure, Simon
See Swinnerton, Frank Arthur

Pushkin, Alexander (Sergeyevich)
1799-1837 .... **NCLC 3, 27; DA; PC 10;
WLC**
See also SATA 61

P'u Sung-ling 1640-1715 .... **LC 3**

Putnam, Arthur Lee
See Alger, Horatio, Jr.

Puzo, Mario 1920-......... **CLC 1, 2, 6, 36**
See also CA 65-68; CANR 4, 42; DLB 6;
MTCW

Pym, Barbara (Mary Crampton)
1913-1980 .... **CLC 13, 19, 37**
See also CA 13-14; 97-100; CANR 13, 34;
CAP 1; DLB 14; DLBY 87; MTCW

Pynchon, Thomas (Ruggles, Jr.)
1937- . . . . . CLC 2, 3, 6, 9, 11, 18, 33, 62, 72; DA; SSC 14; WLC
See also BEST 90:2; CA 17-20R; CANR 22; DLB 2; MTCW

Qian Zhongshu
See Ch'ien Chung-shu

Qroll
See Dagerman, Stig (Halvard)

Quarrington, Paul (Lewis) 1953- . . . . **CLC 65**
See also CA 129

Quasimodo, Salvatore 1901-1968 . . . **CLC 10**
See also CA 13-16; 25-28R; CAP 1; DLB 114; MTCW

Queen, Ellery . . . . **CLC 3, 11**
See also Dannay, Frederic; Davidson, Avram; Lee, Manfred B(ennington); Sturgeon, Theodore (Hamilton); Vance, John Holbrook

Queen, Ellery, Jr.
See Dannay, Frederic; Lee, Manfred B(ennington)

Queneau, Raymond
1903-1976 . . . . **CLC 2, 5, 10, 42**
See also CA 77-80; 69-72; CANR 32; DLB 72; MTCW

Quevedo, Francisco de 1580-1645 . . . . **LC 23**

Quiller-Couch, Arthur Thomas
1863-1944 . . . . **TCLC 53**
See also CA 118; DLB 135

Quin, Ann (Marie) 1936-1973 . . . . **CLC 6**
See also CA 9-12R; 45-48; DLB 14

Quinn, Martin
See Smith, Martin Cruz

Quinn, Simon
See Smith, Martin Cruz

Quiroga, Horacio (Sylvestre)
1878-1937 . . . . **TCLC 20; HLC**
See also CA 117; 131; HW; MTCW

Quoirez, Francoise 1935- . . . . **CLC 9**
See also Sagan, Francoise
See also CA 49-52; CANR 6, 39; MTCW

Raabe, Wilhelm 1831-1910 . . . . **TCLC 45**
See also DLB 129

Rabe, David (William) 1940- . . . **CLC 4, 8, 33**
See also CA 85-88; CABS 3; DLB 7

Rabelais, Francois
1483-1553 . . . . **LC 5; DA; WLC**

Rabinovitch, Sholem 1859-1916
See Aleichem, Sholom
See also CA 104

Radcliffe, Ann (Ward) 1764-1823 . . **NCLC 6**
See also DLB 39

Radiguet, Raymond 1903-1923 . . . . **TCLC 29**
See also DLB 65

Radnoti, Miklos 1909-1944 . . . . **TCLC 16**
See also CA 118

Rado, James 1939- . . . . **CLC 17**
See also CA 105

Radvanyi, Netty 1900-1983
See Seghers, Anna
See also CA 85-88; 110

Rae, Ben
See Griffiths, Trevor

Raeburn, John (Hay) 1941- . . . . **CLC 34**
See also CA 57-60

Ragni, Gerome 1942-1991 . . . . **CLC 17**
See also CA 105; 134

Rahv, Philip 1908-1973 . . . . **CLC 24**
See also Greenberg, Ivan
See also DLB 137

Raine, Craig 1944- . . . . **CLC 32**
See also CA 108; CANR 29; DLB 40

Raine, Kathleen (Jessie) 1908- . . . **CLC 7, 45**
See also CA 85-88; DLB 20; MTCW

Rainis, Janis 1865-1929 . . . . **TCLC 29**

Rakosi, Carl . . . . **CLC 47**
See also Rawley, Callman
See also CAAS 5

Raleigh, Richard
See Lovecraft, H(oward) P(hillips)

Rallentando, H. P.
See Sayers, Dorothy L(eigh)

Ramal, Walter
See de la Mare, Walter (John)

Ramon, Juan
See Jimenez (Mantecon), Juan Ramon

Ramos, Graciliano 1892-1953 . . . . . **TCLC 32**

Rampersad, Arnold 1941- . . . . **CLC 44**
See also BW 2; CA 127; 133; DLB 111

Rampling, Anne
See Rice, Anne

Ramuz, Charles-Ferdinand
1878-1947 . . . . **TCLC 33**

Rand, Ayn
1905-1982 . . . . . . **CLC 3, 30, 44, 79; DA; WLC**
See also AAYA 10; CA 13-16R; 105; CANR 27; MTCW

Randall, Dudley (Felker)
1914- . . . . **CLC 1; BLC**
See also BW 1; CA 25-28R; CANR 23; DLB 41

Randall, Robert
See Silverberg, Robert

Ranger, Ken
See Creasey, John

Ransom, John Crowe
1888-1974 . . . . **CLC 2, 4, 5, 11, 24**
See also CA 5-8R; 49-52; CANR 6, 34; DLB 45, 63; MTCW

Rao, Raja 1909- . . . . **CLC 25, 56**
See also CA 73-76; MTCW

Raphael, Frederic (Michael)
1931- . . . . **CLC 2, 14**
See also CA 1-4R; CANR 1; DLB 14

Ratcliffe, James P.
See Mencken, H(enry) L(ouis)

Rathbone, Julian 1935- . . . . **CLC 41**
See also CA 101; CANR 34

Rattigan, Terence (Mervyn)
1911-1977 . . . . **CLC 7**
See also CA 85-88; 73-76; CDBLB 1945-1960; DLB 13; MTCW

Ratushinskaya, Irina 1954- . . . . **CLC 54**
See also CA 129

Raven, Simon (Arthur Noel)
1927- . . . . **CLC 14**
See also CA 81-84

Rawley, Callman 1903-
See Rakosi, Carl
See also CA 21-24R; CANR 12, 32

Rawlings, Marjorie Kinnan
1896-1953 . . . . **TCLC 4**
See also CA 104; 137; DLB 9, 22, 102; JRDA; MAICYA; YABC 1

Ray, Satyajit 1921-1992 . . . . **CLC 16, 76**
See also CA 114; 137

Read, Herbert Edward 1893-1968 . . . . **CLC 4**
See also CA 85-88; 25-28R; DLB 20

Read, Piers Paul 1941- . . . . . . **CLC 4, 10, 25**
See also CA 21-24R; CANR 38; DLB 14; SATA 21

Reade, Charles 1814-1884 . . . . **NCLC 2**
See also DLB 21

Reade, Hamish
See Gray, Simon (James Holliday)

Reading, Peter 1946- . . . . **CLC 47**
See also CA 103; DLB 40

Reaney, James 1926- . . . . **CLC 13**
See also CA 41-44R; CAAS 15; CANR 42; DLB 68; SATA 43

Rebreanu, Liviu 1885-1944 . . . . **TCLC 28**

Rechy, John (Francisco)
1934- . . . . **CLC 1, 7, 14, 18; HLC**
See also CA 5-8R; CAAS 4; CANR 6, 32; DLB 122; DLBY 82; HW

Redcam, Tom 1870-1933 . . . . **TCLC 25**

Reddin, Keith . . . . **CLC 67**

Redgrove, Peter (William)
1932- . . . . **CLC 6, 41**
See also CA 1-4R; CANR 3, 39; DLB 40

Redmon, Anne . . . . **CLC 22**
See also Nightingale, Anne Redmon
See also DLBY 86

Reed, Eliot
See Ambler, Eric

Reed, Ishmael
1938- . . . **CLC 2, 3, 5, 6, 13, 32, 60; BLC**
See also BW 2; CA 21-24R; CANR 25; DLB 2, 5, 33; DLBD 8; MTCW

Reed, John (Silas) 1887-1920 . . . . . . **TCLC 9**
See also CA 106

Reed, Lou . . . . **CLC 21**
See also Firbank, Louis

Reeve, Clara 1729-1807 . . . . **NCLC 19**
See also DLB 39

Reich, Wilhelm 1897-1957 . . . . **TCLC 57**

Reid, Christopher (John) 1949- . . . . . **CLC 33**
See also CA 140; DLB 40

Reid, Desmond
See Moorcock, Michael (John)

Reid Banks, Lynne 1929-
See Banks, Lynne Reid
See also CA 1-4R; CANR 6, 22, 38; CLR 24; JRDA; MAICYA; SATA 22, 75

Reilly, William K.
See Creasey, John

Roberts, Kate 1891-1985 . . . . **CLC 15**
See also CA 107; 116

Roberts, Keith (John Kingston)
1935- . . . . **CLC 14**
See also CA 25-28R

Roberts, Kenneth (Lewis)
1885-1957 . . . . **TCLC 23**
See also CA 109; DLB 9

Roberts, Michele (B.) 1949- . . . . **CLC 48**
See also CA 115

Robertson, Ellis
See Ellison, Harlan; Silverberg, Robert

Robertson, Thomas William
1829-1871 . . . . **NCLC 35**

Robinson, Edwin Arlington
1869-1935 . . . . **TCLC 5; DA; PC 1**
See also CA 104; 133; CDALB 1865-1917;
DLB 54; MTCW

Robinson, Henry Crabb
1775-1867 . . . . **NCLC 15**
See also DLB 107

Robinson, Jill 1936- . . . . **CLC 10**
See also CA 102

Robinson, Kim Stanley 1952- . . . . . . **CLC 34**
See also CA 126

Robinson, Lloyd
See Silverberg, Robert

Robinson, Marilynne 1944- . . . . **CLC 25**
See also CA 116

Robinson, Smokey . . . . **CLC 21**
See also Robinson, William, Jr.

Robinson, William, Jr. 1940-
See Robinson, Smokey
See also CA 116

Robison, Mary 1949- . . . . **CLC 42**
See also CA 113; 116; DLB 130

Rod, Edouard 1857-1910 . . . . **TCLC 52**

Roddenberry, Eugene Wesley 1921-1991
See Roddenberry, Gene
See also CA 110; 135; CANR 37; SATA 45

Roddenberry, Gene . . . . **CLC 17**
See also Roddenberry, Eugene Wesley
See also AAYA 5; SATA-Obit 69

Rodgers, Mary 1931- . . . . **CLC 12**
See also CA 49-52; CANR 8; CLR 20;
JRDA; MAICYA; SATA 8

Rodgers, W(illiam) R(obert)
1909-1969 . . . . **CLC 7**
See also CA 85-88; DLB 20

Rodman, Eric
See Silverberg, Robert

Rodman, Howard 1920(?)-1985 . . . . . **CLC 65**
See also CA 118

Rodman, Maia
See Wojciechowska, Maia (Teresa)

Rodriguez, Claudio 1934- . . . . **CLC 10**
See also DLB 134

Roelvaag, O(le) E(dvart)
1876-1931 . . . . **TCLC 17**
See also CA 117; DLB 9

Roethke, Theodore (Huebner)
1908-1963 . . . . . . **CLC 1, 3, 8, 11, 19, 46**
See also CA 81-84; CABS 2;
CDALB 1941-1968; DLB 5; MTCW

Rogers, Thomas Hunton 1927- . . . . . **CLC 57**
See also CA 89-92

Rogers, Will(iam Penn Adair)
1879-1935 . . . . **TCLC 8**
See also CA 105; 144; DLB 11

Rogin, Gilbert 1929- . . . . **CLC 18**
See also CA 65-68; CANR 15

Rohan, Koda . . . . **TCLC 22**
See also Koda Shigeyuki

Rohmer, Eric . . . . **CLC 16**
See also Scherer, Jean-Marie Maurice

Rohmer, Sax . . . . **TCLC 28**
See also Ward, Arthur Henry Sarsfield
See also DLB 70

Roiphe, Anne (Richardson)
1935- . . . . **CLC 3, 9**
See also CA 89-92; CANR 45; DLBY 80

Rojas, Fernando de 1465-1541 . . . . . . **LC 23**

Rolfe, Frederick (William Serafino Austin
Lewis Mary) 1860-1913. . . . . . **TCLC 12**
See also CA 107; DLB 34

Rolland, Romain 1866-1944. . . . . . **TCLC 23**
See also CA 118; DLB 65

Rolvaag, O(le) E(dvart)
See Roelvaag, O(le) E(dvart)

Romain Arnaud, Saint
See Aragon, Louis

Romains, Jules 1885-1972 . . . . **CLC 7**
See also CA 85-88; CANR 34; DLB 65;
MTCW

Romero, Jose Ruben 1890-1952 . . . **TCLC 14**
See also CA 114; 131; HW

Ronsard, Pierre de 1524-1585. . . . . . . **LC 6**

Rooke, Leon 1934- . . . . **CLC 25, 34**
See also CA 25-28R; CANR 23

Roper, William 1498-1578. . . . . **LC 10**

Roquelaure, A. N.
See Rice, Anne

Rosa, Joao Guimaraes 1908-1967 . . . **CLC 23**
See also CA 89-92; DLB 113

Rose, Wendy 1948- . . . . **CLC 85**
See also CA 53-56; CANR 5; NNAL;
SATA 12

Rosen, Richard (Dean) 1949- . . . . **CLC 39**
See also CA 77-80

Rosenberg, Isaac 1890-1918. . . . . . . **TCLC 12**
See also CA 107; DLB 20

Rosenblatt, Joe . . . . **CLC 15**
See also Rosenblatt, Joseph

Rosenblatt, Joseph 1933-
See Rosenblatt, Joe
See also CA 89-92

Rosenfeld, Samuel 1896-1963
See Tzara, Tristan
See also CA 89-92

Rosenthal, M(acha) L(ouis) 1917- . . . **CLC 28**
See also CA 1-4R; CAAS 6; CANR 4;
DLB 5; SATA 59

Ross, Barnaby
See Dannay, Frederic

Ross, Bernard L.
See Follett, Ken(neth Martin)

Ross, J. H.
See Lawrence, T(homas) E(dward)

Ross, Martin
See Martin, Violet Florence
See also DLB 135

Ross, (James) Sinclair 1908- . . . . **CLC 13**
See also CA 73-76; DLB 88

Rossetti, Christina (Georgina)
1830-1894 . . . **NCLC 2; DA; PC 7; WLC**
See also DLB 35; MAICYA; SATA 20

Rossetti, Dante Gabriel
1828-1882 . . . . **NCLC 4; DA; WLC**
See also CDBLB 1832-1890; DLB 35

Rossner, Judith (Perelman)
1935- . . . . **CLC 6, 9, 29**
See also AITN 2; BEST 90:3; CA 17-20R;
CANR 18; DLB 6; MTCW

Rostand, Edmond (Eugene Alexis)
1868-1918 . . . . **TCLC 6, 37; DA**
See also CA 104; 126; MTCW

Roth, Henry 1906- . . . . **CLC 2, 6, 11**
See also CA 11-12; CANR 38; CAP 1;
DLB 28; MTCW

Roth, Joseph 1894-1939. . . . . **TCLC 33**
See also DLB 85

Roth, Philip (Milton)
1933- . . . . . . **CLC 1, 2, 3, 4, 6, 9, 15, 22,**
31, 47, 66; DA; WLC
See also BEST 90:3; CA 1-4R; CANR 1, 22,
36; CDALB 1968-1988; DLB 2, 28;
DLBY 82; MTCW

Rothenberg, Jerome 1931- . . . . **CLC 6, 57**
See also CA 45-48; CANR 1; DLB 5

Roumain, Jacques (Jean Baptiste)
1907-1944 . . . . **TCLC 19; BLC**
See also BW 1; CA 117; 125

Rourke, Constance (Mayfield)
1885-1941 . . . . **TCLC 12**
See also CA 107; YABC 1

Rousseau, Jean-Baptiste 1671-1741 . . . **LC 9**

Rousseau, Jean-Jacques
1712-1778 . . . . **LC 14; DA; WLC**

Roussel, Raymond 1877-1933 . . . . . **TCLC 20**
See also CA 117

Rovit, Earl (Herbert) 1927- . . . . **CLC 7**
See also CA 5-8R; CANR 12

Rowe, Nicholas 1674-1718. . . . . **LC 8**
See also DLB 84

Rowley, Ames Dorrance
See Lovecraft, H(oward) P(hillips)

Rowson, Susanna Haswell
1762(?)-1824 . . . . **NCLC 5**
See also DLB 37

Roy, Gabrielle 1909-1983. . . . . . . **CLC 10, 14**
See also CA 53-56; 110; CANR 5; DLB 68;
MTCW

Rozewicz, Tadeusz 1921- . . . . **CLC 9, 23**
See also CA 108; CANR 36; MTCW

Ruark, Gibbons 1941- . . . . **CLC 3**
See also CA 33-36R; CANR 14, 31;
DLB 120

Rubens, Bernice (Ruth) 1923- . . . **CLC 19, 31**
See also CA 25-28R; CANR 33; DLB 14;
MTCW

Santiago, Danny . . . . **CLC 33**
  See also James, Daniel (Lewis); James,
  Daniel (Lewis)
  See also DLB 122

Santmyer, Helen Hoover
  1895-1986 . . . . **CLC 33**
  See also CA 1-4R; 118; CANR 15, 33;
  DLBY 84; MTCW

Santos, Bienvenido N(uqui) 1911- . . . **CLC 22**
  See also CA 101; CANR 19

Sapper . . . . **TCLC 44**
  See also McNeile, Herman Cyril

Sappho fl. 6th cent. B.C.- . . . . **CMLC 3; PC 5**

Sarduy, Severo 1937-1993 . . . . **CLC 6**
  See also CA 89-92; 142; DLB 113; HW

Sargeson, Frank 1903-1982 . . . . **CLC 31**
  See also CA 25-28R; 106; CANR 38

Sarmiento, Felix Ruben Garcia
  See Dario, Ruben

Saroyan, William
  1908-1981 . . . . . **CLC 1, 8, 10, 29, 34, 56;
                                        DA; WLC**
  See also CA 5-8R; 103; CANR 30; DLB 7,
  9, 86; DLBY 81; MTCW; SATA 23, 24

Sarraute, Nathalie
  1900- . . . . **CLC 1, 2, 4, 8, 10, 31, 80**
  See also CA 9-12R; CANR 23; DLB 83;
  MTCW

Sarton, (Eleanor) May
  1912- . . . . **CLC 4, 14, 49**
  See also CA 1-4R; CANR 1, 34; DLB 48;
  DLBY 81; MTCW; SATA 36

Sartre, Jean-Paul
  1905-1980 . . . . **CLC 1, 4, 7, 9, 13, 18, 24,
                              44, 50, 52; DA; DC 3; WLC**
  See also CA 9-12R; 97-100; CANR 21;
  DLB 72; MTCW

Sassoon, Siegfried (Lorraine)
  1886-1967 . . . . **CLC 36**
  See also CA 104; 25-28R; CANR 36;
  DLB 20; MTCW

Satterfield, Charles
  See Pohl, Frederik

Saul, John (W. III) 1942- . . . . **CLC 46**
  See also AAYA 10; BEST 90:4; CA 81-84;
  CANR 16, 40

Saunders, Caleb
  See Heinlein, Robert A(nson)

Saura (Atares), Carlos 1932- . . . . **CLC 20**
  See also CA 114; 131; HW

Sauser-Hall, Frederic 1887-1961 . . . . **CLC 18**
  See also CA 102; 93-96; CANR 36; MTCW

Saussure, Ferdinand de
  1857-1913 . . . . **TCLC 49**

Savage, Catharine
  See Brosman, Catharine Savage

Savage, Thomas 1915- . . . . **CLC 40**
  See also CA 126; 132; CAAS 15

Savan, Glenn 19(?)- . . . . **CLC 50**

Sayers, Dorothy L(eigh)
  1893-1957 . . . . **TCLC 2, 15**
  See also CA 104; 119; CDBLB 1914-1945;
  DLB 10, 36, 77, 100; MTCW

Sayers, Valerie 1952- . . . . **CLC 50**
  See also CA 134

Sayles, John (Thomas)
  1950- . . . . **CLC 7, 10, 14**
  See also CA 57-60; CANR 41; DLB 44

Scammell, Michael . . . . **CLC 34**

Scannell, Vernon 1922- . . . . **CLC 49**
  See also CA 5-8R; CANR 8, 24; DLB 27;
  SATA 59

Scarlett, Susan
  See Streatfeild, (Mary) Noel

Schaeffer, Susan Fromberg
  1941- . . . . **CLC 6, 11, 22**
  See also CA 49-52; CANR 18; DLB 28;
  MTCW; SATA 22

Schary, Jill
  See Robinson, Jill

Schell, Jonathan 1943- . . . . **CLC 35**
  See also CA 73-76; CANR 12

Schelling, Friedrich Wilhelm Joseph von
  1775-1854 . . . . **NCLC 30**
  See also DLB 90

Schendel, Arthur van 1874-1946 . . . **TCLC 56**

Scherer, Jean-Marie Maurice 1920-
  See Rohmer, Eric
  See also CA 110

Schevill, James (Erwin) 1920- . . . . . . **CLC 7**
  See also CA 5-8R; CAAS 12

Schiller, Friedrich 1759-1805 . . . . **NCLC 39**
  See also DLB 94

Schisgal, Murray (Joseph) 1926- . . . . . **CLC 6**
  See also CA 21-24R

Schlee, Ann 1934- . . . . **CLC 35**
  See also CA 101; CANR 29; SATA 36, 44

Schlegel, August Wilhelm von
  1767-1845 . . . . **NCLC 15**
  See also DLB 94

Schlegel, Friedrich 1772-1829 . . . . **NCLC 45**
  See also DLB 90

Schlegel, Johann Elias (von)
  1719(?)-1749 . . . . **LC 5**

Schlesinger, Arthur M(eier), Jr.
  1917- . . . . **CLC 84**
  See also AITN 1; CA 1-4R; CANR 1, 28;
  DLB 17; MTCW; SATA 61

Schmidt, Arno (Otto) 1914-1979 . . . . **CLC 56**
  See also CA 128; 109; DLB 69

Schmitz, Aron Hector 1861-1928
  See Svevo, Italo
  See also CA 104; 122; MTCW

Schnackenberg, Gjertrud 1953- . . . . . **CLC 40**
  See also CA 116; DLB 120

Schneider, Leonard Alfred 1925-1966
  See Bruce, Lenny
  See also CA 89-92

Schnitzler, Arthur
  1862-1931 . . . . **TCLC 4; SSC 15**
  See also CA 104; DLB 81, 118

Schor, Sandra (M.) 1932(?)-1990 . . . **CLC 65**
  See also CA 132

Schorer, Mark 1908-1977 . . . . **CLC 9**
  See also CA 5-8R; 73-76; CANR 7;
  DLB 103

Schrader, Paul (Joseph) 1946- . . . . . . **CLC 26**
  See also CA 37-40R; CANR 41; DLB 44

Schreiner, Olive (Emilie Albertina)
  1855-1920 . . . . **TCLC 9**
  See also CA 105; DLB 18

Schulberg, Budd (Wilson)
  1914- . . . . **CLC 7, 48**
  See also CA 25-28R; CANR 19; DLB 6, 26,
  28; DLBY 81

Schulz, Bruno
  1892-1942 . . . . **TCLC 5, 51; SSC 13**
  See also CA 115; 123

Schulz, Charles M(onroe) 1922- . . . . **CLC 12**
  See also CA 9-12R; CANR 6; SATA 10

Schumacher, E(rnst) F(riedrich)
  1911-1977 . . . . **CLC 80**
  See also CA 81-84; 73-76; CANR 34

Schuyler, James Marcus
  1923-1991 . . . . **CLC 5, 23**
  See also CA 101; 134; DLB 5

Schwartz, Delmore (David)
  1913-1966 . . . . . . **CLC 2, 4, 10, 45; PC 8**
  See also CA 17-18; 25-28R; CANR 35;
  CAP 2; DLB 28, 48; MTCW

Schwartz, Ernst
  See Ozu, Yasujiro

Schwartz, John Burnham 1965- . . . . **CLC 59**
  See also CA 132

Schwartz, Lynne Sharon 1939- . . . . . **CLC 31**
  See also CA 103; CANR 44

Schwartz, Muriel A.
  See Eliot, T(homas) S(tearns)

Schwarz-Bart, Andre 1928- . . . . **CLC 2, 4**
  See also CA 89-92

Schwarz-Bart, Simone 1938- . . . . **CLC 7**
  See also BW 2; CA 97-100

Schwob, (Mayer Andre) Marcel
  1867-1905 . . . . **TCLC 20**
  See also CA 117; DLB 123

Sciascia, Leonardo
  1921-1989 . . . . **CLC 8, 9, 41**
  See also CA 85-88; 130; CANR 35; MTCW

Scoppettone, Sandra 1936- . . . . **CLC 26**
  See also AAYA 11; CA 5-8R; CANR 41;
  SATA 9

Scorsese, Martin 1942- . . . . **CLC 20**
  See also CA 110; 114

Scotland, Jay
  See Jakes, John (William)

Scott, Duncan Campbell
  1862-1947 . . . . **TCLC 6**
  See also CA 104; DLB 92

Scott, Evelyn 1893-1963 . . . . **CLC 43**
  See also CA 104; 112; DLB 9, 48

Scott, F(rancis) R(eginald)
  1899-1985 . . . . **CLC 22**
  See also CA 101; 114; DLB 88

Scott, Frank
  See Scott, F(rancis) R(eginald)

Scott, Joanna 1960- . . . . **CLC 50**
  See also CA 126

Scott, Paul (Mark) 1920-1978 . . . . **CLC 9, 60**
  See also CA 81-84; 77-80; CANR 33;
  DLB 14; MTCW

Scott, Walter
1771-1832 .... **NCLC 15; DA; WLC**
See also CDBLB 1789-1832; DLB 93, 107,
116, 144; YABC 2

Scribe, (Augustin) Eugene
1791-1861 .... **NCLC 16**

Scrum, R.
See Crumb, R(obert)

Scudery, Madeleine de   1607-1701..... **LC 2**

Scum
See Crumb, R(obert)

Scumbag, Little Bobby
See Crumb, R(obert)

Seabrook, John
See Hubbard, L(afayette) Ron(ald)

Sealy, I. Allan   1951- .... **CLC 55**

Search, Alexander
See Pessoa, Fernando (Antonio Nogueira)

Sebastian, Lee
See Silverberg, Robert

Sebastian Owl
See Thompson, Hunter S(tockton)

Sebestyen, Ouida   1924- .... **CLC 30**
See also AAYA 8; CA 107; CANR 40;
CLR 17; JRDA; MAICYA; SAAS 10;
SATA 39

Secundus, H. Scriblerus
See Fielding, Henry

Sedges, John
See Buck, Pearl S(ydenstricker)

Sedgwick, Catharine Maria
1789-1867 .... **NCLC 19**
See also DLB 1, 74

Seelye, John   1931- .... **CLC 7**

Seferiades, Giorgos Stylianou   1900-1971
See Seferis, George
See also CA 5-8R; 33-36R; CANR 5, 36;
MTCW

Seferis, George .... **CLC 5, 11**
See also Seferiades, Giorgos Stylianou

Segal, Erich (Wolf)   1937- .... **CLC 3, 10**
See also BEST 89:1; CA 25-28R; CANR 20,
36; DLBY 86; MTCW

Seger, Bob   1945-................. **CLC 35**

Seghers, Anna .... **CLC 7**
See also Radvanyi, Netty
See also DLB 69

Seidel, Frederick (Lewis)   1936-..... **CLC 18**
See also CA 13-16R; CANR 8; DLBY 84

Seifert, Jaroslav   1901-1986..... **CLC 34, 44**
See also CA 127; MTCW

Sei Shonagon   c. 966-1017(?) ...... **CMLC 6**

Selby, Hubert, Jr.   1928- ..... **CLC 1, 2, 4, 8**
See also CA 13-16R; CANR 33; DLB 2

Selzer, Richard   1928-............. **CLC 74**
See also CA 65-68; CANR 14

Sembene, Ousmane
See Ousmane, Sembene

Senancour, Etienne Pivert de
1770-1846 .... **NCLC 16**
See also DLB 119

Sender, Ramon (Jose)
1902-1982 .... **CLC 8; HLC**
See also CA 5-8R; 105; CANR 8; HW;
MTCW

Seneca, Lucius Annaeus
4B.C.-65.................. **CMLC 6**

Senghor, Leopold Sedar
1906- .... **CLC 54; BLC**
See also BW 2; CA 116; 125; MTCW

Serling, (Edward) Rod(man)
1924-1975 .... **CLC 30**
See also AITN 1; CA 65-68; 57-60; DLB 26

Serna, Ramon Gomez de la
See Gomez de la Serna, Ramon

Serpieres
See Guillevic, (Eugene)

Service, Robert
See Service, Robert W(illiam)
See also DLB 92

Service, Robert W(illiam)
1874(?)-1958 ...... **TCLC 15; DA; WLC**
See also Service, Robert
See also CA 115; 140; SATA 20

Seth, Vikram   1952-............... **CLC 43**
See also CA 121; 127; DLB 120

Seton, Cynthia Propper
1926-1982 .... **CLC 27**
See also CA 5-8R; 108; CANR 7

Seton, Ernest (Evan) Thompson
1860-1946 .... **TCLC 31**
See also CA 109; DLB 92; JRDA; SATA 18

Seton-Thompson, Ernest
See Seton, Ernest (Evan) Thompson

Settle, Mary Lee   1918- .... **CLC 19, 61**
See also CA 89-92; CAAS 1; CANR 44;
DLB 6

Seuphor, Michel
See Arp, Jean

Sevigne, Marie (de Rabutin-Chantal) Marquise
de   1626-1696 .... **LC 11**

Sexton, Anne (Harvey)
1928-1974 .... **CLC 2, 4, 6, 8, 10, 15, 53;**
DA; PC 2; WLC
See also CA 1-4R; 53-56; CABS 2;
CANR 3, 36; CDALB 1941-1968; DLB 5;
MTCW; SATA 10

Shaara, Michael (Joseph Jr.)
1929-1988 .... **CLC 15**
See also AITN 1; CA 102; DLBY 83

Shackleton, C. C.
See Aldiss, Brian W(ilson)

Shacochis, Bob .... **CLC 39**
See also Shacochis, Robert G.

Shacochis, Robert G.   1951-
See Shacochis, Bob
See also CA 119; 124

Shaffer, Anthony (Joshua)   1926-.... **CLC 19**
See also CA 110; 116; DLB 13

Shaffer, Peter (Levin)
1926-.......... **CLC 5, 14, 18, 37, 60**
See also CA 25-28R; CANR 25;
CDBLB 1960 to Present; DLB 13;
MTCW

Shakey, Bernard
See Young, Neil

Shalamov, Varlam (Tikhonovich)
1907(?)-1982 .... **CLC 18**
See also CA 129; 105

Shamlu, Ahmad   1925- .... **CLC 10**

Shammas, Anton   1951-........... **CLC 55**

Shange, Ntozake
1948- .... **CLC 8, 25, 38, 74; BLC; DC 3**
See also AAYA 9; BW 2; CA 85-88;
CABS 3; CANR 27; DLB 38; MTCW

Shanley, John Patrick   1950-....... **CLC 75**
See also CA 128; 133

Shapcott, Thomas William   1935- ... **CLC 38**
See also CA 69-72

Shapiro, Jane.................... **CLC 76**

Shapiro, Karl (Jay)   1913- .. **CLC 4, 8, 15, 53**
See also CA 1-4R; CAAS 6; CANR 1, 36;
DLB 48; MTCW

Sharp, William   1855-1905 .... **TCLC 39**

Sharpe, Thomas Ridley   1928-
See Sharpe, Tom
See also CA 114; 122

Sharpe, Tom.................... **CLC 36**
See also Sharpe, Thomas Ridley
See also DLB 14

Shaw, Bernard................... **TCLC 45**
See also Shaw, George Bernard
See also BW 1

Shaw, G. Bernard
See Shaw, George Bernard

Shaw, George Bernard
1856-1950 .... **TCLC 3, 9, 21; DA; WLC**
See also Shaw, Bernard
See also CA 104; 128; CDBLB 1914-1945;
DLB 10, 57; MTCW

Shaw, Henry Wheeler
1818-1885 .... **NCLC 15**
See also DLB 11

Shaw, Irwin   1913-1984....... **CLC 7, 23, 34**
See also AITN 1; CA 13-16R; 112;
CANR 21; CDALB 1941-1968; DLB 6,
102; DLBY 84; MTCW

Shaw, Robert   1927-1978 .... **CLC 5**
See also AITN 1; CA 1-4R; 81-84;
CANR 4; DLB 13, 14

Shaw, T. E.
See Lawrence, T(homas) E(dward)

Shawn, Wallace   1943- .... **CLC 41**
See also CA 112

Sheed, Wilfrid (John Joseph)
1930- .... **CLC 2, 4, 10, 53**
See also CA 65-68; CANR 30; DLB 6;
MTCW

Sheldon, Alice Hastings Bradley
1915(?)-1987
See Tiptree, James, Jr.
See also CA 108; 122; CANR 34; MTCW

Sheldon, John
See Bloch, Robert (Albert)

Shelley, Mary Wollstonecraft (Godwin)
1797-1851 .... **NCLC 14; DA; WLC**
See also CDBLB 1789-1832; DLB 110, 116;
SATA 29

Shelley, Percy Bysshe
1792-1822 .... **NCLC 18; DA; WLC**
See also CDBLB 1789-1832; DLB 96, 110

Shepard, Jim 1956-.............. **CLC 36**
See also CA 137

Shepard, Lucius 1947-............ **CLC 34**
See also CA 128; 141

Shepard, Sam
1943-......... **CLC 4, 6, 17, 34, 41, 44**
See also AAYA 1; CA 69-72; CABS 3;
CANR 22; DLB 7; MTCW

Shepherd, Michael
See Ludlum, Robert

Sherburne, Zoa (Morin) 1912-...... **CLC 30**
See also CA 1-4R; CANR 3, 37; MAICYA;
SAAS 18; SATA 3

Sheridan, Frances 1724-1766........ **LC 7**
See also DLB 39, 84

Sheridan, Richard Brinsley
1751-1816 ... **NCLC 5; DA; DC 1; WLC**
See also CDBLB 1660-1789; DLB 89

Sherman, Jonathan Marc.......... **CLC 55**

Sherman, Martin 1941(?)-......... **CLC 19**
See also CA 116; 123

Sherwin, Judith Johnson 1936-... **CLC 7, 15**
See also CA 25-28R; CANR 34

Sherwood, Frances 1940-......... **CLC 81**

Sherwood, Robert E(mmet)
1896-1955 .... **TCLC 3**
See also CA 104; DLB 7, 26

Shestov, Lev 1866-1938......... **TCLC 56**

Shiel, M(atthew) P(hipps)
1865-1947 .... **TCLC 8**
See also CA 106

Shiga, Naoya 1883-1971......... **CLC 33**
See also CA 101; 33-36R

Shilts, Randy 1951-1994 .... **CLC 85**
See also CA 115; 127; 144; CANR 45

Shimazaki Haruki 1872-1943
See Shimazaki Toson
See also CA 105; 134

Shimazaki Toson .... **TCLC 5**
See also Shimazaki Haruki

Sholokhov, Mikhail (Aleksandrovich)
1905-1984 .... **CLC 7, 15**
See also CA 101; 112; MTCW; SATA 36

Shone, Patric
See Hanley, James

Shreve, Susan Richards 1939-...... **CLC 23**
See also CA 49-52; CAAS 5; CANR 5, 38;
MAICYA; SATA 41, 46

Shue, Larry 1946-1985............ **CLC 52**
See also CA 145; 117

Shu-Jen, Chou 1881-1936
See Hsun, Lu
See also CA 104

Shulman, Alix Kates 1932-...... **CLC 2, 10**
See also CA 29-32R; CANR 43; SATA 7

Shuster, Joe 1914-.............. **CLC 21**

Shute, Nevil .... **CLC 30**
See also Norway, Nevil Shute

Shuttle, Penelope (Diane) 1947-..... **CLC 7**
See also CA 93-96; CANR 39; DLB 14, 40

Sidney, Mary 1561-1621 .... **LC 19**

Sidney, Sir Philip 1554-1586.... **LC 19; DA**
See also CDBLB Before 1660

Siegel, Jerome 1914-............ **CLC 21**
See also CA 116

Siegel, Jerry
See Siegel, Jerome

Sienkiewicz, Henryk (Adam Alexander Pius)
1846-1916 .... **TCLC 3**
See also CA 104; 134

Sierra, Gregorio Martinez
See Martinez Sierra, Gregorio

Sierra, Maria (de la O'LeJarraga) Martinez
See Martinez Sierra, Maria (de la
O'LeJarraga)

Sigal, Clancy 1926-............... **CLC 7**
See also CA 1-4R

Sigourney, Lydia Howard (Huntley)
1791-1865 .... **NCLC 21**
See also DLB 1, 42, 73

Siguenza y Gongora, Carlos de
1645-1700 .... **LC 8**

Sigurjonsson, Johann 1880-1919... **TCLC 27**

Sikelianos, Angelos 1884-1951 .... **TCLC 39**

Silkin, Jon 1930-............ **CLC 2, 6, 43**
See also CA 5-8R; CAAS 5; DLB 27

Silko, Leslie (Marmon)
1948-................. **CLC 23, 74; DA**
See also CA 115; 122; CANR 45; DLB 143

Sillanpaa, Frans Eemil 1888-1964... **CLC 19**
See also CA 129; 93-96; MTCW

Sillitoe, Alan
1928-......... **CLC 1, 3, 6, 10, 19, 57**
See also AITN 1; CA 9-12R; CAAS 2;
CANR 8, 26; CDBLB 1960 to Present;
DLB 14, 139; MTCW; SATA 61

Silone, Ignazio 1900-1978 .... **CLC 4**
See also CA 25-28; 81-84; CANR 34;
CAP 2; MTCW

Silver, Joan Micklin 1935- .... **CLC 20**
See also CA 114; 121

Silver, Nicholas
See Faust, Frederick (Schiller)

Silverberg, Robert 1935-........... **CLC 7**
See also CA 1-4R; CAAS 3; CANR 1, 20,
36; DLB 8; MAICYA; MTCW; SATA 13

Silverstein, Alvin 1933- .... **CLC 17**
See also CA 49-52; CANR 2; CLR 25;
JRDA; MAICYA; SATA 8, 69

Silverstein, Virginia B(arbara Opshelor)
1937-....................... **CLC 17**
See also CA 49-52; CANR 2; CLR 25;
JRDA; MAICYA; SATA 8, 69

Sim, Georges
See Simenon, Georges (Jacques Christian)

Simak, Clifford D(onald)
1904-1988 .... **CLC 1, 55**
See also CA 1-4R; 125; CANR 1, 35;
DLB 8; MTCW; SATA 56

Simenon, Georges (Jacques Christian)
1903-1989 .... **CLC 1, 2, 3, 8, 18, 47**
See also CA 85-88; 129; CANR 35;
DLB 72; DLBY 89; MTCW

Simic, Charles 1938-... **CLC 6, 9, 22, 49, 68**
See also CA 29-32R; CAAS 4; CANR 12,
33; DLB 105

Simmons, Charles (Paul) 1924-..... **CLC 57**
See also CA 89-92

Simmons, Dan 1948-.............. **CLC 44**
See also CA 138

Simmons, James (Stewart Alexander)
1933-....................... **CLC 43**
See also CA 105; DLB 40

Simms, William Gilmore
1806-1870 .... **NCLC 3**
See also DLB 3, 30, 59, 73

Simon, Carly 1945-.............. **CLC 26**
See also CA 105

Simon, Claude 1913-....... **CLC 4, 9, 15, 39**
See also CA 89-92; CANR 33; DLB 83;
MTCW

Simon, (Marvin) Neil
1927-.......... **CLC 6, 11, 31, 39, 70**
See also AITN 1; CA 21-24R; CANR 26;
DLB 7; MTCW

Simon, Paul 1942(?)-............. **CLC 17**
See also CA 116

Simonon, Paul 1956(?)-........... **CLC 30**

Simpson, Harriette
See Arnow, Harriette (Louisa) Simpson

Simpson, Louis (Aston Marantz)
1923-.................. **CLC 4, 7, 9, 32**
See also CA 1-4R; CAAS 4; CANR 1;
DLB 5; MTCW

Simpson, Mona (Elizabeth) 1957-... **CLC 44**
See also CA 122; 135

Simpson, N(orman) F(rederick)
1919-....................... **CLC 29**
See also CA 13-16R; DLB 13

Sinclair, Andrew (Annandale)
1935-....................... **CLC 2, 14**
See also CA 9-12R; CAAS 5; CANR 14, 38;
DLB 14; MTCW

Sinclair, Emil
See Hesse, Hermann

Sinclair, Iain 1943-.............. **CLC 76**
See also CA 132

Sinclair, Iain MacGregor
See Sinclair, Iain

Sinclair, Mary Amelia St. Clair 1865(?)-1946
See Sinclair, May
See also CA 104

Sinclair, May .... **TCLC 3, 11**
See also Sinclair, Mary Amelia St. Clair
See also DLB 36, 135

Sinclair, Upton (Beall)
1878-1968 ...... **CLC 1, 11, 15, 63; DA;
WLC**
See also CA 5-8R; 25-28R; CANR 7;
CDALB 1929-1941; DLB 9; MTCW;
SATA 9

Singer, Isaac
See Singer, Isaac Bashevis

Singer, Isaac Bashevis
1904-1991 .... **CLC 1, 3, 6, 9, 11, 15, 23,
38, 69; DA; SSC 3; WLC**
See also AITN 1, 2; CA 1-4R; 134;
CANR 1, 39; CDALB 1941-1968; CLR 1;
DLB 6, 28, 52; DLBY 91; JRDA;
MAICYA; MTCW; SATA 3, 27;
SATA-Obit 68

Souster, (Holmes) Raymond
1921- .... **CLC 5, 14**
See also CA 13-16R; CAAS 14; CANR 13,
29; DLB 88; SATA 63

Southern, Terry 1926- .... **CLC 7**
See also CA 1-4R; CANR 1; DLB 2

Southey, Robert 1774-1843 .... **NCLC 8**
See also DLB 93, 107, 142; SATA 54

Southworth, Emma Dorothy Eliza Nevitte
1819-1899 .... **NCLC 26**

Souza, Ernest
See Scott, Evelyn

Soyinka, Wole
1934- .... **CLC 3, 5, 14, 36, 44; BLC;**
DA; DC 2; WLC
See also BW 2; CA 13-16R; CANR 27, 39;
DLB 125; MTCW

Spackman, W(illiam) M(ode)
1905-1990 .... **CLC 46**
See also CA 81-84; 132

Spacks, Barry 1931- .... **CLC 14**
See also CA 29-32R; CANR 33; DLB 105

Spanidou, Irini 1946- .... **CLC 44**

Spark, Muriel (Sarah)
1918- .... **CLC 2, 3, 5, 8, 13, 18, 40;**
SSC 10
See also CA 5-8R; CANR 12, 36;
CDBLB 1945-1960; DLB 15, 139; MTCW

Spaulding, Douglas
See Bradbury, Ray (Douglas)

Spaulding, Leonard
See Bradbury, Ray (Douglas)

Spence, J. A. D.
See Eliot, T(homas) S(tearns)

Spencer, Elizabeth 1921- .... **CLC 22**
See also CA 13-16R; CANR 32; DLB 6;
MTCW; SATA 14

Spencer, Leonard G.
See Silverberg, Robert

Spencer, Scott 1945- .... **CLC 30**
See also CA 113; DLBY 86

Spender, Stephen (Harold)
1909- .... **CLC 1, 2, 5, 10, 41**
See also CA 9-12R; CANR 31;
CDBLB 1945-1960; DLB 20; MTCW

Spengler, Oswald (Arnold Gottfried)
1880-1936 .... **TCLC 25**
See also CA 118

Spenser, Edmund
1552(?)-1599 .... **LC 5; DA; PC 8; WLC**
See also CDBLB Before 1660

Spicer, Jack 1925-1965 ...... **CLC 8, 18, 72**
See also CA 85-88; DLB 5, 16

Spiegelman, Art 1948- .... **CLC 76**
See also AAYA 10; CA 125; CANR 41

Spielberg, Peter 1929- .... **CLC 6**
See also CA 5-8R; CANR 4; DLBY 81

Spielberg, Steven 1947- .... **CLC 20**
See also AAYA 8; CA 77-80; CANR 32;
SATA 32

Spillane, Frank Morrison 1918-
See Spillane, Mickey
See also CA 25-28R; CANR 28; MTCW;
SATA 66

Spillane, Mickey .... **CLC 3, 13**
See also Spillane, Frank Morrison

Spinoza, Benedictus de 1632-1677 .... **LC 9**

Spinrad, Norman (Richard) 1940-... **CLC 46**
See also CA 37-40R; CAAS 19; CANR 20;
DLB 8

Spitteler, Carl (Friedrich Georg)
1845-1924 .... **TCLC 12**
See also CA 109; DLB 129

Spivack, Kathleen (Romola Drucker)
1938- .... **CLC 6**
See also CA 49-52

Spoto, Donald 1941-.............. **CLC 39**
See also CA 65-68; CANR 11

Springsteen, Bruce (F.) 1949- ...... **CLC 17**
See also CA 111

Spurling, Hilary 1940-............ **CLC 34**
See also CA 104; CANR 25

Squires, (James) Radcliffe
1917-1993 .... **CLC 51**
See also CA 1-4R; 140; CANR 6, 21

Srivastava, Dhanpat Rai 1880(?)-1936
See Premchand
See also CA 118

Stacy, Donald
See Pohl, Frederik

Stael, Germaine de
See Stael-Holstein, Anne Louise Germaine
Necker Baronn
See also DLB 119

Stael-Holstein, Anne Louise Germaine Necker
Baronn 1766-1817 .... **NCLC 3**
See also Stael, Germaine de

Stafford, Jean 1915-1979... **CLC 4, 7, 19, 68**
See also CA 1-4R; 85-88; CANR 3; DLB 2;
MTCW; SATA 22

Stafford, William (Edgar)
1914-1993 .... **CLC 4, 7, 29**
See also CA 5-8R; 142; CAAS 3; CANR 5,
22; DLB 5

Staines, Trevor
See Brunner, John (Kilian Houston)

Stairs, Gordon
See Austin, Mary (Hunter)

Stannard, Martin 1947-........... **CLC 44**
See also CA 142

Stanton, Maura 1946- .... **CLC 9**
See also CA 89-92; CANR 15; DLB 120

Stanton, Schuyler
See Baum, L(yman) Frank

Stapledon, (William) Olaf
1886-1950 .... **TCLC 22**
See also CA 111; DLB 15

Starbuck, George (Edwin) 1931-.... **CLC 53**
See also CA 21-24R; CANR 23

Stark, Richard
See Westlake, Donald E(dwin)

Staunton, Schuyler
See Baum, L(yman) Frank

Stead, Christina (Ellen)
1902-1983 .... **CLC 2, 5, 8, 32, 80**
See also CA 13-16R; 109; CANR 33, 40;
MTCW

Stead, William Thomas
1849-1912 .... **TCLC 48**

Steele, Richard 1672-1729.......... **LC 18**
See also CDBLB 1660-1789; DLB 84, 101

Steele, Timothy (Reid) 1948-....... **CLC 45**
See also CA 93-96; CANR 16; DLB 120

Steffens, (Joseph) Lincoln
1866-1936 .... **TCLC 20**
See also CA 117

Stegner, Wallace (Earle)
1909-1993 .... **CLC 9, 49, 81**
See also AITN 1; BEST 90:3; CA 1-4R;
141; CAAS 1; CANR 1, 21; DLB 9;
DLBY 93; MTCW

Stein, Gertrude
1874-1946 ...... **TCLC 1, 6, 28, 48; DA;**
WLC
See also CA 104; 132; CDALB 1917-1929;
DLB 4, 54, 86; MTCW

Steinbeck, John (Ernst)
1902-1968 ...... **CLC 1, 5, 9, 13, 21, 34,**
45, 75; DA; SSC 11; WLC
See also AAYA 12; CA 1-4R; 25-28R;
CANR 1, 35; CDALB 1929-1941; DLB 7,
9; DLBD 2; MTCW; SATA 9

Steinem, Gloria 1934-............ **CLC 63**
See also CA 53-56; CANR 28; MTCW

Steiner, George 1929-............. **CLC 24**
See also CA 73-76; CANR 31; DLB 67;
MTCW; SATA 62

Steiner, K. Leslie
See Delany, Samuel R(ay, Jr.)

Steiner, Rudolf 1861-1925........ **TCLC 13**
See also CA 107

Stendhal
1783-1842 ..... **NCLC 23, 46; DA; WLC**
See also DLB 119

Stephen, Leslie 1832-1904........ **TCLC 23**
See also CA 123; DLB 57, 144

Stephen, Sir Leslie
See Stephen, Leslie

Stephen, Virginia
See Woolf, (Adeline) Virginia

Stephens, James 1882(?)-1950...... **TCLC 4**
See also CA 104; DLB 19

Stephens, Reed
See Donaldson, Stephen R.

Steptoe, Lydia
See Barnes, Djuna

Sterchi, Beat 1949-.............. **CLC 65**

Sterling, Brett
See Bradbury, Ray (Douglas); Hamilton,
Edmond

Sterling, Bruce 1954-............. **CLC 72**
See also CA 119; CANR 44

Sterling, George 1869-1926....... **TCLC 20**
See also CA 117; DLB 54

Stern, Gerald 1925- .... **CLC 40**
See also CA 81-84; CANR 28; DLB 105

Stern, Richard (Gustave) 1928-... **CLC 4, 39**
See also CA 1-4R; CANR 1, 25; DLBY 87

Sternberg, Josef von 1894-1969..... **CLC 20**
See also CA 81-84

Suskind, Patrick
See Sueskind, Patrick
See also CA 145

Sutcliff, Rosemary　1920-1992 ...... **CLC 26**
See also AAYA 10; CA 5-8R; 139;
CANR 37; CLR 1; JRDA; MAICYA;
SATA 6, 44, 78; SATA-Obit 73

Sutro, Alfred　1863-1933........... **TCLC 6**
See also CA 105; DLB 10

Sutton, Henry
See Slavitt, David R(ytman)

Svevo, Italo .... **TCLC 2, 35**
See also Schmitz, Aron Hector

Swados, Elizabeth　1951- .... **CLC 12**
See also CA 97-100

Swados, Harvey　1920-1972 .... **CLC 5**
See also CA 5-8R; 37-40R; CANR 6;
DLB 2

Swan, Gladys　1934- .... **CLC 69**
See also CA 101; CANR 17, 39

Swarthout, Glendon (Fred)
1918-1992 .... **CLC 35**
See also CA 1-4R; 139; CANR 1; SATA 26

Sweet, Sarah C.
See Jewett, (Theodora) Sarah Orne

Swenson, May
1919-1989 .... **CLC 4, 14, 61; DA**
See also CA 5-8R; 130; CANR 36; DLB 5;
MTCW; SATA 15

Swift, Augustus
See Lovecraft, H(oward) P(hillips)

Swift, Graham　1949- .... **CLC 41**
See also CA 117; 122

Swift, Jonathan
1667-1745 ...... **LC 1; DA; PC 9; WLC**
See also CDBLB 1660-1789; DLB 39, 95,
101; SATA 19

Swinburne, Algernon Charles
1837-1909 ...... **TCLC 8, 36; DA; WLC**
See also CA 105; 140; CDBLB 1832-1890;
DLB 35, 57

Swinfen, Ann .... **CLC 34**

Swinnerton, Frank Arthur
1884-1982 .... **CLC 31**
See also CA 108; DLB 34

Swithen, John
See King, Stephen (Edwin)

Sylvia
See Ashton-Warner, Sylvia (Constance)

Symmes, Robert Edward
See Duncan, Robert (Edward)

Symonds, John Addington
1840-1893 .... **NCLC 34**
See also DLB 57, 144

Symons, Arthur　1865-1945 ...... **TCLC 11**
See also CA 107; DLB 19, 57

Symons, Julian (Gustave)
1912- .... **CLC 2, 14, 32**
See also CA 49-52; CAAS 3; CANR 3, 33;
DLB 87; DLBY 92; MTCW

Synge, (Edmund) J(ohn) M(illington)
1871-1909 .... **TCLC 6, 37; DC 2**
See also CA 104; 141; CDBLB 1890-1914;
DLB 10, 19

Syruc, J.
See Milosz, Czeslaw

Szirtes, George　1948-............. **CLC 46**
See also CA 109; CANR 27

Tabori, George　1914-............. **CLC 19**
See also CA 49-52; CANR 4

Tagore, Rabindranath
1861-1941 .... **TCLC 3, 53; PC 8**
See also CA 104; 120; MTCW

Taine, Hippolyte Adolphe
1828-1893 .... **NCLC 15**

Talese, Gay　1932-............... **CLC 37**
See also AITN 1; CA 1-4R; CANR 9;
MTCW

Tallent, Elizabeth (Ann)　1954- ..... **CLC 45**
See also CA 117; DLB 130

Tally, Ted　1952-................ **CLC 42**
See also CA 120; 124

Tamayo y Baus, Manuel
1829-1898 .... **NCLC 1**

Tammsaare, A(nton) H(ansen)
1878-1940 .... **TCLC 27**

Tan, Amy　1952- .... **CLC 59**
See also AAYA 9; BEST 89:3; CA 136;
SATA 75

Tandem, Felix
See Spitteler, Carl (Friedrich Georg)

Tanizaki, Jun'ichiro
1886-1965 .... **CLC 8, 14, 28**
See also CA 93-96; 25-28R

Tanner, William
See Amis, Kingsley (William)

Tao Lao
See Storni, Alfonsina

Tarassoff, Lev
See Troyat, Henri

Tarbell, Ida M(inerva)
1857-1944 .... **TCLC 40**
See also CA 122; DLB 47

Tarkington, (Newton) Booth
1869-1946 .... **TCLC 9**
See also CA 110; 143; DLB 9, 102;
SATA 17

Tarkovsky, Andrei (Arsenyevich)
1932-1986 .... **CLC 75**
See also CA 127

Tartt, Donna　1964(?)-............. **CLC 76**
See also CA 142

Tasso, Torquato　1544-1595 .... **LC 5**

Tate, (John Orley) Allen
1899-1979 .... **CLC 2, 4, 6, 9, 11, 14, 24**
See also CA 5-8R; 85-88; CANR 32;
DLB 4, 45, 63; MTCW

Tate, Ellalice
See Hibbert, Eleanor Alice Burford

Tate, James (Vincent)　1943- ... **CLC 2, 6, 25**
See also CA 21-24R; CANR 29; DLB 5

Tavel, Ronald　1940-.............. **CLC 6**
See also CA 21-24R; CANR 33

Taylor, Cecil Philip　1929-1981 ..... **CLC 27**
See also CA 25-28R; 105

Taylor, Edward　1642(?)-1729.... **LC 11; DA**
See also DLB 24

Taylor, Eleanor Ross　1920-........ **CLC 5**
See also CA 81-84

Taylor, Elizabeth　1912-1975 ... **CLC 2, 4, 29**
See also CA 13-16R; CANR 9; DLB 139;
MTCW; SATA 13

Taylor, Henry (Splawn)　1942-...... **CLC 44**
See also CA 33-36R; CAAS 7; CANR 31;
DLB 5

Taylor, Kamala (Purnaiya)　1924-
See Markandaya, Kamala
See also CA 77-80

Taylor, Mildred D. .... **CLC 21**
See also AAYA 10; BW 1; CA 85-88;
CANR 25; CLR 9; DLB 52; JRDA;
MAICYA; SAAS 5; SATA 15, 70

Taylor, Peter (Hillsman)
1917- ...... **CLC 1, 4, 18, 37, 44, 50, 71;**
SSC 10
See also CA 13-16R; CANR 9; DLBY 81;
MTCW

Taylor, Robert Lewis　1912-........ **CLC 14**
See also CA 1-4R; CANR 3; SATA 10

Tchekhov, Anton
See Chekhov, Anton (Pavlovich)

Teasdale, Sara　1884-1933......... **TCLC 4**
See also CA 104; DLB 45; SATA 32

Tegner, Esaias　1782-1846........ **NCLC 2**

Teilhard de Chardin, (Marie Joseph) Pierre
1881-1955 .... **TCLC 9**
See also CA 105

Temple, Ann
See Mortimer, Penelope (Ruth)

Tennant, Emma (Christina)
1937- .... **CLC 13, 52**
See also CA 65-68; CAAS 9; CANR 10, 38;
DLB 14

Tenneshaw, S. M.
See Silverberg, Robert

Tennyson, Alfred
1809-1892 .. **NCLC 30; DA; PC 6; WLC**
See also CDBLB 1832-1890; DLB 32

Teran, Lisa St. Aubin de .... **CLC 36**
See also St. Aubin de Teran, Lisa

Terence　195(?)B.C.-159B.C....... **CMLC 14**

Teresa de Jesus, St.　1515-1582 ...... **LC 18**

Terkel, Louis　1912-
See Terkel, Studs
See also CA 57-60; CANR 18, 45; MTCW

Terkel, Studs .... **CLC 38**
See also Terkel, Louis
See also AITN 1

Terry, C. V.
See Slaughter, Frank G(ill)

Terry, Megan　1932-.............. **CLC 19**
See also CA 77-80; CABS 3; CANR 43;
DLB 7

Tertz, Abram
See Sinyavsky, Andrei (Donatevich)

Tesich, Steve　1943(?)-.......... **CLC 40, 69**
See also CA 105; DLBY 83

Teternikov, Fyodor Kuzmich　1863-1927
See Sologub, Fyodor
See also CA 104

Voltaire
1694-1778 ... **LC 14; DA; SSC 12; WLC**

von Daeniken, Erich 1935- .... **CLC 30**
See also AITN 1; CA 37-40R; CANR 17, 44

von Daniken, Erich
See von Daeniken, Erich

von Heidenstam, (Carl Gustaf) Verner
See Heidenstam, (Carl Gustaf) Verner von

von Heyse, Paul (Johann Ludwig)
See Heyse, Paul (Johann Ludwig von)

von Hofmannsthal, Hugo
See Hofmannsthal, Hugo von

von Horvath, Odon
See Horvath, Oedoen von

von Horvath, Oedoen
See Horvath, Oedoen von

von Liliencron, (Friedrich Adolf Axel) Detlev
See Liliencron, (Friedrich Adolf Axel) Detlev von

Vonnegut, Kurt, Jr.
1922- ...... **CLC 1, 2, 3, 4, 5, 8, 12, 22, 40, 60; DA; SSC 8; WLC**
See also AAYA 6; AITN 1; BEST 90:4; CA 1-4R; CANR 1, 25; CDALB 1968-1988; DLB 2, 8; DLBD 3; DLBY 80; MTCW

Von Rachen, Kurt
See Hubbard, L(afayette) Ron(ald)

von Rezzori (d'Arezzo), Gregor
See Rezzori (d'Arezzo), Gregor von

von Sternberg, Josef
See Sternberg, Josef von

Vorster, Gordon 1924- .... **CLC 34**
See also CA 133

Vosce, Trudie
See Ozick, Cynthia

Voznesensky, Andrei (Andreievich)
1933- .... **CLC 1, 15, 57**
See also CA 89-92; CANR 37; MTCW

Waddington, Miriam 1917- .... **CLC 28**
See also CA 21-24R; CANR 12, 30; DLB 68

Wagman, Fredrica 1937- .... **CLC 7**
See also CA 97-100

Wagner, Richard 1813-1883....... **NCLC 9**
See also DLB 129

Wagner-Martin, Linda 1936-....... **CLC 50**

Wagoner, David (Russell)
1926- .... **CLC 3, 5, 15**
See also CA 1-4R; CAAS 3; CANR 2; DLB 5; SATA 14

Wah, Fred(erick James) 1939-...... **CLC 44**
See also CA 107; 141; DLB 60

Wahloo, Per 1926-1975 .... **CLC 7**
See also CA 61-64

Wahloo, Peter
See Wahloo, Per

Wain, John (Barrington)
1925-1994 .... **CLC 2, 11, 15, 46**
See also CA 5-8R; 145; CAAS 4; CANR 23; CDBLB 1960 to Present; DLB 15, 27, 139; MTCW

Wajda, Andrzej 1926-............. **CLC 16**
See also CA 102

Wakefield, Dan 1932-............. **CLC 7**
See also CA 21-24R; CAAS 7

Wakoski, Diane
1937- .... **CLC 2, 4, 7, 9, 11, 40**
See also CA 13-16R; CAAS 1; CANR 9; DLB 5

Wakoski-Sherbell, Diane
See Wakoski, Diane

Walcott, Derek (Alton)
1930- .... **CLC 2, 4, 9, 14, 25, 42, 67, 76; BLC**
See also BW 2; CA 89-92; CANR 26; DLB 117; DLBY 81; MTCW

Waldman, Anne 1945- .... **CLC 7**
See also CA 37-40R; CAAS 17; CANR 34; DLB 16

Waldo, E. Hunter
See Sturgeon, Theodore (Hamilton)

Waldo, Edward Hamilton
See Sturgeon, Theodore (Hamilton)

Walker, Alice (Malsenior)
1944- .... **CLC 5, 6, 9, 19, 27, 46, 58; BLC; DA; SSC 5**
See also AAYA 3; BEST 89:4; BW 2; CA 37-40R; CANR 9, 27; CDALB 1968-1988; DLB 6, 33, 143; MTCW; SATA 31

Walker, David Harry 1911-1992.... **CLC 14**
See also CA 1-4R; 137; CANR 1; SATA 8; SATA-Obit 71

Walker, Edward Joseph 1934-
See Walker, Ted
See also CA 21-24R; CANR 12, 28

Walker, George F. 1947-....... **CLC 44, 61**
See also CA 103; CANR 21, 43; DLB 60

Walker, Joseph A. 1935-.......... **CLC 19**
See also BW 1; CA 89-92; CANR 26; DLB 38

Walker, Margaret (Abigail)
1915- .... **CLC 1, 6; BLC**
See also BW 2; CA 73-76; CANR 26; DLB 76; MTCW

Walker, Ted.................... CLC 13
See also Walker, Edward Joseph
See also DLB 40

Wallace, David Foster 1962-....... **CLC 50**
See also CA 132

Wallace, Dexter
See Masters, Edgar Lee

Wallace, (Richard Horatio) Edgar
1875-1932 .... **TCLC 57**
See also CA 115; DLB 70

Wallace, Irving 1916-1990....... **CLC 7, 13**
See also AITN 1; CA 1-4R; 132; CAAS 1; CANR 1, 27; MTCW

Wallant, Edward Lewis
1926-1962 .... **CLC 5, 10**
See also CA 1-4R; CANR 22; DLB 2, 28, 143; MTCW

Walpole, Horace 1717-1797......... **LC 2**
See also DLB 39, 104

Walpole, Hugh (Seymour)
1884-1941 .... **TCLC 5**
See also CA 104; DLB 34

Walser, Martin 1927-............. **CLC 27**
See also CA 57-60; CANR 8; DLB 75, 124

Walser, Robert 1878-1956........ **TCLC 18**
See also CA 118; DLB 66

Walsh, Jill Paton.................. CLC 35
See also Paton Walsh, Gillian
See also AAYA 11; CLR 2; SAAS 3

Walter, Villiam Christian
See Andersen, Hans Christian

Wambaugh, Joseph (Aloysius, Jr.)
1937- .... **CLC 3, 18**
See also AITN 1; BEST 89:3; CA 33-36R; CANR 42; DLB 6; DLBY 83; MTCW

Ward, Arthur Henry Sarsfield 1883-1959
See Rohmer, Sax
See also CA 108

Ward, Douglas Turner 1930-....... **CLC 19**
See also BW 1; CA 81-84; CANR 27; DLB 7, 38

Ward, Mary Augusta
See Ward, Mrs. Humphry

Ward, Mrs. Humphry
1851-1920 .... **TCLC 55**
See also DLB 18

Ward, Peter
See Faust, Frederick (Schiller)

Warhol, Andy 1928(?)-1987........ **CLC 20**
See also AAYA 12; BEST 89:4; CA 89-92; 121; CANR 34

Warner, Francis (Robert le Plastrier)
1937- .... **CLC 14**
See also CA 53-56; CANR 11

Warner, Marina 1946-............. **CLC 59**
See also CA 65-68; CANR 21

Warner, Rex (Ernest) 1905-1986.... **CLC 45**
See also CA 89-92; 119; DLB 15

Warner, Susan (Bogert)
1819-1885 .... **NCLC 31**
See also DLB 3, 42

Warner, Sylvia (Constance) Ashton
See Ashton-Warner, Sylvia (Constance)

Warner, Sylvia Townsend
1893-1978 .... **CLC 7, 19**
See also CA 61-64; 77-80; CANR 16; DLB 34, 139; MTCW

Warren, Mercy Otis 1728-1814... **NCLC 13**
See also DLB 31

Warren, Robert Penn
1905-1989 .... **CLC 1, 4, 6, 8, 10, 13, 18, 39, 53, 59; DA; SSC 4; WLC**
See also AITN 1; CA 13-16R; 129; CANR 10; CDALB 1968-1988; DLB 2, 48; DLBY 80, 89; MTCW; SATA 46, 63

Warshofsky, Isaac
See Singer, Isaac Bashevis

Warton, Thomas 1728-1790........ **LC 15**
See also DLB 104, 109

Waruk, Kona
See Harris, (Theodore) Wilson

Warung, Price 1855-1911........ **TCLC 45**

Warwick, Jarvis
See Garner, Hugh

Washington, Alex
See Harris, Mark

Washington, Booker T(aliaferro)
1856-1915 .... **TCLC 10; BLC**
See also BW 1; CA 114; 125; SATA 28

Washington, George 1732-1799 ...... **LC 25**
See also DLB 31

Wassermann, (Karl) Jakob
1873-1934 .... **TCLC 6**
See also CA 104; DLB 66

Wasserstein, Wendy
1950- .... **CLC 32, 59; DC 4**
See also CA 121; 129; CABS 3

Waterhouse, Keith (Spencer)
1929- .... **CLC 47**
See also CA 5-8R; CANR 38; DLB 13, 15;
MTCW

Waters, Roger 1944- .... **CLC 35**

Watkins, Frances Ellen
See Harper, Frances Ellen Watkins

Watkins, Gerrold
See Malzberg, Barry N(athaniel)

Watkins, Paul 1964- .... **CLC 55**
See also CA 132

Watkins, Vernon Phillips
1906-1967 .... **CLC 43**
See also CA 9-10; 25-28R; CAP 1; DLB 20

Watson, Irving S.
See Mencken, H(enry) L(ouis)

Watson, John H.
See Farmer, Philip Jose

Watson, Richard F.
See Silverberg, Robert

Waugh, Auberon (Alexander) 1939- .. **CLC 7**
See also CA 45-48; CANR 6, 22; DLB 14

Waugh, Evelyn (Arthur St. John)
1903-1966 ...... **CLC 1, 3, 8, 13, 19, 27,
44; DA; WLC**
See also CA 85-88; 25-28R; CANR 22;
CDBLB 1914-1945; DLB 15; MTCW

Waugh, Harriet 1944- .... **CLC 6**
See also CA 85-88; CANR 22

Ways, C. R.
See Blount, Roy (Alton), Jr.

Waystaff, Simon
See Swift, Jonathan

Webb, (Martha) Beatrice (Potter)
1858-1943 .... **TCLC 22**
See also Potter, Beatrice
See also CA 117

Webb, Charles (Richard) 1939- ...... **CLC 7**
See also CA 25-28R

Webb, James H(enry), Jr. 1946- .... **CLC 22**
See also CA 81-84

Webb, Mary (Gladys Meredith)
1881-1927 .... **TCLC 24**
See also CA 123; DLB 34

Webb, Mrs. Sidney
See Webb, (Martha) Beatrice (Potter)

Webb, Phyllis 1927- .... **CLC 18**
See also CA 104; CANR 23; DLB 53

Webb, Sidney (James)
1859-1947 .... **TCLC 22**
See also CA 117

Webber, Andrew Lloyd .... **CLC 21**
See also Lloyd Webber, Andrew

Weber, Lenora Mattingly
1895-1971 .... **CLC 12**
See also CA 19-20; 29-32R; CAP 1;
SATA 2, 26

Webster, John 1579(?)-1634(?) .... **DC 2**
See also CDBLB Before 1660; DA; DLB 58;
WLC

Webster, Noah 1758-1843 .... **NCLC 30**

Wedekind, (Benjamin) Frank(lin)
1864-1918 .... **TCLC 7**
See also CA 104; DLB 118

Weidman, Jerome 1913- .... **CLC 7**
See also AITN 2; CA 1-4R; CANR 1;
DLB 28

Weil, Simone (Adolphine)
1909-1943 .... **TCLC 23**
See also CA 117

Weinstein, Nathan
See West, Nathanael

Weinstein, Nathan von Wallenstein
See West, Nathanael

Weir, Peter (Lindsay) 1944- .... **CLC 20**
See also CA 113; 123

Weiss, Peter (Ulrich)
1916-1982 .... **CLC 3, 15, 51**
See also CA 45-48; 106; CANR 3; DLB 69,
124

Weiss, Theodore (Russell)
1916- .... **CLC 3, 8, 14**
See also CA 9-12R; CAAS 2; DLB 5

Welch, (Maurice) Denton
1915-1948 .... **TCLC 22**
See also CA 121

Welch, James 1940- .... **CLC 6, 14, 52**
See also CA 85-88; CANR 42

Weldon, Fay
1933(?)- .... **CLC 6, 9, 11, 19, 36, 59**
See also CA 21-24R; CANR 16;
CDBLB 1960 to Present; DLB 14;
MTCW

Wellek, Rene 1903- .... **CLC 28**
See also CA 5-8R; CAAS 7; CANR 8;
DLB 63

Weller, Michael 1942- .... **CLC 10, 53**
See also CA 85-88

Weller, Paul 1958- .... **CLC 26**

Wellershoff, Dieter 1925- .... **CLC 46**
See also CA 89-92; CANR 16, 37

Welles, (George) Orson
1915-1985 .... **CLC 20, 80**
See also CA 93-96; 117

Wellman, Mac 1945- .... **CLC 65**

Wellman, Manly Wade 1903-1986 .. **CLC 49**
See also CA 1-4R; 118; CANR 6, 16, 44;
SATA 6, 47

Wells, Carolyn 1869(?)-1942 ...... **TCLC 35**
See also CA 113; DLB 11

Wells, H(erbert) G(eorge)
1866-1946 .... **TCLC 6, 12, 19; DA;
SSC 6; WLC**
See also CA 110; 121; CDBLB 1914-1945;
DLB 34, 70; MTCW; SATA 20

Wells, Rosemary 1943- .... **CLC 12**
See also CA 85-88; CLR 16; MAICYA;
SAAS 1; SATA 18, 69

Welty, Eudora
1909- ...... **CLC 1, 2, 5, 14, 22, 33; DA;
SSC 1; WLC**
See also CA 9-12R; CABS 1; CANR 32;
CDALB 1941-1968; DLB 2, 102, 143;
DLBY 87; MTCW

Wen I-to 1899-1946 .... **TCLC 28**

Wentworth, Robert
See Hamilton, Edmond

Werfel, Franz (V.) 1890-1945 ...... **TCLC 8**
See also CA 104; DLB 81, 124

Wergeland, Henrik Arnold
1808-1845 .... **NCLC 5**

Wersba, Barbara 1932- .... **CLC 30**
See also AAYA 2; CA 29-32R; CANR 16,
38; CLR 3; DLB 52; JRDA; MAICYA;
SAAS 2; SATA 1, 58

Wertmueller, Lina 1928- .... **CLC 16**
See also CA 97-100; CANR 39

Wescott, Glenway 1901-1987 .... **CLC 13**
See also CA 13-16R; 121; CANR 23;
DLB 4, 9, 102

Wesker, Arnold 1932- .... **CLC 3, 5, 42**
See also CA 1-4R; CAAS 7; CANR 1, 33;
CDBLB 1960 to Present; DLB 13;
MTCW

Wesley, Richard (Errol) 1945- .... **CLC 7**
See also BW 1; CA 57-60; CANR 27;
DLB 38

Wessel, Johan Herman 1742-1785 .... **LC 7**

West, Anthony (Panther)
1914-1987 .... **CLC 50**
See also CA 45-48; 124; CANR 3, 19;
DLB 15

West, C. P.
See Wodehouse, P(elham) G(renville)

West, (Mary) Jessamyn
1902-1984 .... **CLC 7, 17**
See also CA 9-12R; 112; CANR 27; DLB 6;
DLBY 84; MTCW; SATA 37

West, Morris L(anglo) 1916- ..... **CLC 6, 33**
See also CA 5-8R; CANR 24; MTCW

West, Nathanael
1903-1940 ..... **TCLC 1, 14, 44; SSC 16**
See also CA 104; 125; CDALB 1929-1941;
DLB 4, 9, 28; MTCW

West, Owen
See Koontz, Dean R(ay)

West, Paul 1930- .... **CLC 7, 14**
See also CA 13-16R; CAAS 7; CANR 22;
DLB 14

West, Rebecca 1892-1983 .. **CLC 7, 9, 31, 50**
See also CA 5-8R; 109; CANR 19; DLB 36;
DLBY 83; MTCW

Westall, Robert (Atkinson)
1929-1993 .... **CLC 17**
See also AAYA 12; CA 69-72; 141;
CANR 18; CLR 13; JRDA; MAICYA;
SAAS 2; SATA 23, 69; SATA-Obit 75

Westlake, Donald E(dwin)
1933- .... **CLC 7, 33**
See also CA 17-20R; CAAS 13; CANR 16,
44

Westmacott, Mary
See Christie, Agatha (Mary Clarissa)

Weston, Allen
See Norton, Andre

Wetcheek, J. L.
See Feuchtwanger, Lion

Wetering, Janwillem van de
See van de Wetering, Janwillem

Wetherell, Elizabeth
See Warner, Susan (Bogert)

Whalen, Philip 1923- .... **CLC 6, 29**
See also CA 9-12R; CANR 5, 39; DLB 16

Wharton, Edith (Newbold Jones)
1862-1937 ...... **TCLC 3, 9, 27, 53; DA;**
SSC 6; WLC
See also CA 104; 132; CDALB 1865-1917;
DLB 4, 9, 12, 78; MTCW

Wharton, James
See Mencken, H(enry) L(ouis)

Wharton, William (a pseudonym)
.... **CLC 18, 37**
See also CA 93-96; DLBY 80

Wheatley (Peters), Phillis
1754(?)-1784 .... **LC 3; BLC; DA; PC 3;**
WLC
See also CDALB 1640-1865; DLB 31, 50

Wheelock, John Hall 1886-1978 .... **CLC 14**
See also CA 13-16R; 77-80; CANR 14;
DLB 45

White, E(lwyn) B(rooks)
1899-1985 .... **CLC 10, 34, 39**
See also AITN 2; CA 13-16R; 116;
CANR 16, 37; CLR 1, 21; DLB 11, 22;
MAICYA; MTCW; SATA 2, 29, 44

White, Edmund (Valentine III)
1940- .... **CLC 27**
See also AAYA 7; CA 45-48; CANR 3, 19,
36; MTCW

White, Patrick (Victor Martindale)
1912-1990 .. **CLC 3, 4, 5, 7, 9, 18, 65, 69**
See also CA 81-84; 132; CANR 43; MTCW

White, Phyllis Dorothy James 1920-
See James, P. D.
See also CA 21-24R; CANR 17, 43; MTCW

White, T(erence) H(anbury)
1906-1964 .... **CLC 30**
See also CA 73-76; CANR 37; JRDA;
MAICYA; SATA 12

White, Terence de Vere
1912-1994 .... **CLC 49**
See also CA 49-52; 145; CANR 3

White, Walter F(rancis)
1893-1955 .... **TCLC 15**
See also White, Walter
See also BW 1; CA 115; 124; DLB 51

White, William Hale 1831-1913
See Rutherford, Mark
See also CA 121

Whitehead, E(dward) A(nthony)
1933- .... **CLC 5**
See also CA 65-68

Whitemore, Hugh (John) 1936-..... **CLC 37**
See also CA 132

Whitman, Sarah Helen (Power)
1803-1878 .... **NCLC 19**
See also DLB 1

Whitman, Walt(er)
1819-1892 ..... **NCLC 4, 31; DA; PC 3;**
WLC
See also CDALB 1640-1865; DLB 3, 64;
SATA 20

Whitney, Phyllis A(yame) 1903-.... **CLC 42**
See also AITN 2; BEST 90:3; CA 1-4R;
CANR 3, 25, 38; JRDA; MAICYA;
SATA 1, 30

Whittemore, (Edward) Reed (Jr.)
1919- .... **CLC 4**
See also CA 9-12R; CAAS 8; CANR 4;
DLB 5

Whittier, John Greenleaf
1807-1892 .... **NCLC 8**
See also CDALB 1640-1865; DLB 1

Whittlebot, Hernia
See Coward, Noel (Peirce)

Wicker, Thomas Grey 1926-
See Wicker, Tom
See also CA 65-68; CANR 21

Wicker, Tom .... **CLC 7**
See also Wicker, Thomas Grey

Wideman, John Edgar
1941- .... **CLC 5, 34, 36, 67; BLC**
See also BW 2; CA 85-88; CANR 14, 42;
DLB 33, 143

Wiebe, Rudy (Henry) 1934-... **CLC 6, 11, 14**
See also CA 37-40R; CANR 42; DLB 60

Wieland, Christoph Martin
1733-1813 .... **NCLC 17**
See also DLB 97

Wiene, Robert 1881-1938........ **TCLC 56**

Wieners, John 1934-.............. **CLC 7**
See also CA 13-16R; DLB 16

Wiesel, Elie(zer)
1928- .... **CLC 3, 5, 11, 37; DA**
See also AAYA 7; AITN 1; CA 5-8R;
CAAS 4; CANR 8, 40; DLB 83;
DLBY 87; MTCW; SATA 56

Wiggins, Marianne 1947-......... **CLC 57**
See also BEST 89:3; CA 130

Wight, James Alfred 1916-
See Herriot, James
See also CA 77-80; SATA 44, 55

Wilbur, Richard (Purdy)
1921- .... **CLC 3, 6, 9, 14, 53; DA**
See also CA 1-4R; CABS 2; CANR 2, 29;
DLB 5; MTCW; SATA 9

Wild, Peter 1940-.............. **CLC 14**
See also CA 37-40R; DLB 5

Wilde, Oscar (Fingal O'Flahertie Wills)
1854(?)-1900 .... **TCLC 1, 8, 23, 41; DA;**
SSC 11; WLC
See also CA 104; 119; CDBLB 1890-1914;
DLB 10, 19, 34, 57, 141; SATA 24

Wilder, Billy .... **CLC 20**
See also Wilder, Samuel
See also DLB 26

Wilder, Samuel 1906-
See Wilder, Billy
See also CA 89-92

Wilder, Thornton (Niven)
1897-1975 ...... **CLC 1, 5, 6, 10, 15, 35,**
82; DA; DC 1; WLC
See also AITN 2; CA 13-16R; 61-64;
CANR 40; DLB 4, 7, 9; MTCW

Wilding, Michael 1942-.......... **CLC 73**
See also CA 104; CANR 24

Wiley, Richard 1944-............. **CLC 44**
See also CA 121; 129

Wilhelm, Kate .... **CLC 7**
See also Wilhelm, Katie Gertrude
See also CAAS 5; DLB 8

Wilhelm, Katie Gertrude 1928-
See Wilhelm, Kate
See also CA 37-40R; CANR 17, 36; MTCW

Wilkins, Mary
See Freeman, Mary Eleanor Wilkins

Willard, Nancy 1936-.......... **CLC 7, 37**
See also CA 89-92; CANR 10, 39; CLR 5;
DLB 5, 52; MAICYA; MTCW;
SATA 30, 37, 71

Williams, C(harles) K(enneth)
1936- .... **CLC 33, 56**
See also CA 37-40R; DLB 5

Williams, Charles
See Collier, James L(incoln)

Williams, Charles (Walter Stansby)
1886-1945 .... **TCLC 1, 11**
See also CA 104; DLB 100

Williams, (George) Emlyn
1905-1987 .... **CLC 15**
See also CA 104; 123; CANR 36; DLB 10,
77; MTCW

Williams, Hugo 1942-.......... **CLC 42**
See also CA 17-20R; CANR 45; DLB 40

Williams, J. Walker
See Wodehouse, P(elham) G(renville)

Williams, John A(lfred)
1925- .... **CLC 5, 13; BLC**
See also BW 2; CA 53-56; CAAS 3;
CANR 6, 26; DLB 2, 33

Williams, Jonathan (Chamberlain)
1929- .... **CLC 13**
See also CA 9-12R; CAAS 12; CANR 8;
DLB 5

Williams, Joy 1944-.............. **CLC 31**
See also CA 41-44R; CANR 22

Williams, Norman 1952-.......... **CLC 39**
See also CA 118

Williams, Tennessee
1911-1983 ..... **CLC 1, 2, 5, 7, 8, 11, 15,**
19, 30, 39, 45, 71; DA; DC 4; WLC
See also AITN 1, 2; CA 5-8R; 108;
CABS 3; CANR 31; CDALB 1941-1968;
DLB 7; DLBD 4; DLBY 83; MTCW

Literary Criticism Series
Cumulative Topic Index

This index lists all topic entries in the Gale Literary Criticism Series *Classical and Medieval Literature Criticism, Contemporary Literary Criticism, Literature Criticism from 1400 to 1800, Nineteenth-Century Literature Criticism,* and *Twentieth-Century Literary Criticism.*

Topic Index

LC Cumulative Nationality Index

LC Cumulative Title Index

Title Index

Title Index

Title Index

Title Index

Title Index

Title Index

Title Index

Title Index